Looking Unto Jesus

You are holding a reproduction of an original work that is in the public domain in the United States of America, and possibly other countries.You may freely copy and distribute this work as no entity (individual or corporate) has a copyright on the body of the work.This book may contain prior copyright references, and library stamps (as most of these works were scanned from library copies).These have been scanned and retained as part of the historical artifact.

This book may have occasional imperfections such as missing or blurred pages, poor pictures, errant marks, etc. that were either part of the original artifact, or were introduced by the scanning process. We believe this work is culturally important, and despite the imperfections, have elected to bring it back into print as part of our continuing commitment to the preservation of printed works worldwide. We appreciate your understanding of the imperfections in the preservation process, and hope you enjoy this valuable book.

Robert Finley
 given him
By his Worthy Friend
 Job Palmer

LOOKING UNTO

JESUS:

A View of the Everlasting

GOSPEL;

Or, the SOUL's

EYING OF JESUS,

As carrying on the great Work of Man's Salvation, from First to Last.

By ISAAC AMBROSE, Minister of the Gospel.

ISAIAH xlv. 22. *Look unto me, and be ye saved, all the Ends of the Earth.*

BELFAST:

Printed by and for JAMES MAGEE at the BIBLE and CROWN in *Bridge-Street.*
M,DCC,LXIII.

TO the RIGHT HONOURABLE,

WILLIAM,
Earl of BEDFORD,
LORD *RUSSEL*, BARON of *Thornhaugh*.

RIGHT HONOURABLE,

ONCE I made bold to prefix an EPISTLE to your honour, before my book, entitled ULTIMA: since which time, you have continued with increase your wonted favours: as the *sun*, that rejoiceth to run his race, and is unwearied after his many revolutions, so, year after year, have you indefatigably expressed your great *bounty*, whereby both myself, and my family, have been exceedingly refreshed. As I cannot, but, in the way of thankfulness, acknowledge thus much, so I shall be a sincere remembrancer, both of your honour, and your nearest relations, at the throne of GRACE.

My LORD, I have now composed this WORK, containing a necessary practice, and high privilege of every CHRISTIAN; it is by way of supplement to the other duties set down in my BOOK called MEDIA, but because of my large handling it, I reserved it for a tract by itself. Indeed of all other duties, I prefer it as the chief; and I exceedingly wonder, that before this time, it hath not been undertaken by some abler hand. CHRISTIANS ordinarily go to *prayer, sacraments, hearing, reading,* and *meditation* of the *word;* and sometimes, (though more seldom) they set on the exercise of other duties, as *self-trial, self-denial,* the improving of *experiences,* the clearing of *evidences,* extemporary and deliberate *meditation,* &c. But, in the mean time, How is the main, the prime employment, even the duty of duties, OF LOOKING UNTO JESUS, wholly neglected? If many, or most have been ignorant of it hitherto, I think it is high time to discover it to the sleepy world; and it may be, when day is clear, they will walk in the *light,* and bless GOD for

finding

finding out a way wherein they may more immediately have commerce with *Jesus Christ*. I could have wished, that others more able had appeared in this service, in a particular handling of this excellent subject. I find it in print, wished for by a *Godly Brother*, where he complains, That CHRIST's love had been so little studied; men have been very swift in searching after other *truths*, but slow in searching after this. An ample, exact discovery of this love of CHRIST, I say of this love (in carrying on our SOUL's SALVATION from first to last) may well be set down amongst the *desiderata*, the desireables of divines, it having been so little handled (unless in some parts or pieces) by any: surely it is very sad to think, that the knowledge of this love of CHRIST, (in a continued *series*) being of such necessary and high concernment, hath been so little enquired into. O! what a gallant gospel-design were it for some one who is acquainted with the Spirit in a large measure, to go over the whole history of the *Gospel*, (*of the everlasting Gospel of JESUS*) and to observe the glorious shinings of the love of CHRIST to *believers* in all! It would *be precious if some would take it in hand*, and perfect it to the purpose; but it is sad to think it hath been neglected so long. As the LORD hath enabled, I have adventured; and, if for my rashness, in not waiting any longer, to see if any star of a greater magnitude would have appeared, I must be censured, I flee to your honour for patronage, not only for patronage, but I humbly beg of you and yours, to peruse and practise this slender WORK: Who can tell, but some of the golden oil of Grace may come out of JESUS CHRIST, the true *Olive Tree*, even through these pipes; and if so, your own experiences will be satisfactory answers to all other censures. Sure I am, in this exercise, (however the directions may be weak) you will find the advantage of lying at the *well-head*, and so you may drink more sweetly than others, that make use only of the streams. That you, (My NOBLE LORD), and your virtuous *Lady*, with your hopeful issue, may receive spiritual good by this *Treatise*, and all other helps which GOD's good providence may put into your hands, is the hearty *prayer*,

MY LORD,

Of Your Honour's Thankful, Faithful,
Though very unworthy Servant,

ISAAC AMBROSE.

TO THE
READER.

AMONGST all the duties I formerly mentioned, I omitted one, that now I look upon as chief and choice of all the rest: this is the duty I call *Looking unto Jesus*, and if I must discover the occasion of my falling on it, I shall do it truly and plainly, and in the simplicity of the gospel, as thus. In the *Spring* 1653. I was visited with a sore sickness, and as the LORD began to restore my health, it came into my thoughts what my JESUS had done for my soul, and what he was doing, and what he would do for it, till he saved to the uttermost. In my conceptions of these things, I could find no beginning of his actings, but in that eternity before the world was made: nor could I find any end of his actings, but in that eternity after the world should be unmade: only betwixt these two extremities, I apprehend various transactions of JESUS CHRIST, both past, present, and to come. In the multitude of these thoughts within me, my soul delighted itself, and that delight stirring up in me other affections, (for one affection cannot be alone) I began to consider of those texts in Scripture, which seemed at first to impose the working of my affections on so blessed an object, as a gospel-duty: then I resolved, if the LORD JESUS would but restore my health, and prolong my life, I would endeavour to discover more of this gospel-duty than ever I yet knew: and that my pains therein might not hinder my other necessary labours, my purpose was to fall on this subject in my ordinary preaching, wherein I might have occasion both to search into scriptures, several authors, and my own heart. In process of time, I began this work, begging of GOD, that he would help me to finish, as he inclined me to begin, and that all might tend to his glory, and the Church's good. In the progress of my labours, I found a world of spiritual comfort, both in respect of the object that I handled, JESUS CHRIST, and in respect of the act, wherein consisted my duty to him, in *looking unto Jesus*. 1. For the object, it was the very subject whereon more especially I was bound to preach, *Christ in you, the hope of glory,* (saith Paul to the Colossians) and he immediately adds, *whom we preach,* Col. i. 27, 28. And *unto me, who am less than the least of all the Saints, is this grace given,* What grace? *That I should preach among the Gentiles the unsearchable riches of Christ,* Eph. iii. 8. Ministers ought in duty more abundantly to preach CHRIST. Dr Sibbs is clear, 'That the special office of the 'ministry of CHRIST is to lay open CHRIST, to hold up the tapestry, and to unfold 'the hidden mysteries of CHRIST;' And therefore he exhorts, 'That we should

labour

'labour to be always speaking somewhat about CHRIST, or tending that way; when
'we speak of the law, let it drive us to CHRIST; when of moral duties, let them
'teach us to walk worthy of CHRIST: CHRIST, or something tending to CHRIST,
'should be our theme and mark to aim at,' *Sibbs Cantic.* P. 428.' And I may
feelingly say, it is the sweetest subject that ever was preached on; Is it not *as an
ointment poured forth,* whose smell is so fragrant, and whose savour is so sweet, that
therefore all the virgins love him? Is it not comprehensive of all glory, beauty,
excellency, whether of things in heaven, or of things on earth? Is it not a mystery
sweet and deep? Surely volumes are writ of JESUS CHRIST: there is line upon
line, sermon upon sermon, book upon book, and tome upon tome, and yet such
is the mystery, (as one speaks plainly) that we are all but, as yet, at the first side
of the *Single Catechism* of JESUS CHRIST: yea, Solomon, was but at, *What is his
name?* And I fear many of us know neither name nor thing. It is a worthy study
to make farther and farther discoveries of this blessed mystery; and it were to be
wished that all the ministers of CHRIST would spend themselves in the spelling,
and reading and understanding of it. Look as some great point doth require the
abilities of many scholars (and all little enough when joined together) to make a
good discovery thereof; such is this high point, this holy, sacred, glorious mystery,
worthy of the pains of all the learned; and if they would bring all their notes together, and add all their studies together, (which I have in some measure endeavoured in the following treatise) they should find still but a little of this mystery
known in comparison of what remains, and is unknown; only this they should
know, *Quod difficili intellectu, dilectabile inquisitu,* (as Bernard said) 'That which
is hard to understand, is delightful to be dived into,' and so I found it. 2. For
the act of *looking unto Jesus,* as it is comprehensive of *knowing, desiring, hoping,
believing, loving,* so also of *joying :* how then should I but be filled with joy unspeakable and glorious, whilst I was studying, writing, and especially acting my
soul in the exercise of this *looking?* If there be any duty on earth, resembling the
duty of the saints in heaven, I dare say, this is it. Mr Rutherfoord, in his epistle
to CHRIST dying writeth thus, *An act of living in Christ, and on Christ, in the
acts of seeing, enjoying, embracing, loving, resting on him, in that noon-day divinity,
and theology of beatifical vision : there is a* General Assembly *of immediately illuminated divines round about the throne, who study, lecture, preach, praise Christ night
and day : oh! what rays, what irradiations and dartings of intellectual fruition,
beholding, enjoying, living in him, and fervour of loving come from that face, that
God-visage of the Lord God Almighty, and of the Lamb that is in the midst of them?
And, oh! what reflections and reaching forth of intellectual vision, embracing, loving, wondering, are returning back to him again in a circle of glory?* Now, if this
be the saints duty, who are perfect in glory? Do not we imitate them, and feel
something

To the READER.

something of heaven in our imitation, in our *looking also unto Jesus?* I write what in some measure I have felt, and of which I hope to feel yet more: and therefore, whoever thou art that readest, I beseech thee come, warm thy heart at this blessed fire! O come, and smell the precious ointments of JESUS CHRIST! O come, *and sit under his shadow with great delight!* oh! that all men, (especially into whose hands this book shall come) would presently fall upon the practice of this gospel-art of *looking unto Jesus!* if herein they find nothing of heaven, my skill will fail me; only let them pray, that as they *look to him,* so virtue may go out of him, and fill their souls.

READER, one thing more I have to say to thee, if thou wouldst know how to carry on this duty constantly, as thou dost thy morning and evening prayer: it were not amiss every day, either morning or evening, thou wouldst take some part of it at one time, and some part of it at another time, at least for some space of time together. I know some, that in a constant daily course carry on in secret those two necessary duties of *meditation and prayer:* what the subject-matter of their meditation is, I am not very certain; only our experience can tell us, that be it heaven, or be it hell, be it sin, or be it grace, or be it what it will, if we be in the exercise of the self-same subject, either constantly or frequently, we are apt to grow remiss, or cold, or formal; and the reason is, One thing tires quickly, unless that one be all: now, that is CHRIST, for *he is all,* Col. iii. 11. If then but once a day thou wouldst make this *Jesus Christ,* thy subject to *know, consider, desire, hope, believe, joy in, call upon, and conform unto,* in his several respects of plotting, promising, performing thy redemption in his birth, life, death, resurrection, ascension, session, intercession, and coming again; and that one of these particulars might be thy one day's exercise, and so every day thou wouldst proceed from first to last, in thus *looking unto Jesus,* I suppose thou wouldst never tire thyself; And, why so? O there is a variety in this matter to be looked unto, and there is variety in the manner of looking on it. *Ex. gr.* One day thou mightest act thy *knowing of Jesus,* in carrying on the great work of thy salvation in his eternity, the next day thou mightest *consider Jesus* in that respect, and the next day thou mightest *desire after Jesus* in that respect, and the next day thou mightest *hope in Jesus* in that respect; and so on till thou comest to the last day of the work, which (besides * the object handled at large in every period, in these very actings upon the object) would in all amount to the number of eighty one days. Now, would not this variety delight? It is the observation of Mr Lockyer, on Col. i. 16. that *an holy soul cannot tire*

---

* I suppose the reader will at last once read over the whole book; and then, for his constant daily exercise, during eighty one days in a year, I leave the object in every period to be read, or not read, as he pleaseth; unless it may be in whole, or in part, conduce any thing to that one act of *knowing Jesus,* in such or such a respect.

To the READER.

tire itself in the contemplation of Jesus. How much less can it tire itself in *looking unto Jesus,* which is far more comprehensive than contemplating of JESUS? Come, try this duty, and be constant in it, at least for eighty one days in one year, and so for eighty one days in a year during thy life: and then, for thy meditations on any other subject, I shall not take thee quite off, but leave the remainder of the year, which is above three parts more to thy own choice. If thou art so resolved, I shall say no more, but, the LORD be with thee; and if sooner or later, thou findest any benefit by this work, give GOD the glory, and remember him in thy prayers, who hath taken this pains for CHRIST's honour, and thy soul's good. So rests,

Thy Servant in Christ Jesus,

ISAAC AMBROSE.

Psal. xxxiv. 5. *They looked to him, and were lightened.*
Isa. xlv. 22. *Look unto me, and be ye saved.*
Zech. xii. 10. *They shall look upon him whom they have pierced.*
Isa. lxv. 1. *I said, Behold me, Behold me, unto a nation that were not called by my name.*
Micah vii. 7. *Therefore I will look unto the Lord, I will wait for the God of my salvation.*
Numb. xxi. 8. *Every one that is bitten, when he looketh upon it, shall live.*
John iii. 15. *Whosoever believeth on him shall not perish, but have everlasting life.*
Heb. xii. 2. *Looking unto Jesus, the beginner, and finisher of our faith.*
Philip. iii. 20. *We look for the Saviour, the Lord Jesus Christ.*
2 Cor. iii. 18. *But we all with open face, beholding, as in a glass, the glory of the Lord.*

THE CONTENTS.

BOOK I.

Chap. I. The proeme, division, and opening of the words, 1
Chap. II Sect 1 The duty of looking off all other things confirmed and cleared, 2
Sect 2 An exhortation to look off all other things, 5
Sect. 3. Directions how to look off all other things, 7
Chap. III. Sect 1. An explanation of the act and object, 8
Sect. 2. The main doctrine, and confirmation of it, 10
Sect. 3 Use of reproof, 11
Sect 4. Use of exhortation, 14
Sect. 5 Motives from our wants in case of neglect, 15
Sect 6 Motives from our riches in case we are lively in this duty, 17
Sect 7. More motives to encourage us in this work, 19
Sect. 8. Use of direction. 23

BOOK II.

Chap I Sect. 1 Of the eternal generation of our Jesus, 24
Sect. 2. Of our election in Christ before all worlds, 27
Sect. 3. Of that great treaty in eternity betwixt God and Christ to save souls, 29
Sect. 4. The project, 30
Sect. 5. The counsel, ibid
Sect. 6 The foreknowledge, 32
Sect. 7. The purpose, 34
Sect 8. The decree, 35
Sect 9 The covenant. 37
Chap. II. Sect. 1. Of knowing Jesus as carrying on the great work of our salvation in that eternity, 40
Sect 2. Of considering Jesus in that respect, ib.
Sect. 3. Of desiring after Jesus in that respect, 48
Sect. 4. Of hoping in Jesus in that respect, 50
Sect. 5. Of believing in Jesus in that respect, 52

Sect 6 Of loving Jesus in that respect, 54
Sect 7. Of joying in Jesus in that respect, 56
Sect 8 Of calling on Jesus in that respect, 57
Sect. 9 Of conforming to Jesus in that respect. ib.

BOOK III

Chap. I. Sect 1. Of Christ promised by degrees, 60
Sect. 2 Of the covenant of promise, as manifested to Adam, 62
Sect. 3 Of the covenant of promise, as manifested to Abraham, 67
Sect 4 Of the covenant of promise, as manifested to Moses, 73
Sect 5 Of the covenant of promise, as manifested to David, 82
Sect 6 Of the covenant of promise, as manifested to Israel, about the time of their captivity 86
Chap II Sect 1 Of knowing Jesus, as carrying on the great work of our salvation from the creation until his first coming, 95
Sect 2 Of considering Jesus in that respect, 96
Sect. 3 Of desiring Jesus in that respect, 102
Sect 4 Of hoping in Jesus in that respect, 106
Sect 5. Of believing in Jesus in that respect, 108
Sect 6 Of loving Jesus in that respect, 112
Sect 7. Of joying in Jesus in that respect, 115
Sect. 8. Of calling on Jesus in that respect, 116
Sect. 9 Of conforming to Jesus in that respect. 118

BOOK IV. PART I.

Chap. I Sect. 1. Of the tidings of Christ, 123
Sect. 2 Of the conception of Christ, 126
Sect 3. Of the duplicity of natures in Christ, 128
Sect. 4 Of the distinction of the two natures of Christ, 130
Sect. 5 Of the union of the two natures of Christ in one and the same person, 131
Sect. 6 Of the birth of Christ, 140
Sect. 7. Of some consequents after Christ's birth, 146

Chap.

The CONTENTS.

Chap. II. Sect. 1. *Of knowing Jesus, as carrying on the great work of our salvation in his birth,* 149
Sect. 2. Of considering Jesus in that respect, ib.
Sect. 3. Of desiring after Jesus in that respect, 154
Sect. 4. Of hoping in Jesus in that respect, 155
Sect. 5. Of believing in Jesus in that respect, 158
Sect. 6. Of loving Jesus in that respect, 163
Sect. 7. Of joying in Jesus in that respect, 165
Sect. 8. Of calling on Jesus in that respect, 168
Sect. 9. Of conforming to Jesus in that respect. 169

BOOK IV. PART II.

Chap. I. Sect. 1. *Of the first year of Christ's ministry, and therein of the beginning of the gospel,* 175
Sect. 2. Of the preaching of John the Baptist, 176
Sect. 3. Of the baptism of Jesus, 178
Sect. 4. Of the fasting and temptation of Christ, 182
Sect. 5. Of the first manifestations of Christ, 188
Sect. 6. Of Christ's whipping the buyers and sellers out of the temple. 191
Chap. II. Sect. 1. *Of the second year of Christ's ministry, and of his acts in general for that year,* 194
Sect. 2. Of Christ's sermons this year, ib.
Sect. 3. Of Christ's prophetical office, 195
Sect. 4. Of Christ's miracles. 198
Chap. III. Sect. 1. *Of the third year of Christ's ministry, and generally of his actings that year,* 202
Sect. 2. Of Christ's ordination of his apostles, 203
Sect. 3. Of Christ's reception of sinners, 205
Sect. 4. Of Christ's easy yoke and light burden. 211
Chap. IV. Sect. 1. *Of the fourth year of Christ's ministry, and generally of his actings in that year,* 219
Sect. 2. Of the distinctions, or several divisions of Christ's righteousness, 220
Sect. 3. Of the holiness of Christ's nature, ib.
Sect. 4. Of the holiness of Christ's life, 221
Sect. 5. Of the great controversy, Whether we are not justified by the passive righteousness of Christ only, without any consideration had to the righteousness of Christ, either inherent in him, or performed by him? 224
Chap. V. Sect. 1. *Of knowing Jesus, as carrying on the great work of our salvation in his life,* 226
Sect. 2. Of considering Jesus in that respect, 227
Sect. 3. Of desiring after Jesus in that respect, 234
Sect. 4. Of hoping in Jesus in that respect, 237
Sect. 5. Of believing in Jesus in that respect, 240
Sect. 6. Of loving Jesus in that respect, 244
Sect. 7. Of joying in Jesus in that respect, 246
Sect. 8. Of calling on Jesus in that respect, 249
Sect. 9. Of conforming to Jesus in that respect. ib.

BOOK IV. PART III.

Chap. I. Sect. 1. *Of the day of Christ's sufferings, divided into parts, and hours,* 259
Sect. 2. Of the brook over which Christ passed, 261
Sect. 3. Of the garden into which Christ entred, 264
Sect. 4. Of the prayer that Christ there made, 265
Sect. 5. Of the dolours, and agonies, that Christ there suffered, 268
Sect. 6 Of Judas's treason, Christ's apprehension, binding and leading unto Annas, 271
Sect. 7. Of Christ's examination, and condemnation, with their appendices. 275
Chap. II. Sect. 1. *Of Christ's indictment, and Judas's fearful end,* 281
Sect. 2. Of Christ's mission to Herod, and the transactions there, 283
Sect. 3. Of Christ and Barrabas compared, and of the question debated betwixt Pilate and the Jews, 286
Sect. 4 Of Christ stripped, whipped, clothed in purple, and crowned with thorns, 288
Sect. 5. Of Christ brought forth and sentenced, 292
Sect. 6. Of Christ's crucifying, with its appendices, 295
Sect. 7. Of the consequents after Christ's crucifying. 299
Chap. III. Sect. 1. *Of knowing Jesus, as carrying on the great work of our salvation in his death,* 300
Sect. 2. Of considering Jesus in that respect, 301

The CONTENTS.

Sect. 3. Of desiring Jesus in that respect, 306
Sect. 4. Of hoping in Jesus in that respect, 309
Sect. 5. Of believing in Jesus in that respect, 314
Sect. 6. Of loving Jesus in that respect, 320
Sect. 7. Of joying in Jesus in that respect, 322
Sect. 8. Of calling on Jesus in that respect, 324
Sect. 9. Of conforming to Jesus in that respect. 325

BOOK IV. PART IV

Chap I Sect. 1 *Of the time of Christ's resurrection*, 334
Sect 2. Of the reasons of Christ's resurrection, 336
Sect 3. Of the manner of Christ's resurrection, 337
Sect. 4. Of the arguments of Christ's resurrection, 341
Sect 5. Of Christ's apparition to Mary Magdalene, 344
Sect. 6. Of Christ's apparition to his ten disciples, 355
Sect. 7. Of Christ's apparition to all his apostles, 360
Sect 8. Of Christ's apparition to some of his apostles at the sea of Tiberias. 366
Chap II Sect. 1. *Of knowing Jesus, as carrying on the great work of our salvation in his resurrection*, 368
Sect 2. Of considering Jesus in that respect, ib.
Sect. 3. Of desiring Jesus in that respect, 374
Sect. 4. Of hoping in Jesus in that respect, 377
Sect 5. Of believing in Jesus in that respect, 383
Sect. 6. Of loving Jesus in that respect, 387
Sect. 7. Of joying in Jesus in that respect, 389
Sect 8. Of calling on Jesus in that respect, 391
Sect. 9. Of conforming to Jesus in that respect. 392

BOOK IV. PART V.

Chap. I Sect 1. *Of Christ's ascension, and of the manner how*, 400
Sect 2. Of the place whither he ascended, 402
Sect 3. Of the reasons why he ascended, ib.
Sect. 4. Of God's right hand, and of Christ's session there, 405
Sect. 5. Of the two natures wherein Christ sits at God's right hand, 407
Sect. 6. Of the reasons why Christ doth sit on God's right hand, 408
Sect 7. Of the time when the Holy Ghost was sent, 410
Sect. 8 Of the persons to whom the Holy Ghost was sent, 412
Sect 9 Of the manner how the Holy Ghost was sent, ibid
Sect 10. Of the measure of the Holy Ghost now given, 415
Sect 11. Of the reasons why the Holy Ghost was sent 417
Chap II Sect. 1. *Of knowing Jesus, as carrying on the great work of our salvation in his ascension, session, and mission of the Spirit*, 425
Sect 2 Of considering Jesus in that respect, ib.
Sect. 3. Of desiring after Jesus in that respect, 429
Sect 4 Of hoping in Jesus in that respect, 431
Sect 5. Of believing in Jesus in that respect, 438
Sect 6 Of loving Jesus in that respect, 444
Sect 7 Of joying in Jesus in that respect, 446
Sect 8 Of calling on Jesus in that respect, 448
Sect 9 Of conforming unto Jesus in that respect 449

BOOK IV. PART VI

Chap 1. Sect 1 *What the intercession of Christ is*, 453
Sect. 2 According to what nature Christ doth intercede, 454
Sect 3 To whom Christ's intercession is directed, 455
Sect 4. For whom this intercession is made, 456
Sect 5 What agreement there is betwixt Christ's intercessions, and the intercessions of the high priests of old, ibid
Sect 6. What the difference is betwixt Christ's intercessions, and the intercessions of the high priests of old, 458
Sect 7. What the properties of this intercession of Christ are, 459
Sect. 8 Wherein the intercession of Christ consists, 460
Sect. 9 How powerful and prevailing Christ's intercessions are with God his Father, 467
Sect. 10. Of the reasons of Christ's intercession 470

Ch.

The CONTENTS.

Chap. II. Sect. 1. *Of knowing Jesus, carrying on the great work of our salvation in his intercession*, 472
Sect. 2. Of considering Jesus in that respect, *ib.*
Sect. 3. Of desiring after Jesus in that respect, 476
Sect. 4. Of hoping in Jesus in that respect, 478
Sect. 5. Of believing in Jesus in that respect, 481
Sect. 6. Of loving Jesus in that respect, 485
Sect. 7. Of joying in Jesus in that respect, 487
Sect. 8. Of praying to, and praising of Jesus in that respect, 489
Sect. 9. Of conforming to Jesus in that respect. 490

BOOK V.

Chap. I. Sect. 1. *Of Christ's preparing for judgment*, 494
Sect. 2. Of Christ's coming to judgment, 497
Sect. 3. Of Christ's summoning of the elect to come under judgment, 500
Sect. 4. Of Christ and the saints meeting at the judgment-day, 505
Sect. 5. Of Christ sentencing his saints, 507
Sect. 6. Of Christ and the saints judging the rest of the world, 511
Sect. 7. Of Christ and his saints going up into heaven, and of the end of this world, 522
Sect. 8. Of Christ's surrendring, and delivering up the kingdom to God, even the Father, 525
Sect. 9. Of Christ's subjection to the Father, that God may be *all in all*, 529
Sect. 10. Of Christ (notwithstanding this) being *all in all* to his blessed, saved, and redeemed saints, to all eternity. - 531
Chap. II. Sect. 1. *Of knowing Jesus, as carrying on the great work of our Salvation in his second Coming*, 539
Sect. 2. Of considering Jesus in that respect, *ib.*
Sect. 3. Of desiring after Jesus in that respect, 544
Sect. 4. Of hoping in Jesus in that respect, 547
Sect. 5. Of believing in Jesus in that respect, 552
Sect. 6. Of loving Jesus in that respect, 558
Sect. 7. Of joying in Jesus in that respect, 560
Sect. 8. Of calling on Jesus in that respect, 562
Sect. 9. Of conforming to Jesus in that respect, *ib.*
The Conclusion. 566

LOOKING

LOOKING UNTO JESUS.

THE FIRST BOOK.

CHAP. I.

Hebrews, Chap. xii. Verse 2. *Looking unto Jesus, the Beginner, and Finisher, of our Faith.*

The Proeme, Division, and Opening of the Words.

THE most excellent subject to discourse or write of, is JESUS CHRIST. Augustine, having read Cicero his works, commended them for their eloquence, but he passed this sentence upon them, *They are not sweet, because the name of Jesus is not in them.* And Bernard's saying is near the same, *If thou writest, it doth not relish with me, unless I read Jesus there; if thou disputest or conferrest, it doth not relish well with me, unless Jesus found there.* Indeed all we say is but unsavoury, if it be not seasoned with this salt. *I determined not to know any thing among you* (saith Paul) *save Jesus Christ, and him crucified.* He resolved with himself before he preached among the Corinthians, that this should be the only point of knowledge that he would profess himself to have skill in; and that, in the course of his ministry he would labour to bring them to: this he made *the breadth, and length, and depth, and heighth of his knowledge;* yea doubtless (saith he) *and I count all things but loss for the excellency of the knowledge of Christ Jesus my Lord,* Eph. iii. 18. Phil. iii. 8.

In this knowledge of Christ, there is an excellency above all other knowledge in the world; there is nothing more pleasing and comfortable, more animating and enlivening, more ravishing and soul-contenting; only Christ is the sun and centre of all divine revealed truths, we can preach nothing else as the object of our faith, as the necessary element of your soul's salvation, which doth not some way or other, either meet in Christ, or refer to Christ; only Christ is the whole of man's happiness, the sun to enlighten him, the Physician to heal him, the wall of fire to defend him, the friend to comfort him, the pearl to enrich him, the ark to support him, the rock to sustain him under the heaviest pressures, *As an hiding place from the wind, and a covert from the tempest, as rivers of waters in a dry place, and as the shadow of a great rock in a weary land,* Isa. xxxii. 2. Only Christ is that ladder betwixt earth and heaven, the Mediator betwixt God and Man, a mystery, which the angels of heaven desire to pry, and peep, and look into, 1 Pet. i. 12. Here's a blessed subject indeed, who would not be glad to pry into it, to be acquainted with it? *This is life eternal to know God, and Jesus Christ whom he hath sent,* Joh. xvii. 3. Come then, let us look on this sun of righteousness;

ness: we cannot receive harm but good by such a look; indeed by looking long on the natural sun we may have our eyes dazled, and our faces blackned; but by looking unto Jesus Christ, we shall have our eyes clearer, and our faces fairer; if *the light of the eye rejoice the heart*, Prov. xv. 30. How much more, when we have such a blessed object to look upon? As Christ is more excellent than all the world, so this sight transcends all other sights; it is the epitome of a Christian's happiness, the quintessence of evangelical duties, looking unto JESUS.

In the text we have the act and object, the act in the original is very emphatical, [*aphorontes eis*;] the English doth not fully express it; it signifies an averting, or drawing off the eye from one object to another: there are two expressions, [*apo* and *eis*;] the one signifies a turning of the eye from all other objects; the other a fast fixing of the eye upon such an object, and only upon such. So it is both a looking off, and a looking on. On what? That is the object, *a looking unto Jesus*; a title that denotes his mercy and bounty, as Christ denotes his office and function. I shall not be so curious as to enquire why Jesus, and not Christ is nominated; I suppose the person is aimed at, which implies them both; only this may be observed, that Jesus is the purest gospel-name of all other names; Jesus was not the dialect of the old Testament; the first place that ever we read of this title as given to Christ, it is in Matth. i. 21. *Thou shalt call his name JESUS, for he shall save his people from their sins.* Some observe that this name *Jesus*, was given him twice; once till death, Matth. i. 21. and afterwards for ever, Phil. ii. 10. The first, was a note of his entring into covenant with God, to fulfil the law for us, and to die for our sins; the second was a note of so meritorious a person, who for his humility was more exalted than any person ever hath been, or shall be. First, Jesus was the humble name of his deserving grace; now Jesus is the exalted name of his transcendent glory: at first the Jews did crucify Jesus and his name; and the apostle did then distrust, whether Jesus was the true Jesus; but now God hath raised him from the dead, and hath *highly exalted him, and given him a name above every name, that at the name of Jesus every knee shall bow, of things in heaven, and things in earth, and things under the earth*, Luke xxiv. 21. Phil. ii. 9, 10. My meaning is not to insist on this name, in contradiction to other names of Christ, he is often called Christ, and Lord, and Mediator, and Son of God and Emmanuel; why? Jesus is all these, Jesus is Christ, as he is the anointed of God; and Jesus is the Lord, as he hath dominion over all the world; and Jesus is Mediator, as he is the reconciler of God and man; and Jesus is the Son of God, as he was eternally begotten before all worlds; and Jesus is Emmanuel, as he was incarnate, and so God with us. Only because Jesus signifies Saviour, and this name was given him upon that very account, *For he shall save his people from their sins.* I shall make this my design to look at Jesus more especially, as carrying on the great work of our salvation from first to last. This indeed is the glad tidings, the gospel, the gospel-privilege, and our gospel-duty, *Looking unto Jesus*.

CHAP. II. SECT. I.

The duty of looking off all other things, confirmed and cleared.

First Doctrine.

BUT first we must look off all other things, the note is this, We must take off our mind from every thing which might divert us in our Christian race from looking unto Jesus. [*Aphorontes,*] the first word, or first piece of a word in my text, speaks to us thus, hands off, or eyes off from any thing that stands in the way of Jesus Christ. I remember 'twas wrote over Plato's door, "There's none may come hither, that is not a "geometer." But on the door of my text is written clean contrary; *No earthly-minded man must enter here*. Not any thing in the world, be it never so excellent, if it stand in the way of Jesus Christ, is to be named the same day; we must not give a look, or squint at any thing that may hinder this fair and lovely sight of Jesus.

This was the Lord's charge to Lot, *Look not behind thee*, Gen. xix. 17. He was so far to renounce and detest the lewdness of Sodom, as that he must not vouchsafe a look towards it.

At that day shall a man look towards his Maker, and his eyes shall have respect to the holy One of Israel, and he shall not look to the altars, the work of his hands, Isa. xvii. 7, 8. This was the fruit of God's chastisement on the elect Israel, that he should not give a look to the altars, lest they diverted, or drew his eyes from off his Maker.

We look not at the things which are seen, but at the things which are not seen, saith Paul, 2 Cor. iv. 18. A Christian's aim is beyond visible things. O when a soul comes to know what an eternal God is, and what an eternal Jesus is, and what an eternal crown is; when it knows that great design of Christ to save poor souls, and to communicate himself eternally to such poor creatures, this takes off the edge of its desires as to visible temporal things; what are they in comparison?

1. *Question*, But what things are they we must look off in this respect? I answer,——1. Good things. 2. Evil Things.

1. Good Things. The apostle tells us of a cloud of witnesses in the former verse, which no question, in their season, we are to look unto. But when this second object comes in sight, he scatters the cloud quite, and sets up Jesus himself; now the apostle willeth us [*aphoran*] to turn our eyes from them, and to turn them hither to Jesus Christ. *q. d.* If you will indeed see a sight once for all, look to him, the saints though they be guides to us, yet are they but followers to him; he is the arch-guide, the leader of them, and of us all. Look on him. There is a time when James may say, 'Take my brethren the prophets, who have spo-'ken in the name of the Lord, for an example:' But when Jesus comes forth, that said, *I have given you an example*, an example above all examples, then *be silent, O all flesh, before the Lord*, James v. 10. John xiii. 15. Zech. ii. 13. Let all saints and seraphims, then cover their faces with their wings, that we may look on Jesus, and let all other sights go.

2. Evil things, { 1. In general. 2. In special.

1. In general, we must look off all things that are on this side Jesus Christ, and so much the rather, if they be evil things. In a word, we must look off all self; whether it be sinful self, or natural self, or religious self, in this case we must draw our eyes off all these things.

2. In special, we must look off all that is in the world; and that the apostle compriseth under three heads, *The lusts of the eyes, the lusts of the flesh, and the pride of life*, 1 John ii. 16. 1. Pleasures, profits and honours.

1. We must look off this world, in respect of its sinful pleasures; Jude tells us, *such as are sensual have not the Spirit*, Jude verse 18, 19. We cannot fixedly look on pleasures, and look on Jesus at once. Job tells us, *That they that take up the timbrel and harp, and rejoice at the sound of the organ, that spend their days in mirth*, are the same that say unto God, *Depart from us, for we desire not the knowledge of thy ways; what is the Almighty that we should serve him? And what profit should we have if we pray unto him?* Job xxi. 12, 13, 14, 15. We have a lively example of this in Augustine's conversion; he would indeed have had Christ, and his pleasures too, but when he saw it would not be, Oh! what conflicts are within him? In his orchard (as he stories it in his book of confessions) all his pleasures past represented themselves before his eyes, saying, What wilt thou depart from us for ever, and shall we be no more with thee for ever? O Lord, (saith Augustine writing this confession) turn away my mind from thinking that which they objected to my soul! What filth? What shameful pleasures did they lay before my eyes? At length, after this combat, a shower of tears came from him, and casting himself on the ground under a fig-tree, he cries it out, O Lord, how long, how long shall I say, To-morrow, to-morrow? Why not, To-day, Lord, why not, to-day? Why should there not be an end of my filthy life even at this hour? Immediately after this he heard a voice, as if it had been of a boy or girl, singing by, Take up and read, take up and read: and thereupon opening his Bible, that lay by him at hand, he read in silence the first chapter that offered itself, wherein was written, *Let us walk honestly as in the day, not in rioting and drunkenness, not in chambering and wantonness, not in strife and envying, but put ye on the Lord Jesus, and make not provision for the flesh, to fulfil the lusts thereof*, Rom. xiii. 13, 14. Further than this sentence I would not read (saith Augustine) neither indeed was it needful, for presently, as if light had been poured into my heart, all the darkness of my doubtfulness fled away. His eye was now taken off his pleasures, and for ever after it was set on Jesus.

2. We must look off this world in respect of

its sinful profits. A look on this keeps off our looking unto Jesus. *Whosoever loveth the world, the love of the Father is not in him,* 1 John ii. 15. Just so much as the world prevails in us, so much is God's love abated both in us, and towards us. *Ye adulterers and adulteresses,* (saith James) *know ye not that the friendship of the world is enmity with God?* James iv. 4. Covetousness in Christians is spiritual adultery, when we have enough in God and Christ, and yet we desire to make up our happiness in the creature, this is plain whoring. Now there are degrees in this spiritual whoredom, as——

1. The minding of this world; ye know there may be adultery in affection, when the body is not defiled; unclean glances are a degree of lust, so the children of God may have some worldly glances, straggling thoughts; when the temptation is strong, the world may be greatned in their esteem and imagination.

2. The setting of the heart upon the world; this is an higher degree of this spiritual adultery, our hearts are due and proper to Christ, now to set them on the world, which should be chaste and loyal to Jesus Christ, what adultery is this? *Ye cannot serve God and Mammon,* Matth. vi. 24. That woman that is not contented with one husband, must needs be an harlot.

3. The preferring of the world before Christ himself. This is the height of covetousness, and the height of this adultery; what, to make the members of Christ the members of an harlot? Why, worldlings! those admiring thoughts are Christ's, those pains are Christ's, that love is Christ's, that time, that care, that earnestness is Christ's; they are all Christ's, and will you give that which is Christ's unto the world? And prefer the world before Christ with his own? What, live as professed prostitutes, that prefer every one before their husbands? How will this expose you to the scorn of men and angels? At the last day they will come pointing and say, This is the man that made not God his strength, but trusted in the abundance of his riches; this is the Gadaren that loved his swine more than Christ Jesus, Ps. lvii. 2. *Love not the world* (saith John) 1 John ii. 15. Christ is never precious in man's apprehension, so long as the world seems glorious to him. As we begin to relish sweetness in Christ, so the world begins to be bitter to us. The more sweetness we taste in the one, the more bitterness we taste in the other.

4. We must look off the world in respect of its sinful honours; what is this honour but a certain inordinate desire to be well thought of, or well spoken of, to be praised, or glorified of men? As if a man should run up and down street after a feather flying in the air, and tossed hither and thither with the gusts and blasts of infinite men's mouths, it is a question, whether ever he get it. But if he do, it is but a feather; such is this pride of life, honour, vain glory; it is hard to obtain it, but if obtained, it is but the breath of a few men's mouths, that alter upon every light occasion; but that which is worst of all, it hinders our sight of Jesus Christ, *Not many wise men after the flesh, not many mighty, not many noble are called,* 1 Cor. i. 26. Worldly honour keeps many back from Christ, and therefore *Moses, when he was come to years, refused to be called the son of Pharoah's daughter,——Esteeming the reproaches of Christ, greater riches than all the treasures of Egypt,* Heb. xi. 24, 26. If the blind man in the way to Jericho, had depended on the breath or liking or approbation of the multitude, he had never received the benefit of his sight, for *they* (saith the text) *which went before rebuked him, that he should hold his peace,* Luke xviii. 39. They disswaded him from running and crying so vehemently after Christ; experience tells us how these things pull and draw us off from Jesus Christ, *The lusts of the eyes, the lusts of the flesh, and the pride of life.*

2. *Quest.* But why must we look off every thing that diverts our looking unto Jesus?

1. Because we cannot look fixedly on Christ, and such things together, and at once; the eye cannot look upwards and downwards at once in a direct line; we cannot seriously mind heaven and earth in one thought, *No man can serve two masters,* saith Christ, Matth. vi. 24. Especially such as jar, and who have contrary employments, as Christ and mammon have.

2. Because, whilst we look on these things, we cannot see the beauty that is in Christ; suppose a squint look on Christ, whilst we have a direct look on other things, alas! Christ will be of no esteem that while; this was the voice of sinners concerning Christ, *He hath no form nor comliness, and when we see him there is no beauty that we should desire him,*

An Exhortation to look off all other Things.

him, Isa. liii. 2. Indeed beauty is the attractive of the soul, the soul must see a beauty in that which it lets out itself to in desiring: but our wishing looks on other things make Christ but mean and contemptible in our eyes.

3. Because all other things, in comparison of Christ, are not worthy a look, they are but as vile things, as under things, as poor and low and mean and base things, in comparison of Christ. *I count all things but loss* (saith Paul) *for the excellency of the knowledge of Christ Jesus my Lord.—I count them but dung, that I may win Christ,* Phil. iii. 8. [*skubalu,*] some translate it *chaff*; others, *dogs-meat*; others, *excrements, dung*; all agree, it is such a thing as men usually cast away from them with some indignation.

4. Because it is according to the very law of marriage, *Therefore shall a man forsake father and mother, and cleave to his wife,* Gen. ii. 24. The Lord Christ marries himself to the souls of his saints, *I will betrothe thee unto me for ever, I will betrothe thee unto me in righteousness, and in judgment, and in loving kindness, and in mercies,* Hos. ii. 19. And for this cause the soul must forsake all, and cleave unto Christ, as married wives use to do, we must leave off all for our Husband the Lord Jesus; *Hearken, O daughter, and consider and incline thine ear, forget also thy own people, and thy father's house,* Psal. xlv. 10.

5. Because Christ is a jealous Christ. Now, jealousy is a passion in the soul, that will not endure any sharing in the object beloved: the woman that hath a jealous husband, must leave all her old companions: if she cast any amorous looks or glances after them, the husband will be jealous, and *jealousy is cruel as the grave,* Cant. viii. 6. Christians! our God *is a jealous God,* Exod. xx. 5. Our Christ is a jealous Christ, he cannot endure that we should look on any other things, so as to lust after them.

6. Because all other things can never satisfy the eye, *All things are full of labour* (saith Solomon) *man cannot utter it, the eye is not satisfied with seeing,* Eccl. i. 8. It is but wearied with looking on divers objects, and yet still desires new ones: but once admit it to behold that glorious sight of Christ, and then it rests fully satisfied. Hence it is, that the daughters of Zion are called to come forth; *Go forth, O ye daughters of Zion, and behold King Solomon with the crown wherewith his mother crowned him in the day of his espousals, and in the day of the gladness of his heart,* Cant. iii. 11. Go forth, O ye daughters of Zion, lay aside all private and earthly affections, and look upon this glory of Christ. As the daughters of Jerusalem sitting or remaining in their chambers, closets, houses, could not behold the glory of King Solomon passing by, and therefore they were willed to come forth of their doors: even so, if we will behold the great King, Jesus Christ in his most excellent glory (a sight able to satisfy the eye, and to ravish the heart) we must come out of our doors, we must come out of ourselves, otherwise we cannot see his glory; we are in ourselves shut up in a dark dungeon, and therefore we are called upon to come forth into the clear light of faith, and with the eyes of faith to behold, in daily meditation, the glory of Christ Jesus.

SECT. II.

An exhortation to look off all other things.

ONE word of exhortation, Christians! I beseech you look off all other things, especially all evil things. I know I am pleading with you for an hard thing, I had need of the rhetorick of an angel, to persuade you to turn your eyes from off these things; nay, if I had, all were too little, *It is God only must persuade Japhet to dwell in the tents of Shem,* and yet let me offer a few considerations, venture at a persuading of you, and leave the issue with God.

1. Consider that all other evil things are in God's account as very nothing. *Verily every man at his best estate is altogether vanity,* Psal. xxxix. 5. Not only man, but every man; nor every man in his worst condition, but every man at his best estate; nor every man at his best estate is little worth, but every man at his best estate is vanity, emptiness, nothing; it may be so in part, nay, but in every part, he is wholly, totally, altogether vanity. Would any man think, that a great, rich honourable man, whom we look upon with such high admiring thoughts, should be laid thus low in God's esteem? O wonder, wonder! and yet 'tis no such wonder, but one day you shall find the experience of this truth yourselves. *Rich men have*

have slept their sleeps, and none of the men of might have found their hands, or, as others render it, *They have found nothing in their hands*, Pſal. lxxvi. 5. That is, rich men have paſſed over this life, as men do paſs over a ſleep, imagining themſelves to have golden mountains, and rocks of diamond, but when they awake at the day of death, they find themſelves to have nothing. Why Chriſtian, *Wilt thou ſet thine eyes upon that which is not?* Prov. xxiii. 5. 1ſt. Obſerve that riches are not, they are nothing, thoſe things that make men great in the eyes of the world, are nothing in the eyes of God. 2. Obſerve, That God would not have us ſo much as ſet our eyes upon them, they are not objects worth the looking on. 3. Obſerve, with what indignation he ſpeaks againſt thoſe that will ſet their eyes upon theſe vanities, wilt thou ſet thine eyes upon a thing which is not? *q. d.* What a vain, unreaſonable, ſottiſh, ſenſeleſs thing is this?

2. Conſider, That all ſuch things (if they are any thing) they are but trifles, deceits, thorns, miſeries, uncertain things; this is an ordinary theme, it is every man's object, and every man's ſubject, and a very eaſy thing it is, to declaim up the vanity, miſery, uncertainty of the creatures: ay, but do you make it the matter of your meditation, and be you ſerious in it, think of it deeply, and deſire God to be in your thoughts. Oh what work will it then make in your breaſts! Oh how would it wean your loves and deſires off all theſe things! Chriſtians! conſider all theſe adjuncts of all ſublunary things. When the creatures tempt you, be not enticed by the beauty of them, ſo as to forget their vanity: ſay, Here is a flower, fair, but fading: here is a glaſs that's bright, but very brittle.

3. Conſider the difference of theſe objects, Chriſt, and all other things; as thus, all other things are vanities, but Chriſt is a real, ſolid, ſubſtantial, excellent, glorious thing; all other things are temporary, fading things, but Chriſt is an enduring ſubſtance, *The ſame yeſterday, and to day, and for ever, which is, and which was, and which is to come,* Rev. i. 4. All other things are thorns, vexations of ſpirit, but Chriſt is full of joy and comfort, a moſt raviſhing object, all compoſed of loves, or *altogether lovely*. O who would make it his buſineſs to fill his coffers with pebbles, when he may have pearls, or gold or ſilver, or precious things? What, muſt you look off your ſins! Why, ſee before you the graces of the Spirit of Chriſt. Muſt you look off your idle ſinful company? See before you *the fellowſhip of the Father, and the Son, the Lord Jeſus Chriſt*, 1 John i. 3. Muſt you look off your pomp and glory? See before you the privilege of adoption? you ſhall be called *the ſons and daughters of God, heirs and co-heirs with Chriſt*, Rom. viii. 17. Muſt you look off worldly riches? See before you the riches of the graces of Chriſt. Muſt you look off ſinful pleaſures? See before you fulneſs of joy, *at Chriſt's right-hand are pleaſures evermore*, Pſal. xvi. 11. Muſt you look off your own righteouſneſs? See before you the righteouſneſs of Chriſt Jeſus. O what a vaſt difference is there betwixt theſe objects, Chriſt, and all other things!

4. Conſider, that Chriſt looked off heaven and heavenly things for you, how much more ſhould you look off the earth and earthly things, the world and worldly things for him? Chriſt left the glory, the company, the pleaſures of paradiſe for you, and *he made himſelf of no reputation*, he nothing'd himſelf (as it were) for you; *you know the grace of our Lord Jeſus Chriſt, who though he was rich, yet for your ſakes he became poor, that you through his poverty might be rich,* 2 Cor. viii. 9. O let that melting love win you to him, and wean you off all other things!

5. Conſider, that the rational ſoul of man is of too high a birth to ſpend its ſtrength upon other things; the ſoul of man is of the ſame nature with angels; is a kind of divine ſpark. Now, if a man have a golden mill, he will not uſe it to grind dirt, ſtraws and rotten ſticks in. The ſoul, the mind, the thinking faculty of man is too high to be exerciſed in the things of this earth. The ſoul is of a moſt excellent capacious nature, it is fit to converſe not only with angels, but with the eternal God himſelf, with Father, Son and Holy Ghoſt; it is of a tranſcendent being; put all the world into the ballance with it, and it is nothing in compariſon. The ſoul of the meaneſt galley ſlave is more than heaven and earth, than ſun and moon and ſtars, and all the hoſt of heaven. Now, if a man's ſoul be of ſuch an high-born nature, if the Lord hath put ſuch a ſpirit into the boſom of man; for him, to beſtow the ſtrength of it upon low, baſe, mean and earthly things, oh what an evil is this!

6. Con-

6. Confider, how short is the time that you have here in this world: This is the argument of the apostle, *Because the time is short, therefore let us use the world as if we used it not*, 1 Cor. vii. 29, 31. Therefore let our hearts be taken off these things, yet a few days, and you shall be here no more; time passeth on, many hundred diseases are ready to assault you: you that are reading, or hearing, talking, or walking, you must very shortly be carried on men's shoulders, and laid in the dust, and there left to the worms in darkness and corruption; you are almost there already, it is but a few days, or months, or years, and what is that when once they are gone and past? And oh! *What is a man profited if he gain the whole world, and then lose his soul?* Matth. xvi. 26.

7. Consider the great account that you are to give of all earthly things: it is the sin of most of the sons of men, to look on creature-comforts, but they consider not the account they must give for them. Oh here's a prevailing motive to take off your eyes! consider the last accounts; what if ye were now to die, and to go the way of all flesh, and then to make up your reckoning, what good would it do you to remember all those contentments and pleasures you once enjoyed upon the earth? If the factor, after many years spent in foreign countries, at last returns home with this bill of accounts, 'Thus much for singing, so much for dancing, this for courting, that for feasting.' Who would not blame him for so fond a reckoning! oh it will be a sad reckoning, if the bill come in, that you have spent most of your time in looking and gazing upon earthly things.

SECT. III.

Directions how to look off all other things.

1. STUDY every day more and more the vanity of the creature: read over the book of Ecclesiastes well, it is enough that, through the assistance of Christ, to teach you that lesson. A serious and fruitful meditation of that word, *Vanity of vanities, saith the preacher, vanity of vanities, all is vanity*, Eccl. i. 2. What work might it make in your hearts! Men usually look on these things through some false glass, or at a distance, which makes them so admire them; but if they could see them truly in themselves, oh how uncomely would they be? Or if they could see them as compared to Christ, oh how vain would they be? Honours and greatness in that respect, would appear as bubbles, pleasures and delights in that respect, would appear as shadows.

2. Converse but a little with any evil thing on this side Christ; have as little to do with the world, the sinful pleasures, profits, riches, manners of it, as possibly you can; the lesser the better. Things of this world have a glutinous quality, if you let the heart lie any while amongst them, it will cleave unto them, and if it once cleave to them there will be no way, but either repentance or hell-fire must part them.

3. Be more and better acquainted with Jesus Christ; get nearer to him, be more in communion with him, get more tastes of Christ and heaven, and earth will relish the worse for them. Oh! when I look on Christ and consider, That he that was the Lord of heaven and earth, put himself into so poor and low a condition, merely for the redeeming of his elect, how should this but deaden my heart to the world? *I account all things but loss for the excellency of the knowlege of Christ Jesus my Lord; and do count them but dung that I may win Christ*, Phil. iii. 8. If Christ be in view, all the world then is but dung and dross, and loss in comparison; the glory of Christ will darken all other things in the world.

4. Set before us the examples of such saints, who accounted themselves pilgrims and strangers upon earth. The apostle gives you a catalogue of such, *who confessed that they were strangers and pilgrims on the earth*; and see how they are used, *They were stoned, they were sawn asunder, were tempted, were slain with the sword, they wandred about in sheep-skins, and goat-skins, being destitute, afflicted, tormented: Who were these? They were they of whom the world was not worthy*, Heb. xi. 13. 37, 38. Oh! when you read, or hear how joyfully these servants of the most High went thro' their wilderness-condition, methinks this should take off your hearts from earthly things.

5. Go in your meditations to heaven, and keep there a while: the mind that is in heaven cannot attend these earthly things: would a man leave his plough and harvest in the field, to run with

children

children an hunting after butter-flies? No more will a soul that is taking a survey of heaven and heavenly things, fix his eyes on such poor things below: *Non vacat exiguis, &c.* is the character of a truly prudent man: the children of that kingdom above, have no while for trifles, and especially when they are imployed in the affairs of the kingdom. Oh! when a Christian hath but a glimpse of eternity, and then looks down on the world again, how doth he contemn and vilipend these things? *How doth he say of laughter, thou art mad, and of mirth, what is this thou dost?* Eccl. ii. 2. Whilst the saints are tasting heaven, they feel such sweet, that they care not for other things: Christians! how would this meditation wean your hearts? and make you laugh at the fooleries of the world? And scorn to be cheated with such childish toys? If the devil had set upon Peter in the mount, when he saw Christ in his transfiguration, and Moses and Elias talking with him, would he so easily have been drawn to deny his Lord? What, with all that glory in his eye? So if the devil should set upon a believing soul, and persuade his heart to profits, or pleasures, or honours of the world, when he is taken up in the mount with Christ, what would such a soul say? 'Get thee behind me, Satan, wouldst thou persuade me from hence with many trifling toys! wouldst thou have me felt these joys for nothing? Is there any honour or delight like this? Or can that be profit, which loseth me this?' Some such answer would the soul return: Oh! if we could keep the taste of our souls continually delighted with the sweetness of heaven, as a man would spit out aloes after honey, so should we spit out all the baits of the world with disdain.

6. Cry mightily unto God, that he would take off your hearts and eyes, *Turn away mine eyes from beholding vanity,* Psal. cxix. 37. prays David, Either God must do it, or you will be wearied in the multitude of your endeavours: but, if the Lord draw off the eye, it will be drawn indeed. *Incline my heart unto thy testimonies, and not to covetousness,* prays David again, Psal. cxix. 36. If the heart bend downwards, then go to God to erect it, and to incline it heaven-wards; if it be after covetousness, then cry to God, and say, *Lord, not after covetousness, but after thy testimonies incline my heart.*

I have hitherto stood only at the door of the text, to call you in; if now you will enter and be intent, and fix your eyes, I'll shew you a blessed, a most glorious sight. But, *First,* I must explain the act, You must look. *Secondly,* The object, You must look on Jesus.

CHAP. III. SECT. I.

An explanation of the act and object.

1. FOR the act you must look. Looking is either ocular or mental.

First, For ocular vision, there may be some use of that in heaven, for there we shall look on Jesus. *With these eyes shall I behold him,* saith Job, Job xix. 27. *And we shall see him as he is,* saith the apostle, 1 John iii. 2. *Now we see him as in a glass, then we shall see him face to face,* 1 Cor. xiii. 12. But till then, *We must walk by faith, not by sight,* 2 Cor. v. 7.

Secondly, For mental vision, or the inward eye, that is it that will take up our discourse, and that is it which the apostle speaks of in his prayers for the Ephesians, *That the eyes of their understanding may be opened, that they may know,* &c. Eph. i. 18. Now the excellency of this mental sight is far above the ocular sight: for there are more excellent things to be seen by the eye of the mind, than by the eye of the body; we only see a piece of the creation by the eye of the body, but the mind reacheth every thing that is in it, yea, the mind reacheth to him that made it: God is invisible, and yet this eye sees God. It is said of Moses, That *he saw him that is invisible,* Heb. xi. 27. 2d. It is the sight of the mind, that gives light and vigour to the sight of the eyes; take away the inward light, and the light of the external sense is but as darkness and death. 3. It is the sight of the mind that looks into the worth, use, &c. propriety of any thing presented. The eye can see a thing, but not the worth of it; a beast looks on gold, as well as a man, but the sight and knowledge of the worth of it is by the internal light of the mind; so the eye can see a thing, but not the use of it; a child looks on a tool in the hand of a workman, but the sight and knowledge of the use of it, is only by a man of reason that hath internal light to judge of it: and so the eye can see a thing, but not the propriety of of it; a beast looks on his pasture, but he likes it, not because it is his, but because it is a pasture and well furnished. Now, we know that the worth and use and property of a thing, are the very cream of the things themselves, and this the eye of the mind conveys, and not the eyes of the body. 'Tis said of Joseph, that *he saw his brethren and knew them, but they knew not him*, Gen. xlii. 7, 8. This was the reason why Joseph was so exceedingly taken at the sight of his brethren, that his bowels wrought with joy, and a kind of compassion towards them; but they were before him as common strangers; though they saw Joseph their brother a prince, yet they were taken no more with the sight of him, than of any other man, because they knew him not.

Again, this mental looking, is either notional and theoretical, or practical and experimental, the first, we call barely the look of our minds; 'tis an enlightening of our understandings with some measure of speculative light, in spiritual and heavenly mysteries. The 2d. we call the look of our minds and hearts, whereby we not only see spiritual things, but we are affected with them: we desire, love, believe, joy and embrace them. To this purpose is that rule, 'That words of knowlege do sometimes signify the affections in the heart, and the effects thereof in our lives.' And this was the look which Paul longed for, *That I may know him, and the power of his resurrection*, Phil. iii. 10. *i. e.* That he might have experience of that power, that it might so communicate itself unto him, as to work upon him to all the ends of it. And this was the look that Bernard preferred above all looks. 'In reading of books, (saith he) let us not so much look for science, as favourness of truth upon our hearts.' *This I pray* (saith the apostle) *that your love may abound yet more and more, in knowlege and in all judgment*, Phil. i. 9. *i. e.* in knowlege and feeling. And certainly this feeling, this experimental looking on Jesus, is that my text aims at; it is not a swimming knowlege of Christ, but an hearty feeling of Christ's inward workings; it is not heady notions of Christ, but hearty motions towards Christ, that are implied in this inward looking.

2. For the object; you must look on Jesus. It is the blessedest object that the eye of the mind can possibly fix upon; of all objects under heaven Jesus hath the preeminence in perfection, and he should have the preeminence in our meditation. It is he that will make us most happy when we possess him, and we cannot but be joyful to look upon him, especially when looking is a degree of possessing Jesus, for the name signifies Saviour. It is an Hebrew name; the Greeks borrowed it from the Hebrews, the Latins from the Greeks, and all other languages from the Latins. It is used five hundred times in Paul's epistles, saith Genebrard. It comes from the Hebrew word Jehoshuah, or Joshua, which in the books of Ezra and Nehemiah (written after the Babylonian captivity) is Jeshua, and so is our Saviour's name always written in the Syriack translation of the New Testament. This name Jesus was given to Christ the Son of God by his Father, and brought from heaven by an angel, first to Mary, and then to Joseph. And on the day when he was circumcised (as the manner was) his name was given him by his parents, as it was commanded from the Lord, *by the angel Gabriel*, Luke i. 26. 31. Not to stand on the name, for the matter it includes both his offices and his nature; he is the alone Saviour of man, *For there is none other name under heaven, given among men, whereby we must be saved*, Acts iv. 12. And he is a perfect and an absolute Saviour; *He is able to save them to the uttermost that come unto God by him, seeing he ever liveth to make intercession for them*, Heb. vii. 25. I will not deny, but that the work of salvation is common to all the three persons of the trinity; it is a known rule, 'All outward actions are equally common to the three persons:' for as they are all one in nature and will, so must they be also one in operation; the Father saveth, the Son saveth, and the holy Ghost saveth; yet we must distinguish them in the manner of saving. The Father saveth by the Son, the Son saveth by paying the ransom and price of our salvation, the holy Ghost saveth by a particular applying of that ransom unto men. Now, whereas the Son pays the price of our redemption, and not the Father, nor the holy Ghost; therefore, in this special respect, he is called our Saviour, our Jesus, and none but he.

This objection, though contained in a word, is very comprehensive: herein is set forth to our view the offices of Christ, the two natures of Christ, the qualities of Christ, the excellencies of Christ; O what variety of sweet matter is in Jesus? He hath in him *all the powders of the merchants*, Cant. iii. 6.

An holy soul cannot tire itself in viewing Jesus; we know one thing tires quickly, unless that one be all; which so is Christ, and none else, *He is all and in all*, Col. iii 11. All belonging to being, and all belonging to well-being in things below Jesus, some have this excellency, and some have that, but none have all; and this withers contemplation at the root. Contemplation is soul-recreation, and recreation is kept up by variety; but O what variety is in Jesus? Variety of time, *He is Alpha and Omega*; variety of beauty, *He is white and ruddy*; Variety of quality, he is a lion and a lamb, a servant and a son; variety of the excellency in the world, he is man and God. O where shall we begin in this view of Jesus? *Who shall declare his generation? Or who shall count and reckon his age?* Isa. liii. 8. All the evangelists exhibit unto us the Saviour, but every one of them in his particular method. Mark describes not at all the genealogy of Jesus, but begins his history at his baptism. Matthew searcheth out his original from Abraham. Luke follows it backwards as far as Adam. John passeth farther upwards, even to the eternal generation of this *word that was made flesh*. So they lead us to Jesus, mounting up four several steps: in the one, we see him only among the men of his own time; in the second, he is seen in the tent of Abraham; in the third he is yet higher, to wit, in Adam; and finally, having traversed all ages, through so many generations, we come to contemplate him in the beginning, in the bosom of the Father, in that eternity in which he was with God before all worlds. And there let us begin, still looking unto Jesus, as he carries on the great work of our salvation from first to last, from everlasting to everlasting.

SECT. II.

The main doctrine and confirmation of it.

BUT for the foundation of our building take this note.——

Doctrine 2.

Inward experimental looking unto Jesus, such as stirs up affections in the heart, and the effects thereof in our life, it is an ordinance of Christ; a choice, an high gospel-ordinance.

Or thus,

Inward experimental knowing, considering, desiring, hoping, believing, loving, joying, calling on Jesus, and conforming to Jesus, it is a complicate, folded, compounded ordinance of Jesus.

I need not so much to explain the point, you see here is an ordinance, or a gospel duty held forth. Many other duties we have elsewhere described, but this we have kept for this place, and the rather for that, this is a choice duty, a compounded duty, an high gospel-ordinance. No question, but watchfulness, self-trial, self-denial, experiences, evidences, meditation, life of faith, &c. dwell in their place and order; yet as oars in a boat, (though it be carried with the tide) may help it to go faster. It is *Jesus lifted up, (as Moses lifted up the serpent)* which strikes more soundly into the beholder, than any other way. Looking unto Jesus is that great ordinance appointed by God for our most special good. How many souls have busied themselves in the use of other means? And though, in them, Christ hath communicated some virtue to them; yet, because they did not trade more with him, they had little in comparison. Such a one, as deals immediately with Christ, will do more in a day, than another in a year! and therefore I call it a choice, a complete, a complicate, an high gospel-ordinance. Now, what this ordinance is, the text tells you, it is a looking unto Jesus.

1. Jesus is the object, and Jesus is Jesus, as he is our Saviour, as he hath negotiated, or shall yet negotiate, in the great business of our salvation. I ground this on all the texts jointly, as on Isa. xlv. 22. Isa. lv. 1. Micah vii. 7. Zach. xii. 10. Numb. xxi. 8. John iii. 15. Heb. xii. 2. Phil. iii. 20. 2 Cor. iii. 18. Matth. i. 21, &c. 2. Looking unto is the act: but how? It is such a look as includes all these acts, knowing, considering, desiring, hoping, believing, loving, joying, enjoying of Jesus, and conforming to Jesus. It is such a look, as stirs up our affections in the heart, and the effects thereof in our life. It is such a look, as leaves a quickning and enlivening upon the spirit. It is such a look as works us into a warm affection, raised resolution, an holy and upright conversation. Briefly, it is an inward experimental looking unto Jesus.

For confirmation of the point; this was the Lord's charge to the Gentiles of old, *Look unto me,*

An Explanation of the Act and Object.

me, and ye shall be saved, all the ends of the earth. And I said, Behold me, behold me, unto a nation that was not called by my name, Isa. xlv. 22. lxv. 1. And according to this command was their practice. *Mine eyes are ever towards the Lord,* (saith David) *And they looked unto him and were lightned, and their faces were not ashamed,* Psal. xxv. 15. xxxiv. 5. Thus in the gospel after this command, Looking unto Jesus, it follows, *Consider him that hath endured such contradiction of sinners against himself,* Heb. xii. 3. And according to this command is the practice of gospel-believers. *We all with open face, beholding as in a glass the glory of the Lord, are changed into the same image, from glory to glory, even as by the Spirit of the Lord,* 2 Cor. iii. 18. Instead of the vail of Mosaical figures, God hath now given to his church the clear glass of the gospel, and hence all believers under the gospel do, by contemplative faith, behold Christ, together with the glorious light of his mercy, truth, goodness, and the rest of his divine attributes; and by means thereof they are made like unto him, in the glory of holiness, and in newness of life.

The reasons why we are thus to look unto Jesus, will be as so many motives, which we shall reserve to an use of exhortation: but the reasons why this looking unto Jesus, is, 1. An ordinance. 2. An ordinance of Christ, may be these,

1. Why an ordinance? Here is only this reason, the will of the Lord, *Even so, Father, for so it seemed good in thy sight.* Ordinances are certain impositions set forth by an external mandate of a lawgiver, having authority to command. It is the will of Christ to impose this law on all the sons of men, that they should look up unto him; and concerning this, What have we to do to enquire into the reason? It is our duty to obey, and not to know of him; why he commands. If [autos ephe] was enough in Pythagoras his school, to put the business past disputing amongst his scholars, I am sure it should be much more in Christ's school; we will therefore enquire no further reason for it.

2. Why an ordinance of Christ? It is this; because all spiritual ordinances, laws, institutions do hold on Christ. It is not in the liberty of man to erect any new spiritual ordinance in the Church of Christ. I will not deny but the power of man may come in to order such things as are not proper, but rather common to the church with other societies, as to meet together in some place, and at some time, &c. according to that rule, *Let all things be done decently and in order,* 1 Cor. xiv. 40. For this is not an institution, but only the dictate of right reason. But when it comes up to an ordinance, law, institution, *i. e.* when something more shall be put on the thing, than nature hath put on it, when, by virtue of the institution, there is conjoined to it some kind of spiritual efficacy to work upon the soul, this only holds on Christ. Hence, because in the preaching of the word, and in the administration of the sacraments, we expect a virtue, a spiritual efficacy more than they have, or can yield in any natural way, therefore we say, These are ordinances of Christ; and so because, in looking unto Jesus, we expect a virtue, a special efficacy, to go along together with it, more than nature can give it, therefore we call this an ordinance, and an ordinance of Christ, to distinguish it from all other ordinances, rules, constitutions of men whatsoever.

SECT. III.

Use of Reproof.

Use 1. WELL then, is inward experimental Looking unto *Jesus* a choice, an high gospel-ordinance? How may this reprove thousands? How many are there that mind not this duty? The truth is, that as *the whole world lies in wickedness,* 1 John v. 19. So the eyes of the whole world are misplaced; there's few that have a care of this choice, of this high gospel ordinance. I shall therefore reprove both the ungodly and Godly.

1. For the ungodly, *not God, nor Christ, is in all their thoughts,* Psalm x. 4. Alas! they never heard of such a duty as this, they cannot tell what it means to look unto Jesus. Nor speak I only of poor Indians, and other savages of the unchristian world, whose souls are overclouded with the blackest mists of irreligion, that the prince of darkness can possibly inwrap them in, who came into the world, not knowing wherefore, and go out of the world, not knowing whither, an heavy case, which cannot sufficiently be bewailed with tears of blood;

but I speak of such as live within the paradise of the Christian church, that have nothing to distinguish them from the Indian miscreants, but an outward conformity, outward formalities, the charity of others, and their own slight imaginations. Why, alas! these are they that the Lord complains of, that *they have eyes, and see not ; my people have forgotten me days without number,* Jer. ii. 32. They have negligently suffered me to be out of their minds, and that for a long time. You will say, Is there any such here ? Can I tax any of you, that you should not look up to Jesus ? Are not your eyes towards Christ in your prayers, praises, soliloquies, public and private duties ? Nay, are not you now in the duty, whilst I am speaking, and you hearing ?

I answer, however you may deem, that you do this, or that ; yet God reckons it as a thing not done in these respects.

1. When 'tis not done to purpose, as if our look to Christ, makes us not like Christ ; a man may give a thousand glances every day towards Christ, yet if there be no effectual impression upon the heart, Christ takes it, as if he had never looked towards him at all.

2. When 'tis done unwillingly. Sometimes men think of Chirst, but they know not how to shun it ; the Lord breaks in upon their spirits, whether they will or no, whereas their own temper is to follow and to pursue other objects : thus you drop into our assemblies out of custom, or fashion, or for some sinister end, and here is Christ lifted up upon the pole, he his discovered in his beauties, graces, sweetnesses, excellencies, but when you see him, you say, *He hath no form nor comeliness, there is no beauty, that we should desire him,* Isa. liii. 2. Let no man deceive himself, though he cast his eyes towards heaven all the day long, if he love not this work, he doth nothing, he looks not at Jesus.

3. When 'tis not done according to the rule, *This is not to eat the Lord's supper,* said Paul to his Corinthians, 1 Cor. xi. 20. No question they did eat it, but because it was not done after its due manner, he said, *This is not to eat the Lord's supper.* Many think of Christ, and look up to Jesus, but because their thoughts are not holy, awful and subjecting to the Spirit in no way proportionable to the goodness and glory of the Son of God, they look loosly, carelesly and carnally upon him, he therefore reckons it as not done, this is not to look unto Jesus.

4. When a man makes it not his course and trade to look unto Jesus. A man may come into a carpenter's house, and take up his tools, and do something at his work, but this makes him not a carpenter, because it is not their trade. The best saints sin, yet because it is not their trade and course, they are said not to sin, *Whosoever is born of God sinneth not,* 1 John v. 18. And so ungodly men may look, and muse, and meditate, and think of Christ, but because this is not their course and trade, they make it not their work to look to Christ, they are therefore said not to look to him.

Why, now consider, you that plead that you are Christians, and that you mind Christ at this very instant, that you are in the duty, even whilst I am speaking of it, and yet you neither do it to purpose, nor willingly, nor according to rule, nor as it is your trade ; is it not with you, as it was with them of whom Christ spake, Matth vii. 22, 23. *Many will say to me at that day, Lord, Lord, have we not prophesied in thy name ? and in thy name have cast out devils ? and in thy name have done many wonderful works ?* They will plead at the last day as they plead now, but, for all that, you know the answer, *I never knew you, depart from me, ye workers of iniquity.* Surely Christ will say to you one day, I know you not, I was a stranger to you upon earth, I could not have an eye from you, but when your lazy idle spirits pleased ; and now out of my sight, I'll never own you, nor look upon you more.

2. For the godly, are not they careless of this duty ? O their excursions from God ! sad dejections of spirit ! inordinate affections of the world ! and in the mean while, O the neglect of this gospel-ordinance even amongst saints themselves ! I know not whether through want of skill, or thro' want of will, but sure I am this duty lies dormant, neglected of most of the people of God : their faults I may express in these respects.

1. In not sending out their understandings, in not pointing their minds towards Jesus. *I write unto you,* said the apostle, *to stir up your pure minds by way of remembrance,* 2 Pet. iii. 1. It is in the original [*egeirein,*] *to awaken your pure minds,* and it was but need. See how David calls upon himself,

self, *Awake my glory!* Pſal. lvii. 8. And ſee how Deborah calls upon herſelf, *Awake, awake, Deborah, awake, awake, utter a ſong,* Judg. vii. 12. *Awaking,* is a word that imports *rouzing,* as birds that provoke their young ones by flight, to make uſe of their wings. Now, how few are there, that thus call upon themſelves? It was the prophet's complaint, *No man ſtirs up himſelf to take hold of God,* Iſa. lxiv. 7. O what a ſhame is this? Is it fit that our underſtandings, which God hath entruſted us withal, ſhould be no more improved? Is it fit, that our minds (thoſe golden cabinets, which God hath given us to be filled with heavenly treaſure) ſhould either be empty, or ſtuft with vanity, nothing, worſe than nothing? O! that ſuch glorious creatures as our ſouls, ſhould lackquey after every creature, which ſhould be in attendance upon Chriſt, which ſhould be like angels, waiting and ſtanding in the preſence of our God! O that ſuch glorious things as our immortal ſpirits, ſhould run after vanity, and ſo become vain; which if rightly improved, ſhould walk with angels, ſhould lodge themſelves in the boſom of the glorious God! Do we not ſee, how Chriſt is ſending out to us continually? The thoughts of his heart are love, eternal love; and ſhall not we ſend out our thoughts towards him? Shall not we let our minds run out towards him?

2. In not bending of their minds to this work. It may be the mind looks up, but 'tis ſo feeble, that, like an arrow ſhot from a bow weakly bent, it reacheth not the mark. It is the wiſe man's counſel, *Whatſoever thine hand findeth to do, do it with all thy might,* Eccl. ix. 10. O that God's people ſhould be ſo lazy, dull, ſluggiſh, ſlothful in this ſpiritual work! as Jeſus ſaid to the multitudes concerning John, *What went ye out into the wilderneſs to ſee?* Matth xi. 7. So may I aſk believers in their looking unto Jeſus, What went ye out to ſee? When ye crawl, and move, as if you had no hearts, nor ſpirits within you. Whom go ye forth to ſee? What, him that is the Lord of glory? What, him that is *the brightneſs of his Father's glory, and the expreſs image of his perſon,* Heb. i. 3. What, are ſuch heavy and lazy aſpects fit to take in ſuch a glory as this is? You ſee in what large ſtreams your thoughts flie forth to other things, and are you only languiſhing, weak and feeble in things of ſo great concernment? Oh that Chriſtians ſhould be ſo cold in ſpirituals, and hot in the purſuit of earthly temporal things?

3. In not binding of their minds to this object, in not ſtaying the eye on Jeſus Chriſt. Some may give a glance at Chriſt, but they are preſently wheeled off again: but why doth not the eyes abide there, at leaſt till it come to ſome profitable iſſue; Is not Chriſt worthy on whom our ſouls ſhould dwell? Certainly, if we love our Jeſus, that love will hold us: Chriſt then will be in our thoughts and minds, and we cannot off him. As the load-ſtone having drawn the iron, and keeps it faſt to itſelf, ſo, if love draw our hearts, it holds it faſt to the object loved. Chriſt himſelf acknowlegeth ſuch an operation of love upon himſelf, *Turn away thine eyes, for they have overcome me. Thou haſt raviſhed my heart, my ſiſter, my ſpouſe, with one of thine eyes,* Cant. vi. 5. chap. iv. 9. Chriſt was held in the galleries, and captivated with love to his people, ſo that his eye was ever upon them. Nay, he could not get his eyes off them, *Can a mother forget her child? No more can I forget you,* Iſa. xlix. 14. And is Chriſt ſo tender in his love towards us, that he ever minds us, and ſhall our minds be ſo looſe to him; ſo fluttering, and fleeting? Shall there be no more care to bind ourſelves in cords of love to him, who hath bound himſelf in ſuch cords of love to us?

4. In not daily exerciſing this bleſſed duty; it may be now and then they are awakned, and they get up into heaven to ſee their Jeſus, but it is not daily. Oh conſider! Is this now and then going to heaven within the vail, to live the life of friends? Is this to carry ourſelves as children? What, to be ſo ſtrange at home? But now and then? Once in a month, in a year? There to be ſeldom, where we ſhould always be? Is Jeſus Chriſt ſuch a mean thing, that a viſit now and then ſhould ſerve the turn? The Queen of Sheba hearing Solomon's wiſdom, Oh, ſaid ſhe! *Bleſſed are thoſe thy ſervants, that always ſtand before thee, and hear thy wiſdom,* 1 Kings x. 8. If ſhe was ſo taken with Solomon, remember, *That a greater than Solomon is here:* and ſhall we deprive ourſelves of that bleſſedneſs, which we might enjoy, by ſtanding always in the preſence of Chriſt, to hear his wiſdom, and to behold his glory?

Oh! my brethren, let us take ſhame to ourſelves, that to this day we have been ſo careleſs in ſending, bending,

bending, binding our minds to this blessed object Jesus Christ: yea, let us blush, that we have not made it our daily business. David describes the blessed man, by his *delighting in the law of the Lord*, and by his *meditating on that law day and night*, Psal. i. 2. How then is he to be reproved, that neither meditates on the law of the Lord, nor on the Lord, the law-maker, day and night? O alas! we keep not a constant course, we are not daily in the exercise of viewing Jesus. Nay, I fear we look upon this duty of looking unto Jesus, as a questionable thing; it seems to many as a duty unknown, unheard of, unthought of, it is not in their notice, and how should it be in their practice? But I leave this first use.

SECT. IV.

Use of Exhortation.

Use 2. IS inward experimental looking unto Jesus a choice, and high gospel ordinance? One use of exhortation. *I beseech you by the meekness and gentleness of Christ*, 2 Cor. x. 1. *I beseech you, by the mercies of God*, Rom. xii. 1. *I beseech you, brethren, for the Lord Jesus Christ's sake, and for the love of the Spirit, to look unto Jesus*, Rom. xv. 30. Or, if my beseechings will not prevail, why, yet look on me as an ambassador of Christ, consider as though *God did beseech you by me*, I beseech, *I pray you in Christ's stead*, 2 Cor. v. 28. It is a message that I have from God to your souls, to look unto Jesus; and therefore *set your hearts to all the words that I testify to you this day, for it is not a vain thing, but it is for your lives*, Deut. xxxii. 46.

O that I should need thus to persuade your hearts to look unto Jesus! What, is not your Jesus worthy of this? Why then, are your thoughts no more upon him? Why are not your hearts continually with him? Why are not your strongest desires, and daily delights in, and after the Lord Jesus? What's the matter? Will not God give you leave to approach this light? Will he not suffer your souls to taste and see? Why then are these words in the text? Why then doth he cry, and double his cry, *Behold me, behold me*? Ah vile hearts! how delightfully and unweariedly can we think of vanity? How freely and how frequently can we think of our pleasures, friends, labours, lusts? Yea, of our miseries, wrongs, sufferings, fears? And what, is not Christ in all our thoughts? It was said of the Jews, that they used to cast to the ground the book of Esther before they read it, because the name of God is not in it; and Augustine cast by Cicero's writings, because they contained not the name of Jesus. Christians! thus should you humble and cast down your sensual hearts, that have in them no more of Christ: O chide them for their wilful or weak strangeness to Jesus Christ! O turn your thoughts from off all earthly vanities, and bend your souls to study Christ, habituate yourselves to such contemplations, as in the next use I shall present; and let not those thoughts be seldom or cursory, but settle upon them, dwell there, bathe your souls in those delights, drench your affections in those rivers of pleasures, or rather in the sea of consolation. O tie your souls in heavenly galleries, have your eyes continually set on Christ! say not, "You are unable to do thus, this must be God's work only, and therefore all our exhortations are in vain." Baxter's rest. A learned divine can tell you, Though God be the chief disposer of your hearts, yet next under him you have the greatest command of them yourselves: though, *without Christ ye can do nothing*; yet under him you may do much: or else it will be undone, and you undone, through your neglect; do your own parts, and you have no cause to distrust whether Christ will do his. It is not usual with Christ to forsake his own people in that very work he sets them on. Oh but we can do nothing! how! nothing? What, are you neither spiritual nor rational creatures? If a carnal minister can make it his work to study about Christ through all his life-time, and all because it is the trade he lives by, and knows not how to subsist without it: why then, methinks a spiritual Christian should do much more. If a cook can labour and sweat about your meat, because it is the trade that maintains him, though perhaps he taste it not himself, methinks, you for whom it is prepared, should take the pains to taste its sweetness, and feed upon it. Christians! if your souls were sound and right, they would perceive incomparably more delight and sweetness, in knowing, thinking, believing, loving and rejoicing in Jesus Christ, than the soundest stomach finds in his food, or the strongest senses in the enjoyment of their objects,

Now

Now, for shame never say, You cannot reach it; *I can do all things* (faith Paul) *thro' Christ that strengthneth me,* Phil. iv. 13. Oh, it is our sloth, our security, our carnal mind, which is enmity to God and Christ, that keeps us off. Be exhorted! Oh be exhorted in the fear of God.

SECT. V.

Motives from our Wants, in Case of Neglect.

TO quicken us to this duty; I shall propound some moving considerations: ponder and weigh them with an impartial judgment. Who knows, but, through the assistance of Christ, they may prove effectual with your hearts, and make you to resolve upon this excellent duty of looking unto Jesus.

Consider { 1. Our wants, in case of our neglect. 2. Our riches, in case we are lively in this duty.

1. For our wants. If Christ be not in view, there is nothing but wants.

Suppose first a Christless soul, a poor creature, without any beam or ray of the Son of righteousness, and what sad condition is he in? I may say of such a one, that——

1. He is without light. There is no oil of saving knowlege, no star of spiritual light arising in his soul, *Ye were once darkness,* Eph. v. 8. saith the apostle to his Ephesians: not only dark, but darkness itself; they were wholly dark, universally dark, having no mixture nor glimpse (whilst without Christ) of spiritual light in them. Of such carnal wretches, saith our Saviour, *They have not known the Father, nor me,* John xvi. 3. They have not known the Father in his word, nor me in my natures, offices, sufferings, exaltations, communications. Very miserable is the carnal man's ignorance of God and Christ, he hath no saving knowledge of Jesus.

2. Such an one is without grace, without holiness, Christ is our wisdom and Sanctification, as well as righteousness and redemption, 1 Cor. i. 30. Where Christ is not, there is no spiritual wisdom, no inclination to the ways and works of sanctification.

3. Such an one is without contention; the soul in this case finds nothing but emptiness and vanity in the greatest abundance. Let a man have what the world can give; yet, if he have not Christ, he is nothing worth. Christ is the marrow and fatness, the fulness and sweetness of all our endowments: separate Christ from them, and they are bitter, and do not please us; empty, and do not fill us.

4. Such an one is without any spiritual beauty, *There's nothing in him but sores and swellings, and wounds and putrefaction,* Isa. i. 6. From the sole of his foot, to the crown of his head, there is nothing in him, but loathsome and incurable maladies. Hence the greatest sinner is the foulest monster. Bodily beauty without Christ is but as green grass upon a rotten grave. Did man see his uncomliness and deformity without Jesus Christ, he would stile himself, as the prophet stiled Pashor, Magor-missabib, *Fear round about,* every way a terror to himself, Jer. xx. 3.

5. Such an one is without peace. There is no true, spiritual heavenly peace, no joy and peace in the holy Ghost, without Jesus Christ. Joram asking Jehu, *Is it peace?* was answered, *What hast thou to do with peace, so long as the whoredoms of thy mother Jezebel, and her witchcrafts are so many?* 2 King ix. 22. A Christless man asking, Is it peace, O messenger of God? He can look for no other but Jehu's answer, What hast thou to do, O carnal man, with peace, so long as thy lusts are so strong within thee, and thy estrangements from the prince of peace so great? The soul that is without Jesus Christ, is an enemy to the God of peace, a stranger to the covenant of peace, uncapable of the word of peace, an alien to the way of peace, *There is no peace to the wicked, saith my God,* Isa. lvii. 21.

6. Such an one is without acceptation with God the Father. Christ only is God's beloved, and therefore, as Joseph's brethren might not look him in the face, unless they brought their brother Benjamin, so cannot we look God in the face with any confidence or acceptance, unless we bring Christ with us in the arms of our faith. Without Christ man is stubble, and God is a consuming fire to destroy him; man is a guilty malefactor, and God is a severe judge to condemn him; the whole of man without Jesus Christ is a very abomination in God's presence.

7. Such an one is without life; *He that hath*

12. Chrift lives not in that foul; it is a dead foul, *dead in fins and trefpaffes*, Eph. ii. 1. As the dead fee nothing of all that fweet and glorious light which the fun cafts forth upon them, fo the dead in fin have no comfortable apprehenfion of Chrift, though he fhine in the gofpel more glorioufly than the fun at noon. And as *the dead know not any thing*, Eccl. ix. 5. fo the dead in fin know nothing at all of the wifdom of Chrift guiding them, or of the holinefs of Chrift fanctifying them, or of the fulnefs of Chrift fatisfying them, or of the death of Chrift mortifying their lufts, or of the refurrection of Chrift quickning their fouls, or of the dominion of Chrift reigning in their hearts. O what a mifery is this!

All this you may fay is true to a chriftlefs foul, but what evil to him that may have a title to Chrift, and yet minds not Chrift, makes not ufe of Chrift, doth not look unto Jefus?

Such a cafe I confefs may be. Yea, as many duties are neglected by fome Godly, fo this main duty is (I may tremble to think it) exceedingly neglected. But O! the fin and fadnefs of thofe fouls! O the wants attending fuch poor creatures! confider them in thefe particulars;

1. They have not that wifdom, knowlege, difcerning of Chrift, as otherwife they might have; by looking and ferious obferving of Chrift, we gain more and more knowlege of Chrift, but if we will not look, how fhould we underftand thofe great myfteries of grace? Nor fpeak I only of fpeculative knowlege, but more efpecially of practical and experimental, without looking on Chrift we cannot expect that virtue fhould go out of Chrift; there is but a poor character or cognizance of Chrift upon them that are fuch; they have not fo clear, and comfortable, and inward, and experimental a knowlege of Jefus Chrift.

2. They do not fo tafte the goodnefs of Chrift, as otherwife they might. Chrift is no other unto them, whilft neglected by them, but as an eclipfed ftar, with whofe light they are not at all affected; Chrift is not fweet to them in his ordinances, they find not in them that delight and refreshment, that comfort and contentment, which they ufually minifter. They cannot fay of Chrift, as the fpoufe did, Cant. ii. 3. *I fat down under his fhadow with great delight, and his fruit was fweet to my tafte.* They are in the cafe of Barzillai, who could not tafte what he did eat, or what he did drink, nor could hear any more the voice of finging-men, or of finging-women: fo they cannot tafte the things of God, nor hear the fpiritual melody, which Chrift makes to the fouls of them that look up to him.

3. They have not the love to Chrift which Chrift's beholders have; they meditate not upon Chrift as lovers on their love; they delight not themfelves in Chrift, as the rich man in his treafure, and the bride in the bridegroom which they love; their thoughts are rather on the world than Chrift; their palates are fo diftempered, that they have no pleafure in the choiceft wine, they cannot fay, That their fouls long after him; and no wonder, for how fhould they love Chrift, who turn their eyes from him, who is *the faireft of ten thoufands* to other objects? Surely they have no flaming, burning love to Chrift, that will give every bafe thing a kind of preeminence above Chrift.

4. They have not that fenfe of Chrift's love, which thofe that exercife this duty have. Whilft the foul neglects Chrift, it cannot poffibly difcern the love of Chrift; it perceives not Chrift applying the doctrines of his love to the confcience: Chrift appears not in his banqueting-houfe, he enables not the foul to pray with confidence, he makes it not joyful in the houfe of prayer. And hence it is that fuch fouls move fo flowly in God's fervice; they are juft like Pharaoh's chariots, without wheels. O they perceive not the love of Chrift, either in the clear revelation of his fecrets, or in the free communication of his graces, or in the fanctifying and fweetning of their trials, or in fealing up the pardon of their fins: O they feel not thofe ravifhing comforts, which ufually Chrift fpeaks to the heart, when he fpeaks from his heart in love. O the want! O the mifery of this want!

5. They have not that experience of the power of Chrift, which they have that are in the exercife of this duty. Would you know wherein lies the power of Chrift? I anfwer, In cafting down the ftrong holds of fin, in overthrowing Satan, in humbling mens hearts, in fanctifying their fouls, in purifying their confciences, in bringing their thoughts to the obedience of Chrift, in making them able to endure afflictions, in caufing them to grow and encreafe in all heavenly graces; and this power we partake of, who rightly and experimentally look

up

An Explanation of the Act and Object.

up to Chrift. But if this duty be neglected, there is no fuch thing: hence we call this, The duty of duties, the chief duty, the efpecial duty; and for all other duties, means, ordinances, if Chrift be not in them, they are nothing worth. In every duty this is the effential part; that we look thro' all, unto Jefus; it is only from Chrift that virtue, and efficacy is communicated in fpiritual ordinances. There were many people in a throng about Chrift, but the infirm woman that touched him, was fhe alone that felt efficacy come from him; we fee many attend the ordinances, frequent the affemblies, but fome few only find the inward power of Chrift derived unto their fouls. They that neglect, or are grofly ignorant of this great myftery of looking unto Jefus, are no better than ftrangers to the power of Chrift.

6. They have not that fenfe of the worth and excellency of Chrift, that are unacquainted with this duty; they are not fo ravifhed with his beauty, they are not fo taken with his fweetnefs and pleafantnefs of the face of Chrift; he is not the faireft of ten thoufands in their eyes;' and hence it is that they do not pleafure long after, delight or joy themfelves in Chrift. Indeed thefe affections are the evidences of our high efteem; they that rejoice not in Chrift, nor have any longings after Chrift, they put a very unworthy price upon Chrift.

7. They have not that fenfe either of their own wants, or of the world's vanity, who are not in the practice of this duty. In this glafs we fee that man is blind, and no fun but Chrift can enlighten him; that man is naked, and no garment but Chrift's can clothe him; that man is poor, and no treafure but Chrift's can enrich him; that man is indebted, and none but Chrift can make fatisfaction for him; that man is empty, and none but Chrift can fill him; that man is diftreffed, perplexed, tormented, and none but Chrift can quiet him. Why all this, and much more than this appears in this glafs of Jefus. The foul that looks here cannot but comprehend an end of all other perfection; yea, the further it looks on the creature, the deeper and deeper vanities it difcerns. But, alas! there is no obfervation, no fenfe, no feeling, either of man's wants, or of the world's vanity, or of any fuitable good in Chrift to them that are not in this divine and fpiritual contemplation.

Thus far of their wants that neglect this duty of looking unto Jefus.

SECT. VI.

Motives from our riches in cafe we are lively in this duty.

2. FOR our riches, in cafe we are lively in this duty; O the bleffed incomes to fuch! I may reckon up here thofe very particulars, which the others wanted. 1. That Chrift gives light unto them. As the receiving of the fun gives light to the body, fo the receiving of the fun of righteoufnefs gives light, a fpiritual, heavenly and comfortable light to their fouls. 2. That Chrift gives grace and holinefs unto them; *of his fulnefs we receive grace for grace*, John i. 16. As the print upon the wax anfwers to the feal, or as the characters upon the fon anfwers to the father; fo there are certain ftamps of the grace of Chrift upon the faints, that what good they do it fprings not from external motives only, as in hypocrites, but from Chrift working in them an inward principle of new nature: and upon this account doth John tell us, *The law was given by Mofes, but grace and truth came by Jefus Chrift*, John i. 17. 3. That Chrift gives contentment or fatisfaction unto them. As the pearl fatisfied the merchant in the parable with treafure, fo Chrift fatisfieth the foul with wifdom in underftanding, with the fenfe of his love in the heart, with fure and bleffed peace in the confcience. They that rightly look unto Jefus, may fay, as Jacob did, *I have enough*. 4. That Chrift gives glory unto them; *he is the glory of Ifrael*, Luke ii. 32. He is both the author and matter of their glory; he is the glory of their juftification, as the garment is the glory of him that wears it; he is the glory of their redemption, as the ranfomer is the glory of the captive; he is the glory of their fanctification, as Jordan cleanfing him from his leprofy was the glory of Naaman; he is their all in all in whom they glory, and *to whom they give all honour, and glory, and power, and praife*, 2 Cor. v. 19. 5. That Chrift gives peace unto them, *God is in Chrift reconciling the world unto himfelf*, he is the author, and the world is the object of this reconciliation. *Chrift is our peace*, and [...] preached by Jefus

C

sus Christ, Eph. ii. 14. They that hear Christ in the word, or that look unto Christ by the eye of faith, they have this peace, Acts x. 36. for Christ only in ordinances is the revealer, and procurer, and the worker of peace in all the children of peace. 6. That Christ procures acceptation with God for them; he stands betwixt God and such believers; and as they mind him, so he is ever mindful of them, pleading their cause, answering all the accusations of Satan, and praying to his Father in their behalf. 7. That Christ gives life unto them, *He that hath the Son, hath life*, 1 Joh. v. 2. He that hath Christ in his heart as a root of life living in him, or as a king setting up his throne within him, or as a bridegroom betrothing himself in loving kindness to him, *he hath life*, the life of grace, and the earnest of the life of glory. 8. That Christ gives wisdom unto them, *Christ hath in him all the treasures of wisdom*, and therefore he that looks most to Christ, is the wisest man in the world; he that hath the sun, hath more light than he that hath all other lights in the world, and wants the sun. 9. That Christ gives a taste of his goodness unto them. They cannot look unto him, but he makes them joyful with the feeling of himself and spirit; and hence it is that many times they break out into *psalms, and hymns, and spiritual songs, and make melody in their hearts unto the Lord*, Eph. v. 19. O there is a goodness of illumination, regeneration, sanctification, consolation, contentation, pacification, and spiritual freedom flowing from Christ to the souls of his saints, which to carnal men is a sealed well, whose waters their palates never tasted. 10. That Christ gives a sincere and inward love of himself unto their hearts. No sooner is their eye of faith looking unto Jesus, but presently their heart is all on fire. Such a suitableness is betwixt Christ and their souls, as is betwixt the hearts of lovers; their love to Christ is like the love of Jonathan to David, a wonderful love, and *passing the love of women*, 2 Sam. i. 26. They love him as the bridegroom to whom their souls are married, as the choicest pearl by whom they are enriched, as the sun of consolation, by whose beams their souls are comforted, as the fountain by whom their hearts are refreshed, and their desires every way satisfied. 11. That Christ gives the sense of his own love to them; they cannot look on Christ, but they see him loving, and embracing their humble souls; they see him binding up their broken hearts; they behold him gathering to himself, and bearing in the bosom of his love, and comforting with the promises of his word their wounded spirits: they behold him, like Jacob, serving in the heat and in the cold for Rachel, serving in manifold afflictions from his cradle to his cross, to make a spouse unto himself. 12. That Christ gives the experience of his power to them. They that look on Christ, do feel the power of Christ inwardly in their souls, dissolving the works of Satan, casting down his kingdom, and mighty holds within them, healing all their spiritual maladies, sustaining them in all afflictions, filling their souls with all spiritual and heavenly might, making them strong in knowledge, and strong in faith, and strong in love, and strong in motion, and coming to Christ, as a river of much waters is strong in coming home to the ocean. 13. That Christ gives the sense of his own worth and excellency unto them, they see now in Christ his wisdom surpassing the brightness of the sun, even all the treasures of wisdom; in Christ is power excelling the strength of rocks, he is not only strong, but strength itself; in Christ is honour transcending all the kings of the earth, for he is King of kings, and Lord of lords; in Christ is beauty excelling the rose of Sharon, and lilly of the valleys; he is fairer than all the flowers of the field, than all the precious stones of the earth, than all the lights in the firmament, than all the saints and angels in the highest heavens. 14. That Christ gives the sense of their wants, and of the world's vanity, and of his suitable goodness unto them. In looking unto Jesus, they see themselves in themselves miserable, and all other things miserable comforters; they have learned the meaning of that psalm, *Put not your trust in princes, nor in the son of man, in whom there is no help. His breath goeth forth, he returneth to his earth: in that very day his thoughts perish. Happy is the man that hath the God of Jacob for his God, whose hope is in the Lord his God*, Psalm cxlvi. 3, 4, 5. 15. That Christ gives all things, every thing unto them. *All things are yours* (saith the apostle) *whether Paul, or Apollos, or Cephas, or the world, or life, or death, or things present, or things to come, all are yours; and you are Christ's, and Christ*

Chrift is God's, 1 Cor. iii. 22, 23. All things are yours; firft, all the minifters of Chrift from the higheft to the loweft, *whether Paul, or Apollos, or Cephas*; they are your fervants; they are men that watch over you for your falvation. Secondly, *the world is yours*. Indeed the world ftands but for your fakes, if your number were but once completed, quickly would the world be fet on fire. You will fay, Ay! but how is the world ours? We find not this, for who hath the world at will? Why, though you have not, yet the mifery you find in the world, the want of wealth, as well as the enjoying of it is yours, (*i. e.*) it tends to your advantage. Thirdly, *life is yours*. It is a fitting, a preparing, a fquaring of you for a better life, even for eternity. Fourthly, *death is yours*; for you fhall die juft then when it is beft for you; death fhall ferve but as a fervant to your advantage. Fifthly, *things prefent, and things to come are yours; Godlinefs hath the promife of this life, and of that which is to come*, 1 Tim. iv. 8. Sixthly, I will add, the Lord himfelf is yours. Take God, and look on him in his greatnefs, in his mighty power, even this great God the Lord of heaven and earth is yours; he is yours, and all that he hath is yours, and all that he doth is yours, and all that he can do is yours, *I will be thine*, (faid God to Abraham) *I will be to thee an exceeding great reward*, Gen. xv. 1. Here is a catalogue, an inventory of a Chriftian's riches; have Chrift, and have all. When an heathen was but afked, Where all his treafure was, he anfwered, *Where Cyrus my friend is*. And if any afk you, Where all your treafure is, you may anfwer, *Where Chrift your friend is*. In this refpect you may truly fay, There is no end of your riches, they are called *the unfearchable riches of Chrift*, Ephef. iii. 8. Paul could find no bottom of thefe riches; O who would not look unto Jefus? If Chrift be yours (befides thofe particulars enumerated in this text, 1 Cor. iii. 22, 23.) God is yours, the Father is yours, the Son is yours, the Spirit is yours, all the promifes are yours; for in Chrift they are all made, and for him they fhall be performed. Come, let the proud man boaft in his honour, and the mighty man in his valour, and the rich man in his wealth, but let the Chriftian pronounce himfelf happy, only happy, truly happy, fully happy in beholding Chrift, enjoying Chrift, having Chrift, in looking unto Jefus.

You have the motives of your wants, in cafe of neglect; and of our riches in cafe we are active, frequent, ferious, and lively in this duty. But for our further encouragement to fall upon it, I fhall add a few motives more.

SECT. VII.

More motives to encourage us in this work.

1. CONfider your looking on Jefus will maintain your communion with Jefus; and is not this worth the while? Why, Chriftians! what is this communion with Chrift, but very heaven aforehand? Hereby we enjoy his perfon, and all fweet relations to his perfon, his death, and all the faving fruits, privileges, and influences of his death: hereby we are *brought into Chrift's banqueting houfe, held in his galleries, his banner over us being love*, Ca. ii. 4. Hereby we are carried up into the mount with Chrift, that we may fee him (as it were) transfigured, and may fay with Peter, *Mafter, it is good for us to be here; and let us here build tabernacles*. Oh it is an happy thing to have Chrift dwelling in our hearts, and to lodge in Chrift's bofom! Oh 'tis an happy thing to maintain a reciprocal communication of affairs betwixt Chrift and our fouls! as thus; He bare our fins, take we his healing? He endured wounds for us, drink we the fpiritual balfam that fprang out of his wounds? He took upon him our unrighteoufnefs, do we clothe ourfelves with his righteoufnefs? He endured pains for us, come we to him, and take his reft to our fouls? He embraced our curfe and condemnation, do we embrace his blefling, juftification, and falvation? To this end do we look on Jefus? If he hide his face by defertions, reft not till we find him, if we find him, hold him faft, let him not go, difturb him not out of your hearts by our corruptions. Thus, if we would prize the prefence of Chrift, how comfortably fhould we maintain and encreafe our communion with Chrift.

2. Confider that your daily neceffities call for a frequent looking up unto Jefus. You have need of Chrift, y...

need that he pray for you to your heavenly Father; you have need that he work in you, and need that he work for you his own blessed will; you have need that he present you and yours blameless before his Father's presence in life and death, and at the day of judgment: there's not a moment in your life wherein you stand not in continual need of Jesus Christ; and can an hungry man forget his bread? Can the hart that pants for thirst forget the river? Can a man in bonds forget freedom? Can a child in distress forget a father in honour and wealth? Oh then, let your necessities drive you to Christ, and mind you of Christ! is not he the fountain that supplies all wants? Christians! consult your own experiences; when you look up to Jesus, and lean on Jesus, are you not best at rest? O then, why do you not always rest and lean upon him? Sometimes you say, His bread is sweet, and his cup is pleasant, how amiable is his presence? At such a time you have never done wondering at him. O the sweet impressions that are even then on your spirits! why do you not then always look unto him? Or, at least, why are you not frequent in his disciples posture, *who looked stedfastly towards heaven as Christ went up?* Acts i. 10. How richly might your idle hours and spare time be laid out here to the supply of all necessities, bodily, or spiritual?

3. Consider that an eye, an heart on Christ is one of your most unquestionable evidences of sincerity. *Where your treasure is, there will your hearts be also,* Matth. vi. 21. If Christ be your treasure, your hearts will be on Christ; and surely an heart set upon God in Christ is a true evidence of saving grace. External actions are easiest discovered, but those of the heart are surest evidences. When thy learning will be no good proof of thy grace, when thy arguments from thy tongue and hand may be confuted, yet then will this argument from the bent of thy heart prove thee sincere. Take a poor Christian that hath a weak judgment, a failing memory, a stammering tongue; yet if his heart be set on Christ, I had rather die in this man's condition; and have my soul in his soul's case, than in the case of him, without such an heart, tho' he had the most eminent gifts, and parts and abilities of any in the world. Christians! as you would have a sure testimony of the love of God, and a sure proof of your title to glory, labour to get your hearts on Christ, O look on Jesus, you may be sure Christ will acknowledge that you really love him, when he sees your hearts are set upon him.

4. Consider, that your looking on Jesus will strengthen patience under the cross of Christ. This is the very particular motive of the text, *Let us run with patience the race that is set before us, looking unto Jesus the author and finisher of our faith; who for the joy that was set before him, endured the cross, despising the shame, and is set down at the right hand of the throne of God. For consider him that endured such contradiction of sinners against himself, lest you be wearied and faint in your mind,* Heb. xii. 1, 2, 3. It is storied of a martyr, that, having offered him a cup of spirits to sustain him, when he seemed to faint under his greatest trial, he returned this answer, *My Lord and master had gall and vinegar given him to drink;* as if he had been astonished to see himself fare better than Jesus Christ. How may it strengthen your patience in sufferings, to think of Christ's patience? What, are you served ill? Ay, but Jesus Christ was not served so well. Can you suffer so much as he hath done? *I tell you,* nay. O then do you stay your murmurings and repinings, bear with patience the little you endure; and, to this end, *Consider him that hath endured the contradictions of sinners.*

5. Consider that a thorough-sight of Christ will encrease your outward joy in Christ. *Your father Abraham rejoiced to see my day, and he saw it, and was glad,* John viii. 56. A right sight of Christ will make a right-sighted Christian glad at heart. I wonder not that you walk uncomfortably, if you never tried this art of Christ-contemplation; can you have comfort from Christ, and never think of Christ? Doth any thing in the world glad you, when you do not remember it? If you were possessed of all the treasure in the earth, if you had title to the highest dignities, and never thought of them, sure they would never rejoice you. Come, look up unto Jesus, fix your eyes, thoughts, and hearts on that blessed object, and then you may expect David's experience, *My mouth shall praise thee with joyful lips, when I remember thee upon my bed, and meditate on thee in the night-watches,* Psalm lxiii. 5. A frequent access to Christ, in a way of meditation, cannot but warm the soul in
spi-

spiritual comforts. When the sun in the spring draws near our part of the earth, how do all things congratulate its approach? The earth looks green, the trees shoot forth, the plants revive, the birds sing sweetly, the face of all things smiles upon us, and all the creatures below rejoice. Christians! if you would but draw near, and look on this Son of righteousness, Jesus Christ, what a spring of joy would be within you? How would your graces be fresh and green? How would you forget your winter-sorrows? How early would you rise (as those birds in the spring) to sing the praise of our great Creator, and dear Redeemer.

6. Consider that your eye on Jesus will preserve the vigour of all your graces. As the body is apt to be changed into the temper of the air it breathes in, and the food it lives on; so will your spirits receive an alteration, according to the objects which they are exercised about. You that complain of deadness and dulness, that you cannot love Christ, nor rejoice in his loves, that you have no life in prayer, nor any other duty, and yet you never tried this quickening course, or at least you were careless and unconstant in it; what, are not you the cause of your own complaints? Say, *Is not your life hid with Christ in God?* O! whither must you go but to Christ for it? If you would have light and heat, why then are you not more in the sun-shine? If you would have more of that grace which flows from Christ, why are you no more with Christ for it? For want of this recourse to Jesus Christ your souls are as candles that are not lighted, and your duties are as sacrifices which have no fire; fetch one coal daily from this altar, and see if your offerings will not burn; keep close to this reviving fire, and see if your affections will not warm. Surely, if there be any comfort of hope, if any flames of love, if any life of faith, if any vigour of dispositions, if any motions towards God, if any meltings of a softned heart, they flow from hence. Men are apt to bewail their want of desire and hope, and joy, and faith, and love to Jesus Christ, whilst this very duty would nourish all these.

Consider, 'tis but equal that your hearts should be on Christ, when the heart of Christ is so much on you. Christ is our friend, and in that respect he loves us, and bears us in his heart; and shall not he be in ours? Surely this is ill requital; this is a great contradiction to the law of friendship: but Christ is our Lord as well as friend; and if the Lord of glory can stoop so low as to set his heart on sinful dust, one would think we should easily be persuaded to set our hearts on Jesus Christ. Christians! do you not perceive that the heart of Christ is set upon you? and that he is still minding you with tender love, even when you forget both yourselves and him? Do you not find him following you with daily mercies, moving on your souls; providing for your bodies, and preserving both? Doth he not bear you continually in the arms of love, and promise that *all shall work together for your good?* Doth he not give his angels charge over you, and suit all his dealings to your greatest advantage? And can you find in your hearts to cast him by? Can you forget your Lord, who forgets not you? Fie upon this unkind ingratitude! when the Lord speaks of his thoughts and respects to us, he gives this language, *Can a woman forget her sucking child, that she should not have compassion on the son of her womb? Yea, they may forget, yet will not I forget. Behold I have graven thee upon the palms of my hands, thy walls are continually before me,* Isa. xlix. 15, 16. But when he speaks of our thoughts to him, the case is otherwise; *Can a maid forget her ornaments, or a bride her attire? Yet my people have forsaken me days without number,* Jer. ii. 32. *q. d.* You would not forget the clothes on your backs, you would not forget your braveries, your ornaments, your attires, and are these of more worth than Christ? Yet you can forget me day after day.

8. Consider 'tis a command of Christ, that we should look to Jesus. *Behold me, behold me, lo I, lo I.* A command not only backed with authority, but accompanied with special ordinances appointed to this end: what is baptism? And what is the Lord's supper, but the representation of Jesus Christ? Is it not Christ's command in his last supper, *Do this in remembrance of me?* And *this do ye as oft as ye drink in remembrance of me,* 1 Cor. xi. 24, 25. In this ordinance we have Christ crucified before our eyes, and can we forget him? Or can we hold our eyes off him? Can we see the bread broken, and the wine distinctly severed from the bread, and not call to mind (according to the scripture) Christ's agony in the garden, and on the cross? Can we take and eat the bread, and take and drink

drink the cup, and not apprehend Christ stooping down from heaven to feed our souls? At such a time, if we forget the Lord Jesus Christ, it will argue our dissatisfaction, our ingratitude, our disobedience every way.

9. Consider 'tis both work and wages to look unto Jesus. Hence David professed, *It is good for me to draw near to thee*, Psal. lxxiii. 28. And *my meditation of him shall be sweet*, Psal. civ. 34. The word imports a sweetness with mixture, like compound spices, or many flowers. Every thought of Jesus is sweet and pleasant, nay, 'tis better than wine, *we will remember thy love more than wine*. Can. i. 4. There is more content in contemplating on Christ, more refreshing to the spirit, than wine gives to the body, *How precious are thy thoughts unto me, O God!* Ps. cxxxix. 17. Look, in what kind soever you account a thing precious, so precious are the thoughts of God and Christ to a man, whose heart is in right frame. Such a one loves every glance of Christ, and the more it sees, the more it loves. It is said of one Eudoxius, that he wished he might be admitted to come near the body of the sun, to have a full view of it, though it devoured him; he was something rash in his wish, but there is something proportionable in a godly spirit, he so loves Christ, that he could be content to be swallowed up in the beholding of him. Certainly there is a blessing in his work; when we are bid to look unto Jesus, it is but to receive from Jesus. Is it any thing else but to call and invite us to look on the most pleasing and delightful object; that in the beholding of it, it may convey itself unto us, and we be delighted and filled with it? It is all one, as if he should bid us sit down by a well of life, and drink; or if he should bid us be as the angels are, who are blessed in the beholding of this Jesus. Why come then; if this be a blessed work, why will we unbless ourselves? If the work will exalt us, why will we debase ourselves in not closing with it? If we might live above heaven, why will we live below? Certainly when thoughts of Christ are moving in us, Christ himself is not far off, he will come, and enter too: and how sweet is it for Christ to come and take up his habitation in our souls?

10. Consider how the angels exceedingly desire to look on Jesus. They stoop down and pry into the natures, offices, and graces of Jesus Christ, *which things* (saith the apostle) *the angels desire to look unto*, 1 Pet. i. 12. He alludes to the manner of the cherubims looking down into the mercy-seat. This is the study, yea, this is the delight and recreation of the elect angels to look on Jesus, and to look into the several scopes of our salvation by Jesus Christ, to behold the whole frame and fabric of it, to observe all the parts of it from the beginning to the end, to consider all the glorious attributes of God; his wisdom, power, justice, mercy, all shining and glittering in it like bright stars in the firmament; this, I say, is their work, yea, this is their festivity and pastime. And shall not we imitate the angels? Shall not we think it our honour to be admitted to the same privilege with the angels?

11. Consider that looking unto Jesus is the work of heaven; *it is begun in this life*, (saith Bernard) *Vita contemplativa incipit in hoc seculo, perficitur in futuro, but it is perfected in that life to come*; not only angels, but the saints in glory do ever behold the face of God and Christ: if then we like not this work, how will we live in heaven? The dislike of this duty is a bar against our entrance; for the life of blessedness is a life of vision; surely if we take no delight in this, heaven is no place for us.

12. Consider that nothing else is in comparison worth the minding, or looking after. If Christ have not your hearts, who, or what should have them? O! that any Christian should rather delight to have his heart among thorns and briars, than in the bosom of his dearest Jesus! why should you follow after drops, and neglect the fountain? Why should you fly after shadows, and neglect him who is the true substance? If the mind have its current from Christ toward other things, these things are not only of less concernment, but destructive; *They are gone far from me, and have walked after vanity, and are become vain*, Jer. ii. 5. How unworthy the world is of the look of Christians, especially when it stands in competition with Jesus, we have discussed before.

Many other motives might be given, but let these suffice. I have done with the exhortation; in the next place I shall lay open to you the particular way of this duty, which all this while I have been persuading to.

SECT.

SECT. VIII.

Use of Direction.

Use 3. IS inward experimental looking unto Jesus a choice or an high gospel ordinance? Why then some directions how we are to perform this duty. Practice is the end of all sound doctrine, and duty is the end of all right faith; now, that you may do what you have heard in some good measure, I shall prescribe the directions in the next part prescribed.

But first in the work observe those two parts of the text, the act, and object; the act is looking unto; and the object is Jesus.

1. By looking unto, we mean (as you have heard) an inward experimental knowing, desiring, hoping, believing, loving, calling on Jesus, and conforming to Jesus. It is not a bare swimming knowlege of Christ, it is not a bare thinking of Christ. As Christ hath various excellencies in himself, so hath he formed the soul with a power of divers ways apprehending, that so we might be capable of enjoying those divers excellencies that are in Christ; even as the creatures having their several uses. God hath accordingly given us several senses, that so we might enjoy the delights of them all: what the better had we been for pleasant odoriferous flowers, or sweet perfumes, if we had not possest the sense of smelling? Or what good would language, or music have done us, if God had not given us the sense of hearing? Or what delight should we have found in meats, or drinks, or sweetest things, if we had been deprived of the sense of tasting? So what pleasure should we have had even in the goodness and perfection of God in Christ, if we had been without the faculty and power of knowing, desiring, hoping, believing, loving, joying and enjoying? As the senses are to the body, so are these spiritual senses, powers, affections to the soul the very way by which we must receive sweetness and strength from the Lord Jesus.

2. By Jesus, who is the object of this act, we mean a Saviour, carrying on the great work of man's salvation from first to last; hence we shall follow this method, to look on this Jesus as our Jesus in these several periods. 1. In that eternity before all time until the creation. 2. In the creation, the beginning of time, until his first coming. 3. In his first coming, the fulness of time, until his coming again. 4. In his coming again, the very end of time, to all eternity. In every one of these periods, oh what a blessed object is before us! Oh what wonders of love have we to look upon! before I direct you how to look on him in these respects, I must, in the first place, propound the object: still we must lay the colours of this admirable beauty before your eyes, and then tell you the art how you are to look upon them.

You may object, The apostle in this text refers this look only to the passion and cession of Christ. But a worthy interpreter tells you out of these words, *Andr. Ser.* on the words, *That Christ our blessed Saviour is to be looked on at all times, and in all acts; though indeed, then, and in those acts more especially.* Besides, we are to *look unto Jesus, as the author and finisher of our faith.* And why, as the author and finisher of our faith, but to hint out to us that we are to stand still, and to behold, as with a stedfast eye, what he is from first to last? You have called us hither (say they in Canticles) to see your Shulamite, *What shall we see in him?* What, saith the spouse, *but as the company of two armies?* that is, many legions of good sights; an ocean of bottomless depths of manifold high perfections. Or if these words be understood of the spouse, and not of Christ, yet how many words do we find in Canticles, expressing in him many goodly sights? *Myrrhe, aloes, and cinnamon, all the perfumes, all the trees of frankincense, all the powders of the merchants* are in him; *he is altogether lovely:* he is all every whit of him a confluence, a bundle, an army of glorious sights; all in one cluster, meeting and growing upon one stalk. There are many glorious sights in Jesus, I shall not therefore limit myself to those two especial ones, but take all those before me I have now propounded.

And now, if ever, stir up your hearts. Say to all worldly business and thoughts, as Christ to the disciples, *Sit you here, while I go and pray yonder,* Mat. xxvi. 36. Or, as Abraham, when he went to sacrifice Isaac, left his servants and ass below the mount, saying, *Stay you here, and I and the lad I will go yonder and worship, and come again to you;* so say you to all worldly thoughts, *Abide, you below, while I go up to Christ, and then I will return to you again.* Christians! yourselves may be welcome, but such followers may not.

LOOKING

LOOKING UNTO JESUS.

THE SECOND BOOK.

CHAP. I. SECT. I.

Revel. i. 8, 11. *I am Alpha and Omega, the beginning and the ending, saith the LORD, which is, and which was, and which is to come, the Almighty.——I am Alpha and Omega, the first and the last; and what thou seest write in a book, and send it to the seven churches.*

Of the eternal Generation of JESUS.

WE must *look unto Jesus the Beginner and Finisher of our faith:* we must behold Jesus as with a stedfast eye from first to last. As he is *Alpha and Omega, the beginning and the ending, the first and the last*; so accordingly we must *look unto him.* 1. He is *Alpha, the Beginner*, (so it is in the original), *(Archelon)* the beginner, the inceptor, the first wheel of our faith, Heb. xii. 2. and of the end of our faith, the salvation of our souls, 2 Thes. ii. 13. 2 Tim i. 9. Tit. i. 2. Now, Christ may be called a beginner, in respect of the decree, or execution. I shall begin with the decree, wherein he begun before the beginning of time to design our happiness, for the praise of the glory of his grace, Eph. i. 6. Many depths are in this passage. To this purpose we told you, That *Jesus is God's Son, and our Jesus, eternally begotten before all worlds.* In this first period we shall *look on him.* 1. In relation to God. 2. In relation to us.

1. In his relation to God, *Who shall declare his generation*, Isa. liii. 8. He is God's Son, having his subsistence from the Father alone, of which Father by communication of his essence he is begotten from all eternity.

For the opening of this eternal generation of our Jesus, we shall consider; 1. The thing begotten. 2. The time. 3 The manner of begetting. 4. The mutual kindness and love of him that begets, and of him that is begotten, which brings forth a third person, or subsistence, which we call the holy Ghost.

1. For the thing itself, it is Jesus Christ, who must be considered two ways, as he is a Son, and as he is God. Now, as he is a Son, he is the thing begotten, but not as he is a God. As he is God, he is of himself, neither begotten, nor proceeding; the God-head of the Father, and the God-head of the Son is but one and the same thing, and therefore *Essentia filii est a seipso, & hac ratione dici potest (auto Theos,) The Son as he is God, he is God of himself,* without beginning, even as the Father; *Essentia tamen filii non est a seipso, ideo sic non est (auto Theos,) But as he is not of himself,* but the Son of the Father, begotten of him; and hereupon it follows, that the Son is begotten of the Father as he is a Son, but not as he is a God.

2. For the time of this generation, it hath neither beginning, middle, nor end; and therefore it is eternal before all worlds; this is one of the wonders of our Jesus, that the Father begetting, and the Son begotten are co-eternal. Wisdom, in the book of Proverbs (which with one consent of all divines is said to be Christ) affirmeth thus, *When there were no depths, I was brought forth: when there were no fountains abounding with water. Before the mountains were settled; before the hills was I brought forth: while as yet he had not made the earth, nor the fields, nor the highest part*

part of the dust of the world. When he prepared the heavens, I was there: when he set a compass upon the face of the depth, Prov. viii. 24, 25, 26, 27. I was there. And a little before, *The Lord possessed me in the beginning of his way, before his works of old. I was set up from everlasting, from the beginning, or ever the earth was,* Prov. viii. 22, 23. that is to say, from eternity; for, before the world was made, there was nothing but eternity. It may be alledged to the contrary, that the saying of God the Father, *Thou art my Son, this day have I begotten thee,* Psalm ii. 7. is expounded by Paul of the time of Christ's resurrection. *And we declare unto you glad tidings* (saith Paul) *how that the promise which was made unto the fathers, God hath fulfilled the same unto us their children, in that he hath raised up Jesus again,* Acts xiii. 32, 33. *As it is also written in the second Psalm, Thou art my Son, this day have I begotten thee.* But we distinguish betwixt generation itself, and the manifestation or declaration of it. Jesus the Son of God from all eternity was begotten, but when he was incarnate, and especially when he was raised again from the dead, then was he mightily declared to be God's Son by nature. And of this declaration or manifestation of his eternal generation is that of the apostle understood.

3. For the manner of this generation of Jesus the Son of God, understand, there be two manners of begetting, the one is carnal and outward, and this is subject to corruption, alteration and time; the other is spiritual and inward, and such was the the beginning of the Son of God, of whose generation there is neither corruption, alteration, nor time. But, alas! *How should we declare his generation,* Isa. liii. 8. O my soul, here thou mayst admire, and adore with Paul and David, and cry out, *O the depths of the riches both of the wisdom and knowledge of God! how unsearchable are his judgments, and his ways past finding out!* Rom. xi. 33. There is no searching for us into the secret counsels of God, which he never revealed in his word, but so far as he hath revealed himself, we shall in sobriety, according to the light of the scriptures, endeavour a discovery of the manner of this spiritual generation of the Son of God; as thus,———

We must consider in God two things, 1. That in God there is an understanding. 2. That in God this understanding everlastingly acts or works.

For the first, that God hath a most excellent understanding, or that he is understanding itself in the highest degree, is very clear; for he that gives understanding to all his intelligible creatures, must needs have it, and be it most eminently in himself. If fire be the cause of heat in other things, it must needs be, that fire is the hottest of any thing; *Propter quod unumquodque tale, illud est magis tale.* The axiom is common, but the scripture verifies it, *With God is wisdom and strength, he hath counsel and understanding,* Job xii. 13. Nay, that this understanding is his very being, is very plain, *Counsel is mine, and sound wisdom; I am understanding, and I am strength,* Prov. viii. 14.

For the second, that this understanding in God everlastingly acts or works, is very clear; for that understanding (which is the nature, essence and being of God) is a mere act, or the first act; it is all one with *the life of God.* Now, as all life is active in itself, so the chief life (such as in the highest degree is to be attributed to God) must needs be active. What is the life of God, but an essential property whereby the divine nature is in perpetual action, living and moving in itself? And hereof is that speech in scripture so often used, *The Lord liveth,* Jer. xxxviii. 16. Hereof likewise is that asseveration or oath so often used by God, *As the Lord liveth,* Numb. xiv. 21. And, *As I live, saith the Lord,* Rom. xiv. 11. Well then, the understanding of God being active, or working from all eternity, it must needs have some eternal object on which it acts or works; every action requires a suitable object about which it must act or be exercised; so then, if God's understanding act eternally, it must have some eternal object, and if God's understanding act most perfectly, it must have some most perfect object to act upon; and what is that but only God himself? That God's understanding should act out of himself, would argue his understanding to act upon that which is finite and imperfect. Certainly nothing is infinite, eternal and perfect but only himself, and therefore if his understanding will act upon any suitable object, he must act upon nothing but himself.

And now we come to the manner of this high mystical, spiritual generation of Jesus the Son of God.

God. As the understanding of God doth act and reflect upon itself from all eternity, so it works this effect, that it understands and conceives itself; it apprehends in the understanding an image of that object which it looks upon, and this very image is the Son of God. This we shall lay out by some similitudes. A man's soul (we know) doth sometimes muse and meditate on other things; as it thinks of heaven, or it thinks of earth; this we call a right, or direct, or emanant thought; but sometimes the soul doth muse, or meditate on itself, as when it thinks of its own essence, or faculties, or the like; and this we call a reflex thought; why now the soul understands itself, now it hath some idea, or image of itself, now it conceives itself; this is our phrase, *it conceives itself*. There is not only a carnal, but a spiritual conception; as when I understand this or that, I say, *I conceive this or that*, I have the idea or image of this or that within my soul. Or, as in a glass a man doth conceive and get a perfect image of his own face by a way of reflection; so God, in beholding and minding of himself, doth in himself beget or conceive a most perfect, and a most lively image of himself, which very image is that in the trinity, which we call the Son of God. Thus you read in scripture, that Jesus the Son of God is called, *the brightness of his Father's glory, and the express image of his person*, Heb. i. 3. 1. *The brightness of his Father's glory*; herein God the Father is compared unto a lightsom body, and God the Son unto a beam, or splendor sent forth, or issuing out from that glorious body. 2. *The express image of his person*, herein God the Father is compared unto a seal, and God the Son unto an impression resulting from the seal. Now look, as wax upon a seal, hath the ingraven image of the seal; so the Son of God (which the Father has begotten or conceived of his own understanding) is the very image of his Father's understanding; hence not only the Father, but also the Son is called understanding itself. *I have counsel and wisdom*, (saith Christ) *I am understanding*, Prov. viii. 14. Whatsoever the Father is, the Son is; indeed the understanding in men, and the thing understood, are not usually one and the same, but in God it is all one: God's conceivings and begettings are the most inward of all; the Father conceives of himself, and in himself; and his conceiving is a begetting, and his begetting abideth still in himself, because his understanding can no where meet with any thing suitable, but that which he himself is, and that conceiving of himself, or begetting of himself is the second subsistence in the trinity, which we call the everlasting Son of God.

4. For the mutual kindness and loving-kindness of him that begets, and of him that is begotten, we say this brings forth a third person or subsistence in God. Now, for the understanding of this matter, we must consider two things, *First*, That in the essence of God, besides his understanding, there is a will. *Secondly*, That this will doth work everlastingly upon itself, as his understanding doth.

For the *first*, That in the essence of God, besides his understanding, there is a will, is very clear; for he that gives a will to all rational creatures, cannot want it himself. How should he be without will, whose will it is that we will? Of necessity it is that there should be some prime or chief will, on whose will all other wills should be; but the scriptures are plain, *I am God, and there is none else, I am GOD, and there is none like me. ——My counsel shall stand, and I will do all my pleasure*, Isa. xlvi. 9, 10.

For the *second*, That this will in God doth everlastingly work upon itself, is clear: for, as doth the understanding, so doth the will; but the understanding of God doth act upon itself as the chief and most perfect truth: therefore the will of God doth will himself as the chief and most perfect good. Indeed what other suitable object can the will of God have besides himself? An infinite will must needs have an infinite good, and in this sense, as our Saviour tells us, *There is none good but one, that is God*, Matth. xix. 17. Hence it is that the will of God doth reflect upon itself, and acquiesce in itself as in an infinite good.

And now we come to the manner of this high, mystical, spiritual procession of the Spirit from the Father and the Son. As the will of God doth act and reflect upon itself from all eternity; so it works this effect, that it delights itself in the infinite good, which it knoweth in itself, for the action of the will is delight and liking; and this very delight which God or his will hath in his own infinite goodness, doth bring forth a third person, or subsistence in God, which we call *the holy Ghost*: so that indeed

deed if you would know what the holy Ghoſt is, I would anſwer, 'It is the mutual kindneſs and loving-kindneſs, and joy, and delight of the Father and the Son.' The Father by this act of will doth joy and delight in his Son, and the Son by this act of will doth joy and delight in his Father; and this is it which the Son ſaith of himſelf, and of his Father, *I was daily his delight, rejoicing always before him,* Prov. viii. 30. *q. d.* I was from all eternity his delight, and he was from all eternity my delight; the Father (as it were) from all eternity aſpired in his will, and love, and joy unto the Son; and the Son (as it were) from all eternity aſpired in his will, and love, and joy unto the Father; and from this common deſire and aſpiring of either perſon the holy Ghoſt proceeds, which makes up the whole trinity of perſons.

I ſhall lay out this by ſome ſimilitude or reſemblance; as when a man looks in a glaſs, if he ſmile, his image ſmileth too, here's but one face; and yet in this unity we may find a trinity: the face is one, the image of the face in a glaſs is another, and the ſmiling of them both together is a third, and yet all are in one face, and all are of one face, and all are but one face; ſo the underſtanding which is in God is one, the reflection or image of his underſtanding he beholdeth in himſelf as in a glaſs is a ſecond, and the love and liking of them both together, by reaſon of the will fulfilled, is a third; and yet all are in one God, all are of one God, and all are but one God. In this trinity there is neither firſt nor laſt, in reſpect of time, but all are at once, and at one inſtant: even as in a glaſs the face, and the image of the face, when they ſmile, they ſmile together, and not one before nor after another.——For concluſion of all, As we have the Son of the Father by his everlaſting will in working by his underſtanding; ſo we have the holy Ghoſt of the love, and joy, and delight of them both, by the joint working of the underſtanding and will together; whereupon we conclude three diſtinct perſons, or ſubſiſtences, which we call the Father, Son, and holy Ghoſt, in one ſpiritual, yet unſpeakable ſubſtance, which is very God himſelf.——My meaning is not to inſiſt on the Father, or the holy Ghoſt, but only on the Son. Yet thus far I have added, that you may better underſtand the manner of this generation of the Son of God; together with the mutual kindneſs, loving-kindneſs, joy, and delight betwixt the Father and the Son even from everlaſting.

SECT. II.

Of our election in Chriſt before all worlds.

NOW, let us look on Chriſt in his relation to us before all worlds. God being thus alone himſelf from everlaſting, and beſides himſelf there being nothing at all; the firſt thing he did (beſides what ye have heard) or the firſt thing he poſſibly and conceivably could do, it was this; 'A determination with himſelf to manifeſt his glo-'ry; or a purpoſe in himſelf to communicate his 'glory out of his aloneneſs everlaſting unto ſome-'what elſe.' I ſay, unto ſomewhat elſe, for what is communication but an efflux, an emanation, an iſſuing from, or a motion betwixt two terms? I have now brought you to the acts, or actions of God in reference to his creatures; follow me a little, and I ſhall anon bring you to Chriſt in relation to yourſelves.

Theſe acts or actions of God were and are; 1. The decree. 2. The execution of the decree of God. I muſt open theſe terms;

1. The decree is an action of God, out of the counſel and purpoſe of his own will, determining all things, and all the circumſtances, and order of all things from all eternity, in himſelf certainly and unchangeably, and yet freely. *Who worketh all things* (ſaith the apoſtle) *after the counſel of his own will,* Eph. i. 11. And this work, or action of God is internal, and forever abiding within his own eſſence itſelf.

2. The execution of the decree is an act of God, whereby God doth effectually work in time all things as they were foreknown and decreed. And this action of God is external, and by a temporal act paſſing from God to the creatures.

Now, for the decree; that is of divers kinds; As, *Firſt,* There is a decree common and general, which looks to all the creatures; and it is either the decree of creation, or the decree of providence and preſervation. 2. There is a decree ſpecial, which belongs to reaſonable creatures, angels, and men; it is called the decree of predeſtination, and it conſiſts of the decree of election and reprobation. Concerning the common and general decrees we have but little laid down in fcriptures, and it is little or nothing at all to our purpofe; and concerning the fpecial decree of angels, there is not much in fcriptures, and that is as little alfo to our purpofe; we have only to deal with men, and with God's decree in relation to man's falvation before all worlds.

And this we call predeftination, or the decree of election; which is either of Chrift, or of the members of Chrift. Chrift himfelf was firft predeftinated; this appears by that faying of God, *Behold my fervant whom I uphold, mine elect in whom my foul delighted,* Ifa. xlii. 1. *I have put my Spirit upon him, he fhall bring forth judgment to the Gentiles.* Matth. xii. 18. Thefe very words the evangelift interprets of Chrift himfelf. And Chrift being predeftinate, the members of Chrift were predeftinated in him: fo the apoftle, *according as he hath chofen us in him before the foundation of the world,* Eph. i. iv. We are chofen in Chrift as in a common perfon, he was the firft perfon elected in order, and we in him. Suppofe a new kingdom to be fet up, a new king is chofen, and all his fucceffors are chofen in him; why God hath erected a kingdom of glory, and he hath chofen Jefus Chrift for the king of this kingdom, and in him he hath chofen us, whom he hath made kings and priefts unto the moft high God. But obferve we this of the apoftle, *he hath chofen us in him before the foundation of the world.* 1. He hath chofen, (*i. e.*) God the Father hath chofen; not that the Son and Spirit chofe not alfo; for if three of us had but one will common to us all, one could not will any thing, which the will of the other two fhould not alfo will: but becaufe the Son fuftains the perfon of one elected, and the Spirit is the witnefs fealing this grace unto our hearts, therefore the Father only is expreffed, as the Father alone is often named in prayer, not that the other perfons are not to be prayed unto, but becaufe the Son is confidered as the Mediator, and the Spirit as the inftructor, teaching us to pray as we ought; therefore the Father only is expreffed.

He hath *chofen us in him,* this *him,* denotes Chrift God-man; and this *in him,* denotes the fame Chrift God-man, as the head and firft elect, in whom, and after whom in order of nature, all his body are elected: mark here the order, but not the caufe of our election; though Chrift be the caufe of our falvation, yet Chrift is not the caufe of our election; it is only the foreknowledge of God, and his free love that is the caufe thereof.

3 *He hath chofen us in him before the foundation of the world,* (*i. e.*) From all eternity; but becaufe within eternity God doth forefee the things which are done in time; therefore this phrafe, (fay fome) may be extended not only to refpect the actual creation, but the decree itfelf of the world's being; *q. d.* He hath chofen us in order of nature, before his decree did lay the foundation of the world. My meaning is not to enter into controverfies; this all grant, that the ancient love which the Lord hath borne us in Chrift is not of yefterday, but before all worlds. Paul mentions *grace given us before all worlds,* 2 Tim. i. 9. But that which is the moft obfervable in the text, as to our purpofe, is, that we are chofen in him; we read of three phrafes in fcripture fpeaking of Chrift; fometimes we are faid to have bleffings in him, and fometimes for him, and fometimes through him. Sometimes in him, as here, *he hath chofen us in him;* fometimes for him, as elfewhere, *to you it is given for Chrift's fake, not only to believe but to fuffer,* Phil. i. 29. Sometimes through him, as in that of Paul, *Thanks be to God who giveth us the victory through our Lord Jefus Chrift,* 1 Cor. xv. 57. Now bleffings come through Chrift, in refpect that Chrift is a Mediator, not only of impetration, but execution; not only obtaining and receiving from grace all good for us, but in executing and applying efficacioufly the fame unto us: and bleffings come from Chrift, in refpect that Chrift doth by his obedience obtain every good thing, which in time is communicated to us: and we have bleffings in Chrift, becaufe that Chrift, as in a common ftore-houfe, every thing is firft placed, which is to be imparted afterwards to any of us. And thus we are chofen in Chrift as in a common perfon. This grace of election began firft at Chrift our head, and fo defcends downwards to us his members; Chrift is the firft-begotten amongft all his brethren, having the preeminence, or Chrift was *the firft-born among many brethren,* Rom. viii. 19. The firft that opened the womb: Chrift was fealed and fet apart to be prince of our falvation, before (in order of nature) we are elected. Concerning this election, or predeftination of Chrift, the apoftle puts all out of

of question, *Who verily was foreordained before the foundation of the world, but was manifested in these last days for you*, 1 Pet. i. 20.

SECT. III.

Of this great treaty in eternity betwixt God and Christ to save souls.

NOw was it that God the Father called forth his Son to perform the office of Mediator, that in him all those that should be saved might be chosen. Concerning this call of God the Father, in a special sort the apostle is clear, *No man taketh this honour unto himself, but he that is called of God, as was Aaron: so also Christ glorified not himself, to be made an high priest, but he that said unto him, Thou art my Son, to day have I begotten thee*. He called him to this honour; Heb. v. 4, 5. Christ thrust not himself into this office, but he came to it by the will of God the Father, and by his appointment, *For it pleased the Father, by him to reconcile all things to himself*, Col. i. 19, 20. and *him hath God the Father sealed*, John vi. 27. And why? But the more to assure us of the good will of God to save us, seeing he hath called his Son unto it: for therefore will he accept of all that Christ should do for us, as that which he himself hath ordained.

And now was it that God the Son embraced the call of the Father, and undertook the office of Mediator, *Then said I, lo, I come*, Heb. x. 7. No question it was truth from everlasting: *The Lord God opened mine ear, and I was not rebellious, neither turned away back*, Isa. l. 5. And *as the Father gave me commandment, even so I do*, John xiv. 31. and 6. 27. No sooner the Father called, but Christ accepts the office to which he was designed by the Father: this is plain by those words, *Him hath God the Father sealed*; sealed by ordination, and sealed by qualification, and sealed by way of investiture, as public officers are invested in their places by receiving their commissions under seal. And it must needs be so, because whatsoever the Father wills, the Son wills also, *I and my Father are one*, saith Christ, John x. 30. How one? Why, one in will, and one in power, and one in nature. 1. One in will, that appears in the words precedent concerning Christ's sheep, *My Father gave them me,——and I give unto them eternal life*, verse 28. They are both agreed to save Christ's sheep; the Father is willing, and Christ is willing: look, how much the will of the Father is in it, so much the will of the Son is in it, *For he and the Father are one*. 2. One in power; that appears likewise in the words precedent, *Those sheep shall never perish*; (saith Christ) *neither shall any pluck them out of my hands: my Father is greater that all, and no man is able to pluck them out of my Father's hand*, ver. 28, 29. Here is first the power of Christ, and all in him engaged for the salvation of his sheep, that if he have any power in him, and be able to do any thing, not one of them shall perish; and he gives the reason of the prevalency of his power from his Father's power, engaged as much as his own in this business; they are alike fast in his hands and in his Father's hands, *For he and the Father are one*. 3. One in nature, and of this I suppose are the words more especially understood: the Father and Son are both of one nature, of one essence, of one being, and this is not only an argument that they did both agree, and were like to agree in that great transaction of saving souls, but that they can never disagree; two that essentially have two wills, though for the present agreeing in one, yet they may come to disagree, and will not the same things, but if essentially they have but one will, it is impossible then but that they ever must agree.—— So then the Father from everlasting calls the Son to the office of Mediator. *q. d.* 'Come, my Son,
' the Son of my joy, and high delight ; my belov-
' ed Son in whom I am well pleased ; there's a
' thought in my heart to communicate myself out
' of this aloneness everlasting into somewhat else ;
' and my thought, or purpose, or intention lies in
' this order: First, I intend my own glory, then
' Christ, then the church, then the world ; thus
' is my providence to dispose every thing so much
' more principally and timely, by how much it is
' the more excellent ; next to my glory, and the
' manifestation of it, I will have a Christ, and this
' Christ shall be the chief pattern of the election of
' grace ; and next to Christ the head I intend a
' body, and this body I will predestinate to be
' made like, or to be conformed to the image of my
' Son. And now, behold, I call thee to the office
' of Mediator, thou art my Son, to day (even in
' this

'this day of eternity) have I begotten thee; and
'and to day (even this day of eternity) do I call thee
to this honour to be an high priest for ever.' And
as the Father calls, so the Son from everlasting
accepts the office to which he is designed by the
Father, *q. d.* Come, 'Is that the voice of my e-
'verlasting Father? Why, lo I come in the vo-
'lume of thy book it is written of me; to do thy
'will, O God. This is my mind; yea, and this
'shall be my mind for ever; when I am incarnate
'this shall be my meat to do the will of him that
'sent me to finish his work, Heb. x. 7. Glorious
'Father, thy will is my will; I seek not mine own
'will (as if I had a will distinct from thine) but
'the will of my Father, John iv. 34. Now there-
'fore I accept this honour. Be it to me, or be
'it with me, even as thou pleasest,' John v. 30.
This call of the Father, and answer of the Son is
fully confirmed by that saying of Christ, *I was
set up from everlasting*, Prov. viii. 23.

But concerning the particular passages of these
treaties betwixt God and Christ to save souls, I
shall shew. 1. The project. 2. The counsel. 3.
The foreknowlege. 4. The purpose. 5. The degree. 6. The convenant, we shall find all these in
our first period, in that eternity before all times
until the creation.

SECT. IV.

The Project.

THe project to save souls is diversly laid down
by dissenting brethren. Some give it in thus,
1. That there should be a Mediator and Redeemer unto mankind, considered as fallen in the state
of sin. 2. That all such should be received into
favour as shall repent, and believe, and persevere
unto the end. 3. That sufficient and necessary
means of grace should be offered and administred
unto all men without exception. 4. That certain
singular persons should be saved, whom God foresaw would repent, and believe, and persevere.
This way is justly opposed by others, who deny
God's acts in intention to be in the same order as
we see them in production. In order of material
existing it is granted that Christ is revealed, promised, and exhibited after sin, and that we repent,
believe, persevere before we are saved; but in
order of God's intention Christ is before sin, and

salvation before repentance, faith, perseverance.
The apostle reckoned the order in which things
exist thus, 1. *The word.* 2. *You the Elect.* 3.
Christ. 4. *God,* 1 Cor. iii. 22, 23. But he gives
us to understand the order of intention thus; as
first, God intends his own glory, then Christ, then
the elect, then the world. Certainly it is an hard
thing to marshal the eternal emanant acts of the divine understanding, or will it first, second, third,
fourth: all God's projects are like himself, who
is *tota simul et perfecta possessio sui*, a whole and
perfect possession of himself together and at once;
so as in him considered there is no *prius* nor *posteri-
us* in any of his acts; but considered in effects, or in
respect of us, one thing may be said to be first, second, or third in nature, time and being before,
or after another. And thus in respect of us, we
say the end must be in nature before the means to
the end; now the permission of the fall, repentance, faith, perseverance are used by God as means
to bring some to salvation; God therefore doth
first project our salvation, and then the means;
and both the end and the means are the product of
God's election or predestination. Here then is the
project, that *God will glorify his grace, and to
this end he will predestinate Christ, and in Christ
he will choose some of the sons of men to salvation,
whom, notwithstanding sin, he will make holy, and
without blame before him in love*, Eccl. 1. 4. This
project, or plot, or design of God will be further
enlarged in the next passage, *viz.* his counsels.

SECT. V.

The Counsel.

OF the counsels of God concerning man before
all worlds, we read in several texts, *Christ
was delivered by the determinate counsel of God*,
Acts ii. 23. *For of a truth against thy holy child
Jesus, whom thou hast anointed, both Herod and
Pontius Pilate with the Gentiles, and the people if
Israel were gathered together, for to do whatsoever
thy hand, & thy counsel determined before to be done*,
Acts iv. 27, 28. And thus the members of Christ
are said to *obtain an inheritance, being predestinated according to the purpose of him who worketh all
things after the counsel of his own will*, Eph. i. 11.
Of this counsel of God's will we know but little
now, yet this will be made known when we come

to glory; yea, it will be a great part of the glory of heaven for the Lord to make known the counsel of his will, we know his will, but we shall then know the counsel of his will, and praise him to all eternity for it; this shall be the glory of the saints, that they shall see into the counsel of God's will in choosing them and calling them, and passing by others, and letting others go In the mean while thus far we may know, for thus far he hath revealed himself concerning his counsels about man from everlasting.

1. That man should be a reasonable creature, and because that every creature is unavoidably subject to the Creator (for *he made all things for himself*, Pr. xvi 4. and all is to return that glory to him for which he made them), therefore man should serve him as all other creatures must, only his service should be after a reasonable manner, out of judgment, discretion and election; hence David is said to *have chosen the way of truth*, Pf. cxix. 30. and Moses to have *chosen the afflictions of God's people, and the reproaches of Christ before the pleasures of sin, or the treasures of Egypt*, Heb. xi. 25, 26. And hence it is that holiness in the phrase of scripture is called judgment, *He shall convince the world of judgment*, John xvi 11 and *he shall bring forth judgment unto victory*, Matth xii. 20. And hence it is that our service is called, *a reasonable service*, Rom xii 1. God would not set any such determinating law over the operations of man, as over other creatures, that so he might truly work out of judgment, and stand or fall by his own election.

2. That if man should deviate from this reasonable service, and break the law which God would give, and which he himself should have an original power to perform, that then he should incur the displeasure of God; and such a curse, and such a penalty should be inflicted. And here comes in the fall of man into God's consideration; he looks upon it as a wilful transgression of his law, and by how much the law was more just, and the obedience more easy, by so much he judges the transgression more unreasonable, and the punishment more certain and intolerable

3. That sin should not pass unrevenged; and that for these reasons, 1 Because of God's infinite hatred thereof, *He is of purer eyes than to behold evil, he cannot look on iniquity*, Hab. i. 13. It-provokes a nauseousness and abhorrency in him; *for all these are things which I hate, saith the Lord*, ——*they are a trouble unto me, I am weary to bear them*, Zech viii 17. 2 Because of his truth, he hath said, *In the day that thou eatest thereof thou shalt surely die*, or, *thou shalt dying die*, Gen ii. 17 die temporally, and die eternally, and surely God will in no wise abolish his law. *One jot, or tittle shall in no wise pass from the law till all be fulfilled*, Matth. v. 18 3 Because of his terror and fearful majesty, for God will have men always to tremble before him, and by his terror to be persuaded from sinning, *Knowing therefore the terror of the Lord, we persuade men*, 2 Cor v 11. *And fear him who is able to destroy both body and soul in hell, I say unto you, fear him*, Matth. x. 28 and *let us have grace, whereby we may serve God acceptably with reverence and godly fear, for God is a consuming fire*, Heb. xii 23, 29 Upon these reasons God is resolved sin shall not pass unrevenged, lest thereby his justice should be securely abused, his hatred against sin the less declared, his truth questioned, and his dreadful majesty by men neglected.

4. That every man, notwithstanding sin, should not be utterly destroyed: and that for these reasons, 1. Because of that infinite delight which the Lord hath in mercy why? this delight is it that so disposeth him to pardon abundantly, and to exercise loving-kindness on the sons of men; *Who is a God like unto thee, that pardonest iniquity and passest by the transgression of the remnant of thy heritage? Thou retainest not thine anger for ever, because thou delightest in mercy*, Pf ciii. 8. And *I am the Lord which exercise loving-kindness, judgment and righteousness in the earth, for in these things I delight, saith the Lord*, Jer. ix 24. 2. Because of that delight which God hath to be actively glorified by his creatures voluntary service and subjection, *Herein is my Father glorified, if ye bear much fruit*, John xv 8 And *I have no pleasure in the death of the wicked, but that he turn from his way and live*, Ezek xxxiii 11. He delighteth most in unbloody conquests, when by his patience, and goodness, and forbearance he subdueth the hearts, affection, and consciences of men unto himself: he esteemeth himself more glorified in the services, than in the sufferings of men, and therefore in this eternity he resolves a-

to destroy all men, lest there should be no religion upon the earth. When the angels fell, they fell not all, many were still left to glorify him actively in their service to him, but when Adam fell, all mankind fell in him; so that there was no tree in this paradise left to bring forth any fruit unto God; and this is most certain that God would rather have his trees for fruit, than for fewel; hence he resolves that mankind, notwithstanding sin, should not be utterly destroyed.

Hereupon the trinity calls a counsel, and the question is, 'What is to be done with poor man?' The learned here frame a kind of conflict in God's holy attributes, and, by a liberty which the holy Ghost from the language of holy scripture doth allow them, they speak of God after the manner of men, as if he were reduced unto some straits and difficulties, by the cross demands of his several attributes. Justice calls upon him for the condemnation of a sinful, and therefore worthily accursed creature; which demand is seconded by his *truth*, to make good that threatning, *In the day that thou eatest thereof thou shalt surely die the death*; *mercy* on the other side pleads for favour and compassion towards man, wofully seduced, and overthrown by Satan, and this plea is seconded by *love* and *goodness*, and the like attributes; at last, when the business came to a determination, *wisdom* finds out a way, which the angels of heaven gaze on with admiration and astonishment, how to reconcile these different pleas of his attributes together. A *Jesus* is resolved on; one of the same blessed trinity, who by his Father's ordination, his own voluntary susception, and the holy Spirit's sanctification should be fitted for the business. To this purpose this *Jesus* should be both a surety and an head over sinful men; a surety to pay men's debts unto God, and an head to restore God's image unto man; and thus in him *mercy and truth hath met together, righteousness and peace have kissed each other*, Psal. lxxxv. 10.

This is the great mystery of the gospel; this is that which the angels (as I tell you) pry into; nay, that is that which the angels and saints too shall admire, and bless God for to all eternity; this is that which set the infinite *wisdom* of God on work from all eternity. If all the angels in heaven, and all the men in the world, had been put to it to find out a way to answer this question, 'How shall sin ' be pardoned, the sinner reconciled, and God ' glorify his justice?' They could never have done it; this cost God dear, it cost him the heart-blood of his own Son, and that's a sure sign that God's heart was much in it, and indeed we are not Christians, until in some measure we see and have our hearts taken with the glory of God in this mystery. O the wonder of heaven and earth! here's the case, man is fallen through sin, and ever since the fall, man and sin are inseparably joined together as fire and heat; yet God will have mercy on the man, and he will take vengeance on the sin; the eternal *wisdom* of God hath found out a way to translate this man's sins on another person who is able to bear them, and to interest this man's person in another's righteousness, which is able to cover him; so that now all's one in regard of man, as the law had been utterly abrogated; and all's one too in regard of God, as if the creature had been utterly condemned. And all this is done in our *Jesus*; on him was executed the curse of the law, by him was fulfilled the righteousness of the law, for him was remitted the sin of man, and through him were all things made new again. The world was in Christ as in its surety, making satisfaction to the justice of God; and God was in Christ as in his embassador, reconciling the world unto himself again, O *(bathos!) O the depths of the riches both of the wisdom and knowledge of God! how unsearchable are his judgments, and his ways past finding out?* Rom. xi. 33. You have seen the project, and the counsels of God for man's salvation before all worlds; it is but dimly, *For who hath known the mind of the Lord? Or who hath been his counsellor?* Rom. xi. 34.

SECT. VI.

The Foreknowledge.

OF the foreknowledge of God, in this respect we read in scriptures, Christ is said to be *delivered by the determined counsel and foreknowledge of God*, Acts ii. 23. And it is said of Christ's members, *The called according to his purpose, whom he did foreknow*, Rom. viii. 29. And elsewhere in the same epistle, *God hath not cast away his people, which he foreknew*, Rom. xi. 2. And Peter writes *to the strangers, elect according to the foreknowledge of God the Father*, 1 Pet. i. 2. Understand,

Of the eternal Generation of our Jesus 33

derstand, that foreknowlege is ascribed to God in respect of the creature properly, but in respect of God there is nothing past, nothing to come; all things past, and all things to come are present to him; and therefore in that sense he cannot be said to foreknow any thing. Now the Lord in respect of us is said in scripture to foreknow things or persons two ways.

1. *Generally*, by a general knowledge, of which David speaks; *Thine eyes did see my substance, yet being unperfect, and in thy book all my members were written, which in continuance were fashioned, when as yet there was none of them*, Psalm cxxxix 16.

2. *Especially*, By a more special foreknowlege, which is a knowledge with love and approbation, the very same which barely comprehendeth that we call election, so God's choosing is expressed by loving, *Jacob have I loved, and Esau have I hated*, Rom ix 13. And this is that which the apostle speaks of, *The Lord knoweth who are his*, 2 Tim. ii 19. *i e* the Lord from everlasting knoweth his with love and with approbation, *Hath God cast away his people, which he foreknew?* Rom xi 2. *i. e.* which he before loved and approved. Hence we gather, that after the project was laid, and the counsels of God were agreed upon it, then God foreknew or foresaw whom to embrace in his eternal love as his own. At one act he foreknew whom he would choose, and set apart of his own free love, to life and salvation and here you have the cause of God's predestinating his saints to glory, it was the foreknowledge, and free love of God; the Lord from everlasting, and before the foundation of the world fore-ordained, or fore-appointed, some to salvation, nothing moving him thereunto but his own good pleasure and his own free love. This is that in order of nature, and strictly, goes before, and is the cause of our predestination, *for whom he did foreknow, he also did predestinate*, Rom. viii. 29. First he foreknew, and then he did predestinate; first he loved, and then he elected; first he embraced them as his own in the arms of his eternal love, and then of his free love he set them apart to life, and to salvation· hence the apostle calls it, *The election of grace*, Rom. xi 5. signifying that our election springs out of the womb of love, free love, free grace is the cause of our election.

Some object, That we are predestinated and elected according to foreknowledge, *i e* say they, according to the foreknowledge of our faith, and repentance and perseverance; but if that were Paul's foreknowledge, why then would he say, That *those whom he did foreknow, he also did predestinate to be conformed to the image of his Son*, Rom viii. 29. If God did foreknow them first conformed, why did he then predestinate them *to be conformed?* And if that were Peter's foreknowlege, why then would he say, That *they were elect according to the foreknowledge of God the Father,—unto obedience?* 1 Pet. i 3. If God did foreknow them first obedient, how then did he *foreknow them unto obedience?* I know it is a question, 'Whether God in foresight of belief, and perseverance in faith and holiness, do choose us to salvation?' For my part I am for the negative, upon these well known grounds

1 Because election on faith foreseen makes God to go out of himself, looking to this or that in the creature, upon which his will may be determined to elect; now this is against the all-sufficiency of God's knowledge, as if he should get knowledge from the things we know, and against all the all-sufficiency of God's will, as if he must be beholden to something in us, before the business of our election can be determined.

2. Because election on faith or love foreseen, it makes God to choose us when we have chosen him, and to love us when we have loved him first; but this is contrary to scripture, *We love him, because he loved us first; and herein is love, not that we loved God, but that he loved us, and sent his Son to be the propitiation for our sins*, 1 John iv. 19 Ver. 10

3 Because election on faith foreseen, stands not with the freedom of God's will within himself, but God tells us plainly, *I will have mercy on whom I will have mercy, and I will have compassion on whom I will have compassion*, Rom ix 15, 16 See Jo Goodwin's expos on Rom. ix. 15, 16 I know some would not have this text understood of election from eternity, but of justification, adoption, salvation, and yet they grant the truth of it to be alike, whether in reference to election, or justification. The words, *I will have mercy on whom I will have mercy*, are one and the same with those words spoken by God to Moses, *I will be gracious to whom I will be*

F *gra-*

gracious, Exod. xxxiii. 19. Now, to be gracious, as is confessed, properly imports a propensity of mind and will to do some good without any motive or engagement thereunto from without, especially from the person or persons to whom this good is done, or intended; which is a plain argument, that *I will have mercy*, is not of that kind of mercy, the exercise whereof is drawn out, or procured by any thing whatsoever in those to whom it is shewed, but because it pleaseth itself, or him in whom it resideth so to do; and in this respect mercy differs very little or nothing at all from grace: the apostle, exchanging Moses his words, was but his interpreter.

4. Because election on faith foreseen, is all one as to say, We are ordained to eternal life because we believe; but the scriptures speak contrary, *As many as were ordained to eternal life, believed*, Acts xiii. 48. And not as many as believed were ordained to eternal life.

5. Because a prime and eternal cause cannot depend upon the self-same temporal effects which are thereby caused: now, election is the prime and eternal cause whence our faith, repentance, and perseverance were derived, and therefore our faith, repentance, and perseverance cannot be imagined antecedent causes, conditions, or motives unto the divine election.

6. Because election on faith foreseen, or election of men believing and persevering in faith and holiness unto the last gasp, brings with it many absurdities. As, 1. This is to elect men, not considered as in the state of innocency, nor misery, but as in a state of grace, contrary to their own tenets. 2. This is not to bring faith, holiness, perseverance out of the gracious benefit of election, but to bring election out of the foreseen acts of believing, obeying, persevering, quite contrary to scripture, *He hath chosen us in him before the foundation of the world, that we should be holy and without blame before him in love*, Eph. i. 4. 3. This were to say, that election or predestination affords no man any help at all, in the way unto eternal salvation; for how can that be the cause leading infallibly in the way into eternal life, which comes not so much as into consideration, until a man have run out his race (at least in God's foreknowledge) in faith, and godliness, and be arrived at heaven's gates. Such a falsely named predestination might more truly and properly have been called a post-destination. But I have too long stood on this controversy, and indeed it is against my design, *Which is not to minister questions, but rather edifying, which is in faith*, 1 Tim. i. 4. I remember what I have read, and indeed I begin already to feel, that these controversial points will but discompose our spirits, and waste our zeal, our love, our delight in Jesus (this lovely subject and object we are a viewing) even by the interruption and diversion of our contemplations. Not a word more in that kind.

SECT. VII.

The Purpose.

OF the purpose of God concerning man's salvation before all worlds, we read in scriptures, *We know that all things work together for good to them that love God, to them who are called according to his purpose*, Rom. viii. 28. And it is said of Jacob and Esau, that *being not yet born, neither having done any good or evil, that the purpose of God according to election might stand*, Rom ix. 11. And *in Christ we are said to obtain an inheritance, being predestinate according to the purpose of him who worketh all things after the counsel of his own will*, Eph. i. 11. And elsewhere the apostle speaks of *the manifold wisdom of God, according to the eternal purpose, which he purposed in Christ Jesus our Lord*, Eph. iii. 11. And again, *He hath saved us and called us with an holy calling, not according to our works, but according to his own purpose and grace, which was given us in Christ Jesus, before the world began*, 2 Tim. i. 9. All these hold forth this truth, That God purposed in himself from all eternity to bring them whom he foreknew to life and to salvation. This purpose of God, in order of nature, comes before predestination, in that we are said to *be predestinated according to his purpose*, Eph. 1. 11. And yet it must needs follow after his foreknowledge and counsel: for, first, he loves before he will purpose, *And every purpose is established by counsel*. Yea, *without counsel purposes*, saith the wise man, *are disappointed*, Pro. xxx. 18. and xv. 22. Why then, first he counsels (I speak after the manner of men) and then he foreknows, *i. e.* either he knows whom he will chuse, for God doth not blindly

chuse

chuse he knows not whom, or else he sets his love to life on some, he knows them with a knowledge of approbation, and then he settles a purpose to bring them to life, whom he so foreknows, in that especial and unspeakable way.

This purpose of God speaks our stability and certainty of salvation in Christ; when God once purposeth, it is past altering: *Surely as I have thought, so shall it come to pass, and as I have purposed*, saith God, *so shall it stand*. You may write upon it, that God's purposes are immutable. Paul would not lightly alter purposes taken up by him; *When I was therefore thus minded*, saith he, *did I use lightness? Or the thing that I purpose, do I purpose according to the flesh, that with me there should be yea, yea, and nay, nay?* Paul would not, I say, alter his purpose; And will God, think you, alter his? Methinks his word speaks to me, as if I heard God say from all eternity, 'It is my purpose to save a remnant of mankind, 'though all are lost by sin, yet my wisdom hath 'found out a way to choose out some, and tho' those 'some, those few that I have purposed to save, 'stand in very slippery places, yet *I will be the same 'yesterday, and to day, and for ever*, Heb. xiii. '8. I foresee indeed many thousands of failings 'and exasperations, to alter the purpose that I 'have towards my people, I foresee their daily 'provocations of my justice, I foresee their many 'lusts within, and their many enemies without, I 'foresee that grace inherent. I will give them to 'be as mutable in all the progeny, as in their fa- 'ther Adam; and if I leave them in the hands of 'their own counsel, they cannot but depart daily 'from me, even as water, though it could be 'made as hot as fire, yet being left unto itself, it 'will quickly reduce, and work itself to its own o- 'riginal coldness again; I foresee them in their 'best condition, at full sea, at their highest tide 'of grace, to be as changeable and moveable se- 'veral ways, as wheels; to be as perplexed, hin- 'dred and distracted in themselves, as cross wheels 'in one another; grace swaying one way, and flesh 'another way, and what stability can I think in 'such? Why yet *(says God)* yet I purpose to 'bring this little flock to heaven, my purpose is 'in, and from myself, and I am God, and not 'man, and therefore I cannot repent, nor call in 'the purpose which now I have. *Have I said, and* 'shall not I do it? Have I spoken, and shall I not 'make it good?* Numb. xxiii. 19. Yes, yes, my 'purpose must stand, and for this purpose I will 'set my Son betwixt my people and myself, so 'that if they sin, I will look on him, and by that 'means, I will see no iniquity in Jacob, nor trans- 'gression in Israel, Numb. xxiii. 21. And for this 'purpose, I will join to the wheels the living crea- 'tures, *that when the living creatures go, the 'wheels shall go, and when the living crea- 'tures stand, they shall stand; and when the li- 'ving creatures are lifted up from the earth, the 'wheels shall be lifted up against them, for the 'spirit of the living creatures shall be in the wheels,* 'Ezek. i. 21. My meaning is, that my saints shall 'not have their stability from themselves, for they 'are like wheels, but they shall have it from me, 'and from my Son, unto whom, by the same Spi- 'rit of life, they shall be united.' Thus may I imagine the Lord from all eternity to say, and speak, and purpose with himself; and surely his purpose must stand upon this account, *For the gifts and calling of God, are without repentance*, Rom. xi. 29.

SECT. VIII.

The Decree.

THE decree of God concerning man's sal- vation before the foundation of the world, appears in these texts, *I will declare the decree*, saith God. What was that? Why, concerning Christ, and concerning the church, *Thou art my Son, this day have I begotten thee. Ask of me, and I shall give thee the heathen for thine inheritance, and the uttermost parts of the earth for thy possession*, Psalm ii. 7, 8. It was God's decree to give out of Jews and Gentiles a church to Christ; and this decree was made in that day of eternity, when the Son of God was begotten of the Father. This de- cree in scripture phrase hath several titles. 1. It is the very same with that which we usually call predestination; for what is predestination but a decree of God concerning the different preparation of grace, whereby some are guided infallibly unto salvation? Predestination is a decree both of the means and end; a decree of given grace effectual unto some persons here, and of bringing the same persons unto glory hereafter. This decree, this

predestination, this golden chain of the means and end, is set down by the apostle, *Whom he did predestinate, them he also called, and whom he called, them he also justified, and whom he justified, them he also glorified,* Rom. viii. 30. As God hath predestinated some to life and glory, so he hath predestinated them to be called and justified before they be glorified; whomsoever the Lord hath decreed to save, them hath he also decreed to sanctify before they come to enjoy that salvation. *God hath chosen us in Christ before the foundation of the world, that we should be* first *holy,* and then *happy,* Eph. i. 4. See how these are twisted by the apostle once and again, *God hath from the beginning chosen you to salvation, through sanctification of the Spirit, and belief of the truth,* 2 Thes. ii. 13. I have heard of some blasphemous reasonings, ' If ' we are predestinated to be saved, we may live as ' we will, for howsoever we live, though never so ' wickedly, yet we shall be saved.' O fearful! O devilish reasoning! surely this comes from the devil, and not from God, or his word: mark here one of Satan's depths: *In outward things he tempts men to distrust God, and to rely altogether on means: but in heavenly things and matters of salvation he tempts men to lay all on God's decrees, and God's purposes, without any regard had to the means,* Gal. iii. 29. Such men might as well say, The Lord hath appointed that we shall live to such a time, and till then we shall not die, and therefore what need we food in health, or physick in sickness? O take heed in these reasonings! God's decree doth not remove the use of the means, but establish and confirm them.———2. This decree is the same with that *book of life* wherein are written the names of the elect; Paul tells us of *some women, with Clement, and other fellow-labourers, whose names are in the book of life,* Phil. iv. 3. And Christ bids his disciples *rejoice, because their names are written in heaven,* Luke xii. 20. And John saw in his vision *the dead, small and great stand before God, and the books were opened, and another book was opened, which is the book of life,* Rev. xx. 12. As captains have a book wherein they write the names of their soldiers, and citizens have a book wherein they record the names of their burgesses: so God hath his decree or book of life, in which he registers all that belong to him. Some other texts speak of a book of life, *as, Blot me,* *I pray thee, out of thy book which thou hast written,* said Moses in his zeal for Israel, to whom the Lord answered, *Whosoever sinneth against me, him will I blot out of my book,* Exod. xxxi. 32, 33. But this was not the book, say some, of God's eternal decree, but the book of his providences. God hath a double book, and both in a figure, hath a book of his resolved decrees, and a book of his acted providences; this latter is but a transcript, or a copy of the former: those huge original volumes of love and blessings which God hath laid up in his heart for his own people from all eternity, is the book I mean; indeed this book is writing out every day by the hand and pen of providence in the ordering of all those affairs which concern our salvation.———3. This decree is the very same also with God's seal; *The foundation of God standeth sure, having this seal, the Lord knoweth them that are his,* 2 Tim. ii. 19. A seal is used in three cases; 1. To keep things distinct. 2. To keep things secret. 3. To keep things safe: in every of these respects God's decrees are seals; but especially in the last; those souls that are sealed by God, they are safe in the love and favour of God; as when Job tells us that *God sealed up the stars, i. e.* say some, he preserveth the stars in their orbs, in the places where he hath set them they shall never drop out, so God seals up his saints, *i. e.* he secures them to the eternal love of God, so that they shall never drop out of his heart. All these titles speak the immutability of God's eternal emanant acts, *q. d.* ' I decree, I predestinate, I book ' it, seal it, that such and such persons shall be ' eternally saved; and why all this! but to note ' the certainty and stability of the thing. Shall ' great monarchs of the earth do thus? Shall they ' decree and book and seal, to show their great-' ness and wisdom, that they could so resolve, as ' no person or power whatsoever should be strong ' enough to cause them to change their resolutions? ' And shall not I much more? Do not I know, ' or foresee all that can or will follow? Is there ' any power, or ever shall be, to take them out of ' my hands? or is it possible, that ever I should ' have a relenting thought at the saving of these ' souls? Can any thing fall out hereafter, to make ' me more provident, more powerful, more wise, ' more merciful than now I am? It may be in some ' things I may will a change, but can I in any thing
' truly

' truly change my will?' No, no, *I am the Lord, I change not, therefore ye sons of Jacob are not consumed.* Mal. iii. 6.

SECT. IX.

The Covenant.

THE covenant concerning man's salvation, is the last and main particular I instanced in: I dare not be too curious to insist on the order of nature, and the rather, because I believe the covenant betwixt God and Christ from everlasting is interwoven with the decree, foreknowledge and election above. So the Apostle tells us, *He hath chosen us in Christ before the foundation of the world,* Eph. i. 4. Mark that, *in Christ.* There was an eternal plot betwixt the Father and the Son; there was a bargain made (I speak it with reverence) betwixt God and Christ, there was a covenant betwixt the Lord and his Son Jesus Christ, for the salvation of the elect; and of this observe we especially these following texts.

In Isaiah xlix. 1, 2, 3, 4. The prophet seems to set it dialogue-ways; one expresseth it thus; *First,* Christ begins, and shews his commission, telling God how he had called him, and fitted him for the work of redemption, and he would know what reward he should have of him for so great an undertaking. *The Lord hath called me from the womb, from the bowels of my mother hath he made mention of my name, and he hath made my mouth like a sharp sword, in the shadow of his hand hath he hid me, and made me a polished shaft; in his quiver hath he hid me,* Isa. xlix. 1, 2. Upon this God answers him, and tells him what reward he should have for so great an undertaking; only at first he offers low, *viz.* only the elect people of Israel. And he said unto me, *Thou art my servant, O Israel, in whom I will be glorified by thee,* Isai. xlix. 13. Christ who stood now a making his bargain with him, thought these too few, and not worth so great a labour and work, because few of the Jews would come in, but would refuse him, and therefore he says, he should labour in vain, if this were all his recompence, *Then said I, I have laboured in vain, I have spent my strength for nought, and in vain,* Isa. xlix. 4. And yet withal he tells God, that seeing his heart was so much in saving sinners, he would do it howsoever for these few, comforting himself with this, that his work or his reward was with the Lord. Upon this God comes off more freely, and opens his heart more largely to him, as meaning more amply to content him for his pains in dying. *It is a light thing, that thou shouldst be my servant to raise up the tribe of Jacob, and to restore the preserved of Israel,* Isa. xlix. 6. That is not worth the dying for, I value thy sufferings more than so, *I will also give thee for a light unto the Gentiles, that thou mayest be my salvation unto the ends of the earth.* Methinks I imagine as if I heard God speak unto Christ from eternity, ' See, here I have
' loved a remnant of mankind both of Jews and
' Gentiles, with an everlasting love, I know they
' will sin and corrupt themselves, and so become
' enemies to me, and liable unto eternal death;
' now thou art a mighty person, able to do what
' I require of thee for them; if thou wilt take
' upon thee their nature and sins, and undertake
' to satisfy my justice and law, and take away that
' hatred that is in them towards me and my law,
' and make them a believing holy people, then I
' will pardon them, and adopt them in thee for
' my sons and daughters, and make them co-heirs
' with thee, of an incorruptible crown of life.'
And then said Christ, *Lo I come, to do thy will, O God,* Heb. x. 7, 9. Then Christ, as it were, struck hands with God, to take upon him the nature and sin of man, and to do and suffer for him whatsoever God required of him. Certainly thus was the whole business of our salvation first transacted betwixt God the Father and Christ, before it was revealed to us. Hence we are said to be given unto Christ, *I have manifested thy name* (saith Christ) *unto the men which thou gavest out of the world: thine they were, and thou gavest them me,* John xvii. 6. This very giving implies, as if the Father in his eternity should have said to the Son, ' These I take to be vessels of
' mercy, and them thou shalt bring unto me, for
' they will destroy themselves, but thou shalt save
' them out of their lost estate.' And then the Son takes them at his Father's hand, and looking at his Father's will, *This is the Father's will which hath sent me, that of all which he hath given me, I should lose nothing,* John vi. 39. He thereupon takes care of such, he would

should be loft, which his father hath given him, they are more dear than so.

In Isa. liii. 10, 11. and in Psalm xl. 7. Christ is brought in as a surety, offering himself for us, and readily accepting of God's will in this very matter: and hence it is, that he is called God's servant, and his ears are said to be opened.

In Isa. xlii. 1, 6. This very covenant is expresly mentioned. Thus God speaks of Christ, *Behold my servant whom I uphold, mine elect in whom my soul delighteth:——I will give thee for a covenant of the people, for a light of the Gentiles,* Isa. liii. 11. Psal. xl. 6. Yea, this covenant and agreement seems to be confirmed with an oath, in Heb. vii. 28. And for this service Christ is required to *ask of God, and he will give him the heathen for his inheritance,* Psalm ii. 8. Observe how the church of God is given to Christ, as a reward of that obedience which he showed in accepting of the office of a surety for us. This stipulation some make to be that counsel of peace spoken of by the prophet, *And the counsel of peace shall be betwixt them both,* Zech. vi. 13. i. e. between the Lord, *and the man whose name is the branch,* Verse 12. And for this agreement it is that Christ is called the second Adam; for, as with the first Adam God plighted a covenant concerning him and his posterity, so also he did indent with Christ and his seed concerning eternal life to be obtained by him. I deny not but that some promises were made only to Christ in his own person, and not to descend to his children, as, *Sit on my right hand until I make thine enemies thy footstool,* Heb. i. 13. *And he shall see his seed, he shall prolong his days, the pleasure of the Lord shall prosper in his hands,* Isa. liii. 10. *And ask of me, and I will give thee the heathen for thine inheritance, and the uttermost parts of the earth for thy possession,* Psalm ii. 8. But there are other promises made to him and his; as that grand promise, *I will be to him a Father, and he shall be to me a Son,* Heb i. 5. Jer. xxxii. 38. It is first made to him, and then to us: and that special promise of spiritual grace, John i. 16. of justification, Isa. l. 8. of victory and dominion, Psal. cx. 2. of the kingdom of glory, Luke xxiv. 26. They are every one first made to him, and then to us:——The business from eternity lay thus, 'Here is man lost, said God to his Son, but 'thou shalt in the fulness of time go and be born 'of flesh and blood, and die for them, and satis- 'fy my justice, and they shall be thine for a por- 'tion, and they shall be called *the holy people, the* '*redeemed of the Lord,* Isa. lxii. 12. This shalt 'thou do, said the Father, and upon these terms 'they shall live that believe.' This was God's covenant with the Son of his love for us; to whom the Son answered (as it were) again, 'Content, 'Father, I will go, and fulfil thy pleasure, and 'they shall be mine for ever; I will in the fulness 'of time die for them, and they shall live in me:' *Burnt-offerings, and sin-offerings thou hast not required* (no, it was self-offering) *then said I, Lo, I come, in the volume of thy book it is written of me, to do thy will, O my God,* Psal. xl. 6, 7. In what book was it written, that Christ should come to do the will of God? Not only in the book of the law and the prophets, but also in the book of God's decrees. In this sense, *The Lamb was slain from the foundation of the world,* Rev. xiii. 8. His Father from before all time, appointed him to be our high Priest, and he from all eternity subscribed to his Father's pleasure in it.

In Gal. iii. 15. *Brethren, I speak after the manner of men, though it be but a man's covenant, yet if it be confirmed, no man disannulleth or addeth thereto.* Verse 16. *Now to Abraham and his seed were the promises made. He saith not, And to seeds, as of many; but as of one, And to thy seed, which is Christ.* There is a question, whether this covenant here mentioned, was made only betwixt God and Christ, or only betwixt God and us, or both betwixt God and Christ, and betwixt God and us. The occasion of this question is in these words, *Now to Abraham and his seed were the promises made. He saith not, And to seeds, as of many; but as of one, And to thy seed, which is Christ.* 1. Some argue hence, that there is no covenant or promise made to us, but only to Christ, or with Christ. Christ stood for us, and articled with God for us, and performed the conditions for life and glory; so that the promises are made all to him; yet this indeed is confessed, that because we are Christ's, and are concerned in the covenant, it is therefore sometimes called a covenant made with us; *I will make a new covenant with the house of Israel, and with the house of Judah,* Jer. xxxi. 31. Not that the covenant is really made with us, but only with Christ for us, and

and when we feel ourselves under the power of the promise, we begin then to know, that we are in that same covenant. But this is rather, say they, to feel ourselves in that covenant which God hath made with Christ, than to enter into covenant with God ourselves.

2. Others argue hence, that there is no covenant or promise made with Christ personal, but only with Christ mystical, such who are members of Christ, and so united to Christ, for mark the text, say they, *The promise is made first to Abraham, and then to his seed.* This seed is such a seed, as comes to have right to the promise in order from Abraham; now this cannot be Christ personal, but Christ mystical. And whereas the text says, *The promise is not made to seeds, but to one seed, which is Christ.* They distinguish of a double seed of Abraham; first, there is a carnal natural seed according to the flesh, and in this sense Christ speaks to those wicked unbelieving Jews which went about to kill him, *I know ye are Abraham's seed, but ye seek to kill me,* John viii. 37. *Secondly,* there is a spiritual seed, that walk in the faith and steps of Abraham, *Know ye therefore, that they which are of faith, the same are the children of Abraham.* And, *If ye be Christ's, then are ye Abraham's seed, and heirs according to the promise.* Now the promise is made to Abraham and his seed, not seeds, i. e. not to both seeds, both carnal and spiritual; but only to the one, which is the spiritual; and this seed is Christ, i. e. Christ mystical, the body of Christ, the faithful that are knit to Christ by a true and lively faith.

3. Others argue hence, that this covenant is made both betwixt God and Christ, and betwixt God and us; first, betwixt God and Christ: all the work of redemption and salvation was transacted betwixt God and Christ before the foundation of the world; but this doth not hinder but that the same promise is afterwards in time made to us also: Look, as it is in covenants amongst men, while the child is yet unborn the father takes conveyance of an inheritance for his child, which he keeps in his own hand till the child be born and come to years, and then he puts it into his own possession; so it is here, we are for a time hid in the womb of God's election, till we are brought forth by the grace of regeneration; now during this time we are not in ourselves capable of receiving any promise of life made to us; but it is made to Christ in our behalf, and he receives the promise from the Father in our stead: but yet so that when we come to be born anew, the promises are made unto ourselves, and then we are put into possession of them.

Here then is the meaning of the text, *The covenant is made with Christ,* (i. e.) with Christ and his heirs; principally with Christ, and with Abraham's nature in Christ, and yet personally with believers, who are also the seed of Abraham. All the difference is in that term, Christ; What thereby is meant, whether Christ personal, or Christ mystical, or Christ representative? And we say,

1. Not Christ personal, I mean not Christ's person singly considered; for that, 1. Would fight with the scope of Paul, whose bent it is to prove the promise of eternal life to be made to all believers. And that, 2. Would conclude the promise of eternal life to be given only to Christ, and not at all to those that are believers in Christ.

2. Not Christ mystical, for, 1. The promise is made to Christ, *In whom the covenant was confirmed,* Ver. 17. 2. *In whom the nations were blessed,* Ver. 8. 3. *In whom we receive the promise of the Spirit through faith,* Ver. 14. 4. *Who was made a curse for us,* Ver. 13. Now not any of these can agree to Christ mystical; Christ mystical did not confirm the covenant, nor bless the nations, nor give the Spirit, nor was made a curse.

3. It is Christ representative, Christ-mediator, Christ a publick person, to whom the promises are made, for Christ and his heirs are but all of them one confederate family; and as the covenant of works was made with Adam, and all his; and there were not two covenants: so here the covenant is made with the second Adam and his children, *But every man in his own order, Christ the firstfruits, and afterwards they that are Christ's,* 1 Cor. xv. 23.

I have now propounded the object we are to look unto; it is Jesus in that eternity before all time until the creation; Our next business is to direct us in the art or mystery of grace, how we are to look unto him in this respect.

CHAP.

CHAP. II. SECT. I.

Of knowing Jesus as carrying on the great work of our salvation in that eternity.

Looking comprehends knowing, considering, desiring, hoping, believing, loving, joying, calling upon Jesus, and conforming to Jesus: if then we will have an inward experimental look upon Jesus, we must act and exercise all these particulars.

1. We must know Jesus carrying on the great work of our salvation in that eternity before all time. Come, learn what this Jesus is, 1. In his relation to God, and so he is God's Son, eternally begotten before all worlds. See above and learn it thoroughly, who it is that was begotten, for the person, when it was, for the time, how it was, for the manner, and what was the mutual kindness and love of him that begot, and of him that was begotten: O the heighth and depth of this knowledge! 2. Come, learn what this Jesus is in his relation to us before all worlds; and to that purpose study close that great transaction betwixt God and Christ for our salvation. 1. Study that project of God, that he would glorify his grace; and to this end that he would predestinate Christ, and in Christ he would choose some of the sons of men, and amongst the rest that he would choose thee, whom, notwithstanding sin, he will make holy, and without blame before him in love. 2. Study the counsels of God concerning man before all worlds; O 'twas an hard question, how sin should be pardoned, the sinner reconciled, and yet God glorify his justice. None but the wisdom of God could ever find out a way to have had mercy on the man, and yet to take vengeance on the sin; ' but ' herein appeared the depth of the riches both of ' the wisdom and knowledge of God;' he devised the way to translate this man's sin (suppose thine own sins) on another's person who was able to bear them, and to interest this man's person (suppose thine own self) in another's righteousness who was able to cover them. 3. Study the foreknowledge of God, how the Lord knew his from everlasting with a knowledge of love and approbation; after the project was laid, and the counsels of God were agreed upon it, then God foreknew, or foresaw whom to embrace in his eternal love: and, O my soul, if thou art one of his, if God in Christ hath of his own free love set thee apart to life and salvation, then *know it for thyself*, Job v. 27. It is inward experimental knowledge we speak of. 4. Study the purpose of God concerning thy salvation; this purpose of God speaks the stability and certainty of thy salvation in Christ; his purpose is in, and from himself, who is God and not man, and therefore cannot repent; *hath he said, and shall he not do it? hath he spoken, and shall he not make it good?* Numb. xxiii. 19. 5. Study the decrees of God, they are all one with predestination, the book of life, the seal of God. What hath the Lord decreed, predestinated, booked, sealed thee for salvation? *O how blessed are the people that know the joyful sound? They shall walk in the light of thy countenance, O Lord,* Psal. xxxix. 15. 6. Study the covenant of grace; remember how the business of eternity says thus; 'Here is ' every man lost, said God to his Son, but thou shalt ' in fulness of time go, and be born of flesh and ' blood, and die for some of them, and satisfy my ' justice, and they shall be thine for a portion, and ' they shall be called the holy people, the re- ' deemed of the Lord. To whom the Son an- ' swered, Be it so, Lord, I will go and fulfil thy ' pleasure, and they shall be mine for ever.' Observe and be acquainted with this covenant in that very dialogue, first, God demands of his Son that he lay down his life, and for his labour he promiseth that he shall see his seed, Isa. liii. 10. And God shall give him many children. And secondly, the Son consents to lay down his life, and saith, ' Here I am to do the will of God, thou hast gi- ' ven me a body,' Heb. x. 5, 9. What, O my soul, that the Father and Christ should transact a bargain from eternity concerning thee? that there should be any communing betwixt the Father and the Son concerning thy happiness and salvation? Surely this is worthy thy pains and study; 'O hear ' it, and know thou it for thy good, Job v. 27.

SECT. II.

Of considering Jesus in that respect.

2. WE must consider Jesus carrying on this work of salvation in that eternity: it

is not enough to study, and know him, but according to the measure of knowlege we have attained, we must ponder, and muse, and meditate, and consider of him; now, consideration is an expatiating, and enlarging of the mind and heart on this or that subject. Consideration is a fixing of our thoughts, a stedfast bending of our minds to some spiritual matter, till it work on the affections, and conversation. We may know, and yet be inconsiderate of that we do know, but when the intention of our mind and heart is taken up about some one known object, and other things are not for the present taken notice of, this is consideration. O that, if it were possible, we could so consider Jesus in his first period of eternity, as that for a while at least we could forget all other things! Christians, I beseech you be dead to the world, be insensible of all other things, and look only to Jesus. It is said that men in a frenzy are insensible of what you do to them, because their minds are taken up about that which they apprehend so strongly; and if ever there was any object made known to take up the mind of a spiritual man, it is this, even this: not, but that other objects may be deeply and seriously minded of men; it is reported of one Archimedes, who was a great mathematician, that when the city was taken wherein he was, and the warlike instruments of death clattering about his ears, and all was in a tumult, yet he was so busy about drawing his lines, that he heard no noise, nor did he know there was any danger; but if such objects as those could take up the attention of his mind, so as not to regard other things, how much more should this consideration of Christ? If a carnal heart, a man that minds earthly things, be so taken up about them, because they are an object suitable to him; how much more should a gracious heart, that can see into the reality of these things of God and Christ from everlasting be so taken up with them as to mind nothing else? Come then, O my soul, and set thy consideration on work, as thus,

1. Consider Jesus in his relation to God, how he was the eternal son of the Father: I know in some respects we have little reason thus to look on Jesus. As we are sinners and fallen from God, there is no looking on an absolute Deity; alas! that majesty (because perfectly and essentially good) is no other than an enemy to sinners as sinners; so as we are sinners, and fallen from God, there is no looking on the Son of God; I mean on the Son of God, considered in the notion of his own eternal being, as co-equal, and co-essential to God the Father: alas! our sin hath offended his justice, which is himself: and what have we to do with that dreadful power, which we have provoked? But considering Jesus as jesus, which sounds a Saviour to all sinners believing on him; and that this Jesus contains the two natures of Christ, both the Godhead, and manhood; now we have our interests in him, may draw near, and (as we are capable) behold *the brightness of his glory*, Heb. i. 3. to this purpose the scriptures have discovered to us God the Son, how he is the second person in the trinity, having the foundation of personal subsistance from the Father alone, of whom by communication of his essence he is begotten from all eternity; *When there were no depths I was brought forth,—before the mountains were settled, before the hills I was brought forth*, Prov. viii. 24, 25. *Ante colles genitus eram, Before the mountains I was begotten*, as some; or, *Ante colles filiatus eram, Before the mountains I was sonned his Son*, as, others translate it. Why thus, O my soul, consider Jesus the Son of God, but in this consideration be not too curious; thou hearest of the generation of the Son, and the procession of the holy Ghost, but the manner how the Father begets the Son, how the Father and Son do aspire, and send forth the holy Spirit, be not too busy to enquire, thou mayest know a little, and consider a little, but for the depth and main of this great mystery of grace let the generation of the Son of God be honoured with silence. I remember one being too curious, and too inquisitive, 'What God was 'doing in that long *ævum* of eternity before he 'made the world?' It was answered, He decreed 'to make hell for such curious inquisitors,' *Aug. lib.* 1. *Confess. c.* 12. Be not therefore too nice in this consideration, keep within bounds of sobriety and humility; and then as thou art able not to be curious; to comprehend the scriptures will discover, that before God made the world in that long long *ævum* of eternity, he was doing these things.

1. Some things in relation to himself.
2. Some things in relation to his creatures.

1. Some things in relation to himself; and those things were either proper, or common to three persons.

sons. 1. The things proper to each of the persons were those internal, incommunicable actions of God as 1. To beget; and that belongs only to the Father, who is neither made, nor created, nor begotten of any. 2. To be begotten; and that belongs only to the Son, who is of the Father alone, not made, nor created, but begotten. 3. To proceed from both; and that belongs only to the holy Ghost, who is of the Father, and the Son, neither made, nor created, nor begotten, but proceeding. And these were God's actions in that eternity before all worlds: the Father was begetting God the Son: the Son was begotten of God the Father; the holy Ghost was proceeding from God the Father and God the Son. But what, were these actions of God ever in action during all that eternity? Yes, as they are called eternal actions, so they are permanent: look, as the sun doth beget his beams, and both sun and beams do send forth the heats: so the Father from all eternity ever did, and now doth, and ever will beget his Son, and both the Father and the Son ever did, and now do, and ever will aspire and breathe forth the holy Ghost. And therefore *(Orig. hom. B. in Jerem.)* saith well, ' Our Jesus is the brightness ' of God's glory; now the brightness of glory is ' not once begotten, and then afterwards leaves ' to be begotten; but as often as the glory riseth ' from whence the brightness springeth, so often ' doth the brightness of glory arise,' Heb. i. 3. *Before the hills was I brought forth*, Prov. viii. 25. Some translate thus, *Ante colles generat*, and not as others, *generavit me, Before the mountains were settled he begetteth me.* Surely the Son of God is ever begetting, and the holy Spirit ever proceeding.

2. The things common to the three persons in that eternity were those internal actions of God wherein the three persons did communicate; as 1. That one was in another, and possessed one another; the Father remaining with the Son, the Son with the Father, and the holy Ghost in, and with them both; thus we read of Christ, *The Lord possessed me in the beginning of his way, before the works of old*, Prov. viii. 22. And, *In the beginning was the Word, and the Word was with God*, John i. 1. And, *I am in the Father, and the Father in me.* John xiv. 10. 2. That one glorified another; the Father glorified the Son, and the Son glorified the Father, and the holy Ghost glorified both the Father and the Son: *And now, O Father, glorify thou me with thine ownself, with the glory which I had with thee before the world was*, John xvii. 5. 3. That one delighted in another, the Father delighted in the Son, the Son delighted in the Father, and the holy Ghost delighted in them both, *Then I was by him, as one brought up with him, and I was daily his delight, rejoicing always before him*, Prov. viii. 30. *I was daily his delight*, in the original, *delights*, intimating, That the Son was variety of delights unto his Father. Rejoicing always before him. Christ speaks in terms very quaint and familiar, always rejoicing, *q. d.* greatly sporting: it is a metaphor or simile taken from little ones, which sport and play before their parents. O see how the Father and the Son rejoice in one another's fellowship: nay, see how they spend that long eternity before the creation, in nothing but rejoicing and delights: the Father delights in his Son, and the Son rejoiceth in his Father. Consider, O my soul, thou hast sometimes had a tickling to know, what God was doing before the creation. Why, now be sober, and satisfied with this knowlege, God spent all that time (if I may call it time) in delighting himself in Jesus: why this was God's work to delight in his Son, and he so delighted in him, that he desired no other pleasure than the company and beholding of him which accordingly he twice told from heaven, while Christ was on earth, saying, ' This is my beloved Son in whom I am well plea-' sed: in whom I am well pleased.' The first found was at his baptism, Matth. iii. 17. and the second at his transfiguration, Matth. xvii. 5.

2. Some other things God was a doing in relation to his creatures; they will fall in at our next consideration; only this by the way, as God and Christ rejoiced in the fruition of one another, without communicating the notice thereof to any creature; so in the next verse we find them rejoicing in the salvation of men; *and my delights were with the sons of men*, Prov. viii. 31. Amidst the other considerations, O my soul, think of this; what? That God from all eternity should delight in thy salvation. Why! this consideration sets out to purpose the heart and desire of God to save thy soul. For, 1. Delights arise out of the strongest and choicest desires; men are pleased with many

things

things in which they delight not. 2. God and Christ are mentioned here to delight in this work, and in no other work of theirs, not in angels, not in the world, nor in any thing in it. 3. This their delight is mentioned next to their delighting in each other. 4. This delight was still aforehand, whilst God's heart was only in the expectation, and his mind but laying the plot of thy salvation; all these argue how great a matter this was in God's esteem, and how much his heart was in it, even from everlasting. O let all these fall into thy consideration!

2. Consider Jesus merely in his relation to us: consider him in that great transaction betwixt God and him for our salvation: and that we may settle our thoughts, and dwell here;——

1. Consider the project. The great God having entertained thoughts within himself, to communicate himself out of his aloneness everlasting, he lays this plot, that all he would do in that respect, it should be *to the praise of the glory of his grace*, Eph. i. 6. O my soul, consider, meditate and muse on this plot of the Almighty; it is contained by the apostle in a very few words, do thou weigh them all; here is, 1. The *Praise*. 2. *The Glory*. 3. *Of his grace*. 1. *Praise* is a setting forth this or that, by word, or deed, or gesture; it contains in it a reverend respect, an high esteem, a strong admiration. 2. *Glory* is the glorious being, or, essence of God, the glory of God in himself: sometimes we read of the *glory of his power*, 2 Thess. i. 9. that is his glorious essence, which is most powerful; and sometimes of the *glory of his majesty*, Isa. ii. 16. that is, his glorious essence, which is most majestical; and sometimes of the *glory of his grace*, Eph. i. 6. that is, his glorious essence, which is most gracious and merciful. But, 3. Why the glory of his grace? Mercy and grace meet both in love, only they differ thus, mercy is love as it helps the miserable, and grace is love as it gives good things freely without desert: here then is the great design, which God from everlasting carried on, that the glorious essence of his free love, free grace should be especially manifested to his saints, that so they might admire it, esteem it, honour it, and sound forth the praise of it. All the other designs of God were but subservient unto this. Some reckon up three great designs of the Almighty in communicating himself: as 1. The glory of his saints. 2. The glory of Christ. 3. The glory of himself, and especially the glory of his grace. 1. That the saints should be glorious, and to that purpose he made heaven and earth, and he makes them Lord of all, *All things are yours*, 1 Cor. iii. 21, 23. 2. That Christ should be glorious, and to that purpose he makes the saints, and gives them to Christ, *All things are yours, and you are Christ's*. And certainly, saith the apostle, at the last day, 2 Thess. i. 10. *Christ shall come to be glorified in his saints, and to be admired in all them that believe*. 3. That God himself should be glorified: *he made all things for himself,* ——Prov. xvi. 4. *Bring my sons from far, and my daughters from the ends of the earth, even every one that is called by my name; for I have created him for my glory*, Isa. xliii. 6, 7. Now this is the high design of God, to which all the rest are subservient; mark the steps, *All things are yours, and you are Christ's, and Christ is God's*, i. e. For God, and for his glory; the two former designs are to which, but not for which God worketh: he that buildeth an house, that he may lay a sure foundation, and that he may raise the frame, he gives it the due filling which belongs to it; but these are not his proper ends, his main design; but that he may have an house for his habitation: so God works many things to our glory, and that in us Christ may be glorious; but the proper end, that high design which he hath in all, it is his own glory. And yet, O my soul, consider a little further, the plot of our salvation, of the saints glory, and of Christ's glory, as it aims at the glory of God, so especially at the glory of his grace: as if we see that one doth this, or that in wisdom, it is the glory of this wisdom: if he doth it in strength and power, it is the glory of his power: if he do it out of grace, it is the glory of his grace: so God designing the salvation of our souls out of his mere grace, favour, love, he must needs intend to have his grace notified in us, and to have it (being known) accordingly admired, and praised, and honoured by us; not but that God must be glorified in his wisdom, power, justice, holiness, and his other attributes; ay, but especially in this, it is the grace of God in which he most delighteth; even as virtuous kings affect, above all their other virtues, to be had in honour for their clemency and bounty:

so it is with our God, the King of kings, and Lord of lords; all he doth is to this end, that his grace may be manifested to his greater glory. And to this end is the glory of Christ, and the glory of christians referred. Why, Lord, that this should be thy plot, To save my soul, that my soul should praise the glory of thy grace? That thy grace should before all worlds think on me for good? Oh how should I but think on thee, and thy free grace! how should I but admire it, praise it, exalt it above sun, moon and stars! how should I cry out with the apostle, 'Oh the depth of the 'riches of thy grace! for of him, and through him, 'and to him are all things, to whom be glory for 'ever, Amen! Rom. xi. 36.

2. Consider the counsels of God about thy salvation; *He worketh all things after the counsel of his own will*, Eph. i. 11. And with him is counsel, and with him is understanding. This counsel, as we have discovered, was primarily about the reconciliation of the riches of his grace, and the glory of his justice. Consider this, O my soul, thy sins put all the attributes of God to a kind of conflict; hereupon was that great and mighty counsel, how God should make way for his love and goodness, and yet satisfy his truth, and justice! at last the wisdom of God found out that glorious and wonderful expedient, the Lord Jesus Christ: is not this the meaning of the apostle? *Whom God hath set forth to be a propitiation thro' faith in his blood, to declare his righteousness for the remission of sins*, Rom. iii. 25. Ponder and weigh these words; God sets not forth Christ to be a propitiation to declare only his mercy in the forgiveness of sins: how, is there any thing but *mercy* in the forgiveness of sins? Yes, there is something else, there is *righteousness* also; and therefore he hath set forth Christ to be a propitiation, that he might *declare his righteousness*; nay, see it repeated, verse 26. 'To declare, I say, 'his righteousness, that he might be just, and the 'justifier of him which believeth in Jesus:' not that he might be merciful, but that he might be just in justifying him that believeth in Jesus. This text Luther had a great deal ado to understand; and he prayed much before he could get the right meaning of it.

This is the great mystery of the gospel; no wonder if a poor man could not reach it; this is that which set the infinite wisdom of God on work from all eternity, how to find a way to save sinners, and to be infinitely righteous notwithstanding.—— Nay, yet, O my soul, consider a little further; not only is the mercy of God in this way glorified, but the glory of his justice is as much, yea, more than if the sinner were eternally damned:——It is made good thus.——

1. When God appointed a surety, his Son, and charged our debts upon him to satisfy his justice; in that God would not spare his Son the least farthing token, I mean not the least degree of punishment; hereby the Lord shews a stronger love to justice, than if he had damned ten thousand thousand creatures. Suppose a malefactor comes before a judge, the judge will not spare the malefactor, but commands satisfaction to the law; this shews that the judge loves justice, but if the judge's own son be a delinquent, and it appears before all the country that the judge will not spare him; the judge now doth more honour justice in this than in condemning a thousand others: so when the Lord shall cast many thousands into hell, there to be tormented for ever, and ever, and ever, this shews that God loves justice, but when his own Son shall take our sins upon him, and God will not spare him; (that is the very word in scripture, *He spared not his own Son*, Rom. viii. 32.) this, surely this declares God's love to righteousness more than if all the world should be damned.

2. Suppose the sinner that is reconciled had been damned, then the justice of God had been but in satisfying, and never had been fully satisfied: but in that way that God hath found out to save a sinner, his justice is not only in satisfying, but it comes fully to be satisfied, to have enough. As, for instance, suppose a man to be a creditor to one, who owes him 100,000 *l.* This man is poor, and the utmost he can pay is but a penny a day; suppose the creditor should lay him in the goal until he had paid the utmost farthing, it is true he would be receiving day after day, but he would never be paid so long as the debtor lives; now, if another rich man should come, and lay down an 100,000 *l.* at once, the creditor is presently satisfied. Why here is a difference betwixt God satisfying his justice upon sinners and upon Jesus Christ; God comes upon the sinner and requires the debt

of

of punishment, because he did not pay the debt of obedience: God cast him into prison, and the utmost he can pay is but as it were a penny a day; and hence the poor sinner must still be paying, and paying, to eternity: this is the ground of their eternal punishment in hell, because in any finite time they can never pay enough: but now comes Jesus Christ and he fully pays the debt at once, so that justice saith, *I have enough, I am satisfied:* surely this is the greater glory to the very justice of God.

These were the counsels of God from all eternity, how he should make way for his love and goodness, and yet satisfy his truth and justice. O my soul, consider and wonder! Jesus Christ was the expedient, and in Christ not only God's mercy, but his justice is exalted, yea more exalted and more glorified in thy salvation than ever it could have been in thy damnation.

3. Consider the foreknowledge of God; he knew from everlasting whom he would set apart for life and for salvation. All the saints of God from first to last, they were then present to him, and before him, and he did look on them in his beloved Christ. Before there was a world, or a man, or any creature in it, he foreknew Adam, and Abraham, and Isaac, and Jacob, and all the patriarchs, and all the prophets, and all the apostles, and all the disciples of Christ, and believers in Christ: and, O my soul, if thou art one of God's elect, he foreknew thee with a knowledge of love and approbation: he had thee in his eye and heart: he had thoughts on Jacob, when he was *yet unborn, and had done neither good nor evil,* Rom. ix. 11. Assure thyself the Lord works not without provision or foreknowledge of the things effected; that cannot be in God, which is not to be found in a wise and prudent man: he that builds an house hath the frame of it first in himself: and the Psalmist tells thee, that *the eyes of God did see my substance yet being unperfect,* Psal. cxxxix. 16. *In this book of* knowledge *were all my members written, when as yet there was none of them,* Rom. ix. 13. Yea he knew thee with a knowledge of singular love, he embraced thee in his eternal love; as it is written, *Jacob have I loved, and Esau have I hated:* I will not say that this love was actually bestowed on thee till due time, yet it was prepared for thee from all eternity: and hence it is called,

'An everlasting love. The Lord hath appeared of 'old unto me, saying, I have loved thee with an 'everlasting love, therefore with loving-kindness 'have I drawn thee.

O muse, and meditate, and ponder on this love! it contains in it these particulars: as 1. The eternal good will of God: what else is the love of God towards the elect, but his everlasting good will to shew them mercy, and to do them good, and to save their souls? Hence the angels sung that anthem at Christ's birth, *Glory to God in the highest, and on earth peace, good will towards men,* Luke ii. 14. 2 The eternal pleasure and delight of God in the sons of men, the greatest delight that God hath, or ever had, it is in communicating himself to his Son first, and next unto his saints: nay, such delight he takes in letting out his mercy to his saints, as that he was well pleased with the death of his own Son, as a means conducing thereunto. O wonderful! one would think that the death of Christ should be the most abhorring to the heart of God of any thing in the world, and yet, saith the scripture, *it pleased the Lord to bruise him,* Isa. liii. 10. He took a pleasure and delight in the very bruising of Jesus Christ: the Lord saw this was the way for him to communicate himself in the fulness of his grace unto his saints, and therefore tho' it cost him so dear as the death of his own Son, yet he was well pleased with it. 3. This love of God contains in it a foreknowlege and approbation of all those effects of his love, whether they be temporal concerning this life, or eternal concerning the life to come. Concerning these effects of his love, saith John, *Behold what manner of love the Father hath bestowed upon us, that we should be called the sons of God,* 1 John iii. 1. *q. d.* Behold it, stand amazed at it, that children of wrath should become the sons of the most high God: for a beggar on the dunghill, a vagabound, renagade from God, a prodigal, a stranger to God, whom the Lord hath no cause to think on, to be made a son of God Almighty; O divine love! Pause a while, and muse on this, O my soul, that God should foreknow thee from all eternity, with a knowledge of love and approbation, it is admirable to consider. I say, it is admirable to consider.

4. Consider the purpose of God concerning thy salvation; *God hath not appointed* (or purposed) *us*

to wrath, but to obtain salvation by our Lord Jesus Christ, 1 Thess. v. 9. As when we have a will to do any thing, there follows upon this in the mind a settled purpose to effect it; so when God had loved some to life, there is in God a settled purpose of bringing them to it: *That the purpose of God according to election might stand,* Rom. ix. 11. Or be sure, it imports God's stability, and steadiness and constancy, and firmness in saving souls. There is much inconstancy and fickleness in the love of man, or in the love of a woman, but the love of God to his people is a steady love; 'As the bridegroom rejoiceth over the bride, so shall thy God rejoice over thee,' Isa. lxii. 5. Not only so doth thy God, but so 'shall thy God rejoice over thee.' God's purposes are without any alteration, the love of Christ after thousands of years is still as the love of a bridegroom upon the wedding-day; indeed then ordinarily love is hot, and appears much; so is Christ's love, and so is God's love ever hot; there is no moment of time from eternity to eternity wherein God rejoiceth not over his saints, as the bridegroom rejoiceth over his bride; not only as an husband over his wife, but as a bridegroom over his bride, we may say of this purpose of God, 'As it was in the beginning, it is now, and ever shall be, world without end.'

O my soul, muse, and meditate on this purpose of God, and by consequence on *the sure mercies of David,* Isa. lv. 3. It may be it is not always alike sure to thee: the love of God, as the shining of the sun, doth not always in the fruits of it shine out so gloriously, but the sun keeps his course in a steady way: what though it be sometimes clouded? What though at times it shines not so gloriously as at high noon? yet the purpose of God according to election must stand. All the devils in hell cannot frustrate God's purpose concerning only one soul: 'This is the Father's will which sent me, saith Christ, that of all which he hath given me I should lose none.' John vi. 39

5. Consider God's decree concerning thy soul's salvation, and the means to it. As the purpose of God, so the decree of God speaks stability and certainty of the thing decreed. *The foundation of God standeth sure,* 2 Tim. ii. 19 *i. e.* The decree of God touching man's salvation is unchangeable. If the laws of Medes and Persians were so absolute, that they could not be reversed, then much less can the decrees of God be reversed. No man that is not elected, can be elected; and no man that is elected can possibly be damned. *My sheep hear my voice,* saith Christ, *and I give unto them eternal life, and they shall never perish, neither shall any man pluck them out of my hand,* John x. 27, 28. And it must needs be so, for God's decree is grounded on the eternal and unchangeable will of God: and hence we say that there is a certain number of the elect known only to God, which cannot possibly be encreased or diminished, *I know whom I have chosen,* John xiii. 18. saith Christ. And yet thou canst not, O my soul, hence infer that thou mayest be secure, for in this decree the end and the means are joined together of God, and they cannot be separated by any man: if thou beest not godly, never expect to be happy: God's decree of predestination is as well for the giving of grace, as for the giving of glory.

6. Consider the covenant struck betwixt God and Christ for thy salvation. If thou wouldst fain be acquainted with the very articles of it; go on then, take scripture along, and first on God's part thou mayest observe, and meditate, and consider of these particulars.

1. That there was a designation and appointment of Christ from all eternity to the office of Mediatorship: whence Christ is said to be sealed by the Father, *for him hath the Father sealed,* John vi. 27. And chosen of the Father, *Behold my servant whom I uphold, mine elect, or chosen one,* Isa. xlii. 1.

2. There was a commandment from the Father to the Son, which he must obey, and submit unto. As *first,* he had a command what to teach his people, as the prophet of the church, *For I have not spoken of myself,* said Christ, *but the Father which sent me, he gave me a commandment, what I should say, and what I should speak,* John xii. 49. *Secondly,* he had a commandment to lay down his life for those that were given him, 'No man taketh it from me, but I lay it down of myself. I have power to lay it down, and I have power to take it again; this commandment have I received of my Father,' John x. 18.

3. There was a promise from the Father to the Son, the Father covenants with him in these things; 1 That he will give him the Spirit in abundance, 'Behold

'Behold my servant whom I uphold;——I have
'put my Spirit upon him, he shall bring forth judg-
'ment to the Gentiles,' Isa. xlii. 1. And the Spirit
'of the Lord shall rest upon him, the Spirit of wis-
'dom and understanding, the Spirit of counsel and
'might, the Spirit of knowledge, and of the fear of
'the Lord,' Isa. xi. 1, 2. 2. That he will give him
assistance and help in this great work of redemption, 'I the Lord have called thee in righteousness,
'and will hold thine hand,' Isa. xlii. 6. What's
that? Why, I will strengthen thee with my power,
I will so hold thy hand that thou shalt not be discouraged in the work; 'he shall not fail, nor be
'discouraged till he have set judgment upon the
'earth,' Isa. xlii. 4. 3. That he will give him a
blessed success, that he shall not labour in vain,
'He shall see his seed, he shall prolong his days,
'and the pleasure of the Lord shall prosper in his
'hands: He shall see of the travail of his soul, and
'shall be satisfied,' Isa. liii. 10, 11. Christ's sufferings were as a woman's travail, though she suffer
many pains and pangs, yet she sees her child at last;
so shall Christ see many believing on his name:
they are the promise made by the Father to the
Son, that 'nations that know him not shall run un-
'to him,' Isa. v. 5. 4. That he shall give him and
his redeemed ones everlasting glory; to Christ himself there is a promise of glory, *he hath glorified thee.*
And to the members of Christ there is a promise
of glory; and this promise of glory to them was
made known to Christ from everlasting: it was
one of the secrets of God, and Christ brings out
that secret from the bosom of his Father, and reveals it to his disciples. 'It is my Father's pleasure,' said he, 'to give you the kingdom,' Luke
xii. 32. Christ knew his Father's will by the covenant passing betwixt his Father and him, and this
will of the Father concerning glory promised to
the saints, Christ doth bring forth to light. These
were the articles of the covenant on God's part;
now, O my soul, see them on Christ's part in these
particulars.

1. There was an acceptation of the office, to
which he was designed by the Father; he did not
take the office of Mediatorship upon himself, but
first the Father calls him to it, and then the Son
accepts it; 'Christ glorified not himself to be
'made an high Priest, but he that said unto him,
'thou art my Son, to day have I begotten thee,'
he called him, and then the Son answered, 'Lo
'I come,' Heb. v. 5. and i. 10. 7.

2. There was a promise on Christ's part to depend and trust upon God for help, 'and again I
'will put my trust in him,' Heb. ii 13. They are
the words of Christ to his Father. And Isaiah
brings in Christ as looking for help from God, 'for
'the Lord God will help me, therefore shall I not
'be confounded.——And behold the Lord will
'help me, who is he that shall condemn me?'
Whereto agrees that other passage, 'and my God
'shall be my strength,' Isa. l. 7, 8, 9. and xix. 5.

3. There was a promise of submission to his Father's will in bearing the reproaches and injuries
that should be done to him; and to lay down his
life for those that were given to him by the Father.
'The Lord God opened mine ear, and I was not
'rebellious, neither turned away back; I gave my
'back to the smiters, and my cheeks to them that
'plucked off the hair, I hid not my face from shame
'and spitting,' Isa. l. 5, 6. And 'therefore my
'Father loves me, because I lay down my life,' Joh.
x. 17. Christ first thus covenanted with his Father,
and then he was careful to discharge the same,
and at last he tells God, 'I have finished the work
'which thou gavest me to do,' Joh. xvii. 4

There was an earnest expectation of that glory
which the Father promised Christ and his members: 'And now, O Father, glorify thou me with
'thine ownself, with the glory which I had with
'thee before the world was'. And, 'Father, I
'will that they also whom thou hast given me be
'with me where I am, that they may behold my
'glory which thou hast given me; for thou lovedst
'me before the foundation of the world,' Joh. xvii.
5. and xvii. 24. These were the articles of the covenant on Christ's part, and hence it is that God is
called the 'God and Father of our Lord Jesus
'Christ,' Eph. i. 3. *viz.* by reason of the covenant.

O my soul, with what delight mayest thou consider, muse, and ponder on these articles! what!
that God should make a covenant, and enter into
these, and these articles with his own Son for thy
good, for thy eternal good? What, that God
should bring in the second person in the trinity to
be the head of the covenant as on thy part? What
a mercy is this? O run over, and over the meditation, a thousand and a thousand times! O consider thy *hope of eternal life which God, that can-*
not

not lie, *promised before the world began!* Tit. i. 2. If thy soul question, what promise was there made before this world began? To whom was the promise made? Who was there before the world began for God to make any promise to? Why, now thou hast learned it was only to the Son of God, the second person in the trinity. There was a most blessed transaction between God the Father and God the Son, before the world began, for thy everlasting good, and upon that transaction depend all thy hope, and all thy salvation. O! this is worthy of thy deep, and sad, and serious, and inmost meditation. I have been particular and large in this passage of looking into, or considering Jesus, but I shall be brief in the rest.

SECT. III.

Of desiring after Jesus in that respect.

3. WE must desire after Jesus carrying on the great work of our salvation in that eternity. It is not enough to know and consider, but we must desire. Now, 'Desire is a passion looking after the attainments of some good which we enjoy not, and which we imagine to be fitting for us.' In this respect we cannot desire after Jesus, as now to carry on that work of our salvation before the world began, for that work is already perfectly done; but these things we may desire after. As, 1. After the manifestation of that work in us. 2. After God and Christ the complotters and actors of that great work for us. 3. After the full and utmost execution whereby God effectually works in time according to all his workings, or decrees before time.

1. We must desire after the manifestation of this work in us; we have heard of marvellous, excellent, glorious things done by Jesus Christ for his saints from all eternity, and oh! what desires now should be in us to know that we are of that number? When I hear and consider that there was such a project, and such counsels, and such love, and such a purpose, and such decrees, and such a covenant betwixt God and Christ for salvation of souls; and withal, that they are but few in comparison concerning whom God and Christ hath all this care, will not this whet on my desires? and make me cry, and cry again 'Oh that these 'loves were mine! how happy were I, if I had a

'share in these eternal thoughts of God!' Methinks we should not hear of such transactions, but it should stir up our hearts in infinite desires; methinks we should pant after assurance, and still be wishing, 'Oh what is truth! and what is Christ! 'and what did Christ for me before I was, or be-'fore the world was! I would I knew him, I 'would I could enjoy him, I would I were assur-'ed that he had one good thought of me in that 'eternity!' Christians! if you have any share in those transactions, sooner or later you will feel these desires: nay, if my sinful heart deceive me not, upon the very consideration of these things, I feel myself another creature in my desires than I was before. Tell me, you that have took a full view of God, and Christ, and of all these wonders of eternity, do you not sensibly differ from yourselves in your affections? Is not the world, worldly pleasures, worldly profits, and worldly honours fallen too, yea, ten in an hundred with you? Have they not lost their price? Would you not rather be assured that *your names are written in the book of life*, than to have all the world yours, yea, and all the devils in hell subject to your commands? Certainly, if these revelations work nothing in your hearts, if your affections be so strong and hearty to the world, and the vanities of it, if your desires be so impure, and strongly working downwards, that God's ancient loves and eve lasting workings have no power on your hearts, it is a very sad condition. If David may have his wish, it runs thus, *Lord, lift thou up the light of thy countenance upon us*, Psal. iv. 6. He would have the manifestation of God's eternal love; one smile of his countenance (as an image of that countenance which God had towards him before the world began) was more gladness to his heart, than all that which the men of this world had, *in the time that their corn and their wine increased*.

2. We may and must desire after God and Christ, the complotters and actors of that great work for us; what, hath the gospel revealed this truth, that before the creation God and Christ were busied about our good? Yea, and hath Christ especially, that came out of the bosom of his Father, and brought the treasures of his Father's counsel to the world, discovered such loves to men? How then should our desires be after God and Christ? *Whom have I in heaven but thee? And there is none up-*

on earth that I desire besides thee, Psal. lxxiii. 25. A right beholding of Christ in his eternal workings will cause a desire of Christ above all desires; the heart now thirsts for nothing but him that is all, all power, all love, all holiness, all happiness. Tell such a soul of the world, gold, and glory; oh what are these? The soul will quickly tell you, The world is dung, and glory is dung, *all is but loss and dung for the excellency of the knowledge of Christ Jesus my Lord*, Phil. iii. 8. Give me God and Christ, saith the soul, or I die; oh my desires are to him who hath done all this for me. Is not this the period still of thy expression at the end of every discourse, Would Christ were mine? Thou hearest it may be some worldlings talk, such an one, and such an one hath got so much in these times; he that was yesterday as poor as Lazarus, he is this day like that nameless rich man, *clothed in purple, and fine linen, and faring sumptuously every day*, Luke xvi. 19. Ay, but dost not thou reply either in word or heart, 'Would Christ were 'mine, and then I had got more than he?' Poor soul, dost thou not gasp only after Christ, when thou fetchest (as I may say) the very deepest breath? Canst thou read over the generation of Jesus the Son of God, the time when he was begotten, the manner of his begetting, the mutual kindness and love of him that begets, and of him that is begotten; and dost thou not pant, and breathe, and gasp after Jesus at every period? Canst thou read over Jesus his acts and decree in reference to thyself, canst thou turn over those many leaves, in every of which is discovered those everlasting loves of God in his projects, counsels, foreknowledge, purpose, decree, covenant for thy soul's happiness, and art thou not ready at every discovery to sing David's psalm, *As the hart panteth after the water brooks, so panteth my soul after thee, O God. My soul thirsteth for God, for the living God; O when shall I come and appear before God?* Psal. xlii. 1, 2. O my soul, hadst thou but these pantings, thirstings, breathings after God and Christ, thou mightest comfortably conclude, these are the fruits of God's Spirit, it is the Spirit of the Lord Jesus *which makes these sighs and groans in thee, which cannot be expressed*, Rom. viii. 26. He and thee sigh together, one in another, and one after another, O therefore look, look unto Jesus, and sigh, and desire after him.

3. We may and must desire after the full and utmost execution whereby God effectually works in time according to all his workings or decrees before time. God that purposed and decreed from all eternity, he will not have done the full execution of that purpose or decree till that after-eternity, in that world without end. Indeed some part is a fulfilling now, but the main, the great part is yet to come: why then, as we see the plot, let us desire after the full accomplishment, let us desire after that glory without end, to which we were predestinated before the beginning. It was Paul's *desire to be dissolved, and to be with Christ*, Phil. i. 23. As men burthened, so should we desire and groan after the enjoyment of God in the world to come. O my soul, that thou were but cast into the apostle's mould, that thy affections were but on the wing, that they might take the flight, and steer their course towards heaven, and thereupon that thou mightest say, Yonder is the glorious house, the goodly building, made without hands, which God from all eternity decreed to be my home, my rest, my dwelling place to all eternity; and in yon stately fabrick, is many an heavenly inhabitant before I come: there are angels, and there are all the souls of saints that from Adam to this day have had their pass out of this sinful world: yea, there is Jesus the Son of God, and there is God the Father, God the Son, and God the holy Ghost; and if I am predestinated to this fellowship, Lord, when shall I have run through the means that I may come to this end? O my end! Where is my end? Where is my Lord, my God, my comforter? Where is my rest? Where is my end? I cannot be at rest without my end, and therefore come, Lord Jesus, come quickly, *Be like a roe, or a young hart upon the mountains of spices*, Cant. viii. 14. Christians, why are not your spirits always breathing thus after that glory, to which you are predestinated? Why do not you long after full enjoyment, the utmost execution of God's decree? Why are not your hearts, your souls, your spirits already in heaven? Surely there be your relations; your father is there, your elder brother is there, and there are many, I dare say, most of your younger brethren: again, there is your interest, your estate is there, if you believe: and therefore where should your hearts be, but where your treasure is? Come then, come; set in tune those desires of your souls, *Set*

your

your affections on things above, especially on that one thing Jesus Christ: Looking unto Jesus.

SECT. IV.

Of hoping in Jesus in that respect.

4. WE must hope in Jesus, as carrying on that great work of salvation for us in that eternity. It is not enough to know, and consider, and desire; but we must hope, and maintain our hopes as to our own interest. Now, hope is a passion, whereby we expect probably, or certainly, some future good. All the question is, whether that salvation, concerning which the great transaction was betwixt God and Christ, belongs now to me? and what are the grounds and foundations on which my hope is built? I know some exceedingly abuse this doctrine, 'If God had be-'fore all worlds appointed me to salvation, why 'then I may live as I list, I need not hear, or 'pray, or confer, or perform any holy duty; for 'I am sure I shall be saved.' And thus at once they take away all grounds of hope. It is true, God's decrees are unchangeable; but they do not afford any such inferences or deductions as these: you might as well say, The Lord hath appointed me to live such a time, and before that time I shall not, cannot die; and therefore I need no meat nor drink, nor cloaths, nor any other thing: ah silly, foolish, devilish arguing! God's decree is for the means as well as for the end; whom God hath decreed to save, them also he hath decreed to call, to justify, to sanctify, before he save: O my soul, look to the grounds whereupon thy hope is built: if those be weak, thy hope is weak: but if those be strong, thy hope is strong, thy hope will prove most strong, and certain, and prudent.

In the disquisition of these grounds, *Say not in thine heart, who shall ascend into heaven? Or who shall descend into the deep?* Rom. x. 6. Seek not above, or below: it is not possible for thee to go bodily into heaven to see the records of eternity, and to read thy name in the book of life; but search into these fruits and effects of thy election.

1. If thou beest within God's decrees for salvation, then, sooner or later, God will cause the power of his word to come with authority and conviction upon thy conscience: *Knowing, brethren, beloved, your election of God: for our gospel came not unto you in word only, but also in power*, 1 Thess. i. 4, 5. The apostle speaks thus of others; he might know they were the elected of God, either by his judgment of charity, or by a spirit of discerning, which was vouchsafed to some in the apostle's times: but how comes he immediately to know this truth? By this glorious effect, *Our gospel came not in word only, but also in power*. Oh, 'tis good to consider with what power the word preached falls into thy heart. Doth it convince thee? humble thee, mollify thee, soften thee? This argues thou belongest to God. The word preached will be more than the word of a man, more than a mere human oration, or verbal declamation. Where it comes in power, it will be like fire in thy bowels; like a two edged sword in the secret places of thy heart, thou wilt cry out, verily God is here: oh the power! the conviction! the meltings of my soul, that I feel within me!

2. If God hath ordained thee to salvation, then, sooner or later, God will effectually call thee. *Moreover, whom he did predestinate, them he also called*, Rom. viii. 30. This calling is a calling of the soul from sin, from amongst the rest of the world unto Jesus Christ; it is such a call, as enables the soul to follow Christ; as Matthew, being called by Christ. *He arose and followed Christ*, Matth ix. 9. These two are linked together in Paul's golden chain, predestination and effectual vocation. *We are bound to give thanks always unto God for you, brethren, beloved of the Lord:* and why so? *Because God hath from the beginning chosen you to salvation.——Whereunto he called you by our gospel, to the obtaining of the glory of the Lord Jesus Christ*, 2 Thess. ii. 13, 14. All those that belong to God's election, are sometime or other effectually called by the word and Spirit of Christ; and it must needs be so, because, as the Lord hath put a difference betwixt his elect and others, before the world was, and he will make a final difference betwixt them and others, after the end of the world, so he will have them differenced and distinguished whilst they are in this world, by this inward, effectual, operative calling, they are men of other minds, wills, affections, dispositions, conversations;

conversations; they are *called from darkness to light, and from the power of Satan unto God,* Acts xxvi. 18. As the apostle, *Ye were sometimes darkness, but now are ye light in the Lord. Be not ye therefore partakers with them,* Eph. v. 8, 7.

3. If thou art chosen for salvation, then sooner or later thou shalt have true soul-saving, justifying faith; *As many as were ordained to eternal life believed,* Acts xiii. 48. When God hath a people to call home to himself, he either brings them to the means, or the means to them, and those that belong to the election of grace believe. O my soul, hast thou this saving faith? not a fancied faith, dead faith, an easy faith, but saving faith; such a faith as was wrought in thee by the word and Spirit with power; such a faith as was not in thy power to give, nor in thy power to receive until God enabled thee by his Spirit: then here is thy ground that thou art ordained to eternal life: *for whom he calls he justifies,* and *we are justified by faith,* Rom. viii. 30. and v. 1. Not that the essence of faith justifies; but faith justifies instrumentally, in that it lays hold upon that which justifies, even the righteousness of Christ Jesus.

4. If thou art decreed for salvation, then sooner or later the Lord will beget and increase in thee grace, holiness, sanctification: *Elect according to the foreknowledge of God the Father, thro' sanctification of the Spirit,* 1 Pet. i. 2. God predestinates his people unto holiness; *He chose us in Christ before the foundation of the world, that we should be holy, and without blame before him,* Eph. i. 4. If God appoint thee to eternal life, he doth here in this world appoint thee to an holy gracious life. No sanctification, no election; no grace, no glory: thou art to be a precious jewel here, ere God will make thee up at that great day. Observe the chain, Rom. viii. 29, 30. If I be sanctified with the divine nature, in which glory is begun, then I am justified; if justified, then I have been called according to the purpose; if called, then I was predestinate; and if predestinate to means, then I was foreknown, as one whom God would choose to the end, even to immeasurable and eternal glory.

5. If thou art appointed and prepared for glory, then God will give thee a thankful heart for so great a mercy: thou canst no more keep in the heart from overflowing, when thou art sensible of this everlasting love, than thou canst put bounds to the sea: see Paul praising God for the election of himself and others, *After I heard of your faith, and love, I cease not to give thanks;* and *blessed be the God and Father of our Lord Jesus Christ, who hath blessed us with all spiritual blessings in heavenly places in Christ, according as he hath chosen us in him before the foundation of the world,* Eph. i. 15, 16. and i. 3, 4. And what glorious triumphs doth Paul in the person of all the elected make over all kind of enemies that can be thought of? He challengeth every adversary to put forth his sting, and why? Even because God hath elected, and nothing can separate them from this unchangeable love; and this was it that begot his thanksgiving, *I thank God through Jesus Christ our Lord,* Rom. viii. 33, 39. and vii. 25. O my soul, how is thy heart affected with praise and thankfulness in this matter? He that bestoweth great things, looks for great return of thanks, especially this being all thou canst do.

6. If the project, council, love, purpose, decree, and covenant of God with Christ, concerned thee, and thy soul's happiness, then God will crown thee with perseverance, and a stedfast continuance in that way of grace thou wast first set in: final apostasy, and total back-sliding from the ways of God, can never befal those that are thus chosen; *They went from us, because they are not of us,* said the apostle, 1 John ii. 19. And, *If it were possible, they should deceive the very elect,* said Christ, Matth. xxiv. 24. But it is certainly impossible, and why? *I will put my fear in their hearts, that they shall never depart from me,* Jer. xxxii. 40. Oh what a blessed mercy is this, when there are so many hours of temptation in the world, so many blustering storms and tempests that are able to raise up the very roots, did not that immortal seed preserve them. Of this sign we are sure, if any of the former belongs to us; but to this we cannot actually seal till the end of our life.

Come now, are these, O my soul, the grounds of thy hopes? Hath God's word came with power on thy heart? Hath the Lord so effectually called thee, that thou hast left all to follow Christ? Dost thou believe on the Lord Jesus for life and for salvation? Art thou holy? Is thy life holy? dost thou walk exactly, as the grace of God which bringeth to salvation teacheth? Canst thou with enlarged thankfulness amplify the love and grace of God in thy election? Surely these effects are the very fewel of hope, they are the blessed and clear evidences of thy soul's election; and therefore hope well, take strong consolation: it is clear as the sun, that God hath predestinated thee to life, and that thy name is written in the book of life, and that none in heaven, or on earth, or in hell, shall be able to blot it out again. Away with all sad, dumpish, dejected thoughts: look unto Jesus: hope in Christ, That that very salvation, concerning which that great transaction was betwixt God and Christ, belongs even to thee, and that one day thou shalt see it, and enjoy the happiness of it to all eternity.

SECT. V.

Of believing in Jesus in that respect.

5. WE must believe in Jesus, as carrying on that great work for us in that eternity. It is not enough to know, and consider, and desire, and hope: but we must believe. Now, this is the nature and property of faith, to apply all those ancient and future doings and dealings of God to ourselves, as if they were now present. Some difference there is betwixt hope and faith: as hope hath respect to that which the word promiseth, *rem verbi*; but faith respects the word itself, *verbum rei*; hope eyes chiefly the mercy and goodness of the promise, but faith eyes mainly the authority and truth of the promiser; hope looks upon its object as future, but faith only looks upon the object as present; both make a particular application to themselves, but hope in a waiting for it, and faith in a way of now enjoying it. Hence faith is called, *the substance of things hoped for*, Heb. xi. 1. It is the substance, or confidence of things hoped for, as if we had them already in hand; faith gives the soul a present interest in God, in Christ, in all those glorious things in the gospel of Christ, even in the things of eternal life. Faith is an appropriating, an applying, an uniting grace. It is a blessed thing to have the sight of God, there is much power in it; but to see God in his glory as my God; to see all the majesty, greatness and goodness of God, as those things that my soul have an interest in; to see how the eternal councils of God wrought for me, to make me happy; why this is of the nature of faith: and herein lies the sweetness of faith: in that we believe not Christ only to be a Saviour, and righteousness, but my Saviour and my righteousness; and therefore Luther affirmed, that the sweetness of Christianity lay in pronouns; when a man can say, *My Lord, and my God, and my Jesus. I live by the faith of the Son of God, who loved me, and gave himself for me*, Gal. ii. 20.

O my soul! believe for thy self; believe, and be confident of it, that those eternal projects, councils, love, purpose, decree, and covenant betwixt God and Christ, were all for thee; hast thou not a promise? Nay, was there not a promise before the world began? and that very promise of eternal life? Mark the words, *In hope of eternal life, which God, that cannot lie, promised before the world began*, Tit. i. 2. Here's a promise and a promise of eternal life, and a promise of eternal life made by God, by God that cannot lie, and that before there was a world, or any man in the world. If thou enquirest, to whom then was this promise made? Sweet soul, it was made to Christ for thee: many promises thou hast in scripture made more immediately to thyself; but this was the grand promise, and all the other promises they are but a draught of that grand promise that God the Father made to his Son before the world began.

O, cries the soul, I cannot believe. What, is it possible that God in his eternity should have any thought of me? What, of me, *being not yet born, neither having done any good or evil?* Rom. ix. 11. What, of me, born in these last times of the world, the least of saints, the greatest of sinners, lets then the least of all God's mercies? That of such an one the great God, the majesty of heaven and earth, should have a thought, a project, a council, a knowledge of approbation, a purpose, a decree: nay, enter into a covenant with his Son for my salvation? I cannot believe it. Alas! what am I to God? or what need hath God of me? *If all the nations of the earth are to him, but as a drop of a bucket, and as the small dust of the balance*, Isa. xl. 15. O what a minim am I of that drop? or what a little little atom am I of that small dust? And is it probable that the greatness of God, the goodness of God, the power of God, the wisdom of God, the eternal councils of God, should work

for

Of knowing Jesus as carrying on the great Work of our Salvation. 53

for me, to make me glorious, blessed, happy? to make me one with himself, and one with his Son, and one with his Spirit? What care take I of every dust of the earth, or every sand of the sea shore? and yet these are my fellow-creatures: there's a thousand times more disproportion betwixt God and me, and would God take care of me before I was, or before the world was? What, would he busy himself and his Son about such a worthless wretched worm? Would he decree Christ to come from the Father for me, to be my Redeemer, my Jesus, my Saviour? I cannot, I dare not, I will not believe.

O stay, my soul, and be not faithless, but believing; I'll take thy argument in pieces; As, 1. Thou sayest, *Hath God any thoughts of me?* Yes, saith God, *I know the thoughts that I think towards you, thoughts of peace, and not of evil,* Jer xxix 11. And before the world was, my thoughts and my delights were with the sons of men, Prov. viii 31. 2. Thou sayest, 'I have no thoughts, no care of 'my fellow-creatures, as of the dust, or sand, or 'atoms? And what then? *My thoughts are not as your thoughts, neither are your ways my ways, saith the Lord; for as the heavens are higher than the earth, so are my ways higher than your ways, and my thoughts than your thoughts,* Isa lv. 8. What if thou hast no thoughts or care of the smaller creatures, yet God extends his thoughts, and care, and providence not only to thee, but even to them, *Neither can a sparrow fall to the ground, nor an hair from thy head, nor a leaf from the tree, without the providence of our heavenly Father?* Math. x. 29, 30. 3. Thou sayest, I dare not believe, I am astonished at, confounded in these thoughts of God's eternal love; it is too high for me, I cannot believe it I answer, Herein thou sayest something · I know it is an hard thing to believe these great things in reference to thyself: but see now, how God and Christ stoop and condescend to make thee believe. God stands much upon this, that the hearts of his saints should confide in him: he accounts not himself honoured, except they believe And therefore mark, O my soul, how Christ suits himself to thy weakness; what is it that may beget this faith, this confidence in thy soul? What is it (saith God) that you poor creatures do one to another, when you would make things sure between yourselves? Why, thus,———

1 We engage ourselves by promise one to another And so will I, saith God poor soul, thou hast my promise, my faithful promise; I have made a promise both to Jews and Gentiles, and thou art the one of these two sorts; *The promise is to you, and to your children, and to all that are afar off, even as many as the Lord our God shall call.* Acts ii 39 Be only satisfied in that ground of thy hope, that thou art called of God, and then every promise of eternal life is thine, even thine. Thou mayst find a thousand promises scattered here and there in the book of God; and all these promises are a draught of that promise which was made from all eternity, and therefore it so much is the more sure, it is as if Christ should say, ' Wilt thou have engagement by promise? This ' is past long ago; my Father hath engaged him- ' self to me before the world began; yea, and I ' have made many, and many a promise since the ' world began Read in the volume, and thou ' wilt find here and there a promise, here and there ' a draught of that first copy of that great promise ' which my Father made unto me from all eterni- ' ty'

2. When we would make things sure to one another, we write it down; and so will I, saith God: thou hast the scriptures, the holy writ, those sacred volumes of truth and life, and herein thou hast the golden lines of many gracious promises, are they not as the stars in the firmament of the scripture? Thou hast my Bible, and in the Bible thou hast many blessed glorious truths, but of all the Bible methinks thou shouldest not part with one of those promises, no not for a world Luther observing the many promises writ down in scripture, expresseth thus, ' The whole scripture doth ' especially aim at this, that we should not doubt, ' but hope, confide, believe that God is merciful, ' kind, patient, and hath a purpose and delight to ' save our souls '

3 When we would make things sure to one another, we set to our seals. And so will I, saith God: thou hast my seal, the broad seal of heaven, my sacraments, the seals of my covenant; and thou hast my privy seal also, the seal of m, Spirit. *Grieve not the holy Spirit, whereby ye are sealed unto the day of redemption,* Eph iv 30

4 When we would make things sure to one another, we take witnesses. And so will I, saith God:

God: thou shalt have witnesses as many as thou wilt, witnesses of all sorts, witnesses in heaven, and witnesses on earth; *For there are three that bear record in heaven, the Father; the word, and the holy Ghost, and these three are one. And there are three that bear witness in earth, the Spirit, and the water, and the blood, and these three agree in one,* 1 John v. 7, 8.

5. When we would make things sure to one another, we take an oath. And so will I, saith God: *God willing more abundantly to shew unto the heirs of promise the immutability of his counsel, confirmed it by an oath,* Heb. vi. 17. q. d. There is no such need of an oath; but I will be abundant to thee, because I would have thee trust me, and confide in me thoroughly: and as I swear (saith God) so will I swear the greatest oath that ever was, *I swear by myself,* Heb. vi. 13. God swears *by God: he could swear by no greater, and therefore he sware by himself:* and why thus, but for their sakes who are the heirs of promise? *He knows our frame, and remembers that we are dust*; and therefore, to succour our weakness, the Lord is pleased to swear, and to confirm all by his oath.

6. When we would make things sure to one another, we take a pawn. And I will give thee a pawn, saith God: and such a pawn, as, if thou never hadst any thing more, thou shouldest be happy. It is the pawn of my Spirit. *Who also hath sealed us, and given the earnest of the Spirit into our hearts,* 2 Cor. i. 22. q. d. I will send my Spirit into your hearts; and this Spirit shall be a pawn, an earnest in your hearts of all the good that I intend to do for you for ever.

7. When we would make things sure to one another, something it may be is presently done, as an engagement of all that which is to come. And thus will I deal with thee, saith God, who livest in these last of times. Why, thou seest the greatest part of thy salvation already done: I made a promise from all eternity of sending my Son into the world, to be made a curse for sin; yea, and if thou believest, for thy sin; and this is the greatest work of all that is to be done to all eternity. Surely if I would had failed thee in any thing, it should have been in this; it is not so much for me now, to bring thee to heaven, to save thy soul, as it was to send my Son into the world, to be made a curse for sin: but when I have done so great a work, and have been already faithful in that promise, how shouldest thou but believe my faithfulness in making good all other promises? If a man should owe thee a thousand pounds, and pay thee nine hundred, ninety and nine, thou wouldest think surely, he would never break for the rest. Why, God hath paid his nine hundred, ninety and nine; and all the glory of heaven is but as one in comparison of what he hath done: we may therefore well believe, That he who hath done so much for us, will not leave the little undone.

— Come then, rouse up, O my soul, and believe thy interests in those eternal transactions betwixt God and Christ: is not here ground enough for thy faith? If thou art but called, the promise of God is thine: or if thou darest not rely on his promise (which God forbid) thou hast his indenture, his seal and witnesses of all sorts, both in heaven and earth: or if yet thou believest not, thou hast an oath, a pawn, and the greatest part of thy salvation already done to thy hand: nay, I'll tell thee more, poor soul, than this; even Christ himself from all eternity hath engaged for thee, that thou shalt believe: O then put not Christ to be challenged for his engagement, by refusing the gospel! surely when thou believest, thou makest Christ's word good; *He that believeth not, makes God a liar,* though in another sense, and, for ought he knoweth, even in this, That he frustrates Christ's undertaking in the covenant. And therefore believe; yea, and cry, *Lord, I believe, help thou my unbelief;* increase my faith, till I come to full assurance of faith: Faith in this sense is the very eye of the soul, reading its name written in the book of life; it is an apprehension of our particular election. O believe, till thou comest up to this fulness of persuasion of God's love in Christ.

SECT. VI.

Of loving Jesus in that respect.

6. WE must love Jesus, as carrying on that great work of our salvation in that eternity. And this is the fruit, or effect of faith, if once we believe, that all those designs and transactions were for us, even for us; O then how should

should we but love that God, and love that Christ, who thus first and freely loved us? God loved us before we loved him; for he loved us in that eternity before all worlds; surely then we are bound to love him, first and above all things. As the diamond formeth and fashioneth the diamond, so love formeth and fashioneth love; or as fire converteth fewel into fire, so this ancient love of God and Christ may well cause our love again. O Christ!—didst thou not love us? Who doubts it, that but reads over the project, council, foreknowledge, purpose, decree and covenant of God and Christ? Who doubts it, that but reads the eternal design of God, that Christ should go out of himself, and suffer an extasy through the vehemency of his love? That Christ should so far abase his Majesty, as to die for us, that we might not die, but live with him? O then, how should this but kindle in our hearts a most ardent love towards God and Christ? What more effectual motive to work man's love, than to be prevented by the love and bounty of another? That this fruit doth spring from the sense of our election, Bernard observes, Epist. 107. 'Who is righteous, but he that requiteth the love of God with love again? Which is never done, except the holy Ghost reveal unto a man by faith God's eternal purpose concerning his future salvation.' And hence it is, that the heart is most in frame, when it is a considering the eternal love of God in Christ: as David said of Jonathan, *Thou hast been very pleasant to me, thy love to me was wonderful*, 2 Sam. i. 26. So a poor soul, gathering up all the goodness of God in that eternity, and feeding upon it, and the variety of it, breathes out in that expression, *Thou hast been very pleasant to me, O God, thy love to me hath been wonderful*. O my soul, that thou couldest so live by faith on these eternal passages, as that thou mightest attain to the highest fruits of faith, not only to love God and Christ, but love to them with a burning love, with a mighty love, such a love as lies in the most vigorous prosecution after Jesus Christ, and in the most faithful resignation of thyself to God; such a love as works the most delightful aspect of God and Christ, as makes a man to behold God and Christ with all cheerfulness; such a love as works a man to extol the praises of God. O in these things lies the strength of love.

But alas! this is, or at least this should be thy grief, That thou canst not love so well, and so warmly as thou art beloved. Christ comes towards thee, *Skipping like the hart, or roe on the mountains of spices*, Cant. viii. 14. But thy love towards Christ is creeping like the worm in the unwholsom valley. Indeed the best affections have their fits of swooning; it may be for the present thy love is cold: O but come up to this fire; consider how God and Christ loved thee in every of these.——

1. His project to save thy soul sprung out of his love: love was the first wheel that set all the eternal works of God a going; what was that great design of God, but only an expression of his love? It was his pleasure to communicate himself, and the rise of that communication was his love.

2. The councils of God were all in love. Had not love been as president of the council, where hadst thou been? When all the attributes of God were at a stand, it was the love of God in Christ that resolved the question for thy salvation.

3. The foreknowledge of God was a foreknowledge of love and approbation: in his eternal love he embraced thee as his own; he foreknew thee, *i. e.* of his free love he set thee apart to life and to salvation; *God hath chosen us in Christ before the foundation of the world*, Eph. i. 4. He chose us in Christ, but not for Christ; nothing at all moved him to elect thee, but his own good pleasure and free love.

4. The purpose of God was a resolution of love; it speaks his love to be a constant, settled, abiding love: no unkindness shall alter it; *For having loved his own, he loves them unto the end*, John xiii. 1. Nay, he loves them without end: from everlasting to everlasting.

5. The decree of God was an order (as I may call it) or an act of love, to give in that grace unto his elect, which before all time he decreed should be an effectual means to bring them unto glory.

6. The covenant betwixt God and Christ was an agreement of love: God and Christ struck hands to save our souls; *Grace was given us in Christ Jesus before the world began*, 2 Tim. i. 9. Grace was given us, that is, the gracious love and favour of God in Christ was given us before all secular times. This was God's meaning from everlasting, this was the design, yea, the greatest design that

ever

ever God had, to set out the infinite glory, and the riches of his love in Jesus Christ. No question but he had other great designs in doing such great things as he hath done; but above all the designs that ever God had in all his works, this is the chief, to honour his mercy, to glorify the riches of his love and grace: had it not been for this, he would never have made the world; and therefore in that world to come it will be the delight of God, to shew his saints and angels what he is able to do for a creature; yea, he will to all eternity declare to them, to what an height of excellency and glory, his love and mercy is able to raise poor souls; so that the very saints and angels shall admire and adore, and magnify the name of God everlastingly for it.

O my soul, canst thou ponder on this, and not love him dearly, who hath thus loved thee? Come, *stir up the gift that is in thee*; if thou art a Christian, thou hast some sparks, though now (it may be) under the ashes: come, rub, chafe and warm thy affections at this fire: love, like a watch, must be wound up, or else it will fall downwards: what dost thou? *Why stands thou idle in the heat of the day?* Christ hath fire in his hand, 'tis but looking up, and reaching out thy hand to take it from him: O take it with both thy hands; and be thankful for it. Prayer, ejaculations, contemplation, judicious observation of the Spirit's season, are the best instruments to kindle this fire of love in thee.

And methinks thy heart should begin now to melt, methinks it should receive more easy impressions from the object before it; methinks these eternal works and acts of God and Christ towards thy poor soul should begin to *overcome thee*, and to *burn thy heart as with coals of juniper*, Cant. vi. 5. and viii. 6. Why, Lord, is it thus? Was I elected from all eternity in Christ? Was I ordained to a glorious inheritance before there was a world? Was this business, to make me happy, one of the deep councils of God? Was this one of the works of his wisdom, that he was exercised about before the world began? Was this the great design of God in making the world, and in making heaven, that place of glory, to glorify himself, and to glorify such a poor wretch as I am? O then how should this but mightily inflame my heart with the love of God, and love of Christ? How should I choose but say, as the martyr did, 'Oh 'that I had as many lives, as I have hairs on my 'head, to lay them down for Christ?' Ah what flames of divine affection, what raptures of zeal, what ravishments of delight, what extasies of obedience, can be enough for my blessed God and dearest Redeemer?

SECT. VII.

Of joying in Jesus in that respect.

7. WE must joy in Jesus, as carrying on that great work of our salvation in that eternity. This joy is a passion arising from the sweetness of that object we enjoy. O my soul, dost thou believe? And art thou now cast into a pang of love? How then should thy joy come on? As Christ said to the seventy, *In this rejoice not, that the spirits are subject unto you, but rather rejoice because your names are written in heaven*, Luke x. 20. So rejoice not thou in this, that the world is thine, that riches are thine, that thou hast subdued men and devils; but herein rejoice, that thy name is written in the book of life. O what a comfortable point is this! that the Father and Christ should transact a bargain from eternity, concerning thee by name, that the Father and the Son should commune together concerning thy heaven, as if their language had been thus; 'Father, what shall be given to thy justice 'to ransom such an one, Abraham, Isaac, Jacob, 'Matthew, Mark, Luke, John, Mary, Martha, 'Hannah, &c.' Why no more but this, 'Thou 'shalt die, my Son, and whosoever believeth in 'thee shall live for ever.' Why then, saith Christ, 'I will engage for such and such an one; I will 'enter into bond for such and such a person; A-'braham shall believe in time: see I have writ 'down his name in the book of life.' And who art thou that readest? Art thou a believer? Dost thou believe in the Lord Jesus Christ? Christ said the same of thee, and entered into a bond for thee, and entered thy name in the book of life: see the certainty of this in Phil. iv. 3. Thou Thomas, Andrew, Peter, Christ knows thee by name, and thy name is written in the book of life. O go thy way, and rejoice, and take strong consolation! is there not cause? Why, I tell thee, thy name is in the book of heaven; and, if this may add to thy

to thy joy, know that there is none in heaven or earth shall ever be able to blot it out again. No, no, poor soul, *There is no condemnation to them that are in Christ Jesus*, Rom. viii. 1. God hath decreed thy salvation, and God's decree shall stand, let men and devils say what they will to the contrary, *The council of the Lord standeth for ever, the thoughts of his heart to all generations*, Psalm xxxiii. 11. It is as possible for God to deny himself, as it is possible for thee a believer to perish. *We are kept* (saith the apostle) *by the power of God through faith to salvation*, 1 Pet i. 5. And therefore *rejoice, and again rejoice*; Yea, raise up thy joy to that pitch of triumph, which is joy elevated; and elevated so high, that it comes to victoriousness, and magnanimous conquest of heart over all things. Say with the apostle, *What, my name is written in the book of life, who shall lay any thing to the charge of God's elect?——who then shall separate me from the love of Christ? Shall tribulation, or distress, or persecution, or famine, or nakedness, or peril, or sword? Nay, I am persuaded that neither death, nor life, nor angels, nor principalities, nor powers, nor things present, nor things to come, nor height, nor depth, nor any other creature shall be able to separate me from the love of God which is in Christ Jesus my Lord*, Rom. viii. 33, 35, &c.

SECT. VIII.

Of calling on Jesus in that respect.

8. WE must call on Jesus, or on God the Father in and through Jesus. This also is included in looking; as David while praying, *Unto thee do I lift up mine eyes, O thou that dwellest in the heavens*, Psal. cxxiii. 1. Now this calling on God, or looking to God, contains prayer and praise. 1. We must pray that all these transactions betwixt God and Christ may be assuredly ours, and that God would clear up our titles more and more; yea, and seeing all good things tending to salvation were from all eternity prepared for us, we are therefore to pray, that by prayer we may draw them down from heaven; for what though our evidences be clear, yet this must not cast out means; God doth not use to bestow his saving graces on lazy sluggards; those therefore who from the certainty of predestination do pretend that the duty of prayer is superfluous, do plainly shew that they have no certainty at all. *Aquinas Part* 1. q. art. 8. was orthodox in this, 'The predestinate must pray, because by these effects of pre- destination; the salvation of souls is best ascertained.' The same Spirit which witnesseth to our spirit that we are his chosen, is also the Spirit of prayer and supplication; and therefore he that believes that he is one of God's elect, he cannot but pray for those things which he believeth that God hath prepared for him before the foundation of the world.——2. We must praise God? What, that God should look on us, and predestinate us to life? That he should pass by so many on the right hand, and on the left, and that I should be one whom the Lord did elect? What such a vile, and sinful wretch as I am? Was there ever like love? Was there ever like mercy? May not heaven and earth stand amazed at this? O what shall I do to be thankful enough to this dear God? Thus thou that knowest thy interest in Christ, study praise and thankfulness. Say in thy self, Who made me to differ from those cast-away souls? alas! we were all framed of the same mould, hewed out of the same rock. It is storied of one of the late French kings, that in a serious meditation, considering his own condition of being king and ruler of that nation, oh (said he) when I was born, a thousand other souls were born in this kingdom with me, and what have I done to God more than they? O my soul, what difference betwixt thee and those many thousands of reprobates that live with thee in the world at this day? Nothing; surely nothing, but the free mercy, goodness, and love of God in Jesus Christ. O then praise this God, yea found forth *the praise of the glory of his grace*. Remember that was God's design, and that is thy duty.

SECT. IX.

Of conforming to Jesus in that respect.

9. WE must conform to Jesus; we must fix our eyes on Jesus for our imitation: that also is the meaning of this looking in the text. And, in respect of our predestination, the apostle speaks so expresly, *He did predestinate us to be conformed to the image of his Son*, Rom. viii. 29. This is one end of predestination, and this is one end

end of looking unto Jesus, nay it is included in it. A very look on Jesus hath a power in it to conform us to the image of Jesus. *We are changed by beholding*, saith the apostle, 2 Cor. iii. 18. Oh when I see God's love in Christ to me even from all eternity, how should this but stir up my soul to be like Jesus Christ? Where there is a dependence, there is desire to be like even among men; how much more considering my dependence on God in Christ, should I desire to be like Christ in disposition? All the question is, What is this image of Christ, to which we must be conformed? I answer, holiness, and happiness: but because the latter is our reward, and the former is our duty, therefore look to that.

But wherein consists that? I answer, in that resemblance, likeness, and conformity to Christ in all the passages fore-mentioned: and in every of those must we conform to Christ. As——

1. Christ is the Son of God; so must we be God's sons. *As many as received him, to them he gave power to become the sons of God*, John i. 12. O what lies upon us in this respect; *If I be your Father, where is mine honour?* Mal. i. 6. And, *if ye call on the Father, pass the time of your sojourning here in fear*, 1 Pet. i. 17. God looks for more honour, fear, reverence, duty and obedience from a Son than from the rabble of the world: If thou art God's son, thy sins more offend God than the sins of all the reprobates in the world; why, alas! thy sins are not mere transgressions of the law, but committed against the mercy, bounty and goodness of God vouchsafed unto thee; thy sins have a world of unthankfulness joined with them, and therefore how should God but visit? *You only have I known of all the families of the earth, therefore will I visit you for all your iniquities*, Am. iii. 2. O think of this, you that are God's sons, and conform to Christ, for he was an obedient Son.

2. Christ the Son of God delights in the Father, *and his delight is also with the sons of men*; so must we delight in the Father, and delight in his children. *Delight thyself in the Lord, and he shall give thee the desires of thy heart*, Psal. xxxvii. 4. And *the saints that are on the earth are they, in whom is all my delight*, saith David, Ps. xvi. 3. It is storied of Dr. Taylor, That, being in prison, he could delight in God; and he rejoiced that ever he came into prison, because of his acquaintance with that angel of God, as he called Mr. Bradford. O this is heaven upon earth! not only God, but the very saints of God are sweet objects of delight. Mark them, and if they be saints indeed they are savoury in their discourse, in their duties, in their carriages; their example is powerful, their society profitable, how should we but delight in them?

3. God and Christ laid this plot from all eternity, That all the world would do, should be *to the praise of the glory of his grace:* so must we purpose this as the end of all our actions, *Whether we eat, or drink, or whatsoever we do, we must do all to the glory of God*, 1 Cor. x. 31. But especially if from God we receive any spiritual good, then give all again to the glory of his grace. *Blessed be the name of God for ever and ever*, (saith Daniel, ii. 20, 23.) *for wisdom and might are his;*——And *I thank thee, and praise thee, O God of my Fathers, who hast given me wisdom and might.* An excellent spirit of wisdom and might wrought in Daniel, and he acknowledges all to the giver: *wisdom and might are his.* Christians, if you feel grace in your hearts, I beseech you acknowledge it to Christ. He does all; he subdues lusts, heals wounds, stays inward issues, sets broken bones, and makes them to rejoice; and therefore let him have the glory of all; do you acknowledge grace in its latitude to the God of all grace.

4. God and Christ counselled about our salvation; there was a great conflict in the attributes of God; justice and mercy could not be reconciled, till the wisdom of God found out that glorious and wonderful expedient, *the Lord Jesus Christ*; so let us counsel about our salvation: the flesh and the spirit whereof we are compounded, draw several ways; the flesh draws hell-ward, and the spirit heaven-ward; come then, ca'l we in heavenly and spiritual wisdom to decide this controversy; you may hear its language in Job xxviii. 28. *Behold the fear of the Lord, that is wisdom, and to depart from evil, is understanding.* If we would draw heaven-ward, and save our souls, come then, *Let us hear the conclusion of the whole matter, Fear God and keep his commandments, for this is the whole duty of man*, Eccl. xii. 13. Keep his commandments in an evangelical sense, *i. e.* look at the expedient, Jesus Christ, who hath kept them for us, and in whom and through whom

our

our imperfect obedience is accepted with God.

5. God and Christ loved us with an everlasting love, so must we love him who hath first loved us; this is the nature of spiritual love, that it runs into its own ocean, *O love the Lord, all ye his saints!* Psal. xxxi. 23. Who hath more cause to love him than you have? Or who hath so much come under the power of love as you have? Hath not Christ loved you, not only with a love of well-wishing, which is from everlasting (some call it the love of election, the fountain-love, the well-head of salvation) but also with a love of complacency? Hath not Christ shed abroad his love into your hearts, and shall he lose by it? Will not these cords of love draw up your hearts to love him again? Sure 'tis but reason to love him, who hath first loved you, yea, and loved you when you were unlovely, and had nothing in you worthy of love. Christians! then it was that Christ loved you in rags, it is meet therefore that you should love him in robes.

6. God and Christ appointed, or purposed us unto salvation; his love was a sure, and settled and firm and constant love, *The purpose of God according to election must stand*, Rom. ix. 11. So must we love him, and love unto him for ever: *I have inclined my heart to perform thy statutes always, even to the end*, Psalm cxix. 112. David's heart was much taken with the statutes of God, and therefore he gives this expression of the fulness of his heart, *always and even to the end*. It is a kind of *pleonasm*, his resolutions were such, that he would never depart from his God.

7. God and Christ decreed, booked and sealed our salvation. And so must we put to our seal that God is true, *i. e.* we must believe in Christ; for when we believe we make Christ's word good. He that believes not, makes God a liar (as ye have heard) in that he frustrates, or endeavours to frustrate Christ's undertaking in his predestination.

8. God and Christ entered into covenant concerning our salvation: so must we enter into covenant with him; we must take him to be our God, and give up ourselves to be his people: — Why thus in all particulars conform to Christ. The sum of all is this, We must be like Christ in grace, and gracious actings.

O my soul, see to this grace, see to this conformity to Jesus in gracious actings, and this will enable thee to read thy name written in the book of life. O abhor and repel that devil's dart, *I am predestinate, and therefore I may live as I list*, Eph. i. 4. How contrary is this to the apostle, *He hath chosen us in him before the foundation of the world, that we should be holy, and without blame before him in love?* And, *as the elect of God, put on bowels of mercy, kindness, humbleness of mind, meekness, long-suffering, forgiving one another, even as Christ forgave you?* Col. iii. 12, 13. This conformity to Christ in grace is the very effect of our predestination: O look unto Jesus, and be in grace like unto Jesus: why, Christ is full of grace, a vessel filled up to the lip, or very brim, *Thou art fairer than the children of men, and grace is poured into thy lips*, Psal. xlv. 2. Christ was, as it were, grace speaking, Luke iv. 22. Grace sighing, weeping, dying, Heb. ii. 9. Grace living again, and now dropping, or rather raining down floods of grace on his living members, Eph. iv. 11. Christ is the great *apple tree*, dropping down apples of life, Cant. ii. 3. And all that falls from this tree, as apples, leaves, shadow, smell, blossoms, are but pieces of grace fallen down from him, who is the fulness of all, and hath filled all things. Christ is *the rose of Sharon*, Cant. ii. 1. and every leaf of this rose is an heaven, every white and red in it is grace and glory, every act of breathing out its smell from everlasting to everlasting is spotless and unmixed grace; why then, my soul, if thou wilt conform to Christ, conform in this; *be holy as he is holy*; *of that fulness of grace that is in him, do thou receive even grace for grace*, John i. 16.

Christians! where are we? O that ever men should hear of so much grace, and of such acts of grace in that eternity before all worlds, and yet no impression of grace upon their hearts! O that God and Christ should both be in that business of eternity; that heaven, hell, justice, mercy, souls and deep wisdom should be all in that rare piece, and yet that men should think more of a farm, an ox, an house, a pin, a straw, or of the bones of a crazy livelihood! O look up! look up! if thou art Christ's, consider what he hath done for thy soul;

why thou art *predestinate to be conformed to the image of Christ.*

Thus far we have looked on Jesus as our Jesus, in that eternity before all time until the creation: our next work is to look on Jesus, carrying on the great work of man's salvation in the creation, the beginning of time, until his first coming.

LOOKING UNTO
JESUS.

From the Creation until his first Coming.

THE THIRD BOOK.

CHAP. I. SECT. I.

Isaiah xliii. 6, 8. *The LORD will give thee for a covenant of the people,——Hear, ye deaf, and look, ye blind, that ye may see.*

Of CHRIST promised by Degrees.

IN this period, as in the former, we shall first lay down the object; and then direct you how to look upon it.

The object is JESUS, carrying on the work of man's salvation, in that dark time before his coming in the flesh.

No sooner the world made and the things therein, but man was created, that way might be made for God to shew his grace in the salvation of his elect. And now was it that God's eternal project, and counsel, and foreknowledge, and purpose, and decree, and covenant with Christ began to come into execution. Indeed at the first moment was no need of Christ; for man at first was made in holiness to the image of God, and to bear rule over the rest of the visible creatures; but, alas! this his state was but of little standing: it was the received opinion in former ages, that our first parents fell the very same day they were created. Augustin, among the rest, writes, that they stood but six hours: but though we cannot determine the certain time, very probable it is, that it was but short; this we find, that after Moses had set down the creation of man, without the interposition of any thing else, he comes immediately to the fall; and the devil no doubt took the first occasion he possibly could, to bring man to the same damnation with himself. Well then, long it was not, but Adam by his sin deprived himself, and all his posterity of the image of God: as all mankind was in his loins; so, by the order and appointment of God, all mankind partakes with him in the guilt of his sins: hence is the daily and continual cry, not only of Adam, Abraham, David, Paul, but of every saint, *O wretched man that I am, who shall deliver me from the body of this death?* Rom. vii. 24. But, sweet

sweet soul! stay your complaints, here's gospel-news—

In this sad hour of temptation God stepped in: he will not leave man without hope; he tells the devil who begun this mischief, *I will put enmity between thee and the woman, and between thy seed and her seed, it shall bruise thy head, and thou shalt bruise his heel*, Gen. iii. 15. At the very instant, when God was pronouncing judgments upon the several delinquents in the fall; nay, before judgment was pronounced on the persons tempted, a Jesus is hinted, the covenant of grace is proclaimed. O the infinite riches of the mercy of God in Christ!

But you will say, how comes Jesus in? how carried he on the great work of our salvation in this dark time?

I answer, 1. By assuming and taking upon him the form and shape of a man, and so discharging some special offices in that respect: we read often of Christ's apparitions, before his incarnation, and then especially when he had to do with this great negotiation of man's eternal happiness. Some think it not improbable that Christ assumed the form of man when he first created man, and so he made man, not only in his own image, which he had as God, in holiness, and true righteousness but in respect of that form which he had assumed. Howsoever, this we find that after man had sinned, Christ then appeared, first to Adam, then to Abraham, then to Isaac, then to Jacob, then to Moses, &c.——First, he appeared to Adam in the garden, *And they heard the voice of the Lord God, walking in the garden, in the cool of the day*, Gen. iii. 8. God, as he is God, hath neither voice to speak, nor feet to walk, but assuming the form and shape of a man, he exercised both: and so he was the first that published that first promise to the world, *It shall bruise thy head.* 2. He appeared to Abraham *in the plain of Mamre*, where *the Lord talked with Abraham*, and Abraham calls him *the Judge of the earth*, which can be ascribed to none but Christ *the judge of quick and dead*, Gen. xviii. 1, 13, 25. Some from that saying of Christ, *Your father Abraham rejoiced to see my day, and he saw it, and was glad*, John viii. 50. do gather that Abraham saw Christ, not only with the eyes of faith (as all the rest of the patriarchs and prophets did) but also in a visible shape which he assumed like unto that whereunto he was afterwards to be united; and so it was Christ that renewed the covenant with Abraham, saying, *I will establish my covenant between me and thee, and thy seed after thee in their generations, for an everlasting covenant, to be a God unto thee, and to thy seed after thee*, Gen. xvii. 7—3. He appeared to Isaac, Gen. xxvi. 2. and to Jacob, Gen. xxxii. 24, 30. and to Moses, Ex. xx. 1, 2, 3. and to many others, of which I shall comment in order. And these apparitions of Christ were as *preludes* of his incarnation. But this is not the way I shall insist upon.

2. Christ carried on the great work of our salvation in that dark time, not by himself exhibited (as when he was incarnate) but only promised. The great king would first have his harbingers to lead the way, before he himself would come in person. As the Lord had observed this method in creating the world, that first he would have darkness, and then light; and as still he observes this method in upholding the world, that first he will have dawning, and then clear day; so in the framing and upholding of his church, he will first have Christ held forth in ceremonies, rites, figures, types, promises, covenants, and then, like a glorious sun, or like *the day-spring from on high, he would visit the world, to give light to them that sit in darkness*, Luke i. 78. To this purpose we read, that as Christ, so the covenant of grace (which applies Christ to us) was first promised, and then promulgated, the covenant of promise was that covenant, which God made with Adam, and Abraham, and Moses, and David, and all Israel in Jesus Christ; to be incarnate, crucified, and raised from the dead; the covenant promulgated or new covenant (as scriptures call it by way of excellency) is that covenant which God makes with all believers since the coming of Christ, believing in him that is incarnate, crucified, and risen from the dead; and it was meet that the promise should go before the gospel, and be fulfilled in the gospel, that so great a good might earnestly be desired, before it was bestowed. In a time of darkness men desire light; as the morning-watch watcheth and longeth for the morning, so the obscure revelation of Christ in a promise, raised the hearts of the patriarchs to an earnest desire of Christ his coming in the flesh. But in this obscurity we may observe some degrees;

grees; before the law given by Moses, the promise was more obscure; the law being given even to the time of the prophets, the promise was a little more clear; in the time of the prophets even to John the Baptist, it was clearer yet; as the coming of the Messias did approach nearer and nearer, so was the promise clearer and clearer still: just as the approach of the sun is near or further off, so is the light that goes before it greater or lesser; in like manner was the revelation that went before Christ more dim or clear, as the rising of the Sun of righteousness was more remote, or nigh at hand. It was the good pleasure of God to manifest the riches of his grace by degrees, and not all at once; we see to this very day, that God in his several approaches of mercy and goodness draws nearer and nearer to his church: even now in this marvellous light of the gospel we have our divine ceremonies and sacraments, we see him afar off, we know but in part; but time shall come (even before his second coming) that we, or our children shall see him more clearly, perfectly, immediately. My present business is to hold forth Jesus in the covenant of grace as promised, and because the promise receives distinction of degrees according to the several breakings out of it to the dark world, we will consider it as it was manifested.

1. From Adam till Abraham.
2. From Abraham till Moses.
3. From Moses till David.
4. From David till the Babylonish captivity, or thereabout.
5. From the captivity, or thereabout till Christ.

In every of these periods will appear some further and further discoveries of God's mercy in Christ, of the covenant of grace, of our Jesus carrying on the great work of man's eternal salvation in that dark time.

You heard before of the covenants betwixt God and Christ concerning our salvation; but that was not the covenant of grace, which God immediately made with man as fallen; but a particular covenant with Christ to be the Mediator: or so far as it was a covenant of grace, it was then made betwixt God and Christ, and after to be made betwixt God and us: for a time we were hid in the womb of God's election, and not being then capable to enter into covenant with God, Christ undertook for us; but yet so that when we come to be regenerate, we are then to strike covenant ourselves. And hence we read expresly of God's covenanting with sundry particular persons, as with Adam, and Abraham, and Moses, and David, &c. Of which in the next sections.

SECT. II.

Of the covenant of promise, as manifested to Adam.

THE covenant of grace in this sense is nothing else but a compact made betwixt God and man, touching reconciliation, and life eternal by Christ. Now, the first breaking forth of this gracious covenant was to Adam and Eve, immediately after the fall, expressed in these words, *I will put enmity between thee and the woman, and between thy seed and her seed, it shall bruise thy head, and thou shalt bruise his heel,* Gen. iii. 15.

This promise, as it is the first, so the hardest to be understood; it contains in it good news of the overthrow of Satan's kingdom, and of man's freedom by the death of Christ. But the obscurity is such, that Luther exceedingly complains, The text which of all men should rightly be known, is of no man that I know (saith he) especially and accurately unfolded: amongst the ancients there is not one that hath explained this text according to the dignity of it.

The occasion was this: the Lord looking down from heaven, and seeing how Satan had prevailed against man, and in some sort undone the whole fabrick of the creation, he resolves upon Satan's ruin, and man's preservation: *And the Lord God said unto the serpent, Because thou hast done this, thou art cursed,* Gen. iii. 14. This literally is understood of the serpent, but spiritually of the devil; both were as means to draw man unto sin, and therefore they are joined as one in the punishment: ' The Lord cut off the feet of the serpent ' (saith the Rabbi's) and cursed him, and he cast ' Sammael (the devil) and his company out of hea- ' ven, and cursed them,' *R. Eliezer C.* 14. Indeed man, being in the transgression, must also have his punishment, as it follows, Ver. 17, 18, 19. And yet that God might manifest the riches of his grace, he includes in the serpent's malediction

From the Creation until his first Coming.

diction the everlasting gospel, *I will put enmity between thee and the woman*, &c.

For the sense of the words, we shall open these terms, as, 1. Who is the *serpent?* 2. Who is the *woman?* 3. What is the *seed of the serpent?* 4. What is the *seed of the woman?* 5. What is that *Hu*, in our Bible translated *It?* 6. What is the *serpent's head*, and the *bruising of it?* 7. What is the *heel of the seed of the woman*, and the *bruising of it?* 8. Among whom was the *enmity*, or rather enmities? for in the text we find many armies, *I will put enmity between thee and the woman, and between thy seed and her seed*, &c.

1. Who is the serpent? I find diversity of opinions among interpreters: some say, it was only the serpent, and that which belongs unto Satan is but mystically understood: others say, it was only Satan under the notion of a serpent, as sometimes he is called the *great dragon, And the great dragon was cast out, that old serpent called the devil, and Satan, which deceived the whole world*, Rev. xii. 9. Others say, it was both Satan and the serpent; as men are said to be possessed of Satan, so was the serpent possessed of the devil. Satan could not provoke our first parents to sin by any inward temptation, as now he doth by the help of our corruption. Nor could he enter into their bodies, or minds, because of the holiness and glory that was in them; and therefore he presumed to take a beast of the earth, and by disposing of his tongue he speaks within him. But what, must the serpent have punishment, that was only Satan's instrument in the temptation? Yes:

Such was God's love to man, that he condemns both the author and instrument of that evil: as one that in anger breaks the sword wherewith his son, or his friend was wounded; so God breaks Satan's sword: the serpent is punished according to the letter of the text, and Satan is punished in the spiritual meaning of the Lord.

2. Who is the woman? Some are all for allegories, and they will tell you, that the serpent and the woman are the superior and inferior faculties of the soul, and that ever since the fall there hath been a continual war betwixt these: but I look on this commentary as vain and trifling, though it be fathered on some of the ancients, and of no small note; others say this woman is the blessed virgin, in relation to which they read the last words thus, *she shall bruise thy head*; this reading is not only allowed, but confirmed by the council of Trent; and in some of their prayer-books they call her the mother of our Lord, the tree of life, the breaker of the serpent's head, and the gate of heaven. *Antiphona de Domina nostra secundum usum Ecclesf.* Hildenshem. But I look on this commentary as ignorant and idolatrous, and wholly derogatory to the kingdom of Christ. Others are not so easily misled, and therefore say, that the woman wheresoever mentioned in this text, is Eve, and none but Eve; she it was whom the tempter had seduced, and in just judgment for her familiarity with the tempter, God meets with her, *I will put enmity* (saith God) *between thee and the woman*.

3. What is *the seed of the serpent?* In scripture phrase *seed* is sometimes taken collectively, for many at once; as when the Lord said to Abraham, *I will be thy God, and the God of thy seed: and to thee and to thy seed will I give this land: and I will multiply thy seed as the sand of the sea*, Gen. xvii. 17, 18. And sometimes it is taken singularly for one only person; thus, Eve called her son Seth, *For God, said she, hath appointed me another seed instead of Abel*, Gen. iv. 28. And so it is said of Christ, *In thy seed shall all the nations of the earth be blessed*, Gen. xxii. 18. Now, in this place *the seed of the serpent* is taken collectively, for all the families of devils, for the *devil and his angels* (as Christ calls them) and for all the sons of the devil, *i. e.* for all the reprobate men, whose father and prince is the devil, as Christ told the Jews, *Ye are of your Father the devil, and the lusts of your father ye will do*, John viii. 44. And as John tells us, *he that committeth sin is of the devil—In this the children of God are manifest, and the children of the devil*, 1 John iii. 8, 10. And thus both devils and reprobates are reckoned as the seed of the serpent.

4. What is *the seed of the woman?*——The seed of the woman is that posterity of the woman which do not degenerate into the seed of the serpent: That is the meaning of the first sentence, *I will put enmity*;—and then it follows, *between thy seed and her seed*: and for this sense we have these arguments. 1. The opposition of the seeds; for as the seed of the serpent is taken collectively, so the seed of the woman must be taken collectively, that the opposition may be fit. 2. The enmities

mities fore-spoken do strongly evince it, now the enmities pertain both to Eve and to all her posterity, if godly, to the end of the world; hence *all that will live godly in Christ Jesus shall suffer persecution*, saith the apostle, 2 Tim. iii. 12. *And I will put enmity* (faith God) *between thee and the woman*; Is that all? No, but also *between thy seed and her seed*: and who can deny but these enmities have been ever since betwixt Satan's brood and the saints? *We are all wrestlers against principalities, and powers, and rulers of the darkness of this world, and against spiritual wickedness in high places*, Eph. vi. 12.

5. What is that *hu*, in our Bible translated *it?* *It shall bruise thy head*. Some observe this *hu*, *it*, is of the masculine gender; and *zera*, *seed*, is of the masculine gender; and *jesaphera*, *shall bruise* is of the masculine gender; which confutes the translation that render it thus, *She shall bruise thy head*, and which confirms our translation which is thus, *he*, or *it*, or that same *seed*, *i. e.* one singular person of that same seed, *shall bruise thy head*. Well then, who is this *he?* or what one is *he?* even *Jesus the Son of the living God.* Here is the first hint of Jesus that ever was read or heard of in this world. This was the pro-to-evangel, or first gospel that ever was published after the creation. O blessed news! fit for God's mouth to speak, and to break first to the world now fallen. O dear parents! how would you have despaired, if before sentence you had not heard these blessed tidings! O our first parents upon earth, where had you and we been, if this blessed text had not been! come, set a star upon it, write it in letters of gold, or rather write it on the very tables of our hearts: here is the blessedest news that ever was, or ever shall be; but for this we had been all fire-brands of hell; yea, but for this Adam and Eve, and all their sons and daughters that are now gone out of this world, had been smoking and frying in hell-fire, away with all gross mistakes, erroneous conceits, and as you love your souls, yield to this blessed sense! this *it*, or *he*, is one of that same seed, and this one of that same seed is Jesus, and only Jesus, and none but Jesus; and for this sense we have these arguments.

1. Some observe that this sentence is separated from the former with a period, or great stop: however, God goes on to speak of the seed of the woman, yet he says not, *and that seed shall bruise thy head*; for so we might thought he had spoken of that seed collectively as he did before; but stopping there, and not repeating that same word again, he gives it thus, *It*, or *he shall bruise thy head, i. e.* some individual person of that same seed, some singular one of that same common seed of the woman *shall bruise thy head*, as David alone of all the host of Israel goes forth to fight with Goliath, and overcomes him; so Christ alone of all the seed of the woman was so to fight with the serpent by his own power as to overcome him, and to *bruise his head.*

2. The seventy in their translations of this place (with which agrees the Chaldee paraphrast) render it [*autos*] *he*, which needs must denote some singular person, or son of the woman, and the rather because the seed spoken of before is rendered [*to sperma*], to which if the relative had rightly agreed, it should have been [*auto*] or [*touto*] and not [*autos*]. Hereto we may add, that to this *it*, or *he*, the seed of the serpent, is not opposed as it was in the former sentence; but the serpent itself; one singular antagonist; here is *singularis* [*monomachia*], a duel, or a combat of two hand to hand; only Christ and the serpent; *he shall bruise thy head, and thou shalt bruise his heel.*

3. The bruising of the head doth plainly discover this *it*, or *he*, is Jesus Christ: for none can bruise the serpent's head but only God: *The God of peace* (faith the apostle) *shall bruise Satan under your feet shortly*, Rom. xvi. 20. Now, there was none of the seed of the woman, that was ever God but only Christ, God-man, Man-god, blessed for ever; and therefore it must needs be Christ, and only Christ that can bruise this serpent's head. O! there's a divine power, a power and virtue of God in it, to bruise the serpent's head. Observe but the manner of this duel, Christ treads on the serpent: and by this means he comes to have a bruise in the heel, whilst with his heel he bruiseth the serpent's head. A wonderful thing that Christ should lay at the serpent's head with no other weapon, but only with his heel; it were much for any man to strike at any common serpent with a bare and naked foot; rather would he take a dart, or club or any other weapon; but with a foot to bruise Satan's head (that great and fierce and monstrous serpent) this exceeds any man's power, or

any

any man's daring to attempt: hence it is that some one person of more than human strength must do this deed, and who is that of the seed of the woman, but only Jesus Christ?

4. God himself in other places of scripture doth expresly declare, that this seed here promised is Christ, and only Christ. Mark but where this promise is repeated to the patriarchs, as when the Lord said to Abraham, *In thy seed shall the nations of the earth be blessed*, Gen. xxii. 18. And when the Lord said to David, *I will raise up thy seed after thee, which shall be of thy sons, and I will establish his kingdom*, 1 Chron. xvii. 11. And you may see it clear that this seed is Christ, and only Christ; concerning that promise to Abraham, the apostle interprets it, *Now to Abraham, and his seed were the promises made. He saith not, and to seeds, as of many, but as of one, and to thy seed, which is Christ*, Gal. iii. 16. And concerning that promise to David, the prophet interprets it, *He shall sit upon the throne of David, and upon his kingdom to order it, and to establish it,*——Who is that? in the former verse, his name is *Wonderful, counsellor, The mighty God, The everlasting Father, The prince of peace*, Isa. ix. 7, 6. *i. e.* Christ, and none but Christ; *For unto us a child is born, and unto us a son is given*, &c. And who is that but Jesus Christ?

5. The accomplishment of this promise in Christ is expresly and clearly made out in the New Testament. Was not Jesus Christ of the seed of the woman, born of a virgin? Was not his heel bruised, himself crucified? And did he not bruise the serpent's head, break the power and dominion of Satan? What saith the gospel? *For this purpose the Son of God was manifested, that he might destroy the works of the devil*, 1 John iii. 1. *And the seventy returned again with joy, saying, Lord, even the devils are subject unto us through thy name. And he said unto them, I beheld Satan as lightning fall from heaven; behold, I give unto you power to tread on serpents, and scorpions, and over all the powers of the enemy, and nothing shall by any means hurt you*, Luke x. 17, &c. *And now is the judgment of this world; now shall the prince of this world be cast out*, John xii. 31. *And for as much as children are partakers of flesh and blood, he also himself likewise took part of the same, that through death he might destroy him that had the power of death, that is the devil*, Heb. ii. 14. In these and many other places, we find this very promise fulfilled in Christ, and only in Christ; and therefore he, and only he is the seed of the woman (that *hu, it*, or *he*) that shall bruise the serpent's head. Yet I will not deny, but by way of participation this promise may pertain to the whole body of Christ: *through him that loved us we are more than conquerors*, saith the apostle, Rom. viii. 37. We may conquer Satan, though not in our own strength but Christ's: and so, in a secondary sense, by way of communication with Christ, under this *seed* all the faithful are and may be contained. 1. Because the head and members are all one body, *Both he that sanctifieth, and they who are sanctified are all of one*, Heb. ii. 11. 2. Because the faithful are called the seed of Christ, *When thou shalt make thy soul an offering for sin, he shall see his seed*, Is. lii. 10. 3. Because Satan doth not only bruise the heel of Christ, but of all the faithful, *All that will live godly in Christ Jesus shall suffer persecution*, 2 Tim. iii. 12. 4. Because Satan's overthrow, by Christ our head, is diffused to all the members, *And the God of peace shall bruise Satan under your feet shortly*, Rom. xvi. 20. In this sense many of the ancient and modern divines do extend this *seed* to the whole body of Christ; but primarily, originally, especially and properly, it belongs only to Christ, and to none but the Lord Jesus Christ. He only is the seed by whom the promise is accomplished, though the faithful also are the seed to whom, and for whom, the promise was made.

6. What is the serpent's head, and the bruising of it? 1. For the serpent's head, it is the power, rage, reign and kingdom of Satan: it is observed, that in the head of a serpent lies the strength, power and life of a serpent; so by a phrase of speech fitted to the condition of this serpent, that was satan's instrument. God tells the devil of the danger of his head, *i. e.* of his power and kingdom: now, this power and kingdom of Satan consists more especially in sin and death; for the *sting of death is sin*, 1 Cor. xv. 26. And *the power of death is in Satan*, Heb. ii. 14. Hence sin and death are usually called the works and wages of Satan; they are his own, he owns them, and carries them at his girdle. 2. For the bruising of this head, it is the over-

throw-

throwing of Satan's power; *he shall bruise thy head*, *i. e.* Chriſt ſhall break thy power; Chriſt ſhall deſtroy ſin, and death, and *him that had the power of death, that is the devil.* I ſay, Chriſt ſhall do it, though, as I have ſaid, in a ſecondary ſenſe, the faithful ſhall do it; Chriſt overcomes by his own power, and the faithful overcome by the power of Chriſt; the victory is common to all the ſeed, but the author of victory is only Chriſt, the head and chief of all the ſeed: *Ye have overcome the evil one,* 1 John ii. 13. But how? Not of yourſelves, it is *the God of peace that bruiſeth Satan,* Rom. xvi. 20. Well then, here is the ſenſe, the ſerpent's head is bruiſed, *i. e.* the devil, and ſin, and death and hell are overthrown; not only the devil in his perſon, but the works of the devil, which by the fall he had planted in our natures, as pride, vain glory, ignorance, luſt, &c. nor only Satan's works, but the fruits and effects of his works, as death and hell; ſo that all the faithful may ſing with Paul, *O death, where is thy ſting? O grave, where is thy victory? Thanks be to God who giveth us the victory through Jeſus Chriſt our Lord,* 1 Cor. xv. 55, 57.

7. What is the heel of the ſeed of the woman, and the bruiſing of it? 1. For the heel, it is the humanity of Chriſt, according to which Chriſt properly hath an heel: or (as others) it is the ways of Chriſt, which Satan, by all means he could poſſibly, would ſeek to ſuppreſs. 2. For the bruiſing of his heel, it is the miſeries, mockings, woundings, death and burial of Chriſt, all which he endured in his heel, *i. e.* in his humanity: or it extends further to all the hurts, reproaches, afflictions, perſecutions of the faithful, by the devil and his agents: all which are but as a bruiſe in the heel, which cannot endanger the ſpiritual life of their ſouls. It is obſerved, that the ſerpent hath but one head, but the ſeed of the woman hath two heels; ſo that the one may be ſome help, while the other is hurt; beſides an hurt in the heel is far from the head and heart; though it may be painful, it is not mortal. Indeed, Chriſt's heel was bruiſed, *i. e.* he was delivered to death, even to the death of the croſs; yet he roſe again from the dead; neither had the devil any advantage by his death, for as angry bees ſtinging once, make themſelves drones, ſo the devil now he may hiſs at us, but he cannot hurt us: by that wound which Chriſt received at his death, he wounded all his enemies irrecoverably; the very ſight itſelf was Chriſt's triumph; even then was the kingdom of darkneſs utterly overthrown; ſin, death and Satan were conquered, and taken captive, and whatſoever might be brought againſt us was taken away, as the leaſt bill or ſcroll. O bleſſed riddle! *Out of the eater came forth meat, and out of the ſtrong came forth ſweetneſs,* Jud. xiv. 14. In reference to this promiſe, thou ſhalt bruiſe his heel, Chriſt is ſaid to be *the Lamb ſlain from the foundation of the world,* Rev. xiii. 8. Here's good news betimes.

8. Amongſt whom was the enmity, or this hoſtile war? We find in the text three hoſts, and three battles: as,——

1. Betwixt Satan and the woman; *I will put enmity between thee and the woman;* i. e. betwixt the ſeducer and her whom thou haſt ſeduced. This enmity is oppoſed to the amity and familiarity which had been between the woman and the ſerpent, and upon that account the woman, and not the man is named; not but that enmity muſt be betwixt the devil and the man, as well as betwixt the devil and the woman, but becauſe the woman had more tampered with Satan, and being deceived by Satan, was firſt in the tranſgreſſion, therefore is ſhe only named, *I will put enmity between thee and the woman.*

2. Betwixt Satan's ſeed, and the ſeed of the woman: *I will put enmity,* not only between thee and the woman, but alſo *between her ſeed and thy ſeed. q. d.* This enmity ſhall not ceaſe with the death of the woman, but it ſhall continue to her ſeed, and to her ſeed's ſeed, even to the end of the world. We ſee to this day how the ſerpent and ſerpent's ſeed are ſtriving and warring againſt the church; and a wonder it is (conſidering the malice of the enemy) that there is a church upon earth, but only that we have Chriſt's promiſe, *the gates of hell ſhall not prevail againſt it: and lo I am with you always, even to the end of the world,* Matth. xvi. 18. and xviii. 20.

3. Betwixt Chriſt and the ſerpent; O this is a bloody conflict on both ſides; *he ſhall bruiſe thy head, and thou ſhalt bruiſe his heel.*

1. *He ſhall bruiſe thy head,* Chriſt ſhall break thy power, *i. e.* the power of the ſerpent, or of the devil himſelf; he fights not ſo much with the

ſeed

feed, as with the serpent; if Satan be overthrown, his feed cannot stand. 2. *Thou shalt bruise his heel;* thou shalt afflict him and his; thou shalt cast out of thy mouth a flood of perfecutions; thou shalt *make war with him and all them which keep the commandments of God, and have the testimony of Jesus Christ,* Rev. xii. 17.

I have held you a while in the explication of this first promife, and the rather becaufe of the darkness of it, and the much sweetness that is contained in it; it is full of gospel-truths, strike but the flint, and there will fly out these glorious sparks.

1. That a Saviour was promifed from the beginning of the world. 2. That this Saviour should free all his faints from sin, death and hell, the head, and power of the devil. 3. That to this end this Saviour should be a Mediator, for God would not grant an immediate pardon, but the promifed feed muft firft intervene. 4. That this Mediator should be of the feed of the woman, that is, a man; and yet ftronger than the devil, endued with a divine power, and fo he is God. 5. That this man-god fhould according to his prieftly office be a facrifice for fin, the ferpent fhould *bruife his heel,* he fhould fuffer and die for the people, and yet according to his kingly office he fhould overcome Satan, for *he fhould bruife his head,* overthrow his kingdom, and make us more than conquerors in him that loved us. 6. That this promife of Chrift, and of our juftification is free; God of mere mercy, and free grace brings forth this promife; there could be now after the fall no merit in man; and even now he promifeth remiffion of fins, and life eternal in, for, and through the Lord Jefus Chrift. No queftion but in belief of his promife, the patriarch and fathers of old obtained life, glory, and immortality: *By faith the elders obtained a good report: by faith Abel obtained witnefs that he was righteous: by faith Enoch was tranflated that he fhould not fee death: by faith Noah became heir of the righteoufnefs of Chrift,* Heb. xi. 2, 4, 5, 7. And how fhould it but revive us in thefe laft times, to hear, that the firft thing that ever God did after the world was fallen, it was this act of mercy, to make a promife of Chrift, and to reconcile loft man to himfelf through the fame Jefus Chrift! furely he began to do that foon, which he meant to be always a doing, even to the end of the world. Thus far of the promife as it was manifefted from Adam to Abraham.

SECT. III.

Of the covenant of promife, as manifefted to Abraham.

THE fecond breaking forth of this gracious covenant, was to Abraham, and now it fhines in a more glorious light than it did before; at firft it was propofed in very dark and cloudy terms not eafy to be underftood, and moft things fparingly expreffed, but in this rife and manifeftation, we have it laid down in plainer terms, *I will eftablifh my covenant between me and thee, and thy feed after thee in their generations for an everlafting covenant, to be a God to thee, and to thy feed after thee.——*Gen. xvii. 7. For the right underftanding of this, we fhall examine thefe particulars.——

1. What a covenant is?
2. What is the eftablifhing of this covenant?
3. Betwixt whom is the covenant to be eftablifhed?
4. For what time is the eftablifhed covenant to endure?
5. What are the privileges of this covenant?
6. What is the condition of this covenant?
7. Who is the head both as undertaker, and purchafer, and treafurer upon whom this covenant is eftablifhed?

1. What is a covenant? It is a contract of mutual peace and good will, obliging parties on both hands to the performing of mutual benefits and offices. Thus was the covenant betwixt God and Abraham; there was a mutual ftipulation in it; on God's part to perform his promifes of temporal, fpiritual, and eternal grace; and on Abraham's part to receive this grace by faith, and to perform due obedience and thankfulnefs to God. Hence a little nearer, and we fay the covenant is a mutual compact, or agreement betwixt God and man, whereby God promifeth all good things, efpecially eternal happinefs unto man; and man doth promife to walk before God in all acceptable, free, and willing obedience, expecting all good from God, and happinefs in God, according to his promife; for the praife

praise and glory of his grace. Others describing the covenant of grace (for with the covenant of works we will not meddle) they give it thus. 'The covenant of grace is a free and gracious compact, which God of his mere mercy in Jesus Christ hath made with sinful man, promising unto him pardon of sins and eternal happiness, if he will but repent of sin, and embrace mercy reaching forth by faith unfeigned; and walk before God in willing, faithful, and sincere obedience.'—In this description many things are considerable. As, 1. That the author of this covenant is God; not as our Creator, but as our merciful God and Father in Christ Jesus. 2. That the cause of this covenant is not any worth, or dignity, or merit in man, but the mere mercy, love, and favour of God. 3. That the foundation of this covenant is Jesus Christ, in and through whom we are reconciled unto God, for since God and man were separated by sin, no covenant can pass betwixt them, no reconciliation can be expected nor pardon obtained, but in and through a Mediator. 4. That the party covenanted with, is sinful man; the fall of our first parents was the occasion of this covenant, and God was pleased to permit the fall, that he might manifest the riches of his mercy in man's recovery. 5. That the form of this covenant stands on God's part in gracious and free promises of forgiveness, holiness, happiness; and on man's part on a restipulation of such duties as will stand with the free grace and mercy of God in Christ. 6. That the stipulation on man's part required, is repentance for sin, belief in the promises; and a yielding of fear, reverence, worship and obedience to God according to his word. These I might insist on, but my purposed brevity will not permit.

2. What is the establishing of this covenant? Some say, this speaks the duration of it, of which anon. I suppose it intends also the confirmation of it; we find that the Lord had before made a covenant with Abraham, Gen. xv. 4, 5. And now he doth not abolish the former, and make another, but rather he renews, confirms and establisheth the former. It may be there was some hesitation or doubting in Abraham, so we see, Gen. xv. 2, 3. But now God would assure him infallibly of his will and purpose. O when a man hears, that God will vouchsafe so much favour as to enter into a covenant with him, he is ready to say, as Gideon did, *Alas! my family is poor in Manasseh, and I am the least in all my father's house; and who am I that I should be raised up hitherto? That God should make such promises as these to me,* Judg. vi. 15. And hence to prevent such objections, the Lord will confirm and establish his covenant; as, sometimes by his promises; sometimes by an oath; sometimes by the blood of Christ himself; sometimes by seals. So here, in this very place, God adds the seal of circumcision, *Ye shall circumcise the flesh of your fore-skin* (saith God) *and it shall be a token of the covenant betwixt me and you,* Gen. xvii. 11. As sometimes he said of the rainbow, *I do set my bow in the cloud, and it shall be for a token of a covenant between me and the earth;—That the waters shall no more become a flood to destroy all flesh.—For I will look upon the bow, that I may remember the everlasting covenant,* Gen. ix. 13, 15, 16. After this manner are the signs and seals of the covenant; circumcise yourselves, saith God, and when I see the circumcision, I will remember my covenant, and I will make good to you all the promises thereof. But what is circumcision to the covenant? Much every way; circumcision was not without shedding of blood; because the covenant was not yet established in the blood of the Messiah. Sure there was much in this; howsoever the rite of itself was nothing; yet as it led the faithful patriarchs to the blood of Christ, and as it assured the purging away of sin by the blood of Christ, and as it signed the circumcision of the heart by the Spirit of Christ; so it found acceptance with God. No sooner he looks on it, but he remembers his covenant, and confirms it, and makes it good to Abraham, and to his seed after him.

3. Betwixt whom is the covenant to be established? *Between Me and thee* (saith God) *and thy seed after thee.* The two heads of this covenant are God and Abraham; on God's part are the whole trinity of persons, the blessed angels, and all the host of heaven; on Abraham's part are all his seed, and his posterity, yet with this limitation, that *all are not of Israel, which are of Israel; neither because they are the seed of Abraham, are they all children of Abraham; but in Isaac shall thy seed be called; that is, they which are the children of the flesh, are not the children of God; but the children of the promise are counted for the seed,*

feed, Rom. ix. 6, 7, 8. No queſtion this covenant was not to be extended to the Iſhmaelites, Idumeans or Keturians, Abraham's carnal ſeed; theſe quickly departed both out of Abraham's family and Abraham's faith: no, no, ſaith God, *I will eſtabliſh my covenant with Iſaac for an everlaſting covenant, and with his ſeed after him*, Gen. xvii. 19. With Iſaac, and with his ſeed, *i. e.* with the ſpiritual ſeed of Abraham: Now, under the ſeed, 1. All believing Jews, and 2. All Gentiles are comprehended; all may be called the ſpiritual ſeed of Abraham that walk in the ſteps of the faith of Abraham; and indeed thus runs the promiſe, *In thee ſhall all the families of the earth be bleſſed*, Gen. xii. 3. And *in thee ſhall all the nations of the earth be bleſſed*, Gen. xviii. 18. Theſe families and nations muſt needs comprehend the Gentiles. The apoſtle is very plain, *As it is written, I have made thee a father of many nations*, Rom. iv. 17. *That he might be the father of all them that believe, though they be not circumciſed*, Verſe 11. *That the bleſſing of Abraham might come on the Gentiles through Jeſus Chriſt, that we might receive the promiſe of the Spirit through faith*, Gal. iii. 14. Chriſtians! here is our happineſs, the covenant was not *written for Abraham's ſake alone, but for us alſo, if we believe in him that raiſed up Jeſus our Lord from the dead*, Rom. iv. 23, 24. You may think all this while, we are only diſcovering the privileges of Abraham, Iſaac, Jacob and of the Jews: No, bleſſed be God, heaven is no freer to a Jew, than to a Gentile; *There is neither Jew nor Greek, there is neither bond nor free, male nor female*, &c. *But if ye be Chriſt's, then are ye Abraham's ſeed, and heirs according to the promiſe*, Gal. iii. 28, 29.

4. For what time is the eſtabliſhed covenant to endure? It is not for a few days, or months, or years, but for ever and ever; it is an *everlaſting covenant*; and indeed the word *eſtabliſhed* ſounds this way; *I will eſtabliſh my covenant*, that is (ſay ſome) I will have it ſtand and continue for ever; as it was ſaid of David, *I have made a covenant with my choſen, I have ſworn unto David my ſervant, thy ſeed will I eſtabliſh for ever*, Pſal. lxxxix. 3. And again, *My mercy will I keep for him for ever more, my covenant ſhall ſtand faſt with him*, Pſalm lxxxix. 28.

Now, this covenant is ſaid to be everlaſting *a parte ante* (as we ſay) and *a parte poſt*. 1. *A parte ante*, as being from everlaſting in reſpect of the promiſe made to Chriſt for us, which was done (as you have heard) before the foundation of the world; it is not an infant of days; this covenant bears the ſame date with the divine Being itſelf: as the *mercy of God is from everlaſting*, Pſal. ciii. 17. ſo the covenant of grace is from everlaſting; the writs, evidences and charters of our ſalvation were concluded, and paſſed the ſign and ſeal of the bleſſed trinity from eternity; this goſpel and the covenant is not of yeſterday; no, no, it is an old council of the infinite wiſdom of God.

2. *A parte poſt*, as continuing from everlaſting to everlaſting. Hence it is called, *A covenant of ſalt*, 2 Chron. xiii. 5. Becauſe it corrupteth not, it faileth not; hence all the bleſſings of the covenant are ſaid to be everlaſting: forgiveneſs of ſins is everlaſting, being once forgiven they are *never remembered any more*, Jer. xxxi. 34. Peace and joy is everlaſting: *Your heart ſhall rejoice, and your joy no man taketh from you*, John xvi. 22. Salvation is everlaſting; *Iſrael ſhall be ſaved in the Lord with an everlaſting ſalvation*, Iſa. xlv. 17. Decretal covenant-mercy was not a leaſe, but a making the fee-ſimple (as we call it) of grace and glory to the ſaints for ever: death may put an end to other covenants, as betwixt man and man, or betwixt man and wife; but this covenant betwixt God and us ſtands faſt for ever: though Abraham be dead, yet God is Abraham's God ſtill, and by virtue of this covenant Abraham ſhall be raiſed up at the laſt day.

4. What are the privileges of the covenant? I anſwer, the privileges of the covenant are many; as, they are great things, and great bleſſings which our God promiſeth, ſo they are very many and numerous; the covenant is full of bleſſings, it is a rich ſtorehouſe, repleniſhed with all manner of bleſſings; it is not dry, nor barren, but like the fat olive or fruitful vine; it is a well of ſalvation, a fountain of good things, a treaſure full of goods, of unſearchable riches, which can never be emptied, nor come to an end. Hence it is that our finite narrow capacities can never apprehend the infinite grace that this covenant contains; yet as we may ſee things darkly in a map, ſo let us endeavour, as we are able, to view them in ſome map, or brief

be raised up to the consideration of things not seen, which shall be revealed in due time.

The privileges of the covenant are folded and wrapped up in the promises of it; every promise contains a privilege; but the time of unfolding every promise is not yet come; then only shall the promises of all sorts be unfolded, when the heavens *as a vesture shall be folded up*, Heb. i. 12. In the mean time we have a right and interest in the privileges of eternity by virtue of the promise; and hence the very terms of covenant and promise are taken for the same, Eph. ii. 12. Rom. ix. 4. I shall for the present confine myself only to those promises and privileges of the covenant, which were manifested to Abraham. And they were,

Of Things { Temporal
{ Spiritual

1. Of things temporal. Thus we read God promiseth Abraham, 'I will make of thee a great nation, and I will bless thee, and make thy name great; and thou shalt be a blessing. I will bless them that bless thee, and curse him that curseth thee. And unto thy seed will I give this land,' Gen. xii. 2, 3, 7. We may add hereto the repetitions that God makes of these promises over and over; ' Lift up now thine eyes, and look from the place where thou art, north-ward, and south-ward, and east-ward, and west-ward, for all the land which thou seest to thee will I give it, and to thy seed for ever. And I will make thy seed as the dust of the earth, so that if a man can number the dust of the earth, then shall thy seed also be numbered, Gen. xiii. 14, 15, 16. And the Lord brought forth Abraham abroad, and said, Look now towards heaven, and tell the stars, if thou be able to number them: and he said unto him, So shall thy seed be, Gen. xv. 5. And the Lord again appeared unto Abraham, and said, I will make my covenant between me and thee, and will multiply thee exceedingly: and thou shalt be a father of many nations, neither shall thy name any more be called Abram, but thy name shall be Abraham, for a father of many nations have I made thee. And I will make thee exceeding fruitful, and I will make nations of thee, and kings shall come out of thee. And I will give unto thee, and thy seed after thee, the land wherein thou art a stranger, all the land of Canaan for an everlasting possession, Gen. xvii. 1, 4, 8. By myself have I sworn, saith the Lord, that in blessing I will bless thee, and in multiplying I will multiply thy seed as the stars of heaven, and as the sand upon the sea shore, and thy seed shall possess the gate of his enemies,' Gen. xxii. 16, 17. See here the temporal blessings that God promises Abraham, they are heaped together in Gen. xii. 2, 3, 7. As,

1. ' I will make of thee a great nation;' and this he promiseth once and again; it seemed a thing incredible, because Abraham was old, and Sarah was barren and old, and it ceased to be with Sarah after the manner of women; yet for all this God is all-sufficient; Abraham shall have his desire, he shall be a father, not only of a few children, but of a numerous nation; yea, of many nations, Ishmaelites, and Midianites, and that famous nation of the Jews (of whom it is said, *what nation is so great?* Deut. iv. 7, 8.) must all descend from Abraham. Scripture and heathen authors use three things proverbially, to signify an huge and exceeding great number, the dust of the earth, the sands of the sea, and the stars of heaven; and all these are brought in to resemble the number into which the seed of Abraham should break forth.

2. ' I will bless thee,' saith God; and this blessing had relation to his wealth and riches, ' Abraham was very rich in cattle, in silver, and in gold,' Gen. xiii. 2. No question those riches came from this blessing: ' The blessing of the Lord maketh rich, and he addeth no sorrow with it, Prov. x. 22. This was God's care of the children of Abraham, that he would give them riches, but lest their hearts should be lifted up, and they should forget the Lord in the midst of their riches, he learns them and bids them remember this lesson, ' Say not in thine heart, My power and the might of my hand hath gotten me this wealth; but remember the Lord thy God, for it is he that giveth thee power to get wealth, that he may establish his covenant, which he sware unto thy fathers, as it is this day.' Deut. viii. 17, 18. True riches come from God and by virtue of this covenant: O that none of us had any wealth, but such as comes by virtue of a promise, and of the covenant of grace!

3. I will make thy name great, saith God; no monarch was ever so famous in conquering nations, or the whole world, as Abraham for his faith and obedience; God hath magnified his name amongst the Hebrews, who, for these three thousand years and

From the Creation until his first Coming.

and upward, have acknowledged none (except Moses) greater than Abraham: the Jews could say to very Christ, *Art thou greater than our father Abraham?* —*Whom makest thou thyself?* John viii. 53. And God hath so magnified his name amongst Christians, that all believers look upon it as a glory to be called children of Abraham; nay, we cannot be Christ's, we have no part in Christ unless we be Abraham's *seed, and heirs according to the promise,* Gal. iii. 29.

4. *Unto thy seed will I give this land,* saith God, as *an everlasting possession,* Gen. xvii. 8. But how should that which the Israelites possessed only for a time, be called an everlasting possession? The answer is, That the word translated *everlasting,* doth not ever signify that which shall have no end; but an age, a term, or continuance? as it was said of Samuel, *He should appear before the Lord, and there abide for ever,* 1 Sam. i. 22. *i. e.* As long as he lived. And *I will praise the Lord* (said David) *for ever and ever,* Psalm cxlv. 1, 2. *i. e.* While I live will I praise the Lord. *As long as I shall have any being I will sing praises unto my God,* Psalm cxlvi. 2. And the desolations of the captivity were called, Prepetual desolations, Jer. xxv. 9. *i. e.* Long desolations, even for seventy years.

Touching these blessings, or privileges, I have no more to say but this, that God gave more of the temporal, less of the spiritual to the natural seed in the first ages, but in the latter ages, more of the spiritual privileges, and less of the temporal; yea, and thus it is this day, for the most-what among the Christian seed of the Gentiles; ' For ye see your calling, brethren, how that not many wise men after the flesh, not many mighty, not many noble are called,' 1 Cor. i. 26.

2. Of things spiritual, thus we read, ' Fear not, Abraham, I am thy shield, and thy exceeding great reward; I am God all-sufficient, or omnipotent, the almighty God; and I will be a God unto thee, and to thy seed after thee, Gen. xv. 1. and xvii. 1, 7. O what precious promises are these?

1. I am thy shield, to keep thee from all evil; such a shield as that no creature can pierce thro,' such a shield as shall cover thee over; nay, such a shield as shall cover thee about; as sometimes God spoke of Jerusalem, ' I, saith the Lord, will be unto her a wall of fire round about,' Zech. ii. 5. So here, I will be a shield, a wall of fire round about: not only a wall to keep thee safe, but a wall of fire to consume all them that are against thee; as a fire which stands about like a wall, doth not only defend those that are within, but it burns those that come near unto it; so is God to his people. 2. I am thy exceeding great reward; I am the almighty God; I will be a God unto thee. This is the very soul of the covenant, and of all the promises of God; *q. d. Quantus, quantus sim vester ero;* all I am is thine, myself, my goods, my glory, whatsoever is in me, all that I have, and all my attributes are thine; my power, my wisdom, my counsel, my goodness, my riches, whatsoever is mine in the whole world I will give it thee for thy portion; I and all that I have are thine, for thy use; Christians, was not this an exceeding great reward? Who can understand the heighth, and depth, and length, and breadth of this reward? Surely, ' Happy is the people that is in such a case; yea, happy is that people whose God is the Lord,' Psal. cxliv. 15. But more of this hereafter.

6. What is the condition of this covenant? I answer, The condition of the covenant of grace is faith, and only faith: to this purpose it is said of Abraham, *He believed in the Lord, and he counted it to him for righteousness,* Gen. xv. 6. Rom. iv. 3. Gal. iii. 6. James ii. 23. This text is often alledged by the apostles: the word *believed* imports, That he thought the word of God to be sure, certain, stable and constant; it is such a belief as is opposed to fainting; as it is said of Jacob, when he heard the report of his sons that Joseph was alive, *his heart fainted,* Gen. xlv. 26. because he believed not; but when he believed, his heart revived: and David saith of himself, *I had fainted, unless I had believed,* Psal. xxvii. 13. So that it is a lively motion of the heart, assenting unto, and trusting on God, and in the word of God as firm and constant. This was the very condition of the covenant, which God required of Abraham, *q. d.* Abraham, dost thou believe that such a Messiah shall be sent into the world? Art thou able to believe? Yes, I believe, Lord, said Abraham. Well, said God, I will put thee to the trial; I will give thee a son, though thou art as a dead man, and Sarah as a dead woman; yet I will promise thee a son, art thou able

to believe? Again, thou seest the land of Canaan, thou hast not one foot in it, yet I will give thee this land, in the length and breadth of it for thy possession, art thou able to believe this? You will say, What are these to the condition of the covenant, which is only to believe in God, and to believe in Jesus Christ? O yes, 1. These were shadows of the great promise, Christ; and therefore that act of faith, whereby Abraham believed that he could have a son, and that his children should possess the land of Canaan, was likewise a branch, a shadow, a pledge of that main act of faith, whereby he believed the promised seed, in whom himself and all the nations of the earth should be blessed. But, 2. Let this be remembered, that Abraham did not only believe the temporal promises, but every promise; as, I will be thy shield, and thy exceeding great reward: now, who is our shield but Christ, and who is our reward but Christ? But especially he believed the promise of the seed, and who is the head of the seed but Christ? And who is our reward but Christ? Yea, he believed in that promised seed, in whom all the nations of the earth should be blessed; and who was that but Christ? *Your father Abraham* (saith Christ) *rejoiced to see my day, and he saw it, and was glad,* John viii. 56. He saw it. How could he see it? *Thou art not yet fifty years old* (said the Jews) *and hast thou seen Abraham?* Or could Abraham see thee, or thy day? Yes, even then he saw it, when he believed in Christ; he could see it no other ways but by an eye of faith: and therefore no question he believed in Christ, and that was counted to him for righteousness.

But (may some say) if faith alone be the condition of the covenant, then what need is there of any obedience, or works of holiness?—This was the old plea of loose Libertines in the apostles times, to whom James gave an answer, *But wilt thou know, O vain man, that faith without works is dead,* James ii. 20. *A good tree* (saith Christ) *is known by its fruits;* and so is right and sound faith: let a man believe in truth, and he cannot but love; and if he love, he cannot but be full of good works: thus Abraham was justified by faith, *Abraham believed God,* (saith the apostle) *and it was imputed to him for righteousness.* But was not this faith accompanied with works? Observe but (saith the apostle) when God bad him offer his son, did he not do it? And was not that an exceeding great work? Surely *his faith wrought with his works, and by works was faith made perfect,* James ii. 24. compared with 21, 22.

7. Who is the head, both as undertaker and purchaser, and treasure, upon whom this covenant is established? I answer, Christ and none but Christ, *All the promises of God in him are yea, and amen, unto the glory of God by us,* 2 Cor. i. 20. This was very darkly held forth in the first manifestation of the covenant to Adam; but now in this second breaking forth of it, it is very fully expressed, and often repeated; thus, Gen. xii. 3. ' In thee shall all the families of the earth be blessed. And Gen. xviii. 18. All the nations of the earth shall be blessed in Abraham. And Gen. xxii. 18. In thy seed shall all the nations of the earth be blessed:' See Gen. xxvi. 5. and xxviii. 14. In comparing these texts, we have a clear understanding thereof; *in thee*, in Abraham shall all the families and nations of the earth be blessed; but lest Abraham himself should be thought author of this universal blessing, therefore is the explication, *In thee (i. e.) in thy seed*; and this *seed*, saith the apostle very expresly, is Jesus Christ. *Now, to Abraham and his seed were the promises made. He saith not, and to seeds, as of many; but as of one. And to thy seed, which is Christ,* Gal. iii. 16. So then here is the sense; out of thy posterity shall spring the Messiah, by whom not only thy posterity, but all the nations of the earth shall be blessed. You may remember in the first promise Christ was called *the seed of the woman*; but now the *seed of Abraham*; Christ was the son of Eve, or (if you will) the son of Mary, and so the seed of the woman; and Mary was a daughter of Abraham, and so Christ, and Mary and all upwards were of the seed of Abraham. But where shall we find mention of the passion of Christ in this expressure of his covenant to Abraham? In the first manifestation it was included in that phrase of *bruising his heel*; and surely this is essential to the covenant of grace in any overture of it: some answer, that this is thrice put on the passage of this covenant with Abraham; first, in the federal confirmation, by *the smoking furnace, and burning lamp, that passed between those pieces of the sacrifice,* Gen. xv. 17. As the sacrifice was divided, so was Christ's body torn; and as the smoking furnace, and burning lamp

From the Creation until his first Coming.

lamp paſſed between the divided pieces, ſo the wrath of God run betwixt, (as I may ſay) and yet did not conſume the rent and torn nature of Chriſt. *e*. In that federal confirmation by the ſign of circumciſion: there could not be circumciſion without ſhedding of blood, and where God commands ſhedding of blood in any of his ancient ordinances, it doth certainly reach to the blood of Chriſt, and his everlaſting teſtament. 3. In the reſolved ſacrifice of Iſaac, which was a plain type of the death of Chriſt, Gen. xxii. 10. See it in theſe particulars. 1. Iſaac was Abraham's ſon, his only ſon, his innocent ſon, the beloved ſon of his father, and yet Abraham freely offers up his ſon; ſo Chriſt was the Son of God, his only Son, his innocent ſon, *like to us in all things, ſin only excepted*; and the beloved Son of his Father, *this is my beloved Son in whom I am well pleaſed*; and yet God more freely offers up his Son out of his own boſom. 2. Abraham by God's commiſſion roſe early in the morning to ſacrifice his ſon; and the Jews by God's permiſſion riſe early in the morning to condemn the ſon of God? and hence he is called *the hind of the morning*, Pſal. xxii. 16. compaſſed with dogs that hunted and purſued his life. 3. Abraham muſt offer his ſon upon the mount, the very mount on which Solomon's temple was built, which typified the body of Jeſus Chriſt, John ii. 19. So God offered his Son upon the mount, if not on the ſame mount (as Auguſtin thinks), yet on a mount not far diſtant from it: Golgotha was the very ſkirt of Moriah; the one being within the gate of the city, and the other not far without, the very neareſt to the city of all. 4. Abraham firſt laid the wood on Iſaac, and then he laid Iſaac on the wood; ſo God firſt lays the croſs on Chriſt, *He bearing his croſs, went forth unto a place called the place of a ſcull*, John xix. 17, 18. And then he lays Chriſt on the croſs; there they *crucified him*, ſaith John; or there they bound him to the croſs, and faſtened his hands and feet thereto with nails. 5. Iſaac muſt be offered alone, the ſervants muſt ſtay at the foot of the hill, little knowing the buſineſs and ſorrow in hand, ſo Chriſt *muſt tread the wine preſs alone*, Iſa. lxiii. 3. The diſciples fear and flee, and little conſider the agony of their maſter. 6. Abraham carries in his hand the ſword and fire againſt his ſon; ſo God carries in his hand the ſword and fire, the ſword ſignifying the juſtice of God, the fire his burning wrath againſt the ſins of men; and both theſe were bent againſt Chriſt, in whom the juſtice of God is ſatisfied, and the flame of his wrath extinct and quenched. That this was a plain type of Chriſt's paſſion, is hinted at in the bleſſing that God ſpeaks to Abraham after this trial: *By myſelf have I ſworn, ſaith the Lord, for becauſe thou haſt done this thing, and haſt not withheld thy ſon, thine only ſon, that in bleſſing I will bleſs thee, and in thy ſeed ſhall all the nations of the earth be bleſſed*, Gen. xxii. 16, 17, 18. All believers are bleſſed in the death of Chriſt, who was that ſeed of Abraham, typified by Iſaac Abraham's ſon; for, as Abraham intended, ſo God truly ſacrificed his Son, his only Son to take away ſin.

Thus far of the covenant of promiſe, as it was manifeſted from Abraham to Moſes.

SECT. IV.

Of the covenant of promiſe as manifeſted to Moſes.

THE next breaking forth of this gracious covenant was to Moſes. The revenging juſtice of God had now ſeized on mankind for many generations, even thouſands of years; ſo that now it was high time for God in the midſt of wrath to remember mercy, and to break out into a clearer expreſſion of the promiſe, or covenant of grace. To this purpoſe the Lord calls up Moſes to mount Sinai, and there, of his infinite love and undeſerved mercy, he makes, or renews his covenant with him, and the children of Iſrael, *I am the Lord thy God, which brought thee out of the land of Egypt, out of the houſe of bondage: Thou ſhalt have no other gods before me*, Exod. xx. 2.

For the right underſtanding of this, we ſhall examine theſe particulars.

1. Whether the law was delivered in a covenant-way?
2. In what ſenſe is the law a covenant of grace?
3. How may it appear, That the law in any ſenſe is a covenant of grace?
4. Why ſhould God in the law deal with us in a covenant-way, rather than a mere abſolute ſupreme way?
5. What are the good things promiſed in this expreſſure of the covenant?

K 6. What

6. What is the condition of this covenant on our part, as we may gather it hence?

7. Who was the Mediator of this covenant?

8. What of Christ, and his death do we find in this manifestation of the covenant?

For the first, Whether the law was delivered in a covenant-way? It is affirmed on these grounds. 1. In that it hath the name of a covenant. 2. In that it hath the real properties of a covenant. 1. The name of a covenant, as it appears in these texts. 'And the Lord said unto Moses, Write these words; for after the tenor of these words, I have made a covenant with thee, and with Israel. And he was there with the Lord forty days, and forty nights; he did neither eat bread, nor drink water: and he wrote upon the tables the words of the covenant, the ten commandments, Exod. xxxiv. 27, 28. And he declared unto you his covenant, which he commanded you to perform, even the ten commandments, and he wrote them upon two tables of stone, Deut. iv. 13. When I was gone (says Moses) up into the mount, to receive the two tables of stone, even the tables of the covenant which the Lord made with you, then I abode in the mount forty days and forty nights, I did neither eat bread nor drink water, Deut. ix. 9. And it came to pass at the end of forty days and forty nights, that the Lord gave me the two tables of stone, even the tables of the covenant.' Ver. 11. 'So I turned and came down from the mount, and the mount burned with fire, and the two tables of the covenant were in my two hands.' Ver. 15. It appears plainly and expresly in these texts, that the law is a covenant.

2. The law hath the real properties of a covenant, which are the mutual consent and stipulation on both sides. You may see a full relation of this in Exod. xxiv. 3, 4, 5, 6, 7, 8. 'And Moses came and told the people all the words of the Lord, and all the judgments, and all the people answered with one voice, All the words which the Lord hath said will we do: And Moses wrote all the words of the Lord, and rose up early in the morning, and builded an altar under the hill, and twelve pillars, according to the twelve tribes of Israel. And he sent young men of the children of Israel, which offered burnt offerings, and sacrificed peace-offerings of oxen unto the Lord; and Moses took half of the blood, and put it in basons, and half of the blood he sprinkled on the altar: and he took the book of the covenant, and read in the audience of the people: and they said, All that the Lord hath said, will we do, and be obedient. And Moses took the blood, and sprinkled it on the people, and said, Behold the blood of the covenant which the Lord hath made with you, concerning all these words.' This very passage is related in the epistle to theHebrews, ix. 19, 20. 'When Moses had spoken every precept to all the people, according to the law, he took the blood of calves and goats, with water and scarlet wool, and hysop, and sprinkled both the book, and all the people, saying, This is the blood of the testament (or covenant) which God hath enjoined unto you.' In the words you may observe these properties of a covenant. 1. That God on his part expresseth his consent and willingness to be their God: this will appear in the preface of the law, of which hereafter. 2. That the people on their part give their full consents, and ready willingness to be his servants. Both these appear in that, 1. Moses writes down the covenant covenant-wise. 2. He confirms the covenant by outward signs, as by the blood of calves and goats, whereof one half he puts in basons, to sprinkle it on the people; and the other half of the blood he sprinkles on the altar; that sprinkling on the people signified their voluntary covenanting with God, and the blood sprinkled on the altar signified God's entering into covenant with the people. Thus we have real covenanting when the law is given.

2. In what sense is the law a covenant of grace? I answer, The law may be considered in several senses: as, 1. Sometimes it signifies largely any heavenly doctrine, whether it be promise or precept; and in this sense the apostle tells us, *of the law of works, and of the law of faith,* Rom. iii. 27. 2. Sometimes it signifies any part of the old Testament, in which sense Jesus answered the Jews, *Is it not written in your law, I said, Ye are Gods?* John x. 34. Psa. lxxxii. 6. Now, where was that written but in the book of the Psalms? 3. Sometimes it signifies the whole œconomy, and peculiar dispensation of God's worship unto the Jews according to the moral, ceremonial and judicial law; in which sense it is said to continue until John; *The law*

law and the prophets were until John; but since that time the kingdom of God is preached, Luke xvi. 16. 4. Sometimes it is taken *synechdochically* for some acts of the law only, Gal. v. 23. *Against such there is no law.* 5. Sometimes it is only taken for the ceremonial law, Heb. x. 1. *The law having a shadow of good things to come.* 6. Sometimes it is used in the sense of the Jews, as sufficient to save without Christ; and this the apostle generally takes it in his epistle to the Romans, and Galatians. 7. Sometimes it is taken for that part of the moral law, which is merely mandative and preceptive, without any promise at all. 8. Sometimes it is taken for the whole moral law, with the preface and promises added unto it; and in this last sense we take it, when we say it is a covenant of grace.

3. How may it appear, That the law in this sense is a covenant of grace? It appears, 1. By that contract betwixt God and Israel, before the promulgation of the law. ' If ye will obey my ' voice indeed, and keep my covenant, then ye ' shall be a peculiar treasure unto me above all ' people; for all the earth is mine: and ye shall ' be unto me a kingdom of priests, and an holy ' nation,' Exod. xix. 5, 6. Whereunto the prophet Jeremiah xi. 4. hath reference, saying, ' O-' bey my voice, and do them according to all which ' I command you; so shall you be my people, and ' I will be your God.' Both these scriptures speak of the moral law, or ten commandments, containing the preface and promises; and how should that law be any other but a covenant of grace, which runs in this tenor, ' I will be your God, and ye ' shall be my people; my peculiar treasure; a ' kingdom of priests, an holy nation; if you will ' but hear and obey my commandments?' Surely these privileges could never have been obtained by a covenant of works: what! to be a kingdom of priests, an holy nation, a peculiar treasure to the Lord? What! to be beloved of God as a desirable treasure (for so it is in the original) which a king delivers not into the hands of any of his officers, but keepeth it to himself? This cannot be of works. No, no, these are privileges vouchsafed of mere-grace in Jesus Christ; and therefore Peter applies this very promise to the people of God under the gospel, 1 Pet. ii. 6.

2. It appears by that contract betwixt God and Israel in the promulgation of the law; then it was that God proclaimed himself to be the God of Israel, saying, *I am the Lord thy God, which brought thee out of the land of Egypt, out of the house of bondage.* Some hold this to be the affirmative part of the first commandment; in which the gospel is preached, and the promises therein contained are offered. We say, it is a preface to the whole law, prefixed as a reason to persuade obedience to every commandment. But all universally acknowledge, that it is a free covenant, which promiseth pardon of sin, and requireth faith in the Messiah: when God said to Israel, *I am the Lord thy God which brought thee out of the land of Egypt,* doth he not propound himself as their King, Judge, Saviour and Redeemer? Yea, and spiritual Redeemer from their bondage of sin and Satan, whereof that temporal deliverance from Egypt was truly a type? The Lord begins his commandments with an evangelical promise: and it is very observable, That these words, *I am the Lord thy God,* are prefixed immediately to the first commandment: so in sundry places in scripture they are annexed to all the rest: ' Ye shall fear every ' man his Mother and his father; and keep my ' sabbaths, I am the Lord your God. Ye shall ' not steal, neither deal falsly; neither lie one to ' another; and ye shall not swear by my name ' falsly, neither shalt thou profane the name of ' thy God; I am the Lord.—Neither shalt thou ' stand against the blood of thy neighbour, I am ' the Lord.'—In a word, ' Thou shalt love thy ' neighbour as thyself; I am the Lord.'. Or if that contain only the second table, ' Therefore shall ' ye observe all my statutes, and all my judgments, ' and do them; I am the Lord,' Lev. xix. 3, 11, 12, 16, 18, 37. Add we to this, That in the second commandment God is described to be one shewing mercy unto thousands; all which must needs argue the law to be a covenant of grace.

3. It appears by the contract betwixt God and Israel, after the promulgation of the law: is it not plainly expressed by Moses, *Thou hast avouched the Lord this day to be thy God, and to walk in his ways, and to keep his statutes and commandments.——And the Lord hath avouched thee this day to be his peculiar people, as he hath promised thee, and that thou shouldest keep his commandments,* Deut. xxvi. 17, 18. Yea, and after

this in the land of Moab, Moses was commanded by the Lord to make a covenant with the children of Israel, besides the covenant which he made with them in Horeb; now this was the very same that God made with them on Sinai, only it must be renewed, and it is expresly said, *Ye stand this day to enter into a covenant with the Lord your God:——That he may establish you to be a people unto himself, and that he may be a God unto you as he had sworn to Abraham, Isaac and Jacob,* Deut. xxix. 12, 13. Surely this must needs be a a covenant of grace; how should it be but of grace, that God promised to be the God of Israel? Here are many sweet and precious promises, and they are all free and gracious; and therefore we conclude the law, in the sense aforesaid, to be a covenant of grace.

4. Why should God in the law deal with us in a covenant-way, rather than in a mere absolute supreme way? I answer, 1. In respect of God; it was his pleasure in giving the law not only to manifest his wisdom, and power, and sovereignty, but his faithfulness and truth, and love, and the glory of his grace, *That he might make known* (as the apostle speaks) *the riches of his glory on the vessels of mercy, which he had afore prepared unto glory,* Rom. ix. 15. God's love is a part of his name, *For God is love,* 1 John iv. 8. And God's faithfulness is a part of his name, *I saw heaven opened* (said John in a vision) *and behold a white horse, and he that sat on him was called faithful and true,* Rev. xix. 11. Now, how should we ever have known God's love, at least in such a measure? Or how should we ever have known God's faithfulness and truth at all, if he had not entered into a covenant with us? It is true, if he had given the law in a mere absolute supreme way, if he had given the precept without any promise, he might fully have discovered his illimited supreme power, but his so dear love and faithfulness could not have been known: now, therefore let the world take notice of his singular love, and of his faithfulness, as Moses said to Israel, *Because the Lord loved you, and because he would keep the oath which he had sworn unto your fathers, hath the Lord brought you out with a mighty hand, and redeemed you out of the house of bond men, from the hand of Pharaoh king of Egypt. Know therefore, that the Lord thy God he is God, the faithful God, which keepeth covenant and mercy with them that love him and keep his commandments, to a thousand generations.* Deut. vii. 8, 9.

2. In respect of us, God would rather deal with us in a covenant-way, than in a mere absolute supreme way, upon these grounds.—

1. That he might bind us the faster to himself. A covenant binds on both parts, the Lord doth not bind himself to us, and leave us free; no, *I will bring you* (faith God) *into the bond of the covenant,* Ezek. xx 37. The Lord sees how slippery and unstable our hearts are, how apt we are to start aside from our duty towards him. *We love to wander,* Jer. xiv. 10. And therefore to prevent this inconstancy and unsettledness in us, and to keep our hearts more stable in our obedient walking before him, it pleased the Lord to bind us in the bond of covenant, That as we look for a blessing from God, so we look to it to keep covenant with God. You may say, a command binds as well as a covenant: it is true, but a covenant doth as it were twist the cords of the law, and double the precept upon the soul; when it is only a precept, then God alone commands it, but when I have made a promise to it, then I command it and bind it upon myself.

2. That our obedience might be more willing and free. An absolute law might seem to extort obedience, but a covenant and agreement makes it clearly to appear more free and willing. This is of the nature of the covenant of grace: *First,* God promiseth mercy to be our exceeding great reward, and then we promise obedience, to be his free and willing people; and thus we become God's, not only by a property founded in his sovereign power and love, but by a property growing out of our own voluntary consents; we are not only his people, but his willing people; we give him our hand, when we become his, and enter into covenant with him. See the expression, Ezek xvii. 18. *He despised the oath, by breaking the covenant, when lo he had given his hand.* We are his, as the wife is her husband's, *I entered into covenant with thee,* faith the Lord God, *and thou becamest mine.* Ez. xvi. 8. Now, in marriages, free and mutual consent, you know, is ever given, and so it is here.

3. That our consolation might be stronger; that in all our difficulties and distresses we might ever have recourse to the faithfulness and love of God.

1. To

1. To the faithfulness of God. This was David's stay, 1 Chr. xvii. 27. And this may be ours, though friends be unfaithful, and may deceive, yet the Lord is faithful, and cannot fail his people, *His promises are Yea, and Amen.* 2 Cor. i. 20. We may build upon it. 2. That we might have recourse to the love of God; this indeed was the prime end why God delivered his law in way of a covenant, that he might sweeten and endear himself to us, and so draw us to him with cords of love; had God so pleased, he might have required all obedience from us, and when we had done all, he might have reduced us into nothing, or, at least, not have given us heaven for an inheritance, or himself for a portion; but his love is such, that he will not only command, but he will covenant, that he might further express and communicate his love: how then should this but comfort us in all our troubles? How should this but encourage us to go to God in all distresses? O what thankful loving thoughts should we have of God, that would thus infinitely condescend to covenant with us!

5. What are the good things promised in this expressure of the covenant? Not to reckon up the temporal promises of riches, honour, victory, peace, and protection in a land of oil, olive and honey, the great mercies of God are expressed in these terms, *I am the Lord thy God, which brought thee out of the Land of Egypt, out of the house of bondage.* This is the great promise of the covenant, it is as great as God himself. That we may better see it, and know it, I shall take it in pieces; the gold is so pure, that it is pity the least filing should be lost. Here God describes himself by these notes. 1. By his only, eternal and perfect essence, *I am the Lord.* 2. By the plurality of persons in that one essence, *I am the Lord God, Jehovah Elohim.* 3. By the propriety his people have in Jehovah Elohim, *I am the Lord thy God.* 4. By the fruit of that propriety in reference to Israel, *Which brought thee out of the land of Egypt, out of the house of bondage.*

1. *I am Jehovah:* we read that he *appeared to Abraham, Isaac, and Jacob, by the name of God Almighty,* but now he was known to the Israelites by his name Jehovah, *I am the Lord,* Exod. vi. 3. Why, was it not by that name he appeared to Abraham, Isaac, and Jacob? No; no, saith God: *By my name JEHOVAH was I not known to them.* Gen. xv. 7. This hath occasioned a question, How can this be? Do we not read expresly, That God said to Abraham, *I am the Lord that brought thee out of Ur of the Chaldees?* And again, *I am the Lord God of Abraham thy father, and the God of Isaac?* Gen. xxviii. 13. How then is it said, That by his name Jehovah he was not known unto them? This place hath perplexed many of the learned, but the meaning seems to be this, that though he was known to the patriarchs, by his name Jehovah, as it consists of letters, syllables, and sounds; yet he was not experimentally known unto them in his constancy to perform his promise in bringing them out of the land of Egypt until now. This name Jehovah denotes both his being in himself, and his giving of being, or performance of his word and promise: thus indeed he was not known, or manifested to the patriarchs: they only were sustained by faith in God's Almighty power, without receiving the thing promised: it is said of Abraham, That while he was yet alive, *God gave him no inheritance in Canaan, no, not so much as to set his foot on, yet he promised, that he would give it to him for a possession, and to his seed after him.* Acts vii. 5. And now when his seed came to receive the promise, and to have full knowledge and experience of his power and goodness, then they knew the efficacy of his name Jehovah: So, upon performance of further promises, he saith, they shall know him to be Jehovah, *And thou shalt know that I am the Lord,* Isa. xlix. 2, 3. *Therefore my people shall know my name, they shall know in that day, that I am he that doth speak, Behold it is I,* Isa. lii. 6.

2. *I am Jehovah Elohim,* this denotes the plurality of persons; God, in delivering of the law, doth not only shew his being, but the manner of his being; that is, the three manner of subsistings in that one simple and eternal Being: or the trinity of persons in that unity of essence. The word signifies *strong, potent, mighty;* or if we express it plurally, it signifies *the Almighties;* or *almighty Powers;* hence the scriptures apply the general name, God, to the persons severally; the Father is God, Heb. i. 1, 2. The Son is God, Acts xx. 28. And the holy Ghost is God, Acts v. 3, 4. Now God is said to be Author of these laws delivered in a covenant-way by Moses, that so the

greater

greater authority may be procured to them: and hence all law-givers have endeavoured to perſuade the people, that they had their laws from God.

3. *I am the Lord thy God;* herein is the propriety, and indeed here is the mercy, that God ſpeaks thus to every faithful ſoul, *I am thy God.* By this appropriation God gives us a right in him, yea, a poſſeſſion of him. 1. A right in him, as the woman may ſay of him to whom ſhe is married, This man is my huſband, ſo may every faithful ſoul ſay of the Lord, He is my God. 2. A poſſeſſion of him; God doth not only ſhew himſelf unto us, but he doth communicate himſelf unto us in his holineſs, mercy, truth, grace and goodneſs; hence it is ſaid, *We have fellowſhip with the Father and with his Son Jeſus Chriſt,* 1 John i. 3. And Chriſt is ſaid to *come, and ſup with us,* Rev. iii. 20. And to *kiſs us with the kiſſes of his mouth,* Cant. i. 1, 2. And to be *near to us, in all that we call upon him,* Deut. iv. 7. Surely this is the higheſt happineſs of the ſaints, that God is their God; when they can ſay this, they have enough; if we could ſay, This houſe is mine, this town, this city, this kingdom, this world is mine, what is all this? O but when a Chriſtian comes at length and ſays, This God that made all the world is mine, this is enough; indeed this is the greateſt promiſe that ever was made, or ever can be made to any creature, angels, or men; (if we obſerve it) God gives himſelf to be wholly ours; conſider God eſſentially, or perſonally; conſider Jehovah Elohim, all ours; God in his eſſence and glorious attributes communicates himſelf to us for good; and God perſonally conſidered, as Father, Son and holy Ghoſt, they all enter into covenant with us.

1. The Father enters into a covenant with us; he promiſeth to be a Father to us, hence, ſaith the Lord, *Iſrael is my Son, my firſt-born,* Exod. iv. 23. And again, *Is Ephraim my dear Son? Is he a pleaſant child?* Jer. xxxi. 20. The Lord ſpeaketh, as though he were fond of his children; as delighting in them, for ſo it is ſaid, *The Lord taketh pleaſure in them that fear him,* Pſal. xiv. 11. Or as pitying of them, for ſo it is ſaid likewiſe, *Like as a father pitieth his children, ſo the Lord pitieth them that fear him,* Pſal. ciii. 13.

2. The Son is in covenant with us, and ſpeaks to us in this language, *Thou art mine,* Iſa. xliii. 1. How comes that about? Why, I have redeemed thee, I have called thee by thy name; and therefore *thou art mine;* this is Chriſt's covenant with us; he brings us back to his Father, from whoſe preſence we were baniſhed, and ſets us before his face for ever; he undertakes for us to take up all controverſies, which may fall out between God and us: he promiſeth to reſtore us to the adoption of ſons: and not only to the title, but to the inheritance of ſons, that *we might be where he is,* John xvii. 24.

3. The holy Ghoſt makes a covenant with us. *By one offering he hath perfected for ever them that are ſanctified; whereof the holy Ghoſt alſo is a witneſs and a worker.——This is the covenant, that I will make with them; I will put my law into their hearts, and in their minds will I write them.* Heb. x. 14, 15, 16. I know the Father is implied in this, yet here is the proper work of the holy Ghoſt: what the Father hath purpoſed for us from all eternity, and the Son hath purchaſed for us in his time, that the holy Ghoſt effects in us and for us in our time, he applies the blood of Chriſt for remiſſion of ſins; he writes the law in our hearts; he comforts us in our ſadneſs: he ſupports us in our faintings, and guides us in our wanderings. Now, he that effects theſe things for us, and in our behalf, he is therefore ſaid to make a covenant with us. Thus Elohim, God perſonally conſidered, Father, Son, and holy Ghoſt are in covenant with us.

4. This is the great promiſe; what can be greater? When God ſaid to Abraham, *I will be thy God,* what could he give more? So when God tells us, *I am the Lord thy God,* what could he ſay more? *God having no greater to ſwear by* (ſaith the apoſtle) *he ſware by himſelf,* Heb. vi. 13. So God being minded to do great things for his people, and having no greater thing to give, he gives himſelf. O the goodneſs of God in Chriſt! *I am the Lord thy God.*

5. Let us ſee the fruit of this in reference to Iſrael, *which brought thee out of the land of Egypt, out of the houſe of bondage.* This was God's promiſe long before to Abraham, *Know of a ſurety, that thy ſeed ſhall be a ſtranger in a land that is not theirs, and ſhall ſerve them, and they ſhall afflict them four hundred years; and alſo that nation whom they ſhall ſerve will I judge, and afterwards ſhall they come out with great ſubſtance,* Gen. xv. 13, 14. See here Iſrael muſt be ſtrangers in Egypt, and ſerve the Egyptians four hundred years, but then he will bring them

them out of the land of Egypt, and out of their servile bondage. Why this argues that *God is Jehovah*; now he has performed what he had foretold, and this argues, That God in Christ is our Redeemer. For what was this redemption from Egypt, but a type of our freedom from sin, death, and hell? Here is the work of redemption joined with that great name Jehovah Elohim, to signify that such a redemption is a clear testimony of a true and mighty God. Whether this were laid down only as a peculiar argument to the Jews to keep the commandments, or it belongs also to us being graffed in and become of the same stock with them, I shall not dispute: this is without any controversy, that their bondage was typical, and ours spiritual; you see the good things promised in this covenant.

6. What is the condition of this covenant on our part, as we may gather it hence? The condition of this covenant, is faith in Jesus, which is implied in the promise, *I will be thy God*, or, *I am the Lord thy God*; and commanded in the precept built upon it, *Thou shalt have me to be thy God*, or, *Thou shalt have no other gods before me*. But where is faith in Jesus Christ mentioned either in promise or precept? I answer, If it be not expressed, it is very plainly intended, or meant; God is not the God of Israel, but in and through the Mediator; neither can Israel take God to be their God, but by faith in the Messiah. In the prophets we read frequently these exhortations, *Trust in the Lord*; *Commit thyself unto the Lord*; *lean upon the Lord, and rowl thy burden upon the Lord*; but what the prophets exhort unto, that is commanded in this expressure of the covenant, and who can trust in the Lord, or commit himself to the Lord, or lain upon the Lord, or rowl his burden on the Lord, if he be a sinner, unless it be in and through a Mediator? Israel must walk before God in all well-pleasing; and the apostle tells us, that *without faith it is impossible to please God*, Heb. xi. 6. But to go no further, what is the meaning of the first commandment in the affirmative part, but to *have one God in Christ to be our God by faith*? It is true, There is no mention made of Christ, or faith; but that is nothing, there is no mention of love, and yet our Saviour discovers and commands it there; when the lawyer tempted Christ, *Master, which is the great commandment in the law?* You know Christ's answer, *Thou shalt love the Lord thy God with all thy heart, with all thy soul, and with all thy mind. This is the first, and great commandment*, Matth. xxii. 36, 37, 38. Now, as our Saviour discovers love there, so, in like manner, is faith and Christ, they are the necessary consequents. But you may object, What say we to obedience? Is not that rather the condition of this covenant, thus shining in the law?

Indeed the law and obedience are co-relatives. But in this case we are not to look to the law, as merely mandatory; we gave you the sense of the word, and how it is used as a covenant of grace: remember only this; the law is considered either more strictly, as it is an abstract rule of righteousness, holding forth life upon no other terms but perfect obedience; or more largely, as that whole doctrine delivered on mount Sinai, with the preface and promises adjoined: in the former sense it is a covenant of works; but in the latter sense it is a covenant of grace.—And yet I dare not say, That as the law is a covenant of grace, it doth exclude obedience. In some sort obedience as well as faith may be said to be a condition of the covenant of grace. I shall give you my thoughts in this distinction; obedience to all God's commandments, is either considerable as a cause of life, or as a qualification of the subject; in the former sense it cannot be a condition of the covenant of grace, but in the latter it may: if by condition we understand whatsoever is required on our part, as precedent, concomitant or subsequent to the covenant of grace, repentance, faith and obedience are all conditions; but if by condition we understand whatsoever is required on our part, as the cause of the good promised, though only instrumental; why then, faith or belief in the promises of the covenant is the only condition: faith and obedience are opposed in the matter of justification and salvation in the covenant, not that they cannot stand together in one subject, for they are inseparably united; but because they cannot concur and meet together in one court, as the cause of justification or salvation. Now, when we speak of the condition of the covenant of grace, we intend such a condition as is among the number of true causes; indeed in the covenant of works, obedience is required as the cause of life; but in the covenant of grace, though obedience must accompany faith, yet not obedience, but only faith is the cause of life contained in the covenant.

7. Who

7. Who was the Mediator of this covenant? To this we distinguish of a double Mediator, *viz.* Typical and spiritual; Moses was a typical, but Christ was the spiritual Mediator; and herein was Moses privileged above all before him; he was the mediator of the old Testament, Christ reserving himself to be the *Mediator of a better covenant*, Heb. viii. 6. *i. e.* of the New Testament. Moses received the law from God, and delivered it to the people, and so he stood as a mediator between God and the people: never was mortal man so near to God as Moses was; Abraham indeed was called God's friend; but Moses was God's favourite: and never was mortal man, either in knowledge, love or authority, so near unto the people as Moses was, which makes the Jews (O wonder!) to idolize him to this very day. Moses was called in as a Mediator on both parts, 1. On God's part, when he called him up to receive the law, and all those messages which God sent him to the people. 2. On the people's part, when they desired him to receive the law, for they were afraid by reason of the fire, and durst not go up unto the mount: mark how he stiles himself as a Mediator, *At that time* (saith he) *I stood between the Lord and you, to shew you the word of the Lord*, Deut. v. 5. He was God's mouth to them, and he was their mouth to God; and he was a prevailing Mediator on both parts; he prevailed with God for the suspending of his justice, that it should not break out upon the people, and he prevailed with the people to bind them in covenant unto God, and to make profession of that obedience, which the Lord required and called for; yet for all this, I call him not a mediator of redemption, but relation. A great deal of difference there is betwixt Moses and Christ: as 1. Moses only received the law, and delivered it unto the people, but Christ our true Moses fulfilled it. 2. Moses broke the tables, to shew how we in our nature had broken the law, but Christ our true Moses repairs it again. 3. Moses had the law only writ in tables of stone, but Christ writes in the tables of our hearts. 4. Moses was mere man, but Christ is God as well as man: Moses was only a servant in God's house, but Christ is a son; yea, Christ is Lord of his own house the church: Moses' mediation was of this use, to shew what was the true manner of worshipping God; but he did not inspire force and power to follow it; he could not reconcile men to God as of himself; and therefore it appeared, that there was need of another reconciler, *viz.* The Lord Jesus Christ.

8. What of Christ, and of his death do we find in this manifestation of the covenant? I answer, 1. In delivering the law we find something of Christ; there is a question, Whether the Lord himself immediately in his own person delivered the law? And some conclude affirmatively from the preface, *God spake these words, and said*, Deut. v. 22. And from that passage of Moses, *These words the Lord spake unto all your assembly in the mount out of the midst of the fire — And he wrote them on two tables of stone, and delivered them unto me.* But others are for the negative, and say, This proves that they were not pronounced or delivered immediately by God; for we find in scripture, that when the angels were the immediate persons, yet the Lord himself is reported to have spoken unto me, Gen. xviii. 2, 13. Ex. iii. 2, 6, 7. And Augustin *de Trin. L. 2 C.* 13. is resolute, the Almighty God himself in the time of the Old Testament, did not speak to the Jews with his own immediate voice, but only by Christ, or by his angels, or by his prophets; and for this ministerial voice of his angels some produce these texts, *Who have received the law by the ordinance of angels, and have not kept it*, Acts vii. 53. *And wherefore then serveth the law? It was added because of transgressions, till the seed should come, to whom the promise was made, and it was ordained by angels in the hand of a Mediator*, Gal. iii. 19. *And if the word spoken by angels was stedfast*, &c. Heb. ii. 2. For my part it hath puzzled me at times, whether of these opinions to take; but others say, (and I am now apt to join with them as with any of the former) That Jesus Christ the second person of the trinity, to be incarnate, who is called *the angel of the covenant*, Mal. iii. 1. And *the angel of his presence*, Isa. lxiii. 9. was he that uttered and delivered the law unto Moses; and to this purpose are produced these texts, *This Moses is he that was in the congregation with the angel, which spake to him in the mount Sinai*, Acts vii. 38. Now this angel was Christ, as it is cleared in the following verse 39. *Whom* (or which angel) *our Fathers would not obey; but thrust him from them, and in their hearts turned back again to Egypt.*

gypt. They would not obey the angel, but thrust him from them, *i. e.* they tempted the angel, whom they should have obeyed; and who was that but Jesus Christ? as it is cleared more fully and expresly by the apostle, 1 Cor. x. 9. *Neither let us tempt Christ, as some of them also tempted, and were destroyed of serpents.* Some of the learned are of opinion, That Christ the Son of God did in the shape of a man deliver the law: but I leave that.

2. In the law itself, as it is a covenant of grace, we find something of Christ, in the preface he proclaims himself to be *our God*; and in the first commandment we are bound to take this God to be *our God*; and in the second he gives us a double reason or motive to obey: *For I the Lord thy God am a jealous God, I shew mercy unto thousands of them that love me and keep my commandments.* And in the fifth commandment he gives a promise of long life in Canaan, which is either to be looked at as a type of heaven, or literally for a prosperous condition here on earth; but howsoever it is by virtue of the covenant, and as a testimony of God's love. Now, all these promises are made in Christ: God is not our God but in and through Jesus Christ; God will not shew mercy unto thousands, nor unto one of all the thousands of his saints, but as they are in Jesus Christ; God will not give us long life here, or eternal life hereafter, but in, for, and through the Lord Jesus Christ: what if Moses writ not down the word of Christ: yet certainly Moses wrote of Christ: his words imply Christ, as Christ himself told the Jews, *Had ye believed Moses, ye would have believed me, for Moses wrote of me,* John v. 46. And as Philip told Nathaniel, *We have found him of whom Moses in the law, and the prophets did write, Jesus of Nazareth,* John i. 45. Surely Christ was, if not the only subject, yet the only scope of all the writings of Moses; and therefore in the law itself you see we find something of Christ.

3. In the exposition of the law, as Moses gives it here and there, we find something of Christ. Yea, if we observe it, Moses brought something more to the expression of Christ, and the covenant of grace, than ever was before: in the first promise it was revealed, That Christ should be the feed of the woman; in the second manifestation of the promise it was revealed, That Christ should

be the feed of Abraham; but in Moses' writings, and in Moses' time we learn more expresly, That Christ should be both God and man; or that God was to be incarnate, and to have his conversation amongst men: the promise runs thus, 'And I will 'dwell among the children of Israel, and will be 'their God; and they shall know that I am the 'Lord their God, that brought them forth out of 'the land of Egypt, that I may dwell amongst 'them; I am the Lord their God,' Exod. xxix. 45, 46. The same promise is renewed after, 'And I will set my tabernacle among you and my 'soul shall not abhor you, and I will walk among 'you and will be your God, and ye shall be my 'people,' Lev. xxvi. 11, 12. This promise was punctually fulfilled when Christ was incarnate, for then was *the word made flesh, and dwelt amongst us,* John i. 14. Or if it be referred to the habitation of God by his Spirit amongst the spiritual feed of Abraham, then it implies the incarnation of Christ, because that was to go before the plentiful habitation of Christ's Spirit in the saints. Again, Moses writing of Christ, *The Lord thy God* (faith he) *will raise up unto thee a prophet from the midst of thee, of thy brethren, like unto me, unto him shall ye hearken,* Deut. xviii. 15. Was not this a plain expression? Peter, in his sermon to the Jews, preacheth Jesus Christ, and tells the Jews, that this *Jesus Christ was preached unto them before:* when before? Even in Moses's time; and for proof he cites this very text, *For Moses truly said unto the fathers, A prophet shall the Lord your God raise up unto you, of your brethren, like unto me. Him shall ye hear in all things, whatsoever he shall say unto you,* Acts iii. 20, 22.

4. In the confirmation of the law, we find something of Christ. It was confirmed by seals and sacrifices, &c. What were all these but a type of Christ? In the former expression of the covenant we found the seal of circumcision, but now it pleased God to add unto the former another seal for confirmation of their faith, *sc.* the passover; and was not this a type of Christ, the immaculate Lamb of God, who taketh away the sins of the world? Again, in his manifestation Moses brought in the priesthood, as a settled ordinance to offer sacrifices for the people: and was not this a type of Christ, our true and unchangeable high priest? I have sometimes seen the articles of a believing Jew's creed,

L

creed, collected out of Moses's law; as thus, *I believe that the Messiah should die to make satisfaction for sin:* this they saw in their continued bloody sacrifices; and their deliverance from Egypt by the death of a lamb, taught them no less. 2. *I believe, That he shall not die for his own sins, but for the sins of others;* this they might easily observe in every sacrifice, when (according to their law) they saw the most harmless birds and beasts were offered. 3. *I believe to be saved by laying hold upon his merits.* This they might gather by laying their right hand on the head of every beast that they brought to be offered up, and by laying hold on the horns of the altar, being a sanctuary, or refuge from pursuing vengeance. Thus we might go on: no question the death and resurrection of Christ, the priesthood and kingdom of Christ were prefigured and typed by the sacrifices, and brazen serpent; and the priesthood of Aaron, and the kingdom of Israel: and I cannot but think, That the godly spiritual Jews understood this very well; and that these did not rest in sacrifices or sacraments, but that by faith they did really enjoy Christ in every of them.

5. In the intention of God's giving the law we find something of Christ. The very end of God in holding forth the law, was, That upon the sense of our impossibility to keep it, and of our danger to break it, we should desire earnestly, and seek out diligently for Jesus Christ. To this purpose saith the apostle, *Christ is the end of the law for righteousness to every one that believeth.* Christ is the end of the law, *i. e.* Christ is the end of intention; God, by giving so holy a law, and by requiring such perfect obedience, he would thereby humble and debase the Israelites, so that they should more earnestly fly to Christ. In this sense, *The law is our schoolmaster to bring us unto Christ, that we might be justified by faith:* a schoolmaster (you know) doth not only whip or correct; but also to teach and direct: so the law doth not only threaten and curse, if the work be not done, but it shews where power and help is to be had, *viz.* From the Lord Jesus Christ; if this be so, how much to blame are they that, under pretence of free grace and Christ, cry down the law? Rather let us cry it up, and this is the way to set up free grace in Christ. Surely he that discovers his defects by the perfect rule of the law, and whose soul is imbittered and humbled because of these defects, he must needs prize Christ, desire Christ, advance Christ in his thoughts, above all the men in the world.

And thus far of the covenant of promise, as it was manifested from Moses to David.

SECT. V.

Of the covenant of promise, as manifested to David.

THE next breaking forth of this gracious covenant was to David; and in this manifestation appears yet more of Christ; the expression of it is chiefly in these words, *Although my house be not so with God, yet he hath made with me an everlasting covenant, ordered in all things and sure,* 2 Sam. xxiii. 5.

For the right understanding of this, we shall examine these particulars.

1. Who is the author of this covenant?
2. To whom is the covenant made?
3. What is this, that the covenant is said *to be made*?
4. How is the covenant ordered?
5. Wherein is the covenant sure?
6. Whether is Christ more clearly manifested in this breaking forth of the covenant, than in any of the former?

1. Who is the author of this covenant? David says, *He hath made it: he, i. e.* God the rock of Israel, the everlasting rock; *The rock of their salvation,* Psal. xix. 5. *The rock of their strength,* Psal. lxii. 7. *The rock of their heart,* Psal. lxxiii. 26. *The rock of their refuge,* Ps. xciv. 22. *Their rock and their Redeemer,* Psalm xix. 14. The Psalmist is frequent and ordinary in this stile, to shew that God is the mighty, stable and immutable foundation and defence of all the faithful who fly unto him and will trust in him: he is such a rock as will not shrink, or fail his creatures; man is unstable, but he is God, and not man, who is the author of this covenant.

2. To whom is the covenant made? Why, said David, *He hath made with me an everlasting covenant, i. e.* Either with Christ the antitype, or else with David himself, the type of Christ. To the former sense we have spoken elsewhere; the latter I suppose more genuine; the covenant indeed was first made with Christ, and then with David as a mem-

a member of Jesus Christ. Some are wholly for a covenant betwixt God and Christ; and they deny any such thing as a covenant betwixt God and man; but are not the testimonies express? *Take heed to yourselves, lest you forget the covenant which the Lord hath made with you*, Deut. iv. 23. *And I will make a new covenant with the house of Israel, and with the house of Judah*, Jer. xxxi. 31. And by name do we not see God covenanting with Abraham, and with Isaac, and with Jacob, Gen. xvii. 7. Gen. xxvi. 2. Gen. xxxv. 12. Lev. xxvi. 42. And here do we not see God covenanting with David? *I have made a covenant with my chosen, I have sworn unto David; and once have I sworn by my holiness, that I will not lie unto David;* And the *Lord hath sworn in truth unto David, he will not turn from it*, Psalm lxxxix. 31, 35. and cxxxii. 11. Oh take heed of such doctrines as tend unto liberty and licentiousness! the covenant God makes with us binds us faster to God; and if there be no covenant betwixt God and us, it opens a gap to the looseness of our spirits; for how should we be charged with unfaithfulness unto God, if we have not at all entered into a covenant with God?

3. What is this that the covenant is said *to be made?* This holds forth to us the freeness of God's entering into covenant with us: 'I will make 'my covenant between me and thee, (saith God); 'for I will give my covenant, I will dispose my co-'venant between me and thee,' Gen. xvii. 2. So it is in the original. And elsewhere it is plain, *Behold, I give unto him my covenant of peace*, Numb. xxv. 12. When God makes a covenant, then he gives the covenant of his grace unto all that he takes into covenant with him: *The Lord set his love upon you* (saith Moses to Israel) *to take you into covenant with him, not because ye were more in number than other people, but because he loved you, and chose your fathers*, Deut. vii. 7, 8. As noting out the freeness of his love towards them; he loved them; why? He loved them, because he loved. This freeness of his grace in giving a covenant, may appear in these particulars. As,

1. In that God is the first that seeks after us, to draw us into covenant with him; we seek not him, but he seeks us; we choose not him, but he chooseth us; *He loved us first*, 1 John iv. 19. *I am found of them that sought me not* ——— *I said,*

Behold me, behold me, unto a nation that was not called by my name, Isa lxv. 1.

2. In that there is nothing to us, to draw God into a covenant with us. Many a man seeks first after the unmarried virgin; but then there is beauty, or there is dowry, or there is something or other, which draws on the man; but there is no such thing in us; this made David say, when he heard of God's covenant with him and his, *Who am I, O Lord God? And what is my father's house that thou hast brought me hitherto?* ——— *And is this the manner of man, O Lord God?* 2 Sam. vii. 18, 19. q. d. O Lord God, thou dealest familiarly with me, as a man dealeth with man; or, as it is elsewhere, *Thou hast regarded me according to the estate of a man of high degree*, 1 Chron. xvii. 17. It would make any soul cry out, that deeply weighs the freeness of this covenant, *Lord, what is man that thou art mindful of him, or the son of man that thou visitest him?* Psal. viii. 4.

3. In that there is enough in us to keep off the Lord from ever owning us. We are as contrary to God as darkness to light, or as evil is to good; *The carnal mind is enmity against God*, (saith the apostle) *it is not subject to the law of God, neither indeed can be*, Rom. viii. 7. We are a crooked generation, that cannot abide the straight ways of the Lord; our whole nature is sinful and corrupt before him; and for the most part, when we are most averse and backward, and have least thought of ever seeking after him, then it is that he seeks us to take us unto himself. Thus the Lord called Saul when he was persecuting, and raging, and breathing out slaughter against the Lord, and against his saints; and thus the Lord called those Jews, that mocked the apostles when they spake divers languages, *these men are full of new wine*, Acts ii. 13. Ay, but the next word that they speak, is, *Men and brethren, what shall we do?* Ver. 37. O the free and unexpected grace of our God!

4. In that we are by nature no better than others, that are without God, *and without covenant*, Eph. ii. 12. What makes the difference betwixt us and them, but this free grace of God? Is there any reason in us, why one is taken into a covenant, and another is not? Nay, I'll tell you a wonder: so it pleaseth the Lord, That sometime God chooseth the worst, and leaves those that are better . . . . . We read that publicans and harlots were

were taken in, and the righteous generation, which justified themselves, and were justified by others, were passed by: surely God respects none for any thing in them, his design is, That the freeness of his grace might be seen in those whom he takes to himself. Hence the apostle, *God chooseth the foolish things of this world, and the weak things of this world,* base and despised *things,* while in the mean time he passeth by *the wise and mighty,* 1 Cor. i. 27, 28, 29. And things of high esteem, that all men might see it is the grace of God, and not any thing in man by which we are taken into covenant with him.

5. How is the covenant said to be ordered? The word *ordered* will help us in the answer. It sets out to us a marshalling, and fit laying of things together, in opposition to disorder and confusion; the *Septuagint* renders it [*etoimasas*], which signifies marshalled, disposed, prepared, set forth, as an army in comely order; the same word is in Judg. xx. 22. *And the men of Israel encouraged themselves, and set their battle again in array.* As we see in an army, every one is set in rank and file, so is every thing in this covenant ranked, disposed, ordered, that it stands at best advantage to receive and repel the enemy. A poor Christian that hath a troubled spirit, he sets himself against free grace, and this everlasting covenant; he raiseth thousands of objections against it; but now the covenant is *ordered,* it stands like a marshalled army to receive him, and repel him. Come, let us see a little how it is *ordered in all things.* I shall instance only in these particulars. As,

1. It is well ordered in respect of the root out of which it grew: this (say divines) was the infinite sovereignty, and wisdom, and mercy of God. 1. It was founded in God's sovereignty; he had a right to do what he would with his fallen creatures: he might damn, or save whom he pleased; *Hath not the potter power over the clay, of the same lump, to make one vessel unto honour, and another unto dishonour?* Rom. ix. 21. 2. It was founded in wisdom; the covenant of grace was a result of council; it was no rash act, but a deliberate act with infinite wisdom; God being the sovereign of all his creatures, and seeing mankind in a perishing condition, he determined within himself deliberately to make such a covenant of peace, first with Christ, and then with all the elect in Christ. 3. It was founded in mercy, *i. e.* in the goodness of God flowing out freely to one in misery: for mercy, we say, is made up of these two acts; 1. There must be an object of misery. 2. There must be a free efflux of goodness on that object. Now, the covenant of grace is founded on both these: as, 1. There was an object of misery, lost man, wretched man, undone by sin. And 2. There was an efflux of God's goodness, his very bowels moved within him, and they could not hold, *I have loved thee with an everlasting love* (faith God) *therefore with loving kindness have I drawn thee,* Jer. xxxi. 3. Surely this was well-ordered; a perplexed soul may have its spirit up in arms against the covenant of grace: O cries the soul in its sad condition, ' I am miserable! I shall not live, but die; my sins will damn me! I am lost for ever!' Why, but see how the covenant is ordered in respect of the root or rise; it stands like a well marshalled army to receive, and to repel those doubts: as 1. God acted in a way of sovereignty, and cannot God save thee if he will? 2. God acted in a way of wisdom, and though thou seest no way but one with thee, death and damnation; yet cannot infinite wisdom contrive another way? 3. God acted in a way of mercy, and *O thou afflicted, tossed with tempests, and not comforted,* Isa. liv. 11. is not infinite mercy above all thy misery? Why, see, see, poor soul, how the covenant repels all thy oppositions in respect of its rise.

2. It is well ordered in respect of the persons interested in it from all eternity; and they are God the Father, and Jesus Christ his Son; as for the saints elect, they were not then; and therefore the covenant could not be immediately struck with them. Now there was great need of this order; for should the covenant have been made betwixt God the Father and the elect from all eternity, and that immediately, a troubled soul would have opposed it thus; 1. If it was from all eternity, how then shall I be capable of it? Alas! my being was not so long since. 2. If it were made with me immediately, then I had some part to perform of mine own power and strength; but, alas! I have failed, and can do nothing. O but now the covenant is a well-ordered covenant in these respects: for 1. Christ had a being from all eternity; and thou, as an elect vessel, hadst thy being in him, as he was thy head. 2. Christ is able to per-

perform the covenant, and being contractor, it lies upon his score to satisfy his Father; he that first made the bargain must look to fulfill it; and for thy part, if thou dost any thing it must be through him; *Without me ye can do nothing*, John xv. 5. Why, see now, see how the covenant repels all thy oppositions, in respect of the persons interested in it from all eternity; God hath his place, and Christ his place, and faith his place, and the sinner his place.

3. It is well-ordered in respect of the method of the articles, in their several workings. *First*, God begins, then we come on; *First*, God on his part gives grace and glory, and then, we, on our parts, act faith and obedience: God hath ever the first work; As *First*, *I will be your God*, and then, *you shall be my people*; First, *I will take away the stony heart, and give an heart of flesh*, and then *you shall lothe yourselves for your iniquities, and for your abominations*; First, *I will sprinkle water upon you*, and then, *ye shall be clean from all your filthiness*; First, *I will put my spirit into you, and cause you to walk in my statutes*, and then *ye shall keep my judgments and do them*; First, *I will pour out my Spirit of grace and supplication upon you, and then ye shall mourn as a man mourneth for his only Son*, Jer. xxxi. 33. Ezek. xxxvi. 25, 26, 27, 31. Zech. xii. 10. *First*, I will do all, and then you shall do something: A perplexed troubled spirit is apt to cry out. 'O! alas! I can do 'nothing; I can as well dissolve a rock, as make 'my heart of stone a heart of flesh!' mark now how the covenant stands well-ordered, like an army; I will do all, saith God, and then, thou shalt do something; I will strengthen and quicken you, and then, you shall serve me, saith the Lord.

4. It is well ordered, in respect of the end and aim, to which all the parts of the covenant are referred; the end of the covenant is the *praise of the glory of his grace*, Eph. i 6. The parts of the covenant are the promise, and stipulation. The promise is either principal or immediate, and that is God, and Christ: or secondary and consequential, and that is pardon, justification, reconciliation, sanctification, glorification: the stipulation on our parts is faith and obedience, we must believe in him that justifies the ungodly, and walk before him in all well-pleasing. Observe now the main design and aim of the covenant, and see but how all the streams run towards that ocean; God gives himself *to the praise of the glory of his grace*, God gives Christ *to the praise of the glory of his grace:* God gives pardon, justification, sanctification, salvation, *to the praise of the glory of his grace*, and we believe, we obey *to the praise of the glory of his grace*, and good reason, for all is of grace, and therefore all must tend *to the praise of the glory of his grace:* it is of grace that God hath given himself, Christ, pardon, justification, reconciliation, sanctification, salvation to any soul; it is of grace that we believe; *By grace ye are saved through faith, not of yourselves, it is the gift of God*, Eph. ii. 8. O the sweet and comely order of this covenant! all is of grace, and all tends *to the praise of the glory of his grace*, and therefore it is called *a covenant of grace*; many a sweet soul is forced to cry, I cannot believe, I may as well reach heaven with a finger, as lay hold on Christ by the hand of faith; but mark how the covenant stands like a well-marshalled army to repel this doubt; if thou canst not believe, God will enable thee to believe, *to you it is given to believe*, Phil. i. 29. O the covenant of grace is a gracious covenant: God will not only promise good things, but he helps us by his Spirit to perform the condition, he works our hearts to believe in God, and to believe in Christ; all is of grace, that all may tend *to the praise of the glory of his grace*.

5. Wherein is the covenant sure? I answer, It is sure in the performance and accomplishment of it. Hence the promises of the covenant are called *the sure mercies of David*, Isa. lv. 3. Not because they are sure unto David alone, but because they are sure, and shall be sure unto all the seed of David that are in covenant with God as David was; the promises of God's covenant are not *Yea and nay*, various and uncertain, but they are *Yea and amen*, 2 Cor. i. 20. Sure to be fulfilled. Hence the stability of God's covenant is compared to the firmness and unmovableness of the mighty mountains; nay, *mountains may depart, and the hills be removed by a miracle*, but *my kindness shall not depart from thee, neither shall the covenant of my peace be removed, saith the Lord, that hath mercy on thee*. Isa. liv. 10. Sooner shall the rocks be removed, the fire cease to burn, the sun be turned into darkness, and the very heavens be confounded with the earth, than the promise of God shall fail. *The testimony of the Lord is sure*, saith David,

David, Psal. xix. 7. Christ made it, and writ it with his own blood; to this very end was Christ appointed, and it hath been all his work to ensure heaven to his saints. Some question whether it be in God's present power to blot a name out of the book of life. We say, No; his deed was at first free, but now it is necessary, not absolutely, but *ex hypothesi*, upon supposition of his eternal covenant. Hence it is that the apostle says, *If we confess our sins, he is faithful and just to forgive us our sins,* 1 John i. 9. It is justice with God to pardon the elect's sins as the case now stands: indeed mercy was all that saved us primarily, but now truth saves us, and stands engaged with mercy for our heaven; and therefore David prays, *Send forth mercy and truth, and save me,* Psalm lvii. 3. We find it often in the Psalms, as a prayer of David, *Deliver me in thy righteousness,* and, *Judge me according to thy righteousness,* and, *Quicken me in thy righteousness,* and, *In thy faithfulness answer me,* and, *In thy righteousness,* Psal. xxxi. 1. and xxxv. 24. and cxix. 40. and cxliii. 1. Now, if it had not been for the covenant of grace, surely David durst not have said such a word. The covenant is sure in every respect, *I will make an everlasting covenant with you* (saith God) *even the sure mercies of David,* Isa. lv. 3.

6. Whether is Christ more clearly manifested in this breaking forth of the covenant than in any of the former? The affirmative will appear in that we find in this manifestation these particulars.——

1. That he was God and man in one person; David's Son, and yet David's Lord, *The Lord said unto my Lord, Sit thou on my right hand, until I make thine enemies thy foot-stool,* Psal. cx. 1.

2. That he suffered for us: and in his sufferings, how many particulars are discovered? As, *First,* His cry, *My God, my God, why hast thou forsaken me?* Psal. xxii. 1. *Secondly,* The Jews taunts, *He trusted in the Lord, that he would deliver him; let him deliver him if he delight in him,* Matth. xxvii. 46. *Thirdly,* The very manner of his death, *They pierced my hands and my feet, I may tell all my bones, they look and stare upon me: they part my garments among them, and cast lots upon my vesture,* Psal. xxii. 8.

3. That he rose again for us: *Thou wilt not leave my soul in hell, neither wilt thou suffer thine holy One to see corruption,* Matth. xxvii. 45.

4. That he ascended up into heaven; *Thou hast ascended on high, thou hast led captivity captive, thou hast received gifts for men,* Psal. xvi. 10. and lxviii. 18. Eph. iv. 8. Acts ii. 31.

5. That he must be king over us, both to rule and govern his elect, and to bridle and subdue his enemies; 'I have set my king upon my holy hill of Zion; I will declare the decree, the Lord hath said unto me, Thou art my Son, this day have I begotten thee, Psal. ii. 6, 7. Acts xiii. 33. The Lord said unto my Lord, Sit thou at my right hand, until I make thine enemies thy footstool. The Lord shall send the rod of thy strength out of Zion. Rule thou in the midst of thine enemies,' Psal. cx. 1, 2.

6. That he must be a priest, as well as king; and sacrifice, as well as priest; 'The Lord hath sworn and will not repent, thou art a priest for ever, after the order of Melchizedec, Psal. cx. 4. Thou lovest righteousness, and hatest wickedness, therefore God, thy God hath anointed thee with the oyl of gladness above thy fellows,' Heb. v. 6. Psal. xlv. 7. *i. e.* Above all Christians, who are thy fellows, consorts, and partners in the anointing; 'Sacrifice and burnt-offering thou wouldst not have, but mine ear hast thou bored; burnt-offering, and sin-offering hast thou not required. Then said I, Lo I come, in the volume of the book it is written of me, that I should do thy will, O God,' Psal. xl. 6, 7. Heb. x. 5, 6, 7. Mine ears hast thou bored, or digged open; the septuagint, to make the sense plainer, say, *But a body hast thou fitted to me, or, prepared for me,* meaning that his body was ordained and fitted to be a sacrifice for the sins of the world, when other legal sacrifices were refused as unprofitable. O see how clearly Christ is revealed in this expressure of the covenant! it was never thus before.

And thus far of the covenant of promise, as it was manifested from David till the captivity.

SECT. VI.

Of the covenant of promise as manifested to Israel about the time of the captivity.

THE great breaking forth of this gracious covenant was to Israel about the time of their captivity. By reason of that captivity of Babylon, Israel was almost clean destroyed; and therefore, then

then it was high time, that the Lord should appear like a sun after a stormy rain, and give them some clearer light of Christ, and of this covenant of grace than ever yet. He doth so, and it appears especially in these words, 'Behold, the days come, saith the Lord, that I will make a new covenant with the house of Israel, and with the house of Judah: not according to the covenant which I made with their fathers, in the day that I took them by the hand to bring them out of the land of Egypt, (which my covenant they break, although I was an husband unto them, saith the Lord:) but this shall be the covenant that I will make with the house of Israel, After those days, saith the Lord, I will put my law in their inward parts, and write it in their hearts, and I will be their God, and they shall be my people. And they shall teach no more every man his neighbour, and every man his brother, saying, Know the Lord: for they shall all know me, from the least of them unto the greatest of them, saith the Lord: for I will forgive their iniquity, and will remember their sin no more.' Jer. xxxi. 31, 32, 33, 34. In this expressure of the covenant we shall examine these particulars.——

1. Why it is called a new covenant?
2. Wherein the expressure of this covenant doth excel the former, which God made with their fathers.
3. How doth God put the law into our inward parts?
4. What is it to have the law written in our hearts?
5. How are we taught of God, so as not to need any other kind of teaching comparatively?
6. What is the universality of this knowledge in, *That all shall know me, saith the Lord?*
7. How is God said to forgive iniquity, and never more to remember sin?

1. Why is it called *a new covenant?* I answer, It is called *new*, either in respect of the late and new blessings which God vouchsafed Israel in bringing back their captivity with joy, and planting them in their own land again; or it is called *new* in respect of the excellency of this covenant; thus the Hebrews were wont to call any thing excellent, *new*, *O sing unto the Lord a new song*, Ps. xcvi. 1. That is, an excellent song; or it is called *new*, in contradiction to the covenant of promise before Christ came; in this latter sense the very same words here are repeated in the epistle to the Hebrews, 'Behold, the days come, saith the Lord, when I will make a new covenant with the house of Israel, and the house of Judah. In that he saith, A new covenant, he hath made the first old; now that which decayeth and waxeth old, is ready to vanish away,' Heb. viii. 8, 13. The *new covenant* is usually understood in the latter sense; it is *new* because diverse from that which God made with their fathers before Christ; it hath a new worship, new adoration, a new form of the church, new witnesses, new tables, new sacraments and ordinances; and these never to be abrogated or disanulled, never to *wax old*, as the apostle speaks: yet in respect of those new blessings which God bestowed upon Israel immediately after the captivity, this very manifestation may be called *new:* and in reference to this, 'Behold, the days come, saith the Lord, that they shall no more say, The Lord liveth which brought up the children of Israel out of the land of Egypt, but the Lord liveth which brought up, and which led the seed of the house of Israel out of the north country, and from all countries whither I had driven them, and they shall dwell in their own land, Jer. xxiii. 7, 8.

2. Wherein doth the expressure of this covenant excel the former, which God made with their fathers? I answer,——

1. It excels in the very tenor, or outward administration of the covenant: for this covenant after it once began, continued without interruption until Christ, whereas the former was broken, or did expire. Hence God calls it ' a new cove-
' nant,——not according to the covenant which I
' made with their fathers in the day that I took
' them by the hand, to bring them out of the
' land of Egypt, (which my covenant they break,
' although I was an husband unto them, faith the
' Lord.)' In this respect it might be called *new*, or at least it might be called *an inchoation of the new*, because it continued till Christ, which no other expressure of the covenant did before, and so it excelled all the former.

2. It excels in the spiritual benefits and graces of the Spirit. We find that under this covenant they were more plentifully bestowed upon the church than formerly: mark the promises, 'I will
' set mine eyes upon them for good, and I will
' bring them again to this land, and I will build
' them, and not pull them down, and I will plant
' them,

' them, and not pluck them up; and I will give
' them an heart to know me, that I am the Lord,
' and they shall be my people, and I will be their
' God, for they shall return unto me with their
' whole heart.——Again, I will shake all nations,
' and the desire of all nations shall come, and I
' will fill this house with glory, saith the Lord of
' hosts. The silver is mine, and the gold is mine,
' saith the Lord of hosts: the glory of this latter
' house shall be greater than the former, saith the
' Lord of hosts, Hag. ii. 7, 8, 9. And I will put
' my law in their inward parts, and write it in their
' hearts; and I will be their God, and they shall
' be my people. And they shall teach no more e-
' very man his neighbour, and every man his bro-
' ther, saying, Know the Lord: for they shall
' know me, from the least of them unto the great-
' est of them, saith the Lord: for I will forgive
' their iniquities, and I will remember their sins
' no more,' Jer. xxxi. 33, 34.

3. It excels in the discovery and revelation of the Mediator, in and through whom the covenant was made. In the former expressions we discovered much: yet in none of them was so plainly revealed the time of his coming, the place of his birth, his name, the passages of his nativity, his humiliation and kingdom, as we find them in this.

1. Concerning the time of his coming, *Seventy weeks are determined upon thy people, and upon thy holy city, to finish the transgression, and to make an end of sins, and to make reconciliation for iniquity, and to bring in everlasting righteousness, and to seal up the vision and prophecy, and to anoint the most holy*, Dan. ix. 24.

2. Concerning the place of his birth; *but thou, Bethlehem Ephratah, tho' thou be little among the thousands of Judah, yet out of thee shall he come forth unto me, that is to be ruler in Israel, whose goings forth have been from of old, from everlasting*, Micah v. 2.

2. Concerning his name; ' Unto us a child is
' born, unto us a son is given, and the government
' shall be upon his shoulders; and his name shall
' be called wonderful, counsellor, the mighty God,
' the everlasting Father, the prince of peace; Isa.
' ix. 6. In his days Judah shall be saved, and Is-
' rael shall dwell safely; and this is his name
' whereby he shall be called, the Lord our righ-
' teousness, Jer. xxiii. 6. Behold, a virgin shall
' conceive, and bear a son, and thou, O virgin,
' shalt call his name Immanuel,' Isa. vii. 14.

4. Concerning the passages of his nativity, that he should be born of a virgin, Isa. vii. 14. That at his birth all the infants round about Bethlehem should be slain, Jer. xxxi. 15. That John the Baptist should be his prodrome, or forerunner, to prepare his way, Mal. iii. 1. That he should flee into Egypt, and be recalled thence again, Hosea xi. 1. I might add many particulars of this kind.

5. Concerning his humiliation, ' Surely he hath
' borne our griefs, and carried our sorrows: yet
' we did esteem him stricken, smitten of God, and
' afflicted. But he was wounded for our transgres-
' sions, he was bruised for our iniquities: the chas-
' tisement of our peace was upon him, and with
' his stripes were we healed.——He was oppress-
' ed, and he was afflicted; yet he opened not his
' mouth.—He was taken from prison, and from
' judgment, and who shall declare his generation?
' He was cut off out of the land of the living; for
' the transgression of my people was he stricken.
' ——It pleased the Lord to bruise him; he hath
' put him to grief.—Therefore I will divide him
' a portion with the great, and he shall divide the
' spoil with the strong, because he hath poured
' out his soul unto death, and he was numbered
' with the transgressors, and he bare the sins of
' many, and made intercession for the transgres-
' sors,' Isa. liii. 4, 5, 7, 8. One would think this were rather an history, than a prophecy of Christ's sufferings; you may, if you'll take the pains, see the circumstances of his sufferings; as, that he was sold for thirty pieces of silver, Zech. xi. 12. And that with those thirty pieces of silver there was bought afterwards a potter's field, Zech. xi. 13. That he must ride into Jerusalem before his passion on an ass, Zech. ix. 9. I might seem tedious if I should proceed.

6. Concerning his kingdom; *Rejoice greatly, O daughter of Zion, shout, O daughter of Jerusalem, behold thy king cometh unto thee: he is just, and having salvation, lowly, and riding on an ass, and upon a colt the foal of an ass*, Zech. ix. 9. Isa. lxii. 11. Matth. xxi. 5. Behold a king, behold thy king, behold thy king cometh, and he comes unto thee. 1. He is a king, and therefore able. 2. He is thy king, and therefore willing. Wonderful love, that he would come; but more wonderful

derful was the manner of his coming; he that before made man a soul after the image of God, then made himself a body after the image of man. And thus we see how this covenant excels the former in every of these respects.

3. How doth God put the law into our inward parts? I answer, God puts the law into our inward parts, by enlivening, or qualifying of a man with the graces of God's Spirit, suitable to his commandment. First, There is the law of God without us, as we see it, or read it in scripture, but when it is put within us, then God hath wrought an inward disposition in our minds, that answers to that law without us. For example, this is the law without, ' Thou shalt love the Lord thy God with ' all thy heart, and with all thy soul, and with all ' thy strength,' Deut. vi. 5. To answer which there is a promise, ' I will circumcise thy heart, ' and the heart of thy seed, to love the Lord thy ' God, with all thy heart, and with all thy soul,' Deut. xxx. 6. Now when this promise is fulfilled, when God hath put the affections and grace of love within our hearts, when the habit of love is within, answerable in all things to the command without, then is the law put in our inward parts. Again, this is the law without, ' Thou shalt fear the Lord, ' and keep his ordinances, and his statutes, and his ' commandments to do them,' Deut. xiii. 5. To answer which there is a promise, ' I will make a ' covenant with you, and I will not turn away from ' you to do you good, but I will put my fear in ' your hearts, that you shall not depart from me,' Jer. xxxiii. 40. Now, when this promise is accomplished, when God hath put the affection and grace of fear within our hearts, when the habit of fear is within, answerable to that command without, then is the law put into our hearts. Surely this is mercy that God saith in his covenant, ' I will put my ' law in their inward parts;' many a time a poor soul cries out, it is troubled with such and such a lust, and he cannot keep this and that commandment, he cannot out-wrestle such and such strong inclinations to evil: O but then go to God, and press him with this, ' Lord, it is a part of thy covenant, ' thou hast said thou wilt circumcise my heart; ' thou hast said thou wilt put thy law into my in- ' ward parts; thou hast said thou wilt dissolve ' these lusts: Lord, I beseech thee do it for thy ' covenant's sake.'—— But here's another question.

How may we know this inward work of grace, this law in our inward parts? The best way to satisfy our doubts in this, is to look within; open we the door, and the closet of our hearts, and see what lies nearest and closest there; that we say is intimate, and within a man, which lies next to his heart: *He that loveth father or mother more than me,* (saith Christ) *is not worthy of me,* Mat. x. 37. We know the love of father and mother is a most natural thing; it comes not by teaching, but 'tis inbred in us as soon as we are born, and yet if we love not Christ more than these, if Christ lie not closer to our hearts than father or mother, we are not worthy of Christ. Our natural life is a most inward and deep thing in a man, it lies very near the heart, *Skin for skin* (saith the devil once truly) *and all that a man hath will he give for his life,* Job ii. 4. But *he that hates not father and mother,——yea and his own life also* (said Christ) *he cannot be my disciple,* Luke xiv. 26. Hence the apostle, to express this intimate, inward life of grace, he saith, ' I live, yet not I, but Christ liv- ' eth in me; the life which I now live in the flesh, ' I live by the faith of the Son of God, who loved ' me, and gave himself for me,' Gal. ii. 20. What an emphatical strange expression is this, ' I live, ' yet not I, but Christ liveth in me? *q. d.* I live not the life of sense, I breathe not bodily breath, that is, comparatively to the life of faith; his very natural life, though inward, is said not to be lived in respect of this life of grace, which is more inward. And let this serve for a solution to that question.

4. What is it to have *the law written in our hearts?* This writing contains the former, and is something more, the metaphor is expressed in these particulars —

1. It is said to be written, That there might be something within answerable to the law without, it was written without, and so it is written within. This writing is the very same with copying, or transcribing. The writing within is every way answerable to the writing without; Oh! what a mercy is this, That the same God who writ the law with his own finger in tables of stone, should also write the same law with the finger of his Spirit in the tables of our hearts? As you see in a seal, when you put the seal on the wax, and you take it off again, you find in the wax the same impression that was on the seal: so it is in the hearts of the

faithful, when the Spirit hath once softened them, then he writes the law, *i. e.* he stamps an inward aptness, an inward disposition on the heart answering to every particular of the law; this is that which the apostle calls *the law of the mind, I see another law in my members warring against the law of my mind*, Rom. vii. 23. Now, what is this law in the mind, but a disposition within, to keep in some measure every commandment without? And this is the writing of the law (or if you will) the copying, or transcribing of the law within us.

It is said to be written, that it might be rooted and rivetted in the heart, as when letters are engraven in marble, so is the manner of God's writing; if God write, it can never be obliterated or blotted out; letters in marble are not easily worn out again, no more are the writings of God's Spirit; some indeed would have them as writings in dust: but if Pilate could say, *What I have written I have written*, how much more may God? Hence are all those promises of performance; *My covenant shall stand fast with him*, Psal. lxxxix. 28. and *the root of the righteous shall not be moved*, Prov. xii. 3. And *even to your old age I am he; and even to hoary hairs will I carry you*, Isa. xlvi. 4. I deny not but men of glorious gifts may fall away, but surely the poorest Christian that hath but the smallest measure of grace, he shall never fall away; if the law be written in our hearts, it still remains there; grace habitual is not removable; sooner will the sun discard its own beams, than Christ will desert or destroy the least measure of true grace, which is a beam from the Son of righteousness.

3. It is said to be written, that it might be as a thing legible to God, to others, and ourselves. 1. To God, he writes it that he may read it, and take notice of it, he exceedingly delights himself in the graces of his own Spirit: and therefore the spouse after this writing, after the planting of his graces in her, she desires him to 'come into his garden, and 'eat his pleasant fruits,' Cant. iv. 16. *q. d.* Come, read what thou hast written: come, and delight thyself in the graces of thy own Spirit. The only delight that God has in the world is in his garden, a gracious soul; and that he might more delight in it, he makes it fruitful, and those fruits are precious fruits; as growing from plants set by his own hand, relishing of his own Spirit, and so fitted for his own taste. 2. The law is written that it might be legible to others. So Paul tells the Corinthians, *You are manifestly declared to be the epistle of Christ*, 2 Cor. iii. 2, 3. How manifestly declared? Why, *known and read of all men*. As we are able to read letters graven in stone, so may others read and see the fruits and effects of this law written in our hearts. And good reason, for wheresoever God works the principles of grace within, it cannot but shew itself in the outward life and conversation. It is God's promise, *First, I will put my Spirit within them*, Ezek. xxxvi. 27. And then, *I will cause them to walk in my statutes*, and it is God's truth, *Out of the abundance of the heart the mouth speaketh*, Matth. xii. 34. What the mind thinketh, the hand worketh. 3. The law is written, that it may be legible to ourselves, a gracious heart is privy to its own grace and sincerity, when it is in a right temper: if others may read it by its fruits, how much more we ourselves, who both see the fruits, and feel that habitual disposition infused into us? Nor is this without its blessed use, for by this means we come to have a comfortable evidence both of God's love to us, and of our love to God. You see now what we mean, by this writing of the law within us.

5. How are we taught of God, so as not to need any other kind of teaching comparatively? I answer,——

1. God teacheth inwardly, 'In the hidden 'part thou hast made me know wisdom,' saith David. And again, 'I thank the Lord that gave me 'counsel, my reins also instruct me in the night-'season,' Pf. li. 6. and 16, 17. The reins are the most inward part of the body, and the night-season the most retired, and private time; both the intimacy of divine teaching. Man may teach the brains, but God only teacheth the reins; the knowledge which man teacheth is swimming knowledge; but the knowledge which God teacheth is a soaking knowledge. 'God who command-'ed light to shine out of darkness, hath shined into 'our hearts:' man's light may shine into the head; but God's light doth shine into the heart; *Cathedram habet in coelis qui corda docet*; his chair is in heaven that teacheth hearts, saith Austin.

2. God teacheth clearly: Elihu offering himself instead of God to reason with Job, he tells him, *My words shall be of the uprightness of my heart*,

heart, and my lips shall utter knowledge clearly, Job xxxiii. 3. If ever the word comes home to an heart, it comes with a convincing clearness: so the apostle, 'Our gospel came unto you, not in word 'only, but in power, and in the holy Ghost, and in 'much full assurance,' 1 Thess. i. v. The word hath a triple emphasis, assurance, full assurance, and much full assurance; here's clear work.

3. God teacheth experimentally; the soul that is taught of God can speak experimentally of the truths it knows: *I know whom I have believed,* saith Paul, 2 Tim. i. 12. I have experienced his faithfulness and all-sufficiency, I dare trust my all with him, I am sure he will keep it safe to that day. Common knowledge rests in generals; but they that are taught of God can say, *As we have heard, so have we seen;* they can go along with every truth, and say, It is so indeed; I have experienced this and that word upon my own heart. In this case the scripture is the original, and their heart is the copy of it, as you have heard; they can read over the promises and threatnings, and say, *Probatum est.* David in his Psalms, and Paul in his epistles, speak their very hearts, and find their very temptations, and make their very objections: they can set to their seal, that God is true, John iii. 33. They can solemnly declare by their lives and conversations, that God is true and faithful in his word and promises.

4. God teacheth sweetly and comfortably: *thou hast taught me,* saith David, and then it follows, *How sweet are thy words unto my taste! yea, sweeter than honey to my mouth,* Psalm cxix. 102, 103. He rolled the word and promises as sugar under his tongue, and sucked from thence more sweetness than Sampson did from his honey-comb: Luther said, 'He would not live in paradise, if he 'must live without the word.' *Cum verbo in inferis, facile est vivere,* Tom 4. oper. lat. 'But with 'the word (said he) I could live in hell.' When Christ put his hand by the hole of the door to teach the heart, 'Her bowels were moved, and then 'her fingers drop upon the handles of the lock 'sweet smelling myrrh,' Cant. v. 5. The teachings of Christ left such blessing upon the first motions of the spouse's heart, that with the very touch of them she is refreshed; her fingers drop myrrh, and her bowels are moved at the very moments of his gracious teachings; So, in Can. i. 3. 'Because 'of the savour of thy ointments, thy name is as an 'ointment poured forth; therefore do the vir-'gins love thee.' Christ in ordinances doth, as Mary, open a box of ointments, which diffuseth a spiritual favour in church-assemblies, and this only the spiritual Christian feels. Hence the church is compared to *a garden shut up, a fountain sealed,* Cant. iv. 12. Wicked men are not able to drink of her delicacies, or smell of her sweetness; a spiritual sermon is a fountain sealed up, the spiritual administration of a sacrament is a garden inclosed: 'Sometimes, O Lord, thou givest me a 'strange motion, or affection (said Aug. lib. 16. 'Confess. c. 40.) which if it were but perfected 'in me, I could not imagine what it should be but 'eternal life.' Christians! these are the teachings of God, and in reference to this, *We shall no more teach every man his neighbour, and every man his brother, saying, Know the Lord.* God's teaching is another kind of teaching than we can have from the hands of men, there is no man in the world can teach thus; and therefore they whom God teacheth, need not any other kind of teaching respectively, or comparatively.

6. What is the universality of this knowledge, *They shall all know me from the least of them to the greatest of them, saith the Lord?* The meaning is, that all that are in the covenant of grace, shall be so taught of God, as that in some measure or other they shall every one know God inwardly, clearly, experimentally, sweetly, and savingly. I know there are several degrees of this knowledge; God hath several forms in this school; there are *fathers* for experience, *young men* for strength, and *babes* for the truth and being of grace: as one star differeth from another in glory, so also is the school of Christ: but here I am beset on both sides, 1. Many are apt to complain, *Alas! they know little of God:* sweet babes, consider, 1. It is free grace, you are stars, though you are not stars of the first or second magnitude; it is of the covenant of grace, that God hath let into your souls a little glimmering, though not so much light as others possibly may have in point of holy emulation (as one notes well, *case correc instruct.*) we should look at degrees of grace, but in point of thankfulness and comfort we should look at the truth and being of grace. 2. If you know but a little, you may in time know more; God doth

not teach all his lessons at first entrance; it is true, *The entrance of thy word giveth light,* Psal. cxix. 130. But this is as true, that God lets in his light by degrees; it is not to be despised if God do but engage the heart in holy desires and longings after knowledge, so that it can say in sincerity, *My soul breaketh for the longing that it hath unto thy judgments at all times,* Psal. cxix. 20.

2. Others on the contrary, ground themselves so learned from this very promise, that they exclude all teachings of men. *The anointing* (say they) *teacheth us all things, and we need not that any man teach us,* 1 John ii. 27. *And they shall teach no more every man his neighbour, and every man his brother, saying, Know the Lord, for they shall all,* &c. Jer. xxxi. 34. I answer, The words either relate to the grounds of religion, and so in gospel-times Christians need not to be taught in those fundamental points, for now all know the Lord from the least to the greatest; or else these words are an hebraism, which deny positively, when they intend it only comparatively, or *secundum quid,* as when God and men are compared together, man is vanity, lighter than vanity, and a very nothing: here is a comparison of knowledge in gospel-times with the knowledge of Israel in those dark times when God brought them out of the land of Egypt; then all was dark, and they were fain to teach one another the very principles, the rudiments of religion, there was very little effusion of God's Spirit in those times; 'But in gospel-times (saith the 'prophet) the Spirit of grace and knowledge shall 'be so abundant, that rather God himself shall be 'the teacher, than one man shall teach another.' There shall be such exuberancy and seas of knowledge under the new covenant, above the covenant made with his people, when he brought them out of Egypt, that men shall not need to teach one another comparatively, for all shall know the Lord, who are taught of God from the least to the greatest: 'An highway shall be there, and it shall be 'called the way of holiness; the way-faring men, 'though fools, shall not err therein,' Isa. xxxv. 8.

7. How is God said to 'forgive iniquity, and 'never more to remember sin?'

For the first, God is said to *forgive iniquity,* when guilt of sin is taken away, and for the second, God is said, *never more to remember sin,* in that the sinner after pardon is never more looked on as a sinner. Is not this the covenant? *q. d.* I will remove thy sins, and do them away, as if they had never been; I will blot them out of the book of my memory, I will obliterate the writing, that none shall be able to read it. But you will say, if sin remain still in the regenerate, how are they so forgiven, as to be remembered no more? Divines tell us of two things in every sin, there is *macula et reatus,* the filth and guilt, this guilt some again distinguish into the guilt of sin, which they call the inward dignity and desert of damnation, and the guilt of punishment, which is the actual ordination of a sinner unto damnation. Now, in different respects we say, That sin remains still in believers; and sin doth not remain in believers; First, If we speak of the filth of sin, or of the desert of damnation so it remains still: but if we speak of the actual obligation of a sinner to condemnation, so it remains not after pardon, but the sinner is as free, as if he had never sinned.

But you will say, Is not the filth of sin done away when sin is remitted? I answer, The filth of sin is not done away by remission, but by sanctification and renovation: and because in this life we have not a perfect inherent holiness (sanctification at best being but imperfect and wrought in us by degrees) therefore during this life there is something of the filth of sin, and especially of the effects of original sin, sticking and still cleaving to us. But here is our comfort, and herein lie the sweets of the promise, that when God hath pardoned sin, he takes away the guilt as to condemnation; he acquits the sinner of that obligation; he now looks upon him not as a sinner, but as a just man; and so in this sense he will forgive, and never more remember his sin. Ah, Christians! take heed of their doctrine, who would have justification an abolition of sin in its real essence, and physical indwelling; let us rather say, with scripture, that all the justified saints must take down their top-sail, and go to heaven halting, and that they carry their bolts and fetters of indwelling sin through the field of free grace, even to the gates of glory; Christ daily washing, and we daily defiling, to the end that grace may be grace.

I have run through all the manifestations of the covenant of grace, as we have them discovered in the Old Testament: and yet, that we may see the better how these things concern us, I shall only
pro-

propound these two queries more, and then we have done.

1. Whether is the covenant of grace the same for substance in all ages of the world? We answer, Yea, the fathers before Christ had not one covenant, and we another; but the same covenant of grace belongs to us both. This appears in that, *First*, They had the same promise. *Secondly*, They had it upon the same grounds.

1. They had the same promise, as, *I will be your God, and you shall be my people*, Lev. xxvi. 12. *And happy art thou, O Israel, saved by the Lord*; and, *The Lord is our king, and he will save us*, Deut. xxxiii. 20. They had not only hopes of an earthly inheritance in Canaan (as some fondly imagine) but of an heavenly inheritance in the kingdom of God: and to this purpose our Saviour speaks expresly, *Many shall come from the east, and west, and shall sit down with Abraham, Isaac and Jacob in the kingdom of heaven*, Isaiah xxxiii. 22. Matth. viii. 11.

2. As they had the promise, so they had it upon the same ground that we have, even by faith in Christ Jesus; *Abraham saw my day*, said Christ, John viii. 56. *And Christ is the same yesterday, and to-day and for ever*, Heb. xiii. 8. He is the same not only in regard of essence, but also in regard of efficacy of his office, from the beginning to the end of the world. *We believe* (said Peter) *that, through the grace of the Lord Jesus Christ, we shall be saved even as they*, Acts xv. 11. *And unto us was the gospel preached* (faith Paul) *as unto them*, Heb. iv. 2. Some may think they had no gospel, but only the Law before Christ; but what say you? Have we not observed a thread of the gospel and of the covenant of grace, to run through all the Old Testament, from the first to last? And how plain is the apostle, *For this cause also was the gospel preached also to them that are dead?* 1 Pet. iv. 6. Dead long since; for he speaks of them who lived in the days of Noah. Nay, the apostle to the Hebrews gives us a catalogue of Old-Testament believers, *By faith Abel offered up unto God a more excellent sacrifice than Cain,—By faith Enoch was translated, that he should not see death. —By faith Noah being warned of God, prepared an ark.—By faith Abraham when he was called to go into a place, which he should after receive for an inheritance, obeyed, and he went out, not knowing whither he went.—These all died in faith not having received the promises, but having seen them afar off, and were persuaded of them, and embraced them*, Heb. xi. 4, 5, 7, 8, 13. Besides these, he reckons up the faith of Abraham, and Isaac, and Jacob, and Joseph, and Moses, and Rahab, and Gideon, and Barak, and Samson, and Jephtah, and David, and Samuel, and of all the prophets, who through faith did marvelous things, as it there appears. Surely they had the same doctrine of grace as we have; it is the very same for substance without any difference.

2. Wherein is the difference then betwixt the Old and the New Testament; or betwixt the old and new manner of the dispensation of the covenant of grace?

They are one for substance, but in regard of the manner of dispensation and revealing in the several times, ages, states and conditions of the church, there is a difference. I shall reduce all to these particulars: they are distinguished,

1. In the object. In the old administration Christ was promised, but in the covenant Christ is exhibited: it was meet the promise should go before the gospel, and be fulfilled in the gospel, that so a great good might earnestly be desired before it was bestowed.

2. In the federates. Under the old dispensation they are compared to an heir under age, needing a guardian, tutor or school-master, little differing from a servant; but in the New Testament they are compared to an heir come to ripe years; see Gal. iv. 1, 2, 3. &c.

3. In the manner of their worship; in the Old Testament they were held under the ceremonial law; and oh what an heap of ceremonies, rites, figures and shadows did they use in their worship; certainly these declared the infancy and nonage of the Jews, who being not capable of the high mysteries of the gospel, they were taught by their eyes as well as with their ears. These ceremonies were as rudiments and introductions fitted to the gross and weak senses of that church, who were to be brought on by little and little, through such shadows and figures, to the true image, and thing signified: but in the new covenant or testament, our worship is more spiritual: our Saviour hath told us, That as *God is a Spirit, so they that worship him must worship him in spirit and truth*. The

hour

hour cometh, and now is (faith Chrift) *when the true worſhippers ſhall worſhip the Father in ſpirit, and in truth; for the Father ſeeketh ſuch to worſhip him*, John iv. 23, 24.

4. In the burden of ceremonies: Peter calls the ceremonies of old, *A yoke which neither our fathers nor we* (faith he) *were able to bear*, Acts xv. 10. And no wonder if we confider, 1. The burden of their coftly facrifices; if any had but touched an unclean thing, he muft come and offer a facrifice, as, fometimes a bullock, and fometimes a lamb: you that think every thing too much for a minifter of Chrift, if for every offence you were to offer fuch facrifices now, you would count it an heavy burden indeed. 2. They had long and tedious journies to Jerufalem, the land lay more in length than breadth, and Jerufalem ftood almoft at one end of it, and thither *thrice a year all the males were to go and appear before the Lord*, Deut. xvi. 16. They were tied to the obfervation of many days, the new moons, and many ceremonial fabbaths; and they were reftrained from many liberties, as in meats, and the like; oh what burdens were upon them! but in the new covenant or teftament, the yoke is made more eafy; we are bound indeed to the duties of the moral law as well as they, yet a great yoke is taken off from us; and therefore Chrift inviting us to the gofpel, he gives it out thus, *Take my yoke upon you* (faith he) *for my yoke is eafy, and my burden light*, Mat. xi. 29.

5. In the weaknefs of the law of old; the law then was unable to give life, to purge the confcience, to pacify God's wrath; and therefore, faith the apoftle, *There is verily a difanulling of the commandment going before, for the weakneſs and unprofitableneſs thereof*, Heb. viii. 18. Hence they are called, *weak and beggarly rudiments*, Gal. iv. 9. In comparifon of the new Teftament, there was then a lefs forcible influence of the Spirit accompanying that difpenfation of the covenant: the Spirit was not then given in that large meafure as now; *Becauſe Chriſt was not then glorified*, John vii. 39. It appears in thefe particulars.

1. There was lefs power of faith in the faints before Chrift; when the doctrine of faith was more fully revealed, then was faith itfelf more fully revealed in the hearts and lives of God's people, *Before faith came* (faith the apoftle) *we were kept under the law, ſhut up unto the faith, which ſhould afterwards be revealed*, Gal. iii. 23. Surely this implies there was a time when there was lefs faith in God's people, and that was the time of the law.

2. There was lefs power of love in the faints before Chrift; according to the meafure of our faith, fo is our love; the lefs they knew the loving-kindnefs of God towards them in Chrift, the lefs they loved. It may be they were more drawn by the terrors of the law, than by the promifes of grace; and therefore they had lefs love in them.

3. They had a lefs meafure of comfort to carry them on in all their troubles. Chrift exhibited, is called, *The confolation of Iſrael*, Luke ii. 25. And therefore the more Chrift is imparted, the more means of comfort: hence the primitive faints after Chrift, are faid to *walk in the fear of the Lord, and in the comfort of the holy Ghoſt*, Acts ix. 31. Certainly the Spirit was poured in lefs plenty on the faithful in the Old Teftament, becaufe that benefit was to be referved to the times of Chrift, who was firft to receive the Spirit above meafure in his human nature, and thence to derive grace to his faints.

6. In the darknefs of that adminiftration of old, Chrift was but fhadowed out to the fathers in types, and figures, and dark prophecies, but now we fee him *with open face*, 2 Cor. iii. 18. Obferve the difference in reference to the perfon of Chrift, and to the offices of Chrift, and to the benefits that come by Chrift. 1. Concerning the perfon of Chrift; it was revealed to them, that he fhould be God, Ifa. ix. 6. and that he fhould be man, the fame verfe fpeaks of *a child that is born*, and of a *mighty God*. But how he fhould be God and man in one perfon, it was very darkly revealed. 2. Concerning the offices of Chrift, his mediatorſhip was typed out by Mofes, his priefthood was typed out by Melchizedec among the Canaanites, and Aaron among the Jews, his prophetical office was typed out by *Noah a preacher of righteouſneſs*; his kingly office was typed out by David; but how dark thefe things were unto them, we may guefs by the apoftles, who knew not that he fhould die, who dreamed of an earthly kingdom, and till the holy Ghoft came, were ignorant of many things pertaining to the kingdom of God. 3. Concerning the benefits that came by Chrift; juftification was fignified by the fprinkling of blood, and fanctification

by the water of purification; heaven and glorification by their land flowing with oyl, olive and honey: thus the Lord shewed the Jews these principal mysteries, not in themselves, but in types and shadows, as they were able to see them from day to day: but in the new covenant Christ is offered to be seen in a fuller view; the truth, and substance, and body of the things themselves is not exhibited; Christ is clearly revealed without any type at all to be our 'wisdom, righteousness, 'sanctification, and redemption,' 1 Cor. i. 30.

7. In the number of them that partake of the covenant; at first the covenant was included in the families of the patriarchs, and then within the confines of Judea, but now is the partition-wall betwixt Jew and Gentile broken down, and the covenant of grace is made with all nations, 'He is 'the God of the Gentiles also, and not of the Jews 'only,' Rom. iii. 29. Christians! here comes in our happiness; Oh how thankful should we be! what? That our fathers for many hundreds and thousands of years together should sit in darkness, and that we should partake of this grace? What! that we that were dogs before, should now be set at the childrens table? The very Jews themselves hearing of this, are said 'to glorify God, When they 'heard these things, they held their peace, and 'glorified God, saying, Then hath God also to the 'Gentiles granted repentance unto life,' Acts xi. 8. If they praised God for it, how much more should we do it ourselves? But of that hereafter.

I have now propounded the object we are to look unto, it is Jesus as held forth in a way of promise, or covenant, in that dark time from the creation, till his first coming in the flesh; our next business is to direct you in the art or mystery of grace, how you are to look to him in this respect.

CHAP. II.　　SECT. I.

Of knowing Jesus, as carrying on the great work of our salvation from the creation until his first coming.

Looking comprehends knowing, considering, desiring, &c. as you have heard; and accordingly that we may practise,

1. We must know Jesus carrying on the great work of our salvation in the beginning, and from the beginning of the world: come, let us learn what he did for us so early in the morning of this world; he made it for us, and he made us more especially for his own glory; but, presently after we were made, we sinned and marred the image wherein God made us; this was the saddest act that ever was; it was the undoing of man, and (without the mercy of God) the damning of all souls both of men and women to all eternity; and, O my soul, *Know this for thyself*, thou wast in the loyns of Adam at that same time, so that what he did, thou didst; thou wast partaker of his sins, and thou wast to partake with him in his punishment: but well mayest thou say, *Blessed be God for Jesus Christ*; at the very instant when all should have been damned, Christ intervened; a covenant of grace is made with man, and Christ is the foundation in and through whom we must be reconciled unto God: come, soul, and study this covenant of grace in reference to thyself. Had not this been, where hadst thou been? Nay, where had all the world been at this day? Surely it concerns thee to take notice of this great transaction. After man had fallen by sin, Christ is promised; and that all the saints might partake of Christ, a covenant is entered; this at the beginning of the world was more dim, but the nearer to Christ's coming in the flesh, the more and more clearly it appeared: howsoever dimly, or clearly, thus it pleased God in Christ to carry on the great work of our salvation at that time, *viz.* By a promise of Christ, and by a covenant in Christ; and for the better knowledge of it, study the promise made to Adam, and Abraham, and Moses, and David, and Israel. Come, soul, study these several breakings out of the covenant of grace; it is worth thy pains, it is *a mystery which hath been hid from ages, and from generations, but now is made manifest to the saints*, Col. i. 26. Here lies the first and most firm foundation of a Christian's comfort; if thou canst but study this, and assure thyself of thy part in this, thou art blessed for ever. O how incomparably sweet and satisfying is it to a self-studying Christian, to know the faithful engagements of the Almighty God, through that Son of his loves, in a covenant of grace.

SECT.

SECT. II.

Of confidering Jesus in that respect.

2. WE must confider Jesus as carrying on the great work of our salvation in that dark time; it is not enough to study it, and know it, but we must serioufly muse and meditate, and ponder, and confider of it, till we bring it to some profitable issue. This is the consideration I mean, when we hold our thoughts to this, or that spiritual subject, till we perceive success, and the work do thrive and prosper in our hands. Now, to help us in this,—

1. Confider Jesus in that first promise made to man, *It shall bruise thy head, and thou shalt bruise his heel*, Gen. iii. 15. When all men were under guilt of sin, and in the power of Satan, and when thou, my soul, wert in as bad a case as any other, then to hear the sound of this glad tidings, then to hear of Jesus a Saviour and Redeemer, sure this was welcome news! come, draw the case near to thyself, thou wast in Adam's loins; suppose thou hadst been in Adam's stead; suppose thou hadst ' heard the voice of the Lord walking in the ' garden;' suppose thou hadst heard him call, Adam, *Where art thou*, Peter, Andrew, Thomas, where art thou? What? *Hast thou eaten of the tree whereof I commanded thee that thou shouldest not eat?* Gen. iii. 8, 9, 11. Why then appear and come to judgment, the law is irrevocable, *In the day that thou eatest thereof, thou shalt surely die*, Gen. ii. 17. There is nothing to be looked for but death temporal, and death spiritual, and death eternal. O! what a fearful condition is this, no sooner to come into the world, but presently to be turned over into hell? For one day to be a monarch of the world, and of all creatures in the world, and the very next day to be the slave of Satan, and to be bound hand and foot in a darksome dungeon? For a few hours to live in Eden, to enjoy every tree of the garden, *pleasant to the sight, and good for food*, and then to enter into the confines of eternity, and ever, ever, ever to be tormented with the devil and his angels? 'Tis no wonder, if *Adam hid himself from the presence of the Lord God amongst the trees of the garden*, Gen. iii. 8. O my soul! in that case thou wouldest have cried to the rocks and to the mountains, ' Fall on ' me, and hide me from him that sitteth on the ' throne,' Rev. vi. 16, 17. If God be angry, who may abide it? ' When the great day of his wrath ' is come, who shall be able to stand?' And yet despair not, cheer up, O my soul; for in the very midst of wrath, God is pleased to remember mercy; even now when all the world should have been damned, a Jesus is proclaimed, and promised; and he it is that must die according to the commination, for he is our surety; and he it is that by death must overcome death and the devil, *It shall bruise thy head*, said God to Satan, *q. d.* Come, Satan, thou hast taken captive ten thousand of souls, Adam and Eve are now enfnared, and in their loins all the men and women that ever shall be from this beginning of the world to the end thereof: now is thy day of triumph, now thou keepest holy day in hell; but thou shalt not carry it thus, I foresaw from all eternity what thou hast done; I know thou wouldst dig an hole through the comely and beautiful frame of the creation; but I have decreed of old a counter-work, out of the feed of the woman shall spring a branch, *And he shall bruise thy head*, he shall break thy power, he shall tread thy dominion under foot, he shall lead thy captivity captive, he shall take away sin, he shall paint out to men and angels the glory of heaven, and a new world of free grace. In this promise, O my soul, is folded and inwrapped up thy hope, thy heaven, thy salvation; and therefore confider of it, turn it upside down, look on all sides of it, view it over and over: there's a *Jesus* in it; it is a field that contains in the bowels of it a precious treasure; there's in it a Saviour, a Redeemer,. a Deliverer from sin, death and hell; are not these dainties to feed upon? Are not these rarities to dwell on in our meditations?

2. Confider Jesus in that next promise made to Abraham; ' I will establish my covenant between ' me and thee, and thy seed after thee in their ge- ' nerations for an everlasting covenant, to be a ' God to thee, and to thy seed after thee,' Gen. xvii. 7. In respect of this covenant Abraham is called *the father of the faithful*, Rom. iv. 11. And they which are of the faith, are called the children of Abraham, Gal. iii. 17. And, O my soul, if thou art in covenant with God, surely thou dost by faith draw it through Abraham to whom this promise

was

was made; for *if ye be Chrift's, then are ye Abraham's feed, and heirs according to the promife*, Gal. iii. 29 Confider what a mercy is this, That God fhould enter into a covenant with thee in the loins of Abraham God makes a promife of Chrift, and inclufively a covenant of grace, in his comforting Adam, but he makes a covenant exprefly under the name of a covenant with Abraham and his feed: O mufe, and be amazed! What! that the great and glorious God of heaven and earth fhould be willing to enter into a covenant; this is to fay, That he fhould be willing to make himfelf a debtor to us? O my foul, think of it ferioufly; he is in heaven, and thou art on earth; he is the Creator, and thou art his creature; *Ah what art thou, or what is thy father's houfe, that thou fhouldeft be raifed up hitherto?* The very covenant is a wonder, as it relates to God and us, what is it but a compact, an agreement, a tying, a binding of God and us? When Jehofhaphat and Ahab were in covenant, fee how Jehofhaphat expreffeth himfelf, *I am as thou art, my people as thy people, my horfes as thy horfes*, 1 Kings xxii. 4. So it is betwixt God and us; if once he gives us the covenant, then his ftrength is our ftrength, his power is our power, his armies are our armies, his attributes are our attributes, we have intereft in all; there is an offenfive and defenfive league (as I may fay) betwixt God and us; and if we put him in mind of it in all our ftraits, he cannot deny us. As it was with the nations allied to Rome, if they fought at any time, the Romans were bound in honour to defend them, and they did it with as much diligence, as they defended their own city of Rome; fo it is with the people allied to God, he is bound in honour to defend his people, and he will do it if they implore his aid; how elfe? is it poffible God fhould break his covenant? Will he not ftir up himfelf to fcatter his and our fpiritual enemies? Certainly he will. Thus runs the tenor of his covenant, *I will be a God to thee, and to thy feed after thee*. This is the general promife, I may call it the mother-promife that carries all other promifes in its womb; and we find a Jefus in this promife, confider that; it is God in Chrift that is held forth to us in this phrafe, I will be as a God to thee: O fweet! here is the greateft promife that ever was made, Chrift, God is more than grace, pardon, holinefs, heaven; as the huf-band is more excellent than the marriage-robe, bracelets and rings, fo the well and fountain of life is of more excellency than the ftreams; Chrift Jefus the objective happinefs, is far above a created and formal beatitude which iffueth from him. O my foul! is not this worthy of thy inmoft confideration? But of this more in the next.

3. Confider Jefus in that promife made to Mofes and the Ifraelites, *I am the Lord thy God, that brought thee out of the land of Egypt, out of the houfe of bondage*. Much hath been faid to this promife before, as matter of thy confideration; but, to contract it, confider in this promife the fufficiency, and propriety. 1. Here is fufficiency, it is a promife of infinite worth, an hid treafure, a rich poffeffion, an overflowing bleffing which none can rightly value; it is no lefs than the great and mighty, and infinite God; if we had a promife of a hundred worlds, or of ten heavens, this is more than all; heaven indeed is beautiful, but God is more beautiful, for he is the God of heaven, and hence it is that the faints in heaven are not fatisfied without their God; it is a fweet expreffion of Bernard, ' As whatfoever we give unto thee, Lord, ' unlefs we give ourfelves, cannot fatisfy thee; fo ' whatfoever thou giveft unto us, Lord, unlefs thou ' giveft thyfelf, it cannot fatisfy us;' and hence it is, That as God doth make the faints his portion, fo God is the portion and inheritance of his faints. Confider the greatnefs, the goodnefs, the all-fufficiency of this promife, *I am the Lord thy God!* no queftion but Mofes had many other rich promifes from God, but he could not be fatisfied without God himfelf; *If thy prefence be not with us, bring us not hence*, Exod. xxxiii. 15. And no wonder, for without God all things are nothing; but in the want of all other things, God himfelf is inftead of all: it is God's alone prerogative to be an univerfal good. The things of this world can but help in this or that particular thing; as bread againft hunger, drink againft thirft, clothes againft cold and nakednefs, houfes againft wind and weather, riches againft poverty, phyfic againft ficknefs, friends againft folitarinefs; but God is an all-fufficient good, he is all in all both to the inner and outward man. Are we guilty of fin? There is mercy in God to pardon us Are we full of infirmities? There is grace in God to heal us. Are we ftrong in corruptions? There is power in God

to subdue them in us. Are we disquieted in conscience? There is that Spirit in God that is the comforter, that can fill us with joy unspeakable and glorious: and for our outward man, all our welfare is laid up in God, he is *the God of our life*, Pf. xlii. 8. He is *the strength of our life*, Pf. xxvii. 1. He is a *quickening Spirit*, 1 Cor. xv. 45. Which, though it be in regard of the inner man, yet there it is spoken of the outward man, which the Lord shall quicken after death, and doth now keep alive by his mighty power, for *in him we live, and move and have our being*, Acts xvii. 27.

O my soul, that thou wouldest but ruminate and meditate, and consider this promise in all thy wants and discontents; when means fail, and the stream runs no more, O that thou wouldest then go to the fountain, where the waters run sweeter, and more sure; for as Joseph said to Pharaoh, *It is not in me, God shall give Pharaoh an answer of peace*, Gen. xli. and 16. So may silver and gold, and such things, say to thee, It is not in us; God shall give enough out of himself, have God, and have all; want God, and there is no content in the enjoyment of all: it was the apostle's case, *as to have nothing, and yet possessing all things*; 2 Cor. vi. 18. Surely he lived to God, and enjoyed God, and he was an all sufficient good unto him. God may be enjoyed in any condition, in the meanest as well as the greatest, in the poorest as well as the richest; God will go into a wilderness, into a prison with his people, and there he will make up all that they are cut short of, thy discontents therefore arise not from the want of outward means, but from want of inward fellowship with God: if thou dost not find a sufficiency, it is because thou dost not enjoy him who is thy all-sufficient good. O stir up faith, and consider the covenant, think seriously on this promise, I am God all-sufficient, I am the Lord thy God.

2. Here is the propriety of saints, *the Lord thy God*. O what is this, that God is *thy God*? Heaven and earth, angels and men, may stand astonished at it, What? that the great and mighty God, God Almighty, and God all-sufficient should be called thy God? It is observable what the apostle speaks, *God is not ashamed to be called their God*, Heb. xi. 16. Would not a prince be ashamed to take a beggar, a runnagate, a base and adulterous woman to be his wife? But we are worse than so, and God is better than so; sin hath made us worse than the worst of women, and God is better, holier, higher than the best of princes; and yet God is not ashamed to own us, nor ashamed that we own him as our own, *I am thy God*. It is as if the Lord should say, Use me, and all my power, grace, mercy, kindness, as thine own; go through all my attributes, consider my almighty power, consider my wisdom, council, understanding; consider my goodness, truth, faithfulness, consider my patience, long-suffering, forbearance; all these are thine; as thus, my power is thine, to work all thy works for thee and in thee, to make passage for thee in all thy straits, to deliver thee out of six troubles and out of seven; my wisdom is thine, to counsel thee in any difficult cases, to instruct thee in things that be obscure, to reveal to thee the mysteries of grace, and the wonderful things contained in my law; my justice is thine, to deliver thee when thou art oppressed, to defend thee in thy innocency, and to vindicate thee from the injuries of men. What needs more? O my soul, think of these, and all other God's attributes; say in thyself, all these are mine: nay, more, think of God in Christ (for otherwise what hast thou to do with God in the covenant of grace?) and say in thy heart, Jesus Christ is mine, my Saviour, my Redeemer, my head, my elder brother; his doings are mine, and his sufferings are mine; his life and his death, his resurrection and ascension, his cession and intercession, are all mine; nay, more, if Christ be mine, why then all good things are mine in Christ; I say in Christ, for they come not immediately, but thro' the hands of a sweet Redeemer, and though he be a man who redeemed us, yet because he is God as well as man, there is more of God and heaven, and free-love, in all our good things, than if we received them immediately from God. Ravens have their food, and devils have their being from God by creature-right, but we have all we have from God in Christ by covenant-right; this surely, this very promise is the main and principal promise of the covenant; it is the very substance, soul and life of all; O then how careful shouldest thou be to improve the strength of thy mind, thoughts and affections on this only subject!

4. Consider Jesus in that promise made to David, *He hath made with me an everlasting covenant, ordered in all things, and sure*, 2 Sam. xxiii.

5. 1. An everlasting covenant, consider this in the internal efficacy, and not in the outward administration, it is Christ that hath built and prepared a kingdom that shall never fade, a spiritual and an heavenly kingdom which shall never cease: and as he hath prepared it, so, if thou believest, he hath entered into a covenant with thy soul, to bestow it on thee; it is an everlasting covenant, and he will give thee everlasting life. 2. It is ordered in all things; the covenant of grace is so marshalled and ordered, that it stands at best advantage to receive and to repel all thy objections. Many and many an objection hast thou raised; how often have such thoughts been in thee, 'Oh! I am mi-
' serable, I shall not live but die, my sins will damn
' me, I am lost for ever? And again, If God hath
' made with me a covenant, why then I have some-
' thing to do on my part, for this is of the nature
' of the covenant to bind on both parts; but, alas,
' I have failed! I can do nothing, I can as well
' dissolve a rock as make my heart of stone an heart
' of flesh; I can as well reach heaven with a fin-
' ger, as lay hold on Christ by the hand of faith?'
Have not such arguings, as these been many, and many a time in thy heart? O consider how the covenant is ordered and marshalled in respect of the author of it, of the persons interested in it, of the parts of which it consists, of the end and aim to which it refers; and in some of these, if not in all of these, thou wilt find thy objections answered, removed, routed. 3. It is sure, God is not fast and loose in his covenants, heaven and earth shall pass away, before one jot or tittle of his word shall fail. Consider, O my soul, he both can and will perform his word, his power, his love, his faithfulness, his constancy, all stand engaged. What sweet matter is here for a soul to dwell upon? What needs it to go out to other objects, whilst it may find enough here? But especially, what needs it to bestow itself upon vain things? O that so much precious sand of our thoughts should run out after sin, and so little after grace, or after this covenant of grace!

5. Consider Jesus in that new covenant or promise which God made with Israel and Judah; *I will put my law into their inward parts, and write it in their hearts, and I will be their God, and they shall be my people. And they shall teach no more every man his brother, and every man his neighbour, saying, Know the Lord: for they shall all know me from the least of them to the greatest of them, saith the Lord: for I will forgive their iniquity, and I will remember their sins no more,* Jer. xxxi. 33, 34. Oh what an error is it, that there's no inherent righteousness in the saints, That there's no grace in the soul of a believer, but only in Christ? Is not this the ordinary scripture-phrase, *I will put my Spirit within you,* Ez. xxxvi. 27. And, *the water that I shall give you, shall be in you a well of water springing up unto everlasting life,* John iv. 14. And, *the anointing which you have received of him abideth in you,* 1 John ii. 27. And, *Christ in you the hope of glory,* Col. i. 27. Observe how *the Spirit of the living creatures was in the wheels,* Ezek. i. 20. So that when the Spirit went, they went, and when the spirit was lifted up, they were lifted up; even so is the Spirit of Christ in the saints, acting, and guiding, and framing, and disposing them to move and walk according to his laws. *The kingdom of heaven is within you,* saith Christ, Luke xvii. 21. And, *I delight to do thy will, O my God,* saith David, *yea thy law is within my heart.* Psal. xl. 8. O my soul, if thou art in covenant with God, besides the indwelling of the Spirit, there is a certain spiritual power, or principle of grace, which Christ by his Spirit hath put into thy heart, enabling thee in some measure to move thyself towards God. And this principle is sometimes called *a new life,* Rom. vi. 4. Sometimes *a living with Christ,* Rom. vi. 8. Sometimes, *a being alive to God,* Rom. vi. 11. Sometimes, *a revealing of his Son in man,* Gal. i. 15. And sometimes, *a putting of the law into our inward parts, and a writing of the law within the heart,* Jer. xxxi. 33. O consider of this inward principle, it is an excellent subject worthy of thy consideration.

2. *I will be their God, and they shall be my people*; Consider God essentially, and personally, God the Father, God the Son, and God the holy Ghost; God in himself, and God in his creatures: this very promise turns over heaven, and earth, and sea, and land, bread and clothes, and sleep, and the world, and life and death, into free grace. No wonder if God set this promise in the midst of the covenant, as the heart in the midst of the body, to communicate life to all the rest; this promise hath an influence into all other promises, it is the great pro-

mise of the new covenant, it is as great as God is, though the heavens and the heaven of heavens be not able to contain him, yet this promise contains him, God shuts up himself (as it were) in it. *I will be their God.* 2. *They shall be my people*, i. e. they *shall be to me a peculiar people*, Tit. ii. 14. The word hath this emphasis in it, that God looks upon all other things as accidents in comparison, and his substance is his people; they are his very portion, *For the Lord's portion is his people, Jacob is the lot of his inheritance*, Deut. xxxii. 9. They are his treasure, his peculiar treasure, his peculiar treasure above all people; *If ye will obey my voice indeed, and keep my covenant, then ye shall be a peculiar treasure unto me, and above all people, for all the earth is mine*, Exod. xix. 5. Observe, O my soul, All the earth is mine. *q. d.* All people is my people, but I have a special interest in my covenanted people, they only are my portion, my peculiar treasure. *Blessed be Egypt my people, Assyria the work of mine hands; and Israel mine inheritance*, Isa. xix. 28. I have made all people; Egypt and Assyria, and all the world is mine, but only Israel is my inheritance; the saints are those that God satisfies himself in; the saints are those that God hath set his heart upon; they are children of the high God, they are the spouse that are married to the Lamb; they are nearer God in some respects than the very angels themselves, for the angels are not in a mystical union so married to Christ, as God's people are. Oh the happiness of saints! I will be their God, and they shall be my people.

3. 'They shall teach no more every man his
' neighbour, and every man his brother, saying,
' Know the Lord, for they shall all know me from
' the least of them to the greatest of them, saith
' the Lord.' Consider of this. Oh poor soul, thou complainest many a time of thy weakness, thou knowest little or nothing: why, see here a glorious promise, if thou art but in covenant with God, thou shalt be taught of God, and then thou shalt know God far more clearly than the Jews of old, he will open to thee all his treasures of wisdom and knowledge, he will bestow on thee a greater measure of his Spirit, *So that out of thy belly shall flow rivers of living waters*, John vii. 38. We say, a good tutor may teach more in a day, than another in a week or a month; now, the promise runs thus, *That all thy children shall be taught of God*, Isa. liv. 13. Not that private instruction, or public ministry must be excluded, we know these are appointed under the New Testament, and are subordinate to the Spirit's teaching; but that the teachings of God do far surpass the teachings of men, and therefore the knowledge of God under the New Testament shall far surpass that under the Old: herein appears the excellency of Christ's prophetical office, 'He is such a prophet, as enlightens e-
' very man within, that comes into the world: he'
' is such a prophet as baptizeth with the holy Ghost
' and with fire, John i. 9, 33. He is such a pro-
' phet as makes mens hearts to burn within them,
' when he speaks unto them,' Luke xxiv. 32. He is such a prophet, as bids his ministers, 'Go, teach
' all nations, and I will be with you; and I will make you able ministers, not of the letter, but of
' the Spirit,' Matth. xxviii. 19, 20. He is such a prophet, as teacheth inwardly, clearly, experimentally, and sweetly: no man in the world can say this, or do this, but Jesus Christ the great prophet of the church, whom God hath raised up like unto Moses, or far above Moses. O my soul, consider if thou art thus taught of God!

4. *I will forgive their iniquity, and I will remember their sins no more.* Consider of this, *Blessed are they whose iniquities are forgiven, and whose sins are covered*, Rom. iv. 7. Consider, O my soul, suppose thy case and thy condition thus: as thou livest under laws of man, so for the transgression of those laws thou art called to account; the judge weighs, and gives an impartial and just judgment, he dooms thee to the axe, or rack, or wheel; and because of the aggravation of thy crime he commands thee to be tortured leisurely, that bones, sinews, lights, joints might be pained, for twenty, thirty, forty, fifty years; that so much of thy flesh should be cut off every day; that such and such a bone should be broken such and such a day; and that by art the flesh should be restored, and the bone cured again; that for so many years, as is said, thou mightest be kept every day dying, and yet never die; that all this while thou must have no sleep, nor ease, nor food, nor clothing convenient for thee: that whips of iron, lashes and scourges of scorpions, that racks, wheels, cauldrons full of melted lead should be the prepared instruments of thy continual, horrible, terrible torments; in this case,
sup-

suppose, a mighty prince by an act of free and special grace should deliver thee from this pain and torture, and not only so, but should give thee a life in perfect health, should put thee into a paradise of pleasures, where all the honour, acclamations, love and service of a world of men and angels should await thee, and where thou shouldest be elevated to the top of all imaginable happiness, above Solomon in his highest royalty, or Adam in his first innocency: were not this a mercy? Wouldest thou not think it the highest act of grace and love, that any creature could extend to his fellow-creature? And yet, O my soul, all this is nothing but a shadow of grace in comparison of the love and rich grace of God in Christ in the justification of a sinner. If thou hast a right to this promise, *I will forgive thy iniquity, and I will remember thy sins no more*, that thou art delivered from eternal death, and thou art entitled to an eternal kingdom. O know thy blessedness aright! consider how infinitely thou art engaged to God, and Christ, and mercy, and free-grace! this promise sounds forth nothing but grace and blessing; grace from God, and blessing on us; it is grace, because nothing but grace and mercy can forgive: it is grace, because God, if he will, hath power in his hand to revenge; he doth not pass by sin as men do offences, when they dissemble forgiveness; they may forgive, because they have not power to avenge; it is otherwise with God, *To me belongs vengeance, and recompence, saith God*, Deut. xxxii. 35. He is able to destroy, and yet he chooseth to forgive. This is his name, *Strong and gracious*, Exod. xxxvi. 4.

O my soul, thou art apt to complain, 'What? 'Will the Lord forgive my sins? What reason 'hath God to look on me, to pardon me, to pluck 'me as a fire-brand out of the fire of hell? Why 'should God forgive me?' But now consider (if thy heart be humbled) the Lord will do it.

1. Because he delighteth in mercy, Mic. vii. 18. It is a pleasure to God to forgive sins; never did we take more pleasure, nor so much pleasure in acting and committing of sin, as he doth in the pardoning of sin; he is *the father of mercies*, 2 Cor. i. 3. He delights in mercy, as a father in his children; it doth him good to see the fruits of his own mercy, in taking away the sins of his own people.

2. Because it is his purpose, which he hath purposed within himself from all eternity; this was the great design of God (as you have heard) to make his grace glorious in those whom he intends to save, he will have 'the praise of the glory of his 'grace,' Eph. i. 6 He will not lose his glory; he will be 'admired in his saints,' 2 Thes. i. 10. He will make the world to wonder, when it shall be known what sin hath been committed by them, and pardoned by him. And hence it is that God's people are called vessels of mercy, *That he might make known the riches of his glory on the vessels of mercy*, Rom. ix. 23. For, as vessels are, or may be filled up to the brim, so the vessels of mercy, shall be filled with mercy up to the brim, that the riches of his glory in the pardon of sin may be seen and known to the wonder of all the world.

3. Because it is his nature and inclination to pardon sin. This appears, 1. In the proclaiming of his name, *The Lord, the Lord God, merciful, and gracious, long-suffering, and abundant in goodness and truth, keeping mercy for thousands, forgiving iniquity, and transgression, and sin*, Exod. xxxiv. 6 2. In his gracious invitations, *Come unto me*, saith Christ, Matth. xi. 28. If sin burden you, I will ease you. 3. In his patience and waiting for repentance; he waits to this very end, *That he might be gracious, and that he may have mercy, for the Lord is a God of judgment*, Isa. xxx. 18.

4. Because it is his promise to pardon sin, *I, even I am he that blots out thy transgressions for my own sake, and will not remember thy sin*, Isaiah xliii. 25. This promise of pardon, is one of the great blessings of the covenant of grace; you hear the words in this very expression of it, *I will forgive their iniquity, and I will remember their sins no more*, Jer. xxxi. 34.

Now, come, consider, O my soul, of every particular in this gracious covenant, and, O! be serious in thy consideration; surely there's too much expence of thy spirit upon vain, and transitory and worldly things. Alas! alas! thou hast but a short time to live, and the strength of thy mind that I call for, it is the most precious thing thou hast; O then let the business and activeness of thy mind, let thy inmost thoughts, and deep affections, be acted and exercised on this subject; be careful that none of these waters run beside the mill. If God, and Jesus, and all thy good be included

cluded here, why should not thy whole soul be intent on this? Why shouldest thou spend it on the creature? Why shouldest thou be so subject to carnal grief, and fears? Surely all these are fitter to be fixed on God in Christ, on Jesus in a covenant of grace.

SECT. III.

Of desiring Jesus in that respect.

3. WE must desire after Jesus, carrying on the great work of our salvation in a way of covenant, before his coming in the flesh. It is not enough to know and consider, but we must desire. Thus is the order of God's work; no sooner hath his Spirit clearly revealed the goodness of the promise, that we come to know, but the soul considers of it, turns it upside down, views it in all its excellencies, weighs it in the balance of its best and deepest meditation. This done, the affections begin to stir, and the soul begins thus to reason; O happy I, that I see the goodness of this gracious promise; but miserable I, if I come to see this, and never have a share in it; O! why not I, Lord? Why not my sins pardoned? Why not my corruptions subdued? Why not the law written in my heart, and put into my inward parts; Why may not I say, *My Lord, and my God;* or, *I am my Beloved's, and my Beloved is mine?* Why not this covenant established between God and me? Now, my soul thirsts after this as a thirsty land, my affections hunger after Jesus in a covenant of grace: *Oh, I would fain be in covenant with God; for this is all my salvation, and all my desire,* 2 Sam. xxiii. 5. But here is an objection.

Object. The object of this desire is apprehended as absent and distant; we do not covet those things that we do enjoy; if they are present, we rather rest in them; how then should David, or any soul, already in a covenant of grace, desire after the covenant? What is this? *He hath made with me an everlasting covenant, ordered in all things, and sure, for this is all my salvation and all my desire,* 2 Sam. xxiii. 5.

Answ. It is true, the object of desire, *qua tale,* is something absent; yet not always absent in the whole, but in the parts and degrees of it: the very presence of a good thing does in some sort quicken the desires towards the same thing, so far forth as it is capable of improvements or augmentations: as we see in external riches of the body, none desire them more eagerly than those that possess them; and the more gracious the soul is, the more is the heart enlarged in the appetite for a greater measure of grace, as the putting in some water into a pump doth draw forth more: no man is so importunate in praying, *Lord, help my unbelief,* as he that can say, *Lord, I believe:* things may be desired, in order to improvement and further degrees of them. Again, things present may be the object of our desires unto continuance; as he that delighteth in a good thing that he hath, he desireth the continuance of that delight; so the soul of a man having a reach as far as immortality, it may justly desire as well the perpetuity, as the presence of those good things it enjoyeth.

Come then, O my soul, and whet on thy desires, in every of these respects; as, 1. Desire after thy interest in the covenant. 2. Desire after thy improvement of the covenant. 3. Desire after the continuance of thy covenant-state. 4. Desire after Jesus the great business, or the All in All in a covenant of grace.

1. Desire after thy interest in the covenant; O say in thyself, Is it thus? Is the Lord willing to receive me to his grace? Was that his voice in the streets? *How long, ye simple ones, will ye love simplicity?——Turn ye at my reproof,* Prov. i. 22, 23. Behold I will pour out my Spirit unto you! was that his proclamation, *Ho, every one that thirsteth, come ye to the waters: incline your ear and come unto me ;——And I will make an everlasting covenant with you, even the sure mercies of David,* Isa. lv. 1, 3. And are these the promises offered in the covenant? *I will put my law into your inward parts, and I will write it in your hearts, and I will be your God, and ye shall be my people,* Jer. xxxi. 33. Oh, the blessed condition of those people that are in covenant with God! *Blessed art thou, O Israel, who is like unto thee, a people saved by the Lord?* Deut. xxx. 29. *Oh, happy is the people that be in such a case; yea, happy is the people whose God is the Lord,* Psal. cxliv. 15. But, ah! what can I say? No sin like unto my sin, no misery like unto my misery; alas! I am an alien to God, I am separated from his people, I am out of the covenant; like a poor prodigal, I die for hunger, whilst those that

that are in my Father's house have bread enough: Oh, that I were in their condition! never did David long more for the waters of the well of Bethlehem, than my soul, now touched with the sense of sin, doth desire to be at peace with God, and in covenant with God: oh, I thirst, I pant, I grasp after him, I long for communion and peace with him: 'With my soul do I desire thee in the 'night; yea, with my spirit within me do I seek 'thee early,' Isa. xxvi. 9.

2. Desire after thy improvement of the covenant; it may be God hath given thee an interest in it, but, alas, thy hold is so weak, that thou scarce knowest the meaning of it; the Lord may answer, but yet he speaks darkly, as sometimes he spake to the woman, John viii. 11. *Go thy way, and sin no more:* it is a middle kind of expression, neither assuring her that her sin was pardoned, nor yet putting her out of hope but it might be pardoned; so it may be God hath given thee some little ease, but he hath not spoken full peace; go on and then desire more and more after confirmation. Say in thine heart, O Lord, thou hast begun to shew grace unto thy servant; but, oh, manifest to me all thy goodness. Thou hast given me a drop, and I feel it so sweet, and now I thirst, and long to enjoy the fountain; thou hast given me a kiss of thy mouth and now I pant to be united to thee in a more perfect and consummate marriage; thou hast given me a taste, but my appetite and desire is not hereby diminished, but enlarged; and good reason; for what are these drops and tastes, but only *the first fruits of the Spirit?* Rom. viii. 23. and *earnests of the Spirit,* Ephes. i. 14. Oh then, what are those harvests of joy? What are those treasures of wisdom, and free grace hid in God? I have indeed beheld 'a feast of fat things, of fat things 'full of marrow, of wine on the lees, of wine on 'the lees well refined;' but, O what a famine is yet in my spirit! O Lord, I have longed for thy salvation, I am ready to swoon for further union, and clearer manifestation of my share and interest in this covenant of grace, come, Lord Jesus, come quickly.

3. Desire after continuance of thy covenant-state: many a sweet soul cannot deny but that the Lord hath shewed mercy on him, but he fears that he shall not hold out: he feels within such a power of corruption, such strong temptation, so many lusts, that now he doubts. 'O, what will be'come of my poor soul? What will be the issue 'of this woful work?' Why, come now, and desire after perseverance: when Peter was ravished on the mount, *It is good being here,* (says he) *let us build tabernacles,* Matth. xvii. 4. His desire was to have continued there for ever; and it was the prayer of Christ in Peter's behalf, *I have prayed for thee that thy faith fail not,* Luke xxii. 32. What was this prayer but Christ's vehement desire of Peter's continuing in the faith? Shall Christ desire, and will not thou desire after thy own perfection? O, come with these pantings and breathings after God; put forth thy desires in these and the like expressions, *O Lord, thou hast said, I will betroth thee unto me for ever,* Hos. ii. 19. And what means this, but that the conjugal love of Christ with a gracious soul, shall never be broken? What means this, but that the bond of union in a believer to Christ is fastened on God, and the Spirit of God holds the other end of it, and so it can never be broken? 2. O Lord, thou hast discovered in thy word, that this union is in the Father, who hath laid a sure foundation, *The foundation of God standeth sure, having this seal, The Lord knoweth them that are his,* 2 Tim. ii. 19. And that this union is in the Son, who loves his to the end: and that this union is in the Spirit, who abides in the elect for ever. 3. Thou hast discovered, That 'the mountains shall depart, and the hills be removed, but my kindness shall not depart from thee, neither shall the covenant of my peace be removed, saith the Lord, that hath mercy on thee,' Isa. liv. 10. 4. Thou hast said, That *the saints shall be kept by the power of God,* 1 Pet. i. 5. *q. d.* The special power, I mean, to put forth in this world, it is to uphold the spirits of my saints: the special work I have in the world to exercise my power about, it is to keep Christ and the saints together; it is through the power of God, that heaven and earth is kept up, but if God must withdraw his power from the one of these, sooner should heaven and earth fall in pieces, than God would not uphold one gracious soul that hath union with his Son Jesus Christ. And if these be thy sayings, why then, Lord, I desire the accomplishment? O fulfil what thou hast said: it would break my heart, if ever the covenant should be broken betwixt me

and

and thee; my desire is towards thee, and the more I enjoy thee, the more and more I desire and pant after thee; my desires are like thyself, infinite, eternal, everlasting desires.

4. Desire after Jesus, the great business, or the All in all, in a covenant of grace: the most proper object of desire, especially to man fallen, is Jesus Christ: hence it is, that a poor sinner, under the sense of sin, cries out with that vehemency of desire, Rutherford's trial of faith, 'Christ, and none 'but Christ; give me Christ, or I die; I am un-'undone, I am lost for ever.' But what is Christ, or Jesus to a covenant of grace? I answer, He is the great business, he is the All in all. Christ hath at least a six-fold relation to the covenant of grace. 1. As he is more than a creature, he is the covenant itself. 2. As he deals betwixt parties, he is the messenger of the covenant. 3. As he saw, heard, and testifieth all, he is the witness of the covenant. 4. As he undertaketh for the parties at variance, he is the surety of the covenant. 5. As he standeth between the contrary parties, he is the Mediator of the covenant. 6. As he signeth the covenant, and closeth all the articles, he is the Testator of the covenant. O, here is abundance of fuel for thy desire to work upon. 1. Consider the fuel, and then set on flame thy desire.

1. Christ as the covenant itself, 'I gave thee for ' a covenant of the people, for a light of the Gen-' tiles, Isa. xlii. 7. And, I will preserve thee, and ' give thee for a covenant of the people,' Isa. xli. 9. Christ, God and man, is all the covenant: 1. Fundamentally, he is the original of the covenant; the covenant of grace takes its being and beginning from Christ, he is the covenant maker, undertaker, manager, dispatcher, he doth every thing in the covenant. 2. Materially, the very substance of the covenant standeth in this, ' I will be their God, and ' they shall be my people.' Now, Christ he is both these in himself; he is God unto his people, and he is the people representatively unto God, and before God. 3. Equivalently, many branches or fruits of the covenant are to be fulfilled to believers in their season; but, as soon as ever they are justified, Christ is said to be the covenant, as a present pawn or earnest delivered into the hands of a man at the very instant of his justification; and this pawn is of equal value and worth of the whole covenant when it is fulfilled to the uttermost. Thus Christ in every of these respects, is the covenant itself, he is the very peace and reconciliation itself, ' And this man shall be the peace, when the Assyrian shall come into our land,' Mic. v. 5. As fire is hot for itself, and all things hot for it, as they participate of it; so Christ is the covenant itself, and all we are so far in covenant to Christ, as we have any thing of Christ; want Christ, and want peace, and want the covenant of grace.

2. Christ is the messenger of the covenant, *The Lord, whom ye seek, shall suddenly come to his temple, even the messenger of the covenant whom ye delight in,* Mal. iii. 1. Christ travels with tidings between the parties of the covenant. 1. He reports of God to us, he commends his Father to us, ' My Father is the husbandman, and this is ' the Father's will which hath sent me, that of all ' which he hath given me I should lose nothing,' John xv. 1. John vi. 39, 48. John viii. 12. And he commends himself to us. It became the Lord Jesus to commend himself, ' I am the bread of ' life, I am the light of the world, I am the door, ' I am the good shepherd,' John x. 9, 11. It is a wonderful thing how Christ is a broker (as I may say) for Christ; ' Wisdom crieth out she uttereth ' her voice in the streets, Come, eat of my bread, ' and drink of the wine which I have mingled,' Pro. i. 20. and ix. 5. Ministers cannot speak of Christ, and of his Father, as he can do himself. O my soul, to excite thy desires, come, and hear Christ, speak of Christ, and of his Father, and of heaven, for he saw all. 2. He reports of us to God, he commends us to his Father: ' O righteous Father, the world hath not known thee, but I have known thee, and these have known that thou hast sent me,' John xvii. 25. Christ gives a good report of the saints in heaven; the Father and Son are speaking of them (as I may say) behind back. And surely a good report in heaven is of high esteem; Christ tells over Ephraim's prayer behind his back, ' I ' have surely heard Ephraim bemoaning himself ' thus, Thou hast chastised me, and I was chastised, ' as a bullock unaccustomed to the yoke; turn thou ' me, and I shall be turned, thou art the Lord my ' God:' And thereupon God resolves, ' Is Ephraim ' my dear Son? Is he a pleasant child? for since ' I spake against him I do earnestly remember him ' still, therefore my bowels are troubled for him, ' I will surely have mercy upon him, saith the Lord,' Jer.

Jer. xxxi. 18, 20. Happy souls of whom Christ is telling good tidings in heaven! he is the angel of the covenant.

3. He is the witness of the covenant; he saw, and heard all, 'Behold, I have given him for a witness to the people,' Isa lv. 4. And he is called, 'The faithful witness, The Amen, The faithful and true witness,' Rev. i. 5. and iii. 14. The covenant saith, 'The Son of man came to seek, and to save that which was lost;' Luke xix. 10. Amen, saith Christ, I can witness that to be true. The covenant saith, Christ died, and rose again for sinners; Amen, saith Christ, *I was dead, and behold, I live for evermore,* Amen, Rev. i. 18. There is not any thing said in the covenant, but Christ is a witness to it, and therefore we read in the very end of the Bible, this subscription (as I may call it) in relation to Christ, *He which testifieth these things, saith, Surely I come quickly.* Amen, Rev. xxii. 20.

4. Christ is the surety of the covenant: *In as much as not without an oath he was made a priest: —By so much was Jesus made a surety of a better testament,* Heb. vii. 20, 22. The covenant of works had a promise, but because it was to be broken, and done away, it hath no oath of God as this hath: O doubting soul, thou sayest, Thy salvation is not sure, think on this scripture, thou hast the oath of God for it; it is a sworn article of the covenant, *Believe in the Lord Jesus, and thou shalt be saved.* And to this end is Christ a Surety. 1. Surety for God, he undertakes, that God shall fulfil his part of the covenant, *Fear not, little flock, for it is your Father's good pleasure to give you the kingdom,* Luke xii. 32. And *all that the Father giveth me, shall come to me, and him that cometh unto me, I will in nowise cast out,* John vi. 37. 2. Surety for us; and to this purpose he hath paid a ransom for us, and giveth a new heart to us, and he is engaged to lose none of us, *Those that thou gavest me, I have kept, and none of them is lost,* John xvii. 12.

5. Christ is the Mediator of the covenant: the apostle calls him *Jesus the Mediator of the new covenant,* Heb. xii. 24. He hath something of God, as being true God; and something of man, as sharing with us of the nature of man; hence he is a Mediator by office, and layeth his hands on both parties, as *a days-man doth,* Job ix. 33.

And in this respect he is a friend, a reconciler, and a servant. 1. A friend to both parties, he hath God's heart for man, to be gracious, and he hath man's heart for God, to satisfy justice. 2. A reconciler of both parties; he brings down God to a treaty of peace, he brings up man by a ransom paid, so that he may say unto both, 'Father, come down to my brethren, my kindred and flesh, and thou, my sister, and spouse, come up to my Father, and thy Father, to my God, and thy God.' 3. He is a servant to both parties, *Behold my servant,* saith God, *my righteous servant,* Isa. xxiv. 1. and liii. 11. Yea, and our servant, 'He came not to be served, but to serve, and to give his life a ransom for many,' Matth. xx. 28.

6. Christ is the Testator of the covenant: he died to this very end, that he might confirm the covenant, 'Where a testament is, there must also of necessity be the death of the testator, for a testament is of force after men are dead, otherwise it is of no strength at all whilst the testator liveth,' Heb. ix. 16, 17. Christ then must die, and Christ's blood must be shed, to seal the covenant of grace: it is not every blood, but Christ's blood, that must seal the everlasting covenant, Heb. xiii. 20. And his blood being shed, he is then rightly called the Testator of the covenant.

O what fuel is here to set our desires on flames? Come, soul, and bend thy desires towards Christ, as the sun-flower towards the sun, the iron to the load-stone, and the load-stone to the pole-star: yea, the nearer thou drawest towards Christ, the more and more do thou desire after Christ; true desires never determine or expire: 'He that thirsts let him thirst more, (saith Bernard, *Delect. Evang. Serm.*) and he that desires, let him desire yet more abundantly'. Is there not cause? O what excellencies hast thou found in Christ? Poor soul, thou hast undone thyself by sin, there is but a step betwixt thee and damnation, but, to save thy soul, Christ 'comes leaping on the mountains, and skipping on the hills:' He enters into a covenant with God, he is the covenant, the messenger of the covenant, the witness of the covenant, the surety of the covenant, the Mediator of the covenant, the Testator of the covenant, the great business, the All in all in a covenant of grace. If David could say, *My soul breaks for the longings that it hath to thy judgments at all times,* Psal. cxix. 20. How mayest thou

thou say, 'My soul breaks for the longings that it hath to thy mercies, and my Jesus at all times?' Oh! I gasp for grace, as the thirsty land for drops of rain; I thirst, I faint, I languish, I long for an hearty draught of the *fountain opened to the house of David, and to the inhabitants of Jerusalem.* Oh! that I could see Jesus flying through the midst of heaven, with the covenant in his hand! Oh I long for that angel of the covenant! Oh I long to see such another vision as John did, when he said, *And I saw another angel fly in the midst of heaven, having the everlasting gospel to preach unto them that dwell upon the earth.* What? Is that covenant in the hand of Christ? And is my name written in that roll? Say Lord, is my name written on the heart of Christ? Oh! if I had the glory and possession of all the world, if I had ten thousand worlds, and ten thousand lives, I would lay them all down, to have this poor trembling soul of mine assured of this: Oh my thirst is insatiable, my bowels are hot within me, my desire after Jesus in reference to the covenant is greedy as the grave, the coals thereof are coals of fire, which hath a most vehement flame.

SECT. IV.

Of hoping in Jesus in that respect.

4. WE must *hope* in Jesus carrying on the great work of our salvation, in a way of covenant: now, what is hope but a good opinion of enjoying its object? Indeed a good opinion is so necessary for *hope*, that it makes almost all its kinds and differences; as it is greater, or lesser, so it causeth the strength or weakness, the excess or defect of this passion, *hope*: this good opinion is that which renders *hope* either doubtful or certain; if certain, it produceth confidence, or presumption; presumption is nothing but an immoderate hope without a ground: but confidence is that assurance of the thing hoped for in some measure, as if we had it already in hand. Hence it is, That we usually say we have great, and strong, and good hopes, when we would speak them assured; which hath occasioned some to define it thus, hope is a certain grounded confidence, that the desired good will come. Not to insist on this, all the question is, whether those promises contained in the covenant of grace belong unto me; and what are the grounds and foundations on which my *hope* is built? If the grounds be weak, then hope is doubtful, or presumptuous: but if the grounds be right, then hope is right, and I may cast anchor, and build upon it.

In the disquisition of these grounds, we shall only search into these qualifications, which the scripture tells us they are qualified with, with whom the Lord enters into a covenant of grace; and these we shall reduce, 1. To the condition of the covenant. 2. To the promise of the covenant. As——

1. If thou art in covenant with God, then hath God wrought in thee that condition of the covenant, a true, and lively, and soul-saving, and justifying faith. *Believe on the Lord Jesus, and thou shalt be saved,* Acts xvi. 31. *If thou believest, thou shalt be saved,* Rom. x. 9. The promise of life contained in the covenant is made only to believers. This is so sure a way of trial, that the apostle himself directs us thereunto, *Examine yourselves whether you be in the faith,* 2 Cor. xiii. 5. Ay, but how shall I examine, for there are many pretenders to faith in these days? Why, thus, 1. True faith will carry thee out of thyself, into Christ, *I live, yet not I, but Christ liveth in me,* Gal. ii. 20. A faithful man hath not his life in himself, but in Christ Jesus: he hath his spiritual being in the Father, and in his Son Jesus Christ, he is joined to the Lord, and is one spirit; he seeth the Father in the Son, and the Son within himself, and also the Father within himself thro' the Son; *know ye not that Christ Jesus is in you, except ye be reprobates?* 2 Cor. xiii. 5. *Ye shall know me* (saith Christ) *that I am in the Father, and you in me, and I in you,* John xiv. 20. By faith we enjoy the glory of union; *The glory which thou hast given me, I have given them, that they may be one, even as we are one, I in them, and thou in me,* John xvii. 22, 23. Though we have not the glory of equality, yet we have the glory of likeness; we are one with Christ, and one with the Father by faith in Christ. 2. True faith will carry thee beyond the world; a believer looks on Christ overcoming the world for him, and so by that faith he overcomes the world thro' him; *This is the victory that overcometh the world, even your faith,* 1 John v. 4. Hence it is that the saints are said *to be*

be clothed with the sun, to have the moon under their feet, Rev. i. 12. When through faith they are clothed with *the Sun of righteousness,* the Lord Jesus, then they trample upon all sublunary things as nothing worth in comparison of Christ. 3. True faith is ever accompanied with true love: if once by faith thou apprehendest God's love and Christ's love to thee, thou canst not but love that God, and love that Christ who loved thee, and gave himself for thee; *We love him, because he first loved us,* 1 John iv. 19. He that loveth not God, hath not apprehended God's love to him; if ever God in Christ be presented to thee for thy justification, it is such a lovely object, that thou canst not but love him; *he that loveth not, knoweth not God, for God is love,* 1 Joh. iv. 8. 4. True faith purifies the heart, and purgeth out sin. 'When God discovers this, that 'he will heal back-sliding, and love freely, and 'turn away his anger;' Then Ephraim shall say, *What have I any more to do with idols?* Hos. xiv. 8. If ever Christ reveal himself as the object of our justification, he will be sure to present himself as the pattern of our sanctification: the knowledge of God's goodness will make us in love with holiness; *They shall fear and tremble, for all the goodness, and for all the prosperity, that I procure unto them, faith the Lord,* Jer. xxxiii. 9. The golden chain of mercy let down from heaven, doth bind us faster to the service of our God. 5. Above all observe the rise, true faith, if it be true, it is ever bottomed upon the sense and pain of a lost condition; spiritual poverty is the nearest capacity of believing: this is faith's method, *Be condemned, to be saved, be sick, and be healed.* Faith is a flower of Christ's own planting, but it grows in no soul, but only on the margin and brink of the lake of fire and brimstone, in regard there's none so fit for Christ and heaven, as those who are self-sick, and self condemned to hell. *They that be whole need not a physician* (saith Christ) *but they that are sick,* Mat. ix. 13. This is a foundation of Christ, that because the man is broken, and hath not bread, therefore he must be sold, and Christ must buy him, and take him home to his own fire-side, and clothe him, and feed him there. I know Satan argues thus, 'Thou art not worthy of Christ, and therefore 'what hast thou to do with Christ?' but faith concludes otherwise, I am not worthy of Christ, I am out of measure sinful, I tremble at it, and I 'am sensible of it, and therefore ought I, and 'therefore must I come to Christ.' This arguing is gospel-logic, and the right method of a true and saving faith: for what is faith, but the act of a sinner humbled, weary, laden, poor, and self-condemned? Oh take heed of their doctrine who make faith the act of some vile person never humbled, but applying with an immediate touch, his hot, boiling and smoaking lusts to the bleeding, blessed wounds and death of Jesus Christ.

2. If thou art in covenant with God, then hath God fulfilled in some part the promises of his covenant to thy soul: as——

1. Then hath God put the law into thy inward parts, and writ it in thy heart: look, as indenture answers to indenture, or as face in the glass answers to a face, so the conformity of thy heart is inwardly to the law of God; thou obeyest God's will, and delightest in that obedience; thou sayest, with David, *I delight to do thy will, O God; yea, thy laws is within my heart,* Psal. xl. 8.

2. Thou hast a covenant-relation to God, and a covenant-interest in God; and thou art by covenant as one of the people of God. Christ hath thy soul, thy body, thy affections, thy love to the very uttermost; God hath a propriety and a peculiarity in thee; thou art Christ's by marriage; thou hast past over thyself unto him to be his jewel, his spouse, his diadem, his crown, his servant, his child for ever.

3. Then art thou clearly taught to know the Lord; thou knowest him in another manner than thou didst before; *I will establish my covenant with thee, and thou shalt know that I am the Lord,* Ezek. xvi. 60, 61. There is a double knowledge. 1. A speculative knowledge, and thus men may know much, but they are not affected according to the things they know. 2 A practical knowledge; and thus, if we know the Lord, we shall see in him that excellency and beauty, that our hearts will be affectioned towards him, and we shall be able to say, that we love him with all our heart, and with all our soul, and with all our strength.

4. Then hath God pardoned thy sins, and he will remember thy sins no more. But how should I be assured of that? Why, thus, 1. If thou hast sincerely confessed, bewailed, and forsaken thy sins; *Wash ye, make ye clean, put away the evil of your do-*

doings from before mine eyes, cease to do evil;—And presently it follows, *Come now, and let us reason together, faith the Lord, tho' your sins be as scarlet, they shall be as white as snow, though they be red like crimson, they shall be as wool,* Isa. i. 16, 18. To the same purpose, *Let the wicked forsake his way, and the unrighteous man his thoughts, and let him return unto the Lord, and he will have mercy upon him, and to our God, for he will abundantly pardon,* If. lv. 7. 2. If thy heart after many storms and troubles be calmed and quieted through faith in Christ; *Being justified by faith, we have peace with God*; Rom. v. 1. What? Hast thou peace with God? and hath God stilled thy soul with peace? This is an argument of thy sins pardon. 3. If thine heart be singulary inflamed with the love of Christ; the woman that *had many sins forgiven her by Christ, she loved him much,* Luke vii. 47. Upon that account she wept, and washed his feet with her tears, and so wiped them with the hairs of her head, she kissed his feet, and anointed them with ointment, nothing was too good for Christ who had forgiven her all her sins. 4. If thy heart and soul, and all that is within be singularly enlarged to praise God for his pardons; 'Bless the Lord, O my soul, and for-'get not all his benefits; who forgiveth all thine 'iniquities, Psalm ciii. 1, 2, 3. If thine heart feel his pardons, thy mouth will sing his praises: and hereby thou mayest be assured that God hath pardoned all thy sins.

Come now, are these, O my soul, the grounds of thy hopes; a lively faith in Jesus, an accomplishment in some measure of the promises of the covenant? Why, these are the fuel of hope; if this be thy case, act thy hope strongly on Christ and on the covenant of grace: say not, hope is only of things future; and therefore if I be already in covenant, what need I hope? For whether thou art in covenant or no, it is the main question here, nay, though it be granted, that thou art in covenant, and that hope is swallowed up in the complete presence of its object; yet it is not at all diminished, but rather increased by a partial presence. As in massy bodies, though violent motion be weakest in the end; yet natural motions are ever swiftest towards the centre: so in the hopes of men, though such as are violent and groundless prove weaker and weaker, yet those that are stayed and natural (or rather gracious) are evermore stronger and stronger, till they procure the utmost presence and union of their object. The nearer we come to fruition of a good, the more impatient we are to want it. O then hope in Jesus! draw on thy hope yet more and more in this covenant of grace: be not content only with an hope of expectation, but bring it on to an hope of confidence, or assurance; thou canst not fail if thou hangest thy hope on Jesus: Christ is not fastened as a loose nail, or as a broken rotten hedge in the covenant of grace; he is there, *As a nail in a sure place; and they shall hang on him all the glory of his Father's house; the off-spring and the issue; all vessels of small quantity, from the vessels of cups, even to all the vessels of flaggons,* Isa. xxii. 23, 24. Come, soul, thou art a vessel of small quantity, hang all thy weight on Christ, he is a nail that cannot break.

SECT. V.

Of believing on Jesus in that respect.

5. WE must believe on Jesus carrying on this great work of our salvation in a way of covenant. Many a time Satan comes and hurls in a temptation, what! 'is it likely that God should 'enter into a covenant with thee?' Yea, sometimes he so rivets in this temptation, that he darkens all within, and there's no light of comfort in the soul: O but now believe! now, if ever is the season for faith to act; little evidence and much adherence speaks faith to purpose. We read of some who could stay themselves upon the Lord, whilst they walked in darkness upon the margin and borders of an hundred deaths. David *fears no evil, though he walked thro' the valley of the shadow of death*; for his faith told him, That *God was with him*, Psal. xxiii. 4. Heman could say, *Thy wrath lieth hard upon me, thou hast afflicted me with all thy waves*, Psalm lxxxviii. 7. Sure he thought God could do no more to draw him; not only a wave or two, but all God's waves were on him, and over him, and yet he believes, *Lord, I have called daily upon thee.* ver. 9. Hezekiah's comforts were at an hard pinch, *Mine eyes fail with looking upwards: O Lord, I am oppressed*; yet prayer argues believing, *Lord, undertake for me,* Isa. xxxix. 14. Christ's sense of comforts was ebb and low, when he

he wept, and cried that he was forsaken of God; yet then his faith is doubled, as the cable of an anchor is doubled when the storm is more than ordinary, *My God, my God*, Matth. xxvii. 46.

Poor soul! thou standest wondering at this great condescension of God; 'What, that God should 'enter into covenant with me? What, that God 'should make such great and precious promises 'with me? Surely these comforts, and these pri-'vileges are too high for me, or for any soul 'breathing.'———It may be so, and yet be not discouraged; for God will magnify his grace, and therefore he will do this great thing; all that thou hast to do, and all that God requires of thee, is only to believe: indeed thou hast no part in Christ, no part in the covenant of grace, if thou wilt not believe; faith is the condition of the covenant of grace; and therefore either believe, or no covenant.

I know it is not easy to believe; nay, it is one of the hardest things under heaven to persuade a soul into faith: What! 'will the great God of 'heaven make a covenant with such a wretch as 'I am? I cannot believe it.' Why? what's the matter? 'Ah! my sins, my sins, my sins! God is 'a consuming fire against such, he cannot endure to behold iniquity; little hopes that ever God shall enter into a covenant with me.' But to help on, or to allure a soul in, consider, O thou soul, of these following passages.

1. Consider of the sweet and gracious nature of God: that which undoes broken hearts, and trembling souls, it is misconceivings of God: we have many times low, diminishing, extenuating thoughts of God's goodness: but we have large thoughts of his power and wrath: now to rectify these misapprehensions, consider his name, and therein his nature, *The Lord, the Lord God, merciful, and gracious, long-suffering, and abundant in goodness and truth, keeping mercy for thousands, forgiving iniquity, transgressions, and sins; and that will by no means clear the guilty, visiting the iniquity of the fathers upon the children, and upon the childrens children, unto the third and fourth generation*, Exod. xxiv. 6, 7. O terrible text! says the soul, alas! I am guilty of thousands of sins; and if this be his name, I am undone, wo to me and mine unto the third and fourth generation. But consider again, and in this description of God we shall find an ocean of mercy, to a drop of wrath; a sea of oil, to an half drop of scalding lead. For,———

1. God doth not begin, *The Lord, the Lord, that will by no means clear the guilty:* but *the Lord, the Lord, merciful and gracious, long-suffering*; this is the first and greatest part of his name: God is loth to speak in justice and wrath; he keeps it to the last: mercy lies uppermost in God's heart: if the sentence must come, it shall be the last day of the assize.

2. Many words are used to speak his goodness: *merciful, gracious, long-suffering and abundant in goodness, keeping mercy for thousands, forgiving iniquity, transgression and sin:* here be six several phrases to shew the riches of his goodness; but when he speaks his wrath, what haste makes he over it? There is only two expressions of that; it was a theme he took no delight in; judgment is *his work, his strange work; for he doth not afflict willingly, nor grieve the children of men*, Isa. xxviii. 21. Lam. iii. 33.

3. There's a difference in the expression: when God speaks of mercy, he expresseth it thus, *Abundant in mercy, keeping mercy for thousands*. But in visiting sins, it is not to thousands; but only to the third or fourth generation. Surely *mercy rejoiceth against judgment*, Jam. ii. 13. God would shew mercy to thousands, rather than he would destroy three or four.

4. What if by no means God will clear the guilty, stubbornly guilty; yet never will he destroy humble souls, that lie at his feet, and are willing to have mercy on his easy terms. *How shall I give thee up, Ephraim, how shall I deliver thee, O Israel? How shall I make thee as Admah? How shall I set thee as Zeboim? My heart is turned within me, my repentings are kindled together, I will not execute the fierceness of my anger, I will not destroy Ephraim; for I am God and not man, the holy One in the midst of thee*, Hosea xi. 8, 9. O my soul! why standest thou at a distance with God? Why dost thou fancy a lion in the way? O believe in God, believe in Jesus! and believe thy portion in this covenant of grace! have sweet and delightful thoughts of God's nature, and thou wilt not, thou canst not fly from him: some are of opinion, ' That a soul may fetch more encouragements to believe, from the consideration of God's gracious
' and

'and merciful nature, than from the promise itself.

2. Consider of the sweet and gracious nature of Jesus Christ: our thoughts of God are necessarily more strange than of Jesus Christ; because of our infinite distance from the God-head; but in Christ God is come down into our nature, and so infinite goodness and mercy is incarnate; art thou afraid, O my soul, at his name *Jah*, and *Jehovah?* O remember his name is Emmanuel; the lion is here disrobed of his garment of terror; his rough hair is turned into a soft wool; see thy God disrobed of his terrible majesty, see thy God is a man, and thy Judge is a brother; mince Jehovah with Jesus, and the serpent will be a rod; O that balsamy name, Jesus; that name that sounds healing for every wound, settlement for every distraction, comfort for every sorrow: but here's the misery, souls in distress had rather be poring on hell than heaven; rather frighting themselves with the terrors of justice, than staying themselves with the flaggons of mercy. O my soul, how canst thou more contradict the nature of Christ, and the gospel-description of Christ, than to think him a destroyer of men? But wherein appears the gracious nature of Christ? I answer, In his being incarnate. Oh! How could Jesus have manifested more willingness to save, than that the God-head should condescend to assume our nature? Surely this is ten thousand times more condescension, than for the greatest king to become a fly, or a toad, to save such creatures as toads or flies. 2. In his tender dealing with all sorts of sinners, he professed that he *came into the world, not to condemn the world, but that the world through him might be saved.* He wept over Jerusalem, saying, *O Jerusalem, Jerusalem, how oft would I have gathered thee, as an hen gathereth her chickens under her wings? But ye would not,* Matth. xxiii. 37. I would, but ye would not. And when his disciples would have had fire come down from heaven to consume those that refused him, he reproves them, and tells them, *they knew not of what Spirit they were of.* 3. In his care of his own; not caring what he suffered, so they might be saved. Alas! alas! that the Lord Jesus should pass through a life of misery, to a death more miserable, to manifest openly to the world the abundance of his love; and yet that any soul should suspect him of cruelty, or unwillingness to shew mercy! Ah, my soul, believe; never cry out, *My sins, my sins, my sins*; there is a gracious nature and inclination in Jesus Christ to pardon all.

3. Consider of that office of saving and shewing mercy, which Christ hath set up; this is more than merely a gracious inclination; Christ hath undertaken and set up an office to seek, and to save that which was lost; to bring home straying souls to his Father, to be the great peace-maker, between God and man; to reconcile God to man, and man to God, and so to be the head and husband of his people. Is not here a world of encouragement to believe in Jesus? What? To consider him as one who hath made it his office to heal, and to relieve, and restore, and to reconcile? Among merchants, I remember they have an office of security, that if you dare not adventure on seas, yet there you may be ensured, if you will put in at that office: in this manner Christ hath constituted and assumed the office of being the Mediator, the Redeemer and the Saviour of men; he hath erected, and set up on purpose an office of mere love, and tender compassion, for the relief of all poor distressed sinners, if they dare not venture otherwise, yet, let them put in at this office. O what jealous hearts have we that will not trust Christ, that will not take the word of Christ without an office of security? Surely Christ never so carried himself to any soul, that it need be jealous of his love and faithfulness, yet this dear husband meets with many a jealous spouse; O my soul, take heed of this! Satan hath no greater design upon thee, than to persuade thee to entertain hard thoughts of Christ: Believe! never say, God will not take thee into covenant, for to this purpose he hath erected an office to save and shew mercy.

4. Consider of those tenders and offers of Christ, those intreaties and beseechings to accept of Christ, which are made in the gospel. What is the gospel? Or, what is the sum of all the gospel, but this? 'O take Christ, and life in Christ, that thou 'mayest be saved:' What mean these free offers, *Ho, every one that thirsteth come to the waters, and whosoever will, let him take of the waters of life freely.* And, *God so loved the world, That he gave his only begotten Son,* &c. God is the first suitor and sollicitor, he first prays the soul to take Christ. Hark at the door! who is it that knocks there? Who is it that calls now, even now? *Open unto me, my sister, my love, my dove, my undefiled,*

for

for my head is filled with dew, and my locks with the drops of the night, Cant. v. 2. See him through the windows, this can be none but Christ; his sweet language of *sister, love*, and *dove*, bespeaks him Christ; his suffering language, That *his head is filled with dew, and his locks with the drops of the night*, bespeaks him Christ: but hearken the motion he makes to thy soul, 'Soul! consider what 'price I have given to save thee, this my body 'was crucified, my hands and feet nailed, my heart 'pierced, and through anguish I was forced to cry, 'My soul is heavy, heavy unto death, and now 'what remains for thee but only to believe? See 'all things ready on my part, remission, justifica-'tion, sanctification, salvation; I will be thy God, 'and thou shalt be of the number of my people; 'I offer now my self and merits, and benefits flow-'ing therefrom, and I intreat thee accept of this 'offer, O take Christ, and life, and salvation in 'Christ.' What, is this the voice of my beloved; Are these the entreaties of Jesus? And, O my soul, wilt thou not believe? Wilt thou not accept of this gracius offer of Christ? O consider who is this that proclaimeth, inviteth, beseecheth! if a poor man should offer thee mountains of gold thou mightest doubt of performance, because it is contrary to his nature: but Christ is neither poor, nor covetous; as he is able, so his name is gracious, and his nature is to be faithful in performance; his covenant is sealed with his blood, and confirmed by his oath, That all shall have pardon that will but come in and believe; O then let these words of Christ *(Whose lips like lillies are dropping down pure myrrh)* prevail with thy soul, say *Amen* to his offer, *I believe, Lord, help my unbelief*.

5. Consider of those commands of Christ, which, notwithstanding all thy excuses and pretences, he fastens on thee to believe: *And this is his commandment, That we should believe on the name of his Son Jesus Christ*. Surely this command should infinitely out-weigh and prevail against all other countermands of flesh and blood, of Satan, nature, reason, sense, and all the world. Why, this command is thy very ground and warrant against which the very gates of hell can never possibly prevail. When Abraham had a command to kill his own, only dear son, with his own hand, though it was a matter of as great grief as possibly could pierce his heart, yet he would readily and willingly submit to it; how much more shouldest thou obey, when God commands no more but that thou shouldest *believe on the name of his Son Jesus Christ?* There is no evil in this command; No, no, it comprehends in it all good imaginable, have Christ, and thou hast with him the excellency and variety of all blessings both of heaven and earth; have Christ, and thou hast with him a discharge of all those endless and easless torments of hell; have Christ, and thou hast with him the glorious Deity itself to be enjoyed through him to all eternity. O then believe in Jesus! suffer not the devil's cavils, and the groundless exceptions of thine own heart to prevail with thee against the direct commandment of the Almighty God.

6. Consider of these messages of Christ, which he daily sends by the hands of his gospel-ministers. *Now then we are ambassadors for Christ, as though God did beseech you by us, we pray you, in Christ's stead, be ye reconciled unto God*, 2 Cor. v. 20. What a wonder is here? would not an earthly prince disdain and hold it in foul scorn to send unto his inferior rebellious slaves for reconcilement? It is otherwise with Christ, he is content to put up at our hands all indignities and affronts; he is glad to sue to us first, and to send his ambassadors day after day, beseeching us to be reconciled unto him: O incomprehensible depth of unspeakable mercy and encouragement to come to Christ. That I may digress a little, say thou that readest, Wilt thou take Christ to thy bridegroom, and forsake all others? This is the message which God hath bid me (unworthy ambassador) to deliver to thee; the Lord Jesus expects an answer from thee, and I should be glad at heart to return a fit answer to him that sent me: say then, Dost thou like well of the match? Wilt thou have Christ for thy husband? Wilt thou enter into covenant with him? Wilt thou surrender up thy soul to thy God? Wilt thou rely on Christ, and apply Christ's merits particularly to thyself? Wilt thou believe? for that is it I mean by *taking, and receiving, and marrying of Christ*; Oh, happy I, if I could but join Christ and thy soul together this day! O happy thou, if thou wouldest this day be persuaded by a poor ambassador of Christ! Blame me not if I am an inportunate messenger: if ever I hear from thee, let me hear some good news, that I may return it to heaven.

and give God the glory. Come! say on! art thou willing to have Christ? Wouldest thou have thy name inrolled in the covenant of grace? Shall God be thy God, and Christ thy Christ? Wilt thou have the person of Christ, and all those privileges flowing from the blood of Christ? Sure thou art willing, Art thou not? Stay then, thou must take Christ on these terms, thou must believe on him. *i. e.* Thou must take him as thy Saviour and Lord, thou must take him and forsake all others for him. This is true faith, the condition of the covenant: O believe in Jesus, and the match is made, the hands are struck, the covenant established, and all doubts removed.

SECT. VI.

Of loving Jesus in that respect.

6. WE must love Jesus, as carrying on this great work of our salvation in a way of covenant. I know love is reckoned as the first and fundamental passion of all the rest; some call it the first springing or out-going affection of the soul: and therefore I might have put it in the first place before hope or desire, but I chuse rather to place it in this method, as (methinks) most agreeing (if not to the order of nature, yet) to the spiritual workings, as they appear in my soul: when a God is propounded, first I desire, and then I hope, and then I believe, and then I love. And some describing this spiritual love; they tell me, ' It is an holy disposition of the heart, arising from ' faith.' *Dr. Preston of Love.* But, to let these niceties pass for a spider's web, (curious, but thin) certain it is, that I cannot believe all these transactions of God by Christ in a covenant-way for me, but I must needs love that God, and love that Christ, who hath thus first and freely loved my soul: Go on then, O my soul, put fire to the earth, blow on thy little spark, set before thee God's love, and thou canst not but love, and therein consider, 1. The time. 2. The properties. 3. The effects of God's love. 1. For the time; he loved thee before the world was made: hast thou not heard, and wilt thou ever forget it? Were not these ancient loves from all eternity admirable, astonishing, ravishing loves? 2. He loved thee in the very beginning of the world, was not the promise expressed to Adam, intended for thee? As thou sinnedst in his loins, so didst thou not in his loins receive the promise. *It shall bruise thy head?* And not long after, when God established his covenant with Abraham and his seed, wast thou not one of that seed of Abraham? *If ye are Christ's, then are ye Abraham's seed, and heirs according to the promise,* Gal. iii. 29. 3. He loves thee now more especially, not only with a love of benevolence, as before, but with a love of complacency: not only hath he struck covenant with Christ, with Adam, with Abraham in thy behalf; and O what a love is this? If a woman, lately conceiving, love her future fruit, how much more doth she love it when it is born and embraced in her arms? So if God loved thee before thou hadst a being, yea, before the world, or any creature in it had a being, how much more now? O the height, and depth, and length, and breadth of this immeasurable love! O, my soul, I cannot express the loves of God in Christ to thee; I but draw the picture of the sun with a coal, when I endeavour to express God's love in Christ.

2. For the properties of this love. 1. God's love to thee is an eternal love. He was thinking in his eternity of thee in this manner, ' At such a ' time there shall be such a man, and such a woman ' living on the earth, in the last times such a one ' (I mean thou that readest, if thou believest) and ' to that soul I will reveal myself, and communi' cate my loves; to that soul I will offer Christ, ' and give it the hand of faith to lay hold on Christ; ' and to that purpose now I write down the name ' in the book of life, and none shall be able to ' blot it out again' Oh, eternal love! Oh, the blessed transaction between the Father and the Son, from all eternity, to manifest his love to thy very soul!

2. God's love to thee is a choice love; it is an elective separating love: when he passed by, and left many thousands, then, even then he sets his heart on thee; ' Was not Esau Jacob's brother, ' saith God? Yet I loved Jacob, and hated Esau,' Mal. i. 2, 3. So, wert not thou such a one's brother, or such a one's sister that remained wicked and ungodly? Were not thou of such a family, whereas many, or some, are passed by, and yet God hath loved thee, and pitched his love on thee? Surely this is choice love.

3. God's love to thee is a free love: *I will love them*

them freely, faith God, Hof. xiv. 4. *And the Lord did not set his love upon you, and chuse you, because ye were more in number than any people,—but because the Lord loved you*. Deut. vii. 7, 8. There can be no other reason why the Lord loved thee, but because he loved thee; we use to say, This is a woman's reason; 'I will do it, because I will do it. But here we find it is God's reason, though it may seem strange arguing, yet Moses can go no higher; he loved thee, Why? Because he loved thee.

4. God's love to thee is love of all relations; look what a friend's love is to a friend, or what a father's love is towards a child, or what an husband's love is towards a wife, such is God's love to thee; thou art his friend, his son, his daughter, his spouse; and God is thy All in all.

3. For the effects of his love, 1. God so loves thee, as that he hath entered into a covenant with thee. O what a love was this? Tell me, O my soul, is there not an infinite disparity betwixt God and thee? He is God above, and thou art a worm below: *He is the high and lofty One that inhabiteth eternity, whose name is holy*, and thou art less than the least of all the mercies of God, O wonder at such a condescension! that such a potter and such a former of things should come on terms of bargaining with such clay as is guilty before him! had we the tongues of men and angels, we could never express it.

2. God so loves thee, as that in the covenant he gives thee all his promises; indeed what is the covenant, but an accumulation or heap of promises? As a cluster of stars makes a constellation, so a mass of promises concurreth in the covenant of grace; wherever Christ is, clusters of divine promises grow out of him; as the motes, rays, and beams are from the sun. I shall instance in some few. As—

1. God in the covenant gives the world. *All is yours, whether Paul, or Apollos, or Cephas, or the world,* 1 Cor. iii. 22. *First seek the kingdom of God, and his righteousness, and all these things shall be added unto you*, Matth. vi. 33. These temporary blessings are a part of the covenant, which God hath made to his people, *It is he that giveth thee power to get wealth, that he may establish his covenant which he sware unto thy fathers,* Deut. vii. 18. Others, I know, may have the world, but they have it not by a covenant-right; it may be thou hast but a little, a very little of the world; well, but thou hast it by a covenant-right, and so it is an earnest of all the rest.

2. As God in the covenant gives thee the world, so in comparison of thee and his other saints, he cares not what becomes of all the world. *I loved thee,* faith God, *therefore will I give men for thee, and people for thy life*; Isa. xliii. 4. If the case be so, that it cannot be well with thee, but great evils must come upon others, kindred, people, and nations, 'I do not so much care for ' them, *faith God,* my heart is on thee, so as in ' comparison of thee I care not what becomes of ' all the world;' O the love of God to his saints!

3. God in the covenant pardons thy sins, this is another fruit of God's love, *Unto him that loved us, and washed us from our sins by his own blood,* Rev. i. 5. It cost him dear to pardon our sins, even the heart-blood of Christ, such were the transactions betwixt God and Christ, If thou wilt take upon thee to deliver souls from sin, faith God to his Son, thou must come thyself and be made a curse for their sin: Well, faith Christ, thy will be done in it, though I lose my life, though it cost me the best blood in my heart, yet let me deliver them from sin. This exceedingly heightens Christ's love, that he should foresee their sin, and that yet he should love; many times we set our love on some untoward unthankful creatures, and we say, Could I have but foreseen this untowardness, they should never have had my love; but now the Lord did foresee all thy sins, and all thy ill requitals for love, and yet it did not once hinder his love towards thee, but he puts this in the covenant, *I will forgive their iniquities, and I will remember their sins no more.*

4. God in the covenant gives thee holiness and sanctification, *I will sprinkle clean water upon you, and ye shall be clean from all your filthiness, and from all your idols will I cleanse you,* Ezek. xxxvi. 25. This holiness is our excellency in the eyes of men and angels; this is the crown and diadem upon the heads of saints; whence David calls them, by the name of *excellent ones,* Psal. xvi. 3. Holiness is a *Spirit of glory,* 1 Pet. iv. 14. It is the delight of God; as a father delights himself in seeing his own image in his children, so God delights himself in the holiness of his saints; God loved them before with a love of benevolence and good will, but

P

now

now he loves them with a love of complacency, *The Lord takes pleasure in those that fear him; the Lord takes pleasure in his people,* Pſal. cxlvii. 11. and cxlix. 4. Holineſs is the very eſſence of God, the divine nature of God. O! what is this, that God ſhould put his own nature into thee? You are partakers of the divine nature, O what a love is this, That God ſhould put his own life into thee? That he ſhould enable thee to live the very ſame life that he himſelf lives? Remember that piece of the covenant, *I will put my law into their inward parts, and write it in their hearts.*

5. God in the covenant gives thee the knowledge of himſelf; it may be that thou kneweſt him before, but 'tis another kind of knowledge that now God gives thee than thou hadſt before; when God teaches the ſoul to know him, it looks on him with another eye, it ſees now another beauty in God, than ever it ſaw before, for all that knowledge that it had before bred not love, only covenant knowledge of God works in the ſoul a true love of God. But how doth this covenant-knowledge work this love? I ſhall tell you my own experiences; I go thro' all the virtues, graces, and excellencies that are moſt amiable, and I look in the ſcriptures, and there I find them in God alone; if ever I ſaw any excellency in any man, or in any creature, I think with myſelf there is more in God that made that creature; *he that made the eye, ſhall he not ſee?* And ſo, he that made that lovelineſs, is not he lovely? Now, when by theſe mediums I have preſented God thus lovely to my ſoul, then I begin to feel my heart to warm. As, when I conceive ſuch an idea of a man, that he is of ſuch a carriage, behaviour, diſpoſition; that he hath a mind thus and thus framed, qualified and beautified, why then I love him: ſo when I apprehend the Lord aright, when I obſerve him as he is deſcribed in his word, when I obſerve his doings, and conſider his workings, and learn from all theſe together a right idea, opinion, or apprehenſion of him, then my will follows, my underſtanding and my affections follow them both; and I come to love God, and to delight in God. O here's a ſweet knowledge! ſurely it was God's love in Chriſt to put this bleſſed article into the covenant of grace, *They ſhall all know me from the leaſt of them unto the greateſt of them,* ſaith the Lord.

6. God in the covenant of grace gives thee his Son, *God ſo loved the world, that he gave his only begotten Son, that whoſoever believeth in him ſhould not periſh, but have everlaſting life,* John iii. 16. Nay more, as God hath given thee his Son, ſo he hath given thee himſelf. O my ſoul, wouldeſt thou not think it a marvellous love, if God ſhould ſay to thee, 'Come, ſoul, I will give thee all the world 'for thy portion; or that I may give thee a teſtimony 'that I love thee, I will make another world for thy 'ſake, and will make thee emperor of that world 'alſo.' Surely thou wouldeſt ſay, God loves me dearly; ay, but in that God hath given thee his Son, and given thee himſelf, this is a greater degree of love; Chriſtians, ſtand amazed! O what love is this to the children of men? Oh that we ſhould live to have our ears filled with this ſound from heaven! *I will be a God to thee, and to thy ſeed after thee, I am the Lord thy God, I will be their God, and they ſhall be my people.* O my ſoul! where haſt thou been? Rouſe up and recollect, and ſet before thee all the paſſages of God's love in Chriſt; are not theſe ſtrong attractions to gain thy loves? What wilt thou do? Canſt thou chooſe to love the Lord thy God? Shall not all this love of God in Chriſt to thee conſtrain thy love? It is the expreſſion of the apoſtle, *The love of Chriſt conſtrains us,* 2 Cor. v. 14. God in Chriſt is the very element of love, and whither ſhould love go but to the element? Air goes to air, and earth to earth, and all the rivers to the ſea: every element will to its proper place. Now, *God is love,* 1 John iv. 16. And whither ſhould thy love be carried but to the ocean or ſea of love? *Come, my beloved,* (ſaid the ſpouſe to Chriſt) *let us get up early to the vineyards, let us ſee if the vine flouriſh, whether the tender grapes appear, there will I give thee my loves,* Cant. vii. 12. The flouriſhing of the vine, and the appearing of the tender grapes, are the fruits of the graces of God in the aſſemblies of his ſaints: now, whereſoever theſe things appear, whether in aſſemblies, or in ſecret ordinances, then and there (ſaith the bride) *will I give thee my loves.* When thou comeſt to the word, prayer, meditation, be ſure of this, to give Chriſt thy love: what? Doth Chriſt manifeſt his preſence there? Is there any abounding of his graces there? O let thy love abound; by how much more thou feeleſt God's love towards thee, by ſo much

much more do thou love thy God again. Many sins being forgiven, how shouldest thou but love much?

SECT. VII.
Of joying in Jesus in that respect.

7. WE must joy in Jesus, as carrying on the great work of our salvation in a way of covenant. I know our *joy* here is but in part; such is the excellency of spiritual *joy*, that it is reserved for heaven; God will not permit it to be pure and perfect here below; and yet such as it is (though mingled with cares and pains) it is a blessed duty; it is the light of our souls; and were it quite taken away, our lives would be nothing but horror and confusion. O my soul, if thou didst not hope to encounter joy in all thy acts, thou wouldest remain languishing and immoveable, and wouldest be without action and vigour, thou wouldest speak no more of Jesus or of a covenant of grace, or of God, or Christ, or life, or grace, or glory. Well, then go on, O my soul, and joy in Jesus; if thou lovest him, what should hinder thy rejoicing in him? It is a maxim, That as love proceeds, so if there be nothing which retains the appetite, it always goes from love to joy. One motion of the appetite towards good is to be united to it, and the next appetite towards good is to enjoy it. Now, love consists in union, and joy in fruition: for what is fruition but a joy that we find in the possession of that thing we love? Much ado there is amongst philosophers concerning the differences of love and joy. Some give it thus; as is the motion of fluid bodies which run towards their centre, and think to find their rest there; but being there, they stop not, and therefore they return, and scatter themselves on themselves, they swell and overflow: so, in the passion of love, the appetite runs to the beloved object, and unites itself to it, and yet its motion ends not there; for by this passion of joy it returns the same way; again it scatters itself on itself, and overflows those powers which are nearest to it; by this effusion the soul doubles on the image of the good it hath received, and so it thinks to possess it the more; it distils itself into that faculty which first acquainted it with the knowledge of the object, and by that means it makes all the parts of the soul concur to the possession of it. Hence they say, That joy is an effusion of the appetite, whereby the soul spreads itself on what is good, to possess it the more perfectly.

But, not to stay in the enquiry of its nature, O my soul, be thou in the exercise of this joy. Is there not cause? Come, see and own thy blessedness; take notice of the great things the Lord hath done for thee. As——1. He hath made a covenant with thee of temporal mercies, thou hast all thou hast by free-holding of covenant-grace; thy bread is by covenant, thy sleep is by covenant, thy safety from sword is by the covenant, the very tilling of thy land is by a covenant of grace, Ez. xxxvi. 34. O how sweet is this? Every crumb is from Christ, and by virtue of a covenant of grace. 2. He hath made a covenant with thee of spiritual mercies, even a covenant of peace, and grace, and blessing, and life for evermore. God is become thy God; he is all things to thee; he hath forgiven thy sins, he hath given thee his Spirit to lead thee, to sanctify thee, to uphold thee in that state wherein thou standest, and at last he will bring thee to a full enjoyment of himself in glory, where thou shalt bless him, and rejoice before him with joy unspeakable and full of glory. O pluck up thy heart, lift up thy head, strengthen the weak hands and the feeble knees; serve the Lord with gladness, and joyfulness of spirit, considering the day of thy salvation draweth nigh: write it in letters of gold, that thy God is in covenant with thee to love thee, to bless thee, and to save thee. Yet a little while, and he that shall come will come and receive thee to himself, and then thou shalt fully know what it is to have God to be thy God, or to be in covenant with God. I know these objects rejoice not every heart; a man out of covenant, if he look on God, he is a consuming fire; if on the law, it is a sentence of condemnation; if on the earth, it brings forth thorns by reason of sins; if on heaven, the gate is shut; if on the signs in heaven, fire, meteors, thunder strike in him a terror. But, O my soul, this is not thy case; a man in covenant with God looks on all these things with another eye; if he looks on God, he saith, This is my father; if on Christ, This is my elder brother; if on angels, These are my keepers, if on heaven, This is my house; if on the signs of heaven, fire, meteors, thunder, These are but the effects of my father's power; if on the law, The Son of God hath fulfilled it for me; if on prosperity, God hath better things for me in store; if on adversity, Jesus Christ hath suffered much more for me than this, if on the devil, death and hell, he saith with the apostle, *O death, where is thy sting? O grave, or hell, where is thy victory?* 1 Cor. xv. 55. Come, poor soul, is it not thus with thee? What! art thou in covenant with God? Or art thou not? If yet thou doubtest, review thy grounds of hope, and leave not there till thou comest up to the same measure of assurance; but if thou art persuaded of thy interest, O then rejoice therein, is it not a gospel-duty *to rejoice in the Lord, and again to rejoice?* Phil. iv. 4. The Lord is delighted in thy delights, he would fain have it thy constant frame and daily business to live in joy, and to be always delighting thyself in him.

This one promise, *I am the Lord thy God*, is enough to cause thy appetite to run to it, and to unite itself to it by love, and to scatter itself on it, and to overflow those powers of the soul that are nearest to it, that every part of the soul may concur to the possession of it. *Bless the Lord, O my soul*, (saith David) *and all that is within me, bless his holy name*, Ps. ciii. 1. So rejoice in the Lord, O my soul, and all that is within me rejoice in the name of God: this is true joy, when the soul unites itself to the good possessed in all its parts: and was there ever such an object of true joy as this? Hark, as if heaven opened, and the voice came from God in heaven, *I will be a God to thee, and to thy seed after thee, I am the Lord thy God, and I will be thy God.* What, doth not thy heart leap into thy bosom at this sound? John the Baptist leaped in his mother's womb for joy at the sound of Mary's voice, and doth not thy soul spring within thee at this voice of God? O wonder! some can delight themselves in sin, and is not God better than sin? Others more refined, and indeed sanctified, can delight themselves in remission of sin, in grace, pardon, holiness, fore-thoughts of heaven; how exceedingly have some gracious hearts been ravished with such thoughts? But is not God the objective happiness, the fountain, blessedness more rejoicing than all these? Why, dear soul, if there be in thee any rejoicing faculty, now awake and stir up: it is the Lord thy God, whom thou art to rejoice in: it is he whom the glorious spirits joy in: it is he who is the top of heaven's joy, their exceeding joy: and it is he who is thy God as well as their God: enough! enough! or if this be not enough, hear thy duty as the Lord commands thee, *Rejoice in the Lord*, Phil. iii. 1. *Be glad, ye children of Zion, and rejoice in the Lord your God*, Joel ii. 23. *Rejoice in the Lord, all ye righteous, for praise is comely for the upright*, Psal. xxxiii. 1. *Rejoice in the Lord, ye righteous, and give thanks at the remembrance of his holiness*, Psalm xcvii. 12. *Let all those that put their trust in thee rejoice, let them ever shout for joy, because thou defendest them; let them also that love thy name, be joyful in thee*, Psal. v. 11. *Let the righteous be glad, let them rejoice before God; yea, let them exceedingly rejoice*, Psal. lxviii. 3. *Glory ye in his holy name, let the heart of them rejoice that seek the Lord*, Psal. cv. 3. *Let Israel rejoice in him that made him, let the children of Zion be joyful in their king*, Ps. cxlix. 3. *Be glad in the Lord, and rejoice, O ye righteous, and shout for joy, all ye that are upright in heart*, Ps. xxxii. 11. O what pressing commands are these.

SECT. VIII.

Of calling on Jesus in that respect.

8. WE must call on Jesus, or on God the Father in and through Jesus, in reference to this gracious covenant. Now, this calling on God contains prayer and praise.

1. We must pray, we must use arguments of faith challenging God, *Turn thou me, and I shall be turned:* Why? *For thou art the Lord my God*, Jer. xxxi. 18. This covenant is the ground on which all prayers must be bottomed: the covenant we know contains all the promises, and what is prayer but promises turned into petitions? Thus prayed the prophet Jeremiah, xiv. 21, 22. *Do not abhor us for thy name's sake, do not disgrace the throne of thy glory; remember, break not thy covenant with us.—Why art not thou he, the Lord our God.* And thus prayed the prophet Isaiah, lxiv. 9. *Be not wroth very sore, neither remember iniquity for ever, behold we beseech thee;* and why so? *we are all thy people.* q. d. Every one doth for its own; the prince for his people, the father for his children, and the shepherd for his sheep; and will not God do for his own in covenant with him? Be thy soul in the saddest desertion, yet come and
spread

spread the covenant before God. A soul in the greatest depth, swimming on this covenant of grace, it keeps it from sinking: whence Christ in his blackest, saddest hour prayed thus, *My God, my God, why hast thou forsaken me?* Be thy soul in trouble for sin and prevailing corruption, yet go to God and plead his promise and covenant; say, as Jehoshaphat, *Lord, I am so borne down by the power of my sins, that I know not what to do, only mine eyes are unto thee, O do thou subdue mine iniquities.* Be thy soul troubled for want of strength to do this or that duty, yet go to God and Christ, in the covenant of grace, and say, 'Lord, thou knowest 'I have no strength of myself, I am a barren wil- 'derness, but thou hast entered into a covenant of 'grace with me, that thou wilt put thy law into 'my inward parts, thou wilt cause me to keep thy 'judgments and do them,' Ezek. xxxvi. 27. As sometimes thou saidest to Gideon, *I have sent thee, and therefore I will be with thee,* Judges vi. 16. Many are apt to set upon duties in their own strength; but, O my soul, look thou to the promise of grace, and of the Spirit, and put them in suit, and alledge them unto Christ. Many are apt to work out their sanctifications by their watchfulness, resolutions, vows, promises made unto God; but, alas! were there not more help in God's promises which he makes to us, than in our promises which we make to him, we might lie in our pollutions for ever. O here is the way, in every want, or strait, or necessity, flee to God and Christ, saying, 'Thou art our Father, and we are thy people, O break not thy covenant with us. I confess strong expressions and affections are good in prayer, but surely strength of faith in the covenant of God is the greatest strength of our prayer.

Object. Here it may be some soul will object, O if I were assured that I were in covenant with God, thus would I pray; but, alas! I am a stranger, an alien, and so have been to this very day; I have no part in the covenant.

Answ. I answer, If thou art not actually in covenant, yet thou mayest be in covenant in respect of God's purpose and gracious intention. Howsoever to encourage all to seek unto God, consider these particulars.

1. The freeness of the promise in this covenant of grace, *Come, and buy wine without money, or money-worth,* Isa. lv. 2. *Come, and drink of the waters of life freely,* Rev. xxii. 17.

2. The extent of the promise in this covenant of grace, *I will pour out my Spirit upon all flesh;* hence the gospel is compared to a feast, and God invites universally, *As many as you find, bid to the marriage,* Matth. xxii. 9. As persons are in estate, so they invite and so they feast: now, Christ is a great king over all the earth; he hath one house that will hold all, he hath one table that will hold all; yea, he hath one dish that will serve all; and, answerably he invites all, *Ho every one that thirsteth.*

3. The forwardness of Christ that gives to every one that asketh according to his promise. *Hadst thou but asked,* (said Christ to the Samaritan woman) *I would have given thee living water,* John iv. 10. Mark here the occasion of Christ's words; Christ, being weary and thirsty by reason of his journey, he asked of the woman a cup of water to drink; no great matter, he asks but a cup of water, and the woman stands at the well side where was water enough, yet she gives not, but stands wondering that he, being a Jew, should ask water of her that was a Samaritan: well, saith Christ, thou deniest me a cup of cold water, being weary and thirsty, but hadst thou asked of me, I would have given thee water of life. Wonderful! Christ is more ready to give water of life, the very Spirit of God, to a poor sinner, than we are to give a cup of common water to a thirsty soul: go then, thou that hast denied the least mercy and kindness to Christ in any of his members, yet seek grace from him, O look up unto Jesus! ask his Spirit, intreat him to make thy heart new within thee, plead the promise of his covenant, and wait in hope.

4. We must praise: 1. If we would have the blessing, let us seek it with the same mind that God offers it, *i. e.* with a purpose and desire to have grace exalted; thus Moses sought pardon for this very end, That his mercy might appear; *If thou wilt pardon their sin, thy mercy shall appear, and we shall be thankful unto thee for it,* Ex. xxxii. 32. So the words are made out by expositors, which, in the text, are either passionately or modestly suspended. These are prevailing requests with God, when we plead for the glorifying of his own grace, *Father, glorify thy name,* said Christ, and presently there comes a voice out of the cloud, *I have glorified it, and I will glorify it again,* John xii. 28. 2. If we have the blessing already, then be sure to ascribe the

glory

glory unto him that hath made good his promise unto us, *Who is a God like unto thee, who passest by the transgressions of the remnant of thine heritage?* Micah vii. 18. We should make the praise of his grace to ring through the world, that heaven and earth might take notice of it, and wonder at the grace that hath been shewed unto us. ' I will mention the loving-kindness of the ' Lord, and the praises of the Lord, according to ' all that the Lord hath bestowed on us, and the ' great goodness towards the house of Israel, which ' he hath bestowed on them according to his ' mercies, and according to the multitude of his ' loving-kindnesses,' Isaiah lxiii. 7. See how the prophet mentions the kindnesses, the loving-kindnesses, the multitude of his loving-kindnesses, the goodness, and the great goodness of God; he could hardly get off it, he would have God and grace to have all the glory: O my soul, hath God entered thee into a covenant of grace? Why then, *bless the Lord, O my soul, and all that is within me, bless his holy name*, Psal. ciii. 1. But of this more anon.

SECT. IX.

Of conforming to Jesus in that respect.

9. WE must conform to Jesus, in reference to this covenant of grace, *We are changed by beholding, into the same image*, 2 Cor. iii. 18. If we look unto Jesus in this respect, this look will have such an influence upon us, that we shall conform to Jesus; but wherein consists this conformity? I answer, in these several particulars.

1. God in Christ offers his covenant to us; so we, through Christ, should embrace his offer.

2. God in Christ keeps covenant with us; so we, through Christ, should be careful to keep covenant with him.

3. God in Christ hath highly honoured us, as we are his people; so we, through Christ, should highly honour him, as he is our God.

1. God in Christ offers a covenant of grace to us; so we, through Christ, should embrace this gracious offer. His offers have appeared from first to last, as 1. To Adam. 2. To Abraham. 3. To Moses. 4. To David. 5. To Israel and to Judah. Take notice of it in that great promise of the covenant, *I will be thy God, q d.* ' Come, soul, if ' thou wilt but have me, I am thine; hear, I offer ' myself, my Son, my Spirit, justification, sanctification, adoption, salvation; whatsoever I am, or ' whatsoever I have, all is thine, if thou wilt but ' accept of me: look over all this wide, wide world, ' and if there be any thing in it that can please thy ' soul, and when thou hast gone through all the ' world, then come and take a view of me, and ' see me in my glory, beauty and excellency; view ' me in my attributes, and see if thou findest not ' enough in me worthy of thy acceptance: all this, ' and more than this, nay more than eye can ' see, or ear can hear, or heart conceive, I offer ' to thee if thou wilt but have me; lo, I will be ' thy God,' So, Christians, God is first with us, he is the first mover, he begins with us before we begin with him, *I will bring them* (saith God) *into the bond of the covenant*. Now, in this let us conform; doth he offer? O let us embrace the offer! doth he lead the way? O let us follow him step by step in that very way as he goes before us! let not us prescribe unto God, let not us presume to appoint the conditions of the covenant; let not us seek to wind about the promise of grace to our own mind and will; let not us say, We will have it thus, and thus it shall be, or else we will admit of no conditions of peace: but, O come, take God and Christ upon his own terms; submit to that way of the covenant, and to those conditions of peace which the Lord prescribeth. Why? this is to conform to his gracious offers. There is much in this offer of Christ, and conforming to Christ, therefore give me leave to enlarge. As in the offer God usually scatters some little seeds of faith in the hearts of those that he will bring to himself, so it is worth our while to observe the work of faith in receiving and accepting of this gracious offer: only I shall not herein limit the Lord, but I will shew what some conceive the most usual and ordinary course of faith's working, and of the soul's conforming to Jesus Christ in its closing with Christ, as thus,—

1. Faith hearing the great things proposed in the covenant of grace, it stirs up in the heart a serious consideration of their blessed condition that are in covenant with God, ' Blessed art thou, O Israel, a ' people saved by the Lord, Deut. xxxiii. 29. ' What nation in the earth is like thy people, even ' like Israel, whom God went to redeem for a peo-
' ple

'ple to himself,' 2 Sam. vii. 23. Time was (faith the soul) that I counted the proud blessed, and the rich blessed, and the honourable blessed: time was when I placed my blessedness in other things, in riches, preferments, favour, credit with men; but now these are become vile, and things of no value; faith makes us change our voice, and to speak as the Psalmist, 'Blessed are the people 'whose God is the Lord,' Psal. cxliv. 15.

2. Faith stirs in the heart a longing desire after this condition. Good being believed, cannot but be desired and longed for; desire naturally springs from the apprehension of any good being made known: hence faith (we say) is both in the understanding and in the will; as it is in the understanding, it opens the eye to see, and clearly to discern the blessing of the covenant; as it is in the will, it pursues and desires the attaining of the grace revealed; nor are these desires faint desires, but very earnest, eager, violent; sometimes it is called *a thirsting after God*, and sometimes *a panting after God*, and sometimes *a gasping after God*: It is such a desire, as cannot be satisfied by any thing without God himself.

3. Faith stirs in the heart some hope to enjoy this condition, I say, *Some hope*; for faith being as yet in the bud, or in the seed, though its desire be strong, yet hope of obeying is but feeble and weak: hence faith is taken up with many thoughts; fain would the soul be joined to Christ, but being as yet dismayed with the sense of sin, it stands like the publican afar off; as yet faith can scarce speak a word to God, only, with Jonah, it can *look towards his holy temple*. As a poor weak babe, who lies in the cradle sick, and weak, and speechless, only it can look towards the mother for help; the cast of the eye expresseth in some sort what it would say: thus faith, being weak, it would speak to God, but it cannot; or dares not, only it hath its eye towards heaven; as Jehoshaphat sometimes said, *Our eyes are towards thee*, 2 Chron. xx. 12. It feels a need, and fain would have, but sense of unworthiness, and the sense of the law, strike such a fear into the heart, that it dares not come near. Consider Israel's case, and we shall find it parallel to this: God proclaims on the mount, *I am the Lord thy God*. What was this, but God's offer to be in covenant with Israel? And yet the terror of the thunder was so great, that Israel durst not come near: a poor soul hearing the Lord to offer himself to be in covenant with him, 'Come, soul, I am the 'Lord thy God.' Why, alas! it dares not come near; 'What am I, Lord? or what is my father's 'house, that I should enter into a covenant with 'the Most High God?' The soul is unquiet within itself, it is hurried to and fro, and finds no rest; it hears of peace with God, but feels it not, there is much ado with the soul to sustain its hope; only faith sets the mind again and again to consider the promises, invitations, and all other encouragements which God hath given in his word.

4. Faith stirs in the heart some resolves to go to God's throne, and to sue for grace; faith speaks within as they did, *Who can tell whether the Lord will return?* Jon. iii. 9. And *it may be the Lord God of hosts will be gracious to the remnant of Joseph*, Amos v. 15. So *who can tell?* faith the soul, *It may be the Lord will*, faith the soul. And this begets some resolves, as those lepers in Samaria knew they were sure to perish if they sat still, therefore they resolved to try whether the Aramites would save them; or as Esther, knowing all was undone if she would not stir, she would try whether the king would hold out his golden sceptre; so the poor soul, knowing there is no way but perishing, if it continue in its natural state, therefore it resolves to go to God: doth the Lord say, *Seek my face?* Why! *thy face, Lord, will I seek.*——— Doth the Lord say, *Come unto me?* Why! *behold, Lord, I come unto thee, for thou art the Lord our God*, Jer. iii. 22. And now the soul betakes itself unto God; it sends up complaints of itself, it laments its own sinful rebellions, it puts out a whole volley of sighs, groans and strong cries towards heaven; it confesseth with grief and bitter mourning all its former iniquities: it smites, with repenting Ephraim, upon its thigh; it lies down at God's footstool, it puts its mouth in the dust; it acknowledges God's righteousness, if he should condemn and cast off for ever; and yet withal it pleads for grace, that it may be accepted as one of his; it says unto God, 'Lord, I have nothing 'to plead, why thou mayest not condemn me, but 'if thou wilt receive me, thy mercy shall appear 'in me. O let thy mercy appear, take away all 'iniquity, and receive me graciously.' Thus the soul lies at God's throne and pleads for grace.

5. As faith is thus earnest in suing to God for
grace;

grace; so it is no less vigilant and watchful in observing what answer comes from the Lord; even as the prisoner at the bar not only cries for mercy, but he marks every word which falls from the judge's mouth, if any thing may give him hope; or, as Benhadad's servants lay at catch with the king of Israel, to see if they could take occasion by any thing which fell from him to plead for the life of Benhadad; so the poor soul that is now pleading for life and grace, it watcheth narrowly to see if any thing may come from God, any intimation of favour, any word of comfort, that may tend to peace, *O let me hear joy and gladness.—I will hear what the Lord will say, for he will speak peace unto his people.*

6. As faith waits for an answer, so accordingly it demeans itself.

1. Sometimes God answers not, and faith takes on, and follows God still, and cries after him with more strength, as resolving never to give over, till the Lord either save or destroy: nay, if the Lord will destroy, faith chooseth to die at God's feet, as when Joab was bidden to come forth from the horns of the altar, and to take his death in another place; Nay, saith Joab, *but I will die here*; or as when Christ saw no deliverance come in his agony, *He prayed more earnestly*, Luke xxii. 44. So a poor soul in the time of its agony, when it is striving as for life and death, if help come not at first call, prays again, and that more earnestly, faith is very urgent with God; and the more slack the Lord seems in answering, the more earnest is faith in plying God with its prayers; it will wrestle with God as Jacob with the angel, it will take no denial, but will crave still, *Bless me, even me also, O send me not away without a blessing.*

2. Sometimes God answers in part, he speaks as it were out of a dark cloud; he gives some little ease, but he speaks not full peace; in this manner he speaks to the woman, *Go thy way, and sin no more,* John viii. 11. He doth not say, *Go in peace, thy sin is forgiven thee.* No; no, but *go thy way and sin no more:* hereby faith usually gets a little strength, and looks after the Lord with more hope; it begins to plead with God, as Moses did, *O Lord, thou hast begun to shew grace unto thy servant, go on, Lord, to manifest unto me all thy goodness.* Here faith takes a little hold on the covenant of grace; it may be the hand of faith is feeble, shaking and trembling, yet it takes a little hold, it receives some encouragement, it finds that its former seeking is not in vain.

3. Sometimes God answers more fully and satisfactorily, and applies some promise of grace to the conscience, by his own Spirit; he lets the soul feel and taste the comforts of himself, or of such and such a promise, more effectually than ever before: *Fear not* (saith God) *for I am thy God*, Isa. xli. 10. Here faith waxeth bold, and with glad heart entertains the promise brought home unto it. The apostle calls this, *The embracing of the promises,* Heb. xi. 13. Now embracing implies an affectionate receiving with both arms opened; so the soul embraceth the promise, and the Lord Jesus in the promise; and having him, like Simeon, in his arms, it lays him in the bosom, it brings him into the chamber of the heart, there to rest and abide for ever. And now is the covenant struck betwixt God and the soul: Now, the soul possesseth God in Christ, as her own; it rests in him and is satisfied with him, it praiseth God for his mercy, as Simeon did when he had Christ in his arms; it commits itself wholly and for ever to that goodness and mercy which hath been revealed to it.

O my soul, hast thou come thus by little and little to touch the top of Christ's golden sceptre? Why, then is thy hand given to God, then art thou entered into a covenant of peace, Christ's offering and thy receiving the covenant of grace, bear a sweet agreement, an harmonious conformity.

2. God in Christ keeps covenant with us; so we through Christ should be careful and diligent to keep covenant with God; in the things of this life, a strict eye is had to the covenants we make; now, is it not enough for us to enter into covenant with God, but we must keep it? The Lord never will, never hath broken the covenants on his part; but, alas! we on our parts have broken the first covenant of works; take heed we break not the second, for then there remains not any more place for any more covenants; as the Lord keeps covenant with us, so let us keep covenant with him; and therein is the blessing, *The mercy of the Lord is from everlasting to everlasting,—to such as keep his covenant,* Psal. ciii. 17, 18.

There is much also in this keeping of the covenant, and therefore give me leave a little to enlarge:

From the Creation until his first Coming.

large: sundry acts of faith are required to this keeping of the covenant. As thus,

1. Faith in keeping the covenant hath always an eye to the rule and command of God. As in the things to be believed, faith looks upon the promise; so in things to be practised, faith looks upon the command: faith will present no strange fire before the Lord; it knows that God will accept of nothing but what is according to his own will.

2. As faith takes direction from the rule, so in keeping of the covenant it directs us to the right end, that is to the glory of God: we are of him, and live in him, and by faith we must live to him, and from him: *For none of us liveth to himself, and no man dieth to himself; for whether we live, we live unto the Lord, whether we die, we die unto the Lord, whether we live therefore or die we are the Lord's*, Rom. xiv. 7, 8. 2 Cor. v. 15. Again, *He died for all, that they which live should not henceforth live unto themselves, but unto him which died for them*, Psal. l. 15 and lxxxvi. 12. This God claims as his right and due, *Thou shalt glorify me*, saith God; yes, saith faith, *I will glorify thee for ever*.

3. Faith in keeping the covenant shields the soul against all hinderances that it meets withal: as for instance, sometimes we are tempted on the right hand by the baits and allurements of the world, all these will I give thee, saith the world, *if thou wilt be mine*, John v. 4. But then faith overcomes the world, by setting afore us better things than these. Sometimes we are tempted on the left hand with crosses, afflictions, persecutions, and sufferings for the name of Christ, but then faith helps us to overcome, and makes us conquerors through Christ that loved us, by setting before us the end of our faith and patience. It is said of Jesus, That, *for the joy that was set before him, he endured the cross, and despised the shame*, Heb. xii. 2.

4. Faith encourageth the soul, that the Lord will have a gracious respect unto its keeping covenant; *In every nation he that feareth him, and worketh righteousness, is accepted with him*, Acts x. 35. Surely this is no small encouragement to well-doing: what, would not a servant do, if he knew his Lord will take it in good part? Now, faith assures the soul, there is not one prayer, one holy desire, or one good thought, or word which is spoken, or done to the glory of God, but God takes notice of it, and accepts it in good part. *Then they that feared the Lord spake often one to another, and the Lord hearkened and heard it, and a book of remembrance was written before him, for them that feared the Lord, and that thought upon his name*, Mal. iii. 16.

5. Faith furnisheth the soul with strength and ability to keep the covenant; by faith we get a power and strength of grace; as thus——

1. By faith we look at Christ, as having all fulness of grace in himself, *It pleased the Father, That in him should all fulness dwell*, Col. i. 19. All others have but their measures, some more, some less, according to the measure of the gift of Christ, but Christ hath received the *Spirit, not by measure, but in the fulness of it*, John iii. 34.

2. By faith we know, that whatever fulness of grace is in Christ, he had it not for himself only, but for us; *he received gifts for men*, Psal. lxviii. 18. said the Psalmist; not for himself merely, but for men; *Of his fulness we receive grace for grace*, saith John i. 16. His wisdom is to make us wise, his meekness is to make us meek, and his patience is to make us patient.

3. By faith we look at Christ, as faithful to distribute such grace unto us, as he received for us; *He is faithful in all the house of God*, Heb. iv. 2. He is faithful in dispencing all the treasures of grace committed unto him for his church's good: he keeps nothing back, his faithfulness will not suffer him to keep that to himself which he hath received for us: hence, as the Psalmist faith, *He received gifts for men*, Psal. lxviii. 18. So the apostle renders it, *He gave gifts unto men*, Eph. iv. 8. As he receives, so he gives, being faithful in all that is committed to him.

4. By faith we seek God, and beg performance of his promises according to our need. Do we want wisdom, meekness, patience, or any other grace? Faith carries us by prayer unto the fountain, and in this way it waits and expects to receive the grace we want. As the child by sucking the breast, draws forth milk for its own nourishment, and thereby it grows in strength; so do we by the prayer of faith suck from Christ, and from the promise of grace, and by that means derive strength to our inner man, to fulfil the covenant which we have made with God.

Q 6. As

6. As faith strengthens, so if at any times by occasion or temptation we fail in our covenant-keeping, faith recovers us, and restores us again to our former estate. I do not say the covenant can be broken betwixt God and us; we may offend God, and fail in the service of God, but till we refuse God, and leave God, and choose another master, Lord, and husband besides God, there is no dissolution of the covenant of grace: now, this a true believer cannot do; he may fall, and fall often, yet he doth not fall, but he rises again, he may turn aside, but yet he turns again into the way of the covenant. What a sweet point is this, Christians! we may, and sometimes we do walk weakly in keeping of covenant, our feet slip, and we step aside out of God's path, yet faith brings us back again to God; it casts shame on our faces, that after all the grace shewed us, we should so ill requite God: it reminds us of these promises, ' Return
' unto me, and I will return unto you, Zech. i. 3.
' Ye have done all this wickedness, yet turn not
' aside from following the Lord.—For the Lord
' will not forsake his people for his great name's
' sake, because it hath pleased the Lord to make
' you his people,' 1 Sam. xx. 22. In the minding of these, and such other promises, faith doth encourage us to return unto God, to take words unto ourselves, and to plead the covenant of his grace towards us; this work of faith brought Peter back to Christ, whereas Judas, wanting this faith, lies down in desperate sorrow, never able to rise up, or to recover himself.

O my soul, art thou acquainted with these acts of faith, enabling thee in some good measure to keep covenant with God! then is there a sweet conformity betwixt thee and Jesus.

3. God in Christ hath highly honoured us: as we are his people, so we through Christ should honour him highly, as he is our God: this is the main end of the covenant, and I shall end with this. O my soul, be like to God, bear the image and resemblance of God thy Father in this respect; he hath humbled himself to advance thee; O then humble thyself to advance him, endeavour every way to exalt his name.

We are all willing to be in covenant with God, that we may set up ourselves, that we may fit upon thrones, and possess a kingdom; but we must think especially of setting up the Lord upon his throne; *Ascribe greatness to our God*, saith Moses, Deut. xxxii. 3. Make it a name, and a praise unto him, That he hath vouchsafed to make us his people, and to take us into covenant with himself; honour him as he is God, but honour him more abundantly as he is our God; who should honour him if his people will not? The world knows him not, *The wicked will not seek after God, God is not in all his thoughts*, Psalm x. 4. And shall God have no honour? Shall he that stretched out the heavens, and laid the foundations of the earth, and formed man upon it, have no glory? O yes! the Lord himself answers, *This people have I formed for myself, they shall shew forth my praise*, Isa. xliii. 21. Surely God will have praise from his own people, whom he hath taken to himself, *He will be glorified in all these that come near to him*, Lev. x. 3.

But how should we honour God? I answer,—

1. We must set him up as chief and highest in our esteem: kings account not themselves honoured, if they be not set above other men, and hence God's people have used such expressions concerning God, as do single him forth beyond the comparison of all creatures: Thus Moses, ' Who is
' like unto thee amongst the Gods? Who is like
' unto thee, glorious in holiness, fearful in praises,
' doing wonders? Exod. xv. 11. Thus David,
' Thou art great, O Lord God, for there is none
' like thee, neither is there any God besides thee, ac-
' cording to all that we have heard with our ears,
' 2 Sam. vii. 22. Thus Solomon, Lord God of
' Israel, there is no God like thee in heaven a-
' bove, or in the earth beneath, who keepest co-
' venant and mercy with thy servants, 1 Kings viii.
' 22. Thus Micah, Who is a God like unto thee,
' which passeth by the transgressions of the rem-
' nant of thine heritage?' Micah vii. 18. And thus should we rise up in our thoughts and apprehensions of God, until we come to an holy extasy and admiration of God.

2. We must count it our blessedness and highest dignity to be a people in covenant with God; are we honourable? Yet esteem this as our greatest honour, that God is our God; are we low and despised in the world? yet count this honour enough, that God hath lifted us up to be his people. Christians, if when we are counted as things of nought, we can quiet ourselves in this, that

God

God is our God, if when we are perfecuted, imprifoned, diftreffed, we can fay, with Jacob, *I have enough, becaufe the Lord hath mercy on me, and hath taken me into covenant with him*; furely then we do bear witnefs of God before heaven and earth, that he is better to us than corn, or wine, or oyl, or whatfoever this world affords.

3. We muft lie under the authority of every word of God, and we muft conform ourfelves to the example of God; that is, we muft labour to become followers of God, and imitate his virtues: tis a part of that honour which children owe to their parents, to obey their commands, and to imitate their godly example; we cannot honour God more, than when we are *humbled at his feet to receive his word*, Deut. xxxiii. 3. Than when we renounce the manners of the world, to become his *followers as dear children*, Eph. v. 1. O think of this! for then we conform indeed; then are we *holy as he is holy, and pure as he is pure*; and then how fhould this but tend to the honour and glory of our God?

Thus far we have looked on Jefus, as our Jefus in that dark time before his coming in the flefh; our next work is to look on Jefus, carrying on the great work of man's falvation in his firft coming or incarnation.

LOOKING UNTO
JESUS.

In His BIRTH.

THE FOURTH BOOK, PART FIRST.

CHAP. I. SECT. I.

Luke ii. 15. *Let us now go even to Bethlehem, and fee this thing.*

Of the TIDINGS of CHRIST.

IN this period, as in the former, we fhall firft lay down the object; and, fecondly, direct you how to look unto it.

The object is Jefus, carrying on the work of man's falvation in his firft coming in the flefh, until his coming again. But becaufe in this long period we have many tranfactions, which we cannot with conveniency difpatch together, we fhall therefore break it into fmaller pieces, and prefent this object, Jefus Chrift. 1. In his birth. 2. In his life. 3. In his death. 4. In his refurrection. 5. In his afcenfion, feffion at God's right-hand, and miffion of his holy Spirit. 6. In his interceffion for his faints, in which bufinefs, he now is, and will be employed till his fecond coming to judgment.

Firft, For the tranfactions of *Jefus in his birth*, fome things we muft propound before, and fome things after his birth; fo that we fhall conclude this period till the time of John's baptifm, or the exercife of his miniftry upon earth. Now, in all the tranfactions of this time, we fhall fpecially handle thefe. 1. The tidings of Chrift. 2. The conception of Chrift. 3. The duplicity of natures in Chrift. 4. The real diftinction in that duplicity. 5. The wonderful union notwithftanding that diftinction. 6. The birth of Chrift. 7. Some confequences after his birth, whilft yet a child of twelve years old.

Q 2

The

The first passage in relation to his birth, is *the tidings of Christ*; this appears, Luke i. 26, 27, &c. *And in the sixth month the angel Gabriel was sent from God*, &c. I shall a little insist on some of these words.

1. The messenger is an angel; man was too mean to carry the news of the conception of God: never any business was conceived in heaven, that did so much concern the earth as the conception of the God of heaven in a womb of earth: no less therefore than an angel was worthy to bear these tidings, and never angel received a greater honour than of this embassage. Angels have been sent to divers, as to Gideon, Manoah, David, Daniel, Elijah, Zachariah, &c. And then the angel honoured the message, but here's a message that doth honour the angel; he was highly glorious before, but this added to his glory. Indeed the incarnation of God could have no less a reporter than the angel of God; when God intended to begin his gospel, he would first visit the world with his angel, before he would visit the world with his Son; his angel must come in the form of man, before his Son must come in the nature of man.

This angel salutes the virgin, *Hail, thou that art highly favoured, The Lord is with thee, blessed art thou among women*, Luke i. 28. Many men and women have been and are the spiritual temples of God; but never was any the material temple of God, but only Mary, and therefore *blessed art thou amongst women*; and yet we cannot say, that she was so blessed in bearing Christ, as she was in believing in Christ; her bearing indeed was more miraculous, but her believing was more beneficial to her soul: that was her privilege, but this was her happiness. Christians! if we believe in Christ, and if we obey the word of Christ, we are the mothers of Christ. *Whosoever doth the will of my Father which is in heaven, he is my brother, and sister, and mother*, Matth. xii. 50. Every renewed heart is another Mary, a spiritual sanctuary of the Lord Jesus. It was the woman's acclamation, *Blessed is the womb that bare thee, and the paps that gave thee suck*, Luke xi. 27. True, said Christ, but that blessing extends only to one; I will tell you how many are blessed, and rather blessed, yea, *rather blessed are they that hear God's word and keep it*, Ver. 28. Blessed are they that so incarnate the written word, by doing it, as the blessed virgin gave flesh to the eternal word by bearing it; those that hear and keep God's word, are they that *travail in birth again until Christ be formed in them*, Gal. iv. 19. Hearing, they receive the immortal seed of the word, by a firm purpose of doing they conceive, by a longing desire they quicken, by an earnest endeavour they travail, and when the work is wrought, then have they incarnate the word, and Christ is formed in them. In this respect was Mary blessed; and I make no question but in this respect also the angel calls her blessed, and Elisabeth calls her blessed, and Simeon calls her blessed, and she calls herself blessed, and all generations call her blessed, and God himself calls and makes her blessed; yea, as Paul said, *Cometh this blessedness on the circumcision only?* Rom. iv. 9. So cometh this blessedness on the virgin only? No, even *blessed are the poor in Spirit, blessed are they that mourn, and blessed are the meek, and blessed are they whose sins are not imputed*, Matth. v. 3, 4, 5. Psal. xxxii. 2. Even these hath God blessed with spiritual blessings in heavenly places, and these shall Christ entertain with a, *Come, ye blessed of my Father*.

3. This virgin is *troubled at this salute*, Luke i. 29. She might well be troubled; For, 1. If it had been but a man that had come in so suddenly, when she expected none, or so secretly, when she had no other company, or so strangely, the doors being properly shut, she had cause to be troubled; how much more, when the shining glory of the angel so heightened the astonishment? 2. Her sex was more subject to fear; if Zachary were amazed with the sight of this angel, how much more the virgin? We flatter ourselves how well we could endure such visions, but there is difference betwixt our faith and our senses; to apprehend here the presence of God by faith, this goes down sweetly; but should a glorious angel appear among us, it would amaze us all. But for this the angel comforts her, *Fear not, Mary, for thou hast found favour with God*, Ver. 30. The troubles of holy minds ever end in peace or comfort: joy was the errand of the angel, and not terror; and therefore suddenly he revives her spirit with a cheerful exhortation, *Fear not*, q. d. ' Let those fear who
' know they are in displeasure, or know not they
' are gracious; thine happy-estate calls for confi-
' dence, and that confidence calls for joy; What
' should

'should they fear, who are favoured of him, at 'whom the devils tremble? O Mary, how should 'joy but enter into thy heart, out of whose womb 'shall come salvation?' I question not but these very words revived the virgin; what remote corner of her soul was there into which these beams of consolation did not shine?

4. Here is the foundation of her comfort and our happiness; *Behold, thou shalt conceive in thy womb, and bring forth a Son, and shall call his name Jesus*, Luke i. 31. Never was mortal creature thus honoured, that her womb should yield that flesh, which was personally united to the Godhead, that she should bear him that upholds the world. There's one wonder in the conception, another in the fruit, both are marvellous, but the latter I take it is more mysterious, and fuller of admiration: the fruit of the womb is Jesus, a Saviour, *the Son of the Highest*, a king, *God shall give him a throne*, and he shall reign for ever, *for of his kingdom there shall be no end*, Ver. 31, 32, 33. Here was a son, and such a son as the world never had before, and here was the ground of Mary's joy; how could she but rejoice to hear what her son should be before he was? Surely never was any mother so glad of her son born, as this virgin was of her son before he was conceived.

The ground of this joy lies more especially in that name, Jesus. Here, Christians! here is the object that you are to look unto; the first title that the angel gives our Saviour, it is Jesus, a Saviour. O come, let us dwell a little here, without Jesus we had never known God our friend, and without Jesus, God had never known us for any other than his enemies. This name Jesus is better to us than all the titles of God; indeed, there is goodness and greatness enough in the name Jehovah, but we merited so little good, and demerited so much evil, that in it alone there had been small comfort for us, but in the name Jesus there is comfort, and with the name Jesus there is comfort in the name of God. In old times God was known by his names of power, and of majesty, and of his nature, but his name of mercy was reserved till now, when God did purpose to pour out the whole treasure of his mercy, by the mediation of his Son. And, as this name is exalted above all names, so are we to exalt his mercy above all his works. O it is an useful name in all depths, distresses, miseries, perplexities, we beseech God by the name of Jesus to make good his own name, not to bear it for nought, but, as he is a Saviour, so to save us, and this is our comfort, that God will never so remember our wretched sins, as to forget his own blessed name, and especially this name, Jesus. O it is the highest, the dearest, the sweetest name to us of all the names of God.

The reason of this name was given by the angel to Joseph, *Thou shalt call his name Jesus, for he shall save his people from their sins*, Matth. i. 21. But why from their sins? We seem rather willing to be saved from poverty, ignominy, plague, prison, death, hell, the devil; sin is a thing that troubles but a few; O, how few? how very few be there that break their sleep for their sins? Alas! alas! sin (if we understand) is the very worst of evils: there is no poverty but sin, there is no shame but sin, there is no prison, but that prison is a paradise without sin; there is no death that hath any sting in it but for sin, *The sting of death is sin*, saith the apostle, 1 Cor. xv. 55. Take out the sting, and you may put the serpent in your bosom; nay, I'll say more, there is no hell but for sin; sin first kindled the fire of hell, sin fewels it; take away sin, and that tormenting flame goes out: and for the devil, sin is his instrument, whereby he works all mischief; how comes a man to be a slave to Satan, but by sin? But for sin the devil had no business in the world; but for sin he could never hurt a soul.

What abundance of benefits are here in one word, *He shall save his people from their sins?* There is no evil incident to man, but it ceaseth to be evil when sin is gone; if Jesus take away sin, he doth bless our very blessings, and sanctify our very afflictions; he fetcheth peace out of trouble, riches out of poverty, honour out of contempt, liberty out of bondage; he pulls out the sting of death, puts out the fire of hell; as all evils are wrapt up in sin, so he that saves us from sin, he saves us from all sin whatsoever.

But is not Christ as precious a name as Jesus is? I answer, No: For, 1. Christ is not the name of God: God, as he is God, cannot be anointed, but Jesus is the name of God, and that wherein he more especially delights. 2. Christ is communicated to others, princes are called Christs, but Jesus is proper to himself, there is no Saviour but he.

he. 3. Christ is anointed; to what end, but to be a Saviour? Jesus is therefore the end, and the end is always above the means.——Why, this is that Jesus, the Son of God's love, the author of our salvation, *In whom alone God is well pleased*, and whom the angel published before he was conceived, *Thou shalt conceive and bring forth a Son, and shalt call his name Jesus.*

SECT. II.

Of the conception of Christ.

2. THE conception of Christ was the conclusion of the angel's message; no sooner had the virgin said, *Be it to me according to thy word*, but according to that word it was: immediately the Holy Ghost overshadowed her, and forms our Saviour in her womb: now, Christians! now was the time of love, especially if we relate to his conception and birth, well may we say, Now was it that the day brake up, that the sun arose, that darkness vanished, that wrath and anger gave place to favour and salvation; now was it that *free grace* came down from heaven, thousands of angels waiting on her; the very clouds part (as it were) to give her way; the earth springs to welcome her; floods clap their hands for joy; the heavenly hosts sing as she goes along, *Glory to God in the highest, peace be upon earth, good will towards men.* Truth and righteousness go before her, peace and prosperity follow after her, pity and mercy wait on either hand, and when she first sets her face on the earth, she cries, *A Jesus, a Saviour, hear, ye sons of men! the Lord hath sent me down to bring you news of a Jesus; grace and peace be unto you; I will live with you in this world, and you shall live with me in the world to come.* O here was blessed news! why, this is gospel, pure gospel, this is the glad tidings; *free grace* proclaims a Jesus; and a Jesus is made up (as it were) all of *free grace*; O what eternal thanks do we owe to the eternal God? If there had not been a Jesus, (to borrow that expression) made all of grace, of grace itself, we could never had dealing with God; O how may we say, with the angels, *Glory to God, blessed be God for Jesus Christ.*

But in this conception of Christ are so many wonders, That ere we begin to speak them, we may stand amazed, *without controversy great is the mystery of godliness, God manifested in the flesh*, 1 Tim iii. 16. Say, is it not a wonder, a mystery, a great mystery, a great mystery, without all controversy, That the Son of God should be made of a woman, even made of that woman, which was made by himself? Is it not a wonder, that her womb then, and that the heavens now, should contain him whom the heaven of heavens cannot contain? Concerning this conception of Christ, I shall speak a little, and but a little. What can man conceive much of this conception, which was a conception without the help of man? Our greatest light we borrow from the angel, who describes it thus, *The Holy Ghost shall come upon thee, and the power of the highest shall overshadow thee*, Luke i. 35.

Out of these words, observe, 1. The agent or efficient cause. 2. The fruit or effect. 1. The agent or efficient cause of Christ's conception is the Holy Ghost. This agrees with that speech of the angel to Joseph, *That which is conceived in her is of the Holy Ghost*, Matth. i. 20. Here it may be demanded, why the conception of Christ should be ascribed to the Holy Ghost, which is common to all the actions in the trinity? I answer, not to exclude the rest, but first to shew it was the free grace of God, which is often termed, *The Holy Ghost.* 2. Because the Father and the Son effected it by the Holy Ghost, so was it his work immediately, and in a special manner; good reason have we to be thankful to all the three persons, to the Father for ordaining this garment, to the Holy Ghost for weaving it, to the Son for wearing it, to the whole Deity for cloathing us with it, and making us righteous by it.—Neither yet is the Holy Ghost Christ's father, he did not beget him, but form him; he did not minister matter from his own substance whereof Christ was made, but took a part of human nature from the virgin, and of that he made the body of Christ within her: away with all gross opinions and old heresies! this conception of Christ was not by any carnal effusion of seminal humour, but by way of manufacture, *i. e.* by handy-work, or operation, or virtue of the Holy Ghost; or else by the energetical command and ordination of the Holy Ghost, or else by the benediction and blessing of the Holy Ghost, whereby that part of the virgin's gin's blood or seed whereof the body of Christ was to be framed, was so cleansed and sanctified, that in it there should be neither spot nor stain of original pollution.

2. The fruit or effect was the framing of Christ's manhood, in which we may observe the matter and manner. 1. For the matter, observe we the matter of the body, and of the soul of Christ. 1. The matter of the body of Christ, it was the very flesh and blood of the virgin, *He was made of a woman*, saith the apostle, Gal. iv. 4. *i. e.* of the flesh and blood, and substance of the woman, *And he was made of the seed of David*, (saith the apostle) *according to the flesh*, Rom. i. 3. Otherwise he could not have been the son of David according to the flesh; and if it be true which the philosophers say, 'That the seed of the man doth not fall into 'the substance of the child, but only doth dispose 'the seed of the woman (as a workman frameth 'and disposeth his work) to make the same into the 'form of a man:' Why then, I know not wherein the conception of Christ should differ in the matter at all from our conception, save only in the agent, or worker of his substance, who was the holy Ghost. 2. The matter of substance of the soul of Christ was not derived from the soul of the virgin, as a part thereof, but it was made as the souls of other men be, *i. e.* of nothing, by the power of God, and so infused into the body by the hand of God: but of these things (of his body and soul, and human nature) we shall speak more largely in the next section.

2. For the manner of framing Christ's human nature it was miraculous; the angel ascribes two actions to the holy Ghost in this great work, the one to come upon the virgin, the other to overshadow her; by the first is signified the extraordinary work of the holy Ghost in fashioning the human nature of Christ, as it was said of Samson, *The Spirit of the Lord came upon him*, Judg. xiv. 6. *i. e.* The holy Ghost inspired him with an extraordinary strength; so the Spirit of the Lord came upon her, *i. e.* the holy Ghost wrought in her an extraordinary way. As for instance, in ordinary generation our substance and parts are framed successively by degrees, as first the seminal humours become an embrio, then a body inorganical, then are fashioned the liver, heart, and brain, and then the rest one after another; and it is at least forty days before the body of a child be fully formed: now, it was otherwise with the body of Christ, for in the very instant of his conception, he was made perfect in body and soul, void of sin, and full of grace, in the very instant of his conception he was perfectly framed, and instantly united into the eternal word, perfect God, and perfect man. Surely this was extraordinary, and this is the property of the holy Ghost *subito operari*, to work instantly, and perfectly, 'As soon as ever the flesh was conceived, 'it was presently united and made the flesh of the 'Son of God,' Aug. L. *de fide ad et C.* 18. It was suddenly made, perfectly made, holily made.

The second action ascribed to the holy Ghost, is adumbration or overshadowing of the virgin. This teacheth us that we should not search over much into this great mystery, alas! it is too high for us: if the course of ordinary generation be a secret, how past all comprehension is this extraordinary operation? The holy Ghost did cast a shadow over the virgin, and withal a shadow over this mystery; why should we seek a clear light, where God himself will have a shadow? *I know the word was made flesh*, (saith Chrysostome) hom. 5. *but how he was made I know not*.

1. *Use*, In way of confutation, this word *conception* is the bane of divers heresies, 1. That of the *Manichee*, who held he had no true body; if so, as one says well, that had been *virgo decipiet*, not *concipiet*, rather a deceiving of us, than a conceiving of him. 2. That of the *Valentinian* revived lately in the *anabaptist*, who hold that he had a true body, but made in heaven, and sent into the virgin here on earth; and if so, that had been *virgo recipiet* not *concipiet*, rather a receiving, than conceiving; yet I cannot but wonder how confidently the anabaptists tell us, That the flesh of Christ came down from heaven, and passed through the virgin Mary as water through a conduit pipe, without taking any substance from her: their objections are raised out of these texts.——

1. *No man ascendeth into heaven, but he that came down from heaven, even the Son of man which is in heaven*, John iii. 13. I answer, 1. This speech must be understood, first, in respect of his Godhead, which may be said in some sort to descend, in that it was made manifest in the manhood here on earth. 2. This speech may be understood truly of the whole person of Christ, to whom the

pro-

properties of each nature (in respect of the communication of properties) may be fitly ascribed; but this doth no way prove that his flesh which he assumed on earth descended from heaven.

2. *The first man is of the earth, earthy: the second man is the Lord from heaven,—heavenly.* 1 Cor. xv. 47, 48. I answer, 1. This holds forth that Christ was heavenly minded, as sometimes he told the Jews, *You are from below, I am from above; you are of this world, I am not of this world;* Christ was not worldly-minded, or swayed with the lusts of the flesh, or any way earthly affected; as sometimes he could tell his apostles, *Ye are not of the world,* John viii. 23. and xv. 19. So much more might he say of himself, that he was not of this world, but his conversation was in heaven. Or, 2. This holds forth that Christ was heavenly, or from heaven in respect of the glorious qualities which he received after his resurrection: and not in respect of the substance of his body, many glorious qualities was Christ endowed with after he was raised (I shall not now dispute them) which he had not before, and in respect of these he might be called heavenly, or from heaven. 3. This holds forth that Christ also was in some sort heavenly, or from heaven in his human nature, in that the human nature was united to the divine, and withal in that the human nature was formed by the Holy Ghost: so John's baptism is said to be from heaven, though neither he, nor the water wherewith he baptised descended from heaven, but because he received it from God who is in heaven. Christ was conceived (as you heard) by the Holy Ghost, and in that regard his generation was divine and heavenly, or from heaven.

2. *Use.* In way of comfort and encouragement, Christ was thus conceived that he might sanctify our conceptions: as the first Adam was the root of all corruption, so is the second Adam the root of all sanctification: Christ went as far to cleanse us, as ever Adam did to defile us. What? Were our very conceptions defiled by Adam? In the first place, Christ takes course for this; you see he is conceived by the Holy Ghost, and he was not idle whilst he was in the womb; for even then and there he eat out the core of corruption that cleaved close to our defiled natures: so that God will not account evil of that nature that is become the nature of his own dear Son. O the condescensions of our Jesus! O that ever he would be conceived in the womb of a virgin! O that he would run through the contumelies of our sordid nature, that he would not refuse that which we ourselves are in some sort ashamed of! Some think it a reason why the *Anabaptists,* and some others run into such fancies, and deny this conception of Christ, only to decline those foul indignities (as they take them) for the great God of heaven to undergo; but certainly this was for us, and for our sakes, and therefore far be it from us to honour him the less, because he laid down his honour for our sakes. No, no, let us honour him more, and love him more: the lower he came for us, the dearer and dearer let him be unto us: consider, in all these transactions, Christ was carrying on the great work of our salvation, otherwise he had never been conceived, never had assumed to his person human nature, never had been man.

SECT. III.

Of the duplicity of natures in Christ.

3. THE duplicity of natures in Christ appears in that he was truly God, and truly man, *To us a child is born,* saith the prophet. There is a nature human, and *he shall be called the mighty God,* Is. ix. 6. There is a nature divine; *God sent his Son,* saith the apostle, therefore truly God, and this Son *made of a woman,* Gal. iv. 4. Therefore truly man: one would have thought this truth would never have come into controversy in our days; but these are the last days, and that may take off the wonder; *In the last days shall come perilous times,* 2 Tim. iii. 1. *Men shall resist the truth,* &c. Zech. xii. 8. In the last days I know there will be abundance of truth revealed, *The knowledge of the Lord shall be as the waters that cover the sea, and every child shall be as David,* Dan xii. 4. And the book that was sealed, must be opened, and knowledge shall be increased; but Satan even then will be as busy to sow his tares, as God in sowing of his wheat: then is Satan active to communicate errors, when he sees God begin to discover truths; he hopes in the heat of the market, to vend his own wares, and I believe this is one reason why now the devil sets on foot so

many

many dangerous errors, that so he may prejudge the hearts of God's people in the receiving and entertaining so many glorious truths. But that we may not pass over such a fundamental error as this, some saying with Martian, That he is God, but not man; and others, with Arius, That he is man, but not God; I shall therefore confirm this truth of the two natures of Christ against the adversaries of both sides.

And, 1. That Christ is true God, both apparent scriptures, and unanswerable reasons drawn from scriptures do plainly evince.

1. The scriptures call him God. *In the beginning was the word, and the word was with God, and the word was God,* John i. 1. And *unto the Son he saith, Thy throne, O God, is for ever,* Heb. i. 18. And *Thomas answered and said unto him, My Lord, and my God: and take heed to yourselves, and to all the flock.——To feed the church of God which he hath purchased with his own blood,* John xx. 28. Acts xx. 28. *And hereby perceive we the love of God, because he laid down his life for us,* 1 John iii. 16. *And we know that the Son of God is come.—This is the true God, and eternal life,* 1 John v. 20. And *without controversy, great is the mystery of godliness; God was manifested in the flesh,* 1 Tim. iii. 16.

2. Unanswerable reasons drawn from scriptures prove him God; thus it appears,

1. From those incommunicable properties of the Deity, which are properly ascribed unto him: he is eternal as God, Rev. i. 17. He is infinite as God, Matth. xxviii. 20. He is omniscient as God, Mat. ix. 4. He is omnipotent as God, *He that cometh from above, is above all,* John iii. 13. *He is able to subdue all things unto himself,* Philip. iii. 21. *He hath the keys of hell and death,* Rev. i. 18.

2. From those relations he hath with God, as to be the only begotten Son of God, John i. 18. The image of the Father, 2 Cor. iv. 4. Col. i. 15.

3. From those acts ascribed to him, which are only agreeable to the divine nature, as to be the author of our election, John xiii. 18. To know the secrets of our hearts, Matth. ix. 4. To hear the prayers of his people, John xiv. 14. To judge the quick and the dead, John v. 22. And thus he creates as God, John i. 4. He commands as God, Matth viii. 26. He forgives as God, Mat. ix. 6. He sanctifies as God, John i. 12. He glorifies as God, John x. 28.

4. From all those acknowledgements given to him by the saints, which are only proper unto God, and thus he is believed on as God, John iii. 18 He is loved as God, 1 Cor. xvi 22. He is obeyed as God, Matth. xvii. 5. He is prayed to as God, Acts vii. 59. He is praised as God, Rev. v. 13. He is adored as God, Heb. i. 6. Phil. ii. 10. Surely all these are strong demonstrations, and prove clearly enough that Jesus Christ is God, But why was it requisite that our Saviour should be God? I answer, 1. Because none can save souls, nor satisfy for sin but God alone; *There is none,* (saith the Psalmist, Psal. xlix. 7, 15.) *that can by any means redeem his brother, or give God a ransom for him.—But God will redeem my soul from the power of hell.* 2. Because the satisfaction which is made for sin, must be infinitely meritorious: an infinite wrath cannot be appeased but by an infinite merit; and hence our Saviour must needs be God, to the end that his obedience and sufferings might be of infinite price and worth. 3. Because the burden of God's wrath cannot be endured and run through by a finite creature: Christ therefore must needs be God, that he might abide the burden, and sustain the manhood by his divine power. 4. Because the enemies of our salvation were too strong for us! how could any creature overcome Satan, death, hell, damnation? Ah! this required the power of God; there's none but God that could destroy *him that had the power of death, that is the devil.*

2. As Christ is God, so he is true man, he was born as man, and bred as man, and fed as man, and slept as man, and wept as man, and sorrowed as man, and suffered as man, and died as man; and therefore he is man.

But more particularly, 1. Christ had a human body; *Wherefore when he came into the world, he said, sacrifice and offering thou wouldest not, but a body hast thou prepared me,* Heb. x. 5. And when the apostles thought they had seen a phantasm, or a spirit, he said unto them, *handle me and see, because a spirit hath not flesh and bones, as you see me have,* Luke xxiv. 39. Here's a truth clear as the sun, and yet, O wonder! some in our times, (as Cochlaeus witnesseth) do now avouch, That he had but an imaginary body, an aerial body, a phantasm, only in shew, and no true body.

2. Christ had an human reasonable soul, *My soul is heavy unto death*, said Christ, Matth. xxvi. 38. And, again, *Father, into thy hands I commend my Spirit*, Luke xxiii. 46. Surely, (saith Nazianzen) *either he had a soul, or he will not save a soul*. The Arians opposed this, saying, *Christ had no human soul, but only a living flesh*; because the evangelist saith, that *the word was made flesh*, John i. 14. But this is a *synechdoche* very useful in scripture to put the part for the whole, and signifieth as much, as though he said, *The word was made man*. I know some reasons are rendered why the evangelist saith, *he was made flesh*, rather than *he was made man*. As, 1. To shew what part of Christ was made of his mother; not his Deity, nor his soul, but only his flesh. 2. To express the greatness of God's love, who for our sakes would be contented to be made the vilest thing, *flesh*, which is compared to grass. *All flesh is grass*, Isa. xl. 6. 3. To shew the greatness of Christ's humility, in that he would be named by the meanest name, and basest part of man; the soul is excellent, but the flesh is base. 4. To give us some confidence of his love and favour towards us, because our flesh, which was the part most corrupted, is now united to the Son of God.

3. Christ had all the properties that belong either to the soul or body of a man: nay, more than so, Christ had all the infirmities of our nature, sin only excepted: I say the infirmities of our nature, as cold and heat, and hunger and thirst, and weariness and weakness, and pain, and the like; but I cannot say, That Christ took upon him all our personal infirmities: infirmities are either natural, common to all men, or personal, and proper to some men, as to be born lame, blind, diseased; as to be affected with melancholy, infirmity, deformity; how many deformed creatures have we amongst us? Christ was not thus, his body was framed by the Holy Ghost of the purest virgin's blood, and therefore I question not, it was proportioned in a most equal symmetry and correspondency of parts, *He was fairer than the sons of men*, his countenance carried in it, 'An hidden vailed 'star—like brightness, (saith Jerome) which being 'but a little revealed, it so ravished his disciples 'hearts, That, at the first sight thereof they left 'all, and followed him: and it so astonished his 'enemies, that they stumbled, and fell to the 'ground.' So then he had not our personal infirmities, but only our natural, and good reason, for indeed he took not upon him an human person, but only an human nature united to the person of his Godhead.

But why was it requisite, that our Saviour should be man? I answer, 1. Because our Saviour must suffer and die for our sins, which the Godhead could not do. 2. Because our Saviour must perform obedience to the law, which was not agreeable to the law-giver; the Godhead certainly is free from all manner of subjection. 3. Because our Saviour must satisfy the justice of God in the same nature wherein it was offended, *For, since by man came death, by man came also the resurrection of the dead*, 1 Cor. xv. 21. 4. Because *by this means we might have free access to the throne of grace, and might find help in our necessities, having such an high priest, as was in all things tempted like unto us, and was acquainted with our infirmities in his own person*, Heb. iv. 15. and v. 6.

SECT. VI.

Of the distinction of the two natures in Christ.

4. A Real distinction of these two natures is evident, 1. In regard of essence, the Godhead cannot be the manhood, nor can the manhood be the Godhead. 2. In regard of properties, the Godhead is most wise, just, omnipotent, yea, wisdom, justice, omnipotency it self, and so is not the manhood, neither can it be. 3. They have distinct wills. *Not my will, but thy will be done, O Father*, Luke xxii. 42. Plainly differencing the will of a creature from the will of a Creator. 4. The very actions in the work of redemption are indeed inseparable, and yet distinguishable, *I lay down my life and take it up again*, John x. 18. To lay it down was the action of man, not of God; and to take it up was the action of God, not of man. In these respects, we say, each nature remains in itself intire, without any conversion, composition, commixion, or confusion: there is no conversion of one into the other, as when he changed water into wine, no composition of both, no abolition of either, no confusion at all. It is easy to observe this real distinction of his two natures, from first to last; as, first, he was conceived

as

as others, and so he was man; but he was conceived by the Holy Ghost, as never was man, and so he is God. 2. He was born as others, and so he was man: but he was born of a virgin, as never was man, and this speaks him a God. 3. He was crucified, he died, and was buried, and so he was man; but he arose again from the dead, ascended into heaven, and from thence shall come at last to judge the quick, and the dead, and so he is God.——Or, if from the apostles symbol, we go to the gospel, which speaks both natures at large, we find there, 1. He was born of his mother, and wrapped in swaddling clouts, as being a man, and the star shines over him, and the wise men adore him as being a God. 2. He was baptized in Jordan, as being a man; but the Holy Ghost from heaven descended upon him as being a God. 3. He is tempted of Satan as being a man, but he overcame Satan, and dispossessed devils as being a God. 4. He travelled, and was thirsty and hungry, and weary, as being a man, but he refreshed the weary, and fed the hungry, and gave drink, even water of life to the thirsty, as being a God. 5. He slept in the ship, and his disciples awoke him, as being a man; but he rebuked the winds, and stilled the raging of the tumultuous seas, as being a God. 6. He was poor and needy, had not an house to put his head in, as being a man; but he was and is rich and mighty, and cannot be contained in the heaven of heavens, as being a God. 7. He was sorrowful and sad, he wept, and he prayed, as being a man; but he comforts the sorrowful, and heareth the prayers of all his saints, as being a God. 8. He was whipped, and rent, and torn, and crucified, as being a man; but he rent the vail of the temple, and caused the sun to hide his face for shame when he was crucified, as being a God. 9. He cried out on the cross, *Eli, Eloi, Lamasabachthani*, as being a man; but he could say to the thief, *To-day shalt thou be with me in paradise*, as being a God. 10. He died and was buried, and lay in the grave, as being a man; but he overcame death, and destroyed the devil, and raised up himself to life again, as being a God. 11. After his resurrection, he appeared to his disciples, and eat with them, and talked with them, as being a man but he provided meat, and vanished out of their sight, as being a God. 12. He ascended into heaven, and the heavens now contain him as he is man; but he sustains the heavens, and commands all therein, and rides on the same as being a God. Thus, we see all along two real distinct natures still continuing in Christ; God being become man, the Deity was not abolished, but the human nature was adjoined, according to the old distick, *Sum quod eram, nec eram quod sum,* &c. I am that I was, but I was not that I am. You will say, How then is it said, *The word was made flesh*, or God became man? I answer, One thing may become another either by way of change, as when the water was turned into wine, but thus was not Christ, the Godhead was for a time concealed, but it was never cancelled; or one thing may become another by way of union, as when one substance is adjoined unto another, and yet is not transferred or changed into the nature of the other. Thus, a soldier putting on his armour is an armed man, or a man wearing his own garments, is no more a naked but a cloathed man; and yet the armour of the soldier, the man and his apparel are distinct things, and thus it was with Christ; the flesh is said to be deified, and the Deity is said to be incarnate; not by the conversion of either into the nature of the other, but by assuming and adjoining the human nature to the divine, and yet still the human nature and the divine are distinct things; both the natures in Christ do remain entire and unconfused; indeed the humanity is much magnified by the divinity; but the divinity is nothing altered by the humanity. Thus much for the distinction of his two natures.

SECT. V.

Of the union of the two natures of Christ in one and the same nature.

5. THE union of two natures of Christ, in one and the self-same person, is that great wonder, which now we must speak as we are able; but, alas! how should we speak this union, and not be confounded in ourselves? It is a great mystery, a secret, a wonder, many wonders have been since the beginning of the world, but all the wonders that ever were, must give place to this, and, in respect thereof, cease to be wonderful. Neither the creation of all things out of nothing, nor the

the restoration of all things into their perfect being; I mean, neither the first work, nor the last work of God in this world, (tho' most admirable pieces) may be compared with this. The union of the two natures of Christ, into one person is the highest pitch, (if any thing may be said highest in that which is infinite) of God's wisdom, goodness, power and glory: well therefore said the angel to Mary, *The power of the highest shall overshadow thee.* And if God did overshadow this mystery with his own vail, how should we presume with the men of Bethshemish to look into it? Christians, if you will needs put it to the question, How that wonderful connection of two so infinitely differing natures, in the unity of one person, should be effected? I must answer you with the apostle, *Who is sufficient for these things?* Certainly these are the things which *the angels desire to stoop and look into,* 1 Pet. i. 12. It is an inquisition fitter for an evangelical intelligence than for our shallow capacity; and yet, as Moses could not choose but wonder, though he must not draw nigh to the bush burning with fire, and not consumed; so, though we dare not draw nigh to see this great sight, *how poor dust and ashes should be assumed into the unity of God's own person, and that in the midst of those everlasting burnings, the bush should remain unconsumed, and continue fresh and green for evermore,* Isa. xxxiii. 14. Yet what doth hinder but we may stand aloof off, and wonder at it? This is one piece of our duty, to recite all the longbefore passed acts and benefits of God, (as well as we may, scripture still going along) that thereby we may admire, and adore, and express our love and thankfulness unto God.

For the untying of this knot, I cannot but wonder what a world of questions have been tossed in schools. As,

1. Whether the union of the word incarnate was in the nature?—2. Whether the union of the word incarnate was in the person?—3. Whether the human nature was united to the word by way of accident?——4. Whether the union of the divine and human nature be some thing created?— 5. Whether the union of the word incarnate be the same with assumption?——6. Whether the union of the two natures of Christ be the chief of all unions?——7. Whether the union of the two natures of Christ was made by grace?——8. Whether it was convenient for the divine person to assume a created nature?—— 9. Whether a divine person could assume the nature human?——10. Whether more persons divine could assume one nature human?——11. Whether it was more convenient, that the person of the Son should assume human nature than any other of the persons in the Godhead?—12. Whether the human nature was more assumptible by the Son of God than any other nature?——13. Whether the Son of God did not assume the person of man?——14. Whether the Son of God assumed the human nature in all its individuals, or abstracted from all individuals?—— 15. Whether the Son of God assumed a true body, soul, and all its intellects?——16. whether the Son of God, in respect of nature, though not of time, did first assume the soul, and then the body of man?—17. Whether the Son of God in human nature assumed all the defects of the body?—18. Whether the Son of God assumed all the defects of the soul of man?——19. Whether by virtue of this union, those things which are agreeable to the son of man, may be predicated of the Son of God, and *e converso?*——20. Whether Christ be one or two? And whether in Christ be one or two wills, one or more operations? These and many other like questions are raised, that in their discussions make up large volumes, but I shall leave them all to the schools.

In the explication of this union, that which I shall insist on (as the most necessary for our understanding) is, 1. The union itself. 2. The effects or benefits of it.

1. For the union itself we shall discuss, 1. Of the sorts of union, and of what sort this is. 2. Of the very thing itself wherein this union consists. 3. Of the scriptural texts that confirm this union. 4. Of the similitudes that hold forth this union. 5. Of the person assuming, and of the nature assumed, and of the reason of this way. And of these as briefly as I may; I would rather say much in a little, than a little in much.

1. Union is of divers sorts, as natural and mystical, accidental and substantial, essential and integral. But I shall pass these by, and speak only of these sorts. 1. When one of the things united is turned into the other, as when a drop of water is poured into a vessel of wine. 2. When both the things united are changed in nature and essence,

as when the elements are united to make mixt or compounded bodies. 3. When there is no change of things united, but the constitution of a third nature out of them both, as is the union of the soul and body. 4. When there is neither a change of the natures united, nor a constitution of a third out of them both, but only the founding, settling, and staying of the one of the things united in the other, and the drawing of it into the unity of the personal being or subsistence of the other: so the branch of a tree being put upon the stock of another tree, it is drawn into the unity of the subsistence of that tree into which it is put: and whereas, if it had been set in the ground, it would have grown as a separate tree in itself, now it groweth in the tree, into which it is graffed, and pertaineth to the unity of it: and this kind of union, doth of all others most perfectly resemble the personal union of the two natures of God and man in Christ, wherein the nature of man, that would have been a person in itself, if it had been left to itself, is drawn into the unity of the divine person, and subsisteth in it, being prevented from subsisting in itself, by this personal union and assumption.

2. For the thing wherein this union of two natures consists, we say, That this union consists in that dependence of the human nature on the person *of the word*, and in that communicating of the person, or subsistence *of the word*, with the human nature that is assumed; so that it is an hypostatical or a personal union, that is, such an union, as that both natures do make but one person of Christ; for the better understanding of this, we must consider what the difference is betwixt *nature and person*, and what makes an individual *nature* to be a *person*, briefly thus, ' To be this or ' that, we say, is an individual nature; to be this ' or that, in, and for itself, is a person or subsist-' ence; to be this or that, in, and for another, ' is to pertain to the person or subsistence of ano-' ther.' Now, amongst those created things, which are naturally apt to make a personal being, or to subsist in and for themselves, there is a very great difference. For,—

1. Some things of this kind may become parts of another more entire thing of the same kind; as we see in all those things wherein every part hath the same nature that the whole hath; as every drop of water is water, and being left to itself, it is a subsistence in itself, and hath its quality, nature and being in, and for itself, but if it be joined to a greater quantity of water, it hath now no being, quantity, nor operation, but in and for that greater quantity of water into which it is poured.

2. Other things of this kind cannot naturally put themselves into the unity of any other thing, and yet by the help of some foreign cause they may be united; as the branch of a tree of one kind, (which put into the ground, would be an entire distinct tree in itself) may by the hand of a man be put into the unity of a tree of another kind; and so grow, move, and bear fruit, not distinctly in and for itself, but jointly in, and for that tree into which it is planted.

3. Other things of this kind cannot by force of natural causes, nor by the help of any foreign thing, even become parts of any other created thing, or pertain to the unity of the subsistence of any such thing; as the nature of man, and the nature of all living things; and yet by divine and supernatural working, it may be drawn into the unity of the subsistence of any of the persons of the blessed trinity, wherein the fulness of all being, and the perfection of all created things, is in a more eminent sort than in themselves; for though all created things have their own being, yet seeing God is nearer to them than they are to themselves, and they are in a better sort in him than they are in themselves, there is no question, but that they may be prevented and stayed from being in, and for themselves, and caused to be in, and for one of the divine persons of the blessed trinity.

So that, as one drop of water, that formerly subsisted in itself, if it be poured into a vessel containing a greater quantity, it becomes one in subsistence with the greater quantity of water; and as a branch of a tree that being set in the ground, and left to itself, would be an entire and independent tree, becomes one in subsistence with that tree into which it is graffed; so the individual nature of man assumed into the unity of one of the persons of the blessed trinity, it loseth that kind of being, that naturally, left to itself, it would have had, and it becomes one with the person; for now it is not in, and for itself, but hath got a new relation of dependence and being in another.

But you will say, All the creatures in the world have their being in God, and dependence on God, and therefore all creatures, as well as man, may pertain to the person, or subsistence of God.

I answer, It is not a general being in and dependence on God, but a strict dependence on man's part, and a communicating of the subsistence on God's part, that makes up this union. Hence we say, That there are four degrees of the presence of God in his creatures: the *first* is the general presence, whereby he preserves the substances of all creatures and gives unto them *to live, and to move, and to have their being*, Acts vii. 28. And this extends itself to all creatures good and bad. The second degree is the presence of grace whereby he doth not only preserve the substance of his creature, but also gives grace unto it; and this agrees to the saints, and God's people on earth. The third degree is the presence of glory peculiar to the saints and angels in heaven, and hereby God doth not only preserve their substances, and give them plenty of his grace; but he also admits them into his glorious presence, so as they may behold him face to face. The fourth and last degree, is that whereby the Godhead of the Son is present with, and dwells in the manhood, giving unto it in some part his own subsistence; whereby it comes to pass, That this manhood assumed, is proper to the Son, and cannot be the manhood of the Father, or of the holy Ghost, or of any creature whatsoever. And this is a thing so admirable, and unspeakable, that, though we may find some similitudes, yet there cannot be found another example hereof in all the world.

Hence it follows, That in the manhood of Christ, consisting of body and soul, there is a nature only, and not a person; because it doth not subsist alone as other men, Peter, Paul and John do, but it wholly depends on the person of the word, into the unity whereof it is received; and this dependence of the human nature on the person of the word, and the communicating of the person or subsistence of the word, with the human nature is the very thing itself wherein this union consists.

3. For the scriptural texts that confirm this union. You see the well is very deep, but where is your bucket? What texts of scripture have we to confirm this wonderful union of two natures in one person? Amongst many, I shall only cite these;

When Christ asked his apostles, *Whom do men say that I the Son of man am?* Simon Peter answered, *Thou art the Christ the Son of the living God*, Matth. xvi. 13, 16. Now, if but one Christ, then surely but one person; and if the Son of man be the Son of the living God, then surely there is two natures in that one person: observe how the Son of man, and the Son of God, very man and very God, concentre in Christ; as the soul and body make but one man, so the Son of man and the Son of God make but one Christ: *Thou art Christ*, saith Peter, *the Son of the living God*.

So Paul, speaking of *Jesus Christ the Son of God*, He tells us, Rom. i. 3, 4. That *he was made of the seed of David according to the flesh, and declared to be the Son of God with power according to the Spirit*. 1. *Made of the seed of David* of the substance of the virgin, who was David's posterity. 2. *Declared to be the Son of God*; not made the Son of God, as he was made the Son of man, *but declared to be the Son of God:* the word in the original signifies a declaration by a solemn sentence or definitive judgment. *I will declare the decree, the Lord hath said unto me, Thou art my Son*, Psal. ii. 7. That which I point at, he as the Son of David, *(Kata sarka)* in respect of his manhood, and he is the Son of God, *(kata pneuma)* in respect of his Godhead. Here be the two natures; but in the words before, these two natures make but one Son, Jesus Christ the Lord; and in the very words themselves he is declared to be the Son of God: he doth not say, *Sons*, as of two, but *his Son Jesus Christ, First*, before, and then after; to shew unto us, That as before his making, so after his making, he is still but one Son, or one person of the two distinct natures subsisting.

To the same purpose is that same text, *In him dwelleth all the fulness of the Godhead bodily*, Col. ii. 9. By the union of the divine nature with the human, in the unity of his person, the Godhead dwelleth in Christ, as the soul in the body: *It dwelleth in him bodily*; not seemingly, but really, truly, and indeed; not figuratively, and in shadow, as he dwelleth in the temple; not by power and efficacy, as he dwells in all the creatures; not by grace, as in his people; nor by glory, as in his saints above; but essentially, substantially, personally, the human nature being assumed into union with the person of the word. Observe the passages; he in whom that fulness dwells, is the person; that fulness, which doth so dwell in him, is the nature, now, there dwells in him not only the fulness of the Godhead, but the fulness of the manhood also: for we believe him to be both perfect God, begotten of the substance of his Father before all worlds; and perfect man made of the substance of his mother in this world; only he in whom the fulness of the Godhead dwelleth is one, and he in whom the fulness of the manhood dwelleth, is another; but he in whom the fulness of both these two natures dwelleth, is one and the Emmanuel, and consequently one and the same person; in him, *i. e.* in his person dwelleth all the fulness of the Godhead, and all the fulness of the manhood; *In him dwelleth all the fulness of the Godhead bodily.*

4. For the similitudes that resemble, or set forth this mystery, many are given, but for our better understanding, let us consider these few;

The *first* is of the soul and body, that make but one man: as the soul and body are two distinct things, and of several natures, yet being united by the hand of God, they make one person; so the Godhead and manhood are two distinct things, and of several natures, yet being united by the hand of God, they make but one person. Indeed herein is the similitude defective: *First*, In that the soul and body being imperfect natures, they concur to make one full and perfect nature of a man. *Secondly*, In that one of them is not drawn into the unity of the substance of the other, but both depend of a third subsistence, which is that of the whole.

The *second* is of the light and sun; as after the collection and union of the light with the body of the sun, no man can pluck them asunder, nor doth any man call one part the sun, and another part the light; but both of them jointly together we call the sun: Even so after the union of flesh with that true light the word, no man doth call the word apart to be one Son of God, and the Son of man another Son of God, but both of them jointly together we call one, and the self-same Christ. I know in this similitude are many defectives, yet if hereby we be not altogether able to attain the truth of this great mystery, certainly 'we have 'herein a most excellent similitude, which will 'greatly help, and contentedly suffice the godly 'and moderate searchers of this divine truth,' *Justin Martyr, de recta Confess. de Coessent. Trin.*

The *third* is of a fiery and flaming sword; as the subsistences of the fire and sword are so nearly conjoined, that the operations of them for the most part concur; for a fiery sword in cutting burneth, and in burning cutteth; and we may say of the whole, That this fiery thing is a sharp piercing sword, and that this piercing sword is a fiery thing, even so in the union of the two natures of Christ, there is a communication of properties from the one of them to the other, as shall be declared, if the Lord permit; only this similitude is defective in this, in that the nature of the iron is not drawn into the unity of the subsistence of fire, nor is the nature of the fire drawn into the unity of the subsistence of iron; so that we cannot say, This fire is iron, or, this iron is fire.

The *fourth* is of one man having two qualities, or accidental natures; as a man that is both a physician and a divine, he is but one person, and yet there are two natures concurring and meeting in that same one person; so that we may rightly say of such a one, This physician is a divine, and, this divine is a physician; this physician is happy in saving of souls, and this divine is careful in curing bodies: even so is Christ both God and man, and yet but one Christ; and in that one Christ, according to the several natures, are denominations of either part, as, that this man is God, and, this God is man; or, that this man made the world, and, this God died upon the cross; but in this similitude is this defect, in that the different natures are accidental, and not essential or substantial.

The *fifth* and last is of the branch and tree into which it is ingraffed; as suppose a vine-branch, and an olive-tree. Now, as this olive-tree is but one, but hath two different natures in it, and so it beareth two kinds of fruit, and yet between the tree and the branch there is a composition, not *hujus ex his*, but *hujus ad hoc*, i. e. Not of a third thing out of the two things united, but of one of the two things united or adjoined to the other; even so Christ is one, but he hath two different natures, and in them he performs the different actions pertaining to either of them; and yet between the different natures (the divine and the human nature) there is composition, not *hujus ex his*, but *hujus ad hoc*, not of a third nature arising out of these, but of the human nature added, or united to the divine, in unity of the same person: so that

that now we may say, as, this vine is an olive-tree, and this olive-tree is a vine, or, as this vine bears olives, and olive-tree bears grapes, so the Son of man is the Son of God, and the Son of God is the Son of man; or this Son of man laid the foundation of the earth, and this Son of God was born of Mary, and crucified by the Jews. This similitude (I take it) is the aptest and fullest of all the other, though in some things also it doth fail; for the branch hath first a separate subsistence in itself, and losing it after, then it is drawn into the unity of the subsistence of that tree into which it is implanted; but it is otherwise with the human nature of Christ, it never had any subsistence of its own, until it was united to the person, or subsistence of the Son of God.

5. For the person assuming, and the nature assumed, and for the reason of this way, we say, 1. That the person assuming was a divine person; it was not the divine nature that assumed an human person, but the divine person that assumed an human nature; and that of the three divine persons, it was neither the first, nor the third, neither the Father, nor the holy Ghost that did assume this nature, but it was the Son, the middle person, who was to be the middle one, That thereby, 1. He might undertake the mediation between God and us. 2. He might better preserve the integrity of the blessed trinity in the Godhead. 3. He might higher advance mankind by means of that relation which the second person, the Mediator, did bear unto his Father: for this very end, saith the apostle, Gal. iv. 4, 5, 6. *God sent his own Son made of a woman, That we might receive the adoption of sons; wherefore thou art no more a servant but a son, and, if a son, then an heir of God thro' Christ*; intimating thereby, That what relation Christ hath unto God by nature, we being found in him, have the very same by grace: he was God's Son by nature, and we are his sons by grace: he was in a peculiar manner *the first born among many brethren*, Rom. viii. 29. And in him, and for him, the rest of the brethren by grace of adoption are accounted as *first born*, Heb. xii. 23. Exod. iv. 22, 23.

2. The nature assumed was the seed of Abraham.; *For verily he took not on him the nature of angels, but he took on him the seed of Abraham*, Heb. ii. 16. Elsewhere the apostle calls it the seed of David, *He was made of the seed of David according to the flesh*, Rom. i. 3. And elsewhere it is called the seed of the woman, *I will put enmity between thee and the woman, and between thy seed and her seed*, Gen. iii. 15. And *when the fulness of time was come, God sent forth his Son made of a woman*, Gal. iv. 4. No question she was the passive, and material principle, of which that precious flesh was made, and the holy Ghost the agent and efficient cause; that blessed womb of hers was the bride-chamber, wherein the holy Ghost did knit that indissoluble knot betwixt our human nature and his Deity; the Son of God assuming into the unity of his person that which before he was not, even our human nature. O with what astonishment may we behold our dust and ashes assumed into the unity of God's own person!

3. For the reason of this way; why did the person assume a nature? or rather, why did not the person of the Son of God join itself to a perfect person of the Son of man? I answer,

1. Because then there could not have been a personal union of both natures, and so Christ had not been a perfect Mediator.

2. Because then the work of each of the natures of Christ could not have been counted the works of the whole person; whereas now, by this union of both natures in one person, the obedience of Christ performed in the manhood is become of infinite merit, as being the obedience of God; and thereupon God is said *to have purchased the church with his own blood*. Acts xx. 28.

3. Because, if the person of the Son of God had been joined to the person of man, there should have been four persons in the trinity, It is very observable how for the better preservation of the integrity of the blessed trinity in the Godhead, the human nature was assumed into the unity of the second person; for if the fulness of the Godhead should have dwelt in any human person, there should then have been a fourth person necessarily added to the Godhead; and if any of the three persons, besides the second, had been born of a woman, there should then have been two sons, in the trinity; whereas now the Son of God and the son of man, being but one person, he is consequently but one son; and so no alteration at all made in the relations of the persons of the trinity; but they are still one Father, one Son, and one holy Ghost.

These are the deep things of God, and indeed

so

so exceedingly myſtical, that they can never be perfectly declared by any man. Bernard compares this ineffable myſtery of the union of two natures, with th t incomprehenſible myſtery of the trinity in unity: in the trinity are three perſons, and one nature, in Chriſt is two natures, and one perſon; that of the trinity is indeed the greateſt, and this of the incarnation is like unto it; they both far exceed man's capacity; *For his way is in the ſea, and his path is in the great waters, and his footſteps are not known*, Pſal. lxxvii. 19.

2. For the effects and benefits of this hypoſtatical union, they are either in reſpect of Chriſt, or in reſpect of Chriſtians.

1. Thoſe in reſpect of Chriſt, are 1. An exemption of all ſin. 2. A collation of all graces. 3. A communication of all the properties.

1. We find, That although Chriſt appeared as a ſinner, and that he was *numbered among the wicked, or with the tranſgreſſors,* Iſa. liii. 12. Yet in very deed and truth *he did no ſin, neither was any guile found in his mouth,* 1 Pet. ii. 22. The apoſtle tells us, *He was holy, harmleſs, undefiled, ſeparate from ſinners,* Heb. vii. 26. He aſſumed the nature of man; yet by reaſon of his pure conception, and of this hypoſtatical union he was conceived, and born, and lived without ſin: he took upon him the ſeed of man; but not the ſin of man, ſave only by imputation. But on this point I ſhall not ſtay.

2. The graces collated unto the humanity of Chriſt, by reaſon of this union, are very many; I ſhall inſtance in ſome: as——.

1. That the manhood hath ſubſiſtence in the ſecond perſon of the trinity, whereof itſelf (as of itſelf) is deſtitute.

2. That the manhood is a peculiar temple for the Deity of Chriſt to dwell in, it is the place wherein the Godhead ſhews itſelf more manifeſtly, and more gloriouſly, than in any other creature whatſoever. It is true, That by his providence he ſhews himſelf in all his creatures, and by his grace in his ſaints; but he is only moſt gloriouſly, eternally, according to the fulneſs of his Deity, and by an hypoſtatical union in the humanity of Jeſus Chriſt. *In him dwelleth all the fulneſs of the Godhead bodily.* Some are of opinion, That as now in this life, *No man cometh unto God, but by Chriſt,* Col. ii. 9. So hereafter, in the next life, no man ſhall ſee God, but in the face of Jeſus Chriſt.

3. That the manhood is in a nearer familiarity with the Godhead than any other creature, whether men, or angels, as ſometimes he ſaid, *My Father and I are one, i. e.* one eſſence; ſo he may as truly ſay, The manhood and I are one, *i. e.* one perſon for ever.

4. That the manhood of Chriſt, according to its meaſure is a partner with the Godhead in the work of redemption and mediation: as he is Immanuel in reſpect of his perſon, ſo he is Immanuel in reſpect of his office. He muſt needs be a man as well as God, that he might be able to ſend this comfortable meſſage to the ſons of men, *Go to my brethren, and ſay to them, I aſcend unto my Father and your Father, and to my God and your God,* John xx. 17. I, as man, am in the work of redemption, and in the work of mediation as well as God, *My fleſh is indeed the bread of life.*

5. That the manhood of Chriſt, together with the Godhead, is adored and worſhipped with divine honour; as, in like caſe, the honour done to the king, redounds to the crown upon his head; not that we worſhip the manhood alone, as merely a creature, but that we adore the perſon of Chriſt, which conſiſteth of the manhood and of the Godhead.

6. That the manhood hath an extraordinary meaſure, without meaſure, of habitual graces poured into it; in this he excels the very angels, for to them was given grace only by meaſure, but to the humanity of Chriſt was given grace without meaſure, even ſo much as a creature is anyways capable of. I know it is ſaid, That *Jeſus increaſed in wiſdom, and ſtature, and in favour with God and man,* Luke ii. 52. But this increaſe or growth in wiſdom is not to be underſtood in reſpect of the eſſence or extinction of the habit, (for that he had from the beginning, even from the firſt moment of his incarnation, and he brought it with him out of the womb) but in reſpect of the act and uſe of it, or in reſpect of his experimental knowledge, ſo he increaſed, and not otherwiſe; never was there any but Chriſt, whoſe graces were no way ſtinted, and that was abſolutely full of grace. Divines tell us of a double grace in Chriſt, the one of union, and that is infinite; the other of unction, (which is all one with grace habitual) and that is in a ſort infinite: for, howſoever it be

but a finite and created thing, yet in the nature of grace, it hath no limitation, no bounds, no stint, but includeth in itself whatsoever any way pertains to grace, or that cometh within the compass of it. The reason of this illimited donation of grace bestowed on the nature of man in Christ, was, for that grace was given to it as to the universal cause, whence it was to be derived unto all others; he is the fountain of grace, *And of his fulness we receive grace for grace*, John i. 16.

3. For the communication of the properties. It is a kind, or phrase of speech peculiar to the scriptures, when the properties of either nature of Christ considered singly and apart, are attributed to the person of Christ, from whichsoever of the natures they may be denominated; for the understanding of this, observe, 1. That words are either abstractive or concretive; the former speaks the nature of things, the latter speaks the person that hath that nature, as the Godhead, and God, the manhood, and man, holiness, and holy. 2. Observe, That abstractive words noting precisely the distinct natures, cannot be affirmed one of the other. We cannot say, The Godhead suffered, or the manhood created; but we may truly say, that God suffered, and man created; because the persons which these concretive words imply, is one; and all actions, passions, and qualities agree really to the person, though in respect sometimes of one nature, and sometimes of another: thus, *God purchased the church with his own blood*, Acts xx. 28. Not that the Godhead shed blood, but the person which was God: and thus the *son of man* talking with Nicodemus, is said to be in heaven, John iii. 13. Not that the manhood was in heaven while he was on earth; but the person of the Son of man. Thus we may say, That God was born of a virgin, and that God suffered, and God was crucified, not simply in respect of his Godhead, but in respect of his person, or in respect of the human nature which God united to himself, because God here is a concrete word, and not an abstract, and signifieth the person of Christ, and not the divine nature of Christ. And thus we may say, That the man Christ is almighty, omniscient, omnipresent, yet not simply in respect of its manhood, but in respect of the person, which is the same God and man; or in respect of the divine nature of the man Christ Jesus, for that here also *man* is a concrete word, and not an abstract, and signifieth the whole person of Christ, and not the human nature; but, on the contrary, we may not say, That the Godhead of Christ was born of a virgin, or suffered, or was crucified; nor may we say, That the manhood of Christ is almighty, omniscient, omnipresent, because the Godhead and manhood are abstract words, *i. e.* such words, as note to us the two natures of Christ, the one divine and the other human, and not the person of Christ.

And this I think is the mind of Luther, and his followers, and yet (O wonder) what a deal of objections are made to the multiplying of needless and fruitless contentions; the Lutherans confess, (however they hold the ubiquitary presence of the humanity of Christ) that his body is only in one place locally: *If we ask them,* (saith Zanchius, *in judicio de dissidio caenae Dominicae) whether Christ's body be every where? They answer, That locally it is but in one place, but that personally it is every where. Now, if they mean,* saith he, *That in respect of essence, his body is finite, and confined to one certain place; but in respect of the being of subsistence, or of his person, it is infinite, and every where, they say the truth; and there is no difference amongst us.* Happy are the reconcilers of dissenting brethren: *unto their assembly, mine honour be thou united.*

2. The effects or benefits of this hypostatical union, in respect of Christians, or their spiritual union and communion with God and Christ.

1. There is a spiritual union of Christians with God in Christ; O the wonder of these two blessed unions! First, Of the personal or hypostatical union. Secondly, Of this spiritual or mystical union: in the personal union it pleased God to assume and unite our human nature to the Deity; in this spiritual union, it pleased God to unite the person of every believer to the person of the Son of God. This union is mystical, and yet our very persons, natures, bodies, souls, are in a spiritual way conjoined to the body and soul of Christ; so that *we are members of the body of Christ, and of the flesh of Christ, and of the bones of Christ*, Eph. v. 30. And, as this conjunction is immediately made with his human nature, so thereby we are also united to *the divine nature*, 2 Pet. i. 4. Yea, the person of the believer is indissolubly united to the glorious person of the Son of God.

Now,

Now, concerning this union, for our better understanding, observe these four things.

1. It is a most real union, it is not a mere notional and intellectual union, that consists only in the understanding, and without the understanding is nothing; it is not an imaginary thing, that hath no other being but only in the brain; no, no, it is a true, real, essential, substantial union: in natural unions, I confess, there may be more evidence, but there cannot be more truth; spiritual agents never have, nor put forth less virtue, because sense cannot discern their manner of working; even the load-stone, though an earthen substance, yet when it is out of sight, whether under the table, or behind a solid partition, it stirreth the needle as effectually, as if it were within view. Shall not he contradict his senses, that will say, *It cannot work, because I see it not?* Oh, my Saviour! thou art more mine than my body is mine, my sense feels that present, but so as that I must lose it; but my faith so feels, and sees thee present with me, as that I shall never be parted from thee.

2. It is a very near union; you will say, How near? If an angel were to speak to you, he cannot fully satisfy you in this; only as far as our understanding can reach it, and the creatures can serve to illustrate these things, take it thus, whatsoever by way of comparison can be alledged concerning the combination of any one thing with another; that, and much more may be said of our union with Jesus Christ. To give instance out of the scripture, see what one stick is to another being *glewed together*, 1 Cor. vi. 17 See what one friend is to another, as Jonathan and David, 1 Sam. xviii. 1. Who were said to be woven and knit, each one to another; see how near the father and the child are, how near the *husband and the wife are*, Isa. lxii. 2. See what union is between the *branches and the vine*, the members and the head: nay, one thing more, see what the soul is to the body; such is Christ, and so near is Christ, and nearer to the person of every true believer, *I live, yet not I,* saith Paul, *but Christ liveth in me,* John xv. 5. 1 Cor. xii. 12. Gal. ii. 20. *q. d.* As the soul is to the body of a natural man, that acts and enlivens it naturally, so is Jesus Christ to my soul and body. O there is a marvellous nearness in this mystical union.

3. It is a total union, *i. e.* whole Christ is united to the whole believer, soul and body, if thou art united to Christ, thou hast all Christ, thou art one with him in his nature, in his name, thou hast the same image, grace and spirit in thee, as he hath; the same precious promises, the same access to God by prayer, as he; thou hast the same love to the Father; all that he did or suffered, thou hast a share in it; thou hast his life and death, all is thine: so, on thy part, he hath thee wholly, nature, thy sins, the punishment of thy sin; thy wrath, thy curse, thy shame; yea, thy wit and wealth, and strength, all that thou art or hast, or canst do possibly for him. It is a total union, *My beloved is mine, and I am his*; whole Christ from top to toe is mine, and all that I am, have, or can do for evermore is his.

4. It is an inseparable union, it can never be broken. *I will make,* saith God, *an everlasting covenant with them, and I will not turn away from them to do them good, I will put my fear in their hearts, that they shall not depart from me,* Jer. xxxii. 40. This is a glorious promise, some poor souls may say; 'True, Lord, thou wilt not 'turn away from me, I know thou wilt not; Oh, 'but I fear I shall turn away from thee: oh, alas! 'I turn every day towards him and Satan!' *Nay,* saith God, *I will put my fear into thy heart, that thou shalt not turn away from me, q. d.* We shall be kept together for evermore, and never be separated. Hence Paul triumphantly challenges all enemies on earth, (or rather in hell) to do their worst to break this knot, *Who shall separate me from the love of God in Christ? Shall tribulation, distress, famine, nakedness, peril, or sword?* Rom. viii. 35. Come, all that can come, and see if that blessed union betwixt me and Christ shall ever be broken by all that you can do. Thus for this union.

2. There is a spiritual communion with God in Christ. Both these are the effects of Christ's personal or hypostatical union; first, union to his person, and then communion with his benefits; union, in proper speaking, is not unto any of the benefits flowing to us from Christ; we are not united to forgiveness of sins, holiness, peace of conscience, but unto the person of the Son of God himself: and then, secondly, comes this communication of all the benefits arising immediately from this union to the Lord Jesus; that as Christ was priest,

priest, prophet, and king, so we also by him are, after a sort, priests, prophets, and kings; for being made one with him, we are thereby possessed of all things that are his, as the wife is of the wealth of her husband, *Now, all things are yours*, saith the apostle, *whether Paul, or Cephas, or the world*, &c. 1 Cor. iii. 21, 23.

Hitherto we took a view of Christ in his mother's womb, and O what a marvel's there! Did ever womb carry such a fruit? Well might the angel say, *Blessed art thou amongst women*, and well might Elisabeth say, *Blessed is the fruit of thy womb*; but the blessing is not only in conceiving, but in bearing, and therefore we proceed.

SECT. VI.

Of the birth of Christ.

1. THE birth of Christ now follows. Now was it that the Son of righteousness should break forth from his bed, where nine months he hid himself as being a fruitful cloud: this was the world's wonder, a thing so wonderful, that it was given for a sign unto believers seven hundred and forty years before it was accomplished: *therefore the Lord himself shall give you a sign, Behold a virgin shall conceive, and bear a Son*, Isa. vii. 14. A wonder indeed, and great beyond all comparison, that the Son of God should be born of a woman; that he who is the true Melchisedec, *without father, and without mother*, Heb. vii. 3. must yet have a mother virgin; that he that is before Abraham was, should yet be born after Abraham, a matter of two thousand years; that he who was David's son, and therefore born in Bethlehem, should yet be David's Lord, *wonderful things are spoken of thee, O Son of God*; before he was born the prophets sing, the sybills prophecy, the patriarchs typify, the types foretel, God promiseth, and the Son of God performeth; when he was born, angels run errands, Gabriel brings tydings, the glory of heaven shines, a star displays, and wise men are the heralds that proclaim his birth. But come yet a little nearer, *Let us go to Bethlehem*, as the shepherds said, *and see this thing which is come to pass*, Luke ii. 15. If we step but one step into his lodging, heaven's wonder is before our eyes. Now look upon Jesus! look on him as in fulness of time he carried on the great work of our salvation; here now you may read the meaning of Adam's covenant, Abraham's promise, Moses's revelation, David's succession; these were but vails; but now shall we draw aside the curtains. Come take a view of the truth itself; O wonders of wonders, whom find we in this lodging? A babe in a cratch, a mother maid, a father-virgin; is this the babe whom we look unto as our Jesus? Is this a mother *(as Austin)* scarce fourteen years of age? Is this the father that *knew her not until she had brought forth her first born son?* Matth. i. 25. What a strange birth is this? Look on the babe, there is no cradle to rock him, no nurse to lull him, no linens to swaddle him, scarce a little food to nourish him; look on the mother, there's no midwife's help, no downy pillows, no linen hangings, scarce a little straw where she is brought a-bed: look on Joseph, the reputed father, he rather begs than gives a blessing; poor carpenter, that makes them a chamber of an ox's stall, and carves him a cratch to be his cradle; Mary, that sees with her eyes, and ponders all in her heart, how doth modest shamefulness change her colours, so often as her imagination works? *She must bear a Son*, an angel tells her, the Holy Ghost overshadows her, the days are accomplished, and she is delivered; each circumstance is enough to abash a modest virgin: but who will not wonder? A maid believes, a maid conceives, a maid brings forth, and a maid still remains; how might we descant on this subject? But I shall contract myself, and reduce all wonders to this word, *I am the vine*, John xv. 5.

It is a blessed parable, in which under the shadow of a vine, Christ elegantly sets forth himself, Christ in many resemblances is a precious vine. But why a vine rather than a cedar, oak, or some of the strongest, tallest trees? Many reasons are given. As, 1. Because of all trees the vine is lowest, it grovels as it were on the ground. 2. Because of all trees the vine is the weakest, hence they that have vines, have also their elms to support them, and hold them up. 3. Because of all trees the vine hath the meanest bark and outside, it is of little worth or reputation. 4. Because of all trees the vine is fruitfullest; and therefore it is called *the fruitful vine*, Psal. cxxviii. 3. In every of these respects, Christ is called *a vine*, who by his incarnation

Carrying on the Work of Man's Salvation in his Incarnation.

nation took upon him the lowest condition, and made himself, by emptying himself, *of no reputation*, Phil. ii. 7. But he was the fruitfullest vine that ever the earth bore, and in this respect no vine, nor all the vines on the earth were worthy to be compared with him, or to be so much as resemblance of him. I shall not prosecute the resemblance throughout; for so I might pass from his birth to his life, and from his life to his death, when the blood of the grapes were pressed out, only for the present we'll take a view of this vine, 1. In its plant. 2. In its bud. 3. In its blossom. 4. In its fruit; and so an end.

1. For the plant: the way of vines is not to be sowed, but planted, that thus translated they might better fructify: so our Jesus, first sprung from his Father, is planted in a virgin's womb; God from God, coeternal with God; but by his incarnation made that he was not, and yet remaining that he was; God of his Father, and man of his mother; before all time, yet since the beginning: *Bernard, de Passione Dom.* tells us, 'That 'this vine sprung of the vine, is God begotten of 'God, the Son of the Father, both coeternal and 'consubstantial with the Father; but that he might 'better fructify, he was planted in the earth; *i. e.* 'He was conceived in a virgin's womb.' There is indeed a resemblance in this; yet in this resemblance we must be careful to observe, That communication of properties, of which I told you, we may truly say, That God was planted, or conceived, but not the Godhead; God is a concrete word, and signifies the person of Christ, and his person was planted or conceived, not simply as God, but in respect of the manhood united to it; and thus he that is infinite was conceived; and he that is eternal, even he was born; the very fulness of all perfection, and all the properties of the divine essence are by this communication given to the nature of man in the person of the Son of God; no wonder therefore, that we say, that this vine (the Son of God) is planted in Mary; I know some would have the plant more early, and therefore they say, That Christ was a vine planted in Adam, budded in David, and flourished in Mary: But I take this but for a flourish; all before Mary were but types, now was the truth; now in Mary was Christ planted, and not before; as in the beginning *there was not a man to till the ground,——But out of the ground the Lord made to grow every tree;—And a river went out of Eden to water the garden:* so there was no man that tilled this ground, but out of this ground (the virgin) the Lord made to grow this plant, watering it by his Spirit; *The holy Ghost shall come upon thee, and the power of the Highest shall overshadow thee,* Luke i. 35. Of this conception and of the holy Ghost's efficiency, I believe, spake the prophet, when there was such longing after Christ's coming in the flesh, *Drop down, ye heavens, from above, and let the sky pour down righteousness, let the earth open, and bring forth salvation,* Isa. xlv. 8. But of this conception before.

2. For the bud, the nature of vines is to bud, before it blossom or bring forth its fruit; so was it said of Christ before he came, *Truth shall bud out of the earth,* Psal. lxxxv. 11. Now, what was this budding of truth out of earth, but Christ born of a woman? 'What was the truth (saith *Irenæus* L. 3. C. 5. and *Augustin*) but Christ? And what 'the earth but our flesh? And what truth budding, 'but Christ being born?' Here let us stay a while. surely it is worth the while (as the spouse said in another case) to *get up early to the vineyard, and to see how the vine did flourish, and how the tender grape did open,* Cant. vii. 12.

In Christ's carrying on the great work of our salvation before all worlds, we told you of God's counsels, as if he had been reduced to some straits and difficulties by the cross demands of his several attributes, but wisdom found out a way how to reconcile these differences by propounding a Jesus; and in him *mercy and truth met together, righteousness and peace kissed each other,* Psalm lxxxv. 10. That reconciliation was in the counsel of God from all eternity; but for the execution of this counsel it was now in the fulness of time, even at this time when Christ was born. Now indeed, and in truth in execution in performance, was the reconciliation of all differences; and of this time was the Psalmist's prophecy more especially meant, *Mercy and truth shall meet together, righteousness and peace sha'l kiss each other: truth shall bud out of the earth, and righteousness shall look down from heaven,* Psal. lxxxv. 10, 11.

In these words we find *first*, a meeting of God's blessed attributes, and, *secondly*, This meeting at a birth, the birth of truth; at which meeting, *thirdly*, was that glorious effect, That *righteousness*

ness looked down, and indeed came down *from heaven*. I desire a little to invert the words, and shall *first* speak to Christ's birth; *secondly*, to the effects of his birth, of *righteousness looking down from heaven*. Thirdly, To the meeting and agreement of all God's attributes, as the issue and effect of all; *When mercy and truth met together, and righteousness and peace kissed each other*.

1. For his birth, our vine doth bud; *truth shall bud out of the earth*, i. e. Christ shall be born upon the earth, or Christ shall be born of a woman, for truth is Christ, bud is *born*, and *the earth* is a woman. 1. *Truth* is Christ, *I am the way and the truth*, said Christ, John xiv. 6. He is the truth of all types, and the truth of all prophecies, and the truth of all promises *For in him are all the promises, Yea and Amen*. 2. *Bud* is born; the vine budding is the first putting forth of the grape, so Christ being born, was truth budding out of the earth, he then first shewed himself to the world, and was first seen (like the vine springing forth) above ground. 3 The *earth* is the woman, thus we render that text, *Let the earth bring forth a Saviour*, Isa. xlv. 8. Look how the field-flowers spring forth of themselves without any seed cast in by the hand of man, so the virgin brings forth Christ. It is observable, that in the creation of Adam was laid the prognosticks of this future birth: begin with the first man, Adam, and you may see him paralleled in this second Adam, Christ. Adam was created of the virgin-earth, Christ was born of a virgin-mother; the earth had no husband-man, yet brought forth without seed, Mary had no husband, yet brought forth without seed of man; in the creation God said, *Let us make man*, Gen. i. 26. And now saith the holy Ghost, *The word is made flesh*, John i. 14. Or the word is man indeed; those were but types, but Christ is the truth; he is the vine that buds, the Messias born; the angels own him, the star designs him, the prophets fore-shew him, the devils confess him, his miracles declare him, and heaven and earth rings with the news, That *truth is budded out of the earth*.

2. For the effect of his birth; *righteousness shall look down from heaven*. No sooner Christ born, but righteousness looked down from heaven; she cast her eye upon earth, and seeing truth freshly sprung there, she looked and looked again; certainly it was a sight to draw all the eyes of heaven to it. It is said of the angels, That *they desired to look into these things*, 1 Pet. i. 12. They looked wishfully at them, as it they would look through them; no question, but righteousness looked as narrowly, and as piercingly as the angels: some observe, That the Hebrew word, *she looked down*, signifies that *she beat out a window*; so desirous was righteousness to behold the sight of the vine budding, of Christ being born, That she could not hold, but she beats out a window in heaven: before this time, she would not so much as look down towards earth; righteousness had no prospect, no window open this way; she turned away her eyes; and clapped to the casement, and would not abide to much as to look on such sinful, wretched, forlorn sinners as we are; her eye was purer than to behold iniquity, she abhorred it, and us for it, and therefore would not vouchsafe us once the cast of her eye. O but now the case is altered! no sooner doth our vine bud upon the earth, but she is willing to condescend, and so willing that she breaks a window through the walls of heaven to look down upon this bud; and no marvel: for, what could righteousness desire to see, and satisfy herself in, that was not to be seen in Jesus Christ? He was all righteous, there was not the least spot of sin to be found in him, his birth was clean, and his life was holy, and his death was innocent; both his soul and body were without all sin; both his spirit and his mouth were without all guile; whatsoever satisfaction righteousness would have, she might have it in him, *Lay judgment to the line, and righteousness to the balance*, and there is nothing in Jesus but straight for the line and full weight for the balance.

3. For the meeting and agreement of all God's attributes, as the issue and the last effect of this budding vine, the verse before tells us, That *mercy and truth are met together, righteousness and peace have kissed each other*; this meeting pre-supposeth a distance before they met, for they that meet come from divers coasts: here then are two things considerable; *First*, the distance, and *secondly*, the meeting. But you will say, How came this distance? Are they not all the attributes of God's undivided essence? Are they not all four in the bosom of God from all eternity? I answer, Yes: They are undivided in themselves, but they
were

were divided about us; it was Adam's sin, and ours in him, that first divided heaven, yea, the very attributes of God, and in a sort God himself. I shall speak to both these. That you may first see the differences, and then the agreement and blessed harmony of these glorious attributes.

1. The difference; immediately after the fall, the great question (which before you heard of in the decree and councils of God) was actually propounded, What should be done with sinful man? In this case we must speak of God after the manner of men; and I hope you will give me the liberty that others (I suppose warrantably) take: *Come,* saith God, *What shall be done with sinful man?* He hath violated my law, broken my command, and, as much as lies in him, unpinned the fabrick of the world, spoiled my glorious work of heaven, and earth, and sea, and all therein; undone himself for ever and ever, and ever. 'O 'what shall be done with this sinful, rebellious, 'forlorn, unhappy creature, man?' Silence being a while in heaven, and all struck into amaze to see the great God of heaven stirred up in wrath, at last *mercy and peace* stand up, and they seek with sweet gentle entreaties to pacify God's anger; but righteousness and truth are on the contrary side, and they provoke God Almighty to go on and to manifest himself (as he is indeed) *a consuming fire,* a sin-revenging God. The plea is drawn up, and reported at large by Bernard, Andrews, and others.

1. Mercy began, for out of her readiness to do good, she is ever foremost; her inclination is to pity, or rather she herself is an inclination to pity those that are in misery; and if she can but relieve them, let them deserve what they will, be sure she will relieve them; for she looks not to the party, what he is, nor what he hath done, nor what he deserves; but (which is the comfort of us miserable sinners) she looks at what he suffers, and in how woful and wretched a case he is. Her plea was thus, 'What, Lord, hast thou made all men 'in vain? Wilt thou now destroy him for whom 'thou madest the world? Shall the housholder be 'cast out, and thrown into prison, and there re-'main till he hath paid the utmost farthing? Shall 'all the men and women in the world, from first to 'last, be damned for ever and ever? Alas! what 'profit is in their blood? What will it avail to 'crowd men and devils together in hell-flames?

'Will not those devils, the grand enemies of God, 'rejoice at this? And what then will become of 'thy great name on earth? Is not this thy name,' *The Lord, the Lord, merciful, and gracious, long-suffering, and abundant in goodness and truth, keeping mercy for thousands, forgiving iniquity, transgression and sins?* 'What will the Lord undo his 'name? Will the Lord cast off for ever? And 'will he be favourable no more? Is his mercy 'clean gone for ever? Will he be no more en-'treated? Hath God forgotten to be gracious? 'Hath he in anger shut up his tender bowels?' With these, and such like holy whisperings, or mutterings, did mercy enter into God's bowels, and make them yearn and melt again into compassions.

But, 2. *Truth* must be heard as well as *Mercy*; and she lays in matter of exception, and her plea was thus; *What is God, but his word? Now, this was thy word to Adam,* In the day that thou eatest thereof thou shalt die the death, *and this was thy word to all the sons of Adam,* The soul that sinneth, that soul shall die, Gen. ii. 17. *And God may not falsify his word; his word is truth; falsify truth, that may not be; all men are liars, but God is true, even truth itself,* Ezek. xviii. 20. This plea of truth is seconded by righteousness; and thus she bespeaks God, *Shall not the Judge of all the world do right? Thou hast declared thyself over and over to be just and righteous;* O Lord God of Israel, thou art righteousness, Ezra ix. 15. Righteous art thou, O Lord, and upright are thy judgments, *Psal. cxix. 13.* Thou art righteous, O Lord, which art, and wast, and shall be, *Rev. xvi. 5, 7.* Even so, Lord God Almighty, true and righteous are thy judgments,——Yea the Lord is righteous in all his ways, and holy in all his works, *Psal. cxlv. 17. And wherein consists this righteousness; but in rendering to every one according to his due? And what is the sinner's due, but death?* The wages of sin is death, *Rom. vi. 13. What shall not these sinners die the death? That were (as before) to make truth false, so here to do right wrong.*

These were the controversies at that time, so that *Peace* could not tell how to speak a prevailing word amongst them: nay, the controversy grew so high, that they made it their own cases, *What shall become of me,* (said Mercy) *if God spare not sinners?* And, *What shall become of me,* (said Justice)

Justice) *if God do spare sinners? What shall become of me,* (said Mercy) *if God will shew no mercy?* And, *what shall become of me,* (said Justice) *if God will do no Justice? Why, alas! I perish,* (said Mercy) *if thou wilt not pity; if man die, I die also.* And *I perish,* (said Justice) *if thou wilt have mercy; surely I die, if man die not.* To this it came, and in these terms brake up the assembly, and away they went one from another; *Truth* went to heaven, and was a stranger upon earth; *Righteousness* went with her, and would not so much as look down from heaven; *Mercy,* she stayed below still, for where should mercy be if not with the miserable? As for *Peace,* she went between both, to see if she could make them meet again in better terms: in the mean while our salvation lies a bleeding, the plea hangs, and we stand as prisoners at the bar, and know not what shall become of us; for, though two be for us, yet two are against us, as strong, and more stiff than they; so that much depends upon this meeting, for either they must be at peace between themselves, or they cannot be at peace with us, nor can we be at peace with God.

Many means were made before Christ's time for a blessed meeting, but it would not be, *Sacrifice and burnt-offering thou wouldest not have,* Heb. x. 5. These means were not prevalent enough to cause a meeting. Where stuck it, you will say? Surely it was not long of *Mercy,* she was easy to be entreated? she looked up to heaven, but *Righteousness* would not look down; and, indeed here was the business, *Righteousness* must and will have satisfaction, or else *Righteousness* should not be righteous, either some satisfaction for sin must be given to God, or she will never meet more; better all men in the world were damned, than that the righteousness of God should be unrighteous. And this now puts on the great transaction of our Saviour's birth.

Well then, our Saviour is born, and this birth occasions a great meeting of the attributes; such an attraction is this birth, this *bud of Christ,* that all meet there; indeed they cannot otherwise but meet in him, in whom all the blessed attributes of God do meet: it is Christ is *Mercy,* and Christ is *Truth,* and Christ is *Righteousness,* and Christ is *Peace.* 1. Christ is *Mercy;* thus Zacharias prophesied, That *through the tender mercy of our God,* the day-spring, (or branch) *from on high hath visited us,* Luke i. 7, 8. And God the Father of Christ, is called the Father of mercies; as if *Mercy* were his son, who had no other son but his dearly beloved Son *in whom he is well pleased,* 2 Cor. i. 3. 2. Christ is *Truth, I am the way, and the truth, and the life,* John xiv. 6. That *Truth* in whom is accomplished whatsoever was prefigured of the Messiah, *God shall send forth his mercy and his truth,* Psal. lvii. 3. And, *O prepare mercy and truth,* Psal. lxiv. 7. And this is his name, *The Lord, the Lord—abundant in goodness and truth,* Exod. xxxiv 6. *He is a God of truth,* saith Moses, Deut. xxxii. 4 *Plenteous in mercy and truth,* saith David, Psal. lxxxvi. 15. *Full of grace and truth,* saith John, i. 14, 17. *For the law was given by Moses, but grace and truth came by Jesus Christ.* He is *Truth* by name, and *Truth* by nature, and *Truth* by office.——3. Christ is *Righteousness. This is his name, whereby he shall be called the Lord our righteousness,* Jer. xxiii. 6. And, *Unto you that fear my name, shall the Son of righteousness arise with healing under his wings,* Mal. iv. 2. And, *Christ of God is made unto us wisdom, righteousness, and sanctification, and redemption,* 1 Cor. i. 30. And according to his type, Melchisedec, this was his stile, *King of righteousness,* Heb. vii. 2.—4. Christ is *Peace.* This is his *name wherewith he is called, wonderful, counsellor, The mighty God, The everlasting Father, The Prince of peace,* Isa. ix. 6. And, *Christ is our peace, who hath made both one, and hath broken down the middle wall of partition between us,* Eph. ii. 14. And therefore prays the apostle, *Now the lord of peace himself,* (or the Lord himself who is peace) *give you peace always by all means,* 2 Thes. iii. 16. And according to his type Melchisedec, as he was *king of righteousness, so a so he was king of Salem, which is king of peace,* Heb. vii. 2 —Thus Christ is *Mercy,* and Christ is *Truth,* and Christ is *Righteousness,* and Christ is *Peace.* Now, where should all these meet but in him, who is them all? Surely, there they meet, and at the meeting they all ran first and kissed the Son; and that done, Truth ran to Mercy and embraced her, and Righteousness to Peace, and kissed her; they that so long had been parted, and stood out in difference, now they meet and are made friends again: O the blessed effect of this birth of Christ!

it

Carrying on the Work of Man's Salvation in his Incarnation. 145

it is Christ that reconciled them, and that reconciled us and them. *He reconciled all things*, faith the apostle, *whether they be things in earth, or things in heaven*, Col. i. 20. Now is heaven at peace with itself, and heaven and earth at peace with one another; and that which glues all, and makes the peace, is this birth of Christ; the budding of this vine. *Truth shall bud out of the earth, and then mercy and truth shall meet together*, &c.

3. For the blossom: the nature of vines is in its season, to blossom, or to bear sweet flowers. Pharaoh's butler, you know dreamed of a vine, that not only budded but blossomed, *Her blossoms shot forth*, Gen. xl. 10. And thus Christ our vine both budded and blossomed; he was full of the sweetest flowers: now, what were these flowers and blossoms of Christ but his virtues and blessed graces? In this only Christ differs from the vine, in that in him was seen not only one sort or kind of flowers, but every kind. *Bernard, de Passione Dom.* reckons up, 'The violet of humility, the lily of chastity, 'the rose of patience, the saffron of abstinence;' I may not so far enlarge myself, but in reference to his birth, I cannot but admire at his humility, patience and infinite condescensions; that the Creator should become a creature, though an angel; it were a great gulph, which no creature understanding could measure, that he should reject angels, and take the seed of Abraham; that he should be made lower than the angels, who is God over all; that he would be conceived, who is the uncreated wisdom, in the dark prison of the womb, who is the light of the world; and that of a woman, the weaker, first sinning sex, who is the holy One, and Power of God; that he would be born, who beareth all things; the Lord of all, of a lowly hand-maid; in fulness of time, who is eternity; in the night time, who is *the Sun of righteousness*; in the winter, who gives life and heat; in a time of publick taxation, who is Lord of lords; and that not at Rome, the lady of nations, nor at Jerusalem the glory of the East; but at Bethlehem, the least of the thousands of Judah; not in a palace prepared, nor in his mother's house; but in an inn; not in the best room, nor in any room of the house, but in a stable of beasts; not attended there with a royal guard, but with Joseph and Mary; not adorned in robes, but swaddled in clouts; not stately enthroned, but laid in a manger; nor, lastly, his birth proclaimed by the kings at arms, but by poor shepherds.

That *the word* should be an infant not able to speak a word; that life should be mortal; that power should be subject to a poor carpenter; that the Lord of the covenant should be circumcised; that the God of the temple should be presented in the temple, that wisdom should be instructed, infiniteness should grow in stature; that the Feeder of all things should be fed; that all these are preludes, and but beginnings of his sufferings; O wonderful condescension! O admirable patience! O rare humility! how strange are the blossoms of this vine?

4. For the fruit: the nature of vines is to cast sweet savours, but to bear sour grapes: Christ was blameless before God and man, yet bore the heavy burden of our sin. O the sweetness of his savours! *Because of the savour of thy good ointments, thy name is as ointment poured forth*, Cant. i. 3. Whether by savours we mean his words, the very officers of the Jews can say, *Never man spake like this man*, John vii. 46. Or, whether by savours, we mean his deeds, his very enemies confess him a just man, so Pilate's wife could send her husband word, *Have thou nothing to do with that just man*, Matth. xxvii. 19. The wise men that brought their offerings, *Gave him gold, frankincense, and myrrh*, Matth. ii. 11. Gold is given him, as to a potent king; frankincense, as to a gracious God; and myrrh, as to an holy priest: he is a king to rule, a God to save, and a priest to mediate; thus far he casts sweet savours, but digest them better, and they prove sour grapes; a king he was, but mockt with the title, *Hail king of the Jews*, Mat. xxvii. 29. A God he was, but he emptied himself, *He made himself of no reputation*, Phil. ii. 7. An holy priest he was, but such a priest as must offer up himself for a sacrifice; the wise men that came from the East, they saw his infirmity, yet adore his wisdom; they saw his poverty, yet adore the riches of his mercy; they saw him whom they enquired after, *Where is he that is born king of the Jews?* Matth. ii. 2. The very titles cast sweet savours, but it bears sour grapes; he is a king, that is a title of honour; but he is *king of the Jews*, that's a word of reproach.

All along his life you may see these two; *sweet savours, but sour grapes*, *Vidisti vilia, audisti mirifica,*

T

rifica, said Ambrose; the things you see are mean, but the things you see and hear are wonderful; mean it was to see a sort of shepherds, wonderful it is to see a troop of angels: mean it was to hear one say, *Laid in the cratch below*; wonderful it is to hear many sing, *Glory to God on high*: mean it was to see him man, wonderful it is to know him God. Here's a little child fainting and groaning, yet a powerful God ruling and commanding; hungry himself to shew our nature, yet feeding five thousand to shew his power; dying on the cross as the son of Adam, disposing of paradise as the Son of God. As it was said of Bethlehem, *Minima, & non minima; the least of the thousands*, Mat. ii. 6. So we say of this Bethlemite, *Minimus, & non minimus; He shall sit upon the throne of David*, Isa. ix. 7. Yet he hath borne our griefs, and carried our sorrows, Isa. liii. 4. *His kingdom is an everlasting kingdom*, Dan. vii. 27. *Yet his end shall be, and he shall have nothing*, Dan. ix. 26. Thus all along from his cratch to his cross, *sweet savours but sour grapes*: at last, indeed the grapes grew to a ripeness, and then he was pressed, and his dearest heart-blood run out in abundant streams: this was the sweet juice of our garden vine, God planted it, the heavens water it, the Jews prune it, What remains now but that we abide in it? But of that when we come to the directions, how we are to look.

SECT. VII.

Of some consequences after Christ's birth.

7. Some consequences after the birth of Christ may be touched, whilst yet he was but a child of twelve years old.—

1. When he was but eight days old, he was circumcised, and named Jesus. As there was shame in his birth, so there was pain in his circumcision; a sharp razor passeth through his skin, presently after he is born; not that he needed this ceremony, but that for us he was content legally to be impure; in this early humiliation, he plainly discovers the riches of his grace; now he sheds his blood in drops, and thereby gives an earnest of those rivers, which he after poured out for the cleansing of our nature, and extinguishing the wrath of God; and for a farther discovery of his grace, at this time his name was given him, which was Jesus: this is the name which we should engrave in our hearts, rest our faith on, and place our help in, and love with the overflowings of charity, and joy, and adoration; above all things we had need of a Jesus, a Saviour for our souls, and from our sins, and from the everlasting destruction which sin will otherwise bring upon our souls; hence this name Jesus, and this sign, circumcision, are joined together, for by the effusion of his blood, he was to be our Jesus, our Saviour; *Without shedding of blood is no remission of sins*, Heb. ix. 22. No salvation of souls, *circumcision was the seal*, Rom. iv. 11. And now was it that our Jesus was under God's great seal to take his office, we have heard how he carried on the great work of our salvation from eternity; this very name and office of Jesus, a Saviour, was resolved on in God's fore-counsel, and given forth from the beginning, and we have heard of late how it was promised and foretold by an angel; but now it is signed and sealed with an absolute commission and fulness of power, *him hath God the Father sealed*, John vi. 27. It is his office and his very profession to save, that all may repair unto him to that end, *Come unto me all ye that are weary*, Matth. xi. 28. And *him that cometh unto me I will in noways cast out*, John vi. 37. In which respect he is called *the Saviour of the world*, John iv. 42. *i. e.* Of Samaritans, Jews, Gentiles, kings, shepherds, and of all sorts of men.

2. When he was forty days old, *He was brought to Jerusalem, and presented to the Lord, as it is written in the law of the Lord, Every male that openeth the womb, shall be called holy to the Lord*, Luke ii. 22, 23. O wonder! there was no impurity in the Son of God, and yet he is first circumcised, and then he is brought and offered to the Lord, he that came to be sin for us, would in our persons be legally unclean, that by satisfying the law he might take away our uncleanness; he that was above the law, would come under the law, that he might free us from the law, we are all born sinners; but O the unspeakable mercies of our Jesus, that provides a remedy as early as our sin. First, He is conceived, and then he is born, to sanctify our conceptions and our births; and after his birth he is first circumcised, and then he is presented to the Lord, that by two holy acts, that which

which was naturally unholy might be hallowed into God; Christ hath not left our very infancy without redress, but by himself thus offered, he cleanseth us presently from our unholiness.—Now Christ brought in his mother's arms to his own house, the temple; and as man, he is presented to himself as God. O how glorious did that temple seem, now the owner was within the walls of it? Now was the hour, and guest come, in regard whereof the second temple should surpass the first; his was the house built for him, and dedicated to him, there had he dwelt long in his typical presence, nothing was done there whereby he was not resembled; and now the body of these shadows is come, and presents himself where he had ever been represented. You will say, What is this to me, or to my soul? O yes, Jerusalem is now every where, there is no church assembly, no Christian heart which is not a temple of the living God; and there is no temple of God wherein Christ is not represented to his Father. Thus we have the benefit of Christ's fulfilling the law of righteousness; *God sent his Son, made of a woman, made under the law, that he might redeem them that were under the law, that we might receive the adoption of sons*, Gal. iii. 4, 5. It is as if his Father should have said to Christ, ' Come, my dear Son, here ' are certain malefactors under the law to suffer ' and to be executed; what say you to them? ' Why I will become under the law, (saith Christ) ' I will take upon me their execution, and suffer ' for them;' and to this purpose he is first circumcised, and then he is presented to the Lord.

3. When he was yet under one year old, as some, or about two, as others, he fled into Egypt. As there was no room for him in Bethlehem, so now there is no room for him in all Judea; no sooner he came to his own, but he must fly from them, what a wonder is this? Could not Christ have quit himself from Herod, a thousand ways? What could an arm of flesh have done against the God of spirits? Had Jesus been of the spirit of some of his disciples, he might have commanded fire from heaven on those that should have come to have apprehended him; but hereby he taught us to bear the yoke, even in our youth, thus would he suffer, that he might sanctify to us our early afflictions, he flies into Egypt, the slaughter-house of God's people, the sink of the world, the furance of Israel's ancient afflictions; what a change is here? Israel, the first-born of God flies out of Egypt into Judea; and Christ the first-born of all creatures flies out of Judea into Egypt; *Euseb. de Demonst. L. 6. C. 20.* reports, That the child Jesus arriving in Egypt, and being by a design carried into a temple, all the statues of the idol-gods fell down, like Dagon, at the presence of the ark; and to this purpose he cites Isaiah's prophecy, *Behold, the Lord shall come into Egypt, and the idols of Egypt shall be moved at his presence*, Isa. xix. 1. Now is Egypt become the sanctuary, and Judea the inquisition-house of the Son of God; surely he is every where the same, knows how to make all places alike to his; he knows how to preserve Daniel in the lions den; the three children in a fiery furnace; Jonah in a whale's belly; and Christ in the midst of Egypt.

4. When he was now some five years old, say some; or but two years and a quarter old, say others, an angel appears again in a dream to Joseph, saying, *Arise, and take the young child and his mother, and return again into the land of Israel, for they are dead which sought the young child's life*, Matth. ii. 19, 20. Herod, that took away the lives of all the infants in, or about Bethlehem, is now himself dead, and gone to his own place; and by this means, the coast is clear for the return of that holy family; O the wonderful dispensation of Christ in concealing of himself from men! all this while he carries himself as an infant, and tho' he knows all things, yet he neither takes, nor gives any notice of his removal, or disposing, but appoints that to be done by his angel, which the angel could not have done but by him. As Christ was pleased to take upon him our nature, so in our nature he was pleased to be a perfect child, for that is the word, *Take the young child and his mother*; he suppressed the manifestation and exercise of that Godhead, whereto the infant-nature was conjoined; as the birth of Christ, so the infancy of Christ was exceeding humble. Oh how should we magnify him, or deject ourselves for him; who himself became thus humble for our sakes?

5. When he was twelve years old, *He with his parents went up to Jerusalem, after the custom of the feast*, Luke ii. 42. This pious act of his younger years intends to lead our first years into timely devotion; but I shall not insist on that; I would rather

rather observe him *sitting in the midst of the doctors, both hearing them, and asking them questions,* ver. 46. Whilst the children of his age were playing in the streets, he is found of his parents sitting in the temple, not to gaze on the outward glory of that house, of the golden candlesticks, or tables, or cherubims, or the pillars, or the molten sea, or the altar of gold, or the vessels of pure gold; no, no, but to hear and oppose the doctors. He, who, as God, gave them all the wisdom they had, doth now as the son of man hearken to the wisdom he had given them; and when he had heard, then he asks, and after that, no doubt, he answers; his very questions were instructions, for I cannot think, that he meant so much to learn, as to teach those doctors of Israel. Surely these Rabbins had never heard the voice of such a tutor; they could not but see the very wisdom of God in this child, and therefore, saith the text, *They all wondered,* or they were all astonished, *at his understanding and answers,* ver. 47. Their eyes saw nothing but a child, but their ears heard the wonderful things of God's law; betwixt what they saw, and what they heard, they could not but be distracted and amazed. But why did ye not (O ye Jewish teachers) remember now the star, and the sages, and the angels, and the shepherds? Why did ye not now bethink yourselves of Herod, and of his inquiry, and of your answer, That *in Bethlehem of Judea Christ should be born?* You cited the prophets, and why did you not mind that prophecy now, That *unto us a child is born, and unto us a son is given, and his name shall be called wonderful, counsellor, The mighty God, the everlasting Father, the prince of peace?* v. 56. Fruitless is the wonder that endeth not in faith; no light is sufficient, where the eyes are held through unbelief and prejudice.

6. After this, from the twelfth to the thirtieth year of his age, we read nothing of the acts of Christ; but that *he went down with his parents into Nazareth, and was subject to them,* Luke ii. 51. As he went up to Jerusalem to worship God, and in some sort to shew himself God; so now he goes down to Nazareth, to attend his particular calling. This is the meaning of those words, *And he was subject to them.* Christ's subjection to his parents extends to the profession, and exercise of his life: certainly Christ was not all that time from twelve to thirty years idle; as he was educated by his parents, so of his reputed father he learned to be a carpenter; this I take it is plain in these words, *Is not this the carpenter the son of Mary?* Mark vi. 3. *It appears* (says our English annotations) *that Christ exercised that trade in his younger years.* I know Matthew renders it thus, *Is not this the carpenter's son? Is not his mother called Mary?* Matth. xiii. 55. But Mark thus, *Is not this the carpenter,* &c. Some comment thus, That while Joseph was alive Christ wrought with him in the trade of a carpenter, and when Joseph died, which happened before the manifestation of Jesus unto Israel, he wrought alone, and was no more called the carpenter's son, but the carpenter himself: here's comfort for men of the meanest callings; as husbandry was honoured in the person and condition of the first Adam before his fall; so now the handicraft. O the poverty, humility, severity of Jesus? It appears at this time especially in his labouring, working, hewing of wood, or the like; here's a sharp reproof to all those that spend their time in idleness, or without a particular calling; that take no pains at all, unless in pursuit after vain, foolish, superfluous, sinful things. What! are they wiser than Christ? Our Jesus would not by any means thus spend his time. Indeed for the while he did nothing famous, or of publick note; but neither was this without a mystery, *Nihil faciendo, fecit magnifica,* saith one, *in doing nothing public, he atchieved great and sumptuous, and praise-worthy acts.* There is a season and time to every purpose under heaven: as there is a time of silence, and a time to speak; so there is a time for publick, and a time for private negotiations; as yet Christ conceals his virtues, and conforms himself to the conversation of men, that the mystery of his incarnation might not be thought a phantasm; then he would have his virtues and graces to shine out, when men usually come to their vigour and strength both of body and mind: and besides, as it was said of a divine (Mr. Bolton) that he would never preach a sermon, but he would first endeavour to practise it himself. So I am sure did Christ. He would not teach the world, saying, *Learn of me, for I am meek and lowly in heart,* Matth. xi. 29. But first he would practise, do, and then teach, as Luke tells Theophilus, *He had writ of all that Jesus began both to do and teach,* Acts i. 1.

But

But concerning this time of his youth, because in scripture there is so deep a silence: I shall therefore pass it by.

Thus far I have propounded the object, we are to look unto: it is Jesus, in his first coming or incarnation; whilst yet a child of twelve years old; our next work is, to direct you in the art and mystery, how we are to look to him in this respect.

CHAP. II. SECT. I.

Of knowing Jesus, as carrying on the great work of our salvation in his birth.

WHat looking comprehends, you have heard before: and that we may have an inward experimental look on him, whom our souls pant after, let us practise all these particulars. As——

1. Let us know Jesus, carrying on the great work of our salvation in his first coming or incarnation. Come, let us learn what he did for us when he came among us. There is not one passage in his first appearing, but it is of mighty concernment unto us; is it possible, that the great God of heaven and earth should so infinitely condescend, (as we have heard) but on some great design? And what design could there be, but only his glory and the creature's good? O my soul! if thou hast any interest in Christ, all this concerns thee; the Lord Jesus in all these very transactions had an eye to thee: he was incarnate for thee; he was conceived, and born for thee: look not on these things as notionals or generals; look not on the bare history of things, for that is but unprofitable: the main duty is in eying the end, the meaning and intent of Christ; and especially as it relates to thee, not to others, but to thyself. Alas! what comfort were it to a poor prisoner, if he should hear, that the king or prince, of his mere grace and love, visited all the prisoners in this and that dungeon, and that he made a goal-delivery, and set all free; but he never came near the place where he poor wretch lies bound in fetters and cold irons? Or, suppose he gives a visit to that very man, and offers him the tenders of grace and freedom, if he will but accept of it; and, (because of his waywardness) perswades, entreats, commands him to come out, and take his liberty, and yet he will not regard or apply it to himself; what comfort can he have? What fruit, what benefit shall he receive? Dear soul, this is thy case, if thou art not in Christ, if thou hast not heard the offer, and embraced and closed with it, then what is Christ's incarnation, conception, nativity unto thee? Come, learn, not merely as a scholar, to gain some notional knowlege; but as a Christian, as one that feels virtue coming out of Christ in every of these respects: study close this great transaction in reference to thyself. I know not how it happens, whether out of the generality of some preachers, handling this subject, or whether out of the superstition of the time, wherein it usually hath been handled, it either favours not with some Christians, or it is seldom thought of by the most: O God forbid we should throw out of the doors such a blessed necessary truth! if rightly applied, it is a Christian's joy, *Behold, I bring you glad tidings of great joy, that shall be to all people, for unto you is born in the city of David, a Saviour, which is Christ the Lord,* Luke ii. 10, 11. Sure the birth of Christ is of mighty concernment unto thee, *Unto us a child is born, unto us a son is given,* Isa. ix. 6. There is not any piece of this transaction but it is of special use, and worth thy pains. How many break their brains, and waste their spirits in studying arts and sciences, things in comparison of no value; whereas Paul otherwise *determined not to know any thing among you but Jesus Christ?* 1 Cor. ii 2. To know Jesus Christ in every piece and point, whether in birth, or life, or death, it is saving knowledge: O stand not upon cost, whether pains or study, tears or prayers, peace or wealth, goods or name, life or liberty, fell all for this pearl: Christ is of that worth and use, that thou canst never over-buy him, though thou gavest thyself and all the world for him; the study of Christ is the study of studies; the knowledge of Christ is the knowledge of every thing that is necessary, either for this world, or for the world to come. O study Christ in every one of the aforesaid respects.

SECT. II.

Of considering Jesus in that respect.

2. LET us consider Jesus, carrying on this great work of our salvation at his first coming or incarnation. It is not enough to study, and

and know these great mysteries, but, according to the measure of knowledge we have, we must muse, and meditate, and ponder, and consider of them. Now this consideration brings Christ nearer and closer to the soul; consideration gathers up all the long-fore-passed acts and monuments of Christ, and finds a deal of sweetness and power to come flowing from them; consideration fattens Christ more strongly to the soul, and, as it were, rivets the soul to Jesus Christ, and fastens him in the heart; a soul that truly considers and meditates of Christ, thinks and talks of nothing else but Christ; it takes hold and will not let him go. *I will keep to thee,* (saith the soul in meditation) *for thou art my life,* Prov. iv. 13. Why thus, O my soul, consider thou of Christ, and of what he did for thee when he was incarnate? And that thou mayest not confound thyself in thy meditations, consider apart of these particulars. As,

1. Consider Jesus in his forerunner, and the blessed tidings of his coming in the flesh: now the long looked for time drew near, a glorious angel is sent from heaven, and he comes with an olive branch of peace. First, He presents himself to Zacharias, and then to Mary; to her he imparts the message, on which God sent him into the nether world, *Behold, thou shalt conceive in thy womb, and bring forth a son, and shalt call his name Jesus,* Luke i. 13. Till now human nature was less than that of angels, but by the incarnation of the word, it was to be exalted above the cherubims. What sweet news? What blessed tidings was this message? The decree of old must now be accomplished, and an angel proclaims it upon earth: hear, O ye sons of Adam, this concerns you as much as the virgin; were ye not all undone in the loins of your first father? Was not my soul and your soul in danger of hell-fire? Was not this our case and condition, that, after a little life upon earth, we should have been thrown into eternal torments, where had been nothing, but weeping, wailing and gnashing of teeth? And now that God and Christ should bid an angel tell the news, 'Ye shall not die; lo, here a virgin 'shall conceive and bear a son, and he shall be 'your Jesus; he shall save you from this hell, and 'death, and sin: he shall deliver your souls, he 'shall save you to the utmost; his name is Jesus, 'and he shall not bear his name for nought; be- 'lieve in him, and you shall live with him in glory.' O blessed news! men may talk what they will of this and that news, every one gapes after it, but there's no news so welcome to one even now ready to perish, as to hear of a Saviour. Tell a man in sickness of one that will make him well again; tell a man in captivity of one that will rescue him, and set him free again; tell a man in prison condemned to die, of one with a pardon that will save his life; and every one of these will say, This is the best news that ever was heard. O then if it be good tidings to hear of a Saviour, where is only a matter of loss of life, or of this earth; how much more, when it comes to the loss of heaven, to the danger of hell, when our souls are at stake, and like to be damned for evermore? What glad tidings would that be to hear of one that could save our souls from that destroyer? Is not such a Saviour worth hearkening after? Were not the birth of such an one good news? O my soul, ponder on these words, as if an angel seeing thee stand on the brim of hell, should speak to thee, even to thy soul.

2. Consider Jesus in his conception, no sooner the news heard, but Christ is conceived by the Holy Ghost in the virgin's womb; this conception is worthy our consideration; what, that the great God of heaven should condescend so far as to take our nature upon him, and to take it in the same way, and after the same manner that we do? The womb of the virgin was surely no such place, but he might well have abhorred it; true, but he meant by this to sanctify our very conceptions: and to that purpose, he is conceived in an holy manner, even by the Holy Ghost; we must not be too curious to enquire after the manner of the Holy Ghost's operation, who therefore overshadowed the virgin: this is work for our hearts and not merely for our heads; humble faith, and not curious iniquisition, shall find the sweetness of this mystery. It was David's complaint, *Behold, I was shapen in iniquity, and in sin did my mother conceive me,* Psal. li. 5. O my soul, this was thy case, in thy very first being or beginning, and hadst thou died in that condition, the word is express, That, *nothing defiled nor unclean shall enter into the city of glory.* But here's the remedy, thy sinful conception is sanctified by Christ's holy conception: the holiness of thy Jesus serves as a cover to hide thy

thy original pollutions from the eyes of God. O consider of this! Jesus Christ was not conceived in vain, he was not idle, doing nothing, whilst he was in his mother's womb; he that from all eternity began, he was then carrying on the great work of our salvation for us; O consider this conception thus, till thou bringest it near and close to thy soul, till thou feelest some sweetness and power coming and flowing from Jesus in the womb.

3. Consider the duplicity of natures in Jesus Christ: *The word was made flesh*, John i. 14. No sooner was he conceived, but he was God-man, man-god; he was perfectly framed, and instantly united to the eternal word: *God sent his Son*, there is the nature divine; *made if a woman*, Gal. iv. 4. there's the human nature. Certainly great is this mystery, that the word is made flesh; that the Son of God is made of a woman; that a star gives light to the Son; that a branch doth bear the vine; that a creature gives being to the Creator: that the mother was younger than what she bare, and a great deal less than what she contained. Admire, O my soul, at this! but withal consider, that all this was for us, and our salvation; he was man, that he might die for us; and he was God, that his death might be sufficient to save us; had he been man alone, not God, he might have suffered, but he could never have satisfied for sin, he could not have been Jesus a Saviour of souls; and had he been God alone, not man, he had not been of kin to our nature offending, and so he could not have satisfied the justice of God in the same nature wherein it was offended; neither could he as God alone have died for sin; and the decree was out, that our Redeemer must die for sin, *For without shedding of blood there is no remission*, Heb. ix. 22. And no shedding of blood, no passion could possibly befal the Godhead of Jesus Christ. I shall not dispute the power of God, whether he is able to lay down another kind of way of man's redemption, than by the incarnation of the Son of God: without controversy this was the will of God, and he appointed no other way, because he could not. O my soul, consider of this in relation to thyself, he is God-man, that he might suffer and satisfy for thy sins; he is God-man, that he might be able, and fit most fully to finish the work of thy salvation; as God, he is able, and as man, he is fit to discharge the office of Mediator; as God, he is able to bear the punishment of sin, and as man, he is fit to suffer for sin; O the wisdom of God in this very way? Man's nature can suffer death, but not overcome it; the divine nature can overcome death and all things, but he cannot suffer it; and hence there is a duplicity of natures in Jesus Christ; O muse on this, it is a matter worthy of thy serious consideration.

4. Consider the real distinction of these two natures in Christ. As the unapproachable light of the Godhead was put into the dim and dark lanthorn of human flesh; so these two natures remained intire without any conversion, commixion or confusion; they were not as wine and water that become one by mixing, there is no such blending the divine and human nature, they were not as snow and water, that become one by the dissolving of the snow into the water; there is no such changing of the human nature into the divine, or of the divine nature into the human; some say indeed, That the Godhead was more plentifully communicated with the manhood after his resurrection, than now at his conception; but howsoever, it did not then swallow up the truth of his manhood, as a whole sea would swallow up one drop of oil; look, as at first moment of his conception, he was God and man, so these two natures continued still distinct in substance, properties and actions. Why, consider this, O my soul, in reference to thyself; O there is comfort in this! by this means thou hast now free access unto the throne of grace, that thou mayest find help in thy necessities; and as thou hast free access, so thou mayest boldly draw near; his Deity indeed confounds, but his humanity comforts faint and feeble souls; his divine nature amazeth, but his human nature encourageth us to come unto him; even after his resurrection, he was pleased to send this comfortable message to the sons of men, *Go to my brethren, and say unto them, I ascend to my Father and your Father, and to my God and your God*, John xx 17. Now as long as he is not ashamed to call us brethren, *God is not ashamed to be called our God*, Heb. xi. 16. O the sweet fruit that we may gather off this tree, *The real distinction of two natures in Christ*. As long as Christ is man as well as God, we have a motive strong enough to appease his Father, and to turn his favourable countenance towards us; here is our happiness, That
these

there is one Mediator between God and man, the man Christ Jesus, 1 Tim. ii. 5.

5. Consider the union of the two natures of Christ in one and the same person, as he was the branch of the Lord, and the fruit of the earth, so these two natures were tied with such a gordian knot, as sin, hell, and the grave were never able to untie. Yea, though in the death of Christ, there was a separation of the soul from the body, yet in that separation, the hypostatical union remained firm, unshaken and indissoluble: in this meditation, thou hast great cause, O my soul, to admire and adore; wonderful things are spoken of thee: O Christ! he is God in a person of a Godhead, so as neither the Father, nor the Holy Ghost were made flesh; and he is man in the nature of man, not properly the person; the human nature of Christ never having any personal subsistence out of the Godhead; this is a mystery, that no angel, much less man, is able to comprehend: we have not another example of such an union, (as you have heard) only the nearest similitude or resemblance we can find, is that of the branch and tree into which it is ingraffed; we see one tree may be set into another, and it groweth in the stock thereof, and becometh one and the same tree, though there be two natures or kinds of fruit still remaining therein; so in the Son of God made man, though there be two natures, yet both being united into one person, there is but one Son of God, and one Jesus Christ. If thou wilt consider this great mystery of Godliness any further, review what hath been said in the object propounded, where this union is set forth more largely and particularly; but especially, consider the blessed effects of this union in reference to thyself; as our nature in the person of Christ is united to the Godhead, so our persons in and by this union of Christ are brought nigh to God. Hence it is, that God doth set his sanctuary and tabernacle among us; and that he dwells with us, and which is more, that he makes us houses and habitations, wherein he himself is pleased to dwell by his holy Spirit. *Ye are the temple of the living God; as God hath said, I will dwell in them, and walk in them, and I will be their God, and they shall be my people*, 2 Cor. vi. 16. Was not this Christ's prayer in our behalf? *I pray not for these alone, but for them also which shall believe on me through their word, That they all may be one, as thou, Father, art in me, and I in thee; that they also may be one in us, That the world may believe that thou hast sent me, I in them, and thou in me, That they may be perfect in one, and that the world may know that thou hast sent me, and hast loved them as thou hast loved me*, John xvii. 20, 21, 22, 23. By reason of this hypostatical union of Christ, the Spirit of Christ is given to us in the very moment of our regeneration, *And because ye are sons, God hath sent forth the Spirit of his Son into your hearts, crying, Abba, Father, and hereby we know, that we dwell in him and he in us, because he hath given us of his Spirit*, Gal. iv. 6. As the members of the body however distinct among themselves, and all differing from the head, yet by reason of one soul informing both the head and members, they all make but one *compositum*, or man; so all believers in Christ, however distinct persons among themselves, and all distinct from the person of Christ, and especially from the Godhead, which is incommunicable, yet by one and the same Spirit abiding in Christ and all his members, they become one, *There is one body and one Spirit*, Eph. iv. 4. *He that is joined to the Lord is one spirit*, 1 Cor. vi. 17. O my soul, consider of this, and in considering, believe thy part in this, and the rather, because the means of this union on thy part is a true and lively faith; faith is the first effect and instrument of the Spirit of Christ, disposing and enabling thy soul to cleave unto Christ, and *for this cause I bow my knees unto the Father of our Lord Jesus Christ, that Christ may dwell in your hearts by faith*, Eph. iii. 14, 17.

6. Consider the birth of Christ, this man-god, God-man who in his divine generation was the Son of God, in his human generation was born in a stable, for the saving of the children of men who were as the ox and mule having no understanding. It were a fruitful meditation to consider over and over that sweet resemblance of Christ being a vine; methinks I hear the voice of my beloved, *Rise up, my love, —— the fig tree putteth forth her green figs, and the vine with the tender grapes give a good smell; arise, my love, my fair one, and come away*, Cant. ii. 10, 13. If Christ knocks at the door, who will not awake, and arise? If Christ comes in view, who will not look unto Jesus! If Christ the vine calls us to come see the vine with the tender grape, who will taste the goodness, smell

smell the sweetness? And after a little taste of that goodness, and sweetness that is in him, who would not long after more, till we come from the first-fruits, to the last fruits of the Spirit, even to those visions and fruitions of Christ in glory? Consider, O my soul, of this vine till thou hast brought Christ near and close unto thyself! suppose thy heart the garden, wherein this vine was planted, wherein it budded, blossomed, and bare fruit; suppose the Holy Ghost to come upon thee, and to form and fashion in thee Jesus Christ; (thus Paul bespeaks the Galatians, *My little children of whom I travail in birth again until Christ be formed in you*) Would not this affect? Would not the whole soul be taken up with this? Come, receive Christ into thy soul, or if that work be done, if Christ be formed in thee, O cherish him! (I speak of the spiritual birth) O keep him in thy heart! let him there bud, and blossom, and bear fruit; let him fill thy soul with his divine graces; O that thou couldst say it feelingly, *I live, yet not I, but Christ liveth in me*, Gal. ii. 20. O that this were the issue of thy meditation on Christ's birth! even whilst thou art going with the shepherds to Bethlehem, and there findest thy Saviour lying in a cratch, That thou wouldest bring him thence, and make thy heart to be his cradle! I would not give a farthing for a meditation merely on the history of Christ's birth; either draw virtue from him, by feeling him within, or thy meditation will be fruitless.

7. Consider those few consequences after Christ's birth; every action of Christ is our instruction, here are many particulars, but none in vain; Christ is considered under much variety of notion, but he is still sweet under all. Is it possible, O my soul, That thou shouldest tire thyself in the contemplations of Jesus Christ? If one flower yield thee not pleasure, or delight, go to a second, a third; observe how the bees gather honey, after a while that they have sucked one flower, they go to another; so for a while observe the circumcision of Jesus Christ, and suck there, and gather some honey out of that flower: Christ had never been circumcised, but that the same might be done to our souls, that was done to his body; O that the same Christ would do that in us that was done to him for us. Again, observe Christ's presentation in the temple, this was the law of those that first opened the womb, now Christ was the first-born of Mary, and indeed *the first-born of all creatures*; and he was consecrate unto God, that by him we might be consecrate, and made holy, and that by him we might be accepted, when we are offered unto the Lord. Again, observe Christ's flight into Egypt; though the infancy is usually most quiet, and devoid of trouble, yet here life and toil began together; and see how speedily this comes after dedication unto God: alas! alas! we are no sooner born again, than we are persecuted; if the church travail, and bring forth a male, she is in danger of the dragon's streams. Again, observe Christ's return into Judea; *He was not sent but to the lost sheep of the house of Israel*, Matth. xv. 24. With them alone he was personally to converse in his ministry, in which respect he was called *a minister of circumcision*, Rom. xv. 8. And where should he be trained, and shew himself, but amongst them to whom God had sent him? The gospel first began there, and as a preparation to it, Christ now in his childhood returns thither. Again, observe Christ disputing with the doctors in the temple; in his very non-age, Christ gives a taste of his future proof; see how early his divine graces put forth themselves, *In him were hid* (faith the apostle) *all the treasures of wisdom and knowledge*, Col. ii. 3. All the treasures were hid in him, and yet some of those treasures appeared very early betimes: his wisdom in his very infancy is admired at, nor is it without our profit; *for of God he is made wisdom unto us*, 1 Cor. i. 30. Again, observe how he spent the remainder of his youth, in all his examples he meant our instructions, *He went down with his parents, and was subject to them*; he was not idly bred, but serves his generation in the poor way of a carpenter; *It is every way good for a man to bear God's yoke even from his infancy*, Lam. iii. 27. Christ is enured betimes to the hardship of life, and to the strict observation of the law both of God and nature.

See, O my soul, what a world of matter is before thee to consider of; here is Jesus under many a notion, here's the annunciation of Jesus, the conception of Jesus, the duplicity of natures in Jesus, the real distinction, the wonderful union, the nativity of Jesus, together with some consequences after it. Go over these with often and frequent thoughts, give not over till thou feelest thy heart begin

begin to warm: true meditation is as the bellows of the soul, that doth kindle and inflame holy affections, and by renewed, and more forcible thoughts, as by renewed and stronger blast it doth renew and encrease the flame.

SECT. III.

Of desiring after Jesus in that respect.

3. LET us desire after Jesus, carrying on the great work of our salvation at his first coming, or incarnation. It is not enough to know, and consider, but we must desire. 'Now, what 'is desire, but a certain motion of the appetite, by 'which the soul darts itself towards the absent 'good, purposely to draw near, and to unite itself 'thereunto?' The incarnation of Christ according to the letter, was *the desire of all nations*; so the prophet, *I will shake all nations, and the desire of all nations shall come*, Hag. ii. 7. O how they that lived before Christ, desired after this coming of Christ! Abraham desired to see my day, two thousand years, and more before it came: it was the expectation of all the patriarchs, *O when will that day come?* And surely the incarnation of Christ in the fruit, or efficacy, or application, is or should be the desire of all Christians. There is merit and virtue in Jesus Christ, in every passage of Christ, in his conception, incarnation; in his birth, and in those consequences after his birth; now to make these ours, that we may have our share, and part, and interest in them, we must here begin; O my soul, do thou desire, do thou seek to possess thyself of Christ, set thy desire (as the needle point) aright, and all the rest will follow: never will union be with the absent good, but the soul by desire must dart itself towards it; true it is, and pity it is, millions of souls stand at a distance from Jesus Christ; and why? They have no desire towards him: but, O what, my soul, and thy soul (whosoever thou art that readest) would desire! O that we could desire, and long after him until we languish, and be compelled to cry out, with the spouse, *Stay me with flaggons, and comfort me with apples, for I am sick of love*, Cant. ii. 5.

Is there not good reason for it? What is there in Christ that is not desirable? View over all those excellencies of his conception; of his two natures, really distinguished, and yet wonderfully united; of his birth, of these few consequences after his birth; but, above all, see the fruit of all; he was conceived that our conceptions might be sanctified; he was the Son of man, that he might suffer for us, and the Son of God, that he might satisfy divine justice: he was God and man in one person, that we might be one with him, *Members of his body, and of his flesh, and of his bones*, Ephes. v. 30. He was born of the virgin, that there might be a spiritual conception and birth of Christ in our virgin-hearts; or he was conceived and born, That we might conceive the grace of Christ in our hearts, and bring it forth in our lives! what! are not these desirable things? Never tell me of thy present enjoyments, for never was Christ so enjoyed in this life, but thou hast cause to desire yet more of Christ: it is worth thy observation, *That spiritual desires after Christ, do neither load nor cloy the heart, but rather open, and enlarge it for more and more.* Who was better acquainted with God than Moses? And yet, who was more importunate to know him better? *I beseech thee shew me thy glory*, Exod. xxxiii. 18. And who was more acquainted with Christ than Paul? And yet who was more importunate to be with him nearer? *I desire to be dissolved, and to be with Christ*, Phil. i. 23. Further, and further union with Christ, and communion with Christ are most desirable things, and are not these the fruits of his incarnation? The effects of his hypostatical, personal union? More and more peace, and love, and reconciliation betwixt God and us are desirable things; and are not these the fruits of Christ's birth, the effects of his budding out of the earth? was it not then, *That righteousness looked down from heaven? That mercy and truth met together, and righteousness and peace kissed each other?* An higher degree of holiness, sanctification, likeness to God and Christ are desirable things; and are not these the fruits of his circumcision, and presentation to the Lord? The effects of all those consequences that follow after his birth? Come, soul, and stir up thy desires, true desires are not wavering and dull, but resolute and full of quickness; observe how the nature of true desires in scripture is set forth by the most pathetical and strong similitudes of *hunger, and thirst*, and those not common neither, but by 'the panting of a ti-
'red

'red hart after the rivers of waters, and by the gap-
'ing of dry ground after some seasonable showers.'
O then how is it that the passages of thy desires
are so narrow, and almost shut up: nay, how is
it that thy vessels are so full of contrary qualities,
that there is scarce any room in thy soul for Christ,
and all his train? Will not the desires of the patriarchs witness against thee? How cried they after
Christ's coming in the flesh, *Bow the heavens, O
Lord, and come down*, Psal. cxliv. 5. *Oh that thou
wouldest rent the heavens, that thou wouldest come
down*, Isa. lxiv. 1. *Drop down, ye heavens, from a-
bove, and let the skies pour down righteousness, let
the earth open and bring forth salvation*, Isa. xlv. 8.
Is it possible that their desires should be more vehement after Christ than ours? They lived on the dark
side of the cloud, but we on the bright side; the
vail was upon their hearts, which vail is done away
in Christ; they saw Christ afar off, and their sight
was very dim and dark; *But we all, with open face,
as in a glass, behold the glory of the Lord*, 2 Cor. iii.
18. One would think, the less any thing is known,
the less it should be desired; O my soul, either thou
art more ignorant of Christ than the patriarchs of
old, or thy heart is more out of frame than theirs;
suspect the latter, and blame thy heart; may be
thy torpid and sluggish nature hath laid thy desires
asleep: if an hungry man will sleep, his hunger
will sleep with him; but O stir up, and awake thy
desires! present before them that glorious object,
The incarnation of Jesus Christ; it is an object
which the very angels desire to look into, and art
not thou more concerned in it than the angels? Is
not the fruit of the incarnation thine, more especially thine? Come then, stir up those motions of
thy appetite, by which the soul darts itself towards
the absent good, draw nearer, and nearer, till thou
comest to union and enjoyment; cry after Christ,
*Why is his chariot so long in coming? Why tarry the
wheels of his chariots?* Judges v. 28.

SECT. IV.

Of hoping in Jesus in that respect.

4. LET us hope in Jesus, carrying on the
great work of our salvation at his first
coming, or incarnation, only here remember, I speak
not of every hope, but only of such an hope, as is
grounded on some certainty and knowledge; this
is the main question, whether Christ's incarnation
belongs unto me? The prophet tells, That *unto
us a child is born, and unto us a son is given*, Isa.
ix. 6. But how may I hope that this child is born
to me? And that this son is given to me? What
ground for that? Out of these words of the prophet, I shall draw a double evidence, which may
be instead of all: our first evidence from the former words, *Unto us a child is born:* our second
evidence from the latter words, *Unto us a son is
given.* 1. From the former words, I lay down
this proposition, *Unto us a child is born, if we are
new born.* The surest way to know our interest
in the birth of Christ, it is to know Christ born in
us, or formed in us, as the apostle speaks, Gal.
iv. 19. The new birth is the effect of Christ's birth,
and a sure sign that Christ is born to us. Say then,
O my soul, art thou born anew? Is there in you
a new nature, a new principle? Is the image of
God and Christ in my soul? So the apostle stiles
it, *The bearing of the image of the heavenly*, 1 Cor.
xv. 49. Why then was Christ incarnate for thee,
if thy new birth be not clear enough? Thou mayest
try it further by these following rules.

1. Where this new birth is, there are new desires, new comforts, new contentments: Sometimes with the prodigal thou wast content with
husks, but now nothing will satisfy thee but thy
Father's mansion, and thy Father's feast; sometimes thou mindest only earthly things, but now
the favour of God, the light of his countenance,
society with him, and enjoying of him, are thy
chief desires: this is a good sign, David's heart
and flesh, and all breathed after God: *My soul
longeth, yea, even fainteth for the courts of the
Lord, My heart and my flesh crieth out for the living God*, Psal. lxxxiv. 2. Men truly regenerate do
not judge it so happy to be wealthy, great and honoured in the world, as to have the light of God's
favour shine upon them. O my soul, dost thou
see the glory of the world, and thou fallest down
to worship it? Dost thou say in the increase of
worldly comfort, it is good to be here? Then fear
thyself, but if these things compared with Christ,
are vain, and light, and of poor, and mean esteem,
then hope well, and be assured that thou art born
again, and that Christ is formed in thee.

2. Where this new birth is, there are new words,
new works, new affections, a new conversation,

Old things are passed away, behold, all things are become new, 2 Cor. v. 17. Paul once a persecutor, but *behold now he prayeth*, Acts ix. 11. And *such were some of you, but now ye are washed, now ye are sanctified, now ye are justified, in the name of the Lord Jesus, and by the Spirit of our God*, 1 Cor. vi. 11. As every man is, so is he affected, so he speaks, and so he lives; if thy life be supernatural, so is thy affections, so is thy words, so is thy conversation; Paul lived a life once of a bloody persecutor, he breathed out threatnings against all the professors of the Lord Jesus: but now it is otherwise, *The life which I now live in the flesh, I live by the faith of the Son of God, who loved me, and gave himself for me*, Gal. ii. 20. O my soul, hast thou the old conversation, the old affections, the old discourse, the old passions thou usedst to have? What! is thy heart a den of lusts, a cage of unclean imaginations? Then fear thyself, there cannot from a sweet fountain come forth bitter streams; there cannot from a refined spirit, as refined, come forth corrupted acts or imaginations; *A thorn cannot send forth grapes*, saith Christ; so neither can a vine send forth thorns, say we. I know there is in the best something of flesh, as well as of the Spirit; but if thou art new born, then thou canst not but strive against it, and will endeavour to conquer it.

3. Where this new birth is, there is a new nature, a new principle, Peter calls it, *The hidden man of the heart, The divine nature*, 1 Pet. iii. 4. 2 Pet. i. 4. Paul calls it, *The inward man, the new creature*, Rom. vii. 22. It is compared to a root, to a fountain, to a foundation, 2 Cor. v. 17. And for want of this foundation, we see now in these sad times so much inconstancy and unsettledness in some professors themselves, many have gotten new and strange notions, but they have not new natures, new principles of grace; if grace were but rooted in their hearts, though the winds did blow, and storms arise, they would continue firm and stable, as being founded upon a rock. Never tell me of profession, shew, outward action, outward conversation, outward duties of religion; all this may be, and yet no new creature; you have some brutes that can act many things like men, but because they have not an human nature, they are still brutish; so many things may be done in way of holiness, which yet come not from this inward principle of renovation; and therefore it is but copper and not gold: mistake not, O my soul, in this, which is thy best and surest evidence, though I call the new birth a new creature, my meaning is not, as if a new faculty were infused into him that is new born, a man when he is regenerate hath no more faculties in his soul than he had before his regeneration, only, in the work of regeneration, those abilities which the man had before, are now improved, and made spiritual; and so they work now spiritually which before wrought naturally. As in the resurrection from the dead, our bodies shall have no more, nor other parts and members than they had before, only those parts and members which now are natural, shall then by the power of God be made spiritual. *It is sown a natural body, it is raised a spiritual body; there is a natural body, and there is a spiritual body*, 1 Cor. xv. 44. So the same faculties, and the same abilities, which before generation were made natural, are now spiritual, and work spiritually; they are all brought under the government of the Spirit of Christ. A lively resemblance of this change in the faculties of the soul, we may discern in those natural and sensitive faculties, which we have common with beasts, as, to live, to move, to desire, to feel: the beasts having no higher principle than sense, use them sensually; but a man enjoying the same faculties under the command of a reasonable soul, he useth them rationally: so is it in a regenerate man, his understanding, will, and affections, when they had no other command but reason, he only used them rationally, but now, being under the guiding of the Spirit of Christ, they work spiritually, and he useth them spiritually; and hence it is, that a regenerate man is every where in scripture said to *walk after the Spirit*, Rom. viii. 1. *To be led by the Spirit, to walk in the Spirit*, Gal. v. 18, 25. The Spirit by way of infusing or shedding, gives power, an ability, a seed, a principle of spiritual life, which the soul had not before; and from this principle of spiritual life planted in the soul, flows or springs those spiritual motions or operations, (as the Spirit leads them out) according to the habit or principle of the new creature, the divine nature, the spiritual life infused. Come then, look to it, O my soul, What is thy principle within? Consider not so much the outward actions, the outward duties of religion, as

that

that root from whence they grow, that principle from whence they come: are they fixed ones, settled ones by way of life in thee? Clocks have their motions, but they are not motions of life, because they have no principles of life within. Is there life within? Then art thou born again, yea, even *unto thee a child is born.* This one evidence.

4. From the latter words, I lay down this position; *Unto us a son is given, if we are God's sons.* The best way to know our interest in the Son of God, it is to know ourselves to be God's sons by grace, as Christ was God's Son by nature; Christians, to whom Christ is given, are coheirs with Christ, only Christ is the first-born, and hath the preeminence in all things; our sonship is an effect of Christ's sonship, and a sure sign, that *unto us a son is given.* Say then, O my soul, art thou a son of God? Dost thou resemble God, (according to thy capacity) being holy, even as he is holy? Why then, Christ was incarnate for thee, he was given to thee, if thy sonship be not clear enough, thou mayest try it further by these following rules.

1. The sons of God fear God, *If I be a Father, where is my honour?* (saith God) *If I be a master, where is my fear?* Mal. i. 16. If I be a son of God, there will be an holy fear and trembling upon me in all my approaches unto God. I know there is a servile mercenary fear, and that is unworthy and unbeseeming the son of God; but there is a filial fear, and that is an excellent check and bridle to all our wantonness. What son will not fear the frowns and anger of his loving father? *I dare not do this,* (will he say) *my father will be offended, and I, whither shall I go?* Agreeable to this is the apostle's advice, *If ye call on the Father, pass your sojourning here with fear,* 1 Peter i. 17.

2. The sons of God love God, and obey God out of a principle of love. Suppose there were no heaven or glory to bestow upon a regenerate person, yet would he obey God out of a principle of love, not that it is unlawful for the child of God to have an eye unto the recompence of reward; Moses his reason of *esteeming the reproach of Christ greater riches than the treasures of Egypt, was for that he had respect unto the recompence of reward,* he had respect in the original, *he had a fixed intent eye,* Heb. xi. 26. There was in him a love of reward, and yet withal a love of God, and therefore his love of the reward was not mercenary: but this I say, Tho' there were no reward at all, a child of God hath such a principle of love within him, that for love's sake he would obey his God; he is led by the Spirit, and therefore he obeys; now the spirit that leads him is a spirit of love; and *as many as are led by the Spirit of God, are the sons of God,* Rom. viii. 14.

3. The sons of God imitate God in his love and goodness to all men. Our Saviour amplifies this excellent property of God, *He causeth his sun to shine upon good and bad;* and thence he concludeth, *Be ye perfect as your heavenly Father is perfect,* Matth. v. 48. Goodness to bad men is the highest degree of grace, and as it were the perfection of all: O my soul, canst thou imitate God in this? Consider how thy Father bears it, though the wicked provoke him day by day, yet for all that he doth not quickly revenge; vengeance indeed is only his, and he may in justice do what he will that way; and it is the opinion of some, that if the most patient man in the world should but sit in God's throne one day, and see and observe the doings and miscarriages of the sons of men, he would quickly set all the world on fire; yet God seeth all, and for all that he doth not make the earth presently to gape and devour us; he puts not out the glorious light of the sun, he does not dissolve the work of the creation, he doth not for man's sin presently blast every thing into dust: what an excellent pattern is this for thee to write after? Canst thou but forgive thy enemies? Do well to them that do evil to thee. O this is a sure sign of grace and sonship! It is storied of some Heathens, who beating a Christian almost to death, asked him, ' What great matter Christ ' did ever do for him?' Even this, (said the Christian) ' That I can forgive you though you use me ' thus cruelly.' Here was a child of God indeed, it is a sweet resemblance of our Father, and of our Saviour Jesus Christ, to *love our enemies, to bless them that curse us, to do good unto them that hate us, to pray for them that despitefully use us and persecute us,* Mat. v. 44. O my soul, look on this, consult this ground of hope; if this law be written in thy heart, write it down amongst thy evidences, that thou art God's son, yea, that even unto thee a son is given.

To

To review the grounds: what is a child born to me, and a son given to me? What, am I indeed new born? Am I indeed God's son or daughter? Do I upon the search find in my soul new desires, new comforts, new contentments? What are my words, and works, and affections, and conversation new? Is there in me a new nature, a new principle? Hath the Spirit, by way of infusing or shedding, given me a new power, a new ability, a seed of spiritual life which I had not before? Do I upon the search find, that I fear God, and love God, and imitate God in some good measure in his love and goodness towards all men? Can I indeed and really forgive an enemy, and, according to opportunity and my ability, do good unto them that do evil unto me? Why should I not then confidently and comfortably hope, that I have my share and interest in the birth of Christ, in the blessed incarnation and conception of Jesus Christ? Away, away, all despairs, and dejections, and despondencies of spirit! if these be my grounds of hope, it is time to hold up head, and heart, and hands, and all with cheerfulness and confidence, and to say with the spouse, *I am my beloved's, and my beloved is mine.*

SECT. V.

Of believing in Jesus in that respect.

5. LET us believe on Jesus carrying on the great work of our salvation at his first coming or incarnation. I know many staggerings are oft in Christians, 'What is it likely that Christ 'should be incarnate for me? That such a God 'should do such a thing for such a sinful, woful, 'abominable wretch as I am?' Ah! my soul, put thy propriety in Christ's incarnation out of dispute, that thou mayest be able to say, *As God was manifest in the flesh, and I may not doubt it; so God is manifest in me, and I dare not deny it.*

But, to help the soul in this choice duty, I shall first propose the hinderances of faith. 2. The helps of faith in this respect. 3. The manner how to act our faith. 4. The encouragements to bring on the soul to believe its part in this blessed incarnation of Jesus Christ.

For the first there are but three things that can hinder faith; As

1. The exceeding unworthiness of the soul; and to this purpose are those complaints, 'what! 'Christ incarnate for me! for such a dead dog as 'I am? What king would dethrone himself, and 'become a toad to save toads? And am not I 'at a greater distance from God, than a toad is 'from me? Hath not sin made my soul more ugly 'in God's eye, than any lothsome toad can be in 'my eye? O! I am less than the least of all God's 'mercies, I am fitter for hell and devils, than for 'union and communion with God and Christ, I 'dare not, I cannot believe.'

2. The infinite exactness of divine justice which must be satisfied; a soul deeply and seriously considering of this, it startles thereat, and cries, O what will become of my soul? one of the least sins that I stand guilty of deserves death, and eternal wrath, the wages of sin is death; and I cannot satisfy; though I have trespassed to many millions of talents, I have not one mite of mine own to pay; O then how should I believe? What thoughts can I entertain of God's mercy and love to me-ward? God's law condemns me, my own conscience accuseth me, and justice will have its due.

3. The want of a Mediator, or some suitable person, which may stand between the sinner and God. If on my part there be unworthiness, and on God's part exact, and strict, and severe justice; and withal I see no Mediator, which I may go unto, and first close withal before I deal with the infinite glory of God himself, how should I but despair, and cry out? 'O wretched man that I am! 'O that I had never been! or if I must needs have 'a being, Oh that I had been a toad, or serpent, 'or any venomous creature, rather than a man; 'for when they die they perish, and there's an end 'of them, but the end of a reprobate sinner, is tor-'ments without end: O wo and alas! I cannot 'believe, there's no room for faith in this case!' These are the hinderances.

2. The helps of faith in this sad condition are these.

1. A consideration that God is pleased to pass by, and to overlook the unworthiness of his poor creatures; this we see plain in the very act of his incarnation; himself disdains not to be as his poor creatures, to wear their own flesh, to take upon him human nature, and in all things to become like unto man, sin only excepted.

2. A

2. A consideration that God satisfies justice, by setting up Christ, who is justice itself; now was it that *mercy and truth met together, and righteousness and peace kissed each other*; now was it that free grace and merit, that fulness and nothingness were made one; now was it that all things become nothing, and nothing all things; our nature which lay in rags, was enriched with the unsearchable treasures of glory; now was it that God was made flesh; and so that flesh which was so weak, as not able to save its own life, was now enabled to save millions of souls, and to bring forth the greatest designs of God; now was it that truth ran to mercy, and embraced her, and righteousness to peace and kissed her; in Christ they meet, yea, in him was the infinite exactness of God's justice satisfied.

3. A consideration that God hath set up Christ as a Mediator, That he was incarnate in order to reconciliation, and salvation of souls, but for the accomplishment of this design Christ had never been incarnate; the very end of his uniting flesh unto him, was in order to the reconciliation of us poor souls! alas we had sinned, and by sin deserved everlasting damnation, but to save us, and to satisfy himself, God takes our nature, and joins it to his Son, and calls that *Christ a Saviour:* this is the gospel-notion of Christ; for what is Christ, but God *himself in our nature, transacting our peace?* In this Christ is that fulness, and righteousness, and love, and bowels to receive the first acts of our faith; and to have immediate union and communion with us; indeed we pitch not our faith first or immediately on God himself; yet at last we come to him, and our faith lives in God (as one saith sweetly) before it is aware, through the sweet intervention of that person which is God himself only called by another name, *The Lord Jesus Christ,* and these are the helps of faith in reference to our unworthiness, God's justice, and the want of a Mediator betwixt God and us.

3. The manner how to act our faith on Christ incarnate is this.

1. Faith must directly go to Christ: we indeed find in the Bible some particular promises of this and that grace: and in proper speaking the way to live by faith, it is to live upon the promises in the want of the thing, or to apprehend the thing itself contained in the promise: but the promises are not given to the elect immediately without Christ. No, no, first Christ, and then all other things; *incline your ears, and come unto me.* 1. Come unto Christ, and then *I will make an everlasting covenant;* (which contains all the promises) *even the sure mercies of David,* Isa. lv. 3. As in marriage, the woman first consents to have the man, and then all the benefits which necessarily follow; so the soul by faith, first pitcheth upon Christ himself, and then on the privileges that flow from Christ. Say, soul, dost thou want any temporal blessing? Suppose it be the payment of debts, thy daily bread, health, &c. Why, look now through the scripture for promises of these things, and let thy faith act thus, *If God hath given me Christ, the greatest blessing, then certainly he will give me all these things, so far as they may be for my good.* In the twenty third Psalm we find a bundle of promises, but he begins thus, *The Lord is my shepherd,* saith David, Psal. xxiii. 1. And what then? *Therefore I shall not want;* the believing patriarchs through faith *subdued kingdoms, wrought righteousness, obtained promises, stopped the mouths of lions,* Heb. xi. 33. Did wonders in the world; but what did they chiefly look to in this their faith? Surely to the promise to come, and to that better thing, Christ himself, verse 39, 40. And therefore the apostle concludes, *Having such a cloud of witnesses,* that thus lived and died by faith, *Let us look unto Jesus, the author and finisher of our faith,* Heb. xii. 2.

2. Faith must directly go to Christ as God in our flesh; some think it a carnal apprehension of Jesus Christ, to know him as in flesh: I confess to know him only so, and absolutely so, to consider Jesus no other way, but as having flesh, and going up and down in weakness, it is no better than a carnal apprehension; but to consider Christ as God in flesh, and to consider that flesh as acted by God, and filled with God, it is not a carnal, but a true and spiritual apprehension of Jesus Christ; and hither is faith to be directed immediately, and in the first place; suppose a case of danger by some enemies, and I find a promise of protection from my enemies, I look on that; but in the first place, thus I argue, if the Lord hath given me Christ (God in the flesh) to save me from hell, then much more will he save me from these fleshly enemies. Thus Judah had a promise, That Syria should not

not prevail against Judah. They doubted of this; but how doth the Lord seek to assure them? Why, thus, *A virgin shall conceive and bear a Son, and his name shall be Emmanuel,* Isa. vii. 14. This seems a strange reason to flesh and blood: I knew one turn infidel, and deny Jesus Christ upon this very argument; *ah* (thought he) 'what a 'grand imposture is this, that Christ's conception, 'and Christ's birth many years after should be a 'present sign of the ruin of Rezin king of Aram, 'and of the preservation of Ahaz king of Judah?' Alas, poor soul, he was not acquainted with this art of living by faith; he might have seen the very same reason elsewhere, *The yoke of their burthen, and the staff of their shoulder, and the rod of their oppressor shall be broken,——For unto us a child is born, and unto us a son is given,* Isa. ix. 4, 6. If their faith had not first respected Christ incarnate, they could never have expected any temporal deliverance by that promise of deliverance first laid down; but in this way they might, and so may we.——You will say, What's this to us? They looked for Christ to come in the flesh, but now he is come, and that time and design is gone and past many a year since. I answer, no; the time is gone, but the design is not: Christ remains God in the flesh to this very day; he came not as once to manifest himself in the flesh, to satisfy God's justice in the flesh for sin, and so to lay it down again; that flesh remains, and shall remain; nor is it without use; for all the spirit and life which the saints now have, or which the saints shall have unto the end of the world, it is to be conveyed thro' that flesh; yea, the spirit itself dwells in it, and is conveyed through it; and therefore if they had so much gospel-spirit in the time of the old Testament (which indeed was rare) how much more should we go to Christ, as God in the flesh, and look upon it as a standing ordinance, and believe perfectly on it?

3. Faith must go and lie at the feet of Christ; faith must fix and fasten itself on this God in our flesh: some go to Christ, and look on Jesus with loose and transient glances, they bring in but fleshly, secondary, ordinary actings of faith, they have but coarse and common apprehensions of Jesus Christ. Oh! but we should come to Christ with solemn serious spirits; we should look on Jesus piercingly, till we see him as God is in him, and as such a person thus and thus qualified from heaven; we should labour to apprehend what is the riches of this glorious mystery of Christ's incarnation; we should dive into the depths of his glorious actings; we should study this mystery above all other studies. Nothing is so pleasant, and nothing is more deep; than one person should be God and man, that God should be man in our nature, and yet not assume the person of a man; that blessedness should be made a curse, that heaven should be let down into hell, that the God of the world would shut himself up (as it were) in a body; that the invisible God should be made visible to sense; that all things should become nothing, and make itself of no reputation: that God should make our nature, which had sinned against him, to be the great ordinance of reconciling us unto himself; that God should take our flesh, and dwell in it with all his fulness, and make that flesh more glorious than the angels, and advance that flesh into oneness with himself, and through that flesh open all his counsels, and rich discoveries of love and free grace unto the sons of men; that this man-god, God-man should be our Saviour, Redeemer, Reconciler, Father, Friend; Oh what mysteries are these! no wonder if when Christ was born, the apostle cries, *We saw his glory, as of the only begotten Son of God,* Joh. i. 14. Noting out, that at first sight of him, so much glory sparkled from him as could appear from none but a God walking up and down the world. O my soul, let not such a treasury be unlook'd into; set faith on work with a redoubled strength; surely we live not like men under this great design, if our eye of faith be not firmly and stedfastly set on this. O that we were but insighted into these glories! that we were but acquainted with these lively discoveries! how blessedly might we *live by the faith of the Son of God, who loved us, and gave himself for us?* Gal. ii. 20.

4. Faith must look principally to the end and meaning of Christ, as God coming in the flesh. Now what was the design and meaning of Christ in this? The apostle answers, Rom. viii. 3. *God sent his Son in the likeness of sinful flesh, to condemn sin in the flesh,* i. e. God the Father sent into the world his eternal and only begotten Son, whom in his eternal council, he had designed to the office of a Mediator, to take away or abolish, in the first place,

place, original sin. Mark these two words, *he condemned sin in the flesh*, the first word *condemned*, is by a metonomy put for that which follows condemnation, namely for the abolishing of sin; as condemned persons used to be cut off, and to be taken out of the world, that they may be no more; so Christ hath condemned or abolished this sin. For the second word, *in the flesh*, is meant that human nature which Christ assumed; he abolished sin altogether in his own nature; and that flesh of his, being perfectly holy, and the holiness of it being imputed unto us, it takes away our guilt in respect of the impureness of our nature also. Some may object, If this were so, then were we without original sin? I answer, the flesh, or the nature which Christ took upon him, was altogether without sin, and by imputation of it, we are in proportion freed from sin; Christ had not the least spot of original sin; and if we are Christ's, then is this sin in some measure abolished, and taken out of our hearts. But howsoever the filth of this sin may remain in part, yet the guilt is removed: in this respect the purity of Christ's human nature is no less reckoned to us for the curing of our defiled nature, than the sufferings of Christ's are reckoned to us, for the remission of our actual sins. O my soul, look to this end of Christ, as God in the flesh; if thou consider him as made flesh and blood, and laid in a manger, think withal, that his meaning was to condemn sin in our flesh; there flows from the holiness of Christ's nature, such a power, as countermands the power of our original sin, and acquits and discharges from the condemnation of the same sin, not only the death and life, but also the conception and birth of Christ hath its influence into our justification. Oh! the sweets that a lively faith may draw from this head!

4. The encouragements to bring on souls to believe on Christ incarnate we may draw,

1. From the excellency of this object. This very incarnation of Christ is the foundation of all other actings of God for us; it is the very hinge, or pole on which all turn; it is the cabinet wherein all the designs of God do lie: election, redemption, justification, adoption, glorification, are all wrapt up in it; it is the highest pitch of the declaration of God's wisdom, goodness, power, and glory; Oh what a sweet object of faith is this! I know there are some other things in Christ which are most proper for some acts of faith, as Christ dying is most proper for the pardon of actual sin, and Christ rising from the dead is most proper for the evidencing of our justification: but the strongest, purest acts of faith are those which take in Christ as such a person, laid out in all this glory. Christ's incarnation is more general than Christ's passion, or Christ's resurrection, and (as some would have it) includes all; Christ's incarnation holds forth in some sort Christ in his fulness, and so it is the full and compleat subject of our faith; or if it be only more comprehensive, why, then it requires more comprehensive acts of faith, and by consequence we have more enjoyments of Christ this way than any other way; come, poor soul, I feel, I feel thy eyes are running to and fro the world, to find comfort and happiness on earth, O come! cast thy eyes back, and see heaven and earth in one object! look fixedly on Christ incarnate, there is more in this than all the variety of this world, or of that world to come. Here is an object of faith, and love, and joy, and delight; here is a *compendium* of all glories; here is one for all heart to be taken with to all eternity. O lay thy mouth to this fountain, *Suck and be satisfied with the breasts of his consolation, milk out and be delighted with the brightness of his glory*, Isa. lxvi. 11.

2. From the suitableness of this object. Christ incarnate is most suitable for our faith to act upon. We are indeed to believe on God, but God essentially is the utmost object of faith; we cannot come to God but in and through Christ; alas, God is offended, and therefore we cannot find ground immediately to go to God: hence you heard that *faith must directly go to Christ, as God in our flesh*. O the infinite condescensions of God in Christ! God takes up our nature, and joins it to himself as one person, and lays out that before our faith; so that here is God, and God suited to the particular state and condition of the sinner. Oh, now with what boldness may our souls draw nigh to God? Why art thou strange, poor soul? Why standest thou afar off, as if it were death to draw nigh? Of whom art thou afraid? Is God come down amongst men, and canst thou not see him, lest thou die and perish? Oh, look once more, and be not discouraged. See, God is not come down in fire, God is not descended in the armour of justice and everlasting burning. No, no, he is clothed

with the garments of flesh, he sweetly desires to converse with thee after thine own form; he is come down to beseech thee, to see with thine own eyes thy eternal happiness, *q. d. Come, poor soul, come, put in thy hands, and feel my heart how it beats in love towards thee.* O the wonder of heaven! it is the cry of some poor souls, *Oh that I might see God!* lo, here God is come down in the likeness of man, he walks in our own shape amongst us; it is the cry of others, *O that I might have my heart united to God!* Why, he is come down on this very purpose, and hath united our nature unto himself. Surely God hath left all the world without excuse: oh, that ever there should be an heart of unbelief, after these sensible demonstrations of divine glory and love. Why, soul, wilt thou now stand off? Tell me what wouldest thou have God do more? Can he manifest himself in a more taking, alluring, suitable way to thy condition? Is there any thing below flesh wherein the great God can humble himself for thy good? Come, think of another and a better way, or else for ever believe. Methinks, it is hard to see believers shy in their approaches to God, or doubtful of their acceptance with God, when God himself stoops first, and is so in love with our acquaintance, that he will be of the same nature that we are. O let not such a rock of strength be slighted, but every day entertain sweet and precious thoughts of Christ being incarnate; enure thy heart to a way of believing on this Jesus, as he carries on the great work of thy salvation at his first coming or incarnation.

3. From the gospel-tenders and offers of this blessed object to our souls. As Christ is come in our nature to satisfy, so he comes in the gospel freely and fully to offer terms of love; therein are set out the most rich and alluring expressions that possibly can be; therein is set out that this *incarnation of Christ*, was God's own acting, out of his own love, and grace, and glory; therein is set out the birth, and life, and death of Christ, and this he could not do but he must be incarnate: God takes our flesh, and useth that as an organ or instrument whereby to act: he was flesh to suffer, as he was Spirit to satisfy for our sins. Methinks I might challenge unbelief, and bid it come forth, let it appear, if it dare before this consideration: what is not God incarnate enough to satisfy thy conscience? Come nigh, poor soul, hear the voice of Christ inviting, *Come unto me all ye that are weary, and heavy laden with sin,* Matth. xi. 28. And O let these rich and glorious openings of the heart of Christ overcome thy heart. Suppose the case thus, What if God should have done more than this? Had he only looked down from heaven, and hearing sinners cry out, ' O wo, wo unto us for ' ever! we have broke God's laws, incurred the ' penalty, damned our own souls: O who shall ' deliver us? Who will save us from the wrath ' to come? Who will keep us out of hell, our ' deserved dungeon, where the fury of the great ' Judge burns in a fiery brimstone, and his revenge ' boils in a fiery torrent, limitless and unquench' able?' In this case, if God hearing sinners thus crying out, had he, I say, only looked down and told them in sweet language, *Poor souls, I will pardon your sins by mine own prerogative; I made the law, and I will dispense with it; fear not, I have the keys of life and death, and upon my word you shall not perish.* What soul would not have been raised up even from the bottom of hell at this very voice? I know a poor soul would have scrupled at this, and have said, What shall become of infinite justice? Shall that be dishonoured to save my soul? This would have been scruple indeed, especially considering that great controversy, as we have heard of mercy and truth, and righteousness and peace: but to remove all controversies, God hath not only spoken from heaven by himself, but he himself is come down from heaven to earth to speak unto us: O see the miracle of mercy! God is come down in flesh, he is come as a price; he himself will pay himself, according to all the demands of his justice and righteousness before our eyes; and all this done, now he offers and tenders himself unto thy soul. Oh! my soul, why shouldest thou fear to cast thyself upon thy God? I know thy objection of vileness; notwithstanding all thy vileness, God himself offers himself to lead thee by the hand; and to remove all doubts, God himself hath put a price sufficient in the hands of justice to stop her mouth: or if yet thou fearest to come to God, why come then to thy own flesh; go to Christ as having thy own nature; it is he that calls thee; how? Go to flesh, go to thy own nature; what can be said more to draw on thy trembling heart? If God himself, and

God

God so fitted and qualified, (as I may say) will not allure; must not men die and perish in unbelief? What, O my soul, (give me leave to chide thee) is God come down so low to thee, and dost thou now stand questioning, whether thou shouldest go or come to him? What is this but to say, All that God is, or does, or says, is too little to perfuade me into faith? I cannot tell, but one may think, that unbelief should be strangled, quite slain upon this consideration; all this, O my soul, thou hearest in the gospel; there is Christ incarnate set forth to the life; there is Christ suing thy loves, and offering himself as thy beloved in thy own nature: there it is written, That God is come down in the flesh, with an olive branch of eternal peace in his hand, and bids you all be witness, he is not come to destroy but to save. Oh that this encouragement might be of force to improve Christ's glorious designs, to the supplying of all thy wants, and to the making up of all thy losses! believe, Oh believe thy part in Christ incarnate.

SECT. VI.

Of loving Jesus in that respect.

6. Let us love Jesus, as carrying on the great work of our salvation at his first coming or incarnation. Now, what is *love*, but *an expansion or egress of the heart, and spirits to the object loved, or to the object whereby it is drawn or attracted?* Mark, O my soul, whatsoever hath an attractive power, it is in that respect an object or general cause of love. And canst thou possibly light on any object more attractive than the incarnation of Jesus Christ? If love be the load-stone of love, what an attractive is this before thee? Methinks the very sight of Christ incarnate is enough to ravish thee with the apprehension of his infinite goodness: see how he calls out, or, (as it were) draws out the soul to union, vision and participation of his glory! O come, and yield up thyself unto him; give him thyself, and conform all thy affections and actions to his will: O love him, not with a divided, but with all thy heart.

But to excite this *love*, I shall only propound the object, which will be argument enough. Love causeth love; now, as God's first love to man was in making man like himself, so his second great love was in making himself like to man; stay then a while upon this love, for (I take it) this is the greater love of the two: nay, if I must speak freely, I believe this was the fullest visible demonstration of God's love that ever was; the evangelist expresseth it thus, *God so loved the world, that he gave his only begotten Son*, John iii. 16. He gave him to be incarnate, to be made flesh, and to suffer death; but the extension of his love lies in that expression, *he so loved*. So how, Why so fully, so fatherly, so freely, as no tongue can tell, no heart can think: in this love God did not only let out a mercy, give out a bare grace in itself, but he took our nature upon him. It is usually said, That it is a greater love of God to save a soul than to make a world; and I think it was a greater love of God to take our nature than simply to save our souls; for a king to dispense with the law, and by his own prerogative to save a murderer from the gallows, is not such an act of love and mercy, as to take the murderer's cloaths, and to wear them as his richest livery: why, God in taking our nature hath done thus, and more than thus; he would not save by his mere prerogative; but he takes our cloaths, our flesh, and in that flesh he personates us, and in that flesh he will die for us, that we might not die, but live through him for evermore. Surely this was love, that God will be no more God, as it were simply; but he will take up another nature, rather than the brightness of his glory shall undo our souls.

It will not be amiss, (whilst I am endeavouring to draw a line of God's love in Christ, from first to last in saving souls) that here we look back a little, and summarily contract the passages of love from that eternity before all worlds unto this present. 1. God had an eternal design to discover his infinite love to some besides himself; O the wonder of this, was there any need or necessity of such a discovery? *Deus unus, licet solus, non solitarius: Though God was one, and in that respect alone,* (as we may imagine) *yet God was not solitary.* In that eternity within his own proper essence or substance, there were three divine persons, and betwixt them there was a blessed communication of love; Christ on earth could say, *I am not alone, because the Father is with me*, John xvi. 32. And then before earth was, might the Father say, *I am not alone, for the Son is with me*; and the Son might say, *I am not alone, for the Father is with* me; and the Holy Ghost might say, *I am not alone, for both the Father and the Son are with me.* Though in that eternity there was no creature to whom these three persons should communicate their love; yet was there a glorious communication, and breaking out of love from one to another; before there was a world, the Father, Son, and Holy Ghost did infinitely glorify themselves, John xvii. 5. Surely they loved one another, and they rejoiced in the fruition of one another, Prov. viii. 30. What need was there of the discovery of God's love to any one besides himself? O my soul, I know no necessity for it, only thus was the pleasure of God; *Even so, Father, for so it seemed good in thy sight.* Such was the love of God, that it would not contain itself within that infinite ocean of himself; but it would needs have rivers and channels into which it might run and overflow.

2. God, in prosecution of his design, creates a world of creatures, some rational, and only capable of love, others irrational, and serviceable to that one creature, which he makes the top of the whole creation; then it was that he set up one man, Adam, as a common person to represent the rest; to whom he gives abundance of glorious qualifications, and him he sets over all the works of his hands, as if he were the darling of love; if we should view the excellency of this creature, either in the outward or the inner man, who would not wonder? His body had its excellency, which made the Psalmist say, *I will praise thee; for I am fearfully and wonderfully made,——and curiously wrought in the lowest part of the earth,* Psalm cxxxix. 14, 15. It is a speech borrowed from those who work arras-work; the body of man is a piece of curious tapestry or arras-work, consisting of skin, bones, muscles, sinews, and the like, what a goodly thing the body of man was before the fall may be guessed by the excellent gifts found in the bodies of some men since the fall; as the complexion of David, 1 Sam. xvi. 12. The swiftness of Ahasel, 2 Sam. ii. 18. The beauty of Absalom, 2 Sam. xiv. 25. If all these were but joined in one, as certainly they were in Adam, what a rare body would such a one be? But what was this body in comparison of that soul? The soul was it that was especially made after the image of God; the soul was it that was tempered in the same mortar with the heavenly spirits; the soul was God's sparkle; a beam of his divine glory, a ray or emanation of God himself; as man was the principal part of the creation, so the soul was the principal part of man: here was it that God's love and glory were centred for the time; here was it that God's love set and fixed itself in a special manner, whence flowed that communion of God with Adam, and that familiarity of Adam with God.

3. Within a while, this man, the object of God's love, fell away from God, and, as he fell, so all that were in him, even the whole world, fell together with him; and hereupon God's face was hid, not a sight of him, but in flaming fire ready to seize on the sons of men. And yet God's love would not thus leave the object, he had yet a further reach of love, and out of this dark cloud he lets fall some glimpses of another discovery: these glimpses were sweet; but, alas! they were so dark, that very few could spell them, or make any sense or comfortable applications of them: but by degrees God hints it out more, he points it out with the finger by types and shadows, he makes some models of it in outward ceremonies; and yet so hid and dark, that in four thousand years, men were but guessing, and hoping through promises for a manifestation of God's love. This is the meaning of the apostle, who tells us of *the mystery that was hid from ages and from generations, but now is made manifest to his saints,* Col. i. 26. This love of God was hid in the breast of God from the sons of men for many an age; so that they knew not what to make of this great design: I speak of the generality of men, for in respect of some particulars, as to Adam and Abraham, and Moses and David, and the patriarchs, you have heard the Lord made his loves clear to them in a covenant way; and still the nearer to Christ, the clearer and clearer was the covenant of grace.

4. At last, God fully opens himself in the fulness of time, God takes the flesh of those poor sinners, which he had so loved, and joins it to himself, and he calls it Christ, a Saviour; O now was it that God descended, and lay in the womb of a virgin; now was it that he is born as we are born; now was it that he joined our flesh so near to himself, as that there is a communication of properties betwixt them both, that being attributed to God, which is proper to flesh, as to be born, to suffer, and that being attributed to flesh, which is proper

to

to God, as to create, to redeem: who can choose but wonder when he thinks of this phrase, That a piece of flesh should be called God, and that God should be made flesh, and dwell amongst us? That flesh should infinitely provoke God, and yet God in the same flesh should be infinitely pleased? That God should vail himself and darken his glory with our flesh, and yet unvail at the same time the deepest and darkest of his designs in a comfortable way to our souls? O my soul, how shouldest thou contain thyself within thyself? How shouldest thou but leap out of thyself, (if I may so speak) as one that is lost in the admiration of his love? Surely God never manifested himself in such a strain of love as this before; herein was love manifested and commended indeed, that God would come down in our nature to us. One observes sweetly, That 'God 'did so love the very nature of his elect, that, 'though for the present he had not them all with 'him in heaven, yet he must have their picture in 'his Son to see them in, and love them in.' In this respect, I may call Christ incarnate, a statue and monument of God's own infinite love unto his elect for ever.

Well, hitherto we have followed the passages of his love; and now we see it in the spring, or at full sea: if any thing will beget our love to God surely Christ incarnate will do it: come then, O my soul, I cannot but call on thee to love thy Jesus, and to provoke thy love; O fix thy eye on this lovely object; come, put thy candle to this flame; what, doth not thy heart yet burn within thee? Dost thou not at least begin to warm? Why, draw yet a little nearer, consider what an heart of love is in this design. God is in thy own nature, to take upon him all the miseries of thy nature. Mark it well, this is none other than God's heart leaping out of itself into our bosoms, q. d. 'Poor souls, 'I cannot keep from you, I love your very na-'ture; I will be nothing, so you may be some-'thing; my glory shall not hinder me, but I will 'vail it rather than it shall hurt you; so I may but 'shew myself kind and tender to you, and so I 'may have but communion with you, and you with 'me; I care not if I become one with you, and 'live with you in your very flesh.' Oh, my heart, art thou yet cold in thy loves to Jesus Christ? Canst thou love him but a little who hath loved thee so much? How should I then but complain of thee to Christ? And for thy sake beg hard of God. 'Oh, thou sweet Jesus, that clothest 'thyself with the clouds as with a garment, and 'as now clothest thyself with the nature of a man, 'O that thou wouldest inflame my Spirit with a 'love of thee, that nothing but thyself might be 'dear unto me, because it so pleased thee to vilify 'thyself, thine own self for my sake.'

SECT. VII.

Of joying in Jesus in that respect.

7. LET us *joy* in Jesus, as carrying on the great work of our salvation for us at his first coming or incarnation. If it be so, that by our *desire*, and *hope*, and, *faith*, and *love*, we have indeed, and in truth reached the object which our souls pant after, how then should we but joy and delight therein? The end of our motion is to attain quiet and rest. Now, what is joy, but *a sweet and delightful tranquillity of mind, resting in the fruition and possession of some good?* What, hast thou in some measure attained the presence and fruition of Christ, (as God incarnate) in thy soul? It is then time to joy in Jesus; it is then time to keep a sabbath of thy thoughts, and to be quiet and calm in thy spirit; but you will say, How should this be before we come to heaven? I answer, There is not indeed any perfection of joy while we are here, because there is no perfection of union on this side heaven; but so far as union is, our joy must be; examine the grounds of thy hope, and the actings of thy faith, and if thou art but satisfied in them, why, then lead up thy joy, and bring it up to this blessed object; here is matter for us to work upon, if thou canst possibly rejoice in any thing at all, *O rejoice in the Lord, and again, I say, rejoice.*

Is there not cause, read and spell what is the meaning of the gospel of Christ? What's gospel? But good spell or good tidings. And wherein lies the good tidings according to its eminency? Is it not in the glorious incarnation of the Son of God? *Behold I bring you a gospel,* so it is in the original; or, *Behold I bring you good tidings of great joy, which shall be to all people: for unto you is born this day, in the city of David, a Saviour, which is Christ the Lord,* Luke ii. 10, 11. The birth of Christ to them that have but touched hearts,

hearts, is the comfort of comforts, and the sweetest balm and confection that ever was. O my soul, what ails thee? Why art thou cast down and disquieted within me? Is it because thou art a sinner? Why, *unto thee is born a Saviour*, his name is Saviour, and therefore Saviour, because *he will save his people from their sins*. Come then, and bring out thy sins, and weigh them to the utmost aggravation of them, and take in every circumstance both of law and gospel, and set but this in the other scale, that *unto thee is born a Saviour*, surely all thy iniquities well seem lighter than vanity, yea, they will be as nothing in comparison thereof. *My soul doth magnify the Lord*, (faith Mary) *and my spirit rejoiceth in God my Saviour*, Luke i. 46, 47. Her soul and her spirit within her rejoiced at this birth of Christ; there is cause that every soul and every spirit should rejoice that hath an interest in this birth of Christ, O my soul! how shouldest thou but rejoice if thou wilt consider these particulars;

1. God himself is come down into the world, because it was impossible for thee to come to him, he is come to thee; this consideration made the prophet cry out, *Rejoice greatly, O daughter of Zion, shout, O daughter of Jerusalem, behold thy king cometh unto thee*, Zech. ix. 9. He is called a king, and therefore he is able, and he is thy king, and therefore he is willing; but in that thy king cometh unto thee, here is the marvellous love and mercy of God in Christ: kings do not usually come to visit, and to wait upon their subjects, it is well if poor subjects may come to them, and be admitted into their presence to wait on them; O but see the great king of heaven and earth, the King of kings, and Lord of lords stooping, and bowing the heavens to come down to thee: surely this is good tidings of great joy, and therefore *rejoice greatly, O daughter of Zion*. A little joy is too scant and narrow for this news; hearts should be enlarged, the doors and gates should be set wide open for this king of glory to come in; as Balaam said of Israel, *God is with him, and the shout of a king is amongst them*; so now we may say, God is with us, and the shout of a king is amongst us, *Rejoice, Zion, shout, O daughter of Jerusalem*, Numb. xxiii. 21.

2. God is come down in the flesh, he hath laid aside, as it were, his own glory, whilst he converseth with thee; when God manifested himself as on mount Sinai, he came down in thunder and lightning, if now he had appeared in thunder and lightning, if now he had been guarded with an innumerable company of angels, all having their swords of vengeance and justice drawn, well might poor souls have trembled, and have run into corners, for who could ever be able to endure his coming in this way? But lo, poor soul! God is come down in the flesh, he hath made his appearance as a man, as one of us, and there is not in this regard the least distance betwixt him and us. Surely this is fuel for joy to feed upon; O why should God come down so suitably, so lowly as in our nature, if he would have thy poor soul to be afraid of him? Doth not this very design intend consolation to thy soul? O gather up thy spirit, anoint thy heart with the oil of gladness; see, God himself is come down in flesh to live amongst us, he professeth he will have no other life but amongst the sons of men; see what a sweet way of familiarity and intercourse is made betwixt God and us, now he is come down in human frailty.

3. God hath taken on him our nature, as a vast pipe to his Godhead, that it may flow out in all manner of sweetness upon our hearts; if God had come down in flesh only to have been seen of us, it had been a wonderful condescension, and a great mercy: *If I have found favour in thy eyes*, (said Moses) *shew me the way that I may know thee*, Exod. xxxiii. 12. But to come down, and to come down in flesh, not only to be seen, but to dispatch the great business of our soul's salvation, here's comfort indeed: with what joy should we draw water out of this well of salvation? Surely the great reason of the shallowness of our comforts, the shortness of our hopes, the faintness of our spirits, the lowness of our graces, is from the not knowing or the not heeding of this particular; Christ in flesh stands not for a cypher, but it is an organ of life and grace unto us, it is a fountain of comfort that can never run dry. In this flesh there is laid in one purpose, such a fulness of the Godhead, that of his fulness we might receive in our measure, grace for grace. O my soul! thou art daily busy in eying this and that, but, above all know that all the fulness of God lies in Christ incarnate to be emptied upon thee: this was the meaning of Christ taking on him flesh, that through his flesh he
might

might convey to thee whatsoever is in himself as God. As for instance, God in himself is good, and gracious, and powerful, and all-sufficient and merciful; and what now? Now by his being in flesh he suits all this, and conveys all this to thee; observe this for thy eternal comfort, God in and through the flesh makes all his attributes and glory serviceable to thy soul.

4. God, in our nature, hath laid out the model and draught of what he will do unto all his saints for ever; human nature was never so advanced before. What, to be glorified above the angels! to be united in a personal union with the second person of the Godhead? Surely, hence may be expected great matters, here's a fair step for the bringing of our persons up to the enjoyment of God; if God be come down in the likeness of man, why then he will bring us up unto the likeness of God; look what was done to our nature in Christ, the very same (as far as we are capable) shall be done to our persons in heaven. Think of it, O my soul, why hath God made flesh so glorious, but to shew that he will by that make thee glorious also? Christ is the great epitome of all the designs of God, so that in him thou mayest see what thou art designed unto, and how high and rich thou shalt be in the other world. *Beloved, now are we the sons of God, and it doth not yet appear what we shall be, but we know when he shall appear, we shall be like him,* 1 John iii. 2. He is now like us, but then (saith the apostle) we shall be like unto him, *he shall change our vile body, that it may be fashioned like unto his glorious body,* Phil. iii. 21. Oh! consider what a frame of eternal comfort may we raise up from this ground of Christ incarnate; God in the flesh.

5. God in the flesh is the first opening of his eternal plot to do us good; *the seed of the woman* was the first word of comfort that ever was heard in this world after man was fallen; the plot was of old, but the execution was not till after the creation, and then was a dim discovery of it, even in the beginning of time, though no clearer manifestation till the fulness of time. Well, take it as you please, whether in the beginning of time, or in the fulness of time; whether in the promise or in the performance; this discovering of Christ incarnate is the first opening of all God's heart and glory unto the sons of men; and from this we may raise a world of comfort, for if God in the execution of his decrees begins so gloriously, how will he end? If God be so full of love as to come down in flesh now in this world, oh, what matter of hope is laid up before us, of what God will be to us in that world to come? If the glory of God be let out to our souls so fully at first, what glorious openings of all the glory of God will be let out to our souls at last? Christians, what do you think will God do with us, or bring us unto, when we shall be with him in heaven? You see now he is manifested in the flesh, and he hath laid out a world of glory in that: but the apostle tells us of another manifestation, for *we shall see him as he is*; he shall at last be manifest in himself, *Now we see through a glass darkly, but then face to face, now we know in part, but then shall we know even as also we are known,* 1 John iii. 2. To what an height of knowledge or manifestation this doth arise, I am now to seek, and so I must be whilst I am on this side heaven, but this I believe, the manifestation of God and Christ is more in heaven, than is, or ever hath been, or ever shall be upon earth; *Thine eyes shall see the king in his beauty, or in his glory,* saith Isaiah, xxxiii. 17. There's a great deal of difference betwixt seeing the king in his ordination, and seeing him in his robes, and upon his throne, with his crown on his head, and his scepter in his hand, and his nobles about him in all his glory; the first openings of Christ are glorious, but O what will it be to see him in his greatest glory that ever he will manifest himself in? We usually say, That workmen do their meanest work at first, and if the glorious incarnation of Christ be but the beginning of God's works in reference to our souls salvation, what are those last works?

O my soul, weigh all these passages, and make an application of them to thyself, and then tell me, if yet thou hast not matter enough to raise up thy heart, and to *fill it with joy unspeakable and full of glory.* When the wise men saw but *the star of Christ, they rejoiced with an exceeding great joy,* Matth. ii. 10. How much more when they saw Christ himself? *Your Father Abraham* (said Christ to the Jews) *rejoiced to see my day, and he saw it, and was glad,* John viii. 56. He saw it indeed, but afar off, with the eyes of faith; they also had the promise, but we see the performance; how then should we rejoice? How glad shouldest thou be, O my soul, at the sight, and the effect of Christ's incarnation? If John the Baptist could leap for joy in his mother's belly, when Christ was but yet in the womb, how should thy heart leap for joy, who can say with the prophet, *Unto me a child is born, and unto me a son is given?* If Simeon, waiting *for the consolation of Israel, took him up in his arms for joy, and blessed God,* Luke ii. 28. How should thou with joy embrace him with both arms, who knowest his coming in the flesh, and who hast heard him come in the gospel, in the richest and most alluring expressions of his love? If the angels of God, yea, if multitudes of angels could sing for joy at his birth, *Glory to God in the highest, and on earth peace, and good will towards men,* Luke ii. 14. How much more should thou, whom it concerns more than the angels, join with them in concert, and sing for joy this joyful song of *good will towards men?* Awake, awake, O my soul, awake, awake, utter a song! tell over these passages, That God is come down into the world, that God is come down in flesh, that God is come down in flesh in order to thy reconciliation; that God is come down in the likeness of man, that he may bring thee up into the likeness of God, and that all these are but the first openings of the grace, and goodness, and glory of God in Christ to thy soul: and oh what work will these make in thy soul, if the Spirit come in who is the comforter!

SECT. VIII.

Of calling on Jesus in that respect.

8. LET us call on Jesus, or on God the Father in and through Jesus: Now this calling on Jesus contains prayer, and praise. 1. We must pray, That all these transactions of Jesus at his first coming or incarnation may be ours; and is not here encouragement for our prayers? If we observe it, this very point of Christ's incarnation opens a door of rich entrance into the presence of God; we may call it a blessed portal into heaven, not of iron, or brass, but of our own flesh; this is that *new and living way, which he hath consecrated for us, through the vail, that is to say, his flesh,* Heb. x. 20. With what boldness and freeness may we now enter into the holiest, and draw near unto the throne of grace? Why, Christ is incarnate, God is come down in the flesh; though his Deity may confound us (if we should immediately and solely apply ourselves unto it) yet his humanity comforts our faint and feeble souls; God in his humility animates our souls to come unto him, and to seek of him whatsoever is needful for us. Go then to Christ; away, away, O my soul, to Jesus, or to God the Father, in and through Jesus; and O desire that the effect, the fruit, the benefit of his conception, birth, and of the wonderful union of the two natures of Christ may be all thine. What! dost thou hope in Jesus, and believe thy part in this incarnation of Christ? Why, then pray in hope, and pray in faith: what is prayer, but the stream and river of faith, an issue of the desire of that which I joyfully believe? *Thou, O Lord God of hosts, God of Israel, hast revealed to thy servant, saying, I will build thee an house, therefore hath thy servant found in his heart to pray this prayer unto thee,* 2 Sam. vii. 27.

2. We must praise. This was the special duty practised by all saints and angels at Christ's birth, *My soul doth magnify the Lord* (said Mary) *and my spirit rejoiceth in God my Saviour,* Luke i. 46. *And blessed be the Lord God of Israel* (said Zachary) *for he hath visited and redeemed his people,* ver. 68. And *glory to God in the highest,* said the heavenly host; only an angel had before brought the news, *Unto you is born this day in the city of David, a Saviour, which is Christ the Lord,* Luke ii. 11. But immediately after there were many to sing praises: not only six cherubims, as Isaiah saw; not only four and twenty elders, as John saw, but a multitude of heavenly angels like armies, that by their heavenly hallelujahs gave glory to God. O my soul, do thou endeavour to keep concert with those many angels. *O sing praises, sing praises unto God, sing praises.* Never was like case since the first creation: never was the wisdom, truth, justice, mercy and goodness of God so manifested before: I shall never forget that last speech of a dying saint upon the stage, *Blessed be God for Jesus Christ.* O my soul, living and dying let this be thought on. What, Christ incarnate! and incarnate for me! why, *bless the Lord, O my soul, and all that is within me, bless his holy name.*

SECT.

SECT IX.

Of conforming to Jesus in that respect.

9. LET us conform to Jesus in reference to this great transaction of his incarnation. Looking to Jesus contains this, and is the cause of this; the sight of God will make us like to God; and the sight of Christ will make us like to Christ; for as a looking-glass cannot be exposed to the sun, but it will shine like the same, so God receives none to contemplate his face, but he transforms them into his own likeness by the irradiation of his own light; and Christ hath none that dive into these depths of his glorious and blessed incarnation, but they carry along with them sweet impressions of an abiding and transforming nature. Come, then, let us once more look to Jesus in his incarnation, that we may conform, and be like to Jesus in that respect.

But wherein lies this conformity or likeness? I answer, in these and the like particulars,

1. Christ was conceived in Mary by the Holy Ghost, so must Christ be conceived in us by the same Holy Ghost. To this purpose is the seed of the word cast in, and principles of grace are by the Holy Ghost infused; *he hath begotten us by the word*, saith the apostle, James i. 18. How mean, contemptible or impotent, men may esteem it, yet God hath appointed no other means to convey supernatural life, but after this manner: *Where no vision is the people perish:* where no preaching is, there is a worse judgment than that of Egypt, when there was one dead in every family. By the word and spirit the seeds of all grace are sown in the heart at once, and the heart closing with it, immediately Christ is conceived in the heart.

Concerning this spiritual conception or reception of Christ in us there is a great question, whether it be possible for any man to discern how it is wrought? But for the negative are these texts, *Our life is hid with Christ in God*, Col. iii. 3. And *the wind bloweth where it listeth, and thou hearest the sound thereof, but canst not tell whence it cometh, or whither it goeth*, John iii. 8. It is a wonderful, hidden and secret conception. The Holy Ghost sets out that state of unregeneracy in which Christ finds us by the name of *death*, Eph. ii. 1. So that it must needs be as impossible for us to discover how it is wrought, as it is impossible for one to know how he receives his own life. Some say the first act of infusing or receiving Christ, or grace (they are all one) is wrought in an instant, and not by degrees, and therefore it is impossible to discern the manner: and yet we grant, That we may discern both the preparations to grace, and the first operations of grace. 1. The preparations to grace are discernible; such are those, terrors, and spiritual agonies, which are often before the work of regeneration; they may be resembled to the heating of metals before they melt, and are cast into the mould to be fashioned; now by the help of natural reason we may discern these. 2. Much more may the first motions and operations of grace be discerned by one truly regenerate, because that in them his spirit works together with the Spirit of Christ; such are sorrow for sin, as sin, and seeking rightly for comfort, an hungering desire after Christ and his merits; neither do I think it impossible for a regenerate man to feel the first illapse of the spirit unto the soul, for it may bring that sense with itself, as to be easily discerned; although it doth not always see, nor perhaps usually see: it is true that the giving of spiritual life, and the giving of the sense of it, are two distinct acts of the spirit; yet who can deny but that both these acts may go together, though always they do not go together? Howsoever it is, yet even in such persons, as in the instant of regeneration may feel themselves in a regenerate estate, this conclusion stands firm, viz. *They may know what is wrought in them, but how it is wrought they cannot know nor understand.* We feel the wind, and perceive it in the motions and operations thereof, but the originals of it we are not able exactly to describe; some think the beginning of winds is from the flux of the air, others from the exhalations of the earth, but there is no certainty; so it is in the manner of this conception, or passive reception of Christ, and grace into our hearts; we know not how it is wrought, but it nearly concerns us to know that it is wrought; look we to this conformity, that as Christ was conceived in Mary by the Holy Ghost, so that Christ be conceived in us in a spiritual sense by the same Holy Ghost.

2. Christ was sanctified in the virgin's womb, so must we be sanctified in ourselves, following the commandment of God, *Be ye holy, as I am holy:*

souls regenerate must be sanctified, *Every man (saith the apostle) that hath this hope in him, purifieth himself even as he is pure*, 1 John iii. 3. I know our hearts are (as it were) seas of corruptions, yet we must daily cleanse ourselves of them by little and little: Christ could not have been a fit Saviour for us unless first he had been sanctified, neither can we be fit members unto him, unless we be in some measure purged from our sins, and sanctified by his Spirit. To this purpose is that of the apostle, *I beseech you, brethren, by the mercies of God, that ye present your bodies a living sacrifice, holy, acceptable unto God*, Rom. xii. 1. In the Old Testament they did, after a corporal manner, slay and kill beasts, presenting them, and offering them unto the Lord; but now we are in a spiritual manner to crucify and mortify the flesh, with the affections and lusts, all our inordinate passions, and our evil affections of anger, love, joy, hatred, are to be crucified; and all that is ours must be given up unto God; there must be no love in us but of God, and in reference to God; no fear in us but of God, and in reference to God; and thus of all other the like passions. O that we would look to Jesus, and be like to Jesus in this thing! if there be any honour, any happiness, any excellency, it is in this, even in this, we are not fit for any holy duty, or any religious approach unto God without sanctification, *This is the will of God* (saith the apostle) *even your sanctification*, 1 Thess. iv. 3. All the commands of God tend to this, and for the comfort of us Christians, we have under the gospel promises of sanctification to be in a larger measure made out unto us, *In that day there shall be upon the bells of the horses, holiness unto the Lord.—Yea, every pot in Jerusalem, and in Judah, shall be holiness unto the Lord*, Zech. xiv. 20, 21. Every vessel under Christ and the gospel must have written upon it, *holiness to the Lord*; thus our spiritual services, figured by the ancient ceremonial services, are set out by a larger measure of holiness than was in old times: it is a sweet resemblance of Christ to be holy, for he is still *the holy child Jesus*, Acts iv. 27. He was sanctified from the womb, and sanctified in the womb for our imitation: *For their sakes I sanctify myself*, (saith Christ) *that they might be sanctified*, John xvii. 19.

3. Christ the Son of man is by nature the Son of God; so we poor sons of men must by grace become the sons of God, even of the same God and Father of our Lord Jesus Christ. *For this very end, God sent his own Son made of a woman, that we might receive the adoption of sons.—Wherefore thou art no more a servant but a son, and if a son, then an heir of God thro' Christ*, Gal. iv. 4, 5, 7. This intimates, that what relation Christ hath unto the Father by nature, we should have the same by grace; by nature, *He is the only begotten Son of the Father, and as many as received him*, (saith John i. 21, 14.) *to them he gave power to become the sons of God, even to them that believe on his name*. It is true, Christ reserves to himself the preeminence; he is in a peculiar manner *the first-born among many brethren*, Rom. viii. 29. Yet in him, and for him all the rest of the brethren are accounted as first-borns: so God bids Moses say unto Pharaoh, *Israel is my son, even my first-born; and I say unto thee, Let my son go, that he may serve me, and if thou refuse to let him go, behold I will slay thy son, even thy first-born*, Exod. iv. 22, 23. And the whole church of God consisting of Jew and Gentile, is in the same sort described by the apostle to be, *The general assembly and church of the first-born inrolled in heaven*, Heb. xii. 23. By the same reason that we are sons, we are first-borns; *if we are children, then are we heirs, heirs of God, and joint heirs with Christ*, Rom. viii. 17. O who would not endeavour after this privilege? Who would not conform to Christ in this respect?

4. Christ the Son of God was yet the son of man; there was in him a duplicity of natures really distinguished, and in this respect, the greatest majesty, and the greatest humility that ever was, are found in Christ; so we though sons of God, must remember ourselves to be but sons of men, our privileges are not so high, but our poor conditions, frailties, infirmities, sins may make us as low: who was higher than the Son of God? And who was lower than the son of man? As he is God, he is in the bosom of his Father; as he is man, he is in the womb of his mother; as he is God, his throne is in heaven, and he fills all things by his immensity; as he is man, he is circumscribed in a cradle, I mean a manger, a most uneasy cradle sure; as he is God, he is clothed in a robe of glory; as he is man, he is wrapped in a few coarse swaddling bands; as he is God, he

is

is incircled with millions of bright angels; as he is man, he is in company with Joseph, and Mary, and the beasts; as he is God, he is the eternal word of the Father, all-sufficient, and without need; as he is man, he submits himself to a condition imperfect, inglorious, indigent and necessitous: well, *Let this mind be in you, which was also in Christ Jesus, who being in the form of God, thought it not robbery to be equal with God, but he made himself of no reputation, and took upon him the form of a servant, and was made in the likeness of men, and being found in fashion as a man, he humbled himself,* Phil. ii. 5, 6, 7, 8. He that thought it no robbery to be equal with God, humbled himself to become man; we should have found it no robbery to be equal with devils, and are we too proud to learn of God? What an intolerable disproportion is this, to behold an humble God, and a proud man? Who can endure to see a prince on foot, and his vassal mounted? Shall the Son of God be thus humble for us, and shall not we be humble for ourselves? I say, ourselves that deserve to be cast down amongst the lowest worms, the damnedest creatures? What are we in our best condition here upon earth? Had we the best natures, purest conversations, happiest endowments that accompany the saints, pride overthrows all; it thrust proud Nebuchadnezzer out of Babel, proud Haman out of the court, proud Saul out of his kingdom, proud Lucifer out of heaven: poor man, how ill it becomes thee to be proud, when God himself is become thus humble? *O learn of me* (saith Christ) *for I am meek, and humble, and lowly in Spirit, and you shall find rest unto your souls,* Mat. xi. 29.

5. The two natures of Christ, though really distinguished, yet were they inseparably joined, and made not two, but one person; so must our natures and persons, though at greatest distance from God, be inseparably joined and united to Christ, and thereby also to God. *I pray* (said Christ) *that they all may be one, as thou Father, art in me, and I in thee, that they also may be one in us,* John xvii. 21. That union of Christ's two natures we call a personal hypostatical union; and this union of Christ with us, we call, a mystical and spiritual union; yet though it be mystical and spiritual, this hinders not but that it is a true, real, essential, substantial union, whereby the person of the believers is indissolubly united to the glorious person of the Son of God. For our better understanding we may consider (if you please) of a threefold unity, either of persons in one nature, or of natures in one person, or of natures and persons in one Spirit; in the first is one God; in the second is one Christ; in the third is one church with Christ; our union unto Christ is the last of these, whereby he and we are all spiritually united to the making up of one mystical body: O what a privilege is this! a poor believer, be he never so mean, or miserable in the eye of the world, yet he is one with Christ, as Christ is one with the Father; *Our fellowship is with the Father, and with his Son Jesus Christ,* 1 John i. 3. Every saint is Christ's fellow; there is a kind of analogical proportion between Christ and his saints in every thing: if we take a view of all Christ, what he is in his person, in his glory, in his Spirit, in his graces, in his Father's love, and the access he hath to the Father, in all these we are in a sort fellows with Christ; only with this difference, That Christ hath the preeminence in all things; all comes from the Father first to Christ, and all we have is by marriage with Jesus Christ; Christ by his union hath all good things without measure, but we by our union have them only in measure, as it pleaseth him to distribute. But herein if we resemble Christ, whether in his union with the Father, or in his union of the two natures in one person of a Mediator; if by looking on Christ, we come to this likeness, to be one with Jesus Christ; oh what a privilege is this! had we not good warrant for so high a challenge, it could be no less than a blasphemous arrogance to lay claim to the royal blood of heaven: but the Lord is pleased so to dignify a poor worm, that every believer may truly say, *I am one with Jesus Christ, and Jesus Christ is one with me.*

To sweeten this union to our thoughts, I shall acquaint you with the privilege flowing from it, and let the same stir you up to conform.

Hence it is that Christ lives in us, and that Christ both gives life, and is our life. *When Christ which is our life shall appear; Christ is to me to live; and I live, yet not I, but Christ liveth in me.* Col. iii. 4. Phil. ii. 21. Gal. ii. 20. There is a spiritual and natural life; for the natural life what is it but a bubble, a vapour, a shadow, a dream, a nothing? But this spiritual life is an excellent life, it is wrought in us by the Spirit of Christ; there is a world of difference betwixt the natural and the spiritual life, and that makes the difference betwixt what I do as a man, and what I do as a Christian; as a man I have eyes, ears, motions, affections, understanding, naturally as my own; but as a Christian I have all these from him with whom I am spiritually one, the Lord Jesus Christ; as a man I have bodily eyes, and I behold bodily and material things, but as a Christian I have spiritual eyes, and see invisible and eternal things, as it is said of Moses, That *he endured, as seeing him who is invisible,* Heb. xi. 27. As a man I have outward ears, and I hear outwardly sounds of all sorts, whether articulate, or inarticulate; but as a Christian I have inward ears, and so I hear the voice of Christ, and of God's Spirit, speaking to my soul; as a man I have bodily feet, and by them I move in my own secular ways, but as a Christian I have spiritual feet, and on them I walk with God in all the ways of his commandments; as a man I have natural affections, and so I love beauty, and fear pain, and hate an enemy, and I rejoice in outward prosperity or the like; but as a Christian I have renewed affections, and so I love goodness, and hate nothing but sin, and I fear above all the displeasure of my God, and I rejoice in God's favour, which is better than life. Surely this is a blessed life; and as soon as ever I am united to Christ, why then *I live, yet not I, but Christ liveth in me:* first, Christ is conceived, and then Christ is formed, and then Christ is born, and then Christ grows in me to a blessed fulness: *My little children, of whom I travail in birth again, until Christ be formed in you.* Gal. iv. 19. Formation follows conception, and travail implies birth: then after this we are *babes in Christ,* 1 Cor. iii. 1. Or Christ is as a babe in us, from thence we grow up to strength of youth, *I have written unto you, young men, because ye are strong,* 1 John ii. 14. And at last we come to gospel perfection, even towards the *measure of the stature of the fulness of Christ,* Eph. iv. 13. Is this all? Nay, if my union be firm, and Christ live in me, Why then I go on, and in this condition *I am dead with Christ; and I am buried with Christ; and I am alive again unto God through Christ; and I am risen with Christ; and I am glorified with Christ.* Rom. vi. 8. and vi. 4. 11. Col. iii. 1. Rom. viii. 17. Nay, yet more, my sufferings are Christ's, Col. i. 24. And Christ's sufferings are mine; I am in Christ an heir of glory, Rom. viii. 17. And Christ is in me the hope of glory, Col. i. 27. O my Christ is my life, what am I, or what is my father's house, that thou shouldest come down into me, that thou shouldest be conceived in the womb of my poor sinful heart, that thou shouldest give my soul a new and spiritual life, a life begun in grace, and ending in eternal glory? I shall not reckon up any more privileges of this union, methinks I should not need; if I tell you of grace and glory, what can I more? Glory is the highest pitch, and Christ tells you concerning it, *The glory which thou gavest me, I have given them, that they may be one, even as we are one,* John xvii. 22. Ah, my brethren! to be so like Christ as to be one with Christ, it is near indeed; O let us conform to Christ in this; he is one with our nature in an hypostatical, personal union; let us be one with him in a spiritual, holy and a mystical union; if God be not in our persons as truly, though not as fully as in our nature, we have no particular comfort from this design of his personal, hypostatical and wonderful union.

6. Christ was born, so must we be new-born; to this I have spoken when I laid it down as an evidence, That *unto us a child is born, and unto us a Son is given,* only one word more; we must be new-born; as once born by nature, so new born by grace; there must be some resemblances in us of Christ born amongst us. As, 1. Christ born had a Father in heaven, and a mother on earth; so in our new birth we must look on God as our Father in heaven, and on the church as our mother on earth: It was usually said, *Out of the church no salvation,* and to this the apostle alludes, *Jerusalem which is above is free, which is the mother of us all,* Gal. iv. 26. Indeed out of the church there is no means of salvation, no word to teach, no sacraments to confirm, nothing at all to hold forth Christ to a soul, and without Christ how should there be the salvation of souls? so that we must look on the church as our mother, and on God as our Father; not that we deny some to be as spiritual fathers unto others, Paul tells the Corinthians, that he was their father, *Though ye have ten thousand instructors in Christ, yet have ye not many fathers, for in Christ Jesus I have begotten you through the gospel,* 1 Cor. iv. 15. but alas! such

such fathers are but ministerial fathers, and therefore Paul seems to correct himself, *Who is Paul? And who is Apollos? But ministers by whom ye believed, even as the Lord gave to every man?* 1 Cor. iii. 5. It is God only is our Father principally, originally, supremely; God only puts grace and virtue into the womb of the soul; it is not possible that any creature should be a creator of the new creature. O then let us look up unto heaven and say, *O Lord, new-make me, new-create me, O be thou my Father.*

2. When Christ was born, all Jerusalem was troubled; so when this new birth is, we must look for it, That much commotion, and much division of heart will be, the devil could not be cast out of the possessed person, but he would exceedingly tear, and torment, and vex the possessed person; the truth is, we cannot expect that Christ should expel Satan from those holds and dominions he hath over us, but he will be sure to put us to great fear and terror in heart. Besides not only the evil spirit, but God's Spirit is for a while a Spirit of bondage, to make every thing as a mighty burthen unto us; there are many pretenders to the grace of God in Christ, but they cannot abide to hear of any pains or pangs in this new birth; O this is legal! but I pray thee tell me, dost thou ever know any woman bring forth in her sleep or in a dream, without feeling any pain? And how then should the heart of man be thus new and changed and moulded without several pangs? Look, as it is in the natural, there are many pangs and troubles, *In sorrow shalt thou bring forth children*; so it is, and must be in our spiritual birth, there is usually (I will not say always, to such or such a degree) many pangs and troubles, there's many a throb, and many an heart-ach 'ere Christ can be formed in us.

3. When Christ was born, there was a discovery of many of the glorious attributes of God; then *Mercy and truth met together, and righteousness and peace kissed each other*; then especially was a discovery of the goodness, and power, and wisdom, and holiness of God. So when this new birth is we must look upon it as a glorious discovery of those lovely attributes. As, 1. Of his mercy, goodness, love; how often is this called his grace, and the riches of his grace? Christians! you that know what the new birth means, do not you say, The goodness of God appears in this. Surely it was God's goodness to make a world, but this is the riches of his goodness to create a new heart in you, when man by sin was fallen, he might have been thrown away as refuse, fit fuel for everlasting flames; it might have been with mankind as it was with devils, in their deluge God did not provide an ark to save so many as eight persons, not one angel that fell was the object of God's grace; and that God should pass by all those angels, and many thousands of the sons of men, and yet that he should look upon you in your blood, and bid you live, O the goodness of God!

2. As of the goodness, so in this new birth there's a discovery of God's power; and hence it is called, *A new creature*, Gal. vi. 15. The very same power that framed the world is the Framer of this new creature; the work of conversion is set forth by the work of creation: God only creates man, and God only converts man; in the creation God said, *Let there be light, and there was light*; in our conversion, God saith, *Let there be light,* and presently the same God shines in our hearts: nay, this power of conversion, in some sense, far passeth the creation, *To whom is the arm of the Lord revealed*, Isa. liii. 1. The Lord puts to his arm, his power, his strength indeed in conversion of souls; when he made the world, he met with nothing to resist him, he only spake the word, and it was done; but, in the conversion of a sinner, God meets with the whole frame of all creatures opposing and resisting him, the devil and the world without, and sin and corruption within; here then must needs be a power against all power.

3. As of the power and goodness of God, so in this new birth there is a discovery of the wisdom of God. I might instance in many particulars; as, 1. In that the regenerate are most what of the meanest and contemptiblest persons, *Not many wise, not many noble*, &c. 1 Cor. i. 27. 2. In that many times God takes the worst weeds and makes the sweetest flowers, thus Paul, Zacheus, the publicans and harlots. 3. In that the regenerate are of the fewest and least number, *Many are called, but few are chosen.* 4. In that God chooseth such a time to be his time of love, wherein he usually discovers many concurrences of strange love meeting together, read Ezek. xvi. 4, 5, 6, 8, 9. In all these particulars, is his wisdom wonderful.

4. As of the goodness, power and wisdom of God, so in this new birth there is a discovery of the holiness of God. If a clod of earth, or piece of muck should be made a glorious star in heaven, it is not more wonderful than for a sinner to be made like an angel, doing the will of God; it argues the holiness of God, and his love of holiness, to make man holy; he tells us, *That without holiness none shall see God*; and therefore first he will make us holy, and then he will bring us to himself. O here is a blessed conformity! as Christ was born let us be new born.

7. Christ, after his birth, did and suffered many things in his childhood, (I should be too large to speak to every particular) so should we learn to *bear God's yoke even in our youth*, Lam. iii. 27. It is good to imitate Christ even betimes, *Remember now thy Creator in the days of thy youth, while the evil days come not, nor the years draw nigh, when thou shalt say, I have no pleasure in them*, Eccles. xii. 1. Do we not see by experience, what a blessed thing a gracious and an holy education is? *Train up a child in the way he should go, and when he is old he will not depart from it*, Prov. xxii. 6. O ye parents, that ye would do your duties, and in that respect imitate Joseph and Mary, in their care and nurture of the holy child Jesus; and O ye children, that ye would do your duties, and imitate Jesus, the blessedest pattern that ever was, that as you grow in stature, you also might *grow in favour with God and man*, Luke ii. 52. Observe him in the temple, when he was but twelve years old, see him in the midst of the doctors, both hearing them and asking them questions; children whilst little, (if but capable of instruction) should with their parents wait on God in the midst of our assemblies; Moses told Pharoah, they must have their young ones with them to the solemn worship, Exod. x. 9. And when Joshua read the law of God to the children of Israel, they had their little ones with them on that solemn assembly, Joshua viii. 35. Observe Christ also in Nazareth, where, during his minority, he was ever subject to his parents; so, *Children, obey your parents in the Lord, for this is right*, Eph. vi. 1, 2. Not only the law of God, but the gospel of Christ makes mention of this, *Honour thy father and mother, which is the first commandment with promise*; I know the subjection of Christ extends to his particular calling, and this also is for your imitation; in obedience to his supposed father, the holy child would have a particular employment; something must be done for the support of that holy family wherein Jesus lived, and to that purpose he puts to his own hands, and works in the trade of a carpenter; such as will live idle, and without a calling, that serve for no other use but to devour God's creatures, and to make a dearth, O unlike are they to Christ Jesus! It is noted for a grievous sin, and a chief part of the corruption of our nature, to be unprofitable to the generation with whom we live; *They are altogether become unprofitable, there is none that doth good*, Rom. iii. 12. Religion and grace wherever it prevaileth, makes men profitable, and, in this respect the poorest servant and drudge may have more comfort in his estate, than the greatest gentleman that hath nothing to do but to eat, and drink, and play.

'Thus far we have looked on Jesus as our Je-
' sus in his incarnation, or his first coming in
' the flesh. Our next work is to look on Je-
' sus carrying on the great work of man's sal-
' vation during his life, from John's baptism,
' until his suffering and dying upon the cross.

LOOKING UNTO
JESUS.
IN HIS LIFE.

THE FOURTH BOOK, PART SECOND.

CHAP. I. SECT. I.

1 John i. 2. *For the Life was manifested, and we have seen it.*

Of the Beginning of the Gospel.

IN this piece, as in the former, we must first lay down the object, and then direct you how to look upon it.

The object is Jesus carrying on the work of man's salvation during the time of his life. Now, in all the transactions of this time, we shall observe them as they were carried on successively in those three years and an half of his ministerial office, or if you will in those four complete years before his passion and death.

For the first year, and his actings therein, the evangelist Mark i. 1. begins thus, *The beginning of the gospel of Jesus Christ the Son of God*, q. d. The beginning of that age of the world, which the prophets pointed out for the time of good things to come; or the beginning of the exhibition and completion of that gospel, which, in respect of the promise, figures and signification was from the beginning of the world. This beginning of the gospel, the prophets sometimes expressed by the term of the last days. *And it shall come to pass in the last days*, Isa. ii. 2. Micah iv. 1. Sometimes by the term of the acceptable year of the Lord, *The Spirit of the Lord is upon me to proclaim the acceptable year of the Lord*, Isa. lxi. 1, 2. Sometimes by the term of the kingdom of God, *And in the days of these kings, shall the God of heaven set up a kingdom, which shall never be destroyed*, Dan. ii. 44. Sometimes by the term of a new heaven and a new earth, *Behold I create new heavens and a new earth, and the former shall not be remembered, nor come in mind*, Isa. lxv. 17. Howsoever it is called, this is concluded, that the beginning of the gospel is not to be reckoned from the birth of Christ, but from the beginning of the ministry and preaching of John the Baptist; *From the days of John the Baptist*, (saith Christ) *the kingdom of heaven suffereth violence; for all the prophets, and the law prophesied until John*, Matth. xi. 12, 13. And when the apostles were ready, in the room of Judas, to choose a new apostle, it is said, That *of those men which companied with them all the time that the Lord Jesus went in and out amongst them, beginning from the baptism of John, unto the day that he was taken up, must one be ordained to be a witness*, Acts i. 21, 22. And Peter preaching to Cornelius, and his friends, he tells them, *That the word*, (or gospel) *was published throughout all Judea, and began from Galilee, after the baptism which John preached*, Acts x. 37. And see but how immediately these words follow, *The beginning of the gospel of Jesus Christ, the Son of God; as it is written in the prophets, Behold I send my messenger before thy face, which shall prepare the way before thee*, Mark i. 1, 2. I know that John's ministry was six months before Christ's; and yet that now was the beginning of the gospel; it appears, 1. In that baptism, (which was only used among the Jews, for the admission of proselytes or Heathens to their church) is now published and proposed to the Jews themselves; shewing, 1. That now they were to be entered and transplanted into a new profession. And, 2. That the Gentiles and they now were to be knit into one church and body. And, 3. It appears, in that the doctrine and preaching of John, was of a different strain from the literal doctrine of the law, as it is taken in the sense of the Jews; for that called all for works, and for exact performance, *Do this and live*; but John called for repentance, and for renewing of the mind, and for belief in him that was coming after, disclaiming all righteousness by the works of the law; so that here were new heavens, and a new earth begun to be created, a new commandment given, a new church founded, justification by works cried down, and the doctrine of faith and repentance advanced and set up.

Hence one observes. (*Lightf. har. of the four Evan*). That the evangelist Luke iii. 1, 2. points out this year in a special manner; it was the fifteenth year of Tiberius Cesar, at which time, (says he) Pilate was governor of Judea, Herod was tetrarch of Galilee, Philip was tetrarch of Iturea, Lysanias was tetrarch of Abilene, and Annas and Caiaphas were high priests. And then, even then the word of God came unto John the son of Zacharias in the wilderness. See how exact the evangelist seems, that so remarkable a year of the beginning of the gospel might be fixed and made known to all the world. In this respect I shall begin the first year of Christ's life, with the beginning of John's preaching, which was six months current before the ministry of Christ, and in the compass of this first year, I shall handle these particulars.

1. The preaching of John Baptist. 2. The baptism of Christ Jesus. 3. The fasting and temptation of Christ in the wilderness. 4. The first manifestation of Jesus by his several witnesses. 5. Christ's whipping the buyers and sellers out of the temple. Observe, that every of these four years, I shall end at one of the passovers, of which we read during Christ's ministry; as of the first passover, John ii 13. Of the second passover, in John v 1. Of the third passover, John vi. 4. Of the fourth passover, John xiii. 1. And first of the first year to end at the first passover.

SECT. II.

Of the preaching of John the Baptist.

2. FOR the preaching of John the baptist, now was it that the gospel began to dawn, and John, like the morning star, or the blushing day, springing from the windows in the east, foretels the approaching of the Son of righteousness; now was it that he laid the first rough, hard and unhewn stone of the building in mortification, self-denial, and doing violence to our natural affections. I read not that ever John wrought a miracle, but he was a man of an austere life; and good works convince more than miracles themselves. It is storied of one Pachonius, a soldier under Constantine the Emperor, that his army being well near starved for want of necessary provision, he came to a city of Christians; and they of their own charity relieved them speedily and freely: he wondering at their so free and chearful dispensation, enquired what kind of people those were whom he saw so bountiful? It was answered, They were Christians, whose profession it is to hurt no man, to do good to every man. Hereupon the soldier conceived of the excellency of this religion, he threw away his arms, and became a Christian and a saint. To this purpose, I suppose John the baptist spent his time in prayer, meditations, affections, and colloquies with God, eating flies and wild honey in the wilderness, that he might be made a fit instrument of preparation and dissemination of the gospel of Christ.

In his sermons, he sometimes gave particular schedules of duty to several states of persons; he sharply reproved the Pharisees for their hypocrisy and impiety; he gently guided others into the ways of righteousness, calling them the *straight way of the Lord*; and by such discourses and baptism, he disposed the spirits of men for the entertaining of the Messias, and the doctrine of the gospel. John's sermons were to the sermons of Jesus, as a preface to a discourse.

But observe this, That his most usual note was *repentance, The ax to the root, the fan to the floor, the chaff to the fire:* as his raiment was rough, so was his tongue; and thus must the way be made for Christ in stubborn obstinate hearts: plausibility,

or

or pleasing of the flesh is no fit preface to regeneration; if the heart of man had continued upright, Christ might have been entertained without contradiction; but now violence must be offered to our corruptions, 'ere we can have room for grace; if the great way-maker do not cast down hills, and raise up valleys in the bosoms of men, there is no passage for Christ; never will Christ come into that soul, where the herald of repentance, either on one motive or other hath not been before him.

Shall we hear that sermon which John preached in his own words? Matth. iii. 2. in brief gives it in thus, *Repent ye, for the kingdom of heaven is at hand:* these are the words when he first began to preach the gospel of Christ; and indeed we find Christ himself doth preach the same doctrine in the same words, *Jesus began to preach, and to say, Repent, for the kingdom of heaven is at hand,* Mat. iv. 17. And when Christ sent out his disciples to preach the gospel, he commanded them to preach the same doctrine also, *Go ye, preach, saying, repent; for the kingdom of heaven is at hand,* Matth. vi. 12. Mat. x. 7. In this sermon we must observe these two parts, here's 1. A duty. And 2. A motive to this duty. 1. The duty is, *Repent*; it is not a legal but an evangelical repentance that is here meant; indeed the law strictly takes no notice of repentance, but the gospel: true, and thorough, and consummate repentance is a gospel-grace. 2. The motive is this, *For the kingdom of heaven is at hand.* This phrase, *The kingdom of heaven,* hath several acceptations, and accordingly it hath occasioned some differences. 1. Sometimes it is taken for that glorious condition of the other world: this may be implied; but this I suppose few understand to be this sense of the place. 2. Sometimes it is taken for the church of Christ; Repent, for now the pedagogy of the Jews is expiring, or breathing its last, and the church of Christ is at hand, a people that shall bear the very stile of Christians; that shall profess Christ, and close with Christ as their Saviour and Messiah; of which church that you may be a part, prepare for it, *repent.* 3. Sometimes it is taken for the spiritual kingdom of Christ, in opposition to those earthly temporal kingdoms, which bore the sway, and domineered over all the world with cruelty and tyranny, before Christ's coming; of this Daniel, ii. 44. prophesied, *And in the days of these kings,* *shall the God of heaven set up a kingdom, which shall never be destroyed:* Now, what was this kingdom, but the kingdom of grace? It is by an *hebraism* called, *The kingdom of heaven,* that is, an heavenly kingdom: The Jews expected the Messiah, and dreamed of an outward, glorious, and pompous kingdom: now, saith John, The Messiah is come, and his kingdom is come, but 'tis not earthly, but an heavenly kingdom; and therefore repent. 4. Sometimes it is taken for the preaching of the gospel, or for the preaching of the kingdom of grace, and mercy of God in Christ unto men: *q. d.* 'O 'firs! look about you, there's now a discovery made 'of the glory and grace of God, in another way 'than ever formerly; and therefore prepare for it, 'repent.' 5. Sometimes it is taken for the gospel of Christ, as it is published and preached unto all nations; observe, I do not only say for the gospel as it is preached; but as it is preached to the Gentiles, or among all nations; and this shews how proper and pregnant an argument this was to enforce the doctrine and practice of repentance upon the Jews, because the calling of the Gentiles was near at hand, which would prove their rejection and casting off, if they did not repent.

Oh how unseasonable is this sermon to us? Christians! hath not the kingdom of heaven approach'd unto us? Take the kingdom of heaven for the kingdom of glory, are we not near to the door of glory, to the confines of eternity; *what is our life, but a vapour that appeareth for a little time, and after it vanisheth away?* We know not but 'ere the sun have run one round, our souls may be in that world of souls, and so either in heaven or hell. Or take *the kingdom of heaven* for the church of Christ, and what expectations have we now of the flourishing state of Christ's church here upon earth? *Then shall the children of Israel and Judah be gathered together—for great shall be the day of Jezreel,* Hos. i. 11. A time is at hand, that Israel and Judah shall be called together, that the fulness of the Gentiles shall come in; and what is this, but *the great day of Jezreel?* O then what manner of persons ought we to be? How spiritual? How heavenly-minded? *Arise, arise, shake off thy dust, for thy light is coming, and the glory of the Lord is rising upon thee.* Or, take *the kingdom of heaven,* for the preaching of the gospel of grace, mercy and goodness of God in Christ, what preachings are now

now in comparison of what have been formerly? How doth the Lord set forth his free love, and free grace in the churches of Christ? No question but many former ages have enjoyed their discoveries in some sweet measure, and yet after-ages wonder that they have known no more; and how much of *the kingdom of heaven* do saints find in this age, as if there were a new manifestation of God unto the world? And yet I must tell you, that the ages to come shall know more of this kingdom, there shall be further and further openings of this great mystery of grace unto the sons of men: mark the apostle, *That in the ages to come he might shew the exceeding riches of his grace, in his kindness towards us thro' Jesus Christ*, Eph. ii. 7. How is this? Had not God revealed grace enough in the former ages? Or had not God revealed grace enough in that present age? Did he not then call in the Gentiles? Were not many thousands converted at one only sermon? What a deal of that grace had Paul himself received? He tells us that *the grace of our Lord Jesus was exceeding abundant to him-wards*, 1 Tim. i. 3. And is there yet more grace to be revealed? O yes! herein lies the mystery of grace, That he hath reserved exceeding riches of grace for the ages to come; grace that never saw light before; and I believe there is yet a fuller magazine of the riches of his grace for latter ages, even for the ages to come to be discovered, than ever was yet. Oh then repent, repent! Why, *For the kingdom of heaven is at hand*; the very openings of God's love and grace unto souls, is a way and motive to draw our souls unto God. Or take the kingdom of heaven for the preaching of the gospel to all nations, Jews, and Gentiles, what fears and jealousies may this breed in us as well as the Jews? O boast not against the branches! it may be thou wilt say, 'The 'branches were broken off, that I might be graffed in. Well, because of unbelief they were broken off, and thou standest by faith; be not high 'minded, but fear. For if God spared not the 'natural branches, take heed lest he also spare 'not thee: behold therefore the goodness, and severity of God; on them which fell, severity; but 'towards thee goodness, if thou continue in his 'goodness, otherwise thou shalt be cut off.' But I must not dwell on this; my design is to consider of Jesus and of the transactions of Jesus in reference to our souls health; now, John's sermons were only a preparative to the manifestation of Jesus; he was only the fore-runner of Christ, and not Christ himself, as himself witnesseth.

SECT. III.

Of the baptism of Jesus.

2. FOR the baptism of Christ. He that formerly was circumcised would now be baptised, he was circumcised to sanctify his church that was, and he was baptized to sanctify his church that should be; we find him in both testaments opening a way into heaven. This was the first appearing of Christ in reference to his ministerial office; he that lay hid in the counsel of God from all eternity, and he that lay hid in the womb of his mother for the space of forty weeks, and he that lay hid in Nazareth for the space of thirty years, now at last he begins to shew himself to the world, and *he comes from Galilee to Jordan, to John to be baptized of him*, Matth. iii. 13. The day was but a little broke in John the baptist, but Christ the sun of righteousness soon entered upon our hemisphere; indeed now was the full time come, that Jesus took leave of his mother, and his trade, to begin his Father's work, in order to the redemption of the world. For the clearer understanding of Christ's baptism, we shall examine these particulars.——

1. What reason had Christ to be baptised?
2. How was it that John knew him to be Christ?
3. Wherein was the glory of Christ's baptism?
4. What was the prayer of Christ, at, or after his baptism?
5. Why was it that the Holy Ghost descended on Jesus?
6. Upon what account was it that the Holy Ghost should reveal himself at this time? And why in the form of a dove, rather than some other form?

1. What reason had Christ to be baptised? we find John himself wondering at this, *I have need to be baptized of thee, and comest thou to me?* Matth. iii. 14. Many reasons are given for Christ's baptism; as, 1. That by this symbol he might enter himself into the society of Christians; just like a

king,

king, that to endear himself to any city of his subjects, he condescends to be made a free-man of that city. 2. That he might bear witness to the preaching and baptism of John, and might reciprocally receive a testimony from John. 3. That by his own baptism, he might sanctify the water of baptism to his own church. 4. That he might give an example himself of the performance of that, which he enjoined others. 5. That he might receive testimony from heaven, that he was the Son of God. 6. That he might *fulfil all righteousness*: not only the moral but the figurative, ceremonial and typical: some think that the ceremony, which our Saviour looked at in these words, was the washing of the priests in water, when they entered into their functions, *And Aaron, and his sons thou shalt bring to the door of the tabernacle of the congregation, and shalt wash them with water*, Exod. xxix. 4. Lev. viii. 6. And surely this was the main reason of Christ's being baptised, That by the baptism he might be installed into his ministerial office.

2. How did John know him to be Christ? It is very probable he had never seen his face before, they had in their infancy been driven to several places, and they were designed to several employments, and never met (as we may well conceive) till now; besides the baptist speaks expresly, *I knew him not, but he that sent me to baptize with water, the same said unto me, on whomsoever thou shalt see the Spirit descending, and abiding on him, the same is he that baptizeth with the Holy Ghost*, John i. 33. Now this descent of the Holy Ghost, was not till after baptism; how then did he know him to be Christ?

The answer is given by some, thus; That John knew Christ in some measure before his baptism, but he knew him not so fully as after, when the Holy Ghost had descended on him. Others thus; That John knew Christ before his baptism, by a present revelation, and after baptism by a present sign; it is not unlikely, but John knew Christ at his first arrival by revelation: for if whilst he was in his mother's womb he knew Christ being yet unborn, how much more might he know, and acknowledge him now at his baptism? Thus Samuel knew Saul, and thus John might know Christ. But for that knowledge he had after baptism, it was a further confirmation of that same knowledge that he had

before baptism, and that not so much for his own sake, as for the people's, *I saw and bear record that this is the Son of God*, John i. 34.

3. Wherein was the glory or excellency of Christ's baptism? The ancients gave many encomiums to it, and in some respects prefer it to the birth of Christ: thus *Aug.* Serm. 36. 'Many great 'miracles were at Christ's birth, but they were 'far greater at his baptism; the Holy Ghost over-'shadowed him in the womb, but he brightly 'shone on him in the river; then was the Father 'silent, not a word from him; but now a loud 'voice is heard from heaven, This is my beloved 'Son, in whom I am well pleased; then was the 'mother under suspicion, because she was found 'with child without a father, but now is the mo-'ther greatly honoured, in that the holy child 'is fathered by God himself:' Then was Christ hid to the world, and this made John the baptist say, *There stands one amongst you whom ye know not*: he was before his baptism, as a sun in a cloud, or a pearl in a shell, or a gold mine in a field, but now he appears in public, and to manifest his glory, the heavens open, and from the heavens the Holy Ghost descends, and alights upon his sacred head, and God the Father gives a voice from heaven, declaring his divinity to the world. If the Jews require a sign, here is not one, but many signs at once, which as beams do discover a sun, so they discover this sun of righteousness to be risen amongst them: and herein was the glory of Christ's baptism.

4. What was the prayer of Christ, at, or after his baptism? The evangelist Luke speaks of his prayer, *It came to pass that Jesus being baptized, and praying, the heavens were opened*, Luke iii. 21. This was the manner of those that were baptized, as soon as they were baptized, to come out of the water and pray, and some think that these words, *They were baptized of him in Jordan, confessing their sins*, Mat. iii. 36. hath reference to this: if so, then Christ having no sins to confess of his own, the tenor of his prayer must needs be to some other purpose: but to what purpose? Some say to the same purpose as his prayers were usually, as in Joh. xvii. ' That his Father would preserve his church 'in unity and truth, and that he would glorify 'his church, that they also might be one, even as 'he and his Father are one; and especially that

'many might be converted by his ministry, which 'he was now beginning.' Others think that this prayer at this time, was for that which followed upon his very prayer, *i. e. That the Holy Ghost might descend, and that the Father would glorify the Son by a testimony from heaven.* Indeed the text hath laid his prayer, and the opening of the heavens so close together, as that it seems to point out what was the tenor of his prayer by the consequence of it. Before the heaven was immured up, no dove to be seen, no voice to be heard, but straight upon it (as if they had but waited the last word of his prayer) all of them follow: and in another place, we find the like return upon the like prayer, *Father, glorify thy name. Then came there a voice from heaven, saying, I have both glorified it, and I will glorify it again,* John xii. 28. One reason more, if we consider that Christ was now to enter upon the great work of our redemption, and the preaching of the gospel, it will be less strange to conceive, That he prayed for the visible sealing of him to that work and office, by the coming of the Holy Ghost. To this purpose is that of the evangelist, *For him hath God the Father sealed,* John vi. 27. It is a phrase borrowed from them, who give their commissions under hand and seal; and this is certain, That upon his prayer God sent the holy Spirit, who sealed him, or allowed, and confirmed him to the office of our redemption; and therefore very probable it is, That his prayer might tend to that purpose: but herein take heed of excluding what was mentioned in the former opinion. For my part I suppose Christ's prayer was both for himself and all believers; that the Holy Ghost might now be joined to the water, and that all others, as should ever after believe in his name (as afterwards he enlargeth his prayer) might have the Holy Ghost descend upon them, John xvii. 20.

5. Why was it that the Holy Ghost descended on Jesus? I answer, for these reasons; 1. That John the baptist might be satisfied; for this token was given John, when he first began to preach, *that upon whom he should see the Spirit descending, and remaining on him, the same is he which baptizeth with the Holy Ghost,* John i. 33. It was a sure sign to the baptist, whereby to know the Christ, whose harbinger and *prodromus* he was. 2. That Christ himself might be anointed, or installed into his function, *The Spirit of the Lord is upon me; because the Lord hath anointed me, to preach good tidings to the meek,* &c. Isa. lxi. 1, 2. As Aaron and his sons were anointed with material oil, when they entered into their offices, so Christ was by the Spirit (as it were) anointed, that so he might receive his consecration, and institution for the office, that he was to enter on, *viz.* The preaching and ministry of the gospel.

6. Upon what account was it, That the Holy Ghost should reveal himself at this time? And why in the form of a dove, rather than some other form?

To the *first,* I answer, The Holy Ghost now revealed himself, because the spiritual kingdom and sceptre of Christ, in and by which he was to rule all nations for ever, was now at hand. It was agreeable (faith my Author, Dr. *Lightf. harm. of the Evang.*) That the spiritualness of this kingdom should be sealed and confirmed by the holy Spirit's shewing himself even in the beginning of it. The carnal rites of Moses were now to vanish, and his corporal and ceremonial observances were now to be changed into a spiritual worship; and *neither at Jerusalem, nor at mount Gerazim, nor elsewhere,* must there be any more adoration with fleshly and earthly ceremonies, but he that will worship *God, must worship him in spirit and truth,* John iv. 21, 24. And therefore it is no wonder, if now the Holy Ghost do reveal himself: I say now, when his spiritual dominion by sanctification is to begin. *Secondly,* Because the Holy Ghost was now in especial manner to be restored again. Some observe, That he was visibly departed from Israel, after the death of the last prophets: and therefore now at his restoring, he comes in a visible and apparent form; and he lights on him, to whom it belongs to give the Spirit, and his gifts to whom he pleaseth. As John had preached, That Christ should baptize with the Holy Ghost; so now the Holy Ghost comes, and abides on Jesus Christ in the sight of John; as if the Father should have said, 'Now I seal that power and 'privilege to Christ my Son, which John hath spo-'ken; now the Holy Ghost is upon himself, and 'hereafter he shall baptize others with the same 'Holy Ghost.' *Thirdly,* Because at the beginning of the gospel, it was most suitable, That a full, clear and sensible demonstration of the whole trinity should be made. The learned observe, That the Holy Ghost in scripture hath a special regard to express this mystery of the trinity upon singular occasions; so the very first thing that is taught in all the Bible is this same mystery; *In the beginning God created*, there is the Father; and *God said*, there is the word, or the Son; and *the Spirit of God moved*, Gen. i. 1, 2, 3. there is the Holy Ghost. And the very first word of the Bible, that speaks of man, it holds out the trinity as creating him; *And God said, Let us make man in our own image*, Gen. i. 26. He saith, *Let us*, to shew the trinity of persons; and he saith, *In our Image*, not in *our images*, to shew the unity of essence. And when Moses begins to rehearse the law to Israel, the first thing he teacheth them, is, The trinity in unity, and unity in trinity. *Hear, O Israel, the Lord our God, the Lord is one*, Deut. vi. 4. The last word *One* denotes the unity; the three words, *The Lord our God*, answer the three persons; and the middle word, *Our God*, decyphers fitly the second person, who assumed our nature. How fit then was it, that the beginning of the new world, and the new law, and the baptism of Christ, the three persons should be revealed; especially since he ordained baptism to be administered in all their names? *Baptizing them in the name of the Father, and of the Son, and of the Holy Ghost*, Matth. xxviii. 19 But where is it revealed? See Matth. iii. 16, 17. where the Father speaks from heaven, the Son comes out of the water, and the Holy Ghost appears in the likeness of a dove. This was the greatest meeting that ever was upon the earth; every person of the trinity gives some sensible evidence of his presence at it.

To the *Second*, Why in the form of a dove rather than some other form? Many reasons are given: as,

1. To shew Christ's innocency, purity, simplicity, charity and love.

2. To shew what innocency and harmlesness should be in those that are baptized.

3. To answer the figure in Noah's flood; for as a dove at that time brought tidings of the abating of the waters, so now it brings tidings of the abating of God's wrath upon the preaching of the gospel: the first dove we find in the Bible is Noah's dove, with the olive branch in her bill, proclaiming peace; the next is David's dove, with feathers, silver white, as noting sincerity; then Isaiah's dove, mourning with her voice, as signifying patience. And, *lastly*, Christ's dove, innocent and harmless; now all these properties meet in this dove, the spirit of God. Much more might I add to these, but I desire to hasten to some more edifying truths.

Use. From this baptism of Christ, we may learn a practical necessary truth; there is a generation that cries down baptism of water, and upon this score; because they suppose it was proper to John, to *baptize only with water*, and to Christ, *to baptize only with the holy Ghost, and with fire*. Indeed, Christ in his own person baptized none otherwise but with the Holy Ghost; immediately after his ascension, he sent his Spirit upon the church, and baptized them with fire, the Spirit appearing like a flame; and to this day, (though not visibly) he baptizeth all his saints with the Holy Ghost, and with fire: but for all this, he appointed John, and not only John, but all his apostles, and their successors for ever to baptize with water; and they did so, and yet do so, obeying the preceptive words of Christ, which were almost the last words that he spake upon the earth. And though Christ himself did not baptize with water, yet Christ himself, (we see here) was baptized with water; he himself enters at that door, by which his disciples must for ever follow after him; and indeed therefore he went in at the door of baptism, that he might hallow or sanctify the entrance, which himself made to the house he was now a building. And for the difference they make betwixt Christ's baptism and John's baptism; what's this to the purpose! we all know that in baptism are two parts: the outward part and the inward part, you may call them, (if you please) the outward baptism and the inward baptism: the outward baptism is of the minister, but the inward baptism is of Christ. But must we separate these, or rather join them, (if these in ordinary must be joined) as we find them in Christ, and as we desire they may be in us? I cannot see but the baptism we use and the baptism of John, are in nature and substance one, and the very same. For, 1. *John preached the baptism of repentance for the remission of sins*, Mark i. 4. They have therefore the same doctrine, and the same promise. 2. Baptism ministered by John, pertained *to the fulness of all righteousness*, Matth. iii. 15. and Luke vii. 29, 30. testifies

testifies, that the publicans and people being baptized of John, they *justified God; but the Pharisees despised the counsel of God against themselves, and were not baptized.* Only herein lies the difference, that John baptized in Christ that should die and rise again; but we baptize in the name of Christ, that was dead and risen again. It is a difference in respect of circumstance but not of the substance. Oh, take heed of throwing away the baptism of water, upon the pretence of baptism only with fire! Christ, (we see) hath joined them together, and let no man separate them asunder; Christ himself was baptized with fire, and yet Christ himself was baptized with water.

SECT. IV.

Of the fasting and temptations of Christ.

3. FOR the fasting and temptation of Christ in the wilderness. No sooner is Christ come out of the water of baptism, but he presently enters into the fire of temptation; no sooner is the Holy Spirit descended upon his head, but he is led by the same Holy Spirit to be tempted in the wilderness; no sooner doth God say, *This is my Son,* but Satan puts it to the question, *If thou be the Son of God.* All these are but Christ's preparatives to his prophetical office. In the former section, Christ was prepared by a solemn consecration, and now he is to be further prepared by Satan's temptations; there is much in this particular, and therefore in the same method as the evangelist lays it down, Matth. iv. 1, 2, 3, to Verse 12. I shall proceed, *Then was Jesus led up of the Spirit into the wilderness to be tempted of the devil,* &c. In the whole, we may observe these several branches, as *first*, The place where the temptation was, *to wit*, the wilderness. *Secondly*, The cause of Christ's going into the wilderness, *the Spirit's leading*. *Thirdly*, The end of the Spirit's leading Christ into the wilderness, *to be tempted of the devil*. *Fourthly*, The time and occasion of the devil's onset, *at the end of forty days fast, and when he was an hungered*. *Fifthly*, The temptations themselves, which are in number three, to which are added as many victories which Christ had over the tempter; who therefore *left him, and so the angels come, and ministered unto him.* I shall begin first with the place where the temptation was, *to wit*, in the wilderness.

This wilderness was not that same wilderness, or not that same place of the wilderness wherein John the Baptist lived, Matth. iii. 1. For that wherein John the Baptist lived was a place inhabited, there were in that place cities and towns, and a number of people to whom John preached, but this wilderness was devoid of men, full of wild beasts, so saith Mark i. 13. *He was tempted of Satan, and was with the wild beasts.* As Adam in his innocency lived with wild beasts, and they hurt him not, so Christ the second Adam lives here in a wilderness with wild beasts, and he has no hurt at all: He is Adam-like in his safety and security, but above Adam in resisting of temptation. Some say, That in this wilderness during his forty days abode, Christ was perpetually disturbed and assaulted with evil spirits, however the last brunt is only expressed, because it was most violent. Now whether they appeared in any horrid and affrighting shapes during that time, it is not certain; but it is most likely, that to a person of so great sanctity and high designation as Jesus was, they would appear more angelical and immaterial, and in representments intellectual, because Jesus was not a person of those low weaknesses, to be affrighted or troubled with any ugly phantasms; it is not much material to enquire of this, but in this wilderness, (say they) Christ was perpetually tempted; and, in this respect, I know not but the devil had more advantage now he had Christ in a wilderness; solitariness is no small help to the speed of a temptation, *Wo to him that is alone, for if he fall, there is not a second to take him up.* Others say, That in this wilderness during his forty days abode, Christ was continually exercised in prayer and fasting, all that while he had his immediate addresses and colloquies with God; he knew he had a great work of redemption to promote; and therefore his conversation for this interval must be preparatory to it: in this respect, I know not but the wilderness might be an advantage to Christ's design: In this solitary place, he could not but breathe out more pure inspiration; heaven usually is more open, and God usually more familiar and frequent in his visits in such places. I know not what others experiences may be, but if I have found any thing of God, or of his grace, I may thank

thank a wood, a wildernefs, a defart, a folitary place for its accommodation; and have I not a bleffed pattern here before me? 'It was folitude 'and retirement in which Jefus kept his vigils, 'the defert places heard him pray; in privacy 'he was born in the wildernefs; he fed his thou-'fands upon a mountain apart; he was tranf-'figured upon a mountain, he died, and from a 'mountain he afcended to his Father. I make no queftion but in thofe retirements, his devotion received the advantage of convenient circumftances, efpecially of time and place. And yet I dare not deny the firft opinion, for I fuppofe both Chrift and the devil had their advantages of this wildernefs, the one to pray, and the other to tempt.

2. The caufe of Chrift's going into the wildernefs, was the Spirit's leading. *Then was Jefus led of the Spirit into the wildernefs.* Chrift was led by the good Spirit to be tempted by the evil fpirit. O wonder! that fame Spirit which was one with the Father and the Son, that fame Spirit whereby Chrift was conceived, now drives him or leads him into the wildernefs to be tempted of the devil; the manner of Chrift's leading is a queftion; fome think he was led or catch'd away from Jordan, in fome vifible rapture towards the wildernefs; but to leave that, and to come to truths more neceffary, Chrift taught us to pray unto his Father, *Lead us not into temptation,* and yet he himfelf is now led into the fame temptation, which we muft pray againft, furely this was for our inftruction; we are not to thruft ourfelves upon temptation, Chrift himfelf would not go into the combat uncalled, unwarranted; how then fhould we, poor weaklings, prefume upon any abilities of our own? Who dares grapple with the devil in his own ftrength? O take heed, if we are to pray not to be led into temptation, much more are we to pray not to run into temptation before we are led; and yet for the comfort of God's people, if it be fo that we are led, if by divine permiffion, or by an infpiration of the holy Spirit, we are engaged in an action, or in a courfe of life that is full of temptations, and empty of comforts; let us look upon it as an iffue of divine providence, in which we muft glorify God, but no argument of disfavour or diflove of God; and why? Becaufe Chrift himfelf, who could have driven the devil away by the breath of his mouth, yet was by the Spirit of his Father led to a trial by the Spirit of darknefs. *My brethren, count it all joy,* (faith James) *when ye enter into divers temptations, knowing that the tryal of your faith worketh patience,* James i. 2.

3. The end of the Spirit's leading Chrift into the wildernefs, it was either immediate or remote. 1. For the immediate end; it was to be tempted of the devil: to this purpofe was Chrift brought thither that Satan might tempt him. One would think it a very ftrange defign, that the Son of God fhould be brought into a wildernefs to be fet on by the devils in hell: but in this alfo God had another remote end, *i. e.* his own glory and our good. 1. His own glory appeared in this. Had not Satan tempted Chrift, how fhould Chrift have overcome Satan? The firft Adam was tempted and vanquifhed, the fecond Adam to repay and repair that foil, doth vanquifh in being tempted; now herein was the power of Chrift exceedingly manifefted; the devil having the chain let loofe, he lets fly at Chrift with all his might; and Chrift, that without blows, could not have got a victory, by this furious affault of Satan, he both overcomes him and triumphs over him. And herein were the graces of Chrift exceedingly manifefted; how was the faith, patience, humility, zeal, and favour of Chrift fet forth, which they could not have been if he always had lain quiet in Garrifon, and never had come into the fkirmifh? Who could have felt the odoriferous fmells of thofe aromatic fpices, if they had not been pounded and bruifed in this mortar of temptation? It was by this means that the graces of Chrift clearly fhined forth to his eternal praife. 2. As it was for his glory, fo alfo for our good. now we fee what manner of adverfary we have, how he fights, and how he is refifted, and how overcome; now we fee the dearer we are to God, the more obnoxious we are to a trial of temptation; now we fee that the beft faints may be tempted or allured to the worft of evils; fince Chrift himfelf is follicited to infidelity, covetoufnefs and idolatry; now we fee, *That we have not a Saviour and high Prieft, that cannot be touched with the feeling of our infirmities, but fuch an one as was in all things tempted in like fort, yet without fin; and therefore we may go boldly to the throne of grace, that we may receive mercy, and find grace to help in time of need,* Heb. iv. 15, 16

4. The time and occafion of the devil's onfet,

it was *at the end of forty days fast, and when he was an hungered*. Some say, (as you have heard) that all those forty days, when Christ was in the wilderness he was tempted only invisibly: for Satan during that time assumed not any visible or conspicuous shape, which at the end of the forty days, (say they) he did: my meaning is not to controvert these points. Howsoever for his tempting, yet for his fasting forty days and forty nights, there is no controversy; and of that we had some types before Christ came into the world; thus, Moses fasted forty days at the delivery of the law; and Elias fasted forty days at the restitution of the law; and to fulfil the time of both these types, Christ thinks it fit to fast forty days at the accomplishment of the law and the promulgation of the gospel. In fasting so long, Christ manifests his almighty power, and in fasting no longer, Christ manifests the truth of his manhood and of his weakness; that he might prove that there was no difference betwixt him and us but sin, he both fasted and was an hungered; we know well enough, that Christ could have lived without meat, and he could have fasted without hunger; it had been an easy matter for him to have supported his body without any means of nourishment of life; but to shew that he was man, as well as God, and so a fit Mediator betwixt God and man, he would both feed and fast; make use of the creature, and withal suffer hunger.——And now our Saviour is an hungered, this gives occasion to Satan to set upon him with his fierce and violent temptations; he knows well what baits to fish withal, and when, and how to lay them; he hath temptations of all sorts, he hath apples to cozen children, and gold for men; he hath the vanities of the world for the intemperate, and the kingdoms of the world for the ambitious; he considers the temper and constitution of the person he is to tempt, and he observes all our exterior accidents, occasions and opportunities; but of this hereafter.

5. The temptations themselves are in number three; whereof the first was this, *If thou be the Son of God, command that these stones be made bread*, Matth. iv. 3. What an horrible enterance is this? *If thou be the Son of God*: no question Satan had heard the glad tidings of the angel, he saw the star, and the journey, and the offering of the sages; he could not but take notice of the gratulations of Zachary, Simeon, Anna; and of late he saw the heavens open, and heard the voice that came down from heaven, *This is my beloved Son, in whom I am well pleased*. And yet now that he saw Christ fainting with hunger, as not comprehending how infirmities could consist with a Godhead, he put it to the question, *If thou be the Son of God*. Oh! here's a point, in which lies all our happiness. How miserable were we, if Christ were not indeed and in truth the Son of God? Satan strikes at the root in this supposition, *If thou be the Son of God*. Surely all the work of our redemption, and all the work of our salvation, depends upon this one necessary truth, that *Jesus Christ is the Son of God*. If Christ had not been the Son of God, how should he have ransomed the world? How should he have done, or how should he have suffered that which was satisfactory to his Father's wrath? How should his life or his death have been available to the sins of all the world? If Christ be not the Son of God, we are all gone, we are lost, we are undone, we are damned for ever: O, alas! farewel glory, farewel happiness, farewel heaven, if Christ be not the Son of God, we must never come there. Well, Satan, thou beginnest thy assault like a devil indeed, *If thou be the Son of God*; but what then? *Command that these stones be made bread*. He knew Jesus was hungry, and therefore he invites him to eat bread only of his own providing, that so he might refresh his humanity, and prove his divinity. *Come*, says he, *break thy fast upon the expence of a miracle; turn these stones into bread, and it will be some argument that thou art the Son of God*. There is nothing more ordinary with our spiritual enemy, than by occasion of want to move us to unwarrantable courses: *If thou art poor, then steal; if thou canst not rise up by honest means, then use indirect means*. I know Christ might as lawfully have turned stones into bread as turned water into wine; but to do this in a distrust of his Father's providence, to work a miracle of Satan's choice and at Satan's bidding, it could not be agreeable with the Son of God. And hence Jesus refuses to be relieved, he would rather deny to manifest the divinity of his person, than he would do any act, which had in it the intimation of a different spirit. O Christians! it is a sinful, impious, wicked care, to take evil courses to provide for

our

our necessities. Come, it may be thou hast found a way to thrive, which thou couldest not before; O take heed, was it not of the devil's promoting to change stones into bread, sadness into sensual comforts? If so, then Satan has prevailed. Alas! alas! he cannot endure thou shouldest live a life of austerity, or self-denial, or of mortification; if he can but get thee to satisfy thy senses, and to please thy natural desires, he then hath a fair field for the battle: it were a thousand times better for us to make stones our meat, and tears our drink, than to swim in our ill-gotten goods, and in the fulness of voluptuousness.

But what was Christ's answer? Why, thus *it is written, Man shall not live by bread alone, but by every word that proceedeth out of the mouth of God,* 1. It is written, he easily could have confuted Satan by the power of his Godhead; but he rather chose to vanquish him by the sword of the spirit. Surely this was for our instruction, by this means he teacheth us how to resist and to overcome; nothing in heaven or earth can beat the forces of hell, if the word of God cannot do it. O then how should we pray with David? *Teach me, O Lord, the way of thy statutes.——And take not from me the words of truth. —— Let them be my songs in the house of my pilgrimage.——So shall I make answer to my blasphemers.* 2. *Man shall not live by bread,* &c. Whilst we are in God's work, God hath made promises of the supply of all provisions necessary for us; now this was the present case of Jesus, he was now in his Father's work, and promoting of our interest; and therefore he was sure to be provided for according to God's word. Christians, are we in God's service? God will certainly give us bread; and till he does, we can live by the breath of his mouth, by the light of his countenance, by the refreshment of his promises, by *every word that proceedeth out of the mouth of God*; every word of God's mouth can create a grace, and every grace can supply two necessities, both of the body and of the spirit. I remember one kept straitly in prison, and sorely threatened with famine, he replied, That if he must have no bread, God would so provide that he should have no stomach; if our stock be spent, God can lessen our necessities; if a tyrant will take away our meat, God our Father knows how to alter our faint, and feeble, and hungry appetites,

The second temptation is not so sensual; the devil sees that was too low for Christ, and therefore he comes again with a temptation something more spiritual; verse 5, 6. *He sets him on a pinacle of the temple, and saith unto him, If thou be the Son of God, cast thyself down, for it is written, He shall give his angels charge concerning thee,* &c. He that was content to be led from Jordan into the wilderness for the advantage of the first temptation, he yields to be led from the wilderness to Jerusalem, for advantage of the second; the wilderness was fit for a temptation arising from want, and Jerusalem is fit for a temptation arising from vain glory; Jerusalem was the glory of the world, the temple was the glory of Jerusalem, the pinacle was the highest piece of the temple, and there is Christ content to be set for the opportunity of temptation. O that Christ would suffer his pure and sacred body to be transported, and hurried thro' the air by the malicious hand of the old tempter! but all this was for us, he cared not what the devil did in this way with him, so that he might but free us from the devil. Methinks it is a sweet contemplation of a holy divine; he supposed, as if he had seen Christ on the highest battlements of the temple, and Satan standing by him with his speech in his mouth, [Dr. Hall] ' Well then, since in ' the matter of nourishment, thou wilt needs de-
' pend upon thy Father's providence, take now a ' farther trial of that providence in thy miraculous ' preservation, cast down thyself from this height; ' behold, thou art here in Jerusalem, the famous ' and holy city of the world; here thou art on the ' top of the pinacle of the temple, which was de-
' dicated to thy Father; and if thou beest God, ' why now the eyes of all men are fix'd upon thee! ' There cannot be a more ready way to spread thy ' glory, and to proclaim thy Deity, than by casting ' thyself headlong to the earth; all the world will ' say, There is more in thee than a man; and for ' danger, (if thou art the Son of God) there can be ' none: what can hurt him that is the Son of God? ' And wherefore serves that glorious guard of an-
' gels, which have, by divine commission, taken ' upon them the charge of thy humanity?' Come, cast thyself down; here lies the temptation; *come, cast thyself down,* (saith Satan) but why did not Satan cast him down? He carried him up thither; and was it not more easy to throw him down thence?

thence? O no, the devil may persuade us to a fall, but he cannot precipitate us without our own act; his malice is infinite, but his power is limited; he cannot do us any harm but by persuading us to do it ourselves; and therefore saith he to Christ, *Cast thyself down.*

To this Christ answers, verse 7. *Thou shalt not tempt the Lord thy God.* Though it is true, that God must be trusted in, yet he must not be tempted; if means be allowed, we must not throw them away upon a pretence of God's protection. We read of one Heron, an inhabitant of the desart, that he suffered the same temptation, and was overcome by it; he would needs cast himself down, presuming on God's promise, and he sinfully died with his fall. Christ knew well enough, that there were ordinary descents by stairs from the top of the temple, and therefore he would not so tempt God to throw himself headlong: what, to make trial of God's power, and justice, and mercy, and extraordinary preservation, where there was no need? All the devils in hell could not so tempt Christ, as to make him tempt his God.

The third temptation is yet more horrid: the temple was not high enough, so that now Satan takes him up to the top of an *exceeding high mountain, and sheaws him all the kingdoms of the world, and the glory of them, saying, All these will I give thee, if thou wilt fall down and worship me,* verse 8, 9. Not to insist on those many queries, How should all the kingdoms of the world be presented to Christ's eye, or if they were only presented to his imagination, why could not the valley have served the devil's turn as well as an hill? Or whether was not Rome the object that the devil presented? Because at that time, Rome was the top of all the kingdoms of the world, and the glory of them? For my part, I think in this temptation the devil united all his power of stratagems, and by an angelical power, he drew into one centre the several species and ideas, from all the kingdoms, and glories of the world, and he made an admirable map of beauties, and represented them to the eye of Jesus: he thought ambition more likely to ruin him, because he knew it was that which prevailed upon himself, and all these fallen stars, the angels of darkness; and therefore, *come,* (saith Satan) *All these will I give thee, if thou wilt fall down and worship me.* How? God worship the devil. Was ever the like blasphemy since the creation? Indeed now we have many fearful, execrable, cursed blasphemies belched out, and idolatry, I believe, is the spreading sin in the world; but was ever the like blasphemy or idolatry to this, that not only a creature, but the Creator himself, must fall down before the devil, and give worship unto him? The Lamb of God that heard all the former temptations with patience, he could by no means endure this. Our own injuries are opportunities of patience, but when the glory of God, and his immediate honour is the question, then our zeal should be all on a flame. Now Christ bids him avoid, as soon as he observes his demands, so impudent and blasphemous, he commands him away, and tells him, verse 10. *It is written, Thou shalt worship the Lord thy God, and him only thou shalt serve.* Now was the devil put to flight, and in his stead, *the angels came and ministered unto Jesus,* (i. e.) after his fast, they ministered such things as his necessities required of them.

Use. O Christian, what shall we say to this? If Christ was thus tempted by Satan, what may we look for? Sometimes it cheers my heart to think that Christ was tempted, because thereby he knows how to succour those that are tempted: and sometimes it affrights my soul to think that Satan durst be so bold with Jesus Christ. Oh! what may he do with me? How easily might he prevail against my soul? When he came to tempt Christ, he found nothing in him to join with him in the temptation; but in my heart is a world of corruptions, and unless the Lord prevent, I am quickly gone. I may not here fall under the doctrine of temptations, only a few words. 1. Of Satan's stratagems. 2. Of some general means to withstand his stratagems; and I have done.

1. His stratagems are very many, and very dangerous; as——

1. He observes, and fits his temptations to our dispositions; for example, if he find a man ambitiously affected, then he covers his hook with the bait of honours; and thus he tempted Abimelech to murder his brethren, that he might obtain the sovereignty; or if he find a man voluptuously given, then he tempts him with the baits of pleasures; and thus he allured Noah to drunkenness, David to adultery, Solomon to idolatry; or if he find a man covetously given, then he lets in the golden hook;

hook; and thus he enticed Balaam, by offering him money to curse the people whom God had blessed; and thus he allured Judas, for thirty pieces of silver, to betray his Master. But what need we instance, when we see this day so many thousands intangled in this golden net?

2. He observes, and fits his temptations to our complections; and thus he tempts the cholerick to quarrels and brawls; the phlegmatic to idleness and sloth; the melancholy to malice and revenge; the sanguine to pleasure and fleshly lusts: and hence it is that the apostle tells us, James i. 14. that *Whosoever is tempted, he is drawn away by his own concupiscence.* Satan nevers assaults us, but he is sure there is something within us, that will further him in his temptations.

3. He observes, and fits his temptations to our outward conditions; thus, if we are in prosperity, then he tempts us to pride and forgetfulness of God, to contempt of our brethren, to the love of the world, to coldness in religion, carnal security, and the like: or, if we are in adversity, then he tempts us to the use of unlawful means, to the distrusting of God's all-ruling providence, and never-deceiving promises; or, it may be, to despair, murmur, and repining against God: by this temptation he confidently presumed to have moved Christ to distrust God's providence, and to shift for himself, by turning stones into bread.

4. He observes, and fits his temptations to our spiritual estate; thus if we are notoriously wicked, then he tempts us to atheism, contempt of God's worship, swearing, blaspheming, prophaning of the Lord's day, disobedience, murders, adulteries, drunkenness, theft, covetousness, and all devilish practices; or if we are civilized, and run not with others into such an excess of riot and sin, why, then he tempts us to a good opinion of such a condition, *I thank thee, O Father, that I am not as other men,* &c. 'I deal justly and uprightly with
'all my neighbours; I have a good meaning to-
'wards God, though I am ignorant of scripture,
'and of the principles of religion;' or if we are professors of God's truth, and can tip our tongues with glorious words of religion, holiness, Christ; why, then he tempts us with resting on this;
'What needs more? If I can but outwardly per-
'form the duties of piety, as the hearing of God's
'word, receiving of the sacraments, publick and
'private calling on God? In this I am a true pro-
'testant, that charity, love, good works, and all
'the duties of the second table can never justify
'me, or save me, but only faith; I believe, and
'I make a profession of religion, and I hope this
'will suffice:' Or, if we are sincere professors, and but weak in the faith, why, then he tempts us with sad thoughts of our sins; he sets before us their number and nature, and odiousness in every aggravation; and if therewith he cannot overwhelm us, he adds (it may be) unto them some of his own sins. Thus he casteth into our minds many outrageous blasphemies, such blasphemies as he propounded to Christ, to worship him for our God, to deny Jesus Christ as our God, our Lord, our Saviour, our Redeemer; to say in our hearts, there is no God but nature, no scripture, no Holy Ghost: many a precious soul feels these injections of Satan, and I cannot wonder at it, when I see the devil tempting Christ himself to diffidence, presumption, vain glory, yea, and to the worshipping of the devil himself: or, if we are strong Christians, grown men, and still growing towards the fulness of Christ; why, then he tempts us to sins of presumption against knowledge; or if he cannot so prevail, he will *transform himself into an angel of light*, 2 Cor. xi. 14. and tempt us to the doing a less good that we may neglect a greater; or to the doing of a greater good, but very unseasonable, when as some other duties, in respect of present occasion, are more necessary far: thus many times in the hearing of God's word, he will cast into our minds meditations of this or that excellent subject, on purpose to distract our minds, and to make us hear without profit; and in prayer to God he will bring into our memories this or that profitable instruction, which we have heard at such, or such a sermon, on purpose to disturb our spirits in that holy exercise, and to keep us from lifting up our hearts wholly and purely unto God. I might add a thousand of these stratagems of the devil, and yet not perhaps tell one of a thousand: the apostle could say indeed, that he *was not ignorant of his devices,* 2 Cor. ii. 11. Eph. vi. 11. Rev. ii. 24. Eph. vi. 16. And of some of his devices you see we are not ignorant; but, alas! who can discover all his *methods, wiles, depths, fiery darts?* For my part I cannot do it, I am yet to learn.

2. The general means to withstand his stratagems are such as these.

1 A continual reminding of Christ's commands in this very thing, Eph. vi. 10, 11. 1 Pet. v. 8. *Be strong in the Lord, and in the power of his might; put on the whole armour of God, that ye may be able to stand against the wiles of the devil; him resist in the faith.*

2. An avoiding of the first suggestions of Satan; if this gliding serpent can but thrust in his head, he will easily make room for his body, and therefore we must nip and bruise him in the head, Eph. iv. 27. *Give no place to the devil.*

3. An objecting of Christ against all his temptations; for example, if Satan tell us, that we are miserable sinners, we may answer, that *Christ came into the world to save sinners; and that he was wounded for our transgressions, and broken for our iniquities,——and with his stripes are we healed,* Matth. ix. 13. Isa. liii. 5. If Satan tell us, that we are subject to God's wrath, we may answer, that Christ did bear his Father's wrath, that he might make our peace; if he tell us, that we are subject to the curse of the law, we may answer, that *Christ hath redeemed us from the curse of the law, when he was made a curse for us,* Gal. iii. 13. If he tell us, that we are his bond slaves, we may answer, that we were so indeed in times past, but Christ had paid his Father the price of our redemption, and hath set us free; if he tell us, that we are unjust, and therefore shall be condemned before God's judgment-seat; we may answer, that Christ who was innocent, was therefore condemned, that we who are guilty might thereby be acquitted; and that he that came to save us, will himself judge us, and therefore we need not doubt of mercy, if we plead the merits of Christ: or if Satan will not be thus answered by us, why then, Christians! there's no other way but to send him to Christ: to this purpose we may tell him, that Christ is our advocate, and if he will needs dispute, let him go to Jesus; he is both able to plead our cause, and to answer all the suits that are made against us.

4. I may add hearing, reading, meditating, on God's word, holy conferences, busy employment in the works of our particular callings, living by faith. I must not stay on all these means, only remember amongst the rest that one of Christ, Mat.

xxvi. 41. *Watch and pray, that ye enter not into temptation*; praying against it, is a denying of it, and a great part of the victory; for it is a disclaiming the entertainment of it; it is a positive rejection of the crime, it is a calling in auxiliaries from above, to make the victory more certain to us. Hence one sweetly adviseth, ' If temptation ' sets upon thee, do thou set upon God; for he ' is as soon overcome as thou art, as soon moved ' to good, as thou art to evil; he is as quickly ' invited to pity thee, as thou art to ask him, pro- ' vided thou dost not finally rest in the petition, ' but pass into action, and endeavour by all means ' to quench the flame newly kindled in thy bow- ' els, before it come to devour the marrow that ' is in thy bones:' indeed a strong prayer, and a lazy, incurious, unobservant walking are contradictions in religion; and therefore *watch, and pray; and pray, and watch.*

SECT. V.

Of the first manifestations of Christ.

4. FOR the first manifestation of Jesus by his several witnesses; now it was time that *the Sun of righteousness should arise,* and shine in the view of the world: and (because of unbelief which had blinded the world) that some especial witnesses should be chosen out, both to anoint our eyes, and to point to the light, saying, *This is he of whom Moses in the law and the prophets did write, Jesus of Nazareth, the son of Joseph,* John i. 45. To this purpose we read much of *the manifestations of Jesus; God was manifest in the flesh.* 1 Tim. iii. 16. and Christ *verily was foreordained before the foundations of the world, but was manifest in these last times for you.* 1 Pet. i. 20. In that first miracle that ever he wrought, this is written upon it, *He manifested forth his glory,* John ii. 11. And John the divine in his setting out of Jesus, he tells us, that *the life was manifested, and we have seen it, and bear witness, and shew unto you that eternal life which was with the Father, and was manifested unto us,* 1 John i. 2.

And there is reason for this manifestation; 1. Because every manifestation was an approbation of his mission and divinity. 2. Because, in the manifestation of Christ, there was a manifestation of the grace of God; and this was the will of God, that he would not only act free grace, but he would have it known, and published to the world: this is the glory of grace, and sets it out; and therefore saith the apostle, Tit. ii. 11. *The grace of God that bringeth salvation, hath appeared to all men.* At the opening and discovery of Jesus Christ, Tit. iii. 4. *The kindness, and pity, and love of God our Saviour towards men appeared.* 3. Because this manifestation hath something in it of the removal of sin; it is the voice of Christ unto such as are in sin, Isa. lxv. 1. *Behold me;* the first step towards the remission of sins is the beholding of Christ: now, we cannot behold him that will not come into view; and therefore, saith the apostle, 1 John iii. 5. *Ye know that he was manifested to take away our sins.* 4. Because this manifestation hath something in it to the overthrow of Satan; for the while that Christ hid himself, Satan blinded the minds of men, but when once *Christ the image of God shone forth,* then Satan, like lightning, fell down from heaven, 1 John iii. 8. *For this purpose the Son of God was manifested, that he might destroy the works of the devil.* 5. Because this manifestation tends to our believing in Christ, and by consequence to our salvation through Christ, John ii. 30, 31. *Many signs Christ did in the presence of his disciples which are not written; but these are written* (saith John) *that ye might believe that Jesus is Christ the Son of God, and that believing, ye might have life through his name.*

Well, but wherein was this first manifestation of Jesus? I answer, in those several witnesses that held him forth, John viii. 1. *It is written in the law,* (saith Christ) *that the testimony of two men is true,* but to manifest Christ were many witnesses. As, 1. From heaven the Father is witness, for see, saith Christ, John viii. 18. *The Father that sent me beareth witness of me;* and the Son is witness, for so saith Christ, John viii. 14. *I am one that bear witness of myself, and though I bear record of myself, yet my record is true, for I know whence I came, and whither I go;* and the Holy Ghost is witness, so saith Paul, Heb. x. 19. *The Holy Ghost also is a witness to us:* and to that purpose he descended like a dove, and alighted upon him. 2. On earth John the Baptist is witness, for so saith Christ, Matth. iii. 16. John v. 33. John i. 7. *Ye sent unto John, and he bare witness unto the truth,——He came for a witness, to bear witness of the light, that all men through Christ might believe.* No sooner was John confirmed by a sign from heaven, that Jesus was the Christ, but he immediately manifests it to the Jews; and first to the priests and Levites sent in legation from the sanhedrim, he professed indefinitely, in answer to their question, that himself was not the Christ, nor Elias, nor the prophet, whom they by a special tradition expected to be revealed, though they knew not when; and secondly to all the people he professed definitely, wheresoever he saw Jesus Christ, *This is he;* yea, he points him out with his finger, John i. 29. *Behold the Lamb of God that takes away the sins of the world.* Then he shews him to Andrew, Simon Peter's brother, and then to another disciple with him, *who both followed Jesus, and abode with him all night.* Andrew brings his brother Simon with him, and Christ changes his name from Simon to Peter, or Cephas, *which signifies a stone,* Ver. 42. Then Jesus himself finds out Philip of Bethsaida, Ver. 43. and bad *follow him;* and Philip finds out Nathaniel, and bids him *come and see,* Ver. 45. for the Messiah was found; when Nathaniel came to Jesus, Christ saw his heart, and gave him a blessed character, Ver. 47. *Behold an Israelite indeed, in whom there is no guile.* Thus we see no less than five disciples found out at first, which must be as so many witnesses of Jesus Christ.

And yet we find more witnesses, *The works* (saith Christ) *that I do, in my Father's name, they bear witness of me,* John x. 25. These works or miracles of Christ were many, but because we are speaking of his first manifestation, I shall instance only in his first work, which was at a marriage in Cana of Galilee. The power of miracles had now ceased since their return out of the captivity; the last miracle that was done by man till this very time, was Daniel's tying up the mouth of the lions, and now Christ begins. He that made the first marriage in paradise, bestows his first miracle upon a marriage-feast; O happy feast where Christ is a guest! I believe this was no rich or sumptuous bridal; who ever found Christ at the magnificent feasts or triumphs of the great? The state of a servant (in which state Christ was) doth not well agree with the proud pomp of the world. This poor needy bridegroom wants drink for his guests; and as soon as the holy virgin hath notice of it, she com-

complaints to her son; whether we want bread, or water, or wine, necessaries or comforts, whither should we go but to Christ? Psal. xxiii. 1. *The Lord is my Shepherd*, and if that be so, it will surely follow, *I shall not want*. John ii. 4. *But Jesus answered her, woman what have I to do with thee? Mine hour is not yet come.* This shews that the work he was to do, must not be done to satisfy her importunity, but to prosecute the great work of divine designation: in works spiritual and religious, all outward relation ceaseth: matters of miracle concerned the Godhead only, and in this case, *O woman, what have I to do with thee?* We must not deny love and duty to relations; but in the things of God natural endearments must pass into spiritual, and, like stars in the presence of the sun, must not appear. Paul could say, 2 Cor. v. 16. *Henceforth we know no man after the flesh, yea though we have known Christ after the flesh, yet now henceforth know we him no more.*

At the command of Jesus the water-pots were filled with water, and the water by his divine power is turned into wine; where the different dispensation of God and the world is highly observable: *Every man sets forth good wine at first, and then the worse*; but Christ not only turns water into wine, but into such wine, that the last draught is most pleasant. The world presents us with fair hopes of pleasures, honours, and preferments, but there's bitterness in the end; every sin smiles in the first address, *but when we have well drunk, then comes that which is worse*; only Christ turns our water into wine: if we fill our water-pots with water; if with David we water our couch with our tears for sin, Christ will come in with the wine of gladness sooner or later; and he will give the best wine at the last: O how delicate is that new wine, which we shall one day drink with Christ in his Father's kingdom? These were the first manifestations of Jesus. You see he had several witnesses to set him forth: some from heaven, and some on earth; the Father, Son, and Holy Ghost witness from heaven; the Baptist, disciples, and his works witness on earth; and there's no disagreement in their witness, but all bring in this testimony of Jesus, that he is *the Messiah, which is, being interpreted, the Christ,* John i. 41.

Use. But what are these manifestations to us? Or to that great design of Christ in carrying on our soul's salvation? Much every way. For either must Christ be manifested to us even by these witnesses, in the preaching of the gospel, and manifested in us by that one witness, his holy Spirit, or we are undone for ever.

1. Christ must be manifested to us in the preaching of the gospel; this mercy we have this day; nay, you see every Sabbath-day all the witnesses speak in us; what do we but in God's stead, in the Baptist's stead, in the disciples stead, manifest Christ to you in every sermon? It is the commission which Christ hath given us of the ministry, *Go preach the gospel to every creature*, Mark xvi. 15. Observe but how open Christ's heart is towards you; he cannot contain his love, and grace within himself; he cannot keep his own counsels that are for the good of your souls, but all must be manifest, and that in the openest way, by preaching, and proclaiming them to the world; Christ must be laid out to open view; Christ will have nothing of his love kept back: He wills and commands us of the ministry, in the stead of all those former witnesses, to make all known what he is, and what he hath done and suffered for you. Oh Christians! how cheap are the mysteries of the gospel to you-ward? You may know them, if you will but lend an ear, and listen to them, the word is nigh you, even in your mouths; Christ is proclaimed in your very streets; you may have him if you will, without money or money-worth, Isa. lv. 1. *Come buy wine, and milk, without money, and without price.* Do you not hear? Christ is laid open for every man's good, and profit; Christ deals not under-hand with you; he must be manifested that you may see what you buy: if I should tell you the meaning of the commission, which Christ hath put into our hands, he bids me say thus to your souls, ' Come, poor creatures, you that ' stand in need of Jesus Christ, here is Christ for ' you, take him, and do with him in an holy man- ' ner what you will; he is of infinite use for wis- ' dom, righteousness, sanctification, and redemp- ' tion.' What is our preaching but a manifesting of Christ in this manner? What is the sum of all our sermons, but a discovery of this, that life and light is in Christ for you, that eternal love waits and attends on you, that whatever may do you good is provided and made ready for you? Oh! will

will souls now refuse Christ, when thus, and thus manifested? God forbid.

2. Christ must be manifested in us by his holy Spirit. Christians! look to your hearts, what manifestations of Christ are there? When Paul speaks the gospel in general, he adds in particular, That *it pleased God to reveal Christ in me*, Gal. i. 16. And when Peter speaks of the word of God, he adds, That *we take heed thereunto*, 2 Pet. i. 10. ——*until the day dawn, and the day-star* (that is Christ, Rev. xxii. 16.) *arise in our hearts;* till then, though we be circled with gospel-discoveries, our hearts will be full of darkness; but when Christ, whom the prophet calls *the Son of righteousness*, Mal. iv. 2. and Peter the *day-star*, shall arise within us, we shall be full of light. Sometimes, I confess, I wonder that in those days there should be such glorious discoveries of the beauties, and sweetness, and excellencies of Jesus Christ, and yet that mens hearts are generally full of darkness: but this takes off the wonder; hearts are carnal, John i. 5. *Light shines in darkness, but darkness comprehendeth it not:* lead a blind man through a glorious city, and though there be such and such things in it, yet he tells you, he cannot prize them, he sees them not; though *Jerusalem should come down from God out of heaven* (as John saw it in his vision) *prepared as a bride adorned for her husband*, Rev. xxi. 2. yet the natural man sees neither walls nor gates, nor streets: you may tell him, *All is gold, and jasper, and precious stones*, but for all this he cannot prize them, alas, he sees them not: how many glorious objects do the unregenerate slight? They see no beauty in Jesus Christ, they feel no sweets in his ordinances; the Sabbath is a trouble, and no delight to them; and whence all this? It is because there is no light, no manifestation of Christ within them; the Spirit of Christ hath not witnessed Christ, hath not manifested Christ within their souls, and therefore they remain in darkness.

SECT. VI.

Of Christ's whipping the buyers and sellers out of the temple.

5. COncerning Christ's whipping the buyers and sellers out of the temple, we read in the gospel, *that the Jews passover being at hand, Jesus went up to Jerusalem*, John ii. 23. Thither if we follow him, the first place that we find him in, is the temple, whereby the occasion of the national assembly was an opportune scene for Christ's transactions of his Father's business. In that temple Christ first espies a mart; there were divers merchants and exchangers of money, that brought beasts thither to be sold for sacrifice against that great solemnity; at the sight of which Jesus being moved with zeal and indignation, he makes a whip of cords, and according to the custom of the Zealots of the nation, he takes upon him the office of a private infliction of punishment; he drives all out of the temple; he overthrows the accounting tables, and commands them that sold the doves to take them from thence: and being required to give a sign of this fact, he only foretels the resurrection of his body after three days death, expressing it in the metaphor of the temple, which was never rightly understood till it was accomplished.

In this heroical act, we may see how Christ is carried on with a zeal for God, insomuch as that it brings to mind that saying of the Psalmist, Psal. lxix. 9. *The zeal of thine house hath eaten me up;* a metaphor taken from men that receive nourishment, which after its several concoctions is assimulated into the nature of them that receive it. Zeal doth not totally surprize us in what concerns God; in our zeal we do so mind the things of God, as if we minded nothing else. To what dangers, hazards, and censures did Christ here in the exercise of this zeal expose himself; His eminent zeal appears,

1. In the weakness of his means whereby he did both attempt, and effect the work; we find him not armed with any weapons, that might carry dread and terror with them, at most but with a whip made of a few small cords, which probably were scattered by the drovers which came hither to sell their cattle ——2. In the strength that the opposite power did hold out, which makes the encounter so much the more dangerous; as, 1. A garrison of soldiers ready at hand to appease occasional tumults *(Chem. in loc.)* 2. The temper of those men's spirits with whom the business was; they were men set upon gain, the world's God. 3. The great confluence of the people, it being the most solemn mart of the passover; oh! what a

zeal was this, that neither the weakness of the means on the one side to effect it, nor the greatness of the power of the other side to hinder it, did at all dismay him, or cause him to desist: seem he never so weak, or be they never so strong, he whips them out of the temple, and bids them, be gone.

This action of Christ fulfils that prophecy of Malachy, Mal. iii. 1, 2, 3. *The Lord whom ye seek shall suddenly come to his temple; but who may abide the day of his coming? And who shall stand when he appeareth? For he is like refiner's fire, and like fuller's soap; and he shall sit as a refiner and purifier of silver, and he shall purify the Sons of Levi, and purge them as gold and as silver, that they may offer unto the Lord an offering in righteousness.*

From the main we may observe, that 'a persuasion of Christ's presence in our church-assemblies, is a special means or motive to bring all into order.'

But what is this presence of Christ in church-assemblies? If by Christ's presence we mean his bodily presence: it is true, that Christ, in his humanity, whipped the buyers and sellers out of the temple of Jerusalem; then in his manhood he was upon earth, and accordingly he vouchsafed his bodily presence to their assemblies, and public places; but now his manhood is in heaven, and *the heavens must contain him till the times of restitution of all things*, Acts iii. 21. Now, therefore we cannot expect his bodily presence, unless we will maintain the doctrine of transubstantiation, or of contubstantiation; which far be it from us.

2 If by Christ's presence we mean his spiritual presence, then the question is, what is this spiritual presence of Christ? For, if we say it is his presence as he is God, I should then *quere*, how God is said to be present with men in one place more than another? God in his essence is fully every where, and inclusively no where; heaven is his throne, and earth is his footstool; and yet, nor earth, nor heaven, nor the heaven of heavens is able to contain him: whilst we speak spiritually of Christ's presence in the assemblies of his people, we cannot mean his universal presence, but his especial presence; and therefore as yet, I suppose, we have not the meaning of it.

3. If by Christ's presence, we mean the presence of his Spirit, either in himself, or especially in his workings, stirrings, actings, and movings in our spirit, I should then subscribe; only I think this is not all that is included in his especial presence. True it is, that when Christ was upon earth, he told his disciples that he must go away; for if he went not away, the comforter would not come unto them, *But if I depart* (said he) *I will send him unto you*, John xvi. 7. And accordingly, when that church assembly was convened at Pentecost, God sent the Holy Ghost, much people being then gathered at Jerusalem, that it might be divulged to all the world. To all the assemblies of the saints, Christ promised his Spirit, tho' not always in a visible manner, *Where two or three are gathered together in my name* (saith Christ) *there I am in the midst of them*, Matth. viii. 20. Christ in his Spirit is in the midst of us, stirring and moving in our spirits: or the spirit of unity is with united spirits. O he is a sweet Spirit, a Spirit of love, and concord, and peace, and glory; and therefore, Where should he be but with those that make harmony upon earth? He is with them, and amongst them, and in them, 1 Cor. iii. 16. *Know ye not that ye are the temple of God, and that the Spirit of God dwelleth in you?* And worketh in you?

4. If by Christ's presence, we mean the presence of his angels, I shall then say, we have said enough; as a king is said to be where his court is, where his train or retinue are, so Christ, the King of kings, is there especially present, where the heavenly guard, the blessed angels keep their sacred station and rendezvouz, wheresoever it is. Now, that this is Christ's special presence, it will appear in sundry texts.

1. When Jacob saw that vision in Bethel, of the ladder reaching from earth to heaven, and of the angels of God ascending and descending upon it; Gen. xxviii. 16, 17. *Surely* (saith Jacob) *the Lord is in this place, and I knew it not; and he was afraid, and said, how dreadful is this place? This is none other but the house of God, and this is the gate of heaven.* He calls it *God's house*, where God and his holy angels, who are of his houshold, are especially present; and he calls it *the gate of heaven*, heaven's guild-hall, heaven's court, namely because of the angels; for the gate, guild-hall or court, was wont to be the judgment-hall, and

the

the place where kings and senators used to sit, attended by their guard and ministers. The Chaldee addeth, 'This is no common, or private place, 'but a place wherein God taketh pleasure; and 'over-against this place is the gate of heaven.'

2. When the Lord descended upon mount Sinai, to give the law; some place the specification of God's presence in the angels, to which purpose are alledged these texts, Acts vii. 53. *Who have received the law by the disposition of angels, and have not kept it:* and again, Gal. iii. 19. *The law was ordained by angels in the hand of a Mediator.* Again, the apostle calls the law, Heb. ii. 2. *The word spoken of angels.* I have already delivered my thoughts concerning these angels: but some (I say) conclude from hence, That the special presence of the divine majesty consists in the encamping of his sacred retinue, the blessed angels; for that the Lord of himself, who filleth heaven and earth could not descend, or be in one place more than another. There's yet another text, very pertinent to this, Deut. xxxiii. 2. *And he said, the Lord came from Sinai, and rose up from Seir unto them; he shined forth from mount Paran, and he came with ten thousands of his saints, from his right hand went a fiery law for them:* the words translated, *Ten thousands of his saints,* are, in the original, *Ten thousands of his sanctity,* or *holy ten thousands,* or *holy myriads;* which, in my apprehension, points to the angels, rather than the saints; and the Psalmist puts it out of question, Ps. lxviii. 17. *The chariots of God are twenty thousand, even thousands of angels, the Lord is among them, as in Sinai, in the holy place.*

3. After the law given, this presence of God was fixed to the temple, and what that was, Isaiah describes thus, Isa. vi. 1, 2. *I saw also the Lord sitting upon a throne, high, and lifted up, and his train filled the temple; about it stood the seraphims;* they were God's train, and they filled the temple. And hence David's addresses to God were said to be in the presence of angels, Psal. cxxxviii. 1, 2. *Before the Gods will I sing praises to thee, I will worship towards thy holy temple.* The Septuagint translates it thus, [*enantion aggelon*], *before the angels.* I know, in the time of the gospel, we do not fix God's presence to our temples, or places of public assembling for the worship of his name; but to our church-assemblies in such places, why may we not? Were the rudiments of the law worthy of an attendance of angels, and are the churches of the gospel destitute of so glorious a retinue! did the blessed spirit wait upon the types, and do they decline the office at the ministration of the substance? Is the nature of man made worse, since the incarnation of the Son of God? Or have the angels purchased an exemption from their ministry, since Christ became our brother in the flesh? We have little reason to think so. The apostle treating of a comely and decent demeanour to be observed in church-assemblies, and in particular of womens being covered, or vailed there, he enforces it from this presence of angels, 1 Cor. xi. 10. *For this cause ought the woman to have a covering on her head, because of the angels,* namely, which are there present. Upon this ground Chrysostome reproves the irreverent behaviour of his auditory, *(Chry. hom. 16. in 1 Cor. hom. 15. in Hebr.)* 'The 'church *(saith he)* is not a shop of manufactures, 'or merchandize, but the place of angels, and of 'archangels, the court of God, and the image or 'representation of heaven itself.——I know thou 'seest them not, but hear, and know that the 'angels are every where, and especially in the 'house of God, where they attend upon their 'king, and where all is filled with incorporeal 'powers.' By this time I hope we know what is the meaning of Christ's presence in church-assemblies; to wit, the presence of his Spirit, and the presence of his angels.

And if it be so, would not a persuasion of this presence of Christ in our church-assemblies, be a special means or motive to bring all into order? Sometimes I wonder at the irreverent carriage of some hearers, laughing, talking, prating, sleeping, in our congregations: what, is this a demeanour beseeming the presence of angels, and the Spirit of Christ? Would thou carry thyself thus in the presence of a prince, or of some earthly majesty? *(Chri. ib.)* 'If thou goest but into a king's palace, '(as Chrysostome speaks) thou composest thyself 'to a comeliness in thy habit, look, gait, and all 'thy guise; and dost thou laugh?' I may add, dost thou any way carry thyself indecently in God's presence? Some there are, that in the very midst of ordinances, the devil usually rocks them asleep; but oh! dost thou not fear that thy damnation sleeps not? How justly might Christ come against thee in his wrath, and whip thee out of the temple into hell? Surely we should do well to behave ourselves in such a presence, with the thoughts and apprehensions of heaven about us: our business here is an errand of religion, and God himself is the object of our worship: how then should our actions bear at least some few degrees of a proportionable address to God, and Christ, and the Spirit of Christ? What? Is Christ's presence in his Spirit, and his angels here? Oh! let us *walk with God*, as Enoch did, Gen. v 22. Let us do all we do as in the presence of Christ, and his holy angels.

And now was the first passover after Christ's baptism; as it is written, John ii. 13. *And the Jews passover was at hand, and Jesus went up to Jerusalem.*

This was the first year of Christ's ministry; whereof the one half was carried on by his prodromus, or forerunner, John the baptist: and the other half (betwixt his baptism and this first passover) was carried on by himself. And now hath Christ three years to his death. According to the method propounded, I shall come on to the second year, and to his actions therein, in reference to our souls salvation.

CHAP. II. SECT. I.

Of the second year of Christ's ministry, and of his acts in general for that year.

NOW was it that the office of the baptist was expired; and Christ beginning his prophetical office, he appears like the sun in succession of the morning-star; he takes at John, and preaching the sum of the gospel, faith and repentance, *Repent ye, and believe the gospel*, Mark i. 15. Now, what this gospel was, the sum and series of all his following sermons expressed and declared. It is fully contained in the new covenant, of which we have spoken: for what is the gospel but a covenant of grace, wherein all the imperfections of our works are made up by the perfection and grace of Jesus Christ? The gospel is not a covenant of works, (i. e.) it is not an agreement upon the stock of innocence, requiring strict and exact obedience, without any allowance of repentance: no, no, be holy, faith the gospel; and where that fails, repent and believe. By this time the work in his hand was grown high and pregnant, and Jesus saw it convenient to choose more disciples: with this family he goes up and down the whole Galilee, preaching the gospel of the kingdom, healing all manner of diseases, curing demoniacs, cleansing lepers, giving strength to paralytics, and to lame people.

It is not my purpose to enlarge on all the sermons, miracles, conferences, or colloquies of Christ with men: I am not for large volumes; and I suppose, with John, that if all the acts of Christ should be written, with commentaries on them, that even *the world itself could not contain the books that should be written*, John xxi. 25.

In this year therefore I shall contract and limit myself to the consideration of Christ in these two particulars; as 1. To his preaching. 2. To his miracles: both these relate to the use and exercise of his prophetical office.

SECT. II.

Of Christ's sermons this year.

1. HIS preaching this year was frequent, and amongst others his sermons, now it was that he delivered that first sermon, *Repent, for the kingdom of heaven is at hand.*

2. Now was it that he delivered that spiritual and mystical sermon of regeneration, at which Nicodemus wonders, John iii. 4. *How can a man be born when he is old? Can he enter the second time into his mother's womb and be born?* But Jesus takes off the wonder, in telling him, This was not a work of flesh and blood, but of the Spirit of God, *for the Spirit bloweth where it listeth*; and is as the wind certain and notorious in the effects, but secret in the principle and manner of production. Then Christ proceeds in his sermon, telling him yet of higher things, as of the descent from heaven, of his passion and ascension, and of the mercy of redemption, which he came to work and effect for all that believe; of the love of the Father, the million of the Son, the rewards of faith, and glories of eternity. And this was the sum of his sermon to Nicodemus, which was the fullest of mystery and speculation that ever he made, except that

3. Now was it that the throng of auditors forcing Christ to leave the shore, he makes Peter's ship his pulpit, Luke v. 1, 2, 3, 4. Never was there any such nets cast out of that fisher boat before: whilst he was upon land, he healed the sick bodies by his touch, and now he was upon sea, he cured the sick souls by his doctrine: he that made both sea and land, causeth both to conspire to the opportunities of doing good to the souls and bodies of men.

4. Now was it that he preached that blessed sermon on that text, Luke iv. 18. *The Spirit of the Lord is upon me, because he hath anointed me to preach the gospel to the poor.* No question but he preached both to poor and rich. Christ preached to all, but for the power and fruit of his preaching, it was only received and entertained by the poor in Spirit. In the following particulars, his office is set out still in a higher tenor, *To heal the broken-hearted, to preach deliverance to the captives, and recovery of sight to the blind;* or as it is in Isaiah, lxi. 1. *The opening of the prison to them that are bound.* A sad thing to be bound in captivity, but sadder to be bound in chains or locked up in a prison there; but it is most sad of all to be imprisoned, having one's eyes put out; as it was the case of Samson and Zedekiah. Now the evangelist willing to render the prophet to the highest comfortable sense that might be, he useth an expression that meets with the highest mystery; that is, when a man is not only shut up in a blinded prison, but when he himself also hath his eyes put out; and to such Christ should preach: preach what? Not only deliverance to the captives, but also of restoring of light to captive prisoners; nay, yet more, *recovering of sight to blinded prisoners,* as the evangelist renders it, Luke iv. 18.

5 Now it was, that he delivered the admirable sermon, called, *The sermon upon the mount.* It is a breviary of all these precepts which are truly called Christian: it contains in it all the moral precepts given by Moses, and opens a stricter sense, and more severe exposition than the Scribes and Pharisees had given: it holds forth the doctrine of meekness, poverty of Spirit, Christian mourning, desire of holy things, mercy and purity, and peace, and patience, and suffering of injuries: he teacheth us how to pray, how to fast, how to give alms, how to contemn the world, and how to seek the kingdom of God, and its appendent righteousness.

And thus Christ being entered upon his prophetical office; in these and the rest of his sermons, he gives a clear testimony, that he was not only an interpreter of the law, but a law-giver; and that this law of Christ might retain some proportion at least with the law of Moses, Christ in this last sermon went up into a mountain, and from thence gave the oracle. I cannot stand to paraphrase on this, or any other of his sermons, but seeing now we find Christ in the exercise of his prophetical office, let us observe, 1. His titles in this respect. 2. The reasons of his being a prophet. 3 The excellency of Christ above all other prophets; and then we have done.

SECT. III.

Of Christ's prophetical office.

1. THE titles of Christ, in respect of his prophetical office, were these. 1. Sometimes he is called doctor, or, master, Matth. xxiii. 10. *Be ye not called master, for one is your master, even Christ:* the word is [*Kathegetes*], which signifies a doctor, moderator, teaching-master, a guide of the way. Sometimes he is called a law-giver, James iv. 12. *There is one law-giver, who is able to save and to destroy.* The apostle speaks of the internal government of the conscience, in which case the Lord is our judge, Isaiah xxxiii. 22. *The Lord is our law giver, the Lord is our king, he will save us.* We must hear no voice in our conscience, but God's: no doctrine in the church, but Christ's: no offices, institutions and worship must be allowed, but such as he hath appointed; and therefore, when men brought in foreign doctrines, it is said, *That they did not hold the head,* Col. ii. 19. 3. Sometime he is called a counsellor, *And his name shall be called, Wonderful, counsellor,* Isa. ix. 6. *Counsel is mine and sound wisdom,* saith Christ, *I am understanding, and have strength,* Proverbs viii. 14. Christ, by his office, counsels men how to fly sin, and how to please God, and how to escape hell, and how to be saved. 4. Sometimes he is called the apostle of our profession, Heb. iii. 1. *Wherefore, holy brethren, partakers of the heavenly calling, consider the apostle,*

and high priest of our profession, Christ Jesus. God sent him as an ambassador to make known his will; he came not unsent: the very word imports a mission, a sending, Rom. x. 15. *How shall they preach except they be sent?* Let all those who run before they be sent take notice of this, for this would not Christ do; he was sent; he was the apostle of our profession. 5. Sometimes he is called the angel of the covenant, Mal. iii. 1. *Even the angel of the covenant whom ye delight in.* Christ was the publisher of the gospel-covenant, he declared the gracious purpose of God towards the elect held forth in the covenant; and, in this respect, he is called *a prophet*, Acts iii. 22. and *the prophet*, John vii. 40. and *that prophet*, John vi. 14. *This is of a truth that prophet that should come into the world*; whose office it was to impart God's will unto the sons of men, according unto the name, *angel*. 6. Sometimes he is called the Mediator of the new covenant, Heb. ix. 15. *For this cause he is the Mediator of the new Testament*, saith the apostle; now, a Mediator is such a one as goes betwixt two parties at variance, imparting the mind of the one to the other, so as to breed a right understanding, and thereby to work a compliance betwixt both. And thus Christ is a Mediator betwixt God and us: by him it is that the mind and will of God is imparted to man, John i. 18. *No man hath seen God at any time; the only begotten Son, which is in the bosom of the Father, he hath declared him*; and by him it is that we impart our mind unto God, Rev. viii. 4. *The smoke of the incense which goes with the prayers of the saints, ascends up before God out of the angels hand.* This was typified in Moses, Deut. v. 5. *I stood between the Lord and you at that time, to shew you the word of the Lord.* The vulgar renders it thus, *Ego sequestor et medius,* I was a mediator, a midler betwixt God and you: and so Christ Jesus is a Mediator, a midler, an interpreter, an inter-messenger betwixt God his people.

2. The reasons of Christ's being a prophet were these; 1. That he might reveal and deliver to his people the will of his Father. 2. That he might open and expound the same, being once delivered. 3. That he might make his saints to understand, and to believe the same, being once opened.

1. As a prophet, he delivers to the people his Father's will, both in his own person, and by his servants, the ministers: in his own person, when he was upon earth as a *minister of the circumcision*, Rom. xv. 8. and by his servants the ministers, from the beginning of their mission till the end of the world: thus the gospel is called, Heb. ii. 3. *A great salvation, which at the first began to be spoken by the Lord, and was confirmed unto us by them that heard him.* Christ in his personal preaching, is said but *to have begun to teach*, Acts i. 1. And the consummate publication was the sending of the Holy Ghost to these select vessels, who were to carry abroad this treasure unto all the world; it was begun by the Lord, and it was confirmed by them that are the disciples of the Lord. In this respect, we cannot look on the publishing of the gospel to the world, but as very glorious: was there not a resemblance of state and glory in the preaching of Christ? You have heard how a forerunner was sent to prepare his way, as a herald to proclaim his approach, and then was revealed the glory of the Lord; but, because the publication was not consummate till afterwards, Christ carries it on in greater state afterwards than he did before, Eph. iv. 8. *When he ascended up on high, he then led captivity captive, and gave gifts unto men*; as princes, in the time of their solemn inauguration do some special acts of magnificence and honour, they proclaim pardons, open prisons, create nobles, fill conduits with wine; so Christ, to testify the glory of the gospel at the day of his instalment, and solemn re-admission into his Father's glory, he proclaims the gospel, gives gifts unto men, verse 12. *For the perfecting of the saints, for the work of the ministry, for the edifying of the body of Christ.*

2. As a prophet, he opens and expounds the gospel. Thus, being in the synagogue on the sabbath-day, Luke iv. 17, 18, 21. ' He opened the ' book, and he found the place where it was writ- ' ten, The Spirit of the Lord is upon me, because ' he hath anointed me to preach the gospel to the ' poor,' &c. and then *he closed the book,——— and said, This day is this scripture fulfilled in your ears.* And thus joining himself with two of his disciples, going towards Emmaus, Luke xxiv. 27. *He began at Moses, and all the prophets, and he expounded unto them in all the scriptures, the things concerning himself.* The prophecies of Christ were dark and hard to be understood, and therefore Christ came down from heaven to discover

ver such truths, John iii. 13. *No man hath ascended up to heaven,* (i. e.) to be acquainted with God's secrets, *but he that came down from heaven.* The gracious purpose of God towards lost mankind, was a secret locked up in the breast of the Father; and so it had been even to this day, had not Christ, who was in the bosom of the Father, and one of his privy council, revealed it unto us; hence, Christ is called *The interpreter of God, no man knoweth the Father save the Son, and he to whomsoever the Son will reveal him,* by his interpretation, Matth. xi. 27.

3. As a prophet, he gives us to understand, and to believe the gospel, Luke xxiv. 45. *Then opened he their understanding, that they might understand the scriptures:* and thus was the case of Lydia, *whose heart the Lord opened,* Acts x. 14. He that first opens scriptures, at last opens hearts, John i. 9. *He is that true light which enlighteneth every man that cometh into the world.* He enlighteneth every believer, not only with a common natural light, but with a special supernatural light, of saving, spiritual and effectual knowledge: now, there is no prophet can do this save only Jesus Christ; he is only able to cause our hearts to believe and to understand the matter, which he doth teach and reveal. Other prophets may plant and water, Paul may plant, and Apollos may water, but he, and only he can *give the increase:* other prophets may teach and baptize, but unless Christ come in by the powerful presence of his Spirit, they can never be able to save any one poor soul, 1 Pet. ii. 5. *We, as lively stones, are built up a spiritual house,* saith Peter: but, Psal. cxxvii. 1. *Except the Lord do build the house, they labour in vain that build it.* O alas! who is able to breathe the Spirit of life into these dead stones, but he of whom it is written, John v. 25. *The hour is coming, and now is, when the dead shall hear the voice of the Son of God, and they that hear it shall live?* Who can awaken a dead soul out of a dead sleep? And who can give light unto these blind eyes of ours, but he of whom it is written, Eph. v. 14. *Awake, thou that sleepest, and arise from the dead, and Christ shall give thee light?*

3. The excellencies of Christ above all other prophets, are in these respects.—

1. Other prophets were but shadows and types of this great prophet; even Moses himself was but a figure of him, Acts vii. 37. *A prophet shall the Lord raise up unto you of your brethren, like unto me,* saith Moses: these words, *like unto me,* do plainly shew, that Moses was at first but an image and shadow of Christ: now, as substances do far excel shadows, so doth Christ far excel all the prophets; they were but shadows and forerunners to him.

2. Other prophets revealed but some part of God's will, and only at some times. *God,* saith the apostle, *at sundry times, and in divers manners, spake in times past unto the Fathers by the prophets,* Heb. i. 1. (i. e.) He let out light by little and little, till the day-star and Son of righteousness arose; *But in these last days he hath spoken by his Son,* Verse 1. (i. e.) He hath spoken more fully and plainly: in this respect, saith the apostle, Gal. iv. 1, 2. The heirs of life and salvation were but children before Christ's incarnation. As now we see but through a glass darkly, towards what we will do in the life to come, so did they of old in comparison of us; their light in comparison of ours, was but an obscure and glimmering light: Christ's discovery of himself then was but *a standing behind the wall, a looking forth of the window, a shewing himself through the lattice,* Cant. ii. 9.

3. Other prophets spake only to the ears of men, but Christ spake, and still speaks to the heart; *He hath the keys of David, that openeth and no man shutteth, that shutteth and no man openeth,* Rev. iii. 7. It is a similitude taken from them that keep the keys of a city or castle, without whom none can open or shut; no more can any man open the heart or break in upon the Spirit, but Christ: he only is able to open the eyes of the mind by the secret, kindly and powerfully working of his own Spirit.

4. Other prophets preached wisdom unto men, but only Christ preacheth men wise; other prophets warned men, by telling them of their sins, and denouncing the judgments of God; but Christ reclaimed them, and turned them from sin: hence it is said, That *he taught as one having authority, and not as the scribes,* Matth. vii. 29. It came dryly and coldly from them, but it came from him as being full of conviction and reproof, full of the evident *demonstration of the Spirit, and of power,* 1 Cor. ii. 4.

5. Other

5. Other prophets might not preach themselves; the apostle inveighs against self-commenders, *We dare not, (saith he) make ourselves of the number, or compare ourselves with some that commend themselves,* 2 Cor. x. 12. Yea, Christ himself, relating to himself, as a mere man, saith, That *his witness is not true, if he bear witness of himself,* John v. 31. But, in another place, relating to himself as mediator, he speaks clean contrary, *Tho' I do bear record of myself, yet my record is true,* John viii. 14. Here then is a quite difference betwixt other prophets in respect of their office and Christ; they might not preach themselves, but he bears witness of himself, because he hath not a greater in the point of our justification, sanctification and salvation, to bear witness of than himself. And hence, are those self-predications of his which we find in scriptures, as, Isa. xlv. 22. *Look unto me, and be ye sav d, ye ends of the earth.* Matth. xi. 28. *Come unto me, all ye that labour and are heavy laden.* And, conferring with the two disciples, it is said, That *beginning at Moses, and all the prophets, he expounded unto them in all the scriptures, the things concerning himself,* Luke xxiv. 27. Surely it commends us to the prophecy of Christ, that he might preach, and commend himself without any blot or arrogancy, or taking too much upon him.

6. Other prophets had their commission and authority from him, Ecclef. xii. 11. *The words of the wise are as goads and nails fastened by the masters of the assemblies, which are given from one shepherd,* (i. e.) the words of the wise are divine and heavenly instructions; the masters of assemblies are gospel-ministers, and Christ is that one Shepherd from whom these words are given, and from whom these masters have their authority: are they not called *ambassadors for Christ?* 2 Cor. v. 20 And doth not Ezekiel tell us, that he must *drop his word towards the south?* Ezek. xx. 46. Now what is the meaning of that dropping? It is a phrase borrowed from rain, as the clouds from whence the rain descends, have not their water originally and natively in themselves but from the sea: so have not the prophets a spirit of prophecy of themselves, but all is drawn up out of Christ, as out of a full sea of all-excellent wisdom and knowledge. In him are all the treasures, a sea, an ocean of knowledge, and from him all the prophets derived whatsoever they had.

SECT. IV.

Of Christ's miracles.

2. THE miracles of Christ this year were many. Now what were these miracles? But a pursuance of the doctrines delivered in Christ's sermons. One calls them a verification of Christ's doctrine, a signal of Christ's sermons: if we observe, we shall find him to work most of his miracles in actions of mercy. Indeed once he turned water into wine, and sometimes he walked upon the waters, and all the rest were actions of relief, according to the design of God, who would have him manifest his power, in shewing mercy and relief to men.

Amongst all his miracles done this year, now was it that at Cana, where he wrought the first miracle, he does a second; *a certain nobleman,* or courtier, or little king (as some would have it) *came to Jesus, and besought him to come down to his house, and to heal his son, who was at the point of death,* John iv. 47. We do not find Christ often attended with nobility, but here he is, 1 Cor. i. 26. *Not many wise men after the flesh, not many mighty, not many noble are called;* yet God forbid but that some are, and many be: this noble ruler listens after Christ in his necessity; happy was it for him that his son was sick, for else he had not been so well acquainted with his Saviour: O, we are loth to come to Christ till we see a need, a necessity for it; and hence it is, that Christ sends weakness, sicknesses, infirmities, oppositions, and many afflictions, that he may be sought unto: come then, are we afflicted? Whither should we go but to Cana, to seek Christ? Whither should we go but to that Cana of heaven, where our water shall be turned into wine, where our physician lives, that knows how to cure souls, and bodies, and all; that we may once say, *It is good for me that I was afflicted.* The first answer Christ gives this nobleman is a word of reproof, John iv. 28. *Except ye see signs and wonders, ye will not believe:* incredulity was the common disease of the Jews, which no receipt could cure but wonders, *A wicked and adulterous generation seeks after signs.* The doctrine of Christ, and all the divine words that he spake, must be made up with miracles, or they will

not

not believe: it was a foul fault, and a dangerous one, *Ye will not believe*. What is it that condemns the world but unbelief? Here's a noble Capernaumite, that probably had heard many a sermon of Jesus Christ, and yet he is taxed with unbelief. If such as we that live under the clear sunshine of the gospel shall not believe, O what a sin is this; Christ's next answer to this nobleman, is a word of comfort, Ver. 50. *Go thy way, thy son liveth*: oh the meekness, and the mercy of Jesus Christ! when we would have looked that he should have punished this suitor for not believing, he condescends to him that he may believe: as some tender mother that gives the breast to their unquiet children instead of the rod, so usually deals Christ with our perverseness, *Go thy way, thy son liveth*: with one word doth Christ heal two patients, the son and father, the son's fever, and the father's unbelief. We cannot but observe here the steps of faith; he that believed somewhat 'ere he came, and more when he went, he grew to more and more faith in the way; and when he came home, he enlarged his faith to all the skirts of his family. *And the man believed the word that Jesus had spoken unto him*, and he went his way; and in the way one meets him and tells him, *Thy son liveth*, Ver. 51. Which recovery he understands to be at the same time that Christ had spoken those salutary and healing words, and *himself believed and his whole house*, Ver. 53.

2. (If I mistake not in the year, I shall not contend, because in this year only I shall mention his miracles.) Now was it that *a centurion came unto Christ, beseeching him, and saying, My servant lyeth at home, sick of the palsy, grievously tormented*, Matth. viii. 5, 6. Many suitors came to Christ, one for a son, another for a daughter, a third for himself; but I see none come for his servant, but this one centurion; and if we observe Christ's answer to his suit, we see how well pleased is Christ with his request, *And Jesus saith unto him, I will come and heal him*, Ver. 7. When the ruler entreated him for his son, *Come down 'ere he die*, Christ stirred not a foot, but now this centurion complains only of his servant's sickness, and Christ offers himself, *I will come and heal him*. He that came in the shape of a servant, would rather go down to a sick servant, than to the ruler's son, Acts x. 34, 35. *He is no respecter of persons, but he that feareth him, and worketh righteousness is accepted of him*: It may be this poor sick servant had more grace, or very probable it is he had more need, and therefore Christ (to choose) will go down to visit this poor sick servant. Nay, says the centurion, *I am not worthy, Lord, that thou shouldest come under my roof*, Ver. 8. *q. d.* Alas, Lord! I am a Gentile, an alien, a man of blood, but thou art holy, thou art omnipotent, and therefore, *Only say the word, and my servant shall be whole*. Mark this, O my soul, it is but a word of Christ, and my sins shall be remitted, my soul healed, my body raised, and soul and body glorified for ever. The centurion knew this by the command he had over his own servants, Ver. 9. *I say to this man, Go, and he goes; and to another man, Come, and he comes, and to a third, Do this, and he doth it*. In way of application, oh! that I were such a servant to my heavenly master: alas, every of his commands says, *Do this*, and I do it not, every of his prohibitions says, *Do it not, and I do it*: he says, *Go from the world, and I run to it*: He says, *Come to me, and I run from him*. Wo is me, this is not service, but enmity: Oh that I could come up to the faith and obedience of this example, that I could serve my Christ as these soldiers did their master! Verse 10. Jesus marvels at the centurion's faith. We never find Christ wondering at gold, or silver, or costly and curious works of human skill; yea, when the disciples wondered at the magnificence of the temple, he rebuked them rather: but when he sees the grace or acts of faith, he so approves of them, that he is ravished with wonder. He that rejoiced in the view of his creation, rejoiceth no less in the reformation of his creature, *Behold thou art fair, my love, behold thou art fair, there is no spot in thee. My sister, my spouse, thou hast wounded my heart, thou hast wounded my heart with one of thy eyes*, Ca. iv. 7, 9. To conclude, he that both wrought this faith, and wondered at it, doth now reward it, *Go thy way, and as thou hast believed, so be it unto thee: and his servant was healed in the self same hour*.

3. Now it was, even *the day after, that Jesus goes into the city of Nain*, Luke vii. 11. The fruitful clouds are not ordained to fall all in one field: Nain must partake of the bounty of Christ, as well as Cana, or Capernaum. Thither come, he no sooner enters in at the gate of the city, but he meets a func-

a funeral; a poor widow, with her weeping friends, is following her only son to the grave; Jesus observing her sad condition, he pities her, comforts her, and at last relieves her; here was no sollicitor but his own compassion; in his former miracles he was sought and sued to; his mother at the marriage-feast begged a supply of wine; the ruler came to him for a son; the centurion came to him for a servant; but now Christ offers a cure, to give us a lesson, 'That whilst we have to do with the 'Father of mercies, our miseries and afflictions are 'the most powerful suitors.' Christ sees and observes the widow's sadness, and presently all parts of Christ conspire her good; his heart melts into compassion of her; his tongue speaks cheerfully and comfortably unto her, *Weep not*; his feet carry him to the bier; his hand toucheth the coffin, *And he said, Young man, I say unto thee, Arise.* Ver. 14. See how the Lord of life speaks with command: the same voice speaks to him that shall one day speak to us, and raise us out of the dust of the earth: neither sea, nor death, nor hell, can detain their dead, when he charges them to be delivered: we see not Christ stretching himself on this dead corps, as Elijah and Elisha upon the sons of the Shunamite, and of the widow of Sarepta; nor see we him kneeling down and praying, as Peter did for Dorcas; but we hear him so speaking to the dead, as if the dead were alive; and so speaking to the dead, that by the word he speaks, he makes him alive, *Young man, I say unto thee, Arise. And he that was dead sat up, and began to speak,* Ver. 15. So at the sound of the last trumpet, by the power of the same voice, we shall arise out of the dust, and stand up gloriously, *This mortal shall put on immortality, and this corruptible shall put on incorruption.* And lest our weak faith should stagger at the assent of so great a difficulty, by this he hath done, Christ gives us tastes of what he will do. The same power that can raise one man, can raise a thousand, a million, a world: Christ here raised a widow's son, and after Jairus's daughter, and then Lazarus, and, lastly, at his resurrection, he raised a great many at once; he raised one from her bed, another from his bier, another from his grave, and many at once from their rottenness, that it might appear no degree of death can hinder the efficacy of his Almighty power.

4. Now it was that *in the synagogue he finds a man that had a spirit of an unclean devil,* Luke iv. 33. This, I take it, is the first man that we read of, as possessed with a devil. *And he cried, Let us alone, what have we to do with thee?* &c. Ver. 34. In these words, the devil dictates, the man speaks; and whereas the words are plural, *Let us alone,* it is probable he speaks of himself, and the rest of the men in the synagogue with him.

So high and dreadful things are spoken concerning the coming of Christ, (Mal. iii. 2. *Who may abide the day of his coming, and who shall stand when he appeareth?*) that the devil by this takes opportunity to affright the men of the synagogue with the presence of Christ: He would dissuade them from the receiving of Christ, by the terrors of Christ, as if Christ had come only to destroy them, Ver. 34. *Thou Jesus of Nazareth, art thou come to destroy us? I know thee, who thou art, the holy One of God.*

And Jesus rebuked him, saying, Hold thy peace, and come out of him, Ver. 35. The word, *Hold, thy peace,* is in the original, *(phimoethti)* be muzled: it was not a bare command of silence, but there was such power in it, that it cast a muzzel upon the mouth of Satan, that he could speak no more, Mark i. 26. *And when the unclean spirit had torn him,* not with any gashes in his flesh, or dismembering of his body, for he hurt him not, but with some convulsion fits (as it is supposed) then *he threw him in the midst,* Luke iv. 35. and made an horrid cry, and so *came out.*

From this miracle, they all take special notice of the doctrine attested by so great a miracle, *What a word is this?* Ver. 36. Or, as the other Evangelist, Mark i. 27. *What a thing is this? What a new doctrine is this?* Surely this was the great design of all the miracles of Christ, to prove his mission from God, to demonstrate his power unto men, to confirm his gospel, to endear his precepts, to work in us faith, to help us heaven-ward, John xx. 31. *These signs are written that we might believe,—And that believing we might have life thro' his name.*

Use. I have given you several instances of the miracles of Christ in this second year of his ministry; only a few words on this doctrine of miracles for our information, as

1. What they are?

2. Why

2. Why they are?

3. Whether they are chained and continued in this great transaction of our souls salvation? And I have done.

For the first, What they are? Miracles are unusual events wrought above the course or possibility of nature; such were the miracles of Christ, and such were the miracles of the prophets, and of the apostles of Christ; for what they did was above nature; and all the difference betwixt their miracles and the miracles of Christ, was only in this, *viz.* They wrought them not in their own name and power as Jesus Christ did: Thus when Elisha with twenty loaves, and some full ears of corn, fed an hundred men, 2 Kings xiv. 42, 43. *Give unto the people* (says he) *that they may eat: and his servant said, What, should I set this before an hundred men?* He said again, *Give the people that they may eat, for thus faith the Lord, They shall eat, and shall leave thereof.*

And when Peter cured Æneas, which had kept his bed eight years, and was sick of a palsy, Acts ix. 34. *Peter said unto him, Æneas, Jesus Christ maketh thee whole.* And when he cured that man that was lame from his mother's womb, whom they laid daily at the gate of the temple, Acts iii. 6. 'Silver and gold have I none, (said Peter) but such as I have give I thee, In the name of Jesus Christ of Nazareth, rise up and walk.' But our Saviour speaks in an higher strain to the dead damsel, Mark v. 41. *I say unto thee, Arise.* And, in an higher strain to the stormy winds and seas, Mark iv. 39. *Peace, be still.* And, in an higher strain to the raging devil in the possessed, Luke iv. 35. *Be muzzled, and come out of the man.* Here's the difference betwixt the Lord and his servants; but in this they agree, their miracles were not *miranda* but *miracula*; not only wonders but miracles indeed: they were unusual events wrought above nature, or the course of nature.

For the second, Why they are? Many reasons are given, of which I hinted before, but, in reference to scriptures, (which is the great controversy) this is the main, and the only true reason, 'Miracles are wrought for the grounding or confirming of some divine truth or doctrine at its first settling.' To this purpose, miracles were as the trumpeters or heralds, by which the gospel was first commended unto us; as the law of Moses was first authorized by manifold miracles wrought in Sinai, and in the desert, which afterwards ceased when they came to and were settled in the promised land; so the gospel of Christ was first authorized by manifold miracles; but the sound thereof having gone through all the world, these miracles cease: if new additions of miracles for the confirmation of scriptures should be expected in every age, the former miracles of Christ and his apostles would be slighted of all. Indeed Christ tells us, *of great signs and wonders that shall be in the last days*, Matth. xxiv. 24. But withal he tells us of false Christs and false prophets, that must work them. It may be disputed whether these are true miracles or mere deceptions, and magical pretences: but because they are such as the people cannot discern them from miracles really such, therefore it is all one as to them. Here then is Christ's rule, verse 23, 25. *Believe them not,——Behold, I have told you before.* He that foretold us of the man, foretold us also of the impostor, and commanded us not to trust him: in this respect it had been more likely for antichrist to have prevailed upon Christians by doing no miracles, than by doing any; for if he had done none, he might have escaped without discovery, but by doing miracles or wonders, he both verified the wisdom and prescience of Christ, and he declared to the elect, that he was the very enemy of Christ. All the prophets that spake of Christ, bad us believe him for his miracles; so all that foretold of antichrist bad us disbelieve him for his miracles; which occasioned Augustine to say, *Contra mirabularios istos cautum me fecit Deus meus*, Aug. in Johan. Tract. 3. which is, 'Against such miracle-mongers God hath armed me to take heed. *Go not forth unto such*, faith Christ, Matth. xxiv. 26. And therefore, *brethren, stand fast*, faith Paul, 2 Thess. ii. 15. *The great beast deceiveth them that dwell on the earth by means of miracles:* these are the words of John, Rev. xiii. 14. But *if any man have an ear let him hear, i. e.* let him beware, Rev. xiii. 9. True miracles that proceed from God, are wrought for the grounding of doctrine at the first settling, but being once grounded and settled, and a platform described for the right continuing of it, then we are left to the scripture, and are not to expect any new miracles for the confirming of it.

For the third, Whether they are chained and con-

continued in this great transaction of our soul's salvation? I answer, yea; in this respect miracles cease not. It is without controversy, that Jesus Christ, in carrying on our soul's salvation, is adding miracle to miracle: there is a chain of miracles in the matter of our salvation, from first to last; as,——

1. It was a miracle, that God, in his eternity, before we had a being, should have one thought of us; especially that the blessed trinity should sit in council, and contrive that most admirable and astonishing plot of the salvation of our souls; oh, what a miracle was this!

2. It was a miracle, that God, for our sakes, should create the world, and after our fall in Adam, that God should preserve the world, especially considering that our sin had unpinned the whole frame of the creation; and that God even then sitting on his throne of judgment, ready to pass the doom of death for our first transgression, should unexpectedly give a promise of a Saviour, when justly he might have given us to the devil, and to hell, according to his own law, Gen. ii. 17. *In the day that thou eatest thereof, thou shalt die the death.*

3. It was a miracle, that God's Son should take upon him our nature, and that in our nature he should transact our peace; that he should preach salvation to us all if we would believe; and to the end that we might believe, that he would work so many signs and miracles in the presence of his disciples, and of a world of men. Was not Christ's birth a miracle? And Christ's life a miracle? And Christ's death a miracle? And Christ's ascension a miracle? Was not Christ's ministry a miracle? And was it not a miracle, that Christ's word should not be credited without a world of miracles to back it, and confirm it to the sons of men? 1 Tim. iii. 16. *Without controversy, great is the mistery, as well as the mystery of godliness, God manifest in the flesh, justified in the Spirit, seen of angels, preached unto the Gentiles, believed on in the world, received up into glory.*

4. It was a miracle, that God should look upon us in our blood: what a sight was it for God, when, Ezek. xvi. 4, 5, 6. *Thy navel was not cut, when thou wast not salted at all, nor swaddled at all, when thou wast cast out in the open field to the lothing of thy person?* Yet that then, even the Lord should *pass by thee, and see thee polluted in thy own blood, and should say unto thee when thou wast in thy blood, live; yea, say unto thee, when thou wast in thy blood, live.* O miracle of mercies! if creation cannot be without a miracle, surely the new creature is a miracle indeed. So contrary is our perverse nature to all possibilities of salvation, that if salvation had not marched to us all the way in a miracle, we should have perished in the ruins of a sad eternity. Election is a miracle, and creation is a miracle, and redemption is a miracle, and vocation is a miracle; and indeed every man living in that state of grace is a perpetual miracle: in such a one his reason is turned into faith, his soul into spirit, his body into a temple, his earth into heaven, as water into wine, his aversations from Christ into intimate union with Christ, and adhesions to Christ. O what a chain of miracles is this? Why, Lord, *if thou wilt, thou canst make me clean;* say thus, You that are yet in your blood, Why, Lord, *if thou wilt, thou canst make me clean. O Lord, I believe, help thou my unbelief.*

After this *there was a feast of the Jews, and Jesus went up to Jerusalem,* John v. 1. Some would have the feast to be Pentecost; and, to speak truly, the most of our commentators run that way: others take this for the feast of the passover, and the rather, because the evangelist John reckons the time of Christ's public ministry by the several passovers: now, if this feast were not a passover, we cannot find in the gospel so many passovers as to make up Christ's ministry three years and an half. On this ground I join with the latter opinion; and so here I end the second year of Christ's ministry, and come to the third, and to his actions therein, in reference to our souls salvation.

CHAP. III.   SECT. I.

Of the third year of Christ's ministry, and generally of his actions in that year.

Hitherto all is quiet; neither the Jews, nor the Samaritans, nor Galileans did as yet malign the doctrine or person of Jesus Christ; but he preached with much peace on all hands till the beginning of this year. I shall not yet speak of his sufferings; neither shall I speak much of his doings;

doings: many things were done and spoken this year, which I must pass, lest I be too prolix; only such things as refer more principally to the main business of our souls salvation, I shall touch in these particulars. As, 1. In the ordination of the apostles. 2. In his reception of sinners. 3. In the easiness of his yoke, and the lightness of his burden which he imposeth on men.

SECT. II.

Of Christ's ordination of his apostles.

1. IN the ordination of his apostles, are many considerable things: the evangelist Luke lays it down thus, Luke vi. 12, 13. 'And it came 'to pass in those days, that he went out into a 'mountain to pray, and continued all night in pray-'er to God; and when it was day, he called unto 'him his disciples, and of them he chose twelve, 'whom also he named apostles.' Till now Christ taught alone; but because after his ascension he must needs have a ministry to the end of the world; in the first place, he chooseth out some whom he would have on purpose to wait upon him all the time of his ministry, till he was taken up into heaven. 1. In the election or ordination, here is, first, the person by whom they are chosen, Jesus Christ. 2. The place where they are chosen, *viz.* in a mountain. 3. The time when they were chosen, after his watching and praying all night, and when it was day. 4. The company out of whom they were chosen, they were his disciples, and out of them he makes his election. 5. The number of them that were chosen, they were twelve, nor more nor less. 6. The end to which they were chosen, it was to an apostleship: *he chose twelve, whom he also named apostles.*

1. The person by whom they are chosen is Jesus Christ. They chose not themselves but were chosen of Christ. This call was immediate, and therefore most excellent; but now we look not after such calls, and therefore I shall not insist on that: only, by the way, ministers of the gospel must be ministers of Christ, either immediately or mediately called.

2. The place where they were chosen, it was on a mountain: mountainous places have their situation nearest to heaven, which shews, that they were called to high and heavenly things. Mountains are open in view, which shews their ministry must be public: they cannot lie hid in a mountain, a city that is set upon a hill is exposed to the view of all. Again, mountains are subject to winds and tempests, which shews their callings must meet with many oppositions; and this occasioned Christ to hold up their heart with cordials, Matth. v. 11, 12. 'Blessed are ye when men shall revile you, 'and persecute you, and say all manner of evil a-'gainst you falsly for my sake,——for so persecu-'ted they the prophets which were before you.' The ministers of Christ are sure of opposition; 'the disciple is not above his master, nor the ser-'vant above his Lord; if they have called the mas-'ter of the house Beelzebub, how much more 'shall they call them of his houshold?'

3. The time when they were chosen, when it was, 'and after he had continued all night in pray-'er to God;' he goes not to election, but first he watches and prays all the night before. This shews the singular care that Christ had in this great employment; what? to set men apart to witness his name, and to publish to the world the gospel of Christ? This he would not do without much prayer. Sometimes we find Christ praying alone, as elsewhere, *He went up into a mountain to pray,* Matth. xiv. 23. And here on this mountain, without any of his disciples or domestics about him, he prays alone: thus, Matth. vi. 6. *When thou prayest, enter into thy closet,* (saith Christ) *and when thou hast shut thy door, pray to thy Father which is in secret, and thy father, which seeth in secret, shall reward thee openly.* Sometimes we find Christ praying at night, Luke xxi. 37. *In the day-time he was teaching in the temple, and at night he went out, and abode in the mount, that is called the mount of Olives.* See Christ in the exercise of his double office; he preacheth all day, and prays all night. This text tells us, *He continueth all night in prayer.* Night prayers have their special spiritual advantages. 1. It is a time fitter for compunction and heart contrition, Ps. vi. 6. *All the night make I my bed to swim, I water my couch with my tears,* As some things are by heat parched in the day, but cooled in the night; so, many sins contracted in the day, are seasonably repented at night: night-tears are as sweet dews that cool the heat and pride of our spirits. 2. It is a time of silence, and

and free from distraction. Then all tumults cease, and in the secret of our souls, we may silently go and speak with our heavenly Father. In this respect we have a blessed example of Christ praying at night, and especially now. O! he was about the great work of sending his ministers through all the world, and therefore he now spends all the night long in prayer to his Father. A great and extraordinary work is not to be set upon without extraordinary prayer.

4. The company out of whom they are chosen, 'He called unto him his disciples, and out of them 'he chose twelve.' A disciple of Christ is one thing, and an apostle of Christ is another thing; those were Christ's disciples that embraced Christ's doctrine of faith and repentance; it was not material to the constituting of a disciple of Christ, whether they followed Christ as many did, or they returned to their own homes, as some others did. The man out of whom the legions of devils were cast, *Besought Christ that he might be with him, but Jesus sent him away, saying, Return to thine own house, and shew how great things God hath done to thee*, Luke viii. 38, 39. I make no question but Christ at the election of his apostles, had many disciples both waiting on him and absent from him; and out of them that waited on him his apostles were chosen. Christ's ministers should first be disciples. O how unfit are any to take upon them the ministry of Christ, that were never yet the disciples of Christ! first the grace of God within us, and then must that grace of God be discovered by us.

5. The number of them that were chosen, they were twelve; very probable it is, there was some peculiar reason in this account; the number, (say some) was figured out to us in many particulars, as in the twelve patriarchs, Gen. xxxv. 22. In the twelve wells of Elim, Exod. xv. 27. In the twelve precious stones on the breast of the priest. In the twelve tribes of Israel. In the twelve hours of the day. Christ tells them of *sitting on twelve thrones, and judging the twelve tribes of Israel*, Matth. xix. 28. But I delight not curiously to descant on these things. This I am sure, that the doings of Christ were done in weight, measure and number.

6. The end to which they were chosen, it was to an apostleship, *i. e.* That they might be Christ's legates to the sons of men, that they might be sent up and down the world to persuade men to salvation. ' The dispensers of God's word must look ' to their mission, they must not intrude upon so ' sacred a business before they are sent.' Now, this mission is either extraordinary, by immediate instinct and revelation from God, which is ever accompanied with immediate and infused gifts, and this was the case of the apostles: or ordinary, by imposition of hands and ecclesiastical designation; and, in this likewise is required fidelity and ability. 1. Fidelity; it is required of stewards, that a man be found faithful, that he defraud not Christ of his purchase, which is the souls of men, nor men of their price and privilege, which is the blood of Christ: that he watch as a seer, that he speak as an oracle, that he feed as a shepherd, that he labour as a husbandman, that he be instant in season and out of season, to exhort, rebuke, instruct, to do the work of an evangelist, to make full proof of his ministry, because he hath an account to make. 2. Ability both for right information of the consciences of men, and for the seasonable application of truth to particular circumstances, which is that which makes a wise builder. Ah! *Who is sufficient for these things?* 2 Cor. ii. 16. How should we but detest the presumption of those men, who run before they be sent, who leap from their manual trades into this sacred and dreadful office, unto which heretofore the most learned and pious men have trembled to approach?

Use. This may inform us of our duty, and this may inform you of your happiness, 1. Here's our duty, I mean ours of the ministry; Christ ordained his apostles to preach the gospel; and Paul's motto may be ours, 1 Cor. ix. 16. *Wo unto me if I preach not the gospel: what though I preach the gospel, I have nothing to glory of, for a necessity is laid upon me*. This day hath Christ sent me on this errand, Matth. x 7. *Go preach, saying, Repent, for the kingdom of heaven is at hand*. Surely the Lord hath put this message into my mouth, ' Repent, swearers, repent, drunkards, repent, sin- ' ners, for the kingdom of heaven is at hand.' Gospel-discoveries are made every day; Christ is a-rising and shining in our horizon more and more clearly: that great design of God's love to our souls is manifested in every sermon, on every Sabbath; Is not this gospel preaching? What is the gospel, but the treasure of God's love in Christ o-

pened

pened to us? Oh! it is a pleafant work in this refpect to be a minifter of the gofpel, to be always fearching into the treafures of love, and to make them known to poor fouls for the gaining of them unto God. 2. Here is your happinefs, Chrift hath not erected any ftanding fanctuary or city of refuge for men to fly to for their falvation, but he hath appointed ambaffadors to carry this treafure unto mens houfes, where he invites them, and intreats them, and requires them, and commands them, and compels them to come in. Oh, the unfearchable riches of Chrift! 1. In refpect of the meffengers. 2. In refpect of their meffage.

1. In refpect of the meffengers, they were firft apoftles, now minifters, poor earthen veffels. Had Chrift himfelf come in his glorified body, attended with his angels, it might in fome meafure have reprefented his majefty; but, alas! how would this have dazzled your weaknefs? Or if Chrift had made ufe of his angels, as he did at his birth to preach the gofpel; had they continually come in ftate and proclaimed falvation to the fons of men, this would have fhewed more glory; but, alas! how unfuitable had this been to your weak conditions? Here then is the riches of his grace, that earthen veffels fhould carry this treafure, that falvation fhould come out of the mouths of finful creatures, that hearts fhould be broken, fouls fhould believe, life fhould be infufed by the minifterial breath of a weak, worthlefs man, 2 Cor. iv. 7. 'We have this 'treafure in earthen veffels, that the excellency of 'the power may be of God, and not of us.' God's power is more honoured this way than if an angel had come in perfon: it may be in that cafe, a finner's converfion would have been attributed to the power and efficacy of the angel; but, to prevent this, and to preferve the power of his glory and grace, Chrift takes the treafure, and he puts it into earthen veffels: it is in the original, *Veffels of fhell*; as precious pearls are found in fhells, fo the pearl is the gofpel, and the fhell or mother of pearl, are the apoftles and paftors: it is true, they are veffels of fmall price, and fubject to many knocks and falls, yet in them are the moft excellent treafures of the wifdom of God, and of the gofpel of Chrift. And it is in them on purpofe, that the excellency may reflect on God, and not on them.

2. In refpect of the meffage; O the unfearchable riches of Chrift! what is the meffage of thefe men? What is the treafure they bring, but the blood of Chrift, the promifes of the gofpel, the word of grace? I might fum up all in one word, *They bring unto men an invitation from heaven, to heaven*. Obferve it, Chriftians, the gofpel is a meffage; the Lord fends his Son up and down; carries him from place to place; he is fet forth before mens eyes; he comes, and ftands, and calls, and knocks at their doors, and befeecheth them to be reconciled: O the free grace of God! O that mercy, pardon, preferment, eternal life and falvation fhould go a begging, and fuing for acceptance: O the love of fin, and madnefs of folly in wicked men, to trample on fuch pearls, and to neglect fo great falvation when it is tendered unto them! O what a heavy charge will it be for men at the laft day, to have the mercy of God, the humility of Chrift, the entreaties of the Spirit, the proclamations of pardon, the approaches of falvation, the days, the years, the ages of peace, the miniftry of the word, the book of God, the great myftery of godlinefs, to rife up in judgment, and to teftify againft their fouls! O the condefcenfions of Chrift; who are ye that the Lord fhould fend after you? What need hath God of you? Suppofe you fhould go on in the ways of death, and perifh everlaftingly, what fhall God lofe by it? Chrift might fay, 'If you will go on, go on and perifh; if you love 'fin fo well, take you pleafure in it, and be damn'ed evermore.' Ah, no, faith the mercy of God, and the mercy of Chrift, before that be, meffage after meffage, 'Precept upon precept, precept 'upon precept; line upon line, line upon line; 'here a little and there a little,' Ifa. xxviii. 10. This was the defign of Chrift's choofing his apoftles, Mark xvi. 15. 'Go ye into all the world, 'and preach the gofpel to every creature.' that poor finners may turn from fin, and be faved.

SECT. III.

Of Chrift's reception of finners.

2. FOR Chrift's reception of finners; I cannot limit this only to one year of Chrift's miniftry, but I fhall only mention it this year. Now this will appear, 1. In the doctrine of Chrift. 2. In the practice of Chrift.

1. In his doctrine, Chrift lays it down expreffly, Matth.

Mat. xi. 28. *Come unto me, all ye that labour, and are heavy laden, and I will give you rest.* It is no more, but come and welcome. The gospel shuts none out of heaven, but those that by unbelief lock the door against their own souls. Again, *All that the Father giveth me shall come unto me, and him that cometh unto me, I will in no wise cast out,* John vi. 37. Here is laid down the full intent and purpose of God and Christ, to pardon and receive sinners. The Father is willing, and the Son is willing. 1. The Father is willing, John vi. 39. *This is the Father's will which hath sent me, that of all which he hath given me, I should lose none.* The Father is engaged, in that, *first*, he sent Christ on that errand, to receive sinners. Secondly, In that he gave unto Christ all that he would have to be saved by Christ, with a charge to lose none. Sinners were given to Christ, by his Father, as so many jewels to look to, and to save. 2. The Son is willing, for *He that cometh unto me* (saith Christ) *I will in no wise cast out.* Christ is so willing to receive sinners, as that he sets all his doors open, he keeps open house, and he casts out none that will but come in: and why so? *For I came down from heaven, not to do mine own will, but the will of him that sent me,* John vi. 38. 1. *I came down from heaven*; it was a great journey from heaven to earth, and this great journey he undertook, for no other purpose but to save sinners. Great actions (as one says well) must needs have great ends; now this was the greatest thing that ever was done, that the Son of God should come down from heaven; and what was the end, but the reception and salvation of sinners? Luke xix. 10. *For the Son of man is come to seek and to save that which was lost:* Had not Christ come down, sinners could not have gone up into heaven, and therefore that they might ascend, he descends. 2. *I came down from heaven, not to do mine own will, but the will of him that sent me.* His Father had sent him on purpose to receive, and to save sinners; and to this purpose he is called the *apostle of our profession,——Who was faithful to him that appointed him, as also Moses was faithful in all his house:* his Father could not send him on any errand, but he was sure to do it : his Father's mission was a strong demonstration, that Christ was willing to receive those sinners that would but come to him.

Again, John vii. 37. *Jesus stood and cried, saying, If any man thirst, let him come unto me and drink.* The very pith, heart, and marrow of the gospel is contained in these words: the occasion of them was thus; on that last day of the feast of tabernacles, the Jews were wont with great solemnity to draw water out of the fountain of Siloam, at the foot of mount Sion, and to bring it to the altar, singing out of Isaiah, Isa. xii. 3. *With joy shall ye draw water out of the wells of salvation.* Now, Christ takes them at this custom, and recalls them from earthly to heavenly waters, alluding to that of Isaiah, Isa. lv. 1, 3. *Ho, every one that thirsteth, come ye to the waters,—Incline your ears, and come unto me, and your souls shall live.* The Father saith, *Come,* the Son saith, *Come,* the Spirit saith, *Come* ; yea, *The Spirit and the bride say, Come, and let him that heareth say, Come, and let him that is athirst come, and whosoever will, let him drink of the water of life freely,* Rev. xxii. 17. All the time of Christ's ministry, we see him tiring himself in going about from place to place, upon no other errand than this, to cry at the markets, ' Ho, every one that thirsteth, come ye to ' the waters! if any sinners love life, if any will ' go to heaven, let him come to me, and I will ' shew them the way to my Father's bosom, and ' endear them to my Father's heart.'

Again, hither tend all those arguments of God and Christ, to draw souls to themselves. Thus God draws arguments, 1. From his equity, Ezek. xviii. 25. ' Hear now, O house of Israel, is not my way equal? Or, are not your ways unequal?' *q. d.* I appeal to your very consciences, is this equal, That sinners should go on in sin, and trespass against him that is so willing to receive and save poor sinners? 2. From our ruin, in case we go on in sins (Ezek. xviii. 31. ' Cast away from you ' all your transgressions, whereby ye have trans- ' gressed, and make you a new heart, and a new ' spirit, for why will ye die, O house of Israel?') 3. From his own dislike and displeasure at our ruin, Ver. 32. ' I have no pleasure in the death of ' him that dieth, saith the Lord God, wherefore ' turn your souls, and live ye.' 4. From his mercy and readiness to pardon sinners, Isaiah lv. 7. ' Let the wicked forsake his way, and the unrigh- ' teous man his thoughts, and let him return unto ' the Lord, and he will have mercy upon him, and ' to

' to our God, for he will abundantly pardon. 5. From the freeness of his love, Hof. xiv. 4. 'I will 'love him freely.' And, John iii. 16. *God so loved the world, so fully, so fatherly, so freely, that he gave his only begotten Son,* &c. *And I will give unto him that is athirst of the fountain of the waters of life freely,* Rev. xxi. 6. 6. From the sweetness of his name, Exod. xxxiv. 6, 7. *The Lord, the Lord, merciful and gracious, long-suffering, and abundant in goodness and truth, keeping mercy for thousands, forgiving iniquity, transgression, and sin.* 7. From the benefits that would follow, Isa. xlviii. 18, 19. *O that thou hadst hearkned to my commandment, then had thy peace been as a river, and thy righteousness as the waves of the sea, thy seed also had been as the sand, and the offspring of thy bowels like the gravel thereof.* 8. From his oath, Ezek. xxxiii. 61. *As I live, saith the Lord, I desire not the death of a sinner, but rather that he should turn from his wickedness and live.* O happy creatures (saith Tertullian) for whom God swears! O unbelieving wretches, if we will not trust God swearing! 9. From his expostulations, Ezek. xxxiii. 11. *Turn, yea turn ye from your evil ways, for why will ye die, O house of Israel?* Mic. vi. 3. *O my people, what have I done to thee? And wherein have I wearied thee? Testify against me.* Isa. v. 3. *What could I have done more for my vineyard than I have done? Wherefore, when I looked that it should bring forth grapes, brought it forth wild grapes?* 10. From his appeals. Mic. vi. 2. *Judge now, O ye inhabitants of Judah and Jerusalem.——And hear, O ye mountains, the Lord's controversy, and, ye strong foundations of the earth; for the Lord hath a controversy with his people, and he will plead with Israel.* 11. From his groans, Deut. v. 29. *Oh, that there were such an heart in them, that they would fear me, and keep my commandments always, that it might be well with them, and their children for ever.* Deut. xxxii. 29. *And oh! that they were wise, that they understood this, that they would consider their latter end.* 12. From his loathness to give men up, Hof. x. 8. *How shall I give thee up, Ephraim? How shall I deliver thee, O Israel? How shall I make thee as Admah? How shall I set thee as Zeboim? My heart is turned within me, my repentings are kindled together.* O the goodness of God!

And as God the Father, so God the Son draws arguments to win souls to himself. 1. From his coming; it was the very purpose and design of his coming down from heaven to receive sinners, 1 Tim. i. 15. *This is a faithful saying,* (says Paul) *and worthy of all acceptation, that Christ Jesus came into the world, to save sinners.* 2. From his fair demeanour and behaviour towards sinners: this was so open and notorious, that it was turned to his disgrace and opprobry, Matth. xi. 19. *Behold a friend of publicans and sinners:* and the scribes and pharisees murmured at him, and his disciples, saying, *Why do ye eat and drink with publicans and sinners?* Luke v. 30. 3. From his owning of sinners, and answering for them in this respect, *And Jesus answering, said unto them, They that are whole need not a physician, but they that are sick; I came not to call the righteous, but sinners to repentance,* Luke v. 31, 32. 4. From his rejoicing at sinners conversion: indeed we never read of Christ's laughter, and we seldom read of Christ's joy; but when it is at any time recorded, it is at the conversion of a poor soul; he had little else to comfort himself in, being a man of sorrows: but in this he rejoiced exceedingly, Luke x. 21. *In that hour Jesus rejoiced in Spirit*; it was in that hour when he saw an handful of the fruit of his disciples ministry, as an earnest of the many thousands that should afterwards come in, John xi. 15. *And I am glad for your sakes that I was not there,* (said Christ when Lazarus was dead.) But why was he glad? It follows, *to the intent you may believe.* He rejoiced if any of his got faith, a little more faith, more and more faith. 5. From his grief in case of sinners not repenting: witness his tears over Jerusalem, and those speeches of his, Luke xix. 41, 42. *And when he was come near, he beheld the city, and wept over it, saying, If thou hadst known, even thou, at least in this thy day, the things which belong to thy peace; but now they are hid from thine eyes.* Look, as it is with a man carrying to be buried, his wife weeps, his children weep, his friends weep; so our Saviour follows Jerusalem to the grave, and when he can do no more for it, he rings out this doleful passing bell, *O that thou hadst known,* &c. 6. From his wishes, groanings, Matth. xxiii. 37. *O Jerusalem, Jerusalem, thou that killest the prophets, and stonest them which are sent unto thee, how often would I have gathered thy*

thy children together, even as a hen gathers her chickens under her wings, and ye would not! In this argument, before we pass it, observe we the several passages. Here's *first,* the groan, oh! this aspiration argues a compassionate pang of grief: it ran to the very heart of Christ that Jerusalem had neglected their souls salvation. Oh Jerusalem! Secondly, Here's an ingemination, or a double calling on Jerusalem, *O Jerusalem, Jerusalem!* the name doubled expresseth great affection in the speaker; as when David doubled the name of Absalom, it is said, *The king was much moved,* and so he cried, *O my son Absalom, my son, my son Absalom,* 2 Sam. xviii. 33. Thirdly, Here's the monstrous sin wherewith the Lord charges Jerusalem, *Thou that killest the prophets, and stonest them which are sent unto thee.*

Jerusalem was the very slaughter-house of the prophets, insomuch that very few of the prophets had been murdered elsewhere; and so, comparatively, Christ speaks, *It cannot be that a prophet perish out of Jerusalem,* Luke xiii. 33. Fourthly, Here Christ's willingness to save Jerusalem, which he discovers; 1. In his frequent applications to it. How often? *q. d.* not once, nor twice, nor thrice, but many and many a time have I come to Jerusalem, and spoke to Jerusalem, and wooed Jerusalem, *How often?* 2. In the acting, exercising, and putting forth of his will; *how often would I have gathered thy children together?* The will of Christ was serious, though not absolute: I know his divine will, absolutely considered, could not have been resisted; but this was not his absolute will, but only a will of divine complacency. There is *voluntas absoluta, efficax, decernens, & infalliliter producens effectum volitum: & voluntas conditionata, revelata, approbationis, & simplicis complacentiae,* August. Tract. 15. in Joh. And so he would not have the death of any, but that all should live; or he speaks here of his human ministerial will (say some) and not of his divine: many a sermon had he preached, and many an exhortation had he dropped; and every sermon, and every exhortation, proclaimed his willingness, *I would, yea that I would, have gathered thy children together.* 3. In resemblance of his willingness, Christ would have gathered Jerusalem's children, 'As the hen gathers her chickens under her wings.' In the metaphor Christ's care is admirably displayed. 1. As the hen with her wings covers the unfeathered chickens. 2. As the hen provides for their food, not eating herself till they are filled. 3. As the hen defends her chickens from the ravenous birds, so that to blood she will fight in their defence: so hath Christ's care been for Jerusalem. 'No bird (saith Austin) expresseth such tender love to her young ones, as the hen doth.' No fowls so discover themselves to be mothers, as hens do; other birds we know to be mothers when we see them in their nests, but no other way; only the hen discovers herself to be a mother, when her chickens do not follow her; for then her feathers stand up, her wings hang down, she clocketh mournfully, and goeth feebly: now, in respect of this singular love, Christ compares himself to an hen; *As an hen gathers her chickens, so would I have gathered Jerusalem.* 4. In that he adds so doletully, *but ye would not;* I would, but ye would not, *q. d.* In me no care so great as to save your souls, in you no care so little as your souls salvation; I strove towards you in acts of love, and you strove towards me in acts of ingratitude; I would have done you good, but you would not receive it; *I would,* yea, *how often would I, but ye would not.*

2. Christ's reception of sinners appears yet more in his practice. How welcome were all sorts of sinners unto him? He casts out none that acknowledged him for the Messiah; he turned none away that gave up their souls to be saved by him in his own way. This he manifests. 1. Parabolically. 2. Really.

1. Parabolically, especially in those three parables, of the lost goat, and of the lost sheep, and of the lost son. I shall instance in this last, which may well serve for all the rest.—— Luke xv. 20. *When the prodigal was yet afar off, his father saw him, and had compassion on him, and ran, and fell on his neck, and kissed him.* In these words observe, 1. His father sees him before he sees his father: no sooner a sinner thinks of heaven, but the Lord spies him and takes notice of him. 2. The Lord sees him whilst he was yet a great way off; he was but in the beginning of his way: his father might have let him alone till he had come quite home to his house, and it had been a singular mercy to have bid him welcome then; but he takes notice of him yet a great way off; sinners may

may be far off from God in their own apprehensions, and yet the Lord even then draws near, whilst thus they apprehend. 3. His father had pity or compassion on him; the Lord's bowels even yearn, and work, and stir within him at the sight of his returning prodigals; when Ephraim had bemoaned himself, Jer. xxxi. 18, 19. *Thou hast chastised me, and I was chastised, as a bullock unaccustomed to the yoke;* why then, cries God, verse 20. *Is Ephraim my dear son? Is he a pleasant child? For since I spake against him, I do earnestly remember him still, therefore my bowels are troubled for him, I will surely have mercy upon him, faith the Lord.*———4. *His father ran:* there is much in this. As, 1. It had been mercy though his father had stood still, till his son had come. 2. What a mercy is this, that his father will go, and give his son the meeting? 3. But, above all, O, what abundant mercy call we this, that the father will not go, but run? If he would needs meet his son, might he not have walked towards him in a soft slow pace? O no, if a sinner will but come, or creep towards Christ, mercy will not go a foot-pace, but run to meet him; bowels full of mercy, out-pace bowels pinched with hunger; God's mercy is over his works, and so it is over all our needs, and over all our sins. 5. He ran, *and fell on his neck*; (i. e.) he hugged, and embraced him; O wonder! who would not have been loth to have touched him? Was he not in his lothsome stinking rags? Smelt he not of the hogs and swine he lately kept? Would not some dainty stomachs have been ready to have cast all up upon such embracements? We see mercy is not nice, Ezek. xvi. 6. *When I passed by* (faith God) *I saw thee polluted in thy blood, and I said unto thee when thou wast in thy blood, live; yea, I said unto thee when thou wast in thy blood, live;* that very time of her blood, was the time of love; then the Lord *spread his skirt over her, and covered her nakedness, and sware unto her, and entered into a covenant with her, and she became his,* ver. 6, 8. He ran, and fell on his neck, and kissed him; who would have brooked a person in so filthy a pickle? What? Kiss those lips that have been so lately lapping in the hog's trough? Those lips that had so often kissed those base, and beggarly, and abominable harlots? One would think he should rather have kicked, than kissed them.

There is a passage somewhat like this, and *Esau ran to meet Jacob, and he embraced him, and fell on his neck, and kissed him,* Gen. xxxiii. 4. Before he had thought to have killed him, but now he kissed him; 'tis not to tell how dear the father was to his prodigal son, when *he ran, and fell on his neck, and embraced, and kissed him.* The scope of the parable is this, That Christ is willing and glad to receive sinners, Ezek. xxxiii. 11. *Turn ye, turn ye, from your evil ways, for why will ye die, O house of Israel.*

2. Christ manifests this willingness in his practice really. Amongst many instances, I shall insist on one, a notable instance of this year: one of the Pharisees named Simon, invited Christ to eat with him, Luke vii. 37. Into whose house when he had entered, a certain woman, that was a sinner abiding there in the city, heard of it; a widow she was, and, prompted by her wealth and youth to an intemperate life, she came to Jesus in the Pharisee's house; and no sooner come, but she lays her burden at Jesus' feet, and presents him with a broken heart and weeping eye, and an alabaster box of ointment, verse 38. *She stood at his feet behind him weeping, and began to wash his feet with her tears, and to wipe them with the hairs of her head; and she kissed his feet, and anointed them with ointment.* 1. *She stands at his feet,* a sign of her humility; O what a change! she that was before married to a noble personage, a native of the town and castle of Magdal, from whence she had her name of Magdalene; and she that now was a widow, and therefore took her liberty of pride and lust; who so proud and vile as Mary Magdalene? At this time, she comes in remorse and regret for her sins, and throwing away her former pride, she stoops and waits, and humbly stands at Jesus' feet. 2. *She stood at his feet behind him;* a blushing sign of faith: it comprehends in it a tacit confession of her sins; she knew herself unworthy of Christ's presence, she durst not look him in the face, but believingly she waits behind! her shame speaks her repentance, and her waiting on him, and not flying from him, speaks her faith. 3. *She stood at his feet behind him weeping,* her grief burst out in tears: she heeds not the feast or feaster, tho' usually they are accompanied with joy, and mirth, and music; and such feasts attended with such vanities, she

many a time had probably observed, yet now she comes in trembling to this feast, and falling down before Christ, she weeps, and weeps bitterly for her sins. 4. *She began to wash his feet with tears*; her tears were not feigned but fruitful; she wept a shower of tears: one considering her tears, cries it out, *Terra rigat coelum*, The very earth bedews heaven; her eyes that before were abused to lust, are now fountains of tears; she pours out a flood, great enough to wash the feet of our blessed Jesus: this was the manner of the Jews, to eat their meat lying down, and leaning on their elbows; or if many eat together, leaning in the bosoms of one another: thus at the passover, it is said, That *there was leaning on Jesus' bosom, one of his disciples whom Jesus loved.* John xiii. 23. And in this posture, Jesus sitting or lying at meat, Mary had the convenience to weep on his feet, which he had cast behind his fellow; and, O how she weeps amain! the tears so trickle, that she begins to wash Christ's feet; she not only waters them, but washes them. That which Jeremy wished, Jer. ix. 1. *O that my head were waters, and mine eyes a fountain of tears!* Mary fulfils, for her head is waters, and her eyes are fountains; rivers of tears run down her eyes; Oh! she had pierced Christ with her sins, and now she weeps over him whom she had pierced; crying out, as we may imagine, ' O my sins! and, O my Christ! O foul ' sins! and O sweet Jesus!' 5. *She wipes his feet with the hair of her head*; her hair added to her beauty, sometimes curling rings, or inseemly shed; she made it a snare for men, but now she consecrates it to her Lord, and makes it a towel to wipe Christ's feet withal: O here's a worthy fruit of serious repentance, the apostle calls it *an holy revenge*, 2 Cor. vii. 11. 6. *She kissed his feet*, in token of her new choice, and new love, and new affections: her kisses had been formerly to wantons, but now she bestows them on the feet of Christ. 7. *She anointed them with ointment*, which expression was so great an extasy of love and sorrow, and adoration, that to anoint the feet of the greatest monarch, was long unknown, and in all the pomp of Roman prodigality, it was never used till Otho taught it Nero. When Simon observed this sinner so busy in the expresses of her religion, he thought within himself, that Christ was no prophet, that he did not know her to be a sinner; for, altho' the Jews religion did permit harlots to live and to enjoy the privileges of the nation, save that their oblations were refused, yet the Pharisees, who pretended to a greater degree of sanctity than others, would not admit them to civil usages, or the benefits of ordinary society; and, hence Simon made an objection within himself, which Jesus knowing, (for he understood his thoughts as well as his words) first, he makes her apology, and then his own; the scope giving us to understand that Christ was not of the same superciliousness with the Pharisees, but that repenting sinners should be welcome to him; and this welcome he published first to Simon, Luke vii. 47. ' Her sins, which are ' many, are forgiven;' and then to the woman, ver. 48. ' Thy sins are forgiven thee, ver. 50. ' Thy faith hath saved thee, go in peace.

Use. I have been long in the proof: but a word of use, and I have done. What, is Christ most willing to receive sinners? O then be exhorted, Who would not come to Jesus Christ? Methinks, now all sinners of all sorts should say, Though I have been a drunkard, a swearer, an unclean person, yet now I hear Christ is willing to receive sinners, and therefore I will go to Jesus Christ. This is my exhortation, O come unto Christ, come unto Christ! behold, here in the name of the Lord I stand, and make invitation to poor sinners; Oh, will not ye come? How will you answer it at the great day, when it shall be said, The Lord Jesus made a tender and offer of mercy to you, and you would not accept of it: Oh, come to Christ, and believe on Christ; as Christ is willing to receive you, so be you willing to give up your souls to him. The motives to this I may lay down in these particulars.——

1. The doctrine of Christ, *Come unto me,——and him that cometh unto me I will in no ways cast out.* All the arguments of God and Christ, of which you have heard the practice of Christ while he was upon earth, and the heart of Christ now in heaven; lay these together, and apply them to your own souls; Oh, what work will they make!

2. The calls of God and Christ, as they are frequent in the scriptures: consider that text, *Ho, every one that thirsts, come ye to the waters*, Isa. lv. 1. [*Ho.*] He begins proclamation-ways: we usually say, vocations, interjections speak very affectionate motives towards the distressed. Certainly

ly Christ's love is a very affectionate love: he lays his mouth to the ears of those that are spiritually deaf, and cries aloud, [*Ho,*] *every one*, Christ invites all: *As many as ye shall find, bid them to the marriage*, Matth. xxii. 9. As the heavens are general in their influence, not one grass on the ground but is bedewed; so are Christ's invitations to his feasts: not one man in all the world but he is invited; [*Ho, every one that thirsteth*] so the apostle, *Let him that is athirst, come; and whosoever will, let him take the water of life freely*, Rev. xxii. 17. A thirst and a will is one and the same; it is your will that makes up the match: if you will but sit down at God's table, if you will but have the honey-comb with the honey, if you will drink his wine with his milk; if you will drink, yea, drink abundantly of the flaggons of the wine of his kingdom; why, then, *Come ye to the waters, come unto me and drink*. Christ's arms are spread abroad to receive sinners: he calls and knocks, and calls and waits, and calls and beseeches; every word here hath so much sweetness and dearness in it, as it plainly speaks him free and willing to receive you if you will but come.

3. The wooings of Christ are to gain your hearts: consider him bowing the heavens, and coming down, and laying aside his robes of majesty: consider him going about from place to place, on no other errand, but to gain your hearts and win your souls: and, whoever spake such effectual words as Christ spake when he was upon earth? Who ever gave such precious jewels to a bride, as Christ gave to his spouse? Who ever put on such an apparel as Christ did when he wooed his church? The prophet wonders at it, *Who is this that cometh from Edom, with dyed garments from Bozrah?——Wherefore art thou red in thine apparel, and thy garments like him that treadeth in the wine-fat?* Isa. lxiii. 1, 2. Who ever gave such a love-token as Christ gave when he laid down his life? Oh, consider him living or dying, and say, *Never love like to this*. Ah, poor sinner! see your Jesus hanging on the cross, dropping out his last breath, stretching out his dying arms to incircle sinners; and come, oh, come and throw yourselves into his bleeding arms! away with all prejudiced opinions! who will say, Christ is not willing to save him, and not blaspheme eternal love? Speak truth, corrupt hearts, speak truth, say not Christ is unwilling, but you are unwilling; I would, but ye would not.

4. The weepings of Christ if he cannot prevail. Thus we find him in the gospel expressing himself, not only in words but in tears. And when he was come near Jerusalem, he beheld the city, and wept over it, Luke xix. 41. Christ coming to the city, and seeing it, and foreseeing the desolation that should come upon it, his bowels yearned within him towards his people, and he mourned secretly within himself, *q. d.* O Jerusalem, thou hast had many priests to advise thee, and many prophets to instruct thee in the way of life, but now these days are gone and past; nay, the great prophet of the world is come to woo thee, but yet thy heart is hardened, and thou wilt not receive the things belonging to thy peace, and therefore I will turn my preaching into mourning and sighing, *Oh that thou hadst known, even thou, at least in this thy day, the things belonging to thy peace.——*And then his heart even breaks, and he weeps again, *But now they are hid from thine eyes!* sinners, suppose Christ should come and weep over you, as he did over Jerusalem, saying, 'O ye sinful souls, 'had but you known, even you in this your day 'the things belonging to your peace!' And, suppose you should see one tear trickling down after another: what, Christ to weep for you, over you! methinks, if you had hearts of stone, it should melt your hearts: surely it is no light matter that makes Christ weep: children weep often, but wise men seldom, yet here the wisest of men weeps for them that would not weep for themselves: Oh Jerusalem, Jerusalem!

SECT. IV.

Of Christ's easy yoke and light burden.

3. FOR the easiness of Christ's yoke, and the lightness of Christ's burden, Christ delivers it in these words, Matth. xi. 29, 30. *Take my yoke upon you, and learn of me,——For my yoke is easy, and my burden is light*. See the actions of Christ this year in reference to our souls health. 1. He commissionates his apostles to call sinners in. 2. He stands ready to receive them if they will but come in. 3. He sweetens the way of Christianity to them when they are come in. Many fears

D d 2

and

and jealousies are in the hearts of men, of the difficulty, austerity and severity of Christ's institutions; and therefore, to remove that objection, he tells them plainly, there is no such thing, but rather clean contrary, *For my yoke is easy, and my burden is light.*

My yoke, (i. e.) my commandments: so the apostle John gives the interpretation, 1 John v. 3. *His commandments are not grievous.* My yoke is easy, (i. e.) My commandments are without any inconveniency: the trouble of a yoke is not the weight, but the uneasiness of it, and Christ speaks suitably, *My yoke is easy, and my burden,* (i. e.) my institutions: the word *(primarily)* signifies the freight or ballast of a ship, which cuts through the waves, as if it had no burden; and without which burden there was no safety in the ship, [*Phortion para topheresthei*], *a ferendo,* a burden, which either is laid upon the shoulder, or rather which is put into a ship, that it may go steadily and safely. My burden is light: the yoke of the law was hard, and the burden of the Pharisees was heavy, but Christ's yoke is easy, and his burden is light, every way sweet and pleasant.

Christian religion, and the practice of it, are full of sweetness, easiness and pleasantness: My yoke is easy, and my burden is light.

The prophets prophesying of this, say thus, Isaiah xl. 4. *Every valley shall be exalted, and every mountain and hill shall be laid low, the crooked shall be made straight, and the rough places plain.* The meaning is, That the ways of Christianity should be levelled and made even; and that all lets and impediments should be removed out of the way, that so we might have a more easy and convenient passage unto heaven: to the same purpose is that other prophecy, *And an high way* (or causeway) *shall be there; and a way, a causeway, or a way;* (that is, a way cast up) Isaiah lii. 10. *And it shall be called the way of holiness,* (or a way for the saints of God, and not for the wicked, Matth. vii. 14). *The unclean shall not pass over it, but it shall be for those:* (Or, he shall be with them, or be a guide unto them by his word and Spirit, Isa. xxx. 21). *The wayfaring men, though fools, shall not err therein.* Christ's way is so easy, that the simplest so conducted by his word and Spirit, shall not miss of it, Psal. xxv. 9. *The meek will he guide in judgment, and the meek will he teach his way.*

The apostles are yet more clear, 1 John v. 3. *For this is the love of God, that we keep his commandments, and his commandments are not grievous,* Rom. viii. 2. And *the law of the Spirit of life in Christ Jesus hath made me free from the law of sin and death.* Rom. vii. 6. *And now are we delivered from the law, that being dead wherein we were held, that we should serve in newness of spirit, and not in the oldness of the letter.* Christ Jesus came to break off from our necks those two great yokes; the one of sin, by which we were kept in fetters and prisons; the other of Moses' law, by which we were kept in pupilage and minority: and now Christ having taken off these two, he hath put on a third: he quits us of our burden, but not of our duty: he hath changed the yoke of sin, and the yoke of the law strictly taken, into the sweetness of his fatherly regimen, whose very precepts carry part of their reward in hand, and assurance of glory afterward.

The reasons of the sweetness, easiness, and pleasantness of Christian religion, and the practice of it, I shall reduce into these heads.

1. Christian religion is most rational. If we should look into the best laws that the wisest men in the world ever agreed upon, we shall find that Christ adopted the quintessence of them all into this one law: the highest pitch of reason is but as a spark, a taper, a lesser light, which is involved and swallowed up in the body of this great light, that is made up by the Son of righteousness. Some observe, that Christ's discipline is the breviary of all the wisdom of the best men, and a fair copy and transcript of his Father's wisdom. There is nothing in the laws of Christian religion, but what is perfective of our spirits; rare expedient of obeying God, and of doing duty and benefit to all capacities and orders of men. Indeed the Greeks, whom the world admired for their human wisdom, accounted the preaching of the gospel foolishness, and thereupon God blasted their wisdom, as it is written, *I will destroy the wisdom of the wise, and will bring to nothing the understanding of the prudent,* 1 Cor. i. 19. The gospel may be as foolishness unto some, but *unto them which are called ——Christ the power of God, and the wisdom of God.* 1 Cor. i. 24.

2. Chri-

2. Christian religion hath less trouble and slavery in it than sin, or any thing that is contrary to it; as for instance, he that propounds to himself to live a low, a pious, an humble and retired life, his main employment is nothing but sitting religiously quiet, and undisturbed with variety of impertinent affairs; but he that loves the world entertains a thousand businesses, and every business hath a world of employments: how easy a thing is it to restore a pledge? But if a man means to defeat, or to cozen him that trusts him; what a world of arts must he use to make pretences? As first to delay, then to excuse, then to object, then to intricate the business, then to quarrel; and all the way to palliate the crime, and to represent himself an honest man: the ways of sin are crooked, desert, rocky, and uneven ways; the apocryphal book of Solomon brings in such men, as if in hell they were speaking this language, Wisd. v. 7. 'We wearied ourselves 'in the way of wickedness, yea we have gone 'through deserts, where there lay no way; but 'as for the way of the Lord we have not known 'it.' Wicked men are in thraldom, but *where the Spirit of the Lord is, there is freedom.* 2 Cor. iii. 17. O the pains, troubles, expences that men are at to serve their sensuality! see how the ambitious man riseth early, and goes to bed late; see how he flatters, dissembles, solicits to obtain nothing but a little wind, a puff, a breath of vain mens mouths! see how the covetous man toils, as if he were tied in a galley by the leg, with a chain to serve, by rowing for ever; so I have heard, that Turks use some Christians: but this is a thousand times worse servitude; for such a one is in servitude to a more base creature than a Turk; and he lies bound not only by the feet, but also by the hands, ears, eyes, heart, and all. Only the Christian is at liberty; only Christian religion, and the practice of it, set men at liberty, John viii. 31, 32. 'If ye continue in my word, (saith Christ) then 'are ye my disciples indeed, and ye shall know '.the truth, and the truth shall make you free.'

3. Christian religion is all composed of peace, ' Her ways are the ways of pleasantness, and all ' her paths are peace,' Prov. xvii. 3. Christ framed all his laws in compliance of this design of peace;. peace within, and peace at home, and peace abroad: 1. It holds forth a certain heavenly peace, and tranquillity within, Psalm cxix. 165.] ' Great 'peace have they which love thy law, and nothing. 'shall offend them.' But on the contrary, ' The 'wicked are like the troubled sea when it cannot 'rest, whose waters cast up mire and dirt; there 'is no peace, saith my God, to the wicked,' Isa. lvii. 20, 21. Their passions were never yet mortified; and such passions usually rage in wicked men, as are most contrary, and demand contrary things: the desire of honour cries, spend here; but the passion of avarice cries, hold thy hands; lust cries, venture here; but pride saith, no such thing, it may turn to thy dishonour; anger cries, revenge thyself here; but ambition says, 'tis better to dissemble. And here is fulfilled that of the Psalmist, *I have seen violence and strife in the city*, Psal. lv. 9. The vulgar renders it, *I have seen iniquity and contradiction in the self same city.* First, Iniquity, for all the demands of these passions are unjust. And, 2. Contradiction, for one passion cries out against another. But now, ' Great peace have 'they that love thy law;' for by the aid of Christ and his grace, their passions are in some sort subdued; and they pass on their life most sweetly and calmly, without any perturbations much troubling their spirits: they have that 'peace which passeth all un- ' derstanding; which the world can neither give, ' not taste of,' as Christ affirmeth, John xiv. 27.

2. It holds forth peace at home: the laws of Jesus teach us how to bear with the infirmities of our relatives; and indeed whosoever obeys the laws of Jesus Christ, he seeks with sweetness to remedy all differences; he throws water upon a spark; he lives sweetly with his wife, affectionately with his children, discreetly with his servants; and they all look upon him as their guardian, friend, and patron; but look upon an angry man not subject to these Christian laws, and when he enters upon his threshold, it gives an alarm to his house: every little accident is the matter of a quarrel, and every quarrel discomposes the peace of the house, and sets it on fire, and no man can tell how far it may burn. O the sweetness, easiness, pleasantness of Christian religion! where that is embraced and followed, the man is peaceable, and charitable, and just, and loving, and forbearing, and forgiving; and how should there be but content in this blessed family?

3. It holds out peace abroad; it commands all offices of kindness, gentleness, love, meekness, humility,

mility, lowliness of mind towards others; and such sweet dispositions are usually received with fondness, and all the endearments of the neighbourhood: it prescribes an austere, and yet a sweet deportment: it commands all those labours of love, as to relieve the stranger, to visit the sick, to wash the feet of the poor: it sends us upon charitable embassies, to unclean prisons, nasty dungeons, and in the cause of Christ, to lay down our lives one for another: it teacheth us how to return good for evil, kindness for injuries, a soft answer for the rough words of an enemy: oh! when I think of this, I cannot but think of him who said, that 'either this was not the Christian religion, or we 'were not Christians.' For my part, I am easily persuaded, that if we would but live according to the discipline of Christian religion, one of those great plagues that vexeth the world (I mean the plague of war) would be no more: certainly this was one of the designs of Christianity, That there should be no wars, no jars, no discontents amongst men: and if all men that are called Christians, were indeed charitable, peaceable, just, loving, forbearing one another, and forgiving one another, what sweet peace should we have? How would this world be an image of heaven, and of that society of saints and angels above in glory?

4. Christian religion affords to us all assistances, both outward and inward, in some respects: I know the duties of Christianity are hard and heavy, but whatsoever Christ hath imposed as heavy and hard, he hath made it light in aids. I shall shew the helps in these particulars. As,

1. The holy scriptures be our helps: this was the very scope and aim for which the sacred volume was sent from heaven, *viz.* That we might decline from evil, and do good; that we might die to old Adam, and live to Christ; that we might crucify sin, and follow virtue: what are the scriptures but the register of God's will, the letters of God's love, to invite us to grace, and to dehort us from vice? O the persuasions, directions, and commands of God that we might become holy? and, O the dissuasions, diversions, threatnings, and terrifying of God, that we might flee prophaneness.

2 The ministers of Christ be our helps: thou hast the scriptures, but it may be thou canst not read, or thou canst not understand the sense and meaning thereof; Christ therefore, for thy help, hath set up a ministry, *for the edifying of the body of Christ,* Eph. iv. 12. These are the watchmen over the house of Israel, to cry like trumpets, and to blazon the sins of the house of Israel: these are the suitors of God and Christ, to speak out his goodwill in thine ears; They call, they cry, they wait, they woo, they *pray you in Christ's stead, that you will be reconciled unto God.* 2 Cor. v. 20.

3. The lives of saints be our helps: we have not only teachers in word, but the saints in all ages, as so many stars, have given us light how to walk in the darkness of this life. The examples of the godly are very drawing, and much for our imitation; and therefore the Psalmist bids us, Psalm xxxvii. 37. *Mark the perfect man, and behold the upright, for the end of that man is peace.* O! 'tis a blessed help to a Christian life to read over, much more to mark, and observe the holy and godly lives of the saints of God: how doth their zeal condemn our coldness, their diligence, our negligence, their watching and prayer, our sluggishness and indevotion? And how are they as spurs to quicken us forwards in our spiritual voyage towards heaven?

4. Christ's ordinances be our helpers: as the word, and sacraments, and prayer, and meditation, and conference, &c. What are they but fountains of grace, conduits and conveyances of the blood of Christ? To what end were they instituted, but for the watering of our souls, to the increase of grace, and to supplanting of sin and vice, and all manner of evil?

5. The encouragements of reward be our helps. Now, in the practice of Christian religion, there is a double reward, 1. The reward of duty, Psalm xix. 11. *In the keeping of thy commandments there is great reward:* he saith not, For keeping them, but *in keeping them there is great reward;* there is a grace, a beauty, an excellency in every gracious acting. 2. The reward according to the duty: to this exercise of religion Christ hath annexed many sweet and gracious promises both for this life, and that to come; and these promises may be used as helps; Heb. xi. 26. *He had a respect unto the recompence of reward.* To this purpose are the glorious things of heaven set open before us, that we may have an eye to them, and be encouraged by them. *So run that ye may obtain,* 1 Cor. ix. 24.

6. The

6. The openings and discoveries of the pains of hell are as helps to restrain us from sin, and to keep us in the way to Christ. This, some call legal, but Christ in the gospel tells us of this; in the gospel we find a description of hell-pains, set out by *weeping and wailing, and gnashing of teeth*; by *a worm never dying, and a fire never going out*, Matth. viii. 12. and Mark ix. 44. Oh! when I think of those unquenchable flames, those remediless torments, without hope of recovery, remission, or mitigation: when I think of that privation and loss of the light of God's face, prepared only for those that serve him in holiness, how should I but look about me, and prepare for my reckoning? Nay, how easy should I think any pains in comparison? Some persons in affrightment have been seen to carry burdens, and to leap ditches, and to climb walls, which their natural power could never have done; and if we understood the sadness of a cursed eternity, from which we are commanded to fly, and yet knew how near we are to it, and likely to fall into it, if we continue in sin, it would be able to create fears greater than a sudden fire, or a midnight alarm.

7. A principle of love (wheresoever it is planted) is our help: be the yoke never so uneasy, yet love will make it light: Solomon compares the estate of the church to a chariot, and it is described to have *pillars of silver, and a bottom of gold, and a covering of purple, the midst thereof being paved with love*, Cant. iii. 10. A strange expression, that the midst of a chariot should be paved with love, but 'tis plain, the chariot wherein Christ carries his people up and down in the world, and brings them to himself, is such a chariot as the midst thereof is paved with love: in this case, if there were neither heaven, nor hell, yet a soul would be in the duties of Christianity. I remember how Ivo, bishop of Chartres, meeting a grave matron on the way, with fire in one hand, and water in the other, he asked her, what those symbols meant? And what she meant to do with her fire and water? She answered, ' My purpose ' is, with the fire to burn paradise, and with the ' water to quench the flames of hell, that men ' may serve God *(said she)* without the incentives ' of hope and fear, and purely for the love of God, ' and Jesus Christ.' Surely it was an high expression; for my part, I dare not separate those things which God hath joined together; only this I say, that where true love is, there is an excellent help in our way heaven-wards.

8. The angels be our helps: *They are ministering spirits, sent forth to minister for them who shall be heirs of salvation*, Heb. i. 14. And the kind of their administration is excellently set forth by the Psalmist, *They shall keep thee in all thy ways, they shall bear thee up in their hands, lest thou dash thy foot against a stone,* Psal. xci. 11, 12. In this place the angels are compared to nurses that have a charge over weak children, to keep them and guard them; so the angels do all the offices of a nurse, or mother; they keep us, guard us, instruct us, admonish us, correct us, comfort us, preserve us from evil, and provoke us to good.

9. The motions, inspirations, blessed influences of the Spirit of Christ be our helps: many a time the Spirit cries, and calls on our hearts, saying, ' This is the way, walk therein;' Isa. xxx. 21. As the evil spirit, or devil in wicked men is continually moving, and inclining them to all evil thoughts, affections, and desires; so the good Spirit of God in good men doth incline, and move them to good thoughts, good affections, good actions; and hence they are said *to be led by the Spirit*, Rom. viii. 14. There are indeed several acts of the Spirit; as sometimes, there is a breathing or stirring; sometimes a quickening or enlivening; sometimes a powerful effectual inclining, or bending of our hearts unto good things: now, in some of these works the Spirit is most what, for in the progress of sanctification, we need a continual help and influence from God's holy Spirit, and when we obey these conducts, we are said to *walk in the Spirit*, Gal. v. 24. And as all these are helps in the ways of Christianity, so by these helps, and assistance of Christ's holy Spirit, Christianity is made very easy unto us.

10. The grace of God is our help: many feeling the strength of corruption, cry out, with Paul, *O wretched man that I am, who shall deliver me from this body of death?* O! *I find a law in my members warring against the law of my mind*, Rom. vii. 24. and 23. But they consider not the comfortable saying of Christ to Paul, 2 Cor. xii. 9. *My grace is sufficient for thee:* by the assistance of grace Paul could do any thing; *I can do all things through Christ that strengtheneth me*, Phil. iv. 13. Yea, *In all*

all these things we are more than conquerors thro' him that loved us, Rom. viii. 37. The Psalmist hath a notable expression to this purpose, 'I will run the way of thy commandments, when thou shalt enlarge my heart,' Psal. cxix. 32. This enlargement of heart was by the grace of God: grace is compared to oil; as a dry purse is softened and enlarged by anointing it with oil, so the heart drawn together by sin, is opened and enlarged, by the pouring of Grace into it; and if grace be present, then, saith David, ' I will run the way of thy commandments;' not walk, but run: it is an allusion to a cart-wheel, which crieth and complaineth under a small burden, being dry, but when a little oil is put into it, it runs merrily, and without noise; and if David could say thus in his time, how much more should we that live in these gospel-times, when grace in greater measure is effused, and poured out? 'By the grace of Christ (should we say) we will walk, and run, and fly in the way of his commandments.'

Use. 1. Well, then, is the Christian religion and the practice of it, full of sweetness, easiness, and pleasantness? In the first place for conviction, this may take away the cavils of some men: what is said in way of objection, I shall reduce to these particulars.

1. They object, that Christ himself confesseth it to be a yoke, and a burden; but to that we answer, with Christ, *His yoke is easy, and his burden is light.* Certainly there are burdens which grieve not the bearers at all, as the burden of feathers upon a bird's back; it is nothing grievous to her, but rather bears her up; and a burden of gold and jewels upon a man's back (supposing it the reward of his porterage, and the hire of his labour) it is nothing grievous to him, but rather cheers him up. Men, brethren, and Fathers, if we will but come and close with Christ, the Spirit is given to enable us, and heaven is promised to encourage us; the one gives power, and the other stirs up our affections, and how then should we complain of pressure? O, it is a sweet burden! sweetned by his grace, and sweetned by his Spirit, and sweetned by a principle of love, Psal. cxix. 97, 174. *O how love I thy law?* and sweetned by a principle of delight, *Thy law is my delight;* and sweetned with a promise of reward, Psal. xix. 11. *In keeping of thy commandments there is great reward.*

2. They object, We feel no such thing; you tell us of sweetness, easiness, pleasantness; but if we must speak out our own experiences, Mal. i. 13. *O what a weariness is it?* Amos viii. 5. *When will the new moon be gone, that we may sell corn? And the sabbath, that we may set forth wheat?* We feel a sweetness in these present enjoyments of the world; but as for holiness, grace, religion, the discipline of Christ, we wonder where the sweetness is: we can find no such secret golden mines in these spiritual diggings.

I answer, 1. This indeed is the speech of carnal and profane men; they feel no sweetness, easiness, pleasantness in God's ways, 1 Cor. ii. 14, 15. *The natural man receiveth not the things of the Spirit of God, for they are foolishness unto him, neither can he know them, because they are spiritually discerned: but he that is spiritual judgeth or discerneth all things.* Poor souls! till God speak to your hearts, you cannot understand this hidden manna: it is observed that God never sent the pleasant manna unto Israel so long as their flour and bread of Egypt lasted, so never will you taste how good the Lord is, so long as you doat on sin and vanity.

2. Though you feel not these things for the present, yet in time you may do; yea, certainly, if you belong to God, in time you will do; O but when? you will say, When? I answer, The first taste of this sweetness, is usually at the first taking of Christ's yoke upon us: as merchants desirous to sell their wares, are content, in the first place, to let you see, and handle, and taste, thereby to induce you to buy: so Jesus Christ, willing (as it were) to part with heaven, he is content, in the first place, to impart a certain taste before hand, and to sweeten the ways of Godliness unto us, Hosea ii. 14. *Behold, I will allure her* (saith God) *and bring her into the wilderness, and speak comfortably unto her.* What is it that God means by alluring of his people? I answer, It contains these things, As,

1. A discovery of the beauty of holiness; when God first effectually calls the soul home to himself, he sets open the beauty of his service: naturally the heart is possessed with much prejudice against the ways of religion. Oh! what a strict rule is this to carnal men, to pull out their right eyes, to cut off their right hands, to hate father and mother, and wife, and lands, and life for the name of Christ,

to cross their own desires, to deny their own selves, to mortify their earthly members, to follow the Lamb through evil report and good report, thro' afflictions, and persecutions, and manifold temptations whithersoever he goeth; to war with principalities, and powers, and spiritual wickednesses in high places? And hence it is, that the Lord is forced to set forth the ways of Christ as beautiful, even under crosses and afflictions: thus, when the watchmen smote the church, and wounded her, and took away her vail, yet she still acknowledged Christ (for whose sake she suffered) to be *white and ruddy, the fairest of ten thousands*, Cant. v. 7, 10. Christ sets forth himself and his ways in all the grace, and goodness, and beauty, and sweetness, and loveliness that possibly may be; *q. d.* By these I will allure them that belong unto me.

2. An out-bidding of all the temptations of other lovers; before Christ come, souls go a whoring from Christ, their hearts are allured by other lovers; the world, the flesh, and the devil come in, and they proffer souls such and such contentments; but when Christ comes, he deals with souls in a more powerful way, and he out-bids all their former lovers, *q. d.* Did their lovers proffer them comfort? I will bid more comfort. Did their lovers proffer gain? I will bid more gain. Did their lovers proffer honour and respect? I will out-bid them in that also. And indeed, then hath the gospel a true, and full, and gracious work upon the heart, when it yields to the proffers of the gospel, as finding that all that the world can bid is now out-bidden. You know, when one comes to offer so much for a commodity, and another out-bids him, he carries it away; so when the world, and lust, and sin proffers to the soul such and such contents, then comes Christ and out-bids all, and so the bargain is made up, and Christ carries the heart away: sinners! it may be as yet you feel none of these things, but in time you may do, and in the mean time you see here is a word for it, *Behold, I will allure her*, &c.

3. They object, the saints themselves feel no such things for ought appears to the world; whose spirits are more heavy and sad; as it is said of Christ himself, that he never laughed; and as David said of himself, Psalm lxii. 5. 'Why art 'thou cast down, O my soul, and why art thou 'disquieted within me?' So it may be said of some Christians, if they are strict, that they are seldom merry, or pleasant.

But I answer,———1. Christians that keep indeed close to the rule, are for the most part serious, and the world may suppose them as sad.

2. It may be, they are not in their element in the acts of religion, and therefore they cannot express their spiritual chearfulness; a fish cannot delight itself on earth, but when it is in the water; a bird doth not sing on the ground, but when it is got up into the air; God's people cannot rejoice in sin, as drunkards and revellers do, but when their hearts are in religious exercises, and in communion with God, they are merry and pleasant.

3. It may be, they are in such company as may make them sad: the men of the world object against saints, that they are heavy, and sour, and melancholy men, but, in the mean time, they consider not that their swearing, reviling, and dishonouring of God hath made them so pensive. Why, sinners; your carriage grieves the very Spirit of God, *You grieve God at the heart*, as it is expressed, Gen. vi. 6. And therefore, no wonder if the Godly cannot rejoice in your sinful society; you are the cause of their sadness: but admit them once into the company and fellowship of the saints, and they know how to be joyful.

4. If it be so, that usually they are pensive and sad, it is not because of religion, but because they are not more religious; because they find so much want of Godliness in their own hearts. This was the case of Paul's heaviness, Romans vii. 24. ' O wretched man that I am, who shall deliver ' me from this body of death?' And yet know, that all these sadnesses are true preparatives of joy: and therefore in the very next words, the apostle breaks out into that sweet doxology, *I thank God through Jesus Christ our Lord*. Never was true sorrow for sin, but it ended in rejoicings and praises, and thanksgiving to God.

Why then be convinced, ah, deceived souls; say not that God is an hard master, reaping where he sowed not, and gathering where he strawed not; say not that his ways are tedious, and irksome, and uncomfortable ways; but rather taste, and see, and try how good the Lord is; experience the truth of these words, *My yoke is easy, and my burden is light*; what is lighter than that

E e

bur-

burden, which, instead of burdening, cheers up the party on which it is laid? just like those burdens of Cinnamon that refresh those that carry them through the deep sands of Arabia. A holy divine, once endeavouring to convince men of the sweetness and pleasantness of God's ways by his own experiences, 'I call heaven and earth to record '*(faith he)* that these things are truths of God; 'they are not notions or conceits, but certain rea- 'lities:' another flies somewhat higher, ' If men 'would in earnest *(says he)* abandon the devil's 'service, and give up their names to Christ in truth, 'and try, I dare assure them, in the word of life 'and truth, they would not exchange the saddest 'hour of all their life afterward with the prime 'and flower of all their former sensual pleasures, 'might they have ten thousand worlds to boot; 'her ways are ways of pleasure,' saith Solomon, Prov. iii. 17.

Use 2. You that are so convinced, I beseech you carry on the work of God sweetly, comfortably, and with delight: the Psalmist says, Psal. i. 2, 3. ' Blessed is the man that delights in the law of ' the Lord.' And Psalm cxix. 1. ' Blessed are the ' undefiled in the way, who walk chearfully in the ' law of the Lord. And blessed is the man that ' delighteth greatly in his law.' And it was written upon the heart of Christ, Psalm xl. 8. ' I de- ' light to do thy will, O my God, yea, thy law ' is within my heart;' as God loves a cheerful giver, so a cheerful server, *Come, take my yoke upon you*, saith Christ, *for my yoke is easy*; it is not an iron yoke of bondage, but a chain of heavenly pearls to adorn your souls.

Quest. 1. Oh, but how should we carry on the work, the yoke, the duty, the practice of piety, and of religion pleasantly? I answer,

Ans. 1. Be sure to keep the heart right and upright within; let all we do be in sincerity, and let all we are, in respect to the inner man, be at peace within: sense and reason can tell us, that, according to the temper within, so there is the relishing of things without: he that acts in sincerity, and hath peace within, can easily go through the duties that are required without, with joy and comfort.

2. Exercise faith in the work and office of the Holy Ghost; I mean that work and office to which the Holy Ghost is designed by the Father and the Son; both to help his people, and to be the comforter of his people. 1. The holy Ghost is designed to help his people, Rom. viii. 26. *Likewise the Spirit helpeth our infirmities*; the word in the original, [*sunanplamthetai*] doth properly imply such an help, as when another man of strength and ability steppeth in, to sustain the burden that lieth upon weak shoulders; why, this makes Christ's burden light: we do not bear all the weight, for the Holy Ghost puts under his shoulder. 2. The Holy Ghost is designed to comfort his people. Christ calls him *the Spirit, the Comforter*, John xiv. 26. and xv. 26. because he brings in a kind of spiritual joy and spiritual comfort. Mark, it is not a natural but a spiritual joy: Oh! what a vast difference is there betwixt the comforts of a carnal heart and the comforts of the godly? The one comes from a little meat, or drink, or creature-vanity; but the other comes from the exercise of faith, about the office of the Holy Ghost, who is designed to this work. Surely here is the way to carry on duty sweetly and comfortably, and with delight, (*i. e.*) to be in the exercise of faith on the work and office of the holy Ghost, as he is our helper and comforter. 1 Pet. ii. 9.

3. Understand what is in Christian religion, and in the practice of it to cause delight. As,——

1. In every duty and gracious acting of it there is more of the glory of God than in the whole frame of heaven and earth besides; *Herein is my Father glorified that you bear much fruit*, John xv. 8. Oh, if we but thus looked at the profession and practice of Christian religion, we could not but take pleasure in it.

2. In every duty and gracious acting of it, there is the seed of glory and eternal life; sometimes there breaks out in the very exercise of duty, a joy in the Holy Ghost, a foretaste of glory; but, howsoever, there is the seed of glory; and though the seed of glory be not seen, but lie, as it were, under ground dead and unseen, yet in time it will spring up unto eternal life: why, thus look at the practice of religion, and it will be sweeter to us than honey and the honey-comb; it will be more precious than gold, yea, than much fine gold.

Quest. 2. But how should we know the difference betwixt the natural pleasantness and this spiritual pleasantness in religion? I know Christians may put a lustre upon the ways of God by

their

their nature pleasantness and cheerfulness of spirit; but because we speak of a spiritual joy and comfort, and not of a natural, wherein lies the difference? I answer,——

Ans. 1. If it be a spiritual pleasantness, it will be serious, Eccl. ii. 2. *I have said of laughter, it is mad, and of mirth, what doth it?* There is much lightness and vanity in such breakings out of natural pleasantness; but, in pleasantness spiritual, all is grave, and sober, and exceeding serious.

2. If it be a spiritual pleasantness, it can stand with repentance and humiliation, and the fear of God, Psal. ii. 11. *Rejoice with trembling*, saith the Psalmist: spiritual rejoicing may consist with trembling: and *blessed is the man that feareth the Lord, that delighteth greatly in his commandments*, Psalm cxii. 1. The fear of God may consist with these spiritual delights in the commandments of God.

3. If it be spiritual pleasantness, it is our strength, Neh. viii. 10. *The joy of the Lord is our strength,* saith Nehemiah: nothing animates souls more in duties than joy doth; it carries on the soul more fully: it is as oil, that causeth the wheels of Christian practice to go on more freely: we may be naturally pleasant, and then coming to spiritual duties our hearts are dead, but if our pleasantness be spiritual, our hearts will be strengthened in the ways of God.

4. If it be a spiritual pleasantness, it will bear up the heart in want of all outward pleasantness, Hab. iii. 17, 18. 'Although the fig-tree shall not 'blossom, neither shall fruit be in the vines, the la-'bour of the olive shall fail, and the fields shall yield 'no meat, the flocks shall be cut off from the fold, 'and there shall be no herd in the stalls, yet I will 'rejoice in the Lord, I will joy in the God of my 'salvation.' When all is dark abroad in the world, the soul in this frame will rejoice in God alone; on the contrary, the soul that hath only a natural pleasantness of spirit, when affliction comes, it is all amort and down. I appeal to you that have the most delightful spirits, when you have friends and means, and all you like, you are jocund and merry, but when affliction comes, how quickly are your spirits down? Surely your pleasantness is not spiritual, for, if so, it would bear up your hearts joyful in affliction.

And now again *the passover, a feast of the Jews, was nigh*, John vi. 4. Our English annotations on these words can tell us, 'That this seems *to be the third passover after Christ's baptism.* [So Aretius, and others.] And therefore here I conclude the third year of Christ's ministry: there is but one year more before Christ's death, to which now I come, and to some passages therein, most observable, in reference to our souls salvation.

CHAP. IV. SECT. I.

Of the fourth year of Christ's ministry, and generally of his actions that year.

THIS was the last year of Christ's ministry, in which were thousands of passages: the evangelist John relates more of Christ this year than in all the former; and if I studied not brevity, we might dwell more in his actions for us this year, than hitherto we have done from the beginning of his ministry; now it was that he was transfigured, now it was that he instituted that sacrament called *the Lord's supper*, now it was that after supper he made his farewel sermon, rarely mixt of sadness and joys, and studded with mysteries as with emeralds; now it was that after sermon he blessed his disciples and prayed for them; and then having sung an hymn, he went out into the mount of Olives, where, in a garden he began his sufferings. On these passages I thought to have enlarged, but I see the book swells under my hands, and now that I am drawing nigh Christ's sufferings I shall only touch one point, which hitherto I have pretermitted, and is the most comprehensive of any passage I can touch.

Many questions are about the holiness, or righteousness, or obedience of Christ; as, whether it belongs to us? And, whether it be that matter of our justification? And, whether Christ was bound to observe the law of works, as a Mediator, or only as a mere man? And, whether we are not justified by the passive righteousness of Christ only? And seeing now we are discovering Christ's actions, in reference to our souls salvation, we cannot pass this main business, whereof much relates to Christ's life, as well as to his conception, or birth, or death, or sufferings.

SECT. II.

Of the distinctions, of several divisions of Christ's righteousness.

FOR the better understanding of Christ's righteousness, we usually distinguish, that Christ's righteousness is either that righteousness inherent in him, or performed by him; the righteousness performed by him, is either his fulfilling the commandments, or his satisfying the curse of the law. The same distinction is given by others, in these terms, Christ's righteousness is either his original conformity, or his active and passive obedience unto the law: his original conformity, is that gracious inherent disposition in Christ, from the first instant of his conception, whereby he was habitually conformable to the law; and this original righteousness answered for our original unrighteousness; his active obedience, is his doing legal obedience unto the command; and his passive obedience, is his suffering of punishment due unto us for our sins.——I shall yet a little farther enlarge this distinction of the righteousness of Christ, and give it in thus, viz. The righteousness of Christ, is either negative, (if I may speak so) or positive. By the negative, I understand the absence of all sins and vices forbidden in the law. By the positive, I mean both a presence of all virtues and duties required to the perfect fulfilling of the law, as also a voluntary suffering of the penalty, to satisfy the commination and curse of the law.

1. The negative righteousness, is that which we call the innocency of Christ: we read often in scriptures, that he was both blameless and spotless. 1. Blameless, free in himself from all imputation of sin: to this purpose Christ challenged the Jews, John viii. 46. *Which of you convinceth me of sin?* In all his life he was unblameable and unreprovable; and therefore now, towards the end of his life, he asks the people with whom he had conversed, *Which of you convinceth me of sin?* 2. Spotless, free from all infection of sin. Peter calls him, 1 Pet. i. 9. *A lamb without blemish and without spot.* And Paul, Heb. vii. 26. *An high priest, holy, harmless, and undefiled;* one who never did evil, nor spake evil; *he did no sin*, (saith the apostle) *neither was guile found in his mouth*, 2 Pet. ii. 22. One who never offended so much as in thought, but was absolutely, and in all respects [*choris hamartias*], *without all sin*, Heb. iv. 15.

2. The positive righteousness of Christ is twofold, his perfect fulfilling of all things commanded, and his perfect satisfying of the punishment threatned: the former is the holiness of Christ; this also is twofold, the holiness of his nature and the holiness of his life and conversation: the former is that we call his habitual righteousness; the latter is that we call his actual obedience. And thus much of the distinction of the righteousness of Christ.

SECT. III.

Of the holiness of Christ's nature.

NOW, in the first place, for the holiness of his nature, the Psalmist tells us, Psal. xlv. 2. *Thou art fairer than the children of men, and grace is poured into thy lips.* Which is all one with that description of Christ by the spouse, Cant. v. 10. *My beloved is white and ruddy, the chiefest of ten thousands.* As in the fairest beauty, there is a mixture of these two colours of white and ruddy, so in Christ there is a gracious mixture and compound of all the graces of the spirit: there is in him a sweet temper of gentleness, purity, righteousness, meekness, humility, and what not? Col. ii. 3. *In him are hid all the treasures of wisdom and knowledge:* and I may add of all other gifts and graces; not a grace but it was in Christ, and that in an higher way than in any saint in the world, and therefore he is called *fairer than all the children of men.* Observe, ' there was more habi' tual grace in Christ than ever was, or is, or shall ' be in all the elect, whether angels or men.' He received the spirit out of measure; there was in him as much as possibly could be in a creature, and more than in all other creatures whatsoever. As the sun is the prince of stars, as the husband is the head of the wife, as the lion is the king of beasts, so is the sun of righteousness, this head of the church, this lion of the tribe of Judah, *the chiefest of ten thousands.* If we look at any thing in heaven or earth, that we observe as eminently fair, by that is the Lord Jesus in respect of his inward beauty set forth in scriptures, ' He is the son ' of righteousness, the bright morning-star, the ' light of the world, the tree of life, the lily and
' the

' the rofe;' fairer than all the flowers of the field, than all the precious ftones of the earth, than all the lights in the firmament, than all the faints and angels in heaven.

You will fay, What's all this to us? Certainly much every way; the apoftle tells you, Rom. viii. 2. *That the law of the fpirit of life, which is in Chrift Jefus, hath freed me from the law of fin and death:* let us enquire into thefe words, [*the law of the Spirit of life*;] the fpirit of life is here put for life as elfewhere, *After three days and an half, the Spirit of life coming from God fhall enter into them,* Rev. xi. 11. Now, life is that whereby a thing acteth and moveth itfelf, and it is the caufe and beginning of action and motion: and this *Spirit of life,* or life itfelf, being here applied to Chrift, it is that in Chrift, which is the beginning and caufe of all his holy actions, and what was that but his original holinefs, or the holinefs of his human nature; but why is the holinefs of Chrift's nature called *the Spirit of life?* I anfwer, 1. Becaufe it was infufed into his manhood by the Spirit of God, *The Holy Ghoft fhall come upon thee,*——*therefore alfo that holy thing which fhall be born of thee fhall be called the Son of God,* Luke i. 35. 2. Becaufe it is a moft exact, and abfolute, and perfect holinefs; the fcripture-phrafe fetting out the things in perfection or fulnefs, ufually adds the word fpirit unto them; as the fpirit of pride, the Spirit of truth, and the fpirit of error; fo then the meaning of the Spirit of life is all one with the moft abfolute and moft perfect purity and holinefs of the nature of Chrift. It is briefly as if the apoftle had faid, The law of the Spirit of life, or the power of the moft abfolute and perfect holinefs of the nature of Chrift, *hath freed me from the law of fin and death*; hath acquitted me from the power of my finful nature, and from the power of death due to me, in refpect of my finful and corrupt nature. We might draw from hence this condition, 'That——the benefit of
' Chrift's habitual righteoufnefs infufed at his firft
' conception, is imputed to believers to their juf-
' tification.' As the obedience of his life, and the merit of his death, fo the holinefs infufed at his very conception, hath its influence into our juftification: it is by the obedience of his life, that we are accounted actually holy, and by the purity of his conception, (or having grace) that we are accounted perfonally holy. But I muft not ftay here; thus much of the holinefs of Chrift's nature.

SECT. IV.

Of the holinefs of Chrift's living.

2. FOR the holinefs of Chrift's life, the apoftle tells us, 'That by the obedience of
' one, many fhall be made righteous,' Rom. v. 19. Here's the obedience of Chrift, and its influence on us. 1. The obedience of Chrift, is that whereby he continued in all things written in the book of the law to do them: obferve, Chrift's life was a vifible commentary on God's law. For proof, Mat. v. 17. *Think not that I am come to deftroy the law, or the prophets,* (faith Chrift) *but to fulfil them,* And, John viii. 29. *The Father hath not left me,* (faith Chrift) *for I do always thofe things that pleafe him.* Hence Chrift in the fcripture is called, Acts iii. 14. *Holy and juft,* and, Acts ii. 27. *The holy One,* Dan. ix. 24. *The moft holy.* By his actual holinefs Chrift fulfilled in act every branch of the law of God: he walked in all the commandments of God; he performed perfectly, both in thought, word and deed, whatfoever the law of the Lord required.——I do not, cannot limit this obedience of Chrift to this laft year of his miniftry, for his whole life was a perpetual courfe of obedience; he was obedient unto death, faith the apoftle, [*mechri thanatou*] *even until his death,* Phil. ii. 8. And yet becaufe we read moft of his holy actions this year, and that this was the year wherein both his active and paffive obedience did moft eminently fhine and break forth; the year wherein he drew up all the difperfions of his precepts, and caft them into actions, as into fums total; therefore now I handle it, and I fhall make it out by the paffages following, only in this one year. As,——

1. Now he difcovered his charity in feeding the hungry, as at once five thoufand men, with five loaves and two fifhes, John vi. 9, 10, 11. And, at another time, four thoufand men, with feven loaves and a few fmall fifhes, Matth. xv. 32.

2. Now he difcovered his felf-denial and contempt of the world, in flying the offers of a kingdom when the people were convinced that he was

the

the Messiah, from that miracle of feeding five thousand men with five loaves, presently they would needs make him a king; but he that left his Father's kingdom for us, he fled from the offers of a crown and kingdom from them, as from an enemy; 'When Jesus perceived that they would come and take him by force, to make him a king, he departed again into a mountain himself alone,' John vi. 15.

Now he discovered his mercy, in healing the woman's daughter that had an unclean spirit; the woman was a Greek, a Syrophenician by nation; and, in that respect, Christ called her *a dog*, Mark vii. 26, 27. And yet Christ gave her the desire of her soul; O the rich mercy of Christ, that he would admit a dog to his kingdom! O grace! O mercy! that Christ should black his fair hands in washing foul and defiled dogs! what a motion of free mercy was this, that Christ should lay his fair, spotless, and chaste love upon the black, defiled, and whorish souls? O what a favour, that Christ maketh the leopard and Ethiopian white for heaven?

4. 'Now he discovered his bounty, in giving the *keys of the kingdom of heaven*, Matth. xvi. 19. to the apostles, and to their successors: this was a power which he had never communicated before; it was a gift greater than the great charter of nature, and the donative of the whole creation. Indeed, at first God gave unto man, Gen. i. 26. *a dominion over the fish of the sea, and over the fowl of the air, and over the cattle, and over the earth*; but till now, heaven itself was never subordinate to human ministration; herein was the acting of Christ's bounty, he gives unto his ministers the keys of heaven, that ' whatsoever they shall bind 'on earth, shall be bound in heaven, and whatsoever they shall loose on earth, shall be loosed 'in heaven.'

5. Now he discovered his patience in suffering all injuries: from hence forward to the death of Jesus we must reckon his days like the vigils, or eves of his passion; for now he began, and often did ingeminate those sad predictions of the usage he should shortly find, that he should be *rejected of the elders, and chief priests, and scribes, and suffer many things at Jerusalem, and be killed, and be raised up the third day*, Matth. xvi. 21. And, in the mean time, he suffers both in word and deed: they call him a glutton, a drunkard, a deceiver, a madman, a Samaritan, and one possessed with a devil; sometimes they take up stones to stone him, and sometimes they lead him to an hill, thinking to throw him headlong; and all this he suffered with patience; yea, with much patience he possessed his soul.

6. Now he discovered his glory, in being transfigured on the mount: however, the person of Christ was usually depressed with poverty, disgrace, ignominy; so that neither Jews nor Gentiles, nor the apostles themselves, could at first discern the brightness of his divinity; yet now Christ gave an excellent probation of that great glory, which in due time must be revealed to all the saints, Luke ix 28, 29, 30, 31. *For taking with him, Peter, James and John, he went up into the mountain to pray, and while he prayed, he was transfigured before them, and his face did shine like the sun, and his garments were white and glistering; and there appeared talking with him Moses and Elias, speaking of the decease which he should accomplish at Jerusalem:* the embassy of Christ's death was delivered in forms of glory, that so the excellency of the reward might be represented together with the sharpness of his sufferings: now, if ever whilst he was upon earth, was the beauty of Christ seen at height, Peter saw it, and was so ravished at the sight, that he talked he knew not what: in respect of this glorious beauty, his face is said to *shine like the sun*. I cannot think but his shining exceeded sun, moon and stars; but the sun is the brightest thing we know, and therefore it is spoken to our capacity: Here's one strain of exaltation, though mostly all Christ's life was but a state of humiliation: it learns us to be content with, yea, to expect humiliation, little exaltation here: we may have a taste, but no continued comforts till we come to heaven.

7. Now he discovered his meekness, *in riding upon an ass, and a colt, the foal of an ass*, Mat. xxi. 5. which was according to the prophecy; *Behold, thy king cometh unto thee, meek*; and especially in rebuking the furious, intemperate zeal of James and John, who would fain have called for fire from heaven, to have consumed the inhabitants of a little village, who refused to give Christ entertainment. Ah, saith Christ, Luke ix. 55. *Ye know not what spirits ye are of*. *q. d.* You must

learn

learn to distinguish the Spirit of Christianity from the Spirit of Elias; why, *Christ cometh with a purpose to seek, and to save mens lives, and not to destroy them,* Verse 56. It were rashness indeed to slay a man on some light displeasure, whose redemption cost the effusion of the dearest heart-blood of the Son of God. See here the meekness of Christ in opposition to the fury and anger of his own disciples.

8. Now he discovered his pity and compassion, in weeping over Jerusalem, Luke xix. 41, 42. *And when he was come near, he beheld the city, and wept over it, saying, If thou hadst known, even thou,* &c. We read of Joseph, that there was in him such a brotherly and natural compassion, that *his bowels yearned upon his brethren,* Gen. xliii. 30. *and he could not refrain himself before all them that stood by him,* Gen. xlv. 1. His love was like an hot furnace. Now Jesus Christ hath the same heart and bowels of a man, and I conceive, as Christ was a man void of sin, so the acts of natural virtues, (as to pity the afflicted, to compassionate the distressed) were stronger in him than possibly they could be in any other man. Sin blunteth natural faculties, especially such as incline to laudable and good acts, as to love, and pity, and compassionate the miserable; in this respect, Joseph was nothing to Christ, when Christ saw Jerusalem, he wept, and wept; his compassion strangled and inclosed within him, it must needs break out; it may be in some measure it eased Christ's mind, that his bowels of mercy found a vent: we read that pity kept within God's bowels, pains his very heart, so that it must needs come out. Hos. xi. 8. *Mine heart is turned within me, my repentings are kindled together.*

9. Now he discovered his humility in washing his disciples feet, John xiii. 4, 5. *Supper being ended, he laid aside his garments, and took a towel, and girded himself, and poured water into a bason, and began to wash his disciples feet, and to wipe them with the towel wherewith he was girded.* In this ceremony, and in the discourses following, he instructs them in the doctrine of humility; yea, he imprints the lesson in lasting characters, by making it symbolical. But, why should he wash their feet, rather than their hands or heads? I answer, It is probable on this account, that he might have the opportunity of a more humble posture. See how he lays every thing aside, that he may serve his servants: heaven stoops to earth, one abyss call on another, the miseries of man which were next to infinite, are excelled by a mercy equal to the immensity of God. It is storied of one Guercius, that, upon the consideration of this humility of Christ in washing his disciples feet, he cried out, 'Thou hast overcome me, O Lord, thou hast overcome my pride, this example hath mastered ' me.'

10. Now he discovered his obedience to his Father, in preaching the gospel up and down. He foresaw that the night drew on in which no man could work, and therefore now he hastened to do his Father's business, now he pours out whole cataracts of holy lessons: and still the people drew water from this fountain, which streamed out in continual emanations; he added wave to wave, and precept to precept; and at last he gave them his farewel sermon, which is the most spiritual and comfortable piece that ever was uttered: it comprehends the intentions of his departure to prepare places for his saints in heaven; and in the mean while he would send them the Holy Ghost, to supply his room, to furnish them with proportionable comforts, to enable them with gifts, to lead them into all truth, and to abide with them for ever In conclusion of all, he gave them his blessing, and prayed for them, and then, having sung an hymn, he goes away, and prepares for his sufferings.

2. Hitherto of the obedience of Christ; what was it but *a visible commentary of God's law?* But now for its influence on us, Rom. v. 19. *By the obedience of one many shall be made righteous.* Observe, 'The righteousness of the law fulfilled, and ' fully accomplished in the person of Christ, is as ' truly ours, if we believe in Christ, as if it were ' in ourselves, or as if the law had been fulfilled in ' our own persons.' Thus *Christ is the end of the law* (saith the apostle) *for righteousness to every one that believeth,* Rom. x. 4. Christ hath not only determined, and put an end to the ceremonial law, but he is also the end of the moral law, he hath perfectly in his own person accomplished the moral law, and that not for himself, but for righteousness to every one, that truly believes in him. Rom. viii. 4. *And God sent his Son,—that the righteousness of the law might be fulfilled in us;* these words, in us, must trouble interpreters; for though we believe, yet

yet we are imperfectly holy: how then should the law be fulfilled in us? But 'tis answered, That the righteousness of the law is fulfilled in us, not by infusion, or sanctification, but by imputation, and application; (i.e.) in our nature which Christ took upon him; it was in Christ, and is imputed unto us, and so the righteousness of the law is fulfilled in us. It is well observed of Beza, that the apostle saith not, *That the righteousness of the law might be fulfilled by us, or of us, or by any righteousness inherent in our own persons, but in us, because it is to be found in Christ, whose members we are, who walk not after the flesh but after the Spirit.* The point is sweet, but I cannot stay on it. In reference to what I have spoken of the righteousness of Christ, habitual and actual, a great controversy is then in our days; of which in the next sections.

SECT. V.

Of the controversy, Whether we are not justified by the passive righteousness of Christ only, without any consideration had to the righteousness of Christ, either inherent in him, or performed by him?

FOR my part, I am for the negative, upon these well known grounds.

Arg. 1. By what alone the law is not fully satisfied, by that alone we are not justified; but by the passive obedience of Christ alone, the law is not fully satisfied: therefore by his passive obedience only we are not justified. Thus far I grant that the law is fully satisfied by his passive obedience, in respect of the penalty therein threatned, but not in respect of the commandment, for the obtaining of the blessedness therein promised; and the righteousness of the law is thus described, that *the man which doth these things shall live by them,* Rom. x. 5.

Against this are divers exceptions of the adversaries, as, 1. That the law is satisfied either by doing that which is commanded, or by suffering the punishment which is threatned. *Ans.* It is true, in respect of the penal statutes of men, but not in respect of the commandments of God, in which there is not only a penalty threatned, but a blessedness promised: if man had continued in his integrity, the law might have been satisfied by obedience only; but being fallen into a state of disobedience, two things are necessarily required to the fulfilling of the law, (i.e.) The bearing of the penalty, and the performing of the command, the one to escape hell, and the other to obtain heaven. 2. They except, That whosoever are freed from hell, are also admitted to heaven. *Ans.* The reason thereof is, because Christ, who did bear the punishment, to free us from hell, did also fulfil the commands to bring us to heaven; but howsoever these two benefits of Christ do always concur in the party justified, as the causes thereof concurred in Christ, who not only did both obey and suffer, but in obeying suffered, and in suffering obeyed; yet both the causes between themselves, and the effects between themselves, are carefully to be distinguished; for as it is one thing to obey the commandment, and another thing to suffer the punishment; so it is one thing to be freed from hell by Christ his suffering the penalty, and another thing to be entitled to heaven, by Christ his fulfilling the commandments. 3. They except, That God is a most free agent, and therefore he may, if he will, justify men by the passive righteousness of Christ only, without fulfilling of the law. *Ans.* What God may do, if he will, I will not dispute, but sure I am, that he justifieth men according to his will revealed in his word; and there we find, that, as we are justified from our sins by the blood of Christ, so also we are made just by the active (though not only by the active) obedience of Christ, Rom. v. 19. *For as by one man's disobedience many were made sinners, so by the obedience of one shall many be made righteous.* And, Rom. v. 10. *If when we were enemies, we were reconciled to God, by the death of his Son, much more being reconciled, we shall be saved by his life;* by his life, which he lived before his death, and by his life which he lived, and doth live, after his death; by the acts of his life, before his death, meritoriously, and by the acts of his life after his death (as by his resurrection, ascension, session, and intercession) effectually, 1 Cor. i. 30. *Christ is made unto us of God,* (saith the apostle) *both redemption and righteousness,* redemption, to deliver us from sin; and righteousness, *To bring in everlasting righteousness,* Dan. ix. 24. 4. They except, That if we are justified by Christ his fulfilling the law, then we are justified by a legal righteousness, but
we

we are not justified by a legal righteousness but by such a righteousness as without the law is revealed in the gospel. *Ans.* The same righteousness by which we are justified, is both legal and evangelical, in divers respects; legal in respect of Christ, who, being made under the law, that he might redeem us who were under the law, perfectly fulfilled the law for us; and evangelical, in respect of us, unto whom his fulfilling of the law is imputed. And herein stand both the agreement and difference betwixt the law and the gospel; the agreement, in that both require the perfect fulfilling of the law unto justification; the difference, in that the law requireth perfect obedience to be performed in our own persons, but the gospel accepts of perfect obedience performed by Christ, our surety, and imputed to us; and so it is all one as if it had been performed in our own persons.

2. If Christ, by his conformity to the law, fulfilled the law for us, then are we justified by his habitual and actual righteousness, and not merely by his passive; but Christ, by his conformity to the law, fulfilled the law for us, for so we read, 'He was born for us, Luke ii. 11. He was made 'subject to the law for us,' Gal. iv. 4, 5. and 'for our sakes he sanctified himself,' John xvii. 19. And for our sakes he did the will of God, 'Then 'said I, lo, I come to do thy will, O God; by the 'which will we are sanctified.' Heb. x. 7, 10.

Against this are divers exceptions; as, 1. That Christ obeyed the law, or conformed to the law (as need was) for himself, *Christ* (say they) *as he was man was bound to obey the law for himself.* Ans. This assertion detracts from the merit of his obedience, and from the dignity of his person. 1. From his merit, for if his obedience were of duty, then it were not * meritorious, Luke xvii. 10. And if this be true, then have we no title to heaven. 2. From the dignity of his person, as if he needed either to obey for himself, or by his obedience were any way bettered in himself; O that these men would remember that the person who did obey the law was, and is not only man, but God also. Christ fulfilled the law not only as man, but as God-man Mediator; and therefore as his blood was God's blood, so his obedience was the obedience of God, Acts xx. 28. *Who be-*

* *Debitum non est meritum.*

ing in the form of God, thought it no robbery to be equal with God, Phil. ii. 6, 8. *And being found in fashion as a man, he humbled himself, and became obedient unto death,* or until death. We find him here God-man; and from hence we conclude, that all the legal actions of Christ from his incarnation to his passion inclusively, were the actions of Christ, God-man, Mediator, and surety for us in a way of covenant; and consequently they were not performed of duty, nor for himself. 2. They except, That if Christ obeyed the law for us, that by his obedience we might be justified, then shall not we ourselves need to obey the law; but the consequent is absurd, therefore the antecedent. *Ans.* We need not to obey the law; to that end, that we may be justified thereby; for this is impossible to us by reason of the flesh, and therefore our Saviour fulfilled it for us; and yet it follows not, but that we may endeavour to obey the law for other ends; as to glorify God, to obey his will, to testify our thankfulness, to edify our brethren, to assure ourselves of our justification, and so to make our calling and election sure: in this study and practice of piety consisteth our new obedience, which we must therefore be careful to perform, though Christ, as to justification, hath performed it for us. 3. They except, That if Christ by his active obedience, fulfilled the law for us, and that so we are justified from all kind of sin both original and actual, then Christ's suffering was in vain. *Ans.* Christ's active obedience is an essential part of our justification, but not all our justification: the material cause of our justification is the whole course of the active and passive obedience of Christ, together with his original righteousness, or habitual conformity unto the law; I say, together with his original righteousness, because many authors express no more, but only Christ's active and passive obedience; but they are to be understood, as asserting his original righteousness implicitly, the act presupposing the habit. And here observe the difference betwixt the law in case of innocency, and the law in case of sin; the law in case of innocency required only doing, but the law in case of sin cannot be satisfied without doing and suffering, Gal. iii. 10. Gen. ii. 17. Original justice and active obedience was sufficient to justify man in his innocency, but not to justify man fallen; and therefore we do not separate these, the original, the actual, and the passive righteousness of Christ, as to the matter of justification, but we imply all.

Arg. 3. We read in scripture of two parts of justification, *viz.* The absolving of a believing sinner from the guilt of sin and death; and the accepting of a believing sinner as righteous unto life. The former is wrought by the sufferings of Christ imputed as a full satisfaction for sin, the other by imputation of Christ's perfect obedience, as a sufficient merit of eternal life: by the former we are freed from hell; by the latter we are intitled to the kingdom of heaven; of them both the apostle speaks, Rom. v. 9. *We are justified by his blood.* And verse 19. *we are made righteous by his obedience.* Our adversaries deny these two parts of justification, saying, That it consists wholly in remission of sin. But we reply, In every mutation though it be but relative, we must of necessity acknowledge to terms, *Terminum a quo, & terminum ad quem,* the denomination being commonly taken for the latter: as in justification there is a motion or mutation from sin to justice, (from which term justification hath its name) from a state of death and damnation, to a state of life and salvation: but if justification be nothing else but bare remission of sins, then is there in it only a not imputing of sin, but no acceptation as righteous; a freedom from hell, but no title to heaven.—— They say indeed, That to whom sin is not imputed, to them righteousness is imputed; and we grant that these things do always concur, but yet they are not to be confounded, for they differ in themselves, and in their causes, and in their effects. 1. In themselves, for it is one thing to be acquitted from the guilt of sin, and another thing to be made righteous, as we see daily in the pardon of malefactors. 2. In their causes, for the remission of sin is to be attributed to Christ's satisfactory sufferings, and acceptation as righteous unto life, to Christ's meritorious obedience. 3. In their effects, for by remission of sin we are freed from hell, and by imputation of Christ's obedience we have right unto heaven. I will not deny but that to Christ's habitual actual righteousness is sometimes attributed freedom from sin and hell, as in Rom. viii. 2. *The law of the Spirit of life, which is in Christ Jesus, hath made me free from the law of sin and death.* And on the contrary side, to Christ's passive obedience, is sometimes attributed a right unto heaven, as in Heb. ix. 15. *That by means of his death—they which are called might receive the promise of eternal inheritance;* but such places as these are to be understood by a *synechdoche,* which puts only one part of Christ's obedience for the whole obedience of Christ. But I must recall myself: my design in this work was not for controversies; I leave that to others: see Downham, Burges, Norton, &c. For my part I am sure, I have before me a more edifying work, which is to take a view of this Jesus, not only for intellection, but for devotion, and for the stirring up of our affections.

Thus far I have held forth Jesus in his life, or during the time of his ministry, till the last passover, and now was it, *That Jesus knew his hour was come, and that he should depart out of this world unto the Father,* John xiii. 1. but of that hereafter. Our next business is to direct you in the art or mystery, how we are to look unto Jesus in respect of his life.

CHAP. V. SECT. I.

Of knowing Jesus, as carrying on the great work of our salvation in this life.

FROM the object considered, that we may pass to the act.——

1. Let us know Jesus carrying on the great work of our salvation during his life. We have many books of the lives of men, of the lives of Heathens, of the lives of Christians, and by this we come to know the generations of old: oh, but above all, read over the life of Jesus, for that is worth thy knowing. To this purpose we have four evangelists, who, in blessed harmony, set forth his life; and to this purpose, we have *the book of the generation of Jesus Christ,* Matth. i. 1. Now these would be read over and over, Hosea vi. 3. *Then shall we know,* (saith the prophet) *if we follow on to know the Lord.* Ah, my soul! that which thou knewest of Christ already, it is but the least part of what thou art ignorant of, 1 Cor. xiii. 9. *We know but in part,* saith Paul of himself and others: the highest knowledge which the most illuminated saints have of Jesus Christ, is but defective and imperfect. Come then, and *fol-low*

low on to know the Lord: still enquire after him, imitate the angels, 1 Pet. ii. 12. who ever *desire to stoop down, and to pry into the* actings of Christ for us men, and for our salvation; it is their study, yea, it is their delight and recreation: Paul seemed to imitate them, when he said, 1 Cor. ii. 2. *I determined not to know any thing among you but Jesus Christ.* If there be any thing in the world worth the knowing, this is it. And for the better knowledge, that it may not be confused, but distinct, 1. Study over those passages in the first year of Christ's ministry; as the preaching of John, the baptism of Christ, his fasting and temptation in the wilderness, his first manifestation by his several witnesses, his whipping of the buyers and sellers out of the temple. 2. Study over those passages in the second year of Christ's ministry, as those several sermons that he preached; and because his miracles were as signals of his sermons, study the several miracles that he wrought: thou hast but a few instances in comparison of all his miracles, and yet how fruitful are they of spiritual instructions? 3. Study over those passages in the third year of Christ's ministry: as his commissionating his apostles to call sinners in, his readiness to receive them that would but come in; and his sweetening the ways of Christianity to them that are come in, *For his yoke is easy, and his burden is light.* 4. Study over those passages in the last year of his ministry: as the holiness of his nature, and the holiness of his life, which appeared especially in the exercises of his grace of charity, and self-denial, and mercy, and bounty, and meekness, and pity, and humility, and obedience. Oh, what rare matter is here for a Christian's study? Some have taken such pains in the study of these things, that they have wrote large volumes; men have been writing and preaching a thousand six hundred years of the life of Christ, and they are writing and preaching still. O my soul, if thou dost not write, yet study what is written; come with fixed thoughts, and beat thy brains on that blessed subject, that will make thee wise unto salvation; Paul accounted all things but *dung* or dogs meat, *for the excellency of the knowledge of Christ Jesus our Lord,* Phil. iii. 8. If thou didst truly understand the excellency of this knowledge, thou couldst not but account all things loss in comparison of this one necessary thing.

SECT. II.

Of considering Jesus in that respect.

2. LET us consider Jesus carrying on the great work of our salvation during his life. It is not enough to study and know, but we must muse and meditate, and consider of it till we bring it to some profitable issue. By meditating on Christ, we may feel or find a kind of insensible change, we know not how: as those that stand in the sun for other purposes, they find themselves lightened and heated; so in holy meditation our souls may be altered and changed in a secret insensible way; there is a virtue goes along with a serious meditation, a changing, transforming virtue; and therefore look farther, O my soul, have strong apprehensions of all those several passages of the life of Christ.

1. Consider the preaching of John Baptist: we talk of strictness, but shew me among all the ministers or saints of this age, such a pattern of sanctity and singular austerity; 'the sum of his sermons, *was repentance, and dereliction of sin, and bringing forth fruits worthy of amendment of life.* In the promoting of which doctrine, he was a severe reprehender of the Pharisees, and Sadducees, and Publicans, and soldiers, and indeed of all men, but especially of those that remained in their impenitency, for against them he denounced judgment and fire unquenchable: oh! he had an excellent zeal, and a vehement spirit in preaching: and the best commentary upon all his sermons was his own life; he was clothed in camels hair, his meat was locusts and wild honey; he contemned the world, resisted temptations, despised to assume false honours to himself, and in all passages was a rare example of self-denial and mortification; and by this means he made an excellent and apt preparation for the Lord's coming. O my soul, that thou wouldest but sit a while under this preacher, or that thou wouldest but ruminate and chew the cud; think over his sermons of *repentance, and righteousness, and temperance, and of the judgment to come*; and see what influence they have. When Paul preached such a sermon to Felix, it is said, that *he trembled,* Acts xxiv. 25. A sermon of the *chaff's burning with unquenchable fire,* is enough to make thy heart tremble, if power-

fully

fully delivered and affectionately received; but see what effect doth it work on thy heart and life? Dost thou feel in thee a spirit of mortification? Dost thou, with the Baptist, die to the world? Dost thou deny thy will of all its natural sinful desires? Dost thou abstain from pleasures and sensual complacencies, that the flesh being subdued to the spirit, both may join in the service of God? Dost thou kill the lusts of the flesh by taking away the fuel and incentives of lusts? This is the work of meditation: it first employs the understanding in consideration of things, and then the will in reception of things, and both these in order to grace and a pious conversation. This meditation, which determines in notions or speculations of knowledge, is like the winter sun that shines, but warms not. O my soul, consider on the preaching of this prodromus or forerunner of Christ, till thou feelest this consideration to have some warmth in thy heart, and influence on thy soul, in order to holiness, self-denial and mortification.

2. Consider of the baptism of Christ; he that never sinned was made sin for us, and so it was proper enough for Christ to take upon him the sacrament of sinners, or of repentance for sin; but especially was he baptized, that, in that symbol he might purify our nature, whose stains and guilt he had undertaken. Consider of this, O my soul, and bring it home to thyself: surely every soul that lives the life of grace, *is born of water and the spirit*; and to this purpose, Christ, who is our life, went down into the waters of baptism, that we who descend after him, might find the effects of it, as, pardon of sin, adoption unto the covenant of grace, and holiness of life. Had not Christ been baptized, what virtue had there been in our baptism? As *it became him to fulfil all righteousness*, Matth. iii. 15. And therefore he must needs be baptized; so he fulfilled it not for himself but for us: Christ's obedience in fulfilling the law, is imputed to all that believe unto righteousness, as if themselves had fulfilled, so that he was baptized for us, and the virtue of his baptism is derived unto us. O the sweets of this meditation! Christ was baptized, and, when baptized, *the heavens were opened, and the Holy Ghost descended*, and a voice from heaven proclaimed him to be the *Son of God*, and one, *in whom* the Father was *well pleased*; and the same ointment that was cast upon the head of our high priest, went unto his beard, and thence fell to the borders of his garment; for, as Christ our head felt those effects in manifestation, so through Christ do we believe the like effects in our very baptism: the heavens then, (as it were) opened unto us, and the Holy Ghost then descended upon us, and then were we consigned to the inheritance of sons, in whom the Father, through the Son, is also well pleased. O my soul, what a blessing is there in the baptism of Christ? And how mayest thou suck and be satisfied if thou wilt put thy meditation to the right use? The baptism of Christ is a field of flowers, wherein is a world of privileges, as justification, adoption, regeneration, sanctification, glorification. O then fix thy soul, at least on some of these flowers, and leave them not without carrying some honey away with thee: if thou art in Christ, thou art baptized into his death, and baptized into his baptism; thou partakest of the fruit and efficacy, both of his death, and life, and baptism, and all.

3. Consider the fasting and temptation of Christ in the wilderness. Now, we see what manner of adversary we have, how he fights, how he is resisted, how overcome; in one assault, Satan moves Christ to doubt of his Father's providence, in another, to presume on his Father's protection; and when neither diffidence nor presumption can fasten upon Christ, he shall be tried with honour: and thus he deals with us, if he cannot drive us down to despair, he labours to lift us up to presumption; and if neither of these prevail, then he brings out pleasures, profits, honours, temptations on the right-hand, which are indeed most dangerous. O my soul, whilst thou art in this warfare, here's thy condition; temptations, like waves, break one on the neck of another: if the devil was so busy with Christ, how shouldest thou hope to be free? How mayest thou account, that the repulse of one temptation will but invite to another? Well, but here's thy comfort, thou hast such a Saviour, Heb iv. 15, 16. *As was in all things tempted in like sort, y t without sin; how boldly therefore mayest thou go to the throne of grace to receive mercy, and to find grace to help in time of need?* Christ was tempted that he might succour them that are tempted: never art thou tempted, O my soul, but Christ is with thee in the temptation: he hath sent his Spirit into thy heart to make intercession for thee there,

and

and he himself is in heaven, making intercession and praying for thee there; yea, his own experience of temptations hath so wrought it in his heart, that his love and mercy is most of all at work when thou art tempted most. As dear parents are ever tender of their children, but then especially when they are sick and weak, and out of frame; so, though Christ be always tender of his people, yet then especially when their souls are sick and under a temptation. Oh, then his bowels yearn over them indeed.

4. Consider Christ's first manifestations by his several witnesses; we have heard of his witnesses from heaven, the Father, Son, and Holy Ghost, and of his witnesses on earth, the baptist, his disciples, and the works that he did in his Father's name; and all these witnesses being lively held forth in the preaching of the gospel, they are witnesses to us; even to this day is Christ manifested to us; yea, and if we are Christ's, even to this day is Christ manifested within us. O my soul, consider this above all the rest! O! it is this manifestation within that concerns thee most, Gal. iv. 6. *Because ye are sons, God hath sent forth the Spirit of his Son into your hearts.* If Christ be not manifested in thy heart by his blessed Spirit, thou art no son of God; and therefore the apostle puts thee seriously on this trial, 2 Cor. xiii. 5. *Examine yourselves whether ye be in the faith; prove yourselves; know ye not your ownselves, how that Christ Jesus is in you, except ye be reprobates?* Is Christ manifested in thee; Surely this is more than Christ manifested to thee; the bare history is the manifestation of Christ unto thee; but there's a mystery in the inward manifestation. The apostle speaking of the saints, he adds, Col. i. 27. *To whom God would make known what is the riches of the glory of this mystery among the Gentiles, which is, Christ in you the hope of glory.* Oh the riches of the glory of this mystery! consider it, O my soul, God might have shut thee up in blindness with the world, or he might only have given thee parts and gifts; or at most he might have enlightered thy reason, to have taken in the outward notions of the gospel: but hath he revealed Christ in thee! hath he let thee see into the wonders of his glory? Hath he given thee the light of his glory within? Oh, this argues the witness of Christ's Spirit! this only the experimental Christian feels.

Chrysostome, sometimes speaking of the more hidden and choice principles of Christianity, he useth this phrase, *Sciunt initiati quid dico, Those that are initiated or admitted into our mysteries, know what I mean:* So may the ministers of Christ, preaching of these inward manifestations, say, *Sciunt initiati, &c.* It is only the spiritual men can know these things, for they are spiritually discerned. O my soul, meditate on this until thou feelest God's Spirit working in thy spirit these inward, gracious, glorious manifestations. *It is Christ in thee is the hope of glory.*

5. Consider Christ's whipping the buyers and sellers out of the temple. Sometimes, O my soul, thou art in secret, and sometimes thou art in the assemblies of God's people; and if thou art in duty, wheresoever thou art, consider the especial presence of Christ; and what is that but the presence of his Spirit, and the presence of his angels? 1. The presence of his Spirit; this we know by his working in us; certainly the Spirit doth not only hover over us, but worketh in us: how in us? I answer, by his quickning, feeding, cherishing, healing, mollifying, melting, comforting. In this manner he works in us when we are in ordinances. Why now is he (I hope) riding with triumphing in the midst of the assembly; now is he in his chariot; in his throne; in the hearts of his people; and therefore away, away, with all buyers and sellers out of that temple of the Holy Ghost.— 2. The presence of Christ is the presence of his angels; as a king is where his court is, so is Christ, the King of kings, especially present where his blessed angels pitch their tents. And the presence of angels is worthy (O my soul) of thy consideration. Certainly they are ministering spirits, that have a work to do upon thy inward man: I grant the Spirit of Christ can only enlighten the understanding, and determine the will effectually; it is he only can bend and turn, and form the mind which way soever he pleaseth; but the angels can speak also to thy spiritual parts; and though the spirit only determine, yet their speaking carries a power with it.

By way of digression, it is a fine skill to know how the angels can speak to us, and how we may know when they speak, and how we may discern what is spoken by the immediate inspiration of the Spirit, and what by the mediation of the angels.

1. How do the angels speak to us? We must

conceive if we understand this, 1. That the images, or phantasms of things received by the outward senses, are kept and preserved by the inward senses, as the species of sounds, of shapes, or whatsoever else. 2. That the images or phantasms so kept, may be so moved by our spirits, or humours, or some extrinsical things, as that they may move the fancy, and provoke it to represent, and conceive such things as neither appear, nor are at that time perceived by any outward sense at all. This appears, 1. In our ordinary course, as we can sit in the dark, where we hear and see nothing, and yet there we can multiply a fancy *in infinitum*, by an act of our own will. 2. This appears in our dreams, when though we hear or see nothing, yet the humour can stir up the memory of things, and provoke our fancies to the apprehension of this or that. 3. This appears also in sickness, which altering the body, and the humours, and so troubling the fancy, it begets strange fancies, and makes dreadful and fearful representations unto us. Now, this we must know, that whatsoever an inferior power can do, that a superior power can do much more; whatsoever an act of our own will, or natural dreams, or preternatural sickness can do, that the angels can do most orderly and efficaciously: they know exactly how the spirits and humours must be moved, the images or phantasms may be applied to such or such conceptions or apprehensions, most accommodate and fitted for the knowledge of what truth they would suggest. So that to me here is the difference between the converse of men and angels; men can speak to our understandings, by the mediation of our external senses, but angels go a nearer way to work, and speak to the internals first of all; they do no more but come into the memory, (the treasurer of all our phantasms and imaginations) and there make such and such compositions, even as they please; and then the understanding takes them off, and reads what is written, without more ado.

2. How may we know when the angels speak to us? I confess it is an hard question, and easily it cannot be solved; only some conjecture we may have, as in a case of evil; thou art in a way of sin, and near to fall into it, it may be on a sudden thou hearest within thee some contrary whisperings, which also are above the whisperings of a natural conscience, common to the wicked: or in case of good, it may be on a sudden thou hearest within thee, some independent supernatural persuasions and reasonings to this or that good, or to this or that object, which may more easily lead thee to choose the good. In these cases thou mayest conjecturely think that these whisperings or motions are of the angels of God. Boddin tells us a story of one who desired of God a guidance and assistance of an angel; and accordingly he had sensible manifestations of a spirit that assisted him, and followed him till his death; if in company he spake any unwary words, he was sure to be advertised and reproved for it by a dream in the night; or if he read any book that was not good, the angel would strike upon the book, to cause him to leave it.

3. But how should we discern what is spoken by the immediate inspiration of the Spirit, and what by the mediation of the angels? Here indeed we are at a stand, and therefore my best resolution is that of Calvin, ' That in such secrets we should ' keep one rule of modesty and sobriety,' and that ' we should neither speak, nor think, nor yet de- ' sire to know any other thing than such as hath ' been taught us by God's word.' I know not any great use there may be of this question, and therefore I shall not amuse myself in giving any account of it, only these remain as sure truths. 1. That the things communicated to our inward man, (I mean those inward motions and suggestions to holiness and obedience) are frequently and usually, by the administration of angels. 2. That the same things communicated to our inward man, are ever originally and primarily from the Spirit of Christ; and hence it is, that commonly we put them all on that score, we give them all to Christ's Spirit. 3. That 'tis proper to the Spirit to enlighten the understanding, and to determine the will effectually: the angels are but cisterns, the spirit is the fountain: the angels may speak and move us to our duties, but the blessing, the efficacy is of the Spirit; and in this respect we leave to Christ and his Spirit *the all in all*. Well then, O my soul, consider (especially in church-assemblies, and in the enjoyment of ordinances) the especial presence of Christ, in the presence of his Spirit, and in the presence of his angels: What? Dost thou feel any stirrings, actings, movings in thy spirit? Dost thou feel any quickning, warming, feeding, cherishing,

Carrying on the great Work of Man's Salvation until his Suffering and Dying. 231

rishing, healing, mollifying, melting, comforting, strengthening in thy inward parts? Say then, *Surely the Lord is in this place*, Gen. xxviii. 16, 17. *This is none other but the house of God, this is the gate of heaven.* O here is the Spirit, and here are the angels, ascending and descending; and therefore avoid, Satan! avoid, all prophane thoughts, and earthly-mindedness! avoid dulness, deadness, drowsiness! avoid looseness, lasciviousness, and all irreverence, *Because of the angels*, 1 Cor. xi. 10. And because of the Spirit; and because of the especial presence of Christ, which includes them both.

6. Consider the preaching of Christ. O the admirable sermons of this great prophet? The spouse tells us, Cant. v. 13. *His lips like lilies dropped sweet-smelling myrrh.* His doctrine was sweet as the lilies, and sound as the myrrh. *His lips were like lilies*, as certain odoriferous lilies, that cast forth a sweet-smelling savour. They were full of heavenly grace and sweetness. Grace, saith the Psalmist, *was poured into his lips*, and *they dropped sweet-smelling myrrh*, Psal. xlv. 2. The nature of this herb is to keep from putrefaction; as it is found itself, so it makes other things found: error is of a putrefying nature, corrupting, and defiling the soul; but the doctrine of Christ keeps the soul sound; it is the soul's preservative, it keeps the soul free from all corruption and defilement. See here the prophetical office of Christ held forth in similitudes, his lips were ever dropping, distilling, publishing sweet and sound truths. —— Read and peruse those sermons he hath left on record; yea ruminate and meditate on them in order to piety and an holy life. How sweet was the first sermon of Christ, Matth. iv. 17. *Repent, for the kingdom of heaven is at hand?* And how spiritual was that sermon of Christ, John iii. 3. *Except a man be born again, he cannot see the kingdom of God?* It may be thou art a doctor, a master of Israel, thou art a learned scholar, thou art a man of parts and abilities in other things; it may be thou hast read so long in the Bible, thou hast heard so many, and so many sermons, &c. But, ah miserable soul, it may be all the work is to do still within. Come, say this sermon of Christ unto thine own soul, ' Unless I be born again, I ' cannot enter into heaven. Born again, O Lord, ' what is that? Was ever such a thing done upon ' me? Was ever I cast into the pangs of a new

' birth? And continued I in those pangs until Christ ' Jesus was formed in me? Are old things done ' away, and are all things now become new? Is ' the old man, the old lusts, the old conversation ' quite abandoned and left? Are my principles ' new? My aims and ends new? My life and con' versation new?' Thus I might paraphrase on all the sermons, but I intend brevity; only consider, O my soul, as if this sermon, and all the rest had been preached to thee: relish Christ standing by thee, and opening his mouth, and teaching thee, thus and thus: surely there is a speaking of Christ from heaven, Heb. xii. 25 *See that ye refuse not him* (saith the apostle) *that speaketh from heaven*. And besides, he hath his ministers here on earth, and they are daily preaching over these sermons of Christ, again and again: they preach such things as were *First spoken by the Lord himself*, Heb. ii. 3. *They beseech, and pray thee in Christ's stead*, 2 Cor. v. 20. O then, *Meditate on these things, and give thyself wholly to them, that thy profiting may appear to all*, 1 Tim. iv. 15.

7. Consider the miracles of Christ in pursuance of the doctrines delivered in his blessed sermons. Here's a world of matter to run over; such miracles were done by Christ as never man did before. Moses indeed smote the rock, and the waters gushed out, but he could not turn that water into wine; Elisha raised a child that was dead, to life; but Jesus raised one who had been dead four days, yea who was buried and corrupted: Elias and Samuel, and all the prophets, and the succession of the high priests in both the temples, put all together, never did so many, and so great miracles as Jesus did: he turned water into wine; he healed the nobleman's son even at the point of death; he cured the leprous by his touch; he made the lame man to walk; and the crooked limbs to become straight; he made habitual diseases, and inveterate, of eighteen years continuance, and once of thirty eight years, to disappear at his speaking, even as darkness at the brightness of the sun; he fed thousands of people with two small fishes, and five loaves: he cast out devils, and commanded them whithersoever he pleased; he restored sight to the blind. In a word, he did such miracles as no man else ever did; and the poor blind man proved it by instance of himself, John ix. 23. *It was never heard that any man opened the eyes of one that was born blind.*

blind. O my soul, consider of these miracles, and believe that doctrine which was ratified with arguments from above! how shouldest thou but attent to all those mysterious truths which were so strongly confirmed by an Almighty hand?—What, dost thou think of a meditation needless in this respect? Art thou fully satisfied of the truth of scriptures? It is well; I hope thou art; and yet who knows how soon thou mayest be put to it by an enemy, or a strong temptation? One can tell us in print, 'Some are now talking of a toleration of all religi-'ons; and some desire that the Jews may have a 'free commerce amongst us:' it is good therefore to be well armed at this point; and the best argument to prove the verity of the gospel, next to the inward testimony of the Spirit, is this demonstration, or common place of the miracles of Christ.

8. Consider Christ's ordination of his apostles, Luke vi. 13. *He chose twelve, whom he named apostles:* and what was the office of these apostles, but *to go and teach all nations?* Mat. xxviii. 19. The gospel was first preached in Jewry, but afterwards the sound of it came unto us. Micah iv. 2. *Out of Zion shall go forth the law, and the word of the Lord from Jerusalem.* Gildas affirms plainly, 'That Britain received the gospel in the 'time of Tiberius, under whom Christ suffered: 'and that Joseph of Arimathea, after the disper-'sion of the Jews, was sent of Philip the apostle 'from France to Britain, and here remained in 'this land all his time. Nicephorus adds [Niceph. 'l. 2. c. 40.] That Simon Zelotes did spread the 'gospel of Christ to the west ocean, and brought 'the same into the isles of Britain.' Howsoever it was brought hither, of this we are sure; that Christ was first discovered to his apostles, and from the apostles was discovered to our fore-fathers, and from them unto us, and from us will be the discovery to others to the end of the world. O the goodness of God in Christ! what? That *repentance and remission of sins should be preached in his name, beginning at Jerusalem, and afterwards among all nations,* Luke xxiv. 47. Of what near concernment, O my soul, is this to thee? What art thou but a sinner of the Gentiles? Understand that term; when the apostle would express the greatest sinners that the world had, he calls them *sinners of the Gentiles,* Gal. ii. 15. Why? The Gentiles knew not God, the Gentiles were unacquainted with Christ, the Gentiles walk in nothing but sin; O then what a love is this, that God should ever have a thought of good will towards thee? Surely this is one of *the great mysteries of godliness, God manifested in the flesh, justified in the Spirit, seen of angels, preached unto the Gentiles,* 1 Tim. iii. 16. What? That sinners, and the worst of sinners, should be made the subjects of the utmost discovery of Christ and of the gospel of Christ? This is a mystery indeed; had Christ sent his apostles to proclaim the riches of his grace to some Jews only, or to some unspotted souls among the Gentiles (if any such were) whose hearts might presently have fallen down before it; this had been something suitable, but, that sinners of the Gentiles, that children of wrath should be the subject of this great design, O the mystery! *q. d.* 'Go, my apostles, into all the nations of the world; 'and amongst them all, go into Britain, into that 'corner of the world, England, and there open 'the mystery of Christ, there preach life, and re-'conciliation, and redemption, and glorification to 'those poor souls; lay you (or at least some of you) 'the foundation of the Christian faith amongst 'those heathens, those sinners of the Gentiles; and 'after you, I will raise up some other ministers of 'the gospel to confirm the same: yea, in the last 'times, I will raise up many worthies, as Jewell, 'Usher, Downham, Perkins, Hooker, Rogers, 'Shepherd, Bolton, Ash, Whittaker, &c. Who shall 'be as bright stars in the firmament of that church; 'and after them will I raise up others to discover 'this great design to their generations, amongst 'whom shall live such and such men, such and 'such women.' (And herein, O my soul, think of thyself, and if thou wilt, of thy own family and relations) 'for I owe a good will towards Eng-'land; it shall be said of England, as sometimes 'of Zion, Out of England, the perfection of beau-'ty, hath God shined.' Psal. l. 2. O my soul, how shouldest thou be ravished in this one meditation? What? That Christ should cause the Sun of his gospel to come into this Zodiac, and that now in these latter times (when that sun is set in Zion, where it first arose) it should make a noon with us, and shine more brightly here (for ought I know, or can yet learn) than in any other nation, country, kingdom, throughout all the world. Rom. xi. 33. *Oh the depth of the riches both of the wis-*

dom

dom and counsel of God; how unsearchable are his judgments, and his ways past finding out?

9. Consider Christ's reception of sinners. He sent forth his apostles to call them in, and if they would but come, how ready was he to receive them? This was Christ's errand from heaven, this was the work he came to do, John vi. 38, 39. *I came down from heaven, not to do mine own will, but the will of him that sent me. And this is the Father's will which hath sent me, that of all which he hath given me I should lose nothing.* He must receive all his Father gives him, but he must lose none; Christ must give an account to God the Father of all which he hath given him, and this will be his account, John xvii. 22. *Those that thou gavest me I have kept, and none of them is lost.* Ah, poor soul! why shouldest thou despair because of sin? Look on Christ as spreading out both his arms to receive thee to him; look on the gracious nature and disposition that is in Christ; look on the office of Christ; it is an office of saving and shewing mercy, that Christ hath undertaken; it is an office to receive sinners, yea, to *seek, and to save that which was lost,* Luke xix. 10. To bring home straying souls to God, to be the great Peace-maker between God and man; to reconcile God to man, and man to God, and so to be the Head and Husband of his people. Certainly the devil strangely wrongeth many a poor troubled soul, that he can bring them to have hard thoughts and suspicious thoughts of Jesus Christ. How can they more contradict the office of Christ? How can they more contradict the gospel-description of Christ, than to think him a destroyer of his creatures, one that watcheth for their haltings, and one that hath more mind to hurt than help them? Away, away, with all prejudicate opinions! Resolve, O my soul, to throw thyself on him for life and for salvation: why, if thou wilt but come, he hath promised freely to make thee welcome; all the day long he stretcheth out his arms, and would fain gather thee and all others into his sweet embraces.

10. Consider the easiness of his yoke, and the lightness of his burden. Many a one is willing to take Jesus as their Saviour, but they are unwilling to take him on his sweet terms: oh, they imagine it an hard task, and an heavy burden, *Who may endure it?* It was otherwise with Christ, Psalm xl. 8. *I do delight to do thy will, O my God;* and it is otherwise with Christians, for *his commandments are not grievous,* saith John, 1 John v. 3. And therefore David calls on others to try this truth, Psal. xxxiv. 8. *Oh taste, and see how good the Lord is.* It is said of Mr. Saunders, that a little before his death and martyrdom, he told his wife, 'That he had no riches to leave her, 'but that treasure of tasting how sweet Christ is to 'hungry consciences: and of that, (said he) as I 'feel some part, and I would feel more, so I be-'queath it unto thee, and to the rest of my beloved in Christ,' *Act. & Mon. Folio* 1361. O my soul, if thou canst but taste, thou wilt find a world of sweetness in Christ's ways? there is sweetness in the word, Psal. cxix. 103. *How sweet are thy words to my taste, yea, sweeter than honey to my mouth?* There is sweetness in prayer. Hast thou not known the time that thou hast touched the hem of Christ's garment, and tasted of the joys of heaven in prayer? Hast thou not seen heaven cleft, and Christ sitting at God's right hand? Rom. x. 12. *Surely the Lord is rich to all them that call upon him.* There is sweetness in meditation: some call this very duty, the saints pastime, which re-creates and perfumes the tired spirits: Now, O my soul, thou art in the exercise of this duty, now thou art in the meditation of the easiness of Christ's burden, and of the sweetness of his ways. Tell me, is there nothing of heaven in this meditation? Is it sweet, or is it bitter to thy soul? Thou mayest read in scripture of many admirable effects of meditation, as, that it confirms our knowledge, Psal. cxix. 99. *I have more understanding than all my teachers, for thy testimonies are my meditation:* That it inflames our love, Verse 97. *Oh, how love I thy law? It is my meditation all the day.* That it casts a sweet influence on our lives, Verse 15. *I will meditate on thy precepts, and have respect unto thy ways.* What, is it thus with thee? Canst thou say, with David, Psal. civ. 34. *My meditation of him shall be sweet?* And Psal. xciv. 19. *In the multitude of my thoughts within me, thy comforts exceedingly delight my soul.* Why then, thou hast truly tasted of God's goodness, thou hast actual discoveries of the sweetness of God's ways; thou hast experienced this truth, that *his yoke is easy, and his burden is light,* Matth. xi. 30. *that his ways are ways of pleasantness, and all his paths are peace,* Prov. iii. 17. Oh, if men did but know

G g

what

what ravishing sweetness were in the ways of God, they could not but embrace them, *and esteem one day's society with Jesus Christ*, (as Caracciolus did) *better than all the gold in the world.*

11. Consider the holiness of Christ's nature, and the holiness of Christ's life. 1. For the holiness of his nature, if thou couldest but clearly see it, what work would it make in thy breast? Christ's inward beauty would ravish love out of the devils, if they had but grace to see his beauty; yea, he would lead captive all hearts in hell, if they had but eyes to behold his loveliness. O what a flower? What a rose of love and light is the Lord Jesus Christ? Cant. v. 10. *My beloved is white and ruddy*, (said the spouse) *the chiefest of ten thousand.* Summon before Christ, fair angels, glorified spirits, the azure heavens, the lightsome stars, all the delicious flowers, gardens, meadows, forests, seas, mountains, birds, beasts, yea, and all the sons of men, as they should have been in the world of innocency, and let them all stand in their highest excellency before Jesus Christ, and what are they? The saints in glory now *see the face of Christ*, Rev. xxii. 4. *(i. e.)* They see all the dignity, beauty that is in Christ; and they are so taken with his sight, that they do nothing else but stare, and gaze, and behold his face for ages, and yet they are never satisfied with beholding; suppose they could wear out their eyes, at their eye-holes in beholding Christ, they should still desire to see more. O this loveliness of Christ ravishes the souls of the glorified; how is it, O my soul, that thou art not taken with this meditation? But, 2. Go from the holiness of his nature to the holiness of his life, it may be that will make deep impressions on thy spirit; consider his charity, his self-denial, his contempt of the world, his mercy, his bounty, his meekness, his pity, his humility, his obedience to his Father. A fruitful meditation on these particulars, cannot but cause some resemblance within, and make thee like Christ. O the wonder, that any should disclaim the active obedience of Christ, as to his own justification! away, away with these cavils, and consider the obedience of Christ in relation to thyself, Gal. iv. 4. *God sent forth his Son, made of a woman, made under the law, to redeem them that were under the law, that we might receive the adoption of sons.* It is a sweet note of Dr. Andrews, ' Christ made ' under the law, *(i. e.)* under the whole law, the ' one half of the law, (which is the directive part) ' he was made under that, and satisfied it by the ' innocency of his life, without breaking one jot ' or tittle of the law, and he so answers that part, ' as it might be the principal; the other half the ' law, (which is the penalty) he was under that ' also, and satisfied it, by suffering a wrongful ' death, no way deserved or due by him; and so ' he answered that part, as it might be the forfei- ' ture. But if we come now to ask, for whom is ' all this? It is only for us, that we might be re- ' deemed and adopted; redeemed from all evil, ' and adopted or interested into all good.' If this be so, O who would, for a world of gold, lose the influence and the benefit of Christ's active obedience? Consider of this, O my soul, till thou feelest some virtue to come out of Christ's life into thy self.

SECT. III.

Of desiring after Jesus in that respect.

3. LET us desire after Jesus, carrying on the work of our salvation in his life: it is not enough to know and consider, but we must desire; our meditation of Christ should draw forth our affections to Christ; and amongst all affections, I place this first of all, a desire after Christ.

But what is it in Christ's life that is so desirable? I answer, Every passage or particular named; yea, every thing of Christ is desirable (named or unnamed); all that concerns Christ in any kind whatsoever (if to the former particulars I should add a thousand and a thousand more) it is very precious, and excellent, and necessary, and profitable, and comfortable, and therefore desirable: but to put them in order,

1. The meanest things of Christ are desirable things; the very filings of gold, the dust or sparkles of precious stones are of real price and value, yea of much worth: yea, the very leaves of the tree of life are healing; the very hem of Christ's garment, but even touched, sends forth its virtue: the meanest and worst things of Christ are incomparably to be desired above all things: the dust of Zion; the very ground that Christ's feet treadeth on; any thing that hath the poorest relation to Jesus Christ, it is desirable for him. Hence we read,

read, that one poor woman sought no more of him but to wash Christ's feet, and to kiss them; another woman breathes out these desires after Christ, Matth. ix. 21. *If I may but touch the hem of his garment, I shall be whole.* Mary Magdalene sought only to have her arms filled with his dead body: Joseph of Arimathea was of the same mind. O the bloody winding-sheet, together with the dead and torn body of Christ in his arms are most precious and sweet. Christ's clay is silver; and his brass gold; John the baptist thinks it an honour to *unloose the latchet of his shoes*, John i. 27. David, though he was a great prophet, and appointed to be a king over Israel, yet his soul pants thus, Psalm lxxxiv. 10. *O that I might be so near the Lord, as to be a door-keeper in the house of my God.* Yea, he puts all happiness on the sparrow, and the swallow, that may build their nests besides the Lord's altar, Psal. lxxxiv. 3.

2. The more considerable actions of Christ are especially desirable. Oh my soul, wouldest thou but run through his life, and consider some of his more eminent actions, in relation to his friends, or in relation to his enemies, what desires would these kindle in thine heart after Christ? 1. To his friends, he was sweet and indulgent; where there were any beginnings of grace he did encourage it; so was the prophecy, Matth. xii. 20. *A bruised reed shall he not break, and smoaking flax shall he not quench:* nay, where there was but a representation of grace, he seemed to accept of it: thus, when the young man came and said, Mark x. 17. *What good thing shall I do to inherit eternal life?* he embraced him, and made much of him, verse 21. *Then Jesus beholding him, he loved him.* And so the Scribe, that asked him, *Which is the first commandment of all?* Mark xii. 28 In the conclusion Christ told him, *Thou art not far from the kingdom of God*, verse 34. He laboured to pull him further, in telling him, he was not far from heaven and glory. And so the people that fainted for the bread of life, that were *scattered abroad as sheep having no shepherd*, Matth. ix. 36. *He was moved with compassion on them,* [*eoplagnisthe auton.*] He was bowelled in heart; his very bowels were moved within him. 2. To his enemies, he was kind and merciful; many a time he discovers himself most of all unto sinners; he was never more familiar with any at first acquaintance,

than with the woman of Samaria that was an adulteress: and Mary that had been a sinner, how sweetly did he appear to her at the very first view? How ready was he to receive sinners? How ready to pardon and forgive sinners? How gracious to sinners after the pardon and forgiveness of sin? See it in Peter, he never cast him in the teeth with his apostasy. He never upbraided him with it: he never so much as tells him of it, only he looks upon him, and afterwards, *Lovest thou me? O Peter, lovest thou me? Why, Peter, lovest thou me?* Often he was wronged and injured by men, but what then? Was he all on an heat? Did he call for fire down from heaven to destroy them? Indeed his disciples, being more flesh than spirit, would fain have had it so: but he sweetly replies, *O! you know not what spirits ye are of: the son of man is not come to destroy mens lives, but to save them,* Luke ix. 55, 56. Sometimes we find him shedding tears for those very persons that shed his precious blood, *Oh Jerusalem, Jerusalem, &c. ——If thou hadst known, even thou, at least in this thy day, the things belonging to thy peace,* &c. Why, O my soul, if thou wouldest but run though such passages as these, how desirable are they? Well might *they sing in that day in the land of Judah,* Isa. xxvi. 1, 8. *In the way of thy judgments, O Lord, have we waited for thee, the desire of our soul is to thy name, and to the remembrance of thee.*

3. The ever-blessed and holy person of Christ is desirable above all, Cant. v. 10, 16. *My beloved is white and ruddy, the chiefest of ten thousands,—Yea, he is altogether lovely or desirable:* so Vatablus renders it, *Christus est tota desideria,* Christ is all desires. If the actions of Christ be desirable, what must himself be? If the parings of his bread be so sweet, what must the great loaf, Christ himself, be? Christ is admirable in action and person, but above all, his person is most admirable; no creature in the world yields the like representation of God, as the person of Jesus Christ; *He is the express image of the person of his Father,* Heb. i. 3. As the print of the seal on the wax is the express image of the seal itself, so is Christ the highest representation of God; he makes similitude to him, who otherwise is without all similitudes And hence it is that Christ is called the *standard-bearer of ten thousands,* Cant. v. 10. All excel-

tencies are gathered up in Christ, as beams in the sun. Come, poor soul! thy eyes run to and fro in the world, to find comfort and happiness; thou desirest after worldly honour, worldly pleasure, worldly profits, cast thy eyes back, and see heaven and earth in one; look, if thou wilt, at what thy vast thoughts can fancy, not only in this world, but in the world to come; or, if thou canst imagine more variety, see that, and infinitely more, shining forth from the person of the Lord Jesus Christ. No wonder if the saints adore him. No wonder if the angels stand amazed at him. No wonder if all creatures vail all their glory to him. Oh! what are all things in the world to Jesus Christ? Paul compares them together, [*ta panta*], all things with this one thing, Phil. iii. 8. *And I account all things but loss, for the excellency of the knowledge of Christ.* [*And I count all things*] Surely all things is the greatest count that can be cast up, for it includeth all prices, all sums; it takes in earth, and heaven, and all therein, that are but as created things, *q. d.* Nations, and all nations; gold, and all gold; jewels, and all jewels; angels, and all angels: all these, and every all besides all these; what are they in comparison of Christ, but as feathers, dung, shadows, nothing? If there be any thing worthy a wish, it is eminently, transcendently, originally in the Lord Jesus Christ: there is no honour, no felicity, like that which Christ hath; some are sons, Christ is an only son; some are kings, but Christ is King of kings, some are honourable, none above angels, Christ is above angels and archangels, Heb. i. 5. *To which of the angels said he at any time, Thou art my Son, this day have I begotten thee?* Some are wealthy, Christ hath all the sheep on a thousand hills; the very utmost parts of the earth are his: some are beautiful, Christ is the fairest of all the children of men; he is spiritually fair, he is all glorious within: if the beauty of the angels (which I believe are the beautifullest creatures the world has) should be compared with the beauty of Christ, which consists in the perfection of the divine nature, and in the perfection of his human nature, and in the perfection of the graces of his Spirit, they would be but as lumps of darkness: the brightest cherub is forced to skreen his face from the dazzling and shining brightness of the glory of Christ: alas! the cherubims and seraphims are but as spangles and twinkling stars in the canopy of heaven, but Christ is the Sun of righteousness, that at once illuminates and drowns them all.

Come then, cast up thy desires after Christ, breathe, O my soul, after the enjoyments of this Christ; fling up to heaven some divine ejaculations, ' Oh that this Christ were mine! Oh that the
' actions of Christ, and the person of Christ were
' mine; Oh that all he said and all he did, and
' all he were from top to toe were mine! Oh that
' I had the silver wings of a dove, that in all my
' wants I might fly into the bosom of this Christ!
' Oh, that I might be admitted to his person, Or,
' if that may not be, O, that I may but touch the
' very hem of his garment! if I must not sit at
' table, Oh, that I might but gather up the crumbs!
' surely there's bread enough in my father's house:
' Christ is the bread of life; this one loaf, Christ,
' is enough for all the saints in heaven and earth
' to feed on; and what, must I pine away, and
' perish with hunger? Oh, that I might have
' one crumb of Christ! thousands of instructi-
' ons dropped from him whilst he was on earth;
' Oh, that some of that food might be my
' nourishment! *Oh that my ways were directed
' according to his statutes*, Psalm cxix. 15. Many
' a stream, and wave, and line, and precept flowed
' from this fountain, Christ: oh, that I might drink
' freely of this water of life; he hath proclaim-
' ed it in mine ears, *If any man thirst, let him
' come unto me and drink*, John vii. 37. Oh,
' that I might come, and find welcome! why,
' sure I thirst, I am extremely athirst, I feel in
' me such a burning drought, that either I must
' drink, or die; either the righteousness of Christ,
' the holiness of Christ, the holiness of his nature,
' and the holiness of his life must be imputed un-
' to me, or farewel happiness in another world;
' why, come, come, Lord Jesus, come quickly:
' Oh, I long to see the beauty of thy face! thy
' glory is said to be an enamouring glory; such is
' thy beauty, that it steals away my heart after
' thee; and cannot be satisfied till, with Absalom,
' I see the king's face. Come, Christ; or if thou
' wilt not come,' *I charge you, O daughters of Jerusalem, if ye find my beloved, that ye tell him I am sick of love*, Cant. v. 8.

SECT.

SECT. IV.

Of hoping in Jesus in that respect.

4. Let us hope in Jesus carrying on the great work of our salvation in his life. By this hope I mean not a fluctuating, wavering, doubtful hope, but an assured hope, an hope well-grounded. The main soul question is, Whether Christ's life be mine? Whether all those passages of his life laid open, belong unto me? Whether the habitual righteousness, and actual holiness of Christ be imputed to my justification? And what are the grounds and foundations on which my hope is built? The apostle tells us, 2 Thess. ii. 16. *that God gives good hopes through grace:* if hope be right and good, it will manifest itself by operations of saving grace. O look into thy soul! what gracious effects of the life of Christ are there? Certainly his life is not without some influence on our spirits, if we are his members, and he be our head: the head, we say, communicates life, and sense, and motion to the members; and so doth Christ communicate a spiritual life, and sense, and motion to his members: O the glorious effects flowing out of Christ's life into a believer's soul! I shall lay down these, As,

1. If Christ's life be mine, then I am freed from the law of sin: this was the apostle's evidence, Rom. viii. 2. *For the law of the spirit of life in Christ Jesus hath made me free from the law of sin.* Christ's life is called *the spirit of life,* because of its perfection; and this Spirit of life hath such a power in it, here termed a law, that it works out in believers a freedom *from the law or power in sin.* I cannot think, notwithstanding the influence of Christ's life on me, but that sin still sticketh in me; I am still a sinner, in respect of the inherency of sin, but I am freed from the power of sin, (i. e.) from the guilt of sin, as to its condemning power, and from the filth of sin, as to its ruling, reigning power, Rom. vi. 12. *Let not sin reign in your mortal bodies, that ye should obey it in the lusts thereof.*

I grant there is some difference among divines in their expressions concerning the sins of God's own people, though they mean one and the selfsame thing. Some call them only *sins of infirmity;* and others grant the name of *reigning sins,* but with this limitation, That this is not a total reigning. Sin reigneth as a tyrant over them, not as a king: at sometimes (as in David's case) the will and consent may run along with sin; no actual resistance, may be made against sin at all; and yet at the very same time, *The seed of God remaineth in them,* 1 John iii. 9. though it seem dead, and in God's good time, that very seed will revive again, and throw out the tyrant: there is not, cannot be that antecedent, and consequent consent to sin in the godly as in the wicked: O my soul, consider this, if the virtue of Christ's life come in, it will take down that sovereign high reign of sin which the wicked suffer, and will not strive against: the flesh indeed may sometimes lust against the spirit, but it shall not totally prevail, or get the upper hand, Rom. vi. 14. *Sin shall not have dominion over you.* Sin may tyrannize it in me for a time, but it shall not king in me. Look to this! doth the power and dominion of Christ's life throw out of thy heart and life, that kingly power and dominion of my sin? Here is one ground of hope.

2. If Christ's life be mine, then shall I walk even as he walked. Such is the efficacy of Christ's life, that it will work suitableness, and make our life in some sort like his life. The apostle observes that our communion with Christ works on our very conversations. 1 John ii. 6. *He that abideth in him, walks even as he walked.* And to this purpose are all those holy admonitions, Eph. v. 2. *Walk in love, as Christ also loved us.* And, John xiii. 15. *I have given you an example, that you should do as I have done unto you* And, 1 Pet. i. 15. *As he which hath called you is holy, so be ye holy in all manner of conversation.* Then is Christ's life mine, when my actions refer to him as my copy, when I transcribe the original of Christ's life, (as it were) to the life. Alas! what am I better to observe in the life of Christ, his charity to his enemies, his reprehensions of the Scribes and Pharisees, his subordination to his heavenly Father, his ingenuity towards all men, his effusions of love towards all the saints, if there be no likeliness of all this in my own actions? The life of Jesus is not described to be like a picture in a chamber of pleasure, only for beauty and entertainment of the eye, but like the Egyptian hieroglyphics, whose very feature is a precept, whose image converses with men by sense and signification of excellent discour-

ses: to this purpose saith Paul, 2 Cor. iii. 18. *We all with open face, beholding, as in a glass the glory of the Lord, are changed into the same image, from glory to glory.* Christ is the image of his Father, and we are the image of Christ: Christ is God's master-piece, the most excellent device, and work, and frame of heaven that ever was, or ever shall be; now, Christ being the top excellency of all, he is most fit to be the pattern of all excellencies whatsoever; and therefore he is the image, the idea, the pattern, the platform of all our sanctification. Come then, O my soul, Look unto Jesus, and look into thyself, yea, look and look till thou art more transformed into his likeness: is it so that thou art changed into the same image with Christ? look into his disposition as it is set forth in the gospel; look into his carriage, look into his conversation at home and abroad, and then reflecting on thyself, look there, and tell me, canst thou find in thyself a disposition suitable to his disposition, a carriage suitable to his carriage, a conversation suitable to his conversation? Art thou every way like him in thy measure, in gospel allowance, in some sweet resemblance? Why then, here is another ground of hope; O rejoice in it, and bless God for it.

3. If Christ's life be mine, then shall I admire, adore, believe, and obey this Christ. All these were the effects of those several passages in Christ's life respectively. 1. They admire at his doctrine and miracles; for his doctrine, *All bare him witness, and wondred at those gracious words which proceeded out of his mouth*, Luke iv. 22. And for his miracles, *They wondred and they glorified God, the God of Israel,* Matth. xv. 31. Yea, sometimes their admiration was so great, Mark vi. 51. *That they were sore amazed in themselves beyond measure, and wondred,* Luke ix. 34. *They were amazed at the mighty power of God, and they wondred every one at all things which Jesus did.* And as they admired so they adored, Matth. viii. 2. *There came a leper and worshipped him, saying, If thou wilt, thou canst make me clean.* And there came a ruler and worshipped him, saying, *My daughter is even now dead, come lay thine hand on her, and she shall live,* Mat. ix. 18. And *they that were in the ship came, and worshipped, saying, Of a truth thou art the Son of God,* Matth. xiv. 33. The very worshipping of Christ confesseth thus much, that he is the Son of God 3. And as they adored, so they believed, Mark ix. 23, 24. *If thou canst believe,* (said Christ to the father of the possessed child) *all things are possible to him that believeth: and straightway he cried out, and said with tears, Lord, I believe, help thou my unbelief. And when many of his disciples fell away, then said Jesus to the twelve, Will ye also go away?* Peter answers for the rest, *To whom shall we go?— Why, Lord, We believe, and are sure thou art the Christ, the Son of the living God,* John vi. 66, 69. Not only worshipping of Christ but believing in Christ, is a right acknowledgment that Christ is God. 4. And as they believed so they obeyed; *Ye have obeyed from the heart,* (said Paul to his Romans) *that form of doctrine which was delivered to you,* Rom. vi. 17. No sooner Peter and Andrew heard the voice of Christ, *Follow me,* but they left all and followed him: and no sooner James and John heard the same voice of Christ, *Follow me,* but they left all and followed him, Mat. iv. 19, 20, 22. And no sooner Matthew, sitting at the receipt of custom, heard that voice of Christ, *Follow me,* but he rose and followed him, Mat. ix. 9. Why *then are ye my disciples indeed,* (said Christ to the believing Jews) *if ye continue in my word,* John viii. 31. Come then, put thyself, O my soul, to the test; thou hast seen and heard the wonderful passages of Christ's life; the baptism of Christ, the fasting of Christ, the temptations of Christ, the manifestations of Christ, the doctrine of Christ, the miracles of Christ, the holiness of Christ; and is this the issue of all? Dost thou now begin to admire, and adore, and believe, and to obey this Christ? Is thy heart warmed? Thy affections kindled? Forbes tells us, That the word of God hath three degrees of operations in the hearts of his chosen, *First,* 'It falleth to mens ears like the 'sound of many waters, a mighty great and con-'fused sound, and which commonly brings neither 'terror nor joy, but yet a wondering and acknow-'ledgment of a strange force, and more than hu-'man power.' This is that effect which many felt hearing Christ, when they were astonished at his doctrine, as teaching with authority, what manner of doctrine is this? Never man spake like this man, Mark i. 22. *The next effect is the voice of thunder, which bringeth not only wonder but fear also,* Luke iv. 34. *Not only filleth the ears with sound, and*

the

the heart with astonishment, but moreover shaketh, terrifieth the conscience, John vii. 46. *The third effect is the sound of harping, while the word not only ravisheth with admiration, and striketh the conscience with terror, but also, lastly, filleth it with sweet peace and joy.* In the present case, give me leave to ask, O my soul, art thou struck into amaze at the mighty miracles and divine doctrine of Jesus Christ? Dost thou fall down and worship him as thy Lord and thy God? Dost thou believe in him and rely on him for life and salvation? Dost thou obey him and follow the Lamb which way soever he goes? Dost thou act from principles of grace in newness of life and holiness of conversation? Dost thou walk answerable to the commands of Jesus Christ, or, at least, is there in thee an earnest endeavour so to walk, and is it the sorrow of thy soul when thou obeyest thy failings? And dost thou rejoice in spirit when thou art led by the Spirit? Why, then here is another ground of hope, that virtue is gone out of Christ's life into thy soul.

4. If Christ's life be mine, then *I live, yet not I, but Christ liveth in me,* Gal. ii. 20. Paul speaks out this evidence, *I am crucified with Christ, nevertheless I live,* &c. He conjoins the death of Christ, and the life of Christ, in one and the same soul, q. d. No man knows the benefit of Christ's death, but he that feels the virtue of Christ's life; there is no assurance of Christ's dying for us, but as we feel Christ living in us; if the power of Christ's death mortify my lusts, then the virtue of Christ's life will quicken my soul: but what means he by this, *I live, yet not I, but Christ liveth in me? I live,* It seems some paradox, *I live, yet not I:* but a right interpretation reconciles all; as this, I live to God, and not unto myself, I live to Christ, and not unto the world; I live according to the word of God, and not after my own lust and fancy, or, (as some would have it) I live under grace and not under the law, q. d. 'Sometimes I lived wholly under the law, which made me a persecutor of the church of God, which wrought in me all manner of concupiscence, and slew me, and then I found myself to be dead in sin; but now I have embraced Christ, and I am no more the man I was: Now, I feel Christ quickning, ruling, guiding, and strengthening me by his Spirit; now I live spiritually and holy, not of myself but from another.' The very whole of Christians is from Christ; Christ is both fountain-filling and life-quickning, *I live, yet not I, but Christ liveth in me.* Christ's life hath an influence, infusion, transmission into ourselves in reference to spiritual life: look, as the heavens, by an influence into the earth, do quicken and enliven the heart, and make all the seeds and roots hidden in the earth to revive and put forth themselves, so there is an influence that goes forth from the Sun of righteousness into the souls of men, reviving and quickning them, and making them of dead to become living, and of barren to become fruitful, Mal. iv. 2. *To you shall the Sun of righteousness arise, with healing in his wings, and ye shall go forth and grow up as the calves in the stall.* O my soul! question thyself in these few particulars; dost thou live to God and not to thyself? Dost thou live to Christ and not to the world? Dost thou derive thy life from Christ? And hath that life of Christ a special influence into thy soul? Dost thou feel Christ living in thy understanding and will, are thy imaginations and affections, in thy duties and services? 1. In thy understanding, by prizing the knowledge of Christ, by determining to know nothing in comparison of Christ? 2. In thy will, by making thy will free to choose and embrace Christ, and by making his will to rule in thy will? 3. In thy imagination, by thinking upon him with more frequency and delight, by having more high, and honourable, and sweeter apprehensions of Christ than of all the creatures? 4. In thy affections, by fearing Christ above all earthly powers, and by loving Christ above all earthly persons? 5. In thy duties and services, by doing all thou dost in his name, by his assistance, and for his glory? Why then, here is another ground of thy hope, surely thou hast thy part in Christ's life.

Away, away with all dejecting doubts and perplexing fears! while Christ was in Augustine's eye, he said, 'I dare not despond, I know who hath said it, and I dare build upon it: this anchor of hope thus cast out, and fastening upon Christ, it would be admirably useful when billows of temptation beat upon souls: this helmet of hope thus used would keep off many blows, whereby the comforts of distrustful spirits are many times sadly battered.' O my soul, look to the grounds of thy hope, if thou findest the power of sin dying in thee, if thou walkest as Christ walked; if thou admirest, adorest, believest and obeyest thy Christ; if thou livest and livest not, but indeed, and in truth it is Christ that lives in thee: why then, thou mayest comfortably hope and assure thyself that Christ's habitual righteousness and actual holiness is imputed to thy justification: thou mayest confidently resolve that every passage of Christ's life, (so far as legal or moral) belongs unto thee. What? would ever Christ have come with his power against thy power of sin, if he had not meant to rescue thee? Would Christ ever have set thee a copy, and have held thy hand and thy heart, to have writ legibly after him, if he had not meant thee for *a scribe instructed into the kingdom of heaven!* Matth. xiii. 52. Would Christ in his several actions have set himself before thee as the object of admiration, adoration, belief and obedience, if he had not meant to own thee, and to be owned by thee? Would Christ ever have come so near to thee, as to have lived in thee, to have been the soul of thy soul, and the life of thy life, the *All* of thy understanding and will, imaginations, and affections, duties and services, if he had not purposed to have *saved thee by his life?* Rom. v. 10. Surely, *it is good, that I both hope and quietly wait for the salvation of God*, Lam. iii. 26. I cannot hope in vain if these be the grounds of my hope.

SECT. V.

Of believing in Jesus in that respect.

6. LET us believe in Jesus, carrying on the great work of our salvation in his life. Many souls stand aloof, not daring to make a particular application of Christ and his life to themselves: but herein is the property of faith, it brings all home, and makes use of whatsoever Christ is or does for itself. To ponder Christ's actions during his life, and the influences of his actions to all that are his, what is this to me unless I believe my own part in all this? *Oh, I dare not believe*, (cries many a poor soul.) 'Is it credible, that Jesus 'Christ the Son of God, the brightness of his Fa- 'ther's glory, the express image of his Father's 'person, should be incarnate for me, and lead such 'a life upon earth for my soul? What, to be bap- 'tized, to be tempted, to manifest himself in the 'form of man, to whip the buyers and sellers out 'of his temple, to preach up and down the gospel 'of the kingdom, to work miracles among men, to 'send abroad his apostles with a commission to 'preach, to invite sinners, to ease the burden of 'duties, and, in a word, to publish the righteous- 'ness of his nature and life; and all this, and a 'thousand times more than all this for my soul? 'O what am I? or what is my father's house? 'If God should let me live one year in heaven, it 'were infinite mercy: but that the God of heaven 'should live so many years on earth, and that all 'that while he should employ himself in watching, 'fasting, praying, preaching for my sake; oh the 'depth! Oh the depth! I cannot believe.'

Sweet soul, be not faithless, but believing; I know it is an hard and difficult thing: but, to help on a trembling soul, I shall first direct, and then encourage.

First, For direction, let souls be acquainted how to act their faith on Christ in respect of his life. The manner of its proceedings, I suppose is thus.——

1. Faith must directly go to Christ. Many poor souls humbled for sin, and taken off from their own bottom, they run immediately to the promise of pardon, and close with it, and rest on it, not seeking for or closing with Christ in the promise: this is a common error among thousands: but we should observe, that the first promise that was given, was not a bare word, simply promising pardon, peace, or any other benefit, which God would bestow, but it was a promise of Christ's person, as overcoming Satan and purchasing those benefits, Gen. iii. 15. *The seed of the woman shall bruise the serpent's head.* So, when the promise was renewed to Abraham, it was not a bare promise of blessedness and forgiveness, but of *that seed*, that is, *Christ*, Gal. iii. 6. in whom that blessedness was conveyed, Gen. xxii. 18. *In thy seed shall all the nations of the earth be blessed.* So that Abraham's faith first closed with Christ in the promise, and therefore he is said to see Christ's day, and to rejoice in embracing him. Christ, in the *first* place, and more immediately, is every where made the thing which faith embraceth to salvation, and whom it looks unto, and respects, as it makes us righteous in the sight of God, John iii. 16. *God so loved the world, that he gave his only-begotten Son, that whosoever believeth in him should not perish, but*

but have everlasting life, John xi. 25. *I am the resurrection and the life, he that believeth in me, though he were dead yet shall he live*, Acts xiii. 39. *And by him all that believe are justified from all things, from which ye could not be justified by the law of Moses*, Acts xvi. 31. *And, believe on the Lord Jesus, and thou shalt be saved*, Acts x. 43. *And to him give all the prophets witness, that thro' his name, whosoever believeth in him, shall receive remission of sins.* And hence it is, that faith is called *the faith of Christ*, Gal. ii. 16. Phil. iii. 9. Because it is Christ whom faith apprehends immediately, and as for the other promises they depend all on this, John iii. 36. *Whosoever believeth on him shall receive the remission of sins:* and *he that believeth on the Son of God shall have life everlasting: verily, verily I say unto you, he that believeth on me hath everlasting life*, John vi. 47. O remember this in the first place, faith must go unto Christ; and yet I mean not to Christ as abstractedly and nakedly considered, but to Christ as compassed with all his promises, privileges, benefits.

2. Faith must go to Christ, as God in the flesh. Some make this the difference of faith's acting betwixt believers of the New and Old Testament: under the Old Testament, when Christ was but in the promise, and not as then come in the flesh, their faith had a more usual recourse unto God himself; as for Christ (God-man, Man-God) they had not so distinct, but only a confused knowledge of him, and therefore we read not so frequently, and usually of their recourse unto him, but only unto God. 2 Chron. xx. 12. *O our God, wilt thou not judge them? we know not what to do, but our eyes are upon thee.* Ver. 20. *And hear me, O Judah, and ye inhabitants of Jerusalem, believe in the Lord your God, so shall ye be established.* Psal. lxxviii. 21, 22. And, *the Lord heard this, and was wroth, because they believed not in God, and trusted not in his salvation:* but now, under the New Testament, because Christ as Mediator, who was promised, is come, our faith more usually and immediately addresseth itself unto Christ as God in the flesh. God dwelling in our nature is made more familiar to our faith, than the person of the Father, who is merely God: God in the flesh is more distinctly set forth in the New Testament, and so he is more distinctly to be apprehended by the faith of all believers: *Ye believe in God* (says Christ to his disciples, whose faith and opinion of the Messiah was till Christ's resurrection of the same elevation with that of the Old Testament-believers) John xiv. 1. *Ye believe in God*, but he rests not there, *Believe also in me*; make me the object of your trust and salvation, as well as the Father, *Believe also in me*; not only so, but believe in the first place on me. One sweetly observes, that when faith and repentance came more narrowly to be distinguished by their more immediate objects, it is laid down thus, Acts xx. 21. *Repentance towards God, and faith towards our Lord Jesus Christ*; not but that God and Christ are objects of both, but that Christ is more immediately the object of faith, and God is more immediately the object of repentance, so that we believe in God through believing in Christ first, and we turn to Christ by turning to God first. O remember this! let your faith, in the more direct and immediate exercise of it, be pitched upon Christ as God in the flesh.

3. Faith must go to Christ as God in the flesh, made under the law: and hence it is that the apostle joins these together, Gal. iv. 4. *God sent his Son made of a woman, made under the law:* if Christ had been out of the compass of the law, his being incarnate, and made of a woman had done us no good. Suppose one in debt and danger of the law to have a brother of the same flesh and blood, of the same father and mother, what will this avail, if that same brother will not come under the law, (*i. e.*) become his surety, and undertake for him! It is our case; we are debtors to God, and there is *an hand-writing against us, and contrary to us*, Col. ii. 14. Here is a bond of the law which we have forfeited: now, what would Christ avail, if he had not come under the law? If he had not been our surety, and undertook for us? Our faith therefore must go to Christ, as made under the law, not only taking our nature upon him, but our debt also, our nature as men, and our debt as sinful men; *He hath made himself to become sin for us who knew no sin*, 2 Cor. v. 21. (*i. e.*) He made him to be handled as a sinner for us under the law; though he knew no sin on his part, continued in all things written in the book of the law to do them. If faith be inquisitive, when was Christ made under the law? I answer, Even then when he was circumcised; thus

Paul protests, Gal. v. 3. *I testify to every man that he that is circumcised, is a debtor to do the whole law.* Christ at his circumcision entred into bond with us, and undertook for us; and therefore then, and not till then, he had his name given him, Luke ii. 21. *Jesus a Saviour*; and from that time he was a debtor *to do the whole law*; not only to suffer, but also to do, for he both satisfied the curse, and fulfilled the commandments. O remember this! as Christ, and as Christ in the flesh, so Christ in the flesh made under the law, is principally to be in the eye of our faith: if we put all together, our first view of faith is, to *look on Christ, God in the flesh, made under the law.*

4. Faith going to Christ as God in the flesh, and as made under the law, it is principally to look to the end and meaning of Christ, as being God in the flesh, and as fulfilling the law.

Now, if we would know the meaning of Christ in all this, the apostle tells us of a remote, and of a more immediate end.

1. Of a remote end, Gal. iv. 4, 5. *God sent forth his Son made of a woman, made under the law, to redeem them that were under the law, that we might receive the adoption of sons*: this was Christ's meaning, or the remote end of Christ. Alas! we were strangers from the adoption, and we lay under the law as men whom sentence had passed on: now from this latter we are redeemed; he was under the law, that we might be redeemed from under the law; nor is that all, but as we are redeemed, so are we adopted the children of God: and this end I rather attribute to the life of Christ, *that we might receive the adoption,* (i. e.) from the estate of prisoners condemned, that we might be translated into the estate of children adopted. O the mercy of God! who ever heard of a condemned man to be afterwards adopted? Would not a condemned prisoner think himself happy to escape with life? But the zeal of the Lord of hosts hath performed this; we are in Christ both pardoned and adopted; and by this means the joy and glory of God's heavenly inheritance is estated upon us; O let our faith look mainly to this design and plot of Christ! he was made under the law, yea, and under the directive part of the law by his life; he fulfilled every jot and tittle of the law, by his active obedience, that we might be intitled to glory, that we might be adopted to the inheritance of the saints in glory.

2. For the more immediate end of Christ, the apostle tells us, that Christ was made under the law, or fulfilled all righteousness, Rom. viii. 4. *That the law might be fulfilled in us.* In Christ's life were we represented, and so this fulfilling of all righteousness is accounted ours, *That the law might be fulfilled in us.* O my soul, look to this! herein lies the pith and the marrow of thy justification; of thyself thou canst do nothing that good is, but Christ fulfilled the law in thy stead, and if now thou wilt but act, and exercise thy faith, thou mayest thereby find, and feel the virtue and efficacy of Christ's righteousness, and actual obedience, flowing into thy own soul. But here is the question, how should I manage my faith: Or how should I act it to feel Christ's righteousness my righteousness? I answer, 1. Thy way is to discover and discern this righteousness of Christ; this holy and perfect life of the Lord Jesus Christ in the whole and in all the parts of it, as it is laid down in the written word: much hath been said of it in those four years of Christ's ministry, but especially in the last year; I shall say more anon in our conformity to Christ, whether also thou mayest have recourse. 2. Thy way is to believe, and to receive this discovery, as sacred and unquestionable, in reference to thy own soul, as intended for thee, for thy use and benefit. 3. Thy way is to apprehend, apply, and to improve this discovery, according to that judgment and proposal, to those uses, ends, and benefits, to which thou believest they were designed. Yea, but there lies the question, how may that be done? I answer,

1. Setting before thee that discovery (that perfect life of Christ in the whole, and all the parts of it) thou must first endeavour to be deeply humbled for thy great inconformity thereto, in whole and in part.

2. Still keeping thy spirit intent on the pattern, thou must quicken, provoke, and increase thy sluggish and drowsy soul, with renewed, redoubled vigilancy and industry to come up higher towards it, and (if it were possible) completely to it.

3. Yet having the same discovery, rule, and copy before thee, thou must exercise faith thereupon, as that which was performed, and is accepted on thy behalf. And so go to God, and there represent, offer, and tender Christ's holy life, and active obe-

obedience unto him. And that first to fill up the defects of thy utmost endeavour. Secondly, To put a righteousness, price, value, and worth, upon what thou dost, and attainest to. Thirdly, To make Christ's righteousness thy own, that thou mayest say with the Psalmist, in way of assurance, *O God, my righteousness.* O my soul, if thou wouldest thus live by faith, or thus act thy faith on Christ's life, Christ's righteousness, Christ's active obedience, what a blessed life wouldest thou live? Then mightest thou find and feel Christ's righteousness thy righteousness; I say thy righteousness, in respect of its efficacy, but not in respect of its formality; for so sinners would be their own mediators. But of some of these particulars I shall speak more largely in our conformity to Christ's holy life.

2. For encouragements to bring on souls thus to believe on Christ, consider,

1. The fulness of this object; Christ's life is full, it is very comprehensive; it contains holiness and happiness, sanctification and justification if Christ's garments were healing, how much more so main and essential a part of Christ, even the half of Christ as it were, for so is Christ's life: it is vehemently to be suspected, that the true reason why so much is said of his death, and so little in comparison of his life, it is either because we understand not the fulness of his life, or because we are carnal and selfish, affecting freedom from hell, more than holiness on earth, some benefit by Christ more than conformity to Christ. O come! see the fulness of Christ's life in reference to our sanctification; was it not a most exact model of perfection! A most curious exemplification of God's whole word? An express idea, image, representation of the whole mind of God? A full precedent for all others to walk by, to work by, to live by? And in reference to justification, is not Christ's life the object of faith and justifying? Nay, is not Christ's life the object of justifying faith, as well as Christ's death, resurrection, ascension, session, intercession? The assertors of Christ's active and passive obedience for us, can tell us of two things in the law intended, one principal, *viz.* Obedience; and another secondary, *viz.* Malediction, supposition of disobedience; so that sin being once committed, there must be a double act to justification, the suffering of the curse, and the fulfilling of righteousness anew; the one is satisfaction for the injury we have done unto God as our judge, and the other is a performance of a service which we owe unto God as our Maker. O then how large, and full, and comprehensive is this life of Christ;

2. Consider the excellency, the glory of this object: Christ's life is glorious; and hence it is that the righteousness of Christ, is the most glorious garment that ever the saints of God did wear. It is Marlorat's saying, ' That the church which ' puts on Christ and his righteousness, is more il-' lustrious than the air is by the sun.' John thus sets her out in his vision, Rev. xii. 1. *And there appeared a great wonder in heaven, a woman clothed with the sun, and the moon under her feet.* I take this to be a lofty poetical description of Christ's imputed righteousness. Imagine a garment were cut out of the sun, and put upon us, how glorious would we be? O, but the righteousness of Christ is much more glorious; no wonder if the church clothed with the sun *tread the moon under her feet,* (i. e.) if she trample on all sublunary things, which are uncertain and changeable as the moon, Phil. iii. 8, 9. *I count all things but dung* (saith Paul) *that I may win Christ; and be found in him, not having my own righteousness, which is of the law, but that which is through the faith of Christ, the righteousness which is of God by faith.* When Paul compares Christ's righteousness with the glory of the world, then is the world but dung. O the glory! O the excellency of the righteousness of Christ!

3. Consider the suitableness of this object; Christ's life, and the virtue of it, is most suitable to our condition: thus I might apply Christ to every condition, if thou art sick, he is a physician: if thou fearest death, he is the *way, the truth, and the life:* if thou art hungry, he is the bread of life: if thou art thirsty, he is the water of life. But, not to insist on these words, it is the daily complaint of the best of saints, ' O my sins! I had ' thought these sins had been wholly subdued, ' but now I feel they return upon me again; now ' I feel the springs in the bottom fill up my soul ' again; Oh I am weary of myself, and weary of ' my life! oh! what will become of me?' In this case now Christ's life is most suitable; his righteousness is a continual righteousness; it is not a cistern, but *a fountain open for thee to wash in,* Zech. xiii. 1. As sin abounds, so grace in this gift

of righteousness, abounds much more. Christ's life in this respect is compared to *changes of garments*, Zech. iii. 4. Thou criest, 'O what shall become of me? Oh I feel new sins, and old sins committed afresh:' Why, but these *changes of garments* will hide all thy sins: if thou art but clothed with the robes of Christ's righteousness, there shall never enter into the Lord's heart one hard thought towards thee of casting thee off, or of taking revenge upon any new occasion or fall into sin. Why, here is the blessedness of all those that believe. Oh, then believe; say not, 'would Christ be incarnate for me; would he lead such a life on earth for my soul?' Why? Yes, for thy soul; never speak of thy sins, as if they should be any hindrance of thy faith: if the wicked that apply this righteousness presumptuously can say, *Let us sin that grace may abound*, and so they make no other use of grace but to run in debt, and to sin with licence; how much rather mayest thou say on good ground, 'Oh, let me believe! oh, let me own my portion in this righteousness of Christ! that, as my sins have abounded, so my love may abound; that as my sins have been exceeding great, so the Lord may be exceeding sweet; that as my sins continue and increase, so my thankfulness to Christ, and glory in God, and triumph over sin, death and the grave, may also increase.' Why, thus be encouraged to believe thy part in the Lord Jesus Christ.

SECT. VI.

Of loving Jesus in that respect.

6. LEt us love Jesus as carrying on the great work of our salvation for us during his life. Now what is love, but 'a motion of the appetite, by which the soul unites itself to what seems fair unto it?' And if so, O what a lovely object is the life of Christ? Who can read over his life? Who can think over his worthiness, both in his person, relations, actions, and several administration, and not love him with a singular love? That which set the daughters of Jerusalem in a posture of seeking after Christ, was that description of Christ, which the spouse made of him, Can. v. 10, 11, 12, 13, 14, 15. *My beloved is white and ruddy, the chiefest of ten thousands, His head is as the most fine gold, his locks are bushy, and black as a raven. His eyes are as the eyes of doves, by the rivers of water, washed with milk, and fitly set. His cheeks are as a bed of spices, and sweet flowers: his lips like lilies dropping sweet-smelling myrrh*, &c. By these are intimated unto us the government of Christ, the unsearchable councils of Christ, the pure nature of Christ, without any impurity or uncleanness; the gracious promises of Christ, the soul-saving instructions of Christ; the holy actions, and just administrations of Christ; the tender affections, and amiable smilings of Christ, the gracious, inward, and wonderful workings of Christ; so that he is altogether lovely, or he is composed of loves: from top to toe there is nothing in Christ, but 'tis most fair and beautiful, lovely and desirable.——Now, as this description enflamed the daughters of Jerusalem, so to act our loves toward the Lord Jesus Christ, take we a copy of the record of the spirit in scriptures; see what they say of Christ; this was his own advice, *Search the scriptures, for*——*they are they which testify of me*, John v. 39.

O my soul, much hath been said to persuade thee to faith; and if now thou believest thy part in those several actings of Christ, why let thy faith take thee by the hand, and lead thee from one step to another; from his baptism to his temptations, from his temptations to his manifestations; and so on: is not here fuel enough for love to feed upon? Canst thou read the history of love, (for such is the history of Christ's life) and not be all on a flame? Come, read again!, there is nothing in Christ but 'tis lovely, winning, and drawing; as,

1. When he saw thee full of filth, he goes down into the waters of baptism, that he might prepare a way for the cleansing of thy defiled and polluted soul.

2. When he saw the devil ready to swallow thee up, or by his baits to draw or drag thy soul down to hell, he himself enters into the lists with the devil, and he overcomes him, that thou mightest overcome, and triumph with Christ in his glory.

3. When he saw thee in danger of death, thro' thy own unbelief, for *except thou sawest in his hands the print of the nails, and put thy finger into the print of the nails*; except thou hadst clear manifestations of Christ even to thine own sense, thou

wouldest

wouldest not believe; he condescends so far to succour thy weakness, as to manifest himself by several witnesses; three in heaven, and three on earth; yea, he multiplies his three on earth to thousands of thousands; so many were the signs witnessing Christ, that the disciple which testified of them, could say, John xxi 25. *If they should be written every one, the world could not contain the books that should be written.*

4. When he saw thee buying and selling in the temple, yea, making merchandize of the temple itself, I mean of thy soul, which is the temple of the Holy Ghost; he steps in to whip out those buyers and sellers, those lusts and corruptions: O (cries he) *will ye sell away your souls for trash? O what is a man profited though he gain the whole world, and lose his own soul?*

5. When he saw thee like the horse and mule, Prov xxx. 2, 3. *More brutish than any man, not having the understanding of a man; thou neither learnedst wisdom, nor hadst the knowledge of the most holy*; He came with his instructions, adding line unto line, and precept on precept, *teaching and preaching the gospel of the kingdom*, Matth. iv. 23. And sealing his truths with many miracles, that thou mayest believe, *and in believing thou mightest have life through his name*: and O what is this but to make thee wise unto salvation?

6. When he saw thee a sinner of the Gentiles, a stranger from the commonwealth of Israel, and without God in the world, he sent his apostles and messengers abroad, and bad them preach the gospel to thee, *q. d.* ' Go to such a one in the dark ' corner of the world, an isle at such a distance from ' the nation of the Jews, and set up my throne a-' mongst that people; open the most precious ca-' binet of my love there, and amongst that people, ' tell such a soul, that Jesus Christ came into the ' world to save sinners, of whom he is one.' O admirable love!

7. When he saw thee cast down in thyself, and refusing thy own mercy, crying and saying, *What? Is it possible that Jesus Christ should send a message to such a dead dog as I am? Why, the apostles commission seems otherwise*; Matth. x. 5, 6. *' Go not into the way of the Gentiles, or into any city of the Samaritans enter ye not? but go rather to the lost sheep of the house of Israel.* ' O! I am a lost sheep, but ' not being of the house of Israel, what hope is there ' that ever I should be found?' He then appeared, and even then he spread his arms wide to receive thy soul: he satisfied thee then of another commission given to his apostles, *Go, teach all nations: and he cried even then, Come unto me, thou that art weary and heavy laden with sin, and I will receive thee into my bosom, and give thee rest there.* Matth. xxviii. 19.

8. When he saw thee in suspence, and heard thy complaint, ' But if I come, shall I find sweet ' welcome? I have heard, that his ways are narrow ' and strait: oh! it is an hard passage, and an high ' ascent up to heaven,' Luke xiii. 24. *Many seek to enter in, but shall not be able*: ' oh! what shall ' become of my poor soul?' Why, he told thee otherwise, that *all his ways are ways of pleasantness, and all his paths peace*, Prov. iii. 17. He would give thee his Spirit that should bear the weight, and make all light: he would sweeten the ways of Christianity to thee, that thou shouldest find by experience, that *his yoke was easy, and his burden was light*, Matth. xi. 29.

9. When he saw the wretchedness of thy nature, and original pollution, he took upon him thy nature, and by this means took away thy original sin. O here is the lovely object! what is it but the absolute holiness and perfect purity of the nature of Christ? This is the fairest beauty that ever eye beheld: this is that compendium of all glories: now, if love is a motion and union of the appetite to what is lovely, how shouldest thou flame forth in loves upon the Lord Jesus Christ? This is rendered as the reason of those sparklings, *Thou art fairer than the children of men*, Psal. xlv. 2.

10. When he saw thee actually unclean, a transgressor of the law in thought, word and deed; then said he, Heb. x. 9. *Lo, I come to do thy will, O God*: And wherefore will he do God's will, but merely on thy behalf? O my soul, canst thou read over all these passages of love, and dost thou not yet cry out, *O stay me, comfort me, for I am sick of love*. Can a man stand by a hot and fiery furnace and never be warmed? Oh for an heart in some measure answerable to these loves; surely even good nature hates to be in debt for love; and is there in thee, O my soul, neither grace nor yet goodnature? O God forbid! awake, awake thy ardent love towards thy Lord Jesus Christ! why art thou rock and not flesh, if thou beest

beest not wounded with these heavenly darts? Christ loves thee, is not that enough? Fervent affection is apt to draw love where is little or no beauty; and excellent beauty is apt to draw the heart where there is no answer of affection at all; but when these two meet together, what breast can hold against them? See, O my soul! here is the sum of all the particulars thou hast heard, Christ loves thee, and Christ is lovely: his heart is set upon thee, who is a thousand times fairer than all the children of men: doth not this double consideration, like a mighty loadstone, snatch thy heart unto it, and almost draw it forth of thy very breast? O sweet Saviour, thou could say even of thy poor church, (though labouring under many imperfections) Cant. iv. 9, 10. *Thou hast ravished my heart, my sister, my spouse, thou hast ravished mine heart with one of thine eyes, with one chain of thy neck. How fair is thy love, my sister, my spouse? How much better is thy love than wine, and the smell of thine ointments than all spices?* Couldest thou, O blessed Saviour, be so taken with the incurious and homely features of the church; and shall I not much more be enamoured with thy absolute and divine beauty? It pleased thee, my Lord, out of thy sweet ravishments of thy heavenly love, to say to thy poor church, *Turn away thine eyes from me, for they have overcome me,* Cant. vi. 5. But oh, let me say to thee, ' Turn thine eyes to me, ' that they may overcome me: my Lord, I would ' be thus ravished, I would be overcome, I would ' be thus out of myself, that I might be all in thee.'

Thus is the language of true love to Christ? but, alas! how dully and flatly do I speak it? O my soul, how art thou out of frame? In creature-communion I usually feel thee warm, and vigorous, active, and very strong; but now thy heart is inditing of a good matter, thou art speaking of the things which thou hast made concerning the king: thy words do almost freeze between thy lips; how chill and cold art thou in thy converses with Jesus Christ? Oh! this puts me in mind of my deserts; surely had Christ's love been but like this faint and feeble love of mine, I had been a damned wretch without all hope. O Christ, I am ashamed that I love thee so little, I perceive thy loves are great by all those actions in thy life; come, *blow upon my garden,* persuade me by thy Spirit, that I may love thee much: *Many sins are forgiven me,* O that I may *love thee much.*

SECT. VII.

Of joying in Jesus in that respect.

7. LET us joy in Jesus, as carrying on the great work of our salvation for us during his life. But what is there in Christ's life, or in all the passages of his life to stir up joy? I answer, All his life, and all the passages of his life, if rightly applied, are excellent matter for the stirring up of thy affection: indeed the main of the work is in the application of Christ's life: if ever we rejoice spiritually in Christ, we must bring together the object and the faculty: and this union of the object and the faculty is usually wrought by contemplation, or by confidence, or by fruition: I shall but a while insist on these, that we may come up at last to rejoice in Christ; yea, if it were possible to rejoice and again rejoice.

1. Let us contemplate on this life of Christ, Let us think of it in our minds: there is a kind of delight in knowing some things speculatively, which we would abhor to know experimentally; and therefore the devil's first temptation was drawn from the knowledge of evil as well as good: he knew that the mind of man would receive content in the understanding of that which in its own nature had no perfection at all. Now, if there be a delight in the contemplation of evil, how much more in the contemplation of that which is good? And is not the life of Christ, the graces, the virtues, the holy actions, the dear affections of Jesus Christ to us-ward good, and very good? Come then, stir up our memories, let us be settled men! let us spend our frequent thoughts upon this blessed object: the reason we miss of our joys, is because we are so little in contemplation of our Christ. It is said, ' That he pities us in our sorrows, but he delights ' in us when we delight in him.' Certainly he would have us to delight in him; and to that purpose he way-lays our thoughts, that wheresoever we look, we shall still think on him: O my soul, cast thine eyes which way thou wilt, and thou shalt hardly think on any thing, but Christ Jesus hath taken the name of that very thing upon himself; What, is it day? And dost thou behold the sun?

fun? He is called *the Sun of righteousness*, Mal. iv. 2. Or, is it night? And dost thou behold the stars? He is called a star, Numb. xxiv. 17, 19. *There shall come a star out of Jacob.——Out of Jacob shall he come that shall have dominion.* Or, is it morning? And dost thou behold the morning-star? He is called *the bright morning-star*, Rev. xxii. 16. Or, is it noon? And dost thou behold clear light all the world over in thy hemisphere? He is called *the light*, and *that light that enlightneth every man that cometh into the world*, John i. 7, 8, 9. Or, to come a little nearer, if thou lookest on the earth, and takest a view of the creatures about thee, seest thou the silly sheep? He is called *a sheep*, Isa. liii. 7. *As a sheep before her shearer is dumb, so he openeth not his mouth:* Or, seest thou a lamb bleating after the harmless sheep? He is called *a lamb*, John i. 29. *Behold the Lamb of God which taketh away the sins of the world.* Seest thou a shepherd watching over his flock, by day or night? He is called *a shepherd*, John x. 15. *I am the good Shepherd, and know my sheep, and am known of mine*, Or, seest thou a fountain, rivers, waters? He is called *a fountain*, Zech. xiii. 1. *In that day there shall be a fountain opened to the house of David, and to the inhabitants of Jerusalem, for sin and uncleanness*, Or, seest thou a tree good for food and pleasant to the eye? He is called *the tree of life*, Pro. iii. 18. And *as the apple-tree among the trees of the wood, so is my beloved among the sons*, Cant. ii. 3. Seest thou a rose, a lily, any fair flower in thy garden? He is called *a rose, a lily*, Cant. ii. 1. *I am the rose of Sharon, and the lily of the valleys:* or, to come a little nearer yet, art thou within doors? John x. 9. *I am the door, by me if any man enter in he shall be saved, and shall go in and out, and shall find pasture.* Art thou adorning thyself, and takest a view of thy garments? He is called *a garment*, Rom. xiii. 14. *Put ye on the Lord Jesus Christ.* Art thou eating meat, and takest a view of what is on thy table? He is called *bread, the bread of God, true bread from heaven, the bread of life, the living bread which came down from heaven*, John vi. 32, 35, 51. Why thus Christ way-lays our thoughts, that wheresoever we look, we should ever think of Christ.——Now these thoughts or contemplations of Christ, are they that bring together the object and the faculty of joy: I cannot think of Christ, or the life of Christ, of Christ preaching, or of Christ preached, but I must rejoice in Christ, as sometimes the apostle said, Phil. i. 18. *Christ is preached, whether in pretence or truth, I matter not, but in that he is preached, I therein do rejoice, yea, and will rejoice.*

2. Let us consider in Christ, let us upon good grounds hope our share and interest in the life of Christ; O this would strengthen our joy, yea, fill us with joy unspeakable and glorious: where true joy is, there is 1*st*, a thinking of the good in our minds; and, 2*dly*, an expecting of it in our heart. Hence it is, that whatsoever doth encourage our hope, the same doth enlarge our delight: the apostle joins both these together, Rom. xii. 12. *Rejoice in hope*: hope and joy go both together; if I have but assured hope that Christ's life is mine, I cannot but rejoice therein; on the contrary, if my hope fluctuate, if I am but uncertain, if I look on the influence and benefits of Christ's life as only possibly mine, and no farther, then is my comfort but unstable and weak: sometimes we find Christ compared to a rich store-house; *In him*, (saith the apostle) *are hid all the treasures of wisdom and knowledge*, Col. ii. 3. But, alas! what am I richer for all his treasures, if I have no claim thereto or interest therein? Or what can I joy in another's riches, when I myself am wretched, and miserable, and poor, and blind, and naked? Look to this, O my soul, pursue again and again thy grounds of hope as afore laid down; do not slightly run them over, thou canst not be too sure of Christ: thou readest in the gospel this and that passage of thy Jesus, canst thou lay thine hand on every line, and say, ' This passage is mine, this sermon was preached, and this miracle was wrought ' for me, that I might believe, and that in believing ' I might have life through his name?' O then, how shouldest thou but rejoice? When Zaccheus in the sycamore tree heard but Christ's voice, *Zaccheus, make haste, and come down, for today I must abide in thy house*, Luke xix. 5, 6. O what haste made Zaccheus to receive Christ? He came down hastily and received him joyfully. This offer of Christ to Zaccheus is thine as well as his, if thy hope be right, *Come down, poor soul*, (saith Christ) *this day must I abide in thy house*. O then what joy should be in thy heart when Christ comes in, or

when

when thou feelest Christ come in, John iii. 29. *The friend of the bridegroom rejoiceth greatly, because of the bridegroom's voice:* how much more may the bride herself rejoice?

3. Let us come up to more and more, and make fruition of Christ; all other things work out delight, but as they look towards this: now, in this fruition of Christ are contained these things; First, A propriety unto Christ, for as a sick man doth not feel the joy of a sound man's health, so neither doth a stranger to Christ feel the joy of a believer in Christ: how should he joy in Christ that can make no claim to him in the least degree? But to that we have spoken. Secondly, A possession of Christ, this exceedingly enlargeth our joy. O how sweet was Christ to the spouse, when she could say, Cant. vi. 3. *I am my well-beloved's, and my beloved is mine, he feedeth among the lilies,* q. d. We have took possession of each other, he is mine through faith, and I am his through love; we are both so knit by an inseparable union, that nothing shall be able to separate us two; *he feedeth among the lilies,* he refresheth himself and his saints by his union and communion with them: many are taken up with the joy and comfort of outward possessions, but Christ is better than all; in Christ is comprized every scattered comfort here below, *Christ is mine,* (saith the soul) *and all mine.* 3. An accommodation of Christ to the soul, and this is it that completes our joy: it is not bare possession of Christ which bringeth real delight, but an applying of Christ unto that end and purpose for which he was appointed: it is not the having of Christ, but the using of Christ, which makes him beneficial. O the usefulness of Christ to all believing souls! the scriptures are full of this, as appears by all his titles in scripture: he is *our life, our light, our bread, our water, our milk, our wine; his flesh is meat indeed, and his blood is drink indeed.* He is our father, our brother, our friend, our husband, our king, our priest, our prophet; he is our justification, our sanctification, our wisdom, our redemption; he is our peace, our mediation, our atonement, our reconciliation, our *all in all.* Alas! I look on myself, and I see I am nothing, I have nothing without Jesus Christ: here's a temptation, I cannot resist it; here's a corruption, I cannot overcome it; here's a persecution, I cannot down with it; well, but Christ is mine, I have interest in Christ, and I have possession of Christ, and I find enough in Christ to supply all my wants, he was set up on purpose, to give me grace and to renew my strength, so that if I make my application to Christ, *I can do all things,* Phil. iv. 13. *I can suffer the loss of all things,* Phil. iii. 8. I can conquer all things, nay, *in all things be more than a conqueror through him that loves me,* Rom. viii. 37. Oh the joy now that this accommodation brings to my soul! I see it is nothing but Christ, and therefore I cannot but rejoice in this Christ, or I must rejoice in nothing at all. Surely *we are the circumcision, which rejoice in Christ Jesus, and have no confidence in the flesh,* Phil. iii. 3.

O my soul! where is thy faculty of joy? Come, bring it to this blessed object, the Lord Jesus Christ; if thou knowest not how? First, contemplate on Christ, think on those several passages in his life: those that lived with him, and stood by to see them, it is said of them, That *they all rejoiced for the glorious things that were done by him,* Luke xiii. 17. Or if thy heart be so dull and heavy, that this will not raise it up, then look to thy grounds of hope, and confidence in Christ; so long as thou doubtest of him, or of thy interest in him, how shouldest thou rejoice, or be cheerful in thy spirit? The poor man could not speak it without tears, *Lord, I believe, help thou my unbelief,* Mark ix. 24. A believing unbelief, a wavering, staggering, trembling faith cannot be without some wounds in spirit; O be confident, and this will make thee cheerful: or if yet thou feelest not this affection to stir, aspire to fruition, yea, to more and more fruition of Christ, and union with Christ; and to that purpose, consider thy propriety to Christ, thy possession of Christ, and the accommodation or usefulness of Christ to thy condition, whatsoever it is. What! will not these things move thy spiritual delight? Canst thou not hear Christ say, 'All I am is thine, and all I have done ' is thine, for thy use, and for thy benefit?' And doth not thy heart leap within thee at each word? O my soul, I cannot but check thee for thy deadness: it is said, That when *Christ was at the descent of the mount of Olives, that the whole multitude of disciples began to rejoice, and praise God with a loud voice, for all the mighty works that they had seen,* Luke xix. 37. What? A multitude of

disciples

disciples rejoicing in Christ's acts? And art thou not one amongst the multitude? If thou art a disciple, rejoice thou? surely it concerns thee as much as them, and therefore rejoice; lift up thy voice in harmony with the rest; *rejoice, and again rejoice.*

SECT. VIII.

Of calling on Jesus in that respect.

8. LET us call on Jesus, or on God the Father, in and through Jesus. Thus we read, That looking up to Jesus, or lifting up the eyes to Jesus, goes also for prayer in God's book, Psalm v. 3. *My prayer will I direct to thee* (faith David) *and will look up,* Psal. lxix. 3. And *mine eyes fail with looking upwards.* Faith in prayer will often come out at the eye in lieu of another door; our affections will often break out at the window when the door is closed: thus *Stephen looked up to heaven,* Acts vii. 55. He sent a post, a greedy, pitiful, and hungry look up to Jesus Christ out at the window, at the nearest passage, to tell him, that a poor friend was coming to him; why thus, let us look up to Jesus by calling on him: now this calling on him contains prayer, and praise.

1. We must pray, that all these transactions of Jesus during his life, or during his ministry upon earth, may be ours; we hope it is so, and we believe it to be so, but for all that we must pray that it may be so: there is no contradiction betwixt hope and faith, and prayer, but rather a concatenation, Mark ix. 24. *Lord, I believe,* yet *help my unbelief,* or *be it to me according to my faith, how weak soever:* it will bear that sense.

2. We must praise God for all those passages in Christ's life. Thus did the multitude, *They praised God with a loud voice, for all the mighty works that they had seen, saying,* Luke xix. 37, 38. *Blessed be the king that comes in the name of the Lord, peace in heaven, and glory in the highest.* What (my soul) hath Christ done all this for thee? Was he made under the law, to redeem thy soul, and adopt thee for his son to the inheritance of heaven? Came he down from heaven, and travelled he so many miles on earth, to woo and win thy heart? Spent he so many sermons, and so many miracles to work thee into faith? O how shouldest thou bless, and prize, and magnify his name? How shouldest thou break out into that blessed hymn, *To him that loved us, and hath made us kings, and priests unto God, and his Father, to him be glory and dominion, for ever and ever. Amen.* Rev i. 5, 6.

SECT. IX.

Of conforming to Jesus in that respect.

9. LET us conform to Jesus, as he acted for us in his life. Looking to Jesus intends this especially; we must look as one looks to his pattern; as mariners at sea, that they may run a right course, keep an eye on that ship that bears the light; so, in the race that is set before us, we must have our eye on Jesus, our blessed pattern. This must be our constant quere, 'Is this the 'course that Jesus steered?' Or, that I may enlarge.——

In this particular I shall examine these three queries: 1. Wherein we must conform? 2. Why we must conform? 3. How we must conform to this life of Jesus?

For the first, wherein we must conform? I answer.——

1. Negatively, We must not, cannot conform to Christ, in these works proper to his Godhead, as in working miracles. I deny not but that the works of miracles were by way of privilege, and temporary dispensation granted to the apostles and some others, but this was but for ministry and service, not for their sanctity or salvation; nor must we conform to Christ in those works of his mediation, as, in redeeming souls, in satisfying divine justice for our sin, Psal. xlix. 7. *No man can redeem his brother, nor give to God a ransom for him.* 1 Tim. ii. 5. *There is but one Mediator between God and man, the man Christ Jesus.* Nor must we conform to Christ in those works of his government, and influence into his church, as in his dispensing of his Spirit; in quickening of his word; in subduing of his enemies; in collecting of his members: all these are personal honours, which belong unto Christ, as he is head of the church: and to these works, if we should endeavour to conform, we should crack our sinews, dissolve our silver cords, and never the nearer. —— Nor need we to conform to Christ in some other particulars, in his

his voluntary poverty, *he became poor for our sakes*, 2 Cor. viii. 9. In his ceremonial performances, as in going up to Jerusalem at the feasts; in his perpetual grave deportment; we never read that Jesus laughed, and but once or twice that he rejoiced in spirit. Alas, the declensions of our natures cannot come up to this pattern, nor did I look at these passages as any acts of moral obedience at all.

2. Affirmatively, or positively, we must conform to Christ's life.

1. In respect of his judgment, will, affections, compassions. Look we at his Spirit, observe what mind was in Jesus Christ, and therein do we endeavour to conform, Phil. ii. 5. *Let the same mind be in you* (saith the apostle) *which was in Christ*; and *we have the mind of Christ* (saith the apostle) 1 Cor. ii. 16.

2. In respect of his virtues, graces, habitual holiness, Matth. xi. 29. *Learn of me*, (saith Christ) *for I am meek and lowly in heart*. Christ was of a meek and gentle spirit, *I beseech you by the meekness and gentleness of Christ*, saith Paul, 2 Cor. x. 2. And Christ was of an humble and lowly spirit, Phil. ii. 6, 7. *Being in the form of God, he thought it no robbery to be equal with God: yet he made himself of no reputation, and took upon him the form of a servant*. I might instance in all other graces, for he had them all in fulness, *And of his fulness have all we received, grace for grace*, John i. 16.

3. In respect of his words, talk, spiritual and heavenly language. The very officers of the priests could say of Christ, *Never man spake like this man*, John vii. 46. And sometimes they *all wondred at the gracious words which proceeded out of his mouth*, Luke iv. 22. He never sinned in word, *neither was guile found in his mouth: who, when he was reviled, reviled not again*, 1 Pet. ii. 22, 23. The apostle, speaking thus of Christ, he tells us, That herein *Christ left us an example, that we should follow his steps*, verse 21.

4. In respect of his carriage, conversation, close walking with God. The apostle sets forth Christ as an high priest, who *was holy, harmless, undefiled, and separate from sinners*, Heb. vii. 26. And, in like manner, saith Peter, *Ye are a chosen generation, a royal priest-hood, a holy nation, a peculiar people; that ye should shew forth the virtues of him, who hath called you out of darkness into his marvellous light*, 1 Pet. ii. 9. *that ye should shew forth the virtues*, (i. e.) That, in your lives and conversations, you should express those graces and virtues which were so eminent and exemplary in Jesus Christ: that you should not only have them, but that you should hold them forth; [*exaggelein*], the word signifies properly *to preach*, so clearly should we express the virtues of Christ, as if our lives were so many sermons of the life of Christ.

5. In respect of all his acts, practices, duties of moral obedience: we find in the life of Christ many particular carriages and acts of obedience to his heavenly Father, whereof some were moral, and some ceremonial. Now, all these are not for our imitation, but only such moral acts, as concerning which we have both his pattern and precept: come, let us mark this one rule, and we need no more, ' whatsoever he commanded, and whatso- ' ever he did, of precise morality, we are therein ' bound to follow his steps.' I join together his commands and deeds, because in those things which he did, but commands not, we need not to conform; but in those things which he both did, and commanded, we are bound to follow him. In such a case, his laws and practice differ but as a map and guide, a law, a judge, a rule and precedent.

In respect of all these particulars, and especially in respect of Christ's moral obedience, the whole life of Christ was a discipline, a living, shining and exemplary precept unto men; and hence it is that we find such names given to him in scripture, as signifies not only preeminence, but exemplariness; thus he was called *a prince*, Dan. ix. 25. *A leader*, Isa. lv. 4. *A governor*, Matth. ii. 6. *A captain*, ii. 10. *A chief shepherd*, 1 Peter. v. 4. *A forerunner or conduct into glory*, Heb. ii. 20. *A light to the Jews*, Exod. xiii. 21. *A light to the Gentiles*, Luke ii. 3. *A light to every man that entreth into the world*, John i. 9. All which titles, as they declared his dignity, so his exemplariness, that he was the author and pattern of holiness to his people. And as for all other saints, though they are imitable, yet with limitation unto him, only so far as they express his life in their conversation, 1 Cor. xi. 1. *Be ye followers of me, even as I am of Christ*.

For the second, Why we must conform? Upon what motives? I answer, 1. Because Christ hath done and suffered very much to that end and purpose. Sometimes I have wondred why Christ would

would do so much, and suffer so much, as the evangelists, in their histories, relate? This I believe, that Jesus was perfect God, and perfect man; and that every action of his life, and but one hour of his passion and death, might have been satisfactory, and enough for the expiation and reconcilement of ten thousand worlds. But now I am answered, that all those instances of holiness, and all those kinds of virtues, and all those degrees of passion, and all that effusion of his blood, was partly on this account, that he might become an example to us, that he might shine to all the ages and generations of the world, and so be a guiding star, and a pillar of fire to them in their journey towards heaven. O my soul! how doth this call on thee to conform to Christ? What? that a smaller expence should be enough to thy justification; and yet that the whole magazine should not procure thy sanctification? That, at a lesser sum of obedience, God might have pardoned thy sin; and yet, at a greater sum, thou wilt not so much as imitate his holiness? In a dark night, if an *ignis fatuus* go before thee, thou art so amused with that little flame, that thou art apt to follow it, and lose thyself; and wilt thou not follow the glories of the Sun of righteousness, who, by so many instances, calls upon thee, and who will guide thee into safety, and secure thee against all imaginable dangers? God forbid! if it had not been for thy imitation, I cannot think that Christ should have lived on earth so many years, to have done so many gracious meritorious works. O, think of this!

2. Because Christ is the best and the highest example of holiness that ever the world had; hence we must needs conform to Christ, (as the apostle argues) because *he is the first-born among many brethren*, Rom. viii. 29. The first in every kind is propounded as a pattern of the rest; now, Christ is the first-born, Christ is the head of all the predestinate, as the first-born was wont to be the head in all families. The old saying is, *Regis ad exemplar, &c.* A very deformity was sometimes counted an honour, if it were an imitation of the prince: It is storied of Nero, that having a wry neck, there was such an ambition in men to follow the court, that it became the fashion and gallantry of those times, to hold their necks awry; and shall not Christ, the king of saints, be much more imitated by the saints? Christ is *the head of the body, the beginning, the first-born from the dead, in all things he hath the preeminence*, Col. i. 18. And the rule is general, that, ' That which is first, and best ' in any land, is the rule and measure of all the ' rest.' Why, such is Christ. O! then, let him be the guide of our life, and of our manners.

3. Because Christ doth not only give us an example, but he doth cherish, succour, and assist us by its easiness, complacency, and proportion to us. Some sweetly observe, that ' Christ's piety (which ' we must imitate) was even, constant, unblameable, complying with civil society, without any ' affrightment of precedent, or without any prodigious instances of actions, greater than the imitation of men.' We are not commanded to imitate a life, whose story tells us of extasies in prayer, of abstractions of senses, of extraordinary fastings to the weakning of our spirits, and disabling of all animal operations: no, no; but a life of justice, and temperance, and chastity, and piety, and charity, and devotion; such a life as without which human society cannot be conserved;—— And it is very remarkable, that besides the easiness of this imitation, there is a virtue in the life of Christ; a merit, and impetration in the several passages of Christ's life, to work out our imitation of him. In the Bohemian history, it is reported, that Winceslaus their king, one winter's night going to his devotion in a remote church, his servant Podavivus, who waited on his master, and endeavoured to imitate his master's piety; he began to faint through the violence of the snow and cold; at last the king commanded him to follow him, and to set his feet on the same footsteps which his feet should mark, and set down for him; the servant did so, and presently he fancied, or found a cure. Thus Christ deals with us; it may be we think our way to heaven is troublesome, obscure, and full of objection; well, saith Christ, ' But ' mark my footsteps; come on, and tread where ' I have stood, and you shall find the virtue of my ' example will make all smooth, and easy; you ' shall find the comforts of my company, you shall ' feel the virtue and influence of a perpetual guide.'

4. Because Christ in his word hath commanded us to follow his steps, Matth. xi. 29. *Learn of me, for I am meek and lowly in heart*, John xiii. 13, 14, 15. *And ye call me master, and Lord, and ye say well, for so I am: if I then your Lord*

and master have washed your feet, ye also ought to wash one another's feet, for I have given you an example, that ye should do as I have done to you, Col. iii. 12, 13. *Put on therefore bowels of mercy, kindness, humbleness of mind, meekness, long-suffering, forbearing one another, and forgiving one another; if any man have a quarrel against any, even as Christ forgave you, so also do ye.* 1 Pet. i. 15, 16. *And as he which hath called you is holy, so be ye holy in all manner of conversation; because it is written, Be ye holy, for I am holy.*—— Against this some object, How can we be holy as Christ is holy? First, the thing is impossible; and, secondly, if we could, there would be no need of Christ? But I answer to the first; the thing, if rightly understood, is not impossible: we are commanded to be holy as Christ is holy, not in respect of equality, as if our holiness must be of the same compass with the holiness of Christ; but in respect of quality, our holiness must be of the stamp, and truth, as the holiness of Christ; as when the apostle saith, Rom. xiii. 9. *That we must love our neighbour as ourselves;* the meaning is not, that our love to our neighbour should be mathematically equal to the love of ourselves, for the law doth allow of degrees in love, according to the degrees of relation in the thing beloved, Rom. xii. 9. *Do good unto all men, especially to those of the houshould of faith.* Love to a friend may safely be greater than love to a stranger; or love to a wife, or child, may safely be greater than to a friend; yet in all, our love to others, it must be of the self-same nature, as true, as real, as cordial, as sincere, as solid as that to ourselves; *We must love our neighbour as ourselves,* (i.e.) unfeignedly, and without dissimulation.——Again, I answer, to the second, Christ is needful, notwithstanding our utmost holiness, in two respects: 1. Because we cannot come to full and perfect holiness, and so his grace is requisite to pardon and cover our failings. 2. Because that which we do attain unto, it is not of, or from ourselves, and so his Spirit is requisite to strengthen us unto his service. We must be holy as Christ is holy, yet still we must look at the holiness of Christ, as the sun, and root, and fountain; and that our holiness is but of a beam of that sun, but as a branch of that root, but as a stream of that fountain.

For the third, How we must conform to this life? I answer:

1. Let us frame to ourselves some idea of Christ, let us set before us the life of Christ in the whole, and all the parts of it, as we find it recorded in God's book. It would be a large picture if I should draw it to the full, but, for a taste, I shall give it in few lines. Now then, setting aside the consideration of Christ as God, or as Mediator, or as head of his church,——

1. I look at the mind of Christ, at his judgment, will, affections; such as love, joy, delight, and the rest; and especially at the compassions of Jesus Christ. O the dear affections and compassions which Christ had towards the sons of men! this was his errand from heaven, and while he was upon the earth he was ever acting it, I mean his pitifulness, I mean his affections and compassion *in healing broken hearts,* Luke iv. 18. So the Psalmist, Psal. cxlvii. 3. *He healeth the broken in heart, and bindeth up their wounds.* It is spoken after the manner of a chirurgion: he had a tender heart towards all broken hearts; he endeavours to put all broken bones into their native place again: nor speak I thus only of him in respect of his office; but, as he was man, he had in him such a mind, that he could not but compassionate all in misery: O what bowels, what stirrings, and boilings, and wrestlings of a pained heart, touched with sorrow, was ever, upon occasion, in Jesus Christ! peruse these texts, Matth. xiv. 14. 'And Jesus went 'forth, and saw a great multitude, and he was 'moved with compassion towards them, and he 'healed their sick. Mark vi. 34. And Jesus, when 'he came out, saw much people, and was moved 'with compassion towards them, because they were 'as sheep not having a shepherd. Mark i. 40, 41. 'And there came a leper to him, and kneeling 'down to him, and saying to him, if thou wilt, 'thou canst make me clean: and Jesus, moved 'with compassion, put forth his hand, and touch-'ed him, saying, I will, be thou clean. Matth. 'xv. 32. Then Jesus called his disciples unto him, 'and said, I have compassion on the multitude.' And for the two blind men that cried out, 'Have 'mercy on us, O Lord, thou son of David:' it is said, that 'Jesus stood still,—— and 'he had com-'passion on them, and touched their eyes,' Mat. xx. 34. And the poor prodigal returning, Luke xv. 20. *When he was yet a great way off, his Father saw him, and had compassion, and ran, and*

fell

fell on his neck, and kissed him. How sweet is this last instance! that our sense of sinful weakness should be sorrow and pain to the bowels and heart of Jesus Christ? You that are parents of young children, let me put the case, If some of you, standing in the relation of a father, should see his child, sweat and wrestle under an over-load, till his back were almost broken, and that you should hear him cry, 'Oh, I am gone, I faint, I sink, I die.' would not your bowels be moved to pity? And would not your hands be stretched out to help? Or, if some of you standing in the relation of a mother, should see your sucking child fallen into a pit, and wrestling with the water, and crying for help, would you not stir, nor be moved in heart, nor run to deliver the child from being drowned? Surely you would, and yet all this pity and compassion of yours is but as a shadow of the compassions and dear affections that were and are in the heart of Jesus Christ; O he had a mind devoid of sin, and therefore it could not but be full of pity, mercy, and tender bowels of compassion.

2. I look at the grace in Christ; O he was full of grace, yea, full of all the graces of the Spirit, Cant. i. 13, 14. *A bundle of myrrh is my well-beloved to me:——My beloved is unto me as a cluster of camphire of the vineyards of Engedi.* A bundle of myrrh and a cluster of camphire denote all the graces of the Spirit: as many flowers are bound together in a nosegay, so the variety of the graces of the Spirit concentered in the heart of Jesus Christ, *Ex. gr.*

1. In him was meekness, Matth. xxi. 5. *He cometh unto the meek:* he had a sweet command and moderation of his anger; he was meek as Moses; nay, though Moses was very meek, *and very meek above all men which were upon the face of the earth*, Numb. xii 3. Yet Christ's meekness exceeded Moses's, as the body doth exceed the shadow.

2. In him was humility; he saved not the world by his power but by his humility: in his incarnation Christ would be humble; and therefore he was born of a poor virgin; in a common inn: in his life, his way on earth was a continual lecture of humility: a little before his death, he gave such an example of humility as never was the like, John xiii. 5. *He poured water into a bason and began to wash the disciples feet.* O ye apostles, why tremble ye not at the wonderful sight of this so great humility? Peter, what dost thou? Wilt thou ever yield, that this Lord of majesty should wash thy feet? Methinks, I hear Peter saying, 'What, 'Lord, wilt thou wash my feet? Art not thou the 'Son of the living God, the Creator of the world, 'the beauty of the heavens, the paradise of an- 'gels, the Redeemer of men, the brightness of 'the Father's glory? And I, what am I but a 'worm, a clod of earth, a miserable sinner? And 'wilt thou, notwithstanding all this, wash my 'feet? Leave, Lord, O leave this base office for 'thy servants; lay down thy towel and put on thy 'apparel again; beware that the heavens, or the 'angels of heaven be not ashamed of it, when they 'shall see that by this ceremony thou settest them 'beneath the earth; take heed lest the daughter 'of king Saul despise thee not, when she shall see 'thee girded about with this towel after the man- 'ner of a servant, and shall say, That she will not 'take thee for her beloved, and much less for her 'God, whom she seeth to attend upon so base an 'office.' Thus may I imagine Peter to bespeak his Master, but he little knew what glory lay hid in this humility of Christ; it was for us and our example; an humble Christ to make humble Christians.

3. In him was patience; O when I think of Christ's labours in preaching, weariness in travelling, watchfulness in praying, tears in compassionating; and then I add to all these his submission of Spirit, notwithstanding all the affronts, injuries and exprobations of men; How should I but cry out, *O the patience of Christ!* The apostle tells us, 1 Pet. ii. 23. that *when he was reviled, he reviled not again, when he suffered, he threatened not, but committed himself to him that judgeth righteously.* —I have already given you a touch of the graces in Christ, which now I may set before me.—In him was wisdom, and knowledge, and justice, and mercy, and temperance, and fortitude, and every virtue, or every grace that possibly I can think of; *A bundle of myrrh is my beloved unto me, as a cluster of camphire in the vineyards of Engedi.*

3. I look at the conversation of Christ in word and deed; for his words they were gracious. Not an idle word ever came out of the lips of Christ; himself tells us, that *of every idle word we must give an account*, Matth. xii. 36. O then how freewas

was Christ of every idle word? He knew the times and seasons when to speak, and when to be silent; he weighed every word with every circumstance, time and place, and manner and matter. Eccles. iii. 7. *There is a time to keep silence, and a time to speak,* said Solomon, when he returned again to his wisdom; and hence we read, that sometimes Jesus being accused, *He held his peace, and when he was accused of the chief priests and elders, he answered nothing,* Matth. xxvi. 63. and xxvii. 12. But other whiles he pours out whole cataracts of holy instructions; he takes occasion of vines, of stones, of water, and sheep, to speak a word in season; he is still discoursing of the matters of the kingdom of heaven, and he speaks such words as give grace unto all the hearers round about him; so for his deeds and actions they were full of grace and goodness. The apostle Peter gives him this character, (which I look upon as a little description of Christ's life) *who went about doing good,* Acts x. 38. It was his meat and drink to do all the good he could; it was as natural to him to do good, as it is for a fountain to stream out; he was holy and heavenly, unspotted every way; O the sweet conversation of Christ! How humbly carries he it among men? How benignly towards his disciples? How pitiful was he towards the poor? to whom, (as we read) he made himself most like, 2 Cor. viii. 9. *He became poor, that we might be made rich.* He despised or abhorred none, no not the very lepers that were eschewed of all; he flattered not the rich and honourable, he was most free from the cares of the world, his prescriptions were, *Care not for the things of the morrow;* and in himself he was never anxious of bodily needs; above all, he was most solicitous of saving souls. —Much more I might add if I should go over the particulars in the gospel; but by these few expressions of Jesus Christ, we may conceive of all the rest.—

2. Let us be humbled for our great unconformity to this copy: what an excellent pattern is here before us? And how far, how infinitely do we come short of this blessed pattern? O alas! if Christ will not own me, unless he see his image written upon me, what will become of my poor soul? Why, Christ was meek, and humble, and lowly in spirit; Christ was holy and heavenly, Christ ever went about doing good; and now when I come to examine my own heart according to this original, I find naturally a mere antipathy, a contrariety, I am as opposite to Christ as hell and heaven. 1. For my thoughts; within I am full of pride and malice; I am full of the spirit of the world: what is there in my heart but a world of passions, rebellions, darkness and deadness of spirit to good? And, 2. if the fountain be so muddy, can I expect clear streams? What words are these that come many a time from me? Christ would not speak an idle word, but how many idle, evil, sinful words come daily flowing from my lips? *Out of the abundance of the heart the mouth speaketh.* And if I may guess at my heart by my words, where was my heart this Sabbath, and the other Sabbath, when my discourse was on my calling, or on the world, or it may be on my lusts, or on my Dalilahs, on my right-hand sins, or on my right-eye sins? And, 3. What actions are these so frequently performed by me? If I must read my state by my conversation, *whose image and superscription is this?* The last oath I sware, the last blasphemy I belched out, the last act of drunkenness, idolatry, adultery I committed: (or if these sins are not fit to be named) the last piece of wrong I did my neighbour, the last prank of pride I played on this stage of the world, the last expence of time when I did no good in the world, neither to myself nor others, the last omission of good as well as commission of evil: O my soul, whose image is this? Is it the image of Christ or of Satan? If the worst scholar in the school should write thus untowardly after his copy, would he not be ashamed? If in my heart and life I observe so many blots and stains, so great unconformity and dissimilitude to the life of Christ, how should I but lie in the dust? O wo is me! what a vast disproportion betwixt Christ's life and mine? Why thus, O my soul, shouldest thou humble thyself; each morning, each prayer, each meditation, each self-examination, shouldest thou fetch new, fresh, clear, particular causes, occasions, matters of humiliation: as thus, *Lo, there* the evenness, gravity, graciousness, uniformity, holiness, spiritualities, divineness, heavenliness of Jesus Christ: lo, there the fragrant zeal, dear love, tender pity, constant industry, unwearied pains, patience, admirable self-denial, contempt of the world in Jesus Christ; lo, there those many, yea, continual devout, divine breath-

breathings of soul after God, his Father's glory, after the spiritual and immortal good of the precious souls of his redeemed ones: oh! all the admirable meekness, mercifulness, clemency, charity, with all other excellent temperature, rare composure, wonderful order of his blessed soul! O the sweet expressions, gracious conversation! oh the glorious shine, blessed lustre of his divine soul! oh the sweet countenance, sacred discourse, ravishing demeanour, winning deportment of Jesus Christ! and now I reflect upon myself, oh, alas! oh the total, wide, vast, utter difference, distance, disproportion of mine therefrom! I should punctually answer, perfectly resemble, accurately imitate, exactly conform to this life of Christ, but ah my unevenness, lightness, vanity! ah my rudeness, grossness, deformity, odiousness, slightness, contemptibleness, execrableness! ah my sensuality, brutishness, devilishness! how clearly are these and all other my enormities discovered, discerned, made evident and plain by the blessed and holy life of Jesus? so true is that rule, *Contraria juxta se posita, magis elucescunt.*

3. Let us quicken, provoke and incense our sluggish drowsy souls to conform to Christ. If we will but strictly observe our hearts, we shall find them very backward to this duty, and therefore let us call upon our souls as David did, Ps. ciii. 1. *Bless the Lord, O my soul, and let all that is within me bless his holy name:* let us work upon our souls by reasoning with our own hearts, as if we discoursed with them thus, *O my heart,* or, *O my soul,* if in the deep councils of eternity this was God's great design to make his Son like thee, that thou also mightest be like his Son, how then shouldest thou but endeavour to conform? And what says the apostle? Rom. viii. 29. *For whom he did foreknow, he also did predestinate, to be conformed to the image of his Son:* this was one of his great purposes from eternity; this law of God set down before he made the world, that I should conform to his Son; and what, O my soul, wouldest thou break the eternal bonds of predestination? O, God forbid! again, if this was one of the ends of Christ's coming to destroy the works of the devil, to deface all Satan's works, especially his work in me, his image in me, and to set his own stamp on my soul; how then should I but endeavour to conform? I read but of two ends of Christ's coming into the world in relation to us, whereof the first was to redeem his people, and the other to purify his people; Titus ii. 14 *He gave himself for us, that he might redeem us from all iniquity, and purify unto himself a peculiar people, zealous of good works.* The one is the work of his merit which goeth upward, to the satisfaction of his Father; the other is the work of his Spirit and grace, which goeth downwards to the sanctification of his church; in the one he bestoweth his righteousness on us by imputation, on the other he fashioneth his image in us by renovation: and what, O my soul, wouldest thou destroy the end of Christ's coming in the flesh? Or wouldest thou miss of that end for which Christ came in relation to thy good? O, God forbid! again, consider the example of the saints before thee; if this was their holy ambition to be like their Jesus, emulate them in this; for this is a blessed emulation. It is observable how the heathens themselves had learned a rule very near to this; 'Seneca advised, that every 'man should propound to himself the example of 'some wise and virtuous personage, as Cato or So- 'crates, or the like.' [Senec. ep. 11.] And really to take his life as the direction of all their actions; but is not the life of Jesus far more precious and infinitely more worthy of imitation? We read in history of one Cecilia a virgin, who accustomed herself to the beholding of Christ for imitation, and to that purpose she ever carried in her breast some pieces of the gospel, which she had gathered out of all the evangelists, and thereon night and day she was either reading or meditating; this work she carried on in such a circulation, that at last she grew perfect in it, and so enjoyed Christ and the gospel, not only in her breast, but also in the secrets of her heart; as appeared by her love of Christ, and confidence in Christ, and familiarity with Christ; as also by her contempt of the world, and all its glory, for Christ his sake: there is some resemblance of this in the spouse, when she resolved of Christ, Cant. i. 13. *He shall lie all night betwixt my breasts,* q. d. He shall be as near as near may be; my meditation (and by consequence my imitation) of him shall be constant and continual; not only in the day, but *he shall lie all night betwixt my breasts.* What, O my soul, was this the practice of the saints? And wilt thou not be of that communion? O, God forbid! thus let

us quicken and provoke our souls to that conformity; let us excite, rouse, incense, awake, and sharpen up our wretched, sluggish, drowsy, lazy souls; our faint, feeble, flagging, faultering, drooping, languishing affections, desires, endeavours! let us with enlarged industry engage and encourage our backward and remiss spirits to fall upon this duty of conformity, again and again; let us come up higher towards it, or, if possibly we may, completely to it, that the same mind, and mouth, and life, may be in us that was in Jesus Christ, that we may be found to walk after Christ, that we may tread in the very prints of the feet of Christ, that we may climb up after him into the same heavenly kingdom, that we may aspire continually towards him, and grow up to him, even *to the measure of the stature of the fulness of Christ.*

4. Let us regulate ourselves by the life of Christ; whatsoever action we go about, let us do it by this rule, What, would Christ have done this, or, at least, would have allowed this? It is true, some things are expedient and lawful with us, which were not suitable to the person of Christ. *Marriage is honourable with all men, and the bed undefiled;* but it did not befit his person, who came into the world only to spiritual purposes, to beget sons and daughters. Writing of books is commendable with men, because, like Abel, being dead, they may still speak, and teach these who never saw them, but it would have been deragotory to the person and office of Christ, for it is his prerogative to be in the midst of the seven golden candlesticks, to be present to all his members, to teach by power and not by ministry, to write his law in the hearts of his people, and to make them his epistle. Contrition, compunction, mortification, repentance for sin, are acts and duties necessary to our state and condition; for we are sinners, and sinners of the Gentiles, *To whom God also hath granted repentance unto life,* Acts xi. 18. But these were in no sort agreeable to Christ; for he was without sin, and needed not repentance, nor any part of it. The several states of men, as of governors, kings, judges, lawyers, merchants, &c. are convenient for us, otherwise what a tax and confusion would there be in the world? And yet Jesus never put himself into any of these states, John xviii. 36. *My kingdom* (says he) *is not of this world.* Now, as in these things we must only

respect the allowance of Christ, so in other things we must reflect upon the example of Christ; as, 1. In sinful acts eschewed by Christ. 2. In moral duties that were done by Christ.

1. In sinful acts eschewed by Christ, as when I am tempted of sin, then am I to reason thus with myself; would my blessed Saviour if he were upon earth, do thus and thus? When I am tempted to looseness and immoderate living, then am I to ask conscience such a question as this, would Christ have done thus? Would he have spent such a life upon earth as I do? When I am moved by my own corruption, or by Satan, to drunkenness, gluttony, sinful and desperate society, to swearing, cursing, revenge, or the like; then am I to ask, Is this the life that Christ led? Or, if he were to live again, would he live after this manner? When I fall into passion, peevishness, rash words, or if it be but idle words, then I am to consider, O but would Christ speak thus? Would this be his language? would such a rotten or unprofitable speech as this drop from his honey lips?

2. In case of moral obedience, concerning which we have both his pattern and precept, I look upon Christ as my rule, and I question thus, Did Christ frequently pray both with his disciples, and alone by himself? And shall I never in my family or in my closet think upon God? Did Christ open his wounds for me, and shall I not open my mouth to him? Did Christ serve God without all self-ends, merely in obedience and to glorify him? And shall I make God's worship subordinate to my aims and turns? Did Christ shew mercy to his very enemies? And shall I be cruel to Christ's very enemies? O my soul, look in all thy sins and in all thy duties to thy original, and measure them by the holiness of Christ. Whether in avoiding sin or in doing duty; think, What would my blessed Saviour do in this case? Or, what did he do in the like case when he was upon earth? If we had these thoughts every day, if Christ were continually before our eyes, if in all we do or speak we should still muse on this, What would Jesus say if he were here? I believe it would be a blessed means of living in comfort and spiritual conformity to the commands of God, yea, of acting Christ's life (as it were) to the life.

5. Let us look fixedly on Jesus Christ, let us keep our spiritual eyes still on the pattern, until
we

we feel ourselves conforming to it: it is a true saying, 'That objects and moving reasons kept much upon the mind, by serious thoughts, are the great engine, both appointed by nature and grace, to turn about the soul of man.' If I may deliver it in fewer terms, 'Objects considered much, or frequently, do turn the soul into their own nature.' Such as the things we are most thinking of, and consider of, such will be ourselves; or if we be not so, it is not thro' any imperfection in the object, (especially in such an object as Jesus Christ is) but because it is not well applied, and by consideration held upon the heart till it may work there, indeed the manner of this working may be secret and insensible; yet if we follow on we shall feel it in the issue. The beholding of Christ is a powerful beholding; there is a changing, transforming virtue goes out of Christ, by looking on Christ: can we think of his humility and not be humble? Can we think of his meekness and gentleness of spirit, and yet we continue in our fierceness, roughness, forwardness of spirit? Can a proud fierce heart apprehend a meek, and sweet, and lowly Jesus? No, no, the heart must be suitable to the thing apprehended; it is impossible otherwise, certainly if the look be right, there must be a suitableness betwixt the heart and Christ. Sight works upon the imagination in brute creatures; as Laban's sheep, when they saw the party-coloured rods, they had lambs suitable: now, will sight work upon imagination, and imagination work a real change in nature; and is not the eye of the mind, (especially the eye of faith) more strong and powerful? If I but write after a copy, I shall in a while learn to write like it: if I seriously meditate on any excellent subject, it will leave a print behind it on my spirit; if I read but the life and death of some eminently gracious and holy man, it moulds, and fashions, and transforms, and conforms my mind to his similitude; even so, and much more is it in this case, since the eye of faith works in the matter, which in itself is operative and effectual, and therefore it cannot but work more than where there is only simple imitation or naked meditation. O then let us set the copy of Christ's life (as before described) in our view, and let us look upon it with both eyes, with the eye of reason, and with the eye of faith.

But how should we keep the eye of our faith on this blessed object, until we feel this conformity in us? I answer.——

1. Let us set apart some times on purpose to act our faith in this respect, Eccl. iii. 1. *There is a time for all things under the sun*, saith Solomon. It may be sometimes we are in our civil employments, but then is not the time; yet when they are done, and the day begins to close, if together with our closet-prayer we would fall on this duty of looking unto Jesus by lively faith; how blessed a season might this be? I know not but that some Christians may do it occasionally, but for any that sets some time apart for it every day, and that in conscience, as we do for prayer, where is he to be found?

2. Let us remove hinderances; Satan labours to hinder the soul from beholding Christ with the dust of the world, *The God of this world blinds the eyes of men*. O take heed of fixing our eyes on this world's vanity! our own corruptions are also great hindrances to this view of Christ; away, away with all carnal passions, base humours, sinful desires; unless the soul be spiritual, it can never behold spiritual things.

3. Let us fix our eyes only on this blessed object; a moving rolling eye sees nothing clearly, 1 Peter i. 12. *When the angels are said to look into these things*, the word signifies, that they look into them narrowly, as they, who bowing or stooping down do look into a thing; so should we look narrowly into the life of Christ; our eye of faith should be set upon it in a steady manner, as if all the world could not move us, as if we forgot all the things behind, and had no other business in the world but this.

4. Let us look wishingly and cravingly; there is affection as well as vision in the eye; as the lame man that lay in Solomon's porch looked wishfully on Peter and John, *Expecting to receive something of them*, Acts iii. 5. So let us look on Christ with a craving eye, with an humble expectation to receive a supply of grace from Christ, 'Why, Lord, 'thou art not only anointed with the oil of gladness above thy fellows, but for thy fellows; I 'am earthly minded, but thou art heavenly; I 'am full of lusts, but the image of God is perfect 'in thee: thou art the fountain of all grace, an 'head of influence as well as of eminence: thou 'art not only above me, but thou hast all grace 'for

'for me; and therefore, O give me some portion of thy meekness, lowliness, heavenly-mindedness, and of all other the graces of thy Spirit. Surely thou art an heaven of grace, full of bright shining stars. Oh that of that fulness thou wouldest give me to receive even grace for grace: I pray, Lord, with an humble expectation of receiving from thee: oh let me feel the droppings of the two olive-trees into the golden candlesticks; yea even unto my soul.'

5. Be we assured that our prayer (if it be in faith) is even now heard; never any came to Christ with strong expectations to receive grace, or any benefit prayed for, that was turned empty away. Besides, Christ hath engaged himself by promise to write his law in our hearts; to make us like himself; *As he which hath called us is holy, so should* (yea, and so shall) *we be holy in all manner of conversation*, 1 Pet. i. 15. Oh let us build on his gracious promise; *Heaven and earth shall pass away before one jot or tittle of his word shall fail*; only understand we his promise in this sense, that our conformity must be gradual, not all at once, 2 Cor. iii. 18. *We all with open face, beholding as in a glass the glory of the Lord, are changed into the same image from glory to glory*, (i. e.) from grace to grace, or from glory inchoate in obedience, to glory consummate in our heavenly inheritance.

6. If, notwithstanding all this, we feel not for the present this conformity in us, at least in such a degree, let us act over the same particulars again and again; the gifts of grace are therefore communicated by degrees, that we might be taken off from living upon a received stock of grace; and that we might still be running to the spring, and drink in there: why, alas! we have a continual need of Christ's letting out himself and grace into our hearts, and therefore we must wait at the well-head, Christ; we must look on Christ, as appointed on purpose by his Father to be the beginner and finisher of our holiness; and we must believe that he will never leave that work imperfect whereunto he is ordained of the Father. *We may be confident*, (saith the apostle) *of this very thing, that he which hath begun a good work in us, will perform it, or finish it until the day of Jesus Christ*, Phil. i. 6. Oh then, be not weary of this work until he accomplish the desires of thy soul.

I have now done with this subject: only before I finish, one word more. Sometimes I have observed that many precious souls in their endeavours after grace, holiness, sanctification, have been frequent in the use of such and such means, duties, ordinances; wherein I cannot say but they have done well; and for their help, I therefore composed that piece called *Media*: but of all the ordinances of Christ, this *Looking unto Jesus* is made least use of, though it be chief of all: it is Christ, (when all is done) that is that great ordinance appointed by God for grace and holiness: and certainly those souls which trade immediately with Jesus Christ, will gain more in a day than others in a month, in a year. I deny not other helps, but amongst them all, if I would make choice which to fall upon, that I may become more and more holy, I would set before me this glass, (i. e.) *Christ's holy life*, the great example of that holiness, we were at first created after his image in holiness, and this image we lost thro' sin, and to this image we should endeavour to be restored by imitation: and how should this be done, but by looking on Christ as our pattern? By running through the several ages of Christ, and by observing all his graces and gracious actings? In this respect I charge thee, O my soul, (for to what purpose should I charge others if I begin not at home and with thee)? that thou make conscience of this practical, evangelical duty; Oh be much in the exercise of it! not only in the day intend Christ, but when night comes, and thou liest down on thy bed, let thy pillow be as Christ's bosom, on which John the beloved disciple was said to lean; there lean thou with John, yea, lie thou between his breasts, and *let him lie all night betwixt thy breasts*, Cant. i. 13. Thus mayest thou *lie down in peace and sleep, and the Lord only will make thee to dwell in safety*, Psal. iv. 8. And when day returns again, have this in mind, yea, in all thy thoughts, words and deeds, ever look unto Jesus as the holy examplar, say to thyself, 'If Christ my Saviour were now upon earth, would these be his thoughts, words and deeds? Would he be thus disposed as I now feel myself? Would he speak these words that I am now uttering? Would he do this that I am now putting my hand unto? O let me not yield myself to any thought, word or action, which my dear Jesus would be
'ashamed

'ashamed to own!' Yea, (if it were possible for thee to be so constant in this blessed duty) going and standing, sitting and lying, eating and drinking, speaking and holding thy peace, by thyself or in company, cast an eye upon Jesus; for by this means thou canst not choose but love him more, and joy in him more, and trust in him more, and be more and more familiar with him, and draw more and more grace and virtue and sweetness from him. O let this be thy wisdom, to think much of Christ, so as to provoke thee to the imitation of Christ! then shalt thou learn to condemn the world, to do good to all, to injure no man, to suffer wrong patiently; yea, to pray for all those that despitefully use thee and persecute thee, then shalt thou learn to condescend to the weak, to condole sinners cases, to embrace the penitent, to obey superiors, to minister to all; then shalt thou learn to avoid all boasting, bragging, scandal, immoderate eating and drinking; in a word, all sin. Then shalt thou learn to *bear about in thy body the dying of our Lord Jesus Christ, that the life also of Jesus may be made manifest in thy body:* so the apostle, *for we which live, are always delivered unto death for Jesus sake, that the life also of Jesus might be made manifest in our mortal flesh,* 2 Cor. iv. 10, 11. Why, this is to follow Christ's steps, he descended from heaven to earth for thy sake; do thou trample on earthly things, *Seek after the kingdom of God and his righteousness,* for thy own sake; though the world be sweet, yet Christ is sweeter; tho' the world prove bitter, yet Christ sustained the bitterness of it for thee; and now he speaks to thee, as he did to Peter, Andrew, James and John, *Come follow me*; O do not faint in the way, lest thou lose thy place in thy country, that kingdom of glory.

Thus far we have looked on Jesus as our Jesus in his life, during the whole time of his ministry, our next work is to look on Jesus carrying on the great work of man's salvation, during the time of his suffering and dying on the cross, until his resurrection from the dead.

LOOKING UNTO
JESUS.
IN HIS DEATH.

THE FOURTH BOOK, PART THIRD.

CHAP. I. SECT. I.

Lam. i. 12. *Is it nothing to you, all ye that pass by? Behold, and see.*

Heb. xii. 3. *Consider him who hath endured such contradiction of sinners against him.*

Of the Day of CHRIST's Sufferings, divided into Parts and Hours.

THE Sun of righteousness that *arose with healing,* we shall now see go down in a ruddy cloud: and in this place, (as in the former) we must first lay down the object, and then direct you to *look upon it.*

The object is Jesus, carrying on the work of man's salvation during the time of his sufferings. Now, in all the transactions of this time, we shall observe them as they were carried on successively in those few hours of his passion and death.

As this work of man's salvation was great, so we cannot but observe how every piece of it was carried on in its due time, even from eternity to eternity. The very time of Christ's passion depended not on the will of man, for his enemies sought many a time before to slay him; as Herod in his infancy, Matth. ii. 16. The Jews in his riper age, when sometimes they took up stones to stone him, John viii. 59. and sometimes they would have broke his neck from an hill, Luke iv. 29. but his time was not then come. We read of the paschal lamb that it was to be slain, Exod. xii. 2, 6. *On the fourteenth day of the first month called Abib or Nisan, at the full of the moon, in the evening, or between the evenings:* some think this month answers to our March, others to our April, I shall not be too curious in the inquisition, for I think it not worth the while; only this I cannot but observe, that the same day that the lamb must be slain, must our paschal lamb begin his sufferings: and as then it was full moon, so it notes unto us the fulness of time which now was come: and as it was in such a month, as when light prevails against darkness, and every thing revives and springs, so Christ (by his sufferings) was to chase away our darkness and death; and to bring in light, and life, and a blessed spring of grace and glory: and as it was to be slain in the evening, or between the evenings: so must Christ, the true paschal lamb, be sacrificed about the very same hour that the mystical lamb was slain. To understand which we must know, that the Jews distinguished their artificial day into four parts, from six to nine, from nine to twelve, from twelve to three, from three to six. This last part was counted the evening of the day; and the next three hours the evening of the night: now, in this last part of the day used the paschal lamb to be slain; and after it was slain, some time was taken up to dress it whole for supper: so Christ, at the fourth part of the day, at their ninth hour, that is, at our three of the clock in the afternoon, *between the evenings, with a loud voice yielded up the Ghost*, Matth. xxvii. 50.

For the whole time of these last and extreme sufferings of Christ, I shall reduce them to somewhat less than one natural day; or, if we may take the whole day before us consisting of twenty four hours, and begin with the evening, according to the beginning of natural days from the creation, (as it is said, Gen. i. 5. *The evening and the morning made the first day,*) in this revolution of time, I shall observe these several passages.—As,—

1. About six in the evening, Christ celebrated and eat the passover with his disciples, at which time he instituted the sacrament of the Lord's supper; and this continued till the eighth hour.

2. About eight in the evening he washed his disciples feet, and then leaning on the table, he pointed out Judas that should betray him; and this continued until the ninth hour.

3. About nine in the evening, (the second watch in the night) Judas, that traitor, went from the disciples; and, in the mean time, Christ made that spiritual sermon, and afterwards that spiritual prayer recited only by John, John xiv. xv. xvi. xvii. chapters, and this, together with a psalm they sung, continued at least until the tenth hour. Thus far we proceeded before we had done with the *life of Christ*. That which concerns his passion follows immediately upon this; and of that only I shall take notice in my following discourse.

This passion of Christ I shall divide between the night and day. 1. For the night, and his sufferings therein, we may observe these periods, or thereabouts. As,—

1. From ten to twelve he goes over the brook Cedron to the garden of Gethsamene, where he prayed earnestly, and sweat water and blood.

2. From twelve till three he is betrayed: and by the soldiers and other officers he is bound, and brought to Jerusalem, and carried into the house of Annas, who was one of the chief priests.

3. From three to six, they led him from Annas to Caiaphas, when he, and all the priests of Jerusalem sat upon Jesus Christ; and there it was that Peter denied Christ; and at last the whole sanhedrim of the Jews gave their consent to Christ's condemnation.

2. The night thus dispatched, at six in the morning, about sun-rising, our Saviour was brought unto Pilate, and Judas Iscariot hanged himself, because he had betrayed the innocent blood.—— About seven in the same morning, Christ is carried to Herod, that cruel tyrant, who, the year before, had put John the Baptist to death.——At eight of the same day, our Saviour Christ is returned to Pilate, who propounded to the Jews, whether they would have Jesus or Barrabas let loose unto

unto them.—About the ninth, (which the Jews call the third hour of the day) Chrift was whipped and crowned with thorns. About ten, Pontius Pilate brought forth Jefus out of the common-hall, faying, *Behold the man*; and then in the place called *Gabbatha* he publickly condemned Chrift to be crucified. About eleven our Saviour carried his crofs, and was brought to the place called Golgotha, where he was faftened on the crofs, and lifted up, *as Mofes lifted up the ferpent in the wildernefs*.—About twelve (in that meridian which the Jews call the fixth hour) that fupernatural eclipfe of the fun happened.—And about three in the afternoon, (which the Jews call the ninth hour) the fun now beginning to receive his light, Chrift cried, *It is finifhed*; and commending his Spirit into his Father's hands, he gave up the ghoft.—I fhall add to thefe, That, about four in the afternoon, our bleffed Saviour was pierced with a fpear; and there iffued out of his fide both blood and water.—And, about five, (which the Jews call the eleventh, and the laft hour of the day) he was buried by Jofeph of Arimathea, and Nicodemus.—So that in this round of one natural day, you fee now the wonderful tranfaction of Chrift's fufferings. I fhall take them in order, and begin with his fufferings in that night before his crucifying. *And Jefus faid unto his difciples, All ye fhall be offended becaufe of me this night*, Matth. xxvi. 31. And he faid unto Peter, *That this day, even in this night before the cock crow twice, thou fhall deny me thrice*, Mark xiv. 30.

SECT. II.

Of the brook over which Chrift paffed.

THE firft paffage of that night, was Chrift's going over the brook Cedron to the garden of Gethfemane, *When Jefus had fpoken thefe words, he went forth with his difciples over the brook Cedron, where was a garden, into which he entred, and his difciples*, John xviii. 1.

In this paffage obferve we thefe particulars. 1. The river over which they paffed. 2. The garden into which they entred. 3. The prayer he there made; and the dolours and agonies he there fuffered.

1. He and his difciples went over the brook Cedron. So it was called (fay fome) from the many cedars that grew all along the banks; or (fay others) from the darknefs of the valley: fo Kader fignifies darknefs; and this was done to fulfil a prophecy, *He fhall drink of the brook in the way*, Pfal. cx. 7. By the brook or torrent we may underftand myftically the wrath of God and the rage of men, the very afflictions which befel Jefus Chrift; and by his *drinking of the brook*, we may underftand Chrift enduring afflictions, or (as others) his enduring many afflictions, and not a few.

1. That *afflictions* are underftood by *waters*, we find it very frequently in fcriptures; *The forrows of death compaffed me, and the floods of Belial made me afraid*, Pfal. xviii. 4.——*Deep calleth unto deep, at the noife of the water-fpouts, all thy waves and thy billows are gone over me*, Pfal. xlii. 7.——*And, Save me, O God, for the waters are come in unto my foul*, Pfal. lxix. 1. *And if it had not been the Lord, who was on our fide,—then the waters had overwhelmed us, the ftream had gone over our foul, then the proud waters had gone over our foul*, Pfal. cxxiv. 1, 4, 5.

2. As waters fignify afflictions, fo Chrift drinking of thofe waters, it fignifies *Chrift's fuffering of afflictions*; or, as others, it fignifies *Chrift's fuffering of many afflictions*. Thus we find together two words with relation thereunto, *Are ye able to drink of the cup* (faith Chrift) *that I fhall drink of, and to be baptized with the baptifm that I am baptized with?* Matth. xx. 22. He that drinketh hath the water in him; and he that is baptized, dipped or plunged, hath the water about him: fo it notes the variety or univerfality of afflictions which Chrift fuffered; it was within him, and it was about him; he was every way afflicted.

Not to fpeak yet of thofe fufferings, which yet we are not come to fpeak unto, we find here in the way, betwixt the city and the garden, that Chrift went over the brook Cedron; in the night he wades through the waters, yea, in a cold night he wades through cold waters on bare feet; and as he wades through them, he drinks of them; he doth not fip, but drink: *He fhall drink of the brook in the way*. I know fome would not have this prophecy accomplifhed till after Chrift's apprehenfion, when it is faid, That the rude rout brought him again to Jerufalem, over the brook Cedron; and then he drunk of the brook: but I find no mention of this brook in fcripture at fuch a time; only

now,

now, in this way, I find these passages, 1. His conference with his disciples as they go along. 2. The disciples reply upon his conference. 3. His dolorous passage over the brook, betokening the very wrath of God.

1 In the way * he hath a serious conference with his disciples: so the evangelist, Matth. xxvi. 30, 31. *And when they had sung a hymn, they went out towards the mount of Olives; and then saith Jesus unto them, all ye shall be offended because of me this night, for it is written, I will smite the shepherd, and the sheep of the flock shall be scattered abroad.* Christ now begins the story of his passion; *the shepherd shall be smitten*; and he proves it from God's decree, and from the prophecy of the prophet Zech. xiii. 7. *Awake, O sword, against my shepherd, and against the man that is my fellow,——smite the shepherd, and the sheep shall be scattered abroad.* God the Father is here brought in, as drawing and whetting his sword, and calling upon it, to do execution against Jesus Christ; God the Father had an hand in the sufferings, *It pleased the Lord to bruise him, he hath put him to grief*, Isa. liii. 10.—*I will smite the shepherd*, saith God. It was not a naked permission, but a positive decree, and actual providence of God that Christ should suffer: the plot was long since drawn, and lay hid in God's bosom, till he was pleased (by the actions of men) to copy it out, and to give the world a draught of it. This was not a thing of a yesterday: no, no; God spent his eternal thoughts about it! the story was long since written in Zechariah's book; and *in the volume of God's book,* Psf. xl. 8. Christ was ordained to be a Lamb slain from the beginning of the world; *him being delivered by the determinate council and fore-knowledge of God, ye have taken* (saith Peter) *and by wicked hands have crucified and slain,* Acts ii. 23. The enemies of Christ, though they broke commands, yet they fulfilled decrees. *Against thy holy child Jesus whom thou hast anointed, both Herod and Pontius Pilate, with the Gentiles, and people of Israel, were gathered together, for to do whatsoever thy hand and thy council determined before to be done,* Acts iv. 27, 28. The story of Christ's sufferings was long since taken up, and resolved on in the councils of heaven. And now in the way, *The only begotten Son, which lay in the bosom of his Father,* reveals this story, he tells the disciples, *It is written, I will smite the shepherd, and the sheep of the flock shall be scattered.*

2. The disciples hearing this discovery of 'the 'shepherd being smitten, and the sheep being scat- 'tered,' they are amazed; what shall Christ die? And shall we, like cowards, run away, and leave him alone in the combat? Peter, who seems boldest, he speaks first, *Though all men shall be offended because of thee, yet will I never be offended.* O rash presumption! it appears in these particulars;
——1. Peter prefers himself before the rest, as if all the other disciples had been weak, and he only strong, *Though all should be offended, yet will not I.* 2. Peter contradicts Christ's great discovery of his Father's great design from all eternity, with a few bragging words; *q. d.* What, though Zechariah hath said it, and God hath decreed it, yet, on my part, I will never do it, *Though I should die with thee, I will not deny thee.* 3 Peter, in his boast, never mentions God's help, or God's assistance; whereas, in relation to future promises, and future purposes, the apostle's rule is, *Ye ought to say, if the Lord will, we shall live, and do this, and that,* James iv. 15. So Peter should have said, 'By God's 'assistance I will not be offended; by the Lord's 'help I will not deny thee; if the Lord will, I 'will do this, and that; I will live with thee, 'and die with thee, rather than I will deny thee;' but we find no such word in all the story; and therefore Christ takes him off his bottoms in the first place, *Verily I say unto thee, Peter, that this night, before the cock crow twice, thou shalt deny me thrice:* Oh no, saith Peter, he will not, of his presumptuous confidence, Matth. xxvi. 35. *Tho' I should die with thee, I will not deny thee; likewise also said all his disciples.* But I must not dwell on these passages.

3. His dolorous passage over the brook succeeds; *He went forth with his disciples over the brook Cedron*; I never read of this brook Cedron, but some way or other, it points at the sufferings of our Saviour; I shall instance in some places: 1. When David fled from Absalom out of Jerusalem, it is said, That *all the country wept with a loud voice, and all the people passed over: the king also himself passed over the brook Cedron.——towards the way of the wilderness,* 2 Sam xv. 23. In this story

* Vide *Aretius in locum.*

story we find David passing over this brook Cedron with bare head and bare feet; and he and all his men *weeping as they went up by the ascent of mount Olivet*, ver 30. I cannot think, but in this, king David was a type of king Jesus; Christ, as another David, with his soldiers or disciples, goes out of Jerusalem, bare head and bare foot (as this type seems to speak) what weeping was in the way I cannot tell; but probably sadness was in the hearts both of him and his disciples, whose conference was of fleeing, suffering, dying, the most grievous death that ever was: all the difference that I find betwixt the type and antitype in this passage is, in that David fled from the face of Absalom; but Christ goes out of Jerusalem, not to flee from Judas, or the Jews, but rather to commit himself into their hands.

2. When Solomon confined Shimei to his house in Jerusalem, saying, *Dwell there, and go not forth thence any whither, for it shall be, that on the day thou goest out, and passest over the brook Cedron, thou shalt know for certain that thou shalt surely die*, 1 Kings ii. 36, 37. Now, two of the servants of Shimei running away from him, he follows after them, and passing over this brook Cedron it became his death; why, here was a type of Jesus Christ: we were those fugitive servants that ran away from God, and to fetch us home, Jesus goes over the brook Cedron; rather than he will lose his servants, he will lose his life. All the difference that I find betwixt Shimei and Christ in this, is, in that Shimei was but a wicked man, and yet he died an honourable death, not for his servants, but for his own transgression; but Christ being a just man (so Pilate's wife sent her husband word, *have nothing to do with that just man*) he died a most ignominious shameful death, even the death of the cross, and that not for himself, but for us; Isa. liii. 5. *He was wounded for our transgressions, he was bruised for our iniquities.*

3. When the good kings, Hezekiah and Asa and Josiah, had purged the city and the temple of idolatry, they burnt the cursed things at the brook Kidron, and cast them therein. *And Asa cut down the idol, and he brought out the grove from the house of the Lord without Jerusalem unto the brook Kidron, and burnt it at the brook Kidron*, 2 Kings xxiii. 6.——*And the priests went into the inner parts of the house of the Lord to cleanse it,* and brought all the uncleanness that they found in the temple of the Lord into the court of the house of the Lord; and the Levites took it to carry it out abroad into the brook Kidron, 2 Chron. xxix. 16. ——*And they arose, and took away the altars that were in Jerusalem, and all the altars for incense took they away, and cast them into the brook Kidron, or Cedron,* 2 Chron xxx. 14. All these note unto us, that the brook was, as it were, the sink of the temple, into which all the *purgamenta*, and uncleanness of God's house, and all the accursed things were to be cast: and here again was a type of Christ; upon him were cast all the filths of our sins, that, as a river or fountain, he might cleanse us from them; in this respect he is said to be *made sin for us who knew no sin, that we might be made the righteousness of God in him*, 2 Cor. v. 21. He was made sin for us, and a curse for us, that so he might swallow up sin and death, and might be the destruction of hell, and all.

I cannot pass over this passage of the book, without some use or application to ourselves.

Use. 1. It informs. Methinks this valley, and this brook of Cedron, is a right representation of a Christian's life; Jesus went forth with his disciples over the brook Cedron; what is our life if we are Christ's, but a passage thro' a vale of tears, and over a brook of several afflictions? *Many are the troubles of the righteous*, Psal. xxxiv. 19. The very word Cedron, which signifies darkness, denotes this state: an horror of great darkness was said to fall on Abraham; and then said God, *Know of a surety, that thy seed shall be a stranger in a land that is not theirs, and shall serve them, and they shall afflict them four hundred years*, Gen. xv. 12, 13. As God made the evening and the morning the first day, and second day, and third day, &c. See, O the life of God's saints is as the evening of troubles, and their happiness hereafter is as the morning of glory; God's worst is first, with those that are his; the way to Canaan is through the wilderness; *The way to Zion is through the valley of Bacca*, Psalm lxxxiv. 6. *Through much tribulation we must enter into the kingdom of God*, Acts xiv. 22. *In the world ye shall have tribulation*, saith Christ, John xvi 33. Yea, *all that will live godly in Christ Jesus must suffer persecution*, saith the apostle, 2 Tim. iii. 12.——Our rest is not here in this world; what is this world, but an ark of travail,

travail, a school of vanities, a fair of deceits, a labyrinth of error, a barren wilderness, a stony field, a tempestuous sea, a swelling brook, a vale of tears full of all miseries?

2. It reproves. It is the first passage of Christ when he begins his sufferings, to go over the brook Cedron, and it is the A, B, C, of Christianity (as Bradford said) to learn the lesson of taking up the cross, and following Christ. Surely this world is no place, and this life, it is no time for pleasure; God hath not cast man out of paradise, that he should find another paradise on this side heaven. Oh! why do we seek the living among the dead? Why do we seek for living comforts, where we must expect to die daily? It is only heaven that is above all winds, and storms, and tempests, and seas, and brooks, and waves; Oh! why do we look for joys in a vale of tears? It was an heavy charge that the apostle James laid upon some, that *they lived in pleasure upon earth*, James v. 5. *q. d.* Earth is not the place for pleasure; earth is the place of sorrow, of trouble, of mourning, of affliction, *Remember that thou in thy life-time receivedst thy good things, and Lazarus evil things, but now he is comforted, and thou art tormented*, Luke xvi. 25. All the pleasure that wicked men have, it is upon earth, but the condition of the Godly is clean contrary; Oh! it is sad to out-live our happiness; and when we should come to live indeed, then to want our comforts and our joys, Matth. vi. 2. *Verily I say unto you, they have their reward*, said Christ of hypocrites, their heaven is past, *They spend their days in wealth, or in mirth* (saith Job of the wicked) *and in a moment go down to the grave*, Job xxi. 13. Alas their best days are then past, and they must never be merry any more. Ah, fond fools of Adam's seed, to lose heaven for a little earthly contentment! How should this sour your carnal joys, when you remember, all this is only upon earth, it cannot be for ever? There must be a change of all these things, here you laugh, and hereafter you must howl! no sooner death comes, but then you will cry, 'Farewel, world, oh into what a gulph am I now 'falling!'

3. It instructs. Ah, my brethren! let us remember, we are pilgrims and strangers upon earth, and our way lies over the brook and valley of Cedron; we cannot expect to enter with Christ into glory, but we must *first drink of the brook in the way*, (i. e.) we must endure many afflictions, variety of afflictions.——You will say, *This is an hard saying, who can bear it?* I remember, when Jesus told his disciples of his sufferings to be accomplished at Jerusalem, Peter takes the boldness to dehort his master, *be it far from thee, Lord, this shall not be unto thee*, Matth. xvi. 22. But Jesus thereupon calls him *Satan*, meaning, that no greater contradictions can be offered to the designs of God and Christ, than to dissuade us from sufferings. There is too much of Peter's humour abides amongst us; Oh! this doctrine of afflictions will not down with libertines, antinomians, or the like; and hence I believe we have our congregations so thin in comparison of some of theirs, they that can break off the yoke of obedience and untie the bands of discipline, and preach a cheap religion, and present heaven in the midst of flowers, and strew palms and carpets in the way, and, offer great liberty of living under sin, and reconcile eternity with the present enjoyment, shall have their schools filled with disciples; but they that preach the cross, and sufferings, and afflictions, and strictness of an holy life, they shall have the lot of their blessed Lord, (i. e.) they shall be illthought of, and deserted and railed against. Well, but if this be the way that Christ hath led us, whilst others abide at ease in Zion, let us follow him in the valley, and over the brook that is called Cedron.

Thus far have we observed Christ in the way, together with his passage over Cedron; we come now to the garden, into which he entred and his disciples.

SECT. III.

Of the garden into which Christ entered.

Matthew relates it thus, Matth. xxvi. 36. *Then cometh Jesus with them unto a place called Gethsemane*, [*:ifchorion*], it signifies in special, a field, a village; but more generally a place, as we translate it; and this place was called Gethsemane, (i. e.) *a valley of fatness*; certainly it was a most fruitful and pleasant place, seated at the foot of the mount of Olives: accordingly John relates it thus, John xviii 1. *Jesus went forth with*

with his disciples over the brook Cedron, where was a garden; many mysteries are included in this word, and I believe it is not without reason that our Saviour goes into a garden.—As, 1. Because gardens are solitary places, fit for meditation and prayer; to this end we find Christ sometimes in a mountain, and sometimes in a garden. 2. Because gardens are places fit for repose and rest; when Christ was weary with preaching, working of miracles, and doing acts of grace in Jerusalem, then he retires into this garden. 3. Because a garden was the place wherein we fell, and therefore Christ made choice of a garden to begin there the great work of our redemption: in the first garden was the beginning of all evils; and in this garden was the beginning of our restitution from all evils; in the first garden, the first Adam was overthrown by Satan, and in this garden the second Adam overcame, and Satan himself was by him overcome; in the first garden sin was contracted, and we were indebted by our sins to God, and in this garden sin was paid for by that great and precious price of the blood of God: in the first garden man surfeited by eating the forbidden fruit, and in this garden Christ sweat it out wonderfully, even by a bloody sweat; in the first garden, death first made its entrance into the world; and in this garden life enters to restore us from death to life again; in the first garden Adam's liberty to sin brought himself and all us into bondage; and, in this garden, Christ being bound and fettered, we are thereby freed and reduced to liberty. I might thus descant in respect of every circumstance, but this is the sum, in a garden first began our sin, and in this garden first began the passion, that great work and merit of our redemption. 4. Christ goes especially into this garden, that his enemies might the more easily find him out; the evangelist tells us that this garden was a place often frequented by Jesus Christ, so that Judas, *which betrayed him, knew the place, for Jesus oftentimes resorted thither with his disciples,* John xviii. 2. Sure then he went not thither to hide himself, but rather to expose himself; and, like a noble champion, to appear first in the field, and to expect his enemies. Thus it appears to all the world, that Christ's death was voluntary. *He poured forth his soul unto death,* (faith the prophet) Isa. lii. 12. *He gave himself for our sins,* (faith the apostle) Gal. i. 4. Nay, himself tells us, *Therefore doth my Father love me, because I laid down my life: no man taketh it from me, but I lay it down of myself, I have power to lay it down, and I have power to take it up again,* John x. 17, 18. But I will not stay you at the door; let us follow Christ into the garden, and observe his prayer, and his sufferings there.

SECT. IV.

Of the prayer that Christ there made.

JESUS entring the garden, he left his disciples at the entrance of it, calling with him Peter, James and John; they only saw his transfiguration, the earnest of his future glory; and therefore his pleasure was, that they only should see of how great glory he would disrobe himself even for our sakes.——In the garden we may observe, *first*, his prayer, and *2dly*, his passion.

1. He betakes himself to his great antidote, which himself, (the great physician of our souls) prescribed to all the world: he prays to his heavenly Father: he kneels down, and not only so but falls flat upon the ground: he prays, with an intention great as his sorrow; and yet with a submission so ready, as if the cup had been the most indifferent thing in the world. The form of his prayer runs thus, *O my Father, if it be possible, let this cup pass from me, nevertheless not as I will, but as thou wilt,* Mat. xxvi. 39. In this prayer, observe we these particulars. 1. The person to whom he prays, *O my Father.* 2. The matter for which he prays, *let this cup pass from me.* 3. The limitation of this prayer, *if it be possible,* and *if it be thy will.*

1. For the person to whom he prays, it is *his Father*; as Christ prayed not in his Godhead, but according to his manhood, so neither prayed he to himself as God, but to *the Father*, the first person of the Godhead: hence some observe, that as the Father sometimes saying, *This is my beloved Son*, he spake not to himself but to the Son; so the Son usually saying, *O my Father*, he prays not to himself but to the Father.

2 For the matter of his prayer, *Let this cup pass from me*, some interpret thus, *Let this cup pass from me, Oh that I might not taste it,* But others thus. *Let this cup pass from me, though I*

must taste it; yet, *Oh that I may not be* too long or tediously annoyed by it!* that which leads us unto this last interpretation, is that of the apostle, *Christ in the days of his flesh offered up prayers and supplications, with strong cries and tears unto him, that was able to save him from death, and he was heard in that which he feared*, Heb. v. 7. How was he heard? Not in the removal of the cup, for he drank it up all; but, in respect of the tedious annoyance or poisoning of the cup; for though it made him sweat drops of blood, though it grieved him, and pained him, and made him cry out, *My God, my God, why hast thou forsaken me?* Tho' it cast him into a sleep, and laid him dead in the grave, and there sealed him for a time, yet presently, within the space of forty hours, or thereabouts, he revived, and awakened as a lion out of sleep, or as a giant refreshed with wine; and so it passed from him, as he prayed in a very short time; and by that short and momentary death, he purchased to his people everlasting life.

3. For the limitation of his prayer, *If it be possible, if it be thy will*; he knows what is his Father's will, and he prays accordingly, and is willing to submit unto it: *if the passing of the cup* be according to the last interpretation, we shall need none of those many distinctions to reconcile the will of God and Christ: *if it be possible*, signifies the earnestness of the prayer; and *if it be thy will*, the submission of Christ unto his Father. The prayer is short, but sweet: how many things needful to a prayer do we find concentered in this one instance? Here is humility of spirit, lowliness of deportment, importunity of desire, a fervent heart, a lawful matter, and a resignation to the will of God. Some think this the most fervent prayer that ever Christ made on earth, *If it be possible, O, if it be possible, let this cup pass from me*; and I think it was the greatest dereliction and submission to the will of God that ever was found upon the earth, for whether the cup might pass or not pass, he leaves it to his Father; *nevertheless, not as I will, but as thou wilt.* q. d. Though in this cup are many ingredients, it is full red, and hath in it many dregs; and I know I must drink and suck out the very utmost dreg; yet, whether it shall pass from me in that short time, or continue with me a long time, I leave it to thy will. I see, in respect of my humanity, there is in me flesh and blood; O I am frail and weak, I cannot but fear the wrath of God, and therefore I pray thus earnestly to my God, *O my Father, if it be possible, let this cup pass from me, nevertheless not as I will, but as thou wilt.*

But what was there in the cup, that made Christ pray thus earnestly that it might pass from him? I answer.——

1. The great pain that he must endure, buffetings, whippings, bleedings, crucifying; all the torments from first to last throughout all his body; why, all these came now into his mind, and all these were put into the cup, of which he must drink.

2. The great shame that he must undergo; this was more than pain, as *a good name is better than precious ointment, and loving favour better than silver and gold*, so is shame a greater punishment to the mind, than any torture can be to the flesh. Now came into his thoughts, his apprehending, binding, judging, scorning, reviling, condemning; and, oh, what a bloody blush comes into the face of Christ, whilst in the cup he sees these ingredients!

3. The neglect of men, notwithstanding both his pain and shame, I look upon this as a greater cut to the heart of Christ, than both the former, when he considered, that after all, his sufferings and reproaches few would regard. O this was a bitter ingredient, naturally men desire, if they cannot be delivered, yet to be pitied; it is a kind of ease, even to find some regard among the sons of men; it shews that they wish us well, and that they would give us ease if they could; but, oh! when it comes to this, that a poor wretch is under many sufferings and great shame; and that he finds none so much as to regard all this: now, verily, it is an heavy case, and hence was Christ's complaint, *Have ye no regard, O all ye that pass by the way? Consider and behold, if ever there was sorrow like unto my sorrow, which was done unto me, wherewith the Lord hath afflicted me in the*

---

* *Quod dicit, transfer calicem istam a me, non hoc est, non adveniet mihi: nisi enim advenerit, transferri non poterit; sed sicut quod petierit, nec intactum est, nec permanens; sic salvator leviter invadentem tentationem flagitat pelli. Sic*, Dionysius Alexandrinus.

days

Carrying on the great Work of Man's Salvation during the Time of his Sufferings. 267

days of his fierce anger, Lam. i. 12. Christ complains not of the sharp pains he endured; but he complains of this, *Have ye no regard?* He cries not out, *Oh deliver me and save me*; but, *Oh! consider and regard me*, q. d. All that I suffer I am contented with, I regard it not, only this troubles me, that you will not regard; why, it is for you I endure all this, and do you look so upon it, as if nothing at all concerned you? Suppose a prince should pay some mighty price to redeem a slave from death, and the slave should grow so desperate, as, after the price paid, to throw himself upon his death, yea, with all the strength and might he hath, to offer a death upon his very Redeemer: Would not this trouble? Why, thus it was; Christ is willing to redeem us with his own precious blood, but he saw many to pass by without any regard, yea, ready to trample his precious blood under their feet; and *to account the blood of the covenant as an unholy thing*, Heb. x. 29. Oh! this was another spear in the heart of Christ, or a bitter ingredient in this cup.

4. The guilt of sin which he was now to undergo; *upon him was laid the iniquity of us all*, Isa. liii. 6. All the sins of all believers in the world, from the first creation to the last judgment, were laid on him; Oh! what a weight was this? Surely if one sin is like a talent of lead; oh then, what were so many thousands of millions? The very earth itself groans under the weight of sin until this day; David cried out, *That his iniquities were a burden too heavy for him to bear*, Ps. xxxviii. 4. Nay, God himself complains, *Behold I am pressed under you, as a cart is pressed that is full of sheaves*, Amos ii. 13. Now then no wonder, if Christ bearing all the sins of Jews and Gentiles, bound and free, cry out, *My soul is heavy*, for sin was heavy on his soul.——In that I say, all the sins of all believers were laid on Christ, understand me soberly; my meaning is not that believers sins were so laid on Christ, as that they ceased to be believers sins according to their physical and real indwelling, but only that they were laid on Christ by law-imputation, or by legal obligation to satisfactory punishment. I make a difference betwixt sin and the guilt of sin; for sin itself is *macula*, the blot, defilement, and blackness of sin, which I conceive is nothing but the absence and privation of that moral rectitude and righteousness which the law requireth: but the guilt of sin is somewhat issuing from this blot and blackness, according to which the person is liable and obnoxious to eternal punishment. Some indeed give a distinction of the guilt of sin, there is *reatus culpae*, the guilt of sin as sin; and this is all one with sin, being the very essence, soul, and formal being of sin; they call it a fundamental or potential guilt; and there is *reatus penae, reatus personae, reatus actualis*, the guilt or obligation to punishment, the actual guilt, or actual obligation of the person who hath thus sinned to punishment; and this guilt is a thing far different from sin itself, and is separable from sin; yea, and is removed from sin in our justification. Now, this was the sin or guilt which was laid on Christ, in which sense the apostle speaks, *Who his ownself bare our sins in his own body on the tree*, 1 Pet. ii. 24. How, bare our sins on the tree, but by his suffering?——*And he hath laid on him the iniquity of us all*, Isa. liii. 6.—How laid on him but by imputation?—*And he hath made him to be sin for us who knew no sin*, 2 Cor. v. 21. How made sin for us? Surely there was in Christ no fundamental guilt; no, no, but he made sin by imputation and law-account: he was our surety, and so our sins were laid on him in order to punishment, as if now in the garden he had said to his Father, *Thou hast given me a body, as I have taken the debts and sins of all believers in the world upon me; come now, and arrest me, as the only paymaster; lo here I am to do and suffer for their sins whatsoever thou pleasest*, Psal. xl. 6, 7, 8. Heb. x. 4, 5, 6, 7, 8, 9. Or as if he had said to the Father thus, *I am the sinner, O Father, I am the surety, all my friends wants, and all their debts let them be laid on me; my life for their lives, my soul for their souls, my glory for their glory, my heaven for their heaven*. Now, this was no small matter; little do we know or consider, what is the weight and guilt of sin. And this was another ingredient of Christ's cup.

5. The power and malice of Satan; the devil had a full leave and licence, not as it was with Job, *Do what thou wilt, Satan, but save his life*; no, no, he had a commission without any such restriction or limitation; the whole power of darkness was let loose to use all his violence; and to afflict him as far possibly he could: and this our Saviour intimates, when he saith, *That the prince of this*

world

world cometh, John xiv. 30. Now was it that the word must be accomplished, *Thou shalt bruise his heel*, Gen iii. 15. The devil could go no higher than the heel of Christ, but whatever he could do he was sure to do; he had been nibbling a great while at his heel; no sooner he was born, but he would have killed him, and after he fell fiercely on him in the wilderness; but now, all the power and all the malice of hell conjoins. If we look on the devil in respect of his evil nature, he is compared to *a roaring lion*; not only is he a lion but a roaring lion, his disposition to do mischief is always wound up to the height; and if we look on the devil in respect of his power, there is no part of our souls or bodies that he cannot reach; the apostle, describing his power, he gives him names above the highest comparisons, as *principalities, powers, rulers of the darkness of this world, spiritual wickedness above*, Eph. vi. 12. Devils are not only called princes, but *principalities*; not only mighty, but *powers*; not only rulers of a part, but of *all the darkness of this world*; not only wicked spirits, but *spiritual wickedness*; not only about us, but *above us*; they hang over our heads continually; you know what a disadvantage it is to have your enemy get the hill, the upper ground; and this they have naturally, and always. Oh then, what a combat must this be, when all the power and all the malice of all the devils in hell, should (by the permission of God) arm themselves against the Son of God? Surely this was a bitter ingredient in Christ's cup.

6. The wrath of God himself; this (above all) was the most bitter dreg; it lay in the bottom, and Christ must drink it also; *Oh! the Lord hath afflicted me in the day of his fierce anger*, La. i. 12. God afflicts some in mercy, and some in anger; this was in his anger, and yet in his anger, God is not alike to all, some he afflicts in his more gentle and mild, others in his fierce anger: this was in the very fierceness of his anger. It is agreed upon by all divines, that now Christ saw himself bearing the sins of all believers, and standing before the judgment-seat of God; to this end are those words, *Now is the judgment of this world, and the prince of this world shall be cast out*, John xii. 31. Now is the judgment of this world, *q. d.* Now I see God sitting in judgment upon the world; and as a right representative of all the world of believ-

ers, here I stand before his tribunal, ready to undergo all the punishments due to them for their sins; why, there is no other way to save their souls, and to satisfy justice, but that the fire of thy indignation should kindle against me; *q. d.* 'O I 'know it is a fearful thing to fall into the hands of 'the living God; Oh I know God is a consuming 'fire: who can stand before his indignation? and 'who can abide in the fierceness of his anger? His 'fury is poured out like fire, and the rocks are 'thrown down by him,' Neh. i. 6. But for this end came I into the world; O my Father, I will drink this cup, lo here an open breast, come prepare the armory of thy wrath, and herein shoot all the arrows of revenge.——And yet, O my Father, let me not be oppressed, subverted or swallowed up by thy wrath; let not thy displeasure continue longer than my patience or obedience can endure; there is in me flesh and blood in respect of my humanity; 'and my flesh trembleth for fear of thee, I am 'afraid of thy judgments: oh! if it be possible, if 'it be possible, let this cup pass from me.'

SECT. V.

Of the dolours and agonies that Christ there suffered.

2. CHRIST's passion in the garden was either before, or at his apprehension; his passion before is declared. 1. By his sorrows. 2. By his sweat.

1. For his sorrow; the evangelists diversely relate it, *He began to be sorrowful, and very heavy*, saith Matthew, Mat. xxvi. 37. *He began to be sore amazed, and to be very heavy*, saith Mark, Mark xiv. 33. *And being in an agony, he prayed more earnestly*, saith Luke, Luke xii. 44. *Now is my soul troubled, and what shall I say? Father, save me from this hour, but for this cause came I into this hour*, saith John, John xii. 27. All avow this sorrow to be great, and so it is confest by Christ himself: *then saith he unto them, My soul is exceeding sorrowful, even unto death*, Matth. xxvi. 38. Ah Christians! who can speak out this sorrow? *The spirit of a man will sustain his infirmity, but a wounded spirit who can bear?* Prov. xviii. 14. Christ's soul is sorrowful; or if that be too flat, his soul is sorrowful, exceeding sorrowful; or if that language be too low, his soul is exceeding sorrowful, even
unto

unto death; not only extensively, such as must continue for the space of seventeen or eighteen hours, even until death itself should finish it; but also intensively, such, and so great, as that which is used to be at the very point of death; and such as were able to bring death itself, had not Christ been reserved to a greater and an heavier punishment. Of this sorrow is that especially spoken, *Consider, and behold if ever there was sorrow like unto my sorrow*, Lam. i. 12. Many a sad and sorrowful soul hath, no question, been in the world, but the like sorrow to this, was never since the creation; the very terms of the evangelists speak no less, he was sorrowful and heavy, saith one; amazed and very heavy, saith another; in an agony, saith a third: in a soul-trouble, saith a fourth. Surely the bodily torments of the cross were inferior to this agony of his soul; the pain of the body is the body of pain; oh! but the very soul of sorrow and pain is the soul's sorrow, and the soul's pain. It was a sorrow unspeakable, and therefore I must leave it, as not being able to utter it.

2. For this sweat, Luke only relates it, 'And his sweat was as it were, great drops of blood falling down to the ground,' Luke xxii. 44. In the words I observe a climax. 1. His sweat was as it were blood; Ethymius and Theophilact interpret those words as only a similitude or figurative hyperbole; an usual kind of speech to call a vehement sweat a bloody sweat; as he that weeps bitterly is said to weep tears of blood; Augustine, Jerom, Epiphanius, Athanasius, Irenens, and others, from the beginning of the church, understand it in a literal sense, and believe it was truly and properly a bloody sweat; nor is the objection considerable, that it was, *Sicut guttae sanguinis, as it were drops of blood*; for if the Holy Ghost had only intended that *sicut* for a similitude or hyperbole, he would rather have expressed it, as it were drops of water, than as it were drops of blood. We all know sweat is more like to water than to blood; besides, a *sicut* in scripture-phrase doth not always denote a similitude, but sometimes the very thing itself, according to the variety of it; thus we *beheld his glory, the glory, as it were of the only begotten Son of the Father*, John i. 14.— *And their words seemed to them as it were idle tales, and they believed them not*, Luke x. 11.

The words in the original [*hos hostoi*,] are the same; here is the first step of this climax, his sweat was a wonderful sweat, not a sweat of water, but of red gore-blood.

2. Great drops of blood, [*thenombo'aimatos*] There is *sudor diaphoreticus*, a thin faint sweat; and *sudor grumosus*, a thick, concrete, and clotted sweat; in this bloody sweat of Christ, it came not from him in small dews, but in great drops, they were drops, and great drops of blood, crassy and thick drops; and hence it is concluded as preternatural, for though much be said for sweating blood in a course of nature; * Aristotle affirms it; † and Augustine grants, 'That he knew a man that could sweat blood even when he pleased:' in faint bodies, a subtile thin blood like sweat, may pass through the pores of the skin; but that thro' the same pores, crassy, thick and great drops of blood should issue out, it was not, it could not be without a miracle: some call them *grumes*, others *globes* of blood; certainly the drops were great, so great, as if they had started through his skin, to outrun the streams and rivers of his cross.

3. Here is yet another climax, in that these great drops of blood did not only *distilare* drop out; but *decurrere*, run a stream down so fast, as if they had issued out of most deadly wounds; they were great drops of blood falling down to the ground; here is magnitude and multitude; great drops, and those so many, so plenteous, that they went through his apparel, and all streaming down to the ground; now was it that his garments were dyed with crimson red; that of the prophet, tho' spoken in another sense, yet, in some respect, may be applied to this; 'Wherefore art thou red in thine apparel, and thy garments like him that treadeth in the wine-fat?' Isa. lxiii. 2. Oh what a sight was here! his head and members are all in a bloody sweat; this sweat trickles down, and bedecks his garments, which stood like a new firmament studded with stars, portending an approaching storm: nor stays it there, but it *falls down to the ground*: Oh happy garden, watered with such tears of blood! how much better are these rivers *than Abana and Pharpar, rivers of Damascus, yea, than all the waters of Israel*, yea, than all those

---

* *Arist. L. III. de Hist. animal. c. 29.*
† *Aug. L. X.V d. Civit. dei. c. 24.*

rivers that water the garden of Eden?——— *Use.* 1. This may inform us of the weight and burden of sin, that thus presseth Christ under it till he sweat and bleed; when the first Adam had committed the first sin, this was the penalty, *In the sweat of thy face shalt thou eat thy bread,* Gen. iii. 19. but now the second Adam takes upon him all the sins of all believers in the world; he sweats not only in his face, but in all his body; O then how was that face disfigured, when it stood all on drops, and those drops not of a watry sweat, but of a gore-blood? we see in other men, that when they are disquieted with fear or grief, the blood usually runs to the heart, indeed that is the principal member, and therefore leaving the other parts, it goes thither as of choice to comfort that; but our sweet Saviour contrariwise (because he would suffer without any manner of comfort) he denies to himself this common relief of nature; all the powers of our souls, and parts of our bodies were stained with sin, and therefore he sweats blood from every part: we sin, and our eyes will scarce drop a tear for sin; but his eyes, and ears, and head, and hands, and feet, and heart, and all run rivers of tears of blood for us, even for our sins. —— Let jesuits and friars, in meditating of Christ's sufferings cry out against the Jews: in this bloody sweat of Christ, I see another use; alas! here is no Jew, no Judas, no Herod, no Pilate, no Scribe, no Pharisee; here are no tormentors to whip him, no soldiers to crown his head with thorns; here are neither nails, nor spear to fetch his blood out of his body; how comes it then to pass? Is there any natural cause? Ah no! the night is cold, which naturally draws blood inwards; in the open air he lies groveling on the ground, and there *he sweats and bleeds,* 2 Sam. xii. 5. O my heart, who hath done this deed? *As the Lord liveth, the man that hath done this thing, shall surely die,* ver. 5. So said David, when Nathan replied upon him, *Thou art the man.* O my heart! my sinful heart! O my sinful, deceitful, abominable heart! thou art the murderer; thy sin sat upon the heart of Christ as heavy as a mountain of lead or iron, when none was near, but a few dull, heavy, sleepy disciples; then all the sins of believers (and amongst them thy sins) fell upon the soul of Christ, as so many murderers, and squeezed blood, and made him cry out, *My soul is heavy, heavy unto death.* Go thy ways now, and weep with Peter, and say with David, *I have sinned against the Lord,* ver. 13. O how should these eyes of mine look upon Christ thus sweating, bleeding, streaming out blood, clouds of blood, great drops of blood, from all the parts and members of his body, but I must *mourn over him, as one that mourneth over his only son; but I must be in bitterness, as one that is in bitterness for his first-born,* Zech. xii. 10.

2. This may inform us of the extraordinary love of Christ. It is said of the pelican, that when her young ones are struck with the tail of some poisonous serpent, she presently strikes her breast with her beak or bill, and so lets out her own blood as a medicine for them, that they may suck and live; even so Christ seeing us struck with the poison of sin, he is impatient of delay, he would not stay till the Jews let him blood with their whips, and thorns, and nails; ' I have a baptism ' to be baptized with, (saith Christ) and how am I ' straitened till it be accomplished?' Luke xii. 50. He is big with love; and therefore he opens all his pores of his own accord, he lets blood gush out from every part, and therefore he makes a precious balsam to cure our wounds. O the love of Christ! As Elihu could sometimes say, ' Be- ' hold, my belly is as wine which hath no vent, it ' is ready to burst like new bottles,' Job xxxii. 19. so the heart of Christ was full, even full of love, so, full, that it could not hold, but it burst out through every part and member of his body, in a bloody sweat. I will not say, but that every drop of Christ's blood was very precious, and of sufficient value to save a world; but certainly that blood which was not forced by whips, or thorns, or spear, is to be had in singular honour; as the myrrh, that by incision of the tree flows out, is very precious, yet that which drops out of its own accord, is accounted as the first and choice; and as the balsam which way soever it come, is sweet, yet that which falls of its own accord is held the most pure and odoriferous; to this aludes that apocryphal saying in Ecclesiasticus, *I gave a sweet smell like cinamon, and I yielded a pleasant odour like the best myrrh,* Eccl. xxiv. 15. The vulgar translate it thus; *Quasi libanus non incisus vaporavi,* as the myrrh-tree that is not cut I evapoured; as if Christ should have said, Without any lancing, cutting, pruning, out of mere love, I poured out my blood upon the earth: this

is

is certain, at this time, no manner of violence was offered him in body, no man touched him or came near him; in a cold night (for they were fain to have a fire within doors) lying abroad in the air, and upon cold earth, he casts himself into a sweat of blood; surely love is hot, he had a fire in his breast that melts him into this bloody sweat; O wonderful love;

3. This may inform us of the design of Christ in these very sufferings; '* Christ weeps, (saith ' Bernard) not only in his eyes, but in all his ' members, that with the tears of his body he ' might wash and purify his body, which is the ' church.' Or Christ weeps blood, that he might give us a sign of the enemies ruin; sweat in sickness is as a crisis, or promising sign, that nature, with all her force, hath strove against the peccant humour, and hath now overcome it; so this bloody sweat is a blessed crisis, or argument of sin decaying, and that the Lamb hath overthrown the lion. As Christ sometimes said, *Now is the judgment of this world: now shall the prince of this world be cast out. And I, if I be lifted up from the earth, will draw all men unto me*, John xii. 31, 32.

Thus far of Christ's passion, before his apprehension. And now we may suppose it about midnight, the very time which Christ called *the hour, and power of darkness*, Luke xxii. 53. What followed from twelve till three at night, we shall discover in the next section.

SECT. VI.

Of Judas's treason, Christ's apprehension, binding and leading unto Annas.

BY this time the traitor Judas was arrived at Gethsemane; and being near the garden door, Jesus goes to his disciples, and calls them from their sleep, by an irony (as some think) he bids them *sleep on now, and take their rest*, meaning, if they could for danger, that now was near; but withal, he adds, *Behold the hour is at hand; and the Son of man is betrayed into the hands of sinners: Rise, let us be going: behold, he is at hand that doth betray me*, Matth. xxvi. 45, 46.

* Bern. Serm. in dom. palm.

That it might appear he undertook his sufferings with choice and free election; he not only refused to fly, but he calls his apostles to rise, that they might meet his murderers. And now they come *with swords and staves*, or, as John adds, *with lanthorns and torches, and (Judas going before them, and drawing near unto Jesus to kiss him) they took him, and bound him, and led him away to Annas first*, Mat. xxvi. 47. John xviii. 3, 12, 13.

In this period I shall observe, 1. Judas's treason. 2. Christ's apprehension. 3. Christ's binding. 4. Christ's leading to Annas, one of the chief priests, as to his first station.

1. Judas's treason. *And while he yet spake, behold, a multitude, and he that was called Judas, one of the twelve, went before them, and drew near unto Jesus to kiss him*, Luke xxii. 47. This traitor is not a disciple only, but an apostle; not one of the seventy, but one of the twelve. Augustine speaks of many offices of love, that Christ had done to Judas in especial manner; he had called him to be an apostle, made him his friend, his familiar, caused him to eat of his bread, sit at his table, and to dip his hand in the dish with him; yea, if his tradition be true, † ' Jesus had deliver- ' ed Judas often from death, and for his sake ' healed his father of a palsy, and cured his mo- ' ther of a leprosy, and next to Peter honoured ' him above all other his apostles.' Of this we are sure, that he kissed him, and washed his feet, and made him his treasurer, and his almoner; and that now Judas should betray Christ; O how doth this add to the sufferings of Christ, and to the sin of Judas? *Behold a multitude*, and Judas in the front; he went before them, *tam pedibus quam moribus*; in his presence, and in his malice. The evangelist gives the reason of this, that he might have the better opportunity to kiss him; that this was the sign, he gave the rout, *Whomsoever I shall kiss, that is he, lay hold on him*; he begins war with a kiss, and breaks the peace of his Lord by a symbol of kindness: Jesus takes this ill, What, Judas, *betrayest thou the Son of man with a kiss?* Luke xxii. 48. *q. d.* What, dost thou make the seal of love the sign of treachery? What, must a kiss of thy mouth be the key of treason? O what a friendly reproof is here! by way of use.———

† Aug. Serm. 28. ad fratres.

Use.

Use. † 'It were well for the world (faith Chrysostome) especially for the children of God, that Judas were alone in this transgression, that there were no more perfidious, treacherous persons in it besides himself. But, Oh! how full is the world of such miscreants? There was never yet an Abel, but he had a Cain to murder him; never yet a Moses, but he had a Jannes and Jambres to resist him; never yet a Joseph, but he had unkind brothers to envy him; never yet a Sampson, but he had a Dalilah to betray him; never yet a David, but he had an Achitophel to hurt him; never yet a Paul, but there was an Alexander to do him much evil; nay, it is well if in every assembly we meet not with a Judas: in civil affairs how many are there that live and make gain by lying, swearing, cheating, cozening, selling away Christ, and their own souls, for a lesser matter than thirty pieces of silver: and in religious affairs, how many secure and drowsy professors have we amongst us, that salute Christ, both by hearing the word, and receiving the seals, and yet in their lives and conversations, they deny Christ? *They honour God with their lips, but their hearts are far away from him*, Mark vii. 6.

2. For Christ's apprehension, *Then came they, and laid hands on Jesus, and took him*; they apprehended him whom the world cannot comprehend? and yet before they took him, he himself begins the enquiry, and leads them into their errand; he tells them, that he was *Jesus of Nazareth, whom they sought*; this was but a breath, a meek and gentle word, yet had it greater strength in it than the eastern wind, or the voice of thunder; for God was in that still voice, and it struck them down to the ground. O the power of Christ! they come to him with clubs, and staves, and swords, and he does no more, but let a word fly out of his mouth, and presently they stagger, run *backward and fall to the ground*, John xviii. 6. Oh! if we cannot bear a soft answer of the merciful God, how dare we so provoke, as we do, the wrath of the Almighty Judge? And yet he suffers them to rise again, and they still persist in their enquiry after him; and he tells them once more, *I am he*; he offers himself, he is ready, and desirous to be sacrificed, only he lets them their bounds; and therefore he secures his apostles to be witnesses of his sufferings: in this work of redemption, no man must have an active share besides himself, he alone was to tread the wine-press; *If therefore ye seek me* (saith Christ) *let these go their way*, Joh. xviii. 8. thus he permits himself to be taken, but not his disciples.

And now they have his leave; oh! with what fierce and cruel countenances, with what menacing and threatening looks, with what malicious and spightful minds, do they invade and assault our Saviour? They compass him round; then they lay their wicked and violent hands upon him, in the original, [*epethelon*] signifies a violent taking. One speaks the manner of his apprehension in these words, ' * Some of them lay hold on his garments, ' others on the hairs of his head; some pluck him ' by the beard, others struck him with their impi- ' ous fists, and, being enraged, that with a word ' he had thrown them backwards on the ground, ' they therefore threw him on his back, and basely tread him under their dirty feet.' Another ' Author gives it thus, ‡ As a roaring ramping lion ' draws along the earth his prey, and tears it, ' and pulls it, so they hawled Christ all along the ' earth, spitting, buffeting, pulling him by the ' hair.' Another, in like manner thus, '§ They ' all rush violently upon him, they fling him to the ' ground, they kick him, tear him, spurn him, ' pull off the hair, both of his head and beard.' Of every of these passages, we find scriptures full, *Many bulls have compassed me, strong bulls of Bashan have beset me round, they gaped upon me with their mouths, as a ravening and roaring lion*, Psal. xxii 12, 13.

Use. We are apt to cry out on Judas and the Jews; and we think, Oh if we had been in their stead, we should never have done this; but lay aside a while those instruments, and look we at the principal cause; had not we an hand in all these actions? Did not we conspire his death, and ap-

---

† *Utinam Judas solus sic peccasset* Chrysof. * *Quidam apprehendebant vestes ejus, alii mittebant manus in capillos capitis, &c.* Homil. Johan. Carthag. Hispan. ‡ *Sicut leo rugiens et rapiens trahit prædam per terram et lacerat, et laviat, &c.* Jacob. *de valenti* in Psal. xxi. § *Omnes impetum faciunt in eum, &c.*

prehension

prehension in reference to it? Oh, my sins, my sins! these were the band, the captain, and the officers; these were the multitude, a multitude indeed, if I should tell them, I might tell a thousand, and yet not tell one of a thousand, these were the soldiers that beset him round, the bulls that compassed him about, the roaring lions that gaped upon him with their mouths: O my heart, why shouldest thou rise up against the Jews, when thou findest the traitor, and the whole rout of officers in thyself? Oh that thou wouldest turn the edge of thy detestation into its right stream and channel! oh that thou wouldest 'remember thy own ways, 'and all thy doings, wherein thou hast been defiled,' and that thou wouldest 'lothe thyself in thy own 'sight, for all the evils that thou hast committed!' Ezek. xx. 43.

3. For Christ's binding, the evangelist tells us, That *the band, and the captain, and the officers of the Jews took Jesus, and bound him*, John xviii. 12. [*edesan*], they bound his hands with cords; a type of this was Sampson, whom Dalilah bound with ropes or cords, foreshewing hereby, that he must die, they never using to bind any with ropes or cords, but those whom undoubtedly they purposed to crucify: and so they bound him with ropes or cords: some add the circumstances of this binding, that they bound him with three cords, and that with such violence, that they caused blood to start out of his tender hands; certainly they wanted no malice, and now they wanted no power, for the Lord had given himself into their hands. Binding argues baseness; it is storied of Alexander, that when some arrow that was shot into him was to be drawn out, his physicians advised to bind him, for that the least motion, (as they said) would do him hurt; but he answered, * *Kings were not fit to be bound, the power of a king was ever free and safe:* And David in his lamentation over Abner, said, *Died Abner as a fool dieth? Thy hands were not bound, nor thy feet put into fetters*, 2 Sam. ii. 33, 34. Fools and slaves were accustomed to be bound, and so were thieves; they that open their hands to receive others goods, it is fit their hands should be bound and tied up;

but is our Saviour numbered amongst any of these? O yes, 'In that same hour said Jesus to the multi- 'tude, Are ye come out as against a thief, with 'swords and staves?' Matth. xxvi. 55. 'He made 'himself of no reputation, and took upon him the 'form of a servant,' Phil. ii. 7. O wonderful condescension of Christ! O admirable exinanition! he that was eminently just is reputed a thief; he that was equal with God is become a servant; he that was stronger than Sampson, and could have broken his cords from off his arms like a thread, he is bound with cords; and as a poor Lamb he continues bound for the slaughter: and thus began our liberty, and redemption from slavery, and sin, and death, and cursings.

But besides these cords, the word [*edesan*] signifies a binding with chains, Mark v. 3, 4. and some are of opinion, that they shackled both his hands and feet, *pedibus et catenis vinctus*, Mark v. 4. and others say, that they put about his neck † *a chain of iron*; and it is not altogether improbable but they might be as cruel to the master as to the servants; I cannot think they were so enraged against Peter, as they were against Christ, and yet they laid on him *two chains*, Acts xii. 6. Nor can I think they were so enraged against Paul, as they were against Jesus, and yet *the chief captain took him, and commanded him to be bound with two chains*, Acts xxi. 33. And that this might be their dealing with Christ, Judas, by his counsel, seems to speak, *Hold him fast*, Matth. xxvi. 48.——*Take him, and lead him away safely*, Mark xiv. 44. *q. d.* Make him sure, that he escape not out of your hands, he hath deceived you often, and therefore chain him with an iron chain that will be sure to hold. I cannot pass this without some word to ourselves.

Use. Christ undergoes this restraint, that all sorts of persecution might be sanctified to us by his susception. Again, Christ was faster bound with his cords of love, than with iron fetters, his love was strong as death, it overcame him who is invincible, and bound him who is omnipotent; the Jews cords were but the symbols and figures, but the dear love, the tender bowels of Jesus Christ were the morals and things signified: again, Christ

---

* *Non decet vinciri regem, cum libera sit regis et semper salva potestas.* Bern. Serm. de pas.
† *Quidam existimaverunt catena ferrea collum ejus alligasse, quod mihi certe incredibile non est.* Hom. Joh. Carthag.

was bound that we might be free; the cords of Christ were so full of virtue, that they loosed the chains of our sins, and tied the hands of God's justice, which were stretched out against us for our sins. Again, he was bound for us, that so he might bind us to himself. *I drew them with cords of a man, with bands of love,* Hosea xi. 4. A strange thing it was, to see the king bound for the thieves offence; but such was Christ's love, that he might draw sinful mankind to the love of him again. Lastly, One good lesson we may learn from wicked Judas, *Take him, and lead him away safely;——hold him fast.* Come, Christians! here is good counsel from a Judas, like another Caiaphas, he prophesies he knows not what; *take him and lead him away, and hold him fast.* It is of necessity, that those which spiritually seek after Christ, should take him by faith, and hold him fast by love; *I will rise now,* (saith the spouse) *I will seek him whom my soul loveth;* ——— and anon, ' I found him whom my soul loveth, I held him, and ' would not let him go, until I had brought him in- ' to my mother's house, into the chamber of her ' that conceived me,' Cant. iii. 2, 4. We must arise out of the bed of sin, we must seek Christ in the use of ordinances; and there if we find him, we must take him, lay hold on him by the hands of faith, and not let him go, but lead him safely until we have brought him into our mother's house, into the assemblies of his people; or, if you will, until we have brought him into our souls, where he may sup with us, and we with him.

4. For his leading to Annas, John records it, That ' they led him away to Annas first, for he was ' father-in-law to Caiaphas, who was the high ' priest that same year,' John xviii. 13. 1. They led him away, [*apegagon*], it refers to the place whence they led him; the garden was the *terminus a quo,* there they apprehended him, and bound him, and thence led him away; but the word [*Apago*] is something more than merely *abduco*; sometimes it signifies *abigo,* to drive away, whether by force or fraud; sometimes *rapio ad supplicium, ad judicandum,* to snatch away either to punishment or judgment: it is said, * ' They drew him away ' by the hairs of the head, and that they led ' him in uncouth ways, and through the brook Ce- ' dron, in which the ruder soldiers plunged him, ' and passed upon him all the affronts and rudeness ' which an insolent and cruel multitude could think ' of.' So that now again was the fulfilling of the prophecy, *He shall drink of the brook in the way,* Psal. cx. 7. I dare not deliver these things as certain truths, only this they affirm, that they led him, snatched him, hauled him from the garden back again to Jerusalem, over the brook and valley called Cedron. ——— 2. They led him first to Annas; why thither, is a question, the cognizance of the cause belonged not properly to Annas but to Caiaphas; all that can be said for Annas, is, that he was the chief of the sanhedrim, and father-in-law to Caiaphas, and to be high priest the next year following.

Use. Oh! when I think of Jesus thus led away to Annas first, when I think of him partly going, and partly hauled forwards, and forced to hasten his grave pace; when I think of him thrown into, or plunged in the waters of the brook, and so forced to drink of the brook Cedron in the way; when I think of him presented by a deal of soldiers, and rude catch-poles to this mercenary Annas; and withal, think that I had an hand as deep as any other in these acts, my heart must either break, or I must proclaim it an heart of flint, and not of flesh: come, Christians, let us lay our hands upon our hearts, and cry, ' Oh, my pride! and oh, my covetous- ' ness! and oh, my malice and revenge! oh, my ' unbelief! and oh my unthankfulness! and oh, ' my uncharitableness to the needy members of ' Christ Jesus! why, these were the rout, these ' were they that led, and dragged, and drew Je- ' sus (as it were) by the hair of his head; these ' were they that took hold of the chain, and pull- ' ed him forwards, and shewed him in triumph ' to this bloody Annas; nay, these were the Judas, ' Jews, Annas, and all: oh! that ever I should ' lodge within me such an heart, that should lodge ' in it such sins, such betrayers, such murderers of ' Jesus Christ.'

But I must remember myself, *Watchman, what of the night? Watchman, what of the night?* Isa. xxi. 11, 12. *If ye will enquire, enquire, return, come,* Matth. xiv. 25. We may now suppose it about the third hour, or last watch:

---

* *Ecce trahebatur passis Priamidia virgo crinibus,* Virg. Aeneid 1.

in gospel it is called the *fourth watch of the night*, Exod. xiv. 24. Elsewhere it is called *the morning watch*, Psalm cxxx. 6. which continueth *till the morning*. And of the acts done in this interval of time, we are next to treat.

SECT. VII.

Of Christ's examination and condemnation, with their appendices.

NOW it was, that they led him from Annas to Caiaphas; and presently a council is called of the high priests, scribes and elders; these were the greatest, gravest, learnedest, wisest men amongst them, and they all conspire to judge him, who is the greatest judge both of quick and dead.—In their proceedings we may observe. 1. The captious examination of the high priest. 2. The sacrilegious smiting of one of the servants. 3. The impious accusations of the witnesses. 4. The sentence of the judges. 5. The perfidious denial of perjured Peter. 6. The shameful delusion and abuses of the base attendants.

1. For the captious examination of the high priest, *The high priest then asked Jesus of his disciples, and of his doctrine*, John xviii. 19. 1. Of his disciples; what the questions were it is not expressed; but probably they might be such as these, ' How many disciples he had? And where they ' were? And what was become of them? Why ' he should take upon him to be better guarded ' than others of greater place and calling? Whe-' ther it did not favour of sedition and disturbance ' of the state, to lead about such a crew of disciples ' and followers after him? And what was the rea-' son of their flight, whether it were not a token ' of their guiltiness of some disorder, or of riotous ' practices?' It is not for me to speak how many queries the high priest might make to tempt Jesus, but certainly he was sifted to the brain, examined to the full, of all such circumstances as either might trap Christ, or, in the least degree, advance and help forward his condemnation: to this question concerning his disciples our Saviour answered nothing; alas! he knew the frailty of his followers, he might have said, ' For my disciples, you see ' one hath betrayed me, and another will anon ' forswear me, he stays but for the crowing of ' the cock, and then you shall hear him curse and ' swear, that he never knew me; and for all the ' rest, a panic fear hath seized upon their hearts, ' and they are fled, and have left me alone to tread ' the wine-press.' Ah, no, he will not speak evil of the teachers of his people; it was grief to him, and added to his sufferings, that all had forsaken him: once before this *many of his disciples went back, and walked no more with him*, which occasioned Jesus to say to the twelve, *Will ye also go away?* Why, no, said Peter then, *Lord, whither shall we go, thou hast the words of eternal life; and we believe, and are sure, that thou art that Christ, the Son of the living God?* John vi. 67, 68, 69. Oh, Peter! what a strong faith was that? *We believe, and we are sure*; but how is it now that ye have no faith? Or why are ye so fearful, O ye of little faith? I believe this sat upon the heart of Christ, and yet he would not accuse them who now stood in their places, and was accused for them, and for us all; and therefore to that question of his disciples he answered nothing.

2. He asked him of his doctrine; what his questions were of that, are not set down neither, but probably they may be such as these, ' Who ' was his master and instructor in that new doctrine ' he had lately broached? Why he did seek to in-' novate and alter their long practised and accus-' tomed rites? And what ground had he to bring ' in his own devices in their steads? As baptism ' for circumcision, the Lord's supper for the pass-' over, himself and his apostles for the high priests ' and Levites, when neither he, nor most of them ' were of that tribe? Why he was so bold and sau-' cy, (being but three and thirty years of age) to ' declaim so bitterly and satyrically against the ' Pharisees and Saducees, and Scribes, and priests, ' and elders of the people?' Much of this stuff he might bring out in his interrogatories, that so, by his questioning him in many things, he might trap him in something to his confusion and destruction.——And this question our Saviour answers, but, oh, how wisely! *I spake openly to the world*, (said he) *I ever taught in the synagogue and in the temple, whither the Jews always resorted; and in secret have I said nothing, why askest thou me, ask them which heard me, what I said unto them, behold they know what I said?* John xviii. 20, 21. *q. d.*

I appeal to the testimony of the very enemies themselves; thou suspectedst me to be a seditious person, and one that plots mischief against the state in secret; I tell the truth, *I speak nothing in secret*, (i.e.) nothing in the least manner tending to sedition; my doctrine I brought with me from the bosom of my Father, it is the everlasting gospel, and not of yesterday; and it contains nothing in it of sedition, faction, rebellion, treason; ask these mine enemies, these who have apprehended, and bound me, and brought me hither; *They know what I said*, let them speak, if they can, wherein I have transgressed the law.

2. For the stroke given Christ by that base servant; 'one of the officers who stood by, struck 'Jesus with the palm of his hand, saying, Answerest 'thou the high priest so?' John xviii. 22. that holy face, which was designed to be the object of heaven, in the beholding of which, much of the celestial glory doth consist; that face which the angels stare upon with wonder, like infants at a bright sun-beam, was now smitten by a base varlet, in the presence of a judge; and howsoever the assembly was full, yet not one amongst them all reproved the fact, or spake a word for Christ; nay, in this the injury was heightened, because the blow was said to be given by * Malchus, an Idumean slave; it was he whose ear was cut off by Peter, and cured by Christ; and thus he requites him for his miracle.—Amongst all the sufferings of Christ, one would think this but little, and yet when I look into the scriptures, I find it much; thus Jeremy, *He giveth his cheeks to him that smiteth him, he is filled full with reproach*, Lam. iii. 30. Thus Micah speaking of Christ, *They shall smite the Judge of Israel with a rod upon the cheek*, Mic. v. 1. There was in it a world of shame; the apostle lays it down as a sign of suffering and reproach, 2 Cor. xi. 20. *If a man smite you on the face, nothing more disgraceful*, † (saith Chrysostome) *than to be smitten on the cheek*; the divers reading of the word speaks it out farther, *He struck him with a rod*, or *he struck him with the palm of his hand*, ‡ [*edone rapisma*] the word [*rapisma*] say some, refers to his striking with a rod, or club, or shoe, or pantoffle; or, as others, it refers to his striking with the palm of his hand; of the two, the palm of the hand is judged more disgraceful than either rod or shoe; and therefore in the text we translate it, *With the palm of the hand he struck at Jesus*, (i.e.) with open hand, with his hand stretched out.

* The ancients commenting on this cuff; 'Let 'the heavens be afraid, (saith one) and let the 'earth tremble at Christ's patience, and this servant's impudence. † O ye angels, how were 'ye silent? How could you contain your hands, 'when you saw his hand striking at God?——If 'we consider him, (saith another) who took the 'blow, was not he that struck him worthy to be 'consumed of fire, or to be swallowed up of earth, 'or to be given up to Satan, and thrown down into hell?' If a subject should but lift up his hand against the son of an earthly sovereign, would he not be accounted worthy of punishment? How much more in this case, when the hand is lifted up against the King of kings, and Lord of lords, whom not only men, but the *cherubims* and *seraphims*, and all the celestial powers above, adore and worship? § Bernard tells us, 'That his hand 'that struck Christ was armed with an iron glove; '╪ and Vincentius affirms, That by the blow 'Christ was felled to the earth;' ‡ and Lodovicus adds, ' That blood gushed out of his mouth; and ' that the impression of the varlet's fingers remain-' ed on Christ's cheek, with a tumour and wan ' colour.' I need say no more of this, only one word in reference to ourselves.

Use. Come, look upon this lively and lovely picture of patience; he was struck on the face, but he was never moved in his heart; notwithstanding the abuse, he shewed all mildness and gentleness towards his enemies; O what art thou that canst not brook a word, that canst not bear a distasteful speech, that canst not put up the least and smallest offence, without thy wrath and fury? O proud man! O impudent wretch! How art thou so suddenly moved at the least indignity, when thou seest

---

*Chrys. hom. 82. in Joh. † Chrys. hom. 82. in Joh. ‡ [*rapos*] & *virgam* & *crepidam significat*. Lei. crit. Sacr. * [*Kolaphos*] *pugno*, [*rapis*] *palmi*. Idem Chrys. hom. 81. in Joh. C. 18. † Aug. in Tract. 113. § Ber. Serm. *de pass*. ╪ Vinc. Serm. *de pass*. ‡ Lodo. *de vita Christi*.

thy

thy Saviour quietly suffer great affronts? Come, learn of Christ, if ever we mean to have a share and interest in his sufferings, let us conform to him in meekness and patience, in gentleness and lowliness of mind; and so we shall find rest unto our souls.

3. For the accusation of the witnesses; he is falsly accused, and charged with the things that he never knew; in his accusation I observe these things. 1. That they sought false witnesses, for true witnesses they could have none; *Now the chief priests, and elders, and all the council sought false witnesses against Jesus to put him to death*, Mat. xxvi. 59. They were resolved in a former council, that he should not live, but die; and now palliating their design with a scheme of a tribunal, they seek out for witnesses; O wonder! who ever heard that judges went about to enquire for false witnesses, and suborned them to come in against the prisoner at the bar? 2. *Though many false witnesses came in to testify against him, yet they found none*, Ver. 60. because *their witness did not agree together*. Mark xiv. 56. O the injustice of men in bringing about the decrees of God! the judges seek out for witnesses, the witnesses are to seek out for proof, those proofs were to seek for unity and consent; and nothing was ready for their purpose. 3. At last, after many attempts, *came two false witnesses, and said, This fellow said, I am able to destroy the temple of God, and to build it in three days*, Ver. 61. They accuse him for a figurative speech, a trope which they could not understand, which if he had affected, according to the letter, it had been so far from a fault, that it would have been an argument of his power; but observe their false report of the words he had spoken, for he said not, *I am able to destroy this temple of God, and to build it in three days*; but, *Destroy this temple, and in three days I will raise it up*, John ii. 19. The allegation differs from the truth in these particulars, 1. *I am able to destroy*, say they; ay, but, *destroy ye*, saith Christ.
2. *I am able to destroy this temple of God*, say they; ay, but, *destroy ye this temple*, saith Christ; simply this temple without addition. 3. *I am able to destroy this temple of God, and to build it in three days*, say they; ay, but, *destroy ye this temple, and in three days I will raise it up*, said Christ; he spoke not of building an external temple, but of raising up his own body, which he knew they would destroy. These were the accusations of the false witnesses, to all which *Jesus answered nothing*; he despised their accusations, as not worthy an answer; and this vexed more.

——But, 4. Another accusation is brought in; Caiaphas had a reserve, which he knew should do the business in that assembly, he adjured him by God, to tell him if he were the Christ, *I adjure thee by the living God, that thou tell us whether thou be the Christ the Son of God*, Matth. xxvi. 63. The holy Jesus being adjured by so sacred a name, would not now refuse an answer, but he confessed himself to be *the Christ, the Son of the living God:* and this the high priest was pleased (as the design was laid) to call blasphemy; and in token thereof, he rends his cloaths, prophetically signifying, that the priest-hood should be rent from himself.

Use. We are taught in all this quietly to suffer wrong, *If my adversary should write a book against me, surely I would take it upon my shoulder* (saith Job) *and bind it as a crown to me*, Job xxxi. 35, 36. It is impossible, if we are Christ's servants, to live in this world without false accusations; come, let us take heart, and in some cases say not a word; since he that was most innocent was most silent, why should we be too forward in our excuses? I know there is a time to speak, as a time for silence; if it may tend to God's honour, and to the spreading of God's truth, and that right circumstances do concur, it is then time to open our mouths, though we set in death. So did our blessed Saviour; O let us learn of him, and follow his steps.

4. For the doom or sentence of these judges, Caiaphas prejudging all the sanhedrim, in declaring Jesus to have spoken blasphemy, and the fact to be notorious, he then asked their votes; *What think ye? And they answered and said, He is guilty of death*, Matth. xxvi. 66. They durst not deny what Caiaphas had said, they knew his faction was very potent, and his malice great, and his heart was set upon the business; and therefore they all conspire, and say, as he would have them, *He is guilty of death*. Oh! here is Jesus's sentence, which should have been mine, *He is guilty of death*. But this sentence was but like strong dispositions to an inraged fever? they had no power at that time to inflict death, or such a death as that of the cross,

cross, they only declared him apt, and worthy, and guilty of death.

In the multitude of counsellors there is safety, said Solomon, Prov. xi. 14. But we must take this in, *If it be of good men, and to good purpose;* for otherwise the meetings, assemblies and councils of the wicked are dangerous and deadly; *The kings of the earth set themselves, and the rulers take counsel together against the Lord, and against his anointed,* Psal. ii. 2. Such counsels we had many in our times; I know not whether we may call them councils, or *struta tantum civitatis,* an ulcerous bunch, raised by the disorder and distemper of the city.

5. For Peter's denial and abjuration; whilst these things were thus acting concerning Christ, a sad accident happened to his servant Peter; at first a damsel comes to him, and tells him, *Thou wast with Jesus of Galilee,* Matth. xxvi. 69. And then another maid tells the by-standers, *This fellow was also with Jesus of Nazareth,* Verse 71. And after a while, they that stood by spake themselves, *Surely thou art one of them, for thy speech bewrayeth thee,* Verse 73. *q. d.* Thy very idiom declares thee to be a Galilean; thou art as Christ is, of the same country and sect; and therfore thou art one of his disciples; Peter thus surprized, without any time to deliberate, he shamefully denies his Lord. And, 1. He doth it with a kind of subterfuge, *I know not what thou sayest,* Ver. 70. He seems to elude the accusation with this evasion, I know not thy meaning, I understand not thy words, *I skill not what thou sayest,* Verse 72. 2. At the next turn, he goes on to a licentious boldness, *denying Christ with an oath, I know not the man.* And, lastly, he aggravates his sin so far, that he grows to impudence, and so denies his Lord with *cursing and swearing, I know not the man,* Verse 74. Here is a lie, an oath, and a curse; the sin is begun at the voice of a woman, a silly damsel, not any of the greatest ladies, she was only a poor serving maid that kept the doors; but it grew to ripeness, when the men-servants fell upon him; now he swears, and vows, and curses himself if he knew the man. O, Peter, is the man so vile that thou wilt not own him? hadst thou not before confest him to be Christ, the Son of the living God? And dost thou not know him to be man, as well as God? Say, Is not this the Man-God, God-man, that called thee and thy brother Andrew at the sea of Galilee, saying, *Follow me, and I will make you fishers of men.* Is not this he whom thou sawest in mount Tabor, shining more gloriously than the sun? Is not this he whom thou sawest walking on the waters, and to whom thou saidst, *Lord, if it be thou, bid me come unto thee on the waters?* Matth. xiv. 28. How is it then that thou sayest, *I know not the man?* Surely here is a sad example of human infirmity; if Peter fell so foully, how much more may lesser stars? And yet, withal, here is a blessed example of serious thorough repentance; no sooner the cock crew, and Christ gave a look on Peter, but he goes out and weeps bitterly, Verse 75. The cock was the preacher, and the look of Jesus was the grace that made the sermon effectual; O the mercy of Christ! he looked back on him that had forgot himself; he revives his servant's memory to think on his Master's words; he sends him out to weep bitterly, that so he might restore him mercifully to his favour again.

Use. Let us learn hence, to think modestly and soberly of ourselves, yea, *Let him that thinketh he standeth, take heed lest he fall,* 1 Cor. x. 12. If Peter could first dissemble, and then lie, and then forswear, and then blaspheme and curse, O let *not us be high-minded but fear,* Rom. xi. 20. —And in case we fall indeed, as Peter did, yet let us not despair as Judas did, but still, upon our repentance, let us trust in God. When Christ looked on Peter, he wept bitterly; notwithstanding our sins are great, yet one look of Christ is full of virtue, and enough to melt us into tears: O let us not sink in despair, but look up to him, that he may look down to us. * Pliny tells us of some rocks in Phrygia, that when the sun doth but shine upon them, they send out drops of water, as if they wept tears; Peter signifies a rock, and whilst Peter persisted in his sin of denying Christ, his heart was hard as the rock; but when Christ the Sun of righteousness looked upon him, his heart was softened, and he dropped tears continually. Such is the virtue of Christ's look, *It turns the rock into a standing water, and the flint into a fountain of waters,* Psal. cxiv. 8. —Lastly, Let us not decry repentance, but rather be in the

* *Pliny's History.*

use and practice and exercise of it: is not here a gospel precedent? * Clement, an ancient writer, of whom Paul makes mention, Phil. iv. 3 expresseth Peter's repentance to have been so great, that 'in his cheeks he made (as it were) furrows, in 'which, as in certain channels, his tears run down.' The text tells us ' he wept bitterly,' and Clement adds, That while he lived, ' As often as he heard 'a cock crow, he could not but weep, and bewail 'his denial.' David is another like example, *All the night*, laid he, *I make my bed to swim, I water my couch with tears*, Psal. vi. 6 David makes mention of his bed and couch, because there most especially he had offended God: it was on his bed that he committed adultery; and it was in his couch, that he designed and subscribed with his own hand, that Uriah must die; and hence it is, that he waters his bed and couch with his tears; the very sight of his bed and couch brings his sin into his remembrance, as the very hearing of the crowing of a cock ever after awakened Peter to his task of tears: that repentance is a gospel-duty, we have spoke elsewhere, O take heed of decrying it! as we are often sinning, so let us often repent, it concerns us near to be frequent in this duty of bewailing sin, and turning to God.

6. For the abuses and derisions of the base attendants offered to Christ, the evangelist tells us, 'Then did they spit in his face, and buffeted him, 'and others smote him with the palms of their 'hands, saying, Prophesy unto us, thou Christ, 'who is he that smote thee?' Mat. xxvi. 67, 68. And as Luke adds, ' Many other things blasphemously spake they against him,' Luke xxii. 65. What those many things were, it is not discovered, only some ancient writers say, That Christ in that night suffered so many, and such hideous things, † 'That the whole knowledge of them is reserved 'only for the last day of judgment.' Mallonius writes thus, ' After Caiaphas and the priests had 'sentenced Christ worthy of death, they committed him to their ministers, warily to be kept till 'day; and they immediately threw him into the 'dungeon in Caiaphas's house, there they bound 'him to a stony pillar, with his hands bound on his 'back, and then they fell upon him with their palms 'and fists.' Others add, ' That the soldiers not yet 'content, they threw him into a filthy dirty puddle, 'where he abode for the remainder of that night;' of which the Psalmist, ' Thou hast laid me in the 'lowest pit, in darkness, and in the deeps, Psal. 'lxxxviii 6. And I sink in the deep mire, where 'there is no standing, Psal lxix. 2. Behold the bed 'which is Solomon's,' Cant. iii. 7. or rather which is Christ's, for a greater than Solomon is here; behold the flourishing bed, wherein the King of saints doth lie, surely a place most sordid, full of stench; his other senses had their pain, and his smell felt a loathsome savour, in this noisome puddle.

But we need not borrow light from candles, or lesser stars; the scripture itself is plain; observe we these particulars.———

They spit in his face; this was accounted among the Jews a matter of great infamy and reproach; ' And the Lord said to Moses, If her 'father had but spit in her face, should she not be 'ashamed seven days?' Num. xii. 14. We ourselves account this a great affront, and so did Job, Job xxx. 9, 10 *I am their song, yea, and their byword; they abhor me, they flee far from me, and spare not to spit in my face.* Oh that the sweet face of Christ, so much honoured and adored in heaven, should be defiled and deformed by their spitting! Oh that no place should be thought so fit for them to void their excrements and drivel in, as the blessed face of Jesus Christ. *I hid not my face* (saith Christ) *from shame and spitting*, Is. l. 6. I used no mask to keep me fair, though I was fairer than the sons of men, I preserved not my beauty from their nasty flegm, but I opened my face, and I set it as a butt for them to dart their spittle at.

2. They buffet him; we heard before, that one of the officers struck Jesus with the palm of his hand, but now they buffet him; some observe this difference betwixt [*rapisma, kolaphos:*] the one is given

---

* *Flevit quidem tanta lachrimarum inundatione ut in maxillis profundos sulcos haberet, per quos quasi per quosdam canales aut aquæductos lachrimæ ejus defluebant.* Clem. *Quoties galli cantum audiebat, in lachrimas prorumpebat, per totum vitæ tempus negationis culpam frequenter adeo planxit* Idem.
† *Hier ut citat Guliel, statione tertia Christi patientis. Mallon de flagellatione Christi. c. 6. Landul. de pass. & alii.*

with

with the open hand, but the other with the fist shut up; and thus they used him at this time, they struck him with their fists, and so the stroke was greater, and more offensive; 'By this means they made his 'face to swell, and to become full of bunches all o-'ver.' One gives it in thus, ‡ By these blows of their 'fists, his whole head was swollen, his face be-'came black and blue, and his teeth ready to fall 'out of his jaws.' Very probable it is, that with the violence of their strokes, they made him reel and stagger, they made his mouth, and nose, and face to bleed, and his eyes to startle in his head.

3. They covered his face, Mark xiv. 65. Several reasons are rendered for it, As, 1. That they might smite him more boldly, and without shame. 2. That they might not have that object of pity in their view; it is supposed, that the very sight of his admirable form, so lamentably abused, would have mollified the hardest heart under heaven; and therefore they vailed and hoodwinkt that alluring, drawing countenance. 3. That they might not see their own filth in his face; however, his beauty was winning, yet they had so bedaubed it with their beastly spitting that they began to lothe to look upon him, ' † It was a nauseous sight, (saith 'one) and enough to make one spue to look upon 'it.' But whether his splendor or his horror occasioned this vail over his face, this is most certain, that it vailed not their cruelty, but rather revealed it, and made it manifest to all the world.

4. They smote him with the palms of their hands, saying, *Prophesy unto us, thou Christ, who is he that smote thee?* To pass away that doleful tedious night, they interchangeably sport at him, first one, and then another give him a stroke, (we usually call it a box on the ear) and being hoodwinkt, they bid him *aread, who it is that smote him.* Some reckon these taunts amongst the bitterest passages of his passion, nothing is more miserable, even to the greatest misery, than to see itself scorned of enemies. It was our Saviour's case, they used this despight for their disport; with a wanton and merry malice, they aggravate their injury with scorn, *q. d.* ' Come on, thou 'sayest thou art Christ, the Son of the living 'God, and therefore it is likely thou art omni-'scient, thou knowest all things; tell now, who is 'it that strikes thee; we have blindfolded thee, 'that thou canst not see us with thy bodily eyes. 'let thy divinity aread, guess, tell, prophesy, who 'is it now that smote thee last? Who gave thee 'that blow?' O impiety without example! surely if his patience had been less than infinite, these very injuries would have been greater than his patience. In way of application.

Use 1. Consider, Christians, whether we had not a hand in these abuses: For, 1. They spit in the face of Christ, who defile his image in their souls, who reject his holy and heavenly motions in their hearts.——2. They buffet him with their fists who persecute Christ in his members, *Saul, Saul, why persecutest thou me? It is hard for thee to kick against the pricks.* 3. They cover his face that do not readily and willingly confess their sins, that extenuate their frailties and imperfections with counterfeit pretexts.——4. They mock and scoff at Christ, that scorn and contemn his messengers and ministers, Luke x. 16. *He that despiseth you, despiseth me,* saith Christ, O that we would lay these things to our hearts, and see and observe wherein we stand guilty of these sins, that we may repent.

2. Consider, Christians, and read Christ's love in all these sufferings; O unheard of kindness, and truly paternal bowels of pity and compassion! who ever heard before, of any that would be content to be spit upon, to wipe their filths who spit upon him? That would be content to be beat and buffeted, to save them from buffets who were the buffeters? That would be content to be blindfolded, that he might neither take notice of, nor see the offences of them that blindfolded him? That would be content to be made a scorn, to save them from scorn that shall scorn him?——Christians! you that take your name from Christ! how should you admire at the infiniteness and immensity of this love of Christ? Was it a small thing, that the wisdom of God should become the foolishness of men, and scorn of men, and ignominy of men, and contempt of the world for your sins sake. O think of this!

‡ *Colaphis illi tuber totum caput, facies livida forte & excussae dentes.*
† *Nauseam ipsis spectatoribus fœdites illa provocabat.*

And

And now the dismal night is done, what remains, but that we follow Christ, and observe him in his sufferings the next day. The Psalmist tells us, *Sorrow may endure for a night, but joy cometh in the morning,* Psal. xxx. 5. Only Christ can find none of this joy neither morning nor evening, for after a dismal night, he meets with as dark a day; what the passages of the day were, we shall observe in their several hours.

CHAP. II. SECT. I.

Of Christ's indictment, and Judas's fearful end.

ABOUT six in the morning, Jesus was brought unto Pilate's house; ' Then led they Jesus ' from Caiaphas unto the hall of judgment, and it ' was early, John xviii. 28.—When the morning ' was come, all the chief priests and elders of the ' people took counsel against Jesus to put him to ' death. And when they had bound him, they led ' him away, and delivered him to Pontius Pilate ' the governor. Then Judas which had betrayed ' him hanged himself,' Mat. xxvii. 1, 2, 3, 4, 5. O the readiness of our nature to evil! when the Israelites would sacrifice to the golden calf, *They rose up early in the morning,* Exod. xxxii. 6. If God leave us to ourselves, we are as ready to practise mischief, as the fire is to burn, without all delay. But on this circumstance I shall not stay; the transactions of this hour I shall consider in these two passages, Christ's indictment, and Judas's fearful end.

In Christ's indictment we may observe, 1. His accusation. 2. His examination.

In his accusation we may observe, 1. Who are his accusers. 2. Where he was accused. 3. What was the matter of which they do accuse him.

1. His accusers were *the chief priests and elders of the people,* Matth. xxvii. 12. The very same that before had judged him *guilty of death,* are now his accusers before the temporal judge; but why must our Saviour be twice judged? Was not the sanhedrim or ecclesiastical court sufficient to condemn him? I answer,——he is twice judged, 1. That his innocency might more appear; true gold often tried in the fire, is not consumed, but rather perfected; so Christ's integrity, though examined again and again by divers judges wholly corrupt, yet thereby it was not hurt, but made rather more illustrious. 2. Because his first judgment was in the night, and a sentence pronounced then, was not reputed valid; it is said of Moses, that *he judged the people from the morning unto the evening,* Exod. xviii. 13. for until night no judgment was protracted. 3. *Because,* said the Jews, *It is not lawful for us to put any man to death,* John xviii. 31. These words had need of exposition; we know Moses's law prescribed death to the adulterers, idolaters, blasphemers, manslayers, sabbath-breakers; but now the Romans (say some) had come and restrained the Jews from the execution of their laws; others are of another mind, and therefore the meaning of these words, *It is not lawful for us to put any man to death,* may be understood (say they) in a double sense. 1. That it was not lawful for them to put any man to such a death, as the death of the cross; Moses's law was ignorant of such a death; and the words following seem to favour this interpretation, *That the saying of Jesus might be fulfilled which he spake, signifying what death he should die.* John xviii. 32. We read only of four sorts of death that were used among the Jews, as strangling, stoning, burning, and killing with the sword; crucifying was the invention of Romans, and not of Jews.——2. That it was not lawful for them to put any man to death at such a time; on this day was celebrated the Jews passover, which was in memory of their deliverance out of Egypt; so that now they had a custom to deliver some from death (the case of Barabbas) but they could not now condemn any one to death; hence it was, that after Herod the Jew had killed James, he proceeded further to take Peter also; yet, during the days of unleavened bread, he delivers him to be kept in prison, *intending* (saith the text) *after Easter to bring him forth to the people,* Acts xii. 4. Pilate, a Gentile, was not tied to these laws; and therefore they led Jesus from *Caiaphas, unto the hall of judgment,* or *unto Pilate's house.*

2. The place of the accusation was at the door of the house; *They would not go into the judgment hall, lest they should be defiled, but that they might eat the passover,* John xviii. 28. See what a piece of superstition and gross hypocrisy is here! they are curious of a ceremony, but make no strain to shed innocent blood; they are precise a-

N n bout

bout small matters, but for the weightier matters of the law, as mercy, judgment, fidelity, and the love of God, they let them pass; they honour the figurative passover, but the true passover they seize upon with bloody and sacrilegious hands.

3. The matter of which they accused him, 1. That he seduced the people. 2. That he forbad to pay tribute to Cæsar. 3. That he said he was a king. How great, but, withal, how false were these their accusations? For the first, Christ was so far from stirring up seditions, that he strove and endeavoured to gather the people into one. 'O Jerusalem, Jerusalem, how often would I have gathered thy children together, even as a hen gathers her chickens under her wings, and ye would not?' Matth. xxiii. 37. For the second, instead of denying to pay tribute to Cæsar, he paid it in his own particular; *Take twenty pence out of the fish's mouth,* (said he to Peter) *and give it unto them for me and thee,* Mat. xvii. 27. And, *give unto Cæsar the things that are Cæsar's,* (said he to the people) *and to God the things that are God's.* Luke xx. 25. For the third, instead of making himself a king, he professeth that *his kingdom is not of this world,* John xviii. 36. And when they would have made him a king, instead of flattering them, he fleeth from them, and that into the wilderness; or, *into a mountain himself alone,* John vi. 15.——Thus much of the accusation.

2. For his examination, Pilate was nothing moved with any of the accusations, save only the third; and therefore, letting all the rest pass, he asked him only, *Art thou the king of the Jews?* To whom Jesus answered, *My kingdom is not of this world,* &c. John xviii. 33, 36. He saith not, my kingdom is not *in this world,* but my kingdom is not of *this world,* by which Pilate knew well that Christ was no enemy unto Cæsar; Christ's kingdom is spiritual, his government is in the very hearts and consciences of men; and what is this to Cæsar?——Hence Pilate useth a policy to save Jesus Christ, they tell him that Christ was of Galilee, and therefore he takes occasion to send him to Herod, who was governor of Galilee. But of that anon.

Use. How many lessons may we learn from hence? 1. Christ was accused, who can be free? The chief priests and elders of the Jews accused Christ, no wonder if those that are chief and great amongst us accuse poor Christians: oh! there's a perpetual enmity between the seed of the woman and the seed of the serpent; there is an everlasting, irreconcilable, implacable enmity and antipathy between grace and prophaneness, light and darkness, Christ and Belial: as it is reported of tigers, that they rage when they smell the fragrancy of spices, so it is with the wicked, who rage, at the spiritual graces of them that are sincere for God.

2. Christ's accusers would not go into the judgment-hall, lest they should be defiled; the very prophane can learn to be superstitious in lesser matters; how many amongst us, will make conscience of outward ceremonies (as of eating meats, observing days) but as for the weightier matters of the law, judgment and mercy, they leave them undone?

3. Christ is most falsly accused of sedition, seduction, and usurpation; it were indeed to be wished, that they who take upon them the name of Christianity were guiltless of such crimes; but let them look to it who are such: this I am sure was Christ's rule and practice, *Be subject to every constitution and authority of man, for the Lord's sake,* 1 Pet. ii. 13. If any dare to resist the power that is of God, *They shall receive to themselves damnation,* Rom. xiii. 2. Nor can we excuse ourselves, because our governors are not godly; for all the governors to whom Christ and his apostles submitted themselves, and to whom all those strict precepts of duty and obedience related in the new Testament, were no better (for ought I know) than tyrants, persecutors, idolaters, and heathen princes.

4. Christ is examined only of his usurpation, *Art thou the king of the Jews?* Phil. iii. 19. The men of this world mind only worldly things; the apostle so describes them, *Who mind earthly things.* Pilate regards not Christ's doctrine, but he is afraid, lest he should aspire the kingdom; and concerning this, our Saviour puts him out of doubt, *My kingdom is not of this world.* As Pilate and Christ, so worldlings and Christians are of different principles, they mind earthly things, *but our conversation* (saith the apostle) *is in heaven,* ver. 20. our conversation, (i. e.) the aim, and scope of our hearts in every action, is only for heaven, whatsoever we do, it should, some way or other, fit us for heaven; we should still be laying in for heaven against the

the time that we should come and live there; we should have our thoughts and hearts set upon heaven; so it is said of holy Mr Ward, That being in the midst of a dinner very contemplative; and the people wondering what he was musing about, he presently breaks out, *For ever, for ever, for ever;* and tho' they endeavoured to still him, yet he still cried out, *for ever, for ever, for ever;* oh eternity! to be for ever in heaven with God and Christ, how shall this swallow up all other thoughts and aims? And especially all worldly, careful, sinful thoughts, aims or ends?

2. Pilate having dismissed Jesus, this hour is concluded with a sad disaster of wicked Judas; *Then Judas which had betrayed him, when he saw that he was condemned, repented himself,* &c. Mat. xxvii. 3. Now his conscience thaws, and grows somewhat tender, but it is like the tenderness of a boyl, which is nothing else but a new disease; there is a repentance that comes too late; Esau wept bitterly, and repented him, when the blessing was gone; the five foolish virgins lift up their voices aloud when the gates were shut; and in hell men shall repent to all eternity; and such a repentance was this of Judas; about midnight he had received his money in the house of Annas, and now betimes in the morning, he repents his bargain, and throws his money back again; the end of this tragedy was, That Judas died a miserable death; he perished by the most infamous hands in the world (i. e.) by his own hands; *He went and hanged himself,* Matth. xxvii. 5. And as Luke, *he fell headlong, and burst asunder in the midst, and all his bowels gushed out.* In every passage of his death, we may take notice of God's justice, and be afraid of sin; it was just that he should hang in the air, who for his sin was hated both of heaven and earth; and that he should fall down headlong who was fallen from such an height of honour; and that the halter should strangle that throat through which the voice of treason had sounded; and that his bowels should be lost, who had lost the bowels of all pity, piety and compassion; and that his Ghost should have its passage out of his midst, (he burst asunder in the midst) and not out of his lips, because with a kiss of his lips he had betrayed his Lord, our blessed Jesus.

Use! Here's a warning-piece to all the world; who would die such a death for the pleasure of a little sin? Or, who would now suffer for millions of gold, that which Judas suffered, and yet suffers in hell for thirty pices of silver? Now, the Lord keep our souls from betraying Christ, and from despairing in God's mercy through Christ. Amen, Amen.

I see one sand is run, and I must turn the glass; now was the seventh hour, and what are the passages of that hour, I shall next relate.

SECT. II.
Of Christ's mission to Herod, and the transactions there.

About seven in the morning, Jesus was sent to Herod, *who himself also was at Jerusalem at that time.* Luke xxiii. 7. The reason of this was, because Pilate had heard that Christ was a Galilean, and Herod being tetrarch of Galilee, he concludes, that Christ must be under his jurisdiction; Herod was glad of the honour done to him, for ' he was desirous to see Christ of a long season, ' because he had heard many things of him, and he ' hoped to have seen some miracle done by him, ver. 8. That which I shall observe in this passage is, 1. Herod's questioning of Jesus Christ. 2. Christ's silence to all his questions. 3. Herod's derision; and Christ's dismission back again to Pilate.

1. *Herod questioned him in many words,* ver. 9. What those words were are not expressed, only we have some conjectures from Luke xxiii. 8. *q. d.* ' What, art thou he, concerning whom my ' father was so mocked of the wise men? and for ' whose fake my father slew all the children that ' were in Bethlehem? I have heard thou hast ' changed water into wine, and hast multiplied ' loaves, whereon so many thousands fed; come, ' do something at my request, which elsewhere ' thou hast done without request of any; come, ' satisfy my desire, work now but one miracle be- ' fore me, that I may be convinced of thy divini- ' ty.' I dare not deliver these words as certain truths, because of that silence that is in scripture, only we read, that *he hoped to have seen some miracles done by him.* Herod could not abide to hear his word, and to bear his yoke: but he was well content to see the works and miracles of Jesus Christ.

2. Whatever his questions were, *he answered him nothing,* verse 9. Many reasons are given in

for this, as, 1. Because he enquired only in curiosity, and with no true intent or end; concerning which, saith the wise man, *answer not a fool according to his folly*, Prov. xxvi. 4. and *ye ask and receive not* (saith James) *because ye ask amiss*, Jam. iv. 3. 2. Because Christ had no need of defence at all; let them go about to apologize that are afraid or guilty of death; as for Christ, he despiseth their accusations by his very silence. 3. Because Herod had, the year before, put John the Baptist to death, who was that voice crying in the wilderness; now that voice being gone, Christ the word will be silent, he will not give a word. 4. Because Herod had been sottishly careless of Jesus Christ, he lived in the place where Jesus more especially had conversed, yet never had seen his person, or heard his sermons. It gives us to learn thus much, that if we neglect the opportunities of grace, and refuse to hear the voice of Christ in the time of mercy; Christ may refuse to speak one word of comfort to us in our time of need; if we, during our time, stop our ears, God will, in his time, stop his mouth, and shut up the springs of grace that we shall receive no refreshment, no instruction, no pardon, no salvation. 5. Because Christ was resolved to be obedient to his Father's ordinance, he was resolved to submit to the doom of death with patience and silence; for this purpose he came into the world, that he might suffer in our stead, and for our sins; and therefore he would not plead his own cause, nor defend his own innocency in any kind; he knew that we were guilty, tho' himself was not.

3. This silence they interpret for simplicity: and so, 1. They despised him; and, 2. They dismiss him; *and Herod with his men of war set him at nought, and mocked him, and arrayed him in a gorgeous robe, and sent him again to Pilate*, Luke xxiii. 11. They arrayed him with a white, glittering, gorgeous raiment: [*lampros*] signifies *gorgeous, bright, resplendent*, such as nobles and kings used to wear: the Latins sometimes render it *splendidam vestem*; and sometimes *candidam*, or *albam vestem*: we translate it *a gorgeous robe*, and the ancients call it *a white robe*; in imitation whereof, the baptised were wont to put on a white raiment, which they called [*lamproriphoan*], but whether it were white or no, I shall not controvert: the original yields thus far, that it was *a bright and resplendent garment, such as came newly from the fulling*, many mysteries (if it be white) are found out here; some say, this held forth the excellency or dignity of Christ; white colour is most agreeable to the highest God, he many times appeared in white, but never in any other colour; and the saints in heaven are said to be *clothed in long white robes*, Rev. iv. 4. and peers, kings, and Cæsars were usually clothed in white, saith Jansenius: others say, this held forth the innocency of Christ, and that they were directed herein by divine providence, declaring plainly against themselves, that Christ should rather have been absolved as an innocent, than condemned as a malefactor.———But to leave these mysteries, the meaning of Herod was not so much to declare his excellency, or innocency, as his folly, or simplicity; certainly he accounted him for no other than a very fool, an ideot, a passing simple man. 'The philosophers (says Tertullian) drew him in 'their pictures, attired by Herod, like a fool, with 'long asses ears, his nails plucked off, and a book 'in his hand,' &c. Oh marvellous madness! oh the strange mistakes of men! in his lifetime they *account Jesus a glutton, a drinker of wine, a companion of sinners, a blasphemer, a sorcerer, and one that cast out devils through Belzebub prince of devils; yea, and one that himself was possessed with a devil*, Matth. xii. 19. Mark ii. 7. Matth. xii. 24. John viii. 48. And now towards his death, he is bound as a thief, he is struck in the house of Caiaphas, as an arrogant and saucy fellow; he is accused before the sanhedrim, of blasphemy; he is brought before Pilate as a malefactor, a mover of sedition, a seducer, a rebel, and as one that aspired to the kingdom; he is transmitted unto Herod, as a jugler to shew tricks; and now in the close of all, he is accounted of Herod, and his men of war, as a fool, an ideot, a brute, not having the understanding of a man. But soft, Herod, is Christ therefore a fool, because he is silent? And art thou wise, because of thy many words, and many questions? Solomon, a wiser man than Herod, is of another mind: *in the multitude of words there wanteth not sin, but he that refraineth his lips is wise*, Prov. x. 19. Again, *He that hath knowledge spareth his words, and a man of understanding is of a cool spirit; even a fool when he holdeth his peace, is counted wise; and he that shutteth his*

his lips, is esteemed a man of understanding, Prov. xvii. 27, 28. Ah, poor Herod, consult these texts, and then tell me who is the fool. What, thou that speakest many words, and questionest about many things, which in time will turn to thy greater condemnation; or Christ Jesus that was deeply silent to the world's eternal salvation. Paul was of another spirit, and of another judgment concerning Christ, in him was knowledge; nor is that all, in whom was wisdom and knowledge; nor is that all, in him were treasures, and all treasures of wisdom and knowledge; *In him are hid all the treasures of wisdom and knowledge*, Col. ii. 3. And yet that is not all neither, not only is wisdom in him, but he is wisdom itself (for that is his name, and title to the book of Proverbs) and yet by Herod and his courtiers, he is reckoned, arrayed, and derided as a mere simple man.

2. They dismiss him; in this posture they sent him away again to Pilate, to all their former derision they added this, that now he was exposed, in scorn, to the boys of the streets. Herod would not be content, that he and his men of war only should set him at nought, but he sends him away through the more public and eminent streets of Jerusalem, in his white garment, to be scorned by the people; to be hooted at by idle persons: and now was fulfilled the prophecy of Christ, Lam. iii. 14. *I was a derision to all my people, and their song all the day.*

Use. Of this let us make some use. Was the eternal word of God, and the uncreated wisdom of the Father reputed a fool? No wonder if we suffer thousands of reproaches; *We are made a spectacle unto the world, and to angels, and to men; we are fools for Christ's sake,* saith the apostle.—— *we are made as the filth of the world, and are the off-scouring of all things unto this day,* 1 Cor. iv. 9, 10, 13. Christians must wear the badge and livery of Jesus Christ; we cannot expect to fare better than our master, why then should we despond? I never knew Christians in better heart than when they were stiled by the name of puritans, precisians, hypocrites, formalists, or the like.

2. Let us not judge of men and their worth, by their out-side garments; wisdom may be, and often is, clad in the coat of a fool; as beggarly bottles oftimes hold rich wines, so poor robes contain sometimes many precious souls; in right judgment, we should look only to the mind, and soul, and in-side of a man: yea, to the hidden man of the heart: and for ourselves, we should look to the inward, and not to the outward adorning: men and women especially have rules for this, *your adorning, let it not be that outward adorning, of platting the hair, and of wearing of gold, or of putting on of apparel; but let it be in the hidden man of the heart, in that which is not corruptible,* 1 Pet. ii. 3, 4. Oh what is it for a man to be clothed in gold, whilst his soul is *wretched, and miserable, and poor, and blind, and naked?*

3. Let us admire at the condescension of Christ, who for our sakes came down from heaven to teach us wisdom; and for us, who were fools indeed, was content to be accounted a fool himself; yea, and if need had been, would have been ready to have said with David, *I will yet be more vile than thus, and will be base in my own sight,* 2 Sam. vi. 22. I know this doctrine is an offence to many, *Christ crucified, is unto the Jews a stumbling-block, and unto the Greeks foolishness,* 1 Cor. i. 23. To tell natural men (such as Herod, and his men of war) that this same Jesus whom they mock, and set at nought, is the Son of God, and Saviour of the world, they cannot believe: it is plainly evident, that *not many wise men after the flesh, not many mighty, not many noble are called; but God hath chosen the foolish things of the world, to confound the wise,* 1 Cor. i. 26, 27. Why is this, the fruit of Christ's condescension, called the *foolishness of God?* ver. 25. Wisdom itself was content to be counted a fool, that those who are accounted the foolish things of the world, might be wise to salvation.

4. Let us search whether Herod and his men, do not keep a rendezvous in our hearts; do not we set Christ at nought? Do not we mock him, and array him in a gorgeous robe? Whatsoever we do to one of the least of his saints, he tells us that we do it to himself, Matth. xxv. 40, 45. And have we not dealt thus with his saints? Have we not dealt thus with his ministers? When Elisha was going up to Bethel, *there came little children out of the city, and mocked him, and said unto him, go up thou bald-head, go up thou bald-head,* 2 Kings ii. 23. A reproach of *bald-head, round-head,* given to a faithful Elisha, or minister of Christ, proclaims you as bad as those little children; yea, as

bad.

bad as Herod and his men of war; such Herods were a little before the destruction of Jerusalem, some there were then, that *mocked the messengers of God, and despised his words, and misused his prophets, until the wrath of the Lord arose against his people, till there was no remedy*, 2 Chron. xxxvi. 16. O take heed of this sin, banish Herod out of your hearts, or Christ will never lodge there: ruin without remedy will seize on those souls that, Herod like, mock the messengers of God; what is it, but to mock the messenger, the angel of the covenant, even Christ himself? as Herod sent Christ away, so let us send Herod away, and give him a dismission out of our doors.

The hour strikes again, and summons Christ and us to another station, let us follow him still, as Peter did, when he went into the high priest's palace, *and sat with the servants to see the end*, Matth. xxvi. 58.

SECT. III.

Of Christ and Barabbas compared; and of the question debated betwixt Pilate and the Jews.

About eight in the morning, our Saviour Christ is returned to Pilate, who propounded to the Jews, whether they would have Jesus or Barabbas let loose unto them. *Ye have a custom* (said he) *that I should release unto you one at the passover, will ye therefore, that I release unto you the king of the Jews? then cried they all again, saying, Not this man, but Barabbas: now Barabbas was a robber*, John xviii. 39, 40. It is supposed, that in this passage Pilate endeavoured Christ's liberty, *he knew, that for envy they had delivered him*, Matth. xxvii. 18. And he saw that Herod had sent him back again uncondemned, and therefore now, he propounds this *medium*, to rescue him from their malice, *Whom will ye that I release unto you, Barabbas or Jesus which is called Christ?* In the prosecution of this passage, I shall observe, 1. Who this Barabbas was. 2. What is the difference betwixt him and Christ. 3. How they vote. 4. Pilate's quere upon the vote. 5. Their answer to his quere. 6. His reply unto their answer. 7. Their reduplication upon his reply.

For the first, what was this Barabbas, but a notable prisoner? Matth. xxvii. 16. *One that had made insurrection, and who had committed murder in the insurrection?* Mark xv. 7. *One that for a certain sedition made in the city, and for murder was cast into prison?* Luke xxiii. 19. *One that was a robber, or an high-way thief?* John xviii. 40. One that was the greatest malefactor of his time? And must he be taken, and Jesus cast? Must he be saved, and Christ condemned?

For the second, what the difference is betwixt him and Christ, let us weigh them in the balance, and we may find, 1. Barabbas was a thief, and by violence took away the bread of the needy, but Christ was a feeder and supplier of their needs. 2. Barabbas was an high-way thief, wounding them that travelled by the way, but Christ was the good Samaritan that healed such, binding up their wounds, and pouring into them wine and oil. 3. Barabbas was a murderer, and had slain the living, but Christ was the Saviour, restoring life unto the dead. 4. Barabbas was a seditious tumult raiser, he made a certain sedition in Jerusalem, but Christ was a loyal tribute payer, and his commands were, *Give unto Cæsar the things that are Cæsar's*. 5. Barabbas was a bloody revenger, a man of blood, that hunted after blood, but Christ was of a meek and quiet spirit, and what with sweating, binding, buffeting, bleeding, was now become almost a bloodless Redeemer: light and darkness have not less fellowship, Christ and Belial no lesser discord; here is a competition indeed, the author of sedition with the Prince of peace; a murderous mutineer with a merciful Mediator; a son of Belial with the son of God.——

3. For their votes, they gave them in thus; *Not this man, but Barabbas*, John xviii. 40. q. d. '* Let us have him crucified who raised the 'dead, and him released who destroyed the liv-'ing: let the Saviour of the world be condemned 'to death, and the slayer of men be released from 'prison, and have his pardon.' A strange vote, to desire the wolf before the lamb, the noxious and violent, before the righteous and innocent; here was the prophetic parable of Jotham fulfilled, *The trees of the forest have chosen the bramble, and refused the vine*, Judg. ix. 14.——But there is something more observable in this vote; the Jews had a custom not to name what they held

* *Aug. trac. 15. in Johan. Leo. Serm. de pass.*

accursed;

accurſed; *I will not make mention of their names within my lips*, Pſal. xvi. 4. and ſurely this ſpeaks their ſpight, that they will not vouchſafe to ſpeak the name of Jeſus; the cry is not thus, *Not Jeſus, but Barabbas*; but thus, *Not this man, not this fellow, but Barabbas*, as if they meant firſt to murder his name, and then his perſon.

4 For Pilate's quere upon the vote, *What ſhall I do then with Jeſus, which is called Chriſt?* Mat. xxvii. 22. Pilate gives him his name to the full, *Jeſus, who is called Chriſt*; his name is *Jeſus Chriſt*. There is more pity in a Gentile Pilate, than in all the Jews; in ſome things Pilate did juſtly, and very well; as firſt, he would not condemn him before his accuſations were brought in, nor then neither, before he was convicted of ſome capital crime; becauſe he perceives, that it was envy all along, that drove on their deſign, he endeavours to ſave his life by balancing him with Barabbas; and now he ſees that they prefer Barabbas before Jeſus, he puts forth the queſtion, *What ſhall I do then with Jeſus, which is called Chriſt?* q. d. I know not what to do with him, it is againſt my light to condemn him to death, who is of innocent life: I could tell what to do with Barabbas, for he is a thief, a mutineer, a murderer, a notable malefactor; but there is no ſuch thing proved againſt Jeſus, who is called Chriſt, *what then ſhall I do with him?*

5. For their anſwer to his quere, *and they all ſaid unto him, let him be crucified*, Matth. xxvii. 22. This was the firſt time that they ſpake openly their deſign; it had long lurked within them, that he muſt die a curſed death; and now their envy burſts, and breaks out with unanimous conſent, and cry, *Let him be crucified*. O wonder! muſt no other death ſtint their malice, but the croſs? Other deaths they had in practice, as the towel, ſtoning and beheading, more favourable and ſuitable to their nation: and will they now pollute a Jew with a Roman death? * *Magna crudelitas*, &c. 'a great cruelty; they ſought not only to kill him, 'but to crucify him, that ſo he might die a ling-'ring death.' The croſs was a gradual and ſlow death, it ſpun out pain into a long thread, and therefore they make choice of it, as they made choice of Jeſus; let him die, rather than Barab-bas, and let him die that death of the croſs, rather than any other ſpeedy, quick, diſpatching death.

6. For Pilate's reply unto their anſwer, *Why, what evil hath he done?* Matth. xxvii. 23. he was loth to ſatisfy their demands, and therefore he queſtions again, *What muſt he die for?* Was it meet that he ſhould condemn one to death, and eſpecially to ſuch a death, and no crime committed? *Come on* (ſaith Pilate) *what evil hath he done?* † Auguſtine upon theſe words, aſk (ſaith he) ' And let them anſwer with whom he converſ-'ed moſt, let the poſſeſſed who were freed, the 'ſick and languiſhing who were healed, the leprous 'that were cleanſed, the deaf that hear, the dumb 'that ſpeak, the dead that were raiſed, let them 'anſwer the queſtion, *What evil hath he done?* Sometimes the Jews themſelves, could ſay, *He hath done all theſe things well; he maketh both the deaf to hear, and the dumb to ſpeak*, Mark vii. 37. Surely he had done all things well, he ſtilled the winds, and calmed the ſeas; with the ſpittle of his mouth he cured the blind, he raiſed the dead, he prayed all night, he gave grace, and he forgave ſins, and by his death he merited for his ſaints everlaſting life: why then ſhould he die, that hath done all things well? No wonder if Pilate object againſt theſe malicious ones, *What evil hath he done?*

7. For their reduplication on his reply, *They cried out the more, ſaying, let him be crucified*. Ibid. Inſtead of proving ſome evil againſt him, *they cried out the more*; as Luke, *they were inſtant with loud voices*, Luke xxiii. 23. they made ſuch a clamour, that the earth rang with it, the cry was doubled and redoubled, *Crucify him, crucify him*, twice *crucify him*, as if they thought one croſs too little for him. O inconſtant favour of men! their anthems of *Hoſanna*, and *Benedictus* not long ſince joyfully ſpoken, are now turned into jarring hideous notes, *Let him be crucified*. And now is Pilate threatned into another opinion, they *require* his judgment, and the voices of them, and *of the chief prieſt prevailed*, ver. 23. ſo it follows, and when *he ſaw he could prevail nothing, but that rather a tumult was made*, Matth. xxvii. 24. why then Barabbas is releaſed unto them, and Jeſus is delivered to be ſcourged.

* Beda. † Aug. tract. 15. Super Joh.

I would

I would not dwell too long on Pilate, the high priests, and Jews, the application is the life of all. ——Now then——

Use 1. Give me leave to look amongst ourselves, Is there not some or other amongst us, that prefer Barabbas before Jesus? O yes! those that listen to that old mutinous murderer in his seditious temptations, those that reject the blessed motions of God's own Spirit, in his tenders and offers of grace, those that embrace the world, with its pleasures and profits, and make them their portion, all these choose Barabbas and reject Jesus Christ; little do we think, that every wilful act of sin is a sedition, a mutiny against our souls, another Judas Galileus, that stirs up all the passions of our mind against our Jesus. I cannot but think what drawing and soliciting of our souls is made by *virtue and vice* in our passage towards that other world; on the one hand stands *vice*, with all her false deceits and flatteries, her temptations are strong. ' Come let us enjoy the good things that
' are present, and let us speedily use the creatures
' as in youth, let us fill ourselves with costly wine
' and ointments, and let no flower of the spring
' pass by us, let us crown ourselves with rose buds
' before they be withered, let none of us go with-
' out his part of jollity, let us leave tokens of our
' joyfulness in every place, for this is our portion,
' and our lot is this.' Wisd. ii. 6, 7, 8, 9. On the other hand stands *virtue*, or grace with all the promises of future happiness, she points at Jesus, and cries, ' O come unto Christ and live; wisdom is better than rubies, her fruit is better than gold,
' yea, than fine gold, and her revenue than choice
' silver; they that love Christ shall inherit sub-
' stance, and he will fill them with treasures, e-
' ven with durable riches,' Prov. viii. 11, 18, 19. But oh! how many thousands, and ten thousands neglect this cry, and follow *vice?* What millions of men are there in the world that prefer Barabbas before Jesus? If we proclaim it in our pulpits, that, ' Christ is the chiefest of ten thousands,
' that he is fairer than all the children of men, that
' he is the standard-bearer, and there is none to
' him:' that if you will but have Jesus Christ, you need no more, yet do not many of you say in your hearts, as Pilate here, ' What shall I do with
' Jesus that is called Christ?' Or as the devils said elsewhere, ' what have we to do with thee, Je-
' sus thou Son of God?' Nay, hath not many times the secret grudgings of your reluctant souls, accounted the gracious offers of speedy repentance, to be but as a coming of Christ to torment you before your time? Why, alas! what is this now but to prefer Barabbas before Jesus? You that swear as the devil bids, and as Christ forbids; you that prophane Sabbaths, that revel, that drink to excess, or it may be to drunkenness, surely your vote goes along with the Jews, *Not this man, but Barabbas.*

2. Give me leave to look on the love and mercy of God in Christ; our Jesus was not only content to take our nature upon him, but to be compared with the greatest malefactor of those times; and by publick sentence; yea, votes and voices of the people, to be pronounced a greater delinquent, and much more worthy of death than wicked Barabbas. O the love of Christ! we read in Leviticus, Lev. xiv. 4, 5, 6, 7. that in the days of the cleansing of the leper, the priest was to take two birds, (or two sparrows) alive, and the one of them must be killed, and the other being kept alive, must only be dipt in the blood of the bird that was slain; and so it must be let loose into the open field. Barabbas, say some, but all believers say we, are that live sparrow, and Jesus Christ was the sparrow that was slain, the lot fell upon him to die for us, all our sins were laid upon his soul; so that in this sense Jesus Christ was the greatest sinner in the world, yea, a greater sinner than Barabbas himself; and therefore he must die, and we being dipt in the blood of Christ, must be let loose and set at liberty! was not this love? He died that we might live; it was the voice of God as well as men, *Release Barabbas, every believing Barabbas, and crucify Jesus.*

Another hour is gone, let us make a stand for a while; and the next time we meet, we shall see farther sufferings.

SECT. IV.

Of Christ stripped, whipped, clothed in purple, and crowned with thorns.

ABout nine, (which the Jews call the third hour of the day) was Christ stripped, whipped, clothed with purple, and crowned with thorns:

in this hour his sufferings came thick, I must divide them into parts, and speak of them severally by themselves.

1. When Pilate saw how the Jews were set upon his death, he consented and delivered him first to be stripped. *Then the soldiers of the governor took Jesus into the common hall, and gathered unto him the whole band of soldiers, and they stripped him,* Mat. xxvii. 27. They pulled off his clothes, and made him stand naked before them all; he that adorns the heavens with stars, and the earth with flowers, and *made coats of skins to clothe our first parents in,* Gen. iii. 21. is now himself stripped stark naked. I cannot but look on this as a great shame; it appears so by our first parents, Adam and Eve, who no sooner had sinned, and knew themselves naked, but they *sewed fig-leaves together, and made themselves aprons,* Gen. iii. 7. If Adam was so ashamed of his nakedness before his own wife, (who was naked too as well as he) what a shame and blush was it in the face of Christ, when in the common hall, in the view of the whole band or company of soldiers, he stands all naked? *My confusion is continually before me, and the shame of my face hath covered me,* saith David in the person of Christ, Psal. xliv. 15. It is reported, in the ecclesiastical story, that when two martyrs, and holy virgins, (they call them Agnes and Barbara) were stripped stark naked for their execution, God pitying their great shame and trouble, to have their nakedness discovered, made for them a vail of light, and so he sent them to a modest and desired death; but our Saviour Christ, who chose all sorts of shame and confusion, that by a fulness of suffering, he might expiate his Father's wrath, and consecrate to us all kinds of sufferings and affronts, he endured the shame of his nakedness at the time of his scourging; see here a naked Christ, and therein see the mercy of Christ to us; he found us like the good Samaritan, when we were stripped, and wounded, and left half dead, and that we might be covered, he quietly suffered himself to be divested of his own robes, he took on him the state of sinning Adam, and became naked, that we might first be clothed with righteousness, and then with immortality: oh! what a blessed use may we make of the very nakedness of Christ?

* Hi—. . t'h(um, Tom. IX.

2. Pilate gave him to be scourged; this some think he did upon no other account, but that the Jews being satiated and glutted with these tortures, they might rest satisfied, and think themselves sufficiently avenged, and so desist from taking away his life: that he was scourged is without controversy, for so the evangelist relates, *Then Pilate therefore took Jesus and scourged him,* John xix. 1. And that Pilate might give him to be scourged on that account, is very probable, because, that after the scourging, he brings him out to the Jews, proclaiming, *I find no fault in him,* verse 6. and before his scourging, he speaks it more expresly, *he hath done nothing worthy of death, I will therefore chastise him and release him,* Luke xxiii. 15, 16. And it adds to this, that howsoever the custom was, that those that were to be crucified must first be whipped, 'yet * if they were ad-'judged to die, their stripes must be less, and if 'they were to be set at liberty, they must be bea-'ten with more stripes.' And Pilate endeavouring to preserve his life, they scourged him above measure, even almost to death.

In this scourging of Christ I shall insist on these two things. 1. The shame. 2. The pain.

1. For the shame, it was of such infamy, that the Romans exempted all their citizens from it. *Is it lawful for you,* (said Paul) *to scourge a man that is a Roman?* ——— *And when the centurion heard that, he went and told the chief captain, saying, Take heed what thou dost, for this man is a Roman,* Acts xxii. 25, 26. The Romans looked upon it as a most infamous punishment, fit only for thieves and slaves, and not for free-born or privileged Romans; and the Jews themselves would not suffer it above so many stripes, lest a brother should seem vile unto them; *If a wicked man be worthy to be beaten, that the judge shall cause him to lie down, forty stripes he may give him, and not exceed, lest if he should exceed, and beat him above these with many stripes, then thy brother shall seem vile unto thee,* Deut. xxv. 2, 3. Whipping is so unworthy a punishment, that only children, bound slaves and rogues, were used to be corrected therewith, especially if they exceed the number of forty stripes. When Paul was thus used he tells us, *Of the Jews five times received I forty stripes, save one,* 2 Cor. xi. 24. Theophilact says, They

They would not exceed that number, left Paul should have become infamous, and ever after uncapable of public office, and hoping they might have regained him, they would not brand him with that note of infamy. O then, if one stripe above forty was so infamous amongst the Jews, what shame, what infamy was this, when so many scores, hundreds, and thousands of stripes, (as some reckon them) were laid on Jesus Christ? And yet our Lord doth not disdain to undergo them for our sakes, he bears in his body those wounds and stripes that we had deserved by our sins.

2. For the pain, this kind of punishment was not only infamous but terrible; no sooner the soldiers had their commission, but they charged and discharged upon him such bloody blows, as if he had been the greatest offender and basest slave in all the world. †Nicephorus calls these whippers, bloody hangmen, by the fierceness of whose whipping, many had died under their hands; ‘‡ The manner of their whipping is described thus, After they had stripped him, they bound him to a pillar, whither came six young and strong executioners, scourgers, varlets, hangmen, (saith Jerome) to scourge him, and whip him while they could, whereof two whipped him with rods of thorns; and when they had wearied themselves, other two whipped him with ropes or whip-cords, tied and knotted like a carter's whip; and when they were tired, the other two scourged off his very skin with wires or little chains of iron; and thus they continued till by alternate and successive turns, they added stripe upon stripe, and wound upon wound, latter upon former, and new upon old, that he was all over in a gore-blood.' The scripture tells us, That *he was wounded for our transgressions, and bruised for our iniquities; the chastisement of our peace was upon him, and with his stripes we are healed*, If. liii. 5. He was wounded, bruised, chastised, whipped with stripes; if you would know with how many stripes, some reckon them to the number of the soldiers, six hundred and sixty, or a thousand stripes; others reckon them according to the number of the bones compacted in a man's body, which say Anatomists, are two hundred and sixty: and Christ having received for every bone three stripes, according to the triple manner of his whipping, they amounted in all to seven hundred and eighty stripes; others reckon them to five thousand above the forty, which the Jews were commanded not to exceed in.——And the truth is, if the whole band of soldiers were the whippers of Christ, (as some would have it) I cannot see but his stripes might be more than so: when the Son of an Israelitish woman blasphemed God, the Lord said unto Moses, *Bring forth him that hath cursed without the camp, and let all that heard him, lay their hands upon his head, and let all the congregation stone him*, Lev. xxiv. 14. Now Christ had said before all the band, *That he was the Son of God*, which they called blasphemy; and therefore why might they not all (according to this law) lay their hands upon him, and fall upon him, if not with stones, (which was now turned into whipping) yet with rods, whip-cords, and little chains?

I shall not contend about the number of his stripes, but this is certain, that the soldiers, with violence and unrelenting hands, executed their commissions; they tore his tender flesh, till the pillar and pavement were purpled with a shower of blood; and if we may believe Bernard, ' They plowed with their whips upon his back, and made long furrows; and after that, they turned his back upon the pillar, and whipt his belly and his breast, till there was no part free from his face unto his foot.' A scourging able to kill any man, and would have killed him, but that he was preserved by the Godhead to endure and to suffer a more shameful death.

Use. We may read here a lecture of the immense love of God in Christ to us poor Gentiles; he is therefore whipped, that he might marry us to himself, and never reject us, or cast us off: we read of a law in Moses, that if a man took a wife, and hated her, and gave occasions of speech against her, and brought an evil name upon her undeservedly, that then *the elders of the city should take that man and chastise him,——and she should be his wife, he might not put her away all his days*, Deut. xxii. 18, 19. There is a great mystery in this ceremony, for that man, (say some) was Christ, who, by his incarnation, betrothed unto himself the Gentile church; but he seems to hate

† Nicep. 1. C. 3. ‡ Bosq. de pass. domini, pag. 840

her

her, and to give an occasion of a speech against her, and to bring an evil report upon her, as *into the way of the Gentiles ye shall not go, and into the city of the Samaritans ye shall not enter,* Mat. x. 5. *And it is not meet to take the childrens bread, and cast it unto dogs,* Matth. xv. 26. And now he is accused before the elders, now he is whipt and chastised, and commanded by his father, to take her to his wife, and not to put her away all his days. I know there is much unlikeliness in this mystery, for Christ was not whipt for calling the church adulterous, that indeed was chaste, but he was whipt to present the church as a chaste virgin to his Father that indeed was adulterous: *Oh he loved the church, and gave himself for it.—That he might present it to himself a glorious church, not having spot, or wrinkle, or any such thing, but that it should be holy, and without blemish,* Eph. v. 25, 27. This was the meaning of Christ's whipping, *the chastisement of our peace was upon him, and with his stripes are we healed,* Isaiah liii. v. Come then, and let us learn to read this love-letter sent from heaven in bloody characters, Christ is stripped, who clothed the lilies of the field; Christ is bound hand and foot, his hands that multiplied the loaves, and his feet that were weary in seeking the straggling sheep: Christ is scourged all over, because all over we were full of *wounds and bruises, and putrifying sores,* Isa. i. 6. And there was no way to cure our wounds but by his wounds, our bruises but by his bruises, our sores but by his sores: O read, and read again, Christ is whipped, belly, back, side, from his shoulders to the soles of his feet, the lashes eating into his flesh, and cutting his very veins, so that, (as some say with much confidence, though I know not with what truth) the gashes were so wide, that you might have seen his ribs, and bones, and very inwards: what, was these ever love like unto this love? Had he not been God as well as man, he could never have had in his heart such a love as this; O it was a divine love, it was the love of a Jesus, a love far surpassing either the love of men, or women, or of angels.

3. They put upon him *a purple robe,* or *a scarlet robe,* John calls it purple, John xix. 2. and Matthew, scarlet, Matth. xxvii. 28. Howsoever, some difference may be, yet, because of their likeness, they are put sometimes one for another: they put on him *a scarlet robe,* it is in the original, * *A scarlet cloke;* it was a loose short garment, at first used only by kings or emperors; and the colour of it was suitable to Christ's condition, for he was now purple all over, as well within it as without it; his body and his garment were both of a deep dyed sanguine colour. Some out of Zachary, where it is said, *That Joshua was clothed with filthy garments,* Zach. iii. 3. Conclude the old ragged, threadbare filthiness of his robe; so that every thing shall have its office and several share in his abuse; the colour and the manner of the garment denote his kingdom; the bareness, his outward estimation with the people, the raggedness, his late scattered retinue, the sulliedness, his stained spotted life, as they pretended, saying, *He was a friend of publicans and sinners.*——— But out of this darkness the Lord can bring light, he hath his mysteries wrapt up in the malice of his enemies; for both *on his garment and on his thigh* was written a *mystery,* Rev. xix. 16. And in this sense, what other is his garment but the emblem of his humanity? And what is his scarlet garment but the emblem of his wounded body? That as he spake of the woman, *She anointed him aforehand unto his burial,* John xii. 7. So Pilate in the mystery, clothes him aforehand unto his bloody death.

4. They *platted a crown of thorns, and put it upon his head,* Matth. xxvii. 29. a goodly crown for the King of kings; we read of many sorts of crowns, as of the triumphal, laural, naval, mural, &c. but never till this, did we read of a crown of thorns; a crown it was to delude him, and a crown of thorns to torment him: in this we may read both his pain and shame. 1. For his pain, it bored his head, saith Osorius, with seventy and two wounds; ‡ Bernard speaks of many more, *melli puncturis, &c.* I know not what ground they have to number them; but certainly many wounds they made; and the rather may we say so, because, that after they had put it upon his head, *They took a reed, and smote him on the head,* Matth. xxvii. 30. (i. e.) They smote him on the head, to fasten the crown of thorns upon him surer, and to imprint it deeper, till, as some think,

* [*Klamula kokrinen*]

‡ *Ber. Serm. de pass. dom.*

it pierced his very scull. 2. Nor was it only pain, but shame; when Jotham put out his parable to the men of Shechem; 'The trees (said he) went 'out, on a time, to anoint a king over them, and 'they said unto the olive tree, reign thou over us. 'But the olive tree said unto them, should I leave 'my fatness, wherewith by me they honoured God 'and man, and go to be promoted over the trees? 'And the trees said unto the fig-tree, come thou and 'reign over us. But the fig-tree said unto them, 'should I forsake my sweetness, and my good fruit, 'and go to be promoted over the trees? Then said 'the trees unto the vine, Come thou and reign over 'us. And the vine said unto them, should I leave 'my wine, which cheereth God and man, and go to 'be promoted over the trees? Then said all the trees 'unto the bramble, come thou and reign over us. 'And the bramble said unto the trees, if in truth ye 'anoint me king over you, then come, and put your 'trust in my shadow; and if not, let fire come out of 'the bramble, and devour the cedars of Lebanon,' Judg. ix. 8, 9, 10, 11, 12, 13, 14, 15. As Jotham put out his parable in scorn of Abimelech, so the soldiers in scorn, put on Christ's head this bramble crown, q. d. 'Come, thou sayest thou 'art king of the Jews, and therefore we will make 'thee a crown of brambles, king of trees;' by which means they protest against Christ as a feigned fabulous king, as if he were no fitter to be king of the Jews, than the bramble was to be king of all the trees in the forest.

Use. How many lessons might we draw from hence? They put upon his head a crown of shame, of death, of torture, who came to give us a crown of victory, of life, of glory 2. Our sins caused the earth to bring forth thorns and briars; and our Saviour must wear them, both to take away our sins, and in the issue, to take away sin's curse, thorns or briars, or whatsoever. 3. From the crown of the head to the sole of the foot, we were full of sin, and Christ accordingly must shed his blood from head to foot; their whips did not reach his head, their nails could not pierce it without an end of torture, but now they draw blood from it with thorns; Isa. i. 5. *The whole head is sick,* saith the prophet of us; and the whole head of Christ is bruised with thorns to cure our sickness. 4. Christ is not crowned with thorns without a prophesy or a type; here he is *a true lily among thorns.* Cant. ii. 2 here he is, as Isaac's ram, *tied fast by the head in thorns,* Gen. xxxiii. 13. he was ever intended to be a sacrifice, and a ransom for our sins; and to that purpose he was caught in a thicket, he was crowned with thorns. 5. O what a shame is it, for any of us to crown our heads with rose-buds, (as the wanton worldlings could say) afore they were withered, to spend our time in vanity, folly, sin, when Christ our Lord had such a grove of thorns growing on his sacred head? *The disciple is not above his master, nor the servant above his Lord: it is enough for the disciple to be as his master, and the servant as his Lord,* Matth. x. 24, 25. If our Lord and master was crowned with thorns, surely the members of Christ should not be soft, delicate, and effeminate, wholly sensual, or given up to pleasures. 6. 'As every bird sitteth upon the thorns in the 'orchard,' Baruch vi. 7. so let us draw near, and make our nest in these blessed bushes; let us abandon all the colours of other captains, as the world, flesh, and devil; and let us keep close to the royal standard of our king; under these thorns we may find shelter against all our enemies; from these thorns we may undoubtedly gather grapes, even a vintage of spiritual joy and gladness.

Now, the hour sounds again, and calls us to go forth, and to behold king Jesus, with the crown wherewith he was crowned in the day of his espousals. And this we shall do the next hour.

SECT. V.

Of Christ brought forth and sentenced.

About ten, Christ was brought forth and sentenced. 1. For his bringing forth, I shall therein observe these particulars. As,——

1. We find Pilate bringing forth Jesus out of the common-hall, and shewing this sad spectacle to all the people, *Then came Jesus forth, wearing the crown of thorns, and the purple robe, and Pilate saith unto them, Behold the man,* John xix. 5. He thought the very sight of Christ would have moved them to compassion; they had lashed him almost unto death, they had most cruelly divided those azure channels of his guiltless blood, they had clothed him with purple, crowned him with thorns;

thorns; and now they bring him out by the hair of the head, (say some) and expose him to the public view of the scornful company, Pilate crying unto them, 'Behold the man, q. d. Behold a 'poor, silly, miserable, distressed man; behold, I 'say, not your king, to provoke you against him, 'nor yet the Son of God, which you say he makes 'himself to be; behold the man, a mean man, a 'worm and no man; behold how he stands disfigured with wounds, behold him weltring and 'panting in a crimson river of his own gore-blood; 'and let this be sufficient, yea, more than sufficient 'punishment; suffice to satisfy your rage; what 'would you have more? If it be for malice that 'you are so violent against him, behold how miserable he is: if for fear, behold how contemptible he is: as for any fault whereby he should 'deserve his death, I find no fault in him; he is a 'Lamb without spot, a dove without gall; O 'come and behold this man, I can find no fault 'in him.' Some doctors affirm, That whilst Pilate cried out, *behold the man*, his servants lifted up the purple robe, that so all might see his torn, and bloody, and macerated body; he supposed his words could not so move their hearts as Christ's wounds; and therefore, said he, *behold the man*, as if he had said again, 'Look on him, and view 'him well, is he not well paid for calling himself 'king of the Jews? Now see him stript, and whipt, 'and crowned with thorns, and sceptred with a 'reed, anointed with spittle, and clothed with 'purple; what would you more?'

2. We find the Jews more enraged against Jesus: *When the chief priests and officers saw him, they cried out, saying, crucify him, crucify him*, John xix. 6. The more Pilate endeavours to appease them, the more were the people enraged against him, and therefore they cry, *away with him away with him, crucify him, crucify him*, ver. 15. Now was fulfilled that prophesy of Jeremy, *My heritage is unto me as a lion in the forest, it crieth out against me*, Jer. xii. 8. The naturalists report of the lion, That when he is near to his prey, he gives out a mighty roar, whereby the poor hunted beast is so amazed and terrified, that almost dead with fear, he falls flat on the ground, and so becomes the lion's prey indeed: and thus the Jews (who were the heritage of the Lord) were unto Christ as a lion in the forest; they hunted and pursued him to his death; and being near it, they give out a mighty shout, that the earth rung again, *Away with him, away with him, crucify him, crucify him.* O ye Jews, children of Israel, seed of Abraham, Isaac and Jacob, is not this he concerning whom your fathers cried, 'Oh that thou wouldest rent the heavens, that thou wouldest come down, that the 'mountains might flow down at thy presence,' Isa. lxiv. 1. How is it, that you should despise him present, whom they desired absent? How is it that your cry and their's should be so contrary? The panther (say they) is of so sweet a savour, that if he be but within the compass of scent, all the beasts of the field run towards him; but when they see his ugly visage, they fly from him, and run away: so the Jews afar off feeling the sweet savours of Christ's ointment, they cried, *Draw me, we will run after thee, come Lord Jesus, come quickly*, Cant. i. 2. but now in his passion, looking on his form, they change their note, *he hath no form, nor comeliness, there is no beauty, that we should desire him, away with him, away with him*, Isa. liii 2.

3. We find Pilate and the Jews yet debating the business; Pilate is loth to pronounce the sentence, and the chiefest of the jews provoke him to it with a threefold argument. As,

1. *They had a law, and by their law he ought to die, because he made himself the Son of God*, John xix. 7. Thus the doctors of the law do accuse the author and publisher of the law; but they consider not the rule concerning laws, * *he may 'lawfully abolish, who hath power to establish;'* nor did they consider that this law concerned not himself, who is indeed, and in truth the Son of God; the text tells us, That Pilate *hearing this argument, was the more afraid.* Pilate (saith Cyril) was an Heathen idolater; and so worshipping many gods, he could not tell but that Christ might be one of them; and therefore in condemning Christ, he might justly provoke all the gods, to be revenged of him. This was the meaning of Pilate's question, *Whence art thou?* What is thy off-spring? Of what progenitors art thou sprung? *And from thence forth Pilate sought to release him.*

2. The Jews come with another argument, they threaten Pilate, *If thou let this man go, thou art not Cæsar's friend*, John xix 12. a forcible reason,

reason, as the case then stood; it was no small matter to be accused by so many audacious impudent men of high-treason-against Cæsar; and therefore, under this obligation Pilate seems to bend and bow; whom the fear of Christ's divinity had restrained, him the fear of Cæsar's frown provoked to go on to sentence and condemnation. Oh! he was more afraid of man, whose breath is in his nostrils, 'Than of God himself, who made 'the heavens, and framed the world.' And yet, before he gives sentence, 'He takes water and 'washed his hands before the multitude, saying, I 'am innocent of the blood of this just person, see 'ye to it, Matth. xxvii. 24.

3. In reference to this, they engage themselves for him, which was their last argument, *his blood be upon us and our children*, Matth. xxvii. 25. q. d. Act thou as judge, let him be condemned to die; and if thou fearest any thing, we will undergo for thee, let the vengeance of his blood be on us, and on our children for ever. Thus far of the first general.

2. For the sentence itself, *When Pilate heard that,——he sat down in the judgment seat, in a place that is called the pavement*, because erected of stones, *but in the Hebrew Gabbatha*, Jon xix. 13.——This word signifies an high place, and raised above; it was so on purpose, that the judges might be seen of men when they pronounced sentence. And here Pilate sitting down, he gave the doom. What was the form or manner of the sentence, is a great question amongst divines; † Chrysostome is of mind, that he pronounced no form at all, but only *delivered Jesus unto them to be crucified*, Mark xv. 15. John xix. 16. Others cannot yield to this, for to what end (say they) should he then *sit down upon the judgment-seat?* And yet amongst themselves they cannot agree on a form; ‡ Anselm gives it thus, 'I adjudge Jesus of Nazareth to that ig- 'nominious and shameful death of the cross.' § 'Vincentius thus, I condemn Jesus, seducing the 'people, blaspheming God, and saying that he was 'Christ, the king of the Jews, to be fastened to the 'cross, and there to hang till he die.' Many other forms are brought in by others, but that of Luke is, I am sure, most authentic. *And Pilate gave sentence, that it should be as they required*, and then *he delivered Jesus to their will*, Luke xxiii. 24, 25. Here's a sentence indeed, a delivery of Jesus, not to his own, but to his enemies liberty; to the boundless bonds, and all the possible tortures of their own wills and wishes. O unjust sentence! *Give me not over to the will of my adversaries*, cries David, Psal. xxvii. 12. the will of malice is an endless wheel, it cares not how long it spins out pain, and therefore they cried, *Crucify him, crucify him, let him be crucified. Amen,* (says Pilate) *do what you please, crucify him, and crucify him as often as you will, it shall be as you require. Lo now I deliver him to your own will.*

We cannot shake this tree without some fruit; from this sight of Christ, and sentence of Pilate, we may learn some good.

Use 1. From this sight of Christ, as he was presented by Pilate to the people, we may learn remorse: not any of us who have crucified Christ by our sins, but we are called on at this time, to *behold the man*; suppose we saw him with our bodily eyes; suppose we had the same view of Christ as the Jews had, where he was thus presented; suppose we saw him in the very midst of us wearing the crown of thorns, and the purple robe, and the cane or reed held in his right hand; suppose we heard the voice of Pilate speaking to us, as he did to the Jews, *Behold the man*; suppose we saw the purple robe lifted up, that we might see all under, how his body was torn; and that some voice from heaven should come to us, saying, 'This 'same is he whom ye have buffeted, scourged, 'crowned, crucified by your sins:' were not this enough to prick us in our hearts, and to make us cry, *Men and brethren, what shall we do?* Acts ii. 37. Oh! we look at the instruments, and we cry, 'Fy on Pilate, fy on the soldiers, fy on the 'Jews;' but we look not on our sins, saying, Fy on them. Could we but realize our sins as the principles of these sufferings of Christ, methinks our hearts should break in very pieces: consider, yesterday in the midst of our markets so many lies were told, and so many oaths were sworn; and this day, so soon as the day-light sprang, so many acts of prophaning the Lord's day were committed by us; little did we think, that all this while we had been stripping Christ naked, whipping Christ

† *Chri.* 1 *Cor. serm. ult. de eleemos.*   ‡ *Ansel. de pass.*   § *Vinc. di pass.*

with

with rods, or little chains, clothing Christ with a purple scarlet robe, platting a crown of thorns, and putting it on his head, sceptring him with a reed, and saluting him in scorn, *Hail king of the Jews*, Men, brethren, and Fathers, be not deceived, Christ is mocked, scorned, and thus abused by you when you sin; your sins thus dealt with Christ, and in God's acceptance your sins thus deal with Christ, even to this very day. Never say it was long since Christ was crucified, and he is now in heaven, for by your sins you crucify again the Lord of glory, you put him again to open shame; you strip him, and whip him, and torment him afresh. Oh look on him whom you have pierced! Pilate thought, that if the Jews would but see the man, *Behold the man*, their hearts would have mollified; and shall not I think as well of you? It is a blessed means to make sin bitter, and to breed in our hearts remorse for sin, if we will but hearken to this voice of Pilate, *Behold the man*.

2. From the sentence of Pilate, that *Christ should be crucified*, as the Jews required, we may learn the deceitfulness of our hearts, in making self the end, and aim of our particular callings. Pilate, as judge, should have glorified God in doing justice; but when he heard the Jews cry, *If thou let him go, thou art not Cæsar's friend*, he then looks to himself and his own interests. Judges can have their ends in the very place of judicature: nay, is not this the very common sin of magistrates, ministers, tradesmen, of all sorts of callings; come what is it you aim at in your several places? Is it not to be great, and rich and high, and honourable? Say truly, is it in your hearts to say, ' That ' by this calling, my chief aim is to glorify God, ' and to serve my generation, with all faithfulness; ' and these two ends I prefer before all worldly ' advantages whatsoever?' O then, what a blessed reformation would be amongst us? If it be not thus, what are you but as so many Pilates, that if you were but threatned into a sentence, you would rather condemn Christ than yourselves of enmity against Cæsar; such would be the cry, *Let Christ be crucified*, and self advanced.

Much more might be said, but the hour strikes again; Pilate is now risen, the court dissolved, and Jesus is delivered into the hands of the Jews for execution. How that went on the next hour will speak, only God prepare your hearts to hear devoutly, and to consider seriously, what Jesus the great Saviour of the world hath suffered for you.

SECT. VI.

Of Christ's crucifying, with its appendices.

ABOUT eleven, they prepare with all speed for the execution: in the revolution of this hour we may observe these several passages. As, 1. Their taking off the robe, and clothing him again with his own raiment. 2. Their leading him away from Gabbatha to Golgotha. 3. His bearing the cross, with Simon's help to bear it after him. 4. His comforting the women who followed weeping after him as he went. 5. Their giving him vinegar to drink mingled with gall. 6. Their crucifying, or fastening him on the cross, whereon he died.

1. The evangelist tells us, Matth. xxvii. 31. *They took the robe off from him, and put his own raiment on him:* Origen observes, ' They took ' off his robes, but they took not off his crown of ' thorns; what served their interest, they pursued still, but nothing of mitigation or mercy to the afflicted Son of man. It is supposed this small business could not be done without great pain; after his sore whipping his blood congealed, and by that means stuck to his scarlet mantle, so that in pulling off the robe, and putting on his own raiment, there could not but be a renewing of his wounds.

2. *They led him away*, Matth. xxvii. 31. Some say, they cast a rope or chain about his neck, by which they led him out of the city to mount Calvary, and that all along the way, multitudes attended him, and a crier went before him, proclaiming to all hearers the cause of his death; namely, ' That Jesus Christ was a seducer, blas' phemer, negromancer, a teacher of false doc' trines, saying of himself, that he was the Messi' as, king of Israel, and the Son of God.'

3. *He bore his cross*, John xix. 17. So John relates, before it bears him, he must bear it; and thus they make good their double cry, *Crucify him, crucify him*; first crucify him with it as a burden, and then crucify him with it as a cross; those shoulders, which had been unmercifully battered with whips before, are now again tormented with the

the weight of his cross. As a true Isaac, he bears the wood for the sacrifice of himself, or Uriah like, he carries with him the very instrument of his own sad death. O the cruelty of this passage! they had scarce left him so much blood or strength as to carry himself; and must he now bear his heavy cross? Yes, till he faint and sink, so long he must bear it, and longer too; did they not fear that he should die with less shame and smart than they intended him, which to prevent, they *constrained one Simon a Cyrenian, to bear his cross after him,* Matth. xxvii. 32. Mark xv. 21. How truly do they, here again, swallow the camel, and strain at a gnat? The cross was a Roman death, and so one of their abominations; hence they themselves would not touch this tree of infamy, lest they should have been defiled, but to touch the Lord's anointed, to crucify the Lord of glory, they make no scruple at all; but why must another bear the cross, but to consign this duty unto man, that we must enter into a fellowship of Christ's sufferings? *If any man will come after me, let him deny himself, and take up his cross and follow me,* Matth. xvi. 24 ——*And therefore Christ hath suffered for us, leaving us an example that we should follow his steps,* 1 Pet. ii. 21.

4. He comforted the women, who followed weeping after him as he went along. *And there followed him a great company of people, and of women, which also bewailed and lamented him; but Jesus turning to them, said, Daughters of Jerusalem, weep not for me, but weep for yourselves, and for your children,* Luke xxiii. 27, 28. In the midst of his misery he forgets not mercy; in the midst of all their tortures and loudest outcries of contumely, of blasphemy, of scorn, he can hear his following friends weeping behind him, and neglect all his own sufferings to comfort them, *Weep not for me.* He hath more compassion on the women that follow him weeping, than of his own mangled self, that reels along, fainting and bleeding unto death: he feels more the tears that drop from their eyes, than all the blood that flows from his own veins. We heard before, that sometimes he would not vouchsafe a word to Pilate that threatned him, nor to Herod that entreated him; and yet unaskt, how graciously doth he *turn about* his blessed bleeding face to these weeping women, affording them looks, and words too, both of compassion and of consolation, *Daughters of Jerusalem, weep not for me, but for yourselves.*——And yet observe, he did not turn his face to them, until he heard them weep; nor may we ever think to see his face in glory, unless we first bathe our eyes in sorrow. It is a wonder to me, that any in our age should ever decry tears, remorse, contrition, compunction: how many saints do we find, both in the Old and New Testament, confuting by their practices these gross opinions? The promise tells us, That *they that sow in tears shall reap in joy;* he that follows Christ, or *goeth forth weeping, bearing precious seed, shall, doubtless, come again with rejoicing, bringing his sheaves with him,* Psal. cxxvi. 5, 6.

But what is the meaning of this, *Weep not for me?* May we not weep for the death of Christ? Do we not find in scripture, that all the people wept at the death of Moses? Deut. xxxiv. 8. That all the church wept at the death of Stephen? Acts viii. 2. That the women lamented the death of Dorcas? and if all Christ's actions be our instructions, (I mean not his miraculous, or meritorious, but his moral ones) did not Christ himself weep for Lazarus, and for Jerusalem? Nay, is he not here weeping showers of blood all along the way? And may not we drop a tear for all those purple streams of his? Oh what is the meaning of this, *Weep not for me, but weep for yourselves?*

I answer, the words are not absolute, but comparative. Christ doth not simply forbid us to weep for our friends, but rather to turn our worldly grief into godly sorrow for sin as sin. Christ herein pointed the women to the true cause and subject of all their sorrow, which was their sins; and thus we have cause to weep indeed. Oh! our sins were the cause of the sufferings of Christ; and in that respect, Oh that our heads were fountains, and our eyes rivers of tears! Oh that our tears were as our meat and drink! Oh that we could feed with David *on the bread of tears,* and that the Lord would give us *plenteousness of tears to drink!* Oh that the Lord would strike (as he did at Rephidem) these rocky hearts of ours, with the rod of true remorse, that water might gush out? Oh that we could thus mourn over Jesus, whom we have pierced, and *be in bitterness for him, as one that is in bitterness for his first-born!* Zech. xii 10.

5. No sooner he was come to the place of execution,

cution, *but they gave him vinegar to drink mingled with gall*, Matth. xxvii. 34. In that they gave him drink, it was an argument of their humanity. This was a custom amongst Jews and Romans that to the condemned they ever gave wine to drink: *Give strong wine unto him that is ready to perish, and wine unto those that be of heavy heart*, Prov. xxxi. 6. But in that they gave him vinegar mingled with gall, it was an argument of their cruelty and envy. * Theophilact speaks plainly, that the vinegar mingled with gall was poisonous and deadly; and therefore, when Christ had tasted it, he would not drink, choosing rather the death of the cross, to which he was destinated by his Father, than any poisonous death.

Use. Ah brethren, are not we apt to think hardly of the Jews for giving Christ so bitter a potion at his time of death? And yet, little do we think, that when we sin we do as much. See but how God himself compares the sins of the wicked Jews to very poison, *For their wine is of the wine of Sodom, and of the fields of Gomorrah, their grapes are grapes of gall, their clusters are bitter, their wine is the poison of dragons, and the cruel venom of asps*, Deut. xxxii. 32, 33. In this respect we may think as hardly of ourselves as of the Jews, because, so oft as we sin against God, we do as much as mingle rank poison, and bring it to Jesus Christ to drink.

6. *They crucified him*, Matth. xxvii. 35. (i. e.) They fastened him on the cross! and then lift him up. A great question there is amongst the learned, whether Christ was fastened on the cross after it was erected, or whilst it was lying on the ground? I would not rake too much into these niceties, only more probable it is, that he was fastened to it whilst it lay flat on the ground; and then, *as Moses lifted up the serpent in the wilderness, so was the Son of man lifted up*, John iii. 14. We may express the manner of their acting, and his sufferings now, as a learned brother hath done before us; ‘ † Now come the barbarous inhuman hangmen, and begin to unloose his hands, but how? Alas! 'tis not to any liberty, but to worse bonds of nails: Then stript they off his gore-glewed clothes, and with them, questionless, not a little of his mangled skin and flesh, as if it were not

* *Theophil. in Mar.*

‘ enough to crucify him as a thief, unless they flea
‘ him too as a beast; then stretched they him out
‘ as another Isaac on his own burden, the cross,
‘ that so they might take measure of the holes:
‘ and though the print of his blood on it gave them
‘ his true length, yet how strictly do they take it
‘ longer than the truth? Thereby at once both to
‘ crucify and rack him? That he was thus stretcht
‘ and rackt upon his cross, David gives more than
‘ probable intimation, Psal. xxii. 17. *I may tell
‘ all my bones;* and again, *All my bones are out of
‘ joint*, Ver. 14. which otherwise, how could it
‘ so well be, as by such a violent stretching and
‘ distortion? Whereby it seems they had made him
‘ a living anatomy: nor was it in the less sensible
‘ fleshly parts of his body that they drive these their
‘ larger tenters, whereon his whole weight must
‘ hang, but in the hands and feet, the most sinewy,
‘ and consequently the most sensible fleshly parts
‘ of all other, wherein rudely and painfully they
‘ handle him, appears too by that of David, *They
‘ digged my hands and my feet, they made wide
‘ holes like that of a spade, as if they had been dig-
‘ ging in some ditch*. The boisterous and unusual
‘ greatness of these nails we have from venerable
‘ antiquity; Constantine the great is said to have
‘ made of them both an helmet and a bridle.——
‘ How should I write on, but that my tears should
‘ blot out what I write, when 'tis no other than he
‘ that is thus used,’ *who hath blotted out that handwriting of ordinances that was against me*, Col. ii. 14.

But the hour goes on, and this is the great business of the world's redemption, of which I would speak a little more: by this time we may imagine Christ nailed to the cross, and his cross fixed in the ground, which, with its fall into the place of its station, gave infinite torture, by so violent a concussion of the body of our Lord. That I mean to observe of this crucifying of Christ, I shall reduce to these two heads, *viz.* the shame and pain.

1. For the shame, it was a cursed death, *Cursed is every one that hangeth on a tree*, Gal. iii. 13. When it was in use, it was chiefly inflicted upon slaves, that either falsly accused, or treacherously conspired their master's death; but on whomsoever it was inflicted, this death, in all ages among

† *Herle contemplat. on Christ's pass.*

the Jews, had been branded with a special kind of ignominy, and so the apostle signifies, when he saith, *he abased himself to the death, even to the death of the cross*, Phil. ii. 8. It was a mighty shame that Saul's sons were hanged on a tree, 2 Sam. xxi. 6. and the reason is more especially from the law of God, *for he that is hanged is accursed of God*, Deut. xxi. 23. I know Moses's law speaks nothing in particular of crucifying, yet he doth include the same under the general hanging on a tree; and some conceive, that Moses in speaking that curse, foresaw what manner of death the Redeemer should die.

2. For the pain it was a painful death, that appears several ways; as —— 1. His legs and hands were violently racked, and pulled out to the places fitted for his fastening, and then pierced through with nails. 2. By this means he wanted the use both of his hands and feet, and so he was forced to hang immoveable upon the cross, as being unable to turn any way for his ease. 3. The longer he lived, the more he endured, for by the weight of his body his wounds were opened and enlarged, his nerves and veins were rent and torn asunder, and his blood gushed out more and more abundantly still. 4. He died by inch-mile (as I may say) and not at once, the cross was a death long in dying, it kept him a great while upon the rack, it was full three hours betwixt Christ's affixion and expiration, and it would have been longer if he had not freely and willingly given up the ghost: it is reported, that Andrew the apostle was two whole days on the cross before he died, and so long might Christ have been, if God had not heightened it to greater degrees of torment supernaturally.

I may add to this, as above all this, the pains of his soul whilst he hanged on the cross, for there also Christ had his agonies and soul conflicts, these were those [*odinasthanatou*] those pains, or *pangs of death*, Acts ii. 24. from which Peter tells us Christ was loosed. The word [*odinas*] properly signifies the pains of a woman in travail; such were the pains of Jesus Christ in death; the prophet calls it *the travail of his soul*, Isa. liii. 11. and the Psalmist calls it the pains of hell, *The sorrows of death compassed me, and the pains of hell gat hold upon me*, Psal. cxvi 3. The sorrows, or cords of death compassed his body, and the pains of hell got hold upon his soul; and these were they that extorted from him that passionate expostulation, *My God, my God, why hast thou forsaken me?* Matth. xxvii. 46. He complains of that which was more grievous to him, than ten thousand deaths, 'My God, my God, why hast 'thou with-drawn thy wonted presence, and left 'my soul (as it were) in the pains of hell!

Use. And now reflect we on the shame and pain! O the curse and bitterness that our sins have brought on Jesus Christ! when I but think on these bleeding veins, bruised shoulders, scourged sides, furrowed back, harrowed temples, digged hands and feet, and then consider that my sins were the cause of all; methinks I should need no more arguments for self-abhorring; Christians! would not your hearts rise against him that should kill your father, mother, brother, wife, husband, dearest relations in all the world? O then, how should your hearts and souls rise against sin? Surely your sin it was that murdered Christ, that killed him, who is instead of all relations, who is a thousand, thousand times dearer to you, than father, mother, husband, child, or whomsoever; one thought of this should, methinks, be enough to make you say, as Job did, *I abhor myself, and repent in dust and ashes*, Job xlii. 6. Oh! what is that cross on the back of Christ? My sins; oh! what is that crown on the head of Christ! my sins; oh! what is the nail in the right-hand, and that other in the left-hand of Christ? My sins; oh! what is the spear in the side of Christ? My sins; oh! what are those nails and wounds in the feet of Christ? My sins. With a spiritual eye I see no other engine tormenting Christ, no other Pilate, Herod, Annas, Caiaphas condemning Christ, no other soldiers, officers, Jews, or Gentiles doing execution on Christ, but only sin: oh my sins, my sins, my sins.

2. Comfort we ourselves in the end and aim of this death of Christ; *As Moses lifted up the serpent in the wilderness, so must the Son of man be lifted up: that whosoever believeth in him should not perish, but have everlasting life*, John iii. 14, 15 The end of Christ's crucifying is the material business; and therefore let the end be observed, as well as the meritorious cause: without this consideration, the contemplation of Christ's death, or the meditation of the story of Christ's sufferings, would be altogether

gether unprofitable; now what was the end? Surely this; *Christ lifted up, that he might draw all men to him,* John xii. 32. *Christ hanged on a tree, that he might bear our sins on the tree,* 1 Pet. ii. 24. This was the plot, which God by ancient design had aimed at in the crucifying of Christ, and thus our faith must take it up; indeed our comfort hangs on this; the intent, aim and design of Christ in his sufferings, is that welcome news, and the very spirit of the gospel! O remember this! Christ is crucified, and why so? That *whosoever believeth in him should not perish, but have life everlasting.*

We are now at the height of Christ's sufferings, and the sun is now in his meridian, or height of ascent; I shall no more count hour by hour, for 'from the sixth hour till the ninth hour' (that is, from twelve to three in the afternoon) *there was darkness over all the land,* Matth. xxvii. 45. But of that, and of the consequents after it, in the next section.

SECT. VII.

Of the consequents after Christ's crucifying.

THE particulars following I shall quickly dispatch. As thus,——

1. About twelve, when the sun is usually brightest, it began now to darken. This darkness was so great, that it spread over all the land of Jewry; some think, over all the world; so we translate it in Luke, *And there was a darkness over all the earth,* Luke xxiii. 44. and many Gentiles, besides Jews, observed the same as a great miracle, Dionysius the Areopagite (as * Suidas relates) could say at first sight of it, 'Either the world is ending, or the God of nature is suffering.' This very darkness was the occasion of that altar erected in Athens, and dedicated unto *the unknown God,* Acts xvii. 23. Of this prophesied Amos, *And it shall come to pass in that day, that I will cause the sun to go down at noon, and I will darken the earth in the clear day,* Amos viii 9.

The cause of this darkness is diversly rendered by several Authors; some think, 'That the sun 'by divine power withdrew and held back its 'beams.' Others say †, 'That the obscurity was 'caused by some thick clouds, which were mira-'culously produced in the air, and spread them-'selves over all the earth.' Others say, 'That 'this darkness was by a wonderful interposition of 'the moon, which at that time was at full, but 'by a miracle interposed itself betwixt the earth 'and sun.' Whatsoever was the cause, it continued for the space of three hours, as dark as the darkest winter's night.

2. About three (which the Jews call the ninth hour) the sun now beginning to receive his light, *Jesus cried with a loud voice, Eli, Eli, Lamasabachthani, My God, my God, why hast thou forsaken me?* Matth. xxvii. 46. —— *And then, that the scripture might be fulfilled, he said, I thirst,*—— *And when he had received the vinegar, he said, It is finished,* John xix. 28, 30.——*And at last, crying with a loud voice, he said, Father, into thy hands I commend my Spirit, and having said thus, he gave up the Ghost,* Luke xxiii. 46. I cannot stay on these seven words of Christ, which he uttered on the cross; his words were ever gracious, but never more gracious than at this time; we cannot find, in all the books and writings of men, in all the annals and records of time, either such sufferings, or such sayings, as were these last words and wounds, sayings and sufferings of Jesus Christ. —*And having said thus, he gave up the ghost:* or, as John relates it, *He bowed his head, and gave up the ghost,* John xix. 30. he bowed, not because he was dead, but first he bowed and then died; the meaning is, he died willingly without constraint, cheerfully without murmur; what a wonder is this? Life itself gives up his life, and death itself dies by his death; Jesus Christ, who is the author of life, the God of life, lays down his life for us, and death itself lies for ever nailed to that bloody cross in the stead of Jesus Christ. And now we may suppose him at the gates of paradise, calling with his last words to have opened, 'That the king of glory 'might come in.'

3. About four in the afternoon, he was pierced with a spear, and there issued out of his side both blood and water. And *one of the soldiers with a*

---

* Suid. in vita S. Djon. Epist. 7 ad Policarpum.

† Hier in Matth. 17. Orig. tract. 35. in Matth. Dionis.

spear pierced his side, and forthwith came thereout blood and water, John xix. 34. How truly may we say of the soldiers, 'That after all his 'sufferings they have added wounds:' they find him dead, and yet they will scarce believe it, until with a spear they have searched for life at the well-head itself, even at the heart of Christ; and 'forthwith there came out blood and water.' This was the fountain of both sacraments, the fountain of all our happiness, *The fountain open to the house of David, and to the inhabitants of Jerusalem for sin and for uncleanness*, Zech. xiii. 1. *There are three that bear witness in earth*, (saith John) *the Spirit, and the water, and the blood*, 1 John v. 8. Out of the side of Christ, being now dead, there issues water and blood, signifying, that he is both our justification and sanctification. Physicians tell us, that about the heart there is a film or skin like unto a purse, wherein is contained clear water to cool the heat of the heart, and therefore very probable it is, that that very skin (or *pericardium*) was pierced through with the heart, and thence came out those streams of blood and water.——
'O gates of heaven! O windows of paradise! O 'palace of refuge! O tower of strength! O sanc-'tuary of the just! O flourishing bed of the spouse 'of Solomon! methinks I see water and blood run-'ning out of his side, more freshly than these gol-'den streams which ran out of the garden of Eden, 'and watered the whole world.' Here, if I could stay, I might lengthen my doctrine during my life; Oh! it were good to be here, it were a large field, and a blessed subject.

4. About five (which the Jews call the eleventh, and the last hour) Christ was taken down, and buried by Joseph and Nicodemus. But enough! I must not wear out your patience altogether.

Thus far we have propounded the blessed object of Christ's suffering and dying for us: our next work is to direct you (as formerly) in the art or mystery, how you are to look unto him in this respect.

CHAP. III. SECT. I.
Of knowing Jesus, as carrying on the great work of our salvation in his death.

1. LEt us know Jesus, carrying on the great work of our salvation during his sufferings and death. This is the high point, which Paul was ever studying on, and preaching on, and pondering on; *For I determined not to know any thing among you, save Jesus Christ, and him crucified*, 1 Cor. ii. 2. Christ crucified, is the rarest piece of knowledge in the world; the person of Christ is a matter of high speculation, but Christ farther considered, as clothed with his garments of blood, is that knowledge, which especially Paul pursues; he esteems not, reckons not, determines not to make any profession of any other science or doctrine, than the most necessary and only saving knowledge of Christ crucified. O my soul, how many days, and months, and years, hast thou spent to attain some little measure of knowledge in the arts, and tongues, and sciences? And yet, what a poor skill hast thou attained in respect of the many thousands of them, that knew nothing at all of Jesus Christ? And what if thou hadst reached out to a greater proficiency? Couldest thou have dived into the secrets of nature? Couldest thou have excelled *the wisdom of all the children of the east country, and all the wisdom of Egypt, and the wisdom of Solomon, who speak of beasts, of fowls, of fishes, of all trees from the cedar-tree that is in Lebanon, even to the hyssop that springeth out of the wall*, 1 Kings iv. 33. Yet, without the saving knowledge of Christ crucified, (Christ suffering, bleeding and dying) all this had been nothing, see Ecc. i. 18. only that knowledge is worth the having, which refers to Christ; and, above all, that is the rarest piece of Christ's humiliation, which holds him forth suffering for us, and so freeing us from hell sufferings. Come then, and spend thy time for the future more fruitfully, in reading, learning, knowing this *one necessary thing*. Study Christ crucified in every piece and part; O the precious truths and precious discoveries that a studying head and heart would hammer out here! much hath been said, but a thousand thousand times more might be yet said; we have given but a little taunting of that which Christ endured; volumes might be written till they were piled as high as heaven, and yet all would not serve to make out the full discoveries of Jesus's sufferings. Study therefore, and study more, but be sure thy study and thy knowledge, be rather practical than speculative; do not merely beat thy brains to learn the history of Christ's death, but the efficacy, virtue and merit of it; I know what thou knowest

knowest in reference to thyself, as if Jesus had been all the while carrying on the business of thy soul's salvation, as if thou hadst stood by, and Christ had spoke to thee, as sometimes to the woman, 'Weep not for me but for thyself; thy sins 'caused my sufferings, and my sufferings were for 'the abolition of thy sins.

SECT. II.

Of considering Jesus in that respect.

2. LEt us consider Jesus, carrying on this great work of our salvation during his sufferings and death. 'They shall look upon me whom 'they have pierced,' saith the prophet Zech. xii. 10. (i. e.) they shall consider me, and accordingly is the apostle 'looking unto Jesus, or considering 'of Jesus the author and finisher of our faith, who 'for the joy of our salvation set before him, endu- 'red the cross, and despised the shame,' Heb. xii. 2. Then indeed, and in that act is the duty brought in; it is good in all respects, and under all considerations, to look unto Jesus from first to last; but above all, this text relates first, to the time of his sufferings; and hence it is, that Luke calls Christ's passion [*theorian*] theory or sight; 'And all the 'people that came together to that sight, — smote 'their breasts and returned,' Luke xxiii. 48. Not but that every passage of Christ is a theory or sight worthy our looking on, or considering of; Christ in his Father's purpose, and Christ in the promise, and Christ in performance, Christ in his birth, and Christ in his life; O how sweet? what blessed objects are these to look upon? But, above all, 'con- 'sider him (saith the apostle) that endured such 'contradiction of sinners against himself,' Heb. xii. 3. —— 'Consider him, who for the joy that was 'set before him, endured the cross, and despised 'the shame,' verse 2. Of all other parts, acts, or passages of Christ, the Holy Ghost hath only honoured Christ's passion (his sufferings and his death) with his name of *theory* and *sight*. Why, surely this is the theory ever most commended to our view and consideration; O then let us look on this, consider of this. As in this manner, ——

1. Consider him passing over the brook Cedron; it signifies the wrath of God and rage of men; the first step of his passion is sharp and sore; he cannot enter the door, but first he must wade through cold waters on bare feet, nor must he only wade through them but drink of them; through many tribulations must they go that will purchase souls, and through many tribulations must they go that will follow after him to the kingdom of glory — Consider him entering into the garden of Gethsemane; in a garden Adam sinned, and in this garden Christ must suffer, that the same place which was the nest where sin was hatched, might now be the child-bed of grace and mercy; into this garden, no sooner was he entred, but he began to be agonized; all his powers and passions within him were in conflict. Consider, O my soul, how suddenly he is struck into a strange fear; never was man so afraid of the torments of hell, as Christ (standing in our room) is of his Father's wrath; fear is still suitable to apprehension, and never man could so perfectly apprehend the cause of fear as Jesus Christ, nor was he only afraid but very heavy; *My soul is exceeding sorrowful, even unto death.* His sorrow was lethal and deadly, it melted his soul gradually, as wax is melted with heat; it continued with him till his last gasp, his heart was like wax burning all the time of his passion, and at last *it melted in the midst of his bowels*, Psal. xxii. 19. Mark xiv. 33. Nor was he only afraid and heavy, but he began to be sore amazed; this signifies an universal cessation of all the faculties of the soul from their several functions; we usually call it a consternation, it is like a clock stopped for the while from going, by some hand or other laid upon it; or if it was not wholly a cessation, yet was it at least an expavefaction, such a motion of the mind, as whereby, for the present, he was disenabled to mind any thing else but the dreadful sense of the wrath of God. O what an agony was this? O what a struggling passion of mixed grief was this? What afflicting and conflicting affections under the sight and sense of eminent peril was in this agony! *And being in an agony, he prayed more earnestly*, Luke xxii. 44. Thrice had he prayed, but now in his agony he prayed more earnestly. *O my Father, if it be possible, let this cup pass from me, nevertheless, not as I will, but as thou wilt.* Tho' I feel the soul of pain in the pain of my soul, yet there is divinity in me, which tell me there is a wage for sin, and I will pay it all. O my Father, sith thou hast bent thy bow, lo, here an open breast,

breast, fix herein all thy shafts of fury, better I suffer for a while, than that all believers should be damned for ever; thy will is mine, lo I will bear the burden of sin, come and shoot here thy arrows of revenge. And thus as he prayed he sweat, *and his sweat was as great drops of blood falling down to the ground*, Luke xxii. 44. Oh! what man or angel can conceive the agony, the fear, the sorrow, amazement of that heart, that without all outward violence, merely out of the extremity of his own passion, bled through the flesh and skin, not some faint dew, but solid drops of blood? Now is he crucified without a cross, fear and sorrow are the nails, our sins the thorns, his Father's wrath the spear, and all these together, cause a bleeding shower to reign throughout all his pores; O my soul, consider of this, and if thou wilt bring this consideration home, say, *Thy sins were the cause of this bloody sweat*, Jesus Christ is that true Adam, that is come out of paradise for thy sins, and thus laboured on earth with his bloody sweat, to get the bread that thou must feed on.

2. Consider his apprehension; Judas is now at hand with a troop following him to apprehend his master, see how without all shame, he set himself in the van, and coming to his Lord and master, gives him a most traiterous and deceitful kiss, *What, Judas, betrayest thou the Son of man with a kiss?* Hast thou sold the Lord of life to such cruel merchants, as covet greedily his blood and life? O, alas! at what price hast thou set the Lord of all the creatures? At thirty pence. What a vile and slender price is this for a Lord of such glory and majesty? God was sold for thirty pieces of silver, but man could not be bought without the dearest heart-blood of the Son of God. At that time, said Christ, *Ye be come as it were against a thief, with swords and staves; I sat daily amongst you teaching in the temple, and ye never laid hands on me; but this is your hour, and the power of darkness*, Luke xxii. 52, 53. Now the prince of darkness exercised his power, now the hellish rout and malicious rabble of ravenous wolves assaulted the most innocent Lamb in the world, now they most furiously hauled him this way and that way; O how ungently did they handle him? How uncourteously spake they unto him? How many blows and buffets did they give him? What cries, and shouts, and clamours made they over him? Now they lay hold on his holy hands, and bind them hard with rough and knotty cords, so that they gall the skin off his arms, and make the very blood spring out: now they bring him back again over Cedron, and they make him once again to *drink of the brook in the way*; now they lead him openly thro' the high streets of Jerusalem, and carry him to the house of Annas in great triumph. O my soul, consider these several passages, consider them leisurely, and with good attention, consider them till thou feelest some motions or alterations in thy affections; is not this he, that is the infinite virtue, the pattern of innocency, the everlasting wisdom, the honour of earth, the glory of heaven, the very fountain of all beauty, whether of men or angels? How is it then, that this virtue or power is tied with bands, that innocency is apprehended, that wisdom is flouted and laughed to scorn, that honour is contemned, that glory is tormented, that he that is fairer than all the children of men, is besmeared with weeping, and troubled with sorrow of heart? Surely there is something, O my soul, in thee, that caused all this; hadst not thou sinned, the sun of righteousness had never been eclipsed.

3. Consider the hurrying of Jesus from Annas to Caiaphas; there a council is called, and Caiaphas, the high priest, adjures our Lord to tell him, *if he was Christ the Son of God*, Mat. xxvi. 63. No sooner he affirms it, but he is doomed guilty of blasphemy, and so *guilty of death*, verse 66. Now, again, they assault him like mad dogs, and disgorge upon him all their malice, fury and revenge; each one, to the outmost of his power, gives him buffets and strokes; there they spit upon that divine face with their devilish mouths; there they hoodwink his eyes, and strike him on the cheek, scoffing and jesting, and saying, *Aread who is he that smote thee*. O beauty of angels! was that a face to be spit upon? Men usually, when they are provoked to spit, turn away their faces towards the foulest corner of the house; and is there not in all that palace a fouler place to spit in than the face of Jesus? O my soul, why dost not thou humble thyself at this so wonderful example? How is it, that there should remain in the world any token of pride, after this so great and marvellous an example of humility? Surely I am at my wits end, and very much astonished to consider how this so great patience overcomes not my anger.

ger, how this so great abasing assuageth not my pride, how these so violent buffets beat not down my presumption. Is it not marvellous, that Jesus Christ by these means should overthrow the kingdom of pride; and yet, that there should remain in me the reliquies of pride? Consider all those night-sufferings of Christ; O cruel night! O unquiet night! now was the season that all creatures should take their rest, that the senses and members wearied with toils and labours should be refreshed; but, on the contrary, Christ's members and senses were then tormented, they struck his body, they afflicted his soul, they bound his hands, they buffeted his cheeks, they spit in his face; O my soul, thou sinnest in the dark, in covert, in secret, when no eye is upon thee, when the sun, that eye of the world, is set or hid; and therefore all the night long is Christ thus tormented by thy sins; not one jot of rest hath Christ, not a wink of sleep must seize on him, whom thou, by the alarm of thy sins disquieted, both at evening, at mid-night, and at the cock crow, and at the dawning.

4. Consider the hurryings of Jesus from Caiaphas to Pilate; now he stands before Pilate, where he was accused of sedition, seduction and usurpation. Not only Jews but Gentiles, have their hands imbrued in the blood of Christ; Pilate was delegated from Cæsar, both of them Gentiles; yet not without a prophesy, *Behold we go up to Jerusalem, and all things that are written by the prophets concerning the Son of man, shall be accomplished, for he shall be delivered unto the Gentiles,* Luke xviii 31, 32. At the Gentiles tribunal he is questioned of his kingdom, and he answers both the Jews and Gentiles, that they need not fear his usurpation, *My kingdom is not of this world,* John xviii. 36. He gives kingdoms that are eternal, but he will take away none that are temporal; Christ came not into the world to be Cæsar's, or Pilate's, or Herod's successor, but if they had believed to have been their Saviour. Look through the chronicles of his life, and we find him so far from a king, that he was the meanest servant of all men; where was he born? But at Bethlehem a little city. Where did the shepherds find him? But in a poor cottage. Who were his disciples? But a deal of fishermen. Who his companions? But publicans and sinners. Is he hungry? Where stands his table? But on plain ground. What are his dainties? But bread and a few fishes. Where is his lodging? But at the stern of a ship. Here's a king without either presence chamber or bed-chamber, *The foxes have holes, and the birds of the air have nests, but the Son of man hath not whereon to lay his head.* Come, fear not Pilate the loss of thy diadem; it may be the people would sometimes have made him a king, but see how he flies from it, *My kingdom is not of this world,* saith Jesus. Oh! that I could but contemn the world as Christ did. Oh! that first, and above all, I could seek the kingdom of God, and his righteousness. Oh, my soul! I feel it, I feel it, unless I can be free from the affections of all creatures, I cannot with freedom of mind aspire unto divine things; unless I be willing with Christ to tread on crowns and sceptres, to be despised and forsaken of all, and to be esteemed nothing at all, I can have no inward peace, nor be spiritually enlightened, nor be wholly united to the Lord Jesus Christ.

5. Consider the hurryings of Jesus from Pilate to Herod; there is he *questioned of many things,* but justly is the Lamb of God dumb, and opened not his mouth to him, that not long before had taken away his voice; upon this *he is mocked and arrayed in a gorgeous robe,* Luke xxiii. 11. Wisdom is taken for folly, virtue for vice, truth for blasphemy, temperance for gluttony, the peace-maker of all the world, for a seditious disturber of the world, the reformer of the law for a breaker of the law, and the justifier of sinners for a sinner, and the follower of sinners. See how he emptied himself, and made himself of no reputation, that he might fill thee with goodness, and make thee spiritually wise unto salvation.

6. Consider the hurryings of Jesus from Herod back again to Pilate; O my Saviour, how art thou now abused? New accusations are forged; and when Pilate sees that nothing will do, but Christ must die, he delivers him to be stripped, whipped, clothed in purple, crowned with thorns, and sceptred with a reed. He that with spittle cured the eyes of the blind, is now blinded with their spittle; who can number those stripes wherewith they flea and tear his body, one wound eating into another, that *there is no health in his bones by reason of my sins?* O Jesus! was that frothy spittle the ointment, those thorns thy crown, that reed thy sceptre, that purple dyed and embroidered with

with blood thy royal robes? Or, because Adam's sin brought forth thorns, must it therefore be thy penance to wear them? Unthankful people, thus watered with his blood, that bring forth nothing but thorns to crown him. But, oh! that the Lord of heaven, the Creator of the world, the glory of the angels, the wisdom of God, should for my sake, be punished with whips and scourges! O my heart, how can I think on this without tears of blood? O joy of the angels, and glory of saints, who hath thus disfigured thee? Who hath thus defiled thee with so many bloody blows? Certainly they were not thy sins but mine; it was love and mercy that compassed thee about, and caused thee to take upon thee this so heavy a burden; love was the cause why thou didst bestow upon me all thy benefits, and mercy moved thee to take upon thee all my miseries.

7. Consider that sad spectacle of Jesus, when *he came forth wearing the crown of thorns, and the purple robe, and Pilate saying unto them, Behold, the man*, John xix. 5. O my soul, fix thy eyes on this sad object: suppose thyself in the case of Jesus: what, if in so sensible and tender a part as thy head is, men should fasten a number of thorns, yea, and those so sharp, that they should pierce into thy scull, why, alas! thou can'st hardly abide the prick of a pin, much less the piercing in of so many thorns. O but thy Jesus was crowned with thorns, and sceptred with a reed, and that reed was taken out of his hands to beat the crown of thorns into his head; and, besides, thy Jesus was whipped with cords, and rods, and little chains of iron, that from his shoulders to the soles of his feet, there was no part free; and being now in this plight, thou art called on *to behold the man*: dost thou see him? Is thy imagination strong? Canst thou consider him at present, as if thou hadst a view of this very man? Methinks it should make thee break out, and say, ' O brightness of thy Fa-
' ther's glory, who hath thus cruelly dealt with
' thee? O unspotted glass of the majesty of God,
' who hath thus wholly disfigured thee? O river
' that flows out of the paradise of delights, who
' hath thus troubled thee? It is my sins, O Lord,
' that have so troubled thee, my sins were the
' thorns that pricked thee, the lashes that whip-
' ped thee, the purple that clothed thee; it is I,
' Lord, that am thy tormenter, and the very cause of these thy pains.'

8. Consider Pilate's sentence, That *Jesus should be crucified as the Jews required*. Now they had him in their will, and they did to him what seemed them good. Follow him from Gabbatha to Golgotha, see how they lay the heavy cross upon his tender shoulders, that were so pitifully rent and torn with whips, accompany him all the way to the execution, and help to carry his cross to mount Calvary, and there, as if thou hadst been frozen hitherto, thaw into tears, see him lifted up on that engine of torture the bloody cross, he hangs on nails, and as he hangs, his own weight becomes his own affliction: O see how his arms and legs were racked with violent pulls, his hands and feet bored with nails, his whole body torn with stripes, and gored with blood: And now, O my soul, run with all thy might into his arms, held out at their full length to receive thee; oh weigh the matter! because sin entred by the senses, therefore his head, in which the senses flourish, is crowned with searching thorns; because the hands and feet are more especially the instruments of sin, therefore his hands and feet are nailed to the cross for satisfaction. O marvellous! What king is he, or of what country, that wears a crown of thorns? What man is he, or where lives he, whose hands and feet are not only bored, but digged into, as if they had been digging with spades in a ditch? Surely here is matter for a serious meditation; be enlarged, O my thoughts, and dwell upon it! consider it, and consider it again!

9. Consider the darkness that spread over all the earth; now was the sun ashamed to shew his brightness, considering that the Father of lights was darkned with such disgrace, the heavens discoloured their beauty, and are in mourning robes, the lamp of heaven is inmantled with a miraculous eclipse, the sun in the firmament will sympathise with *the Sun of righteousness*, it will not appear in glory though it be mid-day, because the Lord of glory is thus disgraced. And now hear the voice that comes from the Son of God, *My God, my God, why hast thou forsaken me?* Christ in the garden tasted the bitter cup of God's fierce wrath, but now he drunk the dregs of it; he then sipped of the top, but now he drunk all off, top, and bottom, and all. O! but what's the meaning of this, *My God, my God, why hast thou for-*
saken

saken me? Surely, 1. This was not a total, but a partial dereliction; this was not a perpetual, but a temporary forsaking of him; the God-head was not taken away from the man-hood, but the union remained still, even now when the man-hood was forsaken. 2. This was not a forsaking on Christ's part, but only on the Father's part; the Father forsook Christ, but Christ went after him; God took away the sense of his love, but the Son of God laid hold upon him, crying, and saying, *My God, my God, why hast thou forsaken me?* 3. This forsaking was not in respect of his being, but in respect of the feeling of God's favour, love and mercy; certainly God loved him still, oh! but his sense of comfort was now quite gone, so as it never was before: in his agony there was some inklings of God's mercy now and then, at least, there was some star light, some little flash of lightning to cheer him up, but now as the sense and feeling of God's love was gone, and not so much as any little star light of the same appeared. Christ now took the place of sinners, and God the Father shut him out (as it were) amongst the sinners; he drew his mercy out of sight, and out of hearing, and therefore he cried out in a kind of wonderment, *My God, my God, why hast thou forsaken me?* After this he speaks but a few words more, and he gives up the ghost. He dies that we might live, he is dissolved in himself, that we might be united to his Father; O my soul, see him now, if thou canst for weeping, his eyes are dim, his cheeks are wan, his face is pale, his head is bowing, his heart is panting, himself is dying; come, come, and die with him, by a most exact mortification; look pale like him with grief, and sorrow, and trouble for thy sins.

10. Consider the piercing of his side with a spear, whence came out a stream of blood and water; O fountain of everlasting waters! methinks I see the blood running out of his side more freshly than these golden streams which ran out of the garden of Eden, and watered the whole world. Consider the taking of his body down by Joseph; the burying of it by Joseph and Nicodemus; O here's excellent matter for our meditation! O my spirit, go with me a little? Christ being dead, it is pity but he should have a funeral; according to the letter, let Joseph and Nicodemus bear his corpse; let the blessed virgin go after; sighing, and weeping, and at every other pace looking up to heaven; let Mary Magdalene follow after with a box of precious ointment in her hand, and with her hair hanging, ready (if need were) to wipe his feet again; or, that in this meditation I may be more spiritual, let the usurer come first with Judas's bag, and distribute to the poor as he goes along; let the drunkard follow after, with the spunge that was filled with gall and vinegar, and check his wanton thirst; let the young gallant, or voluptuous man, come like his master with bare foot, and with the crown of thorns set also upon his head; let the wanton person bear the rods, and whips, and wires wherewith Christ was scourged, and fright his own flesh; let the ambitious man be clad in the purple robe, the angry person in the seamless coat; my meaning is, let every sinner, according to the nature of his sin, draw something or other from the passion of Christ, to the mortifying of his sin; yea, let all turn mourners, let all bow their heads, and be ready to give up the ghost for the name of Christ. And let not Christ be buried without a sermon neither, and let the text be this, *The good shepherd giveth his life for the sheep*, John x. 11. and in the end of the sermon (whether it be in use or no) let the preacher take occasion to speak a word or two in the praise of Christ; let him say with the spouse, *That he was the chiefest among ten thousands, that he was altogether lovely*, Cant. v. 10, 16. That being God above all Gods, he became man beneath all men; that when he spake, he began ordinarily with *Verily, verily, I say unto you*; that he was an holy man, that he never sinned in his life, neither in thought, word or deed; that being endowed with the power of miracles, he lovingly employed it in curing the lame, and blind, and deaf, and dumb, in casting out devils, in healing the sick, in restoring the dead to life; that as he lived, so he died, for being unjustly condemned, mocked, stripped, whipped, crucified, he took all patiently, praying for his persecutors; and leaving to them, when he had no temporal thing to give them, a legacy of love, of life, of mercy, of pardon, of salvation. When the sermon is done, and the burial is finished, let every mourner go home, and begin a new life in imitation of Jesus Christ. O my soul, that thou wouldest thus meditate, and thus imitate, that so thy meditation might be fruitful, and thy imitation

Q q real;

real; I mean, that thy life and death might be conformable to the life and death of Jesus Christ. But of that hereafter.

SECT. III.

Of desiring Jesus in that respect.

3. Let us desire after Jesus, carrying on the work of our salvation in his death. Jesus Christ, to a fallen sinner, is the chief object of desire, but Jesus Christ, as crucified, is the chief piece of that object. Humbled souls look after the remedy, and they find it chiefly in Christ crucified; and hence are so many cries *after bathings in Christ's blood, and hiding in Christ's righteousness, active and passive.* Indeed, nothing doth so cool and refresh a parched, dry and thirsty soul, as the blood of Jesus, which made the poor woman cry out so earnestly, 'I have an husband, and children, 'and many other comforts, but I would give them 'all, and all the good that ever I shall see in this 'world, or in the world to come, to have my poor 'thirsty soul refresht with that precious blood of 'the Lord Jesus Christ.'

But what is there in Christ's blood or death that is so desirable? I answer.——

1. There is in it the person of Christ, he that is God-man, man-God, *The brightness of his Father's glory, and the express image of his person,* Heb. i. 3. It is he that died; every drop of his blood was not only the blood of an innocent man, but of one that was God as well as man, *God with his own blood purchased the church,* Acts xx. 28. Now surely every thing of God is most desirable.

2. There is not a worth or price; Christ considered, under the notion of a sacrifice, is of infinite worth; now *this sacrifice* (saith the apostle) *he offered up,* Heb. ix. 28. He offered up, not in heaven, as the Socinians would have it, in presenting himself before God his Father, but upon earth, *viz.* in his passion upon the cross. No wealth in heaven or earth besides this, could redeem one soul; and therefore the apostle sets this against all *corruptible things,* as silver and gold, the things so much set by amongst the men of this world; *Ye were not redeemed with corruptible things, as silver and gold,* 1 Pet. i. 18.——*But with the precious blood of Christ, as of a Lamb without blemish,*

and without spot.

3. There is in it a merit and satisfaction; the scripture indeed doth not expresly use these words, but it hath the sense and meaning of them, as in the text, *He hath made us accepted in the beloved, to whom we have redemption through his blood,* Eph. vi. 7. I know there is a different notion in these words, for merit doth properly respect the good that is to be procured, but satisfaction the evil that is repelled; but in Christ we stand not on these distinctions, because in his merit was satisfaction, and in his satisfaction was merit. A great controversy is of late risen up, *Whether Christ's death be a satisfaction to divine justice?* But the very words *redeeming and buying,* do plainly demonstrate, that a satisfaction was given to God by the death of Jesus, *He gave himself for us that he might redeem us,* Tit. ii. 14. *Ye are bought with a price,* 1 Cor. vi. 20. And what price was that? Why, his own blood. *Thou was slain, and hast redeemed us to God by thy blood,* Rev. v. 9. (i. e.) by thy death and passion. This was the [*lutson*], that ransom which Christ gave for his elect, *The son of man came to give his life a ransom for many,* Matth. xx. 28. or as the apostle, *He gave himself a ransom for all,* 1 Tim. ii. 6. the word is here [*antilutson*], which signifies an adequate price, or a counter-price; as when one doth, or undergoeth something in the room of another; as when one yields himself a captive for the redeeming of another out of captivity, or gives up his own life for the saving of another man's life; so Christ gave himself [*antilutson*], a ransom, or counter-price, submitting himself to the like punishment that his redeemed ones should have undergone.

The Socinians tell us, that Christ's sufferings and death were not for satisfaction to God, but in reference to us, that we might believe the truth of his doctrine confirmed and sealed (as they say) by his death, and that we might yield obedience to God, according to the pattern that he hath set before us; and that so believing and obeying, we might obtain remission of sins, and eternal life.

But the scripture goes higher; in that mutual compact and agreement betwixt God and Christ, we find God the Father imposing, and Christ submitting to this satisfaction. 1. The Father imposeth it, by charging the sins of his elect upon Jesus Christ, *The Lord hath laid on him the iniquity of us all,* Isa. liii. 6. Not the sins themselves, not the evil in them, or fault of them, but the guilt and penalty belonging to them; this God laid upon his Son, and charged it upon him; he charged it as a creditor chargeth the debt upon the surety, requiring satisfaction. 2. Christ undertook it, *He was oppressed, and he was afflicted,* ver. 7. or as some translate, 'It was exacted, and he answered,' (i. e.) God the Father required satisfaction for sin, and Jesus Christ, as our surety, answered in our behalf; *He bare the sins of many,* ver. 12. He bare them as a porter that bears the burden for another which himself is not able to stand under; he bare them by undergoing the punishment which was due for them; he bare them as our surety, submitting himself unto the penalty which he had deserved; and by that means he made satisfaction to the justice of God. Surely Christ's death was not only for confirmation of his doctrine, but for satisfaction to God.

4. There is in it not only a true, but a copious and full satisfaction, Christ's death and blood is superabundant to our sins; *The grace of our Lord was exceeding abundant,* 1 Tim. i. 14. [*huperepleonase*] it was overful, redundant, more than enough. Many an humble soul is apt enough to complain, 'Oh! if I had not been so great a sinner, if I had not committed such and such transgressions there might have been hope:' This is to undervalue Christ's redemption; this is to think there is more in sin to damn, than in Christ's sufferings to save; whereas all thy sins to Christ are but as a little cloud to the glorious sun, yea, all the sins of all the men in the world, are but to Christ's merits as a drop to the ocean. I speak not this to encourage the presumptuous sinner, for, alas! he hath no part in this satisfaction, but to comfort the humble sinner, who is loadened with the sense of his sins; what though they were a burden greater than he can bear, yet they are not a burden greater than Christ can bear! There is in Christ's blood an infinite treasure able to sanctify thee and all the world; there is in Christ's death a ransom, a counter-price sufficient to redeem all the sinners that ever were, or ever shall be: the price is of that nature, that it is not diminished, though it be extended to ever so many; as the sun hath fulness of light to enlighten all the world, and if the blind do not see by it, it is not any scarcity of light in the sun, but by reason of his own indisposition: so, if all men are not acquitted by Christ's death, it is not because that was insufficient, as if it had not virtue enough to reach them, as well as others, but because they, by their unbelief, do reject this remedy. O what large room hath faith to expatiate in! sit down, and dive, and dive, yet thou canst not come to the bottom of Christ's blood; but as the prophet Ezekiel saw still more and greater abominations, so mayest thou, in the sufferings of Christ, observe more and more fulness. See what a notable opposition the apostle makes, Rom. v. 15, 16, 17, 18, 19, 20, 21. between the first and second Adam, proving at large, that Christ doth superabound in the fruits of his grace, above the first Adam in the fruits of his sins: he calls it *grace,* and *the abundance of grace,* ver. 17. and this abundance of grace reigneth to life, so that these texts should be like so much oil poured into the wounds of every broken-hearted sinner. Oh! is there any thing that can be desired more than this?

5. There is in it remission of sins; so, saith Christ, *This is my blood of the New Testament, which is shed for many for the remission of sins,* Matth. xxvi. 28. Remission of sins is attributed to Christ's death as a cause; it is not thy tears, or prayers, or rendings of heart that could pay the least farthing, *Without shedding of blood* (saith the apostle) *there is no remission,* Heb. ix. 22. God will have tears and blood also, though not for the same purpose; for all thy tears thou must flee to Christ only as the cause; it is true, thou must mourn, and pray, and humble thyself, but it is Christ's blood only that can wash us clean: Oh remember this! God will not pardon, without satisfaction by the blood of Christ. And surely this makes Christ's death so desirable; 'Oh! my sins 'afflict me, (cries many a one) Oh! I am lothe-'some in mine own eyes, much more in God's; 'surely God is offended with my dulness, sloth-'fulness, and my thousand imperfections: I am all 'the day long entangled with this sin, and that sin, 'and the other sin:' but let this contrite spirit look on Christ's death, and therein he may find all sin is pardoned; see here what an argument is put into thy mouth from these sufferings of Christ; well mayest thou say, 'O Lord, I am unworthy, but it 'is just and right that Christ obtain what he died 'for;

'for; O pardon my sins for his death's sake, and for his precious blood's sake.'

6. There is in it reconciliation and peace with God; *In Christ Jesus ye who sometimes were afar off, are made nigh by the blood of Christ, for he is our peace, who hath made both one, and hath broken down the middle wall of partition between us*, Eph. ii. 13, 14.——*When we were enemies, we were reconciled unto God by the death of his Son*, Rom. v. 10.——*That he might reconcile both (viz. Jews and Gentiles) unto God in one body by the cross*, Eph. ii. 26.——*And having made peace through the blood of his cross, by him to reconcile all things to himself*, Col. i. 20. This certainly should admirably support the drooping soul; it may be thou criest, ' My sins have made a breach betwixt ' God and my soul; I have warred against heaven, ' and now God wars against me; and, Oh what ' odds! If the Lord be angry, yea, but a little; ' what will become of my poor soul? is a little ' stubble able to contend with the consuming fire? ' How then should I contend with God?' But come now, and look on Christ's death as the means and meritorious cause of reconciliation, and thou canst not but say, O this death is desirable? when God the Father looks at a sinner in the bloody glass of Christ, then saith God, ' Oh! now fury ' and wrath is not in me; I have no more quarrel ' or controversy with this soul, seeing Christ hath ' suffered, it is enough, I have as much as my jus-' tice can demand, my frowns are now turned in-' to smiles, and my rod of iron into a sceptre of ' grace.' Why, this is it that makes Christ's death and blood so desirable to the soul; what, shall Jacob so rejoice in seeing Esau's face altered to him? shall he say to Esau, *I have seen thy face, as the face of God*? How much rather may the humble and believing sinner be filled with gladness, when, through Christ's blood, God should be thus appeased and reconciled with him.

7. There is in it immunity, and safety from all the judgments and dangers threatned against our sins. Surely, if there were such force in the blood of the type, that by the effusion of it the Israelites lay safe and untouched of the revenging angel, how much more in the blood of Christ? Satan himself is said to be *overcome by the blood of the Lamb*, Rev. xii. 11. And God's revenge due to our sins is said to be removed by the blood of Jesus, therefore it is called, *The blood of sprinkling, that speaks better things than the blood of Abel*, Heb. xii. 24. the blood of sprinkling was for safety, and Christ's blood is for safety, it cries not for revenge, as Abel's blood cried, but for mercy, and for deliverance from all misery.

8. There is in it a blessed virtue to open heaven, to make passage thither for our souls, *Having boldness, or liberty, to enter into the holiest by the blood of Jesus*, Heb. x. 19. It is the blood of Christ that rents the vail, and makes a way into the holy of holies, that is, into the kingdom of heaven; without this blood there is no access to God; it is only by the blood of Christ that heaven is open to our prayers, and that heaven is open to our persons. This blood is the key that unlocks heaven, and lets in the souls of his redeemed ones; *And I looked* (saith John) *and behold a door was open in heaven, and the first voice I heard was, as it were of a trumpet talking with me, which said, Come up hither*, Rev. iv. 1. And no sooner was he in the spirit, and entred in, but he heard the new song of the four beasts, and four and twenty elders, saying to Christ, *Thou art worthy to take the book, and to open the seals thereof, for thou wast slain, and hast redeemed us to God by thy blood*, Rev. v. 9.

Come now, and gather in all these several particulars; there is in Christ's blood inclusively the person of Christ, the price of souls, a merit and satisfaction, a copious and full satisfaction, remission of sins, reconciliation with God, immunity from dangers, a passage into glory: I might add all other privileges, benefits, dignities of the soul, for they all flow from the blood of Jesus, and they are all contained either expresly, or virtually in the blood of Jesus: and is not all this worth the looking after? O my soul, where is thy langour and fainting towards this blessed object? Shall Ahab eagerly desire after Naboth's vineyard; yea, so eagerly desire it, that his desire shall cast him upon his bed? And is not Christ's blood better than Naboth's vineyard? How is it, O my soul, that thou art not sick on thy bed in thy desires after Jesus? When David desired strongly after God's law, he expressed his longings by the breaking and fainting of his soul, *My soul breaketh for the longing that it hath to thy judgments at all times*;——*And my soul fainteth for thy salvation*, Psal.

Psal. cxix. 20, 81. Oh! where be these breakings and faintings? Strength of desire is expressed by the apostle, by *groaning*, 2 Cor. v. 2. which is the language of sickness; Oh! where be these groanings after Christ's death? When I call to mind that Christ's death is my ransom, that Christ's wounds are my salves, that Christ's stripes are my cures, that Christ's blood is my fountain to wash in, and to be clean; how should I but pray in this sense, *His blood be upon us, and on our children?* Oh, I am undone, except I have a share in this blood! why, it is only this blood that can heal my soul, it is only this *fountain opened to the house of David, and to the inhabitants of Jerusalem*, that can quench my thirst? and now I have seen the fountain opened, How should I but thirst, and cry out with the woman of Samaria, *O give me this water, that I thirst no more?* John iv. 15. But alas, I say it, I only say it. Oh that I could feel it! Oh, my Jesus! that thou wouldest breed in me ardent desires, vehement longings; unutterable groans, mighty gaspings: O that I were like the dry and thirsty ground that gapes and cleaves, and opens for drops of rain! when my spirit is in right frame, I feel some desires after Christ's blood, but how short are these desires? How unworthy of the things desired? Come, Lord, kindle in me hot burning desires, and then give me the desirable object.

SECT. IV.
Of hoping in Jesus in that respect.

4. LEt us hope in Jesus, carrying on the great work of our salvation in his sufferings and death. By this hope, I intend only that which the apostle calls *full assurance of hope*, Heb. vi. 11. the main question is, Whether I have any part in Christ's sufferings? They are of excellent use and of great value to believers; but what am I the better for them if I have no part in them? Or if I say, I hope well, Oh! but what grounds of that hope? It is not every hope that is a well grounded hope, full assurance of hope is an high pitch of hope; and every Christian should strive and endeavour after it: now, that we may do it, and that we may discern it, that our hope is not base but right born, that the grounds of our hope in Christ's death are not false but of the right stamp; I shall lay down these signs.——

1. If Christ's death be mine then is Christ's life mine; and converse, if Christ's death be mine then is Christ's life mine. Christ's active and passive obedience cannot be severed; Christ is not divided: we must not seek one part of our righteousness in his birth, another in his habitual holiness, another in the integrity of his life, another in his obedience of death. They that endeavour to separate Christ's active and passive obedience, they do exceedingly derogate from Christ, and make him but half a Saviour. was not Christ our *surety?* Heb. vii. 22. and thereupon was he not bound to fulfil all righteousness for us? (i. e.) As to suffer in our stead, so to obey in our stead. Oh! take heed of opposing or separating Christ's death and Christ's life; either we have all Christ, or we have no part in Christ: now, if these two be concomitants, well may the one be as the sign of the other; search then, and try, O my soul, hast thou any share in Christ's life? Canst thou make out Christ's active obedience unto thy own soul? If herein thou art at a stand, peruse those characters laid down in the life of Christ; the many glorious effects flowing out of Christ's life unto a believer's soul we have discovered before.

2. If Christ's death be mine, then is that great end of his death accomplished in me, viz. *By the sacrifice of himself, he hath put away sin*, even my sin, Heb. ix. 26. —— And, *in him I have redemption through his blood, even the forgiveness of sins*, Eph. i. 7. As on this account he suffered, *to finish the transgression, to make an end of sins, and to make reconciliation for iniquity*, Dan. ix. 24. So, if his death be mine, I may assuredly say, *My sins are pardoned, and my iniquities are done away.* Come then and try by this sign, canst thou assure thyself that thy sins are forgiven thee? Hast thou heard the whispers of God's Spirit, *Son, or daughter, be of good comfort, thy sins are remitted?* There is no question then but thou art redeemed by his blood, thou hast part in his sufferings. Indeed this very character may seem obscure, assurance of pardon is the *hidden manna, the white stone, which no man knoweth saving he that receives it and feels it*; and yet, if thou diligently observest the Spirit's actings, even this may be known, for remission of sin and repentance are twins of a birth; these two, God in scripture hath joined together,

gether, *If we confess our sins, he is faithful and just to forgive our sins,* 1 John i. 9.——And *repent and pray, if the thought of thy heart may be forgiven thee,* Acts viii. 22. And *Christ is a prince and a Saviour to give repentance to Israel, and forgiveness of sins.* Acts v. 31.——And *thus it is written, and thus it behoved Christ to suffer,* Luke xxiv. 46, 47.——*That repentance and remission of sins should be preached in his name.* In this way David assured himself, Psalm xxxii. 5. *I said, I will confess my transgressions unto the Lord, and thou forgavest the iniquity of my sin. Selah.* It is no more than but to ask thy own soul, What are thy repentings kindled together? Hast thou seriously and sincerely repented thee of sin as sin? Hast thou turned from all sin unto God with constancy and delight? Surely this is peculiar and proper to the child of God by virtue of Christ's death.

3. If Christ's death be mine, then am I ingrafted into the likeness of Christ's death, then am I made conformable to Christ in his death; *That I may know him, and the fellowship of his sufferings, being made conformable unto his death,* Phil. iii. 10. The same that was done to Christ in a natural way, is done and performed in the believer in a spiritual way, (i. e.) as Christ died, so the believer dies; as Christ died for sin, so the believer dies to sin; *In that he died, he died unto sin,——likewise reckon ye also yourselves to be dead indeed unto sin,* Rom. vi. 10, 11. Observe here the analogy, and proportion, and resemblance betwixt Christ and us; both die unto sin, Christ by way of expiation, suffering and satisfying for the sins of others; we, by way of mortification, killing, and slaying, and crucifying our own sins. I look upon this sign as the very touchstone of a Christian, and therefore I shall insist upon it.

Two questions I suppose needful to resolve the grounds of our hope concerning our interest in the death of Christ.

1. Whether indeed, and in truth, our sins are mortified?
2. Whether we increase, or grow in our mortification?

For the first, whether indeed and in truth, our sins are mortified? It is a skill worth our learning, because of the many deceits that are within us; sin may seem to be mortified when the occasion is removed; or sin may seem to be mortified when it is not violent but quiet; or sin may seem to be mortified when it is but removed from one sin unto another; or sin may seem to be mortified when the sap and strength of sin is dead, as the lamp goes out when either the oil is not supplied or taken away. Now, that in this scrutiny we may search to the bottom, and know the truth and certainty of our mortification, it will appear by these rules.

1. True mortification springs from a root of faith. Every thing in the world proceeds from some cause or other; and if the cause be good the effect must needs be good, but if the cause be evil, the effect must needs be evil; *A good tree cannot bring forth evil fruit, and an evil tree cannot bring forth good fruit,* Matth. vii. 18. In this case, therefore let us examine the cause, if we can make out this truth that we believe in Christ, that we role ourselves on the Lord Jesus Christ for life and for salvation; and that now we begin to feel in us the decay of sin, we may conclude from the cause or rise, that this decay of sin is true mortification; surely it hath received the deadly wound: it is a blessed effect, arising from a good, and right, and genuine cause.

2. True mortification is general; not only one sin, but all sins are mortified in a true believer. As death is unto the members of the body, so is mortification unto the members of sin; now death seizeth upon every member, it leaves not life in any one member of the body, so neither doth mortification leave life in any one member of sin; my meaning is, it takes away the commanding power of sin in every member: *mortify your members which are upon the earth,* (saith the apostle) your members, not one member; and then he instanceth, *Fornication, uncleanness, inordinate affections, evil concupiscence, and covetousness, which is idolatry,* Col. iii 5. Christians that have their interest in Christ's death, must not only leave pride but lust; not only uncleanness but covetousness; sin must not only be slain in the understanding, but in the will and affections: mortification is general.

You will say this is an hard saying, Doth any man, any believer, leave all sin! Yes, in respect of ruling power, he leaves all sin, all gross sins, and all other sins; only with this difference, all gross sins in practice and actions, and all frailties and infirmities in allowance and affection. It is good to ob-

observe the degrees of mortification. The first is, to forbear the practice of gross and scandalous sins in word and deed, *If any man offend not in word, the same is a perfect man*, Jam iii. 2. And this perfection, by the help of grace, a godly man may reach to in this life. The second is, to deny consent and will to all frailties and infirmities, *the evil which I would not, that do I*, Rom. vii. 19. I may do evil, and yet *I would not do evil*, there is a denial of it in the will. The third is, to be free from any settled liking of any evil motion, not only to deny consent and will, but also to deny the very thought or imagination settledly and deliberately to delight in sin; I know, to be void of all evil motions arising from the flesh, or of all sudden passions within, or of all sudden delights in sin, or of all deadness or backwardness to good things by reason of sin, it is an higher pitch than any man can touch in this present world; for, whilst we live, the law of members will be working, and we shall find cause enough to complain of a body of death; only, if when these motions first arise we presently endeavour to quench them, to reject them, to detest them, and to cast them away from us, therein is true mortification; and thus far we must look to it, to leave all sin.

3. True mortification is not without its present combats, though at last it conquer, many a time corruption may break out, and lust may be strong and violent; but this violent lust is only for the present, whereas a lust unmortified ever reigneth. It is with sin in a believer, as it is with a man that hath received his deadly wound from his enemy; he will not presently fly away, but rather he will run more violently upon him that hath wounded him; yet, be he never so violent, in the middle of his action, he sinks down, because he hath received his deadly wound; so it is with a believer's sin, and with a mortified lust, it may rage in the heart, and seem to bear sway for a time, but the power and strength of sin is mortified, it sinks down and wants ability to prevail: by this sign we may know whether the corruptions and stirrings of our hearts proceed from a mortified or from an unmortified lust; a lust, though mortified, may rage for a time, but it cannot rule; it strives, but it cannot totally prevail; it may be in the heart, as a thief in the house, not to reside or dwell, but to lodge for a night and be gone: and (that which is ever to be observed) after its swing and breaking out, the heart that lodged it abhors itself in dust and ashes, cries nightily unto God for mercy and pardon, repairs the breach with stronger resolution, and more invincible watchfulness against future assaults: but a lust unmortified possesseth itself, and rules and reigns in the heart and soul; it abides there, and will not away: I shall not deny but there may be a cessation of its actings for a time; but that is not any want of good-will, as they say, but only of matter, means, opportunity, enticement, company, provocation, or the like; and after such cessation or forbearance, the heart usually entertains it again with more greediness; it lies and delights in it as much as ever; it hardens itself most obstinately in it, as if it were impossible to leave it, or to live without it with any kind of comfort.

4. True mortification is a painful work. The very word imports no less; to kill a man, or to mortify a member, will not be without pain; hence it is called a crucifying of the flesh, and a cutting off the right hand, a plucking out the right eye, *They that are Christ's have crucified the flesh*, Gal. v. 24. *If thy hand offend thee, cut it off, and if thy eye offend thee, pluck it out*, Matth. v. 29, 30. In this respect, this death unto sin carries with it a likeness to the death of Christ; it is attended with agonies and soul-conflicts, both before and after our conversion.

1. Before conversion, before the first wound be given it; why then, ordinarily there is some compunction of spirit, some pricking of heart, what a case do we find the Jews in, when after Peter's sermon they were pricked at their hearts? Acts ii. 37. And what an agony do we find the jaylor in, when he came trembling in, and falling down at the apostles feet, and crying out, *Sirs, What shall I do to be saved?* Acts xvi. 30. With such agonies as these, is the beginning of mortification usually attended; I do not say they are alike in all, whether for degree or continuance; but, in ordinary, true and sound conversion is not without some of these soul-conflicts.

2. After conversion, after the first round there are some agonies still; for, though a believer be delivered of sin in respect of the guilt and reigning power, yet he hath still some remainders of sinful corruption left within him, which draw many a groan;

groan, and many a sigh from his trembling heart, 'We also which have the first fruits of the Spirit, 'even we ourselves groan within ourselves, 'waiting for the adoption, to wit, the redemption 'of our bodies,' Rom. viii. 23. Such are the groans of mortified saints, saints dying unto sin, like the groans of dying men, whose souls being weary of their bodies, do earnestly desire a dissolution; and thus Paul groaned, when he said, *O wretched man that I am, who shall deliver me from the body of this death?* Rom. vii. 24.

Oh! what a touchstone is this? How will this discover true mortification from that which was counterfeit? Some may think they are dead unto sin, when indeed, and in truth, they are not dead, but sleep unto sin: and it appears by this, because there were no pangs in their death; you know there is a difference betwixt death and sleep, there are pangs in the one but not in the other: O my soul examine, what pangs were there in thy death unto sin? What agonies, what soul-conflicts hast thou felt? What compunction of heart, what affliction of spirit hast thou endured for sin? What trouble hast thou had to find *such a law in thy members rebelling against the law in thy mind, and bringing thee into captivity to the law of sin?* Rom. vii. 23. Why, surely thou art not so mortified as to be freed wholly from the power of sin; it may be it doth not rule in thee as a prince, yet certainly it tyrannizeth over thee; it oftimes carries thee contrary to the bent of thy regenerate mind, to the omitting of what thou wouldest do, and to the committing of what thou wouldest not do; and is not this an affliction of spirit? Doth not this cause frequent conflicts in thy spirit? If not, thou mayest well suspect that sin is not dead but asleep; or, if it be dead to thee, yet thou art not dead to it. I confess, death-pangs are not all alike in all, some have a more gentle, and others a more painful death; so it is in this spiritual death unto sin; and that herein there may be no mistake, I shall propound this question, What is the least measure of these pangs, these soul-agonies and conflicts that are necessarily required to true mortification? I answer,——

1. There must be a sense of sin, and of God's wrath due unto sin; such a sense we find in Jesus Christ, he was very sensible of the weight and burden of those sins, and of that wrath of God that lay upon him, which made him cry out, *My God, my God, why hast thou forsaken me?* Thus souls in the act of mortification, sometimes cry it, *O my sins, and O God's wrath.*

2. There must be a sorrow for sin. Such an affection we find also in Jesus Christ, *My soul is exceeding sorrowful, even unto death,* 2 Cor. vii. 10. [*perilupos,*] he was beset and surrounded with sorrows; so every mortified sinner, at some time or other, he feels an inward sorrow and grief, even that *godly sorrow,* which the apostle speaks of, *a sorrow according to God,* (i. e.) coming from God, well-pleasing to God, and bringing to God back again.

3. There must be a desire of being freed and delivered from sin: such a desire we find also in Jesus Christ, *I have a baptism to be baptized with, and how am I straitned until it be accomplished?* Luke xii. 50. A regenerate soul earnestly desires to be freed, not only from the guilt but also from the power of sin, *O wretched man that I am, who shall deliver me?* &c.

4. There must be answerable endeavours in effectual strivings against sin, *Ye have not resisted unto blood, striving against sin,* Heb. xii 4. How did our Saviour wrestle in the garden, *offering up prayers and supplications, with strong crying and tears?* Heb. v. 7. So will a regenerate soul wrestle with God about the death of sin, praying, watching, going out in the strength of God, and engaging in a continual war, a deadly feud against it; and these are the least of these soul-conflicts, wherewith this mortification or death unto sin is attended.

Now try we the truth of our mortification by these signs; doth it spring from a right root of faith? Is it general and universal in respect of all sins? Is it accompanied with combats? Doth the flesh lust against the Spirit, and the Spirit against the flesh? And in this combat, Doth the Spirit at last prevail and triumph over the flesh? Do we find it a painful work both before and after conversion? Why, then may I say with the apostle, *Now I know Christ, and the fellowship of his sufferings; now, by the grace of Christ, I am made conformable unto his death.* As he died for sin, so I die to sin; and here is the ground of my hope, that Christ's death is mine.

For the *Second,* Whether we increase and grow in our mortification? The question is needful as the former, to satisfy our soul's interest in the death of Christ. As true grace is growing grace, so true mortification is that which grows. Now that we may be resolved in this point also, the growth of our mortification will appear by these following signs.———

1. Growing mortification hath its chiefest conflicts in spiritual lusts. At first, we mortify grosser evils, such as oaths, drunkenness, uncleanness, worldly mindedness, or the like; but when we grow in this blessed duty, we then set ourselves against spiritual wickedness, as pride, presumption, self-carnal confidence in a man's own graces, or the like. This method the apostle sets down, *Let us cleanse ourselves from all filthiness of flesh and Spirit*, 2 Cor. vii. 1. *First*, From all filthiness of the flesh or body, and then from all filthiness of the Spirit or soul; as the children of Israel, in their entrance into the land of promise; *first*, they set upon the frontiers and skirts of the land, and then they fought it out, and prevailed in the heart of the country; so Christians in their mortification, they first set upon worldly lusts, gross evils, outward sins; and when they have encountered them at the frontiers, they then conflict with such corruptions as lie more inwardly in the very heart, spiritual wickedness that is within. Now, if this be our case, here is one sign of our growth.

2. Growing mortification is more even, constant, lasting, durable, when there is in the heart a sudden flowing and reflowing, it comes from those vast seas of corruption that are within us; many souls have their ague fits, sometimes hot and sometimes cold; it may be now they are in a very good frame, and within an hour or two a mighty tide comes in, and they are borne down by sin and corruption, in this case mortification is very weak; but, on the contrary, if we find our standing more firm and sure, if for the main we walk evenly, and keep closely to the Lord, it carries with it an evidence that our mortification grows.

3. Growing mortification feels lust more weak, and the Spirit more strong in its ordinary actings. If we would know the truth of growth, let us look to our usual fits of sinning, for then a man's strength or weakness is discerned most; as a man's weakness to good is discerned when he comes to act it, *to will is present with me, but how to perform that which is good, I find not*, Rom. vii. 18.

So a man's weakness to sin is best discerned when he comes to act it: mark then the ordinary fits (as we call them) of sinning; sometimes God is pleased to appoint some more frequent assaults, as if he would on purpose suffer the law in the members to war and to muster up all their forces, that so we might the rather know what is in our hearts; at such a time, if we find that resistance against sin grows stronger, that sin cannot advance and carry on his army so as formerly, that sin is encountered at first, or met withal at the frontiers, and there overthrown; this is a good sign, that now our mortification grows; as, suppose it to be a lust of fancy, it cannot boil up to such gross fancies as it was wont; or, suppose it to be a lust of pride, it boils not up to such a spirit of pride as formerly; instead of bringing forth fruit it now brings forth blossoms; or, instead of bringing forth blossoms it now brings forth nothing but leaves; why, this is a sure sign that this lust is withering more and more, when the inordinate thirst is not so great in the time of the fit, when the inward lusts pitch upon lower acts than they had wont; when the waters abate, and fall short, and lessen, and overflow less ground, we may conclude certainly that mortification grows.

4. Growing mortification hath more ability to abstain from the very occasions and beginnings of lust, thus, Job, (whom we look on as a man much mortified) *made a covenant with his eyes, that he would not think upon a maid*, Job xxxi. 1. And no question as he made a covenant, so he kept his covenant, oh! when a man cannot endure to come where such a one is that he loves not, when he cannot endure the sight of him, or any thing that puts him in mind of him, not so much as to parley or to speak with him, this is a sign of a strong hatred; and so when a man hates the very garment spotted with the flesh, here is a good sign; I know this height is not easy to attain to, and therefore some, in imitation of Job and David, have bound themselves with vows and promises, as much as might be, to abstain from the appearance of evil, to crush the cockatrice egg before the serpent could creep out of it, to avoid sin in its first rise; but, alas; how have they broken their vows from time to time? For all this I dare not speak against vows, provided that, 1. They be of things lawful. 2 That we esteem them not as duties of absolute necessity.

necessity. And, 3. that we bind not ourselves perpetually, left our vows should become burdens unto us, but only for some short time, and so renew them as occasion requires: in this way, our vows might much help us in our mortification; and if once, through the help of vows, or prayer, or *looking unto Jesus*, or going to the cross of Jesus Christ, or by any other means we feel ourselves more able to resist sin, to hate sin, in its first rise, first motions, first onset, we may assuredly hope, that now our mortification grows.

O my soul, try now the growth of thy mortification by these signs; hast thou overcome grosser sins, and is now thy chiefest conflict with spiritual wickedness? Is thy standing and walking with God more close, and even, and constant, than sometimes it hath been? Are thy lusts more weak, and thy grace more strong in ordinary actings? I say in ordinary actings, for the estimate of thy growth must not be taken for a turn or two, but by a constant course: hast thou now more ability to quench the flame of sin in every spark, to dash Babylon's brats against the stones, even whilst they are little to abstain from sin in its first motion or beginning? Why, then is the promise accomplished, *He will subdue our iniquities*, Micah vii. 19. Surely thou art a growing Christian, thou hast fellowship with Christ in his sufferings, thy ground is solid, firm and stable, thy hope hath a rock foundation, and thou mayest build upon it, that Christ's death, and blood, and sufferings are thine, even thine, *He loved thee, and gave himself for thee*.

SECT. V.

Of believing in Jesus in that respect.

5. LET us believe in Jesus, carrying on the great work of our salvation for us, during his sufferings and death. Every one looks upon this as an easy duty, only the humble soul, the scrupulous conscience cries out, what, 'Is it possible that Christ should die, suffer, shed his blood 'for me? His incarnation was wonderful, his life 'on earth was to astonishment; but that the Son 'of God should become man, live amongst men, 'and die such a death, even the death of the 'cross, for such a one as I am, I cannot believe 'it; it is an abyss past fathoming; the more I con-
'sider it, the more I am amazed at it; suppose I 'had an enemy in my power, man or devil, one 'that provokes me every day, one that hunts my 'soul to take it away, should I not say with Saul, '*If a man find his enemy, Will he let him go well* '*away?* 1 Sam. xxiv. 19 it may be an ingenuous 'spirit (such as David) would do thus much; but 'would David, or any breathing soul, not only 'spare his enemy, but spill himself to save his ene-'my? Would a man become a devil to save de-'vils? Would a man endure hell pains to free all 'the devils in hell from their eternal pains? And 'yet what were these in comparison of what Christ 'hath done or suffered for us. It is not so much 'for us to suffer for devils (for we are fellow crea-'tures) as it is for Christ God-man, Man-God to 'suffer for us: oh! what an hard thing is it, con-'sidering my enmity against Christ, to believe that 'Christ died for me, that he gave himself to the 'death, even to the death of the cross for my soul?'

Trembling soul! throw not away thyself in a way of unbelief. It may be thou wouldest not die for an enemy, an irreconcileable enemy; but are not the mercies of God above all the mercies of men? O believe! and that I may persuade effectually, I shall lay down first some directions. And, 2. Some encouragements of faith.

1. For the directions of faith in reference to Christ's death, observe these particulars.

1. Faith must directly go to Christ, not first to the promise, and then to Christ. But, *first*, to Christ, and then to the promise; the person ever goes before the prerogative.

2. Faith must go to Christ *as God in the flesh*; this was the difference betwixt the New Testament and Old Testament believers; their faith directs only to God, but our faith looks more immediately to Jesus Christ, *Believe in the Lord Jesus and thou shalt be saved*.

3. Faith must directly go to Christ, as God in the flesh, *made under the law*. He continued in all things written in the book of the law to do them, and so our faith must look upon him: but of these before, I shall now say nothing more to these particulars.

4. Faith must go to Christ, not only as made under the directive part of the law by his life, but under the penal part of the law by his death; in both these respects, *Christ was made under the law*;

the one half of the law he satisfied by the holiness of his life, he fulfilled the law in every jot, and every tittle; the other half of the law he satisfied by his enduring the death, even the death of the cross; he paid both the principal and the forfeiture; and though men do not so, yet Christ did so, that the whole law might be satisfied fully, by his being under both these parts of the law, pay, and penalty; come then, and look upon Christ as dying; it was the serpent, *as lifted up*, and so looked at, that healed the Israelites of their fiery stings. Alas! we are diseased in a spiritual sense, as they were, and Christ Jesus was *lifted up* as a remedy to us, as the serpent was unto them; it remains therefore, that as they looked up to the brazen serpent, so we look up to Jesus, believe in Jesus as lifted up for life, and for salvation: *As Moses lifted up the serpent in the wilderness, even so must the Son of man be lifted up: that whosoever believeth in him should not perish, but have eternal life*, John iii. 14, 15. Indeed some difference there is betwixt the serpent and Christ.———

As, 1. The brazen serpent had not power in itself to cure, as Christ hath. 2. The serpent cured the Israelites but only for a time to die again; but whomsoever Jesus cures in a spiritual sense, he cures for ever, *They shall never die*, John xi. 26. 3. The serpent also had its time of curing, it did not always retain the virtue, but during the time they were in the wilderness; only Jesus Christ our brazen serpent, doth ever retain his power and virtue to the end of the world; and hence it is, that in the ministry Christ is still held forth as lifted up, that all that will but look on him by faith may live. 4. The serpent, sometimes a remedy against poison, was after turned, even to poison the Israelites, which made Hezekiah to crush it, and break it, and stamp it to powder; but Jesus Christ ever remains the sovereign and healing God, he is *the same yesterday, and to day, and for ever*. He is unchangeable in his goodness, as he is an holy and divine nature; he can never be defaced, nor destroyed, but he abideth the Saviour of sinners to all eternity; why then, let us rather *look unto Christ, and believe in Christ as lifted up*. (i. e.) as he was crucified, and died on the cross. In this respect he is made a fit object for a sinner's faith to trust upon, and rest upon; *Christ as crucified, as made sin, and a curse for us, is the object of our pardon*: O this is it that makes Christ's death so desirable! why, therein is, virtually and meritoriously, pardon of sin, justification, redemption, reconciliation, and what not? Oh! cries a sinner, 'Where may I set my foot? 'How should I regain my God? My sin hath undone me, which way should I cast for pardon?' Why, now remember, that in seeking pardon, Christ was crucified, Christ as dying is principally to be eyed and looked at; *Who is he that condemneth? It is Christ that died*, Rom. viii. 34. No question Christ's active obedience during his life, was most exact, and perfect, and meritorious, yet that was not the expiation of sin; only his passive obedience (Christ only in his sufferings) took away sin, the guilt of sin, and punishment for sin, *We have redemption through the blood of Christ, even the forgiveness of sins*, Eph. i. 7. If any humble soul would have recourse to that Christ, who is now in heaven, let him first, in the actings of his faith, consider him as crucified, as lifted up, as made sin for us, as through whom (under that consideration) he is to receive pardon of sin, justification, redemption, reconciliation, sanctification, salvation.

5. Faith in going to Christ, as lifted up, it is principally and mainly to look unto the end, meaning, intent, and design of Christ in his sufferings as he was lifted up; we are not barely to consider the history of Christ's death, but the aim of Christ in his death; many read the history, and they are affected with it; there is a principle of humanity in men, which will stir up compassion, and love, and pity towards all in misery; whilst Christ was suffering, the women followed after him weeping, but this weeping, not being spiritual or raised enough, he said to them, *Daughters of Jerusalem, weep not for me, but weep for yourselves*. The way of faith drawing virtue out of Christ's death, it is especially to look to the scope, and drift of Christ in his sufferings; as God looks principally to the meaning of the spirit in prayer; so doth faith look principally to the meaning of Christ in his sufferings: mistake not, my meaning is not that we should be ignorant of the history of Christ's death, or of the manner of Christ's sufferings; you see we have opened it largely, and followed it close from first to last: but we must not stick there, we should above all, look to the mind and heart of Christ in all this: some observe, that both in the

Old and New Testament we find this method; first the history, and then the mystery; first the manner, and then the meaning of Christ's sufferings; as in the Old Testament, we have first the the history in Psal xxii. written by David; and then the mystery in Isa. liii. writen by Isaiah: and in the New Testament we have, first, the manner of his sufferings, written at large by all the evangelists; and then the meaning, written by the apostles in all their epistles. Now, accordingly are the acts of faith, we must first *look on Jesus as lifted up*, and then look at the end and meaning; why was this Jesus thus lifted up? Well, but you may demand, what was the end, the plot, the great design of Christ in this respect?

I answer, some ends were remote, and others were more immediate; but omitting all those ends that are remote, his glory, our salvation, &c. I shall only answer in these particulars.

1. One design of Christ's death, was to redeem us from the slavery of death and hell, *He hath redeemed us from the curse of the law, being made a curse for us, as it is written, cursed is every one that hangeth on a tree*, Gal. iii. 13. Hence it is, that we say, That *by his sufferings Christ hath redeemed us from hell, and by his doings Christ hath given us a right to heaven; he was made under the law, that he might redeem them that were under the law*, Gal. iii. 4, 5. Alas! we were carnal, sold under sin, whereupon the law seized on us, lockt us up as it were in a dungeon; yea, the sentence passed, and we but waited for execution; now to get us rid from this dismal, damnable estate, Christ himself is made under the law, that he might redeem us; redeem us! How? Not by way of entreaty, to step in and beg our pardon, that would not serve the turn; sold we were, and bought we must be; a price must be laid down for us, it was a matter of redemption; but with what must we be redeemed? Surely with no easy price; ah! no, it cost him dear and very dear, *Ye were not redeemed with corruptible things, as silver and gold, but with the precious blood of Christ*, 1 Pet. i. 18. His precious blood was the price we stood him, which he paid when *he gave his life a ransom for many*, Matth. xx. 28. the case stood thus betwixt Christ and us in this point of redemption, we all like a crew or company of malefactors, were ready to suffer, and to be executed now, what said Christ to this? *Why I will come under the law*, said Christ, *I will suffer that which they should suffer, I will take upon me their execution, upon condition I may redeem them:* Now this he did at his death; and this was the end why he died, that by his death we might be redeemed from the slavery of death and hell.

2. Another design of Christ's death, was to free us from sin; not only would he remove the effect, but he would take away the cause also, *whom God hath set forth to be a propitiation—for the remission of sin*, Rom iii. 25 —*B. hold the Lamb of God which taketh away the sins of the world*, John i. 29. —— *He hath made him to be sin for us, who knew no sin, that we might be made the righteousness of God in him*, 2 Cor. v. 21. —— *Once hath he appeared to put away sin by the sacrifice of himself*, Heb. ix. 26. —— *And the blood of Jesus Christ his Son cleanseth us from all sin*, 1 John i. 7. This was the plot which God by an ancient design aimed at in the sufferings of Jesus Christ; that he would take away sin; and thus faith must take it up, and look upon it. When Peter had set forth the heinousness of the Jews sin in killing Christ, he tells them at last of that design of old, *All this was done*, (said he) *by the determinate counsel of God*, Acts ii. 23 His meaning was first to humble them and then to raise them up, *q. d.* it was not so much they that wrought his death, as the decree of God, and the agreement of God and Christ; there was an ancient contrivement that Jesus Christ should die for sin, and that all our sins should be laid on the back of Jesus Christ; and therefore he seems to speak comfort to them in this, that howsoever they designed it, yet God and Christ designed a further end in it than they imagined, even to remission of sins; *Who was delivered to death for our sins, and rose again for our justification*, Rom. iv. 25. The Death of Christ (as one observes) was the greatest and strangest design that ever God undertook; and therefore, sure he had an end proportionable to it: God that willeth not the death of a sinner, would not for any inferior end, will the death of his Son, whom he loved more than all the world besides; it must needs be some great matter for which God should contrive the death of his Son, and indeed it could be no less than to remove that which he most hated, and that was sin. Here then is another end of Christ's

Christ's death, it was for the remission of sin, one main part of our justification.

3. Another design of Christ's death was to mortify our members which are upon the earth. Not only would he remit sin, but he would destroy it, kill it, crucify it; he would not have it *reign in our mortal bodies, that we should obey it in the lusts thereof*, Rom. vi 12. This design the apostle sets out in these words, *He bare our sins in his own body upon the tree, that we being dead unto sin, should live unto righteousness*, 1 Pet. ii. 24. Christ by his death had not only a design to deliver us from the guilt of sin, but also from the power of sin; *God forbid that I should glory, save in the cross of our Lord Jesus Christ, by whom the world is crucified unto me, and I unto the world*, Gal. vi. 14. Paul was a mortified man, dead to the world, and dead to sin, but how came he so to be? Why, this he attributes to the cross of Christ, to the death of Christ; the death of Jesus was the cause of this death in Paul, *How much more shall the blood of Christ — purge your consciences from dead works to serve the living God?* Heb. ix. 15. There is in the death of Christ, first, a value, and secondly, a virtue; the former is available to our justification, the latter to our sanctification; now sanctification hath two parts, mortification, and vivification; Christ's death or passive obedience is more properly conducible to the one, his life or active obedience to the other. Hence believers are said to be *engraffed with Christ in the likeness of his death*, Rom. vi 5. There is a kind of likeness betwixt Christ and Christians: Christ died, and the Christian dies; Christ died a natural death, and a Christian dies a spiritual death; Christ died for sin, and the Christian dies to sin: this was another end of the death of Christ; there issues from his death a mortifying virtue, causing the death of sin in a believer's soul, one main part of our sanctification.

O my soul, look to this, herein lies the pith and marrow of the death of Christ; and if now thou wilt but act and exercise thy faith in this respect, How mightest thou draw the virtue and efficacy of his death into thy soul? But here is the question, How should I manage my faith, or how should I act my faith, to draw down the virtue of Christ's death, and so to feel the virtue of Christ's death in my soul-mortifying, crucifying and killing sin?

I answer, 1. In prayer, meditation, self-examination, receiving of the Lord's supper, &c I must propound to myself and soul the Lord Jesus Christ, as having undertaken and performed that bitter and painful work of suffering, even unto death, yea, that of the cross, as it is held out in the history and narrative of the gospel. 2. I must really and stedfastly believe, and firmly assent, that those sufferings of Christ, so revealed and discovered, were real and true, undoubted, and every way unquestionable as in themselves. 3. I must look upon those grievous, bitter, cruel, painful, and withal opprobrious, execrable, shameful sufferings of Christ, as very strange and wonderful; but especially considering the spiritual part of his sufferings, *viz.* the sense and apprehension of God's forsaking, and afflicting him in the day of his fierce anger, I should even be astonished and amazed thereat; what, that the Son of God should lay his head on the block under the blow of divine justice? That he should put himself under the wrath of his heavenly Father? That he should enter into the combat of Gods heavy displeasure, and be deprived of the sense and feeling of his love and mercy, and wonted comfort? How should I but stand agast at these so wonderful sufferings of Jesus Christ? 4. I must weigh and consider what it was that occasioned and caused all this, *viz.* Sin, yea, my sin, yea, this and that sin particularly. This comes nearer home; and from this I must now gather in these several conclusions. As,——

1. It was the design of Christ, by his sufferings, to give satisfaction to the infinite justice of God for sin. 2. It was intended and meant (at least in a second place) to give out to the world a most notable and eminent instance and demonstration of the horridness, odiousness, and execrableness of sin, sith no less than all this, yea, nothing else but this would serve the turn to expiate it, and atone for it. 3. It holds forth again, as sin is horrid in itself, so it cannot but be exceeding grievous and offensive to Christ; Oh! it cost him dear, it put him to all this pain and torture, it made him cry out, *My God, my God, why hast thou forsaken me?* How then should it but offend him above all, above any thing in the world? 4. If therefore there be in me any spark of love towards Christ, or any likeness to Christ, or, if I would have Christ to bear

bear any affection, love, regard or respect unto me, it will absolutely behove me, by all means, to lothe sin and to cast it away from me, and to root it up, to quit my hands, and to rid my heart of it. The truth is, I cannot possibly give forth a more pregnant proof of my sincere love, entire affection, respect, conformity, resemblance, sympathy to and with Christ, than by offering all violence, using all holy severity against sin for his very sake.

Now, when the heart is thus exercised, God by his Spirit will not fail to meet us. our desire and endeavour of soul to weaken and kill sin in the soul is not without its reward; but especially when sin hath in this way, and by this means, lost the affection of the soul, and is brought in hatred and disesteem, it decays, and dies of itself, for it only liveth and flourisheth by the warm affections, good thoughts, and opinion that the soul hath of it. So that matters going thus in the heart, the influence that should nourish and maintain sin is cut off, and it withers by degrees, till it be finally and fully destroyed.

Thus for directions; now for the encouragements of our faith to believe in Christ's death. Consider,—

1. The fulness of this object, Christ crucified; there is a transcendent all-sufficiency in the death of Christ. In a safe sense it contains in it universal redemption: it is sufficient for the redemption of every man in the world, yea, and effectual for all that have been, are, or shall be called into the state of grace, whether Jews or Gentiles, bound or free. I know some hold, that Christ died for all and every man with a purpose to save; only thus they explicate. 1. That Christ died for all men, considered in the common lapse or fall, but not as obstinate, impenitent, or unbelievers; he died not for such as such. 2. That Christ died for all men in respect of the request or impetration of salvation; but the application thereof is proper to believers. 3. That Christ died not to bring all or any man actually to salvation, but to purchase salvability and reconciliation so far, as that God might and would *(salva justitia)* deal with them on terms of a better covenant. 4. That Christ hath purchased salvability for all men, but faith and regeneration he hath merited for none; because God is bound to give that which Christ hath merited of him, although it be not desired, or craved. I cannot assent to these positions: but thus far I grant, that Christ's death in itself is a sufficient price and satisfaction to God for all the world; and that also it is effectual in many particulars to all men respectively in all the world; every man in one way or other hath the fruit of Christ's death conferred upon him; but this fruit is not of one kind: for, 1. Some fruit is common to every man, as the earthly blessings, which infidels enjoy, may be termed the fruits of Christ's death. 2. Other fruit is common to all the members of the visible church, as to be called by the word, to enjoy the ordinances, to live under the covenant, to partake of some graces that come from Christ. 4. Other fruit is indeed peculiar to the saints of God, as faith, unfeigned regeneration, pardon of sin, adoption, &c. And yet this fruit is universal to all the saints, whether Jews or Gentiles: in which sense speaks the apostle, *He spared not his own Son, but delivered him up for us all*, Rom. viii. 32.—*And he gave himself a ransom for all*, 1 Tim. ii. 6.——*And God hath concluded them all in unbelief, that he might have mercy upon all*, Rom. xi. 32.—And *by the righteousness of one, the free gift came upon all men unto justification of life*, Rom. v. 18.—*He tasted of death for all men*, Heb. ii. 9—or distributively for every man. All which texts are rightly interpreted by Caiaphas, *He prophesied that Jesus should die for that nation: and not for that nation only, but that also he should gather together in one the children of God that were scattered abroad*, John xi. 51, 52. And thus John brings in the four beasts, and four and twenty elders, saying, *Thou art worthy to take the book, and to open the seals thereof, for thou wast slain, and hast redeemed us to God by thy blood, out of every kindred, and tongue, and people, and nation*, Rev. v. 9. and thus Paul rightly argues, *Is he the God of the Jews only? Is he not of the Gentiles also? Yes, of the Gentiles also*, Ro. iii 29. O the fulness of Christ's death!—— Many are apt to complain, 'Would 'Christ die for me? Why, alas, I am an alien, I 'not of the common-wealth of Israel, I am a 'dog, I am a sinner, a grievous sinner, a sinner of 'the Gentiles:' and what then? *Ye who sometimes were afar off, are now made nigh by the blood of Christ, for he is our peace, who hath made both one,*

and

and hath broken down the middle wall of partition between us, that he might reconcile both unto God in one body by the cross, Eph. ii. 13, 14, 16. Oh! what encouragement is this for thee to believe thy part in the death of Christ?

2. Consider the worth, the excellency of this glorious object, Christ crucified. There is an infinity of worth in the death of Christ; and this ariseth, 1. From the dignity of his person, he was God-man; the death of angels and men, if put together, could not have amounted to the excellency of Christ's death: stand amazed at thy happiness, O believer, thou hast gained by thy loss, thou hast lost the righteousness of a creature, but the righteousness of an infinite person is now made thine: hence it is many times called the *righteousness of God*, Rom. x. 3. 2 Cor. v. 21. Both because Christ is God, and because it is such a righteousness as God is satisfied with: he looks for no better, yea, there can be no better. 2. This worth is not only in respect of the dignity of the person, but also in respect of the price offered: O it was the blood of Christ, one drop whereof is of more worth than thousands of gold and silver! it was this *blood* that *purchased* the whole *church of God*, Acts xx. 28. which a thousand worlds of wealth could never have done. 3. This worth is not only in respect of the person and price neither, but also in respect of the manner of the oblation, 1 Pet. i. 18 Christ must die on the cross, as it was determined; the price in itself is not enough, unless it be ordered and proportioned according to the will of him who is to be satisfied: if a man should give for a captive prisoner an infinite sum of money, sufficient in itself to redeem a thousand, yet, if not according to such a way as the conqueror prescribeth, if not according to the condition, it could not be called a satisfaction. Now this was the condition, that Christ must die, and die that death of the cross; and accordingly he undertook, and performed, which set a lustre, and glory, and excellency, and worth upon his death. O the worth, O the excellency of this death of Christ!—Many are apt to complain, O the filth of my sins! 'O the injuries and unkindness that have been in 'mine iniquities! It is not my misery, my destruction that so much troubles me, as that God is displeased!' Sweet soul! turn thine eyes hither; surely this death of Christ is more satisfactory to God, than all thy sins possibly can be displeasing to God, there was more sweet savour in Christ's sacrifice, than there could be offence in all thy sins; the excellency of Christ's death in making righteous, doth superabound the filthiness of sin in making a sinner. Come on then, and close with Christ upon this encouragement; there is a dignity, an excellency in this object of faith, Christ crucified.

3. Consider the suitableness of this blessed object, the death of Christ. There is in it a suitableness to our sinful condition; whatsoever the sin is, it is the cry of some, 'They dare not believe, 'they dare not touch Christ crucified, they dare 'not approach to that precious blood, because of 'this sin, and that sin, and the other sin.' Whereas in the death and blood of Christ (if they could but take a full view of it) they might find something suitable to their state: as for instance, suppose thy sin the greatest sin imaginable, except that against the Holy Ghost, art thou a murderer? Hast thou had thy hands imbrued in the blood of the saints? Why, see now how Christ, for thy sake, was esteemed of the Jews a murderer, and worse than a murderer. Barabbas is preferred before Jesus, Barabbas is released, and Jesus murdered; yea, his blood is shed to wash away thy blood-shed: art thou a sorcerer, a necromancer? Is thy sin the sin of Manasseh, of whom it is said, That *he used enchantments, and witchcrafts; and dealt with a familiar spirit, and with wizards*, 2 Chro. xxxiii. 6. Why, see now how Jesus Christ, for thy sake, was esteemed of the Jews as an impostor, an enchanter; for so some say, that he got the name of God, and sowed it in his thigh; and by virtue thereof, he wrought all his miracles; and they commonly reported of him that he had a devil, and that *he cast out devils, through Belzebub the prince of devils*. Art thou a blasphemer? Hast thou joined with those in these sad times, who have opened their mouths against the God of heaven, enough to make a Christian rend his heart, and weep in blood? Why, see now how Jesus for thy sake was judged of Caiaphas, and all the sanhedrim, for a blasphemer of God, and that in the highest kind of blasphemy, as making himself equal with God; yea, see how *the high priest rends his clothes, saying, He hath spoken blasphemy*, Mat. xxvi. 65. Surely all this he endured, that every blasphemer may find mercy, if they will but come in, and believe

in

in Jesus. I might instance in other sins, Art thou a traitor, a glutton. a drunkard, a wine-bibber, a thief, a seducer, a companion of sinners? Why, see now, how Jesus Christ was, for thy sake thus called, reputed, accounted; whatever the sin is, there in something in Christ that answers that very sinfulness; thou art a sinner, and he is made sin to satisfy the wrath of God even for thy sin; thou art such, and such a sinner, and he is accounted such and such a sinner for thy sake, that thou mightest find in him something suitable to thy condition, and so the rather be encouraged to believe, that in him, and through him, all thy sins shall be done away. Away, away unbelief, distrust, despair! you see now the brazen serpent lifted up, you see what a blessed object is before you; O believe! O look up unto Jesus! O believe in him thus carrying on the work of thy salvation in his death.

SECT. VI.
Of loving Jesus in that respect.

6. LET us love Jesus as carrying on the great work of our salvation for us during his sufferings and death. What, did he suffer and die? *Greater love than this hath no man, that a man should give his life for his friends:——But God commendeth his love towards us, in that while we were yet sinners, Christ died for us,* Rom. v. 8. Why, here is an argument of love indeed, How should we but love him, who hath thus loved us? In prosecution of this I have no more to do, but first to shew Christ's love to us, and then to exercise our love to him again.

1. For his love to us, had not God said it, and the scriptures recorded it, Who would have believed our reports? Yet Christ hath done it, and it is worth our while to weigh it, and consider it in an holy meditation.—Indeed with what less than ravishment of spirit can I behold the Lord Jesus, who, from everlasting, was clothed with glory and majesty, now wrapped in rags, cradled in a manger, exposed to hunger, thirst, weariness, danger, contempt, poverty, revilings, scourgings, persecution? But to let that pass, into what extasies may I be cast, to see the judge of all the world accused, judged, condemned: To see the Lord of life dying upon the tree of shame and curse? To see the eternal Son of God struggling with his Father's wrath? To see him who had said, *I and my Father are one,* sweating drops of blood in his agony, and crying out on his cross, *My God, my God, why hast thou forsaken me?* Oh! whither hath his love to mankind carried him? Had he only sent his creatures to serve us, had he only sent his prophets to advise us in the way to heaven, had he only sent his angels from his chamber of presence to attend upon us, and minister to us, it had been a great deal of mercy; or, if it must be so, had Christ come down from heaven himself, but only to visit us, or had he come only and wept over us, saying, 'Oh! that you had 'known, even you in this your day the things be-'longing to your peace! Oh! that you had more 'considered of my goodness! oh, that you had 'never sinned!' This would have been such a mercy as that all the world would have wondered at it; but that Christ himself should come, and lay down his blood, and life, and all for his people, and yet I am not at the lowest, that he should not only part with life, but part with the sense and sweetness of God's love, which is a thousand times better than life, *Thy loving-kindness is better than life,* Psalm lxiii. 3. That he should be content to be accursed, that we might be blessed; that he should be content to be forsaken, that we might not be forsaken; that he should be content to be condemned, that we might be acquitted; Oh! what raptures of spirit can be sufficient for the administration of this so infinite mercy? Be thou swallowed up, O my soul, in this depth of divine love, and hate to spend thy thoughts any more upon the base objects of this wretched world, when thou hast such a Saviour to take them up.——Come, look on thy Jesus, who died temporally, that thou mightest live eternally, who, out of his singular tenderness, would not suffer thee to burn in hell, for ten, twenty, thirty, forty, an hundred years, and then recover thee; by which, notwithstanding, he might better and deeper have imprinted in thee the blessed memory of a dear Redeemer; no, no; this was the article betwixt him and his Father, 'That thou 'shouldest never come there.' See but, observe but Christ's love in that mutual agreement betwixt God and Christ, 'Oh! I am pressed (saith God) 'with the sins of the world, as a cart is pressed that 'is full of sheaves; come, my Son, either thou

'must

' must suffer, or I must damn the world.' Accordingly I may imagine the attributes of God to speak to God, Mercy cries, I am abused; and patience cries, I am despised; and goodness cries, I am wronged; and holiness cries, I am contradicted; and all those come to the Father for justice crying to him, ' That all the world were opposers of his grace and Spirit; and if any be saved, Christ must be punished.' In this case we must imagine Christ stept in; *Nay, rather than so,* (saith Christ) *I will bear all, and undertake the satisfying of all.* And now look upon him; he hangs on the cross all naked, all torn, all bloody, betwixt heaven and earth, as if he were cast out of heaven; and also rejected by earth: he has a crown indeed, but such a one as few men will touch; none will take from him; and if any rash man will have it, he must tear hair, skin and all, or it will not come; his hair is all clotted with blood, his face is clouded with black and blue; he is all over so pitifully rent, outwards, inwards, body and soul. — I will think the rest, alas! when I have spoken all I can, I shall speak under it, had I the tongues of men and angels, I could not express it. Oh! love more deep than hell! oh! love more high than heaven! the brightest seraphims that burn in love, are but as sparkles to that mighty flame of love in the heart of Jesus.

2. If this be Christ's love to us, What is that love we owe to Christ? Oh now for an heart that might be somewise answerable to these mercies! oh for a soul, sick of love, yea, sick unto death! How should I be otherwise, or any less affected? This only sickness is our health, this death our life, and not to be thus sick is to be dead in sins and trespasses; why, surely I have heard enough, for which to love Christ for ever. The depths of God's grace are bottomless, they pass our understandings, yet they recreate our hearts; they give matter of admiration, yet they are not devoid of consolation: O God, raise up our souls to thee, and if our spirits be too weak to know thee, make our affections ardent and sincere to love thee.

Surely the death of Christ requires this, and calls for this: many other motives we may draw from Christ, and many other motives are laid down in the gospel; and indeed the whole gospel is no other thing than a motive to draw man to God by the force of God's love to man; in this sense the holy scriptures may be called *The book of true love*, seeing therein God both infolds his love to us, and also binds our love to him; but of all the motives we may draw from Christ, and of all the arguments we may find in the gospel of Christ, there is none to this, the death of Christ, the blood of Jesus; Is not this such a love-letter, as never, never was the like? Read the words, *For his great love wherewith he loved us*, Eph. ii. 4. Or, if you cannot read, observe the hieroglyphicks, every stripe is a letter, every nail is a capital letter, every bruise is a black letter; his bleeding wounds are as so many rubricks to shew upon record: oh! consider it, is not this a great love? Are not all mercies wrapt up in this blood of Christ? It may be thou hast riches, honours, friends, means; oh! but thank the blood of Christ for all thou hast; it may be thou hast grace, and that is better than corn, or wine, or oil: oh! but for this thank the blood of Jesus, surely it was the blood of Christ that did this for thee; thou wast a rebellious soul, thou hadst an hard and filthy heart, but Christ's blood was the fountain opened, and it took away all sin and all uncleanness; Christ, in all, and Christ above all, And wilt thou not love him? Oh! that all our words were words of love, and all our labour labour of love, and all our thoughts thoughts of love, that we might speak of love, and muse of love, and love this Christ who hath first loved us, with all our heart, and soul, and might! what, wilt thou not love Jesus Christ? Let me ask thee then, Whom wilt thou love, or rather whom canst thou love, if thou lovest not him? If thou sayest, *I love my friends, parents, wife, children*; Oh! but love Christ more than these; a friend would be an enemy, but that the blood of Christ doth frame his heart; a wife would be a trouble, but that the blood of Christ doth frame her heart; all mercies are conveyed to us through this channel; oh! who would not love the fountain!—Consider of it again and again, our Jesus thought nothing too good for us, he parts with his life and blood, he parts with the sense and feeling of the love of God, and all this for us, and for our sakes; ah! my soul, how shouldest thou but love him in all things, and by all means?

It is reported of Ignatius, that he so continually meditated on the great things Christ suffered for him, that he was brought entirely to love him; and when he was demanded, why, he would not forsake Christ, rather than to suffer himself to be torn and devoured of wild beasts? He answered, That he could not forget him, because of his sufferings; 'Oh! his 'sufferings (said he) are not transient words, or removeable objects, but they are indelible characters, so engraven in my heart, that all the torments of earth can never raze them out.' And being commanded by that bloody tyrant Trajan to be ript and embowelled, they found *Jesus Christ* written upon his heart in characters of gold. Here was an heart worth gold; oh that it might be thus with us! if my hands were all of love, that I could work nothing but love; if my eyes were all of love, that I could see nothing but love; if my mind were all of love, that I could think of nothing but love, all were too little to love that Christ, who hath thus immeasurably loved me; if I had a thousand hearts to bestow on Christ, and they most enlarged and screwed up to the highest pitch of affection; all these were infinitely short of what I owe to my dear Lord and dearest Saviour. Come let us join hands, *He loved us, and therefore let us love him*; if we dispute the former, I argue from the Jews, when he shed but a few tears out of his eyes at Lazarus's grave; *Then said the Jews, behold how he loved him!* John xi. 36. How much more truly may it be said of us, for whom he shed both water and blood, and that from his heart, *Behold, how he loved us!* why then, if our hearts be not iron; yea, if they be iron, How should they choose but feel the magnetical force of this loadstone of love? For to a loadstone doth Christ resemble himself, when he saith of himself; *And I, if I be lifted up from the earth will draw all men unto me*, John xii. 32.

SECT. VII.

Of joying in Jesus in that respect.

7. LET us joy in Jesus, as carrying on the great work of our salvation in his sufferings and death: what hath Christ suffered for us? Hath he drunk off all the cup of God's wrath, and left none for us? How should we be but cheered? Precious souls! why are you afraid? There is no death, no hell, *no condemnation to them that are in Christ Jesus*, Rom. viii. 1. There is no divine justice for them to undergo, that have their share in this death of Christ: oh! the grace and mercy that is purchased by this means of Christ! oh! the waters of comfort that flow from the sufferings and obedience of Christ! Christ was amazed that we might be cheered, Christ was imprisoned, that we might be delivered; Christ was accused, that we might be acquitted; Christ was condemned, that we might be redeemed; Christ suffered his Father's wrath, and came under it, that the victory might be ours, and that in the end we might see him face to face in glory: is not here matter of joy? It may be the law, and sin, and justice, and conscience, and death, and hell, may appear as enemies, and disturb thy comforts; but is there not enough in the blood of Christ to chase them away? Give me leave but to frame the objections of some doubting souls, and see whether Christ's death will not sufficiently answer, and solve them all.

1. One cries thus, 'Oh! I know not what will become of me, my sins are ever before me;' *Against thee, thee only have I sinned, and done this evil in thy sight*, Psal. li. 3, 4. 'I have sinned against a most 'dear, and gracious, and merciful God and Father 'in our Lord Jesus; O the aggravations of my sins! 'are they not sins above measure sinful?'

It may be so, but the blood of Christ is *a fountain opened for sins and for uncleanness*, Zech. xii. 1. *In him we have redemption through his blood, even the forgiveness of sins*, Eph. i. 7.—*He by himself purged our sins*, Heb. i. 3.—*And now once in the end of the world hath he appeared to put away sin by the sacrifice of himself*, Heb. ix. 26 —*And Christ was once offered to bear the sins of many*, Ver. 28. [*Anenegchein*,] to bear away the sins of many. As the scape-goat under the law had upon his head the iniquities of the children of Israel, and so was sent away by the hand of a fit man into the wilderness, Lev. xvi. 21, 22. So the Lord Jesus (of whom that goat was a type) had all the iniquities of his elect laid upon him by God his Father; and bearing them, he took them away, *Behold, the Lamb of God that taketh away the sins of the world*, John i. 29. He bore them, and bore them away; he went away with them into the wilderness, or into the land of forgetfulness. See what comfort is here.

2. Another cries thus, 'Oh! I know not what 'will become of me, that law is mine enemy, I have 'transgressed the law, and it speaks terribly,' *Cursed is every one that continueth not in all things that are written in the book of the law to do them*, Gal. iii. 10.

10. 'Oh! I have offended the law, and I am under the curse.'

Say not so, for by the death of Christ, though the law be broken, yet the curse is removed; the apostle is clear, *Christ hath redeemed us from the curse of the law, being made a curse for us*, Gal. ii. 13. He was made a curse for us, (i. e.) the fruits and effects of God's curse, the punishment due to sinners, the penal curse which justice required, were laid upon Christ; and by this means we are freed from the curse of the law. It is true, that without Christ thou art under this law, do, or die; and if thou offendest in the least kind, thou shalt perish for ever, the curse of the law is upon thee to the uttermost; but on the other side, if thy claim be right to the blood of Christ, thou art freed from penalty, not but that we may be corrected and chastised; but what is that to the eternal curse which the law pronounceth against every sin? We are freed from the curse, or damnatory sentence of the law, *There is no condemnation to them that are in Christ Jesus*, Rom. viii. 1. the law is satisfied, and the bond is cancelled by our surety Christ. Ah! what comfort is this?

3. Another cries thus, 'O! I know not what will become of me, I have offended justice; and what shall I appeal from the seat of justice to the throne of grace? My sins are gone before, and they are knocking at heaven's gates, and crying, justice, Lord, on this sinner; I know not what will be the issue, but either free grace must save me, or I am gone.'

Say not so, for by this death of Christ, free grace and justice are both thy friends. However some do, yet certainly thou needest not to appeal from the court of justice to the mercy-seat; in this mystery of godliness there may be as much comfort in standing before the bar of justice, as at the mercy-seat, (i. e.) by standing therein, and thro' the Lord Jesus Christ; yea, this is the gospel-way, to go to God the Father, and to tender up to him the active and the passive righteousness of Christ his Son for an atonement, and satisfaction for our sins; in this way is the comfort of justification brought; if we go to God in any other way than this, it is but in a natural way, and not in a true evangelical way. A man by nature may know thus much, that when he hath sinned, he must seek unto God for mercy, but to seek unto God for pardon with a price in our hands, to tender up the merits of Jesus Christ for a satisfaction to divine justice: here is the mystery of faith; and yet I speak not against relying on God's mercy for pardon, but what need we to appeal from justice to mercy, when by faith we may tender the death of Christ, and so find acceptance with the justice of God itself? Come soul, and let me tell thee for thy comfort, if thou hast any share in the death of Christ, thou hast two tenures to hold thy pardon and salvation by: 'Mercy and justice, free grace 'and righteousness,' mercy in respect of thee, and justice in respect of Christ; not only in free grace ready to acquit thee, but a full price is laid down to discharge thee of all thy sins: so that now, when the prince of this world comes against thee, thou mayest say in some sense as Christ did, 'He can 'find nothing in me; for how can he accuse me 'seeing Christ is my surety? Seeing the bond hath 'been sued, and Christ Jesus would not leave one 'farthing unpaid. As Paul said to Philemon con-'cerning Onesimus, if he have wronged thee, or 'owe thee any thing, put it on my account, so 'doth Christ say to God, if these have wronged 'thy majesty, or owe thee any thing, put it on 'me.' Paul indeed added, *I Paul have written it with mine own hand;* but Christ speaks thus, *I Jesus have ratified and confirmed it with my own blood.*

4. Another cries thus, 'O! I know not what 'will become of me, the first threat that ever was '(*In the day that thou eatest thereof thou shalt 'surely die,)* Gen. ii. 17. now sits on my spirit; 'methinks I see the grisly form of death standing 'before me; Oh! this is he that is the king of 'fears, the chief of terrors, the inlet to all those 'plagues in another world; and die I must, there 'is no remedy, Oh! I startle, and am afraid of it.'

And why so? *It is Christ that died*, Rom. viii. 34. And by his death he hath taken away the sting of death, that now the drone may hiss, but cannot hurt: come, meditate much upon the death of Christ, and thou shalt find the matter enough in his death, for the subduing of thy slavish fears of death, both in the merit of it, in the effect of it, and in the end of it.——1. In the merit of it, Christ's death is meritorious, and in that respect the writ of mortality is but to the saints a writ of ease, a passage unto glory. 2. In the effect of it,

Christ's death is the conquest of death; Christ went down into the grave to make a back-door, that the grave which was before a prison, might now be a thoroughfare; so that all his saints may with ease pass through, and sing, *O death where is thy sting? O hell, where is thy victory?* 3. In the end of it, Christ's death among other ends, aims *at the ruin of him that had the power of death, that is the devil; and to deliver them, who thro' fear of death were all their life time in bondage,* Heb. ii. 14, 15. Christ pursued this end in dying, to deliver thee from the fear of death; and if now thou fearest, thy fearing is a kind of making Christ's death of none effect. O come, and *with joy draw water out of the wells of salvation!* Isa. xii. 3.

5. Another cries thus, 'Oh! I know not what 'will become of me; the very thoughts of hell 'seem to astonish my heart; methinks I see a little 'peep-hole down in hell, and the devil roaring 'there, being reserved in chains under darkness, 'until the judgment of the great day; and me-'thinks I see the damned flaming, and Judas, and 'all the wicked in the world, and they of Sodom 'and Gomorrah, there lying, and roaring, and 'gnashing their teeth: now, I have sinned, and 'why should not I be damned? Oh! why should 'not the wrath of God be executed on me, yea, 'even upon me?'

I answer, the death of Christ acquits thee of all, *Blessed is he that hath a part in the first resurrection, on such the second death hath no power,* Rev. xx. 6. Christ's death hath taken away the pains of the second death, yea, pains and power too, for it shall never oppress such as belong to Christ. If hell and devils could speak a word of truth, they would say, 'Comfort yourselves, ye 'believing souls, we have no power over you, for 'the Lord Jesus hath conquered us, and we have 'quite lost the cause.' Paul was very confident of this, and therefore he throws down the gauntlet, and challengeth a dispute with all comers, *Who shall lay any thing to the charge of God's elect? It is God that justifieth, who is he that condemneth? It is Christ that died,* Rom. viii. 33, 34. Let sin, and the law, and justice, and death, and hell, yea, and all the devils in hell unite their forces; this one argument of Christ's death, *(it is Christ that died)* will be enough to confute and confound them all.

Come then, and comfort yourselves all believers in the death of Christ; what, do you believe? And are you confident that you do believe? Why then do you sit drooping? *What manner of communication, are these that you have, as ye walk and are sad?* Luke xxiv 17. Away, away dumpishness, despair, disquietness of spirit! Christ is dead, that you might live and be blessed; in this respect every thing speaks comfort, if you could but see it; God and men, heaven and earth, angels and devils; the very justice of God itself is now your friend, and bids you go away comforted, for it is satisfied to the full; heaven itself waits on you, and keeps the doors open that your souls may enter; *We have boldness,* (saith the apostle) *to enter into the holiest by the blood of Jesus, by a new and living way which he hath consecrated for us through the vail; that is to say, his flesh,* Heb. x. 20. Christ's death hath set open all the golden gates and doors of glory; and therefore go away cheerfully, and get you to heaven, and when you come there, be discouraged or discomforted, if you can. O my soul, I see thou art poring on sin, on thy crimson sins and scarlet sins; but I would have thee dwell on that crimson-scarlet blood of Christ; oh! it is *the blood of sprinkling, it speaks better things than the blood of Abel,* it cries for mercy, and pardon, and refreshing, and salvation; thy sins cry, 'Lord, do me justice against such a soul;' but the blood of Christ hath another cry, 'I am 'abased, and humbled, and I have answered all' Methinks this should make thy heart leap for joy; Oh the honey, the sweet that we may suck out of this blood of Christ! come, lay to thy mouth, and drink an hearty draught, it is the spiritual wine that makes merry the heart of man, and it is the voice of Christ to all his guests, *Eat, O friends, drink, yea, drink abundantly, O beloved,* Cant. v. 1.

SECT. VIII.

Of calling on Jesus in that respect.

8. LET us call on Jesus, or on God the Father, in and through Jesus.

1. We must pray, that all these transactions of Christ in his sufferings and death may be ours; if we direct our prayers immediately to Jesus Christ,

let

let us tell him what anguish and pains he hath suffered for our sakes; and let us complain against ourselves, 'Oh! what shall we do, who by our 'sins have so tormented our dearest Lord? What 'contrition can be great enough, what tears sufficiently expressive, what hatred and detestation 'equal and commensurate to those sad and heavy 'sufferings of our Jesus?' And then let us pray, that he would pity us, and forgive us those sins wherewith we crucified him, that he would bestow on us the virtue of his sufferings and death, that his wounds might heal us, his death might quicken us; and his blood might cleanse us from all our spiritual filth of sin; and, lastly, that he would assure us, that his death is ours, that he would persuade us, *That neither death, nor life, nor angels, nor principalities, nor powers, nor things present, nor things to come, nor height, nor depth, nor any other creature, should be able to separate us from the love of God, which is in Christ Jesus our Lord,* Rom. viii. 38, 39.

2. We must praise the Lord for all these sufferings of Christ. Hath he indeed suffered all these punishments for us? Oh! then what shall we render unto the Lord for all his benefits upon us? What shall we do for him, who hath done and suffered all these things? But especially, if we believe our part in the death of Christ, in all the virtues, benefits, victories, purchases, and privileges of his precious death; Oh then! what manifold cause of thankfulness and praise is here? Be enlarged, O my soul! found forth the praises of thy Christ, tell all the world of that warmest love of Christ, which flowed with his blood out of all his wounds into thy spirit; tune thy heart-strings aright, and keep consort with all the angels of heaven, and all his saints on earth; sing that Psalm of John the divine, *Unto him that loved us, and washed us from our sins in his own blood, and made us kings and priests unto God, and his Father, to him be glory and dominion for ever and ever, Amen.* Rev i. 5, 6.

SECT. IX.

Of conforming to Jesus in that respect.

9. LEt us conform to Jesus, in respect of his sufferings and death; looking unto Jesus is effective of this; objects have an attractive power, that do assimilate or make like unto them. I have read of a woman, that by fixing the strength of her imagination upon a blackamore on the wall, she brought forth a black and swarthy child. And no question but there is a kind of spiritual imagination of power in faith to be like to Christ by looking on Christ; come then, and let us look on Christ, and conform to Christ in this respect.

In this particular I shall examine these queries. 1. Wherein must we conform? 2. What is the cause of this conformity? 3. What are the means of this conformity as on our parts?

For the first, Wherein must we conform? I answer, We must conform to Christ in his graces, sufferings, death.

1. In the graces that most eminently shined in his bitter passion; his life indeed was a gracious life, he was full of grace, *And of his fulness have we all received, and grace for grace,* 1 John. i. 16. But his graces shined more clearly and brightly at his death; as a lily amongst the thorns seems most beautiful, so his graces in his sufferings shew most excellent; I shall instance in some of them; as,—

1. His humility was profound; what, that the most high God, that the only begotten and eternal Son of God, should vouchsafe so far as to be contemned and less esteemed than Barabbas a murderer? That Christ should be crucified upon a cross between two thieves, as if he had been the ring-leader of all malefactors; O! what humility was this!

2. His patience was wonderful; in respect of this the apostle Peter sets Christ a blessed example before our eyes, *If when ye do well, and suffer for it, ye take it patiently, this is acceptable with God, for even hereunto were ye called, because Christ also suffered for us, leaving us an example that ye should follow his steps.—Who, when he was reviled he reviled not again; when he suffered he threatned not, but committed himself to him that judgeth righteously,* 1 Pet. ii. 20, 21, 23. O the patience of Christ!

3. His love was fervent; *Herein is love, not that we loved God, but that he loved us, and sent his Son to be the propitiation for our sins,* 1 John iv. 10. This love is an exemplar of all love; it is the fire that should kindle all our sparks, *Be ye followers of God* (faith the apostle) *as dear children; and walk*

walk in love as Christ also hath loved us, and gave himself for us an offering and sacrifice unto God for a sweet-smelling savour, Eph. v. 1, 2. Some observe, that in the temple there were two altars, the brazen and the golden; the brazen altar was for bloody sacrifices, the golden altar was for the offering of incense; now the former was a type of Christ's bloody offering upon the cross, the latter of Christ's sweet intercession for us in his glory; in regard of both, the apostle tells, that Christ gave himself both for an *offering and sacrifice of a sweet-smelling savour unto God.* O! what love was this?

4. His mercy was abundant; he took upon him all the miseries and debts of the world, and he made satisfaction for them all; he acted our redemption immediately in his own person; he would not intrust it to angels, but he would come himself and suffer; nor would he give a low and base price for our souls, he saw the misery was great, and his mercy should be more great; he would buy us with so great a ransom as that he might overbuy us, and none might outbid him in the market of our souls; O! we underbid and undervalue the mercy of God, who overvalued us; we will not sell all to buy him, but he sold all he had, and himself too to buy us; indeed, if he had not done it we had been damned; and to save our souls, he cared not what he did or suffered; O the mercy of Christ!

5. His meekness was passing great; in all the process of his passion, he shewed not the least passion of wrath or anger; he suffered himself gently and quietly to be carried like a sheep to the butchery; and *as a lamb before the shearer is dumb, so opened he not his mouth;* a lamb is a most meek and innocent creature, and therefore Christ is called *the Lamb of God which taketh away the sins of the world,* John i. 19. —— And *he was brought as a Lamb to the slaughter.* Isa. liii. 7. Why, a lamb goes as quietly to the shambles, as if it were going to the fold, or to the pasture field where its dam feedeth; and so went Christ to his cross; O the meekness of Christ!

6. His contempt of the world was to admiration; he tells them, *his kingdom was not of this world,* John xviii. 36. John vi. 15. When a crown was offered him, and forced upon him, he refused it; but, above all, behold the bed where the bridegroom lyeth and sleepeth at noon-day; here's but an hard flock and narrow room; O blessed head of a dear Redeemer! how is it that thou hast not a pillow where to rest thyself? He hangs on the cross all naked, few kings do so; he hath no crown for his head but one of thorns; he hath no delicates but gall and vinegar; he is leaving the world, and he hath no other legacies to give his friends but spiritual things, *Peace I leave with you, my peace I give unto you, not as the world giveth, give I unto you,* John xiv. 27. He had so contemned the world, that he had not a legacy in all the world to give, *not as the world giveth, give I unto you.*

7. His obedience was constant; *He became obedient unto death, even the death of the cross,* Phil. ii. 8 —*He sought not his own will, but the will of him that sent him,* John v. 30. There was a command, that the Father laid on Christ from all eternity, *O my Son, my only begotten Son, thou must go down, and leave heaven, and empty thyself, and die the death, even the death of the cross, and go and bring up the fallen Sons of Adam out of hell.* Mankind, like a precious ring of glory, fell off the finger of almighty God, and was broken all in pieces; and thereupon was the command of God, That his Son must stoop down, though it pain his back, he must lift up again the broken jewel; he must restore it, and mend it, and set it as a seal on the heart of God: all which the Lord Jesus did in time, he was obedient till death, and obedient to death, even to the death of the cross. *Son, thou must die,* said God, *Why, Father, I will do it,* said Christ; and accordingly he freely made his soul an offering for sin.

Now, in all these graces we must conform to Christ. *Learn of me, for I am meek and lowly,* Matth. xi. 29.—And *walk in love as Christ also hath loved us,* Eph. v. 2. It is as if Christ had said, Mark the steps where I have trod, and follow me in humility, in patience, in love, in mercy, in meekness, in contempt of the world, in obedience unto death; in these and the like graces you most conform to Christ.

2. We must conform to Christ in his sufferings, if he calls us to them; this was the apostle's prayer, *That I may know him, and the power of his resurrection, and the fellowship of his sufferings,* Phil. iii. 10. It was his desire, that he might experimentally

perimentally know what exceeding joy and comfort it was to suffer for Christ and, with Christ, Concerning this the other apostle speaks also, *Christ suffered for us, leaving us an example that we should follow his steps*, 1 Peter ii. 21. But the text that seems so pertinent and yet so difficult, is that of Paul, *I now rejoice in my sufferings for you, and fill up that which is behind of the afflictions of Christ in my flesh for his body's sake, which is the church*, Col. i. 24. One wou'd wonder how Paul should fill up that which is behind of the sufferings of Christ; were Christ's sufferings imperfect? And must Paul add to them? No, surely, *For by an offering Christ hath perfected for ever them that are sanctified*, Heb. x. 14. I shall not insist on many commentaries, I suppose this is the genuine sense and meaning of the Spirit. 'Now rejoice I in my 'sufferings for you, whereby I fulfil the mea- 'sure of those tribulations which remain yet to be 'endured of Christ in his mystical body, which I 'do for the body's sake, not to satisfy for it, but 'to confirm it, or strengthen it by my example 'in the gospel of Christ.' The sufferings of Christ are either personal or general, his personal sufferings were those he endured in his own body as Mediator, which once for ever he finished; his general sufferings are those which he endures in his mystical body, which is the church, as he is a member with the rest; and these are the sufferings Paul speaks of, and which Paul fills up.

But wherein is the conformity betwixt our sufferings and the sufferings of Christ? I answer, 1. Negatively. 2. Positively.

1. Negatively, our sufferings have no conformity with Christ in these two things; 1. Not in the office of Christ's sufferings, for his were meritorious and satisfactory, ours only ministerial and for edification. 2. Not in the weight and measure of Christ's sufferings, for his were bitter, heavy, and woful, such as would have pressed any other creature as low as hell, and have swallowed him up for ever; but ours are but in comparison light and tolerable; *There hath no temptation taken you, but such as is common to man, for God is faithful, who will not suffer you to be tempted above that you are able*, 1 Cor. x. 13.

2. Positively, our sufferings must have conformity with Christ. 1. In the cause of them, Christ's sufferings were instrumentally from Satan and wicked men; we must look to suffer by the enemies of Christ, if we have any share of Christ; the enemy continues still, *I will put enmity between thee and the woman, and between thy seed and her seed*, Gen. iii. 15. This was primarily meant between the devil and Christ, but if we conform to Christ, we must expect the very same condition. 2. In the manner of undergoing them, we must suffer with a proportion of that humility, and patience, and love, and meekness, and obedience, which Christ shewed in his very sufferings. 3. In respect of the issue of them, we must look upon Christ's issue, and expect it to be ours; *ought not Christ to have suffered these things, and so enter into glory?* Luke xxiv. 26.—*And if so be that we suffer with Christ, we shall be glorified together with Christ*, Rom. viii. 17.——*If we suffer with him, we shall also reign with him*, 2 Tim. ii. 12.

By reason of this conformity we have that communion and association with Christ in all these particulars: as, 1. We have Christ's strength to bear sufferings. 2. His victories to overcome sufferings. 3. His intercession to preserve us from falling away in sufferings. 4. His compassion to moderate and proportion our sufferings to the measure of strength which he hath given us. 5. His Spirit to draw in the same yoke with us, and to hold us under all sufferings that we sink not. 6. His graces to be more glorious by our sufferings, as a torch when it is shaken shines the brighter. 7. His crown to reward our sufferings, when we shall have tasted our measure of them, *For our light affliction, which is but for a moment, worketh for us a far more exceeding and eternal weight of glory*.

O my soul! study this conformity, and be content with thy portion; yea, comfort thyself in this condition of sufferings; Must we not drink of our Saviour's cup? What not of our Master's own cup? We read of Godfrey of Bolein, that he would not be crowned in Jerusalem with a crown of gold, where Christ was crowned with a crown of thorns, because he would not have such a great disproportion betwixt him and Christ. And we read of Origen, that when Alexander Severus, the emperor sent for him to Rome, that he might take his choice, whether he would ride thither on a mule or in a chariot, that he refused them both, saying, ' He was less than his master Christ, of whom he ' never read that he rode but once.' O the suffer-

ing

ing Christ endured! he was called a wine-bibber, a Samaritan, a devil; he was pursued, entrapped, snared, slain: and surely *they that will live godly in Christ Jesus must suffer persecution*, 2 Tim. iii. 12. Never wonder that thou art hated of men, or persecuted of men; why, I tell thee, if Christ himself was now amongst us, in the form and fashion of a servant, in that very condition that sometimes he was, and should convince men of their wickedness, as searchingly as sometimes he did, I verily think he would be the most hated man in all the world. It is plain enough what carnal men would do, by those very doings of the carnal Jews.

3. We must conform to Christ in his death, carrying in us a resemblance and representation of his death. But what death is this? I answer in a word, *A death unto sin* (so the apostle) *in that he died, he died unto sin;* — *likewise reckon ye yourselves to be dead indeed unto sin*, Rom. vi. 10, 11. There is a likeness betwixt Christ's death and our death in this respect, *We are planted together in the likeness of his death*, Rom. vi. 5. True mortification carries a similitude, a likeness, a resemblance of the death of Christ. As for instance.

* 1. Christ's death was a voluntary death. *I lay down my life, that I may take it again; no man taketh it from me, but I lay it down of myself; I have power to take it again*, John x. 17, 18. Not all men on earth, nor all devils in hell could have enforced Christ's death, if he had not pleased; his death was a voluntary death, a spontaneous act, so is our mortification; *The people shall be willing in the day of thy power*, Psal. cx. 3. many may leave their sins against their wills, but this is not true mortification, it bears not in it the likeness of Christ's death, for he died willingly: it may be thou hast a clamorous conscience, which continually dogs thee, and therefore thou leavest thy sin: thus Judas came in with his thirty pieces of silver, and cast them down in the temple at the high priest's feet, Matth. xxvii. 5. but no thanks to Judas, for they were too hot for him to hold, or it may be there is some penalty of the law, or some temporal judgment that hangs over thy head, like Damocles' sword; and therefore thou leavest thy sin: thus Ahab, for a time, acts the part of a penitent; but no thanks to Ahab, for the prophet had rung him such a peal for his sin, as made both his ears tingle, *In the place where dogs licked the blood of Naboth, shall dogs lick thy blood, even thine*, 1 Kings xxi. 19. Or it may be, there is in thee a fear of hell; in thy apprehension death is come, and is ready to carry thee before the dreadful tribunal of a terrible God; and therefore thou leavest thy sin: thus seamen, in a stress, part with their goods, not because they are out of love with them, but because they love their lives better; they see plainly, that either they must part with them, or perish with them. Now, in these cases, thy leaving off sin bears no similitude with the death of Christ, for his death was voluntary, and a true mortification is a voluntary action.

Quest. But may there not be some reluctancy in this work betwixt the flesh and the Spirit? And if so, is it then voluntary? I answer,——

Answ. Yes; such a reluctancy we find in the human nature of Christ concerning the cup, that it might *pass from him*, Matth. xxvi. 39. and yet his death was a true voluntary death. An action is said to be voluntary or involuntary, according to the superior faculties of the soul, and not according to the inferior; if the reasonable part be consenting, the action may by called voluntary, tho' there be some reluctancy in the sensitive appetite. Thus in the Christian, in whom there is nature and grace, flesh and Spirit, an unregenerate, and a regenerate part; if the superior and better part be willing (I mean advisedly and deliberately willing, with full consent of the inward man) though perhaps there may be some reluctancy in the flesh, in the unregenerate part, yet this is said to be a true voluntary act, *So then with the mind, I myself serve the law of God, but with my flesh the law of sin*, Rom. vii. 25. —— *I delight in the law of God after the inward man; but I see another law in my members, warring against the law of my mind*, Ver. 22, 23. Paul was dead to sin, according to the inward man, the regenerate part, tho' he found a reluctancy in his outward members; and therefore, his death to sin carried with it the resemblance of the death of Christ; it was a voluntary death.

2. Christ's death was a violent death; he died not naturally, but violently; *He was put to death*

---

* See Mr. Brinsley at large, *mystical implantation.*

in the flesh, 1 Pet. iii. 18. *He was brought as a lamb to the slaughter*, Isa. liii. 7. So is our mortification, it is voluntary in respect of us, but violent in respect of sin; and herein is the life (as I may say) of this death: oh! when a man lays violent hands on his sins; when he cuts them off, being yet in their flower, and strength, and power, and vigour; when he pulls up those weeds before they wither in themselves, this is true mortification: many have left their sins, who never mortified them; so the aged adulterer hath left his lust, because his body is dead: and hence it is, 'That late repentance in an aged sinner is 'seldom found true!' alas! he dies not to sin, but his sin dies to him; I will not say but God may call at the eleventh hour, though it be very seldom, but in that case, you had need to be jealous over yourselves with a godly jealousy; what, do you find some sins within you to be dead that were sometimes alive? O be inquisitive, impannel a jury, call a coroner's inquest upon your own souls, enquire how they came by their deaths, whether they died a violent or a natural death: search what wounds they have received, and whether they were deadly wounds, yea or no; enquire what weapon it was that slew them, whether the sword of the Spirit, that two edged sword the word of God; what purposes, what resolutions have been taken up and levelled against them? What prayers and tears have been spent upon them? If you find not these signs, you may give in your verdict, that they died not a violent, but a natural death. And here is a good caveat for others, *Remember now thy Creator in the days of thy youth, while the evil days come not, nor the years draw nigh, when thou shalt say, I have no pleasure in them*, Eccl. xii. 1. Oh! take heed of reprieving your lusts! let them not live till to-morrow; now bring them forth in the sight and presence of God; arraign, condemn, crucify, mortify them whilst they might yet live. Surely this is true mortification, when the body of sin dieth, as Christ died a violent death.

3. Christ's death was a lingering death; he hung divers hours upon the cross, *From the sixth hour to the ninth hour*, (saith Matthew), Matth. xxvii. 45. (i. e) from our twelve to three, before he gave up the ghost; so is our mortification a lingering death; sin is not put to death all at once, but languisheth by little and little. This is looked upon as one main difference betwixt justification and sanctification; the former is a perfect work, admitting of no degrees, but so is not the latter; though a believer is freed perfectly from the guilt of sin, yet not so from the power of it; sin dwelleth in us, though it hath not altogether a dominion over us, *It is no more I that do it, but sin that dwelleth in me*, Rom. vii. 17. like a rebellious tenant, it keeps possession in despight of the owner, till the house be pulled down over his head. True indeed, the body of sin in a regenerate soul hath received its death-wound, and in that respect it may be said to be dead, but it is not quite dead, still it stirreth and moveth, dying but by degrees; what the apostle saith of the renewing of the new man, we may say of the destroying of the old man, *The inward man is renewed day by day*, 2 Cor. iv. 16. and the old man is destroyed day by day: or as Paul said of himself, in respect of his afflictions, we may say of a Christian, in respect of his sins, *I die daily*, 1 Cor. xv. 31. There is not the most sanctified soul upon earth, but it hath some remainders of corruption left in it, which God, in his wise providence permits, for the trying, exercising, and humbling of our souls, and for the making his own rich grace, in renewing and multiplying pardons, so much the more glorious.

And here is a ground of consolation to a drooping and dejected soul; such a one cries out, 'Alas! I feel the stirring and vigorous actings of 'sin, and I am afraid my sin is not mortified, as 'Rebeccah said, when she felt the children struggling within her, *If it be so, why am I thus?* 'Gen. xxv 22. So if sin be mortified, (saith the 'soul) Why am I thus?——Trembling soul! let not this discourage; Jesus Christ was not dead so soon as he was fastened to the cross: but hast thou taken the same course with the body of sin, that the Jews did with the body of Christ; Hast thou arraigned it, accused it, condemned it, and fastened it to the cross? Hast thou arraigned it at the bar of God's judgment, accused it by way of humble and hearty confession, condemned it in passing the sentence of eternal condemnation upon thyself for it, and fastened it to the cross, in beginning the execution of it, in setting upon the mortification of it with a serious and unfeigned resolution to use all means for its mortifying

tifying and killing? Why then, be not disheartened, it may be thou feelest it stirring and struggling within thee, and so will a crucified man do, 'and yet in the eye of the law, and in the account of all men that see him, he is a dead man; surely so is the body of sin when it is thus crucified; though it still move and stir, yet upon a gospel account, and in God's estimation, it is no better than dead, and it shall certainly die; it shall decay, and languish, and die more and more; Is not the promise express? *He that hath begun the good work, he will perfect it to the day of Jesus Christ*, Phil. i. 6. Of this Paul was confident in behalf of his Philippians; and of this, let all true believers rest confident in respect of themselves. Thus far we see wherein we must conform to Christ, *viz.* In his graces, in his sufferings, and in his death.

For the *Second* quere, What is the cause of this conformity? I answer, The death of Christ is the cause of this conformity, and that a fourfold cause.——

1. It is a meritorious cause; Christ's death was of so great a price, that it deserved at God's hands our conformity to Christ, *Christ loved the church, and gave himself for it, that by his death he might sanctify it, and cleanse it:—And present it to himself a glorious church, not having spot or wrinkle, or any such thing, but that it should be holy, and without blemish*, Eph. v. 25, 26, 27.

2. It is an exemplary cause; *He suffered for us, leaving us an example that we should follow his steps*, 1 Pet. ii. 21. he died for us, leaving us an example that we should die to sin, as he died for sin; we may observe in many particulars (besides those I have named) a proportion, analogy, and likeness betwixt Christ's death and ours; Christ died as a servant, to note that sin should not rule or reign over us; Christ died as a curse, to note that we should look upon sin as a cursed thing; Christ was fast nailed on the cross, to note that we should put sin out of ease, yea, crucify the whole body of sin; Christ died not presently, yet there he hung till he died, to note that we should never give over subduing sin, while it hath any life or working in us.

3. It is an efficient cause; it works this conformity by a secret virtue issuing from it. Thus Christians are said to be *engraffed with Christ in the likeness of his death*, Rom. vi. 5. The word [*homoio-mati,*] is of a passive signification, importing not only a being like, but a being made like, and that by a power and virtue out of ourselves, so the apostle elsewhere interprets, *That I may know him,—and the fellowship of his sufferings, being made conformable unto this death,* Phil. iii. 10. not conforming myself, but being made conformable, by a power out of myself.

Quest. But how then is the power of mortification attributed to men? As, *Mortify therefore your members which are upon the earth,* Col. iii. 5.—— *And they that are Christ's have crucified the flesh,* Gal. v. 24.

Answ. I answer, There is a twofold mortification, the one habitual, the other practical; the former consists in a change of the heart, turning the bent and inclination of the heart from all manner of sin. Now, this is the only and immediate work of the spirit of grace, breathing and working where it will; the latter consists in the exercise or putting forth of that inward grace, in the acting of that principle, in resisting temptations, in suppressing inordinate lusts, in watching against sinful and inordinate acts: Now, this is the work of a regenerate person, himself co-operating with the Spirit of God, as a rational instrument with the principal agent; and therefore the apostle joins both together, *If ye, through the Spirit, do mortify the deeds of the body, ye shall live,* Rom. viii. 13.

4. It is an impelling or a moving cause, as all objects are; for objects have an attractive power. Achan saw the wedge of gold, and then coveted it; David saw Bethshebah, and then desired her. As the brazen serpent did heal those who were bitten by the fiery serpent, *Tanquam objectum fidei,* merely by being looked upon, so Christ crucified doth heal sin, beget grace, encourage to sufferings, by being looked upon with the eyes of faith. *Wherefore, seeing we are compassed about with so great a cloud of witnesses, let us lay aside every weight, and the sin which doth so easily beset us; and let us run with patience the race that is set before us; looking unto Jesus the author and finisher of our faith,* Heb. xii. 1, 2. The apostle was to encourage the Hebrews to hold on the well-begun profession of faith in Christ; and to that purpose, he sets before them two sights to keep them from fainting, 1. *A cloud of witnesses,* the saints in heaven; on which cloud, when he had stayed their eyes a while and made them

them fit for a clearer object, he scatters the cloud, and presents *the sun of righteousness*, Christ himself; and he wills them, [aphora], to turn their eyes from it to him, *Looking unto Jesus.* q. d. this sight is enough to make you run the race, and not to faint; why, Jesus is gone before you, and will ye not follow him; O look unto Jesus, and the very sight of him will draw you after him; Christ crucified hath an attractive power, *And I, if I be lifted up, will draw all men to me*, John xii. 32.—Thus of the causes of our conformity; we see how it is wrought.

3. For the last quere, what are the means of this conformity as on our part? I answer,

1. Go to the cross of Jesus Christ. It is not all our purposes, resolutions, promises, vows, covenants, endeavours, without this, that will effect our conformity to Christ in his sufferings and death; no, no, this conformity is a fruit and effect of the death of Christ; and therefore, whosoever would have this work wrought in him, let him first have recourse to Christ's cross; O! go we more immediately to the cross of Jesus.

2. Look up to him that hangs upon it; contemplate the death of Jesus Christ, consider seriously, and sadly his bitter, shameful, painful sufferings: much hath been said, only here draw it unto some epitome: as, 1. Consider who he was. 2. What he suffered. 3. Why he suffered. 4. For whom he suffered. 5. For what end he suffered. 6. With what mind he suffered: every one of these will make some discoveries, either of his graces, or of his gracious actings in our behalf; and who can tell how far this very look may work on us to change us, and transform us into the very image of Jesus Christ?

3. Let us humbly bewail our defects, exorbitancy, irregularity, and inconformity either to the graces, sufferings, or death of Christ. As thus, ' Lo here the profound humility, wonderful pati-
' ence, fervent love, abundant mercy, admirable
' meekness, constant obedience of Jesus Christ!
' lo here the tortures, torments, agonies, conflicts,
' extreme sufferings of Christ for the spiritual, im-
' mortal good of the precious souls of his redeem-
' ed ones! lo here the death of Christ, see how
' he bowed the head, and gave up the ghost! why,
' these are the particulars to which I should con-
' form; but, oh alas! what a wide, vast, utter
' difference, distance, disproportion is there be-
' twixt me and them? Christ in his sufferings shin-
' ed with graces, his graces appeared in his suffer-
' ings like so many stars in a bright winter's night;
' but how dim are the faint weak graces in my soul?
' Christ, in his sufferings, endured much for me,
' I know not how much, by thine unknown sor-
' rows and sufferings felt by thee, but not distinct-
' ly known to us (said the ancient fathers of the
' Greek church in their liturgy) have mercy upon
' us, and save us; his sorrows and sufferings were
' so great, that some think it dangerous to define
' them; but how poor? How little are my suffer-
' ings for Jesus Christ? I have not yet resisted unto
' blood; and if I had, What were this in com-
' parison of his extreme sufferings? Christ in his
' sufferings died, his passive obedience was unto
' death, even to the death of the cross! he hung
' on the cross till he bowed his head, and gave
' up the ghost, *He died unto sin once*, Rom. vi.
' 10. But alas! how do I live in that for which
' he died? To this day my sin hath not given up
' the ghost; to this day the death of Christ is not
' the death of my sin; O! my sin is not yet cru-
' cified, the heart blood of my sin is not yet let
' out; Oh! wo is me, how unanswerable am I to
' Christ in all these respects?'

4. Let us quicken, provoke, and rouse up our souls to this conformity: let us set before them exciting arguments. *ex gr.* The greatest glory that a Christian can attain to in this world, is, to have a resemblance and likeness to Jesus Christ. Again, the more like we are to Christ, the more we are in the love of God, and the better he is pleased with us; it was his voice concerning his Son, *This is my beloved Son, in whom I am well pleased*; and for his sake, if we are but like him, he is also well pleased with us. Again, a likeness or resemblance of Christ is that which keeps Christ alive in the world: as we say of a child that is like his father, ' This man cannot die so long as his
' son is alive:' so we may say of Christians who resemble Christ, that so long as they are in the world Christ cannot die; he lives in them, and he is no otherwise alive in this nether world, than in the hearts of gracious Christians, that carry the picture and resemblance of him. Again, a likeness to Christ in his death will cause a likeness to Christ in his glory, *If we have been planted toge-*
ther

ther in the likeness of his death, we shall be also in the likeness of his resurrection, Rom. vi. 5. As it is betwixt the graft and the stock, the graft seeming dead with the stock in the winter, it revives with it in the spring; after the winter's death it partakes of the spring's resurrection; so it is betwixt Christ and us; if with Christ we die to sin, we shall with Christ be raised to glory; being conformed to him in his death, we shall be also in his resurrection. Thus let us quicken and provoke our souls to this conformity.

5. Let us pray to God, that he will make us conformable to Jesus Christ. Is it grace we want? Let us beg of him, that of that fulness that is in Christ, we may, in our measure, receive grace for grace. Is it patience, or joy in sufferings that we want? Let us beg of him, that as he hath promised, he will send us the comforter, that so we may follow Christ cheerfully from his cross to his crown, from earth to heaven. Is it mortification our souls pant after? This indeed makes us most like to Christ in his sufferings and death; why then pray we for this mortification?——

But how should we pray? I answer, 1. Let us plainly acknowledge, and heartily bemoan ourselves in God's bosom for our sins, our abominable sins. 2. Let us confess our weakness, feebleness, and inability in ourselves to subdue our sins, *We have no might*, (may we say) *against this great company that come against us; neither know we what to do, but our eyes are upon thee*, 2 Chron. xx. 12. 3. Let us put up our request, begging help from heaven; let us cry to God that virtue may come out of Christ's death to mortify our lusts, to heal our natures, to staunch our bloody issues; and that the Spirit may come in to help us in these works, *For by the Spirit do we mortify the deeds of the body*, Rom viii. 13. 4. Let us press God with the merits of Christ, and with his promises through Christ, for he hath said, *Sin shall not have dominion over us, for we are not under the law, but under grace*, Rom. vi. 14. and Paul experienced it. *The law of the Spirit of life in Christ, hath freed me from the law of sin and death*, Rom. viii. 2. 5. Let us praise God, and thank God for the help already received, if we find that we have gotten some power against sin, that we have gotten more ability to oppose the lusts of the flesh, that we are seldom overtaken with any breaking forth of it, that we have been able to withstand some notable temptations to it, that the force of it in us is in any measure abated, that indeed and in truth virtue is gone out of the death of Christ; O then return we praises to God, let us triumph in God, let us lead our captivity captive, and sing new songs of praises unto God, and even ride in triumph over our corruptions, boasting ourselves in God, and setting up our banners in the name of the most High, and offering up humble and hearty thanks to our Father for the death of Christ, and for the merit, virtue, and efficacy of it derived unto us, and bestowed upon us!

5. Let us frequently return to our looking up unto Jesus Christ, to our believing in Christ as he was lifted. How we are to manage our faith, to draw down the virtue of Christ's death into our souls, I have discovered before; and let us now be in the practice of those rules; certainly there is a conveyance of an healing, strengthening, quickning virtue, flowing into the soul in the time of its viewing, eying, contemplating, reflecting upon Christ crucified, Christ lifted up; and this comes from the secret presence of God, blessing this our looking upon Christ, as the ordinance by which he hath appointed to make an effectual impression upon the heart. It is not for us curiously to enquire how this should be; *principles* (we say) *are not to be proved*, save only God hath said it, and experience hath found it out, that when faith is occasioned to act on any suitable sacred object, God, by his Spirit, doth not fail to answer; in such a case he fills the soul with comfort, blessing, virtue; he returns upon the soul, (by, from and through the actings of faith) whatsoever by it is looked for. Indeed none knoweth this but he that feels it, and none feels this that knoweth how to express it; as there is somewhat in the fire, (heat, warmth, and light) which no painter can express; and as there is somewhat in the face, (heat, warmth, and life) which no limner can set forth, so there is somewhat flowing into the soul, while it is acting faith on the death of Christ, which for the rise, or manner of its working, is beyond what tongue can speak, or pen can write, or pencil can delineate. Come then, if we would have grace, endure afflictions, die to sin, grow in our mortification, let us again, and again return to our duty

ty of looking unto Jesus, or believing in Jesus as he was lifted up.

And yet, when all is done, let us not think that sin will die or cease in us altogether, for that is an higher perfection than this life will bear; only in the use of the means, and through God's blessing we may expect thus far that sin shall not reign, it shall not wear a crown, it shall not sit in the throne, it shall hold no parliament, it shall give no laws within us; we shall not serve it, but we shall die to the dominion of it by virtue of this death of Jesus Christ. And this, grant he who died for us. Amen, Amen.

Thus far we have looked on Jesus as our Jesus, in his sufferings and death. Our next work is to look on Jesus carrying on the great work of our salvation during the time of his resurrection, and abode upon earth, until his ascension, or taking up to heaven.

John xx. 1. to 19. *The first day of the week cometh Mary Magdalene early, when it was yet dark, unto the sepulchre, and seeth the stone taken away from the sepulchre,* &c.

John xx. 19, 20. *The same day at evening, being the first day of the week, when the doors were shut where the disciples were assembled, for fear of the Jews, came Jesus, and stood in the midst, and saith unto them, Peace be unto you; and when he had so said, he shewed unto them his hands, and his side.*

John xx. 26, 27, 28. *And after eight days again, his disciples were within, and Thomas with them, then came Jesus, the doors being shut, and stood in the midst, and said, Peace be unto you; then saith he to Thomas, reach hither thy finger, and behold my hands, and reach hither thy hand, and thrust it into my side, and be not faithless, but believing; and Thomas answered and said unto him, My Lord, and my God.*

John xxi. 1. to 15. *After these things, Jesus shewed himself again to his disciples, at the sea of Tiberias; and on this wise shewed he himself,* &c.

Heb. xii. 2. Matth. xxvii. 6. 2 Tim. ii. 7, 8. *Looking unto Jesus the beginner and finisher of our faith.* — *He is not here, for he is risen.* — *Come, see the place where the Lord lay.* — *Consider what I say, and the Lord give thee understanding in all things; remember that Jesus Christ, of the seed of David, was raised from the dead according to my gospel.*

Rev. i. 17, 18. *And when I saw him, I fell at his feet as dead, and he laid his right hand upon me, saying unto me, Fear not, I am the first and the last; I am he that liveth, and was dead, and behold I am alive for evermore. Amen.*

LOOKING

LOOKING UNTO JESUS.

In His RESURRECTION.

THE FOURTH BOOK, PART FOURTH.

CHAP. I. SECT. I.

Matth. xxviii. 6. *He is risen.——Come, see the place where the Lord lay.*

2 Tim. ii. 8. *Remember that Jesus Christ, of the seed of David, was raised from the dead.*

Of the Time of Christ's Resurrection.

THE sun that went down in a ruddy cloud, is risen again with glorious beams of light. In this piece, as in the former, we shall first lay down the object, and then give directions how to look upon it.

The object is Jesus carrying on the work of man's salvation in his resurrection; and during the time of his abode upon earth after his resurrection. Now, in all the transactions of this time, I shall only take notice of these two things. 1. Of his resurrection. 2. Of his apparitions; for, first, he rose, and, secondly, he shews himself that he was risen; in the first is the position, in the second is the proof.

1. For the position, the scripture tells us, That he rose again the third day. In this point, I shall observe these particulars. 1. When he arose. 2. Why he arose. 3. How he arose.

1. When he arose; it was the third day after his crucifying, 'As Jonas was three days and three 'nights together in the whale's belly, so shall the 'Son of man be three days and three nights in the 'heart of the earth,' Mat. xii. 40. This was the time he had appointed, and this was the time appropriated to Christ, and marked out for him in the kalendar of the prophets: of all those whom God raised from death to life, there is not one that was raised on the third day but Jesus Christ; some rose afore, and some rose after; the son of the Shunamite, the son of the widow of Serephtah, the daughter of Jairus, he of Nain, and some others rose afore; Lazarus, and the saints that rose again from the dust when Christ rose, stayed longer in the grave; but Christ takes the day, which discovers him to be the Messiah; 'Thus it 'is written, and thus it behoved Christ to suffer, 'and to rise from the dead the third day,' Luke xxiv. 46. Had he rose sooner, a doubt might have been of his dying, and had he lain longer, a doubt might have been of his rising; he would rise no sooner, because in some diseases, as in the apoplexy, or such like, examples are given of such, as seeming to be dead, have indeed revived; and he would lie no longer in his grave, because, in all dead carcases, (and especially in a wounded body) putrefaction and corruption begins the third day; this may be gathered by the story of Lazarus in the gospel, where Jesus commanding the stone to be rolled from his grave, Martha, his sister, answered, 'Lord, by this time he stinketh, for he hath been 'dead four days,' John xi. 39. Now the body of Christ (as it was prophesied) must not corrupt, *For thou wilt not leave my soul in hell, neither wilt thou suffer thy holy one to see corruption*, Psal. xvi. 10. Mark this text, all men shall rise again, but their bodies must first see corruption; only the

Messiah

Messiah was to rise again before he saw corruption, and therefore he would not delay his resurrection after the third day. Some think this, and that of Hosea, *After two days he will revive us, and in the third day he will raise us up,* Hosea vi. 2. to be the main texts to which Christ refers when he said, *Thus it is written,* Luke xxiv. 46. And to which the apostle refers, when he said, That *Christ rose again the third day according to the scriptures,* 1 Cor. xv. 4.

I dare not be too curious in giving reasons for this set time, and the rather because Christ is a free worker of his own affairs; he doth what he pleaseth, and when he pleaseth; times and actions are in his own power, and he needs not to give us any account of them; and yet, so far as scripture discovers, we may go along, and amongst many others, I shall lay down these following reasons,——

1. Because the types had so prefigured; we see it in Isaac, Jonah and Hezekiah, a patriarch, a prophet, and a king. 1 For Isaac; from the time that God commanded Isaac to be offered for a burnt-offering, Isaac was a dead man, but the third day he was released from death: this the text tells us expresly, that it was the third day when Abraham came to mount Moriah, and had his Son, as it were restored to him again, Gen. xxii. 4. and Paul discovers that this was *in a figure,* Heb. xi. 19. 2. For Jonah; from the time that Jonah was cast into the sea, and swallowed up of the fish, Jonah was in account as a dead man; but the third day the Lord spake unto the fish, *and it vomited up Jonah upon the dry land,* Jonah ii. 10. And that this was a figure of Christ, Christ himself discovers, *For as Jonas was three days and three nights in the whale's belly, so shall the son of man be three days and three nights in the heart of the earth,* Mat. xii. 40. 3. Hezekiah, from the time that Isaiah said unto him, *Set thine house in order, for thou shalt die, and not live,* 2 Kings xx. 1. Hezekiah was in account as a dead man, his bed was to him as a grave, but on the third day he was now miraculously raised up again; and as the prophet said, *On the third day thou shalt go up to the house of the Lord,* verse 5. Surely this was a figure of Christ, and these types prefiguring Christ, are as one reason.

2. Because the prophets and himself had so foretold; for the prophets we have cited, Psal. xvi. 10. Hosea vi. 2. and for himself, he told them very expresly, that *he must suffer many things of the elders, and chief priests, and scribes, and be raised again the third day,* Matth. xvi. 21. Yea, said he, 'The Son of man shall be betrayed into the hands 'of men, and they shall kill him, and the third day 'he shall be raised again,' Mat. xvii. 22, 23. and after this he tells them again, That 'the Son of 'man should be betrayed,—and crucified, and the 'third day he should be raised again.' Mat. xx. 18, 19. so often had he prophesied thus, that the chief priests and Pharisees came to Pilate, after his death, saying, 'Sir, we remember that this deceiver said, 'while he was yet alive, after three days I will rise 'again, command therefore, that the sepulchre be 'made sure until the third day,' Mat. xxvii. 62, 63, 64. And no question his disciples remembered these sayings, for so the two disciples travelling towards Emmaus, after they had said many things concerning him, and that they trusted it had been he which should have redeemed Israel, they added this as a most special observation above all the rest, That 'to-day is the third day since these things were done,' Luke xxiv. 21. Why, all these signify, that his rising on the third day was the accomplishment of prophesies, and a certain evidence that he was the Messiah indeed.

3. Because that time was most suitable for comforting his friends, for confounding his enemies, for clearing the truth both of his humanity and divinity, he would stay no longer, lest his disciples might have been swallowed up with grief; and he would come no sooner, lest his enemies should have urged that he had not died; the watchmen kept the sepulchre till this very time, but then the angels appearing, and the earth trembling, they became as dead men; and as soon as they could, they run away; and with their tidings confounded all Christ's enemies. And withal, as Christ consisted both of a divine and human nature, so in respect of his humanity, he must die; and to shew his death, it was requisite that he should rise no sooner than the third day; and, in respect of his divinity, it was impossible that he should be held of death any longer than three days, for as he must not see corruption, so 'God raised him 'up, having loosed the pains of death, because 'it was not possible that he should be holden of 'it,' Acts ii. 24.

SECT.

SECT. II.

Of the reasons of Christ's resurrection.

2. WHY he rose, We have these reasons,— 1. That he might powerfully convince or confound his adversaries: they that crucified him were mightily afraid of his resurrection, they could tell Pilate, 'Sir, we remember, this deceiver 'said, while he was yet alive, after three days I 'will rise again,' Mat. xxvii. 63, 64. and therefore they desire him of all loves, ' to command the 'sepulchre to be made sure until the third day;' if ever he rise again whom they have killed, then they know they were all ashamed, then 'the last 'error (as they said) would be worse than the first:' all the world would look on them as a cursed generation, to kill the Messiah, to crucify such a one, as after his death and burial should rise again: now then, that he might either convince them, or confound them, notwithstanding their care, their watch, their seal, their making all sure as possibly they could; at the very same time, he had told them before he broke open the gates of death, and made the gates of brass to flee asunder.

2. That he might confirm the faith of all his followers, *If Christ be not risen, your faith is vain,* (saith the apostle) 1 Cor. xv. 14. Christ's resurrection both confirms our faith, as to his person and to his office; for his person, this speaks him to be *the eternal Son of God, by the resurrection from the dead,* Rom. i. 4. and for his office, this speaks him to be the promised Messiah, the great prophet, the chief high priest, the king and Saviour of his church. when the Jews saw Christ purging the temple, and Messiah like, reforming what he saw amiss in the house of God; *What sign* (say they) *shewest thou unto us, seeing that thou dost these things? and he said unto them, Destroy this temple, and in three days I will raise it up.——When therefore he was risen from the dead, his disciples remembered that he had said this unto them, and they believed the scripture, and the word which Jesus had said,* John ii. 18, 19, 22. as the resurrection of Christ argues his Mediatorship, so it confirms their faith, as it is said, *They believed the scriptures, and they believed Jesus Christ.* And thus John writing of his resurrection, tells us, *These things are written that ye might believe, and that believing,* &c. John xx. 31.

3. That it might clearly appear, that he had fully satisfied the justice of God for sin; so it was, that God laid the forfeiture of the bond on Christ, he arrested him, brought him to the goal the grave, and there he was till the debt was paid to the utmost farthing: and then, that it might clearly appear that the bond was cancelled, the prisoner discharged, God's justice satisfied, he rose again from the dead. Some make a question when this bond was cancelled; and they say, as the debt was paid, so the bond was cancelled 'ere he stirred off the cross (only by the cross, I suppose they mean the utmost degree of Christ's humiliation, viz. his being held in captivity and bondage under death) and so *the hand-writing of the law that was against us,* was there delivered him; and there he *blotted it out, cancelled it, took it out of the way, nailing it to his cross.* Col. ii. 14. Others think, that as to the full discharge of a debt, and freeing the debitor, two things are requisite: first, the payment of the debt. Secondly, The tearing or cancelling of the bond; so the payment was wrought by Christ's death, and the cancelling of the bond was at his resurrection; I shall not disprove either of these, I am sure this is without all controversy, that Christ rose, that it might fully appear, that now the bond was cancelled, and God's justice satisfied.

4. That he might overcome and conquer sin, death, and devil; and hence the apostle cries, *victory,* upon the occasion of Christ's resurrection, *O death, where is thy sting? O grave, where is thy victory?* 1 Cor. xv. 55. Now was the day that he broke the prison, and carried the keys of death and hell at his own girdle: now was the day that he spoiled principalities and powers, that he trod on the serpent's head, and all to bruise it; that he came upon him, took from him his armour wherein he trusted, and divided his spoils: now was the day that the Jew lost his rage, and death his sting, and the grave his corruption, and hell his purchase; now was the day of his victory over all his enemies; now was the day that the Phœnix sprung up out of its own ashes, that Jonas came safe out of the belly of the whale, that the tabernacle of David that was fallen was raised again, that the Sun of righteousness, covered with a cloud, appeared and shone with greater lustre than before;

fore; that Sampson took the gates of the city, and carried them away: he rose even upon that account.

5. That he might *become the first-fruits of them that slept*, 1 Cor. xv. 20. Christ is called the first-fruits in a double respect. 1. In respect of the day whereon he rose; Paul was an excellent critic, the very feast carried him to the word; as the day of his passion was the day of the passover, and the apostle thence could say, *Christ is our passover*, 1 Cor. xv. 7. so the day of Christ's rising was the day of the first-fruits; and the apostle thence could say, *Christ is our first-fruits*, 1 Cor. xv. 20. Concerning this feast of the first-fruits we read, Levit. xxii. 10, 11. It was their first harvest of their basest grain barely, but the full harvest of their best grain of wheat, was not till Pentecost. Now, upon this day, the morrow after the Sabbath, the beginning of their first harvest, when the sheaf of their first-fruits was brought unto the priest, and waved before the Lord, Christ arose from the dead; and, in this respect, Paul calls him *the first-fruits of them that slept*, 1 Cor. xv. 20. of all the saints. He rose first as on this day, for the full harvest is not till doomsday, the general resurrection-day. 2. He is called the first-fruits, in respect of them whom he thereby sanctified; for as an handful of the first-fruits sanctified the whole field of corn that was growing, so Jesus Christ, the first-fruits of the dead, sanctifies all those who are lying in the grave to rise again by his power, even when they are in the dust of death, *If Christ be not risen*, (saith the apostle) *ye are yet in your sins.* —— *But now is Christ risen from the dead, and become the first-fruits of them that slept*, 1 Cor. xv. 17, 20.

6. That being formerly abased as a servant, and crucified as a sinner, he might thus be declared to be the Son of God, and exalted to be a prince and Saviour of men; and so his name might be glorified of all the world *He was made of the seed of David, according to the flesh, and declared to be the Son of God with power, according to the Spirit of holiness, by the resurrection from the dead*, Rom. i. 3, 4. It was of necessary consequence, that he that was so humbled, must be thus exalted; *Therefore will I divide him a portion with the great, and he shall divide the spoil with the strong; because he hath poured out his soul unto death*, Isa. liii. 12. agreeable to which is that of Christ, *Thus it is written, and thus it behoved Christ to suffer, and to rise from the dead the third day*, Luke xxiv. 46. When Peter was preaching Christ to the high priest and council, that condemned him to death, he told them, That *the God of our fathers hath raised up Jesus whom ye slew and hanged on a tree; him hath God exalted with his right hand to be a prince and a Saviour*, Acts v. 30, 31. and suitable to this is that of Paul, *he humbled himself, and became obedient to the death, even to the death of the cross. Wherefore God also hath highly exalted him, and given him a name which is above every name*, Phil. ii. 8, 9. It was for his own glory, and his Father's glory that he should rise again from the dead, *God raised him up from the dead, and gave him glory*, 1 Pet. i 21. and he was therefore exalted, *That every tongue should confess that Jesus Christ is Lord, to the glory of God the Father*, Phil. ii. 11. Of all the reasons of Christ's resurrection we must look upon this as the main, for as he hath made all things for himself, so he hath done all things for his own glory, *Christ was raised up from the dead* (saith the apostle) *by the glory of the Father*, Rom. vi 4. By the glory, or to the glory, or for the glory of himself, and of his Father.

SECT. III.
Of the manner of Christ's resurrection.

3. HOW he rose; for the manner of his resurrection we may consider in it these particulars.——

1. That Christ rose again as a common person; he stood in our stead, and therefore when he rose from death, we and all the church of Christ rose together with him and in him. We have formerly observed, that Christ took upon him the person of no man, he took only the nature of man into the union of the second person, that so he might die and rise again, not as a particular, but a common person, that he might be as a representative in our room and stead, that he might be as a spiritual head, and as the second Adam, who could infuse life into all his members. In this respect the apostle makes comparison betwixt Adam and Christ; now Adam, we know, was reckoned, before his fall, as a common public person, not standing singly or alone for himself, but as representing all mankind to come of him; so Jesus Christ is reckoned to us, both before his death, and in his death, and after his death,

death, as a common public person, not living, dying, or rising again, singly, or alone for himself, but as representing all the believers in the world; and hence it is, that Adam is called *the first man*, and Jesus Christ is called *the second man*, 1 Cor. xv. 47. as if there never had been, nor ever should be any more men in the world, save only these two; And why? But because these two between them, had all the rest of the sons of men hanging at their girdles: Adam had all the sons of men born in this world, called *earthly men*, included in him; and Christ had all his elect, whose names are written in heaven, and therefore called *heavenly men*, included in him; so that now whatsoever Christ did, it is reckoned by God, as it done by us, and for us. When Christ arose, he arose as our head, and as a common person, and in God's account we arose with him, and in him. As among all the sheaves in the field, there was some one sheaf, that in the name and room of all the rest, was lift up, and waved before the Lord; so when all were dead, Christ as the first-fruits, rose again from the dead, and by this act of his resurrection, all the elect from the beginning of the world to the end, are risen with him, and in him, *He is the first-fruits of them that slept*, 1 Cor. xv. 20. though the saints are asleep, yet are they virtually risen already with Christ, because he is their first-fruits. Let this ever be remembered, that Christ rose again as the first-fruits, as the second man, as an head, as a common person.

2. That Christ rose again by his own power: this he meant when he said, *Destroy this temple, and in three days I will raise it up*, John ii. 19. He saith not, destroy you, and some other shall raise it up; no, no, but I, even I myself will do it, yea, and I will do it by my own proper power and virtue: here is a plain argument of the divine nature of Christ, for none ever did, ever could do that, but God himself: some were raised before Christ was incarnate, but not any by himself, or by his own proper power; only a power was imparted to some prophet by God, for that time and turn, and so they were raised; but Christ rose again, not by a power imparted to some, but by his own power. The widow's son of Serephtah was raised by Elias, and the Shunamite's son was raised by Elisha, both these were raised by others, and those others that raised them, did it not by their own power, but by a power given them from above; and therefore, though in their lifetime they raised others, yet being dead they could not raise themselves; but Jesus Christ did not only in his lifetime raise others, but also being dead, and laid in his grave, and pressed with stones, and watched by soldiers, and sought to be detained by all the powers of darkness; yet he as a conqueror, by his own power, raised himself to life; he caused all things, by the strength of his own arm, to give way unto himself, *I have power to lay down my life, and I have power to take it up again*, Joh. x. 18. an equal power to take it up as to lay it down.

But against this it may be objected, *The God of our fathers raised up Jesus*, Acts v. 30 — *Whom God hath raised up, having loosed the pains of death*, Acts ii. 24. In many places, the resurrection of Christ is ascribed to his Father; how then is he said to raise up himself by his own power?

I answer, it is true that the Father raised him, and yet this contradicts not, but that he raised up himself, *Whatsoever the Father doth, I do*, saith Christ, John v. 19. Christ's resurrection is the indivisible work of the blessed trinity; it is a work common to all the three persons, there is but one power of the Father, and of the Son; so that of both it is truly verified, the Father raised him, and the Son raised himself.

3. That Christ rose again with an earthquake; *And behold there was a great earthquake, for the angel of the Lord descended from heaven*, Matt. xxviii. 2. The earth shook at his death, and now it trembles again at his resurrection; plainly speaking, that it could neither endure his suffering, nor hinder his rising. As a lion with a roar is said to make the bed wherein he lies, to tremble; so this *lion of the tribe of Judah* was able with his voice, or sight, to make his bed (the earth wherein he lay) to tremble; no sooner he shakes himself, but he shakes the earth; at his first motion the earth moves, and now was fulfilled that prophesy, *Tremble thou earth at the presence of the Lord, at the presence of the God of Jacob*, Psal. cxiv. 7. It is not for us curiously to enquire into the cause of this earthquake: certainly the cause was above nature's reach; it was not any hollow-wind got into the bowels of the earth, but either it was Christ's rising, or the angels descending; the earth either danced for joy that Christ was risen, or it
trembled

trembled for fear that men would not believe his resurrection. The evangelist seems to lay it on the angel, *For the angel of the Lord descended from heaven:* sure the power of angels is very great, they can move all corporeal things almost in an instant, they can stir up tempests, they can shake the earth, move the waters, only all their power is subjected to God's will, *Bless the Lord all ye angels that excel in strength, that do his will,* Psal. ciii. 20. It was the will of God, that now an angel should take hold on the pillars of the earth, and make it shake; no wonder if *for fear of him the keepers shake, and become as dead men,* Matth. xxviii. 4. And, if one angel be able to shake the earth, and to shake the keepers, those armed soldiers that were set to watch the tomb; what then will Christ himself do, when he shall come to judgment the second time, with many thousand thousands of angels? Oh! how terrible and fearful will his coming be? As at Christ's resurrection, so at the last resurrection there will be *earthquakes in divers places,* Matth. xxiv. 7. Christ hath shewed, and he will shew himself to be the absolute Lord of heaven and earth: see how the earth trembling under his feet, doth (as it were) pay him homage: *And behold there was a great earthquake.*

4. That Christ rose again, angels ministering to him; *An angel came and rolled back the stone from the door, and sat upon it,* Matth. xxviii 2. Christ's power was not included in the grave, or on the earth, but extended to heaven, and to the hosts therein; however the chief priests and Pharisees conspired together to close him in the earth, they sealed the stone, and set a watch, they made all as sure as possibly they could; yet the angels of heaven are ready to wait on him as their sovereign Lord *An angel descended to roll away the stone;* not that Christ was unable to do it himself, he shook the earth: and could he not lift up a stone? O yes! but this would manifest his power, by declaring his power over the mighty angels; he needed but to say unto his angel, *do this, and he doth it.* I find some difference amongst authors, why an angel should roll away the stone; some think it was only for the womens sake, that they might go into the sepulchre; and take a view of the empty tomb, and so be satisfied that Christ was not there, but risen, as they said, *Come see the place where the Lord lay,* Matth. xxviii 6.

Others think it was to do their office of duty and service to Christ Jesus, to make way for his body to pass out of the grave without any penetration of other bodies; for my part, I adhere to these, though we need not to exclude the former, for the stone might be removed, both that Christ might shine forth, and that the women might be convinced that he was risen again. But as for the opinion of them who think the stone was not removed till after the resurrection; and that the body of Christ went through the grave-stone when he rose again, it is without all warrant; the very order of nature will not permit that one body should pass through another, without corruption or alteration of either; we say two bodies cannot be together, and at once, in one proper place; no more than one body can be together, and at once, in an hundred, or a thousand places; now that angelical argument is full for this, *He is not here, for he is risen,* Matth. xxviii. 6. He is not in the grave, for he is risen, out of the grave; he could not be in the grave, and out of the grave at one and the same time. But I mean not to dwell on controversial points.

5 That Christ rose again accompanied with others; *And the graves were opened, and many bodies of saints which slept, arose, and came out of the graves after his resurrection, and went into the holy city, and appeared unto many,* Mat. xxvii. 52, 53. It may be the graves were opened when Christ was laid down in his grave, yet the spirits came not into the dead bodies till Christ's resurrection; the text is plain, that they came not out of their graves till Christ was raised, *Christ is the beginning,* (saith the apostle) Col. i. 18. the first-born from the dead; how the first-born? I answer, both in time and efficacy. 1. In time, he rose to eternal life the first of all men. This was the sum of Paul's preaching, that Christ should suffer, *and that he should be the first that should rise from the dead,* Acts xxvi. 2, 3. It is true indeed, that Lazarus, and sundry others rose before Christ, but they rose to live a mortal life, and to die again; Christ was the first of all that rose to eternal life; never any in the world rose before Christ in this manner. 2. In respect of efficacy, Christ rose first, that by his power all the rest might rise, there is in Christ's resurrection a reviving and a quickening virtue; and herein is a main difference

betwixt

betwixt the resurrection of Christ, and the resurrection of any other man: the resurrection of Abraham avails nothing to the resurrection of Isaac, or of Jacob, but the resurrection of Christ avails to the resurrection of all that have believed, or that shall believe in him: Is not Christ called *a quickning Spirit?* 1 Cor. xv. 45. How then should he but quicken all his members? When a man is cast into the sea, and all his body is under water, there is nothing to be looked for but present death; but if he carry his head above the water, there is good hope then of a recovery; now Christ is the head unto his church, and therefore he being raised, all his members must follow in their time: no sooner did Christ arise, but many of the bodies of the saints arose, not all that were dead, but only some, to shew the resurrection of all to come; the time for the whole church's rising being not yet till the great resurrection-day. It is a question, What became of those bodies which now arose? Some think they died again; but it is more probable, that seeing they rose to manifest the quickning virtue of Christ's resurrection, that they were also glorified with Christ; and as they rose with Christ arising, so they ascended up into heaven with Christ ascending.

6. That Christ rose again with a true, perfect, incorruptible, powerful, spiritual, agile, and glorious body.

1. He had a true body, consisting of flesh, and blood, and bone; so he told his disciples, when they supposed him a spirit, *Handle me, and see,* (said he) *for a spirit hath not flesh and bones, as ye see me have,* Luke xxiv. 39. I know his body after his resurrection was comparatively a spiritual body; yet for all that, he never laid aside the essential properties of a true body, as length, and breadth, and visibility, and locality, and the like; he still keepeth these, because they serve to the being of a true body.

2. He had a perfect body; however, he was cut, and bored, and mangled before his death, yet after his resurrection all was perfect: Eusebius tells of one of the children of the Machabees that were put to death for the profession of the truth; and when they cut off his members, says he, 'I have received these from heaven, and now do I give them unto the God of heaven, and I hope I shall have them again.' Not a member of Christ was wanting, not a bone out of joint, but all was perfect.

3. He had an incorruptible, immortal body; *To this end* (saith the apostle) *Christ both died, and rose, and revived,* Rom. xiv. 9. And why revived? But to shew that he rose, never to die again. The apostle is yet more express, *Christ being raised from the dead, dieth no more: death hath no more dominion over him,* Rom. vi. 9. Consonant hereunto is that of Christ, *I am he that liveth, and was dead, and behold, I am alive for evermore,* Amen. Rev. i. 18. And herein the body of Lazarus and the rest, whom Christ raised, differed from his, for after they were raised they died again, but Christ died no more.

4. He had a powerful body: Luther could say of the glorified saints, that they had a power so great, as to toss the greatest mountains in the world like a ball; and * Anselm hath an expression not so much unlike, 'That they have such 'a power, as they are able to shake the whole ' earth at their pleasure.' How much more could Christ cause that great earthquake at the rising of his body? O it was powerful!

5. He had a spiritual body; it needed not meat, drink, and refreshings, as it did before; it is true, that the disciples *gave him a piece of a broiled fish, and of an honey-comb, and he took it, and did eat before them,* Luke xxiv. 42, 43. but this he did only to confirm their faith, that he appeared solidly, and not imaginary; he eat out of power, and not out of necessity, even as the sun sucks up the water out of power, but the earth out of want: he eat not as standing in need of food, but to shew the truth of his being risen again; as the saints in heaven never eat, nor drink, nor sleep, nor have magistrates, nor ministers, but the Spirit of God is all in all to them; so it was with Christ after his resurrection, he was full of the Spirit; he was enlivened immediately by the Spirit of God, which flowed into him, and that supplied the absence of all other things.

6. He had an agile body; it was in his pleasure to move as well upwards as downwards, as it may appear by the ascension of his body into heaven, which was not caused by constraint, or by any violent motion, but by a property agreeing to all bo-

* Ansel Lib. *de simul* Cap. 52.

dies

dies glorified; * Augustine hath an expression concerning the glorified saints, 'That they shall move to any place they will, and as soon as they will,' shall move up and down like a thought; how much more may it be said of the body of Christ.

7. He had a glorious body: this appeared in his transfiguration, 'when his face did shine as the sun, and his raiment was white as light,' Mat. xvii. 2. but especially after his resurrection and ascension, when *his head and his hairs were white like wool, as white as snow, and his eyes were as a flame of fire, and his feet like unto fine brass, as if they burned in a furnace*, Rev. i. 14, 15. The glorified bodies of saints which *are fashioned like unto his glorious body*, Phil. iii. 21. are said to shine like stars, Dan. xii. 3. or like *the sun itself*, Matth. xiii. 43. O then! how glorious is *the Sun of righteousness*, from whence all those suns and stars do borrow their light? It is true, that from his resurrection until his ascension, his body appeared not thus glorious to them that saw it; but whether this glory was delayed, and he was not possessed of it during his forty days abode upon the earth, or whether he so far condescended, for his disciples sake, as to keep in his glory, that it might not dazzle them, and therefore appeared sometimes in the form of *a gardiner*, John xx. 15. and sometimes in the form of *a stranger*, Luke xxiv. 18. and sometimes in *another form*, Mark xvi. 12. and sometimes in his own form, in the same form wherein he lived before he was crucified, John xx. 20, 27. it is hard to determine. I am apt to think, that in some sort he might draw in the beams of his glory, and yet that he was not entred into that fulness of glory, as after his ascension; and so some expound those words of Christ to Mary, 'Touch me not, for I am not yet ascended to my Father,' q. d. Fix not thy thoughts so much upon my present condition, for I am not yet attained to the highest pitch of my exaltation, nor shall I until 'I ascend unto my Father.'

Use. From this resurrection of Christ how are we informed, that Christ is the Son of God? Thus Paul speaks, he *was declared to be the Son of God with power, according to the Spirit of holiness, by the resurrection from the dead*, Rom. i. 4. And how are we informed, that Christ is Lord over all things that are? For *to this end Christ both died*,

* Aug. Lib. 22. de civit. die Cap. ult.

and rose, and revived, that he might be Lord both of the dead and living, Rom. xiv. 9. And how are we informed, that Christ rose again for us, as one that stood in stead and room of all the elect? 'But now is Christ risen from the dead, and become the first-fruits of them that slept,' 1 Cor. xv. 20. And how are we informed, that by his resurrection we are justified? 'Who was delivered for our offences, and was raised again for our justification,' Rom. iv. 25. And that by his resurrection we are regenerate? For 'he hath begotten us again into a lively hope, by the resurrection of Jesus Christ from the dead,' 1 Pet. i. 3. And that by his resurrection we are sanctified? For 'as he was raised up from the dead by the glory of his Father, even so we also should walk in newness of life,' Rom. vi. 4. And that by his resurrection, at the last day we shall be raised? For, 'if the Spirit of him that raised up Jesus from the dead, dwell in you; he that raised up Christ from the dead, shall also quicken your mortal bodies,' Rom. viii. 11. And that by his resurrection, finally we shall be saved? For after we are raised, 'we shall never die any more, but be equal unto the angels, and be the children of God, as being the Children of the resurrection of Christ,' Luke xx. 36.

Thus far of the position, *Christ rose again the third day*. Now for the proof.

SECT. IV.

Of the arguments of Christ's resurrection.

CHRIST *after his passion shewed himself alive by many infallible proofs*, Acts i. 3. And so he had need to persuade men into the faith of so strange a truth; if we consult with antiquity, or novelty, with primitive times, or later times, never was matter carried on with more scruple and slowness of belief, with more doubts and difficulties, than was this truth of Christ's resurrection. Mary Magdalene saw it first, and reported it, *but they believed her not*, Mark xvi. 11. The two disciples that went to Emmaus, they saw it also and reported it, but *they believed them not*, Luke xxiv. 37. Divers women together saw him, and came and told the disciples, but *their words seemed to them as idle tales, and they believed them not*, Luke xxiv. 11. They all saw him, and even seeing him, *yet they believed not for joy, but wondred*, Luke xxi. 41. when the wonder was o-ver,

ver, and the rest told it but to one that happened to be absent, you know how peremptory he was, 'Not he, except he saw in his hands the print of 'the nails, and put his fingers into the print of the 'nails, and thrust his hands into his side, he would 'not believe,' John xx 25 ——In after times, the whole world stopt their ears at this report of the *resurrection of Christ*; it was with the Grecians at Athens a very scorn, 'When they heard of 'the resurrection of the dead, some mocked,' Acts xvii 32. It was with Festus, the great Roman [*mania*,] a sickness of the brain, a plain phrenzy; Festus said with a loud voice, ' Paul, thou art be-' side thyself, much learning doth make thee ' mad,' Acts xxvi. 24.——But come we to our own times, the resurrection of Christ to this day is as much opposed by Jews and Atheists as any one article of our creed. And surely we had need to look to it, for ' if Christ be not risen (as ' the apostle argues) then is our preaching vain, ' and your faith is also vain, 1 Cor. xv. 14. If ' Christ be not risen, ye are yet in your sins; and ' they which are fallen asleep in Christ, are perish-' ed,' 1 Cor. xv. 17, 18. Of all the precious truths in the book of God, we had need to preserve this truth, and to be well skilled in the defending of this truth, of *the resurrection of Christ*. Some talk of a toleration of all religions, and some desire that the Jews may have free commerce amongst us, it will then be time, as I think, to be well armed at this point. Let the ordinary professors of our times, who are of weak judgments, and fiery spirits, look to this point, lest as now, when they cannot answer a separatist, they turn separatists; and when they cannot answer an antinomian, they turn antinomians; and when they cannot answer a seeker, quaker, blasphemer, they turn to them; so when they cannot answer the subtil arguments of a Jew, they should as easily turn Jews, and deny Christ, and the resurrection of Christ.

I mean not to enter into controversies, only I shall declare from what heads, arguments of this nature may be drawn.—As,

1. More generally from Gentiles grants, Jews concessions, typical instructions, prophetical predictions.

2. More especially from these clear demonstrations, that circumstantially and substantially do prove this Christ to have risen again.

1. The arguments in general are,—

1. From Gentiles grants; Pilate that condemned Christ, testified in a letter to * Tiberius Cæsar, that Christ was risen again, and therefore Tiberius desired the senate to admit Christ into the number of their Gods, which, when they refused, Tiberius was incensed, and gave free leave to all Christians to profess Christianity. And to the Gentiles, Sybilla left written these very words, ' He ' shall end the necessity of death by three days ' sleep, and then return from death to life again; ' he shall be the first that shall shew the beginning ' of resurrection to his chosen, for that by con-' quering death, he shall bring us life.'

2. From Jews concessions; Josephus, the most learned amongst the later Jews, acknowledgeth, † ' That after Pilate had crucified him, he appear-' ed unto his followers the third day, according-' ly as the prophets had foretold.' The scribes and Pharisees being astonished with the sudden news of his rising again, confirmed by the soldiers whom they set to watch, found no other way to resist the same, but only by saying, (as all the Jews do unto this day) That his disciples came by night, and stole away his body whilst the soldiers slept: O strange! if they were asleep, How know they that his disciples stole away his body? And if they were not asleep, How could a few weak fishers take away his body from a band of armed soldiers?

3. From typical instructions: such was Adam's sleep, Isaac's lying upon the altar, Joseph's imprisonment, Sampson's breaking of the gates of Gaza, David's escaping out of Saul's hands, Jeremiah's deliverance out of the pit, the raising of the Shunamite's child, of the widow of Screptah's son, of the temple of Solomon, of Jonah from the deep; a thousand of these types might be produced which relate to this antitype, *Christ's resurrection*

4. From prophetical predictions; *Thou wilt not leave my soul in hell, neither wilt thou suffer thine holy one to see corruption*, Psal xvi. 10. *After two days he will revive us, in the third day he will raise us up*, Hosea vi. 2 He will raise us up, (i e.) his Son united to us, our flesh assumed by his Son, *Thou art my Son, this day have I begotten*

---

* Tertul. L. *Contingent* Egesippus *de vita r. su. & Christi.* † Joseph. *Antiq.* Lib. 8. C. 9.

thee,

Carrying on the great Work of Man's Salvation during the Time of his Resurrection. 343

thee, Psalm ii. 7. Acts xiii. 33. *I laid me down and slept, I awaked, for the Lord sustained me,* Psal. iii. 5. Above all, how plain was the prophecy of Christ himself, That *he must go to Jerusalem, and suffer many things of the elders, and chief priests, and scribes, and be killed, and be raised again the third day,* Matth. xvi. 21.

2. The special arguments are exceeding many: as, 1. The angel's assertion: *He is not here, for he is risen, as he said, come see the place where the Lord lay,* Matth. xxviii. 6. 2. The great earthquake; *And behold there was a great earthquake, for the angel of the Lord descended from heaven, and came and rolled back the stone from the door,* Matth. xxviii. 2.

3. The apparitions of raised bodies; and 'the graves were opened, and many bodies of saints which slept arose, and came out of the graves after his resurrection, and went into the holy city, and appeared unto many,' Matth. xxvii. 52, 53.

4. The sudden courage of the apostles; whereas a little before they durst not peep out of doors, they presently after compassed the whole world, and confidently taught, That *there was no other name given under heaven, whereby men may be saved, but the name of Jesus,* Acts iv. 12. 5. The martyrs sufferings even for this truth. 6. The adversaries confessions even to this truth. 7. The Jews punishment even to this day for not believing this saving truth. There is one Rabbi Samuel, who six hundred years since, writ a tract in form of an epistle, to Rabbi Isaac, master of the synagogue of the Jews, wherein he doth excellently discuss the cause of their long captivity and extreme misery: and after that he had proved it was inflicted for some grievous sin, he sheweth that sin to be the same which Amos spoke of, *For three transgressions of Israel, and for four, I will not turn away the punishment thereof, because they sold the righteous for silver,* Amos ii. 6. The selling of Joseph, he makes the first sin; the worshipping of the calf in Horeb the second sin; the abusing and killing of God's prophets the third sin; and the selling of Jesus Christ the fourth sin. For the first, they served four hundred years in Egypt; for the second, they wandered forty years in the wilderness; for the third, they were captives seventy years in Babylon; for the fourth, they are held in pitiful captivity even until this day. 8. The last argument on which only I shall insist, it is the several apparitions that Christ made to others after his resurrection, some reckon them ten times, others eleven times, and others twelve times, according to the number of his twelve apostles.

1. He appeared unto Mary Magdalene apart. As a woman was the first instrument of death, so was a woman the first messenger of life; she brought the first tidings of the resurrection of Christ, which is the surest argument of man's salvation.

2. He appeared unto all the Maries together as they returned homewards from the sepulchre; never any truly sought for Christ, but with these women they were sure to find Christ.

3. He *appeared to Simon Peter alone*; Luke xxiv. 34. he was the first among men to whom he appeared, he first went into the sepulchre, and he first saw him that was raised thence: he was called first, and he confessed Christ first to be the Son of God; and therefore Christ appears first to him: the angel bad the woman to *tell his disciples and Peter,* (that is to say, and Peter especially) *that he was risen, and gone before them into Galilee,* Mark xvi. 7. Of this speaks Paul, *He was first seen of Cephas, and then of the twelve,* 1 Cor. xv. 5.

4. He appeared to the two disciples journeying towards Emmaus; the name of the one was Cleophas, and probable it is the other was Luke, 'Who out of his modesty concealed his own name, saith Theophilact.'

5. He appeared unto the ten apostles when the doors were shut. Some controversy there is in this, because the evangelist saith expresly, That *the eleven disciples were gathered together,* Luke xxiv. 33.——*And as they spake, Jesus himself stood in the midst of them,* ver. 36. Now Judas was hanged, and Matthias was not elected, and Thomas Didymus was not with them when Jesus came, John xx. 24. How then could he appear to eleven apostles, considering at this time there was but eleven in all?——Some say it is a certain number put for an uncertain. Others say, That the eleven might be together when the two disciples came, and when Jesus came, Thomas might be absent and gone from amongst them. And if the text be

be viewed well, there is no contradiction in this saying. But I must not dwell on controversial points.

6. He appeared to all the disciples, *and Thomas with them,* John xx. 26. and then he shewed them his wounds, to strengthen the weak faith of his wavering servants. Thomas would not have believed unless he had seen, and therefore Christ shews him the wounds of his body, that he might cure the wounds of Thomas's unbelieving soul.

7. He appeared *to Peter, and John, and James, and Nathaniel, and Didymus, and two other disciples,* John xxi. 2. when they were a fishing at the sea of Tiberias, there he proved the verity of his Deity by that miracle of the fishes, and the verity of his humanity by eating meat with them. And this was the third time that he shewed himself publickly and solemnly unto all, or to the most part of his disciples, ver. 14

8. He appeared unto more than five hundred brethren at once; of this we read not in the evangelists, but the apostle Paul records it, *After that he was seen of above five hundred brethren at once, of whom the greater part remain unto this present, but some are fallen asleep,* 1 Cor. xv. 6.

9. He appeared unto James the brother of the Lord; (i. e.) the cousin-german of Christ according to the flesh; he was called James the just, in regard of his upright and innocent life. Jerom, in his book, *De viris illustribus,* tells us, That afore Christ's death, this James made a vow, that he would eat no bread till Christ was risen again from the dead; and now Christ appearing to him, he commanded bread and meat to be set on the table, saying to James, 'O my brother, now rise and eat, for now I am risen again from the dead.' Of this apparition Paul makes mention, *After that he was seen of James,* 1 Cor. xv. 7.

10 He appeared to the eleven disciples on mount Tabor in Galilee. And this Matthew intimates when Jesus bad the woman, ' tell his brethren that he was risen, and that they should go into Galilee, and there they should see him; and accordingly in that mountain where Jesus had appointed them, they saw him and worshipped him,' Matth. xxviii 10, 16, 17.

11. He appeared to all his apostles and disciples upon mount Olivet by Jerusalem, when in the presence of them all he ascended up into heaven. This mountain is expressed by Luke, when after Christ's ascension it is said, That *the disciples returned back to Jerusalem from the mount called Olivet,* Acts i. 12.

12. He appeared unto Paul travelling unto Damascus, this indeed was after his forty days abode upon the earth; and yet this Paul mentions amongst the rest of his apparitions; and, *last of all, he was seen of me also, as of one born out of due time,* 1 Cor. xv. 8.

My meaning is not to speak of all these apparitions in order, for some of them we are neither assured of the order nor of the time: but of the most considerable and most edifying we shall treat.

SECT. V.

Of Christ's apparition to Mary Magdalene.

ON the first day were many apparitions, but I shall speak only of one or two, as related by the evangelist John.

1. Christ appeared unto Mary Magdalene apart, *The first day of the week cometh Mary Magdalene early, when it was yet dark, unto the sepulchre,* John xx. 1. She came whilst it was yet dark, she departed from home before day, and by that time she came to the sepulchre the sun was about to rise; thither come, she finds the stone rolled away, and the body of Jesus gone; upon this she runs to Peter and John, and tells them, *They have taken away the Lord out of the sepulchre, and we know not where they have laid him.* Then Peter and John ran as fast as they could to see, they looked into the sepulchre, and not finding the body there, they presently returned. By this time, Mary Magdalene was come back, and howsoever the disciples would not stay, yet she was resolved to abide by it, and to see the issue.

We find this apparition, for our farther assurance, compassed and set about with each needful circumstance; here's the time when, the place where, the persons to whom, the manner how he appeared; together with the consequents after the apparition.

1. For the time when he appeared; *now upon the first day of the week, very early in the morning,* John xx. 1. It was the first day of the week, the next day to their sabbath; I shall speak more particularly to this in the next apparition; and it was

very

very early in the morning: the apparition was early, but Mary's seeking of Christ was so early, that *it was yet dark:* she's going to the grave, when, by course of nature she should have been in her bed; she sought him early whom she loved entirely: giving us to learn, that we should seek Christ betimes, even *in the days of our youth*, Eccl. xii. 1. That in these first days of the week we should rise up early to enquire after Christ; they that will not seek Christ until they have given over seeking other things, may justly fear to miss Christ, *First seek the kingdom of God, and his righteousness, and then* (saith Christ) *all other things shall be added unto you*, Matth. vi. 33.

2. For the place where he appeared, it was in the garden where Christ was buried; in a garden Adam first sinned, in a garden Christ first appeared, in a garden death was first threatned and deserved, and in a garden life is restored and conferred upon us; Christ makes choice of a garden, both for his grave, and resurrection, and first apparition, to tell us where we might seek him, if we have lost him, 'My beloved is gone down into his garden, to the 'beds of spices, to feed in the gardens, and to ga- 'ther lilies,' Cant. vi. 2. That is, Jesus Christ is to be sought and found in the particular assemblies of his people; they are the garden of his pleasure wherein are varieties of all the beds of renewed souls, there he walks, and there he feeds, and there he solaceth himself with those fruits of righteousness and new obedience, which they are able to bring forth to him. O! there let us seek him, and we shall find him.

3. For the person to whom he appeared, it was Mary Magdalene, she that sometimes lived a sinful life, that was no better than a common courtizan, now is first up to seek her Saviour. Let never any despair of mercy, that but hears of the conversion of Mary Magdalene: Dionisius tells us, 'That she 'that was loose and dissolute in her youth, be- 'took herself in her old age to a most solitary 'life; that she sequestred herself from all world- 'ly pleasures in the mountains of Balma, full 'thirty years; in all which time she gave herself 'to meditation, fasting and prayer.' The text tells us, 'That much was forgiven her, and she 'loved much,' Luke vii. 47. Her love to Christ appears at this time, 'But Mary stood without at 'the sepulchre weeping, and as she wept, she 'stooped down, and looked into the sepulchre,' John xx. 11. This scripture we may call *a song of Loves*, or, if you will, *a song of degrees*; every word is a step or degree of love more than another. As,—

1. Mary stood at the sepulchre; she stood by the grave of Christ, it signifies her great love to Jesus Christ; many would stand by him while he was alive, but to stand by him dead, none would do it; those we love most, we will wait on them living, or if they die, we will bring them to the grave, and lay them in the grave, but there we leave them:——Only Mary chooseth Christ's tomb for her best home, and his dead corpse for her chief comfort, she praiseth the dead more than the living, and having lost the light of the sun of righteousness, she desired to dwell in darkness, in the shadow of death.

2. But Mary stood, q. d. others did not, but she did: Peter and John were there even now, and when they could not find Jesus, away they went, but Mary went not, she stood still: their going away commends her staying behind; how many circumstances may we observe in Mary, setting out her love to Christ above them all? To the grave she came before them; from the grave she went to tell them; to the grave she returns with them; and at the grave she stays behind them. Certainly there was in Mary a stronger affection, than either in Peter or John, and this affection fixed her there, that she could not stir; go who would, she would not go, but stay still, but Mary stood without.

3. But Mary stood without at the sepulchre weeping: this was love indeed; see how every word is a degree of love. But Mary stood there weeping: when Christ stood at Lazarus's graveside weeping, the Jews said then, Behold how he loved him; and may not we say the very same of Mary, Behold how she loved him, her very love runs down her cheeks, she cannot think of Jesus as lost, but she weeps; she weeps for having lost him whom she loved; at first she mourned for the departure of his soul out of his body, and now she laments the taking of his body out of the grave; at first she mourned because she could not keep him alive, yet that sorrow had some solace, in that she hoped to have enjoyed him dead; but when she considers that his life was lost, and not so much as his body could be found, Oh! she weeps, and weeps,

weeps. The last office she could do, was to anoint his body, and to bewail his death; and to that purpose she comes now unto his grave; as sometimes she had washed his feet with her tears, now she would shed them afresh upon his feet, and head, and hands, and heart, and all; but when she saw the grave open, and the body gone, and nothing of Christ now left her to mourn over, she weeps the more, she weeps most bitterly. But Mary stood there weeping.

4. And as she wept, she stooped down and looked in the sepulchre. She did so weep as she did seek with all; her weeping hindred not her seeking, she sought and sought; to what purpose? That Christ is not in the tomb, her own eyes have seen; the disciple's hands have felt, the empty winding sheet, doth plainly avouch; Peter and John had looked in before, nay, *they went into the sepulchre, and saw the linen clothes lying, and the napkin that was about his head wrapt by itself*, John xx. 6, 7. and yet for all this she will be stooping down, and looking in; she would rather condemn her own eyes of error, and both their eyes and hands of deceit, she would rather suspect all testimonies for untrue, than not to look after him whom she had lost, even there where by no diligence he could be found; 'It is not enough for love to look in once.' You know this is the manner of our seeking, when we seek something seriously; where we have sought already, there we'll seek again; we are apt to think we sought not well, but if we seek again, we may find it where we sought: and thus Mary sought, and when she could think of no other place so likely to find Christ in, as this, she sought again in this, she will not believe her own senses, she would rather think that she looked not well before, than she will leave off looking. When things that are dearly affected are gone and lost, love's nature, is, never to be weary of searching, even the oftenest searched corners; there must still be an haunt for hope. Oh! love thinks it hath never looked enough; in the first verse she looked, and saw the stone taken away from the sepulchre; and now again, she stooped down and looked into the sepulchre.

4. For the manner how he appeared; it was first by his angels, and secondly by himself.

1. There was an apparition of angels, she seeth *two angels in white, sitting, the one at the head, and the other at the feet where the body of Jesus had lain*, John xx. 12, 13. I will not stay here, only for the opening of the words I shall answer these questions: as, 1. What means the apparition of angels? I answer, It is only a preparation to Christ's apparition. Mary's loss must be restored by degrees; though she saw not Christ at first, yet she saw his angels; it often pleaseth Christ in the desertions of his people, to come to them by degrees, and not at once, he comes first by his angels, so it was at his birth, and so it is at his resurrection.——But, 2. What do angels in a sepulchre? It is a place fitter for worms than angels: we never read of angels being in a grave before this time; they are blessed creatures, and is the grave a fit place for them? O yes! since Christ lay in the grave, that very place is a blessed place; *Blessed are the dead, which die in the Lord from henceforth*, Rev. xiv. 13. *Precious in the sight of the Lord is the death of his saints*, Psal. cxvi. 15. —But, 3. Why are the angels in white? Solomon answers, That white is the colour of joy, *Let thy garments be always white, and let thy head lack no ointment*, Eccl. ix. 8. When Christ was transfigured, his *raiment was all white, no fuller in the earth could come near it*, Mark ix. 3. And the saints in heaven are said to *walk in white robes*, Rev. vii 9. And here the angels are in white, to signify the joy they had in Christ's resurrection from the dead.—But, 4. Why are they one at the head, and the other at the feet, where the body of Jesus had lain? Some answer, That as Mary Magdalene had anointed his head and feet, so at those two places the two angels sit, as it were to acknowledge so much for her sake. Others think it speaks comfort to every one of us; if we are but in Christ, we shall go to our graves in white, and lie between two angels, who are said to guard our bodies even dead, to present them alive again at the day of the resurrection.

But in this apparition we see farther, a question and answer: 1. The angels question Mary, *Woman, why weepest thou?* May I paraphrase upon these words; it is as if they had said, O Mary! what cause is there for these tears? where angels rejoice, it agrees not that a woman should weep; thou couldest before, with a manly courage, arm thy feet to run among swords when thou camest to the grave, and art thou now so much a woman, that thou canst not command thine eyes to forbear tear? *O woman, why weepest thou?* If thy Christ were here in his grave, under this tomb-stone, we might think thy sorrow for the dead enforced thy tears; but now that thou findest it a place of the living, Why dost thou stand here weeping for the dead? If thy tears be tears of love, as thy love is acknowledged, so let these tears be suppressed; if thy tears be tears of anger, they should not here have been shed, where all anger was buried; if thy tears be tears of sorrow, and duties to the dead, they are bestowed in vain where the dead is now revived; and therefore, *O woman, why weepest thou?* Would our eyes be dry, if such eye-streams were behoveful for us? Did not angels always in their visible resemblances represent their Lord's invisible pleasure, shadowing their shapes in the drifts of his intentions? As for instance, when God was incensed, they brandished swords; when he was appeased, they sheathed them in scabbards; when he would defend, they resembled soldiers, when he would terrify, they took terrible forms; and when he would comfort, they carried mirth in their eyes, sweetness in their countenance, mildness in their words, favour, and grace, and comeliness in their presence: why then dost thou weep, seeing us rejoice? Dost thou imagine us to degenerate from our nature, or to forget any duty, whose state is neither subject to change, nor capable of the least offence? Art thou not fervent in thy love, or more privy to the counsel of our eternal God, than we that are daily attendants at his throne of glory? *O woman, why weepest thou?* Thus far paraphrase.

2. For her answer, *She saith unto them, because they have taken away my Lord, and I know not where they have laid him,* John xx. 13. Here was the cause of Mary's tears; 1. *They have taken away my Lord.* 2. *I know not where they have laid him,* q. d. He is gone without all hope of recovery; for they, but I know not who, have taken him away, but I know not whither; and they have laid him, but I know not where; there to do to him, but I know not what. O what a lamentable case is this! she knows not whither to go to find any comfort; her Lord is gone, his life is gone, his soul is gone, his body is gone, yea gone, and carried she knows not whither; and do they ask her, *Woman, why weepest thou?* Why, here is the cause, *They have taken away my Lord,* (i. e.) the dead body of my Lord, *and I know not where they have laid him.* Where a little of Christ is left, and that is lost, it is a lamentable loss. Mary had sometimes a possession of whole Christ, she had his presence, she heard his words, she saw his divinity in his miracles, and in casting seven devils out of her own body; but now she had lost all Christ, his presence lost, his preaching lost, his divinity lost, his humanity lost, his soul lost, and last of all his body lost. Oh! what a lamentable loss was this? Mary would now have been glad of a little of Christ; O ye angels, fill but her arms with the dead body of her Jesus, and she will weep no more; one beam of that Sun of righteousness would scatter all the clouds of Mary's grief.

Quest. But doth Christ ever leave his totally?

Ans. I answer, not indeed, but only in apprehension. In desertions, a Christian may to his own apprehension find nothing of Christ; and this was the case of Mary Magdalene: or, if Christ desert a soul indeed, and in truth, (for desertions are sometimes in appearance, and sometimes real) yet never doth he forsake his own both really and totally, *The Lord will not wholly forsake his people, for his great name's sake,* 1 Sam. xii. 22. the acts of his love may be withdrawn, but his love is still the same, it is *an everlasting love,* Jer. xxxi. 3. Those acts which are for well-being may be withdrawn, but his acts of love that are for being, shall never be removed, *No such good things will God withhold from them that walk uprightly,* Psal. lxxxiv. 11. Or Christ may go away for a season, but not for ever, 'For a moment have I forsaken thee, but 'with great mercies will I gather thee: in a little 'wrath, I have hid my face from thee for a mo-'ment; but with everlasting kindness will I have 'mercy on thee, saith the Lord thy Redeemer,' Isa. liv. 7, 8. It was Christ's promise to his disciples, *I will not leave you comfortless, or as orphans, but I will come again,* John xiv. 18. Tho' his compassions may be restrained, yet they cannot be extinguished; as the sun sets to rise again, and as the tender mother lays down her child to take it up again, so deals Christ with his, only for the present it is a sad thing; O! it is a lamentable thing to lose all Christ, tho' but in our own apprehensions. To hear Mary's pitiful complaints, ' They have taken a-' way my Lord, and I know not where they have ' laid my Lord,' it would make a flint to weep;

me-

methinks I hear her cries, 'O my Lord, what's become of thee? Time was, that my soul was an enclosed garden, and the chiefest of ten thousands did walk in the shadow of the tree; but now the fence is down, my love is gone, and Sharon is become a desert: time was, that I sat at the feet of my Lord, and I received daily oracles from his mouth; but now he hides himself, and will not come at me; I pray, but he hears not; I hearken after him, but he speaks not; I call, but he answers not. O my Lord, if I had never known thee, I could have lived without thee; but this is my misery, not so much that I am without thee, as that I have lost thee; many are well without thee, because they never enjoyed thee; the children of beggars count it not their misery that they are not princes; but Oh! the grief, when the children of princes shall be turned to beggars! O my Lord, once I had thee, but now I have lost thee, yea, I have lost thee every jot, and piece, and parcel of thee; O! ye apostles, where is the dead body of my Lord? Oh! sir angel, tell me if ye saw his torn, his macerated, crucified body? O grave! O! death! shew me, is there any thing of Christ's body (though but a few dead ashes) in your keeping? No, no, all is gone; I can hear nothing of what I would hear, death is silent, the grave is empty, the angels say nothing to the purpose, the apostles are fled, and they (I know not who) have taken away my Lord, and I know not where they have laid him.'

2. After this Christ himself appears, but first as unknown, and then as known. 1. As unknown, *She turned herself back, and saw Jesus standing, and knew not that it was Jesus. Jesus saith unto her, Woman, why weepest thou? Whom seekest thou? She supposing him to be the gardener,* &c. John xx. 14, 15. In this apparition of Christ unknown, I shall only take notice of Christ's question, and Mary's inquisition; his question, is in these words, *Woman, why weepest thou? Whom seekest thou?* 1. *Why weepest thou?* This very question the angels asked her before, and now Christ asks it again; sure there is something in it, and the rather we may think so, because it is the first opening of his mouth, the first words that ever came from him, after his rising again; some say that Mary Magdalene represents the state of all mankind before this day, *viz.* One weeping over the grave of another, as if there were no hope; and now at his resurrection Christ comes in with, weep not: *Woman, why weepest thou?* q. d. There is no cause of weeping now, lo, I am risen from the dead, and am become the first-fruits of them that sleep.

And yet we may wonder at the question, Why should Christ demand of Mary, why she wept? But a while since she saw him hanging on a tree, with his head full of thorns, his eyes full of tears, his ears full of blasphemies, his mouth full of gall, his whole person mangled and disfigured, and doth he ask her, *Woman, why weepest thou?* Scarce three days since she beheld his arms and legs racked with violent pulls, his hands and feet bored with nails, his side and bowels pierced with a spear, his whole body torn with stripes, and gored in blood; and doth he ask her, *Woman, why weepest thou?* She saw him on the cross yielding up his soul; and now she was about to anoint his body, which was the only hope she had alive; but his body is removed, and that hope is dead, and she is left hopeless of all visible help; and yet doth he ask her, *Woman, why weepest thou?* O yes! tho' it may be strange, yet is it not a question without cause? She weeps for him dead, who was risen again from the dead; she was sorry he was not in his grave, and for this very cause she should have been rather glad; she mourns for not knowing where he lay, when as indeed and in truth, he lay not any where; he is alive, and present, and now talks with her, and resolves to comfort her, and therefore, *Woman, why weepest thou?*

2. *Whom seekest thou?* She seeks Christ, and Christ asks her, *Woman, whom seekest thou?* We may wonder at this also, if she seek Christ, Why doth she not know him? Or, if she knew Christ, why doth she seek him still? O Mary! is it possible thou hast forgotten Jesus? There is no part in thee but is busy about him, thy eye weeps, thy heart throbs, thy tongue complains, thy body faints, thy soul languisheth, and notwithstanding all this, hast thou now forgotten him? What, are thy sharp eyes so weak-sighted? That they are dazled with the sun, and blinded with the light? O yes! a shower of tears come betwixt her and him, and she cannot see him; or it may be *her eyes were holden that she should not know him*,

Luke

Luke xxiv. 16. or it may be that he appeared in [*ετερα μορφη*] in some other shape, such as resembled the gardener, whom she took him for; howsoever it was, *she saw Jesus standing, but knew not that it was Jesus, and therefore saith Jesus to her, Woman, why weepest thou? Whom seekest thou?* John x. 14, 15. There is a double presence of Christ, felt, and not felt; the presence felt, is when Christ is graciously pleased to let us know so much, and this is an heaven upon earth: the presence not felt, is that secret presence when Christ seems to draw us one way, and to drive another way: so he dealt with the woman of Canaan; he seemed to drive her away, but at the same time he wrought in her by his Spirit an increase of faith, and by that means drew her to himself. Thus may a soul suppose Christ lost, and seek and weep, and weep and seek, and yet Christ is present.

2. For Mary's enquiry, *She supposing him to be the gardener*, *said unto him, Sir, if thou hast borne him hence, tell me where thou hast laid him, and I will take him away.*

In the words we may observe, *First*, Her mistake. 2. Her speech upon her mistake.

1. Her mistake, *She supposing him to be the gardener*; O Mary! hath Christ lived so long, and laboured so much, and shed so many showers of blood, to come to no higher preferment than a gardener? This was a very strange mistake; and yet in some sense, and a good sense too, Christ might be said to be a gardener: as, 1. It is he that gardens all our souls, that plants in them the seed of righteousness; that waters them with the dew of grace, and makes them fruitful to eternal life. 2. It is he that raiseth to life his own dead body, and will turn all our graves into a garden-plot, *Thy dead men shall live, together with my dead body shall they arise: awake, and sing, ye that dwell in dust, for thy dew is as the dew of herbs, and the earth shall cast out the dead*, Isa xxvi. 19. Besides, there is a mystery in her mistake: as Adam in the state of grace and innocency, was placed in a garden, and the first office allotted to him, was to be a gardener; so Jesus Christ appeared first in a garden, and presents himself in a gardener's likeness: and as that first gardener was the parent of sin, the ruin of mankind, and the author of death; so is this gardener the ransom for our sins, the raiser of our ruins, and the restorer of our life. In some sense then, and in a mystery Christ was a gardener; but Mary's mistake was in supposing him the gardener of that only place; and not the gardener of our souls. ' Souls ' in desertion are full of mistakes, though in their ' mistakes are sometimes many mysteries.

2. Her speech upon her mistake, *If thou hast borne him hence*, &c. we may observe,—

1. That her words to Christ are not much unlike the answer she gave the angels, only she seems to speak more harsh to Christ, than she did to the angels; to them she complains of others, *they have taken away my Lord*; but to Christ she speaks as if she would charge him with the fact, as if he looked like one that had been a breaker up of graves, a carrier away of corpse out of their place of rest, *Sir, if thou hast borne him hence*. But pardon love, as it fears where it needs not, so it suspects very often where it hath no cause; 'When ' love is at a loss, he or any that comes but in ' our way, hath done it, hath taken him away.'

2. That something she spoke now to Christ which she had not mentioned to the angels. She said not unto them, *tell me where he is*, but reserved that question for himself to answer, *Come, tell me where thou hast laid him*; q. d. Thou art privy to the place, and the action of removing Christ my Lord; Oh how she errs, and yet how she hits the truth! Jesus must tell her what he hath done with himself, sure it was fittest for his own speech to utter, what was only possible for his own power to do.

3. That the conclusion of her speech was a mere vaunt or flourish, *and I will take him away*. Alas! poor woman, she was not able to lift him up. there are more than one or two allowed to the carrying of a corpse; and as for his, it had more than an hundred pound weight of myrrh and other odours upon it; sure she had forgotten that women are weak, and that she herself was but a woman; how was it possible that she should *take him away?* She could not do it; well, but she would do it though, *there is no essay too hard for love*; she exempts no place, she esteems no person, she speaks without fear, she promises without condition, she makes no exception, as if nothing were impossible that love suggesteth; the darkness could not fright her from setting out before day; the watch could not fear her from coming to the tomb where Christ was laid; she resolved to break open the seals, and

to

to remove the stone far above her strength; and now her love being more incensed with the fresh wound of her loss, she speaks resolutely, *I will take him away*, never considering whether she could or no; love is not ruled with reason but with love; it neither regards what can be, nor what should be; but only what itself desireth to do.

4. That through all this speech she omits the principal verb, she enquires for Jesus, but the never names him whom she enquires after. She could say to the angels, *They have taken away my Lord*; but now she talks of one under the term of him, *If thou hast borne him hence, tell me where thou hast laid him, and I will take him away:* him, him, him; but she never names him, or tells who he is; this is *solecismus amoris*, an irregular speech, but love's own dialect, *q. d.* Who knows not him? Why, all the world is bound to take notice of him; he is worthy to be the owner of all thoughts, and no thought, in my conceit, can be well bestowed upon any other than him; and therefore, Sir gardener, whosoever thou art, *If thou hast borne him hence*, thou knowest who I mean, thou canst not be ignorant of whom I love, there is not such another among the sons of men, as the Psalmist, *He is the fairest among the children of men*, Psal. xiv. 2. or as the spouse, *He is the chiefest of ten thousand*; and therefore tell me some news of him; of none but him; of him, and only of him; O! tell me where thou hast laid him, and I will take him away? 'A soul sick of 'love, thinks all the world knows her beloved, 'and is therefore bound to tell her where he is;' the daughters of Jerusalem were very ignorant of Christ, Cant. v. 9. and yet *I charge you, O daughters of Jerusalem*, (said the spouse) *if ye find my beloved, that ye tell him I am sick of love*, Cant. v. 8.

2. Christ appears as known; *Jesus saith unto her, Mary; she turned herself, and saith unto him, Rabboni, which is to say, Master*, John xx. 16 *Sorrow may endure for a night, but joy comes in the morning*; she that hitherto had sought without finding, and wept without comfort, and called without answer, even to her Christ now appears; and at his apparition these passages are betwixt them; first he speaks unto her, Mary, and then she replies unto him, *Rabboni, which is to say, Master*.

1. He speaks unto her, *Mary!* it was but a word; but, O what life? What Spirit? What quickning and reviving was in the word? The voice of Christ is powerful; 'If the Spirit of Christ come ' along with the word it will rouse hearts, raise spirits, work wonders. Ah, poor Mary! what a case was she in before Christ spake unto her? She ran up and down the garden, with *O my Lord, where have they laid my Lord?* But no sooner Christ comes, and speaks to her by his Spirit, and with power, but her mind is enlightened, her heart is quickned, and her soul is revived. Observe here the difference betwixt the word of the Lord, and the Lord speaking that word with power and Spirit: we find sometimes the hearts of saints are quickned, fed, cherished, healed, comforted in the use of means, and sometimes again they are dead, senseless, heavy, and hardened; nay, which is more, the very same truth which they hear at one time, it may be affects them, and at another time it doth not; the reason is, they hear but the word of the Lord at one time, and they hear the Lord himself speaking that word at another time; Mary heard the word of the Lord by an angel, *Woman, why weepest thou?* But her tears dropped still; she heard again the word of the Lord by Christ himself, *Woman, why weepest thou?* And yet she weeps, and will not be comforted; but now Christ speaks, and he speaks with power, Mary! and at this word her tears are dried up, no more tears now, unless they are tears for joy: and yet again, observe the way how you may know and discern the effectual voice of Jesus Christ if it be effectual, it usually singles a man out; yea, though it be generally spoken by a minister, yet the voice of Christ will speak particularly to the very heart of a man, with a marvellous kind of majesty and glory stampt upon it, and shining in it; take an humble, broken, drooping spirit, he hears of the free offer of grace and mercy in Jesus Christ, but he refuseth the offers; he hears of the precious promises of God in Christ, but he casts by all promises as things that are generally spoken and applied by man; but when the Lord comes in, he speaks particularly to his very heart, he meets with all his objections, that he thinks *this is the Lord, and this is to me*. Thus Mary before heard the voice of an angel, and the voice of Christ, *Woman, why weepest thou?* It was a general voice, no better title was then afforded, but

but woman; thou weepest like a woman, *O woman*, and too much a *woman*, *why weepest thou?* But now Christ comes nearer, and he singles her out by her very name, *Mary!* oh! this voice came home, he shewed now that he was no stranger to her, he knew her by name; as sometimes God spake to Moses, *Thou hast found grace in my sight, I know thee by name*, Exod. xxxiii. 17. so Christ speaks to Mary, *Thou hast found grace in my sight, I know thee by name*. Why, how should this voice be ineffectual? oh now it works! now she knows Christ, which before she did not; and indeed this is the right way to know Christ, to be first known of Christ; *But now* (saith the apostle) *after that ye have known God*, (and then he corrects himself) *or rather are known of God*, Gal. iv. 9. for till he knows us, we shall never know him aright. Now her dead spirits are raised, which before were benumbed; and no marvel that with a word he revives her spirits, who with a word made the world, and even in this very word shewed an omnipotent power. 'The gardener had done his part (saith one) in making her all green on a sudden.' But even now her body seemed the hearse of her dead heart, and her heart the coffin of her dead soul; and see how quickly all is turned out and in; a new world now; Christ's resurrection is Mary Magdalene's resurrection too; on a sudden she revives, raised (as it were) from a dead and drooping, to a lively and cheerful state.

2. *She said unto him, Rabboni, which is to say, Master*. As she was ravished with his voice, so impatient of delay she takes his talk out of his mouth, and to his first and only word, she answered but one other, *Rabboni, which is to say, Master*. A wonder that in this verse but two words should pass betwixt them two; but some give this reason, ' That a sudden joy rousing all her passions, she could neither proceed in her own, nor give him leave to go forward in his speech.' Love would have spoken, but fear inforced silence, hope framed words, but doubt melts them in the passage; her inward conceits served them to come out, but then her voice trembled, her tongue faultered, her breath failed; why, such is the state of them that are sick with a surfeit of sudden joy; her joy was so sudden, that not a word more could be spoken, but *Rabboni, which is to say, Master*. Sudden joys are not without some doubts or tremblings; when Jacob heard that his son Joseph was alive, *his heart fainted*, Gen. xlv. 26. he was even astonished at so good news; when God restored the Jews out of captivity, they could not think of it otherwise than as *a dream*, Psal. cxxvi. 1. when Peter was by an angel delivered out of prison, he took it only for *a vision*, or apparition, and not for truth, Acts xii. 9. when Christ manifested his resurrection to his disciples, it is said, That *for very joy they believed not*, Luke xxiv. 41. their fears (as it were) kept back, and questioned the truth of their joys. As in the sea when a storm is over, there remains still an inward working and volutation; even so in the mind of man, when its tears are blown over, and there is a calm upon it, there is still a *motus trepidationis*, a motion of trembling, or a kind of solicitous jealousy of what it enjoys: and this might be Mary Magdalene's case; though she suddenly answered Christ, upon the first notice of his voice; yet because the novelty was so strange, his person so changed, his presence so unexpected, and so many miracles were laid at once before her amazed eyes, she found (as it were) a sedition in her thoughts; her hope presumed best, but her fear suspected it to be too good to be true; and while these interchange objections and answers, she views him better, but for the present cannot speak a word more save this, *Rabboni, which is to say, Master*.

5. For the consequents after this apparition, Jesus saith unto her, ' Touch me not, for I am not yet ascended to my Father; but go to my brethren, and say unto them, I ascend to my Father, and to your Father, and to my God, and your God, John xx. 17.

In these words we may observe, a prohibition and a command; the prohibition, *Touch me not*; the command, *but go to my brethren, and say unto them*, &c.

1. *Touch me not*. It seems Mary was now fallen at his sacred feet, she was now ready to kiss with her lips his sometimes grievous, but now most glorious wounds. ' Such is the nature of love, ' that it covets not only to be united, but if it ' were possible, to be transformed out of itself, ' into the thing it loveth.' Mary is not satisfied to see her Lord, nor is she satisfied to hear her Lord, but she must touch him, embrace his feet,

and kiss them with a thousand kisses: oh! how she hangs and clings about his feet! or at least how she offers to make towards him, and to fall upon him!——But on a sudden he checks her forwardness, *Touch me not.*

What a mystery is this? Mary a sinner touched him, and she being now a saint, may she not do so much? She was once admitted to anoint his head, and is she now unworthy to touch his feet? What meaned Christ to debar her of so desired a duty? She had the first sight of Christ, and heard the first words of Christ after his resurrection, and must she not have the privilege of his first embracing; There is something of wonder in these words; and it puts many to a stand, and many an interpretation is given to take off the wonder; I shall tell you of some of them, tho' for my part I shall cleave only to the last.

1. Some think, * that Mary not only essayed to kiss his feet, but to desire the fulfilling of the promise of the Spirit of Christ; this promise Christ made to his disciples at his last supper, *I will send you the comforter*, John xvi. 7. and she expected it to be performed after his resurrection: to which Christ answered, That he would not then give the Spirit unto her, for that as yet he was not ascended into heaven; whence the Spirit should come, q. d. Forbear Mary, if this be the meaning of thy complaint, hands off, O touch me not! *for I am not yet ascended to my Father.*

2. Others think, that † Mary was forbidden to touch because of her unbelief: she had not the least thought till just now, that Christ was risen, or that he should ascend; and therefore she desired not the least favour at his hands, q. d. 'Touch me not, for in thy faith I am not risen, nor shall I ascend unto my Father, thou complainest of me, they have taken away my Lord, thou seekest for the living among the dead, and therefore thou art unworthy of a touch, or any approach, O touch me not!'

3. Others think, that Christ forbad Mary's touch, because she looked upon it as the most manifest confirmation of her faith touching Christ's resurrection. There was a more sure and certain evidence of this thing than touching and feeling, and the discovery of that was to be after his ascension, when the Holy Ghost should be given, q. d. ‡ ' Touch me not, for I would not have my 'resurrection chiefly approved by the judgment of 'sense; rather expect a while till I ascend unto 'my Father in heaven, for then I will send the 'Holy Ghost, and he shall declare the truth and 'certainty of my resurrection, far surer and better.'

4. Others think this touch was forbidden, that Christ might shew his approbation of chastity and sanctity, and inward purity; Mary was now alone with Christ, and that he might give an example of most pure chastity he forbids her to touch, which afterwards in presence of others, he admits her and other women too, for it is said, ' That they 'came and held him by the feet, and worshipped 'him,' Matth. xxviii. 9. And to this exposition the reason affixed doth well agree, for I am not yet ascended to my Father, q. d. * For an example of holy chastity touch me not now, but hereafter in heaven I will give thee leave; when men and women shall be as the holy angels and shall neither marry, nor be given in marriage, then mayest thou touch, there will be no need of the like example then as now; ' Then I will not forbid thee, but 'till then especially if thou art alone, Oh, touch ' me not!

5. Others think, that Mary too much doated upon that present condition of Jesus Christ; she looked upon it as the highest pitch of Christ's exaltation, she desired no more happiness than to enjoy him in that same condition wherein now she

---

* *Quia nondum sanctum spiritum miserat, ideo a tactu suo Mariam prohibebat, dicens, nondum ascendi in cœlum, unde ipse per me spiritum sanctum ad vos mittat.* Ciril. *l.* 12. in Joha. *c.* 50.

† *Noli me tangere, quia in fide tua nondum resurrexi, & ad gloriæ statum perveni.* Hieronym, epist. 95. *c. ad Hedibiam.*

‡ *Noli me tangere; noli meam resurrectionem judicio sensuum comprobare sed parumpar expecta tempus meæ ascensionis & missionis spiritus sanctæ, & tunc longe melius & tenacius percipies veritatem resurrectionis meæ, quam modo me contingens,* Bern. ser. 28. in Cant.

* *Ut ostenderet manifestam, castitatem & sanctimonium per sanctificationem, dixit Mariæ, ne me attingas.* Epipha. haerisi. 26. propesinem.

saw

saw him; and thereupon said Christ, *Touch me not, for I am not yet ascended,* q. d. O Mary! fix not thy thoughts so much upon my present condition, in as much as this is not the highest pitch of my exaltation; I am not as yet attained to that, nor shall I attain to it until I ascend. The degrees of my exaltation are, first, My resurrection. 2. My ascension. 3. My session at God's right-hand, but that is not yet.

6. Others think, * that Mary carried it with too much familiarity towards Christ, she looked upon Christ as she did formerly, she had not that reverence or respect of Christ, as she ought to have had, she differenced not the mortal state of Christ from his new glorified state after his resurrection; whereas with him the case was quite altered; he is risen in a far otherwise condition than he was, for now his corruptible hath put on incorruption, and his mortal hath put on immortality; he died in weakness and dishonour, but he is risen again in power and glory; and as in another state, so to another end, he was not now to stay upon earth, or to converse here any longer, but to ascend up into heaven, q. d. Though I be not yet ascended to my Father, yet I shall shortly ascend; and therefore measure not thy demeanour towards me by the place where I am, but by that which was due to me, and when thou wilt rather with reverence fall down afar off, than with familiarity seem to touch me; Thus, *touch me not.*

7. Others think, † this prohibition was only for that time, and that because he had greater business for her in hand: Christ was not willing now to spend time in complaints, but to dispatch her away upon that errand, *Go to my brethren,* &c. And the reason following suits with this comment, *For I am not yet ascended to my Father,* q. d. Thou needest not so hastily to touch me now, for I am not yet ascended; though I be going, yet I am not gone, another time will be allowed, and thou mayest do it at better leisure, only forbear now; and the first thing thou doest, *go to my brethren;* it will do them more good to hear of my rising than it will do thee good to stand here touching, and holding, and embracing, and therefore in this respect, now *touch me not.*

8. Others think, ‡ that Christ in these words, meant to wean her from all sensual touching, and to teach her a new and spiritual touch by the hand of faith; and to this sense the reason agrees well, for I am not yet ascended, or I shall quickly ascend unto my Father; till Christ were ascended she might be touching with a sensual touch, but that would neither continue, nor do her any good, but if she would learn the spiritual touch, no ascending could hinder that, one that is in heaven might be touched so: and hence it is, that if now we will but send up our faith, we may touch Christ to this day, and there will virtue come out of him. It was Christ's care to wean Mary from the comfort of his external presence, and to teach her how to embrace him by a true and lively faith: he was not long to be seen in his visible shape, being shortly to ascend unto his Father; and therefore the main business was to learn that touch, that would both continue and do her good to her soul's health. And I believe, for this very cause, Christ would not stay long with any of his disciples at any time; he only appeared to manifest himself, and to prove his resurrection, and then to wean them from all sensual and carnal touching, he would quickly have been gone. Observe, that ' a spiritual touch of Christ by faith, is that which ' Christ prefers above all touches;' it is the apostle's saying, ' Henceforth know we no man af-' ter the flesh; yea, though we have known Christ ' after the flesh, yet now henceforth know we him ' no more.' The words have a double interpre-

---

* *Ne pristina illa familiaretate, qua eum in carne mortali intuebatur, per tractaret, judicans post resurrectionem gloriam reverentius, & gravius cum illo agendam esse,* Chrisost. hom. 58. in Johan.

† *Christus non aliud prohibuit Magdalenæ, quam ne nimium temporis absumeret, prout antea solebat, ad pedes ejus, sed quam citius inde se expedirit, ut de ejus resurrectione certiores faceret fratres, suos,* Card. Tolet sup. cap. 20. Joh.

‡ *Christus loquitur de tactu, & de ascensione, non corporali, sed spirituali: Et exinde Magdalena a Christo Domino illuminata fuit, ut deinceps non solum crediderit, sed & alias fæminas ad credendum intraxerit,* Vid Aug. tract. 21. in Joh. serm. 60. de verbis Domini. & 252 and 155. de tempore Ambros. Luc. ult. & lib. de Isaac. & anima. c. 5. & ser. 58.

tation; as, 1. *Henceforth we know him no more*; if we had any earthly carnal thoughts of Christ like unto the rest of the Jews, that he as the king of Israel should begin an earthly temporal kingdom, and that we should enjoy all manner of earthly carnal privileges, as honour, riches, power, yet now we know him no more, we have put off all such carnal imaginations of his kingdom. Or, 2. *Henceforth know we him no more*; we stand no longer affected towards Christ, after any merely human, civil, or natural manner of affections, such as those bear to him, who conversed with him before his resurrection, but altogether in a divine and spiritual manner, agreeable to the state of glory, whereunto he is exalted. Some vilified the ministry of Paul, below that of the rest of the apostles, because he had not been conversant with Christ in the flesh, to which Paul answers, away with this fleshly knowledge, *henceforth know we no man after the flesh*; our way to deal with Christ is in a spiritual manner, yea, the blessing is upon this manner and not on that, *Blessed are they that have not seen, and yet have believed*, John xx. 29. It is said of Mary, his mother, that she had a double conception of Jesus Christ, one in the womb of her body, another in the womb of her soul; the first indeed was more miraculous, the second more beneficial; that this was a privilege singular to herself, but this was her happiness common to all the chosen; it is the work of the inward man that God accepts; a spiritual touch of Christ by faith is that which Christ prefers before all touches.

2. *But go to my brethren, and say unto them, I ascend unto my Father and your Father, and to my God and your God*, this was the command of Christ; instead of touching him, she must go with a message to his apostles, and this was more beneficial both to her and them. The first preacher of this resurrection (besides the angels) was Mary Magdalene; she that before had seven devils cast out of her had now the holy Spirit within her; she that was but a woman is now by Christ made an apostle; *apostolorum apostola*, for to them she was sent, and the message she was to deliver, it was Christ's rising and ascending; and what were they but the gospel, yea, the very gospel of the gospel? This was the first sermon that ever was made by any mortals of Christ's resurrection; and this her fact, had some reference unto Eve's fault; a woman was the first messenger of this our joy, because a woman was the first minister of that our sorrow.

But, what means he to speak of the ascension, when as yet we are but upon the resurrection? I suppose this was to prevent their mistake, who might have thought if Christ be risen, why then we shall have his company again as heretofore; no, saith Christ, I am not risen to make any abode with you, or to converse with you on earth as formerly; my rising is in reference to my ascending; look how the stars no sooner rise but they are immediately in their ascendant; so Christ is no sooner risen but he is presently upon his ascending up.

But whither will he ascend? *To his Father and our Father, to his God and our God*. Every word is a step or round of Jacob's ladder, by which we may ascend up into heaven: as, 1. *Father* is a name of much good-will, there are in it bowels of compassion; Oh! what tenderness is in a father; and yet many a father wants good means to express his good-will unto his child: now therefore *God* is added, that he may not be thought to be defective in that way. Oh, blessed message! this is the voice of a father to his son; *All that I have is thine*, Luke xv. 31. now if this father be also God, and if all that is God's be also ours, what can we desire more than all God hath, or all that ever God was worth? Oh! but here's the question, Whether his Father and God be also ours? That he is Christ's Father, and Christ's God, is without all question; but that his Father should be our Father, and that his God should be our God, this were a gospel indeed; O then! what a gospel is this? *Go to my brethren, and say unto them, That our relations and interests are all but one; the same Father that is mine is theirs, and the same God that is mine is theirs;* his relations are made ours, and our relations are made his interchangeably. No wonder if Luther tell us, That the best divinity lay in pronouns, for as there is no comfort in heaven without God, and no comfort in God without a Father, so neither is there comfort in Father, heaven, or God, without ours, to give us a property in them all. O the blessed news that Christ tells Mary, and that Mary tells us! *I ascend to my Father and your Father, to my God and your God*, Oh! what dull hearts have we that are not affected with this blessed news? No sooner was

Christ

Christ risen from the dead, but he takes care in all haste to appear unto Mary; and no sooner he appears to her, but he sends her away in all haste to others, *go to my brethren, and tell it them*; he would both have Mary, and the rest of the apostles, to hear of his loving-kindness betimes in the morning. Why, alas! they had for some days been amazed with sorrow and fear, but now he provides for their joy; and no sooner they hear the news, but they *joy according to the joy in harvest, and as men rejoice when they divide the spoil*, Isa. ix. 3. Christ's resurrection was a cause of unspeakable joy to them; how is it that we hear the very same glad tidings, and yet we are no more affected with them? Come Christians, sith the occasion extends to us, and is of equal concernment to us, let us tune our hearts to this key; that as upon Christ's absence, we may *weep with them that weep*, so upon his return, we may spring out in joy, and *rejoice with them that rejoice*. So much of the first apparition.

SECT. VI.

Of Christ's apparition to his ten disciples.

ON this day some reckon five apparitions, but of them five, as we have seen the first, so I shall now only take notice of the last, *Then the same day at evening, being the first day of the week, when the doors were shut, where the disciples were assembled for fear of the Jews, came Jesus and stood in the midst, and saith unto them, Peace be unto you, and when he had so said, he shewed unto them his hands and his feet*, John xx. 19, 20. In these words we have the apparition of Christ with all its circumstances: as, 1. When he appeared. 2. Where he appeared. 3. To whom he appeared. 4. How he appeared. So necessary was it to confirm this point, that not a needful circumstance must be wanting. And first is laid down the time, *Then the same day at evening, being the first day of the week.*

How exact is the evangelist in this circumstance of time? It was the same day, the same day at evening, and yet lest the day might be mistaken, it was the same day at evening, being the first day of the week. 1. It was the same day, (i. e.) the very day of rising; he could not endure to keep them in long suspence; the sun must not down before the sun of righteousness would appear. The same day that he appeared to Peter, to the two disciples going to Emmaus, to the woman coming to the sepulchre, and to Mary Magdalene as we have heard; the very same day he appears to the ten. Oh! what a blessed day was this? It was the day of his resurrection, and the day of these several apparitions.

2. It was the same day at evening. Both at morn, noon, and evening, Christ shewed himself alive by many infallible proofs. Early in the morning he appeared to Mary, and presently after to the three Maries, who touched his feet, and worshipped him: about noon he appeared to Simon Peter, in the afternoon he travelled with two of his disciples, almost eight miles to the castle of Emmaus? and, in the evening of the same day, he returned invisible from Emmaus to Jerusalem. At all times of the day Christ is prepared, and preparing grace for his people.

3. It was the same day at evening, *being the first day of the week*, [*Te mia ton sabbatan*], that is in one of the *sabbaths*, but the Greek words are an *hebraism*, and the Hebrews use often by one to signify the first, as in Gen. i. 5. *The evening and the morning were one day* (i. e.) *the first day*. And whereas the Greeks found one of the Sabbaths, [*ton sabbaton*], it must be understood either properly for *Sabbaths*; or else figuratively signifying the whole week; and this acception was usual with the Jews, so the evangelist brings in the Pharisee speaking, [*Nesteuo dis tousabbatou*], *I fast twice in the* sabbath, Luke xviii. 12. (i. e.) in the week, for it is impossible to fast twice in one day; and hence the translators render it thus, *prima die hebdomadis*, on the first day of the week, in which is a discovery of his mercy; Christ took no long day to shew himself to his apostles, nay, he took no day at all, but *the very first day*. When Joseph shewed himself unto his brethren, he would not do it at first, and yet he dealt kindly, and very kindly with them; O! but Christ's kindness is far above Joseph's, for on the first day of the week, the very same day that he rose from the dead he appears unto them. Thus for the time.

2. For the place, it is laid down in this passage, *where the disciples were assembled*. Now if we would know where that was, the evangelist Luke speaks expresly, it was in Jerusalem, Luke xxiv. 33. but

in what house of Jerusalem it is unknown; only some conjecture that it was in the house of some disciple, wherein was an upper room. This upper room, according to the manner of their buildings at that time, was the most large and capacious of any other, and the most retired and free from disturbance, and next to heaven, as having no room above it. § Mede tells us expresly, this was the same room where Christ celebrated the passover, and instituted the Lord's supper, and where on the day of his resurrection he came and stood in the midst of his disciples, the doors being shut; and where eight days after, *the disciples being within*, Joh. xx. 26. he appeared again to satisfy the incredulity of Thomas; and where the apostles met after Christ was ascended, *Then returned they unto Jerusalem from the mount called Olivet,—and when they were come in, they went up into an upper room, where abode both Peter, and James and John, and the rest*, Acts i. 12, 13. If this be true, it should seem that this [*hupesoon*] this upper room, first consecrated by Christ at his institution, and celebration of the * Lord's supper, was thenceforth devoted to be a place of prayer, and holy assemblies: † and for certain the place of the [*hupesoon*] was afterward inclosed with a goodly church, known by the name of the *church of Sion*; to which Jerome made bold to apply that of the Psalmist, *the Lord loveth the gates of Sion more than all the dwellings of Jacob*.

Now of this upper room the doors are said to be shut, and the reason, by way of adjunct, is *for fear of the Jews*; they were shut up as men environed, and beleaguered with enemies; and here a question is raised, Whether Christ could enter, *the doors being shut?* The text is plain, that he came in suddenly, and because of his sudden presence, (the doors being shut) *they were terrified and affrighted, and supposed that they had seen a spirit*, Luke xxiv. 37. The ancients speaking of it, tells us, ‡ ' That he entred while the doors ' were shut, and yet he was no phantasm, but he ' had a true body consisting of flesh and bones.' Now how such a body consisting of crass parts, should enter into the room, and no place at all open, is a great question; but 'tis generally answered, ‡‡ That it was by miracle. As by miracle *he walked on the sea*, Mat. x. 25. ††And as by miracle *he vanished out of their sight*, Luke xxiv. 31. so by miracle he came in, *the doors being shut*. I know it is against the nature of a body, that one should pass through another, both bodies remaining entire; and it is an axiom in philosophy, ' That penetration of bodies is merely ' impossible;' yet for my part I shall not dispute the power of the Almighty; this answer is enough for me to all the objections, either of Papists or Lutherans, ' That the creature might yield ' to the Creator, and the Creator needed not to ' pass through the creature; Christ came in when the doors were shut, either causing the doors to give place, the disciples not knowing how; or else altering the very substance of the doors, that his body might pass through them without destruction; I know not but he that thickened the waters to carry his body, might also extenuate the doors to make way for his body.

3. For the persons to whom he appeared, they were his disciples; they that were shut up in a conclave, not daring to step out of doors for fear of the Jews, to them now Christ appeared. It is Christ's usual course to appear to them who are full of fears, and griefs, and most in dangers, *When thou passest through the waters I will be with thee, and through the rivers they shall not overflow thee*, Isa. xliii. 2.——*Yea though I walk through the valley of the shadow of death, I will fear no evil* (saith David) *for thou art with me*, Psal. xxiii. 4. He was with Joseph in prison, with Jonas in the deep, with Daniel in the lion's den, with the three children in the fiery furnace, *Lo I see four men* (said Nebuchadnezzar) *walking in the midst of the fire, and the form of the fourth is like the Son of God*, Dan. iii. 24. And thus he was with Paul, when he stood before Nero, *Tho' all men forsook me, yet Christ the Lord stood by me, and strengthened me*, 2 Tim. iv. 16, 17. And do not his apparitions this day speak this much? When Mary was full of grief, then Christ appeared to her; when the

---

§ *Mede of churches.* * *Nicephor.* l. 8. ec. *hist.* cap. 30. Psal. l: xxvii. 2.
† Jer. *in Epitabio, Paulæ epist.* 27. ‡ *Aug. Serm.* 59.
‡‡ Aug. *in Serm. Pasch.*
†† *Jest quæst.* 117. *Qui intravit per ostia clausa non erat phantasma*, &c. Chrysot.

two

two disciples travelling towards Emmaus, talking together of all those things which had happened, and were sad, *then Christ appeared to them*, Luke xxiv. 17. And when the apostles were afraid of the Jews, and therefore shut the doors that none might enter, then Christ appeared to them, they were his disciples, his sad, distracted, timerous disciples to whom Christ appeared.

4. For the manner how he appeared; it appears in these passages. 1. *He stood in the midst*. 2. *He said, Peace be unto you*. 3. *He shewed unto them his hands and his side*.

1. *He stood in the midst*. Herein he represents himself as a common good; things placed in the midst are common; and he stands in the midst as a common Saviour, and hence it is that our faith is called a common faith, *To Titus my son after the common faith*, Tit. i. 4. And our salvation is called a common salvation, *I give all diligence to write unto you of the common salvation*, Jude 3. And in that way as salvation is common, Christ Jesus is called a common Saviour, *Behold I bring you glad tidings of great joy which shall be to all people, for unto you* (unto all you) *is born in the city of David a Saviour, which is Christ the Lord*, Luke ii. 10, 11. This posture of Christ (standing in the midst) declares that he despises none, but that he takes care of them all. Some observe, that all the while Christ was on earth, he most stood in this posture; at his birth, he was found in a stable in the midst of beasts; in his childhood he was found in the temple *in the midst of the doctors*, Luke ii. 46. in his manhood, John the Baptist told them, *There standeth one in the midst of you, whom ye know not*, John i. 26. and he said of himself, *I am in the midst of you as one that serveth*, Luke xxii. 27. at his death that very place fell to his turn; for they crucified him in the midst betwixt two thieves, *One on the right-hand, and the other on the left*, Luke xxiii. 33. And now at his rising there we find him again, the disciples in the midst of the Jews, and he in the midst of his disciples. After this in Patmos, John saw him in heaven, *in the midst of the throne*, Rev. vii. 17. and in earth he saw him *in the midst of the seven golden candlesticks*, Rev. i. 13. and in the last day he shall be in the midst too, *of the sheep on his right-hand, and of the goats on his left*, Matth. xxv. 33.

But I find there is yet more in it, *that he stood in the midst*, for the midst is Christ's place by nature, he is the second person in the trinity; and the midst is Christ's place by office, he dealeth betwixt God and man; and the midst is Christ's in respect of his person, he is God-man, one that hath interest in both parties; it was the middle person who was to be the middle one, that undertook this mediation betwixt God and us. We read in the Roman history, that the Romans and Sabines joining battle together, the women being daughters to the one side, and wives to the other, interposed themselves and took up the quarrel; and by their mediation, who had a particular interest in either side, they who before stood upon highest terms of hostility, did now join themselves together into one body and state. God and we were enemies, but Christ stood in the midst to reconcile us unto God, and to slay his enmity; and to this purpose Christ is called [*mesites*,] a mediator, a term peculiar to the scriptures, not to be found among prophane authors. O! what comfort is here to see Jesus Christ stand in the midst? Now may the disciples behold him as their blessed peace-maker, their mediator, as one that hath *slain the enmity*, Eph. ii. 16. not only that enmity betwixt men and men, Jews and Gentiles, but also betwixt God and men. This he did by his death, and now he declares it at his resurrection; for so the apostle there goes on, *Having slain the enmity by his cross, he came and preached peace*, Ver. 17. and so the evangelist here goes on, after his resurrection *Jesus came and stood in the midst, and said unto them, Peace be unto you.* You see how he stood.——

2. What he said, this is the next passage; *He said, peace be unto you*; a seasonable salutation; for now were the disciples in fear and trouble; they had no peace with God or man, or with their own consciences; and therefore more welcome news could not have come; I suppose this peace refers to all these. As,——

1. It speaks their peace with God: sin was it that brought a difference betwixt God and man, now this difference Jesus Christ had taken away by his death, *Behold the Lamb of God which takes away the sins of the world*, John i. 29. he hath taken it away in its condemning power, or as to its separating power betwixt God and them; this was the great design of Christ's coming to make peace betwixt God and man; his Father imposed this

office upon him, and Jesus Christ undertook it, and discharged it, and now, he proclaims it, in the first place to his disciples, *Peace be unto you.*

2. It speaks their peace with man; I know no reason why we should exclude civil peace out of Christ's wish, many, and many a promise and precept we have in the word scattered here and there to this purpose, *And I will give peace in the land, and ye shall lie down, and none shall make you afraid,* Lev. xxvi. 6.—And *thou shalt be in league with the stones of the field, and thou shalt know that thy tabernacle shall be in peace,* Job v. 23, 24. *And seek the peace of the city —— and pray unto the Lord for it; for in the peace thereof shall ye have peace,* Jer. xxix. 7. And *follow peace with all men, and holiness, without which no man shall see God,* Heb. xii. 14. *Orbem pacatam* was ever a clause in the prayers of the primitive church, that *the world might be quiet;* I am sure it is Christ's command, *if it be possible, as much as lieth in you, live peaceably with all men,* Rom. xii. 18.

3. It speaks their peace among themselves, peace one with another. Such is, or should be the condition of the church, *Jerusalem is builded as a city, that is compact together,* or *at unity within itself,* Psal. cxxii. 3. The apostle dwells on this unity, ' There is one body, and one spirit, and ' one hope, and one Lord, and one faith, and one ' baptism, and one God and Father of all, who is ' above all, and through all, and in you all,' Eph. iv. 4, 5, 6. The church is a court, whose very pillars are peace; the building of Christianity knows no other materials to work upon; if we look upon the church itself, *there is one body;* if upon the very soul of it, *there is one Spirit;* if upon the endowment of it, *there is one hope;* if upon the head of it, *there is one Lord;* if upon the life of it, *there is one faith;* if upon the door of it, *there is one baptism;* if upon the father of it, *there is one God and Father of all, who is above all, and through all, and in you all:* it was sometimes Christ's command unto his apostles, *have salt in yourselves, and have peace one with another,* Mark ix. 50. And as a blessed effect of this salutation, (for I look upon them as words full of virtue), the apostles and churches of Christ in primitive times, kept a most sweet harmony, *the multitude of them that believed, were of one heart, and of one soul,* Acts iv. 32.

4. It speaks peace within, peace of conscience; the apostles had exceedingly fallen from Christ; one betrayed him, and another denied him, but all run away, and left him alone in the midst of all his enemies; and yet to them he speaks this salutation, *Peace be unto you;* I know not a better ground for comfort of poor humble sinners, than this is, it may be you have dealt very unkindly with Jesus Christ, you have forsook him, denied him, forsworn him; O! but consider all this hindered not Christ's apparition to his apostles! he comes unexpected, and quiets their spirits; he stays not till they had sued to him for mercy or pardon, but of his mere love and free grace, he speaks kindly to them all, he stills the waves, and becalms their troubled spirits, working in them according to his words, *Peace be unto you.*

O the sweets of peace! it is all wishes in one; this little word is a breviary of all that is good; what can they more have than peace with God, and peace with men, and peace within? Sure there is much in it, because Christ is so much upon it; at his birth the angels sing, *Glory to God in the highest, and on earth peace,* Luke ii. 14 at his baptism the form of a dove lighted upon him, and, what meant this? But peace. In his life this sort of integrity was his court, and what was here but peace? Near his death he gives peace as a legacy to his church, *Peace I leave with you, my peace I give you,* John xiv. 27. at his resurrection his first salutation to his apostles is a wish of peace, *peace be unto you;* what can I say more to make us in love with peace? Why, all Christ did, and all Christ suffered was for peace, he prayed for it. *Neither pray I for these alone, but for them also which shall believe on me, —— that they all may be one, as thou, Father, art in me, and I in thee, that they also may be one in us,* John xvii. 20, 21. And he wept for it, *If thou hadst known, even at least in this thy day, the things which belong unto thy peace,* Luke xix. 42. And he died to purchase it, *But ye who sometimes were afar off, are made nigh by the blood of Christ, for he is our peace,* Eph. ii. 13, 14. Of this we need no other proof or sign, but that of the prophet Jonas; when the sea wrought and was tempestuous, *What shall we do unto thee,* (said the mariners) *that the sea may be calm unto us? And he said, Take me up, and cast me forth into the sea, and so shall the sea be calm,* Jonah i. 11, 12. when that great enmity

mity was betwixt God and us, What shall I do, (said God) that my justice may be satisfied, and my wrath appeased, and that there may be a calm? Why, take me, (said Christ), and cast me forth into the sea, let all thy waves and thy billows go over me, make me a peace-offering and kill me, that when I am dead there may be a calm, and when I am risen I may proclaim it, saying, *Peace be unto you.* You hear what he said.——

3. What he shewed; this is the next passage, *He shewed unto them his hands and his side.* I look upon this as a true and real manifestation of his resurrection: and we find that without this Thomas professed he would never have believed, *Except I shall see in his hands the print of the nails, and put my finger into the print of the nails, and thrust my hand into his side, I will not believe,* Joh. xx 25. But a question or two is here raised, As whether these wounds and prints of the nails and spear, can possibly agree with a glorified body? And why Christ retained those wounds and prints? For the first, Whether those prints could agree with a glorified body? Some affirm it with much boldness; and they say, 'That Christ not only retained those prints whilst he abode upon earth, but now that he is ascended into heaven, he still retains them, for my part I dare not go so far, because scripture is silent; but the day is a coming when we shall see Christ face to face, and then we shall know the truth of this; only I conceive that Christ's body yet remained on earth was not entred into that fulness of glory as it is now in heaven, and therefore he might then retain some scars, or blemishes, to manifest the truth of his resurrection unto his disciples, which are not agreeable to his state in heaven. But this I deliver, not as a matter of faith; reasons are produced both ways by the antient writers, and I refer you to them.

For the second, Why Christ retained these wounds and prints, many reasons are rendered, tho' I shall not close withal.

1. Some think these scars or prints were as the trophies of his victories; nothing is more delightful to a lover, than to bear about the wounds undergone for his beloved; and nothing is more honourable for a soldier, than to shew his wounds undergone for his country's good; what are they but as so many arguments of his valour, and trophies of his victory? This was Beda's sense, * ' Christ reserved his scars, not from any impoten- ' cy of curing them, but to set out the glory and ' triumph of his victory over death and hell.'

2. Others think those scars or prints were for the setting out of Christ's splendour and beauty, as in cut or pink garments the inward silks do appear more splendid, so in Christ's wounds there appears inwardly far more beauty. Aquinas affirms, ' That in the very place of the wounds, there is ' a certain special comeliness in Christ.' And Augustine thinks, '§ That the very martyrs may ' retain some scars of their wounds in glory, be- ' cause there is no deformity, but dignity in them, ' and besides, a certain beauty may shine in their ' bodies answerable to their virtues wherein they ' excelled.'

3. Others think that Christ retains those scars, that he might by them intercede for us: upon these very words, *We have an advocate with the Father, Jesus Christ the righteous,* 1 John ii. 2. they comment thus: ' † That God is appeased by ' Christ's representing to him the prints and scars ' of his human nature.' Christ's wounds are as so many open mouths, which cry at the tribunal of his Father for mercy, as Abel's blood cried for revenge.

4 Others think that Christ retains those scars, that thereby in the day of judgment he might confound the Jews, and all the wicked in the world. It is Augustine's judgment, that as Christ shewed Thomas his hands and his side, because otherwise he would not believe, so at the last day will he shew those wounds to all his enemies, saying, Come, behold the man whom you have crucified, ‡ ' Come, ' see the print of the nails, and the print of the ' spear; these be the hands and feet you nailed and ' clenched to a piece of wood; this is the side you ' pierced; by you and for you was it opened, but ' you would not enter in that you might be saved,' And for this opinion they alledge this text, *Behold he cometh with clouds, and every eye shall see him, and they also which pierced him, and all kindreds,*

---

* Beda. *in* Luc. § Thom. 3 pars q. 53 *a cert.* Aug 22 *de civit Dei.*
† Thom. *in* 1 Joan. *l.* 2. ‡ Aug. *l.* 2 *de symb.* c 8.

of the earth shall wail because of him, even so. Amen. Rev. i. 7.

5. All think that Christ retained his scars, that he might convince the unbelieving disciples of his resurrection; hereby they are assured that Christ is raised, and that the same body of Christ is raised, that before was crucified; and to this we cannot but subscribe, 'The scars of his wounds were for 'the healing of their doubts.' Luke brings in Christ bespeaking his disciples thus, *Behold my hands and my feet, that it is I myself, handle me and see,* Luke xxiv. 39. q. d. ' † Come, let your fingers 'enter into these prints of the nails, and let your 'hands be thrust into the depths of this wound; 'come and open these holes in my hands, open 'this wound in my side; I will not deny that to 'my disciples for their faith, which I denied not 'to mine enemies in their rage; open and feel till 'you come to the very bone, that so both bones 'and wounds may witness.' *That I am he that liveth, and was dead, and behold I am alive for evermore, Amen.* Rev. i. 18.

Use. What testimonies are here to convince the world of Christ's resurrection? Surely this argues the goodness of God that strives thus wonderfully with the weak faith of those that are his. At first he appeared to one, even to Mary Magdalene; and after he appeared to two, saith Matthew, *To Mary Magdalene, and the other Mary,* Mat. xxviii. 1. or to three, saith Mark, *To Mary Magdalene, Mary the mother of James and Salome,* Mark xvi. 1. But of this apparition he is seen of ten at least; and to confirm their faith, not a considerable circumstance must be wanting; here is time, and place, and persons to whom he appears, and the manner how he appears, he stands in the midst to be seen of all, he speaks to them, breathes on them, eats with them, and shews them his hands and his side; O the wonderful condescensions of Christ! what helps doth he continually afford to beget in us faith? If we are ignorant, he instructs us; if we err, he reduceth us; if we sin, he corrects us; if we stand, he holds us up; if we fall down, he lifts us up again; if we go, he leads us; if we come to him, he is ready to receive us; there is not a passage of Christ betwixt him and his, but it is an argument of love, and a means either of begetting, or of increasing faith: O! then believe in Christ, yea believe thy part in the death and resurrection of Jesus Christ; considering that these apparitions were not only for the apostles sake, but if Christ be thine, they were for thy sake, that thou mightest believe, and be saved. But I shall have occasion to speak more of this in the chapter following. So much of the second apparition, as it is recorded by the evangelist John.

SECT. VII.

Of Christ's apparition to all his apostles.

IMmediately after this apparition to his apostles, the next is to all the apostles, not one being absent; and *after eight days, again his disciples were within, and Thomas with them, then came Jesus, the doors being shut, and stood in the midst, and said, Peace be unto you; then saith he to Thomas, Reach hither thy finger, and behold my hands, and reach hither thy hand, and thrust it into my side, be not faithless, but believing; and Thomas answered, and said unto him, My Lord and my God; Jesus saith unto him, Thomas, because thou hast seen me, thou hast believed, blessed are they that have not seen, and yet have believed,* John xx. 26, 27, 28, 29.

In the whole story, we have Christ's apparition, and the fruits of it.

1. For the apparition (as in the former) we have, 1. The time. 2. The place. 3. The person to whom he appeared. And, 4. the manner how he appeared.

1. For the time, *and after eight days,* it was on the same day seven-night after the former apparitions, which was the first day of the week, and now because of his resurrection, and apparitions, called *the Lord's day; I was in the spirit on the Lord's day,* Rev. i. 10. This (in my apprehension) makes much for the honour of the Lord's day: the first assembly of the apostles after Christ's death, was on the first day of the week; and the second church-assembly that we read of, was again on the first day of the week, *and after eight days;* a sign that the Lord's day, sabbath, was on the first day instituted, and that the more solemn assemblies

† Aug. *tract.* 121. *in* Johan.

of God's people, were henceforth to be on the Lord's day. It is an usual observation, That 'things and persons which are named the Lord's, 'are sacred and venerable, in an high degree; as the grace of our Lord, Rom. xvi. 24. the Spirit of the Lord, 2 Cor. iii. 17. the beloved of the Lord, Rom. xvi. 8. the glory of the Lord, 2 Cor. iii. 18. the word of the Lord, 1 Tim. vi. 3. the cup of the Lord, 1 Cor. xi. 27. Augustine tells us, 'That the Lord's resurrection promised us an eter-'nal day, * and that it did consecrate unto us the 'Lord's day.' Surely then this day must needs be venerable, and a solemn day amongst us Christians. Now it was that as the rising of the sun dispelleth darkness, so Christ the sun of righteousness, shined forth unto the world by the light of his resurrection; and hence we read of the apostle's observation of this very day above all others, *The first day of the week, the disciples being come together to break bread, Paul preached unto them*, Acts xx. 7——*and concerning the collection for the saints, as I have given order to the churches of Galatia, even so do ye: upon the first day of the week, let every one of you lay by him in store, as God hath prospered him*, 1 Cor xvi. 1, 2. Charitable contributions, and church-assemblies, were in use and practice on the first day of the week, (i. e.) on the Lord's day. An argument sufficient to me against all the opposers of this sacred truth, that the first day of the week is our Christian-sabbath; why then Christ arose, and at sundry times appeared before his ascension, and after his ascension, Christ sent down the Holy Ghost on that very day; and after sending the Holy Ghost, the apostles then preached, the churches then assembled, charities were then gathered, the Lord's supper was then celebrated: Christ's first apparition was on that day, and after that day finished, not any other apparition before this time, *and after eight days*.

2. For the place, it is said to be within, probably it was the same house wherein the former apparition was; the house wherein Christ celebrated the passover, and instituted the Lord's supper, wherein was the *large upper room made ready for Christ*, Mark xiv. 15. In this upper room immediately after Christ's ascension, was that famous assembly of all the apostles, as we have heard. And in this upper room was that other famous assembly of all the twelve, when the Holy Ghost came down upon them in cloven tongues of fire at the feast of Pentecost, Acts ii. 1. and if we may believe tradition, in this upper room the seven deacons (whereof Stephen was one) were elected and ordained, Acts vi. And in this upper room the apostles and elders of the church at Jerusalem, held that counsel, the pattern of all counsels, for the decision of that question, *Whether the Gentiles that believed were to be circumcised?* Acts xv. In this upper room the apostles and disciples frequently assembled for prayer and supplications; *yea, they continued there with one accord in prayer and supplication*, Acts i. 14. And hence, Cyril, who was bishop of the place, † calls it [*he anotera ekklesia ton apostleon*] the upper church of the apostles; but of this upper room, and of the doors of it being shut, we have spoken before.

3. For the persons, they were his ten disciples, to whom he had appeared formerly, only now Thomas was with them, and so the number is complete, which before was not; his disciples were within and Thomas with them; and, why Thomas with them? Was not Thomas one of them? Was not Thomas a disciple of Christ as well as the rest? I grant; but Thomas is added, because Thomas was not present at the last apparition, and this apparition was more especially for Thomas his sake; O the admirable love of Christ towards poor sinners! observe, *in Christ are bowels of mercy to his straying sheep*; the disciples in danger had fled away from Christ, but he will not fly away from them; no, no, he seeks them, he stands in the midst of them, and he comes again with an olive branch of peace, saying, *Peace be unto you*. Of all these we have touched before, but here is something new, a new mercy breaking out on faithless Thomas; Christ proves it by lively examples, and strong arguments, That *he will not quench the smoaking flax, nor break the bruised reed*, Isa. lxii.

3. That *he came to seek and to save that which was lost*. Luke xix. 10. That he was sent to bind up the broken-hearted, and to heal the sick, to restore the abject, and to bring to the fold the straying sheep; for the sake of one Thomas, Christ appears again, that to him as well as the rest, he might communicate his goodness, bequeathe his peace,

---

* Aug. *de verbi aposto*. Ser. 15.

† Cyr. *Jerus. Cat.* 16.

peace, and confirm him in this necessary point of faith, that he was risen again. O the goodness of Christ! *Like as a father pitieth his children, so the Lord pitieth them that fear him,* Psal. ciii. 13. He that left the ninety and nine in the wilderness to go after that sheep that was lost, declares his desire to save sinners, *Of all that thou hast given me I have not lost one,* Joh. xvii. 12. not one of his sheep; he may suffer them a while to stray as this one disciple, who continued incredulous for one whole week, but a Lord's day comes, and then Christ appears in the midst of the candlesticks, 'The Lord is 'not slack concerning his promise, (as some men 'count slackness) but he is long suffering to usward, 'not willing that any should perish, but that all 'should come to repentance,' 2 Pet. iii. 9. Humbled sinners that despair in themselves, may here find encouragement; it is their usual cry, *O my sins! these sins are heinous, these sins will damn me,* Oh! but consider, hath not the Lord pardoned as great sins? If thou art wicked, consider the Publican, if thou art unclean, remember Magdalene, if thou art a thief, a man-slayer, muse on that thief that was crucified with Jesus Christ, if thou art a blasphemer, call to mind the apostle Paul, who was first a wolf, and then a shepherd; first lead, and then gold; first a Saul, and then a Paul; if thou art faithless, diffident, an unbeliever, one that hath turned thy back on Christ, fled away from thy colours, look on Thomas, he fled away from Christ as soon as any, and he is longest from Christ after his resurrection of all the rest; and though his fellow-disciples say, *They had seen the Lord, and that he was risen indeed,* yet this will not sink into his head, he will not acknowledge it, but is most peremptory, *Except he see in his hands the print of the nails, and put his fingers into the print of the nails, and thrust his hand into his side, he will not believe,* John xx. 25. Oh! why should any sinner despair of mercy? Thou sayest, *I am wicked,* and God saith to thee, *As I live, saith the Lord God, I have no pleasure in the death of the wicked, but that the wicked turn from his way, and live,* Ezek. xxxiii. 11. Thou sayest, 'I am an un- 'believer, I am shut up in the prison of unbelief, 'under bolts and fetters, that I cannot stir one 'inch towards heaven; why, so was Didymus, and yet he obtained mercy; and the apostle tells us, That *God hath concluded all, or shut up altogether in unbelief, that he might have mercy upon all,* Rom. xi. 31. He despiseth none, rejects none, abhors none, unless they continue to despise, reject, and abhor the Lord; Oh! what a sweet point is here to gain sinners, to move, to melt, and thaw hard hearts? The incredulity of this disciple turns to our profit, and tends more to the confirmation of our faith, if we are but weak, than the very faith of all the other disciples of Jesus Christ; had not Thomas disbelieved, we had not received so great encouragements to have believed in Christ, as now we have.

Excuse me, that I speak this much to encourage sinners to come to Christ; I would be sometimes a Boanerges, and sometimes a Barnabas; a son of thunder to rouse hard hearts, and a son of consolation to cheer up drooping spirits. All ministers may learn of the great shepherd and bishop of our souls, to have a respect in their ministry to one sinner, to one incredulous Thomas; we cannot be ignorant of these scriptures, 'Him that is weak in the 'faith receive you, Ro. xiv. 1.—And to the weak I 'became as weak, that I might gain the weak, 1 'Cor. ix. 22.—And we exhort you, Brethren, warn 'them that are unruly, comfort the feeble-minded, 'support the weak, be patient towards all men, 1 'Thes. v. 14.—And some have compassion, making 'a difference; and others save with fear, pulling 'them out of the fire, Jude 22, 23.—And brethren, 'if a man be overtaken in a fault, ye which are spi- 'ritual, restore such a one in the spirit of meekness, 'Gal. vi. 1.—And the servant of the Lord must not 'strive, but be gentle unto all men, apt to teach, pa- 'tient in meekness, instructing those that oppose 'themselves, if God peradventure will give them 'repentance,' 2 Tim. ii. 24, 25. Dear souls! how do we long for your conversion and salvation? How are you in our hearts, in our prayers, in our sermons? 'My little children, how do we travel in birth a- 'gain until Christ be formed in you,' Gal. iv. 19. How gladly would we 'spend and be spent for you, 'though the more abundantly we love you, the less 'we are loved of you?' 2 Cor. xii. 15. If I know but one Thomas in the great assembly of God's people, I should think it as a crown, and the glory of my ministry to persuade this man unto faith. Christ in this apparition eyes one especially above all the rest, *when his disciples were within, and Thomas with them, then came Jesus.*

4. The manner how he appeared. 1. He came, the doors being shut. 2. He stood in the midst. 3. He said peace be unto you. All these we have dispatched in the former apparition; I shall therefore proceed to that which is peculiar to this, *then saith he to Thomas, Reach hither thy finger, and behold my hands, and reach hither thy hand, and thrust it into my side, and be not faithless but believing*, John xx. 27. In this apparition he argues his resurrection, 1. From words. 2. From deeds.

1. From words, Thomas had said, *Except I see in his hands the print of the nails, and put my finger into the print of the nails, and thrust my hand into his side, I will not believe*. Now Christ repeats the very self same words, and therein gives in an argument of his resurrection; for if Christ could know what Thomas had said, How is he but alive, and risen from the dead? The dead have not sense, much less the use of reason, but least of all the knowledge of another's mind; but Christ hath sense, and reason, science and omnisience; observe, ' though Christ be absent as in ' his bodily presence, yet he understandeth all our ' thoughts, and if need were, he could repeat all ' our sayings, word by word;' how then may this convince all unbelievers in the world, that Christ is risen, that he that was dead, now liveth, and that he is alive for evermore?

2. He appears arguing his resurrection from deeds, wherein is an act and object. 1. The act is, Thomas seeing and feeling. *q. d.* Thomas, thou wilt not believe, except thou seest and feelest; now this is against the nature of faith, it consisteth not in seeing or feeling; but, on the contrary, *Faith is the substance of things hoped for, and the evidence of things not seen*, Heb. xi. 1. Indeed in things natural a man must first have experience, and then believe; but in divine things a man must first believe, and then have experience; and yet to help thy unbelief (saith Christ) I am willing thus far to condescend, and to yield unto thy weakness, come feel the print of the nails, and of the spear, *Come, reach hither thy finger, and behold my hands, and reach hither thy hand, and thrust it into my side, and be not faithless, but believing*. Christ compassionates his children, though full of weakness and wants, *He pities them that fear him, for he knoweth our frame, he remembereth that we are dust*, Psal. ciii. 13, 14.

2. The object is Christ seen or felt; his prints and his scars, are the very witnesses of our redemption, and of his resurrection; they declare that Satan is overthrown, that death and hell are swallowed up in victory, that *he hath spoiled principalities and powers*, Col. ii. 15. and to this purpose are these texts, *Who is this that cometh from Edom, with dyed garments from Bozrah?* Isa. lxiii. 1, 2, 3. By Edom is meant death; by Bozrah (the chiefest city of Edom) is meant the state of the dead, or hell, from both which Christ returned at his glorious resurrection, *For thou wilt not leave my soul in hell, neither wilt thou suffer thy holy one to see corruption*, Psalm xvi. 10. Now, saith the prophet, or some angel, *Who is this that cometh from Edom, with dyed garments from Bozrah?* Who is this that cometh so triumphantly, with the keys of Edom and Bozrah, of death and hell at his girdle? To which the answer is given, *I that speak in righteousness, mighty to save*; as much as to say, it is I Jesus Christ, I that am righteous in speaking, and mighty in saving; whose word is truth, and whose work is salvation, it is I, even I: this answer given, another question is propounded, *Wherefore art thou red in thine apparel, and thy garments like him that treadeth in the wine-fat?* q. d. Here are nothing but scars, and wounds, and blood; if thou art so mighty to save, How comes thy apparel to be so red, and sprinkled, or stained with blood? To which Christ answers, *I have trodden the wine-press alone,—and I will tread them in mine anger*. I was trod and pressed till the very blood streamed out of my hands, and feet, and side, so pressed, that they pressed the very soul out of my body. See here, *Behold my hands, and my feet, and my side, that it is I myself, that have trod the wine-press alone*. But as I was trod, so I will tread; up he gets, and he treads on them that trod on him; his enemies of Edom and Bozrah are now like so many clusters under his feet, and he tramples upon them as upon grapes in a fat, till he makes the blood spring out of them, and all to sprinkle his garments, as if he had come out of the wine-press indeed. See here a double sight, his own blood, and his enemies blood; here's the blood of the Lamb that was slain, and the blood of the dragon that was trodden upon; here's a show of his passion and resurrection, of his suffering and triumphing.

——Ano-

—— Another text of this nature, *And one shall say unto him, What are these wounds in thy hands? Then he shall answer, those with which I was wounded in the house of my friends,* Zach. xiii. 6. I know instead of Christ some have applied these words to the false prophets, as if they had passed through the churches discipline, and so had received their wounds. But others refer them to Jesus Christ, of whom, without controversy, the next verse speaks; and of whom the first verse of this chapter speaks, and to whom, after a long parenthesis, the prophet seems to return; 'And one 'shall say unto him, Who was the fountain open-'ed? What are these wounds in thy hands?' Or, as the septuagint, 'In the midst of thy hands?' A wonder it is to see those prints and scars in the hands of Christ; and therefore is the question, What are these wounds? To which Christ answers, *Those with which I was wounded in the house of my friends,* (i. e.) in the house of my beloved, the children of Israel, my brethren according to the flesh, the people of the Jews; why, these are the wounds they gave me, and which now I show as the signs of my victory, and as the marks of my resurrection.

Thus far of the first head, the apparition of Christ.

2. For the fruits of this apparition, they contain Thomas's confession, and Christ's commendation of him in some respects.

1. Thomas's confession, *And Thomas answered and said unto him, my Lord, and my God,* a few words, but of great weight. 1. He acknowledgeth Christ a Lord, into whose hands are put the very keys of heaven, *All power is given unto me in heaven and in earth,* Mat. xxviii. 18. 2. He acknowledgeth Christ God; whom he saw with his eyes, and felt with his hands, he looks on, not as mere man, but as God, and as the second person in the Godhead. 3. He acknowledgeth Christ to be his Lord, and his God; this appropriating of Christ is the right character of faith, by which he brings home all the benefits of Christ unto his own soul, I shall a while insist on all these.

1. He acknowledgeth Christ a Lord; How is he a Lord? I answer, 1. By essence, as God is Lord, so Christ is Lord; the Father is Lord, the Son is Lord, and the Holy Ghost is Lord; and yet they are not three Lords, but one Lord.

2. By creation *Christ is before all things,* (saith the apostle) *and by him all things consist,* Col. i. 17. This very thing is an argument of his Lordship; *To us there is but one Lord, Jesus Christ, by whom are all things and we by him,* 1 Cor. viii 6.

3. By redemption, unction, office, and mediatorship, unto which he was designed by his Father, and therefore the apostle faith, That *God hath made him Lord and Christ,* Acts ii. 36. he is a Lord by his office; and by the accomplishment of his office, in dying, rising, and reviving, he became Lord both of quick and dead, *For to this end Christ both died, and rose, and revived, that he might be Lord both of dead and living,* Rom. xiv. 9. And thus he is a Lord in two respects, 1. A Lord in authority, to command whom and what he will; he only is Lord over our persons, over our faith, over our consciences; to him only we must say, *Lord, what wilt thou have me do? Lord save us, or we perish.* 2. A Lord he is in power, he hath power to forgive, and power to cleanse; he hath power to justify, and power to sanctify; he hath power to quicken, and power to save to the uttermost all that come unto God by him; he hath power to hold fast his sheep, and power to cast out the accuser of the brethren; he hath power to put down all his enemies, and power to subdue all things unto himself; in every of these respects Christ is *a Lord*. True, say blasphemers, he is Lord by office, but he is not Lord *by essence as God is Lord*. No, peruse some texts in the Old Testament, where the title of Lord is essentially spoken of, and we shall find the very same texts and titles applied to Christ in the New Testament. As for instance, in Isa. vi. 5. *Wo is me,* (saith Esay) *for mine eyes have seen the King, the Lord of hosts:* Now this John refers to Christ, *These things said Esaias, when he saw his glory, and spake of him,* John xii. 41. In Psal. lxviii. 17, 18. *The Lord is among them as in Sinai, in the holy place; thou hast ascended on high, thou hast led captivity captive, thou hast received gifts for men:* now this the apostle applies to Christ, *When he ascended up on high, he led captivity captive, and gave gifts unto men,* Eph. iv. 8. In Psal. cx. 1. *The Lord said unto my Lord, sit thou at my right-hand, until I make thine enemies thy foot-stool:* now this Jesus Christ applies to himself, saying, *That David in Spirit called him Lord,*

Lord, saying, The Lord said unto my Lord, Mat. xxii. 43, 44. In Ifa. xl. 3. *The voice of him that crieth in the wilderness, Prepare ye the way of the Lord:* now this the evangelist applies to Christ, *This is he that was spoken of by the prophet Esaias, saying, The voice of one crying in the wilderness, Prepare ye the way of the Lord,* Matth. iii. 3. No wonder, if Thomas call Christ Lord; why, both the Old and New Testament agree in this, that *Christ is Lord,* Lord by creation, and Lord by redemption, Lord by office, and Lord by essence.

2. He acknowledgeth Christ to be God, as well as Lord, *My Lord and my God.* But how is he God? I answer, not only by participation, similitude, or in some respects, as angels and men are called Gods, but simply, absolutely, essentially, and without any restriction. Sometimes we read in scripture, that men or angels, good and bad, are called Gods, *And the Lord said to Moses, see, I have made thee a God to Pharoah,* Exod. vii. 1. —*And thou shalt be instead of God to Aaron,* Ex. iv. 16. Thus Nebuchadnezzar is called the mighty one, or *the God of the heathens,* Ezek. xxxi. 11. and Satan is called *the God of this world,* 2 Cor. iv. 4. Thus magistrates are called Gods, *Thou shalt not revile the Gods,* Exod. xxii. 28. *I have said ye are Gods,* Psal. lxxxii. 6. Angels are called Gods, *Before the Gods will I sing praises unto thee,* Psal. cxxxviii. 1. but in all these there is some restriction, or improper speech; Moses is called Pharoah's God, and Aaron's God, not absolutely, but with restriction to Pharoah and Aaron; Nebuchadnezzar is called the God of the heathen, and Satan the God of this world, not absolutely, but with restriction to the heathen, and this world; magistrates are called Gods, and good angels are called Gods, not absolutely, but in respect of some offices or excellency which they partake of from God. Only Jesus Christ is called God, without any restriction, and not only in respect of some office, or similitude, but absolutely, essentially, properly, as being from all eternity God of God; as being God of the substance of the Father, before all worlds; what is Christ only God, as an angel is God? I challenge here all blasphemers in the world. *Unto which of the angels said he at any time, thou art my son, this day have I begotten thee,* Heb. i. 5. Or, unto which of the angels said he at any time, *Thy throne, O God, is for ever and ever,* Ver. 8. Or, to which of the angels said he at any time, thou art my Son, *my own Son, my only begotten Son,* Rom. viii. 32. John iii. 16. Unto which of the angels said he at any time, *This is the true God, the great God, who is over all, God blessed for ever. Amen.* 1 John v. 20. Tit. ii. 13. Rom. ix. 5. Unto which of the angels are those divine attributes given, as of eternity, immutability, omnipotency, omniscience, omnipresence? And yet are all these given to Christ; for eternity, *I was set up from the beginning, or ever the earth was,* Prov. viii. 23. For immutability, *Thou art the same, and thy years shall not fail,* Heb. i. 12. For omnipotency, *All things are delivered unto me of my Father,* Matth. xi. 27 For omniscience, *He needed not that any should testify of man, for he knew what was in man,* John ii. 25. For omnipresence, *Lo, I am with you always unto the end of the world,* Matth. xxviii. 20.

Men, brethren, and fathers, I am forced to make this defence of the divinity of Christ, because of the blasphemy of those Arians, Photinians, Eunomians, now again raked out of hell. O! who would think that such a generation of men should be amongst us in this island, where the gospel hath shined so brightly for so many years? We maintain Christ is God, and Christ is Lord; we say with Thomas, *my Lord, and my God.* Ay, say blasphemers, ' Christ is God, and Christ is Lord, ' as magistrates and angels are called Gods and ' Lords,' I hope I have said enough to difference betwixt Christ and them; howsoever I conclude with the apostle, *Though there be that are called Gods, whether in heaven or in earth (as there be Gods many, and Lords many) yet to us there is but one God, the Father, of whom are all things, and we in him; and one Lord Jesus Christ, by whom are all things, and we by him,* 1 Cor. viii. 5, 6.

3. He acknowledgeth Christ to be his Lord, and his God, *And Thomas answered, and said unto him, my Lord, and my God.* Now his faith broke out; from the things seen and felt he is raised up to believe things neither seen nor felt; he sees the prints and scars in the manhood of Christ, and now he believes that Christ is God, yea that Christ is his God, *My Lord, and my God.* Observe here, ' That faith gives the soul a propriety in God and ' Christ.' As God loves some with a special and peculiar love, so faith answers God and Christ's

particular love, by a particular application, *My Lord, my God, and my Chrift*. Faith is an appropriating, an applying, an uniting grace; in the actings of faith on God, or on Chrift as God, we may obferve thefe fteps.

1. It fees God in his glory and majefty, in his greatnefs and goodnefs, and all other his attributes; it fees God as the infinite fountain of all good, and it confiders what an infinite dreadful thing it were to be feparated from this God; it fees God, and this fight makes a deep impreffion on that very foul; the love of that God is more to the foul than all the world; and the leaft difpleafure of that God is more trouble to that foul, than all the miferies that all creatures under heaven are able to bring upon it.

2. It difcovers the reality of this glory and majefty, of this greatnefs and goodnefs of God. Before any faith is planted in a foul, the very ufe of reafon may come to underftand much of God and Chrift, but in comparifon it looks upon God and Chrift as notions, conceits, and imaginary things; only faith convinces the foul thoroughly of the certainty and truth of fuch things; where true faith is, the things we believe are more certain to us than the things we fee, or feel, or handle; faith is fo fure in its apprehenfions of God and Chrift, that it will venture foul and body, the lofs of all upon that account; it will bear any hardfhip, yea it will venture the infinite lofs of eternity upon them.

3. It enables the foul to caft itfelf upon God in Chrift for all the good and happinefs it ever expects. Alas! faith the foul, I have formerly refted on worldly things, I looked upon them as the only real fure excellencies that I had to enjoy, but now I find they are but vain things, deceitful things, no better than reeds of Egypt, vanity of vanities; and nothing is real, fure, excellent on this fide God and Chrift; and therefore I will rely upon him, and none but him; it is only God is an all-fufficient good, it is only Chrift that is the rock that will never fail, on him will I roll myfelf, unto him will I make an abfolute refignation of all, I will betruft him with all I have, and all I am, I will commit all unto him for ever and ever.

4. As faith relies all upon God in Chrift, fo it appropriates all God, and all Chrift unto itfelf, *I am my b.loved's, and my beloved is mine*, Cant. vi. 2. There is a mutual propriety betwixt Chrift and the church, and betwixt Chrift and the foul; Chrift hath a propriety in me, and I have a peculiar propriety in Chrift. Chrift is mine, fo as I have none in the world fo mine, *Whom have I in heaven but thee? And there is none upon earth that I defire befides thee*, Pfal. lxxiii. 35. Chrift is mine, and mine in a peculiar manner, there is a propriety with peculiarity, *My Lord, and my God*. O the excellency of faith! this ftep goes beyond all the reft; it is a bleffed thing to have a true fight of God, there is much power in it; but to fee God in his glory, majefty, greatnefs, goodnefs as my God; to fee all the attributes of God as thofe things that my foul hath an intereft in; to fee Chrift coming from the Father for me, to be my Redeemer; to fee Chrift in whom all fulnefs dwells, in whom the treafures of all God's riches are, not only Chrift dying as man, but rifing as God for me, and my falvation; to fee Chrift, and then to lay hold on Chrift, and to fay, *My Lord, and my God*. O! this is the work of precious faith; and to this now is Thomas arrived in this confeffion of his, *My Lord, and my God*.

2. Hereupon follow Chrift's commendation and correction; Jefus faith unto him, *Thomas, becaufe thou haft feen me, thou haft believed; bleffed are they that have not feen, and yet have believed*, John xx. 29. In the firft place Chrift commends Thomas's faith, *becaufe thou haft feen me, thou haft believed*, q. d. Thou feeft me a man, but confidering how I am rifen from the dead, thou believeft in me as God; I commend thy faith, but 'tis a weak faith in refpect of its rife; now therefore to correct it, I pronounce thofe bleffed to all generations, that when I am gone, as in regard of my bodily prefence, yet they will believe in me; *bleffed are they that have not feen, and yet have believed*. I am afraid of tedioufnefs, and therefore I fhall not enlarge any more on this apparition.

SECT. VIII.

Of Chrift's apparition to fome of his apoftles at the fea of Tiberias.

THERE is but one apparition more recorded by John, *After thefe things, Jefus fhewed himfelf again to the difciples at the fea of Tiberias,*

Tiberias, and on this wise shewed he himself, John xxi. 1. In these apparitions, the evangelist useth one and the same method: as in the former, so here again is set down the time when, the place where, the person to whom, the manner how he appeared; not one of these circumstances must be wanting to shew the evidence and certainty of his resurrection.

1. The time, *after these things*; after the three former apparitions, he comes to a fourth, and he concludes with this, as therein making some mention of himself, with which he concludes the whole book, *This is the disciple which testifieth these things, and wrote these things, and we know his testimony is true,* ver. 24.

2. The place, *at the sea of Tiberias*, or at the lake of *Genezareth*, where he had called them to the apostleship, there now he appears to these apostles; they were at first fishers, and now they are at their calling upon the sea, Christ standing on the shore.

3. The persons to whom he appears, they were disciples, their names are in the next verse. All Christ's apparitions were to the disciples of Christ; we read not that ever he shewed himself after his resurrection to any but to his followers; he shewed himself openly, *not to all the people, but unto witnesses, chosen before of God, even to us who did eat and drink with him after he rose from the dead,* Acts x. 41. Strangers to Christ must be no witnesses of Christ's resurrection, and this was his meaning, *Yet a little while, and the world seeth me no more, but ye see me,* John xiv. 19.

4. For the manner of his apparition, on this wise shewed he himself.

1. He shewed himself; so it is in this verse twice repeated, *After these things Jesus shewed himself, and on this wise he shewed himself.* '† Christ now 'was not seen, or known to the bodily eye, (for 'his body was immortal) unless by dispensation he 'condescended thereto.' I deny not, but that glorified bodies are ever actually seen of bodies that are glorified; but of mortal men, who are yet in this vale of tears, those glorious creatures cannot be actually seen, except there be some peculiar and divine dispensation. As the air is too subtil to be seen, or as the sun is too glorious for a weak eye to behold, so are glorified bodies too subtil, too splendid for a mortal eye to pierce; our Saviour tells us, That the bodies of the saints *do shine forth as the sun in the kingdom of their Father,* Mat. xiii. 43. and that they are *as the angels,* Mat. xxii. 30. And the apostle tells us, That their bodies are *spiritual bodies, there is a natural body, and there is a spiritual body,* 1 Cor. xv. 44. Now without dispensation we cannot see spiritual things. And hence it is, that when Christ shewed himself to the two disciples at Emmaus, it is said, That *their eyes were opened, and they knew him, and he vanished out of their sight,* Luke xxiv. 31. Mark, first their eyes were opened; why, no question but their eyes were opened before, they did not walk with him, and talk with him, and sit with him, and eat with him, but their eyes were then opened; ay, but now their eyes were opened in another manner, as it is said of Elisha's servant, that at the prayers of Elisha, ' the Lord opened the eyes ' of the young man, and he saw, and behold the ' mountain was full of horses, and chariots of fire, ' round about Elisha,' 2 Kings vi. 17. in like manner their eyes were so opened, *that they knew Jesus.* And then, 2. He vanished out of their sight; in a strange unusual manner they lost his sight, and they could not tell what was become of him; in a moment he was invisible to them, whose eyes he had opened, it plainly shews, that glorified bodies, as corpulent, and commensurable, may be seen of mortals, but as they are subtil, and spiritual, they cannot be seen actually without dispensation. ‡ ' Christ appeared, (saith Damascene) not by ne- ' cessity, but by his own free will; not by the law ' of nature, but by way of dispensation ' It was his mere condescension and permission, that he would shew himself at any time unto his disciples.

2. He shewed himself on this wise, *there were together, Simon Peter, and Thomas, called Dydimus, &c.* John xxi. 2, 3, 4. *&c.* In the whole narration, we may observe, 1. The occasion, and, 2. The apparition. In the occasion we have a council among the apostles what to do; and 'tis concluded they would go a fishing, they did so, though to no purpose; for they fished all *night, but caught nothing,* ver. 3. In the apparition. 1. Christ is unknown, *he stood on the shore, but the*

† Chrys. hom. 86. in Joh.   ‡ [ougomo phusios alla tik stimas topo,] Damas. l. 4 c. 1.

disciples knew not that it was Jesus, verse 4. In this condition we have Jesus speaking, and then working a miracle; he bids them *cast the net on the right side of the ship*, and then draw, but *they were not able to draw for the multitude of the fishes*, verse 6. 2. Hereupon Christ is known, *therefore that disciple whom Jesus loved, saith unto Peter, it is the Lord*; the alarm given, now all the disciples bestir themselves. 1. Peter, *he casts himself into the sea*, verse 7. 2. The other disciples they came in a little ship to the land, and there they dine, and commune with Jesus, which is the end of the history, and so ends this book of our evangelist John.

Thus far we have propounded the object; our next work is how to direct you how to look unto Jesus in this respect.

CHAP. II. SECT. I.
Of knowing Jesus as carrying on the great work of our salvation in his resurrection.

THAT in all respects we may look on Jesus.

1. Let us know Jesus carrying on the great work of our salvation for us in his resurrection, and during the time of his abode upon earth after his resurrection. This is worth the knowing, on it depends our justification, sanctification, salvation; 'for if Christ be not risen, we are yet in our sins, 'and our faith is in vain, and our hope is in vain:' little hope have we either of heaven, or of resurrection, if Christ be not risen; of all men we are most miserable that believe in Christ, if he whom we believe in be not risen again. O! my soul, study this point; many take it up in gross, they can run over this article of their creed, *the third day he rose again from the dead*; but for a particular understanding of it in respect of the time, or the end, or the manner, or the certainty, how many are to seek? I shall appeal to thyself, are not many discoveries already made, which before thou never tookest notice of? And if thou wouldest but study this point, how much more might yet appear? Especially, how much more might yet appear as to thy own good? It is not enough to know Christ's resurrection, unless thou know it for thyself. Be sure thou hast this in mind, *That Christ rose again, but what is that to me?* Saving knowledge is ever joined with a particular application, if Christ be my head then he could not rise, but I arose with him and in him: and thus, O my soul! look on Christ, and thus search into every particular of Christ's resurrection; come, study when he rose, study the arguments that make out Christ's resurrection sure and certain; study all the apparitions of Jesus Christ; Oh! what delightful studies are these; Hadst thou been with them to whom Christ appeared, Would not thy heart have leaped with joy? Come, study it close, for the benefit of these apparitions extend to thee, the fruit of Christ's resurrection is thine, even thine as well as theirs, *Know this for thyself*, Job v. 27.

SECT. II.
Of considering Jesus in that respect.

2. LEt us consider Jesus carrying on this work of our salvation for us in his resurrection. It is not enough to know a saving necessary truth, but it is required farther that we digest truth, and that we draw forth their strength for the nourishment and refreshing of our poor souls. As a man may in half an hour chew and take into his stomach that meat, which he must have seven or eight hours at least to digest; so a man may take into his understanding more truths in one hour, than he is able well to digest in many; what good those men are like to get by sermons, or providences, who are unaccustomed to this work of meditation, I cannot imagine: it is observed by some, that this is the reason why so much preaching is lost amongst us; why professors that run from sermon to sermon, and are never weary of hearing or reading, have notwithstanding such languishing starved souls, because they will not meditate. And therefore God commanded Joshua, not only to read the law but to consider of it, and dwell upon it, *This book of the law shall not depart out of thy mouth, but thou shalt meditate therein day and night*, Joshua i. 8. Why, this is the duty that I am now pressing to, if thou knowest these things, consider, ruminate, meditate, ponder on them again and again. And because this work requires enlargedness of heart and spirit, therefore take it into parts, and consider of each of them apart by itself. As,——

1. Con-

Carrying on the great Work of Man's Salvation during the Time of his Resurrection. 369

1. Consider of the time when Christ rose again. As Christ had his three days, and no more, so must thou have the same three days like unto his; the first day was called the day of preparation, the second was the sabbath-day, and the third was the resurrection-day; so thy first day is a day of preparation, a day of passion, wherein thou must strive and struggle against sin and Satan, wherein thou must suffer all their bitter darts till thou diest, and give up the ghost. And thy second day is a day of rest, wherein thy body must lie in the grave, and thy flesh rest in hope; wherein thou shalt *enter into peace, and rest in thy bed*, Isa. lvii. 2. until the trumpet sound, and bid thee *arise, and come to judgment*; and thy third day is a day of resurrection unto glory. It is the first day of the week, or the first beginning of a never-ending world. Thus consider the time of Christ's resurrection, and thence mayest thou draw down some use for thy soul's nourishment.

2. Consider of the reasons why Christ arose; was it not to confound the Jews? They could not endure to hear of Christ's resurrection, and therefore, when Peter, and the other apostles preached that point, *They were cut to the heart, and took counsel to slay them*, Acts v. 33. It is the case of them to say, *We will not have that man to reign over us*. They that by their sins crucify Christ every day, cannot without horror think of his exaltation, it cuts them to the heart that Christ is risen to be their judge. Again, was it not to confirm the faith of Christ's followers? Till he was risen their faith was but a weak faith, weak in knowledge, weak in assent, weak in confidence, weak in assurance; much ado had Christ with them, many a time had he chid them, *Why are ye fearful, O ye of little faith?* But after he had shewed himself alive by many infallible proofs, they could then cry it out, *My Lord, and my God*. Again, was it not to evidence that he had fully satisfied all our debts? The apostle tells us, *That Christ was our surety*, Hebrews vii. 22. at his death he was arrested, and cast into prison, whence he could not come till all was paid; and therefore to hear that Christ is risen, and that he hath broken the bolts and fetters of the grave, it is a clear evidence, that God is satisfied, and that Christ is discharged by God himself. Oh! what breasts of consolation are here? Again, was it not to conquer sin, death, and devil? Now he took from death his sting, and from hell his standard; now he seized upon the hand-writing, that was against us, and nailed it to his cross; now he spoiled principalities, and powers, and carried the keys of death and hell at his own girdle; now he came out of the grave as a mighty conqueror, saying, as Deborah did in her song, *O my soul, thou hast trodden down strength, thou hast marched valiantly*, Judg. v 21. Again, was it not to become the first fruits of them that sleep? Christ was the first that rose again from the grave to die no more; and by virtue of his resurrection (as being the first-fruits) all the elect must rise again, *As in Adam all die, even so in Christ shall all be made alive; but every man in his own order, Christ the first-fruits, and afterwards they that are Christ's at his coming*, 1 Cor. xv. 22, 23. Some may wonder, can the resurrection of one, a thousand six hundred years ago, be the cause of our rising? Yes, as well as the death of one, five thousand six hundred years ago, is the cause of our dying; Adam and Christ were two heads, two roots, two first-fruits, either of them in reference to his company whom they stand for. And now, O my soul! thou mayest say with Job, *I know that my Redeemer liveth; and that I shall see him at the last day, not with other, but with these same eyes*, Job xix. 25. If Christ live, then must I live also, if he be risen, then *though after my skin worms shall destroy this body, yet in my flesh I shall see God*, ver. 26. Again, was it not that he might be declared to be the Son of God? Was it not that he might be exalted and glorified? This is the main reason of all the rest; see thou to this; O! give him the glory, and praise of his resurrection; so muse, and meditate, and consider on this transaction, as to ascribe to his name all honour, and glory; what is he risen from the dead? *Hath God highly exalted him, and given him a name above every name?* Psalm ii. 11. O! then let *every tongue confess, that Jesus Christ is Lord, to the glory of God the Father*.

3. Consider of the manner of Christ's resurrection; he rose as a common person; in which respect his resurrection concerns us no less than himself. We must not think that when Christ was raised, it was no more than when Lazarus was raised; his resurrection was the resurrection of us all; it was in the name of us all, and had in it a seed like virtue to

A a a work

work the resurrection of us all. O! the privilege of this communion with Christ's resurrection! if I believe this truly, I cannot but believe the resurrection of my body, and the life everlasting; why, Jesus Christ hath led the dance, and though of myself I have no right to heaven or glory, yet in Christ my head I have as good right to it as any heir apparent to his lands. —— 2. He rose by his own power; and so did none but Jesus Christ: from the beginning of the world it was never heard, that any dead man raised himself; indeed one instance we have that a dead man's corpse should raise up another dead man, *They cast the man into the sepulchre of Elisha, and when the man was let down and touched the bones of Elisha, he revived and stood upon his feet.* 2 Kings xiii. 21. dead Elisha raised up a dead man from the grave, but dead Elisha could not raise up himself from the grave; only Christ arose himself, and at the same time he raised many others; and here was the argument of his Godhead, *I have power to lay down my life, and I have power to take it up again,* John x. 18. How should we but trust him with our life, who is the resurrection and the life? *He that believeth in him though he were dead, yet shall he live.* O my soul! he was able to raise himself, much more is he able to raise thee up; only believe, and live for ever. —— 3. He rose with an earthquake, O the power of Christ in every passage! what ailed thee, O earth, to skip like a ram? Was not the new tomb hewn out of a rock? And was not a great stone rolled to the door of the sepulchre? The ground wherein he lay was firm and solid, *And shall the rock be removed out of his place?* Job xviii. 4. O yes! *the Lord reigneth, and therefore the earth is moved,* Ps. xcix. 1. Oh! what a rocky heart is this of mine? How much harder is it than that rock that moves not, melts not at the presence of God, at the presence of the God of Jacob? The sun (they say) danced that morning at Christ's resurrection; the earth (I am sure) then trembled; and yet my heart is no way affected with this news; I feel it neither dance for joy, or tremble for fear; O my soul! be serious in this meditation, consider what a posture wouldest thou have been in, if thou hadst been with those soldiers that watched Christ; so realize this earthquake, as if thou now felt it trembling under thee.

4. An angel ministred to him at his resurrection. *An angel came and rolled back the stone from the door, and sat upon it,* Matth. xxviii. 2. Angels were the first ministers of the gospel, the first preachers of Christ's resurrection; they preached more of Christ than all the prophets did; they first told the woman that *Christ was risen,* Luke xxiv. 6. and they did the first service to Christ at his resurrection, ' In rolling the stone from the ' door's mouth; O my soul, that thou wert but like the e blessed angels! how is it that they are so forward in God's service, and thou art so backward? One day thou expectest to be equal with the angels, and art thou now so far behind them? What, to be equal in reward, and behind them in service? Here is a meditation able to check thy sloth, and to spur thee on to thy duty.—5. Many of the bodies of the saints arose out of their graves at his resurrection; as the angels ministred, so the saints waited on him. In this meditation trouble not thyself whether David, Moses, Job, Abraham, Isaac and Jacob, were some of those saints, as some conjecture upon some grounds; it is a better consideration, to look upon them as the fruit of Christ's resurrection, and as an earnest of thy own; the virtue of Christ's resurrection appears immediately, and it will more appear at the general resurrection-day. As sure as these saints arose with him, and went into the holy city, and appeared to many; so sure shall thy body rise again at the last day; and (if thou art but a saint) it shall go with him into the heavenly Jerusalem, and appear before God, and his Son Jesus Christ in glory.—6. Christ rose again with a true and perfect body, with an incorruptible and powerful body, with a spiritual and an agile body, with a glorious body, brighter than the sun in his utmost glory. On these things may thy soul expatiate; O! it is a worthy, blessed, soul-ravishing subject to think upon; and the rather if we consider that conformity which we believe, *We look for a Saviour* (saith the apostle) *the Lord Jesus Christ, who shall change our vile bodies, that they may be fashioned like unto his glorious body,* Phil. iii. 20, 21. O my soul, that this clay of thine should be a partaker of such glory! that this body of dust and earth should shine in heaven like those glorious spangles of the firmament; that this body shall rot in dust, and fall more vile than a carrion, should rise, and shine like the glo-

rious

ious body of our Saviour on mount Tabor; surely thou owest much to Chrift's refurrection. O! confider of it, till thou feeleft the influence, and comeft to the affurance of this bleffed change.

4. Confider of the feveral apparitions of Jefus Chrift, efpecially of thofe written by the evangelift John. As,——

1. Mufe on his apparition to Mary Magdalene; Oh the grief before he appeared! and oh the joys when he appeared!——1. Before, fhe apprehended nothing, but that fome or other had taken away her Lord; thefe were all the words fhe uttered before he appeared. *They have taken away my Lord, and I know not where they have laid him*; fo fhe told Peter and John; and when two angels appeared in white, afking her, *Woman, why weepeft thou?* She gives the fame anfwer to them, *they have taken away my Lord, and I know not where they have laid him*. A foul in defertion knows not what to do, but to weep and cry, 'Oh! my Lord is gone, I have loft my Lord, my God, my Jefus, my king;' in this meditation, confider, O my foul! as if thou hadft been in Mary's cafe; was it not a fad cafe, when the angels of heaven knew not how to comfort her? Suppofe any one of confolation had ftood by, and had fuch a one perfuaded, 'O Mary! fupprefs thy fadnefs, refrefh thy heart with this bleffed vifion, thou didft feek but one, and thou haft found two, a dead body was thy errand, and thou haft lit on two alive; thy weeping was for a man, and thy tears obtained angels: obferve them narrowly, the angels invite thee to a parley, it may be they had fome happy news to tell thee of thy Lord: remember what they are, and where they fit, and whence they come, and to whom they fpeak; they are angels of peace, neither fent without caufe, nor feen but of favour, they fit on the tomb, to fhew they are no ftrangers to thy lofs; they come from heaven, from whence all happy news defcendeth; they fpeak to thyfelf, as if they had fome fpecial embaffage to deliver unto thee.' No, no; thefe cordials are in vain; neither man nor angel can do her good, or comfort her drooping foul; either Chrift himfelf muft come in prefence, or fhe cries, 'Miferable comforters 'are ye all. Alas! fmall is the light, that a ftar 'can yield when the fun is down; a forry ex-'change it is to go and gather crumbs after the

'lofs of the bread of life; Oh! what can thefe 'angels do? They cannot perfuade me that my 'mafter is not loft, for my own eyes will difprove 'them; they can lefs tell me where he may be 'found, for themfelves would wait upon him, if 'they knew but where; I am apt to think they 'know not where he is, and therefore they are 'come to the place where he laft was, making 'the tomb their heaven, and the remembrance of 'his prefence the fuel of their joy; alas! what 'do angels here? I neither came to fee them, nor 'defire to hear them; I came not to fee angels, 'but the Creator of angels, to whom I owe more 'than both to men and angels.

2. After he appeared fhe was filled with joy; for fo it was, that when nothing elfe would fatisfy, or comfort this poor creature, Jefus himfelf appears; at firft he is unknown, fhe takes him for the gardener of the place; but within a while he utters a voice that opens both her ears, and eyes, *and Jefus faith unto her, Mary*. It was the fweeteft found that ever fhe heard; many a time had fhe been called by that name, but never heard fhe a voice fo effectual, powerful, inward, feeling as at this time; hereby the cloud is fcattered, and the fun of righteoufnefs appears; this one word Mary, enlightens her eyes, dries up her tears, chears her heart, revives her fpirits that were as good as dead. One word of Chrift wrought fo ftrange an alteration in her, as if fhe had been wholly made new, when fhe was only named. And hence it is, that being ravifhed with his voice, and impatient of delays, fhe takes his talk out of his mouth, and to his firft and only word, Mary, fhe anfwers, *Rabboni, which is to fay, mafter.* q. d. 'Mafter, 'is it thou? With many a falt tear have I fought 'thee, and art thou unexpectedly fo near at hand? 'Thy abfence was hell, and thy prefence is no lefs 'than heaven to me: oh! how is my heart ravifh-'ed at thy found?' If the babe leaped in the womb 'of Elizabeth, when fhe had but heard the falu-'tation of Mary, how fhould my heart but leap 'at thy falutation? I feel I am exceedingly tranf-'ported beyond myfelf. Inftead of my heavy heart 'and troubled fpirit, I feel now a fweet and de-'lightful tranquillity of mind; thou art my folace, 'and foul's delight? whom have I in heaven but 'thee? And whom defire I upon earth in com-'parifon of thee? And yet I am not fatisfied; not 'only

'only fruition of thee, but union with thee, is 'that which my soul longs after; not only thy pre-'sence, but thy embraces, or my embraces of thee 'can give content; come then, and give me leave, 'my Lord, and my God, to run to the haunt of 'my chief delights, to fall at thy sacred feet, and 'to bathe them with my tears of joy; O! my Jesus, 'I must needs deal with thee, as the spouse dealt 'with thee,' *Now I have found thee whom my soul loves dearly, I will hold thee, and I will not let thee go*, Cant. iii. 4.

I know not in all the book of God, a soul more depressed with sorrow, and lifted up with joy! O meditate on this! if Christ be absent, all is night, but if Christ appear, he turns all again into a lightsome day; there is no sorrow like that which apprehends Christ's loss, and therefore in hell it is looked upon as the greatest pain; of the two (say divines) it is a greater torment to lose God, and to lose Jesus Christ, than to endure all those flaming whips, unquenchable fires, intolerable cold, abominable stench; and on the other side, there is no joy in heaven like to that which apprehends Christ's presence, *In thy presence there is fulness of joy, and at thy right-hand there are pleasures for evermore*, Psal. xvi. 11. *I had rather be in hell with Christ*, (said one) *than in heaven without Christ*. This is the very top of heaven's joy, the quintessence of glory, the highest happiness of the saints; O! my soul, seek with Mary, yea seek and weep, and weep and seek, and never rest satisfied till Christ appear, if thou art but in the use of means, he will appear sooner or later; or, what if thou never sawest a good day on earth, one sight of Christ in heaven will make amends. Surely if thou knewest the joy of Christ's presence, thou wouldest run thro' death and hell to come to Christ, it was Paul's saying, *I desire to be dissolved, and to be with Christ, which is far better*, Phil. i. 23. he cared not for death so he might go to Christ, for that was better than very life itself.

2. Muse on his apparition to the ten disciples, *When the doors were shut for fear of the Jews, then came Jesus, and stood in the midst, saying to them, Peace be unto you*, John xx. 19. Before his apparitions sorrow and fear had possessed all their spirits, sometimes they walked abroad, and were sad, and sometimes they kept within, and shut the doors upon them as being exceedingly afraid: in this condition Jesus Christ (that knows best the times and seasons of grace and comfort) comes and stands in the midst of their assembly; he comes in, they know not how, and no sooner he is in, but he salutes them in this manner, *Peace be unto you*. This was the prime of all his wishes; no sooner is he risen, but he wisheth peace to all his apostles; no sooner meets he with them, but the very opening of his lips was with these words; they are the first words, at the first meeting, on the very first day.——— A sure sign that peace was in the heart of Jesus Christ; howsoever it is with us, peace or war, there is a commonweal where Christ is king, and there is peace, and nothing but peace; come, sift, try, and examine, art thou, O! my soul, a member of this body, a subject of this commonweal? Hath the influence of Christ's peace wrought and declared at his resurrection) any force on thee? Hast thou peace with God, and peace within, and peace without? Dost thou feel that ointment poured upon Aaron's head, and running down to the skirts of his garments? Dost thou feel the dew of Hermon, and the dew that descends upon mount Sion, dropping (as it were) upon thy heart? Doth the Spirit assure thee, that Christ, the prince of peace, hath made peace and reconciliation betwixt God and thee, betwixt the king and thee, a rebel to his crown and dignity? *O! how beautiful upon the mountain would the feet of him be, that should publish peace, that should bring these good tidings?* Isa. lii. 7. 'That thou 'art a citizen of that Jerusalem, where God is 'king, and Christ the prince of peace? Where all 'the buildings are compact together, as a city that 'is at unity within itself,' Psal. cxxii. 3.

3. Muse on his apparition to all the apostles, when they were all convened, and Thomas with them, This apparition was occasioned by Thomas's incredulity, 'Except (said he) I see in his hands the 'print of the nails, and put my finger into the print 'of the nails, and thrust my hand into his side, I 'will not believe,' John xx. 25 Now, therefore saith Jesus to Thomas, 'Come, reach hither thy fin-'ger, and behold my hands, and reach hither thy 'hand, and thrust it into my side, and be not faith-'less, but believing,' ver. 27. Methinks I see Thomas's finger on Christ's bored hand, and Thomas's hand in Christ's pierced side. Here's a strong argument to convince my soul that Christ is risen
from

from the dead; why, see, this is the same Christ that was crucified; the same Christ that had his hands bored with nails, and that had his heart pierced with a spear; tho' the wounds are healed as to sense of pain, yet the scars, and holes, and clefts remain as big as ever: the hole in his hand is yet so large, that Thomas may put his finger not only on it, but into it; and the cleft in his side is yet so large, that Thomas may thrust his whole hand into his side, and with his fingers touch that heart that issued out streams of blood for my salvation. In this meditation, be not too curious, whether the print of the nails were but continued till Christ had confirmed his disciples faith, or whether he retains them still for some farther use. It is a better consideration to look upon them so as to confirm thy own faith; is there not too much of Thomas's incredulity in thy breast? Dost thou not sometimes feel some doubtings of Christ's rising? Or, at least, dost thou not question, Whether Christ's resurrection belongs unto thee? Is not Satan busy with a temptation? Is not thy conscience troubled for thy sins, and especially for thy sin of unbelief? If so, (and I know not but it may be so with thee, and the best of saints). ' Come then, ' and reach hither thy finger, and behold Christ's ' hands, and reach hither thy hand, and thrust it ' into his side:' my meaning is, come with the hand of faith, and lay hold on Christ, yea, hide thyself in the holes of the rock, *Be like the dove that maketh her nest in the sides of the hole's mouth*, Jer. xlviii. 28. The dove that would be safe from the devouring birds, or from the fowler's snare, she flies to the hole in a rock, and thus Christ invites his spouse, *O! my dove, that art in the clefts of the rock, in the secret places of the stairs! let me see thy countenance, let me hear thy voice*, Can. ii. 14. In the clefts of the rock, I am safe, (said Bernard) '† There I stand firmly, there I am se-' cure from Satan's prey.' It is storied of a martyr, That writing to his wife where she might find him, when he was fled from home, ' ‡ O my dear! ' (said he) if thou desirest to see me, seek me in the ' side of Christ, in the cleft of the rock, in the ' hollow of his wounds, for there I have made ' my nest, there will I dwell, there shalt thou find ' me, and no where else but there.' O my soul, that thou wouldest make this use of the wounds of Christ! are they not as the cities of refuge, whether thou mayest fly and live? ' * Nothing is more ' efficacious to cure the wounds of conscience, than ' a frequent and serious meditation of the wounds ' of Christ.' Come, be not faithless but believing; these monuments of Christ's resurrection are for the confirmation of thy faith; if well viewed and handled, they will quiet thy conscience, quench the fiery darts of Satan, increase thy faith, till thou comest to assurance, and sayest with Thomas, *My Lord, and my God*. '§ I may be troubled, but I ' shall not be overwhelmed; because I will re-' member the print of the nails, and of the spear, ' in the hands and side of Jesus Christ.'

4. Muse on his apparition to the seven disciples at the sea of Tiberias. First, Christ appears, and works a miracle; he discovers himself to be Lord of sea as well as land; at his word multitudes of fishes come to the net, and are caught by his apostles; nor is this miracle without a mystery, *The kingdom of heaven is like a drawn net, cast into the sea, which when it is full, men draw to land*, Mat. xiii. 47. What is this divine trade of ours, but a spiritual fishing? The world is a sea, souls like fishes swim at liberty in this deep, and the nets of wholsome doctrine are they that draw up some to the shore of grace, and glory. 2. Upon this miracle, *The disciple whom Jesus loved, said unto Peter, it is the Lord*. John is more quick-eyed than all the rest, he considers the miracle, and him that wrought it, and presently he concludes, it is the Lord; O! my soul, meditate on the mystery of this discovery; if ever a soul be converted and brought home to Christ, it is the Lord; but, Oh! whether is Christ gone, that we have lost so long his converting presence? Oh! for one apparition of Jesus Christ? Till then we may preach our hearts out, and never nearer; do what we can, souls will to hell, except the Lord break their career; ministers can do no more but tell, thus and thus men may be saved; and thus and thus men will be damned, *He that believeth on the Son hath eternal life, and he that believeth not the Son shall not see life*, John iii. 36. but when they

† Ber. *ser.* 61. *in Cant.*— ‡ Surius *in vita sancti Elzearij.* * Bern. ibid.
§ *Turbator, sed non perturbator quia vulnerum Christi recordar*, Aug.

have

have said all they can, it is only God must give the blessing: Oh! what is preaching without Christ's presence? One hearing what mighty feats Scanderbeg's sword had done, he sent for it, and when he saw it, 'Is this the sword (said he) that hath done 'such great exploits? What's this sword more 'than any other sword? O! (says Scanderbeg) I 'sent thee my sword, but not my arm that did 'handle it;' so ministers may use the sword of the Spirit, the word of God, but if the Spirit's arm be not with it, they may brandish it every Sabbath to little purpose; when all is done, if ever any good be done, *it is the Lord*. No sooner John observes the miracle, that a multitude of fishes were caught and taken, but he tells Peter of a blessed discovery, *it is the Lord.*——3. Upon this discovery Peter throws himself into the sea; O! the fervent love he carries towards Christ! if he but hear of his Lord he will run through fire and water to come unto him; so true is that of the spouse, *Many waters cannot quench love, neither can the floods drown it; if a man would give all the substance of his house for love, it would utterly be contemned*, Cant. viii. 7. If I love Christ, I cannot but long for communion and fellowship with Christ; ' * Wheresoever thou art, O blessed Saviour, give me no more happiness than to be with 'thee, if on the earth, I would travel day and 'night to come unto thee; if on the sea, with Peter I would swim unto thee; if riding in triumph, 'I would sing Hosanna to thee; but if in glory, 'How happy should I be to look upon thee?' Christ's apparitions are ravishing sights; if he but stand on the shore, Peter throws himself over board to come to Christ; why, now he stands on the pinacles of heaven, wafting and beckoning with his hand, and calling on me in his word, *Rise up my love, my fair one, and come away*, Cant. ii. 10. O! my soul, make haste; in every duty look out for another apparition of Jesus Christ, when thou comest to hear, say, ' Have over Lord by this sermon;' and when thou comest to pray, say, ' Have over ' Lord by this prayer to a Saviour;' neither fire nor water, floods nor storms, death nor life, principalities nor powers, height nor depth, nor any other creature should hinder thy passage to Christ, or separate thy soul from Christ, ' Consider what

' I say (saith Paul) and the Lord give thee understanding in all things; remember that Jesus Christ ' of the seed of David was raised from the dead ' according to my gospel, 2 Tim. ii. 7, 8. That Christ was raised is a gospel truth; ay, but do thou remember it, do thou consider it, and the Lord give thee understanding in all things.

SECT. III.

Of desiring Jesus in that respect.

3. LET us desire after Jesus carrying on the great work of our salvation for us in his resurrection. What desire is, we have opened before, ' Some call it the wing of the soul, where-' by it moveth, and is carried to the thing it ex-' pecteth, to feed itself upon it, and to be satisfied ' with it.

But what is there in Christ's resurrection, that should move our souls to desire after it?

I answer, 1. Something in itself. 2. Something as in reference unto us.

1. There is something in itself; had we but a view of the glory, dignity, excellency of Christ as raised from the dead, it would put us on this heavenly motion, we should *fly as the eagle that hasteth to eat*, Hab. i. 8. The object of desire is good, but the more excellent and glorious any good is, the more earnest and eager should our desires be; now Christ as raised from the dead is an excellent object; the resurrection of Christ is the glorifying of Christ, yea, his glorifying took its beginning at his blessed resurrection; now it was that *God highly exalted him, and gave him a name above every name*, &c. Phil. ii. 9. And in this respect how desirable is he?

2. There is something in reference unto us; as, 1. *He rose again for our justification*, Rom. iv. 25. I must needs grant, that Christ's death, and not his resurrection is the meritorious cause of our justification; but on the other side, Christ's resurrection and not his death is for the applying of our justification; as the stamp adds no virtue, nor matter of real value to a piece of gold, but only it makes that value, which before it had actually, appliable and current unto us; so the resurrection of

* *Ubicunque fueris O domine Jesu, &c.* Aug.

Christ

Christ was no part of the price or satisfaction which Christ made to God, yet it is that which applies all his merits, and makes them of force unto his members. Some I know would go further, Lucius, a learned writer, saith, 'That justification 'is therefore attributed to Christ's resurrection, 'because it was the complete and ultimate act of 'Christ's active obedience:' and from hence inferreth, 'That remission of sin is attributed to 'his passive obedience, and justification or imputation of righteousness, to his active obedience.' Goodwin, no way inferior to him, saith, that justification is put upon Christ's resurrection with a *Rather, Who is he that condemneth? It is Christ that died, yea, rather that is risen again*, Rom. viii. 34. not but that the matter of our justification is only the obedience and death of Christ, but the form of our justification, or the act of pronouncing us righteous by that his obedience and death depends upon Christ's resurrection; for then it was that Christ himself was justified, and then he was justified as a common person, representing us therein, so that we were then justified with him, and in him, and we are said *to be risen with him, and to sit with him in heavenly places*. Burgess, one admirably judicious, saith, 'That justification is given to Christ's resurrection, as a privilege flowing from its efficient cause; 'Indeed Christ's death is the meritorious cause of 'our justification, but Christ's resurrection is, in 'some sense (saith he) the efficient cause, because 'by his rising again, the Spirit of God doth make 'us capable of justification, and then bestoweth it 'on us.' I know there is some difference amongst these worthies, but they all agree in this, that the resurrection of Christ was for our justification, and that by the resurrection of Christ, all the merits of his death were made appliable unto us. As there was a price and ransom to be paid by Christ for the redemption of man, so it was necessary that the fruit, effect, and benefit of Christ's redemption should be applied and conferred; now this work of application and actual collation of the fruit of Christ's death, began to be *in fieri* upon the resurrection-day, but it was not then finished and perfected; for to the consummation thereof, the ascension of Christ, the mission of the Holy Ghost, apostolical preaching of the gospel to Jews and Gentiles, the donation of heavenly grace, and Christ's intercession at the right hand of God, were very necessary. O the benefit of Christ's resurrection as to our justification! *If Christ be not risen again, ye are yet in your sins, and your faith is vain*, 1 Cor. xv. 17. Remission of sin, (which is a part of our justification) though purchased by Christ's death, yet could not be applied to us, or possibly be made ours, without Christ's resurrection; and in this respect, oh! how desirable is it?

2. He rose again for our sanctification. So the apostle, *He hath quickned us together with Christ, and hath raised us up together with Christ*, Eph. ii. 5, 6. Our first resurrection is from Christ's resurrection; if you would know how you that were blind in heart, uncircumcised in spirit, utterly unacquainted with the life of God, are now light in the Lord, affecting heavenly things, walking in righteousness; it comes from this blessed resurrection of Jesus Christ, we are *quickned with Christ*; it is Christ's resurrection that raised our souls, being stark dead, with such a resurrection as that they shall never die more; whence the apostle, *Reckon yourselves to be dead unto sin, but alive unto God through Jesus Christ our Lord*, Rom. vi. 11. We are dead to sin, and alive unto God by the death and resurrection of Jesus Christ; we may reckon thus for ourselves, that if we be in Christ, there comes a virtue from Christ, an effectual working of Christ by his Spirit into our hearts, and it is such a work as will conform us to Christ *dead*, and to Christ risen; why, reckon thus, saith the apostle, go not by guess, and say, I hope it will be better with me than it hath been; no, no, but reckon, conclude, make account, *I must live to God, I must live the life of grace, for Christ is risen*. To the same purpose he speaks before, *Like as Christ was raised up from the dead by the glory of the Father, even so we also should walk in newness of life*, Rom. vi. 4. Christ rose again to a new life, and herein his resurrection differed from the resurrection of those others raised by him, as of Lazarus, Jairus's daughter, the widow of Nain's son, for they were but raised to the same life, which formerly they lived, but Jesus Christ was raised up to a new life; and according to this exemplar we should now walk in newness of life; this is the end of Christ's resurrection, that we should be new creatures, of new lives, new principles,

ciples, new conversations: he rose again for our sanctification.

3. He rose again for our resurrection to eternal life, Christ is both the pattern and pledge, and cause of the resurrection of our bodies, *For since by man came death, by man came also the resurrection of the dead; for as in Adam all die, even so in Christ shall all be made alive,* 1 Cor. xv. 21, 22. There is a virtue flowing from Christ to his saints, by which they shall be raised up at the latter day; as there is a virtue flowing from the head to the members, or from the root to the branches, so those that are Christ's shall be raised up by Christ. Not but that all the wicked in the world shall be raised again by the power of Christ as he is a judge, for *all that are in the graves shall hear his voice, and they shall come forth,* yet with this difference, *They that have done good unto the resurrection of life, and they that have done evil unto the resurrection of damnation,* John v. 28, 29. In this respect the saints shall have a peculiar resurrection; and therefore they are called *the children of the resurrection,* Luke xx. 36. because *they shall obtain a better resurrection,* as the apostle calls it, Heb. xi. 35. And is not Christ's resurrection desirable in this very respect? If we should think, these bodies of ours being dust must never return from their dusts, it might discourage; but here is our hope, Christ is risen, and therefore we must rise; it is the apostle's own argument against those that held ' there was no resurrection of the dead,' why, saith the apostle, *If there be no resurrection of the dead, then is not Christ risen —If the dead rise not, then is not Christ raised ;—But now is Christ risen from the dead, and become the first fruits of them that slept,* 1 Cor. xv. 12, 13, 16, 20. He argues plainly that Christ's resurrection is the principal efficient cause of the resurrection of the just, *I am the resurrection, and the life,* saith Christ, John xi. 25. *(i. e.)* I am the author, and worker of the resurrection to life. *As the Father raiseth up the dead, and quickneth them, even so the Son quickneth whom he will,* John v. 21. and hence it is that Christ is called *a quickning Spirit,* 1 Cor. xv. 45. Christ is the head and stock of all the elect, Christ is the author, procurer, conveyer of life to all his offspring, by the communication of his Spirit. *Christ is a quickning Spirit,* quickning dead souls, and quickning dead bodies, the author both of the first and second resurrection. And is not this desirable?

4. He rose again for the assurance of our justification, sanctification, and salvation. This is the reason why the apostle useth these words to prove the resurrection of Christ, *I will give you the sure mercies of David,* Acts xiii. 34. none of God's mercies had been sure to us, if Christ had not risen again from the dead; but now all is made sure; his work of redemption being fully finished, the mercy which thereupon depended was now made certain, (and as the apostle speaks) *sure unto all the seed,* Rom. iv. 16.

Methinks a thought of this object in respect of itself, and in respect of us, should put our souls into a longing frame; is it not a desirable thing to see the king in his beauty? Were not the *daughters of Sion glad to go forth, and to behold king Solomon with the crown wherewith his mother crowned him in the day of his espousals?* Cant. iii. 11. If Christ incarnate, and in human frailty was the desire of all nations, How much more is Christ exalted, and in his glory? If it was Augustine's great wish to have seen Christ in the flesh, How should we but wish to see Christ as risen again from the dead? *He is altogether lovely,* or *he is altogether desirable,* Cant. v. 16. desirable in the womb, desirable in the manger, desirable on the cross, even when despised and numbered with thieves, desirable in his resurrection, yea, all desirable, yea, above all desirable, as risen, exalted, glorified; in this consideration we cannot fathom the thousand, thousand part of the worth, and incomparable excellency of Jesus Christ. Or, if Christ's resurrection in itself will not stir up our lazy desires, Is it not desirable as in reference unto us? What, that he should rise again for our justification? That by virtue of his resurrection thy soul should appear righteous before the judgment-seat of God? O what a ravishing word is that, what a triumphing challenge? *Who shall lay any thing to the charge of God's elect? It is God that justifieth, who is he that condemneth? It is Christ that died, yea, rather that is risen again,* Rom. viii. 33, 34. Oh! the stings that many have, saying, What shall I do when I die, and go down to the dust? May not the Lord have something against me at the day of reckoning? Why, no poor soul, if thou art in Christ, it is he that died, yea, rather that is risen again

again for thy juſtification; by his reſurrection he hath cleared all reckonings, to that now who ſhall condemn? Not ſin, Chriſt hath taken it away; not the law, Chriſt hath fulfilled it for us; not Satan, for if the judge acquit us, What can the jaylor do; O! my ſoul, that thy portion may be with theirs who hath right and title to this bleſſed reſurrection of Jeſus Chriſt; but thou ſayeſt again, What is it to me if I be juſtified in Chriſt, and yet my heart remain unholy, and unſubdued to Chriſt? It is true thou findeſt a woful, ſinful nature within thee croſs and contrary unto holineſs, and leading thee daily into captivity? Yet remember it is Chriſt that died, yea, rather that is riſen again, and by virtue of his reſurrection he hath given thee a new nature, another nature, which makes thee wreſtle againſt ſin, and ſhall in time prevail over all ſin. But thou ſayeſt again, What if I be juſtified, and ſanctified, if after death I ſhall not be raiſed to life? Why, fear not, O my ſoul, for if Chriſt be riſen thou ſhalt riſe, and riſe to eternal life, *I am the reſurrection and the life*, not only the reſurrection, but life is in him originally, as water is in the fountain, and from him it is derived to us, *becauſe I live, ye ſhall live alſo*, John xiv. 19. But thou ſayeſt again, O! that I were aſſured of this! many doubts and jealouſies are upon me from day to day. Sometimes indeed, I have a comfortable hope of my juſtification, ſanctification, ſalvation, and ſometimes again, I am forced to cry, *Lord, why caſteſt thou off my ſoul? Why hideſt thou thy face from me?* Pſalm lxxxviii. 14. O! conſider of the ends of Chriſt's reſurrection; was it not to give thee the ſure mercies of David? Was it not to apply the merits of Chriſt's active and paſſive obedience, and to bring them home to thy ſoul? Was it not to confirm, and ratify thy faith, *elſe were it in vain?* 1 Cor. xv. 17. O! the perſon of Chriſt! and O the privileges of Chriſt as being raiſed from the dead! O! my ſoul, that thou wert on the wing in thy deſires after Chriſt! O! that thy motions were as ſwift as the eagle that haſteth to eat! O! that feelingly thou kneweſt him, and the power of his reſurrection! that thou wert reſolved to give no ſleep to thine eyes, nor ſlumber to thine eye-lids, until thou couldeſt ſay, 'Chriſt's reſurrection is mine!' Why Lord, that I ſhould long for vanities, trifles, toys, pleaſures, profits, earthly contentments; that I ſhould long like ſome women with child, for a deal of baggage, aſhes, coals, very lothſome food; and yet that I ſhould feel no pantings, breathings, hungerings, thirſtings after Chriſt's reſurrection, to feed upon it, and to be ſatisfied with it! Come, here's a bleſſed object, here's delicious fare, O! ſtir up thy appetite, 'ſuck and be ſatisfied, drink, yea, 'drink abundantly, O my beloved.'

SECT. IV.

Of hoping in Jeſus in that reſpect.

4. LET us hope in Jeſus, as carrying on the great work of our ſalvation for us in his reſurrection: only remember, I mean not a fluctuating, wavering, unſettled, uneſtabliſhed hope, no, no, let us hope firmly, ſuredly, fixedly; let us come up to that plerophory or full aſſurance of hope, that we may conclude comfortably and confidently, Chriſt's reſurrection is ours; and yet that our concluſion may not be raſh, but upon right grounds, we may examine the firmneſs, ſolidneſs, ſubſtantialneſs of our hope in Chriſt's reſurrection by theſe following ſigns —As,

1 If Chriſt's reſurrection be mine, then is Chriſt's death mine, the fruits or effects of Chriſt's death and reſurrection cannot be ſevered; 'If we have 'been planted together in the likeneſs of his death, 'we ſhall be alſo in the likeneſs of his reſurrection, Rom. vi. 5. Mortification and vivification are twins of one and the ſame ſpirit, *Depart from evil and do good*, Pſal. xxxiv. 14.—*Ceaſe to do evil, learn to do well*, Iſa. i. 16, 17. Many may think they have their part in the firſt reſurrection, but can they prove their death unto ſin? As there cannot be a reſurrection before a man die, ſo there cannot be a reſurrection to a new life, but there muſt be a ſeparation of the ſoul from the body of ſin; What, ſhall a man cleave to ſin, be wedded to ſin? Yea, ſhall a man like it, love it, live in it, and yet ſay or imagine that Chriſt's reſurrection is his? O! be not deceived, God is not mocked! come, ſearch, try, examine, Haſt thou any ſhare in Chriſt's paſſion? Knoweſt thou the fellowſhip of his ſufferings? Art thou made conformable to his death; that as he died for ſin, ſo thou dieſt to ſin? If herein thou art at a ſtand, peruſe theſe characters laid down in his ſufferings and death, the truth

and growth of our mortification, or of our death unto sin is discovered before.

2. If Christ's resurrection be mine, then is Christ's Spirit mine, yea, then am I quickned by the Spirit of Christ, 'If any man have not the Spirit of 'Christ, he is none of his.——But if the Spirit of 'him that raised up Jesus from the dead dwell in 'you, then he that raised up Christ from the dead 'shall also quicken your mortal bodies,' (and I may add your immortal souls) ' by his Spirit that dwel- 'leth in you,' Rom. viii. 9, 11. Christ's Spirit (if Christ's resurrection be ours) will have the same operation and effect in our souls, that it had in his body; as it raised up the one, so it will raise up the other; as it quickned the one, so it will quicken the other. But the question here will run on, How shall we know whether we have received this quickning Spirit? Many pretend to the Spirit, never more than at this day; but how may we be assured that the Spirit is ours? I answer,——

1. The Spirit is a Spirit of illumination, here is the beginning of his work, he begins in light; as in the first creation, the first born of God's works was light, *God said, Let there be light, and there was light*, Gen. i. 3. so in his new creation, the first work is light, *God who commanded the light to shine out of darkness, hath shined into our hearts, to give the light of the knowledge of the glory of God, in the face of Jesus Christ*, 2 Cor. iv. 6. Hence the state of nature is called darkness, and the state of grace is called light, *Ye were sometimes darkness, but now ye are light in the Lord*, Eph. v. 8. And *he hath called you out of darkness into his marvelous light*, 1 Pet. ii. 9. There is a light in the mind, and a light in the heart of those who have the Spirit of Christ; there is a speculative and an effective knowledge, not only to know the truth, but to love it, believe it, embrace it. O my soul! wouldst thou know whether Christ's Spirit be thine? Consider, and see then, whether any of this new light of Jesus Christ hath shined into thy heart; take heed, deceive not thyself, thou mayest have a great deal of wit, and knowledge, and understanding, and yet go to hell; this light is a light shining into thy heart, this light is a Christ-discovering light, this light is a sin-discovering light, this light will cause thee to find out thy hypocrisy, deadness, dulness in spiritual duties; if thou hast not this light, thou art near to eternal burnings; darkness is one of the properties of hell, and without this light inward darkness will to utter darkness, where is nothing but *weeping and wailing, and gnashing of teeth*.

2. This quickning Spirit is a Spirit of faith, as is reveals Christ, so it inclines mens hearts to close with Christ upon those gospel terms as he is offered. I know there are degrees and measures of faith, but the least measure of faith is a desiring, panting, breathing after the Lord Jesus; and no sooner hath the soul received that new light from the Spirit of Christ, but it is presently, at the same instant, exceedingly affected with Jesus Christ; O! it desires Christ above all desires. I know not a more undeceiving sign than this, read over the whole *Bible*, and wherever there was any soul-saving discoveries, there ever followed inward desires, soul longings after Jesus Christ; when Paul preached of the resurrection of Christ, some there were that mocked, jeered and slighted that doctrine, but others, (whose hearts the Lord stirred) they were exceedingly taken with it, saying, ' We ' will hear thee again of this matter;' yea, and this very sermon so wrought on some, that *they believed, among whom was Dionysius the Areopagite, and a woman named Damaris, and others with them*, Acts xvii 32, 34. and when he preached another sermon on the same subject at Antioch, the Jews were much offended, but the Gentiles were so exceedingly taken with it, that *they besought Paul, that these words* (the very same resurrection-sermon) *might be preached to them the next Sabbath-day*, Acts xiii. 42. Their very hearts did so long after Christ, whom Paul had preached, that *when the congregation was broken up, many of the Jews and religious proselytes followed Paul and Barnabas; and the next Sabbath-day came almost the whole city together to hear the same sermon*, Verse 43, 44. O my soul! dost thou hear these sermons of Christ's resurrection? Dost thou hear sweet gospel-preaching? Dost thou hear the free tenders and offers of Christ, with all his glory and excellency to poor sinners, to vile, lost, undone souls? And art thou no whit taken with them? Canst thou sleep away such sermons as these! Hast thou no heart-risings, no stirrings, workings, longings, desires in thy soul! Oh! take heed, this is a dangerous case, but, on the contrary, if thou sayest in thy heart, ' Oh! that I ' could hear this sermon again! O! the sweets and ' virtue

' virtue of Chrift's refurrection! I had not thought
' such honey could have dropped out of this rock;
' O! the blessed beginnings and springings of grace
' which I felt in my soul on such a meditation!
' Oh! the desire, the delight! O! the comforts
' of Christ's resurrection! O! the drawings of the
' Spirit, enclining my heart to receive Jesus Christ,
' to close with him, and to rest on him, and to give
' up myself to him!' Why, this Spirit of faith doth
argue thy title and interest to the quickening Spirit
of Christ.

3. Thy quickening Spirit is a Spirit of sanctification; such was the Spirit whereby Christ was raised, ' He was declared mightily to be the Son
' of God, according to the Spirit of sanctification,
' by the resurrection from the dead,' Rom. i. 4.
That same Spirit which raised up Jesus Christ, was that same divine Spirit which sanctified his human nature, wherein it dwelt; and such is this quickening Spirit to all in whom it dwelleth, it is a Spirit of holiness, and it works holiness, changing the heart, and turning the bent of it from sin to holiness, ' If any man be in Christ, he is a new crea-
' ture; old things are passed away, behold all
' things are become new,' 2 Cor. v. 17. q. d. When once the believer is by an act of faith passed over unto Christ, there goes immediately from the Spirit of Christ into his soul an effectual power, which alters and changes the frame of the whole man; now he is not the same that he was, he is changed in his company, in his discourse, in his practice, he is changed in his nature, judgment, will, affections, he is sanctified throughout in soul, body and spirit; O my soul! try thyself by this sign, dost thou find such an inward change wrought in thy soul? Dost thou find the law of God, a law of holiness written on thy heart? Dost thou find a law within thee contrary to the law of sin, commanding with authority that which is holy and good? So that thou canst say with the apostle, ' I
' delight in the law of God after the inward man;
' and with my mind I myself serve the law of God,' Rom. vii. 22, 25. if so, surely this is no other
' but the law of the Spirit of life in Jesus Christ,' Rom. viii. 2. or the law of this quickening Spirit communicated from Christ unto thy soul.

3. If Christ's resurrection be mine, then am I
' planted together in the likeness of Christ's resur-
' rection,' Rom vi. 5. then do I resemble, and am made conformable to Christ in his resurrection; now, if we would know wherein that resemblance is, the apostle tells us, ' That like as Christ was
' raised up from the dead by the glory of the Fa-
' ther, even so we should walk in newness of life,' Rom. vi. 4. Our mortification is a resemblance of Christ's death, and our vivification is a resemblance of Christ's resurrection. In this ground of our hope concerning our interest in the resurrection of Christ, I shall propound these questions.—

1. Whether indeed and in truth our souls are vivified?
2. Whether we encrease and grow in our vivification?

For the first, the truth and certainty of our vivification will appear by these rules.—

1. True vivification is general, both in respect of us, and in respect of grace.

1. In respect of us, it is diffused through the whole man, ' The very God of peace sanctify you
' wholly, (saith the apostle) and I pray God, that
' your whole spirit, soul and body may be preserv-
' ed blameless unto the coming of our Lord Jesus
' Christ,' 1 Thess. v. 23. And, 2. in respect of grace, it is in every grace, I know it is a question, Whether all graces are so connected and chained together, that possibly they cannot be severed? But I suppose it is truly answered, that, in respect of habit, they cannot be severed, though in respect of the act or exercise they may be severed; some graces are more radical than others, as faith and love, and therefore they first appear; but as a man lives first the life of a plant, then of sense, then of reason, though all were radically there at first, so it is in graces; experience tells us, that some Christians are eminent in some graces, and some in other graces; some have more love, and some more knowledge, and some more patience, and some more self-denial; but all that are true Christians have each of these graces, in some measure or other, or, at least they have them in habit, tho' not in the act; if vivification be true, there is a whole work of grace both in heart and life; as the light in the air runs through the whole hemisphere, so the whole work of grace runs through, and is diffused through the whole man, soul, body and spirit. O my soul! this may put thee to thy study, because of the several constitutions or tempers of graces; thou mayest find this or that grace, this or

that image of Christ clearly stampt on thy heart, but thou canst not find such and such graces; in this case fear not, if in truth and sincerity thou hast the whole chain of grace. But to speak to some graces in particular.——

2. True vivification is a new life acting upon a new principle of faith, 'The life which I now live 'in the flesh, I live by the faith of the Son of God,' Gal. ii. 20. They are the words of a man pursued by the law unto Christ, Paul seeing he was dead by the law, he speaks for a better husband; the law finds him dead, and leaves him dead, *Nevertheless I live*, (saith Paul) what! means he a natural life? Why, so he lived before now; no, no, it is a better life than a natural life; such a life is no contentment to a soul pursued by the law; very heathens and infidels have such a life, and in that respect are as happy as the best of saints; Paul's life is a spiritual life, and the spring of his life is the Son of God; Jesus Christ is essentially, radically, fundamentally life itself, and by his incarnation, passion, resurrection, he is life for his saints, they live by him, and in him, and for him, and through him; he is the heart and liver of their spiritual life. But as from the heart and liver there must be arteries and veins for maintainance of life, and the conveyance of blood through all the body; so from Christ there must be a conveyance to bring this life unto us, and this is by faith, 'I live by 'the faith of the Son of God.' O my soul! dost thou live this life of faith on the Son of God? Canst thou make use of Christ in every state, and in every condition? As for instance, in thy particular calling, dost thou look to Christ for wisdom, success, blessing, ability, dost thou say, 'If I have 'ill success, I will go to Christ, it is he that set 'me here, and it is he will enable me?' In case of provision, Dost thou run to Christ, and dost thou hang upon him for all things needful? Dost thou say, 'If I want means, God will create 'means, he commands all means, and he can sud- 'denly do whatsoever he will?' In case of protection, Dost thou look unto Jesus to be thy shield and protector? Dost thou mind the word of God to Abraham? *Fear not, Abraham, for I am God all-sufficient, thy buckler, and thy exceeding great reward*, Gen. xv. 1. In case of thy children, goest thou to Christ, saying, 'Are not my children thy 'children, and wilt thou not provide for thy own?' It is true, thou must do what thou canst, but for the rest despair not, cast thy burden upon him, who hath commanded thee *in nothing to be careful, but in all things to make thy suits known with prayer and supplication*, Phil. iv. 6. *When my father and mother forsake me, God will take me up*, saith David, Psalm xxvii. 10. He is a Father to the fatherless, he provided for them in the womb, he provided breasts for them ere they saw the sun; and therefore, how should he but have care and compassion over thy children? In case of prosperity, dost thou see Christ's love in that state? Dost thou see him in the first place, receiving all, and joining in all as coming from him? Is this it that makes thy prosperity sweet, because thou knowest and believest that thy sins are pardoned? Otherwise what is thy silver and thy gold, so long as thy pardon is not sealed in the blood of Jesus Christ? If a prisoner condemned to die, should abound in all outward plenty, what comfort could he have so long as his pardon were not sealed? It is the life of faith that sweetens prosperity: who are better Christians than they? Who know they enjoy these things with God's favour and blessing? Faith sees God's love in all, and so is abundantly thankful; faith makes a man to eat, and drink, and sleep, and to do all in Christ, as it cost dear to purchase our liberty to the creatures, so faith ever sets Christ in the first place, it receives all his coming from him, it returns all as to the glory of him: in case of disgrace, dost thou commit thy credit to Jesus Christ? Dost thou look up to Jesus, and desirest no more good name, repute, or honour, than Christ will afford thee? Or, in case of death, dost thou like Stephen resign up thy soul to Christ? Dost thou see death conquered in the resurrection of Christ? Dost thou look beyond death? Dost thou over-eye all things betwixt thee and glory? O the sweets of this life of faith on the Son of God! if thou knowest what this means, then mayest thou assure thyself of thy vivification.

3. True vivification is a new life acting upon a new principle of hope of glory, 'Blessed be the God 'and Father of our Lord Jesus Christ, which, ac- 'cording to his abundant mercy, hath begotten us 'again unto a lively hope, by the resurrection of Je- 'sus Christ from the dead, to an inheritance incor- 'ruptible and undefiled, that fadeth not away, re- 'served in heaven for you,' 1 Pet. i. 3, 4 By Christ's

resur-

resurrection we have a lively hope for our resurrection unto glory. Is not Christ our head? And if he be risen to glory, shall not his members follow after him? Certainly there is but one life, one spirit, one glory of Christ and his members, *The glory which thou gavest me, I have given unto them,* said Christ, John xvii 22. The soul that is vivified hath *a lively hope of glory* on several grounds: as, 1. Because of the promises of glory set down in the word; now on these promises, hope fastens her anchor, if Christ hath promised, how should I but maintain a lively hope? 2. Because of the first-fruits of the spirit; there are sometimes fore-tastes of the glory, drops of heaven poured into a soul, whence it comfortably concludes, if I have the earnest and first-fruits, surely in his time Jesus Christ will give the harvest. 3. Because of Christ's resurrection unto glory; now he rose as a common person, and he went up into heaven as a common person, whence hope is lively, saying, Why should I doubt or despair, seeing I am *quickened together with Christ, and raised up together with Christ, and am made to sit together with Christ in heavenly places?* Eph. ii. 5, 6. Try, O! my soul, by this sign; art thou lively in thy hope of glory? Doth thy heart leap and rejoice within at a thought of thy inheritance in heaven? In a lively fountain the waters thereof will leap and sparkle; so if thy hope be lively, thou wilt have living joys, living speeches, living delights; amidst all thy afflictions thou wilt say, these will not endure for ever; I myself shall away e're long, glory will come at last. O! the sweets of this life of hope! if thou feelest these stirrings, it is an argument of thy vivification.

4. True vivification acts all its duties upon a new principle of love to Christ; men not enlivened by Jesus Christ may do much, and go far in outward service, yea, they may come to sufferings; and yet without love to Christ all is lost, all comes to nothing; *Though I speak with the tongues of men and angels,——though I have the gift of prophesy, and understand all mysteries, and all knowledge,——though I bestow all my goods to feed the poor; and tho' I give my body to be burnt, and have not love, it profiteth me nothing,* 1 Cor. xiii. 1, 2, 3. All the rest may be from the flesh, and for the flesh, and fleshly ends; but a true gospel-love is from Christ, and tends to the glory of Christ. *For love is of God, and every one that loveth is born of God, and knoweth God,* 1 John iv. 7 But how may we know that all our actings are out of love to Jesus Christ? I answer,—

1. If we act by the rule of Christ, *If you love me, keep my commandments.——He that hath my commandments and keepeth them, he it is that loveth me.——If any man love me, he will keep my commandments,* John xiv. 15, 21, 23, 24 He that loves Christ, he will look upon every act, every service, every performance, whether it be according to the rule of Christ, and then on he goes with it.

2. If we act to the honour of Christ, we may pray, and hear, and preach, and act self more than the honour of Jesus Christ; whilst Christ shewed miracles, and fed his followers to the full, they cried up Jesus, and none like Jesus; but when Christ was plain with them, 'Ye seek me, not be 'cause ye saw the miracles, but because ye did eat 'of the loaves, and were filled,' John vi. 26. When he pressed sincerity upon them, and preparation for sufferings, 'From that time many of his disciples 'went back, and walked no more with him,' ver. 66. It is no news for men to fall off when their ends fail; only they that love Christ look not at those outward things in respect of the honour of Jesus Christ; and hence it is, that in all their actings they will carry on the design of the Father, in advancing the honour of the Son, whatever it cost them. O! my soul, apply this to thy self! If thou livest the life of love, if in all thy actings, duties, services thou art carried on with a principle of love to Jesus Christ, it is a sure sign of thy vivification.

For the second question, Whether we encrease and grow in our vivification? We may discover it thus,——

1. We grow when we are led on to the exercise of new graces: this the apostle calls adding of one grace unto another, *Add to your faith virtue, and to virtue knowledge, and to knowledge temperance, and to temperance patience, and to patience godliness, and to godliness brotherly kindness, and to brotherly kindness, charity,* 1 Pet. i. 5, 6, 7. At first a Christian doth not exercise all graces; though habitually all graces may be planted in him, yet the exercise of them is not all at once, but by degrees: thus the church tells Christ, *At our gates are all manner of pleasant fruits, new and old, which I have laid up for thee, O! my beloved,* Cant. vii. 13.

she

she had all manner of fruits which she had reserved for Christ, new and old: she had young converts, and more settled professors, as some; or she had new and old graces, as others; she added grace to grace, she was led on from the exercise of one grace, unto another new grace: as wicked men are led on from one sin to another, and so grow worse and worse, so godly men are led from one grace to another, and so they encrease, *Knowing that tribulation worketh patience, and patience experience, and experience hope*, Rom. v. 3, 4.

2. We grow when we find new degrees of the same grace added; as when love grows more fervent, when knowledge abounds, and hath a larger apprehension of spiritual things; when faith goes on from a man's casting himself on Christ, to find sweetness in Christ, and so to plerophory, or full assurance of faith: when godly sorrow proceeds from mourning for sin, as contrary to God's holiness, to mourn for it as contrary to him who loves us, which usually follows after assurance: when obedience enlargeth its bounds, and we abound more and more in the work of the Lord, *I know thy works* (saith Christ to the church of Thyatira) *and the last to be more than the first*, Rev. ii. 19.

3. We grow when the fruits and duties we perform grow more ripe, more spiritual, and more to the honour of Christ; it may be we pray not more, nor longer, than sometimes we used; it may be our prayers have not more wit or memory, than sometimes they had, yet they are more savoury, more spiritual, and more to Christ's honour, than sometimes they were: now, we must know that one short prayer put up in faith, with a broken heart, and aiming at the honour of Christ, argues more of growth in grace, than prayers of a day long, and never so eloquent, without the like qualifications. In every duty we should look at their ends and aims; for, if we debase ourselves in the sense of our own vileness, and emptiness, and inability, and if we aim at God's honour, and power, and praise, and glory, it is a good sign of growth; we call this the spiritual part of duty, when it is from God, and thro' God, and to God.

4. We grow when we are more rooted in Christ; so the apostle describes it, *A growing up unto him in all things*, Eph. iv. 15. This is scripture-phrase; growth of grace is usually expressed by growing unto Christ, *But grow in grace, and in the knowledge of our Lord and Saviour Jesus Christ*, 2 Pet. iii. 18. As if to grow in grace without him were nothing, as indeed it is not. Philosophers, moral men, and others may grow in virtues, but not in Christ. Come then, search, and try whether we are more rooted in Christ; when a young plant is new set, the roots are a small depth in the earth, one may pull them up with his hand; but as the tree shooteth up in height, so it strikes the root deeper and deeper downward, that no force can move it; so it is with us, we have not for degree so firm and near a conjunction with Christ, at our first union; but the more we live in him, like good trees spreading in the sight of all men, and bringing forth the fruits of righteousness, the more we come to root downwards by a more firm faith, and firm confidence. Our union is answerable to that which uniteth us; now at the first, faith is but weak, like a smoaking wick, or a poor bruised reed, but whilst faith is drawing the Spirit from Christ, the more it exerciseth, the more it is strengthened; even as in babes, their powers every day, at first are feeble, but the more they feed and exercise, by so much the more they put forth their strength in all their operations: time was, that Peter's faith was so weak, that at the voice of a damsel, Peter was shaken; but by walking a while in Christ, he was so rooted, that neither threatnings, whippings, imprisonment, covenantings before great powers, nor any other thing, could shake him; you may object, if we are not at first rooted in Christ, a weak faith may be quite overthrown, we may then fall away; true, if we be not rooted in any manner; but this we are at our first setting into Christ by faith; only this I speak of, is an higher degree of rooting, which doth not only shut out falling away, but very shaking, and tottering in a good measure; surely this is not the state of every believer? No, no; it is only the condition of such, who have long walked in Christ, and are grown in grace, holiness, vivification.

O my soul! try now the growth of thy vivification, by these few signs; art thou led on to the exercise of new graces, adding grace to grace? Dost thou find new degrees of the self-same grace? Is thy love more hot? Thy faith more firm? All thy boughs more laden and filled with the fruits of righteousness? Are all thy duties more spiritual?

Are thy ends more raised to aim at God, to sanctify him, and to debase thyself? Art thou more rooted in Christ? In all thy duties, graces and gracious actings, hast thou learned habitually to say, *I live, yet not I, but Christ liveth in me?* Dost thou interest Christ more and more in all thou dost? dost thou know and affect Christ more and more? Oh! when would an ambitious courtier be weary of being graced by his prince? When would a worldling be weary of having the world come in upon him! Why shouldest thou, O! my soul, be weary of insinuating thyself by faith and affection into Christ? Come, search, try, it may be little winds have formerly shaken thee, but so it is, that insensibly, and thou knowest not how, thy root is struck lower and lower into Christ, and now thou art not so soon shaken with every wind; surely thy hope is well grounded; thou hast a part in Christ's resurrection, it is thine, even thine.

SECT. V.

Of believing in Jesus in that respect.

5. LEt us believe in Jesus as carrying on the great work of our salvation for us in his resurrection. This is one main article of our faith, *The third day he rose again from the dead*, and this now I propound as the object of our faith; O! let us believe it, let us believe our part and interest in it. And to that purpose let us look on Jesus as a common person; whatever consideration he passed under, it was in our stead, and in that respect we are to reckon ourselves as sharers with him. Scrupulous souls may object, 'Is it pos-
'sible that Christ should rise, and that I should
'rise with him, and in him? Is it possible that
'Christ should die as a common person for my
'sins? And that Christ should rise, and by his
'resurrection should be justified as a common
'person in my room? O the mystery of this
'redemption! *without controversy, great is the*
'*mystery of Godliness; God was manifest in the*
'*flesh, justified in the Spirit*, 1 Tim. iii. 16. It
'is a mystery beyond my fathoming, that Christ,
'who is God in the flesh, should be justified in the
'Spirit for my justification; that Christ should die
'in my stead as a condemned man, and when he
'had finished his work, that he should rise again
'in my stead as a righteous person. These passages
'are past fathoming, and beyond believing; O!
'what shall I do? I find it hard, very hard to be-
'lieve this point.'

Scrupulous souls, throw not away your confidence, *Ought not Christ to have suffered these things, and to enter into his glory*, Luke xxiv. 26. Was not satisfaction, and justification, payment of debt, and discharge of bonds required of him, and of necessity for us? O believe! and that I may persuade to purpose, I shall lay down, 1. Some directions, and, 2. Some encouragements of faith.

1. For directions of faith in reference to Christ's resurrection, observe these particulars.

1. Faith must directly go to Christ.
2. Faith must go to Christ, as God in the flesh.
3 Faith must go to Christ, as God in the flesh, made under the law.
4. Faith must go to Christ, not only as made under the directive part of the law by his life, but under the penal part by his death; of all these before.

5. Faith must go to Christ as God in the flesh, made under the directive and penal part of the law, and as quickned by the Spirit, *He was put to death in the flesh* (saith Peter) *but quickned by the Spirit*, 1 Pet. iii. 18. And accordingly must be the method, and order of our faith; after we have looked on Christ as dead in the flesh, we must go on to see him as quickned by the Spirit, *if Christ be is not raised, or quickned*, (saith the apostle) *your faith were in vain*, 1 Cor. xv. 17. q. d. To believe in Christ as only in respect of his birth, life, death, and to go no further, were but a vain faith; and therefore soar up your faith to this pitch, that Christ who died, is risen from the dead; to this purpose all the sermons of the apostles represented Christ, not only as crucified, but as raised: in that first sermon after the mission of the Holy Ghost, *Ye have crucified Christ* (said Peter to the Jews) and then it follows, *Whom God hath raised up, having loosed the pains or chains of death, because it was not possible that he should be holden of it*, Acts ii. 23, 24. In the next sermon Peter tells them again, ye have killed the prince of life; and then it follows, *Whom God hath raised from the dead, whereof we are witnesses*, Acts iii. 15. In the next sermon after this, *Be it known to you all* (said Peter) *and to all the people of Israel, that by the name of*

Jesus

Jesus Christ of Nazareth, whom ye crucified, and whom God raised from the dead,——Is this man whole? Acts iv. 10. And in the next sermon after this, *The God of our fathers raised up Jesus, whom ye slew, and hanged on a tree,* Acts v. 30. And as thus he preached to the Jews, so in this first sermon to the Gentiles, he tells them, *We are witnesses of all things which Jesus did, both in the land of the Jews, and in Jerusalem, whom they slew, and hanged on a tree; him God raised up the third day, and shewed him openly,* Acts x. 39, 40. And as thus Peter preached, so in that first sermon of Paul at Antioch, he tells them of the Jews crucifying Jesus, and then it follows, *But God raised him from the dead,* Acts xiii. 30. —*And as concerning that he raised him up from the dead, now no more to return to corruption, he said on this wise, I will give you the sure mercies of David, and thou shalt not suffer thine holy One to see corruption,* ver. 34, 35. And after this, Paul, as his manner was, went into the synagogue at Thessalonica, and three sabbath days reasoned with them out of the scriptures, opening and alledging, *That Christ must needs suffer and rise from the dead,* Acts xvii. 2, 3. This was the way of the apostles preaching; they told them a history (I speak it with reverence) 'Of one Jesus Christ, that was 'the word of God, and that was become man, 'and how he was crucified at Jerusalem, and how 'he was raised from the dead;' and all this in a plain, simple, spiritual way and manner; and while they were telling those blessed truths, the Spirit fell upon the people, and they believed, and had faith wrought in them. 'Faith is not wrought so 'much in a way of ratiocination, as by the Spirit 'of God, coming upon the souls of people by the 'relation, or representation of Jesus Christ to the 'soul.' And this our Lord himself hints, *As Moses lifted up the serpent in the wilderness, even so must the Son of man be lifted up, that whosoever believeth in him should not perish, but have everlasting life,* John iii 14. When the people were stung, God so ordered, that the very beholding of the brazen serpent should bring help (though we know not how) to those that were wounded and stung by those fiery serpents; so God hath ordained in his blessed wisdom, that the discovery of Jesus Christ, as crucified and raised, as humbled and exalted, should be a means of faith; come then, set we before us Christ raised; not only Christ crucified, but Christ raised, is the object of faith; and in that respect we must look up to Jesus.

6. Faith in going to Christ as raised from the dead, or as quickned by the Spirit, it is principally, and mainly to look to the end, purpose, intent, and design of Christ, in his resurrection; very devils may believe the history of Christ's resurrection, *They believe and tremble,* Jam. ii. 19. but the saints and people of God are to look at the meaning of Christ why he rose from the dead. Now the ends are either supreme, or subordinate. 1. The supreme end was God's glory, and that was the meaning of Christ's prayer, *Father, the hour is come, glorify thy Son, that thy Son also may glorify thee,* John xvii. 1. with which agrees the apostle, *He rose again from the dead to the glory of the Father,* Rom. vi. 4. 2. The subordinate ends were many: as, 1. That he might tread on the serpent's head. 2. That he might destroy the works of the devil. 3. That he might be the firstfruits of them that sleep. 4. That he might assure our faith that he is the Lord, and that he is able to keep that which we have committed to him against that day. 5. That he might be justified in the spirit, as he was begotten in the womb by the Spirit, led up and down in the Spirit, offered up by the eternal Spirit, so he was raised from the dead by the Spirit, and justified in his Spirit at the resurrection. Christ was under the greatest attainder that ever man was, he stood publicly charged with the guilt of a world of sins, and if he had not been justified by the Spirit, he had still lain under the blame of all, and had been liable to the execution of all; and therefore he was raised up from the power of death, that he might be declared as a righteous person. 6. That he might justify us in his justification, when he was justified, all the elect were virtually and really justified in him; that act of God which past on him, was drawn up in the name of all his saints; as whatever benefit or privilege God meant for us, he first of all bestowed it on Christ; thus God meaning to sanctify us, he sanctified Christ first! and God meaning to justify us, he justifies Christ first; so whatever benefit or privilege he bestowed on Christ, he bestowed it not on him for himself, but as he was a common person, and one representing us; thus Christ was sanctified instead of us, *For*

their

their sakes I sanctify myself, that they also may be sanctified through thy truth, John xvii. 19. and thus Christ was justified instead of us, *For as by the offence of one, judgment came upon all for condemnation; even so by the righteousness of one, the free gift came on all men unto justification,* Rom. v. 18.

7. That he might regenerate us, and beget us anew by his resurrection, 'Blessed be the God and 'Father of our Lord Jesus Christ, which according 'to his abundant mercy hath begotten us again,— 'by the resurrection of Jesus Christ from the dead,' 1 Peter i. 3. And this he doth two ways. 1. As our pattern, platform, idea, or exemplar, 'Like as 'Christ was raised from the dead,—even so we also 'should walk in newness of life, Rom. vi. 4. and 'likewise reckon ye also yourselves to be alive unto 'God through Jesus Christ our Lord,' ver. 11. 2. As the efficient cause thereof, 'For when we are 'dead in sin, he hath quickened us together with 'Christ, Eph. ii. 5. and, ye are risen with him 'through the faith of the operation of God, who 'hath raised him from the dead,' Col. ii. 12. O! the power of Christ's resurrection in this respect! if we saw a man raised from the dead, how should we admire at such a wondrous power? But the raising of one dead soul is a greater work than to raise a church-yard of dead bodies.

8. That he might sanctify us, which immediately follows after the other,—' But yield ye yourselves unto God as those that are alive from the 'dead, and your members as instruments of righte-'ousness unto God,' Rom. vi. 13. In our regeneration, we are risen with Christ, and it is the apostle's argument, 'If ye then be risen with Christ, 'seek those things which are above,——set your 'affections on things above, and not on things on 'the earth,' Col iii. 1, 2. We usually reckon two parts of sanctification, *viz.* Mortification and vivification, now as the death of Christ hath the special influence on our vivification, 'He hath 'quickened us together with Christ, and hath raised 'us up together with Christ,' Eph. ii. 5, 6.

O my soul! look to this main design of Christ in his rising again, and if thou hast any faith, O! set thy faith on work to draw this down into thy soul! but here is the question, how should I manage my faith? Or, how should I act my faith to draw down the virtue of Christ's resurrection for my vivification? I answer;

1. Go to the well-head, look into the resurrection of Jesus Christ. This one act contains in it these particulars, as, 1. That I must go out of myself to something else, this is that check that lies upon the work of grace, to keep out pride, that faith sees the whole good of the soul in a principle extraneous, even the springs of Jesus Christ. Alas! if this vivification were in me, or in my power, what swellings and excrescences of pride should I quickly nourish? God therefore hath placed it in another, that I may be kept low, and that I may go out of myself to seek it where it is. 2. That I must attribute wholly, freely, joyfully, all that I am to Jesus Christ, and to the effectual working of his grace, *I live, yet not I, but Christ liveth in me,* Gal. ii. 20. And *by the grace of God, I am what I am;* and *I laboured more abundantly than they all, yet not I, but the grace of God which was with me,* 1 Cor. xv. 10. The life of grace springs only from the life and resurrection of Jesus Christ, and therefore, as I must deny myself, so I must attribute all to him from whom it comes. 3. I must lie at his feet with an humble expectation of and dependency upon him, and him alone for the supplies of grace; this was the apostle's practice, 'O! that I may be found in him! O! that I 'may know him, and the power of his resurrection! ——— O! that by any means I might attain 'unto the resurrection of the dead!' He lay at Christ's feet, with an humble expectation to feel the power of Christ's resurrection, in raising him first from the death of sin to the life of grace, and after from the death of nature to the life of glory.

2. Lay to these springs thy mouth of faith; it is not enough to have all the treasures of grace, all the actings of Christ for thee, laid before thee, but thou must act thy faith upon that object; O! then go to Christ's resurrection and believe, make a particular application of those glorious effects of Christ's resurrection upon thy soul. Say, 'Lord 'thou diedst that I might die to sin, and thou 'wast raised from the death that I might be raised 'to newness of life. Come, Lord, and quicken 'my dying sparks, give me to lay hold on Christ's 'resurrection, give me to adhere to it, and to rest 'upon it, and to close with it; I see without faith 'I am never a whit better for Christ's resurrection, 'and thy commands are upon me, *Open thy mouth 'wide, and I will fill it,* Psalm lxxxi. 10. Why,

'Lord,

'Lord, I believe, help thou my unbelief,' Mark ix. 24. This faith is necessary to our vivification as well as Christ. Christ is the fountain of life, but faith is the means of life; the power and origin of life is entirely reserved to Jesus Christ, but faith is the radical bond on our part, whereby we are tied unto Christ, and live in Christ; and thus faith Christ himself, 'I am the resurrection and 'the life,' Is that all? No, 'he that believeth in 'me, tho' he were dead, yet he shall live, John xi. '25. And I am the bread of life,' Is that all? No, 'he that cometh to me shall never hunger, and he 'that believeth on me shall never thirst,' John vi. 35.

3. *Suck and be satisfied, milk out and be delighted*, Isa. lxvi. 11. Christ's resurrection is a breast of consolation; there is in it abundance of life and glory, and therefore we should not believe a little, but much; the word *suck*, is as much as to exact on Christ; draw hard from Christ; the more we exercise faith, the more we have of Jesus Christ and of vivification; there is a depth in Christ's resurrection that can never be fathomed; when the soul hath as much as its narrow hand can grasp, whole Christ is too big to be inclosed in mortal arms; only the longer our arm of faith is, the more we shall grasp of him; and therefore suck, and pull, and draw hard, and to this purpose.

1. Pray for an increase of faith, complain to Christ of the shortness of thy arm; tell him thou canst not believe as thou wouldest, thou canst not get so much of Christ into thy soul as thou desirest, thy vivification is very poor and small; Oh! when Christ hears a soul complain of dwarfishness in faith and grace, then is he ready to let out of his fulness, even grace for grace.

2. Act thy faith vigorously on Christ's resurrection for a further degree of quickning, activity, and lively ability of grace. Christ is an ever-flowing fountain, and he would have believers to partake abundantly of what is in him; he cannot abide that any should content themselves with a present stock of grace; Christ is not as a stream that fails, or as a channel that runs dry; Christ is not as water in a ditch, which hath no living spring to feed it; no, no; Christ is the fountain of life, he is the chief ordinance of life that ever God set up. I know there are other means of Christ's appointment, but if thou wilt leave at the spring and drink in there, yea drink abundantly according to the overflowings of this fountain, O the life, and growth of life that would come in! oh! the virtue of Christ's resurrection (that Christ's Spirit meeting and assisting) would flow into thy soul for thy vivification.

Thus for direction; now for the encouragements of our faith to believe in Christ's resurrection.

1. Consider of the excellency of this object. A sight of Christ in his beauty and glory, would ravish souls, and draw them to run after him; the wise merchant would not buy the pearl, 'till he knew it to be of excellent price; great things are eagerly sought for; Christ raised, Christ glorified, is an excellent object; O! who would not sell all to buy this pearl? Who would not believe?

2. Consider of the power of virtue, and influence of this object into all that golden chain of privileges, 'If Christ be not raised, you are yet in your 'sins; then they also which are fallen asleep in 'Christ are perished,' 1 Cor. xv. 17, 18. From the resurrection of Christ flow all those privileges, even from justification to salvation. The first is clear, and therefore all the rest.

3. Consider that Christ's resurrection and the effects of it are nothing unto us, if we do not believe; it is faith that brings down the particular sweetness and comforts of Christ's resurrection unto our souls: it is faith that puts us in the actual possession of Christ's resurrection; whatsoever Christ is to us before faith, yet really we have no benefit by it until we believe; it is faith that takes hold of all that Christ hath done for us, and gives us the actual enjoyment of it; oh! let not the work stick in us! what, is Christ risen from the dead? And shall we not eye this Christ, and take him home to ourselves by faith? The apostle tells us, That *he that believeth not, hath made God a liar, because he believeth not the record that God hath given of his Son*, 1 John v. 10. Unbelief belies God in all that he hath done for us. O! take heed of this, without faith what are we better for Christ's resurrection?

4. Consider of the tenders, offers, apparitions that Christ raised makes of himself to our souls; when first he rose (to confirm the faith of his disciples) he offers himself, and appears to Mary Magdalene, to the other women, to Peter, Thomas, and all the rest; and all those apparitions were on this

this account that they might believe, *These things are written that ye might believe*, John xx. 31. In like manner Christ at this day offers himself in the gospel of grace; and by his Spirit he appears to souls. Methinks we should not hear a sermon of Christ's resurrection, but we should imagine as if we saw him, *Whose head and hairs are white like wool, as white as snow, whose eyes are as a flame of fire, whose feet are like unto fine brass, as if they burned in a furnace, whose voice is as the sound of many waters*, Rev. i. 14, 15. Or, if we are dazzled with his glory, methinks, at least, we should hear his voice, as if he said, *Fear not, I am the first, and the last, I am he that liveth, and was dead, and behold I am alive for evermore.* Amen. ver. 17, 18. q. d. Come, cast your souls on me; it is I that have conquered sin, death, and hell for you; it is I that have broke the serpent's head, that have taken away the sting of death, that have cancelled the bond of hand-writing against you, that have in my hands a general acquittance and pardon of your sins; come, take it, take me, and take all with me; see your names written in the acquittance that I tender, take out the copy of it in your own hearts; only believe in him who is risen again for our justification.——O my soul! what sayest thou to this still sweet voice of Christ? Shall he who is the Saviour of men, and glory of angels desire thee to believe, and wilt thou not say Amen to it? Oh! how should I blame thee for thy unbelief? What aspersions doth it cast on Christ? He hath done all things well, he hath satisfied wrath, fulfilled the law, and God hath acquitted him, pronounced him just, faith he is contented, he can desire no more; but thou sayest by unbelief that Christ hath done nothing at all, unbelief professeth Christ is not dead, or at least, not risen from the dead: unbelief professeth that justice is not satisfied, that no justification is procured, that the wrath of God is now as open to destroy us as ever it was. Oh! that Christ should be crucified again in our hearts by our unbelief; come, take Christ upon his tenders and offers, embrace him with both arms.

SECT. VI.

Of loving Jesus in that respect.

LEt us love Jesus, as carrying on the great work of our salvation for us in his resurrection; surely if we hope in Christ, and believe in Christ, we cannot but love Christ; if Christ's resurrection be our justification, and so the ground both of our hope and faith, how should we but love him, who hath done such great things for us? She that had much forgiven her, loved much; and if by virtue of Christ's resurrection we are justified from all our sins, how should we but love him much? But that I may let down some cords of love, whereby to draw our loves to Christ in this respect, let us consider thus.——

'Love is a motion of the appetite, by which 'the mind unites itself to that which seems good ' to it.' You may object that Christ is absent, how then should our souls be united to him? but if we consider that objects, though absent, may be united to the powers by their species and images, as well as by their true beings; we may then be said truly to love Christ as raised, though he be absent from us; come then, stir up thy appetite, bring into thy imagination the idea of Christ as in his resurrection; present him to thy affection of love, in that very form wherein he appeared to his disciples; as gazing upon the dusty beauty of flesh, kindleth the fire of carnal love, so this gazing on Christ, and on the passages of Christ in his resurrection, will kindle this spiritual love in thy soul: draw near then, and behold him, *Is he not white and ruddy, the chiefest among ten thousand? Is not his head as the most fine gold; are not his locks bushy, and black as a raven, are not his eyes as the eyes of doves by the rivers of water, washed with milk, and fitly set? Are not his cheeks as a bed of spices, as sweet flowers?* Cant. v. 10, 11, 12, 13. Thus I might go on from top to toe; but that thou mayest not only see his glory and beauty wherein he arose, but that thou mayest hear his voice; doth he not call on thee, as sometimes he did on Mary, on Thomas, on Peter, or on the twelve? As the angel said to the woman, *Remember how he spake, when he was yet in Galilee*, Luke xxiv. 6. so say I to thee, remember how he spake while he was yet on earth; surely *his lips like lilies dropped sweet-smelling myrrh.* As thus,——

1. In his apparition to Mary; Jesus saith unto her, *Woman, why weepest thou? Whom seekest thou?* John xx. 15. Were not these kind words? And hast thou not had the like apparition? Hast not thou

thou heard the like sweet words from Jesus Christ? How often hath thy heart sobbed and sighed out complaints, *O! where is he whom my soul loveth? I charge you, O daughters of Jerusalem, if you find my beloved, that ye tell him I am sick of love,* Cant. v. 8. And then was not Christ seen in the mount? Was not thy extremity his opportunity to do thee good? Did not he bespeak thy comforts with these words, 'Sweet soul, Why weep-' est thou? Whom seekest thou? What wouldest ' thou have that I can give thee? And what dost ' thou want that I cannot give thee? If any thing ' in heaven or earth will make thee happy, it is all ' thine own? Wouldest thou have pardon, thou ' shalt have it, I freely forgive thee all debt? ' Wouldest thou have myself? Why, behold I am ' thine, thy friend, thy Lord, thy husband, thy ' head, thy God.' Were not these thy Lord's reviving words? Were not these the melting, healing, ravishing, quickning passages of Christ his love?

2. In his apparition to the ten; *Jesus stood in the midst, and faith unto them, Peace be unto you,* John xx. 19. Lo, here are more words of love: in midst of their trouble Christ stands in the midst, speaking peace to their souls? And hath not Christ done the like to thee? Hast thou not many and many a time been rapt in troubles, that thou knewest not which way to turn thee? Hast thou not felt the contradictions of men, railings of Rabsheka's? And hast thou not sometimes shut thy doors upon thee for fear of such Jews? And then, even then, Hath not Christ came to thy Spirit with an olive-branch of peace, saying to thy restless soul, *Peace and be still?* Hath he not wrought wonders in the sea of thy restless thoughts? Hath he not made a calm? And more than so, Hath he not filled thee with joy and peace in believing? Hath he not sent thee away from thy prayers and complaints with a piece of heaven in thy soul, so that thou was forced to conclude, *Surely this is the peace of God which passeth all understanding.*

3. In his apparition to the eleven; Jesus faith to Thomas, *Reach hither thy finger, and behold my hands, and reach hither thy hand, and thrust it into my side, and be not faithless, but believing,* John xx. 27. O sweet condescending words! how far, how low would Jesus stoop to take up souls? And O my soul! are not these the very dealings of Christ towards thee? He that called Thomas to come near, hark how he calls on thee, ' Come ' near, poor, trembling, wavering, wandring soul; ' come, view the Lord thy Saviour, and be not ' faithless, but believing; peace be unto thee, fear ' not, it is I.' He that called on them who passed by, to behold his sorrow, in the day of his humiliation, doth now call on thee to behold his glory in the day of his exaltation; look well upon him, Dost thou not know him? Why, his hands were pierced, his head was pierced, his side was pierced, his heart was pierced with the stings of thy sin, and these marks he retains, even after his resurrection, that by these marks thou mightest always know him; Is not the passage to his heart yet standing open? If thou knowest him not by the face, the voice, the hands; if thou knowest him not by the tears, and bloody sweat, yet look nearer, thou mayest know him by the heart, that broken healed heart is his, that dead revived heart is his, that soul pitying melting heart is his, doubtless it can be none but his, love and compassion are its certain signatures. And is not here yet fewel enough for love to feed upon? Doth not this heart of Christ even snatch thy heart, and almost draw it forth of thy breast? Canst thou read the history of love any further at once? Doth not thy throbbing heart here stop to ease itself? if not, go on, for the field of love is large.

4. In his apparition to the seven; *Jesus faith to Simon Peter, son of Jonas, lovest thou me more than these?—And he said to him the second time, Simon, son of Jonas, lovest thou me?—He said to him the third time, Simon, son of Jonas, lovest thou me?* John xxi. 15, 16, 17. Oh! the love of Christ in drawing out man's love unto himself! how often, O my soul! hath Christ come to thy door, and knocked there for entrance? How often hath he sued for love, and begged love, and asked thee again and again, ' Ah soul! dost thou ' love me more than these? Come, tell me, dost ' thou love me, love me, love me? Come, wilt ' thou take me for thy Lord? wilt thou delight in ' me as thy treasure, thy happiness, thy All?' Oh fy! shall Christ raised, a glorious Christ thus wooe, and sue, and call, and wilt not thou answer as Peter did? *Yea, Lord, thou knowest that I love thee.——Yea, Lord, thou knowest all things, thou knowest that I love thee?* Nay, art thou not grieved that Christ should ask the third time for thy love?

love? Art thou not ashamed out of thy stupidity, and forced to say, O! my blessed Lord, I have been too proud, too peevish, but thy free grace, and undeserved love, hath beaten me out of all my pride, so that now I fall down at thy foot stool, and lay myself flat before thee; at first I wondred to hear preachers talk so much of Christ, and I was bold to ask thy friends, What was their beloved more than another beloved? But now I wonder that I could be so long without thee, truly Lord, I am thine, only thine, ever thine, all that I am is at thy command, and all I have is at thy disposing, be pleased to command both it and me.

I might thus go on to consider other passages in other apparitions, But are not these enough to draw thy love? Oh! what love was this? Oh! what humility was this? That Christ, after his resurrection, should converse with men during the space of forty days? Worthy he was, after so many sorrows, sufferings, reproaches, after so cruel, ignominious, and bitter a death, immediately to have rid his triumph to glory; and for the confirmation of his disciples faith, he might have commanded the angels to have preached his resurrection; oh! no, he himself would stay in person, he himself would make it out by many infallible proofs that he was risen again; he himself would, by his own example, learn us a lesson of love, of meekness, of patience, in waiting after sufferings for the reward.

Methinks a few of these passages should set all our hearts on a flame of love; we love earth, and earthly things; we dig in the veins of the earth for thick clay; but if Christ be risen, *Set your affections on things above, and not on things on the earth*, Col. iii. 1, 2. Oh! if the love of Christ were but in us, as the love of the world is in base worldlings, it would make us wholly to despise this world, it would make us to forget it, as worldly love makes a man to forget his God; nay, it would be so strong and ardent, and rooted in our souls, that we should not be able voluntarily and freely to think on any thing else but Jesus Christ; we should not then fear contempt, or care for disgrace, or the reproaches of men; we should not then fear death, or the grave, or hell, or devils, but we should sing in triumph, *O death! Where is thy sting! O grave! Where is thy victory?—— Now thanks be to God, which giveth us victory through Jesus Christ our Lord*, 1 Cor. xv. 55, 57.

SECT. VII.

Of joying in Jesus in that respect.

7. LET us joy in Jesus as carrying on the great work of our salvation for us in his resurrection. This is the great gospel duty, we should *rejoice in the Lord, and again rejoice*, Phil. iv. 4. *yea, rejoice evermore*, 1 Thes. v. 16. A Christian estate should be a joyful and comfortable estate, none have such cause of joy as the children of Zion, *Sing, O daughter of Zion, shout, O Jerusalem, be glad and rejoice with all thy heart, O daughter of Jerusalem*, Zeph. iii. 14. And why so? A thousand reasons might be rendered; but here is one, a prime one, *Christ is risen from the dead, and become the first-fruits of them that slept*, 1 Cor. xv. 20. A commemoration of Christ's resurrection hath ever been a means of rejoicing in God.

Some may object, What is Christ's resurrection to me? Indeed if thou hast no part in Christ, the resurrection of Christ is nothing at all to thee; but if Christ be thine, then art thou risen with him, and in him; then all he did was in thy name, and for thy sake.

Others may object, supposing Christ's resurrection mine, What am I better? How, do not all the privileges of Christ flow from the power and virtue of his resurrection, as well as death? Tell me, what is thy state? What possibly can be the condition of thy soul, wherein thou mayest not draw sweets from Christ's resurrection? As,——

1. Is thy conscience in trouble for sin? The apostle tells thee, *The answer of a good conscience towards God, is by the resurrection of Jesus Christ from the dead*, 1 Pet. iii. 21.

2. Art thou afraid of condemnation? The apostle tells thee, *He was delivered for our offences, and he was raised again for our justification*, Rom. iv. 25.

3. Dost thou question thy regeneration? The apostle tells thee, *He hath begotten us again by the resurrection of Jesus Christ from the dead*, 1 Pet. i. 3.

4. Art thou distressed, persecuted and troubled on every side? The apostle tells thee wherein

in now confists thy confidence, comfort and courage; *to wit*, in the life of Christ, in the resurrection of Christ, 'We always bear about in the 'body, the dying of the Lord Jesus, that the life 'of Jesus might also be made manifest in our body. 'For we which live, are always delivered unto 'death for Jesus' sake, that the life also of Jesus 'might be made manifest in our mortal flesh,' 2 Cor. iv. 10, 11. And thus Beza interprets those following words, 'Knowing, that he which raised 'up the Lord Jesus, shall raise us up also by Jesus,' Verse 14. (*i. e.*) unto a civil resurrection from our troubles; Paul was imprisoned, and in part martyred; but by the virtue of Christ's resurrection he foresaw his enlargement. And this interpretation Beza grounds on the words following, and foregoing, wherein Paul compares his persecutions to a death, and his preservation from them to a life, as he had done before also, Chap. i. Ver. 9, 10.

5. Art thou afraid of falling off, or of falling away? Why, remember, that the immutable force and perpetuity of the new covenant is secured by the resurrection of Jesus Christ, *I will make an everlasting covenant with you, even the sure mercies of David*, Isa. lv. 3. this the apostle applies to the resurrection of Christ, as the bottoming of that sure covenant, *And as concerning that he raised him up from the dead, he said on this wise, I will give you the sure mercies of David*, Acts xiii. 34.

6 Art thou afraid of death, hell, and the power of the grave? Why, now remember that Christ is risen from the dead, and by his resurrection death is swallowed up in victory; so that now thou may'st sing, *O death! where is thy sting? O grave! where is thy victory? Now thanks be to God which hath given us victory through our Lord Jesus Christ*, 1 Cor. xv. 55, 57. It is the voice of Christ, *Thy dead men shall live, together with my dead body shall they arise: awake and sing, ye that dwell in the dust, for thy dew is as the dew of herbs, and the earth shall cast out the dead*, Isa. xxvi. 19. David was so lifted up with this resurrection, that he cries out, *Therefore my heart is glad, and my glory rejoiceth, my flesh also shall rest in hope; for thou wilt not leave my soul in hell, neither wilt thou suffer thine holy one to see corruption*, Psalm xvi. 9, 10 But especially Job was so exceedingly transported with this, that he breaks out into these extasies, *O! that my words were now written,*

O! that they were printed in a book! that they were graven with an iron pen, and laid in the rock for ever! for I know that my Redeemer liveth, and that he shall stand at the latter day upon the earth; and though, after my skin, worms shall destroy this body, yet in my flesh shall I see God, whom I shall see for myself, and mine eyes shall behold, and not another, though my reins be consumed within me, Job xix. 23, 24, 25, 26, 27. No man, ever since Christ did speak more clearly of Christ's resurrection and his own, than Job did here before Christ. Observe in it, O my soul! Job's wish, and the matter wished: his wish was, That certain words which had been cordial to him, might remain to memory; and this wish hath three wishes in one. 1. That they might be written. 2. That they might be registred in a book, enrolled upon record as public instruments, judicial proceedings, or whatsoever is most authentical. 3. That they might be engraven in stone, and in the hardest stone, the rock; records might last long, yet time might injure them, and these words he would have last for ever; O that they were graven in the rock for ever! Moses and Job are said to have lived at one time; now Moses writ the law in stone, and considering that these words were gospel, there was no reason the law should be in tables of stone, and the gospel in sheets of paper; no, no; it were fit that this should be as firm and durable as that, 'Oh; that my words were written, Oh! 'that they were printed in a book, &c.

2. The matter wished, or the words he would have written, are these, *I know that my Redeemer liveth, and that I shall live again.* Here's first his Redeemer and his rising. 2. His own rising and his seeing God. O! this was the matter of his joy, his Redeemer must rise again, and he must rise too, and see his Redeemer; it was a point that exceedingly ravished and revived Job, and therefore he repeats the same thing over and over, 'I shall see God, and I shall see him for myself, 'and I shall see him with my eyes, and not with 'others.' As Christ said of Abraham, *Your Father Abraham rejoiced to see my day, and he saw it and was glad*, John viii. 56. So it appears of his servant Job, he saw Christ's day, both his first day, and his latter day, and he rejoiced and was glad.

Away, away all scrupulous, doubtful, dumpish thoughts!

thoughts! * Consider what joys were of old, at the foresight of Christ's resurrection, but especially what joy was all the world over when he rose again from the dead; then came the angels from heaven, and appeared in white; then the sun danced for joy, (so it is storied) or shone sooner, and brighter than ever it did before, *Then* † (I am sure) *the disciples were exceeding glad, when they saw the Lord*, yea so glad, *that they believed not for joy*, Luke xxiv. 41. It is worthy our observing to see how all the primitive saints were affected with this news, and because of it, with the very day on which Christ rose; some call it ' the first day of joy and ' gladness, and because of the joy occasioned on ' this day, the apostles (say they) devoted the first ' day of the week to the honour and service of Jesus ' Christ.' Augustine applies the words of the Psalm unto this day, *This is the day which the Lord hath made, let us be glad, and rejoice in it*, Psa. cxviii. 24. Ignatius, who lived in the apostles age, and was John's disciple, calls it ' the queen, the princess, the lady paramount among the other weekly days.' Chrysostome calls it ' a royal day,' and Gregory Nazianzen, Orat. 42. saith ' it is higher than the highest, and with admiration wonderful above other days.' Certainly the Lord's day was in high esteem with the ancient church, and the principal motive was because of Christ's resurrection from the dead. O! that on these days we could rejoice in the Lord, and again rejoice: it is observed, ‡ ' That many Christians ' look upon broken-heartedness, and much grieving and weeping for sin, as if it were the great ' thing that God delighteth in, and requireth of ' them; and therefore they bend all their endeavours that way, they are still striving with their ' hearts to break them more, and they think no ' sermon, no prayer, no meditation, speed so well ' with them, as that which can help them to grieve ' or weep; but, O Christians! understand and consider, (saith my author) That all your sorrows ' are but preparatives for your joys, and that it is ' an higher and sweeter work that God calls you ' to, and would have you spend your time and ' strength in, *Delight thyself in the Lord, and he ' shall give thee the desires of thine heart*, Psalm ' xxxvii. 4 —Never take your hearts to be right, ' till they be delighting themselves in their God: ' when you kneel down in prayer, labour so to ' conceive of God, and bespeak him, that he may ' be your delight; do so in hearing, and reading, ' and meditating, and in your feasting on the flesh ' and blood of Jesus Christ at his supper. Especially improve the happy opportunity of the ' Lord's day, wherein you may wholly devote ' yourselves unto this work.' O! spend more of this day in spiritual rejoicing, especially in commemoration of Christ's resurrection, (yea, and of the whole work of redemption) or else you will not answer the institution of the Lord.

SECT. VIII.

Of calling on Jesus in that respect.

8. LET us call on Jesus; that is to say,—— 1. Let us pray that Christ's resurrection may be ours, and that we may be more and more assured of it. Let us say with the apostle, *O! that I may know him, and the power of his resurrection*, Phil. iii. 10. O! that I may find the working of that power in my soul, which was shewed in the resurrection of Christ from the dead! O! that the Spirit of holiness, which quickned Christ from the dead, would, by the same glorious power, beget holiness, and faith, and love, and all other graces in my poor soul! O! that Christ would, by his resurrection, apply his active and passive obedience to me! O! that he would be to me the Lord of the living, and the prince of life! that he would overcome in me the death of sin, and that he would regenerate, quicken, renew, and fashion me by the power of godliness to become like himself. O! that all the virtue, power, privileges, and influences of Christ's resurrection might be conferred on me, and that I might feel them working in me every day more and more.

2. Let us praise God for Christ's resurrection,

---

* Greg. hom. in pas. ca. John xx. 20.

† *Apostoli die dominico exhilerati non solum ipsum festivissimum esse voluerunt verum etiam per omnes hebdomadis frequentandum esse duxerunt*, Juno Cent. 1. Epist. ad. Decent. xi. 4.

‡ Baxter's *method for a settled peace*.

and

and for all the privileges flowing from Chrift's refurrection into our fouls, *Blessed be the God and Father of our Lord Jesus Chrift, who hath begotten us again by the refurrection of Jesus Chrift from the dead,* 1 Pet. i. 3. Chrift is rifen, and by his refurrection he hath juftified, fanctified, quickned, faved our fouls, and therefore *blessed be the God and Father of our Lord Jesus Chrift*; furely God requires a thoufand, thoufand Hallelujahs, and that we fhould blefs him upon a thoufand-ftringed inftrument: here is fewel enough, the Lord kindles a great fire in every one of our hearts to burn out all our lufts, and to enflame all our hearts with a love to Jefus Chrift. Can we ever too much praife him for all his actings in our behalf? Are not all God's creatures called upon to rejoice with us, and to blefs God for his redeeming of us? 'Sing, 'O ye heavens, for the Lord hath done it; fhout, 'ye lower parts of the earth, break forth into fing-'ing, ye mountains, O foreft, and every tree there-'in, for the Lord hath redeemed Jacob, and glori-'fied himfelf in Ifrael,' Ifa. xliv. 23. This is the duty we fhall do in heaven, and I believe we are never more in heaven (whilft on earth) than when we are in this exercife of praifing God, and blefsfing God for Jefus Chrift. Come, let us praife God for Chrift, and efpecially on this day called therefore *the Lord's day,* becaufe of the refurrection of Jefus Chrift: it is the defign of God to glorify Chrift redeeming us, as much, or more than he glorified himfelf creating us; and therefore he purpofely unhinged the *Sabbath* from the laft day to the firft day of the week, that it might be fpent as a weekly day of praife and thankfgiving for the more glorious work of our redemption, that love might not only be equally admired with power, but even go before it. It is the advice of a godly divine, That we fhould * ' improve the happy opportuni-' ty of the Lord's day, wholly to devote ourfelves ' to his work.' And he advifeth minifters and others, ' That they fpend more of thofe days in ' praife and thankfgiving, and be briefer in their ' confeffions and lamentations;—that they would ' make it the main bufinefs of their folemn affem-' blies on thofe days to found forth the high praifes ' of their Redeemer, and to begin here the praifes ' of God and the Lamb, which they muft perfect ' in heaven for ever:—That they would fpend ' a great part of thofe days in pfalms, and folemn ' praifes to their Redeemer;—— and that fome ' hymns and pfalms might be invented, as fit for ' the ftate of the gofpel-church and worfhip, to ' laud the Redeemer, come in the flefh, as ex-' prefly as the work of grace is now expreffed.' O! that thefe directions were but in practice! O! that our churches and families would make our ftreets to refound with the echoes of our praifes! O! that this were the burden of each duty on thefe days, ' Now bleffed be the God and Father ' of our Lord Jefus Chrift, who hath begotten us ' again unto a lively hope, by the refurrection of ' Jefus Chrift, from the dead.'

SECT. IX.

Of conforming to Jefus in that refpect.

9. LET us conform to Jefus in refpect of his refurrection.—— In this particular I fhall examine thefe queries. 1. Wherein we muft conform? 2. How this conformity is wrought? 3. What are the means of this conformity as on our parts?

For the *Firft,* Wherein we muft conform? I anfwer in a word, in our vivification. There is a refemblance of our vivification to Chrift's refurrection; and if we would know wherein the analogy or refemblance of our vivification to Chrift's refurrection doth more efpecially confift, the apoftle's anfwer is very exprefs, *Like as Chrift was raifed up from the dead by the glory of the Father; even fo we alfo fhould walk in newnefs of life,* Rom. vi 4. Chrift's refurrection was to newnefs of life; it was a new life, a life different from that which he lived before, and fo is our vivification a new life; it is a life of a new principle, of new actings, of a new ftate, of a new relation, of a new income, and of a new kind or manner.

1. It is a life of a new principle; before vivification, our principle was the flefh, or world, or devil, *In time paft ye walked according to the courfe of this world, according to the prince of the power of the air, the Spirit that now worketh in the children of difobedience,* Eph. ii. 2. but now we have

Baxter's method of peace and comfort.

a new

a new principle, a Spirit of holiness or sanctification, the Spirit of God, even the same spirit which dwelt in the human nature of Christ, and raised him, *If the spirit of him that raised up Jesus from the dead dwell in you,* Rom. viii. 11. it is an indwelling Spirit; even as the soul dwells in the body, so doth the Holy Ghost dwell in the soul of a regenerate person, animating, and actuating, and enlivening it. This is the new principle that God puts in us after vivification.

2. It is a life of new actings. According to our principle so be our actings, *They that are after the flesh, do mind the things of the flesh; but they that are of the Spirit, the things of the Spirit,* Rom. viii. 5. If some men hear of a good bargain, they mind it, they find their souls going on with much activity; there is something in them proportionable to that which is propounded; but if they hear of divine love, and of the riches of grace, they find their souls flat, unmoveable, and dead, they find no such thing: now, on the other side, they that are vivified, according to their principle, they put forth their power more or less; if they hear of the glorious things of the gospel, they find inward workings, (unless it be under a temptation) they find their souls drawn out to close with the goodness of the thing propounded, *They mind the things of the Spirit (i. e.)* they muse and meditate, and think on these things, they affect them, and love them, and like them, they care for them, and seek after them with might and main, they *live in the Spirit,* Gal. v. 25. They *walk in the Spirit,* they *are led by the Spirit,* Rom. viii. 1. 14. They *serve in the newness of the Spirit,* Rom. vii. 6. How might we try our vivification by these actings of our principle within? What, do we mind the things of the spirit? Do we find things heavenly and spiritual to be sweet, and savoury, and best pleasing to us? Is the *Sabbath* our delight? Do we long for it before it come? Do we rejoice in it when it is come? Do we consecrate it as *glorious to the Lord?* Isa. lviii. 13. Do we come to the exercises of religion, whether publick or private, with much delight, and with cheerfulness, as to a feast? What is this but the life of God? But if these things be harsh and unpleasant, if the *Sabbath* be a burden, if holy exercises be irksome and tedious, if in attending on the word we are heavy and drousy, and we find no relish,

no sweet, no savour in the ointments of Christ, no goings out of the soul with an activity to the things propounded; O! then deceive not ourselves, we have no good evidence of our vivification.

3. It is a life of a new state; before vivification we are in an unjustified estate; sins are unpardoned, we are unreconciled, *And such were some of you,* (said the apostle to his Corinthians) *but now ye are washed, now ye are sanctified, now ye are justified in the name of the Lord Jesu. Christ, and by the Spirit of our God,* 1 Cor. vi. 11. This justification denotes a state, and is universal and unalterable. I know Arminians deny such a state, for as by their doctrine, no man can be absolutely elected till he die, so neither absolutely justified; for (say they) he may fall into such sins, as that though formerly justified, yet now he may be condemned; yea, to-day he may be justified, and to-morrow thrown out of that estate. But against this we hold, that those that are once justified, are never again cast out of God's favour. As Christ once died, but rose again never to die more, death hath no more power over him; so a justified man once allied to God through Jesus Christ, doth from that time forward as necessarily live, as Christ himself by whom he doth live; there is an immortal and indissoluble union betwixt Christ the head and every believer; our justification depends not on our own strength, but it is built on Christ himself, who is the same yesterday, and to-day, and for ever; and hence it is, that a justified man can no more cease to live in this state of justification, than Christ can cease to live in heaven.

4. It is a life of new relations: this immediately follows our state: if once we are justified then we are related to God, and Christ, and to the covenant of grace. 1. To God. Before we were vivified, God and we stood at a distance, God was our enemy, and we were his enemies, *At that time,* (saith the apostle) *ye were without God in the world, but now in Christ Jesus, ye who sometimes were afar off, are made nigh by the blood of Christ,* Eph. ii. 12, 13. God that was a stranger, stands now in near relation, he is a friend, a father, a God all-sufficient to us. 2. We are related to Christ. Before vivification we were a Christless people, *at that time we were without Christ,* Eph. ii. 12. but now we are united to Christ, and (which is more) now we make use of Christ with the Father,

ther, O! the comfort of this relation! a troubled spirit looks on his sins, and they thrust him away from God, what communion hath light with darkness? But then comes the Lord Jesus, and takes him by the hand, and leads him to the Father, and says, 'Come soul, come along with me, and 'I will carry thee along to the Father, wilt thou 'make use of me?' It is the apostle's saying, That *through him we have an access by one Spirit unto the Father*, Eph. ii. 18 we have a leading by the hand, *Christ hath once offered for sins, the just for the unjust, that he might bring us to God*, 1 Pet. iii. 18. By nature we are severed from God, and if he manifest himself, he is dreadful to us, *Your iniquities have separated between you and your God, and your sins have hid his face from you, that he will not hear*, Isa. lix. 2. But in Christ we approach boldly before him, because Christ hath taken away our sins which are the mountains of separation, *In Christ we have boldness and access with confidence by the faith of him*, Eph. iii. 12. Here is the difference betwixt a man related to Christ and a mere stranger; the stranger knows not how to go to God, God stands as a judge, he is a malefactor, the law an accuser, sin. his indictment, and what is the issue? *Every mouth is stopped, and all the world is guilty before God*, Rom. iii. 19. But he that is related to Christ, Christ takes him by the hand, and so he goes with boldness and confidence, and pleads his righteousness before the Father; 'Who shall lay any thing to the charge of 'God's elect? It is God that justifieth:' Who is ' he that condemneth? It is Christ that died, yea, ' rather that is risen again,' Rom. viii. 34. In the very matter and cause of justification, wherein no man can stand, or dare to appear or shew his face; a Christian coming with Christ his advocate, dares to appear, and to plead his case, and to stand upon interrogatories with God himself, yea, and to ask God himself, (humbly and with reverence) What he hath to lay to his charge? What more he will, or can in justice require for satisfaction, than his surety hath done for him?—3. We are related to the covenant of grace. Before vivification we had no such relation, *At that time ye were without Christ, being aliens from the commonwealth of Israel, and strangers from the covenant of promise*, Eph. ii. 12. But now the covenant is ours, that fountain or bundle of promises is ours, God is our God, and we are his people O! the blessedness of this privilege! *Happy is the people that be in such a case, yea, happy is the people whose God is the Lord*, Psal. cxliv. 15. The covenant is reckoned all happiness, it contains in its bowels all benefits in heaven, or under heaven, as a man may say of any thing he hath in possession, This is mine, so may they that are in covenant with God, say, he is mine, I have God himself in my possession. How might we try our vivification even by this communion we have with God and Christ, and the covenant of grace? Christians! look unto your own hearts, have you not felt in your approaches to God some raisings or workings of the Spirit of the Lord, concluding the pardon of your sins? Hath not Christ taken you by the hand, and led you to the Father? It may be your own guilt made you afraid, but the discovery of Jesus, your righteousness made you bold to go to God; you felt boldness coming in on this ground, because all your approaches or drawings to God, were bottomed on Jesus; hath not God married you to himself? Hath he not conveyed himself (through his holy Spirit) into your own hearts by way of covenant? Hath he not sometimes whispered to your souls, thou art mine? And have not your souls echoed back again to the Lord, thou art mine? Much of the truth of all this would appear, if Christians would but daily observe the movings of their own hearts; for as he that hath the spirit of Satan shall ever find him putting on and provoking to evil, so he that hath the Spirit of God, shall most (or at least frequently) find and feel it active and stirring in the heart, to the reforming of the whole man; the holy Spirit is not idle, but he rules and governs, and maintains his monarchy in us, and over us, in spight of the power of Satan, and privy conspiracy of a man's own flesh.

5. It is a life of a new income: I mean of a saving income, as of grace, power, light, &c. Before vivification there was no such income, a man before his conversion might hear, and pray, and do all duties, but, alas! he feels no sweets, no power, no virtue, no communion with Christ. If I might appeal unto such, I beseech you tell me, you have been often at prayer, what have you gotten there? What income hath appeared? If you answer truly, you cannot but say, 'I went to prayer, and I ' was satisfied that I had prayed; I never observ-

' ed,

'ed, whether I had got any power, or strength, any thing of mortification or vivification; I never found any lively work of God on my soul, either in prayer or after prayer:' Or, you have been often at this ordinance of hearing the word; what have you gotten there? What income hath appeared? 'Why, truly, nothing at all; it may be a little more knowledge, but nothing that I can say was a saving work of God. Some one that sat with me in the same seat found much stirrings of God; Oh! what meltings, chearings, warmings of the Spirit had such a one and such a one! The word was to them as honey, and as the honey-comb, but to me, it was as dry bread; I found no sweets, I got no good at all.' Or, you have been often tossing the Bible, and you have observed this or that promise; but, O! what income hath appeared? 'Surely nothing at all. I wonder at saints, that tell of so much sweetness, and comfort, and ravishing of heart, that with joy they should draw water out of these wells of salvation, whereas I find therein no joy, no refreshing at all;' ah! poor soul! thou art in a sad case, thou art not yet vivified, thou hast not the life of God in thee. After vivification thou wilt in the use of ordinances (at least sometimes, if not frequently) feel the saving incomes of God. In prayer, thou wilt feel the Spirit breathing in, and carrying up thy soul above itself; plainly declaring there is another power than thy own, which makes thee not only to exceed others but thyself also; in hearing of the word, thou wilt see the windows of heaven set wide open, and all manner of spiritual comforts showered down upon thee; thou wilt hear the rich treasury of everlasting glory and immortality unlocked and opened, so that thou mayest tumble thyself amidst the mountains of heavenly pearls, and golden pleasures, joys that no heart can comprehend, but that which is weaned from all worldly pleasures, 'As it is written, How beautiful are the feet of them that preach the gospel of peace, and bring glad tidings of good things?' Rom. x. 15. In meditation of the promises, or of divine love, thou wilt find meltings, quicknings, encouragings, filling thy heart with gladness, and glorying, and thy mouth with praises and songs of rejoicings; oh! what fountains of life are the promises to a living man, to a soul that is vivified? What food, what strength, what life is a thought of Christ, of heaven, and of God's love to a spiritual man? Whereas all these glorious things of the gospel are to the natural man but as a withered flower, a sealed book, a dry and empty cistern, he hath no use of them.

6. It is a life of another kind or manner. Before vivification our life was but death, because we ourselves were but dead in sin, even whilst alive, *She that liveth in pleasure is dead while she liveth*, 1 Tim. v. 6. *And you were dead in your sins, and the uncircumcision of your flesh*, Col. ii. 13. But after vivification we live; How live? A spiritual life, *I live by the faith of the Son of God*, Gal. ii. 20. an heavenly life, *For our conversation is in heaven, from whence also we look for the Saviour, the Lord Jesus Christ*, Phil. iii. 20. an immortal life, *Christ being raised from the dead, dieth no more, death hath no more dominion over him;—likewise reckon yourselves to be dead indeed unto sin, but alive unto God through Jesus Christ our Lord*, Rom. vi. 9, 11. You know the meaning of Christ, *Whosoever liveth, and believeth in me, shall never die*, John xi. 26. he shall never die a spiritual death, never come under the dominion of sin, never totally fall away from grace; that incorruptible seed by which he is regenerate shall abide in him for ever, *If Christ be in you, the body is dead because of sin, but the spirit is life because of righteousness*, Rom. viii. 10. the body indeed is subject to corporal death, through the remainders of sin, but the spirit is life, even that little spark of grace, through the most perfect righteousness of Christ imputed, is life here, and shall be life hereafter, even for ever. And herein is our vivification answerable to Christ's resurrection, 'Like as Christ was raised up from the dead by the glory of the Father,' raised up to a new life, 'even so we also should walk in newness of life,' Rom. vi. 4.

For the second question, how is this conformity or vivification wrought? I shall answer only to the state, and so our vivification is usually wrought in us in this manner. As, First, In the understanding. Secondly, In the will.

First, The understanding lets in the verity and truth of what the gospel hath recorded, 'In him was life, and the life was the light of men, John i. 4.——I am the bread of life, he that cometh to me shall never hunger, and he that believeth on me shall never thirst, John vi. 35.——I am the

'resurrection and the life, he that believeth in me,
'though he were dead, yet shall he live, John xi.
'25. I am the way, the truth, and the life, John
'xiv. 6.——And this is the record that God hath
'given to us eternal life, and this life is in his Son;
'he that hath the Son hath life, and he that hath
'not the Son, hath not life,' 1 John v. 11, 12.

2. This light let in, the understanding thence inferreth as to a man's own self, that by the assistance of the Spirit of holiness who raised up Jesus from the dead, it's possible for him to attain to this life; others have attained it, and why not he? *You hath he quickned, who were dead in trespasses and sins;* here's a precedent for a sin-sick soul; *in time past ye walked according to the course of this world, according to the prince of the power of the air, the spirit that now worketh in the children of disobedience,* Eph. ii 1, 2. this was the state of the Ephesians: But were they all so? No, no; ye and we also, 'among whom also we had all our conversation
'in times past.—But God, who is rich in mercy, for
'his great love wherewith he loved us, even when
'we were dead in sins, hath quickned us together
'with Christ,——That in ages to come he might
'shew the exceeding riches of his grace in his kindness towards us through Christ Jesus,' ver. 3, 4, 5, 6, 7. Christ's dealings with some are as flags and patterns of mercy hung forth to tell, and to bring others in: whence the understanding infers, 'It's possible for a dead soul, yea, for my dead soul
'to live; others have lived, and why may not I?
'I discover in those scriptures, even in these pre-
'cedents, a door of hope to myself;' why, Lord, *if thou wilt, thou canst make me clean,* Mat. viii. 2.—
yea, if I may but touch thy garment, I shall be whole, Mat. ix. 21. *if thou wouldest but say, O! ye dry bones, hear the word of the Lord, then breath would enter into me, and I should live,* Ez. xxxvii. 4, 5. 'Surely if Christ be risen again from the dead,
'there's no impossibility but I may rise, if others
'have been raised by the virtue of Christ's resur-
'rection, why may not I?' However, this may seem to be little or nothing, yet considering the soul in a mourning, dark, disconsolate frame, under deep apprehensions of sin, guilt and wrath; full of confusions, distractions, despondencies, staggering and sinking terrors; it will find in it something, yea, it will look on it as a glorious work to discover but the morning star through so much darkness, any thing for life, in such a valley and shadow of death.

3. The understanding hath yet some brighter believing beams; it confidently closeth with this truth, that it is the will of the Lord that he should come, and live, and believe, and lay hold on Christ; it apprehends the particular designs of mercy to him, and doth really principle the soul with this, that God doth particularly call, invite, and bid him come to Christ the fountain of life, for life. Now the understanding takes in general gospel calls in particular to himself. 'It is my poor languishing
'soul which the Lord speaks to, when he says,'
Come to me all ye that are weary, and I will give you rest, Matth. xi. 28 —*Awake thou that sleepest, and rise from the dead, and Christ shall give thee light,* Ephesi. v. 14. Surely this is a great work when set home by the Lord, that the soul acts in its addresses to Christ in the strength of a particular call from God.

2. And now the answer to this call is wrought up in the renewed will; as thus.——

1. The will summons all its confidences, and calls them off from every other bottom, to bestow them wholly upon Christ; and this consists in our voluntary renouncing of all other helps, excepting Jesus Christ alone; now the soul says to idols, 'Get
'ye hence, Ashur shall not save us, we will not
'ride upon horses, neither will we say any more
'to the works of our hands, ye are our Gods,' Hos. xiv. 3. *Ashur shall not save us,* not only cannot, but shall not save us; now as the soul is dissatisfied in judgment, as to the resting on any thing but Christ alone, so the heart and will is disaffected to all other helps but Christ alone; now it renounceth its own righteousness, and worthiness, not only because of their inability to save, but mainly because their glory is swallowed up in that unmatchable excellency, which appears in the way of life and salvation by Jesus Christ. It calls home dependence from every other object.

2. Hereupon there is a willing and cheerful receiving of Christ, and resignation of ourselves to his actual disposal, to quicken us, and save us in his own way. A great part of the answer of faith, to the call of Christ lies in this; for as faith sees life and salvation in the hands of Christ, so it considers it to be given forth in the methods of Christ; and so believing lies not only in assent, but consent of heart, that Christ shall save us in his own way; this

this is called *a receiving of Christ*; *as many as received him to them he gave power to become the sons of God*, John i. 12. Many a soul would be saved by Christ, that sticks and boggles at his methods; they will not pass to happiness by holiness, nor set him up as a king and Lord, whom they could consent to let up as a Saviour: oh! but now Christ that *stood at the door, and knocked*, Rev. iii 10. is received in; consent hath made up the match, and the door is opened that never shall be shut again.

3. Upon this follows the soul's resting and relying; the soul's confidence and dependence upon Jesus Christ for life and for salvation.; this closeth up the whole business of believing unto righteousness; those various expressions used in scripture of 'committing our way and selves to God; of 'casting our care upon God, of rolling ourselves 'on him, of trusting in him, and hoping in his mer-'cy,' &c. wrapt up faith in this affiance, dependence, not without some mixture of confidence, and resolved resting upon Jesus Christ: a clear beholding of God in Christ, and of Christ in the promises, doth present such variety and fulness of arguments to bear up hope and affiance, that the heart is resolved; and so resolved that we commit ourselves, and give our souls in charge to Christ, *I know whom I have believed, and I am persuaded he is able to keep that which I have committed unto him against that day*, 2 Tim. i. 12. 1 Pet. iv. 12.

4. The upshot of all is this, that the same close which the soul makes in believing with Jesus Christ as to justification and righteousness, is not fruitless to this effect of conveying life and virtue from Jesus Christ as to grace and holiness; for that union which then and thereby comes to be enjoined with Christ, is such an union as is fruitful in begetting a quickning power and principle in heart; and this is that which we ordinarily intend by saying, saving faith to be operative; that faith which brings forth nothing of holiness, what is it but a dead faith? *As the body without the spirit is dead, so faith without works is dead also*, James ii. 26. Justification and sanctification are twins of a birth; and hence it is, that vivification (which is one part of sanctification) is wrought, in the soul after the self same manner; as, first. The understanding is enlightened. 2. The will is changed. 3. All the affections are renewed. 4. The internals being quickned, there ensueth the renewing of the body with the outward actions, life, and conversation. And now is fulfilled that saying of Christ in a spiritual sense, *The hour is coming, and now is, when the dead shall hear the voice of the Son of God, and they that hear shall live*, John v. 25. Now is the soul vivified, now it begins to live the life of God, now it feels the power of Christ's resurrection, and is made conformable to it; and immediately upon this, joy is made in heaven by the angels, God himself applauding it, *For this my son was dead, and is alive, he was lost, and is found*, Luke xv. 24.

Thus is the state of vivification wrought. I know it is not in all men after one manner for every circumstance; the methods of God are exceeding various, and we cannot limit the holy One of Israel; I have sometimes concerning this, desired the communications of others thoughts, whom I looked upon as such, who had more than ordinary communion with Christ's Spirit; and from one of such I received this answer, 'I must profess to 'you, I have in all my speculations in divinity, 'found dissatisfaction in the writings of men in no-'thing more, than in the work of clear and dis-'tinct conceptions concerning regeneration; which 'yet is of such a cardinal importance, as that the 'great doors of heaven move upon the hinges of it, 'the Lord enlighten us more, for we see but in 'part, and prophesy but in part.'

For the third question, What are the means of this conformity or vivification which we must use on our parts? I shall answer herein both to the state and growth of our vivification. As,——

1. Wait and attend upon God in the ministry of the word, this is a means whereby Christ ordinarily effecteth this vivification. By this means, it was that those dead bones were quickned in Ezekiel's prophesy, viz. By the prophet's prophesying upon them, *And he said unto me, son of man,—— prophesy upon these bones, and say unto them, O! ye dry bones, hear ye the word of the Lord*, Ezekiel xxxvii 4. And by this means it is that dead souls are quickned, the ministry of the word is the trumpet of Jesus Christ, when that sounds, who knows, but he may quicken the dead? Hearken therefore to this word of God.

2. Act faith upon the Lord Jesus as to justification. As is the clearness and fixedness of our souls in bottoming ourselves on Christ for righteousness;

ousness; so will be our quickness, and successful progress in the work of holiness; because *Mary's sins, which were many, were forgiven her, therefore she loved much; but to whom little is forgiven, the same loveth little*, Luke vii. 47. Many a soul loseth much of vivification, for want of clearness in its justification, or for want of settledness, and stronger measure of acting faith. Oh! what life would be raised as to holiness? What working, binding, filling the laws of love, retribution and thankfulness would there be, when we see ourselves clearly reconciled with God, and wrapt up in the foldings of everlasting love?

3. Trace every ordinance, and every duty for the appearings of the Son of God. Be much in prayer, hearing, reading, and fellowship with the saints, living in the fulness of sacraments; be much in secret conversings with God, in meditation, expostulation, enquiries and searchings? and (which is a precious work) be much in diligent watching of, hearkening and listening to the movings, watchings, hints, and intimations of the Spirit of God; be much in observing the methods, and interpreting the meaning and language of God in all his secret dispensations with the soul certainly there will be abundance of the life of God conveyed to him that walks in these paths. *Blessed are they that dwell in thy house*, might David well say, and one reason is pertinent to this case, because *in your Father's house is bread enough and to spare*, Luke xv. 17. while the prodigal that goes out from it shall feed upon husks, and with Ephraim swallow up the east-wind. Oh! for a spirit of prayer, meditation, &c. Oh! for a spirit even swallowed up in communion with God! *Thou meetest him that worketh righteousness, and those that remember thee in thy ways*, Isa. lxiv. 5.

4. Look much at Christ raised, Christ glorified; Christ's resurrection was the beginning of his glory, and therein is comprehended both the glory that draws desires towards Christ, and the grace and power that established faith in its dependency, 'They looked unto him, and were lightened, Psal. 'xxxiv 5.—Unto thee lift I up mine eyes, O thou 'that dwellest in the heavens; behold, as the eyes 'of the servants look unto the hand of their mas- 'ters, and as the eyes of a maiden unto the hand 'of her mistress, so our eyes wait upon the Lord 'our God,' Psalm cxxiii. 1, 2. It is said of Moses that *he endured affliction, as seeing him who is invisible*, Heb. xi. 27. Oh! could we keep our hearts in a more constant view, and believing meditation of the glory of Christ, our faces would certainly bring some beams of divinity with them from the mount, ' We all with open face, beholding, ' as in a glass, the glory of the Lord, are changed ' into the same image, from glory to glory, 2 Cor. iii. 18. The very beholding of Christ hath a mighty conforming and assimulating virtue to leave the impressions of glory upon our spirits.

5. See our own personal vivification linked unseparably unto, and bottomed unremovably upon the resurrection of Christ: when we can by faith get a sight of this, it is not to speak how courageously and successfully the soul will grapple in the controversies of the Lord against the devil, and our own deceitful hearts; with what strength could Joshuah, Gideon, &c go on, when backed with a promise, and their spirits settled in the persuasion of it? And what use will the promises be in this kind? And (more than all) the life and resurrection of Jesus Christ, when we can clearly and stedfastly rest upon this, that there is an inseparable connection betwixt the resurrection of Christ and our personal holiness, and perseverance to the end? Oh! that I could act my faith more frequently on Christ's resurrection, so that at last I could see it by the light of God to be a destinated principle of my vivification in particular! what a blessed means would this be?

6. Walk as we have Christ Jesus for an example. This example of Christ, though it be not ours, as it is the Socinian's *totum Christi*, yet certainly it yields much to our vivification; who can deny but that acting with the pattern ever in one's eye is very advantageous? Come then, and if we would live the life of God, let us live as Christ lived after his resurrection. But how is that? I answer,—

1. See that we return to the grave no more; take heed of ever returning to our former state, you may say, What needs this caveat? Hath not Christ said, ' He that liveth and believeth in me ' shall never die, or never fall away?' I answer, It is true, they shall never totally and finally fall away, yet they may fall foully and fearfully; they may lose that strength and vigour, that sense and feeling which sometimes they had; they may draw so nigh to the grave, as that, both by
them-

themselves and others they may be accounted amongst themselves that go down to the pit, *Free among the dead*, as Heman faith of himself, Psal. lxxx. 5. The apostle faith something that might even startle Christians; he tells of some, *who have been once enlightened*, (by the word) *and have tasted of the heavenly gift*, (some flashes of inward joy and peace) *and were made partakers of the Holy Ghost*, (the common gifts and graces of the Spirit) *and have tasted the good word of God*, (have found some relish in the sweet and saving promises of the gospel) *and the powers of the word to come*; (have found some refreshing apprehensions of the joys and glory in heaven) *and yet fall away*, (by a total apostacy) Heb. vi. 4, 5, 6. Christians! how far goes this? I know it is said only of such who have a name to live, and no more; but surely it gives a warning to us all that we come not nigh the verge, the brink of the grave again; let us not give way to any one sin, so as to live in it, or to continue in it.

2. Let us evidence our resurrection; Christ being raised, he shewed himself alive by many infallible proofs; so let us evidence our vivification by many infallible proofs, *(i. e.) let us yield up ourselves unto God, as those that are alive from the dead*, Rom. vi. 13. let us walk as men of another world. 'If ye be risen with Christ, seek the things 'which are above, where Christ sitteth on the right-'hand of God,' Col. iii. 1. let us serve God in holiness and righteousness all the days of our life; surely this is the end for which we are delivered out of the hands of our enemies, sin, death, and hell. *Ye were sometimes darkness*, (during your abode in the grave of sin) *but now* (being risen) *ye are light in the Lord, walk therefore as children of light*, Eph. v. 8. Walk, *(i e.)* bestir yourselves in the works of God, *Arise, shine, for thy light is come, and the glory of the Lord is risen upon thee*, Isa. lx. 1. When God doth let the Sun of righteousness arise, it is fit we should be about the business of our souls. We see that the night is dedicated to rest, and therefore God that doth order all things sweetly, he draws a curtain of darkness about us, which is friendly to rest; like a nurse, that when she will have her little one sleep, she casts a cloth over the face, and hides the light every way: but when this natural sun ariseth, then men go out to this work; so must we, though in the darkness of the night we snored in sin, yet now we must bestir ourselves, seeing the sun of the spiritual world is risen over us.

And yet when all is done, let us not think that our vivification in this life will be wholly perfect: as it is with our mortification, so it is but an imperfect work; so it is with our vivification, it is only gardual, and never perfected till grace be swallowed up of glory. Only let us ever be in the use of means, and let us endeavour a farther renovation of the new man, adding one grace to another, *To faith virtue, to virtue knowledge, to knowledge temperance, to temperance patience, to patience godliness*, &c. 2 Pet. i 5, 6 till we *perfect holiness in the fear of God*, Rom. vii. 1. till we shine with those saints in glory at perfect day.

Thus far we have looked on Jesus as our Jesus in his resurrection, and during the time of his abode on earth. Our next work is to look on Jesus carrying on the great work of our salvation in his ascension into heaven; and in his session at God's right hand; and in his mission of the Holy Ghost.

Mark xvi. 19. *So then after the Lord had spoken unto them, he was received up into heaven, and sat on the right hand of God.*

Heb. iv. 14. *Seeing then that we have a great high-priest, that is passed into the heavens, Jesus the Son of God, let us hold fast our profession.*

Heb. viii. 1, 2. *Now of the things which we have spoken, this is the sum; we have such an high-priest, who is set on the right-hand of the throne of the majesty in the heavens; a minister of the sanctuary, and of the true tabernacle, which the Lord pitched, and not man.*

Eph. iv. 8. Psal. lxviii. 18. *When he ascended up on high, he led captivity captive, and gave gifts unto men,——that the Lord God might dwell among them.*

Acts ii. 1, 2, 3, 4. *And when the day of Pentecost was fully come, they were all with one accord in one place, and suddenly there came a sound from heaven, as of a rushing mighty wind, and it filled all*

all the house where they were sitting; and there appeared unto them cloven tongues, like as of fire, and it sat upon each of them, and they were all filled with the Holy Ghost, and began to speak with other tongues as the Spirit gave them utterance.

Heb. xii. 2. *Looking unto Jesus, the author and finisher of our faith; who, for the joy that was set before him, endured the cross, despising the shame, and is set down at the right-hand of the throne of God.*

2 Cor. iii. 18. *We all with open face, beholding as in a glass the glory of the Lord, are changed into the same image, from glory to glory, even as by the Spirit of the Lord.*

LOOKING UNTO JESUS.

In his Ascension, Session, and Mission of his Spirit.

BOOK FOURTH, PART FIFTH.

CHAP. I. SECT. I.

Heb. xii. 2. *Looking unto Jesus, —— who is set down at the right-hand of the throne of God.*

Of Christ's ascension, and of the Manner how.

THUS far we have traced Jesus in his actings for us, *Until the day in which he was taken up,* Acts i. 2. That which immediately follows, is his ascension, session at God's right-hand, and mission of his holy Spirit; in prosecution of which, as in the former, I shall first lay down the object, and secondly direct you how to look upon it.

The object is threefold. 1. He ascended into heaven. 2. He sat down at God's right-hand. 3. He sent down the Holy Ghost.

1. For the ascension of Christ: this was a glorious design, and contains in it a great part of the salvation of our souls. In prosecution of this, I shall shew, 1. That he ascended. 2. How he ascended. 3. Whether he ascended. 4. Why he ascended.

1. That he ascended. 1. The types prefigure it, *Then said the Lord to me, This gate shall be shut, it shall not be opened; — it is for the prince, the prince he shall sit in it to eat bread before the Lord, he shall enter by way of the porch of that gate, and shall go out by the way of the same,* Ez. xliv. 2, 3. As the gates of the *holy of holies* were shut against every man but the high-priest, so was that gate of heaven shut against all, so that none could enter in by their own virtue and efficacy, but only our prince and great high-priest, the Lord Jesus Christ, indeed he hath opened it for us, and entered into it in our place and stead, *Whether the forerunner is for us entered, even Jesus, made an high-priest for ever, after the order of Melchisedec,* Heb. vi. 20. 2. The prophets foretaw it, ' I saw ' in the night visions, and behold one like the Son ' of man came with the clouds of heaven, and ' came to the ancient of days, and they brought ' him near before him, and there was given him ' dominion, and glory, and a kingdom,' Dan. vii. 13, 14. 3. The evangelists relate it, ' He was ' received up into heaven,' Mark xvi. 19. —— ' He was carried up into heaven,' Luke xxiv. 51.

4 The

4. The eleven witness it, 'For while they beheld, he was taken up, and a cloud received him out of their sight,' Acts i. 9. 5. The holy angels speak it, 'For while they looked stedfastly towards heaven, as he went up, behold, two men stood by them in white apparel; which also said, Ye men of Galilee, Why stand ye gazing up into heaven? This same Jesus which is taken up from you into heaven, shall come in like manner as ye have seen him go into heaven,' Acts i. 10, 11. 6. The blessed apostles in their several epistles ratify and confirm it, 'When he ascended up on high, he led captivity captive, and gave gifts unto men,—he that descended, is the same also that ascended up far above all heavens,' Eph. iv. 8, 10 ——' Who is gone into heaven, and is on the right-hand of God, angels, and authorities, and powers, being made subject unto him, 1 Pet. iii. 22.

2. How he ascended. The manner of his ascension is discovered in these particulars.——1. He ascended, blessing his apostles, *While he blessed them, he was parted from them, and carried up into heaven,* Luke xxiv. 51. It is some comfort to Christ's ministers, that though the world hate them, Christ doth bless them; yea, he parted with them in a way of blessing; as Jacob leaving the world, blessed his sons, so Christ, leaving the world, blessed his apostles, and all the faithful ministers of Christ, unto the end of the world. Some add, that in these apostles, not only ministers, but all the elect to the end of the world are blessed: The apostles were then considered as common persons receiving this blessing for all us; and so those words uttered at the same time, are usually interpreted, *Lo, I am with you alway, even to the end of the world,* Matth. xxviii. 20. This was the last thing that Christ did on earth, to shew that by his death he had redeemed us from the curse of the law, and that now going to heaven he is able *to bless us with all spiritual blessings in heavenly places,* Eph. i. 3.

2. He ascended visibly in the view of his apostles, *While they beheld, he was taken up,* Acts i. 9. he was not suddenly snatched from them, as Elijah was, not secretly and privily taken away, as Enoch was; but in the presence of them all, both his apostles and disciples, he ascended up into heaven: but why not in the view of all the Jews, that so they might know that he was risen again, and gone to heaven? Surely this was the meaning, God would rather that the main points of faith should be learned by hearing, than by seeing; however Christ's own disciples were taught the same sight, that they might better teach others which should not see, yet the ordinary means to come by faith is hearing, *How shall they believe in him of whom they have not heard?—So then, faith cometh by hearing, and hearing by the word of God.* And as for the Jews (saith the apostle) *Have they not heard? Yes verily, their sound went into all the earth, and their words unto the end of the world,* Rom. x. 14, 17, 18.

3. He ascended principally, by the mighty power of his Godhead; thus never any ascended up into heaven but Jesus Christ; for though Enoch and Elijah were assumed into heaven; yet not by their own power, nor by themselves, it was God's power by which they ascended, and it was by the help and ministry of angels, *There appeared a chariot of fire, and horses of fire, and Elijah went up by a whirlwind into heaven,* 2 Kings ii. 11.

4. He ascended in a cloud, *While they beheld, he was taken up, and a cloud received him out of their sight,* Acts i. 9. Hereby he shews that he is Lord of all the creatures; he had already trampled upon the earth, walked upon the sea, vanquished hell or the grave, and now the clouds received him, and the heavens are opened to make way for this King of glory to enter in. When Christ shall come again, it is said that he shall *come in the clouds of heaven with power and great glory,* Matth. xxiv. 30.——' Hereafter shall ye see the Son of man sitting at the right-hand of power, and coming in the clouds of heaven, Matth. xxvi. 24. Which verifies that saying of the angel, ' This same Jesus, which is taken up from you into heaven, shall so come in like manner as ye have seen him go into heaven,' Acts i. 11. He went up in clouds, and he shall come again in clouds.

5. He ascended in the sound of a trumpet; not on earth, sounding Hosanna, but in heaven, crying Hallelujah; so the Psalmist, ' God is gone up with a shout, the Lord with the sound of a trumpet,' Ps. xlvii. 5. Certainly great joy was in heaven at Christ's ascending thither; the very angels struck up their harps, and welcomed him thither with hymns and praises.

6 He ascended in triumph, as a Roman victor

F f f   ascend-

ascended to the capitol, or as David ascended after his conquest up to Zion. Now we read of two triumphal acts in Christ's ascension, whereof the first was his leading of his captives, and the second was the dispersing of his gifts; the apostle and the Psalmist join both together, 'When he ascended up on high he led captivity captive, and gave gifts unto men,' Psal. lxviii. 18. Eph. iv. 8. 1. He led them captive who had captivated us, death was led captive without a sting, hell was led captive as one that had lost her victory, the law was led captive, being rent and fastened to his cross (as it were) ensign-ways, the serpent's head being bruised, was led before him in triumph, as was Goliah's head by David returning from the victory; and this was the first act of his triumph. 2. He gave gifts unto men: this was as the running of conduits with wine, or as the casting abroad of new coin, or as the shutting up of Christ's triumph in his ascension up to heaven: what these gifts were, we shall speak in his mission of the Holy Ghost; only thus much for the present.

SECT. II.

Of the place whither he ascended.

3. WHither he ascended; the gospel tells us into heaven; only Paul saith, That 'he ascended far above all heavens,' Eph. iv. 10. But the meaning is, he went above all these visible heavens, into those heavenly mansions, where the angels, and the spirits of the just have their abode. Or, if the highest heavens be included, I see no absurdity in it; the highest heaven, we usually call the kingdom of heaven, which is either heaven material, or heaven spiritual: and first for the material heaven: in some sense he may be said to ascend above that, both in respect of his body, because the body of Christ is more glorious than any material heaven: and in respect of his soul, because the soul of Christ is more blessed than all things else whatsoever. And, 2. For the spiritual heaven *(i. e)* all angelical or heavenly perfections, he is said to ascend above them all, both in respect of his humiliation, because he hath vilified himself below all things, and therefore he is worthily exalted above all things: and in respect of his perfection, because the human nature of Christ is more excellent than any creature, it being joined to the Godhead by an hypostatical union. Some there are that understand this place of *Christ's ascending far above all heavens,* not so much by a local motion, as by a spiritual mutation and exaltation of his person; as earth heightened unto a flame changeth not its place only, but form and figure, so the person of our Saviour was raised to a greatness and glory vastly differing from, and surmounting any image of things visible or invisible in this creation; so it is fitly expressed, 'He was made higher than the heavens,' Heb. vii. 26. He was heightened to a splendor, enlarged to a capacity and compass above the brightest, and beyond the widest heaven; he transcended all in the spirituality of his ascension: but I shall not much insist on that.

SECT. III.

Of the reasons why he ascended.

4. WHY he ascended; the reasons are, 1. On Christ's part, that through his passion he might pass to glory, *Ought not Christ to have suffered these things, and so to enter into his glory?* Luke xxiv. 26. I shall not insist on that controversy, whether Christ merited for himself, this is without controversy, that by his passion, I will not say he properly merited, but he obtained glory, because he humbled himself so low! God exalted him above the grave in his resurrection, above the earth in his ascension, and above the heavens in placing him at his right-hand. And he ascended that all those prophesies, which were foretold of Christ, might be accomplished, *Thou hast ascended on high,* Psalm lxviii. 18. *And his feet shall stand in that day upon the mount of Olives, which is before Jerusalem on the east,* Zach. xiv. 4. The types of this were Enoch's translation, Elijah's ascension, Sampson's transportation of the gates of Gaza into an high mountain, the high-priest's going into the holy of holies, *Seeing that we have an high-priest, that is passed into the heavens, Jesus the Son of God,* Heb. iv. 14. Why, all these prophesies, types and figures, must needs be accomplished, and therefore, on his part, it was necessary that Christ must ascend, and go into heaven.

2. The reasons on our part are,—

1. That in our stead he might triumph over
sin,

in, death and hell. In his refurrection he conquered, but in his afcenfion he triumphed; now: was, that he led fin, death, and devil in triumph at his chariot wheels: and this is the meaning of the Pfalmift, and of the apoftle, *When he afcended up on high, he led captivity captive,* Eph. iv. 8. He vanquifhed and triumphed over all our enemies, he overcame the world, he bound the evil, he fpoiled hell, he weakened fin, he deftroyed death, and now he makes a public triumphal fhew of them in his own perfon; he led the captives bound to his chariot wheels, as the manner of the Roman triumphs was, when the conqueror went up to the capitol. It is to the fame purpofe, that the apoftle fpeaks elfewhere, *Having fpoiled principalities and powers, he made a fhew of them openly, triumphing over them in himfelf,* Col. ii. 5. it is a manifeft allufion to the manner of triumphs after victories amongft the Romans: firft, they fpoiled the enemy upon the place, e'er they ftirred off the field; and this was done by Chrift on the crofs; and then they made a public triumphal fhew, they rode thro' the ftreets in the greateft ftate and had all their fpoils carried before them, and the kings and nobles, whom they had taken, they led to their chariots, and led them as captives; and this did Chrift at his afcenfion, *Then he openly triumphed [enauto] in himfelf,* (i. e.) in his own power and ftrength; other conquerors do not thus; they conquer not in themfelves, and by themfelves, but Jefus Chrift conquered in himfelf, and therefore he triumphed in himfelf. And yet though he triumphed in himfelf, and by himfelf, it was not for himfelf, but for us, which made the apoftle to triumph in his triumph, *O death! where is thy fting? O grave! where is thy victory? The fting of death is fin, and the ftrength of fin is the law; but thanks be to God which giveth us victory through our Lord Jefus Chrift,* 1 Cor. xv. 55, 56, 57. If I may fpeak out what I think was this victory of Chrift; I believe it was that honour given to him after his refurrection by the converfion of enemies, by the amazements of the world, by the admirations of angels, and efpecially by his fitting down at the right hand of majefty on high; for therein is contained both his exaltation, and his triumph over all his enemies to the utmoft.

2. That he might lead us the way, and open to us the doors of glory. It is a queftion, whether ever thofe doors of heaven were opened to any before Chrift's afcenfion? Chrift tells us, 'In 'my Father's houfe are many manfions, if it were ' not fo, I would have told you, but I go to prepare ' a place for you, and if I go and prepare a place ' for you, I will come again, and receive you un-' to myfelf, that where I am, ye may be alfo,' John xiv. 2, 3. Some infer hence, as if there fhould be many outer courts, and many different places or ftates in glory; and yet that there is one place whither the faints fhould arrive at laft, which was not then ready for them, and was not to be entred into, until the entrance of our Lord had made the preparation. *Again,* the apoftle tells us, That *the Fathers received not the promifes, God having provided fome better thing for us, that they without us fhould not be made perfect,* Heb. xi. 40. Whence fome infer that their condition after death was a ftate of imperfection; and that they were placed in an outer court on this fide heaven, called *paradife* or *Abraham's bofom*; and thither alfo Chrift went when he died, and was attended with the bleffed thief. For my part, I fhall not join with fuch who think all fouls of faints fhall go to paradife, where they muft remain till the day of judgment, and then, and not till then muft enter into that heaven, called *the third heaven,* or the kingdom of heaven. Indeed fome of the ancients make heaven, and the immediate receptacles of fouls to be diftinct places, both bleffed, but hugely differing in decrees: and a modern writer is very confident, ' † That no foul could enter into glory before our ' Lord entred, by whom we hope to have accefs;' and to that purpofe he cites thofe texts, John xiv. 2, 3. Heb. xi. 40. * But I fee no ground, why the fouls of faints fhould be excluded heaven, either before, or after Chrift. As for that text of John xiv. 2. Chrift faith, *In my Father's houfe are many manfions,* not many outer courts, nor many different ftates: and as for the fathers mentioned, Heb. xi. 40. *Surely they without us fhall*

† Dr Taylor's great Examplar.
* *Multas dicit non varias aut difpares, fed quæ pluribus fufficiant, acfi diciret non fibi uni, fed omnibus etiam difcipulis locum illic effe* Calvin in loc.

not be made perfect, and we without them shall not be made perfect, in some sense, until the day of judgment. But our perfection is not in respect of a more glorious place, but in respect of that perfection whereof all the faithful shall be made partakers as well in body as in soul, at the resurrection of the just. Thus far I grant, that no soul ever entred into heaven, but by the virtue and power of Christ's ascension; and that no soul and body jointly ever ascended (except Christ's types) before Christ himself opened those doors, and led the way; and in this respect he is called *the forerunner of his people*, Heb. vi. 20.

3. That he might assure us, that now he had run through all those offices which he was to perform here on earth for our redemption, *he that hath entered into his rest, hath also ceased from his own works, as God did from his*, Heb. iv. 10. He was first to execute his office, and then to enter into his rest, though he were a son, and so the inheritance were his own, *yet he was to learn obedience, by the things which he suffered, before he was made perfect, and so to become the author of eternal salvation unto all them that obey him*, Heb. v. 8, 9. This was the argument which Christ used when he prayed to be glorified again with his Father, *I have glorified thee on earth, I have finished the work which thou gavest me to do: and now, O Father! glorify thou me with thy own self, with the glory which I had with thee before the world was*, John xvii. 4, 5. This was the order of the dispensation of Christ's offices; his first work was a work of ministry, and service in the office of obedience and sufferings for his church; and his next work was the work of power and majesty in the protection and exaltation of his church. And there was a necessity in this order. 1. In respect of God's decree, who had so fore-appointed it, Acts ii. 23, 24. 2. In respect of God's justice, which must first be satisfied by obedience before any entrance into glory, Luke xxiv. 26. 3. In respect of Christ's infinite person, which being equal with God, could not possibly be exalted without some preceding descent and humiliation, *That he ascended*, (saith the apostle) *What is it, but that he descended first into the lower parts of the earth?* Eph. iv. 9. 4. In respect of our evidence and assurance; this is the sign that Christ hath finished the work of our redemption upon the earth; first, he was to act as our surety, and then he was to ascend as our head, or advocate; as the first-fruits, the captain, the prince of life, the author of salvation, the forerunner of his people.

4. That he might thoroughly convince the world of believers of their perfect righteousness, *The Spirit when he comes* (saith Christ) *shall convince the world of sin, and of righteousness, and of judgment,—of sin, because they believe not on me,—of righteousness, because I go to my Father, and ye see me no more*, John xvi. 8, 9, 10. If Christ had not fulfilled all righteousness there had been no going to heaven for him, nor remaining there; certainly God would have sent him down again to have done the rest, and the disciples should have seen him with shame sent back again; but his ascension to heaven proclaims openly, 1. That he hath completely finished the work he had to do for us here, that no more was to be done in this world for us, that the satisfactory work to justice was in itself finished. 2. That God was well pleased with Jesus Christ, and with what he had done and suffered for us; yea, God was so infinitely taken with him, and his oblation after his sufferings, as that he thinks it not fit to let him stay above forty days longer in this world; he cannot be without him in heaven, but he takes him up into glory, and gives him a name above every name. 3. That we have our share in heaven with him; he went not up as a single person, but virtually, or mystically, he carried up all the elect with him into glory; or otherwise, how should the Spirit convince the world by his ascension of their righteousness? Or otherwise, how should the Son of God convince his Father by his ascension of his righteousness? I look upon Jesus Christ going into heaven, as a confident debtor after payment going into a court, saying, 'Who 'hath any thing to lay to his charge? All is paid, 'let the law take its course.' When Christ entred into heaven, he seemed thus to challenge justice, 'Make room here for me and mine; Who should 'hinder? Hath the law any thing to say to these 'poor souls for whom I died? If any in heaven 'can make objection, here I am to answer in their 'behalf.' Methinks, I imagine, a silence in heaven (as John speaks) *at this speech*, Rev. viii. 1. only mercy smiles, justice gives in the acquittance, and God sets Christ down at his right-hand. 4. That he hath a new design to be acted in heaven

for

for us; he is taken up into glory that he may act gloriously the second part of our righteousness, I mean that he might apply it, and send down his Spirit to convince us of it. He acted one part in the flesh, in the habit of a beggar, clothed with rags; but now he is gone to act the person of a prince in robes of glory, and all this to manage our salvation in the richest way that may be. Three great things Christ now acts for us in glory. First, He is in place of an advocate for us, *He liveth to intercede for us*, Heb. vii. 25. He is always begging of favour and love for us, he lies there to stop whatever plea may be brought in against us by the devil, or law; yea, he is there to get out fresh pardons for new sins. Secondly, He is the great provider and caterer for us; he is laying in a great stock and store of glory for us against we come there, ' In my Father's house are many mansions. —' I go to prepare a place for you,' John xiv. 2. Jesus Christ went before to take up God's heart for us, and now he is drawing out the riches of love from God his Father, and laying them in bank for us, which made the apostle say, ' My God shall ' supply all your need, according to his riches in ' glory by Christ Jesus,' Phil. iv. 19. Thirdly, He sends down his Spirit to convince us that Christ's righteousness is ours: indeed the means of procuring this was the life and death of Christ, but the means of applying this righteousness are these following acts of Christ's resurrection, ascension, session, intercession, &c. By his death he obtained righteousness for us, but by his ascension he applies righteousness to us, now it is that in special manner he convinceth us of righteousness, ' because he is ' gone to his Father, and we shall see him no more.'

5. That he might receive his kingdom over us in the place appointed for it; look as kings are crowned in the chief cities of their kingdoms, and keep their residence in their palaces near unto them, so it was decent that our Saviour should be crowned in heaven, and there sit down at God's right hand; which immediately follows after his ascension, to which we now come.

SECT. IV.
Of God's right-hand, and of Christ's session there.

2. FOr the session of Christ at God's right-hand, which is a consequent following after his ascension into heaven, I shall examine. 1. What is God's right-hand? 2. What is it to sit there? 3. According to what nature doth Christ sit there? 4. Why is it that he sits at the right-hand of God his Father in glory?

1. What is this right-hand of God? I answer, 1. Negatively, It is not any corporal right-hand of God; if we speak properly, God hath neither right hand, nor left-hand; for God is not a body, but a Spirit, or a spiritual substance. 2. Positively, the right-hand of God, is the majesty, dignity, dominion, power, and glory of God, *The right-hand of the Lord is exalted, the right-hand of the Lord doth valiantly*, Psal. cxviii. 15.—*Thy right-hand, O Lord, is become glorious in power, thy right-hand, O Lord, hath dashed in pieces the enemy*, Exod. xv. 6. *Thou hast a mighty arm; strong is thy hand, and high is thy right-hand*, Psalm lxxxix. 13 — *Mine hand hath laid the foundations of the earth, and my right-hand hath spanned the heavens*, Isa. xlviii. 13. I know some of our divines make this right-hand of God something inferior to God's own power, but others speak of it as every way equal, and I know no absurdity to follow on it.

2. What is it to sit at the right-hand of God? I answer, it is not any corporal session at God's right-hand, as some picture him with a crown of gold on his head sitting on a throne, as if he had no other gesture in heaven but sitting still, which Stephen contradicts, saying, ' I see the heavens o-' pened, and the Son of man standing on the right-' hand of God,' Acts vii. 56. The word sitting, or standing, are both metaphorical, and borrowed from the custom of kings, who place those they honour, and to whom they commit the power of government at their right-hand; more particularly, this sitting at God's right-hand implies two things. 1. His glorious exaltation. 2. The actual administration of his kingdom.

1. Christ is exalted, *Wherefore God also hath highly exalted him, and given him a name above every name, that at the name of Jesus every knee shall bow*, Phil. ii. 9. This session is the supreme dignity and glory given by the Father unto Christ after his ascension; this session is the peerless exaltation of the Mediator in his kingdom of glory. But how was Christ exalted? I answer, 1. In regard of his divine nature, not really, or in itself. Impossible it was that the divine nature should receive

ceive any intrinsical improvement, or glory, because all fulness of glory essentially belonged unto it; but declaratorily, or by way of manifestation; so it was that his divinity, during the time of his humiliation, lay hidden and over-shadowed, as the light of a candle is hidden in a dark and close lantern; but now in his session that divinity in glory which he had always with his Father was shewed forth and declared, *He was declared to be the Son of God with power,* Rom. i. 4. both at his resurrection and at his session. 2. In regard of his human nature; and yet that must be understood soberly, for I cannot think that Christ's human nature was at all exalted in regard of the grace of personal union, or in regard of the habitual perfections of his human soul, because he possessed all these from the beginning; but in regard of those interceptions of the beams of the Godhead, and divine glory; and in respect of the restraints of that sense and sweetness, and feeling operations of the beatifical vision during his humiliation; in these respects Christ was exalted in his human nature, and had all the glory from the deity communicated to it, which possibly in any way it was capable of. There was a time, when the office which Christ undertook for us made him a man of sorrows, but when he had finished that dispensation, then he was filled with unmatchable glory, which before his session he enjoyed not; there was a time when the natural consequence and flowings of Christ's glory from that personal union was stayed and hindered by special dispensation, for the working of our salvation; but when that miraculous stay was once removed, and the work of our redemption fully finished, then he was exalted beyond the capacity, or comprehension of all the angels in heaven, *To which of the angels said he at any time, sit at my right-hand?* Heb. i. 13. in this respect it is said, that *God highly exalted him,* exalted he was in his resurrection, ascension, but never so high as at his session; in his resurrection he was exalted with Jonah from the lower parts to the upper parts of the earth; in his ascension he was exalted with Elijah above the clouds, above the stars, above the heavens; but in his session he is exalted to the highest place in heaven, even to the right-hand of God; *far above all heavens, that he might fill all things,* Eph. iv. 10.

2. Christ reigns, or actually administers his glorious kingdom, and this is the principal part of Christ's sitting at God's right-hand. So the Psalmist, *The Lord said unto my Lord, Sit thou at my right-hand, until I make thine enemies thy footstool: the Lord shall send the rod of thy strength out of Zion; rule thou in the midst of thine enemies,* Psal. cx. 1, 2. The apostle is yet more large, *God set him at his own right-hand in the heavenly places, far above all principality, and power, and might, and dominion, and every name that is named, not only in this world, but also in that which is to come; and hath put all things under his feet, and gave him to be the head over all things to the church, which is his body, the fulness of him that filleth all in all,* Eph. i. 20, 21, 22, 23. Some describe this session at God's right-hand to be all one with his reigning in equal power and glory with the Father; but the Son hath always so reigned, and the Holy Ghost hath always so reigned, who yet is not said in scripture to sit at the right-hand of the father; I believe therefore, there is something in this session or reign of Christ, which doth difference it from that reigning power and glory of the Father, and of the Son as only God, and of the Holy Ghost; and if we would know what this is, I would call it an actual administration of his kingdom, or an immediate executing of his power and glory over every creature as Mediator. There is a natural, and a dispensatory kingdom of Jesus Christ; for the first, the Father reigns immediately by the Son, but by the Holy Ghost the Father doth not reign immediately, but thro' the Son; the same order is to be kept in their power, which is in the persons; the Father reigns not by himself, but of himself, because he is of none; the Son reigneth by himself, not of himself, because he is begotten of the Father; the Holy Ghost reigneth by himself, but from the Father and the Son, from whom he doth proceed. And as in the natural, so in the dispensatory kingdom, the Father reigns immediately by the Son as Mediator; and hence it is that the Son, as Mediator, is only said to sit at God's right-hand, because the right of actual administration, or immediate execution of the sovereign power is appropriate and peculiar to the Son, as Mediator betwixt God and man: and this made Christ to say, *The Father judgeth no man, but hath committed all judgment unto the Son,* John v. 22. as Mediator. You may object, Christ was Mediator immediately after his incarnation, but he did

not

not actually administer his kingdom then. I answer, it is true, Christ for a time did by a voluntary dispensation empty himself, and laid aside the right of actual administration of his kingdom; but immediately after his ascension, the Father by voluntary dispensation resigned it to the Son again, *Come now, saith the Father, and take thou power over every creature, till the time that all things shall be subdued under thee.* This right the one relinquished in the time of that humiliation of himself; and this right the other conferred at the time of the exaltation of his Son.

SECT. V.

Of the two natures wherein Christ sits at God's right-hand.

5. According to what nature is Christ said to sit at the right-hand of God? I answer, according to both natures; first, he sits at God's right-hand as God; hereby his divinity was declared, and his kingdom is such, that none that is a pure creature can possibly execute, *The Lord said to my Lord*, saith David, *Sit thou at my right-hand*, Ps. cx. 1. The Lord said to my Lord, *(i. e.)* God said to Christ: now Christ was not David's Lord merely as man, but as God. And, 2. He sits at God's right-hand as man too; hereby his humanity was exalted, and a power is given to Christ as man, *he hath given him power to execute judgment, in as much as he is the Son of man*, John v. 27. In the administration of his kingdom the manhood of Christ doth concur, as an instrument working with his Godhead. Hence this session at God's right-hand, is truly and properly attributed to Christ, as [*theanthropos*]; and not only to the one nature of Christ, whether divine or human. Or it is attributed to Christ as Mediator; in which respect he is called an high-priest, *We have such an high-priest, who is set on the right-hand of the throne of the Majesty in the heavens,*— Heb. viii. 1. And in which respect he is called a prince, *Him hath God exalted with his right-hand, to be a prince and a Saviour*, Acts v. 31. Now Christ is not a priest and a prince merely according to one nature, whether divine or human. I deny not but Christ had a natural kingdom with his Father as God, before the foundation of the world? but this kingdom as God-man, Christ had not before his ascension into heaven. So then Christ sitteth at the right-hand of God by a mediatory action, which he executeth according to both natures, the word working what pertaineth to the word, and the flesh what appertaineth to the flesh; Christ is Mediator as God and man, and glory hath redounded unto him as God and man, and living in this glory he ruleth and governeth his church as God and man; he ascended indeed into heaven in his humanity only, but he sitteth at the right-hand of God as Mediator in respect of both natures. The Lutherans attribute this session at God's right-hand only to the human nature of Christ; they say this session is nothing else but the elevating of his human nature to the full and free use of some of the divine properties, as of omnipotency, omniscience, and omnipresence; the ground of this error is, that they suppose upon the union of the two natures in Christ, a real communication of the divine properties to follow, so that the human nature is made truly omnipotent, omniscient, and omnipresent, not by any confusion of properties, nor yet by any bare communion and concourse of it to the same effect, each nature working that which belongeth to it with communion of the other, (for this we grant) but by a real donation, by which the divine properties so become the properties of the human nature, that the human nature may work with them no less than the divine nature itself, for the perfecting of itself. Against this opinion we have these reasons, 1. The union cannot cause the human nature to partake more in the properties of the divine, than it causeth the divine to partake in the properties of the human. 2. If a true and real communication did follow of the divine attributes, it must needs be of all the attributes, as of eternity, and infiniteness, seeing these are the divine essence, which can no way be divided. 3. Infinite perfections cannot perfect finite natures, no more than reasonable perfections can make perfect unreasonable creatures. 4. To what end should created gifts serve, which Christ hath received above measure, if no more noble properties should enter and be conferred on Jesus Christ? Other reasons are given in, but I willingly decline all controversial points.

SECT.

SECT. VI.

Of the reasons why Christ doth sit on God's right-hand.

6. Why doth Christ sit at the right-hand of God, his Father in glory? I answer, 1. On Christ's part, that he might receive power and dominion over all the creatures, *All power is given unto me in heaven and in earth,* Mat. xxviii. 18. he speaks of it as done, because it was immediately to be performed; Christ at his session received a power imperial over every creature; that he hath power over the angels is plain, both by the reverence they do him, and by their obedience towards him, at the *name of Jesus every knee must bow,* good angels, and evil angels must yield signs of subjection to Jesus Christ? if the saints shall judge the angels, how much more shall Christ? Oh! what power hath Christ himself this way? And as for the excellencies on earth, they all receive their power from Christ, and are at his disposal; it is Jesus Christ that is *crowned with glory and honour, and all things are put under his feet,* Heb ii. 7, 8. And hence it is, that when the apostle speaks of Christ's session at the right-hand of God, he tells us that he is *far above all pricipalities, and powers* on earth, *and mights and dominions* in heaven, Eph. i. 21. Yea, *that angels and authorities, and powers are made subject unto him,* 1 Pet. iii. 22.

2. On our part many reasons may be given. As,

1. That he might be the head of his church; I mean not head in a large sense, for one who is in any kind before another; for so Christ is the head of angels, and God is the head of Christ; and to this we have spoken before. But in a strict sense, for one that is in a near and communicative sort conjoined with another, as the head is conjoined with the body and members; and so is Christ the head of his church. Look as the king hath a more intimate amiable superiority over the queen than over any other of his subjects; so is it here in Christ our king, he is more amiably tempered, and more nearly affected to his spouse and queen, the church of God, than to any other whomsoever. And to this purpose he sits at God's right-hand, that having now fulness of grace and glory in himself, he might be ready to communicate the same to his church who are as the members of his body, that he might give them grace here, and glory hereafter, when he shall deliver up his kingdom to his Father, and be all in all.

2. That he might be the object of divine adoration; then especially it was said and accomplished, *Let all the angels of God worship him: and let all men honour the Son, as they honour the Father,* Heb. i. 6. John v. 23. After Christ's session, Stephen looked up into heaven, and saw the glory of God, and Jesus standing on the right-hand of God, and then he worshipped, and called upon God, saying, *Lord Jesus, receive my Spirit,* Acts vii. 59. It is true that the ground of this divine adoration is the union of the two natures of Christ, and therefore the Magi worshipped him at his birth, and as soon as ever he came into the world, *the angels of God worshipped him,* Heb. i. 6. but because by his session at God's right-hand the divine nature was manifested, and the human nature was exalted to that dignity and glory which it never had before, therefore now especially and from this time was the honour and dignity of worship communicated to him as God and man. And, hence divines, usually make this one ingredient of Christ sitting at the right-hand of God, *viz.* That Christ, God and man, is the object of divine adoration. ‡ 'O! it is a great thing, and admirable, and full of wonder, that the man Christ 'should sit above, at God's right-hand, and be 'adored of angels and archangels.' Before this was the grace of union conferred on Jesus, and so he was adored before he suffered; but after he *had humbled himself, and was made obedient unto death, even to the death of the cross, then (yea and therefore) God highly exalted him, and gave him a name, which is above every name, that at the name of Jesus every knee should bow, of things in heaven, and things in earth, and things under the earth, and that every tongue shall confess, That Jesus is Lord, to the glory of God the Father,* Phil. ii. 8, 9, 10, 11. He was Lord before, in that he is the Son of God, but now he is Lord again by virtue of his humiliation and session at God's right-hand. Trouble not yourselves with their objection, who say, That

‡ Chry. hom. 5. *in* Heb.

That if adoration be due to Christ as God and man, that then the human nature is to be adored: the person adored is man, but the humanity itself is not the proper object of that worship. There is a difference betwixt the concrete and the abstract, tho' the man Christ be God, yet his manhood is not God, and by consequence not to be worshipped with that worship, which is properly and essentially divine. Certainly if adoration agree to the humanity of Christ, then may his humanity help and save us; but the humanity of Christ cannot help and save us, because *omnis actio est suppositi*, whereas the human nature of Christ is not *suppositum*, a substance or personal Being at all.

3. That he might intercede for his saints. *Now of the things which we have spoken, this is the sum: we have such an high-priest, who is set on the right-hand of the throne of the Majesty in the heavens; and a minister of the sanctuary, and of the true tabernacle, which the Lord pitched and not man,* Heb. viii. 1, 2. He is set on the right-hand of God as an high-priest, or minister to intercede for us, *For as Christ is not entred into the holy place made with hands, which are the figures of the true, but into heaven itself now to appear in the presence of God for us,* Heb. ix. 24. This appearing is an expression borrowed from the custom of human courts; for as in them, when the plaintiff or defendant is called, their attorney appeareth in their names; so when we are summoned by the justice of God to answer the complaints, which it preferreth against us, *We have an advocate with the Father, Jesus Christ the righteous,* John ii. 1. And he standeth up, and appeareth for us: or, it may be, this hath a respect to the manner of high-priests in the time of the law, Exod. xxviii. 9, 10, 11, 12. For as they used to go into the most holy place, with the names of the children of Israel written in precious stones, for a remembrance of them, that they might remember them to God in their prayers; so Jesus being gone up to heaven, he there presents to his Father the names of all his chosen, and he remembers them to his Father in his intercessions. Certainly Christ is not gone to heaven, and advanced to the right-hand of God, only to live in eternal joy himself, but also to procure happiness for his saints. It is to excellent purpose and to the great good of his church, that he sits at the right hand of his Father, for thereby he governs and protects his people, and he continually executes the office of his priesthood, presenting himself, and the sacrifice of himself, and the infinite merit of that sacrifice before the eyes of his Father in their behalf.

4. That true believers may assuredly hope by virtue of Christ's session to sit themselves in the kingdom of glory. It is true, That Christ, and only Christ hath his seat at the right-hand of God, *To which of the saints, or of the angels did he ever say, Sit thou at my right-hand?* Heb. i. 5. It is a prerogative above all creatures, and yet there is something near it given to the saints, *For him that overcometh, I will grant to sit with me in my throne, even as I also am set down with my Father in his throne,* Rev. iii. 21. There is a proportion, though with an inequality; we must sit on Christ's throne, as he sits on his Father's throne, Christ only sits at the right-hand of God; but, the saints are to sit at the right-hand of Christ, and so the Psalmist speaks, *Upon thy right hand did stand the queen, in gold of ophir,* Psal. xlv. 9. It is enough to greaten the spirits of saints, how should they tread on earth, and contemn the world, when they consider, that one day they shall judge the world? *Do ye not know that the saints shall judge the world?* 1 Cor. vi. 2. Nay, when they consider, That one day they shall reign with Christ? *If ye suffer with him, ye shall reign with him,* 2 Tim. ii. 12. Christ sitting in heaven is a very figure of us; Christ's person is the great model and first draught of all, that shall be done to his body, the saints; therefore he is said to be the captain of our salvation that leads us on; he is said to be our forerunner into glory, he breaks the clouds first, and appears first before God, he sits down first, and is glorified first, and then we follow; Christ wears the crown in heaven, as our king, and he is united and married to God, as our proxy.

And yet there is another ground of hope, not only shall we sit with Christ in glory, but even now do we sit with him in glory: Christ is not only gone to heaven, to prepare a place for us, but he sits in heaven in our room, and God looks on him as the great picture of all that body, whereof he is head; and he delights himself in seeing them all glorified as in his Son. To this purpose, the saints are said to sit down with Christ at very present, *He hath made us sit together with him in heavenly*

F f f

heavenly places in Christ Jesus, Eph. ii. 6. Christ in our nature is now exalted, this is that admirable thing, which carried up Chrysostome into an extasy, that the same nature of which God said, 'Dust thou art, and to dust thou shalt return, should now sit in heaven at God's right hand:' but not only the human nature, but Christ in person sits there, as a common person in our stead: he is in his throne, and we sit with him in supercelestial places. O! what structures and pillars of hope are raised up here?

5. That he might defend the church against her enemies, and at last destroy all the enemies of the church. Such is the power of Christ's session, that by it he holds up his saints in midst of their enemies, so that the gates of hell shall not prevail against them: true indeed, that many times they are used as lambs amongst wolves; but so Christ orders, that the blood of martyrs, should be the seed of the church; hereby his church, like a tree, settles the faster, and like a torch shines the brighter for the shaking. And as for the enemies of his church, there is a day of reckoning for them, *He that sitteth in the heavens shall laugh, the Lord shall have them in derision*, the day is a coming, that *he will speak unto them in his wrath, and vex them in his sore displeasure*, Psal. ii. 4, 5. In the mean while Christ is galling and tormenting them, by the sceptre of his word; and at last he will put them all under his feet, *The Lord said unto my Lord, sit thou at my right-hand until I make thine enemies thy foot-stool*, Psal. cx. 1.——*For he must reign till he hath put all his enemies under his feet*, 1 Cor. xv. 25. That the enemies of Christ must be made his footstool, notes the extreme shame and confusion, which they shall everlastingly suffer: in victories amongst men, the party conquered goes many times off, upon some honourable terms, or at worst, if they are led captive they go like men, but to be made a stool for the conqueror to insult over; this is extremity of shame; and as shame, so it notes the burthen which the wicked must bear; the foot-stool bears the weight of the body, so must the enemies of Christ bear the weight of his heavy and everlasting wrath; such a weight shall they bear, that they would gladly exchange it for the weight of rocks and mountains; rather would they live under the weight of the heaviest creature in the world, than under the fury of him, that fitteth upon the throne. And withal it notes an equal and just recompence to the wicked; the Lord useth often to fit punishments to the quality and measure of the sins committed; he that on earth denied a crumb of bread, was in hell denied a drop of water; and thus will Christ deal with his enemies at the last day; here they trample upon Christ in his word, in his ways, in his members, 'They make the saints bow down for them to go 'over; yea, they have laid their bodies as the 'ground, and as the street to them that went over, 'Isa. li. 23. They tread under foot the Son of God, 'the blood of the covenant, Heb. x. 29. They 'tread down the sanctuary, Isaiah lxiii. 18. And 'put Christ to shame,' Heb. vi. 6. And therefore their own measure shall be returned into their own bosom, they shall be constrained to confess with Adoni-bezek, 'as I have done, so God hath requi-'ted me,' Judg. i. 7. Yea, this shall they suffer from the meanest of Christ's members, whom they here insult over; the saints shall be as witnesses, and as it were confessors with Christ, to judge the wicked, both men and angels, and tread them under their feet, ' they shall take them captives, whose captives ' they were, and shall rule over their oppressors; ' all they that despised them shall bow themselves ' at the soles of their feet,' Isa. xiv. 2.

6. That he might send down the Holy Ghost to this purpose Christ told his disciples whilst he was yet on earth, that he must ascend into heaven, and reign there, *It is expedient for you, that I go away, for if I go not away, the comforter will not come unto you, but if I depart, I will send him to you*, John xvi. 7. Christ is now in heaven, and sits at God's right-hand, that he may send us his Spirit by whose forcible working we seek after heaven, and heavenly things, where now Christ sits. But on this I shall insist larger, it being our next subject.

SECT. VII.

Of the time when the Holy Ghost was sent.

7. FOR the mission of his Spirit: no sooner was Christ set down at God's right-hand, but he sends down the Holy Ghost. It was an use amongst the ancients in days of great joy and solemnity, to give gifts, and to send presents unto men; thus, after the wall of Jerusalem was built,

it is said, That *the people did eat, and drink, and send portions*, Neh. viii. 12. And at the feast of Purim, *they made them days of feasting, and joy, and of sending portions one to another, and gifts to the poor*, Eph. ix. 22. Thus Christ, in the day of his majesty and inauguration, in that great and solemn triumph, *When he ascended up on high, he led captivity captive, and did withal give gifts unto men*, Eph. iv. 8.

Concerning this mission of the Spirit, or these gifts of Christ to his church, I shall discover the accomplishment, as it appears in these texts, *And when the day of Pentecost was fully come, they were all with one accord in one place, and suddenly there came a sound from heaven, as of a rushing mighty wind, and it filled all the house where they were sitting; and there appeared unto them cloven tongues, like as of fire, and it sat upon each of them, and they were all filled with the Holy Ghost, and began to speak with other tongues, as the Spirit gave them utterance*, Acts ii. 1, 2, 3, 4. Out of these words, I shall observe these particulars; the time when, the persons to whom, the manner how, the measure what, and the reasons why the Holy Ghost was sent.

1. For the time when the Holy Ghost was sent, it is said, 'When the day of Pentecost was fully 'come,' this was a feast of the Jews, called [*pentekostē a pentechēleka*], from fifty days, because it was ever kept on the fiftieth day, after the second of the passover. We find in scripture sundry memorable things reckoned by the number of fifty. As fifty days from Israel's coming out of Egypt, unto the giving of the law. And the fiftieth year was that great feast of the Jubilee, which was the time of forgiving of debts, and of restoring men to their first estates: and fifty days were in truth the appointed time of the Jews harvest; their harvest being bounded as it were with two remarkable days, the one being the beginning, the other the end thereof, the beginning was [*deutera tou pascha*]; the second of the passover; the end was [*pen tetkostē*], the fiftieth day after, called *the Pentecost*, upon the [*deutera*]; they offered *a sheaf of the first fruits of their harvest*, Lev. xxiii. 10. Upon the Pentecost they offered *two wave-loaves*, Lev. xxiii. 17. the sheaf being offered, all the after-fruits throughout the land were sanctified; and the two loaves being offered, it was a sign of the harvest finished and ended; and now we find, that as there were fifty days betwixt [*deutera*] and the Pentecost, so there were fifty days betwixt Christ's resurrection and the coming down of the Holy Ghost. What was the meaning of this, but to hold harmony, and to keep correspondency with those memorable things? As on the day of Pentecost, (fifty days after the feast of the passover) the Israelites came to mount Sinai, and there received they the law; a memorable day with them, and therefore called the feast of the law; so the very same day is accomplished that prophesy, *Out of Zion shall go forth the law, and the word of the Lord from Jerusalem*, Isaiah ii. 3. now was the promulgation of the gospel called by James, *the royal law*, Jam. ii. 8. as given by Christ our king, and written in the hearts of his servants by the Holy Ghost; it seems to shadow out the great difference betwixt the law and gospel; the law was given with terror, in lightning and thunder; it discovers sin, declares God's wrath, frights the conscience; but the gospel is given without terror, there was no lightning and thunder now; no, no, the holy Ghost slides down from heaven with grace and gifts; and with great joy sits on the heads and in the hearts of his saints. 2. On the Jubilee, or fiftieth year, was a great feast, whence some observe, That the Latins made their word *Jubilo*, to take up a merry song; though the word be derived from the Hebrew, *Jobel*, which signifies a ram's horn; for then they blew with ram's horns, as when they gathered the people to the congregation, they blew with silver trumpets. There were many uses of this feast; 1. For the general release of servants. 2. For the restoring of lands unto their first owners who had sold them. 3. For the keeping of a right chronology and reckoning of times; for as the Greeks did reckon by their Olympiads, and the Latins by their Lustra, so did the Hebrews by their Jubilees; this falls fit with the proclaiming of the gospel, which is an act or tender of God's most gracious general free pardon of all sins, and of all the sinners in the world; now was the sound of the gospel made known unto all, *out of every nation under heaven*, Acts ii. 5. now was that spiritual jubilee, which Christians enjoy under Christ; now was the remission published, which exceeded the remission of the jubilee, as far as the jubilee exceeded the remission of the seventh year,

(i. e.)

(*i. e.*) not only seven times, but *seventy times seven times*, Matth. xviii. 22. 3. On the day of Pentecost, *they offered the two wave loaves, called the bread of the first-fruits, unto the Lord*, Lev. xxiii. 17, 20. In like sort, this very day (the Lord of the harvest so disposing it) the apostles, by the assistance and effectual working of the Spirit, offered the first-fruits of their harvest unto the Lord; for *the same day, there were added unto them about three thousand souls*, Acts ii. 41. We see the circumstance of time hath its due weight, and is very considerable; 'When the day of Pentecost was 'fully come, then came the Holy Ghost.'

SECT. VIII.

Of the persons to whom the Holy Ghost was sent.

8. FOR the persons to whom the Holy Ghost was sent, it is said, *To all that were with one accord in one place*, Acts ii. 1. Who they were it is not here express, yet from the former chapter we may conjecture, they were 'the twelve a-'postles, together with Joseph called Barsabas, and 'the women, and Mary the mother of Jesus, and 'his brethren,' Acts i. 13, 14. These all continued with one accord in one place, for so was Christ's command, 'That they should not depart from Je-'rusalem, but wait for the promise of the Father, 'which, saith he, Ye have heard of me,' Acts i. 4. This promise we read of in the evangelists, 'When 'the comforter is come, whom I will send unto you 'from the Father, even the Spirit of truth, which 'proceedeth from the Father, he will testify of me, 'John xv. 26 —— And behold, I send the promise 'of the Father upon you, but tarry ye in the city 'of Jerusalem, until you be indued with power 'from on high,' Luke xxiv. 49. It was the great promise of the Old Testament, that Christ should partake of our human nature, and it was the great promise of the New Testament, that we should partake of his divine nature; he was clothed with our flesh according to the former, and we are invested with his Spirit according to the latter promise. For this promise, the apostles, and others, had long waited, and for the accomplishment they were now fitted and disposed. 1. They had waited for it from the ascension-day till the feast of Pentecost: he told them at the very instant of his a-scension, That he would send the Holy Ghost, and therefore bad them stay together till that hour; upon which command they waited, and continued waiting until *the day of Pentecost was fully come. He that believeth shall not make haste*, saith Isaiah, Isa. xxviii. 16. surely waiting is a Christian duty, *for the vision is yet for an appointed time, but at the end it shall speak and shall not lie; tho' it tarry, wait for it, because it will surely come, it will not tarry*, Hab. ii. 3. Well may we wait, and wait for him, if we consider how God and Christ have waited for us and our conversion, and especially if we consider, that the comforter will come, and when he comes, that *he will abide with us for ever*, John xiv. 16. But, 2. as they waited for the Spirit, so they were rightly disposed to receive the Spirit; for ' they were all with one ac-' cord in one place.' Mark here the qualifications of these persons, ' they were all with one accord, ' *&c*.' To those that accord is the Spirit given; where is nothing but discord, jars, divisions, factions, there is no Spirit of God; for the Spirit is the Author of concord, peace, unity and amity; he is the very essential unity, love and love-knot of the two persons, the Father and the Son; even God with God: and he was sent to be the union, love and love-knot of the two natures united in Christ, even of God with man; and can we imagine that essential unity will enter but where there is unity? Can the Spirit of unity come or remain but where there is unity of spirit? Verily there is not, there cannot be a more proper and peculiar, a more true and certain disposition to make us meet for the Spirit, that than quality in us, that is likest to his nature and essence; and that is unity, love and concord: do we marvel, that the Spirit doth scarcely pant in us? alas! we are not all of one accord; the very first point is wanting to make us meet for the coming of the Holy Ghost upon us. We see the persons, to whom the Holy Ghost was sent, they were ' they that were together with one accord ' in one place.'

SECT. IX.

Of the manner how the Holy Ghost was sent.

9. FOR the manner how he was sent, or how he came to these apostles; we may observe these particulars.——

1. He

1. He came suddenly, which either shews the majesty of the miracle, that is gloriously done which is suddenly done; or the truth of the miracle, there could be no imposture or fraud in it, when the motion of it was sudden, or the purpose of the miracle, which was to awake and affect them to whom it came; usually sudden things startle us, and make us look up. We may learn to receive those holy motions of the Spirit, which sometimes come suddenly, and we know not how: I am perswaded the man breathes not amongst us Christians, that sometimes feels not the stirrings, movings, breathings of the Spirit of God. Oh! that men would take heed of despising present motions. Oh! that men would take the wind while it blows, and the water while the angel moves it, as not knowing when it will, or whether ever it will blow again.

2. He came from heaven; the place seems here to commend the gift; as from earth, earthly things arise, so from heaven, heavenly, spiritual, and eternal things. And this is one sign to distinguish the spirits, *Beloved, believe not every spirit, but try the spirits whether they are of God*, 1 John iv. 1. If our motions come from heaven, if we fetch our grounds thence from heaven, from religion, from the sanctuary, it is the Spirit of God; or, if it carry us heavenward, if it makes us heavenly-minded, if it wean us from the world, and if it elevate and set our affections on heavenly things, if it form and frame our conversations towards heaven, we may then conclude the motions are not from below but from above. O! that Christians would be much in observation of, and in listening to the movings, workings, hints, and intimations of that Spirit that comes from heaven. Certainly that Spirit is of God, that comes down from heaven, and that lifts up our soul towards heaven.

3. He comes down from heaven like a wind: the comparison is most apt; of all bodily things the wind is least bodily; it is invisible, and comes nearest to the nature of a spirit; it is quick and active as the Spirit is. But more especially the Holy Ghost is compared to a wind in respect of its irresistable workings; as nothing can resist the wind, it goes and blows which way soever it will; so nothing can resist the Spirit of God, wheresoever it hath a purpose to work efficaciously; I will not say, but the heart of a man may resist and reject the work of the Spirit in some measure, and in some degrees; Stephen told the Jews, *They had always resisted the Holy Ghost*, Acts vii. 51. And the apostle tells of *strong holds, and of every thing that exalteth itself against God*, 2 Cor. x. 5. So there is a natural contrariety, a constant enmity, and active resisting of God's Spirit by our spirits; we must therefore distinguish between a prevalent and a gradual resisting; the Spirit in conversion so works, that he takes away the prevalent but not the gradual resisting: a man before he be converted is froward, and full of cavils and prejudices, he is unwilling to be saved; he cannot abide the truth, he doth what he can to stifle all good motions; yet if he belong to the election of grace, God will at last over-master his heart, and make him of unwilling, willing; he will omnipotently bow and change the will, and work on his soul by his mighty power efficaciously, inseparably, and irresistably. Again, the Holy Ghost is compared to wind, in respect of its free actings, *The wind bloweth where it listeth* (saith Christ) John iii. 8. And so the Spirit bloweth where it listeth; who can give any reason why the Spirit breathes so sweetly on Jacob, and not on Esau, on Peter, and not on Judas? Is it not the free grace and good pleasure of God? Springs it not from the mere freedom and pure arbitrariness of his own only workings? *To you it is given to know the mysteries of the kingdom of heaven*, (saith Christ) *but to them it is not given*, Matth. xiii. 11. And *I thank thee, O Father, Lord of heaven and earth, because thou hast hid these things from the wise and prudent, and hast revealed them unto babes, even so, Father, for so it seemed good in thy sight*, Matth. xi 25, 26. These, and the like texts are as so many hammers to beat in pieces all those doctrines of free will, and of the power of man to supernatural things, grace makes no gain of man's work; free-will may indeed move and run, but if it be to good, it must be moved, and driven, and breathed upon by God's free grace. The Spirit blows where it listeth.

4. He came like *a rushing mighty wind:* as the wind is sometimes of that strength, that it rends and rives in sunder mountains and rocks, it pulls up trees, it blows down buildings, so are the operations of the holy Spirit, it takes down all before it, it brings into captivity many an exalting thought; it made a conquest of the world, beginning at Jerusalem,

and

and spreading itself over all the earth; it is mighty in operation, able to shake the stoutest and proudest man, and to break in pieces the very stoniest heart; indeed our words without this Spirit are but weak wind; we may spend ourselves and never waken souls; but if the Spirit blow, he will amaze the consciences of the stoutest peers, and drive away our sins, as the wind drove away the grashoppers and locusts, that overspread the land of Egypt. Some analogy there is betwixt this vehement wind, and the Spirit's workings; the Spirit first comes as a Spirit of bondage, and then as a Spirit of adoption; the Spirit of bondage is as a vehement wind that terrifies, to shew that we are not fit to receive the grace of God, unless the door be first opened by fear and humiliation. Others say, That the vehement rushing of this wind shewed how irresistably the apostles should proceed in preaching the gospel of Jesus Christ; they had a commission to go into all the world, and to teach all nations, and they had a promise, that though many might oppose, yet the gates of hell should not prevail against the church; the Spirit should go along with them, and he in them, and they in him, should prevail mightily like a rushing mighty wind.

5. He filled all the house, where they were sitting; there were none there that were not filled with the Holy Ghost; this room contained a congregation of none but saints. All the men and women (an hundred and twenty, as some think) Acts i. 15. in this room were visited from on high, for the Holy Ghost came upon them, and dwelt in them; well might David say, *Blessed are they that dwell in thy house,——I had rather be a door-keeper in the house of my God, than to dwell in the tents of wickedness*, Psalm lxxxiv. 4, 10. They that abode in this house were under a promise, That the Spirit should come, and now was the promise accomplished; ' For it filled all the house ' where they were sitting; I say, where they were ' sitting,' to signify, that all the other houses in Jerusalem felt none of this mighty rushing wind: there was no assembly of saints in any part of the city, but only in this house; or if any other assembly might be, this Spirit blew upon none of them, where these men were not; that, and only that house it filled, where they were sitting. And this point of blowing upon one certain place, is a property very suitable to the Spirit of God, *The wind bloweth where it listeth, and thou hearest the sound thereof, but canst not tell whence it cometh, nor whether it goeth, so is every one that is born of the Spirit*, John iii. 8. The Spirit blows where it will, and upon whom it will, and they shall plainly feel it, and others about them not one jot: have we not sometimes the experience of this in our very congregations? One soul is heard, one breath doth blow, and it may be one or two, and no more hears the sound, or feels the breath inwardly, savingly; it may be one here, and another there, shall feel the Spirit, shall be affected and touched with it sensibly; but twenty on this side them, and forty on that side them sit all becalmed, and go their way no more moved, than when they came into God's presence. Oh! that this Spirit of the Lord would come daily and constantly into our congregations! oh! that it would blow through them, and through them! oh! that it would fill every soul in the assembly with the breath of heaven; *Come holy Spirit; awake O north-wind, and come thou south-wind, and blow upon our gardens, that the spices thereof may flow out*, Cant. iv. 16.

6. He came down in the form of tongues. As one saith well, ' This wind brought tongues, e-' ven a whole shower of tongues.' The apostles were not only inspired, for their own benefit, but they had gifts bestowed on them to impart the benefit to more than themselves. But why did the Holy Ghost appear like tongues? I answer, 1. The tongue is a symbol of the Holy Ghost's proceeding from the word of the Father; as the tongue hath the nearest affinity with the word, and is moved by the word of the heart, to express the same by the sound of the voice, so the Holy Ghost hath the nearest affinity that may be with the word of God, and is the expressor of his voice, and the speaker of his will. 2. The tongue is the sole instrument of knowledge, which conveys the same from man to man? though the soul be the fountain from whence all wisdom springs, yet the tongue is the channel and the conduit-pipe, whereby this wisdom and knowledge is communicated and transferred from man to man: in like manner the Holy Ghost is the sole author and teacher of all truth; though Christ be the wisdom of God, yet the Holy Ghost is the teacher of this

wisdom

wisdom to men; and hence it is that the Holy Ghost appeared in the form of tongues.

And yet not merely in the form of tongues, but thus qualified; 1. They were *cloven tongues*, to signify, That the apostles should speak in divers languages; if there must be a calling of the Gentiles, they must needs have the tongues of the Gentiles wherewith to call them; if they were *debtors not only to the Jews, but to the Grecians*, not only *to the Grecians, but to the Barbarians also*, Rom. i 14 then must they have the tongues not only of the Jews, but of the Grecians, and Barbarians, to pay this debt, and to discharge this duty off, *Go, and teach all nations*, Mat. xxviii. 19. Surely this gift was bestowed for the propagating of the gospel far and wide: the tongues were cloven, that the apostles might speak all languages, and that all nations of the world, whithersoever they came, might hear them, and understand them speaking in their own tongues. 2. They were *fiery tongues*; to signify, That there should be an efficacy, or fervour in their speaking; the world was so overwhelmed with ignorance and error, that the apostle's lips had need to be touched with a coal from the altar; tongues of flesh would not serve the turn, nor words of air, but there must be fire put into the tongue, and Spirit of life into the words they spake; with such a tongue Christ spake himself, when they said, *Did not our hearts burn within us, while he spake unto us by the way?* Luke xxiv. 32. And with such a tongue Peter spake at this time, something like fire fell from him on their hearts, when they were pricked in their hearts, and said, *Men and brethren, What shall we do?* Acts ii. 37 Oh! that we of the ministry had these fiery tongues! O! that the Spirit would put his live coal into our speeches! O! that our sermons were warming sermons! may we not fear that the Spirit is gone, whilst the people are dead, and we are no more lively in our ministry? It is said of Luther, That when he heard one preach, very faintly, ' Cold, cold, *says he*, this is cold ' preaching, here is no heat at all to be gotten.' Oh! when the Spirit comes, it comes with a tongue of fire; instead of words, sparks of fire will fall from us on the hearts of hearers.

3. These cloven fiery tongues sat upon each of them; to signify their constancy and continuance; they did not light, and touch, and away, after the manner of butterflies; but they sat, they abode still, they continued steady, without any stirring or startling. This was the privy sign, by which John the Baptist knew Jesus to be Christ, *Upon whom thou shalt see the Spirit descending and remaining on him, the same is he which baptizeth with the Holy Ghost*, John i. 33. It was not only the Spirit's descending, but the Spirit's remaining on him, that was the sign. The Spirit of God is a constant Spirit, Psal. li. 10. it abides on the soul to whom it is given; and therefore the Psalmist describes these great transactions of Christ to this very end, that the Spirit might dwell with us, *Thou hast ascended on high, thou hast led captivity captive, thou hast received gifts for men, yea, for the rebellious also, that the Lord God might dwell among them*, Psalm lxviii. 18. Not only that he might stay and lodge for a night as a way-faring man, that comes to his inn, and then is gone in the morning: no, no; but that he might take up his residence, and dwell in them. I know it is a question, Whether the Holy Ghost may be lost? But certainly of the elect he is never totally or wholly lost, only I dare not say, but as touching many gifts, he may be lost even of the elect themselves: David, after his sin, was forced to cry, *Cast me not away from thy presence, O Lord, and take not thy holy Spirit from me; restore unto me the joy of thy salvation, and uphold me with thy free Spirit*, Psa. li. 11, 12. We find here, that in respect of some gifts, even of regeneration, the Spirit is sometimes lost, but that the godly should retain no remnants of the Spirit in their worst declinings, I cannot imagine; John teacheth expresly, *Whosoever is born of God, doth not commit sin*, (a sin unto death) *for his seed remaineth in him, neither can he sin, because he is born of God*, 1 John iii. 9. David in his fall lost the joy of his heart, the purity of his conscience, and many other gifts which he desired to have restored to him; but the Holy Ghost he had not utterly lost; for if so, How could he have prayed, *Cast me not away from thy presence, and take not thy holy Spirit from me?* I have done with the manner of the Spirit's mission.

SECT. X.
Of the measure of the Holy Ghost now given.

4. FOR the measure, What or how much of the Spirit was now given? This question

is

is necessary, because we bring in the Spirit's mission after Christ's ascension, as if the Holy Ghost had not been given before this time. That this was the time of the coming of the Holy Ghost, is very plain, but that the Holy Ghost was not given before this time, we cannot say; certainly the prophets spake by him, and the apostles had him, not only when they were first called, but more fully when ' he breathed on them, and said unto them, ' receive ye the Holy Ghost,' John. xx. 22. So that if ye study the reconciliation of these things, I know not any way better than to put it on the measure, or degrees of the Spirit's mission.——I know some go about to reconcile it thus, that the Holy Ghost was given before secretly with grace, but now he was given in a visible shape with power. Others thus, that the Holy Ghost was before given in respect of grace and ministerial gifts, but now he was given in respect of virtue, or ghostly ability to work wonders, and to speak with divers languages. But we find that the prophets and apostles before this had not only grace, and ministerial gifts, but a miraculous virtue, even the Spirit of powerful and extraordinary operation: only here was the difference, that before this, the Spirit was but sprinkled (as it were) upon them, but now it was poured upon them; before this they were gently breathed on, and refreshed with a small gale; but now they were all blown up with a mighty wind; without controversy a difference there is in the Spirit's mission; and that some lay down chiefly in these three things. As,—

1. In the manner of the Spirit's mission to the old church: the Spirit came usually in dreams, or visions, or in a low still voice, or in some latent ways; but now he came in power, in evidence, and demonstration; and therefore it is called *the Spirit of revelation and knowledge*, Eph i. 17. At the apparition of God to Elijah, it is said, that ' the Lord passed by, and a great, and strong ' wind rent the mountains, and brake in pieces the ' rocks before the Lord; but the Lord was not in ' the wind; and after the wind an earthquake; but ' the Lord was not in the earthquake: and after the ' earthquake a fire; but the Lord was not in the ' fire: and after the fire, a still small voice, and ' then Elijah wrapped his face in his mantle, as ' knowing the Lord's presence was therein,' 1 Kings xix. 11, 12. The Spirit came not of old, save in a vision, or dream, or in a still small voice; but now the Spirit came in a rushing mighty wind, in fiery tongues, in earthquakes, in so much that ' the place ' was shaken where they were assembled, and they ' were all filled with the Holy Ghost,' Acts iv. 31. The Spirit now made choice to come in such apparitions, as should have in them a self-discovering property, which would not be hidden; and here is one difference.

2. Another difference is, in respect of the subjects unto whom he was sent; before now he came only upon the inclosed garden of the Jews, but after the ascension of Christ the Spirit was poured upon all flesh, now every believer is of the Israel of God, every Christian is a temple of the Holy Ghost; now we receive the Spirit too, or else it is wrong with us, for ' if any man have not the Spi-' rit of Christ, he is none of his,' Rom. viii. 9. At Peter's sermon to Cornelius, it is said, that ' the ' Holy Ghost fell on all them which heard the ' word, and they of the circumcision which believed ' were astonished, because that on the Gentiles al-' so was poured out the gift of the Holy Ghost,' Acts x. 44, 45. It was some wonder at first, even to the apostles themselves, but in this sermon Peter acknowledges, ' of a truth, I perceive that God is ' no respecter of persons, but in every nation he ' that feareth him, and worketh righteousness, is ' accepted with him,' Acts x. 34, 35. Mark, ' in ' every nation, upon all flesh, I will pour out my ' Spirit.' Here's another difference.

3. One difference more is in the measure of his mission. At first, he was sent only in drops and dew, but now he was poured out in showers in abundance, *The Holy Ghost* (saith Paul) *was shed on us abundantly through Jesus our Saviour*, Tit. iii. 6. As there are degrees in the wind, *aura*, *ventus*, *procella*, a breath, a blast, a stiff-gale; so we cannot deny degrees in the Spirit; the apostles at Christ's resurrection received the Spirit, but now they were filled with the Spirit; then it was but a breath, but now it was a mighty wind. And indeed never was the like measure of the Spirit given to men as at this time;. the fathers before this, and we and our fathers since this have but (as it were) a hin of the Spirit to their epha; such a Pentecost as this, never was but this, never the like before or since; it was Christ's coronation-day, the day of placing him in his throne, when he gave

these

these gifts unto men, and therefore that day was all magnificence shewed above all other days; thus for the measure of the Spirit now given to the church of Christ.

SECT. XI.

Of the reasons why the Holy Ghost was sent.

1. FOR the reasons why the Holy Ghost was sent; they are several: as,—
1. That all the prophesies, concerning this mission might be accomplished, Isaiah speaks of a time when *the Spirit should be poured upon us from on high, and the wilderness should be a fruitful field,* Isa. xxxii. 15. And Zachary prophesies, *That in that day I will pour upon the house of David and upon the inhabitants of Jerusalem the Spirit of grace and supplication,* Zach. xii. 10. And Joel prophesies yet more expresly, *It shall come to pass, that I will pour out my Spirit upon all flesh, and your sons and your daughters shall prophesy, your old men shall dream dreams, your young men shall see visions; and also upon the servants and upon the hand-maids in those days I will pour out my Spirit, and they shall prophesy,* Joel ii. 28, 29. This very prophesy was cited by Peter in his first sermon after the Spirit's mission, Acts ii 17, 18. in which we read of two pourings of the Spirit, one upon *their sons,* and the other *upon his servants;* the former concerned only the Jews, they should have prophesies, visions, and dreams, the old way of the Jews, but the latter concerns us, we are not of their sons, but of his servants, to whom visions and dreams, are left quite out; and therefore if any now pretend to those visions and dreams, we say with Jeremy, *The prophet that hath a dream, let him tell a dream, but he that hath my word let him speak my word faithfully; What is the chaff to the wheat?* Jer xxiii. 28. But of all the prophesies concerning the mission of the Holy Ghost, our Saviour gives the clearest and the most particular; two great prophesies we find in the Bible, the one is of the old Testament, and the other of the New; that of the old Testament was for the coming of Christ; and this of the New Testament was for the coming of the Holy Ghost: and hence we say, that the coming of Christ was the fulfilling of the law; and the coming of the Holy Ghost is the fulfilling of the gospel. In this respect let us search and see those prophesies of Christ the great prophet in the New Testament, *I will pray to the Father, and he shall give you another comforter, that he may abide with you for ever, even the Spirit of truth,* John xiv. 16, 17.——*But when the comforter is come, whom I will send unto you from the Father, he shall testify of me,* John xv. 26. *And behold I send the promise of my Father upon you, but tarry ye in the city of Jerusalem, until ye be endued with power from on high,* Luke xxiv. 49. *It is expedient for you that I go away, for if I go not away, the comforter will not come unto you: but if I depart, I will send him unto you,* John xvi 7. Why, it was of necessity that all these prophesies, and promises must be accomplished, and therefore was the Holy Ghost sent amongst us.

2. That the holy apostles might be furnished with gifts and graces suitable to their estates, conditions, stations, places. To this purpose, no sooner was the Spirit sent, but *they were filled with the Holy Ghost, and began to speak with other tongues, as the Spirit gave them utterance,* Acts ii. 4. They were filled with the Holy Ghost, not that they were before empty, but now they were more full of the Spirit than ever they were before, and *they spoke with other tongues;* other than ever they had learned; probably they understood no tongue but the Syriac till this time, but now on a sudden they could speak Greek, Latin, Arabic, Persian, Parthian, and what not? The wisdom and mercy of God is very observable herein, that the same means of divers tongues which was the destroying of Babel, should be the very same means, here conferred on the apostles to work the building of Sion; that the curse should be removed, and a blessing come in place; that confusion of tongues should be united to God's glory; that this should be the issue of tongues, that neither speech nor language should be upon all the earth, but his praise, and glory, and gospel should be heard amongst them. And here is something more observable, in that they spake with other tongues *as the Spirit gave them utterance!* the word utterance is in the original [*apophtheggetha*] you have heard of *apothegmes,* (i. e.) wise and weighty sententious speeches: now, such as these, the Spirit gave them to utter, *magnalia Dei,* (as in the eleventh verse) *the wonderful works of God,* ver. 11. they

they spake of those singular benefits God offered to the world by the death of his Son; they spake of the work of our redemption, of the merits of Christ, of the glory and riches of his grace, of the praises due to his name for all his mercies. Others add, That they spake of those admirable works of the trinity, as of our creation, redemption, and sanctification, and of whatsoever generally concerned the salvation of mankind. Their speeches were not crudities of their own brain, trivial, base, or vulgar stuff; but *magnalia*, great and high points, *apothegmas*, or oracles, *as the Spirit gave them utterance*. But these reasons are remote as to us.

3. That he might fill the hearts of all the saints, and make them temples and receptacles for the Holy Ghost, ' Know ye that your body is the tem-
' ple of the Holy Ghost, which is in you, which ye
' have of God, and ye are not your own ?' 1 Cor. vi. 19. It is said here, that after the mighty rushing wind, and cloven fiery tongues, ' they were all fil-
' led with the Holy Ghost, and began to speak with
' other tongues,' Acts ii. 4. First, They were filled with the Holy Ghost, and then they spake with other tongues; the Holy Ghost begins inward, and works outward; it first alters the mind, before it change the speech; it first works on the spirit before on the phrase or utterance; this was the first work of the Spirit, it filled them. And thus for the daily ministrations, such must be appointed as were *full of the Holy Ghost*, Acts vi. 3. And, Stephen, is said, to be *full of the Holy Ghost*, Acts vii. 55. and Barnabas, is called, *a good man, and full of the Holy Ghost*, Acts xi. 24. The Holy Ghost is usually said to fill the saints; only whether it be the person of the Holy Ghost, or the impression of the Holy Ghost, is a very great question; for my part, I am apt to incline to their mind, who say not only the impressions of the Spirit, the qualities of holiness, the gifts and graces of the Holy Ghost, or as some think habitual grace in a special manner, but that the Holy Ghost himself doth fill, and dwell, and reign in the hearts of all regenerate men. And this seems clear to me, 1. By scriptures. 2. By arguments.

1. The scriptures are such as these, *He that believeth on me, as the scripture saith, out of his belly shall flow rivers of living water; but this spake he of the Spirit, which they that believe on him should receive, for the Holy Ghost was not yet given, because that Jesus was not yet glorified,* John vii. 38, 39. for those words, *out of his belly shall flow rivers of living water*; by living water, is meant grace, by rivers of living water, is meant the manifold graces of the Spirit, by the flowing of these rivers, is meant the abounding and communicating of those graces from one to another, and by the belly out of which those rivers should flow, is meant the heart endued or filled with the Holy Ghost; now the spring and rivers, the fountain and streams are divers things, and to be distinguished; the one is the cause, and the other the effect; the one is the tree, and the other the fruit; it is the Holy Ghost filling the hearts of believers, that is the spring and fountain whence all those rivers of living waters flow, and therefore saith the evangelist expresly, ' This spake he of the
' Spirit, which they that believe should receive;' of what spirit? even of the Holy Ghost, which in full measure was not yet given, because that Christ was not yet glorified; it is the same spirit which believers receive, whence all these rivers of living waters flow; but those rivers flow not from habitual grace, not from any of the graces of the Holy Ghost, but from the Holy Ghost himself.

Again, *When the Spirit of truth is come, he will guide you into all truth,———and he will shew you things to come,* John xvi. 13. Now the habits of grace cannot guide or teach, or shew a man things to come; the habits of grace cannot speak and hear, as it is there written, *He shall not speak of himself, but whatsoever he shall hear, that shall he speak*. This can be no other than the Spirit in his own person, this is the comforter, that hears and speaks, and guides into all truth, and shews us things to come.

Again, *the love of God is shed abroad in our hearts by the Holy Ghost, which is given unto us,* Rom. v. 5. Besides, the grace of the Spirit, which is the love of God; the Holy Ghost, or the Spirit itself is said to be given unto us.

And *ye are not in the flesh, but in the Spirit, if so be that the Spirit of God dwell in you,* Rom. viii. 9. Here's a plain distinction betwixt the new man, our being in the Spirit, and the Spirit dwelling in us: *Now, if any man have not the Spirit of Christ,* i. e. the same holy Spirit which dwelleth in our head and Saviour Jesus Christ, ' he is none of his.—But
' if the Spirit of him that raised Jesus from the
' dead dwell in you, he that raised up Jesus from
the

'the dead shall also quicken your mortal bodies, 'by his spirit that dwelleth in you,' ver. 11. This Spirit cannot be meant of habitual grace, for habitual grace did not raise up Jesus from the dead; no, no, it was the same Spirit that dwelt in Christ, and that dwells in us.

Again, 'Know ye not that ye are the temple of 'God, and that the Spirit of God dwelleth in you?' 1 Cor. iii. 16.—And know ye not that your body 'is the temple of the Holy Ghost, which is in you?' 1 Cor. vi. 19. Now gifts and graces are not properly said to dwell in temples; this belongs rather to persons than qualities; and therefore it is meant of the Holy Ghost himself, 'ye are the temples of 'the living God;' surely graces are not the living God, 'but ye are the temples of the living God, as 'God hath said, I will dwell in them, and walk in 'them, and I will be their God, and they shall be 'my people,' 2 Cor. vi. 16.

2. The arguments to confirm this, are such as these.

1. Actions are ascribed to the Holy Ghost, as given unto us, or dwelling in us, 'When the Spi-'rit is come, he will reprove the world of sin. And 'when the Spirit of truth is come, he will guide 'you into all truth, John xvi. 8, 13.——And ye 'have received the Spirit of adoption, whereby ye 'cry, Abba, Father;—and this Spirit beareth wit-'ness with our spirits that we are children of God,' Rom. viii. 15, 16. These actions are usually given to the Holy Ghost, I mean to that Holy Ghost which we receive, and dwelleth in us; it reproves, it guides, it helps, it satisfieth, it witnesseth: now *actiones sunt suppositorum*, actions are of persons and not of qualities; habitual grace cannot reprove, or guide, or teach, or help our infirmities: these are the actions of the Spirit himself, in his own person.

2. The Spirit itself is the bond of our mystical union with Jesus Christ, and therefore it is the Spirit itself that dwelleth in us. Look as it is in our body, there are head and members, yet all are but one natural body, because they are animated and quickned by one and the self-same soul; so it is in the mystical body, Christ is our head, and we are his members, and yet both of us are but one mystical body, by reason of the self-same Spirit dwelling in both. And hence it is said, That Christ dwelleth in us by his Spirit, *Know ye not that Christ Jesus is in you, except ye be reprobates*, 2 Cor. xiii. 5. ——*He that eateth my flesh, and drinketh my blood, dwelleth in me, and I in him*, John vi. 26. ——*And I live*, (saith Paul) *yet not I, but Christ liveth in me*, Gal. ii 20. How in me? Not corporally, for in that sense, *the heavens must receive him until the time of the restitution of all things*, Acts iii. 21. but spiritually according to the testimony of the apostle, *because ye are sons, God hath sent forth the Spirit of his Son into your hearts*, Gal. iv. 6. This is the mystery that should be known among the Gentiles, the glorious mystery, yea the rich and glorious mystery; the apostle gives it all these epithets, *The riches of the glory of this mystery, which is, Christ in you, the hope of glory*, Col. i. 27.

3. As Satan keeps his residence in wicked men, working them unto all manner of sin, and holding them captive to do his will; so the Spirit of God coming and thrusting him out of possession dwelleth in us, leading us into all truth, replenishing us with all grace, and inclining us to all holy obedience. There is little question, but whilst men remain in the state of infidelity, the strong man Satan keeps possession, and dwelleth in them, tho' not after a gross and sensual manner, as in demoniacks, yet invisibly and spiritually, ruling and reigning in them, and making them his slaves to do his will; and therefore by the same reason when a stronger than he cometh, even the good Spirit of God, he casts him out, and takes possession and dwells, and reigns, and rules in our souls and bodies.

4. If the Spirit itself dwell not in us, then how would there be three that bear witness? The apostle tells us, *There are three that bear witness in earth*, (or in our hearts) *the spirit, the water, and blood*, 1 John v. 8. now by water is meant sanctification, it is our sanctification that bears witness with us that we are the children of God; and this sanctification, consists either in the habit of grace, or in the actings of grace; if therefore the Spirit of Christ in a believer were nothing else but grace, then it were all one with the testimony of water; but there are three that bear witness, there's the testimony of the Spirit, of blood, and of water; not only justification and sanctification, which are but two witnesses, but the Spirit is superadded, and that also bears witness in our consciences, that we are the children of God, and that Jesus Christ

is the Son of God.——Chriſtians, think me not tedious in theſe proofs, theſe are not ſpeculative notional points, that tend not to edification, but are exceeding profitable. Only concerning the manner of the indwelling of this Spirit in us, it is moſt difficult to conceive. Certainly it dwells not in us as in Chriſt, viz. *bodily*, Col. ii. 9. *unmeaſurably*, John iii. 34. *originally*, 2 Cor. i. 17. the Spirit is in Chriſt, as light in the ſun, but the ſpirit is in us, as light in the air: * neither dare I affirm, that the Spirit is in us more eſſentially than in any other men or creatures, for the eſſence thereof is individual and omnipreſent, but this I ſay, That the Spirit is in the faithful above all others. 1. In reſpect of covenant: the ſaints have the Spirit by God's free grace and covenant, *I will put my Spirit within you*, Ezek. xxxvi. 27. xxxvii. 14. ſaith God in the covenant, which is not only to be underſtood of the gifts and graces of his Spirit, but alſo of the Spirit itſelf. 2. In reſpect of intimate familiarity and near acquaintance: the Spirit is in the faithful like an inmate-coinhabitant, comforting, directing, ruling, ſtrengthening and cheriſhing them; in which reſpect they are ſaid to be his houſes and temples, in which he dwelleth; whereas contrary-ways, worldlings and infidels to all theſe purpoſes are mere ſtrangers unto him, 'The world 'cannot receive him, (ſaith Chriſt) becauſe it ſeeth 'him not, neither knoweth him, but ye know him, 'for he dwelleth with you, and ſhall be in you,' John xiv. 17. 3. In reſpect of virtue and efficacy; the Spirit works efficaciouſly in his ſaints: he chooſeth them for his own people, he poſſeſſeth them as of his own right, he rules in their hearts as in the chief ſeat of his kingdom, he purgeth and purifieth them from their ſins, he repleniſheth and filleth them with his ſaving graces, he guides and directs them in the way of holineſs, and never leaves them till he brings them to his kingdom. 4. In reſpect of union: it was an old error of the Heathens, that the ſoul remaineth in the body after death, which opinion of theirs, tho' falſe, becauſe it contradicts the word, yet the thing itſelf is poſſible, and doth not contradict reaſon, for the ſoul may have its local being in the body, and yet not give life to the body, for it is not the ſoul's being in the body, but its being united to the body which makes the body live; ſo it is not the ſpirits being locally with the ſoul, but being myſtically united to the ſoul that gives it ſpiritual life. Now in all theſe reſpects the ſpirit is in the faithful above all others.

I know the objections, as, 1. If the Spirit be united to a believer's ſoul, and ſo made one with him, then may a believer ſay, 'I am the Spirit, 'or I am equal with God in reſpect of the Spirit 'in me, tho' not as Peter, Thomas, &c.' But I anſwer, this follows not, tho' the Spirit be really united to a believer's ſpirit, ſo that he may ſay with the apoſtle, *He that is joined to the Lord is one ſpirit*, 1 Cor. vi. 17. or hath one Spirit; yet, firſt, this union is a voluntary act and not a natural act, and in that reſpect the Spirit may unite himſelf to the ſoul as far as he pleaſeth, and no farther: and certainly thus far he is not pleaſed to unite himſelf to a believer, as that a believer ſhould ſay properly, 'I am the ſpirit, or I am equal with God in re-'ſpect of the Spirit;' for then a believer might be worſhipped with divine worſhip. 2. This union is by way of application, and not by way of mixture: if an heap of wheat and a ſtone ſhould be joined together, there is an union, they make both one heap, but the wheat cannot ſay, I am a ſtone, nor can the ſtone ſay, I am wheat, becauſe this union is only by way of application; but, if wine and water ſhould be joined together, then every part may ſay, I am water, and I am wine, becauſe this union is not only by way of application, but by way of mixture. Certainly there is a great union betwixt the Spirit and a believer's ſoul, yet cannot the believer ſay properly, I am the Spirit, or I am equal with God, becauſe their union is only by way of application, and not by way of mixture.

2. *Obj.* No more was the union of Chriſt as God, with our nature as man, any union by way of mixture, yet could he ſay, I am God, and I am man. But I anſwer, Chriſt's union was not only ſpiritual or myſtical, but hypoſtatical or perſonal; and, in that reſpect, though there was no mixture, yet there was an union as cannot be paralleled in all the world. Our ſouls union with the Spirit of Chriſt goes very far, and indeed ſo far as we cannot expreſs it, though we had the tongues, and heads, and hearts of men and angels, yet comes it ſhort of that union betwixt the ſecond perſon

---

* *In Chriſto ut lux in ſole, in nobis ut lumen, in aere.*

in the trinity, and the soul and body of Christ; his union was personal, but so not ours: a believer is a person before he is united to the Spirit of Christ; but now Christ's soul and body were not a person before united to the person of the Godhead. Go we therefore as far as we can, and I shall easily yield that our union with the Spirit is a true, real, essential, substantial, spiritual, invisible, mystical, and intimate union, yet it is not a personal or hypostatical union; the Spirit doth not assume the soul or body of a believer, as the second person assumed the soul and body of Christ. Away, away with these cavils and blasphemies, wherewith too many unstable souls are now infected! I have done with this reason.

4. That the Holy Ghost might, according to his office, endow men with gifts, no sooner he bestows his person, but immediately he fills us with his train.

Now the gifts of the Spirit are of these two sorts, some are common to good and bad, others are proper to the elect only. These gifts which are common, are again twofold, for some of them are given but to certain men, and at certain times, as the gifts of miracles, of tongues, of prophesies, and these were necessary for the apostles, and the primitive church, when the gospel was first to be dispersed; others are given to all the members of the church, and at all times, as the gifts of interpretation, science, arts, prudence, learning, knowledge, eloquence, and such like; the former gifts we have not, but these latter are now given to every member of the church, according to the measure of Christ's gift; as the calling and vocation of every member needeth. As for those gifts and saving graces which are proper to the godly, I shall speak of them anon. Now, here's another reason of the Spirit's mission, *That he might give gifts unto men,* Eph. iv. 8. if you ask, What are those gifts? The apostle tells you in one place, *He gave some apostles, and some prophets, and some evangelists, and some pastors and teachers,* verse 11. Three of these gifts are now gone, and their date is out, but in the same place we find pastors and teachers, and them we have still; Oh! how may this teach us to think of such, (even of pastors and teachers) as of the special gifts and favours of Jesus Christ; if our special friend should but send us from a far country, one of his chief servants, would we not welcome him? Christ now is in heaven, and he sends us ministers, as the stewards of his house; sure if we have any love to Christ, 'The very feet of them would be precious, 'beautiful, who bring us glad tidings of peace,' Rom. x. 15. Again, the apostle tells us in another place, That 'there are diversities of gifts, but the 'same Spirit; and diversities of calling, but the 'same Lord or Christ; and diversities of works, but 'the same God and Father, which worketh all in 'all,' 1 Cor. xii. 4, 5, 6. Christ's errand being done, and he gone up on high, the Spirit came down, and in Christ's stead established order in the church, which order or establishment is here set down, by gifts, callings and works. Here is first, A gift. Secondly, A calling. Thirdly, A work. Gifts are ascribed to the Spirit, callings to Christ, and works to God, even to the Father of our Lord Jesus Christ; where the Spirit ends, Christ begins, and where Christ ends, God begins; if no gift, we must stay there and never meddle with the calling; and if no calling, we must stay there, and never meddle with the work; first, the Spirit comes, and bestows the gift, and then Christ comes, and bestows the calling, and then God the Father comes, and sets us to the work; the gift is for the calling, and the gift and calling are both for the work. And if this be the order established by the Spirit in his church, Oh! what shall we say of them that either have no gifts, yet step into the calling, as if there were no need of the Holy Ghost; or that have no calling, and yet will fall upon the work, utterly against the mind and rule of Jesus Christ? Oh! what the poor church of Christ suffers at this time in these respects? Certainly these men have no commission from the holy Spirit; he was never sent to them that break this order, first gifts, and then calling, and then the work.

But why doth the Spirit endow men with gifts? Surely saith the apostle, to this end, *to profit withal,* 1 Cor. xii. 7. Gifts are given for the good of others, gifts are for edifying: we should not contemn them, gifts are a blessing of God, and therefore we are to endeavour after them, *Let thy profiting appear to all, and covet earnestly the best gifts,* 1 Tim. iv. 15. *and yet* (says Paul) *I shew unto you a more excellent way,* 1 Cor. xii. 31. and that was true grace, of which he discourseth in the next chapter, and this brings in another reason of the Spirit's mission.

5. That

5. That the Holy Ghost might, according to his office, endow men with graces. In doing this, he first gives the inward principle and habit of grace, and then the fruit or actings of grace. 1. He gives a power, an habit, a spiritual ability, a seed, a spring, a principle of grace, whatsoever we call it, I cannot conceive it to be a new faculty, added to those which are in men by nature: a man when he is regenerate, hath no more faculties in his soul, than he had before he was regenerate, only in the work of regeneration, those abilities which the man had, are improved to work spiritually, as before naturally; as our bodies in the resurrection from the dead shall have no more, nor other parts than they have at present, only those which are now natural, shall then by the power of God be made spiritual, 1 Cor. xv. 44. Now this principle is infused or poured in by the Spirit of God; and hence he is called *the Spirit of sanctification*, 2 Thess. ii. 13. 2. He gives the fruit or actings of grace, *but the fruit of the Spirit is love, joy, peace, long-suffering, gentleness, goodness, faith, meekness, temperance*, Gal. v. 22, 23. Some call these the diversifications of the actings of that spiritual principle within us; certainly the Spirit doth not only at first infuse the principles of grace, but he doth also enable us to act and improve those blessed principles; he doth not only give us power to holy actions, but he also works the holy actions themselves, *God worketh in us not only to will, but to do*. Phil. ii. 13. God hath a twofold grace, initial and converting, exciting and quickening: in respect of this last, David prays, *Quicken me after thy loving-kindness, O Lord, and so shall I keep thy testimonies*, Psal. cxix. 88. This is the actuating grace that we need every hour and every moment, and must pray for more earnestly, than we would pray for our daily bread. Two privileges more especially flow from this: as,—1. Hereby the soul will be kept from negligence and dulness, from gross and foul sins; the apostle calls it, *Grace to help in time of need*, Heb. iv. 16. Oh! this is admirable, when grace comes in the very nick of need; it may be some time or other thou wert even falling into such and such a sin, it may be thou wert sometime or other drowning in such and such a wickedness, and this exciting, quickening grace came in and kept up thy head above the waters. 2. Hereby the soul will be kept in a frame for every duty; if the Spirit come but with exciting, quickening grace, then it is ready to say, 'My heart is prepared, O Lord, my heart is prepared, I can now do and suffer thy will.' Sometimes the principles of grace lie still within us, and begin to rust, but then comes the Holy Ghost, and breathes upon our souls, and so it excites, and quickens, and commands faith, patience, zeal, and other graces to be in exercise; and this is as it were the file to take off the rust, it is the whetting of the edge, it is the stirring up of the coals into a mighty flame. Christians! have you not clear experimental demonstrations of this truth? Sometimes you are on the wing of duty, and sometimes you are dull and dead; sometimes the least temptation, the least snare is ready to make you fall, and sometimes again, though strong winds and tempests blow upon you, yet you are able to stand like mount Zion that cannot be removed; Oh! what's the reason of the difference? Surely, according to the incomes of the Spirit of God, this difference comes not from ourselves, but from the Spirit; as this exciting, quickening grace is ready or afar off, so is our condition; you know what changes David usually found in his own heart, sometimes he was able to trust in God, and at other times he was so cast down, as if he had no strength within him, and whence all this, but from the ebbings and flowings of exciting, quickening grace? Well may we cry, Come holy Spirit; Oh! what a comfortable condition would it be, if our Spirits never lay still, but we were always hungering, thirsting or moving after God and goodness?

6. That the Holy Ghost might according to his office, comfort his saints, amidst all their afflictions; this was that which Christ had so often told his apo-'stles, 'I will not leave you comfortless, I will come 'unto you, John xiv. 18.——And I will pray the 'Father, and he shall give you another comforter 'that he may abide with you for ever, verse 16.— 'But the comforter, which is the Holy Ghost, 'whom the Father will send in my name, he shall 'teach you all things, ver. 26 — But when the 'comforter is come, whom I will send unto you 'from the Father, even the Spirit of truth, which 'proceedeth from the Father, he shall testify of 'me, John xv. 26.—If I go not away, the com-'forter will not come unto you, but if I depart I 'will send him unto you,' John xvi. 17.

But

But how is it that the Spirit comforts saints? I answer, in these particulars,

* 1. The Spirit discovers sin, and bends the heart to mourn for sin; and such a sorrow as this, is the seed and matter of true comfort; as Joseph's heart was full of joy, when his eyes poured out tears on Benjamin's neck; so there is a certain seed and matter of joy in spiritual mourning: I know they are contrary, but yet they may be subordinate to each other; as a dark and muddy colour may be a fit ground to lay gold upon. Certainly there is a sweet complacency in an humble and spiritual heart, to be vile in its own eyes; but especially, the fruit of it is joy, and great joy, *A woman when she is in travail hath sorrow, because her hour is come, but as soon as she is delivered of the child, she remembreth no more the anguish, for the joy that a man is born into the world: and ye now therefore have sorrow, but I will see you again, and your heart shall rejoice, and your joy no man taketh from you,* John xvi. 21, 22.

2. The Spirit doth not only discover, but heal the corruptions of the soul, and there is no comfort like to the comfort of a saved and cured man; the lame man that was restored by Peter, expressed the abundant exultation of his heart, by leaping and praising God, Acts iii. 8. and for this cause the Spirit is called, *The oil of gladness,* because by that healing virtue that is in him, he makes glad the hearts of men.

3. The Spirit doth not only heal, but renew and revive again; when an eye is smitten with a sword, there is a double mischief, a wound made, and a faculty perished; and here, though a chirurgeon can heal the wound, yet he can never restore the faculty, because total privations admit no regress or recovery. But the Spirit doth not only heal, and repair, but renew, and re-edify the spirits of men; as he healeth that which was torn, and bindeth up that which was broken, so he reviveth, and raiseth up that which was dead before, Hos. vi. 1, 2. And this the apostle calls, *The renovation of the Spirit,* Tit. iii. 5. Now this renovation must needs be matter of great joy, for so the Lord comforts his afflicted people, *O thou! afflicted, tossed with tempest, and not comforted, behold, I will lay thy stones with fair colours, and lay thy foun-*

* *See at large Dr.* Reynolds *on* Psalm cx.

dations with sapphires; and I will make thy windows of agates, and thy gates of carbuncles, and all thy borders of pleasant stones, Isa. liv. 11, 12. The meaning is, That all must be new, and new built up, as for a goodly, costly, and stately structure.

4. The Spirit doth not only renew, and set the frame of the heart aright, and then leave it to itself, but being thus restored, he abideth with it to preserve and support it, and to make it victorious, against all tempests and batteries; and thus farther multiplieth the joy and comfort of the heart; victory is ever the ground of joy, 'They joy ' before thee,——as men rejoice when they divide the spoil,' Isa. ix. 3. And the Spirit of God is a victorious Spirit, ' A bruised reed shall he not break, ' and smoaking flax shall he not quench, till he send ' forth judgment unto victory,' Matth. xii. 20.

5. The Spirit doth not only preserve the heart, which he hath renewed, but he makes it fruitful and abundant in the work of comfort, ' Sing, O ' barren, thou that didst not bear, break forth into ' singing, and cry aloud thou that didst not travail ' with child, for more are the children of the deso- ' late, than the children of the married wife, saith ' the Lord,' Isa. liv. 1.

6. The Spirit doth not only make the heart fruitful, but gives it the hansel and earnest of its inheritance, and thereby it begets a lively hope, an earnest expectation, a confident attendance upon the promises, and an unspeakable peace and comfort thereupon. Oh! when I feel a drop of heaven's joy, shed abroad into my soul by the Holy Ghost, and that I look upon this as a taste of glory, and a forerunner of happiness, How should I but rejoice with joy unspeakable? In all these respects, the Spirit is our comforter; and this is another reason; why the Holy Ghost is sent, ' I ' will not leave you comfortless,' saith Christ, No, no, ' for I will come unto you by my Spirit.

7. That the Holy Ghost might, according to his office, ' seal us unto the day of redemption,' Eph. iv. 30. By sealing is meant, some work of the Spirit by which he assures a believer, that he is God's: it is all one with the Spirit's witnessing; only under that notion I shall speak of it another time.

But all the question is, What is that work of the Spirit by which he assures?. I answer, This work is manifold. As,——

1. There

1. There is a reflex work of faith: and this is the work of the Spirit too, assuring our souls of our good estate to God-ward and Christ-ward, *He that believeth hath the witness in himself*, 1 John v. 10. He carries in his heart the counterpane of all the promises; this is the first seal, or (if you will) the first degree of the Spirit's sealing; the first discovery of our election is manifested to us in our believing, *As many* (saith the text) *as were ordained to eternal life believed*, Acts xiii. 48.

2. There is a work of sanctifying grace upon the heart: and this is a seal of the Spirit also; for whom the Spirit sanctifieth, he saveth, *The Lord knoweth who are his*, saith the apostle, 2 Tim. ii. 19. Ay, but how should we know? Why, by this seal, as it follows, *Let every one that nameth the name of the Lord depart from iniquity*. None are children of God by adoption, but those that are children also by regeneration; none are heirs of heaven, but they were new born to it, *Blessed be God the Father of our Lord Jesus Christ, who hath begotten us anew—to an inheritance immortal*, 1 Pet. 3, 4. This seal of sanctification leaves upon the soul the likeness of Jesus Christ, even grace for grace.

3. There is a work of assisting, exciting, quickning grace; or of God's gracious concourse with that habitual grace which he hath wrought in his people: now, this is various, according to the good pleasure of his will; the Spirit is more mightily present to some than to others, yea more to the same man at sometimes, and in some condition; sometimes the same Christian is as a burning and shining light, sometimes as a smoaking flax; *The Spirit blows where it listeth*, John iii. 8. Sometimes he fills the soul with fuller gales, sometimes again she is becalmed, a man hath more of the Spirit at one time than another; now when the Spirit comes in thus by exciting, quickening, stirring, and enabling us to act, so that we can say, as sometimes the prophet said, *It was in my heart as a burning fire shut up in my bones, and I was weary with forbearing, and could not stay*, Jer. xx. 9. Why, then the Spirit seals and gives assurance to our souls, that we are his.

4. There is a work of shining upon, or enlightening those graces which the Spirit plants in us, and helps us to exercise, that seals to the purpose; and of this it is that the apostle speaks, *We have received not the Spirit of the world, but the Spirit which is of God, that we may know the things that are freely given us of God*, 1 Cor. ii. 12. The things given to us, may be freely received by us, and yet the receipt of them not known to us, therefore the Spirit for our farther consolation doth (as it were) put his hand and seal to our receipts, he shines upon our graces, or he enlightens our graces, (whereby we may know we believe, and know that we live. Indeed this is rare with God's own people, sometimes (notwithstanding this seal) we may be in such a state as Paul and his company were in the ship, *When they saw neither sun nor star for many days together*, Acts xxvii. 20. So it may be that for a time we may see neither sun nor star, neither light in God's countenance, nor light in our souls, no grace issuing from God, no grace carrying the soul to God; yet in this dark condition, if we do as Paul and his company did, (*i. e.*) if we cast anchor even in the dark night of temptation, and pray still for day, God will appear, and all shall clear up: we shall at last see light without, and see light within; surely the day star will arise in our hearts.

5. There is a work of joy and comfort; and this is a superadded seal of the Spirit; the works of the Spirit you may see are of a double kind; either in us by imprinting, sanctifying grace, or upon us by shining on our souls, and by sweet feelings of joy; habitual grace, or sanctifying grace is more constant, and always like itself; but this work of comfort and joy, is of the nature of such priveleges as God vouchsafeth at one time, and not at another; and hence it is, that a Christian may have grace, and a Christian may know himself to be in the state of grace, and yet, in regard of comfort, God may be gone. Thus it was with Job, he knew his redeemer lived, and he resolved to trust in him, though he killed him; he knew he was no hypocrite, he knew his graces were true; notwithstanding all the objections and imputations of his friends, they could not dispute him out of his sincerity, 'My righteousness I hold fast, and I will not let it go,' Job xxvii. 6. Yet for the present he saw, no light from heaven, but he was in a sore and afflicted condition, till it pleased the Lord to reveal himself in special favour unto him. Now, this work of joy usually comes not till after faith, and many experiences of God's love, and much

much waiting upon God. These are the several works of the Spirit's sealing.

But why is it that we can neither actually believe, nor can know that we believe, nor can enjoy peace and joy in believing, without a fresh and new act of the Spirit?

I answer, Because the whole carriage of a soul to heaven is above nature; where the Spirit makes a stand, we stand, and can go no farther; without the help of the Spirit we can neither make promises, nor conclude for ourselves; it is the Spirit that sanctifies, and witnesses, and *seals our souls unto the day of redemption.* Many other reasons may be rendered, but I shall speak of them in the end of the Spirit's mission.

Thus far we have propounded the object, *viz.* The ascension of Christ, the session of Christ at God's right-hand, and Christ's mission of the Holy Ghost. Our next work is to direct you how to look unto Jesus in these respects.

CHAP. II. SECT. I.

Of knowing Jesus as carrying on the great work of our salvation in his ascension, session and mission of the Spirit.

1. LET us know Jesus carrying on the great work of our salvation for us, in his ascension into heaven, in his session at God's right-hand, and in his mission of the Holy Ghost; these are points of great use, if these transactions had not been, Where had we been? These are points of highest speculation, if these transactions had not been, Where had Christ been? After his humiliation, herein lay the exaltation of his glorious person, he was exalted above the earth, above the clouds, above the stars, above the heavens, above the heaven of heavens; O! the glorious majesty of our King Jesus, as sitting down at God's right-hand! our salvation is the greatest mystery that ever was, it being made up of the various workings of the glory of God; for us men, and for our salvation Christ was incarnate, and came down from heaven; and for us men, and for our salvation Christ was exalted, and went up into heaven. Here is an object of admiration indeed, the very angels at the sight of it stood admiring and adoring; it took up their heart, astonished their understanding; surely it was the blessedest sight that ever the angels did, or could behold; come then, and, O my soul! do thou take a view of that which they admire, the design is not so principally concerning angels, as thyself; they are in it only as afar off, and in general; but it concerns thee in special and particular; and therefore study close this argument, and know it for thyself. Study, 1. the ascension of Christ, how, and whither, and why he ascended. 2. Study the session of Christ at God's right-hand; O! the mines, the riches of that spiritual heavenly knowledge! 3. Study the mission of the Holy Ghost; not a circumstance in it, but deserves thy study; worlds of wealth (ten thousand times better than gold, or silver, or precious stones) may be found in the diggings of these mines; Have not many students beat out their brains on lesser subjects? What endeavours have there been to dive into the secrets of nature? What volumes have been written of physics, metaphysics, mathematics? And is not this subject, Christ? Is not every of these subjects, Christ's ascension, Christ's session, Christ's mission of the holy Spirit of more worth, and value, and benefit, than all those? Come, study that piece of the Bible, wherein these are written; there is not a line or expression of Christ in the scripture, but it is matter enough for a whole age to comment on; thou needest not to leave old principles for new discoveries; for in these very particulars thou mightest find successive sweetness unto all eternity.

SECT. II.

Of considering Jesus in that respect.

2. LET us consider Jesus carrying on this work of our salvation for us, in these particulars: we must not only study to know these things, but we must meditate on them till they come down from our heads to our hearts. Meditation is the poize that sets all the wheels within a going; it were to small purpose to bid us desire, hope, believe, love, joy, &c. if first, we did not meditate; in meditation it is that the understanding works, that the will is inclined to follow, that devotion is refreshed, that faith is encreased, hope established, love kindled; and therefore begin here, O my soul! it is a due consideration that gives both

life, and light, and motion to thy actings in all proceedings.

And to take them in order:——

1. Consider of Christ's ascension into heaven. Methinks souls should put themselves into the condition of the disciples, *When they looked stedfastly towards heaven as Christ went up*, Acts i. 10. What, shall he ascend, and shall not we in our contemplations follow after him? Gaze, O my soul! on this wonderful object, thou needest not fear any check from God or angels, so that thy contemplation be spiritual and divine. No sooner had Christ finished his work of redemption here on earth, but on the mount called Olivet, he assembles with his disciples, where having given them commands, he begins to mount; and being a little lifted up into the air, presently a cloud receives him into her lap. Herein is a clear demonstration of his Godhead; clouds are usually in scriptures put for the house, or temple, or receptacle of God himself. How often is it said, that *the glory of the Lord appeared in the cloud?* Exod. xvi. 10 And that *he came to Moses in a thick cloud*, Ex. xix 9. And that *he called unto Moses out of the midst of the cloud*, Exod. xxiv. 16. And that *the Lord descended into the cloud*, Ex. xxxiv. 5. Is not the cloud God's own chariot? *Behold the Lord rideth on a swift cloud*, Isa. xix. 1.——*And, O Lord my God, thou art very great*, saith David; great indeed, and he proves it thus, *who maketh the clouds his chariot*, Psal. civ. 3. Jesus Christ in his ascension to heaven, enters by the way into a cloud; this was his chariot, led by thousands and ten thousands of his angels, *The chariots of God are twenty thousand, even thousands of angels, the Lord is among them as in Sinai in the holy place, thou hast ascended on high, thou hast led captivity captive, thou hast received gifts for men*, Ps. lxviii. 17, 18. Some are of opinion, that not only thousands of angels led this chariot, but that many of the saints which slept, and rose with Christ at his resurrection, now ascended with him, compassed about this glorious cloud; whence they gave this for the meaning of the text, * 'That when he went up 'through the air, and ascended upon high, he led 'captivity captive; that is, he led a certain number of captives, namely, the saints that were long 'held in captivity of death, whose bodies arose at 'Christ's resurrection, and now they accompanied 'Christ at his triumphant march into heaven.' However he was attended, be not too curious, (O! my soul in this) the bright cloud that covered his body, discovered his divinity; and therefore here is thy duty; to look stedfastly towards heaven, and to worship him in his ascension up into heaven; O! admire and adore.

But stay not thy contemplation in the cloud, he ascends yet higher, through the air, and through the clouds, and through that sphere or element of fire, and through those orbs of the moon, Mercury, Mars; of the Sun, Jupiter, Venus, Saturn; and through that azure heaven of fixed stars, and thro' that first moveable, and through those condense and solid waters of the crystalline heaven; nor stood he still till he came to those doors and gates of the imperial heaven, called *the heaven of heavens*; in all this triumphant glorious march, some tell us of an heavenly harmony made by those queristers of heaven, the blessed angels, † *Some going before, and some going after, they chaunt his praises, and sing halklujahs*; and that is the meaning of the Psalmist, *God is gone up with a shout, the Lord with the sound of a trumpet*, Psal. xlvii. 5. In this meditation pass not over thy duty, which immediately follows, *Sing praises to God, sing praises, sing praises unto our king, sing praises*, ver. 6 ——— *Sing unto God, sing praises to his name, extol him that rideth upon the heav ns, by his name JAH, and rejoice before him*, Ps. lxviii. 4. Thou hast great cause, O my soul! to praise him, and to rejoice before him, especially if thou considerest, that Christ ascended not for himself, but also for thee; it is God in our nature that is gone up to heaven; whatever God acted on the person of Christ, that he did as in thy behalf, and he means to act the very same on thee; Christ as a public person ascended up to heaven; thy interest is in this very ascension of Jesus Christ, and therefore dost thou consider thy head as soaring up? O! let every member praise his name, let thy tongue (called thy glory) glory in this, and trumpet out his praises, that, in respect of thy duty, it may be verified, *Christ is gone up with a shout, the Lord with the sound of a trumpet*.

* *English* Annotations on Eph. iv. 8.

† Cypr. *in Serm. ascens.*

And yet stay not by the way, but consider farther, Christ being now arrived at heaven's doors, those heavenly Spirits that accompanied him, began to say, 'Lift up your heads, O ye gates, even lift up yourselves, ye everlasting doors, and the king of glory shall come in,' Psal. xxiv. 7. To whom some of the angels that were within, not ignorant of his person, but admiring his majesty and glory, said again, *Who is the king of glory?* And then they answered, *The Lord strong and mighty, the Lord mighty in battle*, verse 8. and thereupon those *twelve gates of the holy city, of the new Jerusalem*, opened of their own accord, Rev. xxi. 12. And Jesus Christ with all his ministering spirits entred in. O! my soul, how should this heighten thy joy, and inlarge thy comforts, in that Christ is now received up into glory? Every sight of Christ is glorious, and in every sight thou shouldest wait on the Lord Jesus Christ for some glorious manifestations of himself. Come, live up to the rate of this great mystery, view Christ as entring into glory, and thou wilt find the same sparkles of glory on thy heart. O! this sight is a transforming sight, *We all with open face, beholding as in a glass the glory of the Lord, are changed into the same image from glory to glory, even as by the Spirit of the Lord*, 2 Cor. iii. 18.

2. Consider of Christ's session at God's right-hand: no sooner was Christ entred into heaven, but he is brought before his heavenly Father; and herein was the vision accomplished, *I saw in the night visions, and behold one like the Son of man came with the clouds of heaven, and came to the ancient of days, and they brought him near before him, and there was given him dominion, and glory, and a kingdom*, Dan. vii. 13, 14. This is that we call his session at God's right-hand; a dominion was given him above all creatures, yea, a dominion above the hierarchy of all the angels; O! the glory of Christ at his first entrance into glory! immediately all the angels fell down and worshipped him; immediately his Father welcomed him with the highest grace that ever yet was shewn, Come, (said he) *Sit thou at my right-hand, until I make thy enemies thy foot-stool*, Psal. cx. 1. One sweetly observes, that usually in the several parts of the performance of Christ's office, either God is brought in as speaking to Christ, or Christ is brought in as speaking to his Father; thus when he chose him first to be our Mediator, God speaks to Christ, *Thou art a priest for ever after the order of Melchisedec*, and when Christ came to take upon him our nature, he spake to his Father, *Lo, I come to do thy will, a body hast thou prepared for me*, Heb. x. 7. Again, when Christ hung on the cross he speaks to his Father, *My God, my God, why hast thou forsaken me?* Psal. xxii. 1. But when Christ rose again from the dead, God spake to him, *Thou art my Son, this day have I begotten thee*, Acts xiii. 33. And when Christ ascended into heaven, God spake to him, *Son, sit thou at my right-hand*, Heb. i. 13. This was the highest point of Christ elevated, now was the prophesy accomplished, *He shall be exalted and extolled, and be very high*, Isa. lii. 13. The Chaldee paraphrast reads it thus, 'He shall be exalted above Abraham, he shall be extolled more than Moses, he shall be very high, above the brightest cherubim or Seraphim;' O my soul! meditate on this session of Christ at God's right-hand, and thence draw down some virtue and sweetness into thy self. What? Was Christ exalted? Had he a name given him above every name? Walk then as becomes those that have so glorious a head: O! defile not that nature which in thy Christ was so highly honoured! it was the apostle's arguing, 'Shall I take the members of Christ and make them the members of an harlot?' 1 Cor. vi. 15. So argue thou; Shall I take the nature of Christ, that nature which he in his person hath so highly glorified, and make it in my person the nature of a devil? O my soul! walk worthy of such a Lord, unto all well-pleasing; sith now he is in his throne at God's right-hand, O kiss the Son! honour the Son with divine worship, reverence, and submission; submit cheerfully and willingly to the scepter of his word, bow to his name, as it is written, 'At the name, at the person, the power, the scepter of Jesus Christ, every knee should bow,' Phil. ii. 10.

3. Consider of the mission of the Holy Ghost: no sooner is Christ inaugurated in his throne, but he scatters his coin, and gives gifts, *when he ascended on high, he led captivity captive, and gave gifts unto men*, Eph. iv. 8. He gave gifts, or the gift of gifts, the gift of the Holy Ghost, *If thou knowest the gift of God*, John iv. 10. said Christ to the Samaritan woman, that gift was the water of life, and that water of life was the Spirit, as John who knew

knew best his mind, gave the interpretation, *This spake he of the Spirit,* John vii. 39. O my soul! consider of this princely gift of Christ! such a gift was never before, but when God gave his Son, *God so loved the world, that he gave his Son,* and Christ so loved the world, that he gave his Spirit; but, O my soul! consider especially to whom this Spirit was given; the application of the gift is the very soul of thy mediation, *unto us a Son is given,* said the prophet, Isaiah ix. 6. and *unto us the Holy Ghost is given,* saith the apostle, Rom. v. 5. And yet above all, consider the reasons of this gift in reference to thyself; was it not to make thee a temple and receptacle of the Holy Ghost? Stand a while on this; admire O my soul! at the condescending, glorious, and unspeakable love of Christ in this! it was infinite love to come down into our nature when he was incarnate; but this is more, to come down into thy heart by his holy Spirit, he came near to us then, but as if that were not near enough, he comes nearer now; for now he unites himself unto thy person, now he comes, and dwells in thy soul by his holy Spirit: O my soul! thou hast many incomes of the world, though many are above thee, yet many are below thee; but, oh! what little contentment hast thou in these outward things? Come, here's that which will infinitely content thy vast desires; ' Christ is in thee, really in thee by his Spirit;' will not this content the utmost capacity of an heart? Surely he is too covetous, whom God himself cannot suffice; if thou hast Christ, thou hast all things, and if thou hast the Spirit of Christ, thou hast Christ himself, not notionally, not by the habit of grace only, but really, essentially, substantially by his Spirit; it is the very Spirit of Christ, the Spirit itself; the Holy Ghost itself in his own person that is united to thee, and dwells in thee, not only comes he in person, but he brings along with him all his train; Hath he not endued thee with some gifts? Hath he not divided a portion and measure to thee in thy place and calling? Take notice, observe it, and be thankful, if thou hast a gift of prayer, of prophesy, of wisdom, of knowledge, it comes and flows from his holy Spirit, *Unto every one of us is given grace, according to the measure of the gift of Christ,* Eph. iv. 7. Or, according to the measure of the spirit, who is the gift of Christ, and *all these worketh that one and the self-same Spirit, dividing to every man severally as he will,* 1 Cor. xii. 11. But besides a gift, hath he not endowed thee with his grace? Hath he not planted in thy soul the habit, the power, the seed, the spring, the principle of grace? Hast thou not felt sometimes the excitings, quicknings, stirring of the spirit of God, commanding thy faith, love, zeal, and other graces to be in exercise? Hath he not many a time at some dead lift, at some mighty strait, at some prevailing temptation, when thou wast even ready to yield to Satan, come in as betwixt the bridge and water, and given thee *grace to help in time of need?* Heb. iv. 16. O the sweet incomes of the Spirit of God! as he is an holy Spirit, so he makes holy hearts, and if there be any holiness in thy heart, what is it but an emanation, influence, effect of the spirit of God? If ever thou hadst any flowings of exciting, quickning grace, say, ' This is a- ' bove nature, above flesh and blood, it comes from ' the holy and blessed spirit of God.' Some other effects thou mayest consider of, as of the comforts of the spirit: what, hast thou not sometimes felt thy joys unspeakable and full of glory? Hast thou not sometimes known a morning's joy, after a night's sorrow? An healing of thy broken heart, a reviving of thy dead spirit, a drop of heaven's joy given thee as the hansel, or earnest of thy inheritance? Why, all these are but the workings of the promised comforter, *And I will pray the Father, and he shall give you another comforter, that he may abide with you for ever,* John xiv. 16 Another effect is the seal of the spirit; and, what hast thou not sometimes had the seal of the spirit stamped on thee? I will not say this is absolutely necessary, But hast thou not sometimes been assured of thy salvation, by a reflect act of faith? Or, by a work of grace habitual or actual? Or, by an irradiation of the Spirit on thy graces? Sometimes the spirit is pleased to shine with its bright, and glorious, and heavenly beams into our souls, and then we are assured: hence the apostle prays for the Ephesians, *That they might have the spirit of revelation,* And to what end? *That they might know what is the hope of his calling,* Eph. i 17, 18, 19. (*i. e.*) That they might know upon what certain grounds and foundation their hopes were built; and hence the Psalmist prays for himself, *Cause thy face to shine upon thy servant,* Psal. xxxi. 16. And again, *God be merciful unto us, and bless us, and cause his face*

face to shine upon us, Selah, Psal. lxvii. 1. If the spirit shine upon our graces, then it seals: O! consider of this shining sealing work, and leave it not till the spirit dart in a spiritual light, and give thee a revelation, knowledge, and persuasion of thy effectual calling; many other reasons are of the spirit's mission, but amongst them all, consider, O my soul! and ponder on these few; think over Christ's ascension, session, and mission of the spirit; but in every thought be serious, fruitful, and particular; say, 'Christ is gone up into heaven for me, and 'he is set down at God's right-hand for me; and 'he hath sent down his spirit into my heart.' Oh! what workings would be within, if thou were but lively and active in the meditations of these several passages.

SECT. III.

Of desiring after Jesus in that respect.

3. Let us desire after Jesus, carrying on the great work of our salvation for us in these particulars: who seeing Christ to ascend into heaven, would not be glad to ascend up with him? Who seeing Christ to sit down at the right-hand of his Father, would not be glad to sit down with him? Who seeing Christ to scatter his gifts and spirit amongst his saints, would not cry, 'Come, 'holy spirit, O! Christ give me thy spirit, thou 'that givest gifts unto me, come, and bestow those 'gifts on me, even upon me?' The believing soul cannot hear of Christ in any true discovery of his grace and glory, but it must needs send out many breathings after him, 'Oh! that Christ were mine! 'Oh! that I had any interest in this transaction!' It is true, these transactions are past, but the virtue of them continues still, and accordingly the virtue, power, and influence of these transactions must be the object of our desires. Now, what is the virtue of Christ's ascension, but that we might ascend? And what the virtue of Christ's session, but that we might sit down with him in his throne? And what the virtue of the mission of his spirit, but that we might partake of the Holy Ghost? Oh! let these be the objects of our desires; come, let us pant and breathe after these things. As,——

1. Let us see Christ ascending, and so desire to ascend with him, when Christ ascended, it was not merely for himself, but also in our stead; he ascended as a common person, as the high-priest ascending into the holy of holies, he carried all the names of the twelve tribes on his breast; so Jesus Christ ascending into heaven, he carried the names of all believers in the world on his breast, thereby shewing that they were likewise to come after him; in this case how should we long after him, and cry after him, as Elisha, after Elija, when he saw him ascending, *My father, my father, the chariots of Israel, and the horsemen thereof?* 2 Kings ii. 12. How should we cry after him, 'O my Lord! 'and my God, see that my name, be written in 'thy breast, O! that virtually I may ascend with 'thee, and that really and bodily I may at last a- 'scend after thee!' there are many can say in their heart, *I will ascend above the heights of the clouds, I will be like the most High,* Isa. xiv. 14, 15. But the prophet tells us, *Such shall be brought down to hell, and to the sides of the pit.* O! the desires, and eager pursuits of men, after ambition, what topping and advancing is there of one over another? In the mean time the Psalmist's question is quite forgotten, *Who shall ascend into the hill of the Lord? He that hath clean hands, and a pure heart, who hath not lift up his soul unto vanity,* Psalm xxiv. 3, 4. Down, O my soul! with thy top and top-gallant; strike sail to God and Christ, know that God resists the proud, *How art thou fallen from heaven, O Lucifer! son of the morning?* Isa. xiv. 12. Even he that would *exalt his throne above the stars of God, is brought down to hell;* Come, come! a desire after Christ and his ascension is the way to heaven, if thou wilt ascend after Christ, set thy desires upon Christ; if thou wilt arrive at true glory, breathe after Christ, ascending up into his glory; let others ascend up into their heaven upon earth, but, O my soul! desire thy interest in Christ's ascension into the heaven of heavens, 'Oh! when will it once be, that by 'virtue of Christ's ascension, I shall ascend? Is 'Christ gone up, and am I yet behind? Is my 'head, my husband, my Lord in heaven, and am 'I a poor member of his body grovelling here on 'earth? What, is Christ gone up with a shout, 'the Lord with the sound of a trumpet? Are all 'the angels sounding his praise, and bidding him 'welcome into glory? And am I sinning here on 'earth,' and ' ' ' ' ' ' ' again and again,
'the

'the Lord of glory? O that I might ascend with Christ! Oh! that I were now on the wing toward heaven! Oh! what is it that hinders my ascension, but the clog of clay? So long as this body remains a natural body, I cannot ascend; Oh! therefore that the change were come! Oh! that this natural body were spiritual! that this corruptible had put on incorruption, and this mortal, had put on immortality! then could I move upwards as well as downwards; such is the supernatural property of a glorified body, that it ascends, or descends, with equal ease; or, if this be not possible for my present condition, if this body of mine must first descend, before it ascend, if it must down into the grave, before it go up into glory: why, yet, oh! that my better part were on the wing! oh! that my soul were mounting upwards! O! wretched man that I am, who shall deliver my soul from this body of death? Or, if the union be so strong for a while, that neither soul nor body can really or substantially ascend, yet, O! that I were still ascending in a spiritual way! O! that my affections were still on things above, and not on things beneath! yea, I could wish a nearer union even by a dissolution; why, Christ is ascended, and I would fain be where Christ is, though it cost me dear; I desire to be dissolved, I desire to depart, and to be with Christ, which is far better,' Phil. i. 23.

2. Let us see Christ sitting down at the right-hand of God, and so desire to sit with him: when Christ sat down, it was not in his own pure personal right simply, as it is his inheritance, but with relation to his saints and members, *He hath quickened us together with Christ, and hath raised us up together, and made us sit together in heavenly places, in Christ Jesus,* Eph. ii. 5, 6. I confess Christ's sitting at God's right-hand (as taken for the sublimity of his power) is not communicable unto us, for that is Christ's own prerogative, *To which of the angels said he at any time, Sit on my right-hand?* Heb. i. 13. Yet his sitting in heaven as it is indefinitely expressed, is in some sort communicable unto us, for he sat down as a common person, thereby shewing that we were to sit down with him in our proportion, *Him that overcomes, I will grant to sit with me in my throne, even as I also overcame, and am set down with my Father in his throne,* Revel. iii. 21. Christ sits in his Father's throne, and we sit in Christ's throne; Christ sits at the right-hand of God, and we sit at the right-hand of Christ. O! how desirable is this? The mother of Zebedee's children understood this mystery very darkly, yet worshipping Jesus, *She desired a certain thing of him;* what thing? Why grant, (said she) *that these my two sons may sit, the one at thy right-hand, and the other on thy left-hand, in thy kingdom,* Mat. xx. 21. Christ blamed them, because *they knew not what they asked,* ver. 22. and yet he tells them, that *to sit on his right-hand, and on his left, is given to them for whom it is prepared of his Father,* verse 23. O my soul! desire after this, for this is worthy of thy desire: this is a great thing, an high exaltation, another manner of honour than any that this world affords; courtiers desire no more but to sit at the prince's right-hand; but, O! the virtue of Christ's session, that thereby thou shouldest sit at the right-hand of God; this is the very height and excellency of heaven's glory; only take heed of apprehending it after a carnal and natural way, this very exaltation consists in the image of God, and communion with God; it is the spiritual part, and power, and glory of heaven: if any thing be desirable above another, surely this above all; what, that Christ should be exalted, *above all principalities and powers, and mights, and dominions, and every thing that is named in this world, and in the other?* Eph. i. 20, 21. What, that Christ should sit down in his Father's throne, in the highest part of heaven, *far above all heavens?* Eph. iv. 10. And that I, a poor worm, dust and ashes, should sit with him in heaven, should be one with him in glory, should be as near him in honour and happiness, as such a poor creature is possibly capable of? Oh! how should I but hunger and thirst after this? If I might have a wish, I would not wish low things: why, this is the very top, and height, and quintessence of heaven, *Christ in his Father's throne, and I in Christ's throne;* in desiring this, I desire all; and therefore whatever thou givest or deniest, Lord give me this, and I have enough for ever.

3. Let us see Christ's mission of his holy Spirit, and so desire a share in that gift, we cannot expect to sit with Christ, but we must first have the Spirit of Christ; and therefore, as we would have

that

that, let us desire after this. The greatest gift we can expect in this world is the Spirit of Christ. Consider, O my soul! all things here below are either temporal or spiritual things; and of things spiritual, this is the sum, *the in-dwelling of the Spirit*. O Lord, give me thy self, and that contains all gifts! O! give me thy Spirit, and that thou canst not but with him give me all things, *There be many that say*, (faith the Psalmist) *is ho will shew us any good?* Psal. iv. 6. Earthly things are desired by many; but is any thing on earth to be compared with this gift from heaven? If it were only the beauty of holiness, it were certainly a desirable thing; if we rightly understand it, holiness (though but one effect of the Spirit) is a most rare thing; holiness fills the soul with joy, peace, quietness, assurance; holiness entertains the soul with feasts of fat things, and refined wines; holiness carries the soul into the banquetting house of apples and flaggons; holiness gives the soul a near communion with God and Christ; holiness brings the soul into a sight of Christ, an access to him, a boldness in his presence; holiness admits the soul into the most intimate conferences with Jesus Christ in his bed-chamber, in his galleries of love; and that which is an argument of more beauty than all the creatures in the world have besides; holiness attracts the eye, and heart, and longings, and ravishments, the tender compassions, and everlasting delights of the Lord Jesus; and if holiness be thus lovely, Oh! what is the holy Spirit itself? What is the rise, the spring, the fountain of holiness? What, O my soul! that not only grace, but the Spirit of Christ should dwell in thy spirit? That thou shouldest be God's building? 1 Cor. iii. 9. And that not as the rest of the world is, for his creatures to inhabit, but as *a temple* for himself to dwell in? 2 Cor. vi. 16. As *a gallery*, for himself to walk in? Cant. vii. 5. Oh! what longings? Oh! what pantings and gaspings? Oh! what faintings and swoonings should there be in thy spirit after this Spirit? *Come holy Spirit*, O come and dwell in my soul! I know thou wilt make the place of thy feet glorious; if I have but thy presence, I shall be all glorious within: O come, come holy Spirit.

SECT. IV.

Of hoping in Jesus in that respect.

4 LET us hope in Jesus, carrying on the great work of our salvation for us in these particulars; thus was the apostle's prayer, 'Now the God of hope fill you with all joy and peace in believing; that ye may abound in hope through the power of the Holy Ghost,' Rom. xv. 13. Could we abound in hope that Christ's ascension, session, and mission of his Spirit did belong to us, we should never be ashamed, 'Hope maketh not ashamed,' Rom. v. 5. O! then let us look to our hope, and be sure that it be of the right stamp, which in reference to every of these passages we may examine thus. As,—

1. If Christ's ascension be mine, then am I ascended with Christ; I mean not in respect of any bodily ascension, for that must not be until the last day; nor in respect of any essential, substantial soul-ascension, for that must not be before the separation of soul and body at our death's-day; but in respect of our spiritual ascension, for so we may ascend into heaven by faith, and love, though for the present we are on earth, 'If ye be risen with Christ, seek those things which are above, where Christ sitteth at the right hand of God; set your affections on things above, and not on things on the earth,' Col. iii. 1, 2. If Christ our head be ascended, then we that are his members, must needs follow after him in our affections: Christ tells us, 'Where our treasure is, there will our hearts be also,' Matth. vi 21. If Christ our treasure be ascended into heaven, our loves, our affections, our hearts will follow after him; and if our hearts be in heaven, no question but we ourselves both souls and bodies, shall at last ascend; when Christ ascended, we ascended virtually with him, now we ascend spiritually, and at last we shall ascend bodily, for he that ascended, shall descend, and then 'we shall meet him in the air, and so shall we be ever with the Lord.' 1 Thes. iv 17. In the mean time, to maintain our hope, let us ascend daily by faith and love; and this is our Character that Christ's ascension is truly ours.

2. If Christ's session be mine, then am I set down with Christ in heavenly places: I mean not bodily

bodily, but by faith, which faith makes it as sure to my soul, as if I had a foot already in heaven, 'Faith is the substance of things hoped for, and 'the evidence of things not seen,' Heb. xi. 1. By faith I now sit in heavenly places, in that I verily believe I shall do it one day; my hope is now certain, in that I am as sure of that I look for, as I am of that I have already received; it is the common objection, 'we see it not,' as the apostle said of Christ, 'we see not yet all things put under him,' Heb. ii. 8. but he presently answers, 'We see Je- 'sus who was made a little lower than the angels, 'crowned with glory and honour,' ver. 9. And so we may be sure the thing is as good as done, for if he be above, all must come under; in like manner, we see not ourselves in present possession, but we see Christ crowned, and ourselves sitting with him virtually, and therefore at last we shall see ourselves actually crowned, and sitting together with Christ in heavenly places. In the mean time faith takes possession of the kingdom of heaven; faith makes the soul even now to converse with God, and Christ, and saints, and angels, 'Faith lays hold 'upon eternal life,' 1 Tim. vi. 19. It puts the soul, as it were, into heaven, and sets it down at the right hand of Christ; and this is our character that Christ's session is truly ours.

3. If Christ's Spirit be mine, and sent to me, then have I both the person, and train of the Spirit of Christ; it is the having the Spirit, and the working of the Spirit in me, that is my evidence of the Spirit's mission; I look upon this as the greatest question, and the weightiest, and most important case of conscience, that can be propounded or known of us, *viz.* Whether the Spirit of Christ doth reside in us? Or, whether we have a well-grounded hope to say of ourselves that we have the indwelling of the Spirit of God? 'Know ye 'not that ye are the temple of God,' (saith the apostle) 'and that the Spirit of God dwelleth in 'you?' 1 Cor. iii. 16. And again, 'Know ye not 'that your bodies are the temples of the Holy 'Ghost?' 1 Cor. vi. 19. In this question, he seems to put it out of question, that true Christians should know, and in right temper do know that the Spirit of God dwells in them; if we know not this, we cannot know that we have any part in Christ; because the holy Spirit is the principal bond of our union betwixt Christ and us; if we know not this, we cannot know that we are justified, for we have nothing to do with Christ's righteousness, by which we are justified, until by our spiritual union Christ is made ours; if we know not this, we cannot know we are the adopted children of God, for it is the Spirit of adoption, whereby we *cry in our hearts, Abba, Father,* Rom. viii. 15. If we know not this, we cannot know that we are sanctified, for it is the Spirit which is the beginner and perfecter of our sanctification; if we know not this, we cannot know that our prayers are heard, for it is *the Spirit that helps our infirmities, and that makes intercession for us, with groanings which cannot be uttered,* Rom. viii. 26. If we know not this, we cannot know whether we are in error or truth; or whether our religion which we profess be true, or false, for it is the Spirit who enlightens us, and teacheth us, and leadeth us into all truth, if we know not this, we cannot know our own comforts, for he is the only true comforter, from whom all sound comfort springs. Come then, and put ourselves to the trial; let us search whether we have the Spirit of Christ, which we may resolve (if we will not deal deceitfully with our own heart) by these following signs.——

1. The Spirit of Christ is the Spirit of illumination, if he dwell in us he will enlighten our eyes, reveal to us those saving truths of God as they are in Jesus, *But the comforter, which is the Holy Ghost, whom the Father will send in my name, he shall teach you all things,* John xiv. 26.—*But ye have an unction from the holy One, and ye know of all things,* 1 John ii. 20.—*But the anointing which ye have received of him, abideth in you, and ye need not that any man teach you, but as the same anointing teacheth you of all things,* ver. 27. And hence it is that this holy Spirit is called *the Spirit of wisdom, and revelation, in the knowledge of God,* Eph. i. 17.

2. The Spirit of Christ is the Spirit of adoption, it brings our souls into that blessed estate, that we are the children of God, *Ye have not received the Spirit of bondage again to fear; but ye have received the Spirit of adoption, whereby ye cry, Abba, Father,* Rom. viii. 15. And *because ye are sons, God hath sent forth the Spirit of his Son into your hearts, crying, Abba, Father,* Gal. iv. 6.

3. The Spirit of Christ is a Spirit of prayer, *I will pour upon the house of David, and upon the inhabitants of Jerusalem, the Spirit of grace and of supplication,* Zech. xii. 10.——*Likewise, the Spirit*

Spirit also helpeth our infirmities, for *we know not what we should pray for as we ought, but the Spirit itself maketh intercession for us, with groanings which cannot be uttered*, Rom. viii. 26. It is not said that the Spirit teacheth us words, and fluent phrases, but it teacheth us to pray in the heart and spirit with sighs and groans.

4. The Spirit of Christ is a Spirit of sanctification; the apostle having told the Corinthians, that they had been notorious sinners, saith farther, That *they were washed and sanctified by the Spirit of God*, 1 Cor. vi. 11. Hence the holy Spirit is called *the Spirit of holiness*, Rom. i. 4. Because he makes us holy who were in ourselves corrupt and sinful. If we have this Spirit, it inclines our hearts to the things above, it mortifies our lusts, it brings us nearer unto God; the spirit therefore that is impure, and encourageth men in sin, and cries up carnal liberty, is certainly none of the Spirit of Christ; and by this one sign many carnal pretenders of our times may be justly convicted.

5. The Spirit of Christ is a Spirit of love; *God is love, and he that dwelleth in love, dwelleth in God, and God in him*, 1 John iv. 16. As the Spirit is love, so it begets love in the hearts of his people, *The fruit of the Spirit is love, joy, peace, long-suffering, gentleness, goodness, faith, meekness, temperance*, Gal. v. 22. All these graces are the fruits of the Spirit, but the first grace in the link is love: by his Spirit we are taught to love God, not only for his benefits, but in respect of his nature, for his goodness, mercy, justice, holiness, and all other his saving attributes; by his Spirit we are taught to love any thing that hath but the stamp and image of God upon it, *But as touching brotherly love, ye need not that I write unto you, for ye yourselves are taught of God to love one another*, 1 Thes. iv. 2. The most of the heretical spirits of these times, do hereby shew that they have not the Spirit: their very religion lieth in railing at ministers, and reproaching those that are not in their way; this is far from the spirit of love that is in God's children; certainly where there is malice, hatred, strife, bitter envyings, railings, revilings, for such kind of persons to lay claim to the Spirit of unity, it is a piece of impudent vanity, and a false suggestion from their own corrupt erring spirit, or from the spirit of error himself, who is an hater, reviler, and the accuser of the brethren.'

6. The Spirit of Christ is a leading spirit; 'As 'many as are led by the Spirit of God, they are 'the sons of God,' Rom. viii. 14. But what is this leading of the Spirit? I answer,

1. It is a drawing of the soul Christ-ward; *Draw me*, (saith the spouse) *and we will run after thee*, Canticles i. 4. There must be a drawing of the soul in every duty to Jesus Christ, I say, to Jesus Christ; for a man may be furnished with eminent gifts, and with suitable assistances in the laying out of those gifts from the Spirit, and yet he may be without the leadings of the Spirit; gifts exercised, cannot suppress corruptions in a man's own heart, and hence they that used their gifts are called *workers of iniquity*, Matth. vii. 23. gifts do not carry out the heart towards Christ, but graces do, 'I will cause him to draw near, and he 'shall approach unto me, for who is this that en-'gaged his heart to approach unto me, saith the 'Lord,' Jer. xxx. 21.

2. It is a giving liberty to the soul to walk in the ways of Christ. 'Where the Spirit of the 'Lord is, there is liberty,' 2 Cor. iii. 17. I mean not a liberty to sin, but to duty, nor yet every liberty to duty, for a man may exercise himself in the external part of all duties, and yet be without the leadings of the Spirit; but I mean such a liberty as when a soul accounts it an high favour from the Lord, if he will but use them in any services for himself, when it finds more delectation in these than in any other ways, 'I 'have chosen the way of truth,' (saith David) 'and therein is my delight,' Psal. cxix. 34. 173, 174. And 'I delight in the law of God after the 'inner-man,' (saith Paul) Rom. vii. 22. 'For 'the law of the Spirit of life in Jesus Christ hath 'made me free from the law of sin and death,' Rom. viii. 2.

3. It is a corroborating or strengthening of the soul against all those impediments that would hinder it in the ways of Christ; Israel is said to be *led by the Spirit of the Lord*, And how did he lead them? But *by dividing the waters before them, and by keeping them that they should not stumble*, Isa. lxiii. 11, 12; 13, 14. Many times God's holy ones are beset with temptations, they find their hearts full of deadness, hardness, unbelief, and all manner of distempers; now, if at such a time the mountains have been made plains, if at such a time corruptions

Iii have

have been borne down, and their hearts have been let out towards Christ, certainly there are the leadings of the Spirit, *If ye through the Spirit do mortify the deeds of the body ye shall live; for as many as are led by the Spirit of God, are the sons of God,* Rom. viii. 13, 14. The particle *for,* argues mortification to appertain unto the leadings of the Spirit. There is in the saints a constant opposition between the works of the flesh and the works of the spirit; now when the works of the flesh are kept underneath, and prevailed against, then a soul enjoyeth the leadings of the Spirit, Gal v. 17, 18. I know such oppositions are not in any but saints; carnal men would wonder that any should complain for want of strength unto duties; why, they can easily come up to them, and be in the exercise of them; but, alas! this ariseth either from Satan's not molesting them in the performance of duty, because they look not beyond the external part of it; or from their own insensibleness of the working of corruption, when yet it doth act: only a gracious heart findeth, that if it be not strengthened by a power beyond its own, it cannot act any grace, or perform any duty acceptable to God; and hence the apostle prays, *That they might be strengthened with might by his Spirit in the inner-man,* Eph. iii. 16.

4. It is an enabling of the soul to act in gospel duties for gospel ends; when the spirit leads, the soul never aims at self-advancement, it never looks at its own name and glory, as they did in Matth. vi. 1, 5. But it eyes in all its actings the mortification of corruption, and the attainment of communion with God and Christ, and the increase of all grace, faith, love, patience, meekness, self-denial, &c. Or, if it seek for outward mercies, it seeks them in a subordination to these, and in a way of subserviency to the interest and designs of Christ: in all things whether outward or inward, it seeks the glory of God as the ultimate end, And, in these particulars, consist the leadings of the spirit of Christ.

7. The Spirit of Christ is a witnessing spirit, *The Spirit itself beareth witness with our spirit, that we are the children of God,* Rom. viii. 16. And *every one that believeth hath the witness within himself,* 1 John v. 12. But of this two questions. 1. What is this witnessing work of the Spirit? 2. How doth the Spirit thus witness? For the first, I answer,

1. In general, witnessing is a giving in some evidence upon our knowledge how the matter in question standeth, that thereby others may be ascertained of the truth of the thing, 'At the 'mouth of two or three witnesses shall the matter 'be established,' Deut. xix. 15. These words Christ cited, and said, 'It is written in your law 'that the testimony of two men is true,' John viii. 17. Not but that it was certain in itself before, but that now by the testimony of two, it is rendered certain unto those that question the same; this is witnessing.

2. In special, the witnessing of the spirit is an office of the spirit, whereby it works the soul into a knowledge, persuasion, or conclusion of its acceptation into favour with God in Christ. Now the Spirit witnesseth either objectively, or efficiently.

1. Objectively, when it only affords such special operations as have an aptitude to ascertain the soul, but do not ascertain; thus many a time the spirit comes and brings in such and such assertions or affirmations of our adoption, as if they were but duly observed, might manifest the same; but we overlook these evidences, we will not hear what the spirit speaks to us, *We speak that we know,* (saith Christ) *and testify that we have seen, but ye receive not our witness,* John iii. 11. So may the spirit complain, *I have testified to you that which I know, I have said that ye were children of God, but ye have not received my witness.* Doubtless it is a sinful neglect not to yield attention unto the voice of the spirit, and yet the spirit in this way may be resisted.

2. Efficiently, and if the spirit witness thus, it cannot be resisted; in this way the spirit causeth the soul to conclude of its adoption by its speaking to it: this is not only the assertions or affirmations of our adoption, but the assurances of our souls that we are adopted, *I am persuaded,* (saith the apostle) Rom. viii. 38. *And I know that my Redeemer liveth,* (saith Job) Job xix. 25. And *hereby we know that he abideth in us, by the Spirit which he hath given us,* 1 John iii. 24. But,——

2. How doth the Spirit thus witness? I answer, 1. Immediately. 2. Mediately.

1. Concerning the immediate testimony of the Spirit, there is some controversy: Antinomians would have no other testimony but this; all other evidences (say they) are deceiving evidences; or if not

not deceiving, yet to make use of them, it were but to light a candle to the sun; for what are the graces of the Spirit in comparison of the Spirit's own testimony? And it may be the running into this extreme, hath caused others absolutely to deny any such testimony; or, at least, to say, *For these Enthusiasms or inspirations, let them boast of them that have them, we know no such thing.* Methinks a middle betwixt both these (as it is proved by others) is most consonant to truth; for neither can I reject the graces of sanctification from being grounds of our assurance; neither dare I deny but there is something of the work of the Spirit's testimony, which is an immediate work. Let us hear what others say of it.——

† Certainly there is a work wherein the spirit acts, as in illumination, and infusion of good motions into us, wherein by a secret influence upon the heart, he quiets and calms the troubled soul, concerning its condition by his own immediate power, without any grounds from scripture without, or grace within.

* There is a threefold work of the Spirit; 1. To convey and plant grace in the soul. 2. To act and help us to exercise the graces which are planted here.

3. To shine upon and enlighten those graces: this last work the spirit fulfils two ways; 1. By arguments and inferences, which is a mediate work. 2. By presence and influence, which is an immediate work; this the apostle calls *witness-bearing*, *There are three that bear witness in earth, the spirit, and water, and blood,* 1 John v. 8. The spirit brings in the witness of water and blood, which is his mediate work, but besides and above these, he gives a distinct witness of his own, which is his immediate work, and in a way of peculiarity and transcendency, called *the witness of the Spirit.* ——As it is with the motions of the Spirit, many a time the spirit excites a man to such or such duties, by laying his hand immediately upon the heart, and thereby inclining it to obey those motions; so in this case, when a poor soul sits in darkness, and sees no light, sometimes upon a sudden it is (as it were) taken up into the third heaven; and this is in such a way, that though the spirit of a man really believes it, and is immediately calm by it, yet it cannot tell how it came to pass.

‡ There is a testimony of the spirit, which sometimes the spirit may suggest and testify to the sanctified conscience with a secret still heart-ravishing voice, thus, or in the like manner, *Thou art the child of God; thou art in the number of those that shall be saved; thou shalt inherit everlasting life,* and that as certainly and comfortably as if that angel from heaven should say to thee, as he did to Daniel, *Greatly beloved.*——Mighty and remarkable was the work of the spirit this way, upon the heart of that noble martyr, Robert Glover, upon the first sight and representation of the stake, when he cried, *He is come, he is come.* Such an immediate springing of the Spirit was in the heart. Mr. Peacock, who many days of extremest horror, professed, *The joy which he felt was incredible.* Such an immediate work was upon the heart of mistress Brettergh; who after the return of her beloved, suddenly cried out, *How wonderful! how wonderful! how wonderful are thy mercies, O Lord! O the joys, the joys, the joys that now I feel in my soul!* we feel and acknowledge by daily experience, that Satan doth immediately inject, and shall not the blessed Spirit after his holy and heavenly manner immediately also suggest sometimes?

§ As there is in the eye *lumen innatum*, a certain inbred light, to make the eye see lights and colours without; and as there is in the ear *aer internus*, a certain inbred sound and air, to make it discern the sounds that are without; so is there in a gracious heart, a new nature, an habitual instinct of heaven to discern the consolations of God's Spirit, immediately testifying that we are the sons of God; there are some secret and unexpressible lineaments of the Father's countenance in this child, that the renewed soul at first blush knows and owns it. But for fear of mistakes in this case, observe we these rules.

1. That although the spirit may immediately testify without any express formal application of a word, yet he never testifies but according to the word. If a man that never felt sin a burden, that throws away all duties of religion, that never prays, reads, hears, or meditates, shall say, that he is filled with joy, peace, and the assurance of God's word, it is certain the holy Spirit is not the author

† Ford *of the Spirit.*   * Caryl. *on* Job, *chap.* x.
‡ Bolton's *Direct. for a comfortable walking with C*

of this, becaufe the promife of peace belongs to none of this ftamp; fee Mat. xi. 28. Ifa. lvii. 15. Mal. v. 3, 4, 5, 6, 7, 8.

2. That ordinarily the Spirit brings in his teftimony either in duty, or after duty, *I have seen his way, and I will heal him, I will lead him also, and restore comforts to him and to his mourners; I create the fruit of the lips, peace, peace to him that is far off, and to him that is near, saith the Lord, and I will heal him*, Ifa. lvii. 18, 19. I know there may be a cafe of grievous temptations, and at fuch a time the Spirit of God may come in by a fudden irradiation, and chear the foul wonderfully, tho' it knows not how; yet ufually the fpirit brings in his teftimony either in duty, or not long after outy.

3. That fuch teftimonies of the fpirit beget only an actual affurance during the prefent exigency, or in order to fome prefent defign that God is working thereby; thefe are extraordinary dainties, that God will not have us feed conftantly upon; a gleam of light in a dark winter night, when a man cannot coaft the country, and difcern his way by thofe marks which direct him at other times; or as a lightning from a thunder-cloud, that comes juft in the moment, when a man is ftepping into a pit that would fwallow him up; now a traveller will not depend always upon fuch guides, but rather he will choofe to travel by day, and learn out fuch way-marks as may be ftanding affurances to him, that he is in the way. And therefore,——

2. The fpirit witneffeth mediately; and that either without, or with argumentation; but both from the word.

1. Without argumentation; and that is, when the Spirit applies fome fuitable words to the foul, and without more ado, enables the foul to clofe with that fuitable word. As for inftance, thou are burdened for fin, and thou haft prayed earneftly for pardon of fin, and even then a fecret whifper of the Spirit: caft that word into thy heart, *I will heal thy back-flidings, and love thee freely*, Hof. xiv. 4. Or, fuch a voice as that, *Come unto me all ye that labour, and are heavy laden, and I will give you reft*, Mat. xi. 28. Now this is a direct teftimony, only I dare not leave it without a caution.——Some can relate extraordinary paffages of providence attending the coming in of fuch and fuch a word, as that they did not know there was any fuch fcripture, nor did they know where it was, and yet in opening the book, it was the very firft place their eye was caft upon, or they wanted a book, and in the ufe of fome other means unexpectedly a word was fpoken or remembered, fo put to the cafe as if it had been a very meffage from heaven: certainly the Spirit hinting in of words thus, is very obfervable; yet a bare giving in of a word is no warrant that it comes from the Spirit, unlefs the foul come up to fome end which the word itfelf pointeth at; there muft not only be a word, but a clofing with the word, an improving of the word for the ends it aimeth at, as quickning, comforting, fupporting, acting of fome graces, or fuch like; and, by this, we may know now that teftimony is true, and proceeds from the Spirit of God.

1. With argumentation; and that is when the fpirit brings in the teftimony of blood and water; I may call it a teftimony of faith, and other graces of the fpirit, written in our hearts, and brought out by the fpirit in a way of argument, as thus,—*He that believeth hath everlafting life, but I believe*, Ergo. The firft propofition is the gofpel, and in this way, it is the firft work of the fpirit to open our eyes, for the underftanding thereof. The fecond propofition is thy cafe, or my cafe; and here the fpirit enlightens the foul to fee itfelf under that condition, *but I believe*. Indeed many times this is not fo eafily done, and therefore the fpirit doth elicit and draw forth the foul to an affent by a farther evidence of argument. *True* (fays the foul) *he that believes hath everlafting life, but I am none of thofe believers, and therefore what doth this promife concern fuch an unbelieving wretch as I am?* In this cafe, now the fpirit's work is longer, or fhorter, even as he pleafeth; if it will be no better, the fpirit is fain to produce fome other proofs of fcripture, as evidence faith in the fubject of whom it is; fuch as purifying the heart, love to God, his ways, his people, &c. And poffibly it goes farther yet, and proves thofe graces to be in the foul by farther marks.—I know fome object, if the fpirit fays, thou art a believer, becaufe thou haft love, the foul may doubt ftill whether it hath love or no; and if the fpirit fay, thou haft love becaufe thou delighteft in God's commandments, the queftion may be ftill, whether that delight be fincere, or counterfeit, pure, or mixed; and therefore fay they, *There can be no*
judg-

Carrying on the great Work of our Salvation in his Ascension into Heaven. 437

judgment of a man's justification by his sanctification; or, of his sanctification, by the operation of particular graces.

I answer, it is true, that whilst I endeavour to discover these graces merely by reason, they may be still subject to question, and so they can make no firm assurance; but in the soul that is graciously assured this way, the Spirit of God rests the heart upon an *ultimum quod sic:* he convinceth the soul by that which is most visible in him, and so stops the mouth of cavilling reason, from perplexing the question any more. Indeed it is a fine skill to know whether a true assurance be merely rational, or from the witness of the Spirit of God: whether it be wrought out of a man's own brain, or wrought into his heart by the Holy Ghost. Now in some cases we may discern it as thus, the assurance that the spirit gives, doth sometimes surprize a man unexpectedly, at unawares, as it may be in a sermon that he came accidentally unto, or in a scripture that I cast a transient, glancing eye upon; but thus doth not reason. Again the assurance that the spirit gives, maintains a soul in a way of reliance and dependance, when it sees no reason why he should do so; or it may be when he sees a reason why it should not be so: as it is said of Abraham in another case, *that he believed in hope against hope,* Rom. iv. 18. Faith told him there was hope, that he should be the father of many nations, when reason told him there was none: again, the assurance that the spirit gives, is attended with an high esteem of prayer, duties, ordinances, and in the issue (which is the most principal sure mark) it purifies the soul that hath it, *He that hath this hope purifieth himself, even as he is pure,* 1 John iii. 3. He is even washing himself from sin, and watching against sin, and taking all possible care to keep himself pure and unspotted in this present evil world: it keeps the soul humble, and lowly, it being impossible that such a testimony of the spirit, and so intimate a converse with God, and the light of his countenance should not reflect low thoughts upon a man's self, concerning himself; such a man cannot but say, ' Lord, what am I, that thou hast
' brought me hitherto? What, for such a peevish,
' unbelieving, impatient soul as mine is, to be carried in thy arms, and cheared with thy smiles,
' and to enjoy the comforts of thy spirit? Oh!
' what a wonderful merciful gracious God have I?'

Yet in all this, I exclude not the spirit in drawing a rational evidence from scriptures; certainly the spirit helps in a general way, by making use of our reason, only it elevates and improves our reason to a farther assurance by a supernatural assistance, as in prayer, and in preaching of the word, there may be a common assistance of the spirit of God, but there is another kind of praying and preaching by the spirit, which the scripture often speaks of, and calls *the spirit of supplication, and the demonstrations of the spirit;* and that is not performed by a common or general, but by a special and particular assistance of the spirit of God; so there is a two-fold influence of the spirit in putting forth acts of assurance in the heart, even of a godly and sound Christian; the very same man may act assurance, sometimes rationally, and sometimes spiritually; in the former the spirit acts too, but in a common way, only in the latter is the supernatural, special assistance, which peculiarly is said to be the witness of the spirit. I speak not against rational evidences, only it concerns us to apply ourselves to the spirit to superadd his testimony: O! let us not so content ourselves with rational evidences, but that we labour to elevate the evidences of reason into a testimony of the holy Spirit of God. To wind up all I have said,——

O my soul! try now the hope of the spirit's indwelling by these several signs; art thou enlightened savingly in the knowledge of God, and of Christ? Art thou a child of God, one of his adopted sons, for whom he hath reserved the inheritance? Hast thou a spirit of grace and supplication? A spirit of sanctification? A spirit of love? Art thou led by the spirit? Dost thou feel the drawings of thy soul in every duty to Jesus Christ? Dost thou feel a liberty, or a delight in thy soul to walk in the way to his commandments? Dost thou feel any strength to come in against thy corruptions? Dost thou feel the spirit's help to act in gospel-duties for gospel-ends? Hast thou ever had the immediate testimony of the Spirit? Or, if not so, hast thou ever had the immediate testimony of the spirit without any argumentation? Hast thou unexpectedly dipt and lighted on some place of scripture, that hath satisfied thy soul, as with marrow and fatness? Or, if not so neither, hast thou the mediate testimony of the spirit with argumentation? Canst thou argue thus, *He that believes shall be saved, but I believe,*

there-

therefore I shall be saved. Or, if any doubt be made of the assumption, Canst thou prove it by such other graces as accompany faith, and are the fruits of faith? Canst thou say by the help of the spirit, and shinings of the spirit, that these, and these graces are in me, and have been acted by me; yea, *I do love God and Christ, I do repent of my sins, &c.* Surely then thy hope is well-grounded, thou hast the indwelling of the spirit; it is thine, even thine.

SECT. V.

Of believing in Jesus in that respect.

5. Let us believe on Jesus, as carrying on the great work of our salvation for us in these particulars, many scruples are in many hearts, 'What, is it possible that I should have any share 'in Christ's ascension, Christ's session, Christ's mis-'sion of his Spirit? Was it ever in God's heart 'that I should partake with Christ in all these glo-'ries? If it must be so, that he would let out his 'loves to so unworthy a wretch, was it not suffici-'ent for him to have come down from heaven, and 'to have acted my redemption here below? Is 'it not an high favour that a king should leave 'his court, to give a poor prisoner in the goal a 'visit? But will he take him with him to his own 'home, and bring him into his own presence-'chamber, and set him at his right hand in his 'throne? And so that Christ should not only 'leave his Father's throne, and give me a visit, 'lying in the dark dungeon of unbelief, but that 'he should take off the bolts and set open the prison 'doors, and take me up with him into heaven, 'and there set me down at his right hand, and in 'the mean time give me the earnest and pledge of 'my inheritance, by filling my soul with his own 'Spirit; O! what an admirable incredible thing 'is this? It was the last vision of John, which was 'so full of wonders, *And I John saw the holy city,* 'the new Jerusalem coming down from God out 'of heaven.——*And I heard a great voice out of* 'heaven, saying, Behold the tabernacle of God is 'with men, and he will dwell with them, Rev. 'xxi. 2, 3. Surely it was a miraculous mercy that 'heaven should come down unto earth, and that 'God should come down to men: but, oh! what 'is this, that earth should go up to heaven, that 'men should ascend up to God? Yea, that my 'soul, with Christ, and by Christ, should ascend 'to God, and sit down with God in heavenly pla-'ces? Yea, that my soul should have for its in-'mate the very same Spirit that Christ himself 'hath? Oh! I cannot, I will not, I dare not be-'lieve.'

Scrupulous souls, be not faithless, but believing; there is none of these particulars for which we have not a warrant out of the word of God; and therefore believe: but that I may persuade to purpose, I shall lay down, 1. Some directions, and 2. Some encouragements of faith.

1. For directions of faith, observe these particulars. As,——

1. Faith must directly go to Christ.
2. Faith must go to Christ, as God in the flesh.
3. Faith must go to Christ, as God in the flesh, made under the law.
4. Faith must go to Christ, not only as made under the directive part of the law by his life, but under the penal part of the law by his death.
5. Faith must go to Christ, not only as put to death in the flesh, but as quickned by the Spirit: of all these before.
6. Faith must not only go to Christ as quickned by the Spirit, but as going up into glory, as sitting down at God's right hand, and as sending the Holy Ghost; faith should eye Christ as far as he goes if he be ascended; so should faith, if he go into glory, and sit down there, and act there for his people; so should faith, and so should we in a way of believing follow after him, and take a view of all his transactions where he is; we have heard before how faith should go to Christ as dying, and as rising again, but yet faith is low, while it doth not go within the vail, and see him in glory; it is not enough to have only a faith of justification, but of glorification. O! come let us see Christ in heaven, and we can have no less than a glorious faith! how many are there that never yet came to act faith in Christ as a glorified Christ; we are yet still in the lower form; many of us take in no more of Christ than what was done on the cross, or what some natural, and common resemblances of him can hold forth, we seldom follow Christ into heaven, to see what he is doing there for us. O my soul! and O my faith! mount up, and be

on

on the wing! Christ is gone up to heaven, Christ is set down at God's right hand, Christ hath sent down his holy Spirit: to this purpose, it was expedient that he should go away, and now he is gone away to do something that remains to be done for thee in his kingdom; he had still some glorious peace to frame for thy salvation, and therefore he left this world, and went to his Father, that he might act it in glory; and now he is invested with all the riches of heaven, he hath all the keys of heaven and hell, he hath all power to command, he hath received all the promise to himself, and all that he hath to do, it is to let out of himself again unto his saints; he hath not only got his Father's heart for them, but he hath got all his riches to bestow upon them; when he came to heaven, the Father bad him sit down at his right hand, and take what he would, and bestow what he would upon his saints? and thereupon he gave gifts unto men, yea, he gave the gift of gifts, even the Holy Ghost himself: what, art not thou a partaker of this gift? O! then look up unto Jesus in reference to all these actings; set him before thee, Christ in all these particulars, is a right object for thy faith to act upon.

7. Faith in going to Christ, his ascension, session, and mission of the Spirit, it is principally to look to the purpose, intent, and design of Christ in each of these particulars: Christ did nothing but he had an end, a meaning in it for our good; and here is the life of faith to eye the meaning of Christ in all his doings. Now the ends of Christ's ascension, session, and mission of his Spirit were several; I shall instance only in these few. As,—

1. Christ ascended that we might ascend: look whatever God acted on Christ's person, that he did as in our behalf, and he means to act the same on us; was Christ crucified? So are we; is Christ risen again? So are we risen together with him. Is Christ gone up into glory? So are we; heaven is now opened and possessed by Jesus Christ for us, and, at last, we shall ascend even as he ascended. Christ cannot be content with that glory he hath himself until we be with him, *Father, I will, that those also whom thou hast given me, be with me where I am, that they may behold, or enjoy my glory which thou hast given me,* John xvii. 24. Christ, as our head is in glory, and so we are there already with him, and Christ as our advocate is in glory, and there he is pleading and praying for us, that we may actually be received and brought up to him, *Father, I will, that those whom thou hast given me may be with me.* Christ's crown of glory is, as it were, a burden on his own head, until it be set on the heads of all his saints; O! the blessed end of Christ's ascension; how should faith pry into this? Believers; you see your object, you know his person, never be quiet until you come into his condition, as we must go through all ordinances and creatures till we come to Christ, so through all conditions of Christ until we come to glory.

2. Christ sat down that we might sit with him in heavenly places; what is the end of Christ's session, but that he might invest all his saints with the same privilege? In this height of glory, Christ is the pattern, and platform, and idea of what we shall be; surely this is the very top of heaven, Christ is exalted above the heavens, that we might in our measure and proportion be exalted with Christ; it was Christ's prayer that his Father, and he, and we, might all be one, *As thou Father art in me, and I in thee, that they also may be one in us,* John xvii. 21. Oh! how should faith stand, and gaze on Jesus Christ in this respect? What, is he on God's right hand? And is he there preparing a room, a seat, and mansion for my soul? What, shall I sit at the right hand of Christ? Shall I sit as an assessor on his judgment-seat to judge the world with Jesus Christ? *When the Son of man shall sit on the throne of his glory, ye also shall sit upon twelve thrones, judging the twelve tribes of Israel,* Matth. xix. 28. Oh! what is this? Had not Christ said it, how could I have believed it? Admire, O my soul, at this aim of Christ! the meaning of his exalting himself, it was to exalt thee, and the meaning of his exalting thee on this manner, it is to manifest to all the world, what the Son of God is able to do, in raising so poor a creature, to so rich a glory. O the end of Christ's sitting at God's right hand! hereby the saints are Christ's assessors; lords of the higher house, the king's peers to judge the world with him? Christ divides (as it were) the throne with them, *I appoint unto you a kingdom, as my Father hath appointed unto me, that ye may eat and drink at my table, in my kingdom, and sit on thrones judging the twelve tribes of Israel,* Luke xxii. 29, 30.

3. Christ

3. Christ sent down the Holy Ghost, that he might dwell in our souls, endow us with gifts and graces, that he might comfort us, seal us unto the day of redemption, fit us for glory. Amongst the many ends for which Christ sent down his holy Spirit, I shall insist only on these two——

1. That he might help us *to cry, Abba, Father*, and make us to come boldly to the throne of grace, as children to a Father. It is the Spirit that takes us by the hand, and leads us to the Father, when others stand at a distance, and cannot come near: as a prince's son is admitted at all times, tho' others are kept out by officers and guards; so tho' there be never so much darkness, and fire, and terror about God, yet the adopted child, who hath received the Spirit of adoption, can say, ' Make way there, and ' let me come to my Father, guards are appointed ' to keep out strangers but not sons:' and no wonder, for *the Spirit makes intercession for us with groanings which cannot be uttered*, Rom. viii. 26. The Spirit teacheth us what to pray, and how to pray as we ought; the Spirit puts a courage and boldness into the hearts of his saints, even to admiration; this appears in that sometimes they have beset God with his promises, that he could no way get off, *Quicken me according to thy word*, Psal. cxix. 25.——*And strengthen me according to thy word*, ver. 28. *And be merciful unto me according to thy word*, ver. 58. *And uphold me according to thy word*, ver. 161. *And give me understanding according to thy word*, ver 169. And sometimes they have beset God with their challenges of his justice, faithfulness, and righteousness: so David, *Deliver me in thy righteousness*, Ps. xxxi. 1. *And judge me according to thy righteousness*, Ps. xxxv. 24. *And quicken me according to thy righteousness*, Ps. cxix. 40. *And in thy faithfulness answer me, and in thy righteousness*, Psal. cxliii. 1. Why, this is the Spirit's work, he helps our infirmities, he emboldens our spirits in their approaches to God: surely it is one end of the Spirit's mission, *Because ye are sons, God hath sent forth the Spirit of his son into our hearts, crying, Abba, Father*, Gal. iv. 6. I will not deny that bastards, strangers without the covenant, having no right to God as their Father, may yet petition God, as a subdued people do their conqueror, or as ravens cry to God for food, or as some *howl upon their beds for corn and wine*, Hos. vii. 14. But they cannot pray; in right prayer there are not only required gracious ingredients in the action, but also a new state of adoption and filiation: many speak words to God, who do not pray; many tell over their sins, who confess not their sins to God, many speak good of God, who do not praise God; thousands claim Fathership in God, where there is no sonship, nor ground in the thing itself. A new nature is only that best bottom of prayer that takes it off from being a taking of God's name in vain. Now this is the fruit of the Spirit, and one of those ends of the Spirit's mission.

2. That he might guide us into all truth, I mean into all necessary, fundamental, saving truths; in this respect we have need of the Spirit in these days. He it is that dictates to us which is the true religion; he it is that transcribes upon our hearts, that which was before only written in our books; he it is that not only reveals truth from without, but imprints it also on the soul, as a man doth a seal by impressing it on the wax, to this purpose saith the apostle, *He that believeth on the Son of God hath the witness in himself*, 1 John v. 10. How in himself? I answer, 1. In that the Spirit gives him the habit of faith. 2. In that the Spirit causeth him to bring it forth into act. 3. In that the Spirit stamps on the soul all those other impressions of desire, hope, love, joy, or whatever else we call the new nature, so that now there is a new nature within him, he hath new thoughts, new designs, new desires, new hopes, new loves, new delights, he drives a new trade (as it were) in this world for another world; he is become in Christ a new creature, *Old things are passed away, and all things are become new*, 2 Cor. v. 17. And from hence we may soundly argue the truth of our religion. Mark this, as the written word is the testimony without us, so are these impressions on the Spirit the testimony within us, by which we may know every necessary truth as it is in Jesus; this is the meaning of the apostle, *He that believeth hath the witness in himself*. Unbelievers have indeed a testimony without them, but believers have a double testimony, one without, and one within; and this witness within us, will go with us which way soever we go; it will accompany us through all straits and difficulties. The external testimony may be taken from us; men may take from us our Bibles, our teachers, our friends;

riends; or they may imprison us where we cannot enjoy them; but they cannot take from us the Spirit of Christ; this witness within, is a permanent, settled, habituate, standing witness; O! what an excellent help is here, that a poor Christian hath beyond all the furniture of the most learned men that want this testimony of the Spirit of Christ? Surely this advantage will exceedingly furnish us against all temptations to any error, that is plainly contrary to the essentials of religion. One of our divines puts a case ——

*If the devil, or any seducer, would draw us to doubt, whether there be indeed a Christ, or whether he did rise again, ascended, sat down at God's right hand, and thence sent down the Holy Ghost? What an excellent advantage is it against this temptation, when we can repair to our own hearts, and there find a Christ, or a Spirit of Christ within us? O! saith the sanctified soul, 'Have I felt Christ relieving me in my lost condition, delivering me from my captivity, reconciling me to God, and bringing me with boldness into his glorious presence? And, now after all this, Shall I doubt whether there be a Christ in heaven, or a Spirit of Christ in my heart on earth? Have I felt him new-creating me, opening my dark eyes, and bringing me from darkness into his marvellous light, and from the power of Satan unto God, binding the strong man, and casting him out, and yet shall I question, whether there be a Christ, or a Spirit of Christ? Hath he made me love the things which I hated, and hate that which I loved? Hath he given me such a taste of the powers of the world to come, and possessed me with the hopes of glory with himself, and given me a treasure and portion in God, and set my heart where my treasure is, and caused me in some measure to have my conversation in heaven above, and yet shall I doubt, whether there be a Christ above, or a Spirit within? O! what an impudent lying Spirit is this, that would tempt me against so much experience?' And thus may a believer argue from the testimony that is within.

I know some seeming saints have fallen off into as great blasphemies as these I have named; witness the quakers and ranters, &c. But I may say of such as John did, *They went out from us, but they were not of us, for if they had been of us, they would no doubt have continued with us,* 1 John ii 19 It is no wonder if Satan prevail against those that gave Christ no deeper room but in their phantasy, and that did never heartily close with him in love. But for those that have the Spirit of Christ within them, it is not so with them. If they cannot answer the cavils of Satan, or of any of his instruments, yet they can hold fast the grounds of faith; Christ hath a deep room and interest in their spirits; he is held faster by the heart than by the head alone; love will hold Christ, when reason alone would let him go; his ear is nailed (as it were) unto his door, and because he loveth him, he would not leave him *Who shall separate him from the love of Christ? Shall tribulation, or distress, or persecution, or famine, or nakedness, or peril, or sword?* (*As it is written, For thy sake we are killed all the day long*) *nay, in all these things we are more than conquerors through him that loved us,* Rom. viii. 35, 36, 37. A modern writer brings in a sincere heart, paraphrasing (as it were) on this text, in this manner, †*Who shall separate me from the love of Christ?* O thou malicious devil, thou dost hunt me with thy fiery darts! O you dull heretics, infidels, blasphemers, that fill up my ears with your foolish sophisms, and trouble me with your disputes against my Lord and Redeemer! go to him that knows him only by the hearing of the ear, if thou mean to prevail; but I have known him by the sweet experiences of my soul; go to him that makes a religion of his opinions, and whose belief was never any deeper than his fancy, and whose piety never reached higher than to abstinency and tasks of formal duty; these you may possibly draw away from Christ. But do you think to do so by me? Why, tell me how? With what weapons or arguments can you think to prevail? What, shall tribulation be the means? No, no, I have that promise in the hand of my faith, and that glory in the eye of my hope, that will bring me through all tribulations under heaven: or, shall distress do it? Why, I will rather stick so much closer to him that will relieve me in distress, and bring me to his rest. Or, will you affright me by persecution? I am assured that this is the nearest way to

---

* Mr Baxter's Spirits witness to the truth of Christianity.   † Mr Baxter ibid.

heaven, and I am bleſſed of Chriſt, when I am perſecuted for righteouſneſs ſake. Or, ſhall nakedneſs be the weapon? I had rather paſs naked out of this world to heaven, than to be clothed in purple, and to be ſtript of it at death, and to be caſt into hell; Adam's innocent nakedneſs, and Lazarus's rags were better than that Epicure's gay apparel.—Or, ſhall famine be the means? Why, man liveth not by bread alone, I had rather my body had famiſhed than my ſoul; I have meat to eat that ye know not of, even the bread of life, which whoſo eats ſhall live for ever. Or, will you affright me from Chriſt by the ſword of violence? I know that the Lord whom I believe in, and ſerve, is able to deliver me out of your hands; but if he will not, be it known to you I will not forſake him; your ſword will only be the key to open the priſon doors, and let out my ſoul that hath long deſired to be with Jeſus Chriſt. If ye tell me of peril, I know no danger ſo great as of loſing Chriſt and ſalvation; and of bearing his wrath that can kill both body and ſoul: do I not read in certain hiſtories of that noble army of martyrs, who loved the Lord Jeſus to the death, and gloried in tribulation, and would not by the flames of fire, or jaws of lions, be ſeparated from Jeſus Chriſt? Did not they paſs through the Red-ſea, as on dry ground, to the promiſed land, yea, though *they were killed all the day long, and accounted as ſheep to the ſlaughter?* Did they not ſtick and cleave faſt to the Lord, and to the captain of their ſalvation? Nay, were they not in all this conquerors, and more than conquerors, triumphing in flames, to the confuſion of Satan, and all other enemies; as Chriſt triumphed on the croſs, *deſtroying by death the prince of death,* Heb. ii. 14. Oh! what a bleſſed advantage is it againſt all temptations to have the impreſs of the goſpel of Chriſt on our heart, and the witneſs in ourſelves?

But I hear ſome object, if the witneſs in ourſelves be ſo full and convincing, then what need have we any more to make uſe of ſcriptures or miniſters? Why, ſhould we leave an higher teacher to go to a lower?

But I anſwer, 1. There is more than one thing wanting to enwiſe us to ſalvation, as, *firſt,* An outward word. And, 2*dly,* an outward teacher. And, 2*dly,* an inward light. And accordingly, God ſupplies this threefold want, the *firſt,* by giving us the ſcripture, the *ſecond,* by giving us a miniſtry, and other occaſional teachers; the *third,* by giving us the illumination of the Spirit, to help us to ſee by the former means, and to make the word and miniſtry to us effectual. Now it were a mad thing for a man to ſay, I have eyes to read in a book, and therefore I have no need of the light of candle or of ſun; or I have eyes, and ſun, and therefore I have no need of the light in the air which cometh from the ſun; or I have the light both of the eye, and ſun, and air, and therefore I can read by it without a book; or I have a book, and therefore I can read it without a teacher: certainly if a man would read, he muſt have all theſe, or more then one of theſe; ſo God hath appointed us three neceſſary means for our illumination and direction, the word, the miniſtry, and the Spirit; *What God hath joined, let no man ſeparate*; if any would fooliſhly go, and ſet one of theſe againſt another, when God hath ſet them altogether, and made them all neceſſary, aſſigning to each a ſeveral part in the work of our illumination, they may abuſe God and themſelves, and go without the light, while they deſpiſe the neceſſary cauſes of it, God's evidences muſt not be ſeparated, much leſs muſt one be pleaded to the neglect of all the reſt; as the work within us is not the firſt teſtimony, but a ſecondary confirming teſtimony, ſo doth it not make the firſt unneceſſary or void; beſides that, by the external teſtimony, we muſt convince other men, which by the witneſs within us we cannot do. But this only by the way.

2. For the encouragement of our faith to believe in Chriſt as in reference to his aſcenſion, ſeſſion, and miſſion of his Spirit,

1. Conſider of the excellency of this object; What is it but Chriſt? Chriſt in his aſcending, culminant, regnant power? Chriſt in his marching, conquering, triumphing poſtures? In his free, and large, and magnificent gifts, 'When he aſcended on high, he led captivity captive, and gave gifts unto men.' O the glory! O the excellency of Chriſt in theſe reſpects! verily they are enough to tire out men and angels with the only act of wondering and ſurveying of their vaſtneſs. Here is goſpel-work for all eternity, to dig into this goldmine, to roll and turn this ſoul-delighting precious ſtone, to behold, enquire, and ſearch into theſe depths and heights of Chriſt exalted: and I believe

this

Carrying on the great Work of our Salvation in his Ascension into Heaven.

this the satiety, the top, and prince of heaven's glory to see and wonder at the virtues of him that sits on the throne, at the right hand of God; to be filled but never satiate with the glory of Christ. What, Christ ascended? Christ set down in glory? And Christ sending down his holy Spirit? Here's a compendium of all glories; here is one for an heart to be taken with, made up of nothing, but of several mysteries of glory.

2. Consider the power, virtue, and influence of this object in our souls salvation; oh! what a stately tower have we here erected to see heaven on? faith may stand (as it were) on this mount, and see itself in glory; oh! the flowings, the rich emanations of grace and glory that come from hence! come, let us draw, the well is deep; all the drops and dewings that fall on men or angels are but as chips in comparison of that huge and boundless body of the fulness of grace, that is in Christ: one lily is nothing to a boundless and broad field of lilies; Christ is in these respects the mountain of roses; oh! how high, how capacious, how full, how beautiful, how green? Could we but 'smell him who 'feeds among the lilies, till the day breaks, and 'the shadows fly away?' Could we but dive into the golden veins of these unsearchable riches of Jesus Christ, we should say, *It is good to be here?* Oh! it is good to gather up the fragments that fall from Christ; his crown shines with diamonds and pearls; oh! why do we toil ourselves in gathering sticks, when to-morrow we shall be out of this world and go to Christ? Come, where is our mouth of faith? 'Let us lay it to here, let us suck and be satisfied 'with these breasts of consolation, let us milk out, 'and be delighted with the abundance of his glory.'

3. Consider of the suitableness of these objects to our several conditions; you may remember the first cry, 'Was it not love enough for Christ to 'come down, and to visit us here; but that he 'must go up and take us with him' No, no; his love was so great and vast, that for our sakes he moves up and down; this ravished the spouse, *Behold he comes leaping upon the mountains, and skipping upon the hills,* Ca. ii 8. Gregory that measured his leaps, thus gives them; he first leaps from his Father's mansion to his mother's womb; from her womb to his cratch; from his cratch to his cross; from his cross to his grave; from his grave up again to heaven; great leaps indeed, that shewed both his readiness to love, and willingness to save: infinite love can never be out-tired with greatest actions. But another cries, How should I believe that Christ is exalted, and that by virtue thereof I shall be exalted, when I see myself in a forlorn condition, forsaken of God, an object amongst men; *A'as! man at his best is altogether vanity, yea, men of low degree are vanity, and men of high degree are a lie; to be laid in the balance, I am altogether lighter than vanity; how then should I believe any such a condition? Is a worm a fit or a capable subject to wear a crown?* Psal. lxii. 9. Yes, the Lord is great, and he can do great things, *He raiseth up the poor out of the dust, and lifteth up the beggar from the dunghill, to set them among princes, and to make them inherit the throne of glory; for the pillars of the earth are the Lord's and he hath set the world upon them, he will keep the feet of his saints,* 1 Sam. ii. 8, 9.——Why, there is my sadness, cries another, 'He will keep 'the feet of his saints; if I were but a saint, I 'could believe his power; but alas! I am an un-'holy, an unsanctified piece of clay; I am a sin-'ner, a sinner of the Gentiles, chief of sinners; 'I deserve to be thrown down to hell, rather than 'to be invested with glory, and to sit in heaven' True, but yet the Holy Ghost is given to make thee holy; of thyself, thou art vile, and most vile; but hath not the Holy Ghost entred in, and taken possession of thy Spirit? Hath he not washed thee 'with water? Yea, thoroughly washed away thy 'blood? Hath he not anointed thee with oil, and 'covered thee with silk, and decked thee with 'gold and silver, and made thee comely through 'his comeliness, which he put upon thee?' Why, this is the office of the Holy Ghost, and if thou hast but the indwelling of the Spirit, this is thy state: I know there is a part of thee unregenerate; and it will be so whilst thou art on earth, but withal there is in thee a new nature, another nature; there is something else within thee which makes thee wrestle against sin, and shall in time prevail over all sin, and this is the Spirit of Christ, sanctifying of thee, *Being sanctified* (saith the apostle) *by the Holy Ghost,* Rom. xv. 16.——Other complaints may be thus brought in, but if we understand the meaning, the design of Christ in his ascension, session, and mission of his Spirit, How might a true faith answer all? Oh believe! believe thy

part in Christ's ascension, Christ's session, Christ's mission of his holy Spirit, and thou mayest go singing to thy grave; a lively faith in such particulars would set a soul in heaven, even whilst yet on earth.

SECT. VI.

Of loving Jesus in that respect.

6. LEt us love Jesus, as carrying on the great work of our salvation for us in these particulars; much hath been said already of Christ's conception, birth, life, death, resurrection; such arguments of love, as are enough to swallow up souls in love to Christ again; O! the treasures of love, and wisdom, and that have been opened in former passages! but as if all those were not enough for God, see here new gold-mines, new found-out jewels, never known to be in the world before, opened and unfolded in Jesus Christ. Here are the incomes of the beams of light most inaccessible; here are the veins of the unsearchable glories of Jesus Christ; as if we saw every moment a new heaven, a new treasure of love; the bosom of Christ is yet more opened; the new breathings and spirations of love, are yet more manifested. See! Christ for us, and for salvation is gone up to heaven, is set down at God's right hand, and hath sent down the Holy Ghost into our hearts; in the pouring out of these springs of heaven's love, how should our souls but open the mouth wide and take in the streams of Christ's nectar, honey and milk, I mean his sweet, and precious, and dear love-breathings? We have heard of Christ's invitations, *Come to me all ye that are weary and heavy-laden*, Matth. xi. 28. But suppose Christ had never uttered his love in such a love-expression, *Come to me*, yet Christ himself in these glorious particulars is such a drawing object, (the very beauty of Christ, the very smell of the garments of Christ, the very capacious and wide heaven of Christ's exaltation are intrinsically, and of themselves, such drawing, ravishing, winning objects) that upon the apprehension of them we cannot chuse but love Christ: as gold that is dumb and cannot speak, yet the beauty and gain of it crieth aloud, 'Come hither poor creature, and be thou made 'rich;' so if Christ should never open his lips, if he should never gently move, *Open to me, my sister, my love, my dove, my undefiled, for my head is full of dew, and my locks with the drops of the night*, Cant. v. 2. Yet the glory, the power, the sovereignty of Christ, the exaltation of his person, and the magnificence of his gifts, should even change our souls into a globe or mass of divine love and glory, *as it were by the Spirit of the Lord*, 1 Cor. iii. 18.

Two things I shall instance, which may be as the load-stones of our love to Christ; the first is his glory, and the second his bounty.

1. For his glory; no sooner was he ascended, and set down at God's right hand, but John the divine had a sight of him, and Oh! what a glorious sight! *He was clothed with a garment down to the foot, and girt about the paps with a golden girdle; his head and his hairs were white like wool, as white as snow; and his eyes were as a flame of fire, and his feet like unto fine brass, as if they burned in a furnace, and his voice as the sound of many waters; and he had in his right hand seven stars, and out of his mouth went a sharp two-edged sword, and his countenance was as the sun that shineth in his strength*, Rev. i. 13, 14, 15, 16. When John saw him thus, he swoons at his feet, but Christ for all his glory, holds his head in his swoon, saying, *Fear not, I am the first and the last; I am he that liveth, and was dead, and behold I am alive for evermore, Amen. And have the keys of hell and of death*, ver. 17, 18. A glorious Christ, is good for swooning, dying sinners; would sinners but draw near, and come and see this king in the chariot of love, and come see his beauty, the uncreated white and red in his sweet countenance, he would certainly draw their souls unto him. Nay, say that all the damned in hell were brought up with their burning fiery chains to the utmost door of heaven; could we strike up a window, and let them look in, and behold the throne, and the Lamb, and the troops of glorified spirits clothed in white, with crowns of gold on their heads, and palms in their hands, singing the eternal praises of their glorious king; Oh! how would they be sweetened in their pain, and convinced of their foolish choice, and ravished with the fulness of those joys and pleasures that are in Christ's face for evermore? Surely much more may this glory of Christ warm thy heart: O my soul! what an happiness were it to see the king on his throne; to see the Lamb, the fair tree of life, the branches which cannot, for the

narrow-

narrowness of the place, have room to grow in, *For the heaven of heavens cannot contain him?* What an happiness were it to see love itself, and to be warmed with the heat of immediate love, that comes out of the precious heart and bowels of this princely and royal standard-bearer? As yet thou canst not, must not see these sights, there is no seeing the king thus in his beauty till thou comest to glory; for then, and then must thou see him face to face; and yet the idea and image of his glory is seen and may be seen of every true believing soul; enough may be seen by an eye of faith, to kindle in thine heart a flame of love to the Lord Jesus Christ: Oh! who can think of the glory that is in this dainty delightful one, and not be swallowed up in love? Who can think of Christ's sitting at God's right hand, and sparkling in this glory round about, and casting out beams of glory through east, and west, and north, and south, thro' heaven, and earth, and hell, and not love him with the whole heart, soul and might? I remember one dying, and hearing some discourse of Jesus Christ: 'Oh! *(said she)* speak more of this, let me hear 'more of this; be not weary of telling his praise, 'I long to see him, how should I but long to hear of him?' Surely I cannot say too much of Jesus Christ; in this blessed subject, no man can possibly hyperbolize; had I the tongues of men and angels, I could never fully set forth Christ; it involves an eternal contradiction that the creature can see to the bottom of the Creator. Suppose all the sands on the sea-shore, all the flowers, herbs, leaves, twigs of trees in woods and forests, all the stars of heaven, were all rational creatures, and had they that wisdom, and tongues of angels to speak of the loveliness, beauty, glory, and excellency of Christ, ' as gone to heaven, and sitting at the right ' hand of his Father,' they would in all their expressions stay millions of miles on this side Jesus Christ. O! the loveliness, beauty, and glory of his countenance! can I speak, or you hear of such a Christ? And are we not all in a burning love, in a seraphical love, or at least in a conjugal love? O my heart! how is it thou art not love-sick? How is it thou dost not charge the daughters of Jerusalem, as the spouse did, *I charge you, O daughters of Jerusalem, if you find my beloved, that ye tell him, I am sick of love,* Cant. v. 8.

2. For his bounty; no sooner was he ascended, and set down at God's right hand, but *he gives gifts unto men;* and he sends down the Holy Ghost. This was the gift of gifts; I shall only weigh two circumstances in this gift, either whereof both dignifies, and casts a sparkle of bounty from the giver, into the heart of the receiver to move him to love As,—

1. One circumstance is the greatness of the giver; certainly the preeminence or dignity of any principle ennobleth and enhanceth the effect; a gift coming from a great person carries ever a scent with it of a certain greatness, and relisheth either of excellency, or superiority, or nobility, or all. It is storied of Charles the fifth, that in his wars being ever prest with want of money, and so unable to remunerate the services of divers Dutch captains, and nobles, whom he had entertained; he used after any great exploit performed by them, to call together his nobles, and camp into such a field, and there in the presence of them all, to take a gold chain from about his own neck, and to put it about the neck of such a captain, or such a colonel, and so to embrace him, and to give thanks for his gallant service: why, this they esteemed a greater favour, (being circumstanced by such a person, in such a way) than if in very deed he had given him a sufficient pay, or remuneration. O! they valued that chain more than many bushels of the like gold; the very person of the emperor hanged at the chain such a precious jewel, as in warlike conceits, a million of gold could not countervail; O my soul! if an emperor thus gained the affections of men, how shouldest thou but love Christ, the great emperor of heaven and earth? It was he that gave thee his Spirit, it was he that *took off the spirit which is upon him,* (so is the expression of God to Moses) *and put it upon thee,* Numb. xi. 17. And doth not the person of Christ, the dignity of Christ, enhance the value of the gift? As all gifts are signs of love, so the love of a great personage, and the gifts issuing from such a love, ought more to be accounted than any gifts of any meaner person whatsoever.

2. Another circumstance is the greatness of the gift; this argueth greatness of good will; and consequently deserveth a correspondence of a semblable affection. Now, what greater gift had Christ in store, than to give his own Spirit? The Spirit proceedeth from him, and is the same essence

fence with himself; the Spirit is the third person of the true and only Godhead, proceeding from the Father, and the Son; and co-eternal, and co-equal, and consubstantial with the Father, and the Son; this appears by those divine attributes and properties which are attributed, and communicated to the holy Spirit. as, 1. Eternity. God never was without his Spirit, *In the beginning God created heaven and earth,* —— *and the Spirit of God moved upon the face of the waters*, Gen. i. 1, 2. 2. Omnipotency, because he, with the Father, and the Son, createth and preserveth all things, *By his Spirit he hath garnished the heaven ; the Spirit of God hath made me,* Job xxvi 13 —— xxxiii 4. *And all these things worketh that one and the self-same Spirit, dividing to every man severally as he will,* 1 Cor. xii. 11. 3. Omnisciency, or the knowledge of all things, *For the Spirit searcheth all things, yea, the deep things of God,* 1 Cor. ii. 10. 4. Immutability, or unchangeableness, *Men, and brethren, this scripture must needs have been fulfilled which the Holy Ghost spake,* Acts i. 16. 5. Infinite mercy, or love, *God is love,— and the love of God is shed abroad in our hearts by the Holy Ghost, which is given unto us,* Rom. v. 5. 6. Holy indignation, even against hidden sins, *They rebelled, and vexed his holy Spirit,* Isa. lxiii. 10. *Why hath Satan filled thy heart to lie to the Holy Ghost ?* —— *Thou hast not lied unto men, but unto God,* (a plain text for the divinity of the Holy Ghost)—*How is it that ye have agreed together to tempt the Spirit of the Lord?* Acts v. 3, 4, 9. *Grieve not the holy Spirit of God, whereby ye are sealed unto the day of redemption,* Eph. iv. 30. I might add miracles, and the institution of sacraments, and prophesies, and gifts, and graces, as the effects of his divinity: I cast out devils (saith Christ) *by the Spirit of God, and baptize in the name of the Father, and of the Son, and of the Holy Ghost,* Matt. xii. 28 — xxviii. 19 *And the Spirit speaketh expresly, that in the latter times, some shall depart from the faith,* 1 Tim. iv. 1. *And we are changed into the same image from glory to glory, even as by the Spirit of the Lord,* 2 Cor. iii. 18. See now how the holy Spirit is God, co-eternal, co-equal, and consubstantial with God the Father, and God the Son; is not this a great gift? Yea, as great a gift as possibly can be given? what, can he do more than to give himself, and to give his Spirit? O the bonds of love that are upon man towards Christ in this respect!

Come, my soul, and take a view of the glory and bounty of Jesus Christ? If thy heart be not all brass, and iron, and stone, if there be any fleshiness, softness, or pliableness in it, why; then how shouldest thou choose but love; if either beauty or bounty, if either majesty, or magnificence can draw thy affection, Christ will have it, for in him is all; O let him be thy all! surely if thou hast any thing besides himself, he is the donor of all. he is the beauty of all, the sum of all, the perfection of all, he is the author, preserver, and finisher of all.

SECT. VII.

Of joying in Jesus in that respect.

7. Let us joy in Jesus as carrying on the great work of our salvation for us in these particulars; there is not a particular under consideration, but 'tis the object of a Christian's joy. As,—

1. How should it heighten my joys, and enlarge my comforts, when I do but consider that Christ is ascended into glory? By this it is clear and evident, that Christ is accepted of the Father for me, or otherwise, he should never have been received into heaven; if any frown had been in the face of God, surely Christ coming so near God, he should have had it; if any exception had been against his satisfaction, any flaw in our pardons, surely Christ should have heard of it, yea, without question, he must have been turned out of heaven, until he had made a full payment of our debts. I need not doubt of my acceptance at the throne of grace, when Jesus Christ is accepted for me, and that I stand in such a relation to Jesus Christ. Oh! what joy is in this?

2. How should it heighten my joys, and enlarge my comforts, when I do but consider that Christ is set down at God's right hand. Why, now he hath the keys of heaven delivered into his hands, *All power is given unto him in heaven and in earth,* Matth. xxviii. 18. And now he can do what he will; God the Father hath given away (as it were) all his prerogatives unto Jesus Christ, *All judgment is committed to the Son, for the Father judgeth no man,* John v. 22. Now, he is in a capacity of acting

ing out all his love, and the Father's desire to me in the most glorious way; he is highly advanced, and thereby he hath the advantage to advance me, and to glorify me; God hath given into his hands, all the treasures and riches of heaven, in bidding him, *sit down at his right hand*, he told him that he would have no more to do with the world, but that Christ should have all, and that Christ should bestow all he had amongst his saints; and that this should be the reward of his death, and when once his saints were come about him, and sat with him in his glory, why, then Christ should resign up again his place, *And deliver up the kingdom to God, even the Father*, 1 Cor. xv. 24. Oh! what joy may enter into this poor dark dungeon, disconsolate soul of mine, whilst I but think over these glorious passages of my Christ in glory?

3. How should it heighten my joys, and fill me with joy unspeakable, and full of glory, when I do consider that Christ hath sent down his holy Spirit into my heart? When sorrow hath filled the apostles hearts, because he had told them, *I must go away*, he comforts them with this, *If I go not away, the comforter will not come unto you, but if I depart, I will send him unto you*, John xvi. 7. The Spirit is the comforter, and where he comes he fills souls with comforts; O! what comfort is this to know that the Spirit of Christ is my inmate? That my soul is the temple, the receptacle, the house and dwelling of the Spirit of God? That Christ is in me of a truth, and that not only by the infusion of his grace, but by the indwelling of his Spirit? Surely it is some comfort to a sickly man that he hath a physician always in the house with him; and to a woman that is near her travail, that the midwife is in the house with her; but what comfort is it to a poor soul that the Spirit of Christ is always in him? *I will send you another comforter* (said Christ) *that he may abide with you for ever*, John xiv. 16. Christ in his bodily presence went away, but Christ in his Spirit continues still, *Lo, I am with you always, even unto the end of the world*, Matth. xxviii. 10. He is with us, and which is more, he is in us for our comfort, *Christ in you the hope of glory*, Col. i. 27. Not Christ in sermons which we hear, nor Christ in chapters which we read, nor Christ in sacraments which we receive, nor Christ in our heads by high notions, nor Christ in our mouths by florent

glorious expressions, but Christ in our hearts by his Spirit, is unto us *the hope of glory*. The grounds of our comforts in this respect, are,—

1. Christ's presence. It is said of Paul that after a sad shipwreck, the sight of some Christian brethren so cheared him up, that upon the sight of them *he thanked God, and took courage*, Acts xxviii. 15. It is said of Cæsar, that he cheared the drooping mariners in a storm, by minding them of his presence, *you carry Cæsar*; how much more should the in-being of Christ solace saints? *Lo, I am with you*. O my soul! was it not a cordial to the disciples in a storm, that Christ was with them, whom the winds and waves obeyed? Chear up now, for if the Spirit be in thee, Christ is with thee.

2. Christ's complacency. If his Spirit dwell in us, How should he but be well pleased with us? A man cannot properly be said to dwell in a prison, in which he taketh no delight; the Spirit's indwelling imports a delight of Christ in such a soul, *Here will I dwell, for I have desired it*, or *delighted in it*, saith God of Zion, Psa. cxxxii. 14. tho' many times drooping Christians, viewing their own beggarliness and vileness, judge themselves worthy to be detested and deserted, and would relinquish themselves if they possibly could, yet Christ looketh to the poor and contrite soul, as a meet habitation for himself to dwell in, *I dwell in the high and holy place, with him also that is of a contrite, and humble spirit*, Isa. lvii. 15.

3. Christ's communications. Union is the ground of our communion with Christ; and the nearer our union, the greater is our communion; if Christ were only in a believer by the habit of grace, the union would not be so great, but if Christ be in us by his Spirit, the union is nearer, and therefore the communion will be greater. O my soul! remember this in all thy straits; there can be no creature-want, or danger whatsoever wherein the improvement of this indwelling of the Spirit may not refresh thee, Art thou sick? The physician both of soul and body is within thee; art thou sad? The comforter himself that supplies the stead and room of Christ, inhabits in thee; art thou in exile, in banishment, imprisonment, at greatest distance from thy dearest friends? See Paul's refreshment when they were ready to pull him in pieces, and threw him into the castle, even *the night follow-*

ing

ing the Lord stood by him, and said, be of good cheer, Paul, Acts xxiii. 11. Christ will stand by thee, nay, Christ by his Spirit dwelleth in thee, and will speak to thee comfortable words in thy greatest pressures.

4. Christ's witnessings. If his Spirit dwell in us, we may then be assured of future glory, *Christ in you the hope of glory,* Col. i. 27. 'Tis a sweet note of a divine upon it, '* The existency of Christ's 'Spirit in believers, giveth existence to their hopes 'of glory. The Spirit in us is God's earnest of 'glory, the Spirit in us doth prepare us for parti- 'cipation in that glory.' I look upon this indwelling of the Spirit, as that which no hypocrite in the world can lay any claim unto; as for gifts, or graces, an hypocrite may attain them, or something like; it is said of Simon Magus that he *believed,* Acts viii. 13. It is said of Judas, *that he repented,* Matth. xxvii. 3. And of Esau, that *he sought the birth-right with tears,* Heb. xii. 17. It is said of some, *that partook of the heavenly gift, and of the powers of the world to come, and yet fall away,* Heb. vi. 5, 6. And it is said of such others, *That they trampled upon the blood of Christ wherewith they were sanctified,* Heb. x. 29. Thus we find in scripture-phrase, that in an hypocrite or wicked man, there may be a kind of faith, and repentance, a taste of heaven, and of sanctification; But where do we find in all the Bible, that Christ, or the Spirit of Christ is said to dwell in an hypocrite, or wicked man? This only is the great privilege of a true believer, *Christ in him the hope of glory.*——O the comfort of this indwelling of Christ! if Zaccheus hearing that Christ would abide in his house, *received him joyfully,* Luke xix. How much greater cause of joy have they who have already lodged him in their hearts? *These things have I spoken to you,* (said Christ) *that my joy might remain in you, and that your joy might be full,* John xv. 11.

And now, O my soul, spread thyself on this great good, Christ's ascension, Christ's session, and Christ's mission of his holy Spirit. What is joy but an effusion of the appetite, whereby the soul spreads itself on what is good, to possess it more perfectly? The object is sweet, and large, and therefore the soul had need to spread itself, that it may be more united to the object, and touch the good in more of its parts, yea, if it were possible in every part. There is not any particular here before thee, but it is fuel for joy; O what joy was in heaven, when Christ ascended, and when Christ sat down at God's right hand, and when Christ sent down the holy Spirit? How stood the angels wondering and admiring at these several passages? How did they stoop, and *look with the bowing of the head, and bending of the neck?* 1 Pet. i. 12. As the word implies, And is not thy interest in these transactions more than angels? O rejoice, and again rejoice! suppose thyself in heaven, and that thou hadst a vision of Christ ascended; say, Is not he a pleasant object? *In his face there is fulness of joy,* Psal. xvi. 11. Suppose thyself to have been in heaven when he first entred into it, and when he first sat down at God's right hand, and sent down the comforter to his saints, Was not heaven full of joy! Methinks the very thought of Christ's bright face, and Christ's white throne, and Christ's harpers, and heavenly troops surrounding the throne, and Christ's welcome to his Father, both for himself, and all his saints, and Christ's carrying thy name upon his breast before his Father should fill thy soul as full of joy, as possibly it can hold. O! the first fruits of Emmanuel's land, that lies beyond time and death! O! the joys that were in heaven at Christ's first entrance into heaven! O my soul, why dost thou not check thyself, and lay aside thy sad complaints, and forget this earth and earthly troubles? Why dost thou not look up to Jesus Christ, and rejoice in him who hath done all this for thy salvation? Either the Spirit of God is not thy comforter, or thou canst not but receive comfort in these passages.

SECT. VIII.

Of calling on Jesus in that respect.

8. LET us call on Jesus; I mean——1. Let us pray that we may have our part in these transactions; or let us pray for more and more assurance thereof unto our souls; for though we do believe, yet we may not be without our doubts; and in case of doubts, What better

---

* Mr. *Ash* in his *Serm. of Christ the riches of the gospel.*

means

means than prayer? 'I believe, Lord help my unbelief; Lord strengthen my faith, till I come to that plerophory, or full assurance of faith, that I may know my interest in the ascension of Christ, and session of Christ, and in the mission of Christ's holy Spirit.' And if once we are but assured, then,—

2. Praise God for these great transactions of his Son: are they not mercies like mountains lying one upon another, and reaching up to the very heavens? Did not love break out first in a direct line? And as it went along, Hath it not wound up itself, in such a variety of unthought of discoveries, as that it amazeth men and angels? What, that Jesus Christ should not only act for us here on earth, but also ascend for us into heaven, and sit down there at God's right hand above the heavens. What, that all this should be for us and our salvation! And to that purpose, that he should send down his Spirit into our hearts, to fit us, and prepare us for his glory: Now *bless the Lord, O my soul, and all that is within me bless his holy name, bless the Lord, O my soul, and forget not all his benefits,* Psalm ciii. 1, 2 —— *I will extol thee my God, O King, and I will bless thy name for ever and ever,* Psal. cxlv. 1. *Every day will I bless thee, and I will praise thy name for ever and ever,* Ver. 2 *One generation shall praise thy works to another, and shall declare thy mighty acts,* Ver. 4. *I will speak of the glorious honour of thy majesty, and of thy wondrous works,* Ver. 5. *I will utter the memory of thy great goodness, and will sing of thy righteousness,* Ver. 7. *Thy saints shall bless thee,* Ver. 10 *They shall speak of the glory of thy kingdom, and talk of thy power,* Ver. 11. *And make known unto the sons of men thy mighty acts, and the glorious majesty of thy kingdom,* Ver. 12. *Thy glory is above the earth, and heaven, thou also exaltest the horn of thy people, the praise of all thy saints, and people near unto thyself,* Psal. cxlviii 13, 14. O! that my soul were but in David's temper, thus to breathe out the praises of Jesus, and to bless his name.

SECT. IX.

Of conforming unto Jesus in that respect.

9. LET us conform to Jesus in the aforesaid respects. A serious beholding of Jesus in his ascension, session, and mission of his Spirit, is enough to change us into the same image from glory to glory. It was the sweet saying of an experienced saint, 'View a glorified Christ, see him as in that relation and condition, and you will soon have the sparkles of the same glory on your hearts.' Christ is now exalted, he is now in glory at the right hand of God; O! let all our actings be glorious, let all our walkings, joys, breathings be as in glory, *If ye be risen with Christ, seek those things which are above, where Christ sitteth at the right hand of God; set your affections on things above, and not on things on the earth,* Col. iii. 1, 2. I shall not in this transaction lay out many particular conformities to Christ's actings, but gather all into one, contained in this text, which is *heavenly conversation;* seek things above, set your affections above; Christ is gone up, and Christ is set down at God's right hand; and herein if you will conform, let your hearts be in heaven, let your affections be in heaven, let your conversations be in heaven: it is the apostle's own practice, wherein stood his conformity to Jesus Christ, *For our conversation is in heaven,* Phil. iii. 20. I do not know any one thing wherein we can be more like to Christ exalted, whilst we are upon earth, than to have our hearts, our affections, our conversations with Christ where he is: now then if we be virtually risen with Christ, and ascended with Christ, and set down with Christ in heavenly places, let us spiritually ascend, and sit down with him in these respects: certainly there is a proportion in our heavenly conversation; Oh! let our conversation be in heaven.

In prosecution of this, I shall examine these queries.—

1. What do we mean by our conversation in heaven?

2. Why must our conversation be in heaven?

3. By what means must we come up to this conversation in heaven?

1. By our conversation in heaven, I mean our aim at heaven; as heaven is our home, so our eye is there; whatever we do, our end, our scope is to fit us for heaven, and to lay in for heaven, *We look not* (saith the apostle) *at the things which are seen, but at the things which are not seen, for the things which are seen are temporal, but the things which are not seen are eternal,* 2 Cor. iv. 18. We look not, *that is,* we aim not at things which are seen; invisible things are the only scope and aim of a gracious soul.

2. By our conversation in heaven, I mean our communion with Christ in heaven, *Truly our fellowship is with the Father, and with his Son Jesus Christ*, 1 John i. 3. As it is amongst friends that converse together, they act mutually for the comfort of one another, there is a mutual embracing and opening of their hearts to one another at every turn; so in our conversings with Christ there is a communion, or a mutual acting of the soul upon Christ, and of Christ upon the soul; we let out our hearts to Christ, and he lets out his heart to us, especially when we are with Christ in his ordinances; it is not enough to call upon God, and to use some broken-hearted expressions, but, 'Oh! What communion have I with Jesus Christ? I cannot be satisfied except I taste and see how good the Lord is; I cannot be quiet, except I hear something from heaven this morning.' Why, this is an heavenly conversation.

3. By our conversation in heaven, I mean our living according to the laws of heaven; in all our ways we must still enquire, 'What rule is there from heaven to guide me in these ways? Such and such a thing I have a mind to, But will the law of heaven justify me in this? Have I any word from Jesus Christ to guide me in this? Sometimes indeed my lust, my own ends, and the common course of the world was my rule, but now I dare not act, but according to the will and sceptre of Jesus Christ, now I am guided by the laws of heaven.' Why, this is an heavenly conversation.

4. By our conversation in heaven, I mean our thoughts and meditations of heaven and heavenly things, *When I awake* (saith David) *I am always with thee*, Psal. cxxxix. 18. The hearts of believers are frequently upon their heavenly treasures; as it is storied of queen Mary, that, a little before her death, she told them, 'If they ript her open, they would find Calais in her heart.' So it may be said of them, whose conversation is in heaven, if you rip them up, you shall find heaven in their hearts; not a day passeth over their heads without some converse with heaven, without some thoughts or meditations of heaven, and heavenly things.

5. By our conversation in heaven, I mean our affections on heaven, or on Christ in heaven, *Set your affections on things above*, Col. iii. 2. (i. e) Set your desires, loves, hopes, joys, breathings on heavenly things; our affections are precious things, and are only to be set on precious objects. Oh! what a shame is it to set our affections on the things of this life? Have we a kingdom, a God, a Christ, a crown in heaven to set our affections upon? And shall we set them upon dross, and dung, and such base things? Are not all our pleasures and vanities base in comparison of Christ? O! be not we so base to set our affections on earthly things, but rather on God and Christ; and this is our heavenly conversation.

6. By our conversation in heaven, I mean our tradings, our negotiations for heaven, even whilst we are upon earth: the word in the original points at this, [*hemon gar topiliteuma en ouranois,*] *our trading is in heaven*; though our bodies be not there, yet our tradings are there; we carry and behave ourselves in this life, as free denizens of the city of heaven, our city whereof we are citizens, and whereunto we have right, is in heaven above, in this respect we trade not for trifles, as other men do, but we trade for great things, for high things, we merchandize for goodly pearls, even for God, and for Christ, who sitteth at the right hand of God. We see now what we mean by our conversation in heaven.

2. Why is the conversation of the saints in heaven?

1. Because they know full well, that the original of their souls came from God and heaven; the body indeed was of the dust of the ground, but the soul was the breath of God; so it is said of the first man, *God breathed into his nostrils the breath of life, and man became a living soul*, Gen ii. 7. The soul had a more heavenly and divine original than any of the other creatures that are here in this nether word; and when God works grace in the soul, and so it begins to know itself, and to return to itself, it then looks on all things here below as vile, and as contemptible things; it then looks upwards, and begins to converse with things suitable to its original. As it is with a child that hath a noble birth, if transported into another country, and there used like a slave, there set to rake channels, or (as the prodigal) to feed swine; while he is there, and knows not his original, he minds nothing but to get victuals, and to do his work that he is set about; but if once he come to know from whence he was, that he is indeed born heir to such a prince in such a country; O! then his thoughts,

thoughts, and mind, and longings will be altered; 'O! that I were in my own country! O! that I were with my father in his court!' Even so it is with the souls of the sons of men, they are the birth (as I may so speak) of the great King of heaven and earth, and though by the fall of man they came to be as slaves to Satan, yet when God is pleased to convert the soul, then he discovers thus; 'Oh! man, thou art born from on high, thy soul is (as it were) a sparkle of God himself, thou art come from God, and thou art capable of communion with God, even with God the Father, and God the Son, and God the Holy Ghost. O! consider of thy country whence thou camest at first, certainly thou never hadst such a divine and excellent being given thee, to delight only in the flesh, to be serviceable only to thy body; O! look up unto Jesus.' Why, this is it that turns the heart, and sets the conversation on heavenly things.

2. Because their best and choice things are already in heaven. As their Father is in heaven, and their Saviour is in heaven, thither he ascended, and there now he sits at the right hand of God; their husband is in heaven, their elder brother is in heaven, their King is in heaven, their treasure is in heaven, their inheritance is in heaven, their hope is in heaven, their mansion is in heaven, their chief friends are in heaven, their substance is in heaven, their reward is in heaven, their wages are in heaven: and all these things being in heaven, no marvel their conversations be in heaven.

3. Because they are going towards heaven, even whilst yet they are on earth. If the nobleman, (as we formerly supposed) do once know his condition, and begins his travel homeward towards his Father's court, Will he not every morning that he rises converse with them that come from his Father to conduct him home? Doth it not do him good to hear any man speak of his Father's country? Is it not in his thoughts, in his talk, in his eye, in his aim, at every step? O my soul, if thou art indeed travelling towards heaven, How shouldst thou but have it in thy motions, affections, conversations? How shouldst thou but daily commune with thy own heart, *Heaven is the place that I shall come to?* 'Ere long I shall be there; I know that in this world I am but for a while, but in heaven I shall be for ever and ever; *we shall be caught up into the clouds, to meet the Lord in the air, and so shall we be ever with the Lord*, 1 Thess. iv. 17. Our very travel towards heaven implies an heavenly conversation, *They go from strength to strength, till every one of them in Zion appears before God*, Psal. lxxxiv. 7.

4. Because much of heaven is already in the saints, *The kingdom of heaven is within you*, saith Christ, Luke xvii. 21. *And knowing in yourselves that ye have a better and an enduring substance*, Heb. x. 34. Surely, if the saints have much of heaven within them, it must needs be that their conversation is in heaven; but they know this in themselves; they know it by what God hath revealed in their own hearts; eternal life is already begun in the souls of God's people; heaven is in them, and therefore no marvel if their conversation be in heaven. My meaning is not, as if the saints had no other heaven but that within them; I know there is a heaven above, but some pieces, or earnests, or seeds, or beginnings of that heaven above are within them. Is there not a renewed nature, an image of God, a spark of life, a drop of glory in God's people? Surely, yes; and if so, all these will work heaven-ward; principles of grace will have some actings of grace till we come to glory.

3. By what means should we attain or come up to have our conversation in heaven?

1. Let us watch opportunities for heavenly exercises. God now, by his ministers, calls, *Come ye to the waters; come ye, buy and eat; come, buy wine and milk without money; come to me, and your souls shall live*, Isa. lv. 1, 3. Why, *now is the accepted time, behold now is the day of salvation*, 2 Cor. vi. 2. Whilst ministers call, and we live under the droppings of the word, these are opportunities for heaven; O then! he that never prayed, let him now pray; and he that never heard, let him now hear; the Lord is now come near to us; Christ Jesus is calling, and mercy is entreating, and love is beseeching, and wisdom is even hoarse with crying after us; O! lay hold on these opportunities for heavenly exercises, and then we shall come up to heavenly conversation.

2. Take heed of resting in the formality of duties; many souls that have enlightnings of conscience, dare not but take opportunities for heavenly duties; but then come in the temptations of the devil, and corruptions of their own hearts, and they say, now duty is done, or our task is over, and what needs more? Alas, alas, it is not what have

we done, but where have we been? What, have our souls been in heaven, with God and with Christ? Have we had any communion with the Father and with the Son in our duties? O take heed of formality! it will exceedingly hinder our conversation in heaven; O keep our eye still upon our heart! ask in duty, what affections have been acted? How much are we got nearer heaven thereby? And by this means we shall come to an heavenly coversation.

3. Let us look up unto Jesus, as hanging on the cross, and as sitting on the throne; this is the apostle's rule, *Looking unto Jesus, the author and finisher of our faith, who for the joy that was set before him endured the cross, despising the shame, and is set down at the right hand of the throne of God,* Heb. xii 2. These two are the objects of a Christian's look, who studies an heavenly conversation, viz. Christ's cross, and Christ's session; by the cross he is the author, and by the throne he is the finisher of our faith; in the first, is set down his love to us, in the second, is set down our hope of him; with high wisdom hath the Holy Ghost exhorted us, with these two motives, to run and not to faint; first, here is love, love in the cross, *Who loved us, and gave himself for us a sacrifice on the cross,* Eph. v. 21. 2. Here is hope, hope in the throne, *To him that overcometh will I give to sit with me in my throne,* Rev. iii. 21. After Christ's death he arose again, ascended, and is now set down at the right hand of the throne of God; and the same is our blessed hope, Christ's throne is not only his place, but ours also; the love of his cross is to us a pledge of the hope of his throne, or of whatsoever else he is worth. Come then, and settle your thoughts and looks on this blessed object: a sight of Christ's cross, but especially of Christ's throne, is a blessed means to wean us from the world, and to elevate and raise up our affections to things above, yea, to form and frame our conversations towards heaven.

4. Let us wait for the appearing of Jesus Christ, *Our conversation is in heaven,* (faith the apostle) *from whence also we look for the Saviour, the Lord Jesus Christ,* Phil. iii. 20. Where a man's conversation is, there his expectations may be, and where his expectations are, there a man's conversation is, and will be; if we expect e'er long that the Lord Jesus will appear in glory, and that we shall see him, not with other, but with these same eyes, the very waiting for these things, will help our conversation to be heaven-ward. Certainly the day is a coming, when Jesus Christ shall come with his angels in his glory, and then shall the bodies of the saints shine gloriously before the face of God and Jesus Christ: O the wonder of this day! the glory of Christ shall then darken the glory of the sun and moon, and stars, but my body shall not be darkned, but rather it shall shine like the glorious body of Jesus Christ; if a candle should be raised to have so much lustre and beauty, as if you should put it into the midst of the sun, yet it would shine, you would think it a strange kind of light; surely it shall be so with the bodies of saints, for though they are put into the midst of the glory of God, and of his Son Jesus Christ, yet their bodies shall shine in beauty and lustre there; now, did we believe this, and wait for it every day, how would it change us? How would it work us to an heavenly conversation? 'I have a diseased and lumpish body, and my body hinders me in every duty of 'God's worship, but within a while Christ will 'come in his glory, and then he will make my body 'like unto his glorious body, so that I shall be 'able to look upon the face of God, and to be exercised in holy duties to all eternity without weariness, without intermission: I have many things 'here that trouble my mind and spirit, and that hinder me in my converse with heaven, and heavenly things; but within a while Christ will appear 'with his mighty angels, to be admired of his saints, 'and then shall I sit as an assessor on the throne, 'with Jesus Christ to judge the world, and then 'shall I live for ever with him, to be where he is, 'and enjoy all he has, yea, all that he hath purchased for me by his blood; Oh let me wait for this! 'let me look for it every day! God hath but a 'little work for me here on earth, and when that 'is done, this shall be my condition.' Christians! if but every day we would work these things on our soul, it would be a mighty help to make our conversations, heavenly conversations.

5. Let us observe the drawings, and movings, and windings of the Spirit, and follow his dictates; to this purpose Christ ascended, and sat down at God's right hand, and sent down the holy Spirit, that the Holy Ghost being come down, he might do his office in bringing on our souls towards salvation;

tion ; and if ever our souls get above this earth, and get acquainted with this living in heaven, it is the Spirit of God that must be as the chariot of Elijah, yea the very living principle by which we must move and ascend ; O then take heed of quenching its motions or resisting its workings! take we heed of grieving our guide, or knocking off the chariot wheels of this holy Spirit. We little think how much the life of graces, and the happiness of our souls doth depend upon our ready and cordial obedience to the Spirit of God ; when he forbids us our known transgressions, and we will go on, when he tells us which is the way and which is not, and we will not regard, no wonder if we are strangers to an heavenly conversation ; if we will not follow the Spirit while it would draw us to Christ, How should it lead us to heaven, or bring our hearts into the presence of God?

Oh! learn we this lesson, and let not only the motions of our bodies, but also the very thoughts of our hearts be at the Spirit's beck ; do we not sometimes feel a strong impulsion to retire from the world and to draw near to God? O! let us not despise, or disobey, but take we the offer, and hoise up our sail, while we may have this blessed gale ; if we cherish these motions, and hearken to the Spirit, O! what a supernatural help should we find to this heavenly-mindedness, or heavenly conversation?

Thus far we have looked on Jesus, as our Jesus, in his ascension, session, and mission of his holy Spirit ; our next work is to look on Jesus carrying on the great work of our salvation for us in his intercession, which he makes, and will make to his Father on our behalf, till his second coming to judgment.

LOOKING UNTO JESUS.

In His INTERCESSION.

BOOK FOURTH, PART SIXTH.

CHAP. I. SECT. I.

Heb. iii. 1. Rom. viii. 34. *Consider the Apostle, and high priest of our profession, Christ Jesus,—— who also maketh intercession for us.*

What the Intercession of CHRIST is.

WE have spoken of Christ's entrance into heaven, and of his immediate actings after his entrance there ; that transaction which yet remains, and will remain until his coming again, it is his intercession for the saints. In these actings of Christ in heaven, (if we may follow him) we must go from glory to glory ; no sooner come we out of one room of glory, but presently we step into another, as glorious as that before : one would think enough had been said already of the glory of Christ, and of our glory in Christ ; who would not willingly sit down under the shadow of this happiness, and go no farther? But yet this is not all ; so thick and fast doth the glory of Christ break in upon us, that no sooner out of one, but presently we are led into the bosom of another. Oh! what a blessed thing is it to be viewing Christ, *and to be looking up unto Jesus Christ?* Saints might do nothing else, (if they pleased) but ravish their hearts with the diversity fity of heavenly light and comfort, which breaks forth from the bosom of Jesus Christ. Here is now another mystery as great and amazing as the former, which springs out before our eyes in this transaction of Christ's intercession

And, in prosecution of this, as in the former, I shall first lay down the object, and secondly, direct you how to look upon it. The object is Jesus carrying on the great work of our salvation in his intercession: in ordering of which I shall examine these particulars.——

1. What is this intercession of Christ?
2. According to what nature doth Christ intercede?
3. To whom is Christ's intercession directed?
4. For whom is the intercession made?
5. What agreements are there betwixt Christ's intercessions and the intercessions of the high priests of old?
6. What is the difference betwixt Christ's intercession and the intercession of those high priests?
7. What are the properties of this intercession of Jesus Christ?
8. Wherein more especially do the intercessions of Christ consist?
9. How powerful and prevailing are Christ's intercessions with God his Father?
10. What are the reasons of this great transaction of Christ's intercession for his people?

1. What is the intercession of Christ? Some define it thus, *Christ's intercession is that part of his priestly office, whereby Christ is advocate, and intreater of God the Father, for the faithful.* I shall give it thus, *Christ's intercession is his gracious will, fervently and immovably desiring, that for the perpetual virtue of his sacrifice, all his members, might, both for their persons and duties, be accepted of the Father.* 1. I call the intercession of Christ his own gracious will; for we must not imagine, that Christ in his intercession prostrates himself upon his knees before his Father's throne, uttering some submissive form of words or prayers; that is not beseeming the majesty of him that sits at God's right hand; when he was but yet on earth, the substance of his requests for his saints ran thus, *Father, I will, that they also whom thou hast given me be with me where I am*, John xvii. 24. And how much more now he is in heaven is this the form of his intercessions, *Father I will this,* *and I will that?* 2. The ground or foundation of Christ's intercession is *the sacrifice or death of Christ*; and hence we may make two parts of Christ's priesthood or oblation; the one expiatory, when Christ suffered upon the cross; the other presentatory, when he doth appear in heaven before God for us; the one was finished on earth, when Christ suffered without the gate; the other is performed in heaven; now Christ is within the city, the one was a sacrifice indeed, the other is not so much a sacrifice as the commemoration of a sacrifice; the first was an act of humiliation, and this latter is an act of glory; the first was performed once for all, this latter is done continually; the first was for the obtaining of redemption, and this latter is for the application of redemption; so that the ground of this is, that Christ fervently and immovably desires his Father for the sake and virtue of his sacrifice. 3. The subject matter interceded for, is, That *all the saints, and their services, might find acceptance with God*; first, Christ's intercession is for our persons, and then Christ's intercession is for our works; for as our persons are but in part regenerate, and in part unregenerate, or, in part flesh, and in part spirit, so be our duties, part good, and part evil, in part spiritual, and in part sinful; now by Christ's intercession is Christ's satisfaction applied to our persons, and by consequence the defect of our duties is covered and removed; and both we and our works are approved and accepted of God the Father. And thus much for the nature of Christ's intercession, what it is.

SECT. II.

According to what nature Christ doth intercede.

2. According to what nature doth Christ intercede? I answer, According to both natures; according to his humanity, partly by appearing before his Father in heaven, and partly by desiring the salvation of the elect, *Christ is entered into heaven itself, now to appear in the presence of God for us*, Heb. ix 24. *And I say not unto you, that I will pray, or desire the Father for you, for the Father himself loveth you*, John xvi. 26, 27. Secondly, According to his Deity, partly by applying the merit of his death, and partly by willing the salvation of his saints; and as the effect thereof, by making requests in the hearts of the saints

saints with sighs unspeakable, *Elect, thro' sanctification of the Spirit and sprinkling of the blood of Jesus Christ,* 1 Pet. i. 2. This sprinkling is the applying of the blood of Jesus, and that is an act of intercession: again, *Father, I will, that they whom thou hast given me be with me where I am,* John xvii. 24. he desires as a man, but he wills as God, and as the effect of this he gives the Spirit, *The Spirit itself maketh intercession for us, with groanings which cannot be uttered,* Rom. viii. 26. But what are the intercessions of the Spirit to the intercessions of Christ? I answer, much every way, the spirit's intercessions are as the effect, and Christ's intercessions are as the cause; the Spirit's intercessions are as the eccho, and Christ's intercessions are as the first voice; the Spirit intercedes for men, in and by themselves, but Christ intercedes in his own person; there is a dependance of the Spirit's intercessions in us upon Christ's intercessions in himself. First, Christ by his intercession applies his satisfaction made, and lays the salve to the very sore; and then he sends down his holy Spirit into our hearts, to help our infirmities, and to teach us what to pray, and how to pray as we ought. Now this he doth as God, for who shall give a commission to the Spirit of God, but God himself? It is as if Christ should say, ' See holy Spirit, how I
' take upon me the cause of my saints, I am per-
' petually representing my sacrifice to God my Fa-
' ther, I am ever pleading for them, and answer-
' ing all the accusations that sin or Satan can lay
' against them, and now go thy way to such and
' such, and take up thy dwelling in their hearts,
' and assist them by thy energy, to plead their
' own cause; I am their advocate or intercessor by
' office, and therefore be thou their advocate or
' intercessor by operation, instruction, inspiration,
' and assistance.'

SECT. III.
To whom Christ's intercession is directed.

3. TO whom is Christ's intercession directed? I answer, Immediately to God the Father, *If any man sin, we have an advocate with the Father, Jesus Christ the righteous,* 1 John ii. 1. In the work of intercession are three persons, a party offended, a party offending, and the intercessor distinct from them both; the party offended is God the Father, the party offending is sinful man, and the intercessor distinct from them both, is Jesus Christ, the middle person (as it were) betwixt God the Father, and us men; the Father is God, and not man; and we that believe in Christ are men, and not God; and Christ himself is both man and God; and therefore, he intercedes and mediates betwixt God and man: if any object, that not only the Father is offended, but also the Son, and the Holy Ghost, and therefore there must be a Mediator to them also, the solution is easy; Christ's intercession is immediately directed to the Father, but because the Father, Son and Holy Ghost, have all one indivisible essence, and by consequence one will, it therefore follows, That the Father being appeased by Christ's intercession, the Son and the Holy Ghost are also appeased with him, and in him. I deny not but Christ's intercession is made to the whole trinity, but yet immediately, and directly to the first person, and in him to the rest. — ' But
' if so, then in some sense, (say our adversaries)
' Christ makes intercession to himself, which can-
' not be; because in every intercession there must
' of necessity be three parties:' This point hath sore puzzled the church of Rome, that for the solving of it, they knew no other way but to avouch Christ to be our intercessor only as man, and not as God, which is most untrue; for as both natures did concur in the work of satisfaction, so likewise they do both concur in the work of intercession: and 'tis an ancient and approved rule, ' † That
' names of office which are given to Christ, such
' as Mediator, Intercessor, &c. agree unto him ac-
' cording to both natures;' and can the act of Christ's intercession, be the act of Christ's manhood alone? What, to hear, and offer up prayers? To receive and present the prayers and praises, and other spiritual sacrifices of all believers in the world? To negotiate for them all at one and the same time, according to the variety and multiplicity of their several occasions? Surely this is, and must be the work of an infinite, and not of a finite agent; this cannot be effected without the concurrence of the divine nature with the human: but what needs any farther answer to this objection? Suppose Christ intercede to himself as God; that is not immediately, and directly to the same per-

† *Appellationes officii competunt Christo secundum utramque naturam.*

son God the Son, though to the same God essentially; in Christ, [*Theanthropos*], God-man, in respect of his natures, agreeth with both, being not only God, nor only man, but God-man, man-God blessed for ever; but in respect of his person, being the second person in the trinity, he is distinct from both. 1. From the personality of man, for he hath only the personality of God, and not of man. 2. From the first person of the Godhead, who is God the Father, *For there are three that bear record in heaven, the Father, the Word, and the Holy Ghost; and these three are one*, 1 John v. 7. (i. e.) Three persons, and but one God.

SECT. IV.
For whom this intercession was made.

4. FOr whom is this intercession made? I answer, 1. Negatively, not for the world, *I pray not for the world*, John xvii. 9. saith Christ; whilst Christ was on earth he would not so much as spend his breath, or open his lips for the world, he knew God would not hear him for them; in like manner Christ prays now in heaven, *not for the world*, he never had a thought to redeem them, or to save their souls, and therefore they have no share in his intercessions; I know the objection, that Christ upon the cross, prayed for the bloody Jews, *Father, forgive them, for they know not what they do*, Luke xxiii. 34. but that might be of private duty as man, who in that respect submitted himself to the law of God, which requires, that we forgive our enemies, and pray for them that persecute us, and not of his proper office as Mediator; or if it be referred to the proper mediatory intercession of Jesus Christ (which I rather think) it will not prove that he prayed for them all universally, but only indefinitely, (i. e.) only for them that were present at his crucifying, and that in simplicity of heart, and not of affected ignorance crucified Christ; and accordingly, this prayer was heard, when so many of the Jews were converted at Peter's sermon, Acts ii. 41 What needs more? His own words are express, that Christ's intercessions are *not for the world*, or reprobates. So much negatively.

2. Positively: Christ's intercession is general, and particular; for all, and every faithful man, *I pray for them, I pray not for the world, but for them which thou hast given me, for they are thine*, John xvii. 9. *And the Lord said, Simon, Simon, Behold Satan hath desired to have you, that he may sift you as wheat, but I have prayed for thee, that thy faith fail not*, Luke xxii. 31, 32. As the high priest went into the sanctuary with the names of the twelve tribes upon his breast, so Christ entred into the holiest of all, with the names of all believers upon his heart, and still he carries them upon his breast, and presents his will and desire unto his Father for them; nor doth he only intercede in general, but Simon, Simon, mark that; whatever thy name is, John, Peter, Thomas, Mary, Martha, if thou art a believer, Christ prays for thee; it is our common practice to desire the prayers one of another, but, O! who would not have a share in the prayers of Jesus Christ? Why, certainly if thou believest in Christ, Christ prays for thee, *I have prayed, and I will pray for thee*, saith Christ, *that thy faith fail not*.

SECT. V.
What agreement there is betwixt Christ's intercessions, and the intercessions of the high priests of old.

5. WHat agreement is there betwixt the intercessions of Christ, and the intercessions of the high priests of old? Among the Jews in the times of the Old Testament, they had an high priest, who was in all things to stand betwixt God and them. Now, as the Jews had their high priest to intercede for them, so the Lord Jesus was to be the high priest of our Christian profession, and to intercede for us; it will therefore give some light to the doctrine of intercession, if we will but compare these two, and first consider, What agreement betwixt Christ and the high priests of old; betwixt Christ's intercession, and the high priests intercessions?

1. Christ and the high priests of old agreed in name; not only they, but Christ himself is called an high priest, *We have such an high priest, who is set down at the right hand of the majesty on high*, Heb. viii. 1. —*Consider the apostle and high priest of our profession, Jesus Christ*, Heb iii. 1 — *Thou art a priest for ever, after the order of Melchisedec*, Heb. v. 6. the old priest-hood of Aaron was translated into the priest-hood of Jesus Christ, so that he was a priest as well as they.

2. They

2. They agreed in office; that consisted of two parts, oblation and presentation. 1. They offered a sacrifice; and secondly, they presented it in the holy of holies with prayer and intercession unto God; the one was done without, the other within the holy of holies; and in answer thereunto, there are two distinct parts of Christ's priest-hood. 1. The offering of himself a sacrifice upon the cross. 2. The carrying of himself and of his blood into the holy of holies, or into the heaven of heavens; where he appears and prays on the force of that blood; and this was so necessary a part of his priest-hood, that without this he had not been a complete priest, *For if he were on earth, he should not be a priest*, Heb. viii. 4. that is, if he should have made his abode upon the earth, he should not have been a complete or perfect priest, seeing this part of it, which we call the presentation, or intercession) lay still upon him to be acted in heaven. And indeed, this part of his priest-hood is of the two the more eminent; yea, the top and height of his priest-hood; and therefore, it is held forth to us in the types of both those two orders of priest-hood that were before him, and figures of him, both that of Aaron, and Melchisedec. 1. This was typified in that Levitical priest-hood of Aaron and his fellows; the highest service of that office was the going into the holy of holies, and making an atonement there; yea, this was the height of the high priest's honour, that he did this alone, and it constituted the difference betwixt him, as he was high priest, and other priests; for they killed and offered the sacrifices without as well as he, but only the high priest was to approach the holy of holies with blood, and that but once a year. 2. This was typified by Melchisedec's priest-hood, which the apostle argues to have been much more excellent than that of Aaron's, in as much as Levi, Aaron's father, paid tythes to this Melchisedec in Abraham's loins; now Melchisedec was his type, not so much in respect of his oblation, or offering sacrifice as in respect of his continual presentation and intercession in heaven; and therefore the same clause, *for ever*, still comes in when Melchisedec is named, *Thou art a priest for ever, after the order of Melchisedec*, Heb. v. 6.—vii. 17. Here then is the agreement betwixt Christ and the high priests of old; in respect of name, both were priests, and in respect of office, both had their oblations and presentations, or intercessions with God in glory.

3. In the point of intercession, they agreed in these particulars ——

1. The high priests of old, usually, once a year, went into the most holy place within the vail; and so is Christ, our great high priest, passed into the heavens within the vail, even into the *holy of holies, Christ by his own blood entred in once into the holy place* ——*Not into the holy places made with hands, which are the figures of the true, but into heaven itself, now to appear in the presence of God for us*, Heb. ix. 12, 24.

2. The high priests of old had a plate of pure gold upon their foreheads, which was, *To bear the iniquity of the holy things, that they might be accepted before the Lord*, Exod. xxviii. 38. and so doth Christ bear the iniquity of our holy things. Spiritual Christian! he is your comfort, you are not able to perform any duty to God, there is a great deal of sin in the same; you cannot hear, nor pray, nor confer, nor meditate, without much sin; but Christ bears all these sins, even the iniquity of your holy things, and he presents your persons and prayers without the least spot to his Father; he is *the angel of the covenant that stands at the altar, having a golden censer with much incense, to offer it with the prayers of his saints*, Rev. viii. 3. and so they are acceptable before the Lord.

3. The Jewish high priests *bore the names of the children of Israel on the breast-plate of judgment upon their hearts, for a memorial before the Lord continually*, Ex. xxviii. 29. And so doth Christ, our great high priest, bear the names of his people upon his heart before the Lord continually. But how is Christ said to bear the names of the saints upon his heart? I answer,—

1. Continually, in presenting of them to his Father as they are in him: how is that? Why, he presents them without spot, as righteous in his own righteousness, *Christ loved the church, that he might present it to his Father, and in him to himself, a glorious church, not having spot or wrinkle, or any such thing, but that it should be holy, and without blemish*, Eph. v. 27

2. In his continual remembring of them, *The righteous shall be had in continual remembrance*, Psal. cxii. 6. This is the soul's comfort in a time of desertion, or in an evil day. If any cry out, as sometimes David did, *How long wilt thou forget me, Lord,*

Lord, *for ever? How long wilt thou hide thy face from me?* Pfa. xiii. 1. Let fuch a one remember, that Chrift's redeemed ones are upon his heart, and he cannot forget them, *But Zion faid, The Lord hath forfaken me, and my Lord hath forgotten me* ; Oh no! *Can a woman forget her fucking child, that fhe fhould not have compaffion on the fon of her womb ? Yea, they may forget, yet I will not forget thee; behold I have graven thee upon the palms of my hands, thy walls are continually before me,* Ifa. xl. 14, 15, 16. The fons of Zion are upon Chrift's heart and hands, and they are ever in his fight.

3. In his perpetual loving of them; they are near and dear unto him, he hath fet them as a feal upon his heart; fo was the prayer of the fpoufe, *Set me as a feal upon thine heart, as a feal upon thine arm*; and then it follows, *for love is as ftrong as death*, Cant. viii. 6. Chrift hath an entire love to his faints; he died for them, and now he intercedes for them; he keeps them clofe to his heart, and there is none fhall pluck them out of his hands, *For whom he loves, he loves unto the end*, John xiii. 1. Thus far of the agreement betwixt Chrift's interceffions, and the interceffions of the high priefts of old.

SECT. VI.

What the difference is betwixt Chrift's interceffions, and the interceffions of the high priefts of old.

6. WHAT is the difference betwixt Chrift's interceffions, and the interceffions of the high priefts of old? There is no queftion, but howfoever they might agree in fome refpects, yet Chrift officiates in a more tranfcendent and eminent way than ever any high prieft did before him; now, the difference betwixt Chrift and them, and betwixt Chrift's interceffions and their interceffions, may appear in thefe particulars.——

1. They were called high priefts, but Chrift is called the great high prieft; fuch a title was never given to any but Chrift, whence the apoftle argues for the ftedfaftnefs of our profeffion, *Seeing then that we have a great high prieft, that is paffed into the heavens, Jefus the Son of God, let us hold faft our profeffion*, Heb. iv. 14.

2. The high priefts then, were Aaron and his fons, but Chrift, our great high prieft, is the Son of God; for fo he is ftiled in the fame verfe, the great high prieft that is paffed into the heavens, *Jefus the Son of God*, Heb. iv. 4.

3. The high priefts then, were but for a time, but Chrift is *a prieft for ever, after the order of Melchifedec*, Heb. v. 6. *Melchifedec*, (faith the apoftle) *was without father, without mother, without defcent, having neither beginning of days, nor end of life*, Heb. vii. 3. that is, as far as it is known; and fo is Chrift without a Father on earth, and without a mother in heaven; without beginning and without end; he abides a prieft perpetually, even to the end of the world; yea, and the virtue of his prieft-hood, is infinitely beyond all time, even for ever and ever.

4. The high priefts then entred only into that place that was typically holy; but Chrift is entred into that place that is properly holy; he is entred into the heavens, or (if you will) as into the holy of holies, fo into the heaven of heavens:

5. The high priefts then did not always intercede for the people; only once a year the high prieft entred into the holy of holies, and after that he had fprinkled the mercy-feat with blood, and caufed a cloud to rife upon the mercy-feat with his prayers and incenfe, then he went out of the holy of holies, and laid afide his garments again; but our great high prieft is afcended into the holy of holies, never to put off his princely prieftly garments; nor does he only once a year fprinkle the mercy-feat with his facrifice, but every day; he lives for ever to intercede: oh! what comfort is this to a poor dejected foul? If he once undertake thy caufe, and get thee into his prayers, he will never leave thee out night nor day; he intercedeth ever, till he fhall accomplifh and finifh thy falvation; the fmoke of his incenfe afcends for ever without intermiffion.

6. The high priefts then interceded not for fins of greater inftances; if a man finned ignorantly, there was indeed a facrifice and interceffion for him, but *if a man finned prefumptuoufly, he was to be cut off from among his people*, Numb. xv. 30. No facrifice, no interceffion by the high prieft then, but we have fuch an high prieft as makes interceffion for all fins? every fin, though it boil up to blafphemy, (fo it be not againft the Holy Ghoft) fhall, by virtue of Chrift's interceffion be forgiven,

In

In that day there shall be a fountain opened to the house of David, and to the inhabitants of Jerusalem, for sin and uncleanness, (i. e.) for sins of all sorts, Zech. xiii. 1. *Verily I say unto you, All sins shall be forgiven unto the sons of men,* Mark iii. 28. (i. e.) scarlet sins, or crimson sins; sins of the deepest dye shall by Christ's intercessions be done away; the voice of his blood speaks better things than the blood of Abel; it intercedes for the abolition of bloody sins.

7. The high priests then interceded not without all these miracles, viz. a temple, an altar; a sacrifice of a young bullock for a sin-offering, and a ram for a burnt-offering; a censer full of burning coals of fire taken off the altar, a putting the incense upon the fire, that the cloud of the incense might cover the mercy-seat; a sprinkling the mercy-seat with the blood of the bullock, and of the goat with their finger seven times, Lev. xvi. 3. Such materials they had, and such actions they did which were all distinct as from themselves; but Jesus Christ in his intercessions now, needs none of these materials, but rather he himself and his own merits are instead of all. As, 1. He is the temple, either in regard of the Deity, the gold of the temple being sanctified by the temple; or in regard of his human body, *Destroy this temple,* (saith Christ) *and I will build it again in three days;* it was destroyed, and God found it an acceptable sacrifice, and smelt in it a sweet savour as in a temple. 2. He is the altar according to the Deity, for as the altar sanctifies the gift, so doth the Godhead sanctify the manhood; the altar must needs be of a greater dignity than the oblation, and therefore this altar betokens the divinity of Jesus Christ. 3. He is the sacrifice most properly according to the manhood, for although by communication of properties, the blood of the sacrifice is called the *blood of God,* Acts xx. 28. yet properly the human soul, and flesh of Christ was the holycaust, or whole burnt-offering, roasted in the fire of his Father's wrath. 4 His merits are the cloud of incense, for so the angel Christ is said *to have a golden censer, and much incense, that he should offer it with the prayers of all saints upon the golden altar which was before the throne; and the smoke of the incense which came with the prayers of the saints, ascended up before God out of the angel's hand,* Rev. viii. 3, 4. The merits of Christ are so mingled with the prayers of his saints, that they perfume their prayers, and so they find acceptance with God his Father.—We see now the difference betwixt Christ's intercessions, and the intercessions of the high priests of old.

SECT. VII.

What the properties of this intercession of Christ are

7. WHAT are the properties of this intercession of Jesus Christ? I answer,—
1. It is heavenly and glorious; and that appears in these particulars,
  1. Christ doth not fall upon his knees before his Father, as in the days of his humiliation; for that is not agreeable to that glory he hath received; he only presents his pleasure to his Father, that he may thereto put his seal and consent. Christ doth not pray out of private charity, as the saints pray one for another in this life, but out of public office and mediation, *There is one God, and one mediator between God and man, the man Christ Jesus,* 1 Tim. ii. 5. 3. Christ prays not out of humility, which is the proposing of requests for things unmerited, but out of authority, which is the desiring of a thing, so as withal he hath a right of bestowing it as well as desiring it. 4. Christ prays not merely as an advocate, but as a propitiation too; Christ's Spirit is an advocate, but only Christ is advocate and propitiation; Christ's Spirit is our advocate on earth, but only Christ in his person applieth his merits in heaven, and furthers the cause of our salvation with his Father in heaven. In every of these respects we may see Christ's intercession is heavenly and glorious.

  2. It is ever effectual and prevailing; as he hath power to intercede for us, so he hath a power to confer that upon us for which he intercedes, *I will pray the Father, and he shall give you another comforter,* John xiv. 16. *If I go not away, the comforter will not come unto you, but if I depart I will send him unto you,* John xvi. 7. If Christ prayed on earth, he was ever heard; but if Christ pray in heaven, we may be sure the Father ever heareth and answereth there: when Christ, as man, prayed for himself, he was heard in that which he feareth; but now Christ as mediator praying for us, he is ever heard in the very particular which he desireth.

desireth. We sinful men many a time *ask and receive not, because we ask amiss, that we may consume it upon our lusts,* Jam. iv. 3. But Jesus Christ never asks amiss, nor to wrong ends; and therefore, God, the Father, who called him to this office of being (as it were) the great *master of requests in behalf of his church,* he promised to hear him in all requests. *Father, I thank thee thou hast heard me, and I know thou hearest me always,* (saith Christ) John xi. 41, 42.

3. It is of all other the transactions of Christ till the very end of the world, the most perfective and consummate: indeed so perfective, that without it, all the other parts of Christ's mediatorship would have been to little purpose. As the sacrifices under the law had not been of such force and efficacy, had not the high priest entered into the holy place, to appear there, and to present the blood there unto the Lord; so all that ever Christ did, or suffered upon earth, it had been ineffectual unto us, had he not entred into heaven, *to appear there in the presence of God for us,* Heb. ix. 24. Surely this intercession is that which puts life into the death of Christ: this intercession is that which strikes the last stroke, during this world, in the carrying on of our soul's salvation, and makes all sure. † It is a witty observation that one makes of these several steps of Christ's acting for us; as, first, There was an all-sufficiency in his death, *Who shall condemn? It is Christ that died,* Rom. viii. 34. 2. A rather in his resurrection, yea rather, that is risen again. 3. A much rather in his life and session at God's right hand, *For if when we were enemies, we were reconciled to God, by the death of Christ: much rather being reconciled we shall be saved by his life,* Rom. v. 10. 4. The apostle riseth yet higher, to *a saving to the utmost,* and puts that upon his intercession, *Wherefore he is able to save us to the utmost, seeing he ever liveth to make intercession for us,* Heb. vii. 25. If in the former were any thing wanting, this intercession of Christ supplies all; it is the coronis, which makes all effectual; it saves to the uttermost, for itself is the uttermost and highest step; on earth Christ begins the execution of his office, in heaven he ends it; in his life and death, Christ was the meritorious cause; but by his intercession, Christ is the applying cause of our soul's salvation. In this very intercession of Christ is the consummation and perfection of the priesthood of Christ. O! then how requisite and necessary must this needs be?

4. It is gracious and full of bowels; Christ's intercession, and indeed Christ's priestly office is erected, and set up on purpose for the relief of poor distressed sinners. There is no mixture of terror in this blessed office of Jesus Christ, and this doth distinguish it from his other offices. Christ, by his kingly office, rules over the churches, and over the world; but all obtain not mercy whom he thus rules over; Christ, by his prophetical office, comes to his own, but many of his own received him not; but now wherever the priestly office of Jesus Christ is let forth upon a soul, that soul shall certainly be saved for ever. O this priestly office of Christ, is an office of mere love and tender compassion! Christ (saith the apostle) *is such an high priest, as cannot but be touched with the feeling of our infirmities,* Heb. iv. 15. Oh! he is *a merciful, and a faithful high priest in things pertaining to God, to make reconciliation for the sins of the people,* Heb. ii. 17. He is merciful and exceeding compassionate, *In all our afflictions he is afflicted; —and in his love, and in his pity he redeemed us,* Isa. lxiii. 9. and in his love and pity he intercedes for us.

SECT. VIII.
Wherein the intercession of Christ consists.

8. WHerein more especially doth the intercession of Jesus Christ consist? Some suppose, that Christ's very being in heaven, and putting God in mind of his active and passive obedience by his very presence, is all that intercession that the scripture speaks of. But I rather answer in these particulars. As,——

1. Christ's intercession consists, in the presenting of his person for us; he himself went up to heaven, and presented himself; the apostle calls this, *an appearing for us; Christ is not entered into the holy place made with hands, but into heaven, now to appear in the presence of God for us,* Heb. ix. 24. I believe there is an emphasis in the words, *appearing for us.* But how appears he for us? I answer, 1. In a public manner; whatsoever he did in this kind, he did it openly and publickly; he appears for us in the presence of God the Father;

† Goodwin *Christ set forth.*

ther; he appears for us in the presence of his saints and angels; heaven's eyes are all upon him in his appearing for us. 2. He appears for us as a Mediator, he stands in the middle betwixt God and us; hence it is that he is God-man, that he might be a Mediator betwixt God and man. 3. He appears for us as a sponsor and a pledge; surely it is a comfort to a man to have a friend at court, at the prince's elbow, that may own him and appear for him; but if this friend be both a mediator and a surety: a mediator to request for him, and a surety to engage for him; O! what comfort is this? Thus Christ appeared in every respect; he is a Mediator to request for us; and he is a surety to engage for us: as Paul was for Onesimus a mediator, *I beseech thee for my son Onesimus*, Phil. ix. 10. and a sponsor, *If he have wronged thee, or owe thee ought, put that on my account, I will repay it*, verse 18, 19. So is Jesus Christ for his saints, he is *the Mediator of a better covenant*, Heb. viii. 6. and he *is a surety of a better testament*, Heb. vii. 22. 4. He appears as a solicitor, to present and promote the desires and requests of the saints, in such a way as that they might find acceptance with his Father. He is not idle now, he is in heaven; but as on earth, he ever went about doing good, so now in glory he is ever about his work of doing good; he spends all his time in heaven in promoting the good of his people; as from the beginning it was his care, so to the world's end it will be his care to solicit his Father in the behalf of his poor saints: he tells God, *Thus and thus it is with his poor members, they are in want, in trouble, in distress, in affliction, in reproach*; and then he presents their sighs, sobs, prayers, tears and groans; and that in such a way as that they become acceptable to his Father.—5. He appears as an advocate, *If any man sin, we have an advocate with the Father, Jesus Christ the righteous*, 1 John ii. 1. An advocate is more than a solicitor; an advocate is one that is of counsel with another, and that pleadeth his case in open court; and such an advocate is Jesus Christ unto his people. 1. He is of counsel with them; that is one of the titles given him by the prophet Isaiah, *Wonderful, counsellor*, Isa. ix. 6. He counsels them by his word and Spirit. 2. He pleads for them, and this he doth in the high court of heaven, at the bar of God's own justice, there he pleads their case, and answereth all the accusations that are brought in by Satan or their own consciences; but of this anon.——6. He appears as a public agent or ledger ambassador; what that is, some tell us in these particulars. 1. His work is to continue peace; and surely that is Christ's work, *He is our peace*, Eph. ii. 14. (saith the apostle) that is, the author of our peace; he purchased our peace, and he maintains our peace with God; to this purpose he sits at God's right hand to intercede for us, and to maintain the peace and union betwixt God and us, *Therefore being justified by faith, we have peace with God through our Lord Jesus Christ*, Romans v. 1. 2. His work is to maintain intercourse and correspondency; and surely this is Christ's work also, *By him we have an access unto the Father.* — *In him we have boldness and access with confidence, by the faith of him*, Eph. ii. 18. iii. 12. The word *access*, doth not only signify coming to God in prayer, but all that resort and communion which we have with God, as united by faith to Jesus Christ; according to that, *Christ hath once suffered for sins, the just for the unjust, that he might bring us to God*, 1 Peter iii. 18. This benefit have all believers in and by Christ, they come to God by him, they have free commerce and intercourse in heaven.—— 3. His work is to reconcile and take up emergent differences, and this is Christ's work also, *He maketh intercession for the transgressors*, Isa. liii. 12. He takes up the differences that our transgressions make betwixt God and us. 4. His work is to procure the welfare of the people or state where he negociates: and this is no less Christ's work, for he seeks the welfare of his people, he sits at God's right hand to intercede for them, and commending their estate and condition to his Father, he makes it his request to his Father, that his members may have *a continual supply of the Spirit of Jesus Christ*, Phil. i. 19. that they may be strengthened in temptations, confirmed in tribulations, delivered from every evil work, enabled to every good duty, and finally preserved unto his heavenly kingdom.

2. Christ's intercessions consist in the presenting of his wounds, death and blood, as a public satisfaction for the debt of sin; and as a public price for the purchase of our glory.

There is a question amongst the schools, whether Christ hath now taken his wounds, or the signs, scars,

scars, and prints of his wounds, into heaven with him? And, whether Christ, in representing those wounds, scars, and prints unto his Father, doth not thereby intercede for us? Some, I am sure, are for the affirmative. * Aquinas distinguisheth of Christ's intercession, as being threefold. The first, Before his passion, by devout prayer; and the second, At his passion, by effusion of his blood; and the third, After his ascension, by the representation of his wounds and scars. Howsoever this hold, (for I dare not be too confident without scripture ground) yet this I dare say, that Christ doth not only present himself, but the sacrifice of himself, and the infinite merit of his sacrifice. When he went to heaven, he carried with him absolutely the power, the merit, the virtue of his wounds, and death, and blood, into the presence of God the Father for us; and with his blood he sprinkled the mercy-seat (as it were) seven times. We read in the law, that *when the high priest went within the vail, he took the blood of the bullock, and sprinkled it with his finger upon the mercy-seat eastward: and before the mercy-seat he sprinkled the blood with his finger seven times*, Lev. xvi. 14. Not only was the priest to kill the bullock without the holy of holies, but he was to enter with the blood into the holy of holies and to sprinkle the mercy-seat therein with it; surely these were *patterns of things to be done in the heavens*, Heb. ix. 23. Christ that was slain and crucified *without the gate*, Heb. xiii. 12. carried his own blood into the holy of holies, or into the heaven of heavens, for *by his own blood he entred in once into the holy place, having obtained eternal redemption for us*, Heb. ix. 12. and thither come, he sprinkles it (as it were) upon the mercy seat, (i. e.) he applies it, and obtains mercy by it; by the blood of Christ God's mercy and justice are reconciled in themselves, and reconciled unto us, Christ sprinkles his blood on the mercy-seat *seven times*; seven is a note of perfection; where Christ's blood is sprinkled on a soul, that soul is sure to be washed from all filth, and at last be perfected and saved to the very outmost: Christ's blood was shed upon the earth, but Christ's blood is sprinkled, now he is in heaven; what, is any soul sprinkled with the blood of Christ? Surely this sprinkling comes from heaven; so the apostle, *but ye are come to mount Zion, and unto the city of the living God, the heavenly Jerusalem, — and to Jesus the Mediator of the new covenant*; and then it follows, *to the blood of sprinkling, that speaketh better things than that of Abel*, Heb. xii. 22, 24. It is upon mount Zion where this sprinkling is; there is Jesus at God's right hand, there stands (as it were) upon the mount, and there he sprinkles his blood round about him; heaven is all besprinkled, as the mercy-seat in the holy of holies was, Lev. xvi. 14, 19. The earth is all besprinkled, as the altar out of the holy of holies was; heaven and earth are all besprinkled with the blood of Jesus, so that the saints and people of God are no-where, but their doors, and their posts, and houses (I mean their bodies and souls) are all besprinkled with the blood of the Lamb, slain from the beginning of the world. Why, this is that *blood of sprinkling that speaks better things than that of Abel*. Mark, that Christ's blood hath a tongue, it speaks, it cries, it prays, it intercedes; there's some agreement, and some difference betwixt Christ's blood and Abel's blood.

1. The agreement is in these things; Abel's blood was abundantly shed, for so it is said, *the voice of blood*, Gen. iv. 10. and Christ's blood was let out with thorns and scourges, nails and spear, it was abundantly shed. Again, Abel's blood cried out, yea it made a loud cry, so that it was heard from earth to heaven, *the voice of thy brother's blood crieth unto me from the ground*, Gen. iv. 10. and Christ's blood crieth out, it makes a loud cry, it fills heaven and earth with the noise; yea the Lord's ears are so filled with it, that it drowns all other sounds, and rings continually in his ears.

2. The difference is in these things; Abel's blood cried for vengeance against Cain, but Christ's blood speaks for mercy on all believers; Abel's blood was shed because he sacrificed, and he and his sacrifice accepted; but Christ's blood was shed that he might be sacrificed, and that we thro' his sacrifice might be accepted. Abel's blood cried thus, *See, Lord, and revenge*; but Christ's blood cried thus, *Father, forgive them, for they know not what they do*; and at this very instant Christ's blood cries for remission, and here's our comfort; if God heard the servant, he will much rather hear the son, if he heard the servant for spilling, he will much more hear the son for saving. Yet that I may

---

* Acquinas in John c. 2.

may speak properly, and not in figures, I will not say, that the very blood which Christ shed on the cross is now in heaven, nor that it speaks in heaven; these sayings are merely metaphorical; yet this I maintain as real and proper, that the power, merit, and virtue of Christ's blood is presented by our Saviour to his Father, both as a public satisfaction for our sins, and as a public price for the purchase of our glory.

3. Christ's intercession consists in the presenting of his will, his request, his interpolation for us, grounded upon the vigour and virtue of his glorious merits, *Father, I will that they also whom thou hast given me be with me where I am, that they may behold my glory which thou hast given me,* John xvii. 24. This was a piece of Christ's prayer whilst yet he was on earth, and some say, it is a summary of Christ's intercession which now he makes for us in his glory; he prayed on earth as he meant to pray for us when he came to heaven; he hints at this in the beginning of his prayer, for he speaks as if all his work had been done on earth, and as if then he were even beginning his work in heaven, *I have glorified thee on earth, I have finished the work which thou gavest me to do; and now, O Father! glorify thou me with thy own self, with the glory which I had with thee before the world was,* John xvii. 4, 5.

I know it is a question, Whether Christ now in heaven do indeed, and truth, and in right propriety of speech, pray for us? Some able divines are for the negative, others for the affirmative. For my part (leaving a liberty to those otherwise minded according to their light) I am of opinion, that Christ doth not only intercede by an interpretative prayer, as in the presenting of himself, and his merits to his Father, but also by an express prayer, or by an express and open representation of his will; and to this opinion methinks these texts agree, *I will pray the Father, and he shall give you another comforter, and at that day ye shall ask in my name, and I say not unto you, that I will pray the Father for you,* John xiv. 16. John xvi. 26, 27. When he saith, *I say not, that I will pray for you,* it is the highest intimation that he would pray for them; as it is our phrase, *I do not say that I will do this or that for you, no not I,* when indeed we will most surely do it, and do it to purpose.

Austin confirms this, * *Orat pro nobis, orat in nobis, et oratur, a nobis, &c.* He prays for us, he prays in us, and he is prayed to by us: he prays for us as he is our priest, and he prays in us as he is our head, and he is prayed to by us, as he is our God. † Ambrose tells us, 'That Christ so now prays for 'us, as sometimes he prayed for Peter, *that his faith should not fail.* Methinks I imagine as if I heard Christ praying in heaven, in this language, 'O my Father, I pray not for the world, I will not 'open my lips for any one son of perdition; but I 'employ all my blood, and all my prayers, and 'all my interests with thee, for my dear, beloved, 'precious saints; it is true, thou hast given me a 'personal glory, which I had with thee before the 'world was, and yet there is another glory I beg 'for, and that is the glory of my saints, O that 'they may be saved! why, I am glorified in them, 'they are my joy, and therefore I must have them 'with me where I am; thou hast set my heart 'upon them, and thou thyself hast loved them, 'as thou hast loved me, and thou hast ordained 'them to be one in us, even as we are one, and 'therefore I cannot live long asunder from them, 'I have thy company, but I must have theirs too; 'I will that they be with me where I am; if I 'have any glory, they must have part of it; this 'is my prayer, that they may behold my glory 'which thou hast given me,' John xvii. 10.—xiii. 24. Why, thus Christ prayed while he was on earth, and if this same prayer be the summary of Christ's intercession or interpolation now he is in heaven, we may imagine him praying thus; it were too nice to question, whether Christ's prayer in heaven be vocal or mental? Certainly Christ presents his gracious will to his Father in heaven some way or other, and I make no question but he fervently and immovably desires, that for the perpetual virtue of his sacrifice all his members may be accepted of God, and crowned with glory; not only is there a cry of his blood in heaven, but Christ by his prayer seconds that cry of his blood. An argument is handed to us by Mr. Goodwin thus: '‡ As it was with Abel, so it is with Christ; 'Abel's blood went up to heaven, and Abel's soul 'went up to heaven, and by this means the cry of 'Abel's dead blood was seconded by the cry of 'Abel's living soul: his cause cried, and his soul 'cried;

* Aug. *Prefat.* in Psalm lxxxv.   † Ambr. *super ad* Rom. viii.   ‡ Goodwin *Christ set forth.*

'cried; as it is said of the martyrs, That the souls
'of them that were slain for the testimony which
'they held, cried with a loud voice, saying, How
'long, O Lord! holy and true, dost thou not judge
'and avenge our blood on them that dwell on the
'earth? Rev. vi. 9, 10. Even so it is with Christ;
'his blood went up to heaven, and his soul went
'up to heaven; yea his body, soul, and all his
'whole person went up to heaven; and by this
'means his cause cries, and he himself seconds the
'cry of his cause. Jesus Christ in his own person
'ever liveth to make intercession for us? he ever
'liveth, as the great master of requests, to present
'his desires, that those for whom he died; may be
'saved.'

4. Christ's intercession consists in the presenting of our persons in his own person to his Father, so that now God cannot look upon the Son, but he must behold the saints in his Son: are they not members of his body, in near relation to himself? And are not all his intercessions in behalf of them, and only of them? But how are all the elect carried up into heaven with Jesus Christ, and there set down before his Father in Jesus Christ? I answer, not actually, but mystically; when Christ intercedes, he takes our persons, and carries them in unto God the Father, in a most unperceivable way to us; for the way or manner I leave it to others, for my part, I dare not be too inquisitive in a secret not revealed by God; only this we say, that Christ presents our persons to his Father in his own person: and this was plainly shadowed out by that act or office of the high priest, who went into the holy of holies, with *the names of all the tribes of Israel upon his shoulders, and upon his breast*, Ex. xxviii. 12. And this the apostle speaks out yet more plainly, *By him we have an access unto the Father, and in him we have boldness and access with confidence*, Eph. ii. 18.—iii. 12. I shall a little enlarge on both these texts, recorded for our instruction in the law, and gospel, in the Old and in the New Testament. First, We find in the law, *That Aaron was to put two stones upon the shoulders of the ephod, for stones of memorial unto the children of Israel, and so Aaron was to bear the names before the Lord upon his two shoulders for a memorial*, Exod. xxviii. 14. And again, *Aaron was to bear the names of the children of Israel in the breastplate of judgment upon his heart, when he went in-* *to the holy place, for a memorial before the Lord continually*, ver. 29. Here we find the names of the twelve tribes of Israel engraven in stones, which the high priest usually took with him into the holy place, when he appeared before the Lord; first, upon his humeral, and then upon his pectoral; in both shewing that he entred into that place, not only, or principally, in his own behalf, but in behalf of the tribes whom he presented before the Lord, that they might be a continual remembrance with the Lord; a lively type of Christ's intercession, who being entred into the heavens, he there appears in the behalf of his elect, and he presents their persons to his Father, bearing them (as it were) upon his shoulders, and upon his heart; why, thus Christ takes our persons into heaven, and represents them in his own person to his Father. Secondly, We find in the gospel a gracious promise, *That by Christ we have access unto the Father, and in Christ we have access with confidence*, Eph. ii. 18.—iii. 12. Where the word *access*, [*tirosagoge*], signifies properly a manuduction, or leading by the hand to God, an introduction, or bringing unto God: alluding to the custom in prince's courts, where none may come into the presence-chamber, unless they be led, or brought in by some favourite or courtier there; thus, none may have access into the presence of God, unless they be brought in by this favourite of heaven, the Lord Jesus Christ, whose very office it is to bring men unto God; he takes us by the hand, and leads us to the Father, q. d. 'Come souls, 'come along with me, and I will carry you to the 'Father.' Look how a child that hath run away from his father, is taken by the hand of a friend, or of his elder brother, and so brought again into the presence of his father; even so all we having run away from God, are by the good hand of Christ taken up, and led again into the presence of the Father; he is that ladder that Jacob saw, upon whom we ascend into the bosom of God, and into heaven; he is that high priest, that takes our persons, and bears them on his shoulders and on his heart, sustaining our persons, and presenting our conditions unto his Father, and our Father, unto his God, and our God.

5. Christ's intercession consists in the presenting of our duties unto God. Not only doth he take our persons, and leads and carries them into the
pre-

presence of God, but together with our persons he presents all our services in his own person. Now, in this act he doth these two things.

1. He observes what evil, or what failing is in our duties, and he draws that out, and takes it away, before he presents them unto God; or as a child that would present his father with a posy, he goes into the garden, and gathers flowers and weeds together, but coming to his mother, she picks out the weeds, and binds up the flowers by themselves, and so it is presented to the Father; thus we go to duty, and we gather weeds and flowers together, but Christ comes and picks out the weeds, and so presents nothing but flowers to God the Father: and this is plainly set forth by that ceremony of the high priest, in taking away the iniquity of their holy things, 'And thou shalt make a plate of pure gold, and grave upon it like the ingravings of a signet, holiness to the Lord; and thou shalt put it on a blue lace, that it may be upon the mitre, upon the forefront of the mitre it shall be. And it shall be on Aaron's forehead, that Aaron may bear the iniquity of the holy things, which the children of Israel shall hallow in all their holy gifts, and it shall be always upon his forehead, that they may be accepted before the Lord,' Exod. xxviii. 36, 37, 38. This was the manner of the ceremony, and this was the end of the ceremony, that Aaron might bear and take away the iniquity of their holy things: what was this but a type of Jesus Christ? Who, with his most absolute righteousness, covereth all the defects of our good works, which are still spotted with some defect? alas! 'All our righteousnesses are as filthy rags,' Isa. lxiv. 6. but Christ draws out the evil of duty, and failings in duty, before he will present them unto God.

2. He observes what good there is in any of our duties or performances, and with that he mingles his own prayers and intercessions, and presents all as one work interwoven or mingled together unto God the Father, *And another angel stood at the altar, having a golden censer, and there was given unto him much incense, that he should offer it with the prayers of all saints upon the golden altar, which was before the throne; and the smoke of the incense which came with the prayers of the saints ascended up before God out of the angel's hand*, Rev. viii. 3, 4. I know there is a controversy, Who this angel should be, that with the incense mingles the prayers of all saints? Some conjecture him to be a created angel, in that the incense or odours are said to be given to him, and not to be his own, or to have them of himself. Others say, he could be no other but the angel of the covenant, for no angel does intercede or present our prayers but Jesus Christ; as for that which is spoken concerning the seven angels presenting the saints prayers, *I am Raphael, one of the seven holy angels, which present the prayers of the saints*, Tob. xii. 15. we say it is no canonical scripture, nor is it authorised by any canonical scripture; besides, I cannot think that the priests were types of angels, but only of Christ. Again, howsoever the Greek copies so read that text, yet the ancient Hebrew copy, set forth by Paulus Fagies, and Jerome, who translated it out of the Chaldee, (as Mr. Mead on Zechariah iv. 10. avoucheth) reads it thus, *I am Raphael, one of the seven angels, which stand, and minister before the glory of the holy One.* And certainly in this text of Rev. viii. 3, 4. there is a figurative description of an heavenly service, correspondent to that which was performed in the temple; namely, that the people being without at prayer, the priest offered incense within upon the altar, Luke i. 9, 10. to signify that believers prayers have always need to be helped and sanctified by Christ's intercession; and what though the incense was given him? We know that Christ himself was given of God, *God so loved the world, that he gave his only begotten Son*, John iii. 16. and yet this hinders not but that Jesus Christ gave himself, and that he gave himself for an incense too, for so the apostle, *He hath given himself for us an offering and sacrifice unto God*, Eph. v. 2. for an incense, or for a *sweet-smelling savour*. In this respect the incense might be given him, and yet the incense was his own, they were only Christ's merits, righteousness and satisfaction; they are the sweet odour, by virtue whereof God accepts of his saints persons and prayers; and it is only Christ that presents before God that which he is and hath, he alone being both offering and priest; we can think of no other priest in gospel-times but only Jesus, *The forerunner, even Jesus Christ, made an high priest after the order of Melchisedec*, Heb. vi. 20. It is Jesus, and only Jesus that presents our prayers, and sanctifies our prayers, and mingles our

N n n prayers

prayers with his merits, and so makes them penetrate sweetly before his God.

6. Christ's intercession consists in the presenting of our plea or answer in heaven, to all those accusations that are brought in against ourselves. And this I take to be the meaning of the challenge, *Who shall lay any thing to the charge of God's elect? It is God that justifies, Who is he that condemneth? It is Christ that died, yea rather that is risen again, who is even at the right hand of God, who also maketh intercession for us,* Rom. viii 33, 34. Christ intercedes, and who shall condemn? Christ takes off all accusations, and who shall charge? If the law, or sin, or Satan, shall dare to accuse, our Jesus is ready at God's right hand to answer all. There is a vision in Zechariah representing this, *and the angel shewed me Joshua the high priest standing before the angel of the Lord, and Satan standing at his right hand to resist him,* Zech. iii 1. It was the custom of the accuser to stand at the right hand of the accused, *Set thou a wicked man over him, and let Satan stand at his right hand,* Psal. cix. 6. Now here's Satan standing at Joshua's right hand to accuse him; but whereof doth he accuse him? That appears in the words following, *Joshua was clothed with filthy garments,* Zech. iii. 3. an ordinary sign of sin; as a white garment is a sign of Christ's righteousness, so is a filthy garment, in scripture, a sin of vileness; alas! Joshua was defiled with the pollution which he had gotten by the contagion of Babylon, and now at his return, Satan lays it to his charge, but Jesus Christ, our great high priest steps in, and takes off the accusation, *And the Lord said unto Satan, the Lord rebuke thee, O Satan, even the Lord that hath chosen Jerusalem rebuke thee,* ver. 2. twice he repeats it, to shew the fulness of Christ's intercession, q. d. The Lord my God, my everlasting Father, rebuke, and confound thee, Satan, in this thy malicious opposition against my Joshua; and then he goes on in his apology for Joshua, *Is not this a brand pluckt out of the fire?* ver. 2 q. d. Is not this one, whom, of my grace, I have reserved amongst my people, whom I caused to pass through the fire of mine indignation? And shall not my decree of grace stand firm and inviolable towards such? Or thus, is not this a brand pluckt

newly out of the fire of affliction? Was he not in the captivity of Babylon? And is it likely he should be there, but he would be defiled with the touch of pitch? Take a brand, and pull it out of the fire, and there will be some dust, and ashes, and filth about it; why Lord, (says Christ) this Joshua is newly pulled out of the burning, and therefore he must needs have ashes, and dust, and filth about him: But come, (faith Christ to his holy angels) *take away the filthy garment from him*; and come (says Christ to his servant Joshua) *Behold I have caused thine iniquity to pass from thee, and I will clothe thee with change of raiment,* ver. 4. And thus Christ took off the accusation that was brought against Joshua by Satan for his filthy garments. In like manner doth our blessed intercessor at this instant; if a poor saint falls into any sin, and defiles his garments, Satan comes in, and takes the right hand of him, and accuses him before the Lord, but Christ our great high priest being at the right hand of his Father, he takes up the cause, puts in a plea, and answers all the accusations of the enemy, ' True Lord, ' this poor soul hath filthy garments, but is he not ' a fire-brand newly pluckt out of the fire? Was ' he not in his natural and sinful condition the o- ' ther day? Is he not yet partly regenerate, and ' partly unregenerate? Needs therefore must be ' some ashes, and dust, and filth upon him. O ' my Father! my will is, that thou consider him ' in that respect, thou knowest his frame, and ' thou rememberest that he is but dust, though ' he have filthy garments now upon him, yet I ' will give him change of raiments; I will clothe ' him with the robe of my righteousness, and then ' thou shalt see no iniquity in Jacob, no trans- ' gression in Israel.' Why, thus the Lord steps in and answers to all the accusations that are brought in against us by law, or sin, or Satan, to God his Father; and in this respect he is truly called our advocate, *If any man sin, we have an advocate with the Father, Jesus Christ the righteous,* 1 John ii. 1. We have an advocate that pleads for us, that answers for us; that in a way of equity (grounding all upon his own merits) calls for the pardon of our sins, and for the salvation of our souls.

SECT.

SECT. IX.

How powerful and prevailing Christ's intercessions are with God his Father.

9. HOW powerful and prevailing are Christ's intercessions with God his Father? I answer, Very much, and this will appear, if we consider, As,——

1. That Christ is our great high priest to God, *We have such an high priest who is set down at the right hand of the majesty on high*, Heb. viii. 1. Now it was the way of God to lend his ear in special manner to the high priests; and therefore the people usually run to them, when they would enquire of God, *Beforetime, in Israel, when a man went to enquire of God, thus he spake, Come and let us go to the seer, for he that is now called a prophet, or high priest, was beforetime called a seer,* 1 Sam. ix. 9.——People were wont to repair to the priests, and the priests were wont to go to God; and good reason, for the priests were to mediate for the people, and the people had experience that God would hearken to the cry of the priests, *Samuel called unto the Lord, and the Lord sent thunder and rain that day. And all the people said to Samuel, Pray for thy servants unto the Lord thy God.——And Samuel said unto the people,—— God forbid that I should sin against the Lord, in ceasing to pray for you,* 1 Sam. xii. 18, 19, 23. Now, such an high priest as this, (though with far more eminency) is Christ to God; he intercedes for his people, *God forbid that he should ever cease to pray for his people*; and he hath God's ear in special manner; if ever God lend his ear to any one, it must needs be to this high priest, because of his office to intercede betwixt God and his people. Christ stands in the middle, or indeed next to God, as he is in these gospel times our great high priest; and therefore he must needs prevail with God in every petition he puts up for us.

2. That Christ was called to this office by God, *Christ glorified not himself to be made an high priest*, Heb. v. 4, 5. No, no, but *he was called of God as Aaron was*; it was God, the Father, that designed him to it, and that furnished him for it, and that invested him in it, *The Lord hath sworn, and will not repent, thou art a priest for ever after the order of Melchisedec*, Psal. cx. 4. Now to what purpose should God call him to this office, but especially to intercede for them to whom God was willing to communicate salvation? It was God's mind, as well as Christ's mind, to save his elect; and this was the way whereon they agreed, that an high priest should be appointed, and an office of intercession should be erected, and by that means the salvation purchased should be applied; many times we are apt to conceive legal or law-thoughts of God, the Father, as that he is just and severe, and that Christ his Son is more meek and merciful; but this cannot be, for there are not two infinite wills, nor two infinite mercies, one in the Father, another in the Son, but one will, and one mercy in both. And to that purpose observe but the readiness of God, the Father, to receive Christ honourably into heaven, that he might do the work of the high priest there; no sooner had Christ entred through the gates into the city, but presently, *Sit thou down* (saith God) *at my right hand*; but to what end? Surely not only to rule as king, (of which we have spoken before) but also to intercede as our great high priest; hence we find in scripture, that Christ's session and intercession, his Kingly and Priestly office are joined together, *He is set on the right hand of the throne of the majesty in the heavens*, Heb. viii. 1. He, Who? Why, Christ our high priest, we have such an high priest who is set down. It is, as if Christ at his entrance into heaven, had said, 'My Father, I am come hither as the 'great high priest, having on his breast-plate the 'names of all the elect, and I come to intercede 'for poor sinners; what, shall I have welcome on 'these same terms? to whom the Father replied, 'Welcome my Son, my only Son, on these very 'terms; Come, sit thee down, and intercede for 'whom thou pleasest, I have called thee on pur- 'pose to this very office, and thou shalt prevail.' Surely the Father is engaged to purpose to hear his Son, in that he is an high priest to God, and called to his office by God.

3. That Christ is God's Son, and that is more than Christ's high priest; he is his natural Son, his beloved Son, his Son that never gave him the least offence; sure then, when he comes and intercedes for a man he is most like to speed; if a gracious child do but cry, *My Father, my Father*, he may prevail very much, especially with a Father who is

tender-hearted; Jesus Christ is the gracious, precious Son of God the Father, and God the Father, is a dear and kind-hearted Father; How then should the intercessions of Christ but be most powerful with God? Hence some gather the prevalency of Christ's intercession, because in many places of scripture where this part of Christ's priesthood or intercession is laid down, this Sonship is also expressed or set forth, As *we have a great high priest entred into the heavens, Jesus the Son of God*, Heb. iv. 14 —And *thou art an high priest, for ever, after the order of Melchisedec*, Heb. v. 5, 6. But immediately before, *Thou art my Son, this day have I begotten thee.* O needs must the intercession of such a son be very prevalent: I say, Of such a Son; For was ever any Son like this Son of God? Was ever any Son so like his Father, or so equal with his Father? We know he is a begotten Son, and yet never began to be a Son; he is the Son of the Father, and yet never began to have a Father; he is a branch of the King of ages, and yet in all the ages past was never younger; surely all the relations of son and father in the world, are but a shadow of this relation betwixt God and Christ; it is so near, that though they are two, (as in all relations there must needs be *relatum* and *correlatum*) yet Christ speaks of them, as if they were but one, *I and my Father are one*, John x. 30. If then the Father should deny him any thing, he should deny himself, or cease to be one with his Son, which can never be. Christ is God's Son, his natural Son, his beloved Son, *This is my beloved Son, in whom I am well pleased*, saith God, Matth. iii. 17. Oh then! how prevalent must Christ's intercessions be with God?

4. That Christ is God himself, not only God's Son, but God himself; how powerful in this respect must his intercessions be unto the Father? It is true, that Christ is another subsistence and person from the Father, but Christ is one and the same God with the Father! Christ is the very essential, substantial, and noble representation of God himself; Christ is the very self of God, both God sending and God sent; Christ is the fellow of God; *Awake, O sword, against my shepherd, and against the man that is my fellow*, Zech. xiii. 7. Nay, Christ is 'God, and not another God, but one God, ' God of ' God, light of light, very God of very God, begot-' ten, not made, being of one substance with the Fa-

' ther, by whom all things were made.' Can we imagine now that God himself should be denied any boon of God himself? It God sometimes spake to his servants, *Ask of me, command ye me concerning all the work of mine hands*, Isa. xlv. 11. Will not God much say to God, *Ask of me, and I shall give thee the heathen for thine inheritance, and the uttermost parts of the earth for thy possession?* Psal. ii. 8. We have brought it now so near, that if God be God, and God be omnipotent, that he can do, and can have whatsoever he pleases; then Christ being one God with his Father, he must needs prevail; it is but ask and have, let him ask what he will.

5. That Christ is God's darling upon this very account, because he intercedes for his people, ' Therefore doth my Father love me, because I lay ' down my life, that I might take it again,' John x. 17. I lay it down by suffering, and take it again by rising, ascending up into heaven, and interceding there; and *therefore doth my Father love me.* O the love of God to Christ, and of God in Christ to all his saints! *God so loved the world that he gave his Son*, and Christ so loved the world, *that he gave himself*; and now again because Christ gave himself, and his gift is as a sweet-smelling favour unto God, therefore God loves Christ; O what a round of love is here! ' God loves Christ, and Christ loves us, ' and the Father loves Christ again for loving of us.' There is not an act of Christ in his work of our redemption, but the Father looks on it with love and liking at his baptism. Lo! a voice came from heaven, saying, *This is my beloved Son, in whom I am well pleased*, Matth. iii. 17. at his death, *He seeth of the travail of his soul, and is satisfied*, Isa. liii. 11. at his ascension, he heareth of the intercessions of his soul, and he is delighted; Christ's intercessions are God's musick, and therefore, as sometimes Christ spoke to his spouse, so God speaks to Christ, *Let me see thy countenance, let me hear thy voice, for sweet is thy voice, and thy countenance is comely*, Cant. ii. 14. Now Christ's intercessions must needs prevail, when God loves Christ for his intercessions sake: if before the world was made, the Son was his Father's darling, (for so it is said) *When he appointed the foundations of the earth, then I was by him as one brought up with him, and I was daily his delight*, Prov. viii. 29. 30. In the original, *delights*, intimating that the

eternal

eternal Son was variety of delights to his Father. O then! what delights, what variety, what infinity of delights hath God in Christ now interceding for us? What a dear darling is Christ to God, when not only he stands by him, but he represents to him all the elect from the beginning to the end of the world, *q d* 'See, Father, look on my breast, 'read here all the names of those thou hast given 'me, as Adam, and Abraham, and Isaac, and Ja-'cob; of the twelve tribes, and of the twelve a-'postles, of all the martyrs, professors and con-'fessors of the law and gospel; I pray for them, 'I pray not for the world, but only for them, for 'they are mine. Methinks I hear God answer, 'What my Son! and what the Son of my womb! 'and what the Son of my vows! Hast thou be-'gotten me thus many sons? And are all these 'mine? Why then, ask what thou wilt, and have 'what thou pleasest; I am as strongly inclined and 'disposed to give thee thy asking, as thou wouldest 'have it; it is my joy, my delight, my pleasure 'to save these souls, and surely the pleasure of the 'Lord shall prosper in thy hands'

6 That Christ is God's commander, (I speak it with reverence) as well as petitioner, it is a phrase given to the servants of God, *Command ye me*, Isa. xlv. 11 And may we not give it to the Son of God? Christians! God is as ready to do us service as if we had him at command, *This is the confidence that we have in him, that if we ask any thing according to his will he heareth us*, 1 John v. 14 And, in this sense, we may boldly say, That God, the Father, is as ready to hear Jesus Christ, as if he had him at command; not that in deed and reality he commands God, but that in deed and truth he commands all below God, and he commands all in the stead of God And to this purpose is that voice of God, *I have set my King upon my holy hill of Zion*, Psal ii 6 And why my King? I dare not say he is God's King, as if God were Christ's inferior, or Christ's sub-ject God forbid! why then my King? I answer, He is God's King, because appointed by God; or he is God's King, because he rules in the stead of God, *The Father judgeth no man, but hath committed all judgment unto the Son*, John v 22. God hath given away all his prerogatives unto Jesus Christ, so that now the King of saints can do what he will with God and with all the world;

only it follows, *Ask of me, and I will give thee the heathen for thine inheritance* As if the Father should have said, 'I cannot deny thee, and 'yet, O my Son! I would have thee ask, do what 'thou wilt in heaven, earth and hell, I have not 'the heart, indeed I have not the power to de-'ny thee any thing, only acknowledge this pow-'er to be originally in myself, that all that ho-'nour the Son, may honour the Father, and all 'that honour the Father, may honour the Son' These are the terms betwixt God the Father, and God the Son, oh then! how powerful and prevailing are Christ's intercessions with his Father? If he ask who hath power to command, there is little question of prevailing in his suit, We have heard in our days of a suit managed with a petition in one hand, and a sword in the other, and what the effect is all now can tell. As a King, who sues for peace, backed with a potent army, able to win what he intreats for, must needs treat more effectually; so Christ, suing to his Father for his saints, with a power sufficient to obtain what he sues for, he must needs effect what he desires may be. It is well observed, 'That Christ first is said 'to sit at God's right hand, and then to intercede; 'he treats the salvation of sinners, as a mighty 'prince treats the giving up of some town, which 'lies seated under a castle of his that commands 'the town' Or he treats the salvation of sinners, as a commander treats the surrendering of a person already in his hands; it is beyond God's power (I speak it with submission) to deny his Son in any thing he asks, if the Lord sometimes cried out to Moses, like a man whose hands are held, *Let me alone*, Exod xxxii 10. How much more did Christ's intercession bind God's hands, and command all in heaven, earth and hell? Hence we say, that God the Father hath divested himself of all his power, and given the keys into Christ's own hands. *I am he that liveth and was dead, I am alive for evermore, Amen, and have the keys of hell and death*, Rev i. 18 There is no man goes to hell, but he is lockt in by Jesus Christ, and there is no man goes to heaven, but he is lockt in there by Jesus Christ, he hath the keys of all men's eternities hanging at his own girdle; if he but say, 'Father, I will that this man and that 'woman should inherit heaven,' the Father cannot but ... Son ... power to deny

thy

thy suit, thou hast the keys of heaven in thine own hands, be it even as thou wilt.

7. I shall only add this on the Father's part, That God is Christ's commander to his office, as well as Christ is God's commander in this office. O! why should we have hard thoughts of God the Father more than of God the Son? Is he not as willing of our salvation as Jesus Christ? Surely it was the oath of God, I mean of God the Father, *As I live, saith the Lord, I would not have the death of a sinner, but that the wicked turn from his sin and live,* Ez. xxxiii. 11. Was not this the first salute of God to Christ, when he first entered into heaven, *Sit down here in this throne, and ask what thou wilt of thy Father?* Nay, did not the Father prevent the Son, in laying his commands upon him to ask, before the Son opened his mouth to speak a word, by way of any requests to God his Father? *Thou art my Son, this day* (even this day of thy resurrection, ascension, session) *have I begotten thee, ask of me, and I shall give thee the Heathen for thine inheritance, and the uttermost parts of the earth for thy possession,* Psal. ii. 7, 8. q. d. 'Come Son, thou art my Son, this day 'have I begotten thee, and though I have be-'gotten thee from all eternity, yet this day and 'every day I am begetting thee still: I said to thee 'at thy resurrection, This day have I begotten 'thee; and I said to thee at thy ascension, This 'day have I begotten thee; and now ask, and be 'not shy, or modestly backward in petitioning; I 'command thee to this office, I make thee here 'the great master of requests in heaven; others 'may pray out of charity, but none but thyself in 'a way of justice, authority, and office; and there-'fore ask boldly and largely, open thy mouth wide, 'and I will fill it.' O! what a demonstration of love is this, not only to Christ, but to us in Christ, that when man had offended his God, broke covenant with God, and turned enemy to God, that then God the Father should seek peace with man, offer conditions of peace to man and for that purpose should appoint a Mediator, an intercessor; and call his own Son to that office; and now he is in heaven, that he should bid him do his office, and ask freely, so that if the elect be not saved, it should be laid on the score of Christ, for the Father is most willing: * ' Surely here is more than

* Goodwin, *Christ exalted.*

' intimation of the Father's inclination to accept ' of Christ's intercessions in our behalf.' We may read here, that the Father's heart is as much towards us, as Christ's own heart; Oh! he is full of bowels, he is gentle, and easy to be intreated; Christ needs not much ado to get his grant, ' Christ ' adds not by his intercession one drop of love to ' the heart of God; only he draws it out, which ' otherwise would have been stopt, nor doth he ' broach it before his Father command him to ' it.' Oh then! how powerful and prevailing must Christ's intercessions be?.

SECT. X.

Of the reasons of Christ's intercessions.

10. WHAT are the reasons of this great transaction of Christ's intercession for his people? I answer,——

1. It is the Father's will that it should be so; he called Jesus Christ to this office, the command of God is upon Jesus Christ, 'Ask what thou wilt ' for thy redeemed ones, I willingly engage my-' self to grant, only it is my pleasure thou shouldest ' ask:' as sometimes he said to the house of Israel, *I the Lord have spoken, and I will do it; notwithstanding I will yet for this be enquired of by the house of Israel, to do it for them,* Ezek. xxxvi. 36, 37. So saith God to Christ, 'I the Lord have ' spoken, and I will do it, only, my Son, I will be ' enquired of by thee.' I look upon this as the main reason of Christ's intercession, *Even so Father, for so it seemed good in thy sight;* it's God's will that Christ should intercede.

2. It is the Father's love to engage his Son for his own people. O the comfort of a sound Christian in this respect! what, art thou in temptation, or desertion? Surely Christ is engaged by God to petition for thee; thou hast put up many petitions to Christ, and he hath put them all up unto God; he could do no otherwise, for he is in place an advocate, to mention and plead such cases as are moved to him. Methinks I imagine God thus bespeaking his Son; ' See thou do this poor soul ' good, my Son; here is for him according to all ' he needs, only ask according to what thou know-' est will make him happy; must he have my Spi-
'rit,

'it, my comfortable Spirit? Will no less, no 'cheaper things serve his turn? Then here it is.' Oh! how is Christ engaged now to petition for them, whom God loves, and for whom he gave himself? Surely if Christ should leave to intercede for such, he would displease his Father, which we know he would not do, he would undergo hell first.

3. It is Christ's own inclination to do his office: the power that Christ hath for the good of sinners is necessarily acted; as the sun shines upon all the world, and it cannot do otherwise, so Christ, the Sun of righteousness, shines or intercedes for all his saints, and he can do no less: what is the will of Christ, (I mean the will of Christ naturally, not artificially in a way of self-denial, as God's will is said to be our will) so that what the Father would have Christ own, he cannot but own; for the same Spirit is in Christ, which is in the Father, and in the self same measure: as God is captivated with love towards all captives, so am I, saith Christ; as God would have all to be saved, and to come to the knowledge of the truth, so would I too, saith Christ. The very same bottomless sea of love, that fluctuates in my Father's breast, it is in my breast, for *I and the Father are one*, John x. 30.

4. It is Christ's honour to intercede: hereby is the crown set on Christ's head, much honour and glory redound to Jesus in this very respect. I believe all the work that's done in heaven, it is Christ interceding, and the saints and angels praising; Christ intercedes for ever, and the four beasts, and four and twenty elders sing for ever, Rev. iv. 8, 9, 10, 11 An argument of Christ's honour, by Christ's intercession, is given in thus by ‡ Master Goodwin; if it were not for Christ's intercession, how would the office of Christ's priesthood be out of work? And this reason is more than intimated, Hebrews vii. 24, 25. *This man, because he continueth ever, hath an unchangeable priesthood*; and the work of his priesthood is interpreted, ver. 25. *To make intercession for ever.* The meaning of this is, That God would not have him continue to be a priest in title only, or in respect only of a service past, and so to have only the honour of priesthood perpetuated to him, out of the remembrance of what he once had done: but God would have him to enjoy, as the renown of the old; so a perpetual spring of honour by this new work of intercession, and so to preserve the verdure of his glory ever fresh and green; and the sum of the apostle's reasoning is this, That seeing himself was to be for ever, so his work of priesthood should be for ever, that so his honour might be preserved and continued for ever also.'

5. It is Christ's love to his saints; his heart is so enamoured with his saints, that therefore he intercedes for them for ever; love is as strong as death, it is never weary of doing good for the party beloved; now Christ's saints are Christ's love, *My sister, my love, my dove*, Cant. v. 2. The saints in Christ's books are as so many jewels, *And they shall be mine, saith the Lord of hosts, in that day when I make up my jewels*, Mal. iii. 17. The saints are Christ's only choice, the very flower of the earth, *You have I chosen out of the world*, John xv. 19. and ye are *my people, my chosen*, Isa. xliii. 20. All the world is Christ's refuse, and kings are but mortar to him, only the saints are Christ's chosen, they are they whom the Lord in his eternal counsels hath set apart for himself, *But know* (saith the Psalmist) *that the Lord hath set apart him that is godly*, Psal. iv. 3. The saints are Christ's image, (i. e.) the resemblance of Christ in all that which is his chief excellency, I mean in his righteousness, and holiness; as if I would take the picture of a man, I would not draw it out to resemble his back-parts, but as near as I could, I would draw it to life, the very face and countenance; so are the saints the very picture, the image, the draught of God to his top-excellency. The saints are in covenant with Jesus Christ, and therefore in nearer relation than any others, hence it is that they are called the portion of God, the treasure of God, the peculiar people of God, those that God and Christ doth satisfy themselves in, those that God and Christ have set their hearts on; the children of God the Father, the very spouse and bride of God the Son; in some respect nearer than the angels themselves, for the angels are not so married to Christ in a mystical union, as God's people are: now, is it any wonder that those who are so very dear to Christ, should be in the prayers of Christ? If they were so much in his heart, that sometimes he shed his blood for them, will he not now intercede for them? O yes! to this end he carries them on his breast or heart, as near as near may be,

‡ Goodwin's *Christ set forth*.

be, that they may be in a continual remembrance before the Lord for ever; his very love compels him to his office, to intercede for them.

6. It is Christ's delight to intercede for his saints. Before the world was, *his delights were with the sons of men*, Prov. viii. 31. And when the fulness of time came, then said he, *Lo, I come, in the volume of thy book it is written of me, I delight to do thy will, O my God*, Psal. xl. 7, 8. And what was that, but to be with the sons of men? He knew that was his Father's pleasure, and in respect of himself, he had a delight to live with them, and to die for them: and no sooner he entred into heaven, but there he delights to officiate still in behalf of the sons of men; he carries their names on his heart there, and though some of their persons be on earth, and he in his bodily presence is in heaven, yet distance of place cannot deaden his delights in the remembrance of them; he is ever minding his Father of his people in the nether world; he tells them that they are his all in all upon the earth, and all his joy, and all his delight, all his portion; as men use to give portions to their children, so God having but one Son by eternal generation, he hath given the elect unto him as his portion; and hence he makes it his great business in heaven, to provide mansions for his portion, to take up God's heart for his portion, to beg favour and love for his portion. Here is the joy of Christ in heaven, in going to his Father, and telling him, 'Why Father, I have a small portion yet on earth, 'and because they are on earth, they are still sin- 'ning against thy majesty, but I have suffered and 'satisfied for their sins, and hither am I come to 'mind thee of it, and continually to get out fresh 'pardons for new sins; come, look on my old sa- 'tisfaction, didst thou not promise? Is it not in 'the articles of agreement betwixt thee and me, 'that I should see of the travel of my soul, and 'should be satisfied? Didst thou not say, That 'because I poured out my soul, therefore thou 'wouldest divide me a portion with the great and 'the spoil with the strong? Isa. liii. 11, 12. O 'my Father! now I make intercession for the 'transgressors; give me out pardons for an hun- 'dred thousand millions of sins; thou hast said and 'sworn that thou hast no pleasure in the death of 'sinners, and it is my pleasure, my joy, my infinite 'delight to save sinners, these are my seed, my 'portion, my redeemed ones, and therefore let 'them be saved.' Thus Christ intercedes, and his delight in his saints, as knowing it to be his Father's mind, draws him on to this intercession; indeed this reason hangs upon that primary and first reason; it is God's will that Christ should intercede, and it is Christ's delight to do the will of his Father in heaven, *I delight to do thy will, O my God*.

7. It is Christ's compassion that causeth intercession. *Christ is such an high priest* (saith the apostle) *as cannot but be touched with the feeling of our infirmities. He was in all points tempted like as we are, yet without sin*, Heb. iv. 15. When he was on earth he felt our infirmities, frailties, miseries, and as a man that hath felt the stone, or gout, or fever, or especially that have felt soul-troubles, cannot but compassionate those that are in the like condition; so Christ having had the experience of our outward and inward sufferings, he cannot but compassionate us; and hence is is, (his very compassions moving) that he intercedes to his Father in our behalf. It is observed, That the very office or work of the high priest was to sympathize with the people of God; only in the case of the death of his kindred, he was not as others, to sympathize or mourn; but Jesus Christ goes beyond all the high priests that ever were before him; he doth fully sympathize with us, not in some, but in all conditions, *In all our afflictions, he is afflicted*, Isa. lxiii. 9. I believe Christ hath carried a man's heart up with him to heaven; and though there be no passions in him as he is God, yet the flower, the blossom, the excellency of all these passions, (which we call compassions) are infinitely in him as he is God; he striketh, and trieth and yet he pitieth; when Ephraim bemoaneth himself, God replies, *Is Ephraim my dear son? Is he a pleasant child? For since I spake against him, I do earnestly remember him still, therefore my bowels are troubled for him*, Jerem. xxxi. 20. Surely there's a violence of heavenly passion in Christ's heart as God-man, which makes him to break out into prayer to God, and into compassions towards men: O that tempted souls would consider this! it may be Christ has given you a cup of tears and blood to drink; but who knows what bowels, what turnings of heart, what motions of compassion are in Jesus Christ all the while? Those

who

who feel the fruit of Christ's intercessions know this, and cannot but subscribe to this truth. *O ye of little faith*, Why do ye doubt of Christ's bowels? Is he not our compassionate high priest? Hath not the tenderest, meekest, mildest heart of a man that God possibly can form, met with the eternal and infinite mercy of God himself in Jesus Christ? You have heard that Christ in both natures is our high priest, mediator, intercessor; and if either God or man know how to compassionate, Christ must do it. O the bowels of Christ! *He is touched* (saith the apostle) *with the feeling of our infirmities*, Heb. iv. 15. It is an allusion to the rolled and moved bowels of God, in Jer. xxxi. 20. Christ in heaven is burning and flaming in a passion of compassion towards his weak ones, and therefore he pleads, intercedes, and prays to God for them.

Thus far we have propounded the object, which is Christ's intercession; our next work is to direct you how to look upon Jesus in this respect.

CHAP. II. SECT. I.

Of knowing Jesus, as carrying on the great work of our salvation in his intercession.

1. LET us know Jesus carrying on this great work of our salvation in his intercession. Is it not a rare piece of knowledge to know what Christ is now doing in heaven for us on earth? If I had a weighty suit at court, on which lay my estate and life, If I knew that I had a friend there, that could prevail, and that he were just now moving in my behalf, were not this worth the knowledge? I dare say in the behalf of all believers in the world, Christ is now interceding for us at the right hand of God, ever since his ascension into heaven he hath been doing this work; it is a work already of above sixteen hundred years, and summer, and winter, night and day, without any tiredness of spirit. Christ hath been still praying, still interceding, Christ's love hath no vacation, no cessation at all, yea, even now whilst you read this, Christ is acting as an advocate for you, Christ hath your names engraven as a seal on his heart, and standing right opposite to the eye of his Father, the first opening of the eye-lids of God is terminated upon the breast of Jesus Christ; is not this worth the knowledge? O my soul! leave off thy vain studies of natural things! if they do not conduce some way or other to the right understanding of this, they are not worth the while; what is it for an Aristotle to be praised where he is not, and to be damned where he is? O the excellency of the knowledge of Jesus Christ! such a knowledge (if true) is no less than saving Come, study his intercession in all the former particulars; I have run them over, for the work is swoln under my hands, and I would now abbreviate; only remember this, that in Christ's intercessions are many secrets, which we must never know on this side heaven; Oh! take heed of entring into this labyrinth without the clew of the word; above all desire the guidance of the Spirit to enlighten thy darkness, and whatever thou knowest, *know it still for thyself.*

SECT. II.

Of considering Jesus in that respect.

2. LET us consider Jesus carrying on this work of our salvation in his intercession; many of God's people have found the benefit, and for my part I cannot but approve of it, as an excellent, quickning and enlivening duty, to be much in a way of meditation, or consideration, especially when we meet with such a blessed subject as this is, *My meditation of him shall be sweet*, (saith David) *I will be glad in the Lord*, Psal. civ. 34. It is enough to make a meditation sweet and refreshing, when it is conversant about such a subject, as Christ's intercession; is it not as incense, a sweet odour, and perfume with God himself? And shall not each thought of it be sweet to us? Come, let us be serious in this duty; and that we may do it thoroughly, let us consider it in these several particulars. As, ———

1. Consider of the nature of Christ's intercession: what is it but the gracious will of Christ fervently desiring that for the virtue of his death and sacrifice, thy person and performances might be accepted of God? As Christ on earth gave himself to the death, even to the death of the cross, for the abolition of sin, so now in heaven he prays the Father, *by his agony and bloody sweat, by his cross and*

and passion, by his death and sacrifice, that thy sins may be pardoned, thy service accepted, and thy soul saved. This is the will of Christ, even thy justification, sanctification, and salvation; and accordingly he presents his will, 'Father, I will that 'all those privileges flowing from my death, may 'be conferred on such a person by name; such a 'soul is now meditating and considering of my in-'tercession, and my will is, that his very meditation 'may find acceptance with God.' O! what workings would be in thy heart and spirit, if thou didst but consider, that Christ even now were speaking his will, that thy person and duty might both find acceptance, and be well-pleasing with God.

2. Consider of the person that intercedes for thee, it is Christ in both natures, it is thy Mediator, the middle one betwixt God and man; in this respect thou mayest consider him as one indifferent, and equally inclining to either party, like a pair of scales that hang even, neither side lift up, or depressed more than the other; *a Mediator is not of one*, saith the apostle, Gal. iii. 20 Christ indifferently partook of both natures, God-head, and manhood, that so he might be fit to stand in the gap between his Father and us; he is a priest according to both natures; he is a days-man wholly for God, and a days-man wholly for us, and on our side.

3. Consider of the person to whom Christ intercedes; is it not to his Father? Thou art sure to speed well, O my soul! for God is the Father of thy intercessor. If I had a suit to some majesty, and the prince would but mediate, I might hope to speed; Christ is God's prince, (as I may call him) and in respect of us, *the first-begotten of many brethren.* And herein is thy rejoicing, that the party offended is Christ's own Father, and in Christ thy Father; fathers cannot be cruel to their own dear children, *What man amongst you, whom if his son ask bread, he will give him a stone? Or if he ask a fish, will he give him a serpent? If ye then being evil know how to give good gifts unto your children, how much more shall your Father which is in heaven give good things to them that ask him?* Mat. vii. 9, 10, 11. and especially if Christ himself ask.

4. Consider of the persons for whom Christ intercedes, it is for all the elect, and in particular for thee. O the sweet of this one meditation! if I knew that my name were written in heaven, should I not (as Christ bids me) *rejoice in this?* Luke x. 20 Oh! but what is it to have my name written in the chief part of heaven? What is it to have my name written in the breast-plate of Jesus Christ, Come, read O my soul! is it not thus written? Isaac, or Jacob, 'I have prayed, and I 'am praying for thee that thy faith fail not.' Sure I am, that I would not part with my hope in this privilege for all the wide world; the very consideration of this makes me to esteem of all the world as dross and dogs-meat.

And Oh! that ever the world, or flesh, or devil, should steal this meditation out of my heart! Oh! that ever I should forget that Christ is gone to heaven, that he is entred into the holy of holies, and that he carries my name into the presence of God the Father! I speak the same to thee that readest, if thou art a believer, there is no doubt of it, but Christ is speaking a good word to his Father in thy behalf; he can no more forget thee in his intercessions, than a mother with full breasts can forget her sucking child, that she should not have compassion on the son of her womb; now, if ever, look up to Jesus, yea look, and never leave looking, till thou spiest thy own name writ on his heart; it is enough to fix thy soul, and to make it dwell on Jesus Christ, thus carrying thee on his shoulders, and bearing thee on his breast-plate for a memorial unto his Father in heaven.

5. Consider of the agreement and difference betwixt Christ's intercessions, and the intercessions of the high priests of old; they did both intercede, but Christ's intercessions are ever in a more transcendent eminent way: Christ is more faithful in his office and place than ever high priest was; Christ is more compassionate and pitiful than ever high priest was; and hence it is, that he hath the title of [*poluoplageos*], *One of many commiserations*, Ja. v. 11. All is mercy, and love, and sweetness, and more than motherly affection that comes from Christ. O my soul! why shouldest thou say with Israel, *My way is hidden from the Lord, and my judgment is passed over by my God?* Is. xl. 27. As if Jesus Christ had left thee out of the count of his people, and out of the roll of those whom he is to look after? No, no; he is a faithful and merciful high priest, far above all the high priests of the Old Testament; and if they were so careful not to leave out

of their breast-plate one name of all the twelve tribes, how much more careful is Christ not to leave out thy name in his intercession? From this very argument of Christ's compassion and Christ's faithfulness, the apostle calls on us to *consider the apostle and high priest of our profession, Christ Jesus, who was faithful to him that appointed him,* Heb. iii. 1, 2. above Aaron, or Moses, or any of the high priests; why consider him, O my soul! this gospel high priest is well worthy indeed of thy consideration.

6. Consider of the properties of Christ's intercession; Is it not heavenly and glorious, effectual and prevailing, and of all other the transactions of our salvation whilst this world lasts, the most perfective and consummate? O! give me the intercessions of Christ, above all the intercessions of men or angels. I know the saints on earth pray mutually one for another, but they pray not in their own names, or for their own merits, but in the name and for the merits of Jesus Christ; and as for the saints and angels in heaven, * Cyprian and Jerome seem to grant, that they pray for the state of the church militant; but if so, they do it only of charity as brethren, not of office as mediators; they do it only for the church in general, and not for any particular man or member of the militant church; such an intercession as this, so heavenly, or effectual, so perfective of our salvation, so authoritative and public, founded on the satisfactory merits of the person interceding, is proper only to Christ. I would be glad of all the prayers of all the churches of Christ; O! that there were not a saint on earth, but that I were by name in his morning and evening prayer, (whosoever thou art that readest, I beseech thee pray for me) but above all, let me have a property in those prayers and intercessions that are proper only to Christ? I am sure then I should never miscarry; Christ's prayers are heavenly, glorious, and effectual.

7. Consider of the particulars, wherein more especially Christ's intercession consists; Is it not in the presenting of his person, blood, prayers, interpolations? Is it not in the presenting of our persons, performances, pleas or answers to the accusations of Satan? men little think how busy our mediator, sponsor, solicitor and advocate, is now in heaven for us; men little think that Christ is appearing, and his blood is crying, and his prayers are ascending, and his robe of righteousness is covering us, and the iniquity of our holy things; O my soul! look up, consider Jesus thy Saviour in these respects! I am persuaded, if thou didst but know, if thou couldest but see what a deal of work Christ hath in hand, and how he carries it on for thy salvation, it would melt thy heart into very tears of joy. Whilst Christ was on earth, and his mother had lost him, he could then say, *Wist ye not that I must go about my Father's business?* Luke ii. 29. Now Christ is in heaven, he is about the same business still; all his employment in heaven is to intercede for us, that we may be saved; very true, there is much in this intercession of Jesus Christ, it is a tree of many branches, and every branch fruitful; so that if thou wouldest enlarge thy meditation in this wide ocean of delights, there is room enough; but herein I must leave thee in the duty, for I can but point at the several particulars whereon thou mayest enlarge: O think on't, that Christ, and Christ's blood, and Christ's prayers should be all at work! that Christ should play the advocate, and plead thy cause, and perfume thy duties with his incense, and take thy person in an unperceivable way to God his Father, and cry there, 'O my Father, be merciful to this 'sinner, pardon his sin, and save his soul for the 'sake of Jesus! O blessed mediation! O! bles-'sed is the man, that on this blessed object knows 'how to meditate both day and night.'

8. Consider of the power and prevalency of Christ's intercessions with his Father. Is he not to this purpose a priest to God, and called thereto by God? Is he not the Son of God, yea, God himself? Is he not God's darling, God's commander, as well as petitioner? Nay, Is not the hand of God himself in this design? Is not the Father's heart as much towards us and our salvation, as Christ's own heart? As sure then as Christ is gone into heaven with thy name engraven on his heart, so sure shalt thou follow him, and be with him where he is, 'Who 'shall lay any thing to the charge of God's elect? 'Who is he that condemneth?' Where Christ becomes patron to defend against the sentence of damnation, it is in vain for sin, or law, or Satan, to at-

* Cyprian *Epist.* Hierome *Lib. adverf. vigil.*

tempt any thing; for as an innocent person is safe so long as he hath his learned advocate to answer all objections, so it is with believers, who have Christ himself both judge and advocate; a sure advocate, he ever prevails in whatsoever he undertakes; he was never yet cast in any suit; he hath for these sixteen hundred years carried away all the causes of hundreds, thousands, and millions of souls; why, he is so dear and near to his Father, that he can work him to any thing he will. And, O my soul! if thou hast any relation to Jesus Christ, Is not here comfort? I dare, in the name of Christ, be thy warrant, and give it under my hand, That if Christ pray for thee, Christ will be sure to save thee; he never yet failed, he never will fail in any of his suits to God. Oh! consider of this.

9. Consider of the reasons of Christ's intercession. Many are given, but this may be sufficient, it is God's own ordinance; the very wisdom of God found out this way to save our souls, *viz.* That an high priest should be appointed, who should die for sinners, and afterward present his death to his Father, by way of intercession in their behalf. Some may look upon this as needless; what, could not God have pardoned our sins, and saved our souls without a priest? I shall not dispute God's power, but if any will, let such an one tell me, What way could his own wisdom have found out to heaven, between the wrath of God and the sin of man? I believe it would have posed all the wisdom of the world, (of men and angels) to have reconciled God's mercy in the salvation of man, and his justice in the condemnation of sin; to have poured out hell upon the sin, and yet to have bestowed heaven upon the sinner; now, then if God himself did study to find out this way, and that he hath said, ' That is my pleasure, That Christ my ' Son should be a priest, and that he shall offer ' himself, and present himself and his offering, and ' his prayer to me for my people.' O! No, soul rest on this as the very ordinance of God; admire at the contrivance of God, say, O the depth! question no farther, only meditate, and ponder, and consider of it, till thou feelest Christ's intercession darting its influence and efficacy on thy sin-sick soul.

SECT. III.

Of desiring after Jesus in that respect.

3. LET us desire after Jesus, carrying on this work of our salvation in his intercession. I cannot but wonder what a dulness seizeth on my heart, and on all the hearts of the sons of men, that we have no more longings after Christ, whose heart is ever panting and longing after us. Surely we do not set ourselves to find out experimentally the sweetness that is in Christ; if there were not another object to think upon, but only this one of Christ's intercession, Is not here enough to put us all into a teeming longing frame! O my soul, rouse up, and set this blessed object before thy face! take a full view of it until thy affections begin to warm, and thou beginnest to cry, ' Oh! for my ' part in Christ's intercession! oh, I would not be ' left out of Christ's heavenly prayers for ten thou-' sand worlds!' Come and be serious, the object is admirably sweet and precious; long for it, pant after it! God understands the rhetoric of thy breathing as well as of thy cry. But what is there in Christ's intercession that is so desirable? I answer,—

1. In Christ's intercession lies the present transaction of our soul's salvation. Such passages as hitherto we have spoken of are done and past; the transactions of eternity were at an end when time began; the transactions of Christ promised, had their period when Christ was incarnate; the transactions of Christ's birth, and life, and death, and resurrection, and ascension, are now above a thousand and six hundred years old: I know the virtue and influence of all these transactions continue, and will continue for ever and ever; but the several actings had their periods, and only Christ's session and mission of his Spirit, and his blessed intercession, both were now and are the very present employment of Jesus Christ. If it were possible that we could see into heaven; if, with Stephen, we could look up stedfastly, and see the heavens open; if our eyes, by an extraordinary power, were carried through that azure sky, and through all till we come to the holy of holies, and to Jesus Christ in his glory; What should we see but Christ interceding, Christ busy with his Father in his poor saints behalf? Now he prays, now he presents his person, merits, intercession, interpolation,

polation, *q. d.* 'Father, here are a company of rebels, justly fallen under thy displeasure, they deserve to be set at an eternal distance from thee; but I must needs have them pardoned, and received into thy bosom; come, make thine own terms, let justice require never so great satisfaction, I have paid a price sufficient for all, and effectual for them; give them what laws thou pleasest, I will undertake they shall observe them; and to this purpose, away, away, holy Spirit, go to such and such souls, enable them to their duties, yea, enable them in duty, and sanctify them throughout, in souls, bodies, and spirits.' Why, this is the present transaction of Jesus Christ, and therefore most desirable; methinks, I long to know what Christ is now doing in heaven for my soul, And is it not thus? Is not all his time spent either in reading pardons for redeemed ones, or in presenting petitions for them, and pleading for them? Surely, he is still interceding every day, it is his present work for our souls; O desirable work!

2. In this present transaction lies the application of all Christ's former actings, whether of his habitual righteousness, or of his active and passive obedience. All those passages of Christ's incarnation, conception, circumcision, birth, life and death, which more especially we look upon as the meritorious causes of our salvation, had been nothing to us, if they had not been applied by Christ: they were the means of impetration, but Christ's intercession is the means of application; Christ purchased salvation by those preceding acts, but he possesseth us of our salvation by this perfective and consummate act of his intercession. The order of this is laid down by the apostle, in that first, *He learned obedience, by the things which he suffered*, and then, *being made perfect, he became the author* (or applying cause) *of eternal salvation to all them that obey him*; being to this purpose, *called of God an high priest, after the order of Melchisedec*, Heb. v. 8, 9, 10. Now, is not this the desirable act above all other acts? Alas! what am I the better for a mine of gold, in such, or such, or such a field, in which I have no property at all? I am thoroughly convinced, that Christ's merits are most precious merits, but, oh! that they were mine, oh! that Christ's intercession would bring the salve, and lay it to my sore; oh! that I could hear that voice from heaven, 'My Son, I was incarnate for thee, and conceived for thee, and born for thee, and circumcised for thee, and I did the law, and suffered the penalty for thee; and now I am interceding that thy very soul may have the benefit of all my doings, and of all my sufferings.' Why, if Christ's intercession be the applying cause, if it bring home to my soul all the former transactions of Christ, saying, *All these are thine, even thine*; oh! how desirable must this intercession be?

3. In this application lies that communion and fellowship which we have with the Father and the Son, *I pray for these, that as thou, Father, art in me, and I in thee, that they also may be one in us*, John xvii. 21. Understand this soberly, we cannot think that there should be that oneness in equality betwixt God and us, as betwixt God and Christ; no, no, but there is oneness in similitude and reality, even in this life; by virtue of Christ's intercession we have oneness with God and Christ, not only in comforts, but also in graces; I pray you mark this, when I speak of communion with God in this life, I mean especially the communication of grace between God and the soul; on God's part there's a special influence of grace and favour to man; and on man's part there is a special return of grace and honour to God. Some trembling souls are apt to think, That all communion with God and Christ, consists only in the comforts of the holy Spirit, whereas Christians may as really and advantageously have communion with God in secret conveyances of grace, in inward supports, in a concealed acceptation of service, in the hidden drawings of the soul God-ward; as in the more open and comfortable manifestations of God unto the soul: communion with God is a familiar friendship, (I speak it in an holy, humble sense) now, do we not as usually go to a friend for counsel and advice, as for comfort and cheering? In a friend's bosom we intrust our sorrows, as well as our joys. Suppose a soul, even spiritually overwhelmed and ready to break, betaking itself unto God, and venting itself before the Lord; now, if afterwards the soul hath no more ease than by the bare lancing of the sore, if God pours in no balm at all, but only gives support; Shall we say that this soul, in this case, hath no communion with God? O yes! in God's secret visits of the soul, and in the soul's restless groping after God, though nothing but darkness be apprehended, yet

that

that soul lives in the light of God's countenance; the sun shines, though a cloud interposeth; God smiles, though the soul do not perceive it; or certainly thou hast his strengthening, supporting presence, if not his shining; now, this is the fruit of Christ's blessed intercession, and this is the subject-matter of Christ's intercession, *O! my Father, that these may be one in us, I in them, and thou in me,* John xvii. 23. *I in them by the influence and power of my Spirit, and thou in me by the fulness and power of the Godhead.* And is not this a most desirable thing?

4. In this communion lies the vision and fruition of Jesus Christ's glory; grace brings to glory, if communion here, we shall have communion hereafter: and this also is a part of Christ's prayer and intercession, *Father, I will, that they also whom thou hast given me be with me where I am, that they may behold my glory which thou hast given me,* John xvii. 24. Jesus Christ cannot be in heaven long without his saints, indeed, it is impossible that Christ should be in heaven, and that pieces and bits of Christ mystical should be in hell, or yet long on earth. Christ will draw in his legs and members on earth up nearer to the head; certainly Christ, and you that are believers, must be under one roof 'ere long. Is not he gone before to prepare a place, yea, many mansions for you? John xiv. 2. We think them happy on earth, that have their many stately halls and palaces, their summer and their winter-houses; O Christians! how happy will you be, when you come to be lords and heirs of many stately mansions in the streets of heaven? But what speak I of mansions, now I am naming Christ? Mansions are nothing, many mansions are but little, yea, *many mansions in Christ's Father's house,* are but created chips of happiness, in comparison of that communion, which, by virtue of Christ's intercession we shall have with Christ. It is the saying of an eminently learned, holy divine, * 'I ' should refuse heaven, (saith he) if Christ were ' not there; take Christ away from heaven, and it ' is but a poor, dark, heartless dwelling, heaven ' without Christ would look as the direful land of ' death.' And therefore, after Christ had spoke of many mansions, and of a place that he would prepare for his saints, he adds farther, to encrease their joy, *I will come again,* (saith he) *and receive you unto myself, that where I am, there ye may be also,* John xiv. 3. Mansions are but as places of briars and thorns without Jesus Christ, and therefore I would have heaven for Christ, and not have Christ for heaven; O! this communion with Christ is above all desirable, and this is the subject-matter of Christ's prayer, *Father, I would have the saints to be with me where I am, that they may behold my glory.* Why, this is the communion which the saints shall have with Christ, never will their eyes be off him, never will their thoughts wander after any other object; oh! the intimacy that will be then betwixt Christ and Christians! Oh! what communication of glory will be there to each other? *These shall walk with me,* (saith Christ) *for they are worthy,* Rev. iii. 4.

O my soul! if this be the business of Christ's intercession, if all these particulars are contained in the bowels of this one transaction, how is it that thou art not in a fainting swoon? How is it that thou art not gasping, groaning, sick unto death with the vehement thirst after thy part and portion in Christ's intercession? If there be such a thing as the passion of desire in this heart of mine, O that now it would break out! Oh! that it would vent itself with mighty longings and infinite aspirings after this blessed object! why, Lord, I desire, but help thou my faint desires; blow on my dying spark, it is but little; and if I know any thing of my heart, I would have it more; Oh, that my spark would flame! why, Lord, I desire that I might desire; Oh, breathe it into me, and I will desire after thee!

SECT. IV.

Of hoping in Jesus in that respect.

4. LEt us hope in Jesus, carrying on this work of our salvation in his intercession, *It is good that a man should hope,* Lam. iii. 26. Indeed, if it were not for hope the heart would not hold; only look that our hope be true hope, very hypocrites have a king of hope, but if God's word be true, *The hope of the unjust men shall perish,*—Pro. xi. 7. *What is the hope of the hypocrite?*—*Will God hear his cry when trouble cometh upon him?* Job xxvii. 8, 9. No, no, *The hypocrite's hope shall perish,*

---

* Samuel Rutherford.

Carrying on the great Work of our Salvation in his Intercession. 479

rife, his hope shall be cut off, and his trust shall be as a spider's web, Job viii. 13, 14. O my soul! hope in Jesus, but rest not till thou canst give a reason of thy hope, till thou canst prove that they are the hopes which grace, and not only nature hath wrought; that they are grounded upon scripture-promises and found evidences; that they purify the heart; that the more thou hopest the less thou sinnest; that they depend on sure and infallible causes, as on the truth, power, and mercy of God; on the merits, mediation, and intercession of Jesus Christ; what, is this last amongst the rest (I mean the intercession of Christ) the spring of thy hope? Canst thou follow the stream, till it brings thee to this fountain or well-head of hope, that now thou canst say, *O this intercession is mine!* Come, search, and try, it is worth the pains; and to put thee out of question, and in a more facile way of discerning, I shall lay down these signs, As,—

1. If Christ's intercession be mine, then is the Spirit's intercession mine. Or if thou wouldest rather argue from the effect to the cause, then thus; if the Spirit's intercession be mine, then is Christ's intercession mine. In this case, we need not to ascend up into heaven to learn the truth, rather let us descend into our own hearts, and look whether Christ hath given us of his Spirit, which makes us cry unto God, *with sighs and groans which cannot be expressed*; he that would know whether the sun shine in the firmament, he must not climb into the clouds to look, rather he must search for the beams thereof upon the earth; which, when he sees, he may conclude, that the sun shines in the firmament; O come, and let us ransack our own consciences! let us search whether we feel the Spirit of Christ crying in us, *Abba, Father*; certainly these two are as the cause and the effect: Christ's intercession in heaven, and his Spirit's intercession on earth are as twins of a birth; or rather such is the concatenation of these two, that Christ's intercession in heaven breeds another intercession in the hearts of his saints. It is the same Spirit dwelling in Christ, and in all his members, that moves and stirs them up to cry, *Abba, Father*. Here then is my argument, if Christ hath put his Spirit into thy heart, and if the Spirit hath set thy heart on work to make incessant intercessions for thyself, then is Christ's intercession thine. There is a kind of a round in the carrying on of this great work of intercession; as, 1. Christ intercedes for his people, O that my Spirit might go down! 2. God hearkens to the intercession of Christ, Away, holy Spirit, get thee down, into the hearts of such and such. 3. The Spirit waits on the pleasure of them both, and no sooner down but he sends up his intercession back again: Christ cries to God, and God sends the Spirit, and the Spirit goes and eccchoes in the hearts of saints, to the cries of Christ. Much of this is contained in that one text, *God hath sent forth the Spirit of his Son into our hearts,* [*Krazon*], *crying*, (as if he merely acted our tongues) *Abba, Father*, Gal. iv. 6. Here is God the Father, God the Son, and God the Holy Ghost, and all are acting their parts on the elect people of God: the Son intercedes, *O that my Spirit may be given to these!* the Father willingly grants, *Away, holy Spirit, and, as my Son asketh, enter, and take possession of those sinful hearts:* the holy Spirit obeys, and no sooner in the hearts of the saints, but he cries in them, *Abba, Father*. God hears Christ, and the Spirit hears God, and the elect hear the Spirit; and now, because the Spirit speaks in the elect, God hears the elect. Much like unto this is that of the prophet, *And it shall come to pass in that day, I will hear,* saith the Lord; *I will hear the heavens, and they shall hear the earth, and the earth shall hear the corn, and wine, and oil, and they shall hear Jezreel,* Hosea ii. 21. O my soul to the test! hath God sent forth the Spirit of his Son into thy heart? Hast thou the indwelling of the Spirit? And now by help of the Spirit, canst thou pray with earnestness, confidence, and an holy importunity? Canst thou cry, *Abba, Father?* i. e. Canst thou cry with earnestness, *Father?* With confidence, and *Abba, Father*, or *Father, Father*, with an holy importunity. Why, these are the very signs of the Spirit's intercession. O my soul! that thou wouldest deal faithfully with thy ownself; canst thou by the help of the Spirit go to the Father in the name of Christ? As Christ is gone before into the holy of holies to intercede, so canst thou *with boldness* follow after, *and enter into the holiest by the blood of Jesus,* Heb. x. 19. Canst thou say, God hath given me his Spirit, and his Spirit hath shewed me Christ as my Mediator at the right hand of God; and now under the wing of such a Mediator, I can, by the Spirit's . . . . boldness, [*meta parrefias*],

sias], (with assuming a liberty) to speak any thing I will in the ears of God: surely, this is the fruit, the effect of Christ's intercession, and therefore thou mayest comfortably conclude, *Christ's intercession is mine.*

2. If at any time in the midst of duties I am savingly affected, then is Christ's intercession mine. Sometimes it pleaseth God to appear in ordinances, and the soul is comforted, quickened, enlarged, affected; why, now I look upon this as the efficacy of Christ's blood, and as the power of Christ's intercession? at that very instant that I feel any good in any ordinance of Christ, why then, even then, is Christ prevailing with God his Father; for what I feel, then, even then, may I boldly say *Now is the Lord Jesus, who is at God's right hand in heaven, remembring me a poor worm on earth; Oh! now I feel the fruit of his intercession; Oh! what is this spirit, power, grace, comfort, sweetness I drink of, but a taste of the honey-comb with the end of my rod, dropping from the intercessions of Jesus Christ? And if this presence of Christ's Spirit be so sweet, What is himself then?* I know we had need to be wary in laying down this sign; it is clearly proved by an eminent divine, ‡ *That sweet motions of heart in holy things, are not infallible evidences of grace.* The third kind of hearers are said to *receive the word with joy,* Math. xiii. 22. They found some sweet and power in the ordinances of Christ. And *Herod heard John gladly,* Mark xvi. 20. And many *for a season rejoiced in John's light and ministry,* John v. 35. Certainly affections in holy administrations with delight and joy, may be in those, who yet have no true grace; so it may be, that the novelty and strangeness of a doctrine may much affect and delight; or the nature of the doctrine, as it is comfortable, without any respect to spiritual operation, may exceedingly affect, or the minister's abilities, because of his parts, eloquence, elocution, affectionate utterance, may much delight and stir up the hearers affections; fine head notions may produce some affectionate heart-motions; but what symptom of grace in all this? The sign therefore I lay down of my propriety in Christ's intercessions is not every sweet motion, or every excited affection, but that which is holy, spiritual, heavenly, saving; I may discern much of this, if I will look but into the grounds and effects of my excited, or stirred up affections; if the grounds thereof be fetched from heaven, and in their effect they tend towards heaven, if they wean my heart from the world, if they elevate and raise up my affections to things above, if they form, and frame my conversation heaven-wards, then may I be assured these motions and affections are of the right stamp; for all such motions are but sparks of that heavenly fire, the flame whereof is mindful of its own original; they are the fruits of Christ, and they go back to Christ, they work towards their centre, they tend towards the place from whence they came; and in this respect, O! that I could never hear a sermon without a savoury affection of what I hear! O! that I could never go to prayer without some warmth, and heat, and life, and fervency! Oh! that in every duty I were savingly affected, that I felt the savour of Christ's ointments, whose name, and whose intercession is as an ointment poured forth; in times of the Old Testament, if they offered up a sacrifice, and a material fire came down from heaven, and burnt up the sacrifice to ashes, it was a certain testimony that the sacrifice was accepted: now, in the time of the gospel, we must not expect material fire to come down upon our duties; but hath the Lord at any time caused an inward and spiritual fire to fall down upon thy heart, warming thy Spirit in duty, and carrying it up heaven-ward? Surely if so, thou mayest safely conclude, these are the very effects of Christ's intercession; his intercession is mine.

3. If in my heart I feel a holy frame, disposition, inclination to pray and cry, and intercede for others, especially for the miseries and distresses of the church of God; then is Christ's intercession mine. We should (as near as we may) in every thing conform to Christ; and this conformity is an evidence or sign to us of our interest in Christ: O my soul! go down into the inmost closet of thy heart, look what disposition there is in it towards the members of Christ; and thou mayest conclude, there is in Christ's heart the very same disposition towards thee. Ah! do I think there is love in my bosom towards the saints, and that there is no love in Christ's bosom towards me? What, can I think that my narrow straitened and sinful bowels, are larger than those wide, compassionate and tender

‡ Mr. *Burges of Assurance.*

der bowels of Jesus Christ? As a drop of water is in comparison of the ocean, and as a gravel-stone is in comparison of the sand, so is my heart to Christ's, and my love to Christ's, and my bowels to Christ's. Come then, and try by this sign, *hereby we know that we are translated from death to life, if we love the brethren; he that loveth not his brother, abideth in death*, 1 John iii. 14.—*Hereby perceive we the love of God, because he laid down his life for us, and we ought to lay down our lives for the brethren*, verse 16. Is not this plain, if I love the brethren, Christ loveth me; if I feel in my heart an holy disposition to go to God, and to pray, and cry, and intercede for a saint in misery, surely the Lord Jesus hath as much bowels towards me, to go, and intercede for me, and to present my prayers unto God the Father; his intercession is mine.

4. If I am called, justified and sanctified, then is Christ's intercession mine: are not these the subject-matter of Christ's intercession? *I pray* (saith Christ) *that thou shouldest keep them from the evil*, John xvii. 15.—I pray that thou wouldest *sanctify them through thy truth; neither pray I for these alone, but for them also which shall believe on me through their word, or preaching*; *Father, I will, that those whom thou hast given me, be with me in glory*, ver. 17, 20, 24. He first prays that we may be called and justified, and then he prays that we may be sanctified and saved: he holds at both ends of this golden chain of our salvation; the one end is hanged at his breast, where the names of all his saints are written, and the other end is at his heart that he may be the author and finisher, the first and last, the beginning and ending of our souls salvation; alas! there is nothing in us, in our reach here below; the first stirrings of grace are up in heaven, at the right hand of the Father; and the far end of any gracious thought is as far above us, as the heart of Christ is above the earth: come then, sith all hangs on this great pin of Christ's intercession, let us search and try, are we called? Do we believe on the Son? Are we sanctified in some measure? Are we kept from the evil, that sin may not have dominion over us? Hath Christ put up these prayers in our behalf, that now we feel (as it were) and experience the truth of Christ's prevailings with his Father in our hearts and lives? O sure signs that Christ's intercession is ours! Away,

away, all diffidence, doubting, wavering, fluctuating hopes; a soul thus grounded, may with Paul, cast the gauntlet, and bid defiance to all the world, *Who shall lay any thing to the charge of God's elect? Who is he that condemneth? It is Christ that died, yea, rather that is risen again, who is even at the right hand of God, and who also maketh intercession for us*, Rom. viii. 34.

SECT. V.

Of believing in Jesus in that respect.

5. LEt us believe in Jesus, as carrying on this great work of our salvation in his intercession; wounded spirits are full of scruples, and thus they cry, ' My sins will never be forgiven, ' have not I sinned against God, and Christ, and ' the Spirit of Christ? Had I not my hands imbru-' ed in the blood of his Son? And have not I trod-' den under foot the blood of God? And will that ' blood that I have shed, and trod on, intercede ' for my pardon; Had I but gone so far as the ' Jews did, who indeed killed and crucified Christ, ' I might have had some hopes, because they knew ' not what they did, and therefore Christ prayed, ' *Father, forgive them, for they know not what they ' do*. But alas! I sinned, and I knew well enough ' what, and wherein I have sinned, *Had they known*, ' (saith the apostle) *they would not have crucified ' the Lord of glory*, 1 Cor. ii. 8. But alas! I knew ' it, and I was fully convinced that the commissi-' on of every sin is a crucifying of Christ; and yet ' against knowledge, and judgment, and light, and ' checks of my own conscience, I have crucified ' the Lord of glory; and is not the apostle ex-' press? *It is impossible for those who were once ' enlightened, and have tasted of the heavenly gift,* ' *——if they fall away to renew them again unto ' repentance, seeing they crucify to themselves the ' Son of God afresh, and put him to open shame*, ' Heb. vi. 4, 6. Oh! I fear my name is not in the ' roll of those for whom Christ intercedes, I have ' crucified him afresh, and will he intercede for ' such a dead dog as I am? I cannot believe.' Silence, unbelief! be not tyrannical to thyself, for Christ will not, sin shall do thee no hurt, nor Satan, no nor God himself, for Jesus Christ can work him to any thing; if he but open his wounds in heaven, he will so work his Father, that thy wounds on earth

earth shall close up presently. *O! but I have sinned against light*; and what then? I hope thou hast not sinned wilfully, maliciously, and despitefully against the light: the apostle tells us, That *if we sin wilfully, after we have received the knowledge of the truth, there remaineth no more sacrifice for sins, but a certain looking for of judgment, and fiery indignation,* Heb. x. 26, 27. These two texts in Heb. vi. 4. and x. 26. are parallel, and give light to each other; and therefore unless thy sin be the unpardonable sin, unless wilfully, maliciously and despitefully, thou hast crucified Christ, as some of the Jews did, never pass a doom of final condemnation on thy soul: what, is there no difference betwixt a sin done wilfully, or purposely, of malice with delight, and against the feeling of thy own conscience, and a sin done of mere ignorance, inconsideracy, infirmity, or thro' a strong temptation, tho' against light itself? I know there is a light given in by God's word, and some beam of the Holy Ghost, which yet never penetrated so far as to transform and regenerate the soul wholly to God's image; and in such a case, a man may fall away, even into an universal fall, a general apostasy; but dost thou not hope better things of thyself than so? I suppose thou dost; O then believe! O believe thy part in Christ's intercession! and for the directions of thy faith, that thou mayest know how, or in what manner to believe, observe these particulars in their order. 'As,——

1. Faith must directly go to Christ.
2. Faith must go to Christ as God in the flesh.
3. Faith must go to Christ as God in the flesh, made under the law.
4. Faith must go to Christ made under the directive part of the law by his life, and under the penal part of the law by his death.
5. Faith must go to Christ as put to death in the flesh, and as quickned by the Spirit.
6. Faith must go to Christ as quickned by the Spirit, and as going up into glory, as sitting down at God's right hand, and as sending the Holy Ghost: Of all these before.
7. Faith must go to Christ as interceding for his saints; this act of Christ is for the application of all the former acts on Christ's part; and Christ closing with it, is for the application of this, and all other the actings of Christ on our part. Now is our faith led up very high. if we can but reach this, we may say, that our faith stands very lofty when it may at once see earth and heaven; when it may see all that Christ hath acted for it here, and all that Christ doth act, and will act in heaven for it hereafter. It is not an ordinary, single, particular act of faith that will come up to this glorious mystery; no, no, it is a comprehensive, perfective act; it is such an act as puts the soul into a condition of glorious triumph, 'Who shall condemn? It is 'Christ that will save me to the uttermost, seeing 'he ever liveth to make intercession for me. The 'same word, [*to the uttermost*].is a good word, 'and well put in; *it is a reaching word, and ex-'tends itself so far, that thou canst not look be-'yond it: let thy soul be set on the highest moun-'tain that ever any creature was yet set on, and 'there let thy soul take in, and view the most 'spacious prospect, both of sin and misery, and 'difficulties of being saved, that ever yet any poor 'humbled soul did cast within itself, yea, join to 'these all the objections, and hindrances of thy 'salvation, that the heart of man can suppose, or 'invent against itself; lift up thy eyes, and look 'to the utmost thou canst see, and Christ, by his 'intercession, is able to save thee beyond the hori-'zon, and farthest compass of thy thoughts, even 'to the utmost and worst case the heart of man 'can possibly suppose; it is not thy having lain 'long in sin, or long under terrors and despairs, it 'is not thy having sinned often under many enlight-'nings, that can hinder thee from being saved by 'Christ: do but remember this same word, [*to 'the uttermost*] and then put in what excepti-'on thou wilt, or canst.' O the holy triumphs of that soul that can but act its faith on Christ's intercession! why, this is the most perfect and consummate act of Christ's priestly office, this argues thy Christ to be a perfect Mediator, and being a perfect Mediator, no condition can be desperate, *And being made perfect,* (saith the apostle) *he became the author of eternal salvation unto all them that obey him,* Heb. ix. 5 Now therefore lead up thy faith to this blessed object, and thou hast under consideration the whole of Christ, and the total of Christ's actings in this world from first to last, in respect of mediation this is the coronis, the upshot, the period, the consummation, the perfection of all.

8. Faith

---

* Goodwin's *Christ set forth*.

8. Faith is going to Chrift as interceding for us; it is principally and mainly to look to the purpofe, end, intent, and defign of Chrift's in his interceffion: now the ends of Chrift, as in reference unto us, are thefe.——

1. That we might have communion and fellowfhip with the Father and the Son, *I pray for thefe, that as thou Father art in me, and I in thee, they alfo may be one in us*, John xvii. 21.

2. That we might have the gift of the Holy Ghoft, *I will pray the Father, and he fhall give you another comforter, that he may abide with you for ever, even the Spirit of truth*, John xiv. 16, 17.

3. That we might have protection againft all evil, *I pray* (faith Chrift) *that thou wouldeft keep them from the evil*, John xvii. 15. Some may object, are not the faithful fubject to evils, corruptions, and temptations ftill? How then is that part of the interceffion of Chrift made good unto us? I anfwer, The interceffion of Chrift is prefently available, only it is conveyed in a manner fuitable to our prefent condition, fo as there may be left room for another life; and therefore we muft not conceive all prefently done; it is with us as with malefactors doomed to death, fuppofe the fupreme power fhould grant a pardon to be drawn, though the grant be of the whole thing at once, yet it cannot be written but word after word, and line after line; fo the grant of our protection againft all evil is made unto Chrift at firft, but in the execution thereof, there is line upon line, and precept upon precept, here a little, and there a little: we know Chrift prayed for Peter, *I have prayed for thee, that thy faith fail not*; yet Peter's faith did fhake and totter; the prayer was not, that there might be no failing at all, but that it might not utterly and totally fail; and in that refpect Peter was protected.

4. That we might have free accefs to the throne of grace: fo the apoftle, *Seeing we have a great high prieft that is paffed into the heavens, Jefus the Son of God, let us hold faft our profeffion, and come boldly to the throne of grace*, Heb. iv. 14, 16. And again, *Having therefore boldnefs to enter into the holieft by the blood of Jefus, and having an high prieft over the houfe of God, let us draw near with a true heart, in a full affurance of faith*, Heb. x. 23.

5. That we might have the inward interpolation of the Spirit, which is, as it were, the echo of Chrift's interceffion in our hearts, *The Spirit maketh interceffion for us with groanings which cannot be uttered*, Rom. viii. 26. It is the fame Spirit's groans in us, which more diftinctly and fully in Chrift prayeth for us, *Thefe things I fpeak in the world*, (faith our Saviour) *that they might have my joy fulfilled in themfelves*, Joh. xvii 13. q. d. I have made this prayer in the world, and left a record and pattern of it in the church, that they feeling the fame heavenly defires kindled in their own hearts, may be comforted in the workings of that Spirit of prayer in them, which teftifieth to their fouls, the quality of that interceffion which I make for them in the heaven of heavens; certainly there is a dependance of our prayer on Chrift's prayer; as is with the fun, though the body of it abide in the heavens, yet the beams of it defcend to us here on earth; fo the interceffion of Chrift, though as tied to his perfon, it is made in heaven, yet the groans, and defires of the touched heart, as the beams thereof, are here on earth.

6. That we might have the fanctification of our fervices; of this the Levitical priefts were a type, *For they bear the iniquity of the holy things of the children of Ifrael, that they might be accepted*, Ex. xxviii. 38. *And he is the angel of the covenant, who hath a golden cenfer to offer up the prayers of the faints*, Rev. viii. 3. Some obferve a three-fold evil in man, of every of which we are delivered by Chrift; Firft, An evil of ftate or condition under the guilt of fin. Secondly, An evil of nature under the corruption of fin. Thirdly, An evil in all our fervices by the adherency of fin, for that which toucheth an unclean thing, is made unclean thereby. Now Chrift, by his righteoufnefs and merits, juftifieth our perfons from the guilt of fin; and Chrift, by his grace and Spirit, doth in meafure purify our faculties from the corruption of fin; and Chrift, by his incenfe and interceffion, doth cleanfe our fervices from the adherency of fin; fo that in them the Lord fmells a fweet favour; and both we and our fervices find acceptance with God.

7. That we might have the pardon of all fin. It is by virtue of Chrift's interceffion, that a believer finning of infirmity hath a pardon of courfe, for Chrift is his advocate to plead his caufe; or if he fin of prefumption, and the Lord give repentance, he hath a pardon at the hands of God the Father, by virtue of this interceffion, in a way

of justice. And to this end, rather is Christ called an advocate than a petitioner, *If any man sin, we have an advocate with the Father,* 1 John ii. 1. The work of an advocate differs from the work of a petitioner; an advocate doth not merely petition, but he tells the judge what is law, and what ought to be done, and so doth Christ, 'O my Father! (saith Christ) this soul hath indeed sinned, but I have satisfied for his sins, I have paid for them to the full; now therefore, in a way of equity and justice, I do here call for this man's pardon.' If this were not so, our estate would be most miserable, considering, that for every sin committed by us after repentance, we deserve to be cast out of the love and favour of God our Father, for ever and ever.

8. That we might have continuance in the state of grace, *I have prayed for thee that thy faith fail not,* Luke xxii. 32. Some that dissent from us in the point of perseverance, object, that in our Saviour's prayer for Peter, there was somewhat singular; but we say, That in this prayer there is nothing singular, which is not common to all the faithful, and unto such as are given unto Christ of the Father. They alledge, That this privilege was granted to Peter as an apostle; but we say, That if it was granted to Peter as an apostle, then it was common to Peter and Judas, in that both were apostles. They alledge farther, That Christ prays not for the absolute perseverance of believers, but after a sort, and upon condition. But we say the prayers of Christ are certain and not suspended: in this prayer his desire is not for Peter that he would persevere, but his desire is for Peter that he should persevere; the object of the thing for which Christ prays, is distinct from the thing itself prayed for.

9. That we might have the salvation of our souls in the day of Jesus, *Father, I will, that they also whom thou hast given me, be with me where I am, that they might behold my glory,* John xvii. 24. Why, this is the main end in respect of us, our glory; and indeed herein is the main piece of our glory, to behold his glory! oh! to see the Lord Jesus Christ glorified! as he shall be glorified, must be a glorious thing; What is it to see his glory, but to behold the lustre of his divinity through his humanity? In this respect our very eyes shall come to see God, as much as is possible for any creature to see him; we may be sure God shall appear through the humanity of Christ, as much as is possible for the divinity to appear in a creature; and therefore men and angels will be continually viewing of Christ. I know there is another glory of Christ which the Father will put upon him, 'because he humbled himself, therefore God will exalt him, and give him a name above every name;' and we shall see him in his glory. O the ravishing sight of saints! Christ is so lovely, that the saints cannot leave, but they must, and will *follow the Lamb wheresoever he goes,* Rev. xiv. 4. There shall be no moment to all eternity, wherein Christ shall be out of sight to so many thousand thousands of saints; now this is the glory of the saints above: as a queen that sees the prince in his glory, she delights in it, because it is her glory, so the church when she shall see Christ her husband in his glory, she shall rejoice in it, because she looks upon it as her own. Is not this a blessed end of Christ's intercession? Why, hither tend all the rest; all the other ends end in this; and for this above all, Christ intercedes to his Father, 'Father, I would have my saints with me; O! that all the daughters of Zion may behold King Solomon with the crown wherewith thou hast crowned him in the day of his espousals, and in the day of the gladness of his heart,' Cant. iii. 11.

Only one question, and I have done. How should I set my faith on work to act on Christ's intercession for these ends? I answer,——

1. Faith must persuade itself, that here is a virtue in Christ's intercession. Certainly every passage and acting of Christ hath its efficacy; and therefore there is virtue in this, it is full of juice, it hath a strong influence in it.

2. Faith must consider that it is the design of God, and the intendment of Christ, that this intercession should be for the good of those that are given to Christ. O! there's enough in Christ, enough in Christ's intercession to convey communion, the Spirit, protection, free access to the throne of grace, a Spirit of prayer, pardon of sins, continuance in grace and salvation of souls to the saints and people of God through all the world; and this is the design of God, that Christ's intercession should be as the fountain from whence all these streams must run, and be conveyed unto us.

3. Faith must act dependantly upon the intercession of Christ for these very ends: this is the

very

very nature of faith; it relies upon God in Christ, and upon all the actings of Christ, and upon all the promises of Christ. So then, Is there a desirable end in Christ's intercession which we aim at? O! let us act our faith dependently; let us rely, stay, or lean upon Christ to that same end; let us roll ourselves, or cast ourselves upon the very intercession of Jesus Christ, saying, 'O my Christ! 'there is enough in thee, and in this glorious in-'tercession of thine; and therefore, there will I 'stick, and abide for ever.'

4. Faith must ever and anon be trying, improving and wrestling with God, that virtue may go out of Christ's intercession into our hearts, 'I have 'heard, Lord, that there is an office erected in 'heaven, that Christ as priest should be ever pray-'ing, and interceding for his people; O, that I 'may feel the efficacy of Christ's intercession! am 'I now in prayer? O! that I could feel in this 'prayer the warmth, and heat, and spiritual fire, 'which usually falls down from Christ's intercessi-'on into the hearts of his! Lord, warm my spirit 'in this duty; give me the kisses of thy mouth; 'O! that I may now have communion with thee, 'thy Spirit upon me, thy protection over me! O! 'that my pardon may be sealed, my grace confirm-'ed, my soul saved in the day of Jesus!' In this method, O my soul, follow on; and who knows but God may appear e're thou art aware? Howsoever be thou in the use of the means, and leave the issue to God.

SECT. VI.

Of loving Jesus in that respect.

6. LET us love Jesus as carrying on this great work of our salvation in his intercession. Now, two things more especially will excite our love. 1. Christ's love to us. 2. Our propriety in Christ. For the *First*, many acts of Christ's love have appeared before, and every one is sufficient to draw our loves to him again. As,——

1. He had an eternal love to man; he feasted himself on the thoughts of love, delight, and free grace to man from all eternity; since God was God (O! boundless duration) the Lord Jesus, in a manner was loving and longing for the dawning of the day of the creation; he was (as it were) with child of infinite love to man, before he made the world. Some observe, That the first words that ever Christ wrote, were, *Love to believers*; and these were written with glory, for it was before gold was, and they were written upon his bosom, for then other books were not.

2. In the beginning of time he loved man above all creatures, for after he had made them all, he then speaks as he never did before, *Let us make man in our image, after our likeness, and let him have dominion over the fish of the sea, and over the fowl of the air, and over the cattle, and over all the earth*, Gen. i. 26. And though man at that very instant unmade himself by sin, Christ's love yet was not broken off, but held forth in a promise till the day of performance, *The seed of the woman shall bruise the serpent's head. And in thy seed shall all the nations of the earth be blessed.*

3. In the fulness of time his love was manifested, the seed then blossomed, and the birth came out in an high expression of love; the man-child, the love of Christ, was born, and saw the light, *After that* (saith the apostle) *the kindness and love of God our Saviour towards man appeared*, Tit. iii. 4. I shall not need sure to instance in succeeding passages; so far as we have gone, we have clearly seen Christ's life was a perfect mirrour of his love: as there is no beam in the sun, in which there is no light, so there was no act in the life of Christ, but to a spiritual eye it shines with the light of love. But above all, O the love of Christ in his death! ask a malefactor, if the prince's son should go to his Father, and say, 'Father, I confess this 'wretch hath deserved to die, but I see a willing-'ness in thee, that he should live; only I perceive 'it sticks with thy justice; why, for that, father, 'here I am; and to satisfy thy justice I will die 'myself, only let this poor wretch live to the glo-'ry of thine, and my free grace.' Ask (I say) the malefactor what kind of love were this? Surely Christ died for our sins, and Christ rose again for our justification, and he ascended, and sat down at God's right hand, and sent down his holy Spirit, and all for us: there was not one passage in all these transactions, but held forth the breakings and breathings out of a strong fire of love.

4. At this time there is a coal of burning love in the breast of Christ. This fire was indeed from everlasting, but the flames are as hot this day as ever; now is the Christ loves and lives; And where-

wherefore lives? But only to love us, and to intercede for us. Christ makes our salvation his constant calling; he is ever at his work, *Yesterday, and to day, and for ever:* there is not one hour in the day, nor one day in a year, nor one year in an age, wherein Christ is not busy with his Father in this heavenly employment of interceding for us. He loved us, before he died for us, his love being the cause why he died for us; and he loves us still, in that now he intercedes for us: it is as much as to say, " Christ hath loved us, and he " repents not of his love:" Love made him die for us, and if it were to do again, he would die over again; yea, if our sins had so required, that for every elect person Christ must have died a several death, love, love would have put him willingly upon all these deaths. O the loves of Christ towards our poor souls! if I might but stay, and take some turns in this large field of love, how many thousands of particulars might I draw out of scripture, expressing Christ's love to us in this respect? Though he be in heaven, yet by virtue of his intercession, he bears us in his hands; yea, he leads us by the hand, and arms too, *I taught Ephraim to go, taking them by their arms, but they knew not that I healed them,* Isa. xl. 11. Hof. xi. 3. He dandles us on his knees, he bears us on his wings, *As an eagle stirreth up her nest, fluttereth over her young, spreadeth abroad her wings, taketh them, and beareth them on her wings; so the Lord alone doth lead us,* Deut. xxxii. 11, 12. He carries us on his shoulders, as a man *found his sheep, and laid it on his shoulders rejoicing,* Luke xv. 5. Nay, I must yet come nearer; for Christ by his intercession sets us nearer yet, *His left hand is under us, and his right hand doth embrace us,* Cant. ii. 6. He wears us in heaven as a bracelet about his arms, which made the spouse cry out, *O set me as a seal upon thine arm!* Cant. viii. 6. He stamps and prints us on the palms of his hands, *Behold I have graven thee on the palms of my hand,* Isa. xlix. 16. as if our names were written in letters of blood upon Christ's flesh. He sets us as a seal upon his heart; that is the expression of the spouse too, *O set me as a seal upon thine heart!* Cant. viii. 6. Nay, so precious are the saints to Jesus Christ, that they lodge in heaven in his bowels, and in his heart, for they dwell in Christ, *Hereby we know that we dwell in him,* 1 John iv. 13.

And they dwell in God, and dwell in love, *For God is love, and he that dwelleth in love, dwelleth in God,* 1 John iv. 16. I know not what more to say. You know, the manner of the high priests was to carry the names of the children of Israel into the holy of holies on their shoulders, and on their breasts; but was it ever heard, that any high priest, besides the great high priest of our profession, should carry the names of thousands and millions on his shoulders, and on his arms, and on his hands, and on his wings, and on his bosom, and on his heart; nay in his heart, and in his bowels, as a memorial before the Lord? O unmatchable love!

Methinks this love of Christ should now change my soul into a globe or mass of divine love towards Christ, ' as it were by the Spirit of the Lord.' Methinks a sight of Christ in his presenting himself, and his sacrifice to his Father for me, should so enamour my soul, as that I should delight in no other sight but this. Then is a Christian sweetly exercised, when as the golden ball of divine love is tossed to and again betwixt Christ's bosom and his; and in this respect it is a wonder that before this I am not sickened, and overcome with love, and ready to cry out with the spouse, *O stay me with flaggons, and comfort me with apples, for I am sick of love!* Cant. ii. 5. ' O I am wound-' ed with the arrows of love, so as neither grave, ' nor death, nor hell, neither angels, nor principa-' lities, nor powers, nor things present, nor things ' to come, can ever lick these wounds, or em-' balm, or bind them up. O my Christ, my Lord, ' my Jesus! what should I do, but yield over my-' self as a spouse under the power of her husband? ' What should I do, but lose myself in such a deep o-' cean of loves, stronger than wine, hotter than coals ' of juniper, which hath a most vehement flame?'

2. Another motive of our love to Christ, is our propriety in Christ, *Ye are not your own,* said the apostle of us, 1 Cor. vi. 9. and *he is not his own,* may we say of Christ. If any ask how may this be? I answer, That the soul in loving Christ is not her own, and in regard of loving, Christ is not his own; every one makes over itself to another; and propriety or interest to itself on both sides ceaseth, *My beloved is mine, and I am his,* saith the spouse, Cant. ii. 16. not as if Christ should leave off to be his own, or to be a free God, when he becom-

Carrying on the great Work of our Salvation in his Intercession. 487

becometh ours; no, no, but he so demeans himself, in respect of his loves, as if he were not his own; he putteth on such relations, and assumes such offices of engagement, as if he were all for us, and nothing for himself; thus he is called *a Saviour, a Redeemer, a King, a Priest, a Prophet, a Friend, a Guide, an Head, an Husband, a Leader, Ransomer, and Intercessor*; And what not of this nature?

O my soul! come hither, and put thy little candle to this mighty flame; if thou hadst ten hearts, or as many hearts in one as there are elected men and angels in heaven and earth, all these would be too little for Jesus Christ: only go as far as thou canst, and love him with that heart thou hast, yea, love him with all thy heart, and all thy soul, and all thy might: and as Christ in loving thee is not his own: so let thy soul in loving Christ be not her own: come, love thy Christ, and not thyself; possess thy Christ, and not thyself, enjoy thy Christ, and not thyself, live in thy Christ, not in thyself; solace thyself in Jesus Christ, not in thyself; say with the apostle, *I am crucified with Christ, nevertheless I live, yet not I, but Christ liveth in me*, Gal. ii. 20. Certainly, if ever thou comest to love Christ truly; thou canst not but deny thyself, and all created lovers. This love will screw up thyself so high above the world, and above thy flesh, and above thyself, and above all other lovers, that nothing on this side Christ, whether in heaven or on earth, will come in competition with him. Suppose a man on the top of a castle higher than the third region of the air, or near the sphere of the moon, should look down to the fairest and sweetest meadows, or to a garden rich with roses, and flowers of all sweet colours and delicious smells, certainly he should not see or feel any sweetness, pleasantness, colour or smell, because he is so far above them; so the soul, filled with the love of Christ, is so high above all created lovers, that their loveliness cannot reach or ascend to the high and large capacity of a spiritual soul. O! for a soul filled up with all the fulness of God! O! for a soul stretched out to its widest capacity and circumference for the entertainment of God! O my soul! that thou wert but *able to comprehend with all the saints, what is the breadth, and length, and depth, and height, and to know the love of Christ that passeth knowledge!* Eph. iii. 18.

19. Surely if Christ be mine, if his death be mine, his resurrection mine, his ascension mine, his session mine, his intercession mine, How should I but love him with a singular love? Farewel world, and worldly glory; if Christ come in room, it is time for you to vanish; I shall little care for a candle, when the sun shines fair and bright upon my head: what, is my name written on the heart of Christ? Doth he wear me as a favour and love-token about his arms and neck? Is he at every turn presenting me and my duties to his heavenly Father? *O thou hast ravished my heart, my King, my Jesus, thou hast ravished my heart with one of thine eyes, and with one chain of thy neck*, Cant. iv. 9.

Suppose, O my soul! thou hadst been with Christ when he washed his disciples feet, and that he should have come, and have washed thy feet; would not thy heart have glowed with love to Jesus Christ? Why, Christ is now in glory, and now he takes thy filthy soul, and dirty duties, and washes (as it were) the feet of all, that he may present them to his Father: thou canst not shed a tear, but he washes it over again in his precious blood, and perfumes it with his glorious intercessions. Oh! what cause hast thou to love Jesus Christ? Oh! you that never loved Christ, come, love him now; and you that have loved Christ a little, O! love him more; above all, let me, O my soul! charge upon thee this duty of love; O! go away warmed with the love of Christ, and with a love to Christ.

SECT. VII.
Of joying in Jesus in that respect.

7. LET us joy in Jesus, as carrying on this work of our salvation in his intercession. Surely this is glad tidings of great joy; when wicked Haman procured letters from King Ahasuerus for the destruction of all Jews, then Esther the queen makes request to the king that her people might be saved, and Haman's letters revoked, *And the king said to her, What wilt thou, queen Esther? And what is thy request, and it shall be given thee?* Esther v. 3. O! the joy of the Jews at this happy tidings! *Then the city of Shushan rejoiced, and was glad; then the Jews had light, and gladness, and joy, and honour, in every province, and in every city, whithersoever the king's commandment, and his decree came, the Jews had* [...] *day, [...]*

viii. 15, 16, 17. Is not this our very case? Was there not a law against us, an hand-writing of ordinances, a sentence of a double death, of body and soul; Had not Satan, as wicked Haman, accused us, and sought by all means our condemnation? But yet behold, not only an earthly Esther, but Jesus the Son of God was willing, for our sakes, to come down from heaven; and he it was that took away the hand-writing of ordinances, and cancelled it upon the cross; that ascended into heaven, and there makes requests for us; and he it is in whom his Father is well pleased: never comes he to his Father, but he obtains the grace of the golden sceptre; no sooner he cries, *I will that these poor souls be eternally saved*; but his Father answers, *Amen, be it so, be it, O my Son! even as thou pleasest*. O that we could joy at this! O that we could imitate the Jews! O that light, and gladness, and joy, and honour would possess our souls! if at Christ's birth was such, and so much joy, because a Saviour was proclaimed, is not our joy to be heightened when salvation is effected? If the first act of Christ's mediation was so joyous, shall not the last act of his mediation be much more joyous?—— But I hear many objections, which keep back joy; they are as bars and hindrances at the doors of many heavy hearts, that joy cannot enter in: I shall instance in some.

O! I am much opposed here in this world, (says one) men are as wolves and devils, *dogs have compassed me, the assembly of the wicked have enclosed me*, Psalm xxii. 16. They have no bowels, they persecute, reproach, revile, so that I am killed all the day long.——And what then? What matter oppositions of men, so long as Christ doth intercede for thee in heaven! O remember Christ's bowels; it may be he suffers men to be merciless on earth, that thou mayest look up, and behold how merciful he is who sits above: and tell me, hast thou no experience of this truth? Doth not relief strangely come in now and then? Why, write upon the fore-head of such favours, 'I have a merciful and compassionate Mediator in heaven.'

O! I am much tempted, (says another) that I cannot pray; had I now the key of prayer, I could then unlock the cabinet where all God's treasure lies, and take out what I pleased; but, alas! my prayers are dull, and weak, and dry, and without spirit and life, I cannot pray.——If so, be humbled for it, and yet know this, that when thou canst not pray, Christ then prays for thee, and he prays that thou mayest pray: and tell me, Hast thou no experience of this truth? Hath not thy spirit sometimes been enlarged in prayer? Hast thou not sometimes felt thy heart warmed or savingly affected? Hast thou not sometimes in prayer been lifted up above thyself and above the world? Conclude then, 'My intercessor above hath sent 'me this gift and Spirit; it is not I but Christ's 'intercession, that by an admirable and secret o-'peration hath given me the Spirit to help my in-'firmity; these are the intercessions of the Spirit 'of Christ, and they are the very echo of the 'intercessions of Christ in his own person.'

O but I labour under such and such corruptions! (says another) and the devil is busy, exceeding busy, and he exceedingly prevails; how am I overcome with these corruptions, and with these and these sins? It may be so, and yet do not altogether despond, for Jesus Christ is at God's right hand, and there he sits till his enemies be made his foot-stool; and what, are not thy sins his enemies? O be of good comfort! for Christ will prevail, it is one piece of his prayer that he puts up for thee, *To keep thee from evil*, John xvii. 15. And surely he will either keep thee from it, or keep thee in it, that in the issue thou shalt have the victory; *Those that thou gavest me I have kept*, (saith Christ) *and none of them is lost*, John xvii. 12. If he undertake for thee, thou art safe and sure; *his covenant is everlasting, even the sure mercies of David*, Isa. lv. 3. And therefore if thou dost not, certainly thou shalt feel the virtue of Christ's intercession: sin must be subdued, hell-gates shall not prevail against thee; he will not quench thy sparks until he bring forth judgment unto victory.

Oh, but I am in a suffering condition! (says another) and there is none that regards or takes pity on me, all my friends have dealt treacherously with me, among all my lovers there is none to comfort me: they have heard, that I sigh, and there is none to refresh me; I stand for Christ, but there is none stands by me; I own him, but there is none owns me. Bleeding Christian, bear up! is not Christ's intercession a sufficient answer to this case? alas! thou wouldest be pitied for all thy weaknesses; Why? Know that compassion is natural to Jesus Christ; he is a merciful high priest, and can

be

no other to thee; God ordained him to officiate in such a tabernacle as wherein thou dwellest, he was in all things like unto thee, sin only excepted. It may be thou art in want, and so was Christ, he had no house; thou art persecuted, and so was Christ; sin loads thee, and so it did Christ. A christian's condition needs compassion, and Christ knows how much, and it is his work continually to lay it open above; 'O my Father! thus and thus it is 'with the militant church, not a member in it, but 'he is under sin and affliction; see here the tears, 'hearken to the sighs and groans, and chatterings, 'and mournings of my doves below; I present 'here their persons and performances; and, Oh! 'that they may find acceptance through my me- 'rits!' Some speak of heaven's music, some tell us of saints and angels singing and warbling in lively notes, the praises of Christ in heaven; and if any such thing be, certainly it is ear-tickling, heart-ravishing music; O the melody! O the joys of saints to hear such heavenly airs with heavenly ears! but be it as it will be, of this I am confident, that heaven itself yields no such musick as is the intercession of Jesus Christ; this (if any thing in heaven do it) makes melody in the ears of God, and of all celestial spirits, saints or angels: and O, my soul! suppose thyself within the compass, if now thou couldest but hear what thy Jesus is saying in thy behalf; 'Is not this a brand newly pluckt out of the 'fire? Was not this a poor soul but the other day in 'a state of nature, defiled with sin, within a step of 'hell? And did I not send my Spirit to recal him? 'Was not this precious blood shed for the redemp- 'tion of him? And what though sin stick and cleave 'to him to this day, yet have I not given the charge 'to take away his filthy garments from him, and 'to clothe him with changes of raiment, even 'with the shining robes of mine own righteousness? 'O my Father, let this soul live in thy sight! O 'cast him not away for whom I have suffered and 'done all this! I cannot rest satisfied without his 'society, I am not right till he is with me in glo- 'ry: he is my darling, my purchase, my portion, 'my delight, and therefore let him be saved.' Is not this enough to cause thy very heart leap in thy bosom? Bonaventure fondly reports, That Francis hearing an angel a little while playing on an harp, he was so moved with extraordinary delight, that he thought himself in another world.

O! but suppose thou shouldest hear the voice of Jesus thy intercessor thus pleading for thee; wouldest thou not be cast into an extasy? Would not this fill thee with joys unspeakable and full of glory? ——Come, realize this meditation. Certainly, if thou art Christ's he is thus, or in some other manner interceding for thee; as sure as Christ is in heaven, he is pleading with his Father in heaven on thy behalf: O! the joys, the joys, the joys that I should now feel!—— Tell me, Is it not a comfort for a poor beggar to be relieved at a rich man's door? We are all beggars in regard of heaven, and Jesus Christ doth not only come forth and serve us, but he takes us poor beggars by the hand, and leads us into his heavenly Father. O! what comfort is here?

SECT. VIII.

Of praying to, and praising of Jesus in that respect.

8. LET us pray, and praise our Jesus in this respect.

1. Let us pray or sue our interest in this intercession: it is a question among the schools, Whether we may conveniently pray to Jesus to pray to his Father in our behalf? And thus far is granted, that we may pray to Christ to make us partakers of his intercessions, and to mingle our prayers with his prayers, that they may find acceptance with God his Father. But that we may use such a form, as *Ora pro nobis, O Christ pray for us*, it is looked upon as inconvenient in this respect. 1. Because *we have no such custom, neither the churches of God*, 1 Cor. xi. 6. 2. Because it favours too much of the error of Arrius Nestorius, and indeed of the Romanists themselves. 3. Because our prayers are most-what directed to Christ in his person or divine substance, whose part is rather to give than to ask; or, if they are directed to Christ as Mediator, and not simply, as the only begotten Son of God, then I see no incongruity, though in the former respect some inconveniency, but that we may pray to Christ to intercede for us, for so he is God and man; and he is considered according to both natures, only the difference of both natures is still to be kept and maintained. Intercession is the office of the whole person of Christ, and of the two natures of Christ; but he performs this office

office one way according to his divine nature, and another way according to his human nature. I lift not to quarrel about niceties, it is thus agreed on all hands, and that is enough to our purpose, that we may call on Jesus, or on God the Father in and through Jesus, that Christ's intercession may be ours, and that he would make it out to us in a way of assurance every day more and more.

2. Let us praise, let us bless God, and bless Christ for every transaction in heaven for us. It is a wonder to observe what songs of praises were chaunted to Christ in heaven, for that one transaction of opening the book, and loosing the seals thereof; First, *The four beasts,* and then *the four and twenty elders fell down before the Lamb, having every one of them harps, and golden vials full of odours, which are the prayers of the saints,* Rev. v. 8. *And they sung a new song, saying, Thou art worthy to take the book, and open the seals thereof, for thou wast slain, and hast redeemed us to God by thy blood,*——— ver. 9. And then, *the angels round about the throne, whose number was ten thousand times ten thousand, and thousands of thousands,* verse 11. came on, *saying, Worthy is the Lamb that was slain, to receive power, and riches, and wisdom, and strength, and honour, and glory, and blessing,*——— verse 12. And then, *every creature which is in heaven, and on the earth, and under the earth, and such as are in the sea,* came on, *saying, Blessing, and honour, and glory, and power be unto him that sitteth upon the throne, and unto the Lamb for ever and ever,* verse 13. *And the four beasts, and four and twenty elders fell down and worshipped him that liveth for ever and ever,* verse 14. I cannot tell what other transactions may be in heaven, we have but hints of them here, nor shall we fully or particularly know them till we come to heaven; but for this one transaction of Christ's intercession, we cannot imagine less praise to be given to Christ than for any other. O then let us go do this duty on earth, as it is done in heaven! what, is Christ praying for us? O! let us be on the exercise of praising him! is Christ interceding for us? Let us give him the glory of his intercession; heaven is full of his praises, O! why should not earth ring with the sound thereof? *Praise the Lord, O my soul, and all that is within me, praise his holy name.*

SECT. IX.

Of conforming to Jesus in that respect.

9. LET us conform to Jesus in respect of his intercession I cannot think; but in every action of Christ there is something imitable of us. And as to the present work, I shall instance only in these few particulars. As,———

1. Christ appears in heaven for us, let us appear on earth for him. Is there not equity as well as conformity in this duty? O my soul! consider what thy Christ is doing, consider wherein the intercession of Jesus Christ consists; is not this the first part of it? Why, he appears in heaven before saints, and angels, and before God his Father in thy behalf; and art thou afraid to appear before worms, mortals, dust and ashes in his cause, or for his truth? Shall Jesus Christ own thee in heaven, and wilt thou not own Jesus Christ here in this world? Shall Jesus Christ, as thy great high priest, take thy name, and carry it upon his breast in the presence of God; and wilt not thou take the name of Christ, and hold it forth in profession and practice to all men? Oh! what a mighty engagement is here to stand to Christ, and to appear for Christ, and to own his cause in these backsliding times? In that Christ, who sits at the right hand of God, is willing and ready to appear in person for us, both as a mediator, and sponsor, and solicitor, and advocate, and ledger-ambassador.

2. Christ spends all his time for us and our salvation; let us spend all our time for him, and in his service; the apostle tells us, That *he ever lives to make intercession for us,* Heb. vii. 25. It is not for a day, or a month, or a year, but he lives for ever upon this account; for ever, (i. e.) during all the time from his ascension until the end of the world; he is still interceding, he spends off all that time for us, and shall we think it too much time to spend a few days that we have here to live upon the earth for him? One thinks this is the greatest argument in the world to make us walk closely with God in Christ, ' He spends of his eternity for ' us; and shall not we spend of our whole time ' for him?' Surely people do not think what Christ is adoing in heaven for them; if you who are saints would but seriously consider, that Christ, this sabbath,

bath, this day of rest, is at his work, that without any weariness or intermission, from morning till evening, and from evening till morning, he is ever, ever interceding; How would this engage you in his service? Ah, Christians! if you should continue praying, praising, reading, hearing all this day, without any intermission or breaking off, O! what weariness? Oh! how would you say, 'When 'will the day be done? When will the sabbath 'be at an end?' Well, but Christ is not weary of serving you; this sabbath, and the last sabbath, and the other sabbath, and every sabbath, when you had done your duties, he took your persons and duties, and presented all unto his Father; he prayed over your prayers, and continued praying, and saying, 'Lord, accept of a short, poor, lean, 'imperfect service done on earth for my sake, and 'for these merits sake, which I am continually pre- 'senting to thee here in heaven.' Oh! why do we 'not come up to this conformity? Oh! why are we so unconformable to the actings of Christ? He is preparing mansions for us in heaven, and are we digging in this world? He is making mention of our names to God? And are we sinning against him and God? His blood cries, *O that these souls may be saved!* and shall our sins cry, *It is just that these souls should be damned.* O! mind the examplar, Christ spends all his time for you, do you spend all your time for him: we cannot but judge this to be most equal. 'That they who live 'should not henceforth live unto themselves, but 'unto him who ever lives to make intercession for 'them.'

3. He prays for us and for all believers unto his Father, and let us pray for ourselves, and for all our brethren, and for all sorts of men, though they be our enemies, for we were no better to Jesus Christ: *Learn of me* (saith Christ) and so far as he is imitable let us follow him; doth Christ pray? Let us pray; doth he pray for us and others? Let us pray for ourselves, and then let us pray one for another, *I exhort therefore* (saith the apostle) *that first of all supplications, prayers, intercessions, and giving of thanks be made for all men,* 1 Tim. ii. 1. *And come, lift up thy prayer for the remnant that is left,* said the king to Isaiah, Isa. xxxvii. 4. And *wrestle together in prayer for me,* said Paul, Rom. xv. 30. And, *Give the Lord no rest till he make Jerusalem a praise in the earth,* said the prophet, Isa. lxii. 7. Christ intercedes, and there is no question but we should intercede for the living saints, *Brethren, pray for us,* said the apostle, 1 Thes. v. 25. Whosoever thou art that readest, 'I beseech 'thee remember me in thy prayers, it may be thou 'art nearer God,' and more in favour with God 'than such a poor sinner as I am.' As Mordecai set Esther on work to intercede for him with the king, and for his people; so it is our duty to crave the prayers of such who are upon better terms, possibly with the Lord, than we ourselves are at the present, 'Only I could wish thy prayers at such a 'time, when thy heart is got nearest to God, by 'special stirrings of faith and love.' I suppose, thou canst not have a spirit and power of prayer, but sometimes or other thou art (as it were) in the lap of Christ, upon the spouse's knee, in the beloved's bosom; 'O then make a request for an un- 'worthy one! O then, if ever, intercede for me, 'because then I read Christ's own intercession in 'thy intercession. What is thy prayer then, but 'as the echo of Christ's prayer, the Amen to 'Christ's intercessions, which he makes in heaven?' Christians! it is our duty to put one another upon praying one for another; Christ intercedes for us, and so should we intercede for his, called or uncalled, if so they belong to the election of grace.

4. Christ takes our prayers, and mingles them with his own prayers, intercessions, incense, and so presents all as one work mingled together unto God the Father; O! let this be our care, to put up all our prayers to God in the name of Christ, and to stay ourselves upon the intercessions of Christ; when all is done, let us beg the acceptance of our prayers, not for our sakes, nor for our prayers sake, but for his sake, who perfumes our prayers, by interweaving them with his prayers. Many a poor soul is many a time afraid to pray to God for want of the due consideration of this conformity; such an one goes to prayer, and he looks upon it as it lies upon his own heart, or as it comes from himself, and then he cries, 'O! what a poor, 'weak, sinful, imperfect, impenitent prayer is this?' Well, but if this weak prayer of thine be once mingled with the glorious and heavenly prayer of Jesus Christ, the weakness will soon vanish, and thy prayer will find acceptance with God the Father: it is with your prayers and duties as it is with your fire, your kitchen fire is troubled with abundance

abundance of smoke, but if ever it could ascend into the element of fire above, it would smoke no more; so your prayer, while it lies upon your own hearth, there is a great deal of smoke in it, but if ever it get up into the hands of Jesus Christ, there it is in its own element, and so it is freed from all its smoke, and so the weakness of it is done away. O, conform to Christ in this point! he will not present thy prayers to God, but he will first mingle it with his own prayers; no more shouldest thou present a prayer to God but in Christ's name, considering that all thy prayers find acceptance in, for, and through the intercession of Jesus Christ: if it were not for this, I profess I knew not how to answer the cavils of our dissolute adversaries, who throw down prayers as of no use at all. For thus they object,——

Object. Thou canst not pray, (say they) by thy own confession, without some defect, imperfection, sin: and if so, there is need of a new prayer, to beg pardon for the defects of that prayer; and then another prayer to heal the flaws of that prayer; and then another to do as much for that, and so *in infinitum*: by this means there would be an infinite progression, without any stop at any prayer at all.

Answ. I answer, this objection were valid, if there were no intercession of Christ to stay ourselves and our prayers on: but as we grant requests many times for some friend's sake, rather than for the party's sake; so doth God always grant requests for Christ's sake, never for our own sakes. Thou objectest, There are many defects in our prayers as made by us; but I answer, There are no defects in the merits and intercession of Jesus Christ, for whose sake alone they are granted of God; and therefore our prayers, being made in Christ's name, they may stay their heads in Christ's bosom; in this respect, we need not still to run ourselves in a circle, this being the last resolution, Christ's merits and Christ's intercessions. Christ offers up our persons and wooden prayers in his golden censer to his Father; Christ's intercession therefore is that which doth the deed. Now, to say our prayers are of no use, it is all one as to say, his intercession is of no use; not that we are so good, that he cannot take exception against us and our prayers; but because Christ is so good, and his intercession for us is so good, that he neither can, nor will take exception against him, or his intercession for us; and, in this case, Christ and Christians make one person (as it were) in law; his intercession for us, and our intercession for ourselves are but one intercession; and indeed, he so mingles them that they seem but one, for ' the smoke of the incense, and the ' prayers of the saints, ascend up together before ' God out of the angel's hand,' Rev. viii. 4.

5. Christ pleads the cause of his people, and answers all the accusations of Satan against them; Oh! let us plead for them for whom Christ pleads, and answer the accusation of Satan, or his instruments, against their persons, or their ways. We have a strange generation of men abroad, whose very religion consists in railing, reviling, reproaching the servants of the living God; not the best men, nor the best ministers under heaven escape them. * *Are they not all*, say they, *wolves, dogs, hirelings, priests of Baal, covetous, carnal, damned*; and what not? Are they not all, say they, (as the devil said of Joshua) *clothed with filthy garments, defiled totally, utterly defiled with the pollutions of Babylon?* Christians! when you hear this language, learn you to conform to Christ; go you first to God with the Lord's own plea: *Now the Lord rebuke thee, O Satan, even the Lord that hath chosen Jerusalem rebuke thee*, Zech. iii. 2. And then go on in vindication of their persons and their cause; are they not precious, gracious, holy, able, shining, and burning lights? It may be some of their persons have been faulty; but say of such, *Is not this a brand newly pluckt out of the fire?* Failings and human frailties have been in the best, yea, in most of the prophets and apostles: but shall we therefore condemn to hell the generation of God's dear children? Or, howsoever it may be with their persons, yet is not their cause and office of Christ's own institution? In this respect, *be that despiseth you*,

---

* I lately received a paper, wherein the Quakers gave the ministers of Christ these following names, *Conjurers, thieves, robbers, antichrist, witches, blind guides, devils, liars, Baal's priests, Sir Symonds, dissemblers, upholders of the seven headed and ten horned beasts, a viperous and serpentine generation, bloody Herodians, blasphemers, scarlet-coloured beasts, Babylon's merchants, busy bodies, whited walls, painted sepulchres, ravening wolves, persecutors, tyrants, greedy dogs, Pharisees.*

de-

despiseth me, (saith Christ) *and he that despiseth me, despiseth him that sent me*, Luke x. 16. Are not the ministers of Christ as stars in the right hand of Christ? They that would do them any deadly harm, must pluck them hence. Christians! conform you to Christ in this point; you see how Satan stands at the right hand of our Joshuas to resist them; now then plead you their cause, and answer the adversary's accusations.

6. Christ by his intercession, *saves us to the uttermost*, Heb. vii. 25. O! let us serve him to the uttermost; surely all we can do is too little to answer so great a love as this. Oh, Christians! why should it be esteemed a needless thing to be most rigorously conscionable and exactly circumspect? Christ paid our debt to the uttermost farthing, drunk every drop of our bitter cup, and now presents all unto his Father, by way of intercession, and saves us, [*eis panteles, Thoroughly, to the uttermost*. Why should not we labour to perform his service, and to fulfil every one of his commandments thoroughly, and to the uttermost also? Certainly there is a duty which concerns us Christians, as, to be *hot in religion*, Rev. iii. 16. to be *zealous of good works*, Tit. ii. 14. to *walk circumspectly* or *precisely*, as the word carries it, Eph. v. 15. to be *fervent in spirit*, Rom. xii. 11. to *strive to enter in at the strait gate*, Luke xiii. 24. to *contend for the faith*, Jude. 3. with an holy kind of *violence to lay hold upon the kingdom of heaven*, Matth. xi. 12. Oh! that ever men should be afraid of taking God's part too much, or fighting too valiantly under the colours of Christ, of being too busy about the salvation of their own souls, of being singular (as they call it) in the duties of religion; I observe, men are content to be singular in any thing, save in the service of God; you desire and labour to be singularly rich, and singularly wise, and singularly valourous, and singularly proud? but you can by no means endure singularity or eminency in zeal, and the Lord's service. In matters of religion, you are resolved to do as the most do, though in so doing you damn your own souls, Matth. vii. 13. O come and learn this lesson of Christ! he saves us to the uttermost, and let us serve him to the uttermost, with all our hearts, and with all our souls, and with all our mights.

Thus far we have looked on Jesus in his intercession: our next work is our last work, which is, to look on Jesus, as carrying on the great work of our salvation for us in his coming again, the very end of time, to all eternity; he hath no more now to do but to judge the saints, and to lead them into glory, and to deliver up his kingdom to his Father; and so to live with his redeemed ones, for ever, and ever, and ever.

Mat xxiv. 30, 31. *Then shall appear the sign of the Son of man in heaven: and then shall all the tribes of the earth mourn, and they shall see the Son of man coming in the clouds of heaven with power and great glory. And he shall send his angels with a great sound of a trumpet, and they shall gather together his elect from the four winds, from one end of heaven to the other.*

Mat. xxv. 34, 35. *Then shall the king say to them on his right hand, Come, ye blessed of my Father, inherit the kingdom prepared for you from the foundation of the world. For I was an hungred, and ye gave me meat; I was thirsty, and ye gave me drink, &c.*

Mat. xix. 28. *When the Son of man shall sit on the throne of his glory, ye shall also sit upon twelve thrones, judging the twelve tribes of Israel.*

1 Cor. xv. 24, 28. *Then cometh the end, when he shall have delivered up the kingdom to God, even the Father.——And when all things shall be subdued unto him, then shall the Son also himself be subject unto him, that put all things under him, that God may be all in all.*

Heb. xii. 1. 2 Cor. iii. 18. Phil. iii. 20. Tit. ii. 13. Rev. xx. 12,—21. 1. *Looking unto Jesus, the author and finisher of our faith.——We all with open face beholding as in a glass the glory of the Lord, are changed into the same image from glory to glory——For our conversation is in heaven, from whence also we look for the Saviour the Lord Jesus Christ.——We look for that blessed hope, and the glorious appearing of the great God, and our Saviour Jesus Christ.——And I saw the dead, small and great, stand before God; and the books were opened; and another book was opened, which is the book of life.——And I saw a new heaven, and a new earth; for the first heaven and the first earth were passed away; and t*. . . *no more sea.*

LOOK

LOOKING UNTO JESUS.

In his Second Coming.

BOOK FIFTH.

CHAP. I.   SECT. I.

Job xix 25, 27. *I know that my Redeemer liveth, and that he shall stand at the latter day upon the earth; whom I shall see for myself, and mine eyes shall behold, and not another.*

Of Christ's preparing for Judgment.

AND is yet all done? O the unwearied patience, love, mercy, and free grace of Christ in carrying on this mighty work! he begun it before the beginning of the world, since then he hath been labouring in it about six thousand years; and now the time of restoring being come, he will perfect what he hath begun, and bring on the other end of the golden chain, *Moreover, whom he did predestinate, them he also called; and whom he called, them he also justified; and whom he justified, them he also glorified,* Rom. viii. 30. In this piece also, as in the former, we shall first lay down the object, and then give directions how to look upon it.

The object is Jesus, carrying on the great work of our salvation in his coming again to earth, and taking up with him all his saints into heaven. In this work I shall set before you these particulars.

1. Christ's preparing for judgment.
2. Christ's coming to judgment.
3. Christ's summons of the elect to come under judgment.
4. Christ and the saints meeting at the judgment day.
5. Christ's sentencing or judging the saints for eternal glory.
6. Christ and the saints judging the rest of the world.
7. Christ and his saints going up into heaven; when shall be the end of this world.
8. Christ surrendering and delivering up the kingdom to God, even the Father.
9. Christ's subjection to the Father, that God may be all in all.
10. Christ (notwithstanding this) being all in all to his blessed, saved, and redeemed saints to all eternity.

1. For his preparing for judgment. When once the number of all his elect shall be completed, and the work of his intercession shall be at an end, then immediately will follow these particulars. As,—

1. *A great voice comes out of the temple of heaven, saying, It is done,* Rev. xvi. 17. It comes out of the temple of heaven, that we may understand it to be the voice of Christ. And if this speech be directed unto God, it is as if Christ had bespoke his Father thus, 'And now, O my Fa-
'ther! I have done that office of the priesthood,
'which by agreement we erected, is now at an
'end: here I have sat at thy right hand interced-
'ing for my saints, ever since my ascension; and
'of all that thou hast given me, by thine eternal
'election, I have not lost a saint, John xvii. 12.
'In their several ages I produced them, and gave
'them a being, and in their times I remembered
'them, and presented their conditions and necessi-
'ties before thee; and now I have not a saint more
'in the book of life, there is not another name
                                                                'writ-

'written to be born on earth; and to what pur-
'pose should I now continue the world? The saints
'are they for whom I made the world, the saints
'are they that hold forth the light of my glory in
'the world, the saints are they for whom my e-
'ternal counsels before the world did work, the
'saints are they for whom I was content to shed
'my precious blood when I was in that world be-
'low; and now their number is completed, I am re-
'solved to unpin the fabrick of the world, and take
'it down; it stands but for their sakes, and there-
'fore now let the seventh angel blow his trumpet,
'that the mystery of God may be finished,' Rev. x.
7. *I swear by him that lives for ever, that time shall
be no longer*, Ver. 6.

2. No sooner this said, but the *seventh angel
sounds*, Rev. xi. 15. This seventh angel (saith Pareus) is the archangel that proclaims Christ's coming, with a great and mighty shout, *For the Lord
himself shall descend from heaven with a shout, with
the voice of the archangel, and with the trump of
God*, 1 Thess. iv. 16. The Lord shall descend with
a shout, but before he descend, and I believe upon the very discovery of his coming down, there
will be a shout in heaven; for so it follows, *And
the seventh angel sounded, and there were great
voices in heaven*; if we believe commentaries, *
These are the voices of blessed souls, and blessed
angels in heaven; no sooner Christ bids the angel
[sound] *q. d.* Summon those blessed souls that
were slain for the word of God, and therefore cried, *How long, Lord, holy and true?* Rev. vi. 10.
Summon those blessed souls, that have cried so long,
Come, Lord Jesus, come quickly, Rev. xxii. 20.
Summon all souls, and summon all angels, and bid
them wait on me, now I resolve to go down, and
to judge the world; no sooner, I say, Christ bids
the angels sound, but presently at the joy of this
command, all the voices in heaven gave up a shout;
why, this is the long look'd for day; the day of
perfecting the number of the saints; the day of
joining the souls and bodies of the saints together;
the day of convening all the families both of saints
and angels under one roof; the day of bringing up
the bride unto the Lamb, and of completing the
marriage in its highest solemnity; and therefore
no wonder, if at this news great voices and cries
(such as are used by mariners, or gatherers of the
vintage) were made in heaven. Oh! what an addition of joy is this to heaven's joy itself. The
spirits of the just, and the blessed angels that have
lived together in heaven's bliss, had never such an
adventitious joy as this before; now they shout
and sing a new and blessed song, *The kingdoms of
this world, are become the kingdoms of our Lord,
and of his Christ, and he shall reign for ever and
ever*, Rev. xi. 15. We may call this heaven's triumph for the finishing of God's majesty. Now it
is that Christ will vindicate his kingdom, and o-
verthrow the power of his enemies; they had long
set themselves against the Lord, and against his a-
nointed; the kings of the earth, and the rulers
confederated, they ruled all, and as much as in
them lay, excluded Christ; but now the kingdoms
of the world will return to Christ, and he alone
shall rule; and thence the winged queristers of heaven chaunt forth this anthem, ' The kingdoms of
' the world are become the kingdoms of Christ.

3. After this shout, ' The four and twenty elders
' that sit before God on their seats, fall upon their
' faces, and worship God, saying, We give thee
' thanks, O Lord God Almighty, which art, and
' wast, and art to come, because thou hast taken to
' thee thy great power, and hast reigned, and the
' nations were angry,' &c. Rev. xi. 16, 17, 18. By
these four and twenty elders, we understand all
God's saints of the Old and New Testament, comprehended under the twelve patriarchs, and twelve
apostles; others would have them to be only those
saints of the Old Testament, and therefore called
elders; whosoever they are, we find they are so
glad at this news, that Christ will now judge the
world, that presently they rise off their seats, and
fall on their faces; and first they praise, and then
they pray. 1. They praise God for taking to himself his own power; Christ connived (as it were)
till now at the power of his enemies; antichrist,
and not Christ, seemed to rule, and to sit in the
temple of God, but now Christ is resolved to rule
himself, and to make all his enemies his footstool;
and therefore now *we give thee thanks, O Lord
God Almighty*. 2. They pray Christ to go on to
judgment. 1. Because *the nations were angry*,
Rev. 11. 18. *q. d.* They have been angry long
enough, they have set themselves against Christ,
and against his church; and therefore it is time to
bridle

---

* Pareus *in loco.*

bridle their wrath, and to break them with a rod of iron; *O! let thy wrath come.* 2. Because the time of judgment is now accomplished, which God hath decreed in his eternal counsel, and which the Father hath put in his own power; * 'This time 'was not for mortals to know, but now it was re-'vealed to these celestial spirits by Christ;' and therefore they beg, 'Go on, Lord Jesus; reward 'now thy servants, prophets, and saints, and de-'stroy them which destroy the earth.

4. God, the Father, is well pleased with Christ's purpose of judging the world. *The Lord said unto my Lord, Sit thou at my right-hand, until I make thine enemies thy footstool*, Psalm cx. 1. I know those words were spoke to Christ at his ascension into heaven; yet that hinders not, but that now God speaks them again to Christ; for *as yet* (saith the apostle) *we see not all things put under him*, Heb. ii. 8. And God's purpose was that Christ should rule, until he had put all things in subjection under his feet. Nay, why not those words spoken now, rather than before? Christ indeed reigned as king, ever since his ascension; but now more especially he is to manifest his kingdom, for now he is to *judge among the heathen*; now he is to *wound the heads of many countries*, Psal. cx. 6. Now he is to overthrow Pope, Turk, and all his enemies, and he alone, with the Father and the Spirit, is to reign in his elect saints and angels. Thus all agree, That Christ in the latter days shall be fully honoured in his kingly power; hitherto Christ hath been much honoured in his prophetical and priestly office, but not so much in his kingly, but now he must be fully honoured in his kingly office, now, especially *the kingdoms of this world must become the kingdoms of the Lord, and his Christ, and so he shall reign for ever and ever*, Rev. xi. 15 Certainly, there is a difference betwixt Christ's reign before, and his present reign at the day of judgment; Christ hath a double throne wherein he sits and reigns, *To him that overcomes will I give to sit with me in my throne, as I also overcame, and am set down with my Father in his throne*, Rev. iii. 21. The kingly rule that Christ hath from his ascension is upon his Father's throne, but the kingdom that Christ shall have at the day of judgment, and ever after, it is the joint reign of him with the Father;

he shall have a throne himself, and the saints shall sit with him in his own throne: and now, saith the Father, *Sit thou at my right hand. q. d* Sit on thy own throne by me; go on to judge the nations; I will not judge them but only in thee, and by thee; *Lo! I have committed all judgment unto the Son*, John v. 22. ' and do thou judge them, 'until thou hast rewarded thy friends, and made 'thine enemies thy footstool.' Mark, *he hath committed all judgment unto the Son:* The Father gives the Son a commission, wherein is written (as it were) these words. ' My Son, now is the time 'and season which I had put in my own power, 'and my pleasure is, that all the world shall be 'set on fire; *These heavens under thee shall pass 'away with a great noise, and the elements shall 'melt with fervent heat ; the earth also, and the 'works that are therein shall be burnt up*, 2 Pet. 'iii. 10. *And I will have new heavens, and a new 'earth, wherein shall dwell righteousness*, Verse '13. Go too then, put on thy robes, appear in 'thy glory; empty these heavens of all those glo-'rious Spirits that are therein, and let them wait 'on thee to thy judgment-seat; go pass thy doom 'upon all flesh, and send reprobates to hell, and 'bring up hither all thy saints, that they may live 'with thee, and here behold thy glory for ever and 'ever. Lo! here is thy commission, begone, and 'return no more hither until it be accomplished.

Use. Christians, I cannot but wonder at this joy and exultation in heaven, and that we have so little, or none of this on earth; we say with cold lips, and frozen hearts, *Thy kingdom come, thy will be done in earth as it is in heaven*; but if our prayers were real and fervent, if we could but imitate those heavenly citizens, What longings would be in our hearts after Christ's coming? How should we rejoice at the very thoughts hereof? Christ comforting his disciples in respect hereof, he speaks these words, *When these things begin to come to pass, then look up*, (saith he) *and lift up your heads, for your redemption draweth nigh*, Luke xxi. 28. The fulness of our redemption is a ground of consolation; all the spirits above are sensible of this; God, and Christ, and the angels, and saints rejoice, and again rejoice. *The Spirit and the bride say, Come*, Rev. xxii. 17. and Christ himself saith, *Surely, I come quickly;*

---

* *Mortalibus ignotum, cœlestibus vero nunc revelatum a Christo.* Pareus *in loco.*

Carrying on the great Work of our Salvation in his second coming. 497

quickly; O! let us say, *Amen* to it; *Even so come, Lord Jesus*, verse 20.

SECT. II.

Of Christ's coming to judgment.

2. FOR Christ's coming to judgment, no sooner Christ prepared, and all in readiness, but down he descends from his imperial throne, to the judgment-seat. In this passage I shall observe these particulars.

3. He descends with his train; he comes with his royal attendants out of heaven. This is the glory of a prince, that he hath so many nobles waiting on him; and this is the glory of Jesus Christ, that when he comes to judge the world, he shall have his saints and angels (the glory of the creation) to be his attendants in that work, *Behold the Lord comes with mighty angels*, 2 Thess. i. 7. *Behold, the Lord comes with ten thousands of his saints to execute judgment upon all*, Jude 14. Certainly a numberless number shall wait upon him; Daniel tells us of a thousand thousand that this day minister unto Christ, *a thousand thousands ministred unto him, and ten thousand times ten thousand stood before him*, Dan. vii. 10. Or if heaven have more, I believe heaven will empty itself of all the saints, and all the angels; not one spirit, whether saint or angel, shall stay behind when Christ descends; *The Son of man shall come in his glory and all the holy angels with him*, Matth. xxv. 31. Oh! what a glorious day will this be? If one sun make the morning sky so glorious, what a bright shining and glorious morning will that be, when so many thousands of suns shall shine over all our heads, the glorious body of our Christ surpassing them all in splendor and glory? Here's a new heaven of sun, and stars, such as this nether world never saw: 'Lo, yonder the sun of righteousness with all his morning stars, singing and shouting for joy! heaven now empties itself of all its created citizens, and cleaves asunder to make way for Christ, and all his train.

2. In this descent thro' the heavens, he shakes the heavens, *And the powers of the heavens shall be shaken*, Matth. xxiv. 29. The whole frame of heaven, most strong and immutable in its being and motion; or the mighty bodies thereof, most mighty in their substance, lastingness, motion and operation shall be shaken. I know, *by the powers of heaven*, some mean the angels, who at this wonderful descent of Christ, shall admire and move; but I rather think the heavens themselves are meant hereby, whose very nature shall be moved and shaken at that day, *At his nod the pillars of heaven tremble, and are astonished*, Job xxvi. 11. As yet they are subject to vanity, and therefore it is no wonder if at the coming of Christ, they tremble and are moved. In this moving or shaking the evangelist adds, that the glorious lights of heaven shall be altered, *The sun shall be darkened, and the moon shall not give her light, and the stars shall fall*, Matth. xxiv. 29. Many interpretations are given of this; I am not for allegories, but rather conceive these things as real; * The very coming of Christ shall bring such a light, that the splendor of the sun and moon shall be obscured: † This is most certain, saith Aretius, that both sun and moon shall really be darkened at that day; it is the glory of his majesty, that will dazzle those candles.

3. As he passes through the elementary world, a fire doth usher him, *Our God shall come, and shall not keep silence; a fire shall devour before him, and it shall be very tempestuous round about him*, Psalm l. 3. Whence this fire shall come, I shall not dispute, only one tells us with some confidence, ‡ That 'tis begotten in the middle region of the air by divine command; and that it first goes before him, ushering the judge to the judgment seat, and that there it stays during the judgment, and that ended, and the doom passed on all flesh, then it sets on fire all the world. Let this pass as it may, scripture goes thus far. That *a fire goeth before him*,—Psalm xcvii. 3. *Behold the Lord will come with fire, and with his chariots like a whirlwind,*—Isa. lxvi. 15. *And the Lord Jesus shall be revealed from heaven with his mighty angels in flaming fire,*

---

* *Adventum Christi tantam lucem allaturam, ut ea solis et lunæ splendor obscuretur,* Aretus in loco.
† *Certissimum autem diem judicii magna majestate, fore, ut recte & sol & luna dicantur obscurati,* Aretus in loco
‡ *Suarez de renovatione mundi,* in 2 Part Thomæ

2 Thess. i. 7, 8. In which respect, Daniel saw *his throne like the fiery flame, and his wheels as burning fire; a fiery stream issued and came forth from before him*, Da. vii. 9, 10. And at last, this fire shall have that effect, that the very 'elements shall melt with fervent heat; the earth also and the works that are therein shall be burnt up,' 2 Pet. iii. 10. O Christians? what cause have we to make the apostle's use on this point? 'Seeing all these things shall be dissolved, what manner of persons ought we to be in all holy conversation and godliness, looking for, and hastening unto the coming of the day of God, wherein the heavens being on fire shall be dissolved, and the elements shall melt with fervent heat?' 2 Pet. iii. 11, 12.

4. He descends lower and lower till he is inwrapt with clouds, *Hereafter shall ye see the Son of man sitting on the right hand of power, and coming in the clouds of heaven*, Mat. xxvi. 64. When he went up into heaven, it is said, That *a cloud received him out of their sight*, Acts i. 9. and the angels then said, *Ye men of Galilee, Why stand ye gazing up into heaven? This same Jesus which is taken up from you into heaven, shall so come in like manner as ye have seen him go into heaven*, Acts i. 11, 12. He went up in clouds, and he shall come down in clouds. *I saw in the night visions, and behold, one like the Son of man came with the clouds of heaven*, Dan. vii. 13. Here is the first sight of Christ to men on the earth, when once he is come down into the clouds, then shall they lift up their eyes, and have a full view of Jesus Christ; a cloud first received him out of their sight, and a cloud now discovers him to their sight, *Then shall appear the sign of the Son of man in heaven, and they shall see the Son of man coming in the clouds of heaven with power and great glory*, Mat. xxiv. 30. Is it not plain, that the first appearings and sight of Christ at his second coming from heaven is in the midst of clouds? *Behold, he cometh with clouds, and every eye shall see him, and they also which pierced him*, Re. i. 7. Some controversy there is about these clouds as whether they be angels. When the Psalmist speaks of all sorts of meteors, as of waters, clouds, winds, flames, some say all these are angels; and *of the angels, he saith, Who maketh his angels spirits, and his ministers a flame of fire*, Heb. i. 7. For my part, I take it in the literal sense, that upon the very backs of clouds Christ shall come riding along at the general day; and howsoever this may seem a small matter unto us, yet I cannot look on any circumstance of this transaction as small and trifling; the very clouds on which Christ rides, speak terror and comfort.

1. Oh! what a terror is this to the wicked? 'They shall see the Son of man coming in the clouds, and then shall all the tribes of the earth mourn,' Matth. xxiv. 30. These tribes of the earth are the tribes of the wicked; no sooner shall they look up, * and see Christ in his clouds, but with unconceivable horror will they cry out, O yonder is he whose blood we neglected, whose grace we resisted, whose counsels we refused, whose government we cast off! O yonder is he that comes now in clouds, in tempestuous clouds! O see how he storms! do not these very clouds, in which he rides, speak or threaten a storm? In the eighteenth Psalm is a description of Christ's coming to judgment. But, O! how terrible? in the seventh verse, we find the earth trembling; in the eight verse, a fire devouring; in the ninth verse, the heavens bowing downwards; in the 12, 13, 14, 15 verses, are 'thick clouds darkening the sky, thunders, lightnings, hail-stones flying through the air, the foundations of the world discovered.' Thus the mighty God, our Jesus descends. Oh! how should the wicked but tremble at this, when but a consideration of this hath sometimes startled God's own people? Behold, Habbakuk, with quivering lips, trembling joints, bones mouldering into dust, when he had only a prophetic representation of Christ's second appearance, Hab. iii. 16. All the dreadful things attending the presence of God in Egypt, at the red sea, on mount Sinai, through the wilderness, are made but types, but shadows of the terrible march of the captain of the Lord of hosts, and therefore shall the wicked mourn.

2. Here is the patience, and faith, and joy of saints, 'And all the kindreds of the earth shall mourn over him; even so, Amen,' Revel. i. 7. This I cannot but understand of the wicked; only some tell us of a double mourning on that day, the one of joy and love, and the other of sorrow and despair; I shall not deny but there may be some

---

* *Id de impiis solum intelligo, ad quos placutus & luctus ille miserandus solum pertinet*, Aretius in loco.

sweet

sweet tears upon this sweet subject, Christ's apparition in the clouds: such a shine will be from Christ in the cloud, that the very shine will pierce the hearts of men with the golden-headed arrow of love, and how may this work tears? From this text of John, 'Behold he cometh with clouds, and every eye shall see him, and they also which pierced 'him, and all the kindred of the earth shall wail,' &c. Rev. i. 7. † Some divines gather, that Christ in that day, will shew, in his glorified body, the wounds of his crucifying, as an infallible trophy of his victory over all his enemies; and hence the wicked, who pierced or crucified the Lord of glory, by their sins, will weep, and wail. I can think no less, but that Christ at that day will open his bosom, and shew those wounds of love, which he had in his heart from all eternity, together with those wounds which he received on the cross, as they are glorified in his eternal love. And then, as at the discovery of Joseph, he and his brethren fell upon the necks of each other, and wept; so will this discovery, in the appearances of Christ, bring a sweet confusion upon the spirits of saints; then shall a saint fall at the feet of his Saviour, and weeping, say, O my Jesus! thou art my father, brother, husband, self; while there were other things, I loved other things besides thyself; but, alas! they are everlastingly gone, and have left me alone, yet now thou ownest me; O my Jesus! thou breakest my heart: Oh! I cannot but weep out tears of love, and tears of joy at this appearing; O! welcome, welcome, sweet Jesus, into these clouds! Oh! welcome, welcome, sweet Jesus, into this nether world.

In these clouds I must leave our Saviour for a while, and the rather, because I believe he will descend no lower: only before I pass, one word of use to all his saints.

Use. You see him still upon his old design, tho' the world now end, yet hitherto there is no end of this great transaction; his first coming and his second coming is to save your souls; his first coming was to purchase, his second to give you the possession of salvation. What, are you not glad of this gospel news, that Christ will come at last from his imperial throne to his judgment-seat, to give you the possession of salvation? Is not the promise of his coming comfortable? Is it not comfortable to believe in him, and to hope for him? why, muse then, what comfort will it be to see his person with all his glorious train coming for you? 'The mighty God, the Lord hath spoken, and called the 'earth, from the rising of the sun, to the going 'down thereof; out of Zion, the perfection of 'beauty, God hath shined; our God shall come, 'and shall not keep silence; a fire shall devour 'before him, and it shall be very tempestuous 'round about him; he shall call to the heavens 'from above, and to the earth that he may judge 'his people,' Psal. l. 1, 2, 3, 4. It is indeed a most terrible day unto the wicked, but, Oh! how sweet, and pleasant, and comfortable to his saints? Christians! do we not long to have Christ's Spirit come into our souls with life? Do we not droop whilst Christ is absent from our souls? Are not the feet of them beautiful that bring glad tidings of peace, and of salvation by Jesus Christ? Oh, then! what will it be to see the king, not in his embassadors, but in his own person, coming for us, to fetch us into heaven? If we have but a dear friend returned from some far country, how do all run out to meet him with joy? Oh! saith the child, My father is come; saith the wife, My husband is come; and shall not we, when we see our father, our husband, our head, our Saviour returning with great glory, and glorious majesty, cry out, He is come, he is come? Shall not we at the first view of him in the clouds, cry out, O! yonder is he, whose blood redeemed us, whose Spirit cleansed us, whose prayers prevailed for us, whose law did govern us! Yonder comes he in whom we trusted, and now we see he hath not deceived our trust; yonder is he, for whom we waited long, and now we see we have not waited in vain.

I verily believe, thus it will be with us one day, we shall have comfort then, Oh! let us comfort ourselves with these words; and ever and anon cry, 'Come, Lord Jesus, come quickly; make 'haste, my beloved, and be thou like to a roe, or 'to a young hart, upon the mountains of spices,' Cant. viii 14.

† *Hinc consequitur, Christum in eo judicio cicatrices vulnerum ostensurum tanquam tropheam infallibilem contra omnes suos hostes,* Aretius in loco.

SECT. III.

Of Christ's summoning of the elect to come under judgment.

3. FOR Christ's summons of the elect to come under judgment: no sooner is he in the clouds, his throne of judicature, but there he stands, and thence 'he sends his holy angels with 'a great sound of a trumpet, and they shall gather 'together his elect from the four winds, from one 'end of heaven to another,' Mat. xxiv. 31. Christ's summonses are effectual, if he will have the elect to meet him, they must come; to this purpose he sends his angels, and they return with his saints back again to the judgment-seat. In the carrying on of this affair, we shall discuss these particulars. 1. His mission of the angels. 2. The manner of the mission. 3. The resurrection of the world. 4. The collection of the saints: Wherein, 1. Whence, and, 2. Whither they are gathered.

3. For Christ's mission of his angels, *He shall send his angels.* This was their office from their first creation, they were still sent of God this way and that way; and, indeed, herein is one difference betwixt Christ and the angels, he was to sit on God's right hand, but they were sent abroad to minister to the saints and people of God, 'To 'which of the angels, said he at any time, Sit on 'my right hand, until I make thine enemies thy 'foot-stool? Are they not all ministering spirits, 'sent forth to minister for them who shall be heirs 'of salvation?' Heb. i. 13, 14. Now, according to their office, Christ puts them upon employment at this day, *q. d.* 'O my angels! *You that wait upon 'me, that excel in strength, that do my command-'ments, and hearken unto the voice of my word,* 'Psal. ciii. 20. Go your ways now into all the four 'winds of the world, *gather all my saints together 'unto me, those that have made a covenant with me 'by sacrifice,* Psal. l. 5. Search into all the dusts 'of the earth, and leave not behind one dust that 'belongs unto any saint; search into the bottom 'of the sea, see what becomes of those drowned 'bodies of my dear ones, if either worms have 'eaten those in graves, or fishes have devoured 'them in the deep; why, now restore them; am 'not I as able to recover them, as I was to create 'them? Is it not as easy for me to raise the dead, 'as to make heaven and earth, and all of nothing? 'Go then, and gather together all those dusts, and 'let every dust be brought home to its own pro-'per body, and compact those dusts, as soft as 'they are, into solid bones; and prophesy upon 'those bones, and say unto them, 'O ye dry 'bones! hear the word of the Lord; thus saith 'the Lord, behold, I will cause breath to enter 'into you, and ye shall live; and I will lay sinews 'upon you, and cover you with skin, and put 'breath in you, and ye shall live, and ye shall 'know that I am the Lord,' Ezek. xxxvii. 4, 5, '6. Why, this is my will, and pleasure, and there-'fore be gone, O my angels, do your office, what, 'have not I commanded you?'

2. The mission, or commission, or dismission given, the angels, swift messengers of his will, fall on the execution; and to that purpose immediately they sound the trumpet; so it follows, 'And 'he shall send his angels with a great sound of a 'trumpet.' Here is the manner of their mission; they go, and as they go, they give a shout; what this shout is, or how it is made, is a curious question, and sets many wits on work; in this scripture it is set out by the sound of a trumpet; * Now, some would have it to be a material trumpet, because the scriptures frequently call it a trumpet, *he shall send his angels with the sound of a trumpet,* (saith Christ) Mat. xxiv. 31. 'And in a moment, 'in the twinkling of an eye, at the last trump we 'shall be changed, (saith Paul) for the trumpet 'shall sound, and the dead shall be raised,' 1 Cor. 'xv. 52. And the Lord himself shall descend from 'heaven with a shout, and with the voice of the 'archangel, and with the trumpet of God,' 1 Thess. iv. 16. But whether this trumpet, shall be of silver, or of brass, or of the air, or of the cloud, and meteors whereon Christ rides, they cannot agree. ‡ Others more probably look upon this trumpet as nothing else but a metaphor, or a sound form-

---

* Anselmus, *in elucidario.* Suarez, *tuba ex aera.* Doctor Slator, *who saith, I see not but we may take it properly,* &c. Cornelius a lapide.
‡ Piscator, *estius* Aretius *& alii fere omnes.*

ed in the air, like the sound of a trumpet. A voice it is without all controversy; and metaphorically it may be called a trumpet, both from the clearness and greatness of the sound: so loud shall it be, that it will pierce into the ears of the dead in their graves; '* It will shake the world, rend the rocks, 'break the mountains, dissolve the bonds of death, 'burst down the gates of hell, and unite all spi- 'rits to their own bodies.' An horrible, terrible voice shall it be. But how should angels, who are spirits, make a voice? By a collision of the air, which the angels can move at their pleasure; and who can tell, say some, but there may be some new created instrument, trumpet like, adapted for the angels, at the sides of which, by a force and collision of the air, this great shout may be, to convene all the world? Or, who knows, (say others) but that the Lord Jesus may fill the angels, even as trumpets are filled with a loud blast, and that through them this loud blast shall come rushing like a mighty wind upon the dead saints, and so awaken their bodies out of the dust? We all know this was usual in all the Jews solemnities, to convene the people by the sound of a trumpet, ' And the ' Lord spake unto Moses, saying, Make thee two ' trumpets of silver, — that thou mayest use them ' for the calling of the assembly; —— and when ' thou shalt blow them, all the assembly shall af- ' semble themselves. And if ye go to war, then ' ye shall blow and alarm with the trumpets,' Num. x. 1, 2, 3, 9. And, in the same way, (say they) Christ now will convene all the world with the sound of a trumpet, or with the sound of some such instrument of divine power and virtue, whereby the dead shall be raised, and their bodies and souls re-united. Amidst all those Authors, if I may deliver my opinion, I suppose the text that will clear all to us above all that is written, is that of 1 Thess. iv. 16. *For the Lord himself shall descend from heaven with a shout, with the voice of the archangel, and with the trumpet of God.* Give me leave to insist on it, that we may come up yet to a more full and perfect knowledge of this passage. In these words is shewed, or held forth the coming of Christ in three particulars, *with a shout, with a voice, and with a trumpet*. Some think this to be one and the same set out in variety of expressions;

but I am of another mind. It is agreed by most, that the transactions at the giving of the law on mount Sinai, were a representation of the proceedings which shall be at the great day of judgment; now, in that transaction, we read of a three-fold voice, *The voice of God, the voice of thunder, and the voice of a trumpet*, (Exod. xix. 13. compared with Exod. xx. 1.) And accordingly we find the apostle speaking of a three-fold voice, *Of the voice of Christ, of the voice of thunder, and of the voice of a trumpet*.

1. The Lord himself shall descend *with a shout*. Arius Montanus, and the vulgar, translate it, with a command. Lyra, and others, think this to be the voice of Christ himself, saying, with a loud voice, *Arise ye dead, and come to judgment*. Thus Jesus cried with a loud voice, *Lazarus, come forth*, John xi. 43. And with such a voice, will he call on the dead at the last day. So much Christ himself hath taught us, *The hour is coming, and now is, when the dead shall hear the voice of the Son of God, and they that hear shall live*, John v. 25. The hour is, because by his voice he raised some at his first coming: and the hour is coming, because in the like manner he will raise up all men at the last day, *Marvel not at this*, (saith Christ) *for the hour is coming, in the which all that are in the graves shall hear his voice, and they shall come forth*, John v. 28. As at the creation of the world, he said, *Let there be light, and there was light*; so at the dissolution of the world, he will say, ' Let the dead arise, let the sea give ' up the dead that are in it, and death and hell ' deliver up the dead which are in them;' and it will be so.

2. The Lord shall descend *with the voice of the archangel*. Two questions here, 1. Who is this archangel? 2. What is this voice?

For the first, some argue this archangel to be Gabriel, others Raphael, others Michael. The Jews have an ancient tradition, that there are seven principal angels that minister before the throne of God, and therefore called archangels. The scriptures seem to speak much that way, calling them, *Seven lamps of fire burning before the throne*, Rev. iv. 5. And *seven horns, and seven eyes of the Lamb*; and *the seven spirits of God sent forth into all the*

* *Cui omnia obediunt — mare petras scindit — inferos aperit*, &c. Chrysost. in 1 Cor. xv.

earth

earth, Rev. v. 6. And 'seven eyes of the Lord, 'which run to and fro through the whole earth,' Zech. iv. 10. And yet more plainly, 'Seven angels 'that stand before God,' Rev. viii. 2 Now, which of these seven is the archangel here spoken of, is hard to determine; only probable it is, that all the archangels, and all the angels are hereby understood, as comprehended under that one; to which agrees, Matth. xxiv. 31. Mr Ainsworth observes, That when things are done by a multitude, where one is chief, that the action is frequently ascribed either to the multitude, or to him that is chief, indifferently: as 'Jehoida brought forth the king's 'son, and he put the crown upon him,' 2 Kings xi. 12. or 'They brought forth the king's son, and 'they put upon him the crown,' 2 Chron. xxiii. 11. So David 'offered burnt-offerings,' 2 Sam. vi. 17. or, 'they offered burnt-offerings,' 1 Chron. xvi. 1. And so, 'He shall descend with the voice 'of the archangel;' or, 'He shall send his angels 'with a great sound,' Matth. xxiv. 3.

That there are seven principal angels, Mr. Mede affirms, and that there is one which yet eminently is called the archangel. Some others affirm, as among devils, there is one chief devil, called, The prince of devils; and therefore, the fire is said to be *prepared for the devil and his angels*, Mat. xxv. 41. So from this text of 1 Thess. 16. and of Dan. x. 3. and of Jude, ver 9 Some probably conclude, that the good angels have a prince, even Michael, whom Jude calls the archangel. But of this no more, the Lord keep me from *intruding into those things which I have not seen*, Colos. ii. 18. The day itself will discover it, and so I leave it, as having said enough to satisfy the sober-minded.

For the second, What is this voice of the archangel? I conceive that thereby we are to understand thunder: here is, (as we have said) a manifest allusion to the proceedings at the giving of the law; now, the voices there mentioned, besides the voice of God, and the voice of a trumpet, is the voice of thunder, 'And it came to pass on the third 'day, in the morning, there were thunder,' Exod. xix. 16.——xx. 18. In this sense, some expound these words of the apostle, where the law is said to be *spoken by angels*, Heb. ii. 2 because the angels did raise up those extraordinary thunders, which happily were the matter of the articulate voice, in which the Lord spake to Israel: or, if the law was spoken by Christ (as I have delivered my opinion elsewhere) * he being 'the angel of the 'covenant, Mal. iii. 1. And the angel of his pre-'sence,' Isa. lxiii. 9. Yet this hinders not, but that created angels might speak the law too, if not in respect of the articulate voice, yet in respect of the voice of thunders which attended on it. Thus thunder is often called, 'The voice of God, and 'the voice of his excellency,' Job xxxvii. 4, 5. Psal. xxix. 3, 4, 5, 6, 7, 8, 9.

3. The Lord shall descend with the trump of God. Such a voice was used also at the giving of the law, Ex. xix. 16. and Ex. xx. 18. and so it will be now, when men are called to account for the keeping or breaking of it. For the understanding of this, our last translation tells us, That *Christ shall send his angels with the great sound of a trumpet*, Matth. xxiv. 31. but in four Greek copies, as Beza confesseth, as also in the Hebrew gospel of Matthew, and in the vulgar, and in the margin of our last translation, it is read, That 'Christ shall 'send his angels with a trumpet, and a great voice.' And so the latter words are exegetical, q. d. with a trumpet, that is, with a great voice, like the voice of a trumpet. So that this reading very probably proves, that the last trumpet is to be taken metaphorically. For the more full confirmation whereof, I argue thus, when any thing is ascribed to the angels which is not suitable to their spiritual nature, and which they have no need of for the work they are about, it is to be taken metaphorically, unless the context, or some other scripture force us to a proper acceptation; but a material trumpet of silver, brass, or the like metal, is not suitable to the spiritual nature of the angels; neither have they need of such a trumpet for producing a great sound in the air. It is evident that without a trumpet they can make a great sound like the noise of a trumpet; and that there is nothing at all in the scripture that will force us, or probably lead us to a proper acceptation of the word. Add ye to what hath been said, that sometimes a great voice is set out by the similitude of a trumpet, 'I heard behind 'me a great voice, as of a trumpet, Rev. i. 10. 'and the first voice which I heard, was as it were 'of a trumpet,' Rev. iv. 1.

But why is this sound as of a trumpet, called

the

---
* Book 3. chap i. sect. 4.

the trumpet of God? I anſwer, for the greatneſs of it; for it is uſual in the Hebrew language, for the ſetting forth of greatneſs, excellency, or ſuperlativeneſs of a thing, to add the name of God to the word, whereby the thing is ſignified, as Gen. xxiii. 6. *A prince of God,* i. e. a mighty prince, Gen. xxx. 8. *With the wreſtlings of God,* i. e. with great wreſtlings, Pſal. xxxvi. 5. *Mountains of God,* i. e. great mountains, Pſalm lxxx. 10. *Cedars of God,* i. e. very high cedars, ſo here *the trump of God,* i. e. A very great ſound, like the ſound of a trumpet. It is ſaid in the law, *There were thunders, and lightnings, and a thick cloud upon the mount, and the voice of the trumpet exceeding loud, ſo that all the people that was in the camp trembled,* Exod. xix. 16. And if there was trembling at the giving of the law, oh! what trembling will be at the general aſſize, when ſinners ſhall be condemned for breaking of it?

3. No ſooner the ſhout made, but the ſaints ariſe: 'tis true, the ſaints that are alive need no reſurrection, but upon them will this trumpet have its effect. Something like death ſhall ſeize upon them, and they ſhall be changed. The order of this is given in by the apoſtle from the Lord, 'This ' we ſay unto you, by the word of our Lord, that ' we which are alive, remain unto the coming of ' the Lord, ſhall not prevent them which are aſleep, ' for the Lord himſelf ſhall deſcend from heaven ' with a ſhout, with the voice of the archangel, and ' with the trump of God, and the dead in Chriſt ' ſhall riſe firſt; then we which are alive and remain ' ſhall be caught up together with them into the ' clouds,' 1 Theſſ. iv. 15, 16, 17. The firſt that ſhall be called, are the ſaints that ſleep, and then the ſaints which are alive ſhall be immediately changed. Oh! what a day will this be? What a ſtrange ſight, to ſee all the dead ever ſince the beginning of the world riſe out of their graves? For the wicked, I believe, they ſhall riſe like toads from their holes, in a black, ſwarthy, ugly colour. A queſtion is among the ſchools, whether reprobates ſhall riſe again with all their deformities which they had in this life? As ſome of them being blind, halt, lame, maimed, deaf, dumb, &c. Whether now they ſhall riſe in the ſelf-ſame condition? For my part, I conceive, that whereas God the author of nature, will at that day reſtore human nature, that therefore there ſhall be no defects of natural parts.

Certainly nothing ſhall be wanting in the damned which may impede the ſenſe of torment in any part; now, a defect of any member would hinder theſe univerſal torments, that muſt ſeize on every part of the bodies of the damned in hell: their bodies therefore ſhall be whole, only the bodies of ſuch ſhall be foul, ugly, heavy, lumpiſh bodies, as oppoſed to the glorious qualities of the bodies of ſaints. Why, what bodies (you will ſay) have they? I anſwer, glorious bodies; no ſooner ſhall the bodies of the ſaints ariſe, but they ſhall exceed with ſingular qualities, *They were ſown in corruption, but they are raiſed in incorruption; they were ſown in diſhonour, but raiſed in glory; they were ſown in weakneſs, but raiſed in power; they were ſown natural bodies, but raiſed ſpiritual bodies,* 1 Cor. xv. 42, 43, 44. The ſun in its ſhining, doth but ſhadow forth the glory of their bodies; and this will in ſome meaſure torment rebrobates to ſee the difference of their bodies, and the bodies of the ſaints. O! (will they ſay) yonder are they whom we deſpiſed, and now are they honoured. See a world of ſuns riſing at once out of all parts of the earth; ſometimes we lived on earth, and we never ſaw but one ſun riſing in the eaſt, but, lo! millions of ſuns on eaſt, and weſt, and north, and ſouth; O! thoſe are the glorious ſaints in heaven; ſee with what ſwift and agile bodies they are preparing to fly into the air to meet their Lord and Saviour there, whilſt, in the mean time, we riſe with ſuch heavy, dull, and deformed bodies, that we cannot mount. O! what will come of us? Why, this is the day of reſurrection. The angels have been here to unſeal our graves, to roll away the ſtones, and at their ſhout, and ſound of the trumpet, our ſcattered duſt have met together; and, lo! now we ſtand upon the earth.

4. No ſooner the ſaints raiſed, and their ſouls and bodies reunited with excellent majeſty, but then ſhall all the elect of God, from firſt to laſt, be gathered together. If you aſk, Whence? And whither? I anſwer,——

1. To the queſtion, 'Whence? From the four ' winds, from one end of heaven to another,' i. e. From all parts of the world, from eaſt, and weſt, and north, and ſouth, 'from one end of ' heaven to another.' A vulgar term in regard of our ſight; for in itſelf heaven is round, and hath no end: the meaning is, That not one ſaint in all the world, from Adam to the laſt man, ſhall be

concealed or lie hid; from the most hidden, inward, secret bosom of the earth, all shall be gathered. Howsoever their dust may be scattered into a thousand thousand parts, yet the power of Christ shall restore all those dusts, and bring them together into their several compacted bodies.

2. To the question, Whether they shall be gathered? Some say to the valley of Jehoshaphat, from that text, ' Let the heathen be wakened, and ' come up to the valley of Jehoshaphat, for there ' will I sit to judge the heathen round about,' Joel iii. 12. But I believe, this text hath reference to a particular judgment of God upon Israel's enemies which dwell round about Jerusalem, and not to the general day of judgment. Others say to mount Olivet, from that text, ' This same Jesus which is ta- ' ken up from you into heaven, shall so come in like ' manner as ye have seen him go into heaven; then ' returned they unto Jerusalem from the mount ' called Olivet,' Acts i. 11, 12. But I believe this text speaks only of the manner how Christ shall come, and not of the place to which he shall come. Indeed, it is not probable that either the valley of Jehoshaphat, or mount of Olivet, can be sufficient places to contain all the men that ever were, are, and shall be; and therefore if such a thing can be determined, I should rather appeal to that text, *Then we which are alive, and remain, shall be caught up together with them (that are raised) in the clouds, to meet the Lord in the air*, 1 Thess. iv. 17. When Christ was askt this very question, *Where, Lord?* Whither shall thesaints be gathered? Where shall the general judgment be? He answers, *Wheresoever the body is, thither will the eagles be gathered together*, Luke xvii. 37. By the body, Christ means himself; and by the eagles, Christ meant his elect; because their youth is renewed as the eagles. Now the elect must resort to Christ wheresoever he is, and the apostle is express, that Christ is in the air, and in the clouds: and therefore thither must the elect be gathered; they shall be caught up by the holy angels into the clouds, to meet the Lord in the air.

Use. O my brethren; what sights are these? What changes, wonders, strange face of things will be this day? How is it that we are not as frequent in the meditation of this summons, as Jerome was, who, as he thought, heard daily that sound, *Arise ye dead, and come to judgment?* Methinks a sad and serious consideration of these passages might keep us close to Christ; come, try a little, if in the hurryings of the day we are so distracted, that we cannot reach the spiritual part of a meditation, yet in the evening, or morning, when all is still, or in the night-season, when all is quiet, then labour to prevent the day of doom; so realize it as if then we saw Christ in the clouds, sending his angels on this errand, Away, and bring hither all the men and women in the world; and, in the *first* place, gather my saints together unto me, Adam, and Abraham, those fathers of the world, and of the faithful, let them see all their children, and let all their children see them, and bring them all to my throne: awaken the world, let them who have slept in their graves some thousands of years, be now rouzed and raised. Imagine then, as if we hear the trumpet of God founded by the angels of God, and as the sound of it waxed louder and louder, that we saw the mountains skip like rams, and the little hills like young sheep: that we saw all the graves in churches, or church-yards, in fields, or plains, or seas fly open: that we saw all the bodies of the dead beginning to stir, and to stand upon their feet, and presently the angels coming, and taking all the saints upon their wings, and so flying with them through the air, till they came to the throne and judgment-seat of Christ: is it possible that such a meditation should pass, without some tincture of it on our Spirits? If my ears shall hear that sound, and if my eyes shall see these sights, Is it not time for me to lay these things to heart, that I may be found faithful and well-doing? As sure as I have this book in my hand, I must be one of those that shall hear the sound of the trumpet, and away I must, from the mouth of my grave, wheresoever I shall be buried, to the cloud where Christ doth sit. Come then, How would I rise? As foul as a toad? Or, As an angel of God? O my God! set this home on my soul. O! where's my lamp? And where's my oil? Are all ready? And am I ready, furnished, and prepared to meet the Lord in the air? Christians! if we have any life in us, let us act and realize this to the life. O! this would keep us close to Christ, and to the banner of Christ: who would not march under this banner, and adhere to him, that but reads over these summonses of souls at the last dreadful day?

SECT.

SECT. IV.
Of Christ and the saints meeting at the judgment-day.

4. FOR Christ and the saints meeting at the judgment-day; no sooner are the saints lifted up, and set before the Judge, but these things follow,——

1. They look, and gaze, and dart their beams, and reflect their glories on each other. Oh! the communications! oh! the dartings of beams betwixt Christ and his saints! look as when two admirable persons, two lovers meet together, their eyes sparkle, they look on, as if they would look through one another; so Christ and his saints at first meeting, they look on, as if they would look thro' one another: and such is the effect of these looks, that they give a lustre to each other by their looks. Did not Moses's face shine when he had been with God? And shall not the faces of the elect glitter and shine when Christ also looks on them? Nor stays it there; but as they shine by Christ, so shall their shine reflect on Christ, and give a glory to Christ; and this I take it to be the meaning of the apostle, 'That when Christ shall 'come, he shall be glorified in his saints,' 2 Thes. i. 10. Not only in himself, but in his saints also; whose glory, as it comes from him, so it redounds also to him, 'For of him, and through him, and 'to him are all things,' Rom. xi. 36.

2. They admire at the infinite glory, and beauty, and dignity, and excellency that is in Christ. The glory they reflect on him, is nothing to the glory that is in him. Oh! when these stars, the saints, shall but look upon Christ the Sun of righteousness, they exceedingly admire. So the apostle, 'When he shall come, he shall be glorified in 'his saints, and he shall be admired in all them 'that believe,' 2 Thes. i. 10. All that believe shall break out into admiration of Jesus Christ; they shall at the first sight observe such an excellency in Jesus Christ, as that they shall be infinitely taken with it. Here we speak of Christ, and in speaking we admire; but how will they admire, when they shall not only speak or hear, but see and behold him, who is the 'express image of 'God, and the brightness of his Father's glory?' Heb. i. 3. O the lustre that he casts forth each way! is not his very body more sparkling than the diamond before the sun? Yea, more than the sun itself now shining at noon-day? How should the saints but wonder at this sight? Oh! there is more beauty and glory in Jesus Christ, than ever their thoughts or imaginations could possibly reach; there is more weight of sweetness, joy, and delight in Jesus Christ, than either the seeing *eye*, or hearing *ear*, or the vast understanding *heart*, (which can multiply and add still to any former thoughts) can possibly *conceive*, 1 Cor. ii. 9. Every soul will cry out then, I believed to see much glory in Jesus Christ, whenever I saw him; I had some twilight, or moonlight glances of Christ on earth: but, O blind I! O narrow I! that could never have faith, opinion, thought, or imagination, to fathom the thousand thousand part of the worth, and incomparable excellency that I now see in him. Why, this causeth admiration, when we see more than ever we could expect. The saints shall then cry out, and say, I see more, Ten thousand times more than ever I expected; I see all the beauty of God put forth in Christ, I see the substantial reflection of the Father's light and glory in Jesus Christ, I see thousands of excellencies in Jesus Christ that never were revealed to me before. This is the very nature of admiration, it is ever wondering or admiring at some new and strange thing: the glory of Christ will then exceed all former apprehension. O! they admire to see the King in such a beauty, they admire to see the Judge in such a glittering and glorious robe of majesty; they admire, and they cannot but admire.

3. They adore, and magnify the grace and glory of Jesus Christ; as it is said of the twenty four elders, That 'they fell down before him that sat 'on the throne, and worshipped him that liveth for 'ever and ever, and cast their crowns before the 'throne, saying, Thou art worthy, O Lord, to re-'ceive glory, and honour, and power; for thou 'hast created all things, and for thy pleasure they 'are and were created,' Rev. iv. 10, 11. So all the saints, advanced to come up to Christ, and to stand before the throne, they fall down before Christ, and they worship him that lives for ever, shouting and singing about Jesus Christ, and setting out his glory, grace, and goodness. 'After this I 'beheld, (saith John) and lo, a great multitude, 'which no man could number, of all nations, and 'kindred, and people, and tongues, stood be-'fore the throne, and before the Lamb,——and 'cried

' cried with a loud voice, saying, Salvation to our
' God, which sitteth upon the throne, and unto
' the Lamb; and all the angels stood round about
' the throne, and about the elders, and the four
' beasts, and fell before the throne on their faces,
' and worshipped God, saying, Amen; blessing, and
' glory, and wisdom, and thanksgiving, and honour,
' and power, and might, be unto our God, for ever
' and ever,' Amen, Rev. vii. 9, 10, 11, 12. Saints
and angels will both give glory to Jesus Christ that
day; every elect man will then acknowledge, here is
Christ that shed his blood for me, here is the Saviour that laid down his life for me, here is the sacrifice that gave himself a propitiation for me; here is the person that mediated, and interceded, and made peace for me; here is the Redeemer that delivered, and redeemed me from the wrath to come: and then they begin those hallelujahs, that never, never shall have end, ' Hallelujah; and a-
' gain Hallelujah; and, Amen, Hallelujah, for
' the marriage of the Lamb is come, and his wife
' hath made herself ready, Rev. xix. 7.

4. Christ welcomes them into his glorious presence; if the father could receive his prodigal, but repenting son, with huggs and kisses, How will Christ now receive his saints, when they come as a bride to the solemnization of the marriage? His very heart springs (as I may say) at the sight of his bride; no sooner he sees her, and salutes her, but he welcomes her with such words as these, ' O my
' love, my dove, my fair one, come now and enjoy
' thy husband; many a thought I have had of thee;
' before I made the world I spent my infinite eter-
' nal thoughts on thy salvation; when the world
' began, I gave thee a promise, that I would be-
' trothe thee unto me in righteousness, and in judg-
' ment, in loving-kindness, in mercy, and in faith-
' fulness, Hos. ii. 19, 20. It was I that for thy sake
' was incarnate, and lived, and died, and rose a-
' gain, and ascended; and since my ascension that
' have been interceding for thee, and making ready
' the bride-chamber, where thou and I must live
' for ever and ever. And now I come hither into
' the clouds to meet thee more than half the way;
' and my meaning is to take thee by the hand, and
' to bring thee to my Father. Now do I take thee
' for my own; O my sister, my spouse, thou art as
' dear to me as my own dear heart; come, see into
' my bosom, see here love written in the golden
' letters of free grace; come near, for I must have
' thee with me, and I will never more be so strange
' to thee as to this day; sometimes thy sins have
' made a wall of partition between me and thee;
' sometimes I withdrew and was gone, and I hid
' myself beyond the curtains, and for a time thou
' hast lain hid in the closet of the grave, but now
' we'll never part more, anon I will bring thee to
' my Father, and I will say to him, Father, be-
' hold! here my spouse that I have married unto
' myself: in the mean time welcome to thy Jesus,
' I have purchased thee with my blood, I have paid
' dear for thee, and now I'll wear thee as a crown
' and ornament for ever.'

5. Christ sets them on his right hand, *Upon thy right hand doth stand the queen in gold of Ophir*, Psal. xlv. 9. This is the sign of Christ's love and respect to his saints; when he himself ascended up into heaven, then said the Father to him, *Son, sit thou down at my right hand*; and no sooner the saints are ascended up to Christ, but he speaks the same to them, *Sit thou down at my right hand*. Christ entertains them, as God the Father entertained him; he at the right hand of God, and they at the right hand of Christ. And herein is set forth the great exaltation of the saints; as Christ being set at God's right hand, God highly exalted him, and gave him a name above every name, so now are the saints highly exalted by Jesus Christ, now are they filled with unmatchable perfection, now is the [*pleroma*,] the fulness of perfection, and fulness of honour and glory conferred upon them; *Upon his right hand is set the queen in gold of Ophir*, i. e. in the best, richest, finest gold. The Lord now puts upon his saints heaven's glory, he adorns them with all his ornaments fit for the marriage-day; and indeed here is the beginning of the solemnity of the marriage of the Lamb, not but that the contract was before, but the solemnity was reserved for this day, and all the glory of this day is for nothing else but to set out the solemnity of the marriage. As the bridegroom on the day of nuptials comes forth in his glory, and as the bride on the marriage-day comes forth in her best array; and as the servants, and parents, and friends, and all appear on the marriage-day in as much glory as they can; so Christ on this day comes forth in his glory, with all his angels in their glory; and the saints, the Lamb's wife, *The King's daughter is all*

all glorious without and within, Pſalm xlv. 13. Though ſtars may loſe their ſhining when the ſun ariſeth, yet the glory of the ſaints ſhall be no leſs becauſe of the ſun of righteouſneſs, but rather more. This is the day that Chriſt ſhall honour his ſaints before all the world; come (will he ſay) and ſit you down at my right hand; as a ſhepherd divideth his ſheep from the goats, ſo will I ſeparate you from wicked reprobates: why, you are they for whom the eternal counſels of my Father did work, you are they in whom I am now to be glorified for ever; and therefore, now will I exalt, and advance, and honour you; ſit here, or ſtand here on my right hand; O come! come hither to the right hand of your Saviour.

6. Hereupon Chriſt fully and actually joys in them, and they in him: he joys in them, becauſe now he ſees of the travail of his ſoul; he ſees the iſſue of all his doings and ſufferings here on earth, he ſees now the great work he hath brought about, *to wit*, The glory of his ſaints, and he cannot but rejoice therein. As a man that makes a work that is very curious and glorious, he takes abundance of delight to look upon it; when God made the world, he lookt upon what he had made, and he ſaw it was good, and he delighted in it; ſo Chriſt looks on his ſaints, and when he ſees what he hath done, in raiſing ſo poor a worm to ſo high an excellency, he takes infinite delight therein. Now he ſees that he hath attained his end in that great deſign, and deepeſt counſels that he had before the world; he was then reſolved to ſave a number of ſinners, and to bring them at laſt to himſelf that they might behold him in his glory, and manifeſt the riches of his grace; and to that purpoſe hath he ſtill been carrying on the great work of ſouls ſalvation, as we have heard; and now that he ſees it accompliſhed and fulfilled in them, he muſt needs delight, ' In that day ſhall ' be ſaid to Jeruſalem, Fear thou not; and to Zion, ' Let not thine hands be ſlack: for the Lord thy God ' in the midſt of thee is mighty, he will ſave, he ' will rejoice over thee with joy, he will reſt in his ' love, he will joy over thee with ſinging,' Zeph. iii. 16, 17.

And as he joys in them, ſo they cannot but rejoice in him, as he delights in their glory, ſo they cannot but delight in his glory. Are they not at

* Aug. l. 20. *de civitate Dei*, cap. 14.

Chriſt's right hand? And is not that the place of pleaſure, the paradiſe of God? *In thy preſence is fulneſs of joy, and at thy right hand are pleaſures for evermore*, Pſal. xvi. 11. The very ſetting them on Chriſt's right hand, is the beginning of heaven's joy. *The preſence of* Chriſt makes joy, *exceeding joy*, ſaith Jude, Jude 24. O! but what joy? What fulneſs of joy? What exceeding joy, will it be to be ſet at Chriſt's right hand? Now begins that joy, that never never ſhall have an end. O the complacency which the bleſſed feel in their ſeeing, knowing, loving and being beloved of Jeſus Chriſt! ' O ' my Chriſt! let me have tribulation here, let me ' here ſpend my days in ſorrow, and my breath in ' ſighings; puniſh me here, cut me in pieces here, ' burn me here, ſo that I may there be placed at thy ' right hand.' For then joy will come, and ſorrow will vaniſh; ſorrow is but for a night, this night of life, but joy will come in this morning of the reſurrection, and it never ſhall be night again.

SECT. V.
Of Chriſt's ſentencing his ſaints.

5. FOR Chriſt ſentencing of his ſaints: no ſooner are they ſet on his right hand, but he prepares for ſentence. In the opening of which we muſt conſider, 1. The preparative. 2. The ſentence itſelf.

1. The preparative before ſentence will be ſome exploration or trial of the parties to be ſentenced. As,——

1. The book muſt be opened, *And I ſaw the dead, ſmall and great, ſtand before God, and the books were opened, and another book was opened, which is the book of life*, Rev. xx. 12. It is ſpoken after the manner of men, in whoſe public judgments are produced all the writings of the proceſs, informations, depoſitions of witneſſes, to ſhew that all actions, even the moſt ſecret ones, ſhall then be rehearſed and made manifeſt. * Auguſtine thinks theſe books to be the books of the Old and New Teſtament, wherein all things either to be done, or omitted, are preſcribed by God: and then ſhall theſe books be opened, becauſe, according to them, ſhall ſentence be given, *In that day God ſhall judge the ſecrets of men by Jeſus Chriſt, according to my goſpel*, Rom. ii. 16. † Origen, and almoſt all with him, think theſe books to be the

† Orig. *Com. ad* Rom. 14.

books of our consciences, which now are shut up, and concealed from men, but then shall be made manifest to all the world. Whatsoever those books are, we find here one book opened, which is proper to the saints, called *the book of life:* this book contains in it the names of all that are elected from first to last: thou John, and thou Joseph, and thou Judith, and thou Mary, and thou Elizabeth, &c. you are all booked down, there is the particularity, and there is the certainty, *Your n mes are written in heaven, rejoice in it:* oh! what is the joy of saints, when once they see this book opened, and their names inrolled, engraven there in letters of glory? This very book clears it to me, that God from all eternity made choice of a particular and determinate number of persons, to save them; and that none other can be saved, but those who were so elected, and whosoever are so elected, they shall not fall away; 'All that worship the beast, their 'names are not written in the book of life of the 'Lamb, from the foundation of the world, Rev. '13. 8.—xvii. 8. On the other side, He that 'overcometh, the same shall be written in the 'book of life, and I will not blot out his name, 'but I will confess his name before my Father, 'and before his angels,' Rev. iii. 5. This is the day when that book of life shall be opened, and Christ shall read the names of every elect person before God and angels; not that Christ needs a book, or indeed reads a name, but that his election stands so firm, that he knows every predestinated saint, as well as we know their names, whom for our memories we commit unto our books; and then he will so honour his saints, that he will publish their names to all the world.

2. All the actions, demeanours, graces, duties, and (it may be) sins of saints shall be produced, and laid open; the Holy Ghost tells us, That 'the 'dead were judged out of those things which were 'written in the books.' It appears hence, that not only names, but things were written, and these things were produced, and accordingly they were judged.

1. As to evil things, unfruitful works of darkness. It is a question, and I dare not be too positive in it, viz. Whether the sins of God's people shall be manifest at the day of judgment? Some are for the negative, because God in his promises speaks so expresly 'of forgiving iniquities, of re-
'membering them no more, of blotting them out, 'of throwing them into the bottom of the sea, cast-'ing them behind his back,' Isa. xliii. 25—xliv. 22.—xxxviii. 17. In which respect, say they, the Godly are said *not to come into judgment*, John v. 24. I suppose this last text is ill urged, for by judgment is not meant discussion, but condemnation, and in our best translations so it is rendered: others are for the affirmative, upon those grounds, 1. Because many of the godly and wicked men's sins are mingled together, and there cannot be a judgment of discussion preceding that of condemnation, unless godly men's sins are also produced. 2. Because it is spoken generally in respect of all sorts, that the books were opened; by which books, most understand the consciences of men; and by the opening of those books, they understand the manifesting, clearing, and discovering of consciences at that general day. 3. Because the scriptures are express for the affirmative; not but that those texts are truths, 'That sins are forgiven, blotted out, thrown away, 'to be remembered no more,' (i. e.) as to condemnation; but as for exploration or discussion, the Lord speaks universally, That *of every idle word that men speak, they shall give an account thereof at the day of judgment*, Mat. xii. 36. If the balance weigh down on this side, (for my part I am not peremptory, but shall easily submit to the spirits of the prophets) yet this manifestation shall not be for the shame, grief, trouble, ignominy, or confusion of the godly, but only for the setting up of God's justice, and that the goodness and free grace of God in Christ may be made more illustrious; how will Christ then be exalted, when all the world shall see his righteousness and goodness, his truth and mercy now again meeting together, and kissing each other? It was so at his first coming, and it will be so at his second coming; then shall his justice and mercy, his righteousness and goodness, be manifested to all; in that by his own merits, notwithstanding their sins, he will bring all his saints to his heavenly glory

2. As for good things, whether good works, duties or graces, there is no question but all these that day will be produced and laid open. 1. We see Christ enumerating the good works of them on his right hand; for 'I was an hungered, and ye 'gave me meat; I was thirsty, and ye gave me 'drink; I was a stranger, and ye took me in; na-
'ked,

'ked, and ye clothed me; sick, and ye visited me; in prison, and ye came unto me,' Matth. xxv. 35, 36. It is true, in this catalogue, we find nothing of faith, but all of works; but certainly faith is included, as the life of the tree is included in the fruit; not only, nor principally, are works here mentioned for the goodness of the work considered in itself; but as these works did express our faith and love to Jesus Christ, in that by faith we could see Christ in a poor beggar, or prisoner, and could love Jesus Christ in these poor, better than all our wordly goods or liberties. I do not wonder that Paul adviseth his Corinthians, *See that ye abound in this grace* of contribution to the saints, 2 Cor. viii. 7. And that he prayeth his Philippians, *And this I pray, that your love may abound yet more*, Phil. i. 9. And that he prayeth for his Thessalonians, *Now the Lord make you to increase, and to abound in love, one towards another, and towards all men*, 1 Thess. iii. 12. And that he praiseth God in their behalf, ' We 'are bound to thank God always for you, bre-'thren, as it is meet, because that your faith 'groweth exceedingly, and the charity of every 'one of you all towards each other aboundeth,' 2 Thess. i. 3. Christians! if we did but consider, that every duty done to God or man, that every penny given to a poor naked saint, that every cup of cold water given to a prophet, in the name of a prophet, should not lose his reward; but this day should be reckoned up, or drawn (as it were) into a full inventory; *imprimis*, For this piece of silver, given such a day to such a one; *item*, For this piece of bread, such a day given to such a one, &c. Oh! who would not abound in faith and love? Oh! who would think any thing too much, too good, too dear, to give to the needy members of Jesus Christ? There is a charge laid upon ministers to preach this doctrine, I beseech you give me leave to discharge my duty, and to lay it, and leave it at your doors, where beggars usually stand, *Charge them that are rich in this world,——that they do good, that they be rich in good works, ready to distribute, willing to communicate; laying up in store for themselves a good foundation against the time to come, that they may lay hold on eternal life*, 1 Tim. vi. 17, 18, 19. You to whom God hath given the riches of this world, as you would meet Christ with comfort, learn this lesson; consider whether of these two reckonings will be more comfortable at that day: *item*, so much given to such and such a religious use; or so much given towards such a feast, and for the entertainment of such brave gallants; so much to promote the gospel, or so much at dice, cards, horse-races. If one should tell you, That either you must feed Christ in the poor, or you must starve in hell; you must either clothe naked Christ in the poor, or you must be laid naked to the fiery indignation of the Lord for ever, Oh! what strictness would you call this? But I recollect myself, if Christ set you at his right hand, he will then recount all your charities, and all your labours, of love to the saints; you that are poor, and had nothing to give, he will tell of your good works, if it was no more, but at such a time you cast a mite into his treasure; and, at such a time, you carried a letter for the Lord Jesus; he will produce and commend these pittances of your poor charities to all the world.

2. Not only good works to man, but all the saints duties to God shall come in remembrance. Oh then! it will be known, who served the Lord in spirit and truth, and who did not; then men and angels shall know, ' such a day this poor saint per-'formed such a spiritual service;' every prayer in public or private, every tear shed for sin, every sob, or sigh, every spiritual meditation, or self-examination, every glance, ejaculation, or looking up unto Jesus, shall be recounted by Jesus: it was said of Cornelius, That as well his prayers to God, as his alms to men, *came up for a memorial before God*, Acts x. 4. Certainly every duty, in reference to the first table, is booked in heaven, and at this day the book being opened, it will appear, that such a prayer thou madest such a morning, and such an evening in thy closet, and now will Christ say, ' Did not I tell thee, that if thou wouldest 'pray to thy Father in secret, then he that saw 'thee in secret, should reward thee openly?' Mat. vi. 6. Why, now shalt thou have thy reward in 'a full view, I will divulge here all thy secret du-'ties to men and angels; all the world shall know 'it; thy wanderings I told them, and thy tears I 'bottled them: lo! here, are they not all writ-'ten in my book?' Psalm lvi. 8.

3. Not only duties but graces shall now be rehearsed; thy knowledge, faith, hope, love, and spiritual joy; thy fear, obedience, repentance, humility, meek-

meekness, patience, zeal, and perseverance, shall he fully discovered; time was, that in the incense of such a prayer, many sweet spices were burned together; therein was faith working by love, therein was humility, therein was patience, in submitting to God's will and pleasure, therein was hope of a gracious answer in God's due time, therein was holiness, brokenness of heart, and love to others, &c. 'Time was, saith Christ, That *I gathered my myrrh with my spices, that I eat my honey-comb with my honey*, Ca. v. 1. That I both accepted and delighted myself in thy heavenly graces; I shall never forget how thou didst ravish my heart, my sister, my spouse; how thou didst ravish my heart with one of thine eyes, and with one chain of thy neck.' Why, thus shall the Lord set forth, and tell all the world what gracious children he had; then will appear indeed the meekness of Moses, the faith of Abraham, the patience of Job, the zeal of Phineas, the love of Magdalene; and, according to the measure of grace conferred upon thee, Christ will set thee out; 'We commend the graces of such and such saints at their death; but, Oh! let Christ blazon me, and his graces in me at the resurrection-day?' Thus far for the exploration or trial before sentence.

2. For the sentence itself; then shall the king say to them on his right hand, ' Come ye blessed of my Father, inherit the kingdom prepared for you from the foundation of the world,' Matth. xxv. 24. Every word here is full of life and joy; 1. *Come*. This is the king's invitation of his saints to his court; he had summoned them before to his presence, and now they are about him, he will not part with them, they must come a little nearer yet, they must go with him into his presence-chamber; the mansions are ready, the supper of the Lamb is ready, and now he begins the solemn invitation of his bride, *come*. 2. *Come ye blessed of my Father* Christ blessed them when he went up to heaven, and whilst yet on earth he pronounced them blessed many a time, *Blessed be ye poor, blessed are ye that hunger, blessed are ye that weep*, Luke vi. 20, 21. But now he calls them *the blessed of his Father*; not only Christ, but God the Father hath ever looked upon them as his children; it is the Father's will as well as Christ's, that they should be blessed, *Ye blessed of my Fa-*

ther. 3. *Inherit the kingdom*. Christ had told them before, *It is your Father's pleasure to give you the kingdom*, Luke xii. 32. But then they were only as servants, or as children under age, but now they are heirs, *heirs of God, and joint heirs with Christ*, Rom. viii. 17. and now they are come to full age, *To the measure of the stature of the fulness of Christ*, Eph. iv. 13. and therefore they must have the inheritance in possession? they must all be kings; this very word speaks them kings, and makes them kings; it is the solemn coronation of the saints, it is the anointing, the setting of the crown upon the heads of the saints; *Henceforth there is laid up for me a crown of righteousness, which the Lord the righteous judge shall give me at that day, and not for me only, but unto them also that love his appearing*, 1 Tim. iv. 8. 4. *Inherit the kingdom prepared for you*. As Tophet was prepared of old, so was this kingdom prepared of old; it was the first creature that ever God made, *In the beginning God created heaven*, Gen. i. 1. His first work was to make heaven for himself and his saints to dwell in; he prepared it for them, and then he prepared them for it: but why for them? Were not the angels the first creatures that possessed it? Nay, were they not created in it, or together with it? Yes; but yet the angels are not properly the heirs, sons, members, spouse of God and Christ, as the saints are; the angels are but ministring spirits, and the servants of the bridegroom; but the saints are the bride herself, heirs, and co-heirs with Christ. 5. *Prepared for you from the foundation of the world*. This was the great design of God and Christ from all eternity? before the foundations of the world, and at the first stone laid, and ever since, they have been carrying on this mighty work; it is not a business of yesterday only; no, no, the eternal thoughts of God hath been upon it, *He hath chosen us in him before the foundations of the world*, Eph. i. 4.

Oh! what thoughts are in saints when this sentence is propounded! Oh! what joy enters into them when now they are to enter into their master's joy! methinks if it were possible that tears could be in a glorified estate, the saints should not see Christ reach out a crown to set it on their heads, but they should weep, and hold away their heads, but Christ will have it so; *This honour have all the saints, praise you the Lord*.

SECT.

SECT. VI.

Of Christ and the saints judging the rest of the world.

6. FOR Christ and his saints judging the world: no sooner shall the saints be sentenced, justified, acquitted, anointed, and crowned; but presently they must be enthronized, and sit with Jesus Christ to judge the world. In the unfolding of this we may observe these particulars.——

1. As Christ is on a throne, so now must the elect be set on thrones, 'To him that overcometh will I grant to sit with me in my throne,' Rev. iii. 21. Thrones are for kings and judges; and in that Christ hath now lifted up his saints to this condition, he will have them sit with him as so many judges, and as so many kings; or if it be more honour to have thrones by themselves, than to sit with Christ in his throne, John in his vision saw many thrones, 'And I saw thrones, and they that sat upon them, and judgment was given unto them,' Re xx. 4. And Christ himself told his apostles, 'Verily, I say unto you, that ye which have followed me in the regeneration, when the Son of man shall sit in the throne of his glory, ye also shall sit upon twelve thrones, judging the twelve tribes of Israel,' Mat. xix. 28. Hence some argue, That amongst all the saints, the apostles shall have their thrones seated next to Christ; howsoever the rest shall not be deprived of their thrones; for not only twelve thrones, but twelve and twelve are set about the throne of Christ, 'And round about the throne were four and twenty thrones,' (or seats) 'and upon the throne I saw four and twenty elders, sitting, clothed with white raiment, and they had on their heads crowns of gold,' Rev. iv. 4. Only four and twenty thrones, and four and twenty elders are numbered, but thereby is represented the whole church of Christ: it is plain enough, that all the saints shall appear plainly in the glory of Christ's kingdom, having thrones with him in the air, during the time of his judgment.

2. The goats on the left hand shall then be called to receive their doom: no sooner the saints enthronized, but then shall Christ say, 'Ye blessed angels, bring hither all those mine enemies, who have said, I shall not rule over them, that I may bruise them with my iron-mace, and break them in pieces like a potter's vessel.' O! the fear and trembling that will now seize on reprobates! do but see the case of prisoners, when the judge speaks that word, *Come jaylors, bring hither those prisoners to the bar.* But, alas! what comparison can we make to suit with the condition of these reprobates? Now, shall their hearts fail them for fear; now shall they seek death, (Oh! how gladly would they die again)? but shall not find it; now shall they cry to rocks and mountains, *Fall on us, and hide us from the face of him that sitteth on the throne, and from the wrath of the Lamb,* Rev. vi. 16. As a prisoner in a desperate case had rather remain in his sordid stinking dungeon, than coming into the open air for execution; so the reprobates newly raised from the earth, would fain return again unto the earth, glad to remain, tho' not on the face of it with pleasure, yet in the bowels of it with rottenness and solitude; like malefactors pressing to death, they cry out for more weight, 'Hills cover us, mountains fall upon us, yet more weight, more rocks, more mountains; hide us, press us, cover us, dispatch us.' But all in vain, the command is out, angels and devils will force them to the bar, for the Lord hath spoken it, *Those mine enemies, which would not that I should reign over them, bring them hither,* Luke xix. 27.

3. They shall look on Christ, and his saints, now sitting on their thrones. As prisoners that stand at the bar in the face of the judge; so must these reprobates look the judge and all his assessors in the very face.

1. For the judge, they shall look on him, *Behold he cometh with clouds, and every eye shall see him, and they also which pierced him.* We heard before, That no sooner Christ in the clouds, but they saw him then; as the prisoners that see the judge riding to his judgment-seat; Oh! but now they shall see him in the judgment-seat, ready, with sparkling eyes, and thundring voice, to speak their sentence. Prisoners at the bar must not turn their backs on the judge when he begins their sentence; no more must reprobates; '* They must see him in majes-

---

* *In majestate visuri sunt, quem in humilitate videre noluerunt; ut tanto distinctius virtutem sentiant, quanto contemptius infirmitatem deriserunt.*

'ty, whom they would not deign to look upon in 'humility; that by so much more they may feel 'his power, by how much more they derided his 'weakness.' Oh! the difference betwixt Christ's coming in the flesh, and in his second coming in the clouds; then he came in poverty, now in majesty; then in humility, now in glory; then with poor shepherds, now with mighty angels; then the contempt of nations, now the terror of the world; then crowned with thorns, now with majesty; then judged by one man, now judging all men; then as a lamb, now as a lion. Oh! horror to conceive, how will the sight of this Judge amaze the wicked! and the rather because they shall see him whom *they have pierced*. Is not this the aggravation of their terror? Conceive the guilty man-slayer coming to his trial, Will not the red robes of his Judge make his heart bleed for his bloodshed? Doth not that crimson cloth present a monstrous hue before his eyes? O! then, what sight is this, when the man slain sits in the judgment-seat! The rosy wounds of our Saviour still bleeding (as it were) in the prisoners presence! well may they hang their heads, but they shall not shut their eyes, *They shall see him*, saith the text, yea, *they also which pierced him shall see him*. This very sight will be as convincing, as if they heard Christ say, ' Thou art the man 'didst murder me, thou art the man hast pierced 'me, this wound, this scar, and this print of the 'nails in my hands and feet were thy very doings 'in thy sinning against me.' And who can tell but Christ may speak in some such a manner as this? ' Come all you on the left hand, prepare you for 'the sentence; I am the man whom you did cru-'cify afresh; I am he whose person you despised, 'whose commands you disobeyed, whose ministers 'you abused, whose servants you hated, whose of-'ficers you rejected; and of whom you said, There 'is no beauty in him that we should desire him.' Whatsoever he shall say, this I believe, that Christ's sweet face will be most terrible to the wicked at that day. Oh! it will cut them to see him in the judgment-seat, whom they basely shut out of doors, preferring a lust before his presence; then will they begin, with extremest grief, and bitterness of Spirit, to sigh and say, ' Oh! he that I look upon, 'and must look upon, and cannot choose but look 'upon; he whom I now see sitting in yonder flaming, white, and glorious throne, is Jesus Christ,

'the mighty God, the Prince of peace, that true 'Messiah, whose precious blood was poured out 'as water upon the earth, to save his people from 'their sins: it is he, yea, the self same he, that 'many a time, whilst I lived on earth, invited and 'wooed me by his faithful ministers, that besought 'and entreated me with tears of dearest love, to 'leave my lusts, and to bid the devil adieu; that 'knocked again and again at the door of my heart 'for entrance, offering himself to be my all-suffi-'cient, and everlasting husband, telling me, That 'if I would but have embraced him, at this time 'should have been the solemnity of the marriage, 'and now he would have set an immortal crown 'of bliss and glory upon my head with his own Al-'mighty hand; but, I alas! like a wilful desperate 'wretch, forsook my own mercy, judged myself 'unworthy of everlasting life, and wretchedly and 'cruelly, against my own soul, persecuted all the 'means which should have sanctified me, and all the 'ministers which should have saved me, as instru-'ments in the hands of Christ, and now happy I, if 'I were an hundred thousand millions of miles di-'stant from this sight of Jesus Christ; oh! that 'these eyes in my head were holes again, as they 'were but even now when I was rotting, or rotten 'in the grave! oh! that I could turn any way aside 'from this glorious sight! oh! that I were a stone, 'a tree, or air, or any other thing that wanted 'eyes! Oh! that I had no eye within, nor un-'derstanding faculty to conceive of Christ, or to 'know Christ Jesus as my Judge, now ready to bid 'me go to hell!' Certainly these will be the woful wishes of the wicked, when they shall look on Christ as sitting on his throne of judgment.

2. For the saints, they shall look on them. Indeed they sit so near their Saviour, that they cannot look on him, but they must look on them; the saints are on their thrones, either in the throne or about the throne of Jesus Christ; and the reprobates stand in a direct opposite line to the saints; so that their eyes cannot be off them: it is said in the parable, that the rich man being in hell, *He lift up his eyes, and saw Abraham afar off, and Lazarus in his bosom*, Luke xvi. 23. But the distance being so great as heaven and hell, that cannot be literally understood, but only parabolically; it is otherwise here, for howsoever the separation be already made, yet neither is the sentence, nor execution

ecution past upon the reprobates; and indeed as yet, both the saints and reprobates are in the air, the one on the right hand and the other on the left hand of Jesus Christ, and therefore they cannot but have full view of each other. In the apocryphal book there is a plain description of this view, *Then shall the righteous man stand in great boldness before the face of such as have afflicted him, and made no account of his labours; and when they see it they shall all be troubled with terrible fear, and shall be amazed at the strangeness of his salvation, so far beyond all that they looked for; and they repenting and groaning for anguish of spirit, shall say within themselves, this is he whom we have had sometimes in derision, and a proverb of reproach; we fools, accounted his life madness, and his end to be without honour; how is he numbered among the children of God, and his lot is among the saints?* Wisd. v. 1, 2, 3, 4, 5. Here is a sight that will trouble and amaze the wicked, that those who sometimes were their footstools should now be on thrones; that poor Lazarus, who lay at the gates of that certain rich man, should now shine like a star near the Sun of righteousness; that they which were reproached, reviled, massacred and murdered by them, should now be their Judges, joining with Jesus Christ to sentence them to hell. Oh! who can conceive the terrible thoughts of these mens hearts! now the world cannot help them, their old companions cannot help them, the saints neither can, nor will; only the Lord Jesus can, but oh! there is the soul-killing misery, he will not; 'Ye men 'and devils (saith Christ) joint heirs of hell, fit fuel 'for eternal fire, look on us on our thrones; time 'was we could not have a look from you; Christ 'and Christians were an abhorrency of spirit unto 'you, you trod us under foot, but now we are 'got above you, Oh! see the vast difference betwixt 'us and you; look on us, look on me and my 'saints; see us on our thrones, see us glittering in 'glory, and be confounded and amazed for ever.'

4. A particular strict account shall then be required and given. Of what? you will say; I answer,

1. Of sins; Come (will Christ say) now confess all your sins before all the world; time was that you concealed your sins, but now every sin shall be laid open before God, angels and men, and now is the black book of their consciences opened, wherein appear all their sins, original and actual, of omission and commission. For omissions of duties, all those shall be discovered, 'Christ hungry, 'and I gave him no meat; Christ thirsty, and I 'gave him no drink; Christ a stranger, and I lodg-'ed him not; Christ naked, and I clothed him 'not; Christ sick and in prison, and I visited him 'not.' And for commissions of evils, all those shall be discovered. 'These and these sins I com-'mitted in my childhood, youth, ripe age, and 'old age: these were my gross sins, blasphemy, 'perjury, idolatry, robbery, drunkenness, unclean-'ness, profaneness, &c. And these were my less 'sins, anger, hatred, distrust, impatience, pride, 'presumption, contention, derision, inconstancy, 'hypocrisy, &c Oh! the numberless number of 'evil thoughts, words and deeds that now are laid open; in the black book are not only written all sins done, but all such sins as were intended or purposed to be done'; all the projects of the heart, though never acted, must now be discovered. Men little think of this: if I should tell you of such designs that died in your hearts, and never came out to light, you would be now ready to say, 'Tush, 'I never did such a thing, I only intended it, or had 'some thoughts about it, And what then?' Why, then those very thoughts, secrets, purposes, and projects shall come to light; or, if there be any thing more hidden or secret, as the very bent and frame of our hearts, the very inclinations of our souls to this or that evil, then shall be manifest to all the world. Nay, yet more, such sins as by the sinners themselves were never taken notice of either before or at, or after the commission of them, shall this day come out. Conscience is such a kind of private notary or secretary, that it keeps notes or records of all acts and deeds, whether you observe them or no; conscience hath the pen of a ready writer, and takes in short hand, and in an illegible character, from your mouths as fast as you speak, and from your hearts as fast as you contrive. 'Conscience writ-'ing (saith one) is not now legible: as that which 'is written with the juice of a lemon is not to be 'read by day-light, but against the fire by night 'you may read it; so conscience writing cannot now be read, but in that day when heaven and earth are set on fire, this book shall be opened, 'and the cypher be discovered.' Oh! what a day will this be, when not a sin committed by any reprobate

reprobate from the beginning of the world, but now it shall be rehearsed.

2. As an account of all sins, so an account of all temporal gifts which God hath imparted to reprobates, must now be given. Some have the gifts of the world, as riches, honours, and places of authority; others have the gifts of the body, as health, strength, beauty, and life; others have the gifts of the mind, as understanding, wisdom, policy, and learning; now of all these gifts must they give an account. Come you that are rich, (saith Christ) *render an account of your stewardship;* how have you spent your riches? The like will he say to the honourable, and to those in places of authority; ' oh! remember you were in authority, and office, and place, But what service did you to me, or my members? You had wisdom, and learning, and knowledge, and understanding conferred upon you, But what good had the church or commonwealth by it?' The like will he say to others according to the talent bestowed on them, ' You excelled in strength, beauty, health of body, and length of days; and now tell me; and publish it to all the world, how were these improved.' I believe, many a sad answer will be given to Christ of these things, riches misspent, and health misspent, and wisdom, policy, learning, gifts and parts misspent; O consider it! if the factor, after many years spent in foreign countries, at last returns home without his reckonings, Who will not blame him for his negligence? But when his master calls him to an account, and he finds nothing but a bill of expences, this in courting, that in feasting; who laughs not at so fond a reckoning: thus many pass the time of their life as a time of mirth, then when they return to their Lord again, behold, all their accounts are sins, their profits, vanities.

3. I shall add one thing more : not only of gifts temporal, but of all blessings spiritual, though but tendered and offered, must all give an account. Oh! the sad accounts that many a soul will make of these things. Methinks, I hear some wicked wretch confessing this to Christ, ' True, Lord, I lived at such a time when the sun of the gospel shone bright in my face, and in such a place where all was Goshen; I lived under such a ministry, who set before me life and death; many and many a powerful and searching sermon have I heard, any one passage whereof (if I had not wickedly and wilfully forsaken my own mercy) might have been unto me the beginning of the new birth and everlasting bliss. Sometimes in the use of the means I felt stirrings or strong workings in my heart, and then I was fully purposed to have been another man, to have cleaved to Christ, and to have forsaken the world; I was almost resolved to have been wholly for God, I was almost persuaded to be a real Christian: oh! what thoughts were in my heart when such a faithful minister pressed the truth home? Methinks, every sermon I heard then is now a preaching again, methinks, I hear still the voice of the minister; methinks, I see still his tears dropping down his cheeks. Oh! how fresh is the reproof, admonition, exhortation of such and such a preacher now in my mind? Oh! how earnestly did he intreat me? With what love and tender compassion did he beseech me? how did his bowels yearn over me? How strongly did he convince me, that all was not well with my sin sick soul? How plainly did he rip up all my sores, and open to me all my secrets, and my whole heart? But, alas! within a while I made a jest of all, I hardned my heart against all, I stifled all his convictions, I shut my eyes against his discoveries; I cared neither for the minister, nor any thing he said or did. And yet here is not all, not only the ministers of Christ, but the Spirit of Christ sometimes spake to my heart: I remember at such a time, Christ himself (as it were) condescended and bowed the heavens, and came down to intreat me for my soul's health; oh! the strivings of the Spirit of Christ, as if he had been loath to have taken a denial! O Christ, I remember thy words when thou criedst to me, Open sinner, open thy heart to thy Saviour, and I will come in, and sup with thee, and thou with me, Rev. iii. 20. Why, sinner, are thy lusts better than I? Thy carnal pleasures better than I? Thy worldly commodities better than I? Why, sinner, what dost thou mean? How long shall thy vain thoughts lodge within thee? O take pity on thy Jesus! for here I stand, and wait at the door of thy heart, and my head is filled with the dew, and my locks with the drops of the night. But, alas! I resisted Christ and his Spirit; O thou Judge and Saviour of all thine elect! I dealt churlishly with

thee

'thee, I tired out thy patience, I gave thee a re-
'pulse, I told thee I had entertained other lovers,
'and I would none of thee; I trod on counsel, I
'trampled thy precious blood under my feet, and
'now I am expecting no other but to eat the fruit
'of my own way. Now mayest thou accomplish
'thy word, because I set at nought all thy coun-
'sels, and would none of thy reproof; therefore
'thou mayest laugh at my calamity, and mock now,
'my fear cometh.' Lo, here the confessions of sinners, every thing now comes out, for Christ will
have it so as a preparative to his doom upon them.

5. Christ and his saints proceed to sentence.
First, Christ the chief judge shall pronounce it, *Depart from me, ye cursed, into everlasting fire prepared for the devil and his angels*, Mat. xxv. 41.
Every word breathes out nothing but fire and
brimstone, vengeance and woe; to *depart* from that
glorious presence of Christ were hell enough, but
they must go with a *curse*; not only so, but into
fire, and that must be *everlasting*; and therein they
shall have no other company or comforters but
wicked devils, and they insulting over them with
hellish spite, and stinging exprobrations.

Give me leave a little to enlarge upon these
words. No sooner Christ begins the sentence, *Depart from me*, but methinks, I imagine the reprobates to reply, how? Depart from thee? Why,
O Christ! thou art all things, and therefore the
loss of thee is the loss of all things; thou art the
greatest good, and therefore to be deprived of thee
is the greatest evil; thou art the very centre, and
perfect rest of the soul, and therefore to be pulled
from thee is the most cruel separation. We were
made by thee, and for thee, O let us never be divided from thee! we were made according to thy
image; O never drive us from our glorious pattern! *Away, away*, (saith Christ) ye have no part
in me, or in my merits; never speak or intreat me
any more, but *depart from me*. But, secondly,
They may reply again, If we must depart, and
depart from thee, at least, give us thy blessing before we go; thou hast great stores of blessings to
give, and we hope thou hast one yet in store for us,
we crave but a small thing, but a blessing, O it is a
little one; thou art our Father, (witness our creation) and it is a chief property of a father to bless
his children. 'No, depart from me, ye cursed, in
'place of a blessing take the full curse of your

'father; you have been most prodigal and diso-
'bedient children, you have followed him who
'had my first curse, and now share ye curses with
'him; cursed be you in your souls, and in your
'bodies, and in your thoughts, and in your words,
'and in the heinousness of your sins, and in the
'grievousness of your punishment.' But, Thirdly,
If we must depart from thee, and depart accursed,
yet appoint us some meat and convenient place to
go into; create a fruitful piece of ground, and let
a goodly sun daily shine upon it; let it have a sweet
and wholsome air, and be stored with fruits and
flowers of all forms and colours; give us the variety of creatures for our uses. O! if we must go
from thee, the source and fountain of heavenly
sweetness, afford us some plenty of earthly pleasures, which may in some sort recompence our pain
of loss, speak but the word, and such a place will
presently start up and shew itself. 'No, depart from
'me ye cursed into fire; tho' fire naturally burns
'not spirits, yet I will lift and elevate this fire a-
'bove its nature; you have sinned against nature,
'and I will punish you above nature.' Fire? Alas!
that ever we were born! who is able to rest in fire?
The very thought of it already burns us. Of all the
creatures appointed by God to be the instruments
of revenge, fire and water have the least mercy. But, Fourthly, If we must into fire, let the
sentence stand but a very short time; quench the
fire quickly, half an hour will seem a great while
there. 'No, depart from me ye cursed into ever-
'lasting fire; it was kindled by my breath, and it
'hath this property, among other strange qua-
'lities, that it is an unquenchable fire; as long
'as I am God it shall endure, and ye broil in it;
'and when I cease to be happy, then shall ye cease
'to be miserable.' O woe is us! what, to live in a
fire perpetually, without all end, or hope of end?—
Yet, Fifthly, Allot us then some comforters, whose
smooth and gentle words may sweeten our torments, or somewhat dull the most keen edge of our
extremity; O let the angels recreate us with songs
and hymns of thee, and of thy blessedness, that
we may hear that sweetly delivered which others
fully enjoy! 'No, no, depart from me, ye curs-
'ed, into everlasting fire, prepared for the devil
'and his angels; they shall be your comforters,
'they that will triumph in your miseries, they that
'are your daily desperate enemies; they that will
'tell

'tell you by what deceits and byways they led 'you from me, and what will give you every hour 'new names of scorn and horrible reproach.' O sentence not to be endured, and yet never, never must it be reversed! O my brethren, I tremble at the very mentioning of this sentence! and O what will they do on whom it must pass; I beseech you before we pass from it, will you ask but your souls this one question, What, can you dwell with everlasting fire? If you can, you may go on in sin, but if you cannot, why then stop here, and repent of sin: O now say, 'If this be the effect of sin, Lord 'pardon what is past, and O give me grace that I 'may sin no more, as sometimes I have done.' Methinks, if a temptation should come again for ordinary entertainment, you should fright it away with the remembrance of these powerful words, *Depart from me, ye cursed, into everlasting fire, prepared for the devil and his angels.*

2. The saints shall judge the very self same judgment, *Do ye not know that the saints shall judge the world?* 1 Cor. vi. 2. That they, as well as Christ, shall judge the world, is without controversy, *And judgment was given to the saints of the most High*, Daniel vii. 22. *Ye also shall sit upon twelve thrones judging the twelve tribes of Israel*, Matth. xix. 28. *Behold, the Lord cometh with ten thousands of his saints, to execute judgment upon all*, Jude 14, 15. *Know ye not that we shall judge the angels?* 1 Cor. vi. 3. Not only shall we judge the world, but the God of the world; the principalities and powers that captivate wicked men at their pleasure; even they must be judged by those whom they formerly foiled: so then there is no question but they shall judge.

Only how the saints shall judge together with Christ, is a very deep question; for my part I am apt to think, that it shall not be directly known, 'ere it be seen and done. I shall only relate what others say to this point, and so leave you to your liberty of judging what is right.

1. Some say, That the saints shall judge the world by presenting their persons and actions, by comparing their good examples with the evil examples of all the reprobates; and, so, they shall convince and condemn the world, *Behold, the Lord cometh with ten thousands of his saints, to execute judgment upon all, and to convince all that are ungodly among them*, Jude 14, 15. This I conceive to be a truth; yet surely this is not all truth.

2. Others say, That the saints shall judge the world by way of inditing, impleading, accusing, witnessing, &c. And I conceive it may be thus too; the saints of the law more especially accusing the breakers of the law, by the law; *Do not think that I will accuse you to the Father; there is one that accuseth you, even Moses in whom ye trust*, John v. 45. And the saints of the gospel more especially judging the profaners of the gospel, by the gospel, *In that day, when God shall judge the secrets of men by Jesus Christ, according to my gospel*, Rom. ii. 16. This likewise is truth; but I believe as yet we have not the whole truth.

3. Others say, That the saints shall judge the world after the manner of exultation, glorying, and rejoicing to see the vengeance, *The righteous shall rejoice when he seeth the vengeance, he shall wash his feet in the blood of the wicked*, Psa. lviii. 10. But this their exulting being a constant and perpetual act, not for a time, but for eternity, methinks this present act should be yet somewhat more.

4. Others say, That the saints shall judge the world by way of affection, assent, vote, suffrage, comprobation, and the like subordinate and conformable acts: *And I heard another out of the altar, say, even so, Lord God Almighty, true and righteous are thy judgments,* Rev. xvi. 7. *And after these things I heard a great voice of much people in heaven, saying, Alleluja, salvation, and glory, and honour, and power unto the Lord our God; for true and righteous are his judgments,* Rev. xix. 1, 2. This certainly is truth, and commonly so received; yet neither is this all truth.

5. Others say, That the saints shall judge the world, (*i e.*) Christ in the saints, and the saints in Christ. He in them, by those infallible principles of divine justice, which are imprest in them; and they in him, by those inseparable bonds of union, whereby they wholly relate to him; or he and they together as head and members, the act of the head imputed to the members, and the act of the members acknowledged by the head; his judiciary act (especially as from his mediatorship and manhood) having a peculiar influence upon them; and their judiciary act (in a perfect conformity, tho' not any absolute proportion) having a peculiar reference to him. And methinks, those texts of
Mat-

Matthew xix. 28. Jude 14, 15. speak there of Christ's and of the saints judgment, as of one joint act.

Oh, what terror will it be to all wicked men! when not only Christ, but all the saints shall say of them, *Away with them, away with them, let them be damned.* You that are fathers, it may be your children will thus sentence you; I remember, when the Jews told Christ, That *he cast out devils through Beelzebub, prince of devils*; he answered, *If I through Beelzebub, cast out devils, By whom do your children cast them out? Therefore they shall be your judges,* Matth. xii. 24,—27. They liked well enough of the miracles of their children who were disciples of Christ, but they could not endure them in Christ; and therefore he tells them, that their children whom God had converted, and to whom he had given power to do the same works that he did, even they should be their judges to condemn them. And so it may be with you, if any of your children be converted to the Lord, and you remain still in a natural estate, your very children shall be your judges, and condemn you to hell. But of that anon.

6. In this doom which Christ and his saints shall pass on reprobates, our Saviour tells us of some reasonings betwixt him and them, *I was an hungred,* (saith Christ) *and ye gave me no meat; I was thirsty, and ye gave me no drink,* &c.——Matth. xxv. 42. *Then shall they answer, Lord, when saw we thee an hungred, or athirst, or a stranger, or naked, or sick, or in prison, and did not minister unto thee? And then shall he answer them, Verily, I say unto you, inasmuch as ye did it not to one of the least of these, ye did it not to me,* ver. 44, 45. As if Christ should have said, Time was that I was under reproach, misery, calamity, necessity; I lay at your doors like Lazarus full of sores, and as I thought nothing too much for you, so I expected also something from you, but, Oh! cruelty, to see thy Christ an hungred, and not to feed him! to see thy Christ athirst, and not to cool or quench his thirst! to see thy Christ a stranger, and not to give him a night's lodging! to see thy Christ naked, and not to cover him with a garment, who would gladly have covered thee with the robe of righteousness, the garment of salvation! O monstrous inhuman heart! O prodigious wretch! who among the Heathens ever dealt thus with their idols? Have any of the nations starved their gods, turned them out of doors? And must I only be slighted? Away reprobates! you had no mercy on me, and now I laugh at your calamity; surely *he shall have judgment without mercy, that hath shewed no mercy.* They stand wondering at this, and cannot remember that ever they saw Christ in such a condition, *Why Lord,* (say they) *when saw we thee an hungred, or thirsty, or naked? Art not thou he that rose again from the dead, and ascended on high, and ever since hast been exalted above the highest cherubims, a name being given thee above every name; at which name to this day, but especially now on this day, every knee doth bow, of things in heaven, and things in earth, and things under the earth,* Phil. ii. 9, 10. How then could we see thee in such a condition? Is not this thy second coming in glory? And were we alive at thy first coming in humility? How can this be? Oh! why shouldest thou charge us with unkindness to thyself? Sure, if we had known thee in need, we would have given thee of thy own; thou shouldest never have wanted what things we enjoyed, but thou shouldest have commanded both us and them. To which our Saviour replies, 'O deceitful, ignorant, and stupid souls! have you no 'better learned Christ than so? Am not I head of 'the church, and can the head be without mem- 'bers? Verily, if you had loved, relieved, or 'done good to them, you had done so to me; but 'in being uncharitable to them, you were no less 'unto me.' Never say, you would have been thus and thus kind to Christ, whilst you were unkind to Christians: herein lies the deceitfulness of your hearts, *O! they are deceitful above all things, and desperately wicked, Who can know them? But I the Lord search the heart, I try the reins, even to give to every man according to his ways, and according to the fruit of his doings,* Jer. xvii. 9, 10. In as much as ye did it not to one of the least of my members, ye did it not to me; and therefore get ye down to hell, get ye out of my presence; take them, devils, away with them, angels, to the devil and his angels for ever.

These are the reasonings betwixt Christ and reprobates; and if so, may we not imagine the like betwixt saints and reprobates? Is there not the same reason of reasoning betwixt them and the inferior judges, as betwixt them and the supreme judge?

judge? For my part I cannot conceive, but if we admit of such disputes betwixt Christ and them, well may there be the like disputes, arguings, and reasonings betwixt saints and them: for they had on earth more familiarity, converse, and communion together. Some of them, it may be, were in near and dear relations to each other; and now that the one, shall judge the other to eternal flames, Oh! what passages will be betwixt them? I shall instance in our nearest relations upon earth, as of masters and servants, parents and children, husbands and wives, ministers and people; no question, but in these very relations some shall judge, and others be judged. Our Saviour tells us, *There shall be two men in one bed, the one shall be taken, the other shall be left; two women shall be grinding at one mill, the one shall be taken, and the other left; two men shall be together in one field, the one shall be taken, and the other left,* Luke xvii. 34, 35, 36. Wherein the Lord seems to shew, that God's election doth extend itself to all sorts of persons, and separates the most. They shall not be saved by families, as in Noah's time; but one friend shall be taken by Christ into heaven, and another left for the devil to carry into hell. Give me leave but to enlarge on those reasonings or discourses, that we may imagine will be now betwixt these several relations. As,——

1. Betwixt master and servant. If the master be the saint, and his servant the reprobate, then shall the master say, O! thou wicked servant, how many a time did I call on thee to duty? How often have I told thee, that I would have thee to be God's servant, as well as mine? How often came that word to thy ears, *Servants, obey your masters in all things according to the flesh, not with eye-service, as men pleasers, but in singleness of heart, fearing God?* Col. iii. 22. How often was that precious word laid close to thy conscience, *He that doth wrong, shall receive for the wrong which he doth; but in doing service to me, as to the Lord, thou shouldest of the Lord receive the reward of the inheritance, for in such service thou didst serve the Lord Christ,* Col. iii 23, 24, 25. But thou wouldest not be warned, and now thou art justly condemned; I say amen to Christ's sentence, get thee down to hell and there serve Satan, and receive his wages in fire and brimstone for ever.——Or, if the servant be the saint, and his master the reprobate,

then shall the servant say, O my *quondam* master, how many a time hast thou tyrannized it over me? How didst thou use me, or abuse me, to serve thy own lusts and corruptions? Many a time I have had strong desires to wait upon God in the use of public and private ordinances; this morning, and that evening, I would have served my master the Lord Jesus Christ, but thou wouldest not spare me one hour's time for prayer, reading, meditation, &c I was ever faithful in thy service, going to bed late, and rising early; *The drought consumed me by day, and the frost by night, and my sleep many a time departed from mine eyes; surely God hath seen my affliction, and the labour of my hands, and now he hath rebuked thee,* Gen. xxxi. 40, 42. Dost thou not observe the admirable justice and righteousness of Christ in the sentences past on us both? Remember that thou in thy lifetime receivedst thy good things, and I received evil things; but now I am comforted, and thou must be tormented. I now serve a better master, after my week's work with thee, I shall keep a perpetual Sabbath with God; but go thou with thy old companions from thy glorious mansion, to a lothsome dungeon; from thy table of surfeit, to a table of vengeance; from thy faithful servants, to afflicting spirits; from thy bed of down, to a bed of fire; from soft linen and silken coverings, to wish a rock for thy pillow, and a mountain for thy coverlet.

2. Betwixt parent and child. If the parent be the saint, and the child the reprobate; then shall the parent say, O thou wicked rebellious son! or, O! thou wicked, rebellious, and disobedient daughter! it is I that begot thee, or that brought thee forth; that during thy infancy laid thee in my bosom, and dandled thee on my knee, and carried thee in my arms, and set thee as a seal upon my heart; that during thy minority fed thee, and apparelled thee, and trained thee up in manners, learning, a particular calling, and especially in the nature and admonition of the Lord: and then, when I saw thy untowardness of spirit, and thy breakings out into things forbidden by God and man, O! the admonitions, reprehensions, corrections! O! the many thousands of warnings that I gave thee of this day, and of the wrath to come! and yet thou wentest on in thy stubbornness, till thou becamest many and many a time a grief of mind, a bitterness of spirit unto

me:

me: and then, how often did I mind thee of thy duty? *Children, obey your parents in all things,* Col. iii. 20. *Honour thy father and mother, which is the first commandment with promise,* Eph. ii. 6. *The eye that mocketh his father, and despiseth to obey his mother, the ravens of the valley shall pick it out, and the young eagles shall eat it,* Prov. xxx. 17. But alas! all these expressions made no saving impression on thy hardened heart, thy brow was brass, and thy sinew of iron, thou wast ever stiff-necked, and now thou art justly damned; I cannot but approve of Christ's judgment upon thee, though thou camest out of my bowels, yet now I have no pity, no bowels of compassion towards thee; the glory of God hath swallowed up all my natural affections, that I cannot but laugh at thy calamity, and joy in thy damnation; I gave thee a body, and God himself gave thee a soul; but now let devils have both, and torment them in hell: be gone, I shall never see thee again.——Or, if the child be the saint, and the parent the reprobate; then shall the child say, O! unworthy parent, unworthy of everlasting life! I had my natural being from thee, but my spiritual being was from the Lord: if I had followed thy steps, I had been everlastingly damned; did not I know thy ignorance, thy unbelief, thy worldliness, thy covetousness, thy pride, thy malice, thy lust, thy lukewarmness, thy impatiency, thy discontentment, thy vain-glory, thy self-love? Didst thou not often check me for my forwardness, and zeal, and holiness in religion? Didst thou not ask me, what, art thou wiser than the rest of the neighbourhood? Are there not many gray hairs amongst us, whose wisdom and experience thou hast not yet attained? And canst not thou walk on soberly towards heaven, and either do as the most, or keep pace with the wisest? What, have any of the rulers, or of the Pharisees believed on Christ? Oh! I shall ever remember, to the praise and glory of Christ, what discouragements I had, and yet how the Lord pluckt me as a fire-brand out of the fire; and now hath the Lord set me on the throne, to judge thee according to thy demerits: and therefore I join with him, who is the Father of spirits, against the father of my flesh; depart, go to the gods whom thou hast served, and see if they will help thee in the day of thy calamity.

3. Betwixt husband and wife. Now if the husband be the saint, and the wife the reprobate, then shall the husband say, Thou art she whom I knew in the flesh, whom I dearly affected with my heart and soul; whom I nourished and cherished as my own body; thou art she that was the wife of my bosom, as near and dear to me as my heart in my bosom; thou wast my companion, my yoke-fellow, and my very delight; but Oh! I could never rule thee, lead thee, guide thee in the way of life, in that path that is called holy. Many a time have I wooed, sued, and sought to gain thy soul to that blessed bridegroom, the Lord Jesus Christ; many a time have I prayed with thee, and for thee; many a time have I stirred thee up to hear the word, to wait upon God in the use of all means public and private; and instead of embraces, or yieldings to these blessed motions, I have met with contentions and jars, *As a continual dropping in a very rainy day,* Prov. xix. 13.—xxvii. 15. But death hath dissolved that knot, so that now I am no more thy husband. This is the day of separation, and I shall no more consort with thee; *At the resurrection there is no use of marriage, but now I am to live as an angel in heaven,* Mark xii. 25. And because thou wouldest not draw with me in Christ's yoke, now therefore adieu for ever and ever. We shall never more lie in one bed, or sit at one board, or walk in one field, or grind at one mill: thou hast lost me, and thou hast lost Jesus Christ, two husbands in one day; go now and take thy choice in hell! thou art free from us, but thou shalt be bound there with indissoluble bonds to the devil and his angels.——Or, if the wife be the saint, and the husband the reprobate; then shall the wife say, Thou art he, whom I looked upon as my second-self, my head, my governor, my helper, my husband; for whom I was willing to forsake my native home, father's house, dear relations, of father, mother, brother, sister, and many comforts in that kind; and I expected to have found new matter, and a continued influence of comfort, and delight in a marriage-state: but oh the vexations of spirit I hadst thou not almost drawn me away from Jesus Christ? Was I not forced, through many provocations, sometimes to break out and say, *Surely a bloody husband art thou to me?* Exo. iv. 25. Many a time I cried out, O my husband, when wilt thou set up the rich and royal trade of grace in thy family? When wilt thou exercise prayer, reading, cate-

catechising, conference, days of humiliation, and other houshold, holy duties? Oh, for doing something to assure our souls of meeting together hereafter in heaven! but alas! it would not he; and now see the effect; here I stand like a queen, deckt and adorned with cloth of gold, with raiment of needle-work, with the white robe of Christ's righteousness, so that the king of heaven greatly desires my beauty, and my soul is this day married to Christ; I acknowledge him, and no other husband in the world: and for thee who refused to join with me in the worship of God, now God hath refused thee Farewel or fare ill for ever.

4. Betwixt a minister and some of his people at least: if the people be as so many saints, and the minister the reprobate, then shall the people say, O! thou art the man that undertookest that high and mighty calling of feeding souls with the word of life; but now are thy sins written in thy forehead, for either thou runnest before thou wast sent, or being sent, thou hast been exceeding negligent in the gift that was in thee. Didst thou not prophesy in Baal, and cause God's people to err? Didst thou not studiously and mainly seek for the fleece, not regarding respectively the flock? Didst thou not strengthen the hands of evil-doers, in preaching peace, peace to wicked men? Wast thou not profane, and wicked, and loose in thy life, and by that means leadest many thousands to hell? O thou bloody butcher of souls? hadst thou been faithful in thy ministry, well might those damned companions about thee have escaped the flames! but they are doomed to death, and now thou mayest hear their cries, and grievous groans and complaints against thee; this was the man set over us to give us the bread of life, but O Christ! did he not fail us? Did he not feed us with unprofitable matter, fables, conceits, airy sentences, rather than with any thing tending to godly edifying, which is in faith? Did not our tongues, and the tongues of our children stick to the roof of our mouths, in calling and crying for bread, for the bread of life, and he would not pity us? we gave him the tenths which thou appointed, but he gave not us thy truth which thou didst command him; why, Lord Christ, judge of all the world, didst thou not bid him feed, feed, feed? Didst thou not bid him feed the flock committed to his charge? Didst thou not bid him preach the word, *Be instant in season, and out of season; reprove, rebuke, exhort with all long-suffering?* And notwithstanding all thy commands, did he not miserably starve us? Instead of feeding us to salvation, hath he not starved many thousands of us to our destruction? O Christ! thou art the judge of nations, and the revenger of blood, reward thou this man, as he hath rewarded us; he led us in the ways of wickedness, and (if it must be so) let him be our ring-leader to hell; and upon his soul once buried in hell, let this be the epitaph, *The price of blood, the price of blood.* If thou didst hear the blood of Abel, being but one man, forget not the blood of many, now thou art judging the earth. Why, thus do the damned cry about thine ears; and as for us (say the saints) who were once thy people, but now thy judges, we consent to their cry, and to our Saviour's doom, Go, thou cursed into everlasting fire.

Men, brethren, and fathers, I begin thus with the minister's doom, that you see I would deal impartially; and verily I believe it, if our case come to this, we of the ministry shall be in a thousand times worse condition than any of you: for, besides the horror due to the guilt of our own souls, all the blood of those souls that have perished under our ministry, through our default, will be laid to our charge; little do you know, or consider the burden that lies upon us, a burden able to make the shoulders of the most mighty angel in heaven to shrink under it. Chrysostom was a glorious saint, yet casting his eye upon one only text in the Bible, * *Obey them that have the rule over you, and submit yourselves; for they watch for your souls, as they that must give account,* Heb. xiii. 17. He professeth, That the terror of this text made his heart to tremble Surely it is enough to make our hearts to tremble, if we seriously weigh our terrible doom, in case that we should miscarry.

But now on the other side, if the minister be the elect, and sentenced to salvation, and many of his people prove no better than reprobates; then shall the minister say, O miserable souls! now you feel the truth of those comminations and curses which we opened and unfolded, and discovered to you out of God's word! we dealt plainly with you,

---

* *Hujus comminationis terror animum mihi concutit.* Chrysost. de.

That

That the unrighteous should not inherit the kingdom of God, 1 Cor. vi. 9. We advise you again and again, *Be not deceived, neither fornicators, nor idolaters, nor adulterers, nor effeminate, nor abusers of themselves with mankind, nor thieves, nor covetous, nor drunkards, nor revilers, nor extortioners, shall inherit the kingdom of God*, verse 10, 11. And such were you, and notwithstanding all our threats, warnings, intreatings, beseechings, thus ye lived, and thus ye died; and here is the issue, Christ hath now doomed you to hell, and here am I set on a throne to judge your souls; for the saints shall judge the world as well as Christ himself. Oh! what shall I do? O my bowels, my bowels! here's a case beyond all the former, each of them according to their relations judge another; but here's a multitude, not one, or two, or ten, or an hundred, but many hundreds, or thousands, according to the number of such and such congregations, where I have preached.

In Christ's reasoning with the wicked, we have heard of his sayings, and their answers, and of his replications to their answers, much said on both sides to and again; I may suppose the like here. Oh! what shall I do, (says the minister) what doom shall I pass on this assembly of reprobates? Can I absolve them whom the righteous God hath condemned? Can I say, Come along with me to heaven, now Christ hath said, Go ye cursed into hell? And, oh! now shall I turn my speech from my wonted wooing, beseeching, intreating, exhorting to a direct dooming, damning, condemning these souls to the pit of hell? Sometimes indeed I opened to these souls all the armoury of God's wrath, I thundered and lightned in their congregations, but my design was to fright them out of hell-fire, and knowing the terrors of the Lord, to have persuaded them towards heaven and heavenly things; but now if I speak of condemnation, no sooner shall I speak, but their souls will sink down to hell; O miserable souls! what shall I say, or what can you say for yourselves? Then shall they answer, Oh, Sir! do not you aggravate the torment by your condemnation; the weight of Christ's doom is already unsupportable; But will you add more weight? Why, remember, we are, some of us of your flesh and blood; many a time you told us, That you unfeignedly loved us, and that we were dearer to you than all the worldly enjoyments; many a time you told us that you were willing to spend yourself for us, as the candle that burns itself to give others light; you were pleased to bestow your prayers, tears, sighs, and groans for our souls; your very books and writings were high expressions, and abiding monuments of your dear love to us; you weighed not your strength and spirits in comparison of our souls; And shall this fair comical scene end in a dismal, doleful, bloody tragedy? Would you do, or suffer any thing to save us, and will you now condemn us? Oh, forbear!

Ah, no, (saith the minister) I cannot forbear, all is true that you say, I loved you dearly, and I was willing to spend, or to be spent for you, but this aggravates the more; ah! my travail, pains, books, writings, words, tears, sighs, and groans, are in one volume together, and this volume has been opened this day, and now is the question put, What have you profited by all my words, prayers, tears, sighs, and groans? Is not all lost? And are not your souls lost? And now, do you tell me of love? What, did I ever love you more than Christ loved you? Were the drops of my tears to be compared with the showers of his blood; Were my pains for you equal to the pains of his cross? And hath not he condemned you to hell? And shall not I be like-minded to Jesus Christ? Surely the Lord's will must be my will; he hath already judged you, and he will make me to judge you; so far I am from pitying you, that if he that formed you will shew you no mercy, if he that saves me, and all the elect people of God, will not save you; Can I pity you, or save you, or dissent from Jesus in his sentence upon you? Speak no more of flesh and blood, of labours of love, Christ's sentence must stand, and as I am a member of Christ, I cannot approve of it, and so judge you to hell.

Why then, (say reprobates) we will curse thee and blaspheme Jesus Christ for ever; cursed be the time that ever we heard of Jesus, or that ever we knew thee, or thy ministry. Do not thy sermons send us deeper into hell? Had it not been easier for us at this day of judgment, if we had lived in Tyre and Sidon, where the gospel never was preached? Didst thou not harden our hearts in such and such sermons, when the word came home? Didst thou not deny us the seals which might have been for confirmation of our soul's salvation? Didst thou not estrange thyself from us in respect of any inward,

ward, intimate, and familiar society which thou affordest to others? Doth not the event plainly shew, that all thy tears, prayers, words, and works, as in reference to us, were hypocrisy, flattery, deceit, and diffimulation? Oh! cursed be the day that we lived under such a ministry, or that we ever heard of Jesus Christ.

Nay, then (saith the minister) it is time for us to part, such were your invectives on earth, and now they are, and will be your language in hell; But have I not answered these cavils many a time? Have not I told you that the word would harden some and soften others, the fault being in yourselves? Have I not cleared it, that the seals are not set upon blanks, and that confirmation could not be without a work of conversion to lead it? And were we not commanded in the name of our Lord Jesus Christ to withdraw ourselves from every brother that walketh disorderly? 2 Thess. iii. 16. Did not the wise man tell us, *He that toucheth pitch shall be defiled therewith, and he that hath fellowship with a proud man shall be like unto him? Can a man take fire in his bosom, and his clothes not be burnt? Can a man go upon hot coals and his feet not be burnt?* Prov. vi. 27, 28. As for other cavils, the Lord be Judge betwixt you and us; nay, the Lord hath been Judge betwixt you and us: lo, here we stand on the right hand of Christ; lo, here we sit on our thrones to judge you, and that world of wicked men and angels; let Christ be glorious, and let his sentence stand, and let that word of judgment never be reversed, *He that loveth cursing, let it come upon him; and he that clotheth himself with cursing, as with a garment, let it come into his bowels like water, and like oil into his bones*, Psal. cix. 17, 18. No more, but adieu souls, adieu reprobates, adieu for ever; you must descend, but we must ascend. Go you to hell, whilst we mount upwards to heaven and glory.

At this last word, down they go; the evil angels falling like lightning, and evil men haled and pulled down with them from the presence of God, and Christ, and angels, and all the blessed ones; even from their fathers, mothers, wives, husbands, children, ministers, servants, lovers, friends, acquaintance; who shall then justly and deservedly abandon them with all detestation and derision; and forgetting all nearness, and dearest obligations of nature, neighbourhood, alliance, any thing will rejoice in the execution of divine justice. Oh the shrieks, and horrid cries that now they make, filling the air as they go! oh the wailings and wringings of hands! oh the desperate roarings! oh the hideous yellings, filling heaven, and earth, and hell! but I shall follow them no farther; no sooner do they fall into the bottomless pit, but presently it shuts her mouth upon them, and there I must leave them.

SECT. VII.

Of Christ and his saints going up into heaven, and of the end of this world.

7. FOR Christ and his saints going up into heaven, and so for the end of this world: no sooner are the reprobates gone to their place, but the saints ascend; now Christ ariseth from his judgment seat, and with all the glorious company of heaven, he marches towards the heaven of heavens. Oh! what a comely march is this? What songs of triumph are here sung and warbled? Christ leads the way, the cherubims attend, the seraphims wait on, angels, archangels, principalities, powers, patriarchs, prophets, priests, evangelists, martyrs, professors, and confessors of God's law and gospel following, attend the Judge and King of glory; singing with melody, as never ear hath heard; shining with majesty, as never eye hath seen; rejoicing without measure, as never heart conceived. O blessed train of soldiers! O goodly troop of captains! each one doth bear a palm of victory in his hand, each one doth wear a crown of glory on his head; the church militant is now triumphant; with a final overthrow have they conquered devils, death and hell; and now must they enjoy God, life and heaven; sometimes I have, with much wonder and admiration, beheld some regiments passing our streets; but had I seen those Roman armies, when they returned victors, and made their solemn triumph in the streets of Rome, oh then! how should I have admired, never was the like sight to this of Christ and his army in this world. O the comely march they make through the sky, and through the orbs, and through all the heavens till they come to the heaven of heavens! was ever so many glittering suns together in one day? Was ever so many glories together on this side the

king-

kingdom of glory? Not to speak of Christ, or his angels, *O who is she that looketh forth as the morning, fair as the moon, clear as the sun, and terrible as an army with banners?* Cant. vi. 10. Are not in the head of those regiments, Adam and Abel, and Noah and Abraham, and Isaac and Jacob, and all the patriarchs, and all the prophets, and all the apostles? And (if thou art a faint that readest this) art not thou one sun appointed by God amongst the rest to follow Christ? Here is enough to fill thy heart with joy before-hand, as sure as yonder sun now shines in the firmament, shalt thou that believest pass through that sun in its very orb, and by reason of thy glory it shall lose its shine; oh then! what spreading of beauty and brightness will be in the heavens as all the saints go along? What lumps of darkness shall those glittering stars appear to be, when all the saints of God shall enter into these several orbs and spheres? And thus as they march along higher and higher till they come to the highest, at last heaven opens unto them, and the saints enter into their Master's joy. What is there done at their first entrance, I shall discover another time; only for a while let us look behind us, and see what becomes of this nether world.

No sooner Christ and his company in the imperial heaven, but presently this whole world is set on fire: to this prophane authors seem to assent: as,

1. Philosophers, especially the Stoicks, were of this mind. *Humor primordium, exitus ignis,* said Seneca, 'Moisture was the beginning, and fire shall 'be the end of this world.' And speaking of the sun, moon, and stars, *Mark,* (says he) *Whatsoever now shines in comely and decent order, shall at last burn together in one fire.*

2. The poets grant this. Lucan speaking of those whom Cæsar left unburned at the battle of Pharsalia, *Hos Cæsar populos si nunc non usserit ignis, urent cum terris.*——'If fire shall not now 'burn these, when heaven, and earth, and all 'shall burn, then must they burn.'——Ovid, in like manner, *Esse quoque in fatis*——*quo mare, quo tellus*——*ardent* 'A time shall come, when "sea, and earth, and all the frame of this great 'world shall be consumed in fire.'

3. The Sybills grant this, to which the Roman missal seems to allude, in joining them with the prophet David, though I know not by what warrant. *Dies iræ, dies illa, solvet sæculum in favilla, recte David cum sybilla.*

A day of wrath, a day of fire,
So David with the Sybills doth conspire.

But to wave all these, one text of scripture is to me more than all these.——2 Pet. iii. 10 *The heavens shall pass away with a great noise, and the elements shall melt with fervent heat; the earth also, and the works that are therein shall be burnt up.* Hence all our divines agree, That a fire shall seize on the universe, only some difference is among divines, Whether the world shall be wholly annihilated or renewed by fire? Jerome and Augustine, and many after them say, the end of this fire is for purifying and refining of the heaven and earth, for all corruptible qualities shall be burnt out of them, but they in their substance shall remain still: if we ask them, To what end shall this nether world be renewed? * Some say, for an habitacle of the restored beasts: others, for a fitter accommodation of men and the glorified saints: others, for a perpetual monument of God's power and glory. Polanus, and some of our moderns are of opinion, †
' That these heavens, and this earth, when puri-
' fied with those fires, and superinvested with new
' endowments, they shall be the everlasting habi-
' tations of the blessed saints.' But, on the contrary, others are of the other opinion, that all the world, with all the parts and works, (except men, angels, and devils, heaven and hell, the two mansions for the saved and damned) shall be totally and finally dissolved and annihilated. And of this opinion were Hillary, Clement, and all the ancients before Jerome; and of our moderns not a few. For my part, I rather incline this way, because of the many scriptures that are so express, I shall mention only these.——*Man lieth down, and riseth not till the heavens be no more,*——Job xiv. 12. *Of old thou hast laid the foundations of the earth, and the heavens are the works of thy hands; they shall*

* *Mundus in melius immutatus a parte accommodabitur hominibus in melius immutatis,* August. de civit. Dei. l. 20. C. 16.
† Polan. Syntag. l. 6. C. 70.

perish,

perish, but thou shalt endure, Psal. cii. 25, 26. *All the hosts of heaven shall be dissolved, and the heaven shall be rolled together as a scroll, and all the hosts shall fall down, as the leaf falleth from the vine, and as a falling fig from the fig-tree,* Isa. xxxiv. 4. To which prophecy John seems to allude, *And the heavens departed as a scroll when it is rolled together, and every mountain and island were moved out of their places,* Rev. vi. 14. Again, *Heaven and earth shall pass away,* (saith Christ) *but my word shall not pass away,*—Mat. xxiv. 36. *The day of the Lord will come as a thief in the night, in the which the heavens shall pass away with a great noise, and the elements shall melt with fervent heat, the earth also, and the works that are therein, shall be burnt up,*—2 Pet. iii. 10. *And the world passeth away, and the lusts thereof, but he that doth the will of God abideth for ever,*—1 John ii. 17. *And I saw a great white throne, and him that sat on it, from whose face the earth and the heaven fled away, and there was found no place for them,* Rev. xx. 11. Now I would demand, whether *being no more,* as Job; and *perishing,* as David; *and rolling together, and falling down like a withered leaf,* as Isaiah; and *passing away,* as our Saviour and Peter; and *flying away,* as John; do not include an utter abolition? If to these scriptures I should add one reason, I would argue from the end of the world's creation; Was it not partly for the glory of God, and partly for the use of man? Now for the glory of God, the manifestation of it is occasioned by the manifestation of the world unto man; if man therefore should be removed out of the world, and no creature in it be capable of such a manifestation, What would become of his glory? And for the use of man, that is either to supply his necessity in matter of diet, physick, building, apparel, or for his instruction, direction, recreation, comfort, delight: now, when he shall attain that blessed estate of enjoying God, and seeing God face to face, these ends, or the like, must needs be frustrate. This argument is weighty, and we need no more. Only we shall hear our antagonists objections, and give them their answers, and so conclude.

The texts more especially objected against this opinion, are two: the first is that in Rom. viii. 21. *The creature itself shall be delivered from bondage of corruption, into the glorious liberty of the sons of God.* Here, (say they) is an earnest expectation attributed to brute creatures, that they shall be delivered from the bondage of corruption into the glorious liberty of the children of God. But I answer, That no immortal being of the brute creatures is here promised, but only a simple deliverance and dismission from the servitude they were in to ungrateful men. The birds, beasts, and fishes, do now suffer for our diet; horses, mules, and beasts of that nature, do now groan under the burdens of our pleasures or necessities; their annihilation therefore to them must needs be a kind of deliverance; and, at last, they shall be delivered at the time of the glorious liberty of the sons of God; the text will bear it thus, * [*eis pro dia,*] *The creature shall be delivered by the glorious liberty of the sons of God,* (i. e.) When such a deliverance comes to men, these shall be freed from their servitude, by being not at all, having done all the business for which they were ordained, or created.

The second text is that in 2 Pet. iii. 13. *We look for new heavens, and a new earth wherein dwelleth righteousness.* These words (say some) imply a purging, rather than abolishing; a taking off the corrupt qualities only, not the substance. But I am of another mind, and if I must give my sense of the place, I say,—

1. Negatively, that *by new heavens and new earth,* is not meant renewed heavens and earth; is it not punctually in the seventh verse, That *the heavens and the earth,* which are now, are *reserved unto fire against the day of judgment?* And doth he not descend unto particulars in the tenth verse, That the heavens which are now, *shall pass away with a great noise;* that *the elements shall melt with fervent heat; and that the earth also, and the works therein shall be burnt up?* And doth he not infer thereupon in the eleventh and twelfth verses, that all these things shall be dissolved? And in the thirteenth verse, that we are therefore to *look for new heavens, and a new earth?* 2 Pet. iii. 7, 10, 11, 12, 13. Dissolution mends not a

---

* [*eis pro dia,*] Rom. viii. 21. 1 Cor. x. 2. as sometimes [*dia pro eis,*] Rom. iv. 11. 1 Cor. ii. 15. So Chrysostome expounds it, [*eis pro dia.*]

fabric,

fabric, but destroys it; how then should that which is dissolved, be said to be reserved, and let stand? Surely if Peter had thought of this refining only, some words of his would have intimated so much. The end of these creatures was for man's use, and man's using them no more, To what end should they be reserved? To say for a monument of what hath been, or for the habitation to the saints, or for an out-let for the saints, descending sometimes from the highest heavens to solace themselves here below, are but groundless surmises, and deserve no answer at all.

2. Positively, by *new heavens, and new earth,* is meant the heaven of heavens, and place of glory. Now, these heavens are termed new, not in regard of their new making, but of our new taking possession of them for our new habitation; and they are called heavens and earth, because they come instead of that heavenly covering, and that earthly habitation which we now enjoy; so that the text may well bear this paraphrase, *We look for new heavens,* (i. e.) the supreme court of God's presence, *and a new earth,* (i. e.) a new habitation for us, which shall infinitely exceed the commodities and happiness of those heavens and earth which we now enjoy: thus John in his revelations, *And I saw a new heaven, and a new earth; for the first heaven, and the first earth were passed away, and there was no more sea,* Revel. xxi. 1. This new heaven, and new earth, is the place or habitation prepared for the blessed saints and people of God. *A new heaven,* where the moon is more glorious than our sun, and the sun as glorious as he that made it, for it is he himself, the Son of God, the sun of righteousness, the sun of glory; *a new earth,* where all their waters are milk, and all their milk honey; where all their grass is corn, and all their corn manna; where all their glebe and clods of earth are gold, and all their gold of innumerable carats; where all their minutes are ages, and all their ages eternity; where every thing is every minute in the highest exaltation as good as can be. Of these new heavens, and this new earth, I can never say enough, nor know enough, till I come thither to inhabit it. Something only we shall discover of it in our next sections; for now are the saints entered in with Jesus Christ.

Use. Only one word of use: Christians! what is the matter that we are so busy about this world? Why, look about you, not one of these visible objects shall that day remain, or have a being; those houses wherein we dwell, these temples wherein we meet, this town, this country, this isle, and the seas and waters that surround it, shall be all on fire, and consume to nothing; the sea shall be no more, and time shall be no more: Or, if we look higher, yonder sun, and moon, and stars, shall be no more; that glorious heaven which rolls over our heads, shall be rolled *together as a scroll, and all the host shall fall down as a leaf falleth from the vine, and as a falling fig from the fig tree,*——Isa. xxxiv. 4. *The heavens shall vanish away like smoke,* (saith Isaiah) Isa. li 6. *Comminuentur in nihilum,* (as Hierom reads it) *They shall be battered into nothing.* Alas, alas! what do we toiling all the day (it may be all our life) for a little of this little, almost nothing——earth: You that have an hundred, or two hundred, or a thousand acres, if every acre were a kingdom, all will be at last burnt up; so that none shall say here was Preston, or here was London, or here was England, or here was Europe, or here was the globe of earth on which men trod; let others boast as they will of their inheritances, but Lord give me an inheritance above all these visibles; heaven shall remain, when earth shall vanish; that imperial heaven, those seats of saints, those mansions above, prepared by Jesus Christ, shall never end; but for my riches, lands, possessions, moveables, goods reals or personal, they will end in smoke, in nothing; *What, wilt thou set thine eyes upon a thing that is not?* Prov. xxiii. 5. Upon this the primitive Christians took joyfully the spoiling of their goods, it was but a loss little before the time, *and they knew in themselves that they had in heaven a better, and an enduring substance,* Heb. x. 34. O let this be our care! here we have no abiding city, but, O! let us seek one to come, even that one that will abide for ever and ever. Amen.

SECT. VIII.

Of Christ's surrendering, and delivering up the kingdom to God, even the Father.

8. FOR Christ's surrendering and delivering up the kingdom o. (...), en the Father,

no sooner is he in heaven, but these things follow,——

1. He presents the elect unto his Father; of this the apostle speaks, *You hath he reconciled in the body of his flesh through death, to present you holy and unblameable, and unreprovable in his sight,* Col. i. 21, 22. To this end Christ died, that he might wash us, and cleanse us by his blood, and then that he might present us without spot unto his Father. We may imagine Christ as going to his Father, with his bride in his hand, and saying thus, 'O my Father! here is my church, my spouse, my queen; here are the saints concerning whom I covenanted with thee from eternity, concerning whom I went down from heaven, and died on earth, and ascended up, I have interceded these many hundred years; concerning whom I went down to judge the world, and having sentenced them to life eternal, I now bring them in my hand, to give them the possession of thyself. These are they whom thou gavest me in the beginning of the world, and now I restore them to thyself at the end of the world, for they are thine.' Thus he presents them to his Father. Indeed we read that Christ presents the saints to himself, as well as to his Father, *Christ loved the church, and gave himself for it,——that he might present it to himself a glorious church, not having spot or wrinkle,* Ep. v. 25, 27. But this I take it was done before; when first a soul believes, it is contracted to Christ, when the soul is sentenced to glory, then is the solemnity and consummation of the marriage, then doth Christ present the soul to himself; and I know not but that the ministers of Christ may have a part in this matter, *For I have espoused you to one husband,* (saith Paul to his Corinthians) *that I may present you as a chaste virgin to Christ,* 2 Cor. xi. 2. And after this, when Christ takes the bride home, brings her into heaven, and leads her by the hand into his Father's presence; then is the last presentation, then *he presents her faultless before the presence of his glory with exceeding joy.* The word signifies leaping, springing, and exulting joy: O! what springing, leaping, and exulting is in heaven, when Christ takes the hand of his bride, and gives her into the hand of his Father! *q. d.* 'O my Father! see what a number I have brought home to thee; thou knowest what I have done, and what I have suffered, and what offices I have gone through, to bring these hither; and now my mediatorship is done, I resign all my charge to thee again; see what a goodly troop, what a noble army I have brought thee home; why, all these are mine, and all mine are thine, and all thine are mine, *And I am glorified in them, all those that thou gavest me I have kept, and none of them is lost,* John xvii. 10, 12. See here is Adam, and Abel, and Noah, and Shem, and every saint from the beginning to the end of the world, the nuptial between them and me is solemnized, And whither should I lead them, but to my Father's house, and into my Father's presence? I have already pronounced them blessed, *And the glory which thou gavest me, I have given them, that they may be one, even as we are one; I in them, and thou in me, that they may be made perfect in one,* John xvii. 22, 23. Here take them from mine hands, now give them a welcome into glory, *and let them know that thou hast loved them, as thou hast loved me.*'

2. He presents all his commissions to his Father, as he is a Mediator (at least by destination) from all eternity; were not the saints *chosen in Christ before the foundation of the world?* Eph. i. 4. Then was he a Mediator in the business of election, and then was he predestinated to be a Mediator of reconciliation. *I was set up from everlasting,* Prov. viii. 23. *(i. e.)* I was appointed and designed to be a Mediator from all eternity. Howsoever he was a Mediator virtually and inchoatively from the fall of Adam; then did he undertake that great negociation of reconciling God to man, and man to God, and actually he was a Mediator after his incarnation; for then was he manifested in the flesh, then was he manifested to be what before he was, then did he act that part visibly upon earth, which before he had acted secretly and visibly in heaven, then he entred upon the work of his active and passive obedience, then he discharged his prophetical and priestly office here on earth, which having done, then he entred upon his kingly administration in heaven. Now, as to this work, he was called by God, (*Him hath God the Father sealed,* John vi. 27. *It pleased the Father by him,—to reconcile all things to himself,* Col. i. 19, 20.) And as to these offices severally he had commission from God, (*The Lord hath anointed me to preach good tidings un-

to the meek, Isa. lxi. 1. *And the Lord hath sworn, and will not repent, Thou art a priest for ever*, Psal. cx. 4. *And the Lord said unto my Lord, Sit thou at my right hand until I make thine enemies thy footstool*, Psal. cx. 1.) So now he comes with all his commissions in his hand, and he delivers them all up unto his Father again. In this case it is with Christ, as with some general, whom the king sends forth with regal authority to the war, who having subdued the enemy, he returns in triumph, and all being finished, he makes a surrender of his place; thus Christ having discharged all his offices imposed on him, now the work is finished, he leaves his function, by delivering up his commissions to his Father. *In heaven there is no need of sun or moon*, Rev. xxi. 23. That is, as some interpret, there is no need of preaching or prophesying, of the word or sacraments, *For the Lamb is the light thereof*; Christ is the only means of all the communication that the elect there shall have; and as for his regal office, the apostle is express, *Then shall he deliver up the kingdom to God, even the Father*, 1 Cor. xv. 24. Only here is the question, How is Christ said to resign his kingdom to God the Father? For, saith not the scripture, that *Christ's kingdom shall have no end?* Luke i. 33. And that *Christ's throne is for ever and ever?* Heb. i. 8. For answer, I see no contradiction, but that Christ may both resign his kingdom, and yet reserve it. See a like case, *All power*, (saith Christ) *in heaven and earth is given to me of my Father*, Matth. xxviii 18. Shall we say now, that the Father himself is quite stript of it? No; but as the kingdom which the Father gave the Son, is nevertheless called the Father's kingdom, or *the kingdom of God*, so Christ shall return it, yet return it also. Two things (we say) are contained in the term of reign, *scil.* dominion and execution, to wear the crown, and to bear the sceptre: now, Christ in the former sense shall reign for ever, the honour of dominion, and of wearing the crown, he shall never resign up to his Father, for his Father's throne disturbs not his, there are both their thrones at once, Rev. vii. 11. But the functions of a king, to sit in judgment, to reward deservers, to punish evil doers, to rescue the oppressed, to fight with the enemy, Christ, in this sense, shall cease to reign, and shall deliver up the kingdom to his Father.

More particularly, Christ is said to deliver up the kingdom in three respects

1. Because he ceaseth to execute that authority, which nevertheless he hath; as a judge that goeth from the bench, is a judge still, although he giveth no judgment, but employeth his time in other occasions; so Christ is said to resign his place, not that his authority is subject to diminution, but in that he makes no show, for when his enemies are all put under, there is no need that any more blows should proceed from his kingly power.

2. Because the manner of his kingdom, after the judgment-day shall be wholly changed; he shall not reign in the same fashion that he did before; there is no need in heaven of good laws to keep men from starting into wickedness; the orders of this life are changed into a new kind of government, and in that respect he is said to give over the kingdom.

3. Because he ceaseth to increase his dominion. In this world Christ was still gaining more souls to his kingdom, by the preaching of his word; and so he spread his dominion farther and farther: but when the Lord shall have made up the number of his servants to his mind, then he will end the world, and give up the kingdom, (i. e.) he will cease to enlarge his confines any more, he will be content with the number of his subjects that he hath already. Here is the second thing. Christ presents all his commissions to his Father, he gives up his priestly, prophetical, and regal offices at his first entrance into heaven.

4. He presents himself unto his Father, not only his offices, but Christ himself is presented, and subjected unto God. This I take it is the meaning of the apostle, when he saith, *Then shall the Son also himself be subject to him that put all things under him*, 1 Cor. xv. 28. The words are mystical, and therefore we had need to understand them soberly, and according to the analogy of faith. The Arians hence inferred that the Son was not equal with the Father, because he that is subject must needs be inferior to him whose subject he is. But the answer is easy, Christ is considered either as God, or as man, and Mediator betwixt God and man; Christ as God, hath us subject to him, and is subject to none; but Christ, as man and Mediator, is subject to his Father, together with us. Some would have it, that Christ is subject to his Fa-

Father, in respect of his mystical body, the church; and that this only should be the meaning of the apostle, *Then shall the church be subject to the Father*; but I cannot assent to this exposition. 1. Because the apostle speaks expresly of Christ and of his kingdom. 2. Because tho' Christ be sometimes in scripture read for the church, or for the body of Christ, yet the Son, as opposed to the Father, is never so read or understood. 3. Because we read, that he that is to be subject, must first have all things subject to himself. Now, the Father doth not properly subject or subdue all things to the church of Christ, but only unto Christ, and therefore the apostle speaks of Christ's subjection to the Father: in the same way as Christ delivers up the kingdom to the Father, is Christ also to be subject to his Father; but Christ delivers up his kingdom as man, and as Mediator betwixt God and man: in these respects Christ (as we have heard) must reign no more, at that day his mediatorship shall cease; and by consequence, in respect of his mediatorship, or in respect of his humanity, he shall that day be subject to his Father.

You will say, is not, and was not Christ always subject to his Father, as man, or as Mediator betwixt God and man? How then do we limit this subjection to that day? *Then* (saith the apostle) *shall the Son be subject*.

I answer, This subjection will be then, or at that day, more clearly manifested than ever it was before; then he must surrender his kingdom to his Father, in the sight of men and angels; then he shall lay aside all his offices in the view of all: so that thenceforth God shall not reign by the humanity of Christ, but by himself; nor shall we thenceforth be subject to God through a Mediator Christ, but immediately to God himself; nor shall Christ himself reign over us as Mediator any more: for the very glory of his majesty shall become so illustrious, that all eyes shall see how transcendently eminent the Deity of Christ is above all creatures, even above the humanity of Christ himself. That a fuller view of Christ's subjection shall be at that day then ever before, we may illustrate thus: by night the sun reigns and rules over us, but by the moon; for the light of the moon is borrowed from the sun, though in the night we see not any subjection of the moon to the sun at all: but so soon as the sun riseth, presently the moon surceaseth its office of enlightning others, and becomes subject to the sun itself, not by a new subjection, but by a declaration of its former subjection, so that now all may see what eminency of glory and light the sun hath both above the stars, and above the moon. Thus it is with God and Christ, now it is God reigns over us, but only by Christ as Mediator; God's immediate reign we discern not so clearly for the present, but when the end shall come, and Christ shall surcease his office of mediatorship, then shall the glory of Christ's divinity appear more eminently, not only above all creatures, but above the brightness of Christ's humanity itself; and in this respect Christ then shall be subject, if not by a new subjection, yet certainly by a new declaration and manifestation of his subjection, so as never was before.

Use. O the wonders of this day! O the admirable shews in heaven, at Christ and his saints first entrance into heaven! O my soul! where wilt thou stand, or what wilt thou say, when Christ shall take thee by the hand, and bring thee into the presence of his glorious Father? when he shall present thee, and present all his commissions which he received for thee, and present himself unto his Father with thee, saying, 'O my Father! here are we all
' before thy glorious Godhead; thus far I have
' carried on the great work of man's salvation, and
' now all is done according to the covenant be-
' twixt thee and me; lo! here are all the saints,
' which by decree thou gavest me before the world
' was made; lo! here all the commissions which
' I received from thee, in order to their salvati-
' on; lo! here the humanity which thou gavest
' me when I came into the world; such were
' the sins of my redeemed ones, and grown to such
' an height, *That sacrifice and offering thou woul-
' dest not have, but a body hast thou prepared me*,
' Heb. x. 5. And, lo! here I present all these be-
' fore thee, come take thy commissions, and be thou
' all in all. *We praise thee, O God, we acknow-
' ledge thee to be the Lord.* Come welcome me, and
' welcome mine, we all stand here before thy glo-
' rious throne, and expect every way as high an
' entertainment as heaven, or the God of heaven
' can afford us.' O my soul! what joy will possess thee at this passage? Be sure now thy danger is over, and thy arrival is safe; neither shall it here be heard, *Friend, how camest thou thither?* For the

the Lord himself will run unto thee, he will hug thee, and embrace thee, mouth on thy mouth, eyes on thy eyes, hands on thy hands; and each hand shall clap for joy, each harp shall warble, each knee shall bend and bow, and each heart be merry and glad. O for the day! Oh! when will the day come on, when Christ shall deliver up the kingdom to the Father.

SECT. IX.

Of Christ's subjection to the Father, that God may be all in all.

9. FOR the end of Christ's subjection to his Father, *That God may be all in all,* 1 Cor. xv. 28. Surely this is the meaning, Christ therefore subjects himself unto the Father, that God himself may be *all in all*; that God may no more reign by a deputy, or by a Christ, but that immediately and perfectly he may reign by himself, so that every one may see him face to face. Here we enjoy God (as it were) by means, as in the use of the word, and sacraments, and the like; but when that kingdom (where these administrations are made use of) shall be delivered up, then shall God himself be *all in all,* without means, without defect, without end.

It is observable, that Christ in his Mediatory kingdom hath some such things, as bear an analogy to the means and instruments of governing in the kingdoms of men. 1. He hath his militia and his laws, with threatnings and promises, in the ordinances of the word. 2. He hath his grants and seals, with many privileges to confirm his people in the ordinances of his sacraments. 3. He hath his officers and embassadors, for the management of spiritual affairs in the ordinances of his ministry; but the ceasing of Christ's kingdom, is the ceasing of all these; and he therefore ceaseth his kingdom, that God may immediately succeed all these, without any means, or without any Mediator at all, he himself may be instead of all, or *all in all.*

In prosecution of this, I shall discuss, 1. The meaning, What is it for God to be *all in all?* 2. The particulars, wherein more especially is *God all in all?*

1. For the meaning: it is a periphrasis of our complete enjoyment of God. That God may be *all in all,* is as much as to say, that we may enjoy God alone to all purposes, neither wanting nor willing any thing besides himself; for a person to be *all in all* to me, it is to have an enjoyment of that person to all purposes, so that I neither do, nor need I to enjoy any thing besides himself: thus God is to the saints in glory, he is their exceeding great reward; they need nothing else besides himself, their very draughts of happiness are taken in immediately from the fountain, and they have as much of the fountain as their souls in their widest capacity can possibly hold.

2. For the particulars, wherein more especially is *God our all in all?* I answer,——

1. In our enjoying God immediately. Here we enjoy God by means; either he communicates himself unto us through his creatures, or through his ordinances; and hence it is that we know him but in part, we see him but in a glass darkly; but when he shall be our *all in all* we shall see him *face to face,* 1 Cor. xiii. 12. we shall then *see God as he is,* 1 John iii. 2. clearly and immediately. Oh! how excellent is this enjoyment above all present enjoyments here below? As the enjoyment of a friend in his picture, letters, tokens, is short of what we enjoy when we have his personal presence; or as the heat and light of the sun through a cloud, is beneath that heat and light when the glorious body of it is open to us without any interposition; even so all the enjoyments of God in the use of means, graces, blessings, and ordinances, are infinitely inferior to that enjoyment of God which shall be without all means; all the ravishments of our spirit in prayer, hearing, reading and meditating, is but a sip of those rivers which we shall have in heaven. I know the remembrance of God in a private meditation is sweet, Psal. civ. 34. and communion with God in any ordinance, is *a feast of sweetness, and marrow, and fatness,* Psal. lxiii 5, 6. But when the soul shall immediately possess God, when this kingdom of grace shall expire, and all the administrations of it shall vanish away, Will not the fountain be much more sweet than all the streams? Surely *feasts, and sweetness, marrow and fatness,* are terms exceedingly too diminutive to give us any more than a small hint of that incomprehensible satisfaction by immediate communion. O the wonders of heaven! there shall be light without a candle, and a perpetual

day without a sun; there shall be health without physick, and strength of body without use of food; there shall be knowledge without scripture, and settled government without a written law; there shall be communion without sacraments, and joy without promises to be its fuel; the soul in glory shall go straight unto God, and immediately participate his glory and happiness. It is the comparison of a learned divine, ' Suppose you saw a company of 'crystal globes placed in a parallel line, because 'their posture will not admit the sun's immediate 'beams; we'll suppose another single globe set 'by the middle of them, to transmit the sun beams 'unto all these globes, by this means they all shine, 'though it be only by reflection; but when the 'sun shall so come about, as that they may immediately receive its beams, there is no farther 'use of the single globe then; so here, while we, 'through our distance from God, are uncapable 'of immediate enjoyment, there is a necessity of 'Christ's mediation; but when all things that cause 'that distance are removed, and we brought into 'the presence-chamber of God himself, there is 'no such need of a mediator then.' Now, here is one thing, wherein he is our *all in all*, we shall enjoy him immediately.

2. It consists in our enjoying God fully, *Now I know in part,* (saith the apostle) *but then I shall know, even as I am known*, 1 Cor. xiii. 12. Our enjoyment of God is but here in its infancy, there it will be in its full age; here it is in drops, there it will be in the ocean; here we see God's back-parts, and we can see no more; but there we shall see his face, not his second face, (as some distinguish) which is grace and favour enjoyed by faith; but his first face, which is his divine essence, enjoyed by sight. Yet I mean not so, as if the soul, which is a creature, could take in the whole essence of God, which is incomprehensible: but the soul shall, and must be so full of God, as that it shall not be able to receive or desire any jot more. And, Oh! how excellent is this enjoyment above all present enjoyments! It is now our highest happiness to have some glimpses of his glory shining on us, and some drops of his favour distilled into us: oh! but when God shall be our *all in all*, we shall have as much of God as our souls can hold; we shall have the glory of God so poured in, till we can be able to receive no more. And here is that which gives the soul a full satisfaction; never would it be satisfied till it come to this. Suppose that God should draw out all the beauty, sweetness and goodness that he hath communicated to all creatures in the world, and bring the quintessence of all, and communicate that unto the soul of one poor saint, certainly it would not serve the turn, there must be a greater communication before the soul be fully satisfied and rest content; only once admit it into the glorious presence of him, who is *all in all*, and presently it expires its infinite desire into the bosom of that God: for there is enough to fill his spirit, he cannot desire so much, but there is more, and yet infinitely more. If there be enough in God for the spirits of all just men made perfect with God; if there be enough in God, for angels, whose capacities are greater than the saints; if there be enough in God for Jesus Christ, whose capacity is yet far wider than the angels; if there be enough in God for God himself, whose capacity is infinitely greater than them all: then there must needs be satisfaction enough in God to any one poor soul. Here is another thing wherein God is our *all in all*, we shall enjoy him fully.

3. It consists in our enjoying God solely. Not as if there were nothing else in heaven but only God, but that God in heaven shall be *all in all*, or instead of all; it is God in heaven that makes heaven to be heaven; the saints blessedness and God's own blessedness, doth consist in the enjoyment of God himself. The schoolmen tell us, That we shall not properly enjoy any thing else but only God; we may have some use of the creatures, but no fruition, and therefore is God said to be *all*, or as good as all. And, indeed, what can we imagine to be in heaven, which is not eminently in God himself; If it be greatness, and power, and glory, and victory, and majesty, all these are his: if it be joy, or love, or peace, or beauty, or any thing amiable or desirable, all these are in him. Hence some take it to be David's meaning, when he said, *He had none in heaven but God*, Psalm lxxiii. 25. That the sole enjoyment of God, (of God, and of nothing else but God) is the soul's true happiness, when it is at highest; *Whom have I in heaven but thee?* Whom? Why, there are angels, there are saints, there are the spirits of just and perfect men; Are these nothing with David; O yes! all these are good, but they are not able

Carrying on the great Work of our Salvation in his second coming.

to satisfy a soul without God himself. Whether God will make use of any creatures for our service then, or, if any, or what creatures, and what use, is more than I yet know: but to make a full enjoyment there is required a gracious, glorious presence, a sweet effusion or communication of that presence, a just comprehension of the excellency of that communication, a perfect love, and a perfect rest in the love of whatsoever it is we comprehend: now, this is proper only to God, it is he only that fills the whole capacity of the soul, it is he that so fills it that it can hold no more, it is he only that is the object of love intended to the uttermost; and therefore he only is properly enjoyed, he only is possessed with a full contentment, as portion enough, and as reward enough for the soul for ever.

But shall not the saints have to do with something else in heaven, but only with God? O yes! I believe there shall be in heaven a communion of the blessed spirits of God, an association of the saints and angels of God: yet this shall not take away the sole enjoyment of God, that he should not be their *all in all*: for they shall not mind themselves, or their own good, as created things, but altogether God; they shall not love them, or one another as for themselves, but only for God; here we love God for himself, and it is a gracious love; but there we shall love ourselves for God, and it is a glorious love. Why, this is to enjoy God solely, in this respect, he is *all, and in all; whom have I in heaven but thee?*

Use. Here is a point enough to wean us from the world. Alas! the time is coming on apace, that all this world shall be dissolved, and then *God shall be all in all*. Here lies the saints happiness to have God immediately, God fully, and God solely; and will not saints prepare themselves for such a condition as this? You that have the world, *Use it as if not, for the fashion of this world passeth away,* 1 Cor. vii. 31. And you that have but a little to do with this world, improve that condition; surely it is your own fault if you have not more to do with God, for you have little else to take up your hearts; God may dwell and walk in your hearts without disturbance; *Give me neither poverty nor riches,* (saith the wise man upon that account) a mean condition is more capable of happiness, than that which overloads us with outward things; whilst others are casting up their accounts, you may say with David, *How precious are thy thoughts unto me, O God? How great is the sum of them?* Psal. cxxxix. 17. Whilst others are following their suits at courts of justice, you may follow all you have at a throne of grace, whilst others are numbering their flocks and herds, all your arithmetic may by employed to number your days, whilst others cannot get out of the clutches of the world, you may get into the embraces of your God; why, this is to prepare yourselves for fuller and fuller enjoyments of God, it is God will be *all in all*, and this is the very top of heaven's happiness; surely the less you have of the world now, if you can but improve it, the more you may have of heaven's happiness even upon earth; For what is the happiness of heaven, but the sole enjoyment of God? Christians! If you feel any inclinations, pantings, breathings after this world, give me leave to tell you, That you will never be happy till you have lost all, till you have no friends nor estates, no enjoyment but God alone; when all is done, when this world is nothing, when means shall cease both for bodies and souls, and when Christ shall cease his mediator's office, and the Son of man be subject to his Father then God shall be *all in all*.

SECT. X.

Of Christ's (notwithstanding this) being all in all *to his blessed, saved, and redeemed saints, to all eternity.*

10. FOR Christ's being *all in all*, to his blessed, saved, and redeemed saints to all eternity, we shall dilate in this section. Some may object, If God be *all in all*, What then becomes of Christ? Is not this derogatory to Jesus Christ? I answer, No, in noways: For,——

1. It is not the Father personally and only, but the Deity essentially and wholly, that is our *all in all:* when we say God is *all in all*, we do not exclude the Son, and Holy Ghost; for the whole Godhead is *all in all* to all the saints, as well as the first person in the trinity; the Father is *all*, and the Son is *all*, and the Holy Ghost is *all*; and in that Christ is God, and the Son of God, we may say of Christ, That he is *all in all:* only, the truth of this position is not from the human nature, but from the divine nature of Jesus Christ.

2. It is not derogatory to Christ, but rather it doth

doth exceedingly advance Christ in the thoughts of all his saints; while it was necessary Christ vailed his Deity, and when his work of mediation is fully finished, Christ then shall reveal his Deity to his saints more than ever before. In this respect might I say, If any person in the trinity receives more honour than other, Christ should have most, 'Every 'creature which is in heaven heard I saying, Bles-'sing, honour, glory, and power be unto him that 'sitteth on the throne, and unto the Lamb, for ever 'and ever,' Rev. v. 13. Not only unto God, but particularly *to the Lamb for ever and ever.* It is true, that God only, and God fully, and God immediately, is *all in all;* but doth that hinder that Jesus Christ is not also only, fully, and immediately, *all in all?* See how the scripture joins them together, which plainly argues, that they may consist, 'I saw no temple in the city, for the Lord 'God Almighty, and the Lamb, are the temple of 'it; and the city had no need of the sun, neither 'of the moon to shine in it, for the glory of God 'doth lighten it, and the Lamb is the light thereof,' Rev. xxi. 22, 23.

Now then as I have spoken of God, so that I may speak of Christ, and conclude all with Christ, I assert this doctrine, *That the glory of Christ, which the saints shall behold in Christ to all eternity, is their all in all.* In the discussion of which, I shall open these particulars. 1. What is the glory of Christ? 2. How the saints shall behold his glory? 3. Wherein is the comprehensiveness of this expression, that the beholding of Christ is our *all in all?*

1. What is the glory of Christ? I answer, That the glory of Christ is either human or divine.

1. There is an human glory, which in time was more especially conferred upon his manhood.

2. There is an essential or divine glory, which before time, and after time, even from everlasting to everlasting, issueth from the Godhead; I shall speak to both these, that we may rather take a view of Christ in these glories, (as we are able) wherein he will appear to his saints as their *all in all* to all eternity.

First, For his human glory, that is, either in regard of his soul or body; for his soul, Christ was from the first instant of his conception full of glory, because even then he received grace, not by measure as we do, but as comprehensor; he had the clear vision of God, even as the angels of heaven, which arose from that hypostatical union of two natures at his first conception. It is true, that by the special dispensation of God, the fulness of joy accompanying that glory was withheld from Christ in the time of his passion, and the redundancy of glory from his soul unto his body, was totally deferred until the exaltation of Christ; but Christ no sooner exalted, and set on the right hand of God, but immediately the interruption of joy in his soul, and the interception of glory from his soul to his body, was altogether removed. Then it was that his soul was filled with all joy, solace, pleasure, which could possibly flow from the sight of an object so infinitely pleasing, as is the essence, majesty, and glory of God. And then it was, that his body was replenished with as much glory as was proportionable unto the most vast capacity of any creature; not only his soul, but his body is a glorious creature; it is [*soma tes doxes,*] *A body of glory,* that is, a most glorious body in itself, and the spring of glory unto others, *Ought not Christ to have suffered these things, and so to enter into his glory?* Luke xxiv. 26. It is called *his glory,* as if it were appropriated unto him as the most eminent subject, and principal efficient of glory, as if he had the monopoly of glory: all the glory in heaven is in some sort *his glory.* Surely Christ's manhood is exalted unto an higher degree of glory, than the most glorious saint or angel ever was, or shall be; principalities, powers, mights, and dominions, fall short of his glory.

But some object, that the mediatory office of Christ shall wholly cease, and that the body and soul of Christ shall then be annihilated.

Indeed this was the opinion of Eutiches, That the human nature of Christ should be changed or converted into the divine; and thus he interprets that scripture, *Then shall the son also himself be subject, that God may be all in all,* 1 Cor. xv. 28. * ' What is the subjection, (saith he) but a con-'version of the creature into the very substance or 'essence of the Creator himself?' But we deny the

---

* Ut ipsam subjectionem, communicationem & conversionem credat futuram creaturæ in ipsam substantiam vel essentiam creatoris, Aug. de Trinit. Lib. 1. C. 8. Aret. in loc.

inter-

Interpretation: the Son, as man, shall be subject, and yet the manhood of Christ shall still remain; it is true, that his mediatory office shall wholly cease, but it follows not that therefore the manhood of Christ shall be converted or changed into the Deity. There may be other reasons for the continuation of his human nature, besides the execution of his mediatory office: As, 1. That the lustre of his Deity might shine through his humanity, and that thereby our very bodily eyes may come to see God, as much as is possible for any creature to see him. *I shall see him* (saith Job) *not with other, but with these same eyes*, Job xix. 27. 2. That the saints may see how the power of an infinite God can convey the lustre of his Deity into a creature; upon this account, I verily believe, that angels and men will be continually viewing of Jesus Christ, *He shall come to be admired of the saints*, 2 Thess. i. 10. He shall be admired (as we have heard) at the judgment-day; nor is that all, but the saints in heaven shall see with their eyes such excellencies in Christ, as they shall admire for ever; I say for ever, as much as they did at the first moment when they saw him: here, if we see any thing excellent, we admire at first, but after a while we do not so; but in heaven there will be so much excellency in Christ, that we shall admire as much to all eternity, as we did at the very first moment; there will be no abatement in glory of our being taken with the sight of the glory, in Jesus Christ. 3. That Christ, by his humanity may converse more freely, and familiarly with his brethren in his Father's house; oh! the intimacy that will be there betwixt Jesus Christ and his Christian saints! oh! the mutual rejoicing and delight that will be there betwixt Jesus Christ and his dearest darlings. As Christ from eternity rejoiced in the habitable part of his earth, so will the saints (his habitable earth) to all eternity rejoice in Christ; the eye of the saints in glory can never be off Christ as mediator and God: now the eye of the saints in glory shall never be off Christ as God and mediator then. Thus far of his human glory.

2dly, For his essential divine glory, it is that glory which Christ hath as God: this he never laid aside, but as the sun in a dark gloomy day may not send forth his beams, so Christ, the Sun of righteousness, in the time of his abode upon earth, (except a little glimpse only in his transfiguration) did not send forth his glorious beams; but hereafter the body or humanity of Christ shall not hinder the breaking forth of all his divine glory. No sooner the Son is subjected, and his mediatory office discharged, but Christ, as God, will manifestly put forth his more immediate glory to all his saints, *Behold, now we are the sons of God, and it doth not yet appear what we shall be; but we know when he shall appear we shall be like him, for we shall see him as he is*, 1 John iii. 2. Mark it, *when he shall appear*, at and after the resurrection-day, *we shall see him as he is*, (i. e.) We shall see the very essential glory of Jesus Christ. *Quest.* But what is the essential glory of Christ? *Ans.* I cannot answer, it is a question not to be resolved by all the men in the world; we know little of the glory of saints, How should we know any thing of the essential glory of Christ as God? The scriptures say, That *God spake to Moses face to face*, Exod. xxxiii. 11. yet God tells him, *Thou canst not see my face*, and he favours him so far as to tell him the reason, *For there shall no man see my face and live*, Ver. 20. q. d. No man in this life, he must first die, and be changed, and then he shall have a peculiar revelation of the divine majesty; then he shall *see him as he is*; but how that is, I cannot tell. Come, let us question this no farther; surely it is a mercy that this infinite glory is not discovered to us: for as a weak eye is not able to behold the sun, or to see it in *rota*, (as the school-men speak) in that wheel or circle wherein the sun doth run, but only in the beams of it; no more can we see Christ as God in his glorious essence, or in his essential glory, but only in the beams thereof, in his word and effects. If now we know so little of spirits and spirituals, oh! then, How little do we know of him who is the Father of spirits? I shall say no more therefore, let us be content to be ignorant of these things, till we enter into the confines of eternity.

Quest. But whether shall this glorious essence, or essential glory of Christ be more seen, or manifested, at, or after the day of judgment, than ever it was before? I answer,

Answ. I believe it will. * Some tell us of se-

---
* Dr. Annesly's *communion with God.*

veral

veral periods, wherein the glory of Christ is still more and more seen: as, 1. In this life we may see it in part; thus David speaks of himself, *My soul thirsteth for thee, my flesh longeth for thee, to see thy power and thy glory, as I have seen thee in the sanctuary,* but this sight is very dim, *We see only now as through a glass darkly,* 1 Cor. xiii. 12. The second period is betwixt our dissolution and resurrection; and then shall we see the essential glory of Christ more immediately and fully; our creeping apprehension of God shall then be elevated, and our distance from God shall then be shortened, and all the riddles of grace and of Jesus Christ shall then be opened. This sight is so great, that if a soul should come from heaven to declare it, neither could that soul express it, nor we understand it: we read of Lazarus, whose soul Christ returned unto his body, whom much people of the Jews came purposely to see, that they might hear stories of the other world, but not a word from him of any such matter: Paul's rapture may satisfy with the reason of it, he heard there [*arbreta remata*], *wordless words,* 2 Cor. xii. 4. such words as could not possibly be repeated on earth; and yet all this is but the second step to the full vision of Christ's essential glory. The third period is at the resurrection, and during the time of the last judgment, and then we shall see more of his glory. Camero affirms, 'That it is no curiosity to say, 'that the saints and angels in heaven had a new 'glory of the exhibition of Christ, the great my-'stery of the incarnation being thereby better 'known.' And we may as safely affirm, that the saints shall have a new glory, by new visions of the glory of Christ at the day of resurrection; they shall then see the solemnity of heaven's glory carried on by Christ in his glorious actings; and all that ever the soul saw before in being with Christ in heaven till the resurrection, shall be swallowed up with the sight of this glory of Christ at the resurrection-day. The last period is after the resurrection, and that shall continue even to all eternity; now, all the manifestations of Christ's glory before this, are but as a few green ears rubbed in our hands; so that the full crop, or the full harvest is yet behind. But this is that, (which as we told you before) we cannot tell, tho' we had the tongues of men and angels. Thus far of the first point, What is the glory of Christ?

2. How shall the saints behold this glory? I answer, As Christ hath a twofold glory, so there is a twofold manner of beholding it, (i. e.) Ocular and mental.

1*st.* There is an ocular vision, a sight of Christ with our very eyes, *Whom I shall see for myself, and mine eyes shall behold him,* Job xix. 27. With these eyes in our heads, we shall one day behold the human glory of Christ: I doubt not we shall behold the beauty of heaven, the shining bodies of the saints, but above all, our very eyes shall delightfully contemplate Christ's glorious body; and indeed this shall drown all the other sights. If any think, that Christ's glorious body shall be too intensive, and too extraordinary a brightness for our weak eyes; let such consider. That,—

1. The eye in heaven shall be glorified; now glorification adds a singular excellency to the faculties, it advanceth the faculties, and raiseth them to an higher pitch of excellency: glorification adds a greater capacity to the eye than ever it had before. In this world there is a difference in our eyes and sight; a man of a clear sight sees more things, and more of every thing, than a dark sight doth: so a glorified eye sees more of things, than our eyes now can see. It shall be enlarged exceedingly to take in objects which now it cannot receive; glorification adds strength to the faculties both internal and external, so that the eye shall be able to look on the glory of Christ, not with difficulty, but with contentment; in this world every sense we have is apt to be destroyed by excellent objects, and the more excellent and transcendant the object is, the more it hurts and destroys the sense; as the sun by its brightness darkens the eye, and other things by mighty sounds bring deafness on the ear. Paul indeed had a vision of glory, but because his faculties were not glorified, he was, he knew not how, *whether in the body, or out of the body,* whether alive or dead, he did not know: certainly the sight of the glory of the other world would amaze, distract, and destroy us, if we had a sight of it as now we are; but in heaven the eye shall have great pleasure in beholding the brightest light, because it shall be advanced to the highest pitch of strength that may be.

2. As the eye shall be glorified, so it shall act in a glorified body, and this will make the sight of the glory of Christ instead of hurting us, to leave upon

us a more sweet, enlivening, and powerful impression. By this means all the impediments that hinder the conveyance of divine influences from that heavenly object will be removed. To illustrate this, let the most excellent sight be set before a man that is defective in his bodily state, and it doth not take him, what should a sick man do with such things? He makes nothing of the most pleasant gardens, orchards, buildings, nor of the most glorious sights that are; when he is sick, they are but sick things to him, and of none effect; but in heaven the body shall be glorified, and stript of all corruptions and imperfections; so that there shall be no bar unto the influences of the glory of Christ which shall there be seen.

3. As there shall be a glorified eye acting in a glorified body, so it shall be acted by a glorified Spirit; the eye is but the organ, or instrument of sight, and without the Spirit, would convey no more than a glass doth; it is the spirit of a man that gives life to vision, it is the spirit of a man that discovers things, and sets them forth in their worth, virtues and ends; now in heaven the spirits of men shall be glorified, and enabled to perform all those offices in perfection; so that when a man shall look on the man Christ Jesus, by virtue of a glorified spirit, he shall see more, know more, taste more, than any other can. As a man of understanding, when he looks on a diamond, or a wedge of gold, he hath other apprehensions of it, and a farther touch upon his spirit, than a beast, or a child in a cradle hath; so, where the sight of the eye is acted by a glorified mind, it takes in more from the sight of every thing which is to be seen, (unexpressibly more) than what can be done here by the most sanctified spirit in the world. Now, in these respects Christ's glorified body, (tho' it be the brightest visible thing in the heaven of heavens) yet may it be the object of the eyes of saints, for they shall have glorified eyes in glorified bodies, and acted by their glorified spirits.

2*dly*, There is a mental vision, a sight of Christ by the eyes of our understandings; and surely this exceeds the former, the eye of the body is only on the body of Christ, but the eye of the soul is on the body and soul, on the humanity and Deity of Jesus Christ. This is the very top of heaven, when saints shall be enlightned with a clear and glorious sight of Christ as God; divines usually call it, *Beatifical vision*.

Quest. But how shall saints behold the glorious essence, or Godhead of Christ?

Answ. 1. Some say, Christ as God, or the Godhead of Christ, shall be known by the humanity of Christ; such a lustre of his Deity shall shine thro' his humanity, as that thereby, and by no other means shall the essential glory of Christ appear.

2. Others say, That besides the humanity of Christ, there shall be a species representing the divine essence of Christ, and a light of glory elevating the understanding by a supernatural strength; and that thereby the glorious essence of Christ shall be discovered.

3. Others say, That the divine essence shall be represented to the glorified understanding, not by Christ's humanity, nor by any species, but immediately by itself; yet they also require a light of glory to elevate and fortify the understanding, by reason of its weakness, and infinite disproportion and distance from the incomprehensible Deity.

4. Others hold, That to the clear vision of Christ as God, there is not required a sight of Christ's humanity, as the first suppose; nor a species representing the divine essence, as the second suppose; nor any created light elevating the understanding, as the third suppose; but only a change of the natural order of knowing: it is sufficient. (say they) that the divine essence be immediately represented to a created understanding; which, though it cannot be done according to the order of nature, as experience tells us, (for so we conceive things as first having passed the sense and imagination) yet it may be done according to the order of divine grace. I shall not enter into these scholastical disputes, it is enough for a sober man to know, that in heaven we shall see him *face to face*, 1 Cor. xiii. 12 *His servants shall serve him, and they shall see his face*, Rev. xxii. 3, 4.

Quest. His face, What is that? I answer,

An. 1. They shall see Christ as God, of the same essence with the Father, and the Holy Ghost, and yet a distinct person from them both; they shall see the unity in trinity, and trinity in unity; they shall see how the Son is begotten of the Father, and how the Holy Ghost proceeds from the Father, and the Son; they shall see the difference between the generation of the Son, and procession of the Spirit. These are mysteries in which we are

are blind, and know very little or nothing; but in seeing his face, we shall see all these.

2. They shall see Christ as the first Being, or principle of all the good that is in the world, *They shall see how all things were made by him, and without him was not any thing made that was made*, John i. 3. They shall see all the good in the creature as flowing from Christ, and as contained in the absolute perfection of Christ's divine nature; they shall see in one Christ all the excellencies of all the creatures united, which is indeed to see him in his eminency, if there be any beauty, riches, honour, goodness in any creature, that is eminently, transcendantly, and originally in Christ, and that shall be seen.

3. They shall see Christ, in all his ways, counsels, decrees, executions and transactions, from everlasting to everlasting; that great business of election and reprobation will then be discovered: it is an expression of Augustine, 'They shall then 'see the reason why one is elected, and another 'reprobated; why one is rich, and another poor:' they shall then see all the works that ever God did, or that ever God will do; it is not yet 6000 years since the creation of the world, and what is 6000 years to eternity? Certainly the truth of Origen's opinion, * ' touching the existency of o- ' ther worlds before this, and the future succession ' of other worlds after this,' will then be known. If no worlds before this, yet if God in Christ hath done such great things in only 6000 years, what he may do in the next 6000 years, and so in the next 6000 years, who now can tell? We see not these things, but the saints, in seeing the face of Christ, shall see all things.

4. They shall see Christ in all his glory, ways, counsels, decrees, executions and transactions, as working for their happiness. Now this is more than the former; there is a great deal of difference in seeing an object, as excellent in itself, and in seeing an object, as conducing to my happiness: as one that is a stranger, and another that is an heir, rides over such a demeine; the stranger rides over it, and takes delight to see the situation, rivers, trees and fruits; but the heir looks upon it after another manner, ' This (saith he) is the land ' for which my father laid out so much, and all to ' enrich me, and all to bestow it on me, as my in-' heritance.' So the saints admitted into the glorious sight of Christ, they take not only a view of Christ, of the essential glory of Christ, of the transactions of Christ, things excellent in themselves, but they see, all these as to make them happy; they say of Christ, and of all his actings, *These are mine, and for my happiness*: a stranger may look upon a king, and see beauty, and majesty, and glory, and honour in him; but the queen looks upon the king and his beauty as her own; so the saints look upon the king of heaven, they see Christ, and all in Christ, as their own, to make them happy for ever and ever.

5. They shall *see Christ as he is*, 1 John iii. 2. But what, do we not *see him now as he is*? Oh no! we now see him not as he is indeed and truth, but only as he is in hearsay and report; we now see him only as he is shadowed out to us in the gospel of peace; and what is the gospel, but the portraiture of the king, which he sent to another land, to be seen by his bride? So kings and queens on earth woo one another; whilst the bride is on earth, she never sees him as he is in his best sabbath-royal-robe of immediate glory, she seeth him rather by the second hand, (i. e) by messengers, words, and mediation, he rather sends his portraiture, than comes himself; but in heaven the saints *see him as he is*, they see Christ himself in his own very person, they see the red and white in his own face, they see all the inside of Christ, and thousands of excellencies shall then be revealed, that we see not now, the mysteries of that glorious ark shall then be opened, his incarnation, his two natures in one person, his suffering as man, and his sitting in the seat of God as God, all these shall be seen.

6. They shall see Christ without interruption, and without intermission to all eternity. If once the eye be set on the face of Jesus Christ, it will never be taken off again. Some conceive this to be the reason why the saints in heaven can never fall away, because they shall have a continual view of Christ as God: surely to have but one glimpse of Christ in this respect, though it were gone presently, it were a great happiness beyond all that the world affords; it was sometimes the desire of a philosopher to see the nature of the sun, though he were to be burnt by it; so if Christ should but

grant

---

* Orig. l. *de principiis* 3. c. 5.

grant us this happiness, *You shall come to see me, but the sight of me will destroy you,* this were a desirable thing; but to have such an excellent glorious sight as shall never end, that Christ should not only pass by, but stand still, so as the soul shall never lose his sight; O how glorious is this! if a man do but look upon a delightful object, he is loth to have the eye drawn from it; surely the eyes of saints shall be eternally opened to see the divine nature of Christ; turn them which way they will, they shall never turn aside the busied eyes of their understanding from off the Deity of Christ; he fills heaven; he is that fair tree of life, the branches whereof, in all these huge and capacious borders of heaven, have not room to grow in, *for the heaven of heavens cannot contain him.* O the wonders of heaven! there is Abraham, Moses, Elias, the prophets, the apostles, and all the glorified martyrs; but the saints have neither leisure, nor hearts to feed themselves with beholding of creatures; no, no; all the eyes of heaven (which are a fair and numerous company) are upon (only, only upon) the Lord Jesus Christ; the father hath no leisure to look over his shoulder to his son; the husband hath no leisure to look over his shoulder to his wife; Christ takes all eyes off from such created things; surely it is enough for the saints and angels in heaven to study Christ for all eternity; it shall be their only labour to read Christ, to smell Christ, to hear, see, and taste Christ, to love, joy, and enjoy Jesus Christ for ever and ever. Thus far of the second point, how the saints shall behold the glory of Christ.

3. Wherein is the comprehensiveness of this expression, That *the beholding of Christ is our all in all?* I answer,———

1. It comprehends the immediate seeing and looking upon all that majesty and glory which Jesus Christ hath. In this sense Paul took it when he complained, *We walk by faith, not by sight,* 2 Cor. v. 7. *q. d.* On earth we have faith, and in heaven we have sight; it is some comfort that now I see Jesus Christ by faith, but comparatively to that sight which the saints have in heaven it is as no comfort at all; Alas! I am not, I cannot be satisfied so long as I am absent from the Lord, I look upon myself as one from home: and as a prince in a strange land sits down sadly, because he hath not the sight of his father, so I am forced to complain, O! I cannot see my Lord, *I would fain behold him, I am a stranger on earth, a pilgrim in this world, I am not where I would be, I am absent from him whom I most desire; O! I desire to be dissolved, and to be with Christ; I walk with him here on earth by faith, but to walk with him in the streets of heaven by sight is far better; O! I long, I pant, I breathe, I desire, I think ev'ry day a year, and every year an age, till I be in heaven, at home, in my father's arms, that I may behold and see him, and that immediately, I say immediately in his glory.* This is one way of beholding Christ, it is an immediate sight.

2. It comprehends the fruition and enjoyment of Christ in his glory. Surely the saints shall not be meer idle spectators of the glory of Christ, but they shall enjoy him, and be taken into fellowship with him: it was said of Moses, that he did see the land of Canaan, but he was not admitted into it; it is otherwise with the saints, they shall see heaven, and they shall enter into heaven, *Come thou faithful servant, and enter into thy master's joy,* not only behold it, but enter into it; they must behold Christ, and take possession of Christ, and enjoy him as their own, and thus the word *to see,* or *behold,* is often used in scripture, *Except a man be born again he cannot see the kingdom of God,* John iii. 3. (i. e.) he cannot enjoy it; and *Father, I will, that those whom thou hast given me be with me where I am, that they may behold my glory,* John xvii. 24. (i. e.). That they may enjoy my glory; for Christ is not only glorious in himself, but he is the spring of glory unto others: now, in this respect, more especially is Christ our *all in all;* he is *all* in himself, and if we enjoy him, he is *all in all* unto us: to see a little into the state and condition of the saints in glory in this enjoyment of Christ.———

1. They possess Christ as their own, they go to Christ, and lay hold on him, saying, *Thou art mine.* It was indeed the language of the spouse whilst yet on earth, *I am my beloved's, and my beloved is mine.* There is a right and a propriety made over to her in her betrothing unto Christ; but after the solemnity of the marriage is over, the possession is then more full: when once the spouse comes to behold Christ in his kingdom, she may then go boldly to her beloved, and say, 'All I see is my 'own, I had thee in hope, but now hope is va-
'nished,

'nished, and actual enjoyment comes in place; lo, now I have thee in my eye, and in my heart, and in my hands, and in my arms; and as nothing shall separate us now, for all our enemies are trod under foot, so never will I part with thee, so far as to be out of my eye, I will still behold thee, and in beholding I will still possess thee, for thou art mine own.'

2. They have the use of what they possess, and this is an infinite good to the saints; they shall not only possess Christ, but they shall have what use they will of Christ, and of all in Christ; they shall, as they please, make use of his humanity, and of his Deity, of his glorious essence, and of his glorious attributes; O wonder! that a saint should come to Christ, and say, 'O my Lord, thou art mine, and my pleasure is to make use of thy wisdom, power, and mercy;' and that Christ should reply, and say, *Welcome, sweet soul, use me and all my glory as thou pleasest*. Why, thus it is, even as a friend will say to his friend, 'Make use of all I have as your own;' so will Christ come to his saints, and bid them make use of all his riches, glory and excellency, even as they will, even to the utmost that they are capable of.

3. They have the sweet and comfort of all they use, and this makes up a complete enjoyment. In things below we may have the possession of them, and the use thereof, but if we have not the sweet and comfort of that we use, we cannot be said truly or fully to enjoy those things; what is the possession and use of meat and drink, if we taste not the sweet of them? Hence God is said to *give us all things richly to enjoy*; no creature can give us richly to enjoy another; one may give us such and such things wherein there may be comfort, but he cannot give us comfort in such things, it is only God can give us that; it is so with the saints in glory, God gives them all things, yea, Christ gives himself to them, as *all in all*, to enjoy him richly, fully, sweetly, to the very uttermost. This is another way of beholding Christ, it is a fruition or enjoyment of Christ, wherein, and whereby he is our all in all.

3. It comprehends all the effects and consequents of such a beholding of his glory, which are infinite delight and complacency in the will, and all praise and thanksgiving in the mouths of his saints. For the first, It is disputed, whether eternal happiness be more in the acts of the understanding, or of the will; And some conclude, that it is principally in the will, because that it is an active appetite and predominant in a man, indeed the whole of a man. Oh! the joy, delight, and complacency that will arise in the will, upon the seeing and beholding of Jesus Christ! they shall delight infinitely in the essential glory of Christ, and in the declared glory of Christ; they shall delight in all that glory that is reflected upon Christ by all his creatures in heaven; they shall delight in his presence, and in his love: *Christ is all delights*, and how then should they but delight in Christ? For the second, As they delight in their wills, so will their mouths be filled with praises: we read of saints and angels continually praising God in heaven, there shall be none of our duties of mourning, fasting, praying and humbling; the acts of patience and justifying faith shall cease in heaven; but the duty of praising and glorifying God will continue to all eternity. Methinks I see the saints following the Lamb; methinks I hear the familiar converses betwixt Christ and them, as Christ opens himself to them, so they to him: First, He begins, 'Oh! my dear saints, you are they, for whom, before all time, I decreed this heaven, and now you see the execution of my decrees; whilst the world stood, I was still carrying on the work of your salvation, either in doing or suffering, or in successive works, applying my doings and sufferings, my active and passive obedience to your persons; and now the world is at an end, you see the end of my work, and the end of your faith, which is the eternal salvation of your souls; Oh! now I have my wish, and you have your happiness; here you and I will live together, that I may for ever behold you, and that you may for ever behold me, and my glory.' Which no sooner said, but methinks I hear all those innumerable saints in heaven to answer, *Worthy is the Lamb that was slain to receive power, and riches, and wisdom, and strength, and honour, and glory, and blessing*, Rev. v. 12. *And therefore unto him that loved us, and washed us from our sins in his own blood, and hath made us kings unto God his Father, to him be glory and dominion for ever and ever, Amen*. Rev. i. 5, 6 Yea, methinks I hear every creature in heaven say, *Blessing, honour, glory, and power be unto him that sitteth on the throne*

throne, and unto the Lamb for ever and ever, Amen. Rev. v. 13. Why, this is their continual work in heaven, they have nothing else to do, but with joy and gladness to sing forth the praises of God, and of Christ, and that his mercy endureth for ever. And this likewise is comprehended under that notion of the saints *beholding of Christ,* which completely makes up the proposition asserted, 'That "Christ, or the glory of Christ, which the saints 'shall behold to all eternity, is their all in all.

Thus far we have propounded the object, which is Jesus carrying on the salvation of his saints, in his coming again to earth, and taking them up with himself and his angels into heaven; our next work is to direct you how to look unto Jesus in this respect, and then we have done.

CHAP. II. SECT. I.

Of knowing Jesus as carrying on the great work of our salvation in his second coming.

WHAT looking is, and what it contains, we have often heard, and that in these respects we may look on Jesus.

1. Let us know Jesus, carrying on the saints salvation in his second coming, and taking them to heaven. Many glorious excellent things, many precious passages, many high and heavenly carriages are in this transaction: Is it not of high concernment, that he that now sits at God's right hand interceding for us, should thence come again to judge the world, and after judgment take up his saints with him into glory? Can we read of the several actings of this general assize, and not desire to read on still? Nay, is not all our reading mixt with admiration of every passage? Come! wonder, and sit, and pause, and stop at every word; stay, and wonder, and adore that light, which appears in any beam of truth, and in the admiration of that truth which doth appear, cast thyself down at the feet of Christ, and cry out, *O! the depth of glory, and majesty, and goodness, and grace in thee! O! the riches of love, that thou shouldest let out thyself in these several admirable dispensations!* Come, be exact in this study, gather up all the crumbs and filings of this gold; the least beams of the glory of Christ (especially as it shines and glitters at his second coming) have so much light, and love, and splendor in them, as that they will be very sweet to look upon them: every piece or part of this knowledge will be of very special use and worth; yea, the low and imperfect knowledge of this mystery is of infinite more value than the high and perfect knowledge of ten thousand things besides. And one thing (O my soul!) let me tell thee, it is possible for thee to attain a very sweet and satisfactory degree of this very knowledge. And therefore study close, run over again all that hath been spoken, and dig yet deeper into that glorious mine; content not thyself with a bare discovery of that gold ore, which is only upon the superficies or top of the mind, but go so far as to find out the inward, spiritual, and experimental knowledge, which the saints, by the light of the Spirit, may come to attain. O! study Christ in his second coming to judgment.

SECT. II.
Of considering Jesus in that respect.

2. LET us consider Jesus, carrying on this work of salvation at his second coming. It is not enough to know, but we must meditate, and seriously consider of it. A meer student may know Christ, and study Christ, as he knows and studies other things; he may heap together many notions concerning Christ, and his coming to judgment, but he hath no impression of the holiness of Christ upon his heart; and, in this respect, he is a stranger to Christ, and to all his actings; alas! he studies Christ, but he doth not rightly, seriously, and inwardly consider of Christ; he doth not look unto Jesus, as one that looks to the pattern, or as one that looks to his refuge, hope, and help; true and spiritual consideration is a serious matter; it is not some few and fleeting thoughts that are the discharge of this work, but thoughts resting, dwelling, fixing, and staying upon Christ, until they come to some profitable issue; O! it is another manner of business than many are aware of, it is a thinking with thought upon thought, it is a reiteration and multiplication of the thoughts of the mind upon the subject propounded, so the scripture expresseth it, *I looked on all the works that my hands had wrought;* and, in the next verse, *I returned to see,* Eccles. ii. 11, 12. *He looked upon,* and *considered* his works, and he *returned to behold* them; he thought on them before, but now he returned to think; he renewed his thoughts upon the matter, and took a new view

of them. Indeed when the understanding works seriously and spiritually, it will fetch things into sight, and not only so, but it will hold them there, and fasten upon them, and when they are gone, it will fetch them again, *My soul hath them still in remembrance*, Lam. iii. 20. My soul in remembring doth remember them, and will not off till the end be obtained; so a man eyes Christ, till he have more of Christ, more of his presence, and more of his light, and more of his favour, and more of his image. O! let this be our work, let us thus consider Jesus in reference to his second coming to judgment. And that we may do it in order,—

1. Consider Christ's preparing for judgment; realize it, as if thou sawest or heardest the same; no sooner the time determined which God hath appointed, but Christ commands, 'Make ready ye angels to wait upon me, and make ready, ye glorious souls, that now are with me; it is the Father's pleasure, and it is my pleasure to go down into the nether world, and to call before me all the men and women that ever lived in it; there will I pass my doom upon all flesh, and reward every one, good and bad, according to his works.' Oh! what a shout may I imagine in heaven at this news! what joy is in the souls of saints, that now they must go to their bodies, and enter into them, that both their souls and bodies, which sometimes lived together, may now dwell together with Christ in glory, and never part more? If those that live on earth are commanded by Christ, *To lift up their heads because their redemption draweth nigh*; How much more shall they joy in heaven, who also have *waited for the adoption*, to wit, *the redemption of their bodies?* Rom. viii. 23. That now the long-look'd for day is come, it is come; O! the exultation of the saints and angels at this tidings! this is worthy a pause, a *Selah* to be set upon it.

2. Consider Christ's coming to judgment. All now in readiness, the Son of God comes forth with all his glorious attendants, *For the Son of man shall come in the glory of his Father, with his angels*, Matth. xvi. 27. And with the souls of saints, that for a time have been in paradise. Oh! what a goodly sight is here! in this meditation I may see with John, *the new Jerusalem coming down from God out of heaven, prepared as a bride adorned for her husband*, Rev. xxi. 2. Down comes Christ, and down come the angels, and down come the spirits of the just made perfect; and as they come along, see how they shake the heavens, and dim, and dark the very lights of heaven; see what a flood of fire goes before them, see how they pass into the cloud, where Christ makes a stand, and erects a throne for himself to sit on. Sure it will be a gilded glorious cloud, when Christ, with all his celestial servants, shall sit upon it; a morning's cloud, gilded with the beams of the sun, is admirably fair and shining; But what a shining cloud is that, where the Sun of righteousness, with all his morning stars, do sit and shine? Here is enough to dazzle my eyes, and to take up my thoughts; O my soul think on it!

3. Consider Christ's summons of the elect to come under judgment. No sooner in the cloud, but *he shall send his angels with a great sound of a trumpet, and they shall gather together his elect from the four winds, from one end of heaven to the other*, Matth. xxiv. 31. Will not this be a strange sight, to see Christ a coming, with trumpets sounding before him, causing all the dead to awaken out of their sleeps of death? The very sound of this trumpet was ever in Jerome's ears, *Arise, ye dead, and come to judgment*, and no question but thy ears shall be filled with the blast thereof; the trumpet shall sound that shall be heard over all the world, and then shall the dead arise out of their graves, and every saint's soul shall re-enter into his own body, by virtue of the resurrection of Christ their head. Can I pass this meditation without some reflection on myself! O my soul! how joyfully wilt thou greet thy body, when thou shalt enliven it again? How wilt thou say, O my dear sister! whom I left behind me in the dust when I went to heaven, how sweet is thy carcase, how comely is thy countenance? How do I enter into thee, and animate thee, and I will never more leave thee; thou wast my yoke-fellow in the Lord's labours, and my companion in persecution and wrong; now shall we enter together into our master's joy: see, lift up thy head, behold, Jesus Christ yonder, sitting in the cloud, and, lo! here the angels waiting on us, and coming to take us with the rest of saints into the air, to meet our Redeemer there. Could I but realize the summons, this resurrection, this meeting of the soul and body, and going with the angels into the judgment-seat, oh! how would it work, and what work would it make within!

4. Con-

4. Consider Christ and the saints meeting at the judgment-day. Oh! how shall the saints look, and stare, and gaze at the beauty of Jesus Christ? Oh! how will they break out into admiration at the first view of these glories, which never before appeared on this side heaven? Is not this he *(will they say)* of whom we read so often, That he was fairer than the sons of men? That he was white and ruddy, the chiefest among ten thousands; That his countenance was as Lebanon, excellent as the cedars, glorious as when the sun shineth in his strength? But was ever the half told us, of what now we see and behold? O! the super-excellent transcendent beauty of this Son of righteousness! O! the treasures of loveliness in this Jesus Christ never seen before! and thus as they admire, so they adore; now they begin those Hallelujahs that never, never shall have an end; they fall at the feet of Christ, and the Lord Christ takes them up with his hands, and folds them in his arms: oh! what mutual reciprocal salutations are these betwixt Christ and his members? Oh my head! and, oh my body! oh my husband! and, oh my spouse! oh my dear! and, oh my darling! never two lovers met with such heat of love as Christ and his saints; ' Come, saith Christ, and sit you down here ' at my right hand, and let the world be on my ' left hand; it was otherwise with you in your life-' time, my gold, and my jewels were then cast in-' to the dust; you were then clothed with infamy, ' and the vilest of men were then gilded with ho-' nour; but now I will set all right, now the dust ' shall be swept away, and the jewels of my king-' dom shall be gathered up: now the goats shall ' be driven into the desart, and you, who are the ' sheep, shall be brought into my fold.' Oh my soul! what a meeting is this? What a sight will this be, to behold the saints in this condition, and thyself amongst them? Couldest thou but realize this one very passage, it were enough to quench thy lust, and to kindle a flame of pure love in thy heart to Jesus Christ; it is a quickning, rousing, raising, rejoicing consideration.

5. Consider Christ sentencing his saints for eternal glory. Then shall the books be opened, and all the good works of the saints shall be revealed and made known; and then shall the Judge, from his throne of majesty, (in the sight and hearing of all the world) pronounce that sentence, *Come, ye blessed of my Father, inherit the kingdom prepared for you from the foundation of the world*, Matth. xxv. 34. *q. d.* ' Come my saints, come with me ' into glory; come now from labour to rest, from ' disgrace to glory, from the jaws of death, to the ' joys of eternal life; for my sake ye have been ' railed on, reviled and cursed; but now it shall ' appear to all those cursed Esaus, that you are the ' true Jacobs that shall receive the blessing, and ' blessed shall you be; come now and possess with ' me the inheritance of heaven, where you shall ' be for love, sons; for birth-right, heirs; for ' dignity, kings; for holiness, priests: come, you ' may boldly enter in, for my Father hath prepar-' ed and kept it for you, ever since the first foun-' dation of the world was laid.'

O my soul! dost thou not remember, when sometimes thou hast been at the feet of Christ in the beauty of holiness, and there tookest in those droppings of his Spirit, which were better to thee than the feasts of kings? Dost thou not remember, when sometimes thou hast had the very beams of light darted from the face of Jesus Christ, when he whispered to thy soul the forgiveness of thy sins, saying, *Fear not, thy sins shall not hurt thee, I am thy salvation?* Oh what joy was then! what meltings, movings, stirrings, leapings of heart were then in thy bosom! but was that joy any thing to this, or to be compared with this? That was a drop, but here is an ocean, here is fulness of joy; oh! what leapings of heart, what ravishments will be within, when thou shalt see thyself in the arms of Christ, and shalt receive words of life from the mouth of Christ, in the face of all the world? What a thing will this be, when Christ shall pass a sentence of death on others, and speak words of life unto thee! when thou shalt see him frowning upon the world, (and, oh! those frowns will break the heart) and shall behold him smiling in the fulness of his love upon thyself! that Christ at such a time should be delighting thee with all the embraces of love, and with this sweet invitation to heaven, *Come thou blessed, inherit the kingdom*, it were enough to spirit a soul half dead: the very meditation of this must needs be sweet.

6. Consider Christ and the saints judging the rest of the world. No sooner are the saints sentenced, but Christ turns to the wicked, and bids them *go into everlasting fire*; in which sentence the saints shall

shall join with Christ himself; *Do ye not know that the saints shall judge the world?* 1 Cor. vi. 2. When the saints appear, it is not only by a summons, but with commission; not only to be judged, but to judge; not only shall they stand at Christ's right hand, but they shall sit down on the throne of the Son of God, to judge the wicked angels and the world. O the torment! O the vexation of wicked men and devils, when they shall see those very men whom they scorned, oppressed, and persecuted, to be now advanced not only to glory, but to be their judges! it is as if some nobleman had wronged some poor man, and that the king should therefore deliver the nobleman into the power of the poor man to take his own revenge. Surely *the ungodly shall see this, and be grieved; he shall gnash with his teeth for indignation, and melt away,* Ps. cxii. 10. But on the contrary, *The righteous shall rejoice when he seeth the vengeance, he shall wash his feet in the blood of the ungodly,* Psalm lvii. 10.

O my soul, dost thou believe this truth? And art thou confident that thou shalt sit with Christ on his very throne to judge the world? Why then be joyful in afflictions, exercise thou patience in the censures and judgments of the world, know thou for thy comfort, that there is a turn and time of judging, and therefore say, *With me it is a small matter that I should be judged of you, or of man's judgment,* as the original hath it, *of man's day,* 1 Cor. iv. 3. Is it not enough to command patience, if God's day be at hand, when I shall judge my unjust judges? Hark what the apostle saith, *Be patient, brethren, unto the coming of the Lord; behold, the husbandman waiteth for the precious fruit of the earth, and hath long patience for it, until he receive the early and latter rain: be ye also patient, stablish your hearts; for the coming of the Lord draweth nigh.——Behold, the judge standeth before the door,* James v. 7, 8, 9. Come exercise patience, let the world be judging; if they will needs slander, reproach and persecute thy soul, they had better abuse any judge on earth than thee: tho' thou art the poorest, weakest, meanest, of God's saints upon the earth, they will know one day, that they have abused their own judge in abusing thee; and therefore be thou quiet, silent, patient. Say as David, ' Let him alone, and let him curse, ' yea, let him judge, for the Lord hath bidden ' him; it may be the Lord will look on mine af-' fliction, and will requite good for his judging this ' day: this is his day, but the day of the Lord is ' my day, and then shall I sit with Christ on his ' throne to judge the world.' Oh! the sweet that I may suck from this honey-comb, of Christ and his saints judging the world!

7. Consider Christ and his saints going up into heaven. No sooner hath he done his work with the world, and sent them away, but then he shall conduct all his flock like a faithful shepherd to their fold; then shall he go with all his troops following him into heaven. Hath not Christ said so? *If I go away, I will come again, and receive you unto myself, that where I am, there you may be also,* John xiv. 3. O those songs of joy, and shouts of praise that will fill the world at that day! and thus as they go along, heaven opens unto them, and they enter in; what welcomes they have there is past my telling; if we may imagine and guess, O the welcome that Christ will give! ' Come my spouse, ' and come, my dear, come, all my saints; here ' be those mansions that I went before to prepare ' and make ready for you; here be those ever-' lasting habitations wherein you and I will dwell ' together; here is your father's house, the build-' ing of the wall is all of jasper, and the worst ' piece of it is all of pure gold, like unto clear glass, ' Rev. xxi. 18. Why this is your home, your ' house made without hands; here you and I will ' spend our time, eternity itself, in joying, enjoy-' ing, and beholding each other.' And as thus Christ salutes them, so will the angels, those created citizens of heaven salute them too; for if joy be in heaven at the conversion of one sinner, what joy will there be at the glorification of all these saints? What welcome entertainment will the angels give to these new guests at their first entrance into heaven?

O my soul! if thou art one of them that shall have this welcome, What wilt thou say when thou art admitted in thither, if weeping were in heaven wouldest thou not weep for joy? Sure these things are no fictions of man's brain, but truths and realities; and as they are true and real, so they are exceeding full of joy: all the excellencies of this world are but a dream in comparison of them; even the sun in its brightness is but darkness to this glory that shall then be seen. Come, think over these things, and be so enlarged in thy thoughts,

that

that before they go, thou mayest feel the sweet, and taste of the goodness of the Lord.

8. Consider all the several transactions that will follow in heaven; then will Christ present all his elect to God his Father; then will he give in all his commissions which he hath received from his Father; *Then will the Son himself be subject to the Father, that God may be all in all.* I cannot stay to enlarge on these; only remember, though God be *all in all*, that excludes not Christ, for he also is *all in all* to all his saints, even to all eternity; immediate visions and fruitions of Christ, as God, is the very top of heaven's joy: Christ is *all*, and *in all*; Christ is the centre of heaven's happiness; Christ is the well-spring that fills the capacities of saints and angels; Christ is the object of happiness itself, there is as much happiness in Christ as happiness is; whatever belongs to glory is in Christ, *in him dwelleth all the fulness*. Whatever excellency is in heaven it is in Christ, not only in perfection, but connection; for all those excellencies meet together, and rest in Christ. Christ is all good things to all his saints in heaven; he is beauty to their eyes, musick to their ears, honey to their mouths, perfume to their nostrils, health to their bodies, joy to their souls, light to their understandings, and content to their wills; he is time without sliding, society without lothing, desire without fainting, *Alpha* and *Omega*, the beginning and ending; wanting both, needing neither, yet the author of them both: he is *all in all*, from one, not all. Even all the strength, wit, pleasure, virtue, colours, beauties, harmony, and goodness that are in men, beasts, fishes, fowls, trees, herbs, and all creatures, are nothing but sparkles of those things which are in Christ. Christ himself will then supply their use; so that the best creatures which now serve the saints, shall not have the honour to serve them then; *There will be no need of the sun, nor of the moon to shine in that city; for the glory of God doth lighten it, and the Lamb is the light thereof,* Rev. xxi. 23.

And hence the beholding of Christ is the *all in all* to the glorified saints; this was Christ's prayer, *Father, I will that those whom thou hast given me, be with me where I am;* to what end? *That they may behold my glory,* John xvii. 24. Christ's heavenly presence is conspicuous, he is not present as some things that are not seen, and yet are present, but his presence is, or certainly it shall be conspicuous to all his saints: when he was in the world his glory was covered under a mean outside, he was like a bright light in a dark lantern, and there were very few that knew him then; but in heaven he shall be as a cabinet opened, or as the sun in his full glory, 'We shall know him, as we are known, 'and behold him face to face; we shall see him as 'he is,' 1 John iii. 2. Nor only will he be conspicuous, but his presence shall be vital; a stone may be with us, and seen clearly, but there is little in the sight of that; in the beholding of Christ there will be an acting of kindness upon the saints, there will be visions with life and dear refreshing. O the influences that the sight of Christ will have on his saints in heaven! nor only will he be conspicuous and vital, but his presence shall be fixed; he shall abide with the saints, that they may for ever behold him. O! if there was such running after Christ in this world, some getting on hills, and others on trees, that they might behold him when he passed by, what will the sight of Christ in heaven be, when he shall be always in the eye of his saints, and never out of sight, when they shall be always viewing of him, and be always satisfied with that view? Nor only will he be conspicuous, vital and fixed, but his very presence shall transform; *They shall see his face,—and they shall reign for ever and ever,* Rev. xxii. 4, 5. O the influence of this sight! it is of such a transforming nature, that to see the king will make kings; this vision of glory amounts unto a fruition of glory; if ever thou art a spectator of Christ, thou art sure to be a partaker of Christ in all his glory; *I shall be satisfied when I awake with thy likeness,* Psal. xvii. 15. *It doth not yet appear what we shall be; but we know, that when he shall appear, we shall be like him,* and why so? *For we shall see him as he is,* 1 John iii. 2. And no wonder, for if the imperfect beholding of his glory in the glass of his gospel, *Change the soul into the same image from glory to glory,* 1 Cor. xiii. 12. How much more shall the full view of his glory in heaven, transform both the souls and bodies of his saints into a fulness of glory? Here then is the top of heaven; here is the *all in all*; here is the satisfaction of souls to the very uttermost: if Christ's glory in his transfiguration was so satisfactory to Peter, as that he desired his sight of it might never have end or interruption, *O! it is good* to be here, let us here build tabernacles; and yet Peter was only a spectator of this glory, for he had himself no share in it: O then! what infinite satisfaction mayest thou expect in the beholding of Christ's glory in heaven, which will be accompanied with an everlasting enjoyment? The lustre of his glory will be diffused into all, so that some shall enjoy the glory of the sun, others of the moon, and others of the stars. O my soul! if thou art but a star there, yet if thou art filled with that light that comes from the Sun of righteousness, it is enough. O remember! O consider! O never forget this looking unto Jesus! as it is thy duty on earth, so it is thy privilege and highest happiness in heaven for ever and ever.

SECT. III.

Of desiring after Jesus in that respect.

3. LET us desire after Jesus, carrying on this work of man's salvation at his second coming. It is true, many shrink at the thoughts of death and judgment, and it is an high pitch to desire the dissolution of ourselves, and of this world: the best Christians are compounded of flesh and spirit, and if the spirit long to be in heaven, yet the flesh is loth to leave this earth. Speak out, O my soul! thou prayest daily, *Come Lord Jesus, let thy kingdom come*; but is not the flesh afraid, lest God should hear thy prayers? Oh! that we could lothe our lothness in that respect! Oh! that we could long for this second coming of Christ to judgment? And Christians, this is attainable, or otherwise I should not persuade you to it; *I am in a strait* (said Paul) *betwixt two, having a desire to depart, and to be with Christ; which is far better,* Phil. i. 23. And this is the voice of the desolate bride, *Come*; for the Spirit of Christ within her faith, *Come*; *The Spirit and the bride say, Come,* Revel. xxii. 17. Yea, the whole creation faith, *Come, Waiting to be delivered from the bondage of corruption, into the glorious liberty of the children of God; and not only they, but ourselves also, which have the first-fruits of the Spirit; even we ourselves groan within ourselves, waiting for the adoption, to wit, the redemption of our body,* Rom. viii. 21, 23. Oh that we could groan! Oh! that we could come up to this high pitch, even to sigh out, not our breath, but our spirits even to groan out, not some vapours but our hearts!

I know it is suitable to flesh and blood to tremble at the thoughts of judgment, *When Paul reasoned of righteousness, temperance, and of judgment to come, Felix trembled,* Acts xxiv. 25. Weak Christians, as well as Heathens, may have many terrible fancies and notions of that day; Oh, to think of a time! *When there shall be a great earthquake, when the sun shall become black as sackcloth of hair, and the moon red as blood; when the stars of heaven shall fall unto the earth, and when the heavens shall depart as a scroll when it is rolled together; and every mountain and island shall be moved out of their places. When the kings of the earth, and the great men, and the rich men, and the chief captains, and every bond-man, and every free-man, shall hide themselves in the dens, and in the rocks of the mountains, and shall say to the rocks, and to the mountains, Fall on us, and hide us from the face of him that sitteth upon the throne, and from the wrath of the Lamb, for the great day of his wrath is come, and who shall be able to stand?* Rev. vi. 12, 13, 14, 15, 16, 17. Will it not be terrible? If the people were so afraid when the Lord came without such attendants to give the law upon mount Sinai, certainly much more terrible must such a coming in this manner be, when he shall come like a revenging judge, to take an account of the world, for the keeping, or for the breaking of that law.

In this respect, I wonder not at some weak Christians, that cry out, 'O Lord, thou knowest that 'I have not desired this woful day.' A wise Jew was wont to say, from a deep foresight of the terror of this day. *The Messiah will come, but the Lord let me not live to see his coming.* Now, to conquer this fear, and to abate such slavish terror in such souls, Oh! that they would consider it in the whole notion of it, not only as it shall be a day of blackness and of terror, but as it shall be also a day of rest and of release. Some are apt to take it up in the half notion of it; they look upon it only as a day of judgment, and a day of condemnation, and so they fly from it as from a serpent: but if they would take it up again, and look on the other side, the serpent would be turned into a rod. The day which will be so dreadful to the ungodly, and the beginning

ning of their misery, it will be as joyful to the saints, and the beginning of their glory.

But in what respect is this day of Christ so desirable a day? I answer, in these particulars,——

1. It is *a day of refreshing*, Acts iii. 19. Here the saints work in a furnace, *His fire is in Zion, and his furnace in Jerusalem*, Isa. xxxi 9. But Christ in his second coming, (when all the world shall be on fire) shall fan wind (as I may say) on his saints to cool them: to the wicked it is an hot day, a day of everlasting burning; but to the saints it is a day of cooling, quickning, reviving, and refreshing.

2. It is *a day of restoring of all things*, Acts iii. 21. Every creature is now in its work-day dress, all defiled with sin; but at that day there shall be a restitution of all things: all the disorders and ruins which sin hath brought into the world shall then be repaired, and man himself, whose sin is the cause of all, shall then be restored to his original glory.

3. It is *a day of the manifestation of the sons of God*, Rom. viii. 19. Then shall it be known who are true saints, and who are reprobates: here we live in confusion, and in our most refined churches (if we have none scandalous) yet we may have many hypocrites, and we cannot discern them; but in that day it shall be known who are the Lord's, and who are not. The hypocrite shall then be unmantled, and the sons of God shall shine and glitter as the sun, that all may run and read, *These are God's elect, these are the sons and daughters of the Almighty*.

4. It is *the day of adoption, and of the redemption of our bodies*, Rom. viii. 23. It is the day of our sonship and deliverance: I deny not, but that the saints are adopted and redeemed before this day; but this adoption, and redemption is not consummate nor declared, before Christ come again to judgment; then it is that he takes his saints home to his house, and all the angels and men of the world shall understand the love wherewith he loves them; then shall Christ say, *These are my sons whom I have redeemed, and as I have set them free, so now shall they live and reign with me for ever and ever*.

5. It is *the day of Christ's coming*. He was here not long since, travelling about the earth, and about her business: which done, he went away to heaven upon a special errand for his saints; and there now he is to intercede for them, to attend the court, to be their advocate, and to agitate the business of their souls; and withal, there now he is to take up lodgings for them, and to prepare them mansions for eternity. And no sooner shall he have dispatched his business there, but he will come for earth again, he will bow the heavens, and come down to give a report of his transactions there: hath he not left us a letter to that effect? *I will come again, and receive you to myself, that where I am, there you may be also*, John xiv 3. O! why are his chariots so long a coming? Why tarry the wheels of his chariots?

6. It is *the day of Christ's revealing*, 2 Thess i. 7. Christ to many of his saints here is hidden and withdrawn; it is true, he may be in them, yea, certainly he is in them by his Spirit; but no man knows it, no, nor themselves neither, which makes them cry, *O! where is he whom my soul loveth?* But at this day of Christ's revealing, all curtains shall be drawn aside, Christ shall be unhid, and the saints shall see him face to face, they shall never lose him more; for without any intermission they shall stare, and gaze, and be ever looking unto Jesus.

7. It is *the day of Christ's bright and glorious appearing*, Col. iii. 4. When he was upon the earth he appeared in our dress; many then saw him, who then said of him, *There is no beauty in him that we should desire him*. Oh! it was a sad sight, to see him crowned with thorns, and scourged with whips, and nailed to the cross; but in his next appearing we shall see him in his best attire, arrayed in white, attended with the retinue of glory, riding in his chariot of light, and smiling upon all his saints: now, is not this desirable? The apostle tells us, of the saints *looking for the glorious appearing of the great God, and our Saviour Jesus Christ*, Tit. ii. 13. Therefore surely they desire it.

8. It is the day of Christ's joy. *Then he shall see of the travail of his soul, and he shall be satisfied*, Isa. liii. 11. Now, what is the travail of his soul? Is it not the perfection of his redeemed ones; Oh! when Christ seeth this, when he seeth his spouse as without spot or wrinkle, then shall be fulfilled that prophesy, *As the bridegroom rejoiceth over the bride, so shall thy God rejoice over thee*, Isa. lxii. 5. Look how the joy of a bridegroom is over his bride

upon

upon the wedding day, (surely then, if ever, all is love and joy) so is Christ's joy over his saints at the last day; then begins that joy, that never shall have end, there shall be no moment of time wherein Christ will not rejoice over his saints for ever after.

9. It is *the day of Christ's perfection*. Christ, as Mediator, is not fully perfect till all his members be in glory united to him: as an head that wants an arm, or hand, or leg, we say is lame, so it is a kind of mystical lameness that Christ our head hath not with him all his members; the saints are little pieces of mystical Christ, and it shall not be well till Christ gather in his arms and thighs, and pull them nearer to himself in glory. And is not this desirable, to see the Lord Jesus Christ, as head of the church, in his perfection? To see the sun of righteousness with every beam united to him? O desirable day!

10. It is *Christ's wedding day*, or *the marriage day of the Lamb*. The saints are betrothed to Christ when first they believe in Christ; that is Christ's word, *I will betrothe thee unto me, and thou art my sister, my spouse*, Cant. iv. 10. Not my wife, thou art not yet married, only contracted here; but at that day the marriage of the Lamb will be complete, and then will the voice be heard, *Let us be glad and rejoice, and give honour to him, for the marriage of the Lamb is come, and his wife hath made herself ready*, Rev. xix. 7. O! the joy that Christ, and saints, and angels, and all that belong to heaven will make at this marriage! *Blessed are they that are called into the marriage-supper of the Lamb*, Revel. xix. 9. One of the seven angels that came to John in visions, *talked with him, saying, Come hither, and I will shew thee the bride the Lamb's wife*, Rev. xxi. 9. If the espoused virgin be willing to be married, how is it that we cry not, *Come Lord Jesus, come quickly?*

11. It is Christ's day of presenting his saints unto his Father; *He delivers up the kingdom to God, even the Father*, 1 Cor. v. 24. Then shall he take his bride by the hand and bring her to his house, and present her in all state and solemnity to the Father. Is not this a desirable day? Surely Christ rejoiceth, and his very heart even springs again to present his church unto his Father, ' Father, here behold my bride, that I have married ' unto myself.' It is true, a child may sometimes marry such a one, as he may be ashamed to think of bringing to his father's house; but, how mean and sinful soever we are of ourselves, when once we are married unto Christ, he will not think it any dishonour, no not before his Father, that he hath such a bride, ' Father, (will he say) lo! here ' all my saints, of all that thou hast given me, I ' have lost none, but the children of perdition; ' these are mine, dearly bought, thou knowest ' the price, O welcome them to glory!

12. It is the day of Christ's glory. What glorious descriptions have we in scripture of Christ's coming to judgment? *The Son of man shall come from heaven with power and great glory*, Matth. xxiv. 30. And the work no sooner done, but he shall return again into heaven with power and great glory. Not to mention the essential glory of Christ, O! the glory of Christ as Mediator; all the glory that Ahasuerus could put upon his favourites was nothing to this spiritual and heavenly glory, which the Father will put upon the Son; it is a glory above all the glories that ever were, or shall be; it is an eternal glory, not but that Christ shall at last give up his kingdom to his Father; he shall no more discharge the acts of an advocate or intercessor for us in heaven, only the glory of this shall always continue; it shall to all eternity be recorded that he was the Mediator, and that he is the Saviour that hath brought us to life and immortality, and upon this ground the tongues of all the saints shall be employed to all eternity to celebrate this glory. This will be their everlasting song, *Unto him that loved us, and washed us from our sins in his own blood, and hath made us kings and priests unto God and his Father, to him be glory and dominion for ever and ever, Amen*. Rev. i. 5, 6. Now, is not this a desirable thing? Do we believe there is such a thing as Christ's mediatory glory, and Christ's essential glory, as Christ's human glory, and Christ's divine glory? And have we no desires to behold this glory? Surely Christ himself desired it of God, he would have his saints with him where he is, that they might behold his glory; and shall not we desire it whom it most concerns? O! the sweet temper of the spouse, when she cried out, *Make haste my beloved, and be thou like a roe, or to a young hart upon the mountains of spices*, Cant. viii. 14.

Come now and run over these particulars. Surely

ly every one is motive enough to desire this day; it is a day of refreshing, a day of restoring, a day of manifestation of the sons of God, a day of adoption, and of the redemption of our bodies; a day of Christ's coming, of Christ's revealing, of Christ's appearing, of Christ's joy, of Christ's perfection, of Christ's wedding, of Christ's presenting of his saints, and of Christ's glory. What, are we not yet in a longing frame? The wife of youth that wants her husband for some years, and expects that he should return from over-sea lands, she is often on the shore, her very heart loves the wind that should bring him home; every ship in view, that is but drawing near the shore, is her new joy, and new reviving hopes; she asks of every passenger, 'O! saw you my husband; What is he adoing? When will he come? Is he not yet shipped and ready for a return?' Souls truly related to the Lord Jesus Christ should, methinks, long no less; O! what desire should the Spirit and the bride have, to hear when Christ shall say to his angels, 'Make you ready for the journey, let us go down, and divide the skies, and bow the heavens: I will gather my prisoners of hope unto me, I cannot want my Rachael, and her weeping children any longer, behold I come quickly to judge the nations?' Methinks, every spouse of Christ should love the quarter of the sky, that being rent asunder should yield unto her husband; methinks, she should love that part of the heavens where Christ puts through his glorious hand, and comes riding on the rainbow and clouds to receive her to himself. I conclude this with the conclusion of the Bible, *He that testifieth these things, saith, Surely I come quickly,* Amen. *Even so, come Lord Jesus,* Rev. xxii. 20.

SECT. IV.

Of hoping in Jesus in that respect.

4. LET us hope in Jesus, as carrying on the great work of our salvation for us in his second coming. Hope is of good things to come; hope is an act of the will extending itself towards that which it loves as future; only the future good, as it is the object of hope, it is difficult to obtain, and therein it differs from desire; for desire looks at future good without any apprehension of difficulty, but hope respects the future good, as it is gotten with difficulty. Lazy hopes that will not be in the use of means, though difficult, are not true hopes; we see many desirable things set before us, of which we may say, *Oh! that we had our part and portion of them.* But shall we go on, and search and find out the truth, whether we have any part or portion in them? Or, whether we have any hopes of any such things? Oh! this is worthy our pains. Come then, let us make a farther progress, let us not only *desire that it may be thus and so,* but let us say, on some sure and certain grounds, *We hope it is thus and so, we hope Christ will come again, and receive us to himself, that where he is, there we may be also,* John xiv. 3.

Indeed there is the Christian's stay and comfort, such an hope is a *sure anchor,* Heb. ix. 12. that will hold the ship in a storm; only because our souls lie upon it, we had need to look to it that our hopes be true; the worst can say, *They hope to be saved as well as the best*; but I fear the hopes of many will be lamentably frustrated. Our Saviour brings in many pleading with confidence at the last day for life, who shall be rejected with miserable disappointment, *Many shall say to me at that day, Lord, Lord,* &c. *and I will confess unto them, I never knew them, depart from me.* Now, to clear this point, that our hopes are of the right stamp, and not counterfeit hopes, I shall lay down some signs, whereby we may know that Christ's coming is for us, and for our good, and for the grace that is to be given us at the revelation of Jesus Christ.

1. If we are born again, then will his glorious coming be to glorify us, *Blessed be the God and Father of our Lord Jesus Christ, who, according to his abundant mercy, hath begotten us again into a lively hope, to an inheritance incorruptible,* 1 Pet. i. 3, 4. Whosoever hath the true hope of heaven, he is one that is begotten again; so our Saviour, *Except a man be born again, he cannot see the kingdom of God,* John iii. 3. Many things may be done, as Herod heard John the Baptist, *and did many things*; but except a man be born again, those *many things* are in God's account as nothing. When Peter had told Christ, that he and his fellow disciples had forsaken all, and followed him, *Then Jesus said, Verily I say unto you, That ye which have followed me in the regeneration, when the son of man shall sit on the throne of his glory, ye shall also sit upon*

upon twelve thrones, judging the twelve tribes of Ifrael, Mat. xix. 28. *q. d.* Peter, You have forsaken all, and followed me, but know, that bare forsaking is not enough; but you who have felt the work of God regenerating your souls, upon which ye have followed me, ye shall sit upon twelve thrones. In those who are alive at the last day there will be a change, and this change will be to them instead of death: *Behold I shew you a mystery, we shall not all sleep, but we shall all be changed*, 1 Cor. xv 51. Certainly, in those who at the last day shall sit on thrones with Christ, there must be a change likewise in this life, *(i. e.)* a new spirit, and a new life must be put into them: oh! what a change is this! suppose a rational soul were put into a beast, what a change would be in that creature! suppose an angelical nature were put upon us, what a change would there be in us! oh! but what a change is this, when a man is born again of water and of the spirit? I must tell you, that the highest degree of glory in heaven is not so different from the lowest degree of grace here, as the lowest degree of grace there is different from the highest excellency of nature here; because the difference betwixt the highest degree of the glory of heaven, and the lowest degree of grace is only gradual; but the difference that is betwixt the lowest degree of grace, and the highest excellency of nature, is a specifical difference. Oh! there is a mighty work of God in preparing souls for glory by grace, and this change must they have that must fit on thrones. Come then, you that hope for glory, try yourselves by this; Is there a change in your hearts, words, and lives? Is there a mighty work of grace upon your spirit? Are you experienced in the great mystery of regeneration? Why, here is your evidence that your hopes are sound, and that you shall sit upon thrones to judge the world.

2. If we long for his coming, then will he come to satisfy our longings, *Blessed are they that hunger and thirst, for they shall be satisfied*; How satisfied, but in being saved; *Christ was once offered to bear the sins of many; and unto them that look for him shall he appear the second time, without sin, unto salvation*, Heb. ix 28. Unto them that look for him, or long for him, shall he appear the second time unto salvation: it is very observable, how this *looking for Christ*, is in scripture a frequent description of a true believer in Christ. Who are true, sincere, and sound Christians, but such as live in a perpetual desire and hope of Christ's blessed coming? They are ever *looking for, and hastening unto the coming of the day of God*, 2 Pet. iii. 12. Here are two signs in one verse, *Looking for, and hastening unto:* true believers are not only in a posture looking for the coming of Jesus Christ, but also, as it were, going forth to meet Jesus Christ with burning lamps, Luther could say, That *he was no true Christian, neither could be truly recite the Lord's prayer, that with all his heart, desired not this day of the coming of Christ*, Matth. vi. 10. It is true, that whether we will or no, that day will come; but in the Lord's prayer Christ hath taught us to pray, that God would accelerate and hasten the day of his glorious coming. *Thy kingdom come*, (i. e) the kingdom of glory at the judgment, as well as the kingdom of grace in the church. It is true also, that the day of the Lord is a terrible day, the heavens, and earth, and sea, and air shall be all on a bonfire, and burn to nothing, *Nevertheless, we according to his promise, look for new heavens, and a new earth*; we that have laid hold upon God, and laid hold on him by the right handle, *According to his promises*, we look for this day of the Lord, *we look for it, and hasten unto it*; we are glad it is so near, and we do what we can to have it nearer; with an holy kind of impatience we beg of the Lord, *Come Lord Jesus, come quickly*. This was Paul's character, *We know that the whole creation groaneth, and travaileth in pain together until now; and not only they, but ourselves also, which have the first fruits of the Spirit; even we ourselves groan within ourselves, waiting for the adoption,* to wit, *the redemption of our bodies*, Rom viii. 22, 23. God's children, such as have the first-fruits of the Spirit, the beginnings of true saving grace in them, they constantly look and long for the day of full deliverance, or of the coming of Christ. This the apostle instanceth in his Corinthians, *Ye come behind in no gift, waiting for the coming of our Lord Jesus Christ*, 1 Cor. i. 7 And in like manner he writes to his Philippians, *Our conversation is in heaven, from whence also we look for the Saviour, the Lord Jesus Christ*, Phil. iii. 20. And to Titus himself, he writes the same things, *We look for that blessed hope, and the glorious appearing of the great God, and our Saviour*

viour Jesus Christ, Tit. ii. 13. Now Christians, lay this character to heart; Do you long, pant, and look for this glorious and second coming of Christ? Have you any such wishes, and sayings of heart and mind, as these are? 'Oh that Christ 'would appear! oh that Christ would now break 'the heavens, and come to judgment! oh that I 'could see him in the cloud, and on his throne! 'oh that his enemies were ruined, my sins subdu-'ed, my soul saved, that I might serve him with-'out weariness, for ever and ever!' Surely if these elongations of soul be in you, it is a comfortable evidence that your hopes are sound, and that Christ will come to receive you to himself, and to bring you to glory.

3. If we love Christ's appearing, then will he appear on our side; *Henceforth there is laid up for me a crown of righteousness, which the Lord, the righteous Judge, shall give me at that day; and not to me only, but unto all them also that love his ap-pearing,* 2 Tim. iv. 8. A true Christian loves Christ's appearing in ordinances, and in all the means of grace, How much more in his own person? But how should we love that we see not? O yes! there is a kind of an idea of Christ, and of his glorious appearing in every sanctified soul, and in that respect, we love him, though we cannot see him, 'Who having not seen, ye love,' saith the apostle, 1 Pet. i. 8. And so your 'love and faith, at the 'appearing of Jesus Christ, shall be found unto 'praise, and honour, and glory,' Verse 7. Those that have not seen Christ, and yet love the idea of his sight, even they shall appear, at the appearing of Christ, in praise, and honour, and glory. Is not the crown laid up for them that love the appearing of Christ? Is it not a sign of a good cause, to love a day of hearing? Surely love of Christ's coming cannot consist without some assurance, that a soul shall stand upright in the judgment. He that hath not a confidence in his cause, loves not the coming of the judge; no guilty prisoner loves the sessions, or loves the judge's presence; it is the cry of reprobates, 'O ye mountains! and, O ye rocks! Fall 'on us, and hide us from the face of him that sit-'teth on the throne,' Rev. vi. 16. But as for Christ and his saints, O the mutual loves, and mutual longings in their breasts! The last words that Christ speaks in the Bible, (and amongst us, last words make deepest impressions) are, *Surely I come quick-ly*; and the last answer that is made in our behalf is, *Amen, Even so, come Lord Jesus*. I know this character is near the former, and therefore I shall pass it over.

4. If our works be good, then will he reward us according to our works. At that great day, this will be the trial, works, or no works; 'Then 'will he say to them on his right hand, Come ye 'blessed of my Father, inherit the kingdom prepa-'red for you, for I was an hungred, and ye gave me 'meat; I was thirsty, and ye gave me drink; I was 'a stranger, and ye took me in; naked, and ye clo-'thed me; I was sick, and ye visited me; I was in 'prison, and ye came unto me,' Mat. xxv. 33, 34, 35, 36. Here were works, upon which followed the rewards of heaven, for these *went into eternal life*, Ver. 46. I know works are not meritorious, and yet they are evidences; I know works without faith are but glistering sins; and yet works done in faith are signs and forerunners of eternal glory: I know, that if all the excellencies of all the moralities of all the men in the world were put together, these could never reach glory; and yet *a cup of cold water given to one of Christ's little ones, in the name of a disciple of Christ, shall not lose its reward*, Mat. x. 42. If a Christian doubt, How should I know that my works are of a right stamp? I answer, 1. Look at the principle, Is there not something above nature? Do I not find some new light let out by God, that shews a glory, and excellency, and beauty in good works? Is there not something in me that makes the same to be sweet, or pleasant, or agreeable to me? 2. Look at the end; natural works have no better end than self and creature-respects; but, in my works, Is there no aim at something higher than self? Whatever I do, Is not this in mine eye, that all I do may tend to the honour and glory of God? I had need to take heed of vain glory and self-applause; the godly, at the day of judgment, do not know the good works they did; if my aim be at God, I shall forget myself, as if all I did were swallowed up in God. 3. Look at the manner of my doing works: Uzziah had a good intention, but his work was not good, because the manner was not good; Are my works according to the rule? Do they carry a conformity to the law? 'Let every man try his own work in 'this.' O my soul! bring thy works to the touchstone, the scripture, the rule of goodness, Is not all thy

thy gold then discovered to be dross? The scripture doth not only tell of works, but tells us the manner of performing them; as for instance, if rightly done, they must be done in zeal, in fervency, in activity; thus God's people are called *a peculiar people, zealous of good works*; a formal, customary, superficial performance of all holy works fails in the manner of performing them: what, are my works performed in zeal? Is there not too much of coldness, emptiness, formality in all I do? Why, thus I may know, whether my works are of a right stamp; certainly all works, duties, actings, which are not done by a gracious heart, through a gracious power, to a gracious end, in a gracious manner, are sins, and not such works as shall have the rewards of heaven. Some may object, this is an hard saying, Who then shall be saved? I answer, *First*, By concession very few; 'What is the whole company of Christians, besides a very few, (said Salvian) but a sink of vices?' Are they only good works which are thus and thus qualified? It were enough to make us all fear all the works that ever we have done. But, *Secondly*, Here is all our hope, that, in a gospel-way, Christ looks at our good works in the truth of them, and not in the perfection of them; no man goes beyond Paul, who, *when he would do good, found evil present with him*, Rom. vii. 18, 19. Alas! there is a perpetual opposition and conflict betwixt the flesh and the Spirit, so that the most spiritual man cannot do the good things he would do; and yet we must not conclude, that nothing is good in us, because not perfectly good. Sincerity and truth in the inward parts, may in this case, hold up our hearts from sinking, as he in the gospel cried, *I believe, Lord, help my unbelief*; so if we can but say, 'I do good works, Lord help me in the concurrence of all needful circumstances:' Here will be our evidence that our hopes are sound, and that Christ will sentence us to eternal life. *Come ye blessed*, &c. And, why so? *For I was an hungred, and ye gave me meat*, &c.

5. If we believe in Christ, then shall we live in Christ; if we come to him, and receive him by faith, then will he *come again, and receive us to himself, that where he is, there we may be also*. Good works are good evidences, but of all works, those of the gospel are clearest evidences, and have clearest promises; come then, let us try our obedience to the commandments of faith as well as life; let us try our submission to the Lord, by believing as well as doing. Surely the greatest work of God, that ever any creature did, it is this gospel-work, when it apprehends its own unworthiness, and ventures itself and its estate upon the righteousness of Jesus Christ: if we were able to perform a full, exact, and accurate obedience to every particular of the moral law, it were not so great a work, nor so acceptable to God, nor should be so gloriously rewarded in heaven, as this one work of believing in his Son Jesus Christ. This is the work to which in express terms, salvation, heaven, and glory is promised, ' He that believeth on the Son, hath everlasting life, John iii. 36. ' And he that heareth my words, and believeth on ' him that sent me, hath everlasting life, and shall ' not come into condemnation, but he hath passed ' from death to life,—John v. 24. And this is the ' will of him that sent me, that every one that seeth ' the Son, and believeth on him, may have everlast-' ing life,—John vi. 40. And these things are writ-' ten, that ye might believe that Jesus is the Christ ' the Son of God, and that believing ye might have ' life thro' his name,—John xx. 31. Believe on the ' Lord Jesus Christ, and thou shalt be saved,—Acts ' xvi 31. And if thou shalt confess with thy mouth ' the Lord Jesus, and shalt believe in thine heart, ' that God hath raised him from the dead, thou ' shalt be saved,—Rom. x. 9. And we are not of ' them who draw back unto perdition, but of them ' that believe unto the saving of the soul,—Heb. x. 39. And these things have I written unto you, that ' believe on the name of the Son of God, that ye ' may know that ye have everlasting life,' 1 John v. 13. Why, this, above all, is the gospel work, to which are annexed those gracious promises of eternal life; so that if we believe in Christ, How may we be assured that we shall live with Christ?

O my soul! gather up all these characters, and try by them. Every one can say, That they hope well, they hope to be saved, they hope to meet Christ with Comfort, though they have no ground for it, but their own vain conceits; but hope on good ground is that hope *that maketh not ashamed*, Rom. v. 5. Say then, Art thou born again? Dost thou look and long for the coming of Christ in the clouds? Dost thou love his appearing? Art thou rich in good works, ready to distribute, willing to communicate? Dost thou obey the commandments

Carrying on the great Work of our Salvation in his second coming.

mandments of faith as well as life? Sure these are firm, and sound, and comfortable grounds of an assured hope. Content not thyself with an hope of possibility or probability, but reach out to that plerophory, *or full assurance of hope,* Heb. vi. 11. The hope of possibility is but a weak hope, the hope of probability is but a fluctuating hope; but the hope of certainty is a settled hope, such an hope sweetens all the thoughts of God and Christ, of death and judgment, of heaven, yea, and of hell too, whilst we hope that we are saved from it; And are not the scriptures written to this very purpose, *that we might have this hope?* Rom. xv. 4. Are we not justified by his grace, *that we might be heirs in hope, heirs according to the hope of eternal life?* Tit. iii. 7. And was not this David's confidence, *Lord I have hoped for thy salvation?* Psal. cxix. 166. *Why then art thou cast down, O my soul? And why art thou disquieted within me? Hope thou in God, for I shall yet praise him, who is the health of my countenance, and my God,* Psal xlii. 11.

If I may here enter into a dialogue with my own poor, trembling, wavering soul.——*Person,*——Why art thou hopeless, O my soul! wouldest thou not hope, if an honest man had made thee a promise of any thing within his power? And wilt thou not hope, when thou hast the promise, the oath, and the covenant of God in Christ?—*Soul,*—Yes, methinks I feel some little hope; but, alas! it is but a little, a very little.——*Person,*—Ay, but go on my soul, true hope is called a lively hope, and a lively hope is an efficacious hope; no sooner faith commends the promise unto hope, but hope takes it, and huggs it, and reckons it as its treasure, and feeds on it as *manna,* which God hath given to refresh the weary soul in the desart of sin; go on then, till thou comest up to the highest pitch, even to that triumphant joyful expectation, and waiting for Christ in glory.—*Soul,*--Why, methinks I would hope, I would ascend the highest step of hope, but, alas! I cannot; oh! I am exposed to many controversies, I am prone to many unquiet agitations; though I have a present promise, yet I extend my cares and fears, even to eternity; alas! I cannot comprehend, and therefore I am hardly satisfied; my sinful reason sees not its own way and end; and because it must take all on trust and credit, therefore it falls to wrangling; nay, Satan himself so snarls the question, and I am so apt to listen to him, that I can come to no conclusion

I know not how to extricate myself,——*Person,*—Sayest thou so? Surely in this case there is no cure, no remedy, but only the testimony of God's Spirit; But, saith not the apostle, That *the Spirit itself bears witness with our spirits, that we are children of God?* Rom. viii. 16. If a man, or angel, or archangel, should promise heaven, peradventure thou mightest doubt; but if the supreme essence of the Spirit of God bear witness within, What room for doubting? Why, this voice of the Spirit is the very voice of God; hark then, enquire O my soul! if thou hast but this testimony of the Spirit, thou art sure enough.——*Soul,*——Oh, that it were thus with me! oh, that the Spirit would even now give me to drink of the wells of salvation! oh, that the Spirit would testify it home! oh, that he would shine upon, and enlighten all those graces which he hath planted in me! fain would I come to the highest pitch of hope; oh, that I could look upon the things hoped for, as certainly future!——*Person,*—Thou sayest well, O my soul! and if these wishes be real, then pour out thyself unto God in prayer; this was the apostle's method, *Now the God of hope fill you with all joy and peace in believing, that ye may abound in hope, through the power of the Holy Ghost,* Rom. xv. 13. Let this be thy practice, pray as he prayed, pray thou for thyself, as he prayed for others; if an earthly father will hearken to his child, *How much more will God the Father give the Spirit to them that ask the Spirit of him?* Luke xi. 13.——*Soul,*—Why, if this be it, to thee, Lord, do I come, O! give me the Spirit, the witness of the Spirit, the first-fruits of the Spirit, the sealing of the Spirit, the earnest of the Spirit, O! give me the Spirit, and let the Spirit give me this hope. 'O the hope of Israel, and Saviour thereof, in the time of trouble, Why shouldest thou be as a stranger in my soul, and as a way-faring man that turneth aside to tarry for a night? Come, O come! and dwell in my soul. Come and blow on my garden, that the spices thereof may flow out.' Come and fill me with a lively hope, yea, Lord, excite, and quicken; and stir up my soul to act this hope, yea, so enlighten, or shine upon my hope, that I may know that I hope, and know that I joyfully expect, and wait for the coming of Christ; O let me hear thy voice! *Say unto my soul, I am, and will be thy salvation,* Psal. xxxv. 3.——*Person,*——Well, now thou hast prayed, O my

O my soul! come, tell me, Dost thou feel nothing stir? Is there nothing at all in thee, that assures thee of this assurance of hope? Is there no life in thy affections? No spark that takes hold on thy heart to set it on flame? No comfort of the Spirit, no joy in the Holy Ghost?——*Soul*,—Yes! methinks I feel it now begin to work, the Spirit that hath breathed this prayer into me, comes in as a comforter; Oh! now that I realize Christ's coming, and my resurrection, I cannot but conclude with David, *Therefore my heart is glad, and my glory rejoiceth, and my flesh also shall rest in hope*, Psal. xvi. 9. Oh! what an earnest is this! what a piece hath the Spirit put into my hand of the great sum promised! not only that he, in great mercy, promised me heaven, but because he doth not put me into a present possession, he now gives me an earnest of my future inheritance. Why, surely all is sure, unless the earnest deceive me: and what, shall I dispute the truth of the earnest? Oh, God forbid! the stamp is too well known to be mistrusted; this seal cannot be counterfeit, because it is agreeable with the word; I find in myself an hope, a true sincere hope, though very weak; I find upon trial, that I am regenerate, that I look and long for the second coming of Jesus, that I love his appearance even before hand: that my works, tho' imperfect, are sincere and true; that I believe on the name of the Son of God, and flesh and blood could never work these duties, or these graces in me, it is only that good Spirit of my God, which hath thus sealed me up to the day of redemption. Away, away despair, trouble me no longer with amusing thoughts; I will henceforth (if the Lord enable) walk confidently and chearfully in the strength of this assurance, and joyfully expect the full accomplishment of my happy contract from the hands of Christ, *The Lord is my portion, therefore will I hope in him; the Lord is good to them that wait for him, to the soul that seeketh him; it is good that I both hope, and quietly wait for the salvation of the Lord*,—Lam. iii. 24, 25, 26. *It is good that I hope to the end, for the grace that is to be brought unto me at the revelation of Jesus Christ*, 1 Peter i. 13.

SECT. V.
Of believing in Jesus in that respect.

5. LET us believe in Jesus as carrying on the great work of our salvation in his second coming. Now, this believing in Christ, is more than hoping in Christ; faith eyes things as present, but hope eyes things as future; and hence the apostle describes faith to be *the substance of things hoped for*, Heb. xi. 1. It is the substance, foundation, or prop which upholds the building; or it is the substance, essence, and existence of a thing hoped for, and consequently absent and afar off, to be a firm apprehension of the believer, as already present and real. And this is as necessary as the former; Oh! if we could but see things, now, as they shall appear at that last general day of judgment! how mightily would they work upon our souls? I verily think the want of this work of faith, is the cause, almost of all the evil in the world; and the acting of faith on this subject, would produce fruits, even to admiration. If we could but see that glory of God in Christ, and those glorious treasures of mercies that shall then be communicated; if we could but see those dreadful evils that are now threatned, and shall then be fulfilled; would not this draw the hardest heart under heaven? Come, let us act faith this day, as if this day were the last day; a thousand years are but as one day to faith, it takes hold upon eternal life, whensoever it acts; it takes present possession of the glorious things of the kingdom of God even now.

O then! let us believe in Jesus, as in reference to his second coming to judgment.

But how should we believe? What directions to act our faith on Jesus in this respect? I answer,——

1. Faith must directly go to Christ.
2. Faith must go to Christ, as God in the flesh.
3. Faith must go to Christ, as God in the flesh, made under the law.
4. Faith must go to Christ, made under the directive part of the law by his life, and under the penal part of the law by his death.
5. Faith must go to Christ, as put to death in the flesh, and as quickned by the Spirit.
6. Faith must go to Christ, as going up into glory, as sitting down at God's right hand, and as sending down the Holy Ghost.
7. Faith must go to Christ, as interceding for his saints, in which work he continues till his coming again. Of all these before.
8. Faith must go to Christ, as coming again into

to this nether world, to judge the quick and the dead: this is the last act of faith, in reference to Christ, *from thence he shall come to judge both the quick and the dead.* The coming of Christ, the resurrection of the dead, the change of the living, the last judgment, and the glory of Christ with his saints to all eternity, is that transaction which must be dispatched at the end of the world; now, this is the object of faith as well as the former, Christ's work is not fully perfected, till all these be finished, nor is our work of faith fully completed, till it reach to the very last act of Christ in saving souls. —Oh! what an excellent worker is Jesus Christ! he doth all his works thoroughly and perfectly: the greatest work that ever Christ undertook, was the work of redemption; that work would have broken men and angels, and yet Jesus Christ will carry it on to the end, and then will he say, not only prophetically, but expresly, *I have finished the work which thou gavest me to do,* John xvii. 4. Now, faith should eye Christ as far as he goes; if Christ will not have done till he come again, and receive us to himself, and settle us in glory, no more should faith, it should still follow after him, and take a view of all his transactions from first to last; what, will Christ come again? Will he summon all the elect to come under judgment? Will he sentence, or judge them to eternal life? Will he conduct them into glory, present them to his Father, and be their *all in all* to all eternity? Why then, let our faith act itself upon all these promises; or, if I may instance in one for all, Christ's coming is the most comprehensive of all; and is not the coming of Christ very frequently mentioned in the promises, as the great support, and stay of his people's spirits till then? Do not the apostles usually quicken us to duty, and encourage us to waiting, by the mentioning of this glorious coming of Jesus Christ? Why then, let us act our faith on this glorious object; Christians! what do we believe, and hope, and wait for, but to see this coming? This was Paul's encouragement to rejoicing, and to moderation, *Rejoice in the Lord always,*—*And let your moderation be known to all men, the Lord is at hand,* Phil. iv. 4, 5. To think and speak of that day with horror, doth well beseem the impenitent sinner, but doth ill beseem the believing saint; such may be the voice of an unbeliever, and it may be of a believer in desertion or temptation; but it is not the voice of faith. O! believe on Christ, as carrying on our salvation at his coming again; *for yet a little while, and he that shall come, will come, and will not tarry,* Heb. x. 37.

9. Faith must principally and mainly look to the purpose, design, intent and end of Christ in his second coming to judgment. Now the ends are,—
1. In respect of the wicked, that they may be destroyed, for *he must reign till he hath put all his enemies under his feet.* He shall come with flaming fire, and then he will *take vengeance on them that know not God, and that obey not the gospel of our Lord Jesus Christ; who shall be punished with everlasting destruction from the presence of the Lord, and from the glory of his power,* 2 Thess. i. 8. O miserable men! now it is God's design to be revenged on you. This is the day when the wicked shall suddenly start out of sleep, and meet with ghastly amazedness at the mouth of their sepulchres; above them stands the judge condemning, beneath, hell gaping, on the right hand, justice threatning, on all sides, the world burning; to go forward is intolerable, to go backward is impossible, to turn aside is unavailable; which way then? heaven's gates are shut, hell's-mouth is open where they must end their endless misery; the last torment lasteth ever. Oh the shrieks of the wicked at every passage of this day! when the prophet Joel was describing the formidable accidents of this day, he was not able to express it, but stammered like a child, or an amazed imperfect person, A. A. A. *for the day of the Lord is at hand.* We translate it, *Alas, for the day of the Lord is at hand,* Joel i. 15. But Lyra, Ribera, the vulgar Latin, and others translate it, A A A. in Hebrew it is indeed but one word, and sounds Aha, which howsoever so written, yet it is pronounced without any aspiration as Aharon is pronounced Aaron. The best critics would have it one word, and so they write it, A-a-a. *for the day of the Lord is at hand:* thus they that stammer, and cannot suddenly speak, say, A-a-a. it is not sense at first; the prophet was so amazed, that he knew not what to say; the stammering tongue that is full of fear, can best speak that terror, which will make all the wicked of the world to cry, and shriek, and speak fearful accents; oh the shrieks! oh the fearful sounds, that will then be heard! sure that noise must needs be terrible, when millions

lions of men and women, at the same instant, shall fearfully cry out, and when their cries shall mingle with the thunders of the dying and groaning heavens, and with the crack of the dissolving world, when the whole fabrick of nature shall shake into eternal dissolution, *Now consider this ye that forget God, lest he tear you in pieces, and there be none to deliver you*, Psal. l. 22. Shall not the consideration of these things awake your spirits, and raise you from the death of sin? What, do you believe these things, or do you not? If you do not believe these things, where is your faith? If you do believe them, and sin on, Where is your prudence, and where is your hope? But enough of this, it belongs to the wicked.

2. In respect of the Godly, that they may be saved. Now this contains several steps, As,——

1. They must be regenerated. It is true, they partake of this grace before, but now is the full perfection and manifestation of it; and therefore the last day is called *the day of regeneration*, Mat. xix. 28.

2. They must be redeemed. So they are in this life. Paul could tell his Colossians, That *Christ had delivered them from the power of darkness*; and that *in him they had redemption through his blood*, Col. i. 13, 14. Yet the scripture calls the day of judgment, in a peculiar and eminent manner, the day of redemption, *And grieve not the holy Spirit of God, whereby ye are sealed unto the day of redemption*, Eph. iv. 30.

3. They must be adopted. It is true, they are adopted in this life, *We are now the Sons of God*, (saith the apostle) *yet it doth not appear what we shall be*, 1 John iii. 2. the glory which Christ will put upon us at the last day is far transcendant and superlative to what now we are, that we know not what we shall be, sons, and more than sons; and therefore the apostle calls the last day, *the day of adoption*, Rom. viii. 23.

4. They must be justified. I know they were justified by faith before, and this justification was evidenced to some of their consciences; but now they shall be justified fully by the lively voice of the judge himself; now shall their justification be solemnly and publicly declared to all the world: the Syriac word *to justify*, is also to conquer, because, when a man is justified, he overcomes all those bills and indictments which were brought in against him, now this is manifestly done in the day of judgment, when Christ shall, before men and angels, acquit, and absolve his people: Oh! what a glorious conquest will that be over sin, death and hell, when the judge of the whole world shall pronounce them free from all sin, and from all these miserable effects of sin, death, hell, and damnation!

5. They must inherit the kingdom prepared for them, so is the sentence at that day, *Come ye blessed, inherit the kingdom*, Matth. xxv 34. Not only are they freed from hell, but they must inherit heaven. Now herein is an high step of salvation, and a great part of the design of Christ's coming, to bring his saints into heaven; he went thither before to prepare it for them, and now he comes again to give them the possession of it, *Come, enter into heaven*. Heaven! what is heaven? Surely it is not one single palace, but a city, a metropolis, a mother city, the first city of God's creation: when the angel *carried John in the Spirit to a great and high mountain, he shewed him the great city, the holy Jerusalem, descending out of heaven from God, having the glory of God*, Re. xxi. 10, 11. But a city is too little, therefore it is more, it is a kingdom, *Fear not, little flock, it is your Father's good pleasure to give you the kingdom*: and at this last day he bids his saints to *inherit the kingdom*, Luke xii. 32. Or if a kingdom be too little, it is called a world; *The children of this world marry, and are given in marriage, but they which shall be accounted worthy to obtain that world, and the resurrection from the dead, neither marry, nor are given in marriage, neither can they die any more*, Luke xx. 34, 35, 36. There is another world besides this, and for eminency it is called *the world to come*, Heb. vi. 5. O the breadth, and largeness of that world! as the greater circle must contain the less, so doth that world contain this; alas! all our dwellings here are but as caves under the earth, and holes of poor clay in comparison. In the bosom of that heaven is many a dwelling-place; *In my Father's house are many mansions*, John xiv. 2. There lodge many thousands of glorious kings; O what fair fields, and mountains of roses and spices are there! surely gardens of length and breadth above millions of miles are nothing in comparison. O the wines, the lilies, the roses, the precious trees that grow in Immanuel's lands! an hun-

hundred harvests in one year are nothing there. The lowest stones in every mansion there, are precious stones: the very *building of the wall about it is jasper, and the city is pure gold, like unto clear glass*, Rev. xxi. 18. O glorious inheritance! tell me, Christians, in what city on earth do men walk upon gold, or dwell within the walls of gold? Tho' none such here, yet under the feet of the inhabitants of heaven there is gold; all the streets, and fields of that city, kingdom, world, are pure gold, as it were transparent glass, Rev. xxi. 21. But, alas! what speak I of gold, or glass? All these are but shadows; indeed and in truth there is nothing so low as gold, or precious stones; there is nothing so base in this high and glorious kingdom, as gardens, trees, or roses; comparisons are but created shadows, that come not up to express the glory of the thing. I shall therefore leave to speak this, because unspeakable.

6. They must live with Christ in heaven; they must see, and enjoy Christ there to all eternity. This is a main end of Christ's coming, 'I will come 'again, and receive you unto myself, that where 'I am, there ye may be also.—John xiv. 3. And, 'Father, I will, that those whom thou hast given 'me, be with me, where I am, that they may be-'hold the glory which thou hast given me,' John xvii. 24. O let faith eye this above all the former! What, will my Saviour come again! And shall I see his face? Oh! what a pleasant sight will this same be! if heaven, if the inheritance be such a wonder to the beholders, what a beauty is that which is in the samplar! Oh, what an happiness to stand beside that dainty precious prince in heaven! to see the king on his throne! to see the Lamb, the fair tree of life, the flower of angels, the spotless rose, the crown, the garland, the joy of heaven, the wonder of wonders for eternity! Oh, what a life to see that precious tree of life! to see a multitude, without quantity, of the apples of glory! to see love itself, and to be warmed with the heat of immediate love that comes out from the precious heart and bowels of Jesus Christ! Oh, what a dearness to see all relations meet in one! to see the Saviour, the good Shepherd, the Redeemer, the great bishop of our souls, the angel of the covenant, the head of the body of the church, the king of ages, the prince of peace, the Creator of the ends of the earth, the song of angels and glorified saints! not only must they see Christ, but they shall enjoy him whom they see; they fly with doves wings of beauty after the Lamb, and in flying after him, they lay hold upon him, and they will not leave him; they can never have enough of the chaste fruition of the glorious prince Immanuel, and they never want his inmost presence to the full; they suck the honey and the honey-comb; they drink of the floods of eternal consolations, and fill all empty desires; and, as if the souls of saints were without bottom, afresh they suck again to all eternity. Now this is salvation indeed; the soul that attains this full enjoyment, is saved to the uttermost.

3. In respect of Christ himself, that he may be glorified. Now, in two things more especially will he be glorified at that day. 1. In his justice. 2. In his mercy, or free grace.

1. His justice will be glorified, especially in punishing the wicked: here on earth little justice is done on most offenders; tho' some public crimes are sometimes punished, yet the actions of closets, and chambers, the designs and thoughts of men, the business of retirements, and of the night, escape the hand of justice; and therefore God hath so ordained it, that there shall be a day of doom, wherein all that are let alone by men, shall be questioned by God; *Shall not the judge of all the earth do right?* Gen. xviii. 25. Then all thoughts shall be examined, and secret actions viewed on each side, and the infinite number of those sins which escaped here, shall be blazoned there; all shall have justice, and the justice of the judge will be so exact, that he will account with men by minutes; and that justice may reign intirely, God shall open his treasure, I mean the wicked man's treasure, and tell the sums, and weigh the grains and scruples, ' Is not this laid up in store with me, and ' sealed up among my treasures? I will restore it ' in the day of vengeance, saith the Lord,' Deut. xxxii. 34. Oh! how will God glorify his justice at that day? Surely his justice shall shine, and be eminently glorious in every passage.

2. His mercy, or free grace, will be glorified in rewarding the saints. And this is the main, the supreme end of his coming to judgment, *He shall come* (saith the apostle) *to be glorified in his saints*, 2 Thess. i. 10. Not but that the angels shall glorify the riches of his grace, as well as saints; but

because the angels never sinned, '(They have now 'kept their robes of innocency, their cloth of 'gold above five thousand years, without one 'spark of dirt, or change of colour;') therefore the glory of his grace is more especially fastened on saints, that sometimes were sinners. Oh! what stories will be told at this day of grace's acts? *I was a blasphemer, and a persecutor, and an injurious person,* (said Paul) *but I obtained mercy,* 1 Tim. i. 13. [*All' echeethen*], *but I was he mercied,* as if he had been dipt in a river, in a sea of mercy; it may be he will make the same acknowledgment at the day of judgment, ' I was a sinner, 'but the grace of the Lord Jesus to me was a-'bundant, superabundant; I obtained as much 'grace as would have saved a world.' Certainly free grace shall then be discovered to some purpose; then it shall be known, *where sin abounded, grace far more; it overabounded, or more than overabounded,* Rom. v. 20. [*hupereperirienfen*], it is a word borrowed from fountains, and rivers, which have overflowed with waters ever since the creation; then all the saints shall exalt, and magnify, and with loud voices praise the glory of his grace; they shall look on their debts written in grace's book, and then shall they sing and say, *O the mystery of grace! O the gold mines, and depths of Christ's free love!* why, this was the great design of our salvation: at the first, when God was willing to communicate himself out of his aloneness everlasting, he laid this plot, that all he would do, should be *to the praise of the glory of his grace,* Ep. i. 16. And now at his second coming, having done all he would do, the saints, for whom he hath done all, admire, esteem, honour, and sound forth the praises of his grace. Is not this their everlasting song which they begin at this day, *glory to the Lamb, and glory to his grace, that sitteth on the throne for evermore?* Not but that they glorify him in his wisdom, power, holiness, and his other attributes, ay, but especially in this; it is his grace in which he most delighteth, even as virtuous kings affect, above all their other virtues, to be had in honour for their clemency and bounty; so Jesus Christ, the King of kings, affects above all, the glory of his grace. And to this purpose, heaven itself is an house full of broken men, who have borrowed millions from Christ, but can never repay, more than to read and sing the praises of free grace; *glory to the Lamb, and glory to the riches of his grace for evermore.*

Thus for directions: one word of application, or a few motives to work faith in you in this respect.

1. Christ in his word invites you to believe, these are his letters from heaven, *Come all to the marriage-supper of the Lamb; ho, every one that thirsts come in;* heaven's-gate is open to all that knock, but fools, foolish virgins, foolish souls, which have no faith, nor will have any, to render them fit for heaven. This meets with some that scruple, 'What, will Christ come again to receive me to 'himself? Shall I enter with him into glory? A-'las! no unclean thing shall enter into that holy 'city, and shall such a sinner as I am be admitted?' Oh believe! believe thy part in this coming of Christ, to receive thee to himself; and no sin, that thou feelest a burden, shall keep thee out of heaven. There is Rahab the harlot, and Manasseh the murderer, and Mary that had so many devils; a man that hath many devils, may come where there is not one, *lame, and blind, halt, may enter into heaven, and yet there is room,* Luke xiv. 22. There is great variety of guests above, and yet one table large enough for all; no crowding, and yet thousands, and thousands of thousands sitting together. Ah poor soul! why dost thou make exceptions, where God makes none? Why shouldest thou exclude thyself out of these golden gates, when God doth not? Believe, only *believe in the Lord Jesus,* and the promise is sure, and without all controversy, *thou shalt be saved.*

2. Christ by his ministry intreats you to believe, come, say they, we beseech you believe in your judge: it may be you startle at this, what, to believe in him who is a coming to be your judge? But if your judge be Jesus, if the same person who died for you shall come to judge you, why should you fear? Indeed, if your judge were your enemy, you might fear; but if he who is your Lord, and who loves your souls, shall judge you, there is no such cause: will a man fear to be judged by his dearest friends, a brother by a brother, a child by a father, or a wife by her husband? Consider! is not he your judge who came down from heaven, and who being on earth was judged, condemned, and executed in your stead? And yet are ye fearful, *O, ye of little faith?* Oh! what an unreasonable

able sin is unbelief! nay, say the scrupulous, if I were assured of this, if I knew that my judge were my friend, I should not fear? but is he not my enemy? Have not I provoked him to enmity against my soul? Do I not stand it out in arms against my judge? Am not I daily sinning against him, who justly may condemn me for my sin? Give this for granted, that this and no other, no better is my case, and what say you then? If it be so, hearken then to the voice of our ministry. We poor ministers that love your souls, (say what you will of us) would fain have all this enmity against God, and against Christ done away; and to this purpose, we not only appear many and many a time upon our knees to God for you, but (maugre all your opposition against us) we would be content to come upon our knees from God to you, to beseech you not to provoke your judge against your souls: what, is Christ and you at odds? Is the difference wide betwixt your judge and you? I do now in my master's name, in the name of God, and in the name of the Lord Jesus Christ, beseech you to believe, *I beseech you in Christ's name, in Christ's stead, be ye reconciled unto God.* Is not this the apostle's word? *Now, then we are embassadors for Christ, as though God did beseech you by us, we pray you in Christ's stead,* 2 Cor. v. 20. Christ's ministers are not only God's legates, but Christ's surrogates: to make this plain to you, when a prince sends a messenger to another prince, that messenger is only an ambassador, the prince being not bound to carry the message himself in person; but now Jesus Christ, he is the Father's ambassador, and Christ is thereby bound to bring the message of peace himself; but being necessarily employed elsewhere, (in the same design of grace) he constitutes us his officers, so that we do not come only in the name of God, but in the place of Christ, to do that work which is primarily his, *As the Father hath sent me, even so send I you,* John xx. 21. And this was the commendation of the Galatians, *That they received the apostle Paul even as Jesus Christ,* Gal. iv. 14. Now, weigh our desire, we beseech you to believe; we beseech you to sign the articles of agreement betwixt Christ and you; what, shall some base inconsiderable lust stand in competition with Jesus Christ? Will you not make your peace with your judge whilst you are in the way, and before he sit on the throne? Behold we give the warning, *The judge is at the door, now believe, and be saved,* Oh! how fain would we tempt you (as it were) with glory? We tender Christ, and we offer peace, we come in the judge's name to beseech you to make ready for him, and for heaven; we bring salvation to your very doors, to your very ears, and there we are sounding, knocking, 'Will ye go to heaven, sinners? Will 'ye go to heaven? Oh! believe in him that will 'judge you, and he will save you.'

3. Christ by his Spirit, moves, excites, and provokes you to believe. Sometimes in reading, and sometimes in hearing, and sometimes in meditating, you may feel him stir; have you felt no gale of the Spirit all this while? *It is the Spirit that convinceth the world of sin,* John xvi. 8. especially of that great sin of unbelief; and then *of righteousness,* which Christ procureth by going to his Father. Observe here, it is the work of the Spirit thus to convince, so that all moral philosophy, and the wisest directions of the most civil men, will leave you in a wilderness; yea, ten thousands of sermons may be preached to you to believe, and yet you never shall, till you are overpowered by God's Spirit: it is the Spirit that enlightens and directs you, as occasion is, *saying, This is the way, walk ye in it,* Isa. xxx. 21. It is the Spirit that rouseth and awakeneth you by effectual motions, *Arise my love, my fair one, and come away,* Cant. ii. 10. *He stands at the door and knocks;* he stretches out his hand with heaven in it, and he doth so all the day long, *All the day long have I stretched out my hand,* Rom x. 21. And that you may find his yoke easy, and his burden light, it is the Spirit that draws the yoke with you, and by secret animations, and sweet inspirations, heartens and enables you to do the work with ease; and, in this respect, the saints are said to *be led by the Spirit,* Rom. viii. 14. Even as a mother leads her child that is weak, and enables it to go the better, so the Spirit leads the saints (as it were) by the hand, and strengthens them to believe yet more and more. I speak now to saints, if whilst I press you to believe in Jesus, you feel the Spirit in its stirrings, and impetuous acts, surely it concerns you to believe, it concerns you to be obsequious and yielding to the breathings of God's Spirit, it concerns you to co-operate with the Spirit, and to answer his wind blowing. As you are to take Christ at his word, so you are

to take Christ's Spirit at his work: if now he knocks, do you knock with him; if now his fingers make a stirring upon the handles of the bar, let your hearts make a stirring with his fingers also; O! reach in your hearts under the stirrings of free grace; obey dispositions of grace, as God himself. If now you feel your hearts as hot iron, it is good then to smite with the hammer; if now you feel your spirits docile, say then with him in the gospel, *I believe, Lord, help my unbelief; I believe. What? I believe when Jesus comes again, he will receive me to himself, and that I shall be for ever with the Lord.* Amen, Amen.

SECT. VI.

Of loving Jesus in that respect.

6. LET us love Jesus, as carrying on the great work of our salvation for us in his second coming. In prosecution of this, I must first set down Christ's love to us, and then our love to Christ; that is the cause, and this the effect; that is the spring, and this the stream; in vain should we persuade our hearts to love the Lord, if, in the first place, we were not sensible that our Lord loves us, *We love him,* (saith the apostle) *because he first loved us,* 1 John iv. 19. It is Christ's way of winning hearts, he draws a lump of love out of his own heart, and casts it into the sinner's heart, and so he loves him. Come then, let us first take a view of Christ's love to us, and see, if from thence, any sparks of love will fall on our hearts to love him again. Should I make a table of Christ's acts of love, and free grace to us? I might begin with that eternity of his love before the beginning, and never end till I draw it down to that eternity of his love without all ending: his love is as his mercy, from everlasting to everlasting; he loved us before time, in the beginning of time, in the fulness of time; at this time the flames of his love are as hot in his breast, as they were at first, and when time shall be no more, he will love us still; this fire of heaven is everlasting; there is in the breast of Christ an eternal coal of burning love, that never, never shall be quenched. But I have, in some measure, already discovered all those acts of his grace and love till his second coming: and therefore I begin there.

1. Christ will come; Is not this love? As his departure was a rich testimony of his love, *It is expedient for you that I go away,* so is his returning, *I will not leave you comfortless, I will come unto you,* John xiv. 18. Oh! how can we think of Christ's returning and not meditate on the greatness of his love? Might he not send his angels, but he must come himself? Is it not state and majesty enough to have the angels come for us, but that he himself must come with his angels to meet us more than half the way? What king on earth would adopt a beggar, and after his adoption would himself go in person to fetch him from the dunghil to his throne? We are as filthy Lazarus, from the crown of our heads to the soles of our feet we are full of sores, and yet the King of heaven puts on his best attire, and comes in person with all his retinue of glory, to fetch us from our graves to his own court of heaven. Oh! the love of Christ in this one act, he will come again, he is but gone for a while, but he will come again in his own person.

2. Christ will welcome all his saints into his presence: And is not this love? After he is come down from heaven, he stays for them a while in the clouds, and commanding his angels to bring them thither, anon they come; and, oh! how his heart springs within him at their coming; What throbs and pangs of love are in his heart at the first view of them? As they draw near, and fall down at his feet, and worship him, so he draws near and falls upon their necks, and welcomes them. Methinks I hear him say, ' Come blessed souls, you ' are my purchase, for whom I covenanted with ' my Father from eternity; O! you are dearly ' welcome to your Lord, in that now I have you ' in my arms; I feel the fruit of my death, the ' acceptation of my sacrifice, the return of my ' prayers; for this I was born and died, for this ' I arose again and ascended into heaven; for this ' I have interceded a priest in heaven these many ' years, and now I have the end and design of all ' my actings and sufferings for you; how is my ' joy fulfilled?' Look, as at the meeting of two lovers there is great joy, especially if the distance hath been great, and the desires of enjoying one another vehement; so is the meeting of Christ with his saints; the joy is so great, that it runs over and wets the fair brows, and beauteous locks of

Cherubims and Seraphims, and all the angels have a part of this banquet at this day.

3. Christ will sentence his saints for eternal life. Here is love indeed, every word of the sentence is full of love; it contains the reward of his saints, a reward beyond their work, and beyond their wages, and beyond the promise, and beyond their thoughts, and beyond their understanding; it is a participation of the joys of God, and of the inheritance of the Judge himself: *Come, enter into your Master's joy, inherit the kingdom.* Oh! but if all the saints have only but one kingdom, Where is my room? Fear not, O my soul! thou shalt have room enough, though but one kingdom, yet all the inhabitants there are kings; whole heaven is such a kingdom, as is entirely, and fully enjoyed by one glorified saint, all and every one hath the whole kingdom at his own will, every one is filled with God, as if there were no fellows there to share with him. Oh! that I may come under this blessed sentence. Never was more love expressed in words than Christ expresseth in this sentence, *Come ye blessed,* &c.

4. Christ will take up all his saints with him into glory, where he will present them to his Father, and then be their *all in all* to all eternity. This is the height of Christ's love, this is the immediate love that comes out from the precious heart and bowels of Jesus Christ; this is that Zenith of love, when sensibly and feelingly it burns at hottest; it is true, that Christ's love breaks out in all those precedaneous acts we have already spoken; oh! but what loves will he cast out from himself in glory? The more excellent the soil is, the nearer the sun is, and the more of summer, and the more of day; the more delicious must be the apples, the pomegranates, the roses, the lilies, that grow there: surely Christ in glory is a blessed soil; roses, and lilies, and apples of love, that are eternally summer-green and sweet, grow out of him; the honey of heaven is more than honey; the honey of love that is pure, and unmixed, and glorious in Christ, must needs be incomparable. I cannot say, but that Christ's love, like himself, is *the same yesterday, and to-day, and for ever;* there is no intention, or remission of his love as in itself, for *God is love,* 1 John iv. 8. He is essentially love, and therefore admits of no degrees; yet, in respect of the sense, or manifestation of this love of Christ, there must needs be a difference; thus, if he loved his spouse on earth, How much more will he love her when his bride in heaven? If he loves us while sinners, and enemies to his holiness, How much more will he love us, when we are sons, and perfected saints in glory? He that could spread his arms, and open his heart on the cross, Will he not then open arms, and heart, and all to them that reign with him in his kingdom? It, in this life, such is love's puissance, that we usually say of Christ, 'Though the 'head be in heaven, yet he hath left his heart on 'earth with sinners;' What shall we say of Christ in glory, where love, like the sun, ever stands in the Zenith? Where 'the eternal God is the soul's 'everlasting refuge, and underneath are his ever-'lasting arms?' Deut. xxxiii. 27.

2. And if Christ love thus, How should we love again for such a love? Lord, What a sum of love are we indebted to thee? Is it possible that ever we should pay the debt? Can we love as high, as deep, as broad, as long as love itself, or as Christ himself? No, no, all we can do is but to love a little; and, oh! that, in the consideration of his love we could but love a little in sincerity. Oh! that we were but able feelingly to say, 'Why, 'Lord, I love thee, I feel I love thee, even as I 'feel I love my friend, or as I feel I love myself.' Such arguments of love have been laid before us, as that now I know no more; we have seen whole Christ *cap-a-pee,* we have heard of the loves of Christ from eternity to eternity, we have had a view of the everlasting gospel of Jesus Christ, wherein his love is represented to us as hot as death, or as the flames of God; And do we not yet love him? Hath Christ all this while opened his breast and heart to us, saying, ' Friends, doves, ' come in, and dwell in the holes of this rock?' And do we scratch his breast? Do we turn our backs upon him, and requite his love with hatred? Surely this is more than sin; for what is sin but a transgression of the law? But this sin is both a transgression of the law and gospel. What, to spurn against the warm bowels of love? To spit on grace? To disdain him who is the white and ruddy, the fairest of heaven? Oh! the aggravation of this sin, it is an heart of flint and adamant that spits at evangelic love: law-love is love, but evangelic-love is more than love; it is the gold, the flower of Christ's wheat,

wheat, and of his finest love. Oh! the many gospel passages of love that we have heard. O! the sweet streams of love that we have followed, till now that we are come to a sea of love, to an heaven of love, to an infinite, eternal, everlasting love in heaven. I want words to express this love of Jesus, a sea of love is nothing, it hath a bottom, an heaven of love is nothing, it hath a brim, but infinite, eternal, everlasting love hath no bottom; no brim, no bounds. And do we not yet love him? Do we not yet feel the fire of love break forth? If not, it is time to turn our preaching into praying; 'O thou, who art the element or sun of love! come with thy power, let out one beam, one ray, one gleam of love upon my soul, shine hot upon my heart, cast my soul into a love trance, remember thy promise,' *To circumcise my heart, that I may love the Lord my God, with all my heart, and with all my soul,* Deut. xxx. 6. Surely the great marriage of the Lamb is coming on, he will come, and welcome all his saints into his presence; he will bid them inherit the kingdom, and put them in a possession of the inheritance; and then we cannot chuse but love our Lord Jesus with all our hearts, and with all our souls; only begin we it here, let us now be sick of love, that we may then be well with love; let us now rub and chafe our hearts (our dead, cold hearts) before this fire, till we can say with Peter, *Why, Lord thou knowest all things, thou knowest that I love thee.*

SECT. VII.

Of joying in Jesus in that respect.

7. LET us joy in Jesus, as carrying on the great work of our salvation for us in his second coming. Christ delights to have his people look upon him with delight; for a soul to be always under a spirit of bondage, and so to look upon Christ as a Judge, a Lion, or an offended God, it doth not please God; the Lord Jesus is tender of the joy of his saints, *Rejoice, and be exceeding glad,* saith Christ, Mat. v. 12. *Rejoice evermore,* 1 Thess. v. 16. *Rejoice in the Lord always, and again I say, Rejoice,* Phil. iv. 4. *Let the righteous be glad, let them rejoice before God, yea, let them exceedingly rejoice,* Psalm lxviii. 3. All that Christ doth to his saints tends to this joy, as the upshot or end of all; if he cast down, it is but to raise them up; if he humble, it is but to exalt; if he kill, it is but to make alive; in every dispensation still he hath a tender care to preserve their joy. This is the Benjamin, about which Christ's bowels beat, 'Let my children suffer any thing, but nothing in their joy; I would have all that love my name to be joyful in me.'

Oh! say some, but Christ's day is a terrible day; when Christ appears, he will make the heavens, and the earth, and hell to shake and tremble; *Our God shall come, and shall not keep silence; a fire shall devour before him, and it shall be very tempestuous round about him,* Psalm l. 3. True! but what is all this terror, but an argument of my Father's power, and justice against sinners? If thou art Christ's, and hast thy part in him, not one jot of all this terror belongs to thee; *the Lord knows how to deliver the godly out of temptations, and to reserve the unjust to the day of judgment to be punished,* 2 Pet. ii. 9. He knows how to make the same day a terror to his foes, and a joy to his people; he ever intended it for the great distinguishing and separating day, wherein both joy and sorrow should be manifested to the highest. *O then let the heavens rejoice, the sea, the earth, the floods, the hills, for the Lord cometh to judge the earth; with righteousness shall he judge the world, and the people with equity,* Psalm xcviii. 7, 8, 9. If you find it an hard thing to joy in Jesus, as in reference to his second coming, think of these motives,——

1. Christ's coming is the Christian's encouragement, so Christ himself lays it down, *You shall see the Son of man coming in a cloud, with power and great glory; and when these things begin to come to pass, then look up, and lift up your heads, for your redemption draweth nigh,* Luke xxi. 27, 28. The signs of his coming are the hopes of your approaching introduction into glory; And what should you do then but prepare for your approaching with exceeding joy? Many evils do now surround you every where; Satan hath his snares, and the world its baits, and your own hearts are apt to betray you into your enemies hands; but when Christ comes, you shall have full deliverance, and perfect redemption; and therefore *look up, and lift up your heads.* The apostle speaks the very same encouragement, *The Lord himself shall descend from*

from heaven, with a shout, with the voice of the archangel, and with the trump of God, and the dead in Christ shall rise first; then we which are alive, and remain, shall be caught up together with them in the clouds, to meet the Lord in the air,——Wherefore comfort one another with these words, 1 Thess. iv. 16, 17, 18. Christ's coming is a comfortable doctrine to all believers; and therefore all the elect that hear these words, should be comforted by them, *Comfort ye, comfort ye, my people.*

2. Christ our Saviour must be our Judge, the same Jesus that was born for us, and lived for us, and died for us, and doth now pray for us, will come at last to judge us; is not this comfortable? You that have heard all his transactions, Can you ever forget the unweariedness of Christ's love, in his constant and continual actings for your souls? How long hath he been interceding for his saints? How long hath he been knocking at their hearts for entrance? It is now above a thousand six hundred years that he hath been praying, and knocking, and he resolves not to give over till all be his; till all the tribes in one's and two's be over Jordan, and up with him in the heavenly Canaan. And if this be he that must be our Judge, if he that loves our souls must judge our souls, if he that hath a great interest and increase of joy in our salvation, must pass our sentence, Will not this work us into a rejoicing frame?

3. Christ's sentence is the Christian's acquittance; (I may call it his general acquittance, from the beginning of the world to the end thereof.) Hence some call this the day of the believers full justification; they were before made just, and esteemed just, but now by a lively sentence they shall be pronounced just by Christ himself; now is the complete acquittance, or the full absolution from all sin; now will Christ pardon, and speak out his pardons once for all; now will he take his book, (wherein all our sins, as so many debts or trespasses are written) and he will cancel all; *Your sins shall be blotted out,* (saith Peter) *when the time of refreshing shall come from the presence of the Lord,* Acts iii. 19. And is not this enough to cause our joy? When the Spirit witnessing with our spirits, doth but in part assure us of sin's pardon, Is it not exceeding sweet? Oh! but how sweet will be that sentence, which will fully resolve the question, and leave no room of doubting any more for ever? Consider, O my soul! the day is a-coming, when the Judge of heaven and earth will acquit thee of all thy sins before all the world: it is a part of his business at that day, to glorify his justice and free grace in thy absolution. O Christians! how may we comfort one another with these words?

4. Christ in the issue will lead us into glory. As the bridegroom after nuptials, leads his bride to his own home, that there they may live together, and dwell together; so Christ our Royal Bridegroom will lead us into the palace of his glory. And is not this joy of our Lord enough to cause our joy? Oh! what embraces of love, what shaking of hands, what welcomes shall we have into this city? There shall we see Christ in his garden, there shall we be set as a seal on Christ's arm, and, as a seal upon his heart; there shall we be filled with his love, enlightened with his light, encircled in his arms, following his steps, and praising his name, and admiring his glory; there shall we joy indeed, For *in thy presence there is fulness of joy, and at thy right hand there are pleasures for evermore,* Psal. xvi. 11. there is joy, and full joy, and fulness of joy; there are pleasures, and pleasures evermore, and pleasures evermore at God's right hand. O the musick of the sanctuary! O the sinless and well-tuned psalms! O the songs of the high temple without either temple or ordinances as we have them here! Can we choose to joy at the thought of this joy above? If God would so dispense, that even now we might stand at the utmost door of heaven, and that God would strike up a window, and give us a spiritual eye, and an heavenly heart, so that we could look in and behold the throne, and the Lamb, and the troops of glorified ones, clothed in white; Would not this chear up your hearts, and fill them with joy, unspeakable, and full of glory? Certainly this day will come, when Christ will bring us, not only to the door, *but through the gates into the city;* and then we shall see all these sights, and hear all the musick made in heaven; how then should we but *joy in the hope of the glory of God?* O methinks raised thoughts of our mansion in glory, should make us swim through the deepest sea of troubles and afflictions, and never fear. Come then, O my drowsy soul, and hearken to these motives, if yet thou seest not the sun itself appear, methinks

the twilight of a promise should revive thee; it is but a little while, *and he that shall come, will come, and he will not tarry.* It may be thou art reviled, and persecuted here on earth, And what then? Hath not Christ bid thee to *rejoice in afflictions?* Is it not his word, That in this very case thou shouldest *rejoice, and be exceeding glad?*—Mat. v. 12. Is it not his command, *Think it not strange concerning the fiery trials, but rather rejoice, in as much as ye are partakers of Christ's sufferings, that when his glory shall be revealed, ye may be glad also with exceeding joy?* 1 Pet. iv. 13. We must rejoice now, that we may rejoice then; indeed our present joy is a taste of our future joy, and God would have us to begin our heaven here on earth. Come then, come forth, O my dull, congealed heart! thou that spendest thy days in sorrow, and thy breath in sighing, that minglest thy bread with tears, and drinkest the tears which thou weepest; thou that prayest for joy, and waitest for joy, and longest for joy, and complainest for want of joy; O the time is a-coming, when thou shalt have fulness of joy; the time is a-coming when the angels shall bring thee to Christ, and when Christ shall take thee by the hand, and lead thee into his purchased joy, and present thee unspotted before his Father, and give thee thy place about his throne; And dost thou not rejoice in this? Art thou not exceedingly raised in such a meditation as this? Surely if one drop of lively faith were but mixed with these motives, thou mightest carry an heaven within thee, and go on ever singing to thy grave; say then, Dost thou believe, or dost thou not believe? If thy faith be firm, How shouldest thou but rejoice? If thou rollest thyself on Christ, and on that promise, *I will see you again, and your hearts shall rejoice, and your joy no man taketh from you,* John xvi. 22. How shouldest thou but rejoice, and be exceeding glad? If thou lookest upon the Holy Ghost, as designed by the Father and the Son, to bring joy and delight into thy soul, How shouldest thou but be filled with the water of life, with the oil of gladness, and with the new wine of the kingdom of God? O the blessed workings of faith on such a subject as this! if once we are but *justified by faith,* and that we can act our faith on Christ's glorious coming, then it will follow, that we shall have *peace with God, and rejoice in hope of the glory of God, and not only so, but we shall glory in tribulation also,* Rom. v. 1, 2, 3.

SECT. VIII.

Of calling on Jesus in that respect.

8. LET us call on Jesus, as carrying on our souls salvation, at his second coming; this contains prayer, and praise.

1. Let us pray for the coming of Christ; this was the constant prayer of the church, *Come Lord Jesus, come quickly: the Spirit and the bride say, Come,* Rev. xxii. 17. Well knows the bride that the day of Christ's coming is her wedding-day, her coronation-day, the day of presenting her unto his Father; and therefore, no wonder if she pray for the hastening of it, *Make haste, my beloved, and be thou like to a roe, or to a young hart,* Cant. viii. 14. *Thy kingdom come.* Many prayers are in the bowels of this, as, that Christ, when he comes, may bid us welcome, and give us a place on his throne, on his right hand, and pronounce us blessed, and take us to himself, to live with him in eternal glory, &c. But I mention only this general, and let each soul expatiate on the rest.

2. Let us praise him for his coming, and for all his actings at his coming. Our engagements to Christ, even for this transaction, are so great, that we can never extol his name; at that day the books shall be opened, and why not the book of our engagements to Jesus Christ? If it must be opened, I can surely tell you it is written full; the page and margin, both within and without, is written full; it is an huge book of many volumes; O then let our hearts be full of praises! let us join with those blessed elders that fell down before the Lamb, and sung, *Worthy is the Lamb that was slain, to receive power, and riches, and wisdom, and strength, and honour, and glory, and blessing,* Rev. v. 12. Yea, let us join with all those creatures in heaven, and on earth, and under the earth, and in the sea, whom John heard, saying, *Blessing, honour, glory, and power be unto him that sitteth on the throne, and unto the Lamb for ever and ever, Amen* v. 13.

SECT. IX.

Of conforming to Jesus in that respect.

9. LET us conform to Jesus, as coming again to judge the world. Looking to

Jesus contains this; when the apostle would persuade Christians to patience under the cross, he lays down first the *cloud of witnesses*, all the martyrs of the church of Christ; and, secondly, Jesus Christ himself, as of more virtue and power than all the rest; the martyrs suffered much, but Christ endured more than they all; and therefore, saith the apostle, *Look unto Jesus*, Heb. xii. 2. Surely he is the best examplar, the chief pattern, to whom in all his transactions, we may, in some way or other, conform

But how should we conform to Christ in this respect? I answer,——

1. Christ will, in his time, prepare for judgment; Oh let us at all times prepare for his judging of us; doth it not concern us to prepare for him, as well as it concerns him to prepare for us? If Christ come, and find us careless, negligent, and unprepared, what will become of us? The very thought of Christ's sudden coming to judgment, might well put us into a waiting, watching posture, that we might be still in readiness; it cannot be long, and alas! what is a little time when it is gone? How quickly shall we be in another world, and our souls receive their particular judgments; and so wait till our bodies be raised and judged, to the same condition, or salvation? It is not an hundred years, in all likelihood, till every soul of us shall be in heaven or hell; it may be, within a year, or two, or ten, or thereabouts, the greatest part of this congregation will be in heaven or hell; and I beseech you, what is a year, or two, or ten? What is an hundred, or a thousand years to the days of eternity? How speedily is this gone? And how endless is that time, or eternity that is to come? Is it not high time then to prepare our lamps, to trim our souls, to watch and fast, and pray, and meditate, and to remember, that for all our deeds, good or evil, God will bring us to judgment? Herein is our conformity to Christ's coming; before he comes, he prepares for us, Oh let us, against his coming, prepare for him.

2. Christ at his coming, will summon all his saints to arise, to ascend, and to come to him in the clouds; O let us summon our souls to arise, to ascend, and to go to Christ in the heavens. What Christ will do really at that day, let us do spiritually on this day. It was the prodigal's saying, *I will arise, and go to my father, and say unto him*, Luke xv. 18. We are naturally sluggish, we lie in a bed of sin, and security; and we are loth to arise, to ascend, and to go to God. Oh then, let us call upon our own souls! *Awake, awake, Deborah! why art thou so heavy, O my soul?* Let us stir up our spirits, consciences, wills, affections every day; let us wind them up as a man doth his watch, that it may be in a continual motion. Alas! alas! we had need to be continually stirring up the gifts and graces that are in us; it is the Lord's pleasure that we should daily come to him, he would have us on the wing of prayer, and on the wing of meditation, and on the wing of faith; he would have us to be still arising, ascending, and mounting up to divine contemplation of his majesty; and is it not our duty, and the saints disposition to be thus? *Wheresoever the dead carcase is, thither will the eagles resort*, Mat. xxiv. 28. If Christ be in heaven, where should we be, but in heaven with him? *For where your treasure is, there will your hearts be also.* Oh! that every morning and every evening, at least, our hearts would arise, ascend, and go to Christ in the heavens.

3. Christ will at last judge all our souls, and judge all the wicked to eternal flames; Oh, let us judge ourselves, that we may not be judged of the Lord, in that sad judgment! *If we would judge ourselves*, (saith the apostle) *we should not be judged*, 1 Cor. xi. 31. Good reason we have to conform to Christ in this point; or otherwise, How should we escape the judgment of Christ at the last day? But in what manner should we judge ourselves? I answer,——1. We must search out our sins. 2. We must confess them before the Lord. 3. We must condemn ourselves, or pass a sentence against our own souls. 4. We must plead pardon, and cry mightily to God in Christ for the remission of all those sins, whereof we have judged ourselves, and condemned ourselves.

1. We must search out our sins; *Winnow yourselves, O people! not worthy to be beloved*, Zep. ii.

1. There should be a strict scrutiny to find out all the prophaneness of our hearts and lives, all our sins against light, and love, and checks, and vows, *winnow yourselves*. If you will not, I pronounce to you from the eternal God, that 'ere long the Lord will come in the clouds, and then will he open the black book wherein all your sins are written, he will search Jerusalem with candles, he will

come with a sword in his hand, to search out all secure sinners every where, and then will all your sins be discovered to all the world. O that we would prevent this by our search, and scrutiny aforehand!

2. We must confess our sins before the Lord; we must spread them before the Lord, as Hezekiah did his letter; only in our confessions, observe these rules. As,——

1. Our confession must be full of sorrow, *I will declare mine iniquity*, (saith David) *I will be sorry for my sin*, Psal. xxxviii. 18. His confessions were dolorous confessions, he felt sin, and it wrought upon him as an heavy burden, *They are too heavy for me*, ver. 4. There is nothing in the world can make an heart more heavy, than when it feels the weight and heaviness of sin.

2. Our confession must be a full confession, we must pour it out. Thus David stiles one of his Psalms, *A prayer of the afflicted, when he is overwhelmed, and poureth out his complaint before the Lord*, Psal. cii. preface. We must pour out our complaints, as a man poureth water out of a vessel. ' Arise, cry out in the night; in the beginning of ' the watches pour out thine heart like water before ' the face of the Lord,' Lam. ii. 19. Water runs all out of a vessel, when you turn the mouth downward, never a spoonful will then stay behind; so should we pour out our hearts before God, and (if it were possible) leave not a sin unconfessed, at least for the kinds, if not for the particular sins.

3. Our confession must be with full aggravation; we should aggravate our sins, by all the circumstances that may shew them odious. Thus Peter when he had denied Christ, it is said, That *he thought thereon and he wept*, Mark xiv. 72. He thought thereon, or he cast in his thoughts, one thing upon another, *q. d.* Jesus Christ was my master, and yet I denied him, he told me of this before hand, that I might take heed of it, and yet I denied him; I professed to him that I would never do it, I would never forsake him, and yet I denied him; yea, this very night, and no longer since, I said it again and again, That I would not deny him, and yet I denied him, yea, I said, *Though all others deny thee, yet will not I*; and yet worse than all others, I denied him with a witness, for I affirmed desperately that I knew not the man, nay, I sware desperately that I knew not the man, nay, more than so, I sware, and I cursed too, *If I knew the man let God's curse fall upon me*, and all this I did within a few strides of my Lord, at that very time when I should have stood for my Lord, in that all the world forsook him: why, these were the circumstances of Peter's sin, and meditating on them, *He went out and wept bitterly*. And thus we should aggravate our sins in our confessions; O my sins were out of measure sinful! O they were sins against knowledge, and light, against many mercies received, against many judgments threatned, against many checks of conscience, against many vows and promises; thus oft, and in this place, and at that time, and in that manner, I committed these and these sins; but of all the aggravations let us be sure to remember how we sinned against the goodness, and patience, and love, and mercy of God; surely these circumstances will make our sins out of measure sinful. The angel that reproved the children of Israel at Bochim, after the repetition of his mercies towards them, and of their sins against him, he questions them in these words, *O, why have you done this?* Judge ii. 2 *q. d.* The Lord hath done thus and thus mercifully unto you, Oh! why have you done thus unthankfully towards him? Why was his mercy abused, his goodness slighted, his patience despised? Do you thus requite the Lord, O foolish people, and unwise? In like manner should we confess and aggravate our sins, ' O my God! ' thou art my father; was I ever in want, and thou ' didst not relieve me? Was I ever in weakness, ' and thou didst not strengthen me? Was I ever ' in straits, and thou didst not deliver me? Was ' I ever in sickness, and thou didst not cure me? ' Was I ever in misery, and thou didst not succour ' me! hast thou not been a gracious God to me? ' All my bones can say, Who is like unto thee, ' Lord, who is like unto thee? And shall I thus ' and thus reward the Lord for all his mercies towards me? Hear, O heavens, and hearken, O ' earth; sun, stand thou still, and thou moon be ' amazed at this! hear angels, and hear devils; ' hear heaven, and hear hell, and be you avenged ' on such a sin as this is! O, the sinfulness of my ' sin, in regard of these many circumstances!

3. We must condemn ourselves, or pass a sentence against our own souls: ' Lord, the worst place in ' hell is too good for me; Lord, here is my soul, ' thou

'thou mayest, if thou pleasest send Satan for it, 'and give me a portion among the damned.' This self-judging, or self-condemning is exemplified to the life in Ezra; For,——

1. *He fell on his knees*, Ezra ix. 5. He did not bow down his knees, but like a man astonished, he fell on his knees; he had before rent his garment and mantle, and pluckt off the hair of his head, and of his beard, and sat down astonished; and now at the evening-sacrifice he falls on his knees and on the ground, in great amazement.

2. *He spread out his hands unto the Lord*, ver. 5. *q. d.* 'Here is my breast, and here is my heart-'blood, I spread my arms, and lay all open, that 'thou mayest set the naked point of thy sword of 'justice at my very heart.'

3. He is dumb and speechless (as it were) before the Lord, *And now, O our God! what shall we say after all this, for we have forsaken thy commandments?* ver. 10. *q. d.* 'Shall I excuse the 'matter? Alas! it is inexcusable;' What shall we say after all this? Shall we call for thy patience? We have had it, but how did we abuse it? Should we call for mercy? Indeed we had it, but our stubborn hearts would never come down. O our God! what shall we say? I know not what to say, for we have sinned against thee.

4. He lays down his soul, and all the people's souls at God's feet, *q. d.* Here we are, thou mayest damn us if thou wilt, *Behold, we are all here before thee in our trespass, for we cannot stand before thee, because of this*, ver. 15. Behold, here we are, rebels we are; here are our heads and throats before the naked point of thy vengeance, if now thou shouldest take us from our knees, and throw us into hell, if we must go from our prayers to damnation, we cannot but say, That thou art just and righteous; Oh! it is mercy, it is mercy indeed that we are spared, it is just and righteous with God that we should be damned.

In this more especially lies self condemnation; it makes a man to trample upon his own self, it makes a man freely to accept of damnation, *They shall accept of the punishment of their iniquity, then will I remember my covenant with Jacob*, Levit. xxvi. 41, 42. They save God (as it were) a labour, judging themselves, that they may not be judged.

4. We must plead pardon, and cry mightily to God in Christ, for the remission of all our sins. This the way of judging ourselves, we see nothing but hell and damnation in ourselves; but then we fling down ourselves at God's gate of mercy; we despair not in God, though in ourselves; God in Christ is gracious and merciful, forgiving iniquity, transgression and sin; and hence we make bold to intreat the Lord for Christ's sake, to be merciful to us; surely herein lies the difference betwixt nature and grace; the natural man may see his sins, and confess his sins, and judge himself for his sins, thus Saul did, and thus Judas did; but then they despaired in God, and were damned indeed: now the gracious man hath a conscience within, that represents to him his damned estate, but withal it represents to him the free grace of God in Jesus Christ, and so he only despairs in himself, and not in his God; now thus far good. Come Christians! do we despair in ourselves? Do we fling off all our own hopes, and our own dependencies, hangings, holdings on duties, purposes, graces, performances? And do we go to God in Christ, and tell him, 'We hang upon nothing but 'the mere mercy, the free grace of God in Christ; 'and therefore, Lord pardon, Lord forgive for 'thy name's sake, promise sake, mercy's sake, and 'for the Lord Jesus's sake; O let free grace have 'his work, Lord glorify thy name, and glorify 'the riches of thy grace in saving us.' Why, this is the best hold in the world, though the world cannot abide it; surely if we thus judge ourselves we should not be judged.

4. Christ at coming will be glorified in his saints; not only in himself, but in his saints also, whose glory, as it comes from him, so it will redound to him; Oh! let him now be glorified in us, let us now, in some high way conform to the image of his glory; let us look on Christ till we are like Christ, not only in grace, but in glory; and this glory, as it comes from him, so let it redound to him. I will not say, That the kingdom of heaven and glory is in this life, I leave this opinion to the dreamers of this time, I mean to the familists, quakers, and such like; but this I say, That even in this life the saints of God enjoy a begun and imperfect conformity to Christ's glory, and this is that I would now press upon us, let us so *behold the glory of the Lord in the glass of the gospel, as that we may be changed into the same image from glory to glory,*

glory, 2 Cor. iii. 18. From a lesser measure, to an higher measure of glory. The day is a-coming, that Christ will be glorified in himself, and he will be glorified in his saints; O! the glories that will then be accumulated, and heaped upon Jesus Christ! come now, let us behold this glory of Christ till we are changed in some high measure into the same glory with Christ; Christ's glory rightly viewed, is a changing glory; and herein the views of Christ surpass all creature-views, if we behold the sun, we cannot possibly be changed into another sun; but if, with the eye of knowledge, and faith, we behold Jesus Christ, we shall be changed into the glorious image of Jesus Christ; if the sun of righteousness cast forth his golden beams upon us, and we enjoy this light, why then, *who is she that looketh forth as the morning, (as Aurora, the first birth of the day) fair as the moon, clear as the sun?* Cant. vi. 10.

I know this glorious change is but a growing change by degrees, *from glory to glory*; and yet who can deny but there is some conformity to Christ's glory, even in this life? Do not these very texts speak the self same thing? *These things have I spoken to you, that my joy might remain in you, and that your joy might be full,* John xv. 11. And *these things write we unto you, that your joy may be full,* 1 John i. 4. And *ask, and ye shall receive, that your joy may be full,* John xvi. 24. And *rejoice ye with Jerusalem, and be glad with her, all ye that love her,—that ye may suck and be satisfied with the breasts of her consolation, that ye may milk out, and be delighted with the abundance of her glory,* Isai. lxvi. 10, 11. And *the God of hope fill you with all joy and peace in believing,* Rom. xv 13. Surely *all joy and peace,* are synechdochically put for all other inchoations of glorification. But how is a saint in this life filled with all joy? I answer, 1. In regard of the object, God and Christ. 2. In regard of the degrees; tho' not absolutely, yet so far forth as the measure of joy is in this life attainable; I might instance in the joy of Mr. Peacock, Mrs. Bretturgh, and of some martyrs, who sung in the fires. 3. In regard of duration, *rejoice always,* Phil. iv. 4. not only in the calm of peace, but in the storm of violent opposition. A saint may have his troubles, but these troubles can never totally or finally extinguish his joy, *Your joy no man taketh from you,* John xvi. 22. He rejoiceth always.

O! that some of the glory of Christ might rest upon us! Oh! that having this glory of Christ in our thoughts, we could now feel a change from glory to glory! is it so, that the Lord Jesus will be glorified in all his saints? And shall we have inglorious souls, base and unworthy affections and conversations? Or, shall we content ourselves with a little measure of grace? O be we holy, even as he is holy; let our conversation be heavenly, let us purify ourselves, even as he is pure; let us resemble him in some high measure of grace. And lastly, let us glorify him in bodies and spirits; all our glory is from him, and therefore let all our glory redound to him; let us begin now that gospel-tune of the eternal song of free grace, which one day we shall more perfectly chaunt in glory; *Allelujah! and again, Allelujah! and Amen, Allelujah! salvation, and glory, and power, and praise, and thanksgiving, and obedience, be unto him that sits on the throne, the Lamb blessed for ever and ever.* Amen.

The CONCLUSION.

And now, my brethren, I have done the errand which Christ sent me on, I verily believe, I have now delivered this work of the everlasting gospel, or of Christ's carrying on the great work of man's salvation, and it hath been somewhat long in speaking, but, Oh! how long in acting? May I give you a short view of what I have said, and of what hath been acted from eternity, and will yet be acted to eternity; you may remember, that God, in his eternity, laid a plot or design to glorify the riches of his grace in saving sinners; and to that purpose, 1. He decreed a Christ. 2. Presently after the fall, he promised the Christ he had decreed. 3. In fulness of time he exhibited the Christ that he had promised; then it was, that the same Christ took upon him our nature, and joined it to his Godhead to be one person; and, in that person he was born, and, lived, and died, and rose again, and ascended into heaven; there now he hath been sitting, sending down the Holy Ghost, and interceding for his saints, for above one thousand six hundred years; and, in this last work, he will continue till the end of the world, and then he will come again to judge the world, and to receive his saints to himself, that where he is they may be with him, to see and enjoy him to all eternity. This is the *epitome* of all I have said,

only

only in every particular I have set down Christ's actings towards us, and our actings towards Christ; in various forms, and outgoings of his love he hath acted towards us; and in various forms, and outgoings of our souls we have been taught fitly and suitably to act towards him.

Now, in all these actings, How doth the free grace of God in Christ appear? *Ye are saved by grace*, saith the apostle, Eph. ii. 5. The decree, the means, the end of our salvation is grace, and only grace. The decree is grace, and therefore it is called, *The election of grace*, Rom. i. 5. The means are of grace, and therefore *we are called according to his grace*, 2 Tim. i. 9. and *we are justified freely by his grace*, Rom. iii. 24. And the end is of grace, for *eternal life is the gift of God*, Rom. vi. 23. Both beginning, and progress, and execution is all of grace. This is *the riches of his grace*, Eph. i. 7. *The exceeding, the hyperbolical riches of his grace*, Eph. ii. 7. The conclusion of all is this, God's free grace, which was first designed, will at last be manifested, and eternally praised by saints and angels; the same free grace, which from the beginning of the age of God, from everlasting, drove on the saving plot and sweet design of our salvation, will at last be glorified to purpose; when heaven's inhabitants will be ever digging into this golden mine, ever rolling this soul-delighting and precious stone, ever beholding, viewing, enquiring, and searching into the excellency of this same Christ, and this free grace. Now all is done, Shall I speak a word for Christ, or rather for ourselves in relation to Christ, and so an end? If I had but one word more to speak in the world, it should be this; Oh! let all our spirits be taken up with Christ, let us not busy ourselves too much with toys, or trifles, with ordinary and low things, but look unto Jesus. Surely Christ is enough to fill all our thoughts, desires, hopes, loves, joys, or whatever is within us, or without us; Christ alone comprehends all the circumference of all our happiness; Christ is the pearl hid in the large field of God's word; Christ is the scope of all the scriptures; all things and persons in the old world were types of him; all the prophets foretold him, all God's love runs through him, all the gifts and graces of the Spirit flow from him, the whole eye of God is upon him, and all his designs both in heaven and earth meet in him; the great design of God is this, That *he might gather together in one all things in Christ, both which are in heaven, and which are on earth, even in him*, Ephes. i 10. All things are summed up in this one Jesus Christ, if we look on the creation, the whole world was made by Christ, if we look on providences, all things subsist in Christ, they have their being, and their well-being in him. Where may we find God but in Christ? Where may we see God but in this essential and eternal glass? Christ is *the face of God*, 2 Cor. iv. 6. *The brightness of his glory, the express image of his Father's person*, Heb. i. 3. The Father is (as it were) all sun, and all pearl; and Jesus Christ is the substantial rays, the eternal and essential irradiation of this sun of glory: Christ outs God, as the seal doth the stamp; Christ reveals God, as the face of a man doth reveal the man; so Christ to Philip, *He that hath seen me, hath seen the Father*, John xiv. 9 *q. d.* I am as like the Father, as God is like himself; there is a perfect indivisible unity between the Father and me, *I and my Father are one*; one very God, he the begetter, and I the begotten; Christ is the substantial rose that grew out of the Father from eternity; Christ is the essential wisdom of God; Christ is the substantial word of God, the intellectual birth of the Lord's infinite understanding: Oh the worth of Christ! compare we other things with Christ, and they will bear no weight at all; cast into the ballance with him angels, they are wise, but he is wisdom; cast into the ballance with him men, they are liars, lighter than vanity, but Christ is *the* Amen, *the faithful witness*; cast into the scales kings, and all kings, and all their glory, why, he is King of kings; cast into the scale millions of talents weight of glory; cast in two worlds, and add to the weight millions of heavens of heavens, and the ballance cannot down, the scales are unequal, Christ outweighs all. Shall I yet come nearer home? What is heaven but to be with Christ? What is life eternal but to believe in God, and in his Son Jesus Christ? Where may we find peace with God, and reconciliation with God, but only in Christ? *God was in Christ reconciling the world unto himself*, 2 Cor. v. 19. Where may we find compassion, mercy, and gentleness to sinners, but only in Christ? It is Christ that takes off infinite wrath, and satisfies justice, and so God is a most lovely, compassionate, desirable God in Jesus: all

the

the goodness of God comes out of God through this golden pipe, the Lord Jesus Christ. It is true, those essential attributes of love, grace, mercy, and goodness are only in God, and they abide in God; yet the mediatory manifestation of love, grace, mercy and goodness, is only in Christ; Christ alone is the treasury, store-house, and magazine of the free goodness and mercy of the Godhead. In him we are elected, adopted, redeemed, justified, sanctified and saved; he is the ladder, and every step of it betwixt heaven and earth; he is *the way, the truth and the life*, he is honour, riches, beauty, health, peace, and salvation; he is a suitable and rich portion to every man's soul: that which some of the Jews observe of the *manna*, that it was in taste according to every man's palate, it is really true of Christ, he is to the soul, whatsoever the soul would have him to be. All the spiritual blessings wherewith we are enriched, are in and by Christ; God hears our prayers by Christ; God forgives us our iniquities through Christ; all we have, and all we expect to have, hangs only on Christ; he is the golden hinge, upon which all our salvation turns.

Oh! how should all hearts be taken with this Christ? Christians! turn your eyes upon the Lord; *Look, and look again unto Jesus,* Why stand ye gazing on the toys of this world, when such a Christ is offered to you in the gospel? Can the world die for you? Can the world reconcile you to the Father? Can the world advance you to the kingdom of heaven? As Christ is *all in all,* so let him be the full and complete subject of our desire, and hope, and faith, and love, and joy; let him be in your thoughts the first in the morning, and the last at night. Shall I speak one word more to thee that believest? Oh! apply in particular all the transactions of Jesus Christ to thy very self; remember how he came out of his Father's bosom for thee, wept for thee, bled for thee, poured out his life for thee, is now risen for thee, gone to heaven for thee, sits at God's right hand, and rules all the world for thee; makes intercession for thee, and at the end of the world will come again for thee, and receive thee to himself, to live with him for ever and ever. Surely if thus thou believest and livest, thy life is comfortable, and thy death will be sweet. If there be any heaven upon earth, thou wilt find it in the practice and exercise of this gospel-duty, in *looking unto Jesus.*

A POEM of Mr. GEORGE HERBERT in his *Temple.*

JESU *is in my heart, his sacred name*
  Is deeply carved there; but th' other week
A great affliction broke the little frame,
  Ev'n all to pieces, which I went to seek:
And first I found the corner, where was J,
  After where ES, *and next where* U *was graved,*
When I had these parcels, instantly
  I sat me down to spell them, and perceived
That to my broken heart he was, I ease *you,*
  And to my whole is JESU.

FINIS.

CPSIA information can be obtained
at www.ICGtesting.com
Printed in the USA
BVHW051418030522
635994BV00003B/108

9 781340 663827